Law

Science

Communication

Industry

Commerce

Liam Dunne

THE UNITED STATES

American Democracy in World Perspective

FRANKLIN DELANO ROOSEVELT

THE UNITED STATES

AMERICAN DEMOCRACY IN WORLD PERSPECTIVE

RAY ALLEN BILLINGTON
Professor of History
Northwestern University

BERT JAMES LOEWENBERG
Professor of American History
Sarah Lawrence College

SAMUEL HUGH BROCKUNIER
Professor of History
Wesleyan University

RINEHART & COMPANY INC.
NEW YORK   TORONTO

FOREWORD

This book is dedicated to the fundamental democratic and humane values which were the ultimate stakes in the last and most savage of global conflicts. We accept the proposition that mankind cannot afford a third world war, and we believe that historians have a responsibility for the shaping of a peaceful future. Neither the policies of a country nor the written history of its people can any longer be formulated within a national vacuum. The historic American illusion, the idea of withdrawal, letting the world "stew in its own juice," has been dissipating. But if the scattered peoples in various countries are to seek seriously to tame the forces of nationalism, more is necessary than a verbal substitution of "internationalism" for "isolationism."

The history of each nation must be rewritten. Though old nations—Spain, France, England—have not been "isolated" from the world, their separate histories have been written precisely like American histories—with an insistent accent on national character, national problems, national spirit. In the shrinking world the time has come to recapture the universal spirit. Man's fate hinges upon the recognition of Man as the central theme: Man's character, Man's problems, Man's spirit. If this be the modern accent, we may expect historians in each nation to place less stress on national differences. We may expect them—following cultural anthropologists—to place more stress on evolving similarities in social organization and on the fundamental kinship of human nature. We may see in written history a recovery of the view of the whole, in place of preoccupation with a separate part of mankind as though it were the whole. If Man is made the central preoccupation, a denationalized history in the Humanist tradition may eventually be the product.

According to the classical conception of his role, the historian is passionlessly devoted to objectivity. But the canons of scholarship are implements to fashion a working hypothesis as a means to reach an intelligent conclusion. The historian is and must be today above all a social scientist with a public responsibility. As against the orthodox view that facts speak for themselves, the modern historian as social scientist accepts the responsibility for positive affirmation of those courses of action which the guideposts of social science indicate as valid. There is a difference between polemics and social responsibility; but detachment is a method, not an end in itself. Honest craftsmanship in written history is not a passionless performance; it is "an act of faith."

While it is too early to hope that a single volume can emphasize both American history and world history, we have nevertheless set ourselves the task of telling the American story as a story of man in America. The facts in that story attest the rise of American power; but the historian must be concerned with the rise of mankind, not the power of the few nor the interests of one country.

The present volume represents a synthesis of three central themes:
International linkages and the interdependence of peoples;
Cultural diversity and universal human kinship;
Majority rule and democratic equality.

More comprehensively than is usual in a single-volume history, we have traced both the theory and practice of modern democracy, drawing not merely upon the writings of the "fathers" of the republic but upon the history and comparative studies of the political institutions of other leading democracies. Majority rule is conceived critically and functionally, in terms of national mandates and national party principles as the essential bases for a working democracy. This attention to the history of the process of political management illumines American failures as well as successes. Emphasis upon the idea of responsible party government provides a unifying thesis that clarifies the problem of democracy and leadership.

The liberal tradition presupposes that the struggle for democratic well-being is not alone the political striving for free parties and free elections but a widening struggle for equal freedoms and broader justice in the social relations and economic life of modern man. Accordingly, recurrent challenges to intolerance and authoritarianism, religious ferment, assaults on aristocratic classes, the slavery controversy, the emancipation of women, conflicts over land policy, the growth of collective bargaining, battles against race prejudice, the vision of controls against the ravages of the business cycle, and other great social issues are woven into the history of man's aspiration for a more profound social integration.

While we have unreservedly accepted the international premise, we have assumed that global unity is not incompatible with cultural diversity. The historical method indicates that each culture is composed of many strands; that many culture traits are in the long run less national than international; that "national character" and "national characteristics" are both more imaginary and less national than they are often supposed; and that mankind everywhere, despite differing stages of development, has the same potential capacity for cultural change and human progress. A respect for cultural pluralism is indispensable either for an understanding of the

American story or for the larger story of human diversity. American historians do not assume that their own national culture is necessarily a yardstick for civilized achievement; nor that western European culture has nothing to learn from the East.

The fundamental transition from the agricultural epoch to the industrial era requires special treatment to clarify the vast significance of the changes in the life of the individual and in his relations to society. A straightforward chronological development could not have made the intellectual, moral, and commercial transformation following the change from a rural and small business civilization to the modern urban and industrial life comprehensible. Accordingly we determined on an appropriately large space allotment for a number of chapters on primary aspects of social change initiated by the triumph of industry after 1865. These fundamental changes of the period from 1860 to 1900 were of greater significance than many of the details of political history; the latter have therefore been compressed to harmonize with the general plan of the book. For interpretation of such important phases as the development of urban America, rural America, the role of the immigrant in America, and similar topics, a selected sequence of topics seemed more appropriate than the chronological sequence of chapters that would be normal in a treatment of political history alone.

Our object has been a liberal book that places the story of democratic development in the United States continuously in more universal perspective. To this end we have allocated space for unfamiliar interpretations. Norms or standards set by other countries receive attention as temporal measures of American progress or as challenging forces of international cultural diffusion. "History," as F. W. Maitland observed, "involves comparison." A liberal book necessarily exemplifies belief in the virtue of criticism of historic tendencies. It does not shrink from realistic portrayal of unresolved contradictions in the existing order. Contradictions can be resolved, difficulties surmounted, and realizable goals attained. The idea of progress is essential to democracy. Without accepting a fatalistic optimism, the historian can affirm that regressive tendencies are reversible; that ideas are weapons; that institutions can either dominate and thwart or be mastered and put to work. The historian, as an expert, may—indeed must—analyze the past as the perspective of the future.

R. A. B.
B. J. L.
S. H. B.

March, 1947

CONTENTS

Bert James Loewenberg

Samuel Hugh Brockunier

HALF-TONE ILLUSTRATIONS

OTHER ILLUSTRATIONS

MAPS AND CHARTS

THE UNITED STATES

American Democracy in World Perspective

I

THE TRANSIT OF EUROPEAN CIVILIZATION

1492–1763

In the waning years of the fifteenth century, Europe stood on the threshold of the modern era. Decaying relics of the Middle Ages remained: feudal lords guarded their Lilliputian kingdoms, craft and merchant guilds controlled industry and trade in the growing towns, scholastics in the cells of libraries and monasteries spun out their fine threads of substanceless learning, the papacy's universal authority was supreme. But these institutions were fast crumbling before the onslaught of new forces. Kingdoms, ruled by strong monarchs cooperating with a rising merchant class, were taking shape in Portugal, Spain, England, and France to challenge the local autonomy of feudal overlords and the international pretensions of the church. Scholars were emerging from the darkness of their cells to bask in the light of revived classical learning and to nourish the creative efforts of the Renaissance. And the guilds, which regulated economic life in every town, were giving ground to newer types of business organizations that were better adjusted to the wider commercial horizons then opening before the Continent's traders.

THE SEARCH FOR A NEW ROUTE TO THE EAST

For all of these changes, and particularly the last, expanding trade was responsible. The revival of commerce began in the tenth century when Italian merchants, bursting the chrysalis of localism that had bound each man to his village or to serfdom during the early Middle Ages, first sent their ships to the eastern tip of the Mediterranean. There they found riches undreamed of in drab Europe—spices for flavoring coarse foods, tapestries to brighten gloomy castles, gems to decorate church altars and milady's hair, delicately wrought porcelains to replace crude trenchers on banquet tables. For the next four centuries these exciting luxuries flowed over Europe as Italian shipmasters plied the sea lanes and Italian merchants led their pack trains of richly laden horses along the Alpine trails to Germany, France, and Spain. The goods that could be sent eastward in exchange—rough woolen cloth and metals—paid for only a fraction of these imports and each year more and more gold was carried to the Near East to balance the trade. As this went on an acute money shortage paralyzed the Continent. Monarchs debased the coinage, plundered the church and noblemen, and forced a lower living standard on their people that the flow of Eastern luxuries might continue.

By the middle of the fifteenth century Europeans were casting anxiously about for some way out of the economic plight into which their extravagant tastes had led them. They knew that the exotic goods purchased in the Near East were not produced there but were brought westward by caravan from the fabulously rich lands of the Orient—China, India, Persia, Sumatra, Ceylon, Borneo, and the distant Spice Islands of the Malay Archipelago. This they learned from bold travelers such as Marco Polo, who visited the court of the Tartar emperor, Kublai Khan, in Pekin and returned to tell of the treasures there. They knew, too, that they could not trade directly with the Orient themselves, for Moslem middlemen guarded the caravan routes to India and the fabled lands beyond lest intruders deprive them of their traders' profits. A new route to the Far East was the only answer.

The newly created national states that fringed the Atlantic shore of Europe—Portugal, Spain, France, and England—were best equipped to take up the quest, partly because they had cast off the relics of feudalism sooner than the countries of southern or central Europe and partly because their position at the extremity of the Italian trading routes forced them to pay a higher price for needed Oriental goods. The new routes, their rulers saw, must lie either around Africa or directly west to Asia, for all intelligent men accepted the fact that the world was round and were confident that the newly invented navigation instruments, the compass and astrolabe, made the needed voyages feasible. Portugal took the lead in exploring the southern route, and by 1460 had established colonies in Madeira and the Azores, opened trade with the Guinea coast of Africa, and was pushing slowly down the coast of the Dark Continent. Finally, in 1486, a Portuguese navigator, Bartholomeo Diaz, rounded the Cape of Good Hope and emerged in the Indian Ocean with the path to the Orient before him.

This was the same quest that sent a Genoese sailor named Christopher Columbus westward into the unknown Atlantic on a sunny day in August, 1492, with the flag of Spain flying bravely from the mastheads of his three tiny vessels. When he came scurrying back into Palos on the wings of a mad March wind six months later, he brought news that electrified all Europe. He had found what Spain sent him to find: a direct route to the riches of the Orient. What matter that he brought back only a few

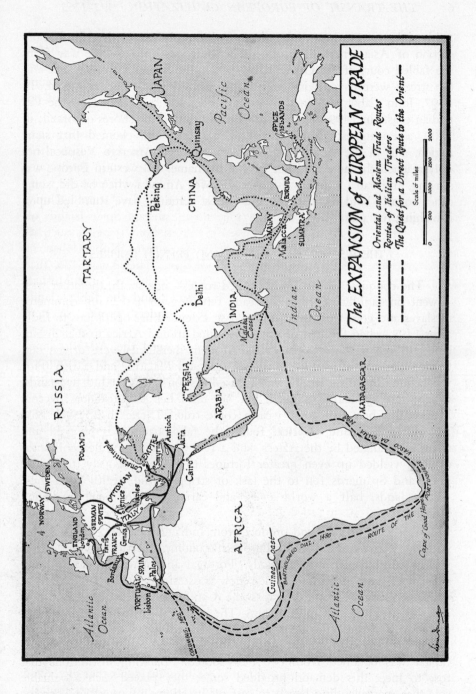

The EXPANSION of EUROPEAN TRADE

Oriental and Moslem Trade Routes ·········
Routes of Italian Traders ————
The Quest for a Direct Route to the Orient — — —

Scale of miles

0   500   1000   1500   2000

gold trinkets? Further exploration would surely reveal that the remote section of Asia where he made his landfall was only a short way from the fabled court of the Grand Khan, where the houses were of silver and the streets were paved with gold. Little wonder that others followed. In 1497, John Cabot, a Venetian in England's service, touched on the Canadian coast; in 1499, the Spaniard Pinzon skirted the shores of Brazil; in 1500, a Portuguese explorer, Cabral, explored and claimed that same region, and in the same year a Florentine named Amerigo Vespucci not only reached the new land but gave it his name. All western Europe was stirring, and had Columbus failed to discover America when he did, some other equally bold navigator would almost certainly have stumbled upon it within a few years.

THE RISE OF THE SPANISH AND FRENCH EMPIRES

The conquest of the newly opened routes—one south, the other west —went on rapidly. Portugal, already fattening on a thriving commerce in slaves and gold from the Guinea coast, extended her operations to India after 1498, when the first of her fleets sailed around Africa to that distant land. In the next two decades the Moslem merchants were driven out, trading posts were established at Malabar and Malacca, and a rich trade was begun. Spain's attention was focused first on the West Indian Islands, which were gradually subdued, but not until her conquistadors overran Mexico did her dreams of wealth come true. There, in 1519, a bold adventurer, Hernando Cortez, found the fabulous hoards of gold and silver accumulated by the Aztecs, and a few years later the peaceful Incas of Peru yielded up even greater fortunes to Spain. Joyously the Portuguese and Spaniards fell to the task of stripping the wealth from these distant lands, half a world away, and carrying it to their prospering homelands.

This flow of gold and produce from India, Africa, and the Americas wrought a transformation in Europe's economy. Particularly noticeable was its effect on business methods. Portugal and Spain, importing gold, silks, dyes, and spices from their new possessions, wished to sell these priceless colonial products across the Continent and to send out new expeditions to harvest more riches. The old local guilds could not adapt themselves to these far-flung operations, for they had neither the vision nor the resources to finance such extended voyages. Instead, the needed capital was obtained from two new sources. Banking institutions that rose to meet this demand provided some; they played such a valuable role that moneylending began to cast off its stigma of usury and become a respectable profession for the first time in the Christian Era. Even these banks, however, were unable to supply the needs of merchants who were fitting out expeditions to trade in the far corners of the world. Associations that would pool the resources of many capitalists were the only answer. These, the joint-stock companies, began to spring up in the first half of the sixteenth century to provide the first adequate financial backing for the expanding commercial ventures. Thus the commercial revolution laid the basis for two institutions indelibly associated with the capitalistic system—banks and corporations.

The wealth from Asia and the New World also helped diversify the economy of agricultural Europe. Some of it fostered new industries, especially hand weaving that could utilize the silk and cotton which traders obtained in the Far East and Africa. Some was used by small landholders who enlarged their estates, enclosed the common fields traditional to medieval farming, and began growing sheep to supply an infant woolen industry. These developments brought some relief to Europe's masses, long bowed under the crushing weight of serfdom, but the principal beneficiaries were members of a newly created middle class —the merchants, traders, bankers, manufacturers, and landholders. This prosperous and ambitious group, which in most countries was distinct from the nobility, gained power most rapidly in the new national states, partly because these nations were less bound by tradition than the older city governments of central and southern Europe, and partly because their monarchs recognized the value of a middle-class alliance and openly wooed merchant support by legislation that would benefit business. Capitalism and nationalism, marching forward hand in hand, were overthrowing the last remnants of feudalism and calling a modern Europe into being.

The changes wrought by the commercial revolution fitted the countries along the Atlantic to transform their initial conquest into permanent colonies. Spain, predestined by Columbus' discovery to play a leading role in peopling the New World, devoted itself largely to Central and South America, where docile natives and rich mines proved more attractive than the forbidding forests north of the Gulf of Mexico. Yet as Spanish galleons, deep with Aztec gold and Inca silver, sailed through the Bahama Channel and northward along the Florida coast before spreading their sails to the westerly winds that would carry them across the Atlantic, Spain's attention was turned to the area of the present United States. For enemy vessels lurking in the inlets of eastern Florida could prey on this rich trade. This danger was brought home in 1564, when an adventurous band of French Huguenots founded the diminutive colony of St. Catherine at the mouth of the St. Johns River and prepared to pounce on Spain's treasure fleets. The intruders were massacred the next spring, but similar threats could be forestalled only by Spanish occupation of the coastal region. Before the year was out Spaniards were busily rearing the first permanent white settlement within the present United States at St. Augustine, and by the end of 1566 their fortifications dominated strategic points as far to the north as Port Royal Sound.

Spain would never have been able to hold these frontier outposts amidst hostile Indians and marauding French raiders without the aid of the Catholic Church. Time and again her little bands of soldiers were driven back or slaughtered, until 1593, when twelve Franciscan friars reached St. Augustine. They pushed at once into the wilderness and founded the first mission stations: crude buildings and a chapel, a few black-robed fathers, a handful of soldiers—these were to be the instruments for Spain's frontier advance in North America. Natives were taught Christianity and agriculture, and were encouraged to abandon their nomadic life to settle in villages about each station. By 1606, when the Bishop of Cuba visited Florida to celebrate their success, missions extended as far north as present Virginia and the whole southeast coast was firmly in Spanish hands.

While brave Spaniards were struggling to win yellow gold and red souls in the south, French pioneers were drifting into the northern lands tributary to the St. Lawrence, lured by the less romantic flesh of the cod and skin of the beaver. Jacques Cartier aroused the interest of his homeland in the New World in 1534, when he explored the St. Lawrence Gulf, but religious wars absorbed French energy during most of the sixteenth century and no official attempt was made to capitalize on his discoveries. Yet during these years France made good her claim to a share of North America, not through haughty servants of the crown in regal ships, but through humble fishermen who flocked to the Newfoundland banks, where the shallow, icy water made an ideal feeding ground for the fish of the North Atlantic. By 1578, 150 French vessels each year were fishing regularly at the banks, three times the number from all other European nations combined. Their effect on American history would have been slight had not an unrecorded event taken place somewhere, sometime, on the bleak Newfoundland coast. There, where the fishermen landed to salt and dry their catch before sailing home, an Indian watched with covetous eyes the gleaming knife of a Frenchman as he skillfully slit open a fat cod. The sailor, seeing that glance, signaled that he would trade for the Indian's fine cloak of beaver skins. Thus was born the fur trade, on which the American empire of France was to rest.

At first this trade was haphazard, carried on by ships' crews and captains, but by the 1580's merchants were entering the field and their traders were pushing far up the St. Lawrence to intercept the furs flowing seaward from the interior tribes. As their activities increased, the thoughts of the French king, Henry of Navarre, turned to the settlement of the river basin before some rival nation captured the rich prize. Two attempts failed, but in 1608 Samuel de Champlain, an agent of the traders, began building the first rude shelters of Quebec beneath the towering cliffs of the lower St. Lawrence. During the next years this outpost served as a center for the *voyageurs* whose canoes penetrated the river routes flowing into the interior and sent a steady stream of shining peltrics across the Atlantic to French markets. France, like Spain, was firmly entrenched in the New World.

ENGLAND'S FIRST AMERICAN COLONIES

England's national ambition was to break the monopoly of these two great Catholic powers. Absorbed in internal reform and the task of welding a united nation from the chaos of feudal days, her monarchs took little interest in affairs beyond the seas until Queen Elizabeth ascended the throne in 1558. This shrewd ruler carried her people into a triumphant war against Spain that raged through the last years of the sixteenth century and sent her sea dogs swarming forth to prey on Spanish treasure fleets Europe-bound with the riches of the New World. So long as war went on, England needed no other way of tapping America's wealth, and not until the first of the Stuart monarchs, James I, mounted the throne in 1603, firmly determined to make peace, did Englishmen have an incentive to leave their tight little isle for homes in the New World. By this time the "monstrous swarm of beggars" loosed by the enclosure of fields for wool growing, the decaying foreign trade, and the religious enthusiasm bred by the long war against Catholic Spain led Englishmen to covet colonies in the belief that they would drain off a surplus population, vitalize commerce, and bring new glory to the crown.

Two years after James became king, two groups of merchants petitioned for the right to found overseas settlements. A charter granted in 1606 brought both together as the Virginia Company, authorized to sell stock and apply the proceeds to "make habitation, plantation, and to deduce a colony of sundry of our people into" America. The company, the charter stated, was to be governed by a royally appointed council meeting in England, and by a local council in each overseas plantation. Under this grant of power, three shiploads of colonists sailed in December, 1606, and, after exploring the southern coast, built their homes on a low-lying peninsula jutting into the James River thirty miles from its mouth—a site they called Jamestown. Starvation and disease reaped a terrible toll during the first years, but a new charter in 1609 that allowed the company to govern itself without royal interference, and the discovery of a staple crop in the form of tobacco three years later, initiated a period of better times. By 1619 Virginia was well established; the homes of its thousand settlers stretched twenty miles up the James and a steady stream of tobacco flowed toward English markets to bring unheard-of prosperity to the planters.

In that year the managers of the Virginia Company, some of them leaders in current parliamentary struggles against the king, took a significant step. Conscious of the middle-class Englishman's desire for self-government, they made their colony more attractive to settlers by authorizing an assembly empowered to make laws subject only to the company's approval. Under this order there gathered at the tiny Jamestown church on July 30, 1619, the twenty-two "burgesses" of the first representative assembly in America. No matter that this first legislature adjourned after passing a few insignificant laws or that its actions had to be validated by the company before they acquired the force of law; liberal Englishmen who sought to perpetuate their ideals in a distant colony had planted a seed of democracy in the New World. There it flourished. When James I, disgusted by the Virginia Company's liberalism and jealous of its growing power, canceled the charter in 1625, the legislature fought tenaciously for its life. James reluctantly gave in, and although he now appointed the governor and the governor's council, the assembly, courts, and agencies of county government continued under local control. Virginia as a royal colony proved more popular than before, and during the next years settlers filled the valleys of the James, York, and Rappahannock rivers with prosperous tobacco farms.

Maryland, Virginia's sister colony to the north, secured its representative institutions after a longer struggle. Granted in 1632 to a prominent English Catholic, George Calvert, Lord Baltimore, and settled in February, 1634, Maryland learned from Virginia's mistakes and was soon so firmly established that it could keep pace with its older sister in the westward march of population. In one respect the two colonies differed, for Lord Baltimore planned to administer his grant as a feudal barony, complete with manor lords and freeholders, over whom he would rule with a baronial hand. These archaic dreams met a speedy death in the New World. The legislature, which was supposed to advise him, insisted on initiating legislation and within fifteen years it was ruling the colony, checked only by the veto power of a governor appointed by the proprietor. This governmental pattern was imitated in other proprietory colonies as they were erected in the West Indies, in Bermuda, and in North America.

The representative forms evolving in the south were matched in the

New England colonies. The settlers who carved their homes from the rock-strewn wilderness of this land were Protestants who remained dissatisfied when Elizabeth effected a compromise settlement to end the squabbles that followed the English Reformation. In their eyes the established Anglican Church that resulted was little better than Catholicism. To separate from this church was unthinkable, for they were too respectful of the established order to take such a radical step; instead, they must purify from within. For years these Puritans labored valiantly, but when James I ascended the throne, pledged to enforce conformity, their last hope seemed gone. They could not stay in an England that seemed to be moving back along the road to Rome; migration to new lands where they could live and worship as they pleased seemed the only answer.

In the vanguard of these swarming dissenters was a little band of religious radicals called Separatists, or Pilgrims, who began building their homes at Plymouth on Christmas Day, 1620. Far more important was the settlement of a group of prominent English Puritans who incorporated themselves as the Massachusetts Bay Company, secured a royal charter in 1629, and in 1630 sailed away, a thousand strong, to found Boston and other tiny outposts about the excellent harbor there. With them they brought their charter, for through an oversight the king had failed to specify that the company must meet in England, and upon it they built their governmental system. The stockholders, called "freemen" according to the custom of that day, became the voters; the president and directors were transformed into a governor and upper branch for the legislature. When increasing population made attendance of all voters at the "general court" inadvisable, a representative system, providing a lower house for the legislature, was devised. The evolution of the structure was completed in 1644, when members of the two legislative branches quarreled so violently over the ownership of a sow claimed by one Goody Sherman that they split apart into two houses.

Thus there developed on American soil a self-governing commonwealth, making and enforcing its own laws, and bound to England only through personal loyalty to the crown. Massachusetts Bay was no democracy, for only "freemen" could vote, only church members could become freemen, and only "Visible Saints," a select few acceptable to the ruling oligarchy of magistrates and clergymen, could become church members. Yet a pattern of self-rule was laid down that became the ideal of every other colony and encouraged a concept of autonomy that found expression in the Revolution.

Undemocratic as this system was, it still attracted some sixteen thousand Puritan migrants from England between 1630 and 1640, for those were the years of "personal rule" when Charles I governed without

Parliament and all hope of reform seemed dead. Many did not stay long in Massachusetts Bay; greater opportunity lay ahead, and the intolerance of the Boston clergy, who believed themselves to be the only divinely appointed interpreters of the Holy Writ, bred a constant stream of rebels who pushed inland to found new colonies where they could worship as their consciences dictated. Boston during these years resembled an inverted funnel through which flowed a stream of English settlers to spread over the rest of New England.

One group went from Cambridge, nestling on the outskirts of Boston. Their lands were wearing thin, their minister was disliked by the orthodox clergy, and they "were moved by a strong bent of their spirits for change" —so westward they moved in 1636 to found Hartford. At their heels were other dissatisfied souls lured by the rich lands of the Connecticut River Valley, until by 1662 the numerous towns there could be united with others along the coast into the colony of Connecticut. Others went south, led by an eccentric divine named Roger Williams, whose tolerant democracy was unpalatable to Zion's saviors in Boston. The town of Providence, which he founded in 1636, became the center of a cluster of settlements that were brought together in 1644 as the colony of Rhode Island. There, alone in all Christendom, men were free to worship the God of their choosing, for while toleration existed elsewhere in the seventeenth century as a political concession, the farseeing Williams made religious freedom an inalienable individual right. This refreshing concept, remarkable as it was amidst the intolerance of the day, was no more revolutionary than the democracy that he preached and installed in his colony. Rhode Islanders had neither a governing hierarchy nor a nose-in-air contempt for other peoples; they ruled themselves and treated all men, whether red of skin or white, as brothers. Roger Williams was far in advance of his time, but the seeds of religious liberty and political freedom that he planted were to blossom in the more enlightened atmosphere of a later generation. New Hampshire was less fortunate in its founder, but still grew rapidly after 1638, when a dissenting Boston clergyman who had been expelled from the Massachusetts Bay Colony laid out the town of Exeter. Sturdy commonwealths, virtually independent of each other and the mother country, these New England colonies turned to the sea for the wealth denied them by their stubborn soil and built their prosperity on commerce, fishing, and shipbuilding.

The first phase of England's colony planting ended in 1640; the second began in 1660. In the twenty-year interim, civil wars and internal disputes so absorbed the mother country's attention that her overseas possessions drifted by themselves, seeking their own markets, expanding their settlements, beating back Indian opposition, and developing such a haughty insularity that Massachusetts could staunchly declare: "Our allegiance binds us not to the laws of England any longer than while we live in England, for the laws of the Parliament of England reach no further." This brief American isolation from Europe's affairs ended for all time in 1660 when Charles II was restored to the throne. With memories of his European exile fresh in mind and anxious not to "go again upon his travels," this Stuart monarch deliberately set out to win the support of England's powerful merchant class. Two things were nearest the hearts of these traders: new colonies and laws welding the empire into an efficient colonial system. Charles II was ready to grant both in a bid for merchant support.

In 1660 England's possessions stretched in a broken arc from Newfoundland across New England, Maryland, and Virginia to Barbados in the Windward Islands of the Caribbean. At intervals along this broad front the colonies of Britain's commercial rivals, Holland and Spain, intruded in a trading area that the London merchants wished for their own, and the principal energies of the Restoration were directed toward filling in these gaps. One was in New York, where the thrifty Dutch, with their usual eye for advantageous sites, had in 1624 established an outpost of their far-reaching empire. Their fur-trading operations, with the Iroquois from Fort Orange (Albany) and along the Connecticut River into the New England back country, had long rankled Englishmen, who only waited an opportunity to drive out the intruders. This came in 1664, when the two nations locked in the second of three great wars fought during the seventeenth century for control of the world's sea lanes. A British fleet forced the New Netherlands to surrender without firing a shot and the area passed into English hands.

Two colonies were erected there, New Jersey on the south and New York along the Hudson. The latter grew rapidly, despite the absolute rule of its reactionary proprietor, the Duke of York, for the fertile valley lands and the trading opportunities attracted numerous English settlers. Although these newcomers soon outnumbered the original inhabitants, New York retained a cosmopolitan population that made it more typically American than any of its neighbors. Observers in the snug little village on Manhattan Island saw a medley of types as they walked the narrow streets: sturdy Dutch burghers, prospering Huguenot merchants who had fled from Catholic persecution, English and Irish Catholics driven from their homes by Protestant intolerance, Jewish storekeepers, Swedish traders visiting from the Delaware Valley, Highland Scots, Welsh farmers, and a sprinkling of Negro slaves. New York was then as now the principal crucible where many racial groups were blended into that new man—the American.

The remaining gaps were filled quickly. Pennsylvania was granted in 1681 to a prominent Quaker named William Penn, who installed such a democratic system of government and allowed such complete religious freedom that his colony prospered. Those settlers who spilled over into the counties west of the Delaware River demanded and received their own legislature in 1701 as the colony of Delaware. More daring was the establishment of new outposts south of Virginia, for these would encroach on lands claimed by Spain. Yet adventurers ready to risk their fortunes for the glory of empire were plentiful, and in the 1670's a group of them began settling the Carolinas under a proprietary grant from the crown. French Huguenots, Scots, Germans, Swiss, and English flocked to the new colony, lured by the liberal political and religious systems and by the chance to reap fortunes from the lowland rice fields or the fur trade. Because settlement clustered around either Charleston or Albemarle Sound, political necessity decreed that Carolina must be divided into two colonies; hence before the end of the seventeenth century North Carolina and South Carolina were in existence. Not until a generation later did England feel strong enough to intrude anew into the Spanish borderlands and found Georgia, the last of the thirteen colonies. This was granted to a group of proprietors in 1732; Savannah was laid out a year later as the center for an expanding society of Scottish Highlanders, Germans, Welsh, and English.

THE COLONIAL SYSTEM

The English commercial leaders responsible for this burst of colony planting also wanted a colonial system that would weld the empire into a compact economic unit, and this, too, Charles II gave them. According to the mercantilist theories then current, national self-sufficiency was the ideal of every nation, and colonies were important only when they contributed to the wealth of the mother country. England's merchants, swayed by this theory and impressed by the example of other nations, wanted a policy that would direct the flow of colonial produce toward English markets: sugar from Barbados and Jamaica, rice and indigo from the Carolinas, tobacco from Virginia and Maryland, grain from the middle colonies, and cod and naval stores from New England. English merchants could then fatten their pocketbooks by exporting surpluses to the Continent rather than permit rising colonial merchants and foreign traders to exchange directly the produce of the empire and the wares of European markets.

This mercantile policy was embodied in a series of laws passed by Parliament between 1660 and 1673 known as the Acts of Trade and Navigation. They aimed at three broad objectives. First, all colonial trade must be in vessels built within the empire and manned by British crews, a measure designed to eliminate Dutch carriers and benefit the shipping interests of mother country and colonies. Second, certain specifically "enumerated" articles could be exported only to England. These included the great staples of colonial agriculture—tobacco, sugar, and cotton—but as the years passed the list was enlarged by the addition of rice, molasses, naval stores, and other vital products. Finally, the Navigation Acts decreed that all goods shipped to the colonies from the Continent must pass through England.

THE COLONIAL ECONOMY

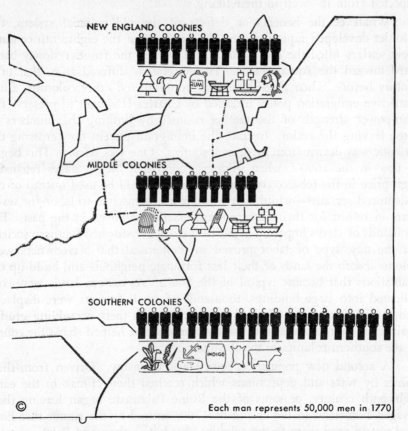

Each man represents 50,000 men in 1770

From Hacker, Modley, and Taylor, *The United States: A Graphic History,* Modern Age Books, Inc. PICTOGRAPH CORP.

The obvious purpose of these laws was to break down colonial economic independence and weld all units of the empire into a compact federation whose parts would contribute to the economic self-sufficiency and national might of the mother country. Yet the switch from free commercial interchange to a protectionist system of empire trade occasioned no alarm in America, for colonial thought was nationalistic so long as no colonist suffered. Virginia planters and New England ship captains hoped for advantages from the new system. American staples might benefit from a monopoly in the British market and American ships could fill the gap left by the exclusion of Dutch carriers, offering promise of new profits for colonial owners and builders. From the swampy rice beds of the Carolinas to the bustling shipyards of New England, Americans found the empire formula of colonies, commerce, and sea power—and the prosperity they expected from it—well to their liking.

Whatever the benefits or defects of the old colonial system, the colonies developed rapidly during the first half of the eighteenth century. New settlers filled the coastal areas and pushed the frontier slowly backward toward the Appalachians. This migration differed from that of a century before, when Englishmen far outnumbered other colonists, for a restrictive emigration policy installed by Charles II sought to preserve the man-power strength of the mother country by limiting the numbers of those leaving the realm. Instead, the immigrant torrent now crossing the Atlantic was drawn from three new sources. One was Africa. This began to flow in the 1690's, when shippers found that Negro slaves fetched a high price in the tobacco colonies, where they could be used instead of the indentured servants—white men who bound themselves to labor for seven years in return for their passage—universally employed in the past. The thousands of slaves imported in the next years transformed southern society, for the new type of labor proved so economical that slaveowners were able to absorb the lands of their less fortunate neighbors and build up the plantations that became typical of the South. As eastern lands were consolidated into large holdings, thousands of small farmers were displaced and forced to move to the interior, bearing with them a rankling grudge against the more successful tidewater planters that helped shape the course of the southern colonies in the Revolution.

A second new population source was Germany. Driven from their homes by wars and depressions which reached their climax in the early eighteenth century, peasants of the Rhine Palatinate began leaving their ravaged homeland in the spring of 1709, enticed by the rumor that England would send them to the colonies. By June a thousand Palatines were reaching the Low Countries each week; there English agents waited to ship the Protestants among them to London. Some fourteen thousand of these immigrants spent the winter of 1709–1710 in crowded taverns and army tents, and in the spring a vanguard of three thousand was shipped at the crown's expense to the Hudson River Valley to produce naval stores. This experiment soon failed and the Germans drifted into the Schoharie River Valley, where cheap lands awaited them. Others followed, both from England and Germany, to build their homes along the Hudson and the Mohawk rivers, but high land prices in New York soon deflected the course of settlement southward to Pennsylvania, where Penn's political liberalism and religious tolerance served as a magnet for Europe's downtrodden. By 1717 they were swarming over the back country in search of cheap lands, filling the Susquehanna Valley with hard-working "Pennsylvania Dutch" farmers, and preparing to turn southward once more down the Great Valley of the Appalachians into Virginia and the Carolinas. By the middle of the century German settlers formed an unbroken line from the Schoharie to the South Carolina backwoods. Their great Palatine barns, their covered Conestoga wagons, and their "kitchen gardens" were adopted by Americans and spread through the west; their thrifty ways and careful conservation of the soil proved less attractive to the wasteful frontiersmen.

The Germans were soon joined in their wilderness homes by a third alien group, from northern Ireland. Made up of lowland Scots and Englishmen who had been planted in the tangled bogs of Ulster a century before in an effort to win that country to civilization and Protestantism, these Scotch-Irish were driven to America by harsh English laws that disrupted their economic life and interfered with the practice of their sacred Presbyterian religion. By the 1720's thousands were crossing the Atlantic weekly, some bound for New England, others for the Mohawk Valley frontier, but most for Pennsylvania. Poverty forced them, as it had the Germans, to seek the cheaper lands on the fringe of settlement, and they spread rapidly over the hilly interior of Penn's colony, then turned southward into the Great Valley along the trail already marked by the Germans. Most of the best lands of the Shenandoah Valley were already under cultivation, so they pushed south beyond the James River, some to burst through the mountain gaps and spread over the Carolina Piedmont, others to build their homes along the maze of westward-flowing streams that made up the headwaters of the Tennessee River. There these robust pioneers learned the frontier technique that equipped them to lead the westward march across the mountains into Kentucky a generation later.

All these immigrants not only gave America a sturdy heterogeneous population and a culture enriched by borrowings from many lands; they stimulated a new independent spirit already developing in the back country. They had no sentimental attachment for an England they had never seen, and their loyalty to a distant king depended on his ability to solve the practical problems facing them in their wilderness homes. These feelings spread rapidly from the Palatines and Scotch-Irish to the English pioneers who lived in the hilly upcountry beneath the long shadows of the Appalachians, for the turbulent streams of the Piedmont offered no easy access to European markets as did the broad coastal rivers, and the frontiersmen's contacts with the mother country were few. What, they asked themselves, did members of Parliament, who basked in the luxury of London life, know of defense against the Indians, or the need of the westerners for cheap lands and transportation outlets for their produce? Obviously the Americans were able to govern themselves better than these rulers far beyond the seas. To these self-reliant sons of the colonial frontier, English rule was acceptable only so long as England did not rule but left them free to solve their own problems.

Fortunately this sentiment fitted well into the prevailing empire philosophy during the first half of the eighteenth century—a period, in Edmund Burke's happy phrase, of "salutary neglect." The mother country, busy at home and on the Continent, was content to let the colonies drift by themselves so long as they did not stray beyond the broad framework of the old colonial system. Royally appointed governors still jealously guarded the king's authority, but the assemblies held the purse strings and used them to usurp a growing list of executive functions. Even the right of veto was seldom used, for the governors soon found that legislatures had a disagreeable habit of withholding salaries unless they had their way. Apparently the relations between the mother country and colonists were harmonious and, in the minds of the colonists if not in those of their English rulers, approaching a system of dominion home rule.

Yet two rankling problems in the imperial relationship were unsolved and would remain so as long as England denied the colonists freedom of trade. One was the shortage of currency. No gold or silver for coinage was produced in the English colonies, and money brought out by new settlers was drained away by an unfavorable trade balance. In vain did the legislatures protest to England. The crown steadfastly refused to allow them to mint money from foreign bullion acquired through trade or to permit English coins to be shipped to America, for this would diminish the gold supply by which Britain measured her national wealth. Time after time assemblies sought to circumvent England's laws by issuing paper money, circulating "bills of credit" that could pass as legal tender, and establishing land banks authorized to emit various types of currency. Each attempt met with rigid disapproval from the king and left the colonists more dissatisfied. As long as prosperity continued they could get along, but any prolonged depression would cause grave discontent.

A more serious problem was the failure of the northern colonies to fit comfortably into the trading structure of the old colonial system. The West Indies could ship sugar and other tropical products to England in

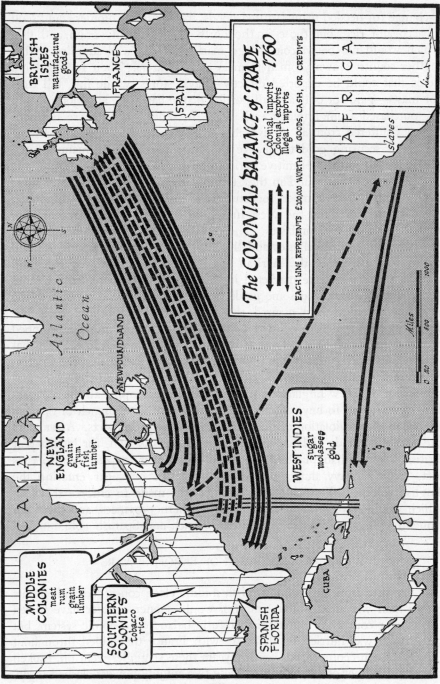

exchange for needed manufactured goods, the southern colonies could send tobacco and rice, but those in the north produced only grain and fish, which would not be welcomed in a market already well supplied by the mother country's own yeoman farmers and seafarers. Their few scattered items that could be exported directly—naval stores, whale fins, tall trees for masts—paid for only a small portion of the hardware and clothing and tea purchased from England each year. In other words, these northern colonies suffered from an unfavorable trade balance and had to find some means of securing gold to finance the large purchases of manufactured goods needed in their primitive agricultural economy.

A remedy was found in the "triangular trade." New England ships loaded with codfish, lumber, foodstuffs, and horses regularly plied between the northern ports and the West Indies, where their prosaic cargoes were traded for sugar and molasses. The molasses was converted into rum in the New England distilleries and this fiery liquor, together with fish and grain, was carried to the African coast to be exchanged for gold and slaves. The slaves were marketed in the West Indies in return for more sugar and molasses, and some gold. So long as this trade continued, the northern colonies were assured the money needed to offset their un-favorable trade balance with the mother country, but it might be stopped at any time, for some day English statesmen would waken to the fact that here was a serious leak in the tight empire structure. Because the English West Indian islands were not large enough to absorb all the grain and slaves that the New Englanders wanted to sell or to supply all the molasses that they wanted to buy, much of their trade was with French or Spanish islands in direct violation of the spirit of the Navigation Acts. After 1733 the triangular trade violated the letter of the law as well, for in that year British West Indian planters persuaded Parliament to pass the Molasses Act, levying heavy duties on foreign molasses or sugar entering the English colonies. Fortunately no attempt was made to enforce this law, which would have brought ruin to the northern provinces, and they con-tinued to purchase English goods with French and Spanish gold.

THE COLONIAL PHASE OF EUROPE'S WARS

Pressure from the rising English middle class, concerned with profits rather than with harmonious empires, would sooner or later have forced the mother country to upset this carefully balanced economic system, but the change was hurried by the wars with France that raged throughout the eighteenth century. For seventy years these struggles went on, broken only by brief periods of peace, as these two mighty powers clashed to de-termine which should control the lion's share of the world's colonies and trade. Their battleground was in Europe, in Asia, in Africa, and on all the seas between. Their weapons were not only their own armies and fleets but those of Spain, Russia, Sweden, Prussia, Austria, Portugal, and most of the German states, for all of these powers sided with the major antagonists in the hopes of sweeping a few crumbs from under the peace tables or of restoring Europe's tottering balance of power when one or the other threatened to become too strong. The Americans, too, were directly involved, not simply because French Canada lay at their doorstep or because they were tied to England's apron strings, but as active participants in a world war that would determine the fate of their trade, their form of government, and their way of life. They learned, during this century of conflict, that even in the eighteenth century isolation from the Old World was impossible; their destiny was decided by naval engagements in the Mediterranean, by encounters between fierce native troops in India, by mammoth battles on the plains of central Europe as well as by the clash of French and English arms along their own frontiers. Their failure to grasp this lesson soon enough eventually cost them their place in the empire, for the reluctance of the colonies to bear a larger share of the burdens of war forced Britain to revise its colonial system, and inadvertently set in motion that chain of events which culminated in the Revolution.

The struggle in America was for the interior of the continent. France gained the first advantage. While the English agricultural frontier was creeping slowly back from the coast in the seventeenth century the French were sweeping westward with breath-taking speed. Before their outpost at Quebec lay two broad highways into the heart of America, one along the St. Lawrence-Great Lakes waterway, the other by way of the Ottawa River-Lake Nipissing portage to Georgian Bay. From the Great Lakes easy water routes tempted explorers to push on to the Ohio and Mississippi River systems, which controlled the continent's interior. New France could not be concerned with agriculture when a vast accessible wilderness teeming with fortunes in fur lay at her door. Her traders flung themselves over the interior, exploring the lakes and rivers, spying out the portages and strategic sites, cementing alliances with the Indian tribes, and returning to Montreal or Quebec with canoes bearing fortunes in peltry. By 1671, when the English had advanced only a few miles from the coast, an official French expedition was at Sault Ste Marie, boldly proclaiming ownership of the whole interior of America. Two years later Louis Jolliet and Father Jacques Marquette entered the Mississippi River and sailed down that majestic stream, in New France's name taking possession of all the lands it drained. By the end of the century France held the heartland of America with strategically located posts at Detroit, Mackinac, Kaskaskia, and Cahokia in the Illinois country, and Louisiana at the mouth of the Mississippi.

This rapid expansion threatened to encircle the English colonies and confine them to the narrow coastal strip east of the Appalachians. England first sensed this threat in the 1680's, when her traders at Albany began encouraging their Iroquois allies to strike at the French communication lines between Quebec and the Great Lakes. France struck back with fire and sword, and by the end of the decade these forest skirmishes had merged into the first of the wars between the two powers. Three of these conflicts—King William's War (1689–1697), Queen Anne's War (1702–1713), and King George's War (1744–1748)—were fought largely in Europe, but the fourth was primarily an American struggle, at least in origin.

The Seven Years' War (1756–1763) climaxed a clash of the fur-trading frontiers of France and England along a front that stretched from Hudson Bay to Georgia. This time the English were the aggressors; their traders were pushing south from Hudson Bay, north from New York, and westward through the Appalachians, bearing superior trading goods from England's factories and threatening to break down the system of Indian alliances by which France controlled the interior of the American continent. The westward advance of the Pennsylvania traders particularly alarmed the French. By 1750 these bold pioneers were swarming about the forks of the Ohio and establishing posts in the Ohio country that threatened to win over the trade, and hence the allegiance, of the important tribes there. The officials of New France swung into action in 1753, when a strong force was sent out from Quebec to build a string of forts from Lake Erie to the forks of the Ohio, where the strongest, Fort Duquesne, was to stand. This barrier, they reasoned, would not only keep the Pennsylvania traders from the Ohio country but would bring New France nearer the Mississippi Valley by allowing her *voyageurs* to use the convenient French Creek-Allegheny River portage rather than the traditional waterways through the Wisconsin and Illinois country. Alarm swept through the colonial back country, for French success would mean the end of English expansion. In the spring of 1754 an American expedition commanded by a youthful Virginia surveyor named George Washington started west to drive out the intruders. This small band was no match for the large force at Fort Duquesne, and after a brief skirmish Washington was forced to surrender. The last and most decisive of the colonial wars had begun.

Until 1757 the English and Americans suffered a series of disastrous defeats, but in that year the tide of battle began to turn, partly because England's control of the seas stopped New France from obtaining trading goods needed to keep the allegiance of the Indians, and partly because of better leadership at home. William Pitt, who took up the reins of government in that dark hour, was endowed with a bold energy and imaginative enthusiasm which made him outstanding as a leader of men. He charmed Parliament into vast expenditures for materials and men, browbeat his fellow ministers into accepting his battle plans, and shook the archaic brass hats from their high posts in the army and navy. In their stead he placed dashing young commanders who had come up from the ranks and sent them over the world to win a series of brilliant victories.

PRINCIPAL CAMPAIGNS
OF THE SEVEN YEARS'
WAR · · · 1758 – 1760

Campaigns of 1758
Campaigns of 1759
Campaigns of 1760

General James Wolfe and Colonel Jeffrey Amherst, who were entrusted with the defense of the American colonies, fell into the spirit of Pitt's grandiose schemes by planning a giant pincers' movement designed to cut New France in two and force the surrender of all Canada. By 1758 they were ready to launch their offensive. One expedition moved northward by sea to capture the powerful French fortress at Louisbourg, which controlled the mouth of the St. Lawrence; another swung west across Lake Ontario and took Fort Frontenac. With Canada cut in half and the Great Lakes country closed to the traders who had kept the interior Indians loyal, France was forced to abandon the west with scarcely a struggle; Fort Duquesne surrendered to an English force under General John Forbes without the firing of a single shot. Only the St. Lawrence Valley remained in French hands in the spring of 1759 and a year later Montreal was crushed between two strong expeditions, one moving up from Quebec and the other northward over the Lake Champlain water route.

Through the rest of the world the story was the same: smashing victories for British arms, crushing defeats for France and her Spanish ally, which entered the war in August, 1761, in a last desperate effort to stop the English juggernaut. One after another the West Indian possessions of Spain fell before Britain's conquering navy until the surrender of rich Cuba in August, 1762, spelled the doom of the once-mighty Spanish empire in the Caribbean. Two months later the Philippines capitulated just as England's continental allies were vanquishing the last of her European foes. Upon a triumphant England fell the pleasant task of dictating the peace. By the Treaty of Paris, finally signed in 1763, France ceded Canada and all lands east of the Mississippi to Britain. Spain relinquished the Floridas as the price for the return of Cuba and received from France compensation in the form of the vast trans-Mississippi territory known as Louisiana.

Yet across the flush of victory fell a shadow, for thinking men on both sides of the Atlantic knew that the war had ended the harmonious relationship between England and her colonies. The Americans, arrogantly proud of their role in the victorious struggle, believed that they should be rewarded by greater control over their own affairs, particularly as the elimination of hostile Canada no longer forced them to cling to the apron strings of the mother country. England, on the other hand, held that the colonists had failed to do their duty and should be compelled to accept more rigid imperial controls for the good of the whole empire. In this conflict of opinion, Britain's case was much the stronger: the Americans had shamefully abused their privileges. New England ship captains refused to give up their triangular trade and openly supplied the French and Spanish West Indies with the food needed to withstand repeated attacks by the British navy. Yankee farmers forced English commanders to import meat from across the Atlantic because they could secure a higher price for their cattle by driving them across the Canadian boundary and selling to French armies there. All the colonies had refused throughout the war to contribute what the home government considered a fair share of the men and money needed for victory. Colonial provincialism and indifference had forced England to fight an American war with English regulars and finance it with money from the pockets of English taxpayers.

It is hardly surprising that English statesmen were alarmed. Clearly the colonies had drifted too far from the mother country for their own or England's good. Long before the war ended, the ministry decided that the period of "salutary neglect" must end and new imperial controls be established. The attempt to reform the colonial system, carried on by a group of blundering British ministers who understood neither American problems nor American temperament, was to lead directly to the disruption of the empire.

II

THE COLONIAL MIND 1607–1763

Revolutions are not made, but born. The chain of events that transformed the loyal British subjects of 1763 to the war-enflamed rebels of 1776 could have wrought no such change had the American people not been ripe for independence. For a century and a half they had grown steadily in numbers, wealth, and self-confidence, until they stood on the eve of the Revolution as a mature, united, and liberty-loving people, physically and intellectually capable of caring for their own affairs. The story of that maturing social order to a point where a sense of unity and a belief in more popular rule were ingrained in the colonists is essential to any understanding of the revolutionary process.

THE INGREDIENTS OF REVOLUTION

Their unity was more real than apparent, for the three million people who inhabited the colonies in 1776 seemingly had little in common. Political differences created a barrier between the more democratically inclined frontiersmen whose small farms hugged the Appalachian foothills and the eastern aristocrats whose wealth derived from tidewater plantations or urban counting houses. Racial differences were just as formidable, for rubbing elbows in the colonies were Englishmen, Scots, Irishmen, Germans, Frenchmen, Dutchmen, Swedes, Jews, and Africans, all peacock-proud of their "national traditions" and many clinging doggedly to their Old World languages and customs. Nor did religion serve as a common bond in a land of Congregationalists, Presbyterians, Anglicans, Huguenots, Lutherans, Mennonites, Dunkers, Baptists, Catholics, Dutch Reformers, and German Reformers who squabbled endlessly among themselves. There seemed little basis for unity in this welter of races, tongues, and faiths; nevertheless, there was a basis for unity, for all the colonists, the Negro slaves alone excepted, shared a great common experience: they traced their origin to the European culture area.

This was decisive. No matter how great the superficial differences separating them, people of a common culture—those, that is, whose inherited ideas, values, habits, technical processes, and artifacts are similar—find unity simpler when faced with a crisis. If the colonists spoke in a babel of tongues, their words expressed a common body of ideas, the European climate of opinion. Whether they earned their living on plantations or in city market places, they all believed in the ethics and techniques of the capitalistic system to which they had been bred in their European homes. While they often carried their theological quarrels to the brink of warfare, Protestant, Jew, and Catholic worshiped the same God and held to the same basic code of public and private morals. They ranted against laxity in their neighbor's behavior, but they all lived in family units on the European model and shared the mores which underlay the social organization of Continental society. The fundamental clash of cultures within the orbit of English colonization was not between European and European; it was between the European—with his family life, his law of private property, his churches, his institutions for representative local government—and the Indian, who clung to very different religious taboos, to tribal organization, and to community of property. If America had been a crossroads for Asiatics, Africans, and other peoples from differing culture areas, cooperation in time of need would have been difficult; actually the basic common folkways of the varying streams of immigrants made unity easy.

The second ingredient of revolution—a faith in a more liberal social order—came less readily to the colonists. The seventeenth-century Europe from which they came was still largely medieval in its intellectual outlook. The masses accepted unquestioningly certain propositions that Europeans had scarcely doubted since the dawn of the Christian Era. All the universe, they believed, had been created by God in six days solely to serve as a habitation for the first human pair, Adam and Eve. For a time these mortals lived in contentment, but eventually they violated their Creator's express command, ate of the forbidden fruit, and were justly driven from their lovely Garden of Eden. As their wickedness and the wickedness of their descendants increased, God moved to blot out all mankind, sparing only Noah's family to repeople the earth after the Flood. The Creator, more pleased with His children, finally sent His son to live among them as their Savior. Christ's sacrifice not only convinced God that some men must be saved; it gave man the Gospel which pointed the road to salvation. Thus began the supreme conflict of history, with God and his angels arrayed against Satan and his sulphurous demons, each determined to secure the souls of as many people as possible.

From this sacred folklore—which Santayana has called the Christian Epic—medieval man derived the basic concepts that shaped his brief earthly existence. He must, he knew, never question the authority of either his religious or secular betters, for they alone could guide him to salvation. He must be wary of unconventional ideas, for these might be devices of the Devil. He must distrust all change or progress, for God had fixed a social order pleasing to His divine wisdom, and the serf who grumbled about his lot in this world might be courting eternal disaster in the next. He must never doubt the validity of existing knowledge, for the Creator had revealed to man all of the truth that man should know. He must be forever concerned with the universe about him, for the stars, planets, animals, and plants had all been created for his benefit; by observing them carefully he might learn the divine will. Complete reliance upon authority, intolerance toward new ideas, abhorrence of all change, preoccupation with the events of nature as they affected each individual—those were the concepts of the medieval mind. As long as they dominated colonial thought, as in the seventeenth century, a democratic revolution was unthinkable. The events of 1776 can be understood only in terms of the intellectual upheaval of the eighteenth century, which prepared the way for political rebellion.

THE MEDIEVAL MIND IN PURITAN NEW ENGLAND

The medieval mind in seventeenth-century America was best expressed in Puritan New England, for the essence of medievalism was authoritarian religious faith, and in no other section were the people so closely held within the bonds of one church. Their God was the God of John Calvin, a wrathful celestial tyrant who constantly reassured men of His concern for their welfare by repeated meddling in their daily affairs. This grim deity, they believed, had been moved by Christ's sacrifice to select certain of the elect for salvation. He had made His decision at that time for all eternity; certain men were predestined to be damned. Others were to be saved. Although they could do nothing to change their fate, they could lead exemplary lives that would fit them to appear before the Heavenly throne if they were fortunate enough to be of the elect. The underlying conviction of sin, the belief that man was evil, made of Puritanism a "thou-shalt-not" religion, a dour faith that forced its disciples to govern their actions and all others to conform to God's revealed will.

Yet Puritanism had its positive as well as its negative aspects. The typical Puritan of seventeenth-century Massachusetts was no sharp-nosed, grim-visaged, crape-garbed joy-killer who gained his earthly pleasure by denying pleasure to others. He was a robust spirit who could enjoy "seasonable merriment" as enthusiastically as the most sophisticated Anglican of Virginia. He might frown on celebrating that "wanton, bacchanalian feast" of the popish church, Christmas Day, but he transformed

Thanksgiving into a day of merriment and laughter. He goaded his legislature into passing laws against cardplaying, mixed dances, stage plays, bowling, shuffleboard, and performing on certain musical instruments (God did not want His chosen people to fritter away their precious time on useless pastimes), but he substituted other amusements that gave him equal pleasure: riotous times at college commencements, boisterous sessions over the rum bowl at the village tavern, joyous communion with his fellows on election day or at the mustering out of the militia. These were simple pleasures, but life was simple everywhere in the seventeenth century.

Puritanism added more than joy to the lives of New Englanders, for the intensity of their religious belief stimulated a vigorous intellectual life which dwarfed that of their fellow colonists. They were passionately devoted to education, believing that trained ministers were needed to interpret the Gospel and that congregations should be able to read and know the Scriptures. Massachusetts led the English-speaking world in 1642 by the enactment of a law requiring parents to teach their children the three R's. Five years later it again pioneered with a bolder measure that ordered all towns of fifty families to hire a schoolmaster, and all of a hundred to establish a Latin grammar school to prepare young men for college. Here, born of Puritanism, was America's first public school system, assuring the Massachusetts Bay Colony literate churchgoers and intelligent citizens. The other Puritan colonies during the next few years followed the example of Massachusetts.

A college was needed to top the educational edifice. In 1636 the Massachusetts General Court set aside four hundred pounds for a university; two years later the new school received its first students at Cambridge and adopted the name of Harvard to honor a Charlestown clergyman who gave it his library and half of his estate. For more than half a century Harvard was the only university in English-speaking America, and was attended by scholars from all the colonies, from Bermuda, and even from England. When the Virginia Anglicans established William and Mary to train ministers in their own faith in 1693 they founded Harvard's first rival. Yale followed in 1701. Two of the three colleges founded in America's first century owed their existence to Puritan zeal.

Nor did New England pioneer in education alone. The first colonial printing press, set up in Cambridge in 1639, issued tracts, sermons, almanacs, and broadsides for the edification of the Puritan fathers. And it was in New England that the first American newspapers were born. *Publick Occurrences Both Foreign and Domestic* came first, a tiny sheet designed to appear monthly "or if any Glut of Occurrences happen, oftener," but this succumbed to Boston censorship after its first issue in September, 1690. Others were more successful; the Boston *News-Letter*

(1704) and the Boston *Gazette* (1719) were both thriving publications before any other colony possessed a single newspaper. Puritanism was clearly no stifling force that hampered intellectual expression; instead it inspired its disciples to unusual efforts so that seventeenth-century New England was truly the intellectual hub of America.

The Puritan authors reacted to the stimulus. Some wrote histories to inform posterity of their sufferings in behalf of the true faith, dull local chronicles most of them, but some rising to the heights of William Bradford's cadenced prose in the *History of Plymouth Plantation*. Others penned theological tracts of enough excellence to attract the attention of churchmen on both sides of the Atlantic. Others compiled almanacs that provided reading matter for rural New England, or dashed off single-sheet broadsides, hawked through city streets, with literary comments upon events of the day. But the one form of expression to which every New England writer aspired was poetry, and countless verses of would-be authors offer an excellent example of intense Puritan conviction and the varying ways in which such a faith was given popular expression. Michael Wigglesworth, Anne Bradstreet, and Edward Taylor were typical of many.

Wigglesworth's dreadful epic, *The Day of Doom* (1662), was a crude description of the Last Judgment written in doggerel with the obvious purpose of frightening New Englanders into strict rectitude. It pictured a cruel God and a merciless Savior sitting in judgment on the world's sinners and visiting upon them horrible condemnation to eternal hell-fire. One well-known passage described the pleas of newborn babes for salvation:

> Then to the Bar, all they drew near who dy'd in Infancy
> And never had or good or bad effected personally,
> But from the womb unto the tomb were straightway carried,
> (Or at the least ere they transgrest) who thus began to plead:

> If for our own transgressions, or disobedience,
> We here did stand at thy left-hand just were the Recompense:
> But *Adam's* guilt our souls hath spilt, his fault is charged on us
> And that alone hath overthrown and utterly undone us.

But this plea availed not, for God answered:

> You sinners are, and such a share as sinners may expect,
> Such you shall have, for I do save none but mine own Elect.
> Yet to compare your sin with their, who liv'd a longer time,
> I do confess yours is much less, though every sin's a crime.
> A crime it is, therefore in bliss you may not hope to dwell;
> But unto you I shall allow the easiest room in Hell.

This message—stanza after stanza of it—was carried into nearly every New England home, for *The Day of Doom* was so popular that one in every twenty-five persons bought a copy.

The power of Puritan faith was illustrated as fully, and in far more pleasant form, in the writings of Anne Bradstreet. Pioneer housewife, mother of eight children, devout believer, she expressed her faith not by denouncing sinners but by worshipfully observing the Divine Hand in the wonders of nature:

> Then on a stately Oak I cast mine Eye,
> Whose ruffling top the clouds seem'd to aspire;
> How long since thou wast in thine Infancy?
> Thy strength, and stature, more thy years admire,
> Hath hundred winters past since thou wast born?
> Or thousand since thou breakest thy shell of horn,
> If so, all these as nought, Eternity doth scorn.

Religion was also the inspiration of Edward Taylor, who preached the Gospel at Westfield, Massachusetts, while patiently writing passionate eulogies to his Savior. His lyrical lines resembled those of no other New England poet:

> Oh! that thy love might overflow my Heart!
> To fire the same with Love: for Love I would.
> But oh! my streightend Breast! my Lifeless Sparke!
> My Fireless Flame! What Chilly Love, and Cold?
> In measure small! in Manner Chilly! See!
> Lord, blow the Coal: Thy Love Enflame in mee.

Taylor's fervent adoration, the gentle simplicity of Anne Bradstreet, the humorless bombast of Wigglesworth were all facets of Puritanism. New Englanders might express their faith in different ways, but express it they did in a volume of output far exceeding the other colonies.

The spiritual ardor that inspired the intellectual outpourings of the Puritans was typical of medievalism; so also was the intolerant attitude with which they viewed dissenters. Like the devout of the Middle Ages, they were absolutely certain that one path alone led to salvation. Why, then, should dissent be tolerated? Liberty of conscience, declared one colonial divine, "is a liberty to blaspheme, a liberty to seduce others from the true God. A liberty to tell lies in the name of the Lord"; another believed that "'tis Satan's policy, to plead for an indefinite and boundless toleration." All who disagreed with them must be converted, banished, or killed. The Puritans tried to convert as many as possible, but when persuasion failed they turned unhesitatingly to harsher alternatives. Better to cause a little suffering, better to spill the blood of a few of Satan's servants, than to risk the salvation of God's chosen people.

Intolerance was expressed both in the Puritans' relations with each other and in their contacts with unbelievers. Within their tightly knit society democracy had no place; the will of the individual was completely subordinate to the will of an authoritarian church and state. This was God's wish according to the divines, who were certain that they alone understood His decrees. Laymen without this sacred knowledge should not be allowed to risk their souls by governing themselves; the ideal state was a theocratic aristocracy rigidly controlled by clergymen and their magisterial allies. "Democracy," wrote the Reverend John Cotton, "I do not conceive that God did ever ordain as a fit government for either church or commonwealth." This distrust of popular government was shown in the rigid moral codes that governed the behavior of everyone to the most trivial detail. Laws prescribed the type of clothing to be worn, regulated the length of men's hair, forbade work or pleasureful pursuits on the Sabbath, compelled church attendance, banned swearing or idle gossip, and in countless other ways shaped the conduct of every individual into a pattern deemed to have the approbation of God. These irksome restrictions were accepted unquestioningly by most Puritans, partly because adherence to authority was inherent in medieval thought and partly because, as hard-working middle-class Englishmen, they welcomed a standard of conduct that sanctified thrift and outlawed "sinful," time-wasting pleasures.

Toward those of other faiths the Puritans were even more intolerant. Some were banished; Roger Williams, Anne Hutchinson, John Wheelwright, and a dozen others were driven from seventeenth-century Massachusetts to seek refuge in other colonies or to found wilderness Zions of their own. Other purveyors of dissent who refused to bow to banishment or exclusion were treated more harshly. Baptists suffered under the lash. The Quaker missionaries who began to invade the colony in 1656, belligerently demanding the right to make converts, were more difficult to suppress. The first to arrive—two women from Barbados—were clapped into a boarded-up jail where they could talk with no one for five weeks, then deported. Eight more who came a month later were treated in the same way, but this time the panic-stricken colonial legislature decreed that any ship captain bringing these "Devil's-disciples" to Boston should be fined a hundred pounds and that the Quakers were to be severely lashed. When this failed to stop their coming, the law was changed to include boring the tongue with a red-hot iron, and finally the death penalty was adopted for any members of the Society of Friends who refused to stay banished. Three were hanged in 1659 and one more was similarly disposed of a year later before rising popular opposition forced the New England fathers to accept a milder means of persecuting these troublesome invaders.

THE WITCH HUNT

Far worse than the Quakers (who, after all, could be detected easily and summarily dealt with) were the Devil's agents who disguised themselves as commonplace New Englanders the better to carry out their satanic master's evil wiles. These were the witches—loathsome men and women who sold their souls to Satan in return for worldly goods and supernatural powers. No one in the Christian world doubted the existence of these fearful creatures, for ever since the dawning skepticism of the Reformation, theologians had sought to scare people back into the fold by conjuring up tales of these dread agents of Satan. For a century before America was settled, witchcraft persecutions occurred with horrible regularity in both the Catholic and Protestant countries of Europe. In France, Italy, and Spain during the late sixteenth century, travelers repeatedly reported the countryside alight with the burning bodies of witches. In England and Scotland hundreds of innocent victims were tortured into gasping out weird tales of midnight rides and secret meetings with their evil master, then hurried away to the waiting faggots. Belief in witchcraft was universal throughout the Christian world.

That witches should appear in America was not strange. One was detected in Virginia long before Massachusetts was settled. Goodwife Wright was her name, and the evidence against her was damning. When she cursed a man, "he having very fair game to shoot at yet could never kill anything"; when she was rejected as midwife by a local woman, the newborn baby died; when a neighbor refused to sell her some chickens, the hen and all her brood fell sick. Many a witch went to the stake in Europe on similar circumstantial evidence, yet Goody Wright was apparently not even convicted. Witchcraft trials became regular features of colonial life, but in the middle and southern colonies all the accused were either acquitted or meted out some punishment milder than execution. On the one occasion outside New England where death was decreed, a practical-minded governor commuted the sentence to life imprisonment after the accused witch agreed to serve as his lifetime servant. Only in the Puritan colonies did the great superstition claim any colonial lives.

There the excitement accompanying the Puritan Revolution in England set the stage for the first executions. Connecticut achieved the dubious honor of hanging the first witch—one Achsah Young of Windsor in 1647 —but Massachusetts soon followed and in the next sixteen years fourteen of the Devil's creatures died on New England gallows. Then followed a period of calm before the unrest accompanying the Glorious Revolution set the witch-hunters on the trail once more. Salem Village, a backward little town north of Boston, was their hunting ground, and their instruments were a handful of young girls who had listened overlong to the voodoo tales of a half-crazed old Negro slave belonging to the local minister. Early in 1692 these "afflicted children" began showing signs of satanic possession, shrieking, casting themselves about, and mumbling meaningless jargon. Learned men who flocked to listen urged them to name their tormentors and they complied so freely that within a few weeks dozens of persons were waiting trial for witchcraft. Then the courts swung into action; witch after witch was summarily tried and hurried away to the hanging post. Before the epidemic wore itself out of its own excesses, nineteen persons and two dogs were hanged, and one brave old man was pressed to death under heavy stones for refusing to accept trial after his plea of not guilty.

INTELLECTUAL PREPARATION FOR REVOLUTION

The Salem persecution was only a minor episode in the tragic story of a great European superstition, yet it actually heralded a new day. For some time before the 1690's thinking colonials were straining against the shackles that restricted their intellectual freedom—the autocratic clerical controls, the atmosphere of intolerance, the authoritarian disapproval of free inquiry—and that were parts of the medieval inheritance. Now the popular reaction against the witch-hunters offered these restive elements new hope. Their quickened efforts during the early eighteenth century gave the colonists a new creed—a creed moving toward democracy, equality, and liberty of conscience, a creed recognizing man as an individual and not as a God-controlled automaton, a creed built upon the broad humanitarian principle that each person should work out his own economic and social destiny, a creed stressing continuous progress and the improvability of man and society. These were the enlightened new concepts that freed the Americans from dependence on medieval authority and prepared them intellectually for the liberal upthrust which brought them independence.

Such an invigorating faith was far from new when it stirred the colonial consciousness in the eighteenth century; for generations advanced thinkers had hammered steadily away at the citadel of indifference that protected the ordinary people from new ideas. This intellectual assault was carried on principally in Europe, but the American pioneers in this movement were not without importance, for their efforts prepared the colonies for acceptance of more modern doctrines when the barriers of ignorance and superstition were at last overrun. The intellectual atmosphere of eighteenth-century America can best be understood by examining the ground-breaking efforts of these few prophets of modernism and viewing the harvest that came when the seeds of the European Enlightenment were finally transplanted to the lands across the ocean.

A supreme object of the seventeenth-century colonial reformers who led the assault on the fortress of medievalism was to secure greater tolerance for unorthodox religious ideas. Most important among them was Roger Williams, whose exile to the wilderness about Narragansett Bay in 1636 provided the opportunity to launch an important experiment in democracy. There, in the colony of Rhode Island, all freeholders were eligible to vote, all men assured an equal division of land, and all "persons distressed for Conscience" freely welcomed. To this oasis in a desert of intolerance came the poor, the oppressed, the persecuted, from both England and America. Pious Puritans shuddered at this reeking "sewer" of heresy and immortality in their midst, little knowing that the very ideas which they most scorned would become the ideals of their own descendants in a future America.

Two other colony founders, although contributing less to the growth of toleration, played a significant role. Lord Baltimore, realizing that well-to-do English Catholics would never migrate to Maryland in sufficient numbers to dominate the colony, took pains to protect his fellow religionists with the famed Toleration Act, adopted by the colonial legislature in 1649. This farseeing measure proclaimed the equality of all faiths when nearly all Christendom accepted the principle that each sect must dominate or be dominated. Even more enduring was the contribution of William Penn, whose intense belief in liberal Quakerism did much to offset his aristocratic background and love of efficiency. His colony of Pennsylvania imitated Rhode Island in its liberal land policy, democratic government, and virtually complete religious freedom, but Penn went beyond Williams in instilling a humanitarian concern for the common man, the outcome of the Quaker principle of universal brotherhood. The liberalism of Penn and Williams set an example for all the European world—one not wholly unnoted among liberal philosophers of eighteenth-century France.

Yet labor as they did in the vineyards of reform, Williams and Penn could have accomplished little had not conditions in America favored their views. Religious toleration made little headway in Europe because each nation was dominated by one favored church which sought to stamp out dissent. In the colonies the situation was different. In the north and the south, state churches reigned supreme—the Puritans in New England and the Anglicans below Maryland—but lying between were the numerous middle colonies where no one sect was powerful enough to impose its will on others. Here Presbyterians, Lutherans, Mennonites, Dunkers, German Reformers, Dutch Reformers, Huguenots, Catholics, Baptists, and Quakers all met and mingled; each had to tolerate the other. To their surprise they found that persuasion won more followers than force, and that voluntary contributions brought the churches as much financial support as did taxes in the regions where one church was officially established. The system of "voluntarism" not only provided a practical basis for separation of church and state but gave the world the first public demonstration that freedom of worship induced rather than diminished popular belief in religion and morality.

An advancing tolerance prepared the colonies for the stimulating thought currents that surged across the Atlantic during the eighteenth century, sweeping aside many of the relics of medieval superstition. A body of refreshing new ideas, collectively known as the Enlightenment, they largely reshaped men's thinking about the universe, about society, and about themselves. And from this new orientation came new doctrines: democracy, rationalism, toleration, liberalism, and equality which, firmly engrained in colonial thought by 1776, provided the intellectual preparation for the American Revolution.

The European scholars who contributed to the Enlightenment attacked concepts as old as Christendom and as unchallengeable as faith. Scientists and philosophers launched the assault, for before improvement in other directions was possible, man had to cast off the concept that the universe had been created for his benefit alone. All medieval men believed that the earth, man's abode, was the center of the heavens. They believed also that each occurrence in the giant structure of creation was especially arranged by the Maker for their benefit; the sun rose, the stars shone, comets flashed through the skies, earthquakes shook the planet in response to specific orders from God. Certain were they that the Creator's will could be learned only by watching these evidences of his handiwork and by searching the Scriptures. They were equally certain that life on earth was brief and unimportant and that they should spend their limited earthly span preparing for eternity instead of attempting to improve their lot on this temporary habitation. For doubt, for inquiry, for progress there was no place in the thought pattern of the static medieval world.

The first breach in this wall of tradition was made in the sixteenth century, when a Polish scholar, Nikolaus Copernicus, publishing a slim little book *On the Revolutions of the Heavenly Bodies* (1543), advanced the startling thesis that the earth revolved about the sun. The implications of this simple theory were staggering, for if ever a belief was undisputed it was that the earth, as man's habitation, was the center of the universe. Such a revolutionary hypothesis could not be accepted at once, but over the next centuries other scientists gradually added proof—Tycho Brahe of Denmark, Johannes Kepler and Gottfried Liebnitz of Germany, Galileo Galilei of Italy, Isaac Newton of England—until by the end of the seventeenth century doubt could no longer be entertained by educated men. A new universe, far different from the medieval world, emerged. The earth appeared as only a minor planet revolving about an obscure sun in a vast cosmic ocean of heavenly bodies. God, it was now supposed, did not rule this vast creation by special decrees but through a body of natural laws. And most important of all, thinking men realized that these truths had been learned not by searching the Scriptures or by reasoning from accepted propositions, but by questioning, investigating, and drawing conclusions. Doubt rather than faith held the key to knowledge; truth could be found in the laboratory as well as in monastic cells.

These exciting scholarly revelations widened the influence of the Enlightenment and permeated every phase of thought. Scientists had questioned one unimpeachable authority—the church itself—to prove that natural laws rather than a special divine dispensation governed the universe. If this were so, why should not laws of nature, rather than arbitrary rules laid down by monarchs, shape the conduct of man? Reasoning in this way, scholars developed a cardinal point in the philosophy of the Enlightenment: that man's character was the product of his natural environment rather than the result of a special creative effort by God. Once this basic concept was accepted, the way was open for a revolution in social thought as epoch-making as the scientific upheaval. The result was a slow recasting, during the seventeenth and eighteenth centuries, of archaic ideas on man's relation to society, to government, and to the economic structure. Where the sixteenth century had stressed the relation of man to God, the eighteenth tended to stress the relation of man to man. This new emphasis moved toward a more democratic conception of the age-old problem of the relative claims of the individual and society.

In his *Essay Concerning Human Understanding* (1690), a seventeenth-century English philosopher, John Locke, blazed the intellectual trail into one unexplored field. Man, he held, possessed no innate ideas —no ideas, that is, either of good or of evil specifically implanted within him by the Creator. If a man were bad he owed his sad state to his own weakness and poor training, and not to any initial depravity inherited from Adam's fall. If a man were good he could thank the happy combination of experiences that made up his life rather than divine guidance. From this proposition Locke argued that faulty institutions and an inhumane social order would warp human nature toward injustice and evil. From the same proposition he advanced the idea of progress eventually to become basic in democratic thought: the conclusion that any improvement in environment would also improve man. By bettering social and economic conditions, by sweeping away the poverty and ignorance which bred evil in man, human nature could be changed and society advanced toward perfection. Here was a challenge to reformers: man could add a cubit to his stature, reform could assure progress toward a higher and better civilization.

The impact of the Enlightenment on political thought was reflected in Jean Jacques Rousseau's *Social Contract* (1762), which summed up the ideas of a whole generation. Rousseau and his fellow theorists rebelled against the concepts of divine right and inherited authority just as Locke revolted against innate ideas. Rousseau held that men, when emerging from an "original" state of nature, had entered into social contracts with a central authority to secure legal protection and had surrendered certain of their freedoms in return. As men had created the state, they could expect their governments to protect certain of their natural rights which they had not given up. If any ruler interfered with their rights to life, liberty, or property, they could legally overthrow him by revolution. Thus the Enlightenment taught men a new theory of government and provided them with a technique for redress.

The economic doctrines of the new philosophy were also voiced by countless theorists before they were put in classic form by Adam Smith in *The Wealth of Nations* (1776). Basic to Smith's thinking was the natural right of all individuals to improve themselves economically as well as morally and politically. This they could do only if they were allowed to operate in an unrestricted environment where the sole controls were natural laws such as the law of supply and demand. Hence Adam Smith favored a laissez-faire policy on the part of governments: the abolition of all laws restricting interest rates, the stoppage of meddling in economic affairs, the dissolution of monopolistic trading concerns that controlled foreign commerce, the removal of trade barriers which hampered the free movement of goods, and the adoption of a hands-off attitude toward business in general. Stimulation of trade and industry would certainly follow in a free society governed by the natural laws so dear to the hearts of eighteenth-century liberals.

Adam Smith was only one of a distinguished group of moral philosophers whose prime concern was the relation of the individual to society; equally prominent was the school of French economists, the physiocrats, who added the term "laissez faire" to the world's vocabulary. As they employed the phrase, laissez faire did not equate with the later nineteenth-century fetish of immunity of private property from public controls. Classic economic liberalism in the tradition of Adam Smith simply signified free trade; this required the destruction of mercantile monopolies and economic nationalism, and elimination of governmental interference which stifled the growth of free competition. Adam Smith himself, friendly toward trade unions, opposed the mercantilist defense of low wages and was fearful not of unions but of high prices fixed by a "conspiracy" of businessmen in restraint of competition.

Although the proponents of the Enlightenment in the main were spokesmen for the propertied middle class rather than the masses, there were democratic seeds in their social criticism. Certainly their intention was not to strip governments of the power to govern. The eighteenth-century assault was not on governmental power to protect the public interest but upon perversion of that power by powerful privileged interests, whereby the economic and political masters of monarchies, exploiting consumers and workers, had prevented the nations from achieving a greater total wealth and their peoples from gaining higher standards of living. Underlying the protest of the Enlightenment against mercantile nationalism were liberal implications—a revival of demand for public policies to protect the neglected consumer, a revolutionary conception of progress away from the regime of rule for the few toward a more responsible government, and an economy dedicated to the common welfare.

These doctrines, developed and formalized by European philosophers, found ardent advocates in America. The lack of hampering restrictions, the absence of an established church, the temptation to experiment natural in a new country, and the predominance of a middle-class population accelerated the revolution on the American side of the Atlantic. By the time of the colonial political revolt, its impact had transformed scientific thought, weakened the hold of the churches, stimulated educational progress, recast economic theory and institutions, and inspired so deep a respect for liberty and equality that the struggle for independence was almost inevitable.

In the scientific realm progress in America was necessarily slow— material tasks in any new country left little time for theorizing—but a few scholars demonstrated the extent to which the principles of the Enlightenment had won acceptance. The greatest strides were made in the natural sciences, where discoveries could be applied by a nation of farmers. The leading experimenter in this field was John Bartram, whose careful observation of New World plants laid the basis for future botanical study in America. Typical of his inquiring attitude were his microscopic studies of "the male and female parts in vegetables"— observations later used by Linnaeus for important work in systematic classification. Only slightly less notable were the experiments of Cadwallader Colden, versatile lieutenant governor of New York, which disclosed sex differences in plants and the value of cross-fertilization; and the labors of James Logan, Pennsylvania official, who pioneered in the study of physiological botany.

Even more remarkable was the progress in the physical sciences, where the material rewards of experimentation were less obvious. One of the enlightened investigators who reflected his fellow scientists' broadening vision was David Rittenhouse, a Philadelphia mechanic and clockmaker. He constructed a workable orrery—a mechanical model of the planetary system—which was the marvel of his age. He observed the effect of diffraction grating on light, recorded significant astronomical observations, and advanced a molecular theory of magnetism that smacked of the twentieth rather than the eighteenth century:

Magnetical particles of matter are a necessary constituent part of that metal which we call iron. . . . These magnetical particles I suppose have each a north and a south pole, and that they retain their polarity, however the metal may be fused or otherwise wrought. In a piece of iron which shews no signs of magnetism these magnetical particles lie irregularly, with their poles pointing in all possible directions, they therefore mutually destroy each other's effects. By giving magnetism to a piece of iron we do nothing more than arrange these particles. . . .

Few scientists of that day, even in Europe, had the vision to state so bold a hypothesis of the constitution of matter.

Yet Rittenhouse was no bolder than his contemporary, Professor John Winthrop of Harvard, whose experiments in mathematics, astronomy, and physics won him membership in the austere Royal Society of London. One of his outstanding contributions was inspired by an earthquake which shook New England in 1755. For centuries clerics and scientists alike had agreed that these disastrous rumblings occurred only when God demonstrated His infinite strength as a warning to earthly sinners, but Winthrop discarded this medieval notion and in 1759 advanced the first modern theory of earthquakes. They were caused, he said, by the expansion of subterranean gases and took place whenever natural conditions were favorable. This precise statement was notable both for its reliance upon natural law as an explanation of a terrifying phenomenon and for the method used by Winthrop to reach his hypothesis: he observed the pendulumlike movement of houses during the quake, reasoned that their motion could only be caused by energy transmitted through the earth's crust, and concluded that these could be formed by the expansion and contraction of gases alone. An example of inductive logic, it presaged the expansion of science and the emergence of the scientific method.

But modern as Winthrop was, he was dwarfed as an intellectual figure by the greatest scientist of colonial America—Benjamin Franklin. Franklin's contributions, as significant in thought as in statecraft, won him an even wider reputation in Europe than in America. His interests were all-embracing and his inquiring mind was ever active. He mapped the Gulf Stream, studied the interaction of oil and water, invented bifocal lenses, proposed steam engines for water navigation, noted the varying ability of different materials to conduct solar heat, built a glass harmonica, experimented with balloon flights, propounded methods of cooling by evaporation, and carried on a dozen other experiments in as many branches of knowledge. All his research was carried on at the highest theoretical level, yet Franklin showed the effect of his environment by constantly seeking practical applications for his discoveries. From his study of hot and cold air movements came his invention of the Franklin stove and a wealth of sound advice on how to cure smoking chimneys; from his studies of solar heat, warnings against wearing dark clothes in summer. Blending of the speculative and material typified all America's reaction to the Enlightenment.

Franklin's greatest contributions were in the field of electricity. Approaching this little-known medium with a fresh mind, he reconducted all the experiments described in the limited scientific literature of Europe. His careful observations convinced him that electricity existed in a fluidlike state in many substances. When some of this fluid was drawn into another body, that body became "electrified positively—or plus," while the material losing fluid was "electrified negatively—or minus." This was the first statement of the "single fluid" theory that underlay later research and the first use of the descriptive terms, "plus" and "minus," to replace the awkward phraseology used by European scientists. Franklin was now prepared to perform his best-known and most awe-inspiring experiment. In 1753, on a field near Philadelphia, he brought down electricity from the skies through the string of his famous kite, a startling discovery indeed. Lightning was no "Heaven's arrow" unleashed by a wrathful God to smite sinners, but a phenomenon explainable by natural laws. No single experiment in the history of eighteenth-century science better illustrated the skepticism with which scholars of that day viewed the superstitions of the past.

Mounting scientific proof of a universe governed by laws of nature greatly influenced religious thought. For centuries Calvinistic churchmen had pictured an omnipotent Deity who ruled His universe by divine decree; now scholars pictured God as a supreme architect who allowed natural laws to govern His creation. Theologians had constructed a wrathful Divinity who sat on high and who predestined most men to eternal damnation for Adam's sin; eighteenth-century thinkers constructed a new God, no angry tyrant but a kindly friend who took joy in saving as many of His creatures as His benevolence could avail. On these two fundamental doctrines the Calvinistic churches and the Enlightenment completely disagreed; one or the other must back down.

The orthodox churches finally divided; their ministers retreated gradually to a rationalistic position in which God was viewed as a reasoning and kindly Savior who had demonstrated His essential goodness by the creation itself as well as by endowing man with a portion of His own divine nature. By the middle of the eighteenth century even the more enlightened Puritan clergy began to modify the concepts of total depravity, predestination, and a meddlesome Deity who constantly interfered in man's daily affairs. The less orthodox among the congregations went beyond this point to embrace deistic doctrines then gaining ground among European intellectuals. That reason was the sole basis for belief became their cardinal creed. Rejecting those portions of the Scriptures that could not stand the test of rational examination, they refused to believe the Biblical miracles or prophecies, and worshiped a Supreme Being who ruled His universe by reasonable laws without interfering in human activities. Long before the Revolution these liberal beliefs gained wide acceptance among the upper middle-class group in the colonies, although the lower classes were largely within the orthodox fold, in part the result of a powerful revival—the Great Awakening—staged in the 1730's.

The liberalization of colonial theology facilitated the spread of more enlightened economic beliefs. To a people who lived in a land of opportunity, where systems of free labor and free enterprise were already deeply implanted, and where cheap land offered a constant means of escape from urban poverty, such beliefs came naturally. Americans had already developed an occupational mobility unknown to Europe; farmers were not bound to the land by feudal relics but drifted constantly westward with the frontier, while city artisans were equally ready to move to any job that promised greater returns. Class lines, although clearly drawn, were not so rigidly fixed as in the older countries of Christendom; many a respected farmer or merchant had come to America as an indentured servant. Freedom of opportunity and the inevitability of progress—two fundamental doctrines of the Enlightenment—were firmly ingrained in American thought even before their revolutionary impact began to transform European economy.

Hence prophets of the new freedom could express themselves as openly on economic as on religious subjects. During the eighteenth century their pamphlets, widely published by colonial presses, all stressed the twin themes that man's will rather than God's shaped economic developments, and that improvement was both desirable and inevitable. Benjamin Franklin was the best known—and the most typically middle class—of these writers. His pleas for an elastic paper currency not only gladdened the hearts of artisans and small farmers, but contributed to a world understanding of the quantitative theory of money. Land or labor, Franklin insisted, represented the true measure of value rather than any precious metal, and he argued that in colonial America, where land was abundant, wages should be higher than they were. Like Adam Smith, he denounced tariffs as a handicap to international trade and urged taxes that would benefit society as a whole rather than protect special property interests. These theories of the Enlightenment made Franklin the darling of the colonial working people.

PRELIMINARY SKIRMISHES AGAINST THE ESTABLISHED ORDER

The underlying American faith in freedom and progress was shown in the refusal of shippers or manufacturers to obey laws that hampered their trade. When England tried to restrict tobacco shipments to the mother country, so much of the golden weed was taken to Glasgow that the Scottish city became one of the leading tobacco marts of Europe. When importation of Spanish wines was forbidden, so much was smuggled in that these wines frequently sold more widely and cheaply than legally imported beverages. When tea was taxed just before the Revolution, the illegal imports were so large that in 1765 only 150,000 of the 1,500,000 pounds consumed by the colonists entered through regular customs ports. When in 1750 Parliament ordered the Americans to stop all iron manufacturing, they ignored the restrictive decree so generally that twenty-five years later only 3,500 of the 30,000 tons of raw iron mined were exported while colonial home industry consumed the rest. When the mother country tried to check any inflation in the colonial currency hurtful to her own creditor classes, the colonies responded with so many devious devices to get money into circulation—laws establishing mints, laws forbidding the export of coins, laws raising the value of specie in circulation, laws authorizing the use of commodities as money, laws providing for the circulation of short-term bills of credit, laws setting up "land banks" to issue paper currency with mortgages as security—that Parliament finally was forced to admit defeat. By 1750 so much paper money circulated in the colonies that its value in relation to gold coins varied from one to eight in Connecticut to one to twenty-six in Rhode Island. One Virginian wrote admiringly of his fellow Americans: "They have a great dexterity at palliating a perjury so well as to leave no taste of it in their mouth, nor can any people like them slip through a penal Statute."

The colonists, clearly, had reached a point at which they refused to recognize any external authority on economic matters. They would accept English laws if certain that their own trade would not suffer; they would refuse to obey any measures that threatened their prosperity. Although something of the mercantile spirit of economic nationalism survived, the medieval spirit of servile obedience was gone; the colonies were in open rebellion on commercial and economic issues long before the Revolution. There remained only the question: would they resort to political revolt if the mother country seriously attempted to enforce any of its unpopular economic legislation?

For this possibility the Enlightenment was also a preparation. The forward-looking political doctrines advanced by European scholars during the eighteenth century were readily accepted by countless Americans who found that the natural rights philosophy fitted well into their spiritual and physical environment. They knew, as did Locke or Rousseau, that the first duty of all rulers was to protect the life, liberty, and property of their subjects. They accepted unquestioningly the right of any people to overthrow a tyrant who failed in this prime duty. They believed implicitly in certain basic rights: government by consent of the governed, the justice of revolution, the control of the state by popular majorities. These doctrines were popularized in America by ministers and pamphleteers all through the eighteenth century. Particularly active in their behalf were the Puritan clergymen who had learned their revolutionary doctrine in the school of Locke and Milton and Sidney. Any uprising of any people against a tyrant, one declared, "is but a reasonable way of vindicating their liberties and just rights . . . . a making use of the means, and the only means, which God has put into their power, for mutual and self defense. And it would be highly criminal of them not to make use of this means." Rebellion against autocracy was a religious duty in America long before Thomas Jefferson enshrined that doctrine in the Declaration of Independence.

As on economic questions, this rebellious spirit was shown more by action than by words. When eastern-dominated legislatures tried to inflict their will on back-country settlers, the frontiersmen protested so vehemently that in one case a pitched battle resulted—the Battle of Alamance (1771) fought between easterners and westerners in North Carolina. Even more indicative of the dawning liberalism were the efforts in the colonies to shake off the shackles of censorship that had long restricted freedom of the press throughout the European world. The first assault on this undemocratic system came in New York during 1735, when the colonial officials arrested John Peter Zenger, editor of the New York *Weekly Journal,* for daring to criticize their tyrannical policies. Zenger's attorney, the eminent Andrew Hamilton of Philadelphia, astounded the trial court: he admitted that his client had written the libelous remarks, then asked the jury to agree with him that the damning words were not "false, scandalous, and seditious." "The question before the court . . .," he said, "is not of small nor private concern; it is not the cause of the poor printer, nor of New York, alone. . . . It is the cause of liberty . *. . the liberty both of exposing and opposing arbitrary power by speaking and writing Truth." This moving plea, the verdict of "not guilty" that followed, and the "huzzas in the hall" when the jury's finding was announced, all showed the growing spirit of liberty in the colonies. The Zenger case did not change the old libel laws, but it did assure critics of the government a chance of immunity from persecution by their victims, and marked an important step forward toward eventual freedom of the press.

Despite these gains, the American people were far from free—socially, economically, or politically—in 1763. An established church still dominated many colonies, Jews and Catholics were mildly persecuted in all, Americans still purchased Africans snatched from their homeland and sold them, property qualifications barred fully half the people from the franchise, restrictions on freedom of expression remained, a vast gulf separated the upper from the lower classes. Yet thinking men were already convinced that these autocratic vestiges must be swept away and knew that the assault had begun. Disciples of the Enlightenment, thoroughly committed to the principles of freedom, equality, and rationalism, only awaited a favorable opportunity to translate their theories into action. The spadework for revolution was completed.

III

THE AGE OF REVOLUTION 1763-1787

From the close of the Seven Years' War (1763) to the inauguration of George Washington as President of the United States one problem before the American people overshadowed all others: how could they reconcile authority and personal liberty? England tried to find an answer between 1763 and 1776, but her formula so overemphasized authority that the colonists would have none of it, not because they wanted independence but because their fundamental English rights were threatened. After 1776 the struggle was transferred to America, where patriots built new governments and tore them down again in their quest for a workable political organization that would not infringe on their sacred liberties. Not until the federal Constitution was drafted in 1787 and the Bill of Rights added in 1791 did they find a partial answer.

CLASH OF AUTHORITY AND LIBERTY

That this problem faced the Americans or that they found a solution difficult is not surprising, for the issue is age-old and as pertinent today as in the eighteenth century. England had been groping for an answer since feudal barons wrung from a reluctant King John a Magna Carta that assured them certain rudimentary liberties. Over the next centuries these noblemen, joined eventually by leaders from the growing middle class, took other steps to protect themselves from the tyranny of their monarchs—steps aimed at building up a strong legislature to check royal power. Their progress was slow but sure: the summoning of the first Commons by a rebellious baronial squire in 1265, the substitution in the fifteenth century of parliamentary legislation by "bill" for the older "petitions" to the king, the "Petition of Right" in 1628 which demanded that taxes should not be levied without legislative consent, the Puritan rebellion against Charles I's autocracy, the "Glorious Revolution" engineered by Parliament in 1689 to install William of Orange on the throne and to establish the "Bill of Rights" which guaranteed the perpetuation of legislative authority, the refusal of kings to veto laws after 1707—

The father of American Democracy. A portrait of Thomas Jefferson from the brush of Gilbert Stuart, portraitist of the Revolutionary era. *(Courtesy Chicago Historical Society)*

The father of his country. *Above*—George Washington as seen by Charles Willson Peale, a representative of the nationalism that Washington symbolized. *(Courtesy New-York Historical Society) Below*—"Parson Weems' Fable." An early national myth in twentieth-century satirical reproduction by Grant Wood. *(Courtesy Mrs. John P. Marquand)*

Cotton Mather, priest of a Puritan past and herald of a scientific future, lived on the threshold of the Enlightenment. *(Courtesy Chicago Historical Society)*

John Locke, philosopher of the Enlightenment at home and in the colonies, rationalized England's revolution and aided Americans in rationalizing theirs.

(Bettmann Archive)

Thomas Paine, appealing to the common sense of common men, spread the concepts of rationalism and democratic liberty on both sides of the Atlantic.

(Bettmann Archive)

The American Revolution, appealing both to force and reason, allowed colonists to protest seeming wrongs with tar and feathers and pens. *Left*—Bostonians, resorting to vigilante justice, vent their spleen on a helpless royal official. (London print, 1774, *courtesy Metropolitan Museum of Art*) *Below*—John Hancock writes out his defiance with a gentlemanly flourish of the pen. (Early nineteenth-century Currier & Ives print, *courtesy Library of Congress*)

these were the landmarks in Parliament's rise to supreme power. When colonists spoke of the "rights of Englishmen" they meant the rights of Parliament to rule itself without royal interference.

By the middle of the eighteenth century, however, Englishmen who had embraced the liberalism of the Enlightenment saw that their struggle to create a strong legislature as a check on the executive had called into being a Frankenstein monster as dangerous to popular liberty as an unrestrained monarch. Few of the people were represented in Parliament, for the Lords Temporal and Spiritual held their offices by right of birth or position, while franchise restrictions and archaic election laws kept all but a handful of wealthy landowners and merchants from voting for members of the Commons. Yet its power over all was virtually unlimited; no written constitution bridled the acts of the eighteenth-century oligarchy. Most Britons failed to take alarm; so accustomed were they to authority and so impressed with the oft-voiced platitudes from the ruling class about English liberty that they accepted subjugation without question. Only a few liberals, led by John Cartwright, John Wilkes, and others, saw the danger. That the situation could be remedied by making Parliament truly representative never occurred to them, for the concept of universal suffrage was alien to the eighteenth century. Instead, as true disciples of the Enlightenment, they sought to protect the people's liberty by insisting that Parliament's authority was limited by an unwritten constitution which guaranteed to each man his natural rights. These included, they said, protection for his life and property, and freedom from arbitrary decrees—whether of Parliament or king.

This doctrine was almost universally accepted by the upper-class group that ruled the American colonies, although their devotion to its principles was based on practical rather than on theoretical grounds. These men—the merchants, the large landholders, the southern planters—sincerely believed that no outside authority could manage their affairs for them. Whether this external control came from king or Parliament made no difference; they simply wanted to be let alone. When Parliament tried to treat them not as competent rulers of their own provinces but as insignificant cogs in a trading machine geared to the needs of the empire as a whole, they naturally resisted. In casting about for justification, they hit upon the same doctrines of the Enlightenment that English liberals were already popularizing. Parliamentary authority, they insisted, was restricted by an unwritten law that guaranteed all men their natural liberties. Thus the voice of protest was raised on both sides of the Atlantic—a voice that cried for liberty against authority. Few realized its significance at the time, for none could foresee that the handful of English liberals would gain strength until they democratized their nation's government in the nineteenth century, or that the colonial protests would lead to revolution. One thing was clear, however: in England those who challenged parliamentary authority were in a minority; in America they were in the majority. This was the situation that made Britain's problem so difficult.

Moreover, all attempts at a solution were complicated by two factors. One was the need of defending an amazingly expanded empire. Merchants could no longer be trusted to protect colonies that straddled the globe; Parliament must levy men, money, and ships from the West Indies, India, and North America. The centralized authority needed to coordinate this vast system of defense would infringe on local autonomy, but what colony would be unwilling to surrender a portion of its self-rule · for the protection of empire? British statesmen spent millions of dollars and thousands of lives to find that the Americans preferred the unrestrained right to manage their own affairs to any amount of security England could offer them. Their habit of self-government was too strong to be broken now, and they saw no reason to change simply because the king of a distant land they had never·seen chose to meddle in matters he could not understand.

The second complicating factor made England's problem even more difficult. In 1763 poorer people in America—the upland farmers, the recent immigrants, the mechanics and laborers, the nonslaveholders of the south—were on the verge of a rebellion against the aristocratic social structure that had been transferred to the colonies with the English migration. They resented the rigid property qualifications that excluded more than five sixths of the adult males from the franchise and limited officeholding to the well to do, the underrepresentation of the interior counties in the colonial legislatures, the antiquated guild system that hindered the rise of artisans in the cities, the threat of an expanding slave economy, the engrossing of the best lands by speculators, the laws of primogeniture and entail that kept the great estates intact, and the need of supporting an established church. These relics of the Old World seemed outworn in a land where greater opportunity for economic advance blurred class lines and made all men equal. Men who believed this were interested not only in the division of authority between their colonial legislatures and Parliament but in who should rule at home. They looked on the period of Revolutionary agitation as a golden opportunity to wring not only political and social equality from the local vested interests but home rule as well. This dual contest complicated the situation and made England's problem virtually insoluble.

PREFACE TO REVOLUTION

Yet it was to this stupendous task that the British government turned its attention as the clash of French and English arms died away. Before a policy could be worked out its hand was forced by an Indian war. The western tribes, alarmed by the defeat of their French allies and by the land speculators who swarmed across the Appalachians with the close of hostilities, found a leader in an able Ottawa chieftain named Pontiac. They fell on the frontier in May, 1763, with such savage fury that all but four of the trans-Appalachian posts were wiped out. Pontiac's Rebellion convinced England that the colonists were unable to protect themselves and that immediate action rather than a well-thought-out policy was demanded. The hurriedly prepared program proclaimed in October, 1763, stopped all settlement west of the mountains, set up elaborate controls for the fur trade, and planted an army of ten thousand men in America.

This elaborate establishment would be expensive to maintain. Why not let America pay part of the cost and why not raise this money by revising the Navigation Acts? This seemed logical to a debt-ridden English people still resentful of Yankees who had sacrificed the welfare of empire to trade with the enemy during the Seven Years' War. Parliament reflected this sentiment by passing two important acts, one in 1764 and the other in 1765. One, the Sugar Act, reduced the tax on foreign molasses from six to three pence a gallon, levied new duties on sugar, wines, coffee, and other luxuries, and provided for the rigorous enforcement of the Navigation Acts. The other, the Stamp Act, ordered that revenue stamps, costing from a halfpenny to twenty shillings, be affixed to all legal forms, commercial papers, newspapers, wills, and similar documents. These measures would raise about one third of the money needed to defend the colonies. England was willing to provide the rest and saw no reason for colonial objection to measures long used for tax purposes within Britain.

The storm of American protest distinctly shocked the home government, for the British ministers, who had been goaded on by the strong mercantile pressure group at home, did not know that they had unwittingly erected a series of laws which together threatened the entire colonial economy. The Sugar Act would end the triangular trade and stop the flow of currency into the northern colonies, while the Stamp Act would drain away their gold and leave a money shortage that might paralyze all commerce. To make matters worse, a postwar depression convinced thousands of sufferers that the fruit of England's laws was hard times and commercial stagnation. But what doomed all chances of patching up the differences between mother country and colonies were the cleavages in American society that were brought to the fore by these measures. Parliament's action aroused not one protest but a chorus of dissent from a variety of groups and classes. This was significant, for these divisions were to shape the whole Revolutionary agitation and, in the postwar years, provided a basis for the social conflicts that spawned the new nation's democratic institutions.

The upper-class objections were voiced by commercial leaders, ministers, newspaper editors, lawyers, and lawmakers. Of these, the merchants were most vociferous in their outcry. The interest of this group—shipowners, wholesalers, importers, shopkeepers—was largely selfish. Abstract principles of liberty meant nothing to them and most of them abhorred democracy; they were only anxious to buy and sell without parliamentary restraint. In casting about for a weapon that could be used against laws that threatened their trade, they hit upon the boycott. Nonimportation agreements spread along the coast in the wake of England's measures as the merchants in town after town voluntarily banded together and agreed to purchase no more British goods until the obnoxious acts were repealed. This was the most effective form of protest, for London business houses soon felt its effects and began clamoring for relief.

Three other groups drawn from the colonial upper classes joined the merchants enthusiastically: the clergymen, the editors, and the government officials, many of whom were lawyers who liked nothing better than a constitutional argument. The ministers, particularly in New England, were steeped in the rebellious doctrines of the Puritan Revolution and had long preached that man's natural, God-given rights transcended the authority of any ruler. These principles could easily be applied now: Parliament had justified resistance by infringing on these sacred liberties. This was the message that rang from many a pulpit and was re-echoed in many a newspaper, for the editors, too, had their grievances. The hated revenue stamps which the law required for all publications threatened to cut seriously into their own revenue. Nor could the lawyers and government leaders stand aside amidst this tumult. Colonial legislatures resounded with the voices of newly risen prophets—Patrick Henry, John Dickinson, Christopher Gadsden, James Otis, and a host more—who urged Americans to resist this attempt of Parliament to tax free-born Englishmen without their own consent. Their prodding forced the assemblies of nine of the provinces to name delegates to a Stamp Act Congress that met in October, 1765, and solemnly resolved that "no taxes ever have been, or can be constitutionally imposed on them, except by their own legislatures."

The great mass of the American people—the artisans and the trades-men of the cities, the small farmers of the countryside—watched this mounting tide of upper-class protest with interest. Some were directly affected by England's laws; city dwellers who worked for importers or distillers were threatened with loss of their jobs, farmers feared declining markets for their produce if trade was regulated out of existence. Others were stirred by the warnings of the merchants who, seeking support for their boycotts, told the people that if Parliament could tax sugar or legal documents it could also tax houses and personal property. But all were motivated by a stronger force than the fear of personal loss; to the masses this agitation was an opportunity to strike for the social and political equality so long denied them. A few of their leaders, notably Samuel Adams of Boston, saw this, and set out to organize lower-class discontent with a definite leveling idea in mind. This proved difficult among the scattered farm dwellers, but the masses in the cities could and did unite. Some formed themselves into a radical society, the Sons of Liberty, with the twin purpose of opposing English measures and wringing democratic concessions from their local rulers. Others gave vent to their feelings by joining mobs that stormed the houses of royal officials and hounded the luckless stamp agents so effectively that by September, 1765, all but one had resigned to save their skins. By this time nearly all of the colonists, who two years before had cheered the mother country's triumphant victories in war, were talking glibly of "taxation without representation" and "tyrannical laws," and were muttering that they must protect their rights as Englishmen.

Parliament repealed the Stamp Act in March, 1766, not because it was impressed by the Americans' constitutional arguments, but because British exporters were objecting. Hard times in England, caused by the same postwar depression that helped shape colonial sentiment, were blamed on the nonimportation agreements, and when Parliament finally bowed before popular pressure London celebrated as enthusiastically as Boston. In their jubilation the Americans failed to note two significant steps. One was the passage of a Declaratory Act flatly asserting Parliament's right to tax the colonies, the other a new tax of one pence a gallon on all foreign and domestic molasses imported into America. The triumph of victory blinded them to the dangers of a statement and a revenue measure more embracing than the Stamp Act. Constitutionally the colonists emerged from the controversy far weaker than when they entered, but practically they were convinced that economic pressure gave them a firm hand over Parliament which could be used to protest future tyrannies.

Nor did they wait long before trying their weapon. During the summer of 1767, Parliament, goaded by the Minister of the Exchequer, Charles Townshend, passed a new series of customs acts levying heavy duties on glass, red and white lead, painters' colors, tea, and other items imported into the colonies. These, Townshend reasoned, would provide revenue without arousing objections, for the colonists had insisted throughout the Stamp Act controversy that Parliament had the right to levy customs duties for the control of commerce, but not direct taxes. At the same time he reconstructed the customs service until it was really effective for the first time since 1660. To his amazement he found that the colonists disliked tariffs that had to be paid as thoroughly as they did direct taxes. Once more a wave of resistance swept over America: legislatures passed resolutions, merchants entered into nonimportation agreements, mobs roamed the seaport towns harrying customs agents, burning revenue ships, and forcibly unloading contraband goods under the noses of the crown's officials. Resistance reached its height at Boston in 1768 when John Hancock's sloop, the *Liberty,* was unjustly confiscated on the charge of smuggling Madeira. Two regiments of troops were hurried there, but the presence of the redcoats only tempted the people to further disorder. This came to a climax in the spring of 1770, when a mob taunted the soldiers until someone gave the order to fire. Four persons were left dead in that Boston Massacre.

England repealed the Townshend Acts that year, but neither the rioting nor the 45 per cent decline in trade caused by the nonimportation agreements was responsible for this move. Instead a more enlightened economic theory convinced Parliament that goods produced by British manufacturers should not be taxed. With all the obnoxious measures except the tax on tea wiped from the statute books during the summer, peace descended once more along the colonial front. For three years of calm and prosperity loyalty to England ran high and agitators were in bad repute—at Salem two Sons of Liberty were tarred and feathered by a mob shouting the praises of George III. Even John Adams, staunch patriot though he was, enjoyed tea at John Hancock's and confided to his diary that he hoped it had been smuggled from Holland but that he had not taken the trouble to inquire.

But in 1773 the applecart was upset once more. Mismanagement of the East India Company, a powerful monopolistic concern that supplied all the empire with tea, was responsible. Its London warehouses clogged with a seventeen-million-pound surplus piled up through inefficiency, the company petitioned Parliament to lower the colonial tax on tea in the hopes of opening new markets. In the Tea Act of 1773 Parliament responded by cutting the tax from seven to three pence a pound and gave the company the right to export and sell the tea directly to the colonies, rather than through the local merchants who had handled sales in the past. This seemed fair to Englishmen, who paid a tax of twelve pence themselves and were long accustomed to old-style mercantile promotion of monopoly. But not so the Americans, who distrusted monopolistic concerns with all the sincerity bred by the equality of opportunity of a new country. Tea merchants whose business was ruined by the measure protested first, but they were soon joined by others who feared monopolies in their own enterprises, and by smugglers driven from business by the new low price. England had unwittingly thrown the whole colonial merchant class into the radical camp. Agitators such as Boston's Sam Adams, who had labored for three years to stir up opposition that might lead to social reform, could again walk down Beacon Street arm in arm with John Hancock. A united America once more faced the mother country.

Nonimportation agreements spread again, but the radicals saw that something more was needed, for boycotts would not solve the problem of dealing with the East India Company's tea ships already on their way to the colonies. Committees of Correspondence—little groups of patriots that had been formed in each town during the past three years to exchange revolutionary sentiments and unite colonial protests—swung into action, determined that the obnoxious beverage should never be landed. When the ships arrived these groups were ready. At New York, Philadelphia, and Charleston the captains were forced to turn back or store their cargo in warehouses, but at Boston, where the royal governor refused to compromise, the radicals took matters into their own hands. On December 16, 1773, the night before the tea was to be landed, an organized and well-disciplined mob, its members disguised as Indians, stormed aboard the company's ships and dumped the offending tea into Boston Harbor.

Wise handling of the situation by England at the time would have nipped agitation in the bud, for the merchant class was horrified by this destruction of property and hurriedly bolted from the radical camp. Instead Britain's blundering ministers took the one step that would unite the colonists once more. They determined to punish Boston. During the spring of 1774 Parliament passed a series of "Intolerable Acts" that closed the port to all commerce, reshaped the Massachusetts charter along less democratic lines, ordered that royal officials be henceforth tried in England, and forced towns to quarter troops against their will. A panic of fear swept over the colonies. If one port could be closed and one charter summarily altered, Parliament could stamp out liberty anywhere in America. Not trade and commerce, but the freedom of the people and their institutions was now at stake; something more than nonimportation agreements was needed. The Committees of Correspondence saw this, and their pressure on the legislatures forced action. Virginia moved first when its burgesses, ousted from their chambers by an irate governor, met at the Raleigh Tavern on May 27, 1774, and issued a call for a Continental Congress. Massachusetts seconded the cry with the doors of its assembly hall locked and the governor vainly shouting through the keyhole that the legislature was dissolved. Under these conditions fifty-six delegates to the Continental Congress from every colony but Georgia assembled at Philadelphia in the late summer of 1774 to shape the protest of the American people.

The time had come for all men to take sides. Two groups found the decision easy. One, made up of crown officials, Anglican clergymen, and wealthy merchants, strongly pro-British from the beginning, did not waver. Another, firmly supporting the American cause, boasted a more heterogeneous membership. Included in its ranks were northern farmers and workers, a radical group with little property to lose and social equality to gain by a revolution. Included too were the southern planters, who were swung to the patriot side by the hope that independence would cancel their long-standing debts to British merchants, by their resentment when England closed the west to their speculative land purchases, and especially by their intense individualism, which rebelled against interference by the crown. The third group, made up of the mass of middle-class merchants, tradesmen, and lawyers, wavered at this critical point. These people had led the agitation with clear consciences as long as the purpose was to remedy specific ills within the structure of the empire, but when the political motive gained precedence over the economic, they began to split from the patriot camp. Like men of wealth through the ages, these influential colonials feared the devastating effect of war on property and the leveling tendency inherent in all revolutions. Better in their eyes for Boston to pay for its Tea Party than risk a conflict that might topple them from their pedestals. One by one they drifted into the pro-British faction as the radical temper of the colonists mounted.

The conservatism of the merchant class complicated the problem of the patriots who controlled the Continental Congress, for these delegates, chosen by provincial assemblies or popular conventions, represented the popular will, which by this time was ready to resort to extralegal methods to bring the mother country to its senses. Yet effective boycotts were impossible so long as the leading importers insisted on trading with England and preaching the need of conciliation. In this emergency Congress took matters into its own hands by setting up a Continental Association that made the import or export of English goods illegal and provided for enforcement by Committees of Correspondence in each colony. This was far different from voluntary nonimportation agreements; now a separate American revolutionary government was making and enforcing laws. Yet few among the members of Congress who voted for the Continental Association dreamed of separation from England. They wanted not freedom, but liberty; not independence, but something like dominion status within the empire.

Only the uncompromising attitude of a blundering British Parliament and a stupid British king drove the colonists to the final point of rebellion. The first bloodshed started the process. British troops, marching inland from Boston to destroy ammunition stored by the patriots at Concord, were met by a determined little band of Americans as the sun rose on the village green at Lexington on the morning of April 19, 1775. There, amidst the confusion of shouted orders and insults, the shot ultimately "heard round the world" was fired. When the redcoats, their task completed, returned to Boston they left the land in flames behind them. Militiamen who had been secretly drilling during the winter gathered from all over New England to besiege the English garrison in Boston, and the Second Continental Congress, which assembled on May 10, 1775, named Colonel George Washington as their commander. The drift toward independence was now rapid, for England showed no tendency to conciliate. An "Olive Branch Petition" was haughtily rejected and in December, 1775, Parliament closed all American ports to British trade. Congress, in desperate need of outside aid, opened the colonies to the ships of all nations in April, 1776. The next step was inevitable. On July 4, 1776, the Declaration of Independence was adopted.

THE WAR FOR INDEPENDENCE

This immortal document climaxed a decade of democratic ferment, and served as a beacon light for liberals throughout the world for another hundred years. Its inspiration was the Enlightenment, its doctrines were revolutionary, its words dynamite-charged blasts against tyranny and hereditary privilege: ". . . all men are created equal . . . . governments are instituted among men, deriving their just powers from the consent of the governed. . . . it is the right of the people to alter or abolish" an unjust government and form a new one that "shall seem most likely to effect their safety and happiness." George III's government had abused its sovereign privileges, and the Declaration listed its misdeeds at length; therefore continued obedience was neither necessary nor wise. Here, summed up in a few vibrant words, was the liberal political theory of the host of thinkers who had contributed to the Enlightenment.

The Declaration of Independence launched the colonies into the Revolutionary War. Their task seemed hopeless. Against the world's greatest military and naval power they must array a straggling population of less than three million, without arms, industries, or even unity, for only about a third of the people actively supported the patriots, an equal number were loyal to England, and the remainder were indifferent. Even the most enthusiastic disliked military service and expected to do nothing but repel local raids. They were governed by a rebel Congress with no legal authority and thirteen states that were jealous of the central government and of each other. Victory seemed impossible under these circumstances. Yet England's obstacles were also great. All America from Quebec to the Floridas was in rebel hands and must be won back by troops transported three thousand miles in slow sailing vessels. The British must fight over unfamiliar terrain and must conquer not one but thirteen rebellious governments. Little wonder that many influential Englishmen favored· a blockade rather than risk military operations under these conditions, or that many Americans preferred appeasement to a war that seemed certain to end in defeat.

That war was already in full swing when the Declaration of Independence was adopted. Washington, having forced the British to evacuate Boston in March, hurried to New York to await the inevitable British invasion of that key city. This came in mid-August, when a mighty force of thirty thousand men under Sir William Howe landed on Long Island and drove the outnumbered Americans backward across New Jersey into Pennsylvania during the fall and winter of 1776–1777. By the spring of 1777 the British were ready to launch their decisive campaign: Howe would march on Philadelphia; a smaller force would move northward along the Hudson River Valley to meet General John Burgoyne, who was advancing southward along Lake Champlain; and the combined armies would then subdue the southern colonies one by one. Fortunately for Washington, these well-laid plans went astray. Howe occupied Philadelphia successfully in the fall of 1777, and settled down to a comfortable winter there while the ragged Americans spent a most uncomfortable one at near-by Valley Forge; but "Gentleman Johnny" Burgoyne fared less well. His seven thousand regulars advanced slowly in the face of stiffening resistance as far as Saratoga, where word finally reached them that the British column supposed to come north along the Hudson had never started. Disheartened by this news and hemmed in by a solid ring of determined Yankees, Burgoyne on October 17, 1777, surrendered his entire command to General Horatio Gates, the leader of the American forces.

The victory at Saratoga was the most decisive of the Revolution, for it not only bolstered sagging morale and swung to the patriot side thousands who hesitated to embrace a losing cause, but transformed a colonial re-

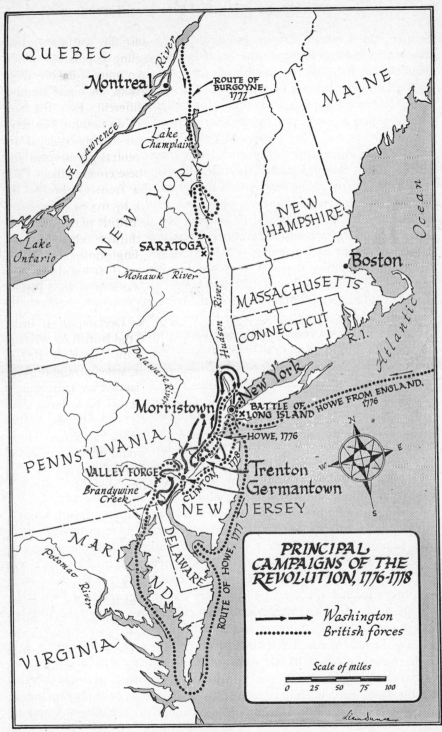

QUEBEC

Montreal

River

ROUTE OF
BURGOYNE,
1777

MAINE

St. Lawrence

Lake
Champlain

NEW YORK

Lake
Ontario

SARATOGA
x

Mohawk River

NEW
HAMPSHIRE

•Boston

MASSACHUSETTS

Hudson River

CONNECTICUT

R.I.

Delaware River

New York

Atlantic Ocean

Morristown

BATTLE OF
xLONG ISLAND

HOWE FROM ENGLAND,
1776

PENNSYLVANIA

VALLEY FORGE
x

HOWE, 1776

*Brandywine
Creek*

CLINTON,
1777

Trenton
Germantown

N

W   E

S

NEW   JERSEY

MARYLAND

DELAWARE

ROUTE OF HOWE, 1777

Potomac River

VIRGINIA

PRINCIPAL
CAMPAIGNS OF THE
REVOLUTION, 1776-1778

→ Washington
•••• British forces

Scale of miles

0   25   50   75   100

Liam Dunne

bellion into a world war by bringing France into the struggle. That nation had been straining at the leash for some time, for British defeat would mean not only the humbling of an ancient enemy and restoration of the European balance of power, but the opening of trading areas long closed to French ships and a triumph for Enlightened principles that were deeply rooted among both the people and some of the king's ministers. Vivid memories of 1763 prevented France from giving more than secret aid until the Americans demonstrated that they could stand against England's might. Saratoga turned the tide. Benjamin Franklin, sent to Paris by Congress early in the war, seized the opportunity to point out that his countrymen could care for themselves and that such a crushing defeat would probably force England to adopt a conciliatory policy that would lure the colonists back into the empire. These prophecies seemed borne out when Parliament in November, 1777, began debating a bill to grant the Americans dominion status if they would abandon demands for independence. France, convinced that her hopes for a dismembered Britain would go glimmering unless she gave the colonists open aid, let Franklin know that she was willing to accept his terms. On February 6, 1778, the two nations signed a formal treaty of alliance in which they agreed to make common cause until American independence was won. England immediately declared war on France, and English arms, instead of being concentrated against the colonists, were spread over the world to defend the straggling empire.

Despite this the next two years were indecisive. Sir Henry Clinton, who replaced Howe as British commander, withdrew to New York in the spring of 1778 and stayed there until a broad new plan of conquest was launched a year and a half later. Six thousand regulars under Lord Cornwallis were sent southward by water, captured Charleston in May, 1780, and began a relentless march northward. By the summer of 1781 the Carolinas and Virginia were in their hands, and the triumphant English were busily fortifying the naval base at Yorktown before moving on to join Clinton in New York. Washington realized that the American cause would be lost if these two armies were reunited; his only hope was to destroy one or the other before this could take place. Both were temptingly located at coastal points where they were open to a joint land-sea attack, but the tiny American navy could never undertake such an operation. Hence Washington sent a hurried plea to Louis XVI for aid, and the French monarch responded by ordering a powerful French fleet to the American coast. In late August, 1781, this strong force slipped into Chesapeake Bay, scattered the British naval vessels that were hurried against them and, in full command of the sea about Yorktown, began ferrying across the bay to Cornwallis's stronghold the fifteen thousand

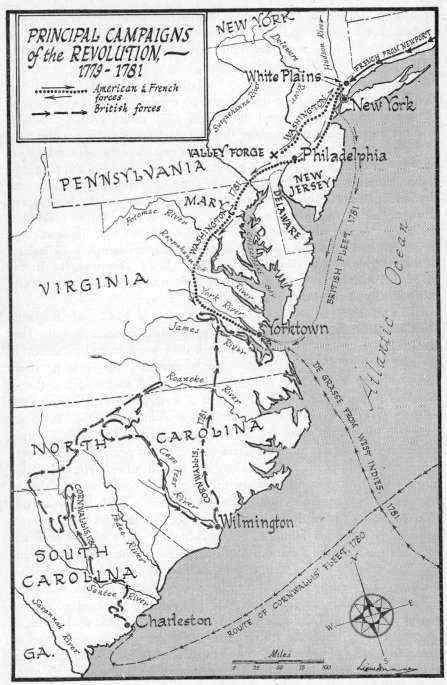

PRINCIPAL CAMPAIGNS
of the REVOLUTION,—
1779 - 1781

••••••► American & French
          forces
————► British forces

NEW YORK

White Plains

New York

FRENCH FROM NEWPORT

Delaware River

Hudson River

Susquehanna River

WASHINGTON

VALLEY FORGE ✕ Philadelphia

PENNSYLVANIA

NEW JERSEY

DELAWARE

MARY

WASHINGTON 1781

Potomac River

Rappahannock River

CHESAPEAKE Bay

BRITISH FLEET 1781

VIRGINIA

York River

James River

Yorktown

Roanoke River

Atlantic Ocean

DE GRASSE FROM WEST INDIES 1781

NORTH CAROLINA

CORNWALLIS 1781

Cape Fear River

CORNWALLIS 1780

Pedee River

Wilmington

SOUTH CAROLINA

Santee River

Savannah River

Charleston

ROUTE OF CORNWALLIS' FLEET, 1780

GA.

N
W   E
S

Lucidien

Miles
0 25 50 75 100

59

French and American troops that had marched southward under Washington. For a month and a half the stout old Britisher held out, but on October 17, 1781, he surrendered his entire force as his bands blared forth "The World Turned Upside Down."

Important as was this victory, it would not have ended the Revolution had not England been discouraged by crushing defeats elsewhere in the world. Spain had entered the war in 1779 under French prodding, and her armies were overrunning the Floridas and pounding at the gates of Gibraltar; the people of the Netherlands cast their lot against England in 1780 and sent a swarm of privateers against English shipping; the Baltic countries were united in a League of Armed Neutrality and threatened to enter the contest to avenge British attacks on their neutral shipping. The empire was a source of weakness now, for so many men and ships were needed to defend its far-flung shores that England could not afford to keep thirty thousand soldiers at the apparently hopeless task of pinning down the elusive Washington. With Yorktown the British realized that they must talk peace on American terms if they were to save more valuable portions of their dominions.

Negotiations began at Paris in the spring of 1782 with Benjamin Franklin, John Jay, and John Adams representing the new nation. They soon found that their allies, so valuable in war, were an embarrassment at the peace table. The United States had agreed in 1778 not to lay down its arms until France was ready; France in 1779 assured Spain that it would continue fighting until the ancient Spanish fortress of Gibraltar was wrested from England. Now, with independence won, the Americans found the war still going on, for Gibraltar remained in British hands, France could not back out until Spain was ready for peace, and the Americans must continue to fight beside their French allies. The move that allowed the United States to escape this apparent impasse was initiated by the Comte de Vergennes, foreign minister to Louis XVI. Knowing that his own nation was ready for peace, he set out to find some means to compensate Spain for her failure to retake Gibraltar. Why not, he reasoned, offer her lands in the American southwest between the Appalachians and the Mississippi? To Jay and Adams, already distrustful of the French minister, this seemed an act of treachery that justified a break with their former allies. They decided to seek immediate peace with England without consulting France. The British ministers were so delighted at this turn of events that they instructed their agents to proceed with a treaty based on the recognition of American independence. Preliminary articles were signed on November 3, 1782, and the definitive peace treaty was approved in September, 1783.

VICTORY AND ITS PROBLEMS

If ever a nation won a peace it was the United States in the Treaty of Paris, whatever may be said of the ethics that permitted the desertion of France. England not only conceded independence, but agreed on the Mississippi boundary and granted American fishermen the same rights in Canadian waters that they had enjoyed under George III. The southern boundary, according to a secret provision, was to be the thirty-first parallel if Spain secured the Floridas in the final Anglo-Spanish settlement; a line drawn east from the mouth of the Yazoo River should they be returned to England. The United States agreed to place no obstacles in the way of British merchants seeking to collect debts owed them by Americans and to "earnestly recommend" that the states restore Loyalist property confiscated during the war. No matter that nearly every clause of the treaty was to breed disputes that would plague the new nation for many years—a glorious victory had been won on the battlefield and in the council chamber.

Yet independence plunged the American people into a new struggle more trying than the military phase of their Revolution. Even before the peace they began to grapple with three problems of unprecedented difficulty. To what extent should they reshape their institutions along the democratic lines forecast in the Declaration of Independence? How much power should the thirteen sovereign states surrender to a national government? How could the nation's borders be freed from foreign intrigue? To a generation born of revolution the first question overshadowed all others, and to this the Americans turned in what has been termed the trying "critical period" after the Treaty of Paris.

The answer was determined by fundamental changes in the social structure carried out through the Revolution. All during the war a steady stream of refugees left the United States, accompanying each British army returning home or taking passage on any ship that would carry them to England, Canada, or the West Indies. These were the Tories or Loyalists —wealthy conservatives who had cast their lot with Britain rather than with the patriots—and fled now before popular wrath. Some were banished, others left voluntarily rather than risk life in a land ruled by "dirty democrats" and the "irresponsible rabble." The exodus of these seventy thousand Loyalists sheered off almost the whole upper crust of society and deprived America of its most influential conservatives who could serve as a brake on radical action. Moreover, their going led to a redistribution of landholdings that stimulated the democratic surge, for their great estates were confiscated by the states and divided among small independent owners. Long before the Revolution was over the new spirit of equality stemming from these changes in land tenure was encouraging attacks on other relics of aristocracy, all of which had stifled the freedom of individuals to express themselves socially, spiritually, or economically.

There were many to arouse patriotic ire: an established church, aristocratic landholding systems, slavery and the slave trade. The battle against them was carried on largely in the South, partly because the plantation system had perpetuated feudal practices and partly because of the able leadership of Thomas Jefferson and James Madison of Virginia. The established Anglican Church, which was supported by taxation in all the states south of Pennsylvania, was the first target of the reformers. Maryland and North Carolina led the way in 1776, Georgia followed in 1777, and South Carolina in 1778, but the battle was most decisive in Virginia's stronghold of orthodoxy. There Jefferson and Madison won a bitter controversy in January, 1786, when the legislature adopted a Statute of Religious Freedom proclaiming that no man could be compelled to attend or support any church not of his own preference. The middle states had proclaimed freedom of conscience long before, but New England Congregationalists were reluctant to bow before the new forces. They modified their strict laws to allow tithes to go either to the established church or to some dissenting sect, but complete liberty of worship was not realized until well into the next century.

Obsolete systems of land tenure, embodied in the laws of primogeniture and entail that were designed to perpetuate an aristocracy of landed gentry, proved less enduring. Jefferson's Virginia again took the lead by abolishing entails in 1776 and decreeing that henceforth landholders could not regulate the descent of their property for generations to come. Primogeniture, which awarded to his eldest son the estates of a man dying intestate, was less easy to overthrow, but Jefferson's steady pressure forced Virginia to adopt a new law in 1785 providing for an equal division of property. Georgia abolished entails in 1777, North Carolina in 1784, and the other states soon afterward, until by the end of the century these antiquated relics of a former day no longer interfered with democratic methods of inheritance.

Slavery, too, aroused the ire of reformers, for human bondage could not be reconciled with the promises of life and liberty to all men contained in the Declaration of Independence. The slave trade was attacked first when, led by Delaware in 1776, the states began passing laws forbidding further importations; within ten years after independence only Georgia permitted the trade to continue. Freeing the slaves already in bondage was more difficult. The northern states, where only a few were held as servants, launched the process; Vermont in 1777 and Massachusetts in 1781 abolished slavery by law and the others followed. Pennsylvania set the pattern for the middle states by setting up a program of gradual emancipation that prevented the introduction of more slaves and freed the children of those in bondage when they reached maturity. Even the South would gladly have followed this course had not the large number of slaves there raised social and political problems that white men did not have the courage to face. The burst of Revolutionary liberalism left the area north of Mason and Dixon's line a free territory and the Southerners convinced that slavery was a necessary evil saddled on them by their ancestors.

These social reforms caught the spirit of the day no more than the political changes that accompanied them. Here the Americans faced a dual problem: the extent of popular control of the government, and the division of authority between the states and the nation. The first was settled by the state constitutions adopted during the Revolution, and in most states settled in a way that was disheartening to the believers in true democracy. For few of these frames of government reflected the political advances of the Enlightenment by assuring complete liberty and equality to the common people; instead, nearly all were based upon the theory that only those whose ownership of property gave them a stake in society should have political influence. Vermont alone opened the ballot box to all adult males; Pennsylvania, Georgia, and New Hampshire allowed poll-tax payers to vote; Virginia, Rhode Island, and Delaware extended the franchise to landholders; the remainder decreed that only larger holders of property should share in the government. In all of the states, too, officeholding was restricted to the wealthy. These conservative features, which seemed so out of tune with the times, were partly the result of tradition; many of the states, hurrying to adopt the written constitutions that they looked upon as bulwarks against tyranny, were too much influenced by their colonial charters and unthinkingly accepted outworn clauses from these documents. More important were the intentions of the upper-class group whose members alone had sufficient education to draw up frames of government. Leaders such as John Adams of Massachusetts might favor the Revolution but they still had little love for popular rule.

Yet democracy made some significant gains in these constitutions. All of them contained bills of rights which, in the best tradition of the eighteenth-century Enlightenment, assured the people freedom of speech, speedy trials, the judgment of their peers, liberty of conscience, and other natural rights. Some—notably those adopted in Pennsylvania and North Carolina—vested virtually all power in the legislature, where the popular will was best represented; and in all the constitutions save those of New York and Massachusetts the governor was given little authority. Only that of Massachusetts granted him the power to veto legislative acts. All the frames of government embodied the principles of separation of powers. Division of power was a decentralization formula which in later practice was to prevent a cohesive joint leadership and to deprive the executive of the power to coordinate the branches of government. According to such writers of the Enlightenment as Locke and Montesquieu, however, the splitting into many hands of the power to govern was the appropriate device to trip up an absolute monarch or to pull down an arbitrary oligarchy that had established mastery over the legislature, executive, and judiciary. The constitution of Massachusetts stated the current doctrine clearly: "In the government of this commonwealth, the legislative department shall never exercise the executive and judicial powers or either of them; the executive shall never exercise the legislative and judicial powers or either of them; the judicial shall never exercise the legislative and executive powers or either of them; to the end it may be a government of laws and not of men." The objectives of the framers of this document and of the others drawn up at that time were not to ensure popular rule by the people but to erect barriers to prevent control of the government either by leveling populist parties or by corrupt aristocratic factions.

The Continental Congress made an attempt to solve the second problem—how to divide authority between the states and the national government—when in 1781 it adopted the Articles of Confederation. This first American constitution was based on the theory that colonial radicals insisted underlay the British Empire: it set up a central government with adequate control over external affairs but with no right to meddle in the internal matters of any state. National authority was vested in a congress that combined legislative, executive, and judicial functions. It could make war or peace, draft treaties and alliances, maintain an army and a navy, regulate the Indian tribes, standardize coinage and measures, and borrow money; these were external matters requiring centralized administration. All other powers were reserved by the states, including the right to levy taxes and regulate commerce, for a people who had rebelled against parliamentary meddling in these matters would not surrender them to any new government, even of their own creation.

The Articles of Confederation were remarkable for both their merits and their defects. They marked a distinct step forward in the creation of a satisfactory federal government that would allow two sovereignties, one within the other, to function harmoniously. Yet three outstanding faults led to their downfall. One was their failure to achieve a proper balance between national and state power; they gave the states too much authority, the federal government too little. Another was the unsatisfactory nature of the central government, for concentration of all functions in one congress without separate executive and judicial branches soon proved unworkable. Most serious of all was their failure to provide the national government with any compulsive power. Congress could not *force* the states or the people to do anything; it could ask them for money or request them to adhere to treaty obligations, but if they refused, it could not enforce its own decrees. In other words, Congress enjoyed adequate *powers* but suffered from insufficient *power,* and this more than any other factor caused its failure.

That the powers of the central government were sufficient to produce excellent legislation was shown by the passage of two monumental laws during the "critical period"—the Ordinances of 1785 and 1787. Both dealt with the trans-Appalachian West, where twenty-five thousand pioneers were living in Kentucky and Tennessee when the Revolution ended. The first ordinance to be passed set up a land system by which settlers could acquire sound title to their homes. When Congress turned to debate on this subject two points of view were apparent: Southerners and Westerners wanted a free-and-easy system of land warrants that would encourage a haphazard settlement by individuals; Northerners wanted a system of prior survey and group occupation of large tracts purchased as a unit. The former program encouraged the peopling of the public domain but would lead to poor surveys and confusion; the latter was orderly but discriminated against the individual pioneer. In the end

TYPICAL SECTION OF THE PUBLIC DOMAIN UNDER THE ORDINANCE OF 1785 the ordinance passed on May 20, 1785, effected a compromise. It ordered the survey of the trans-Appalachian territory into townships six miles square, which were to be divided into sections, each containing 640 acres. Alternate townships were to be sold as a whole to satisfy the New Englanders, while individuals could purchase sections in the remainder at a minimum price of one dollar an acre. This Ordinance of 1785 established an orderly system of surveys that was to be used across the entire United States, but its immediate results were few, for no settler needed or could afford a whole section of land. The first territory surveyed in eastern Ohio found no purchasers, and in 1787 Congress abandoned hope of selling directly to settlers and began parceling out its holdings to great speculating companies.

This reversal of policy was responsible for the second western ordinance, for the Ordinance of 1787 was passed at the insistence of one of the land companies formed to exploit the western country. This concern, the Ohio Company, was made up of Revolutionary veterans from New England who proposed to use the depreciated currency in which they had been paid to purchase a million acres along the Muskingum River in eastern Ohio. Its agent drove a hard bargain with Congress in July, 1787, obtaining the desired lands for about nine cents an acre, but insisted that his company could never sell its holdings until a government was extended over the area. Congress responded on July 13 by passing the Ordinance of 1787, or the Northwest Ordinance.

All lands north of the Ohio and east of the Mississippi, this stated, should be divided into from three to five territories. At first these would be governed directly by Congress through an appointed governor, but as the population increased, so would the amount of self-government. Five thousand male inhabitants would entitle each territory to a legislature and a delegate to Congress; when its population reached sixty thousand it could enter the Union on terms of full equality with the other states. The ordinance also contained a bill of rights guaranteeing freedom of speech and worship, trial by jury, and other protections for individual liberty so dear to eighteenth-century Englishmen. Here was the most liberal colonial system the world had known. The colonies were not to be kept subject to the mother country, but were eventually to share equally in the shaping of imperial affairs. This doctrine, which assured the success of the expanding Union by decreeing that the West should not remain subject to the East, was evidence both of the wisdom of its framers and the adequate powers vested in Congress under the Articles of Confederation.

THE ARTICLES OF CONFEDERATION

Yet important as the Articles were in the evolution of a satisfactory federal government, their doom was predestined by their one weakness: they failed to grant the national government sufficient power over states or individuals. This became clear when a serious depression that gripped the country between 1785 and 1787 demonstrated the impotency of ·Congress: it could neither take needed steps to alleviate the suffering of the poverty-ridden masses nor force the states to deal equitably with the problems that arose from it. This depression was caused partly by the deflationary process inevitable in postwar years, and partly by the failure of commerce to revive with peace, for England closed her colonial ports to American vessels, Spain refused to enter into a commercial treaty, and the Mediterranean trade was blocked by fierce Algerian pirates, who could now pounce on American ships without fear of English retaliation. To make matters worse, business was stifled by floods of depreciated currency sweeping over the country from the printing presses of the several states and Congress. Thousands of farmers and merchants who had expanded their holdings during the war prosperity now were unable to meet their mortgage payments and faced the grim prospect of debtors' prisons.

Little wonder that in this situation the demands of the lower classes became stridently vocal. They had been promised much by the Declaration of Independence and had achieved little. Why not abolish all taxes? Why not divide all property equally among the people? Why not renounce government and return to the state of "natural rights" painted so temptingly by the Revolutionary agitators? This seemed logical, for what did the government give them? Only high taxes they could not pay, courts that confiscated their property for the benefit of hated creditors and cast them into debtors' prisons, protection for property when they had no property to protect. Why endure these hardships when a little action would bring justice and equality for all?

The action of these depression-burdened masses took two forms: legal and illegal. In seven states they secured control of the legislatures and launched a program designed to aid their class. Printing presses were set running to turn out paper money, backed only by the tottering credit of the states, and mortgage stay laws were passed to relieve debtors of both interest and principal payments by preventing creditors from foreclosing on their mortgages. In most of the states the inflation was moderate, but in some, such as Rhode Island, it went beyond all reason. There the paper money declined so rapidly that merchants refused to accept it until the legislature passed a "Force Act" providing for the punishment of all who discriminated against the legal currency of the state. Shop-keepers shut their stores rather than take worthless money for their goods or risk heavy fines—payable only in gold—for refusing it, while to avoid repayment in a currency that would buy nothing, creditors fled the state with their debtors at their coattails. Business and trade came to a standstill and a numbing paralysis descended over the economic life of the commonwealth.

In the six states where the creditors retained control, the situation was just as bad. The debtors, confronted by unsympathetic legislatures and ruthless moneylenders who foreclosed mortgages with a heartless in-difference to the sufferings of the poor, resorted to illegal action to save themselves from judicial tyranny. The situation was particularly grave in Massachusetts, where mobs began forming during the summer of 1786. Courts at Worcester, Springfield, and Northampton, where mortgage-foreclosure proceedings were in progress, were forcibly closed, and when the conservative governor retaliated by declaring them outlaws, these irate farmers determined to march on the state capital. They set out during the cold winter of 1786–1787, armed with staves and pitchforks and led by a Revolutionary veteran named Daniel Shays. When news reached them that a hastily recruited army was moving out from Boston to meet them, they fell back to the wooded country in the western part of the state, where they were hunted down like animals. Shays' Rebellion did little but show the temper of the people, and that clearly was dangerous.

Congress struggled manfully with these problems but could do little, for it had no power to interfere in affairs of the states to protect either creditors or debtors. It is hardly surprising that the conservative class, terrified by the prospect of a spreading rebellion against men of property, resolved that the Articles of Confederation had outlived their usefulness. What was needed now, they agreed, was a strong central government that could stamp out this growing anarchy and adjust the inequalities that had fostered the rebellious tendencies. As radicalism spread and threatened to engulf all the state governments, this group gained recruits until it was strong enough to strike. From the conservative reaction came the new frame of government known as the Constitution of the United States.

IV

THE CONSTITUTION AND CONSERVATISM

1787–1800

Shays' Rebellion in 1787 marked the high point in the rising Revolutionary democracy; for the next thirteen years the course of American thought was to the right as alarmed conservatives captured the reins of government and swept the nation back toward a point where their social and economic privileges would be preserved. By 1787 men of property were thoroughly alarmed. Creditors were menaced by mortgage stay laws, merchants by paper money, shipowners by dwindling trade, and all by a democratic revolution that threatened to dislodge them from power. Swept together by the current of the times, they staged a series of adroit maneuvers that forced Congress to call a special convention designed to strengthen the national government by amending the Articles of Confederation. This was the background for the Constitutional Convention, which met in Independence Hall, Philadelphia, on May 25, 1787.

CONSTITUTIONAL MECHANICS

The fifty-five men who gathered on that spring day to frame a new constitution reflected the conservative view of the legislatures that chose them, for the one state controlled by the paper-money agrarians, Rhode Island, refused to participate. The great Revolutionary liberals—Thomas Jefferson, Sam Adams, John Hancock, Patrick Henry—were not there; the propertied legislators no longer trusted them. Instead, a majority were lawyers, and all were men of wealth who had invested heavily in mortgages, government securities, commerce, or land; not one in his personal economic interests represented the small farmer-artisan class. Moreover, the radicalism of the "critical period" had dimmed what little faith they had ever had in popular rule. Some believed a limited monarchy "one of the best governments of this world"; others spoke bitterly of the "excess of democracy," or maintained that "the people immediately should have as little to do as may be about the government." Even George Washington, who presided over the convention, reluctantly concluded that "mankind, when left to themselves, are unfit for their own government." Yet the framers were wise enough to know that the people would not accept even a rigidly limited monarchy. Their objective was a workable national government strong enough to curb democratic "excesses"; indeed, so absolute that it would circumscribe popular liberty. They realized that such a "government with energy" could be achieved only by granting the new central authority not only broad *powers* but far more *power* than that vested in Congress under the Articles of Confederation.

But was this possible? Could the thirteen states be persuaded to surrender enough of their sovereignty to endow the central government with sufficient power over the people? And, what was more important, could the people, who looked on the states as bulwarks against centralized autocracy, be made to part with a shield that had guarded their liberties since 1776? This was the principal problem, and in solving it the framers made use of three effective devices. They agreed to incorporate enough democratic features into the frame of government to soothe some of the popular apprehension. They decided to concede the states enough power to win them over to ratification. They agreed to install an intricate system of checks and balances between the three branches— executive, legislative, and judicial—which, although ostensibly to protect liberty against monarchical usurpation, would actually deflect and weaken the pressure of democratic majorities and "factious combinations" that might lead to national majority rule. At the same time they would award the national government enough actual power over both individuals and states to curb local tendencies toward the "excesses" of democracy.

There was little dispute on the *powers* to be vested in the national government, for the conservative framers agreed that the states, which had overstepped their privileges during the "critical period," should no longer be allowed to interfere in matters essential to the economic and political welfare of the nation. They decided that the central government should have exclusive control over domestic and foreign commerce, that it alone should make treaties, levy customs duties, and coin money, that it should have the power to raise money by borrowing and taxation, and that its jurisdiction should extend to such purely national questions as the maintenance of an army and a navy, the establishment of post offices, the granting of patents, the regulation of weights and measures, and the like. The framers agreed, too, that national harmony required the states to surrender some of the powers they had abused in the past. They wrote into the Constitution a number of specific restrictions: states could not impair the obligation of contracts, or coin money or issue bills of credit, they could not enter into treaties or alliances or compacts with other states, they were forbidden to levy customs or tonnage duties or to pass ex post facto laws. Thus national control of economic affairs, dear to the hearts of the conservatives, was assured. Stay laws and state paper monies were unlawful. The central government operated under delegated powers and with or without state cooperation could do those things the Constitution said it could do. Here was a clear division of authority, a division sadly lacking under the Articles.

The problem of ensuring sufficient *power* in the national government proved difficult, for the framers had to find some means of clothing it with real authority over the people and the states without offending either. Many of them wanted to grant national compulsive power over the states, either directly through the use of an army, or indirectly by calling on the other states to coerce recalcitrant members. Others pointed out that this would lead to the same resistance that followed Parliament's attempt to coerce the colonies. In the end this wiser counsel prevailed, and the framers decided to give the central government the power to compel not states but individuals. By the device of "dual citizenship," which they wrote into the Constitution, every person was made a citizen both of his state and of the United States and was forced to obey each within its own sphere. More than any other, this monumental step in the development of a workable federal system allowed the new nation to survive its formative years by assuring the central government a safe compulsive power acceptable to the states.

Yet even now the framers' task was not completed, for they must erect some machinery that would allow the national government to take precedence over the states in any direct conflict between the two. Suppose, for example, that each adopted laws on a certain subject, and that these laws were at cross-purposes. Who would decide when such a conflict existed, and how could the supremacy of the national law be secured? Some of the framers would have given Congress the right to veto state laws in conflict with its own measures, but the states would have objected to this as they did to the overriding of their acts by the English Privy Council. The device adopted was far more acceptable. The national Constitution, acts of Congress, and treaties were made the "supreme law of the land," taking precedence over conflicting state laws. The judges in each state, rather than any federal agency, were to determine when a law of that state violated a national law and must bow before this greater authority. This removed a possible source of grievous friction between the two branches, for states would grow less angry when their own judges negated their own laws. This concept and the doctrine of dual citizenship together laid the basis for a successful federal union and assured the strong central government desired by its authors.[1]

The unanimity with which the framers settled these fundamental principles contrasted markedly with divisions that arose when they turned to concrete details in the erection of a frame of government. Here the framers divided into such antagonistic factions that successive compromises were necessary between large and small states, agrarian and commercial interests, Northerners and Southerners. The governmental system that emerged from these bitter conflicts provided for a separation of powers between three branches, executive, legislative, and judicial. The executive branch was to be headed by a president, chosen for four years by a cumbersome "electoral college" whose members were to be selected by the state legislatures. The framers, condemning parties as "factions," failed to foresee the rise of a two-party system. They supposed that the electors would seldom cast the majority vote needed for any one candidate and provided that in this case the final choice should be made by the House of Representatives from among the three having the highest number of votes. The President was given adequate powers, including the right to veto acts of Congress.

The legislative branch was to be made up of two houses. In the upper house, or Senate, each state was to be represented by two delegates; in the lower, or House of Representatives, representation was based on population. The framers intended the Senate to be the more important body, but the large states that would dominate the House of Representatives refused to accept the Constitution until that body was given the vital function of initiating all money bills. Judicial power was vested in a supreme court and in any lesser courts that Congress might create, and these were granted jurisdiction over cases arising under the Constitution or national laws and treaties, as well as over disputes between the states, between citizens of different states, and similar types of litigation.

The Constitution as later interpreted and venerated was very different from the document devised by the framers. The original Constitution was not designed for a democratic system of national parties or dedicated to the democratic proposition of majority rule. Many of the framers, though confused in their conceptions of the future exercise of power by the judicial branch, voiced their belief that the courts would serve as a conservative curb on popular majorities. More important, the strategic design of the separation of legislative and executive powers was heavily weighted against mastery of the government by a democratic majority. The avenue to presidential office by way of the electoral college was intended to ensure the dominance in the executive branch of men who represented substantial

---

[1] For the later evolution of judicial review see Chapter VI.

property interests; for the electors, chosen by state legislators who themselves held office under state property tests, would be men of affluence who would naturally favor for president a man of safe, conservative temper. To prevent popular election of senators, as of presidents, the Constitution provided that the two senators from each state would be "chosen by the Legislature thereof." The staggered terms of senators, further implementing the aristocratic design of separation of powers, was a shrewd barrier against a popular upheaval in state governments; even a popular sweep of all the state governments could capture no more than one third of the Senate seats at any one time. In the three branches, only the members of the House of Representatives were directly accountable to the nation's voters; and the voters were restricted under suffrage laws that allowed no vote to a vast proportion of ordinary citizens.

When, on September 17, 1787, the framers ended their sixteen weeks of debate and adjourned to the City Tavern for a last dinner together they had every reason to view with pride the document that emerged from their labors. The Constitution welded thirteen sovereign states together into the first durable federal government in the world's history. Some might object that it was far from a democratic document. They could point out that the President was far removed from the people, that federal judges were selected for life, that the qualifications for voting gave the wealthy classes a decisive influence over the national government. They could argue that the system of checks and balances inherent in the separation of powers was designed to frustrate the popular will, for the President could veto acts of Congress, the Senate could block appointments and treaties made by the President, and the Senate could likewise defeat legislation desired by the more popular body, the House of Representatives. But even the most carping critics would admit that the Constitution embodied liberal features undreamed of in the monarchical world of the eighteenth century, and time was to show that it could be adapted to the more democratic society of the nineteenth and twentieth centuries. As Judge T. M. Cooley, prominent constitutional lawyer, was to note a century later: ". . . for practical purposes the Constitution is that which the Government in its several departments and the people in the performance of their duties as citizens recognize and respect as such; and nothing else is."

THE CONFLICT OVER RATIFICATION

The framers, in a bold *coup d'état* that ignored a clause in the Articles of Confederation preventing amendment except by unanimous consent, had provided that the new government would go into operation as soon as conventions in nine of the states acted favorably upon it. When elections for the delegates got under way, American opinion split into two camps. On the one side were the small farmers and artisans who formed the great debtor class. Many of these men, the farmers especially, owned enough property to vote, and all heartily disapproved of the new document. What, they asked, had become of the liberty they fought for during the Revolution, for this new central government possessed more power over them than had Parliament! Why had authority been stripped from the states where the masses had at least some voice? Where was there any democracy in a government that denied the people a direct participation in the selection of their judges, president, and legislators? Why was there no bill of rights to guarantee them protection from oppression? The upcountry farmers and city laborers who asked these questions wanted none of this new Constitution. "These lawyers, and men of learning and moneyed men," one of them declared, "that talk so finely, and gloss over matters so smoothly, to make us poor illiterate people swallow down the pill, expect . . . to be managers of this Constitution, and get all the power and all the money into their own hands, and then they will swallow up all of us little folks like the great *Leviathan;* yes, just as the whale swallowed up *Jonah!*" On the other side were the so-called Federalists: the wealthy merchants, lawyers, and landowners who would benefit most from the new frame of government. From the first they enjoyed a distinct advantage in the ratification contest. Concentrated in their ranks were the educated gentry and the wealth of the country; they could flood the nation with newspaper articles and pamphlets arguing the merits of the Constitution. Just as important was the fact that they were better organized, accustomed to political leadership, and lived along the seaboard in thickly settled communities where voters could reach the polls more easily than they could in the sparsely peopled interior. But with all of these advantages, proponents of the Constitution recognized that they were vastly outnumbered and that their sole hope lay in pushing ratification through before the unorganized majority could unite.

The action of the small states helped the strategists in the big states. The smaller states were so pleased with equal representation in the Senate that they accepted the whole document and ratified at once. One of the big states, Pennsylvania, followed with such unseemly haste that the back-country farmers had no chance to express their opposition, for a Federalist mob dragged doubters into the legislative chambers by force, watched over them while they decided that the ratifying convention should meet in only five weeks, stifled the few dissenting voices that could be raised in this scant period, and pushed their state into line by a vote of 46 to 23. In another big state, Massachusetts, Federalists won over their opponents by dangling the vice-presidency before one of their leaders, John Hancock, and by promising to add a bill of rights, but even then the vote of 187 to 168 was uncomfortably close for the Federalists. By practices such as these the necessary nine states were persuaded to ratify by June, 1788, but Virginia and New York remained to be heard from. The battle was bitter in these two key states, for both sides had able leaders with firm convictions; but Virginia finally succumbed to the arguments of the conservatives and accepted the Constitution by a vote of 89 to 79 on June 25, while New York followed a month later by a margin of 3 votes. With Rhode Island and North Carolina alone remaining obdurate, the process of establishing the new government could begin. Ratification was a triumph for an organized minority; they had outargued and outmaneuvered the lethargic mass of the people. Probably not more than 100,000 men, or about one sixth of the adult males eligible to vote, actually cast their ballots for delegates to the ratifying conventions that favored the new form of government.

UNIFYING FACTORS

As soon as the success of the Constitution was assured, the Congress of the Confederation arranged for the election of the President and Congress in the fall of 1788 and decreed that the successful candidates should take office on March 4, 1789. Not until April 30 did enough congressmen straggle into New York to inaugurate George Washington, whom the electoral college had unanimously chosen first President of the United States. A staggering task faced these pioneering officeholders. Only debts and empty coffers had been inherited from the old government—no precedents on which to found the new government, no revenue or tax system, no means of enforcing laws, no civil officials. Yet stabilization took a surprisingly short time. Congress immediately levied customs and tonnage duties that sent a stream of needed revenue flowing into the national coffers. A workable court system was set up, consisting of a supreme court, thirteen district courts each with a federal judge, and three circuit courts to be presided over by judges from the district courts and the Supreme Court. Executive departments of state, war, and treasury were created, together with an attorney general to enforce the laws, and when the President began meeting informally with the heads of these branches he created the American type of presidential Cabinet. Congress strengthened the executive department by allowing the President to select and dismiss these advisors and to make treaties subject only to the subsequent approval of two thirds of the senators. Thus, step by step, a more energetic governmental mechanism was set in motion.

Two things, in addition to Washington's able leadership, assured the permanence of the new system. One was the lifting of the depression that had plagued the nation during the postwar period. By 1789, when the deflationary process had run its course, new sources of trade began pouring wealth into the commercial states—from France, where crop failures created a demand for American grains; from the West Indies, where British planters encouraged smugglers; and from the Far East, where Yankees plied a rich trade in exotic Oriental goods. The new government had almost nothing to do with the return of good times, but the association between the Constitution and prosperity was fixed in many minds. The second factor was the spirit of fair play with which the members of the opposition decided to give the new system a proper trial whether they liked it or not. Patrick Henry reflected this spirit when he announced his willingness to accept the Constitution while working to remove its defects "in a constitutional way." No vigorous opposition party embarrassed the founding fathers; not until trouble brewed over whisky taxes in Washington's second term was the ruling gentry again to be alarmed by a new manifestation of the spirit of the Shays Rebellion.

THE WISDOM OF THE PEOPLE

Partially responsible for this graceful acceptance was the decision of members of Congress to live up to their promise and add a series of constitutional amendments in response to popular demand for a bill of rights to protect the common people from arbitrary federal action. The conservative "Federalists" did so reluctantly, for many hesitated to curb the government's authority over the masses and others sincerely believed that no restraint was necessary; as the Constitution was a grant of power, they insisted, Congress had no authority except that actually bestowed upon it and hence could not deprive its citizens of their liberty—an argument that its own sponsors themselves were to prove false before the end of the decade by enactments against sedition. Signs of popular discontent finally forced action, however, and in August, 1790, under the prodding of Congressman James Madison of Virginia, the obviously unwilling House agreed to recommend to the states seventeen of the seventy-eight amendments proposed by the ratifying conventions. These were reduced to twelve by the still more conservative Senate; of these, ten were eventually ratified; and on December 15, 1791, the Bill of Rights became part of the Constitution, to serve as a cherished bulwark against government encroachment on individual liberty. Embodying the wisdom of the people rather than the wish of the ruling orders, the new amendments reaffirmed the Jeffersonian spirit of the Declaration of Independence. The

Bill of Rights provided that Congress could not prohibit freedom of worship, freedom of speech, or freedom of the press. All people were guaranteed adequate legal protection in the federal courts, speedy and impartial justice, jury trial, and freedom from excessive fines or cruel and unusual punishments. They were assured that their persons and property would be secure against unreasonable search and seizure, that proper compensation would be given them for any property that was taken in the public good, and that they would not be deprived of "life, liberty, or property, without due process of law."

THE RULING CLASS DIVIDES

The differences that had marked the ratification contest and the division over the new amendments were too deep to remain long under the surface. The agrarian-debtor class, with its sincere belief that equality and democracy were the ultimate ends of government, was willing to accept the Constitution only in the hope of eventually attaining broader justice under its operation. As the first years of Washington's administration passed, such hope dimmed, for it was plain that the government was dominated by members of the creditor-capitalist class who were interested primarily in the preservation of order and privileges for the propertied. This narrowness of vision was demonstrated clearly by the early Congresses. Conservatives who controlled those bodies set out to impress the people with the power of the new government and the obedience it demanded. Aspiring architects of aristocratic rule considered the device of conferring awe-inspiring titles on high public officials. The Senate solemnly debated whether to address the President as "Your Majesty," or "Your Electoral Majesty," or "Your Excellency," or "Your Highness," or "Your Highness the President of the United States and Protector of the Rights of the Same." The President's wife was called "Lady Washington," and their home "The Great House," or "The Palace." Senators insisted on being addressed as "Your Highness of the Senate," and when debating precedents they "began with the House of Commons, then the House of Lords, then the King, and then back again," as one disgusted democrat put it. These men were not monarchists, but they had lost what little faith in democracy they had ever had and believed that a government must rule the people rather than be ruled by them. "The people who own the country ought to govern it"—so declared one of the more exalted of Washington's associates.

Both President Washington and John Adams, his successor in 1796, were Federalists, as these conservatives called themselves, but the high priest of the group was Alexander Hamilton. This aristocrat from the

West Indies, only thirty-two years old in 1789 when he became Secretary of the Treasury, was convinced that the government could survive only by remaking the "frail and worthless fabric" of the Constitution. In the Constitutional Convention he had been frustrated in his demand for a stronger executive on the English model. As Secretary of the Treasury he deliberately conceived of his office as like that of a Prime Minister who in England's government was the leader both of the Cabinet and of the Parliament. Winning ascendancy over Federalists in Congress, Hamilton proceeded with his plans for a "government with energy." He proposed first to place the central government securely in the hands of the propertied few and, second, to extend that government's authority until the states and the mass of the people were safely subordinate to it. That the framework he pictured was not democratic did not deter Hamilton. An aristocrat to the core—a man who loved system rather than his fellow men—he was willing to sacrifice individual liberty on the altar of efficiency and national power.

Hamilton's program as Secretary of the Treasury aimed always at these larger objectives and to a remarkable extent his purposes were accomplished. His plans were embodied in a series of brilliant "Financial Reports" that he attempted to present in person in the House of Representatives. Opponents in Congress prevented acceptance of this normal and sensible English procedure; but the Secretary's proposals, when laid before Congress, were adopted one by one. These provided that the national debt, both foreign and domestic, be paid off at face value; that the federal government assume the debts of all the states; that additional revenue be raised by a tariff and by a tax on whisky; and that a national bank similar to the Bank of England be chartered by the United States.

Sound as were these measures financially, Hamilton's ulterior purpose in proposing each bulked larger in his own mind than their fiscal benefits. Funding the national debt would not only restore credit and place the country on its feet financially, but would please wealthy speculators who could redeem at full value government bonds purchased for as little as from eight to twelve cents on the dollar. Similarly, assumption of the state debts would force the creditor class to look to the United States for payment and break down local attachment to state governments. An excise tax on whisky would both bring in needed revenue and extend the authority of the new government over the western farmers who produced this commodity. A national bank would please the nation's businessmen by giving them adequate credit facilities, and—equally important —would establish a vital constitutional principle. Nowhere, Hamilton reasoned, did the Constitution specifically grant Congress the authority to charter a bank. It did have the power to tax, to coin, and to borrow

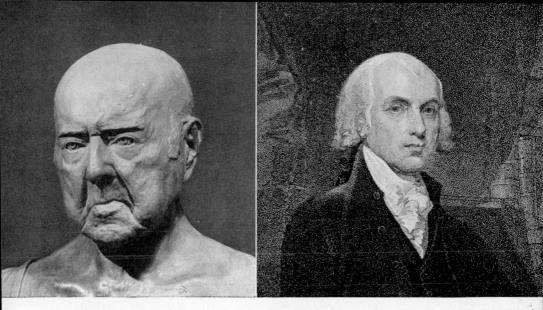

The last Federalist and a triumvirate of Republicans whose ruffles and lace symbolized the gulf between Jeffersonian theory and complete democracy. *Above, left*—John Adams *(courtesy New York State Historical Association)*; *right*—James Madison (engraving by W. A. Wilmer, *Bettmann Archive*). *Below, left*—James Monroe; *right*—Albert Gallatin, Switzerland's contribution to the American Enlightenment (portraits by Gilbert Stuart, *courtesy Metropolitan Museum of Art*).

Revolutionary nationalism sent American architects to the classical republics for examples. *Above*—Washington's Mount Vernon home. (A nineteenth-century print of the national shrine by Currier & Ives, *courtesy Chicago Historical Society*) *Below*—Jefferson's beloved Monticello in the Virginia Piedmont, a transplanted Greek temple designed by Jefferson himself. *(Courtesy Thomas Jefferson Memorial Foundation)*

The search for companionship, divine and human: individual salvation through religious revival and social salvation through mutual aid. *Above* —A romanticized portrayal of an unusually sedate western camp meeting. *(Courtesy Chicago Historical Society)* *Below*—A typical frontier "play party," the husking bee. *(Courtesy Library of Congress)*

Above—Benjamin Franklin, first American citizen of the world and international trail blazer for the Enlightenment, demonstrates that lightning operates through natural laws rather than divine intercession (nineteenth-century print by Currier & Ives). *Below*— The Yankee contraption of Eli Whitney that enslaved the South. An early cotton gin pictured by a nineteenth-century artist. *(Courtesy Library of Congress)*

money, and to take any "necessary and proper" step to carry out its delegated powers. Because a national bank was a "necessary and proper" means of caring for the nation's fiscal problems, it was implied in the Constitution that Congress had the right to issue a charter. Hamilton knew that if this doctrine of "implied powers" or "loose construction" were accepted, the scope of congressional power would be vastly enlarged, and to this device for stretching the Constitution he devoted himself.

As Congress debated these proposals between the fall of 1789 and the spring of 1791, grumbling protests began to be heard from the rural regions. Why, homespun spokesmen asked their fellows, should taxes be increased so that wealthy speculators could fatten on ill-gotten gains? Why should Congress fasten on the nation a giant credit-monopoly that would benefit the few at the expense of the many? This vague discontent was translated into action when the Antifederalists found a leader in the person of Thomas Jefferson, Secretary of State in Washington's Cabinet. Born in back-country Virginia, Jefferson was agrarian in tradition, suspicious of business and finance, and liberal in philosophy. Government, he believed, should be servant and not master of the people; efficiency was less important than liberty, and even periodic revolution was preferable to tyranny. Because his optimism taught him that men were good, he wanted them to share in their own rule; because history taught him that strongly centralized governments not accountable to the people tended toward absolutism, he held that the states should be wary of surrendering power to an aristocratic order entrenched in the national government. Jefferson's ideal was an agrarian republic with a weak national government and strong local governments democratically administered by the people. His views placed him at the opposite end of the scale from Hamilton, who favored a stratified society in which the upper classes controlled a powerful central government in the interests of diversified economic activity.

The break between these two men, each of whom became the symbol of the broad internal division within the country, came at the close of 1790. Jefferson reluctantly accepted Hamilton's proposal to fund the national debt and was won to the assumption of state debts by the promise of northern support for a southern capital, but when the plan for a national bank was laid before Congress in December, 1790, he rebelled. From his vigorous protests to Washington emerged the "strict constructionist" view of the Constitution; he not only held that Congress was strictly limited to the powers specifically delegated to it, but that every measure enacted must be both "necessary" *and* "proper." Washington, more impressed by Hamilton's argument than by Jefferson's, signed the bill creating the bank, but Jefferson was not silenced. With James Madison of Virginia as his ally he launched a sustained attack on Hamilton's measures, which, he believed, were designed to "prepare the way for a change from the present republican form of government to that of monarchy." Behind him rallied thousands of farmers and workers whose dislike for the Constitution, expressed first in the ratifying conventions, had become vocal with Hamilton's financial reports. Despite all of Washington's efforts for harmony, by the end of 1791 he presided over a cabinet and a nation that were split.

THE PARTIES RESHAPE THE CONSTITUTION

The establishment of an opposition party radically modified the constitutional framework established by the founders. Their purpose had been only thinly disguised: they would use a system of "federalism" to prevent the agrarian majorities from forcing equalitarian reforms on the states, and the device of "checks and balances" to forestall similar popular reforms through congressional legislation. To these conservatives, separation of powers was an antidote to majority rule, for the independence of each of the government agencies—Senate, House, executive, and courts—made them successive barricades against pressure from majorities. Even James Madison had acquiesced in this view when he expressed his fear of "a majority of the whole" and described political parties as "factious combinations." Now, in 1791, Madison was willing to admit his error and to help Jefferson build a party that, by seeking control over all branches of the national government, would offset the division of power. The rapid evolution of parties in the next few years introduced changes so fundamental that they amounted in effect to amendments to the Constitution. Circumventing the aristocratic purpose of the framers, they made the presidency an elective office despite the electoral college, brought Congress under some popular control, and even subjected the courts to pressure from the majority. The introduction of party technique made it possible gradually, without formal amendment, to broaden the Constitution into an instrument for democracy.

The depth of the gulf between the first two parties was shown by the opposition to one of Hamilton's measures, the excise tax on whisky. This tax fell heavily on the frontier farmers living along the western fringe of settlement; for they could export their staple crop, grain, only by concentrating it into a less bulky and more renumerative product— whisky. By 1794 discontent in western Pennsylvania reached such proportions that mobs were hunting down the excise agents, threatening governmental officials at Pittsburgh, and talking of seceding from the United States. Washington, foreseeing the danger of making martyrs of these rebellious backwoodsmen, handled the situation wisely. He called out the militia of four states, formed an army of fifteen thousand men, and marched this slowly across Pennsylvania. The rebels melted away before this display of force and bloodshed was avoided, but the Whisky Insurrection showed the spirit of the people. Hatred of the government had reached a danger point when a powerful minority could rise in rebellion.

WASHINGTON'S CONDUCT OF FOREIGN AFFAIRS

These party and class differences were further magnified by diplomatic difficulties during the Washington and Adams administrations. The outbreak of the French Revolution brought these problems to the fore and demonstrated that the United States was no more isolated from Europe in the eighteenth century than it was to be in the twentieth. In 1789, just a week after Washington's inauguration, the Estates-General began the fateful sessions that launched the Revolution. Within three years the Republic was proclaimed and the Revolution transformed into a "war of all peoples against all kings." The first stage of the French uprising aroused boundless rejoicing in America, for Federalists and Antifederalists alike felt a proprietary interest in revolutions everywhere and were delighted to welcome a new republic into the monarchy-ridden world. With the execution of Louis XVI and the beginning of the Reign of Terror, opinion began to divide; when France and England went to war in 1793 the division was completed. Federalists insisted that the choice was between French anarchy, atheism, and bloodshed, and English stability and legality; Antifederalists held that the people must choose between the liberty and equality of France and the tyranny of England. Almost to a man the Antifederalists supported France; the Federalists, England. This was the division in American opinion that made Washington's task so difficult when he sought to unravel the tangled European relations.

In the nation's dealing with France, the problem was complicated by the Treaty of Alliance of 1778, which bound the United States to aid that country in case of attack. The Federalists insisted that this had been made with the king and was no longer binding; the Antifederalists, while not advocating war, were still determined to give republican France all possible aid even at the risk of involvement. The President characteristically steered a middle course. In April, 1793, he issued a proclamation of American neutrality—which angered the Antifederalists—and officially recognized the existence of the French Republic—which aroused the ire of the Federalists. But even this compromising policy did not avoid all difficulties. The minister sent by France proved to be a fiery revolutionist named "Citizen" Edmond Genêt, who, misled by the enthusiastic reception tendered him when he landed at Charleston, believed all Americans were solidly behind his country. When Washington received him coldly and reminded him that the United States must preserve its neutrality, he refused to take warning, but went boldly ahead fitting up privateers to raid British shipping, plotting expeditions against Spain's possessions, and intriguing against the pro-English Federalists who controlled the government. Washington was left with no choice but to ask his recall and "Citizen" Genêt departed, but his brief stay had deepened the rift between the parties. The Federalists were more than ever sure that France could not be trusted; the Antifederalists, or Jeffersonian Republicans as they were called, were equally certain that the American government was in the hands of reactionaries who were ready to stab republicanism in the back.

This divided opinion vastly complicated pending negotiations with England relating to the Treaty of 1783 and the northwest posts. When the Revolution ended, English troops occupied a number of these frontier forts south of the border: at Dutchman's Point on Lake Champlain, and at Oswego, Niagara, Detroit, and Mackinac on the Great Lakes. England hesitated to give them up, fearing an end of the profitable fur trade in the lake country and the outbreak of an Indian uprising that would endanger both British and American settlers. Excuse to hold outposts clearly within the United States was found by English diplomats in the sections of the Treaty of Paris that pledged the states to place no obstacles in the path of English merchants or Loyalists seeking to collect their lawful debts. American states refused to abide by this treaty provision, and Washington faced the problem of expelling a stubborn and powerful nation from American soil. To make matters worse, settlement flowed into the West during these years, filling Kentucky and Tennessee so rapidly that they became states in 1792 and 1796, respectively; but as other settlers pushed north into the Ohio country, Indian tribes had to be removed if the expansion were to continue. Both the frontiersmen and the governmental officials were convinced that this would be difficult as long as the savages were supplied and encouraged by the British garrisons.

The western anti-British sentiment bred of these conflicts was matched in the East by resentment against England's attacks on American shipping. These began with the Anglo-French War in 1793, when the powerful English navy set out to cripple France by squashing the thriving trade between the United States and French colonial possessions. In November, 1793, an order in council ordered the detention of all ships, neutral or enemy, laden with French goods or carrying provisions to French possessions, and British men-of-war fell joyously to the task of preying on American commerce. As news of captured ships and condemned cargoes drifted back to the United States, a demand for war flamed along the seaboard as well as in the back country. By 1794 the two nations seemed on the point of hostilities.

Washington, however, wanted peace, and he determined on two actions to ease the tense situation. One was to fit out a well-trained expedition under General Anthony Wayne to crush the Ohio Indians and convince the British that war in the West would be unprofitable. This challenge was immediately accepted by the English officials, and while Wayne was drilling his troops in southern Ohio, a British expedition moved south from Detroit to the Maumee River and began constructing a new post—Fort Miami—in undisputed American territory. From this outpost word flew through the forest that the redcoats would fight on the side of the Indians, and by the spring of 1794 some two thousand tribesmen were gathered there, confidently waiting the approach of the American army. Wayne wisely delayed his attack until many of the impatient Indians drifted away, then fell on the remainder and decisively defeated them at the Battle of Fallen Timbers. In the actual combat the English did not dare aid their savage allies, and the red men crept back to their forest homes, discouraged and broken by the realization that England's nebulous promises meant nothing. Wayne gathered the remnants of the scattered western tribes and forced them to sign the Treaty of Greenville (August, 1795), ceding southern Ohio and southeastern Indiana to the United States.

Washington's second step was to make a last desperate bid for peace by diplomacy. John Jay, Chief Justice of the Supreme Court, was dispatched to England in the spring of 1794 with orders to wring whatever concessions he could from the British. He found England in a conciliatory mood, for her carefully built European alliance against France was crumbling, and the League of Armed Neutrality again threatened from the north. But before Jay could capitalize on this momentary weakness the attitude of the British negotiators changed; instead of making concessions they suddenly demanded favors from the United States. Ill-advised remarks by Alexander Hamilton were responsible for this abrupt about-face; this pro-English Federalist had assured the English minister that rumors of American entry into the League of Armed Neutrality were false and that England need not fear a war with the United States under any conditions. The enormity of this blunder was shown by Jay's Treaty, which was concluded in November, 1794. The British did agree to evacuate the northwest posts by June, 1796, but in return Canadian fur traders were to be allowed to operate south of the border and to use the important portages there; moreover, the United States agreed to England's contentions on the right of search and seizure of neutral ships on the high seas. Those critical of England and of Washington's administration could assert that the United States had made disgraceful concessions on trade and commerce in order to get back its own property. Yet Washington believed that this treaty was better than war and reluctantly affixed his signature to it in June, 1795. With the Treaty of Greenville, Jay's Treaty ended disorder in the West and flung open the frontier gates to a growing stream of pioneers.

Westward migration was further stimulated by the settling of a dispute with Spain that was even more troublesome. During these years, the Spanish monarchy was briefly tasting the glories of old, with a thriving commerce, an ample treasury, and a lusty nationalism which an able foreign minister, the Count of Floridablanca, easily translated into an aggressive foreign policy. Why not, he reasoned, restore a portion of Spain's lost empire at the expense of the weak United States? Excuse was found in the disputed Yazoo strip, claimed by both nations as a result of the ambiguous statements in the Treaty of 1783. Spain's ownership of the mouth of the Mississippi River, down which flowed the produce of the trans-Appalachian settlements on its way to markets in the East or in Europe, provided the opportunity. If Spain could strangle the economic life of the West by closing the Mississippi to navigation by Americans and at the same time encourage her Indian allies along the southern borderland to fall on the pioneer settlements, the frontiersmen might desert the impotent United States and seek refuge within the Spanish empire. Some, perhaps, could be encouraged to migrate to Louisiana or to the Floridas, and favorable immigration laws were passed to entice them; others, Floridablanca hoped, would grow sufficiently disgusted to carry Kentucky and Tennessee out of the Union and into Spain's eager arms. Confidently the Spanish foreign minister looked forward to the day when his empire would embrace the entire Mississippi Valley.

This intrigue went merrily on for a decade, reaching its boiling point in 1791, when a rash new governor of Louisiana, Hector, Baron de Carondelet, determined to bring it to a successful conclusion. He built up a powerful Indian confederation hostile to the United States; erected Fort Confederation on the Tombigbee River in undisputed American territory to hold his savage allies; offered remarkable inducements to frontiersmen who would move to Louisiana; opened negotiations with a number of prominent Kentuckians—including General James Wilkinson, who commanded the western army—and promised them favorable commercial concessions if they would encourage their countrymen to swing the West into Spain's hands. By 1794 his intrigue seemed on the verge of success and the West on the point of separating from the Union. The frontiersmen saw little reason to remain loyal to a United States that had failed to open the Mississippi River to their commerce or to crush the Indian tribes that plundered their settlements, that had placed a crushing tax on the whisky they exported, and that proved to be unfriendly to the French Revolutionists who were struggling for liberty dear to western hearts. Rumblings of this discontent reached the East and convinced Washington that he must act or face the threat of secession.

His solution was a new diplomatic bid for peace. Thomas Pinckney, American minister to London, accepted the assignment to Madrid with little enthusiasm, for he expected to be no more successful than the other agents had been who had battered against Spanish smugness for the past years. Yet when he arrived in June, 1795, he found Madrid ready not only to listen to reason but to back down completely. Both the European situation and the failure of Spain's policy in the Mississippi Valley were responsible. In Europe her war against revolutionary France proved disastrous, bringing only an empty treasury, military defeats at the hands of the French legions, and the threat of internal collapse. By the spring of 1795 Spain was forced to accept a humiliating peace and face the wrath of England, for the two nations were bound together by treaties that pledged both to fight until France was subdued. English retaliation would probably mean an attack on the Floridas and Louisiana. Friendship with the United States was vital in this tense situation, for if the irate Westerners joined with the British navy, Spain would certainly lose her North American possessions. Better to surrender on the questions in dispute with the Americans than lose everything, particularly as Spain now realized that her policy in the Mississippi Valley was a failure. The carefully built up Indian alliances were crumbling, the immigration laws failed to attract settlers, and the Kentucky intrigue cost much in bribes but accomplished little.

Spain's decision to yield made the Treaty of San Lorenzo, which was concluded by Pinckney in October, 1795, a complete victory for the United States. The Spaniards abandoned all claims to the Yazoo strip, granted Americans the free navigation of the Mississippi, the right of deposit at New Orleans, and extended commercial concessions in Spain itself although refusing to open colonial ports to American traders. Pinckney's treaty not only fostered expansion into the Southwest by ending turmoil there, but demonstrated that even in that day of snaillike transportation America's course was shaped by events in Europe.

The events of 1794 and 1795—Jay's Treaty, Pinckney's Treaty of San Lorenzo, Wayne's victory at Fallen Timbers, the Treaty of Greenville, the defeat of the Whisky Insurrection—brought Washington's administrations to a successful conclusion, allowing him to retire gracefully when he announced to the country that he would not seek re-election. He had every reason to survey his eight years in the presidency with pride: the nation's borders were freed of Indian attack and intrigue, its foreign problems were settled, its commerce was thriving. Yet one of Washington's ambitions—a united nation—was far from fulfilled. By 1796 the people were arrayed in two camps, following Hamilton, England, and commerce, or Jefferson, France, and agriculture, and the din of bitter party strife resounded through the land. After the resignation of Jefferson from the Cabinet in 1793 Washington himself was an actual party leader, governing through the Federalists whom he headed. His influence was enough to secure the election of 1796 for his party's candidate, John Adams, but Jefferson received the second highest number of electoral votes and became vice-president.

THE ADAMS ADMINISTRATION

Scarcely had Adams taken office than he found a new controversy boiling about his ears. France was the villain in this international drama. Powerful and aggressive under a five-man Directory that retained little revolutionary republicanism, the French government was roused to anger by Jay's Treaty. Until this amicable settlement with England the French clung to the hope that the United States would belatedly waken to its responsibilities under the agreement of 1778, but now they threw off all pretext of friendship and sent their corsairs against American shipping with a vengeance unrivaled by England. By 1797 some three hundred vessels had fallen to French raiders and the war cry was ringing through Federalist ranks. Adams, like Washington, was willing to go to any extreme rather than subject the young nation to trial by battle, and he sent three agents to Paris in the fall of 1797 with orders to patch up the differences in any way they could. Unfortunately for the President's hopes, the French foreign minister, Talleyrand, had an unsavory practice of exacting bribes from weak nations before dealing with them, and he tried his tactics now. The Americans were met by three French agents who informed them that they would not be received until the United States loaned France $10,000,000 and presented Talleyrand with an additional $250,000. They hastened back to their own country, where Adams, in the spring of 1798, laid the records of the whole disgraceful episode before Congress, substituting the letters X, Y, and Z for the names of the French agents.

The "XYZ affair" sent a wave of resentment surging across the United States. France had treated the country like a third-rate power; the national honor must be avenged. Stump orators and newspapers demanded "millions for defense but not one cent for tribute," and urged immediate war against the "atheistic, blood-steeped French." As more and more people took up the cry, what amounted to a national hysteria swept over the land; rumors flew of French armies bound for America, of Jeffersonian plots to overthrow the government, and of foreign legions in Canada and Louisiana drilling to fall on the United States. Amidst this atmosphere of fear and uncertainty two significant political developments occurred. One was a marked decline in the strength of the Jeffersonians, as sober folk deserted that party in droves to cast their lot with the anti-French Federalists. The other was a division of the Federalist party into a moderate wing headed by Adams and a more extreme faction led by Hamilton. Adams' followers were inclined to discount the French danger; Hamilton's magnified it beyond reason and preached the glories of a war with France, for their astute leader saw that hostilities would both strengthen the national government and discredit the Jeffersonians. When the congressional elections of 1798 went overwhelmingly Federalist, Hamilton was able to seize the reins of party power and extend his control even into the Cabinet, where ministers looked to him rather than to President Adams for advice.

In this situation the extreme Federalists made a few wise moves and a number of very foolish ones. They created a navy department, and by the end of 1798 had fourteen men-of-war in service, including such famous frigates as the *Constitution,* the *Constellation,* and the *United States.* They equipped privateers to prey on French commerce, and for more than two years an undeclared naval war raged between the two nations—the French Naval War of 1798. They authorized an army of ten thousand men with Hamilton in command and levied new taxes for its support. But most foolish of all was the passage of the Alien and Sedition Acts in the summer of 1798.

Three of these measures were designed to check the flow of immigrants into the United States, for the Federalists, believing that all foreigners were so steeped in the doctrines of French "anarchy" and "atheism" that they made dangerous citizens, were alarmed by the drift of aliens into Jefferson's party. One of the acts extended the period of residence before naturalization from five to fourteen years, another authorized the President to deport dangerous aliens, and the third allowed him to deport or imprison all noncitizens in times of war. The Sedition Act was even more repressive. Not only did it punish conspiracies against the government, but it provided that any person making a false or scandalous statement against Congress or the President, or stirring up hatred against them, could be imprisoned and fined.

This was going too far. The Alien Acts ran contrary to the spirit of a nation that had gained its strength by immigration; the Sedition Act violated the freedom of speech and press guaranteed by the first amendment to the Constitution. Jeffersonians pictured the laws as the crowning achievement in a Federalist plot to force a monarchy on America: they had captured the federal government, vastly extended its power, and now were protecting their tyrannical system from the criticism so indispensable to a democracy. This must not go unchallenged. But an attack even on the hated laws themselves was dangerous, for prejudiced Federalist judges might interpret this as an attempt to bring Congress into disrepute. In this emergency the Jeffersonians hit on a clever device. They persuaded the legislatures of the two states under Antifederalist control, Virginia and Kentucky, to pass resolutions denouncing the Alien and Sedition Acts and the whole tyrannical trend of the administration. These were sent to the legislatures of the other states for action. That most of the Federalist-dominated assemblies denounced the resolutions did not consign them to oblivion. The debate and editorial comment which they inspired showed the people that a strong opposition party was not willing to sit idly by while the flame of democracy was quenched.

The Virginia and Kentucky resolutions were well timed, for a popular reaction against Federalism was developing, nursed by rumors that Hamilton intended to use the army to stamp out opposition and that he planned an alliance with England which would turn the Franco-American naval skirmish into a full-blown war. The widely publicized resolutions trumpeted the challenge to liberty, and honest people who had had misgivings began to desert the Federalist party. The exodus went on through the winter of 1798–1799 as the anti-French hysteria died of its own excesses, and objections mounted to the direct taxes levied to support the army. President Adams was one of the first to sense the error of Federalist ways. He had never sympathized with the rabid anti-French faction of his party or shared their fear of attack; he often said that he no more expected to see a French army in America than in heaven. Popular hysteria had stayed his hands in the past, but now he dismissed Hamilton's followers from his Cabinet and unexpectedly announced that he had appointed a commission to seek peace with France. Hamilton was furious, but any move would subject him to the charge of prolonging the war, and he had to content himself with delaying the commission's sailing until early in 1800.

Adams' negotiators arrived in Paris at an opportune time, for Napoleon was now First Consul of France and his European ambitions overshadowed any wish to continue the minor war with the United States. Seven months of conversations resulted in the Convention of 1800. France accepted the abrogation of the Treaty of 1778, agreed that neutral ships made neutral goods, and received from the United States a promise not to press for indemnities for vessels illegally seized by French raiders. When the treaty was signed on September 30, 1800, it ended all current difficulties with France.

While news of the Convention of 1800 was sweeping the country, the election of 1800 took place. No time could have been more inopportune for the Federalists. Their program of centralized national authority, suitable to a national emergency, loomed as tyrannical in time of peace. Many people resented the party's having shamed them into an absurd hysteria two years before; others remembered the Alien and Sedition Acts and the contrast with the more liberal sentiments of the Virginia and Kentucky resolutions. To make matters far worse, the Federalists, hopelessly divided into two factions—one supporting Hamilton, the other Adams—dissipated their energies during the campaign by hurling pamphlet abuse at each other rather than at Jefferson. But most important of all was the fact that the people were weary of regimentation and discipline; they were contented and prosperous, and wanted to be let alone. The result was foreordained. On the first ballot in the electoral college Jefferson received seventy-three votes against sixty-five for Adams. The reign of the Federalists was over.

The party that passed from power with Jefferson's triumph could well take pride in its accomplishments. Its program of centralized authority and diversified economic life, though ill-suited to the United States of the eighteenth century, had nevertheless strengthened an infant nation in its most trying years. The cold indifference of the Federalists to the popular will snatched order from chaos, their talented leaders tided the Republic over its most critical years, and their philosophy, although oligarchical, had broadened the base upon which the federal government could expand its powers under later democratic leadership. The Americans were wise when they threw their support behind Hamilton for the first decade of the nation's existence; they were equally wise when they repudiated his leadership as soon as the United States was firmly established. Hamilton gave his country security; Jefferson was to start it along the long path to the democracy promised by the Declaration of Independence.

V

ENLIGHTENMENT AND REACTION

1783–1800

The political squabbles between Federalists and Republicans that culminated in the Jeffersonian triumph of 1800 had little effect on American thought. Instead, the intellectual impetus of the postrevolutionary decades was provided by two other forces, each more enduring than any quarrel over the presidency. One of these—the pride felt by the people in their newborn country—was expressed in a conscious effort to write books, paint pictures, design buildings, and even worship God in a distinctly American way. The other—the continuing struggle for more democratic political and social institutions—led to such a vigorous attack on religious and economic orthodoxy that long before the turn of the century an alarmed band of reactionaries entered the field to combat changes threatening the old social structure. These conservatives gained strength so rapidly that by 1800 their ideas were generally accepted by the upper classes, and the United States was launched on a period of patrician control which lasted for a quarter of a century.

ADOLESCENT NATIONALISM

The influence of cultural nationalism was pervasive. The Revolutionary generation was inordinately proud of its country—of its victories in war, its republican government, its limitless prospects. Moreover, the years of combat made Americans aware, for the first time, of the boundlessness of their land; provincial New Englanders learned of the beauties of the Chesapeake, of the riches of the Carolina tidewater, of the magnificence of the Hudson River Valley; Virginians, having traveled far afield, brought home tales of the green Vermont hills, of the rolling Pennsylvania countryside, of the hospitable taverns in Boston's crooked lanes. More important was the realization, born of the war, that the people of this vast country—Americans all—had much in common. Many a Connecticut farm lad, fresh from the wars, awed his neighbors with tales of other soldiers who spoke with Dutch accents, or worshiped at Anglican

90

churches, or carried the long rifles that were the badges of the over-mountain men, yet were just as friendly and just as human, though perhaps not as fortunate, as if they had been born in the Nutmeg State. These were startling stories for a people whose horizon scarcely extended beyond the range of hills that lay across the valley from their farmlands. In consequence their provincialism somewhat abated and a new national patriotism began to take shape.

Even before the war was over a fervent pride in the American homeland found expression. Celebrations of Independence Day were held long before independence was won, with orations, enthusiastic renditions of "Yankee Doodle," and the traditional thirteen toasts to freedom, unity, and Brother Jonathan—the Revolutionary version of Uncle Sam. With the end of the war such fervor reached new heights. In books and pamphlets, newspapers and magazines, sermons and Fourth of July speeches, self-appointed patriots told the Americans that they were the chosen people, selected by a benevolent God from among the unworthy left in Europe, to enjoy life in a modern Eden under the most perfect government ever devised. A people who listened to such enthusiastic outbursts day after day naturally grew proud of themselves and their country. "The national vanity of the United States," wrote one disgusted English traveler, "sur-passes that of any other country, not even excepting France. It blazes out everywhere and on all occasions—in their conversation, newspapers, pamphlets, speeches, and books."

Amid the glow of self-adulation, a sense of inferiority, seldom expressed, haunted American gentry and added to the warmth of their patriotic fervor. The psychological drives of nationalism demanded an American character, a national folklore, a culture stamped out in a unique American mold. Unconsciously moving away from the cosmopolitan spirit of the Age of the Enlightenment, patriotic mythmakers were haunted by doubts that America possessed a culture of its own; the infant nation, they concluded, must evolve a national heritage independent of Europe, purged of English influences, worthy of a free people. The young republic, with the self-consciousness of precocious youth, conceived itself as carrying the torch of liberty which aged Europe had let slip from her grasp.

"For America in her infancy to adopt the present maxims of the old world," declaimed a patriot, "would be to stamp the wrinkle of decrepit age upon the bloom of youth, and to plant the seed of decay in a vigorous constitution." So the people reasoned, looking hopefully to the future, for genius was bound to flourish among a liberty-loving people. A nation that could produce a Washington could certainly produce a Shakespeare; only a little time was needed to make the United States "the seat of the Muses, the Athens of our age, the admiration of the world." In such characteristic hyperbole the vision of American grandeur encouraged the nation's first expression in the world of arts and letters; any writer, any painter, any architect who could contribute to a national culture was assured a sympathetic audience and judgment by patriotic rather than critical standards.

Some carried the new worship of nationalism to imbecilic naïveté. One New York doctor, alarmed lest children be infected by the Old World ideas contained in English nursery rhymes, proposed rewriting Mother Goose in the American idiom. The well-known verse from the "Four and Twenty Blackbirds" was revised to read:

> When the pie was opened
> The Birds they were songless,
> Was not that a pretty dish
> To set before the Congress?

"While I discard the King of England with whom we have nothing to do," he wrote, "I give [the children] some knowledge of our general government by specifying our Congress, as well as correcting their childish impressions of the musical functioning of cooked blackbirds." Another zealot would have revised the monetary system along lines less reminiscent of the "British intricate mode of reckoning." "Their mode," said he, "is suited to the genius of their government, for it seems to be the policy of tyrants, to keep their accounts in as intricate and perplexing a method as possible; that the smaller number of their subjects may be able to estimate their enormous impositions and exactions. But Republican money ought to be simple and adapted to the meanest capacity." Others, rebelling against using even the language of George III, talked seriously of substituting Hebrew or German in schools and public documents. Those not willing to go this far took pains to emphasize the differences between American English and the English of England; one French traveler noted that the people avoided such expressions as "You speak English well," using instead "You speak American well," or "American is not hard to learn."

To translate into tangible form these prejudices against the English language became the lifework of Noah Webster, a Connecticut-born schoolmaster and editor. "As an independent nation," he wrote early in his career, "our honor requires us to have a system of our own, in language as well as government. Great Britain, whose children we are and whose language we speak, should no longer be *our* standard; for the taste of her writers is already corrupted, and her language on the decline." Recognizing the differences between English and American speech, he set out to give his nation a language of its own by rewriting the written language to conform to the oral. This reform would, he believed, accomplish a triple good: writers would be encouraged to use the native idiom as a means of glorifying the national scene, children would find it easier to master the mysteries of reading so essential for democratic voters, and provincial differences which kept apart the people of different sections would be weakened by national uniformity in spelling and speaking. With these goals in mind, Webster produced a number of spelling books and dictionaries, using phonetic spelling and simplified American grammatical forms. Although many of his more radical innovations were not adopted—his last great dictionary, the monumental *American Dictionary of the English language* (1828), abandoned such earlier spellings as "wimmen," "fether," "thum," and "groop"—Webster did popularize a proud conviction among his countrymen that the American idiom was truly their own.

Historians, poets, and novelists were as much influenced by the spirit of cultural nationalism abroad in their land as were the revisers of nursery rhymes or the disciples of language reform. Histories of the Revolution, appearing by the dozens in the years just after the war, were all compounded of that remarkable blend of imagination and plagiarism which passed for historical writing in those uncritical days. Biographies of military leaders were even more popular, with lives of Washington leading the list; works ranged from the pious eulogy of Mason L. Weems (where the delightful fiction of little George and the cherry tree first appeared) to the ponderous five-volume tome by Chief Justice John Marshall which was so strongly biased that the first President appeared as the father of the Federalist party rather than of his country. From the historical point of view little can be said of the effusions of this period; that they appealed to a generation which liked patriotism in strong doses is suggested by the forty editions of "Parson" Weems' *Life of Washington* published during these years.

Equally in demand were the works of the misguided gentry who tried to glorify the United States in verse. Among the hundreds who expressed their nationalistic ardor in rhyme was a small group of Connecticut educators, lawyers, and businessmen who were known to an admiring audience as the "Hartford Wits." They wrote voluminously, and the majestic cantos that rolled endlessly from their pens were viewed by awed Americans as masterpieces beside which the clumsy stanzas of Shakespeare or Milton sank to insignificance. Actually their writings were crude and imitative, yet these weaknesses were more than offset by the patriotism resounding from every line. For they had a purpose, these inspired poets; their one objective was, in the words of Joel Barlow, to "exhibit the importance of this country in every point of view as the noblest and most elevated part of the earth." Barlow reflected this spirit in his famous "Vision of Columbus" (1787); so did Timothy Dwight, who in "Greenfield Hill" (1794) proclaimed that the United States was

> by heaven design'd
> th' example bright, to renovate mankind.

Again, in his poem "Columbia," Dwight spoke of his native land with a devotion almost religious:

> Thy reign is the last and noblest of time;
> Most fruitful thy soil, most inviting thy clime;
> Let the crimes of the East ne'er encrimson thy name;
> Be freedom and science and virtue thy fame.

The writer was no emotional schoolboy; he was a sober, conservative clergyman and president of Yale.

The novelists, exploring a daring new medium frowned upon as a time waster throughout colonial days, also capitalized on cultural nationalism to gain their first American audiences. Using American scenes and American characters, they paraded their books before the people as truthful, morally sound, and thoroughly national, and had the satisfaction of seeing a taste for fiction gradually develop. Best known among these early writers was Charles Brockden Brown, who glorified his native Pennsylvania in *Wieland* (1798) and in half a dozen other romances. To pioneer in this way among people who had either scorned novel reading altogether or preferred romantic pictures of aristocracies in European settings required the boldness of patriotism. Brown, conscious of the part he was playing on the literary frontier, wrote bluntly in the preface to one of his later works: "Puerile superstition and exploded manners, Gothic castles and chimeras, are the materials usually employed for this end. The incidents of Indian hostility, and the perils of the western wilderness, are far more suitable; and for a native of America to overlook these would admit of no apology."

American painting likewise was pervaded by the stimulus of nationalism, and all could agree with the artist who maintained that art in a new country was justified only when it was used to "preserve and diffuse the memory of the noblest series of actions that have ever presented themselves in the history of mankind"—by which, of course, he meant the American Revolution. With an audience for patriotic canvases assured, painters labored to preserve the features of Revolutionary heroes and a pictorial record of their victorious battles. Gilbert Stuart, a Rhode Island genius who deserted his father's snuff mill for a career as a portrait painter, achieved immortality for himself and his subjects; his magnificent paintings of George Washington, his faithful likenesses of John Adams, Thomas Jefferson, James Madison, James Monroe, Samuel Adams, James Otis, Fisher Ames, and a host of other patriots assured him international fame. Comparable to Stuart in a closely allied medium was John Trumbull, a Connecticut-born artist whose brilliant, miniaturelike paintings of scenes from Revolutionary history—"Battle of Bunker Hill," "Signing of the Declaration of Independence," "Capture of the Hessians at Trenton," "Surrender of Cornwallis," and dozens more—made him the leading illustrator of high school textbooks for several subsequent generations.

Similarly, architects, casting about for a means of glorifying America's unique institutions, devised a method which actually changed the physical appearance of the United States. They drew inspiration from the popular identification of the new nation with the ancient republics of Greece and Rome, an identification memorialized in the place names of towns in western New York settled at this time—Troy, Ithaca, Rome, Syracuse, and Utica. Why not visibly symbolize the parallel by scattering replicas of Greek temples or Roman colosseums across the countryside? An army of designers and builders during the prosperous 1790's, of whom Thomas Jefferson was the most famous, put these plans into execution. Jefferson was as skilled in architecture as in statecraft. His own home at Monticello, the buildings he designed for the University of Virginia, and the gracefully domed Massachusetts State House (the work of America's first professional architect, Charles Bulfinch), all indicated a faithful duplication of Roman forms. So also did the new capital city of Washington, where the government established itself in 1800, for despite the fact that this new metropolis was laid out by a Frenchman, its capitol building designed by architects trained in France and England, and its President's mansion created by an Irishman, the guiding genius was Jefferson, who insisted on rigidly classical designs throughout. During the early nineteenth century the vogue of Roman architecture gave way to a Greek revival that lasted until the Civil War. Throughout this period there was scarcely a statehouse, a factory, or a farm dwelling built in the United States without resplendent Ionic columns, Doric friezes, or Corinthian pilasters, all painstakingly wrought in wood, tin, or cast iron. These classical imitations were artificial and prevented the United States from developing a distinctive building style of its own, but an immature generation might conceivably have committed worse aesthetic offense.

THE ENLIGHTENMENT DEEPENS

Cultural nationalism gave the new nation farmhouses like temples and textile mills crowned with domes, but other factors helped to shape the climate of American opinion during the postrevolutionary years. The eighteenth-century Enlightenment continued to exert a profound influence upon men and women already prepared for its invigorating effects by their own Revolutionary experience. The rebellion against authority, the reliance on a philosophy of natural rights, the emphasis on humanitarianism that characterized the Enlightenment were just as deeply imbedded in Revolutionary theory. So also was the idea of progress that had driven the colonists to rebellion against restrictive economic legislation and that still stirred their dreams as they looked forward to a glorious future. Under these conditions the doctrines of the Enlightenment were certain to find favor with Americans, especially after 1789, when the outbreak of the French Revolution—based on the same theories of natural rights— focused the attention of the whole Atlantic basin on man's struggle for liberty, equality, and democracy.

Every phase of life in America responded to the impact of this stimulating philosophy. In religion the reaction was immediate. The attack on outworn creeds was not new; for half a century progressive thinkers, rebelling against concepts of God as a celestial busybody who constantly interfered in the affairs of His universe, had substituted instead an orderly Creator who obeyed natural laws of His own design. Remarkable now was the spread of such deistic ideas among ordinary people. Deism became, in the postrevolutionary years, a national fad, and thousands upon thousands of Americans embraced rationalism, joined cults to study its principles, and reveled in ridiculing orthodox Christianity.

Responsible for the remarkable advance of this new creed was the propaganda spread by three disciples of the Enlightenment. One was Ethan Allen, the Revolutionary patriot from Vermont. His contribution, a crudely written but militant defense of deism entitled *Reason the Only Oracle of Man* (1784), probably attracted few readers, but its vigorous attack on revealed religion reflected the temper of that day. Allen rejected the doctrine of revelation, dismissed Biblical miracles as incompatible with natural law, and scoffed at the Old Testament account of the creation. He said nothing new, but his unflinching defense of an extreme deistical position encouraged others to follow in his footsteps. This was what Allen wished, for he sincerely believed that Americans, as a free republican people, must find a faith more in keeping with their enlightened thought than were the autocratic religions of Europe.

More influential than Ethan Allen's outburst was Thomas Paine's *Age of Reason* (1796), a fiery popularization of deism from the pen of the excitable patriot whose *Common Sense* had helped foment the Revolution. This passionate, well-written summary dismissed the book of Genesis, discarded miracles as unreasonable, criticized the historical accuracy of the Old Testament, and explained God as the First Cause whose well-ordered universe required no celestial interference. In language understandable to laymen, Paine presented an intelligent condensation of the views of Europe's most outspoken deists, and the enthusiasm with which the American people welcomed the *Age of Reason* showed their receptivity to this viewpoint. Newspapers opened their columns to its arguments, booksellers hawked it through the towns, clubs were formed in city and country to debate its merits. In candle-lighted drawing rooms, about the cracker barrels of village stores, before the blazing fires of frontier cabins, men and women discussed Tom Paine's flaming words and weighed conversion to the new cult. Leaders of orthodoxy, horrified, heaped such abuse on Paine through sermon and printed page that future generations were misled into the belief that he was "a filthy little atheist"; yet in his own time every attack advertised and popularized his liberal message.

While hundreds of converts to deism were won by Ethan Allen and thousands by Tom Paine, much of its success was due to the organizing ability of Elihu Palmer. A former Baptist minister, Palmer left his church, convinced that formal religion was a tool of the aristocracy to force despotism on the people. He not only wrote widely but set up deistic clubs in many eastern cities. Publications of these societies, their speakers, newspapers, and Palmer's own *Temple of Reason* bore an impressive fruit by the end of the 1790's. No one will ever know how many Americans were deists, but the number was certainly large and included such governmental leaders as Thomas Jefferson, Benjamin Franklin, John Adams, and probably George Washington. Most of Palmer's followers, however, were the oppressed members of the lower classes who believed, with Paine, that deism best comported with democracy.

The connection between oppressive authority in religion and in government did not escape the attention of the economic overlords of the United States, and was alone enough to damn deism. Why foster a cult that would encourage the downtrodden masses to expect to have greater control of their own affairs—religious or secular—than in the past? Reasoning in this way, many of the nation's wealthy, especially in the Northeast, refused to countenance deism because they feared its disturbing influence on the existing social order. Yet these same men were ready to reject orthodox Christianity, not because they had been won over by such "rabble-rousers" as Paine or Palmer, but because their conversion to the doctrines of the Enlightenment convinced them that traditional religion was irrational. These men sought intellectual and emotional refuge in two new sects—Universalism and Unitarianism.

The Universalist Church owed its American existence to an outcast English clergyman, the Reverend John Murray, who fled to New England to escape a ruined life in the Old World. Discovering that his faith in universal salvation appealed to many, he organized the first Universalist congregation at Gloucester, Massachusetts, in 1779 and another at Boston in 1793. More congregations followed, until by 1794 a church organization was formally established on a national scale with Murray and one of his converts, Hosea Ballou, as its outstanding leaders. Universalism was a liberal creed that sparkled with doctrines drawn from the Enlightenment: rejection of the divinity of Jesus and of belief in human depravity, acceptance of the fatherhood of God and the brotherhood of man, emphasis on the cheerful promise "that *every individual* shall in due time be separated from sin, and rendered fit to associate with the denizens of heaven." Such an optimistic faith, pledging universal salvation through the good offices of a benevolent Creator, appealed especially to New England's successful upper classes, among whom Universalism made numerous converts.

Even more attractive among the well to- do of the Northeast were the teachings of Unitarianism. A European importation, Unitarianism gained its first foothold in the United States in 1785, when the Episcopal congregation of King's Chapel in Boston chose a young Unitarian, James Freeman, as its pastor and revised the prayerbook to emphasize the subordinate position of Christ in the Trinity. Freedom of conscience and inquiry, the discovery of God through reason, the belief that divine man was too good to be damned by God—these were the new teachings. A hymn, written in 1795, caught the spirit of the Unitarian revolt against traditional authority:

> Absurd and vain attempt to bind
> With iron chains, the freeborn mind!
> To force conviction, and reclaim
> The wandering, by destructive flame.

So tuned to the times were such beliefs that the new church made rapid progress; Harvard was won over in 1805 when it chose its professor of divinity from among the Unitarians, and during the next years so many converts were made that New England seemed on the verge of deserting the Congregational churches bequeathed by the Puritans.

While liberalism in theology, manifested in new churches, demonstrated the influence of the Enlightenment, so also did the rapid spread of tolerance among older faiths. The separation of church and state in Virginia and in the other newborn commonwealths could be expected from a people in rebellion against authority, but more startling was the kindly spirit with which American Protestants began to view their former enemies, the Catholics. They still held no brief for Catholic teaching, but persecution had no place in an age when, in the words of Thomas Jefferson, "reason and free inquiry are the only effectual agents against error. Give a loose to them, they will support the true religion by bringing every false one to their tribunal, to the test of their investigation." State after state swept away its colonial inheritance of antipapal legislation; Vermont dropped its constitutional restrictions on Catholics in 1786, Georgia opened her legislature to all regardless of creed, Delaware abolished religious tests for voters. This same spirit led the framers of the Constitution to agree, with only one dissenting vote, on a clause assuring men of all faiths an equal right to federal offices. From that day forward no single faith could seek pre-eminence by government support; in the best tradition of the Enlightenment each must stand or fall upon its merits.

The drive for freedom of conscience was paralleled by a struggle to abolish colonial restraints on freedom of social action. This was concentrated in New England, where a residue of restrictive laws, left behind by the receding wave of Puritanism, still controlled individual conduct. Few frontal attacks were made, but popular indifference soon reduced most of these narrow injunctions to unheeded laws on the statute books. Thus dancing, frowned upon as immoral in the past, was Boston's "principal and favorite amusement" by 1790; secular music was increasingly performed by orchestral societies in eastern cities and even invaded the sacred precincts of the churches; theaters, long considered the certain path to perdition, were springing up everywhere. Philadelphia repealed its laws against state plays in 1789, Boston followed a few years later, and the rest of the country soon fell into line. Religious conservatives bemoaned the laxness of the times and gloomily prophesied a decay in morality, but the majority of the people hailed with enthusiasm the overthrow of restraints on individual conduct.

The quest for freedom—of conscience and action—was typical of the expanding Enlightenment; so was the humanitarian crusade to improve the lot of the common people which was pressed vigorously by forward-looking leaders of the Revolutionary generation. Thomas Jefferson reflected the leveling humanist spirit as clearly as any. His concern was for ordinary Americans—small farmers, artisans, laborers, tenants—who were struggling to secure a stake in society. Jefferson did not believe that all social distinctions should be stripped away or that the masses should be granted immediate political equality, for he realized that they were ill-prepared for such responsibilities. Instead, he proposed a training program, to be carried on through the schools, to fit them for a share in the burdens of government. In the meantime they must be protected from exploitation by legal means and provided with every opportunity for economic betterment. Only in this way, Jefferson and his followers insisted, could the United States attain that ultimate equality which was the goal of every believer in natural rights.

Basic in this program was a reform in the educational system, which had been, in both Europe and America, the exclusive property of the churches. Voices were raised to demand that the state, which would benefit most from an enlightened electorate, assume the task of educating its people free of charge. "Larning," wrote one New England farmer, "is of the greatest importance to the report of a free government, and to prevent this the few are always crying up the advantages of costly collages, national acadimys & Grammer schools, in order to make places for men to live without work, & to strengthen their party. But are always opposed to cheep schools & woman schools, the ondly or prinsaple means by which larning is spred amongue the Many." These crudely spoken words were echoed in more grammatical (but no more sincere) form by dozens of the country's leaders. John Adams urged instruction for "every class and rank of people, down to the lowest and poorest"; James Madison counseled that a "people who mean to be their own governors must arm themselves with the power that knowledge gives"; George Washington cautioned that "in proportion as the structure of government gives force to public opinion, it is essential that public opinion should be enlightened."

Yet of all these public officials, Thomas Jefferson alone proved willing to render more than pious lip service to free education. His plan for an educational system for his native Virginia, advanced in 1779, provided for locally supported public schools to assure three years of free elementary instruction for all boys in the state. In addition, talented students were to be sent to academies and colleges under a scholarship system that offered equal opportunity to all. Although not adopted, Jefferson's proposals reflected the advanced thinking of liberal reformers. So also did the more daring plans of a few revolutionaries who courageously advocated public education for girls as well as boys on the ground that the future mothers of America should be equipped to train their children in the duties of citizenship. At least two coeducational schools—one opened at Greenfield Hill, Connecticut, and the other at Boston in the 1780's—testified to a dawning belief that both men and women had a natural right to intellectual careers.

The reformers who advocated these changes realized that, until the masses were educated to a point where they could care for themselves, they must be protected from exploitation. This could be accomplished only by a broad program of humanitarian legislation, and to this laudable end the enlightened few who sincerely believed in democracy turned during the postwar years. Particularly objectionable in their eyes was the harsh legal system inherited from the past, for this bore brutally upon the lower classes, who might be driven by the lash of poverty to commit minor offenses. The law in most colonies failed to distinguish between insignificant transgressions and major crimes; at the time of the Revolution the death sentence could be imposed for twenty types of crime in Pennsylvania, fourteen in Connecticut, twenty-seven in Virginia, and sixteen in New York. Punishment meted out for less serious violations was scarcely less cruel, with whipping, mutilation, and branding still in common use. Many a victim of this vicious system, guilty of no worse offense than stealing a few pennies' worth of bread, was ruined for life by the shame of a public lashing or by the searing scars of the branding iron upon his cheek, stigmatizing him forever with the mark of a criminal.

Reformers—led once more by Thomas Jefferson—were quick to point out that the very barbarism of this harsh system defeated its purpose, for judges would often release known criminals rather than inflict the cruel sentences prescribed by law. The answer, they insisted, anticipating the well-known words of the Gilbert and Sullivan opera, was to "make the punishment fit the crime"; imprisonment or fines for minor offenses, jail sentences at hard labor for serious transgressions, and the death penalty for murder or high treason where the crime against society was so great that radical social surgery was justified. Pennsylvania adjusted its criminal code to these ideals in 1794, Virginia did so two years later, and the rest of the states slowly followed.

Reforms such as these forced humanitarians to focus their attention on the jails of America, for under the new codes penal institutions were no longer simply places to confine criminals awaiting punishment but had become possible mediums for the reform of prisoners. An English pioneer, John Howard, whose important book on *State of the Prisons in England and Wales* was widely circulated in the United States, first called attention to the problem. Inspired by his pleas, an American group formed the Society for Alleviating the Miseries of Public Prisons (1787) and first began to disclose conditions within their own jails. Their reports shocked the nation. Prisons, far from reforming criminals, were actually turning them into degenerates to be cast out eventually on society. Minor offenders were thrown into crowded cells with little furniture, no heat, and insufficient food, where all ages and both sexes were confined together in squalid conditions sufficient to break the will of the strongest. Such revelations goaded a horrified public to demand far-reaching change. Pennsylvania acted first; by 1800 its legislature enacted laws separating witnesses from convicts, segregating the sexes, and providing that "the most hardened and atrocious offenders" should be kept in separate cell blocks. At the same time work was introduced to relieve the monotony of prison life and to hasten rehabilitation. Few other states followed this laudable example, but the movement toward reform was marked and conditions gradually improved during the next generation.

As offensive to the humanitarians as the conditions within the jails were the universal laws making debt a crime and providing that any person unable to meet his obligations should be thrown into prison until he was able to do so. The victims of this unfortunate legal system were legion—in 1785 half the prisoners in Philadelphia were debtors—and their fate was a sordid one. Cast into foul cells with confirmed criminals, forced to depend upon charity for food and clothing, destined to rot in confinement unless some friend paid off the sums that they owed, the debtors were miserable examples of the worst features of archaic legal codes. Reformers began their attack on imprisonment for debt soon after the Revolution, but they accomplished little except the passage of a few laws providing for the segregation of debtors from other criminals. As late as 1815 two thousand debtors clogged the jails of New York, seven hundred of them for debts of less than twenty-five dollars. Not until a generation later did an awakened people abolish this inhuman system that bore so heavily upon the nation's poor.

Underlying the whole reform movement in education and in the law were the postulates of the Enlightenment: that progress was inevitable and that man could improve himself by reshaping his environment. Belief in an ideal future was an elixir, but favorite panaceas were ignored by an indifferent public or pigeonholed by hostile upper-class legislatures. Prophets of progress regarded such setbacks as temporary, for they were confident that the American struggle for independence would serve as an impetus for continuous reform, leading eventually to the abolition of poverty, absolutism, feudalism, war, and all special privileges. Philip Freneau, a great poet of democracy, caught the spirit of his reforming generation in the lines:

> And men will rise from what they are;
> Sublimer, and superior, far,
> Than Solon guessed, or Plato saw;
> All will be just, all will be good—
> That harmony, "not understood,"
> Will reign the general law.

All things were possible in a democratic, enlightened self-governing nation.

If this progress was to benefit the greatest number, careful planning by the federal government was inescapable. Dr. Benjamin Rush, prominent Philadelphia physician, spoke for a whole group in 1783 when he said that "the American war is over but that is far from being the case of the American Revolution." If the national government adopted a vigorous program designed to improve the manners, morals, and economic well-being of the people, the revolution would continue for generations. Among other liberal leaders, Thomas Jefferson called for positive governmental action against such obstacles to progress as aristocratic land laws, slavery, and snobbish educational systems; while Thomas Paine in his *Rights of Man* (1791) envisaged a not-too-distant future when graduated income taxes and ground taxes would eliminate poverty and provide security for the masses. To these men and a host of others, progress implied a broadened democracy, a society reoriented toward equality and liberty.

THE COUNTERREVOLUTIONARIES

Unfortunately for the immediate future of the United States, this progressive point of view was embraced by only a small minority of government leaders, and as the years of the Revolutionary era passed, their numbers steadily decreased. For rising to power in America was a new aristocracy, formed of men whose wealth and social prestige were gained during the war. As the postwar events unfolded before their eyes—the unrest of the "critical period," the strident protests of Daniel Shays' followers, the liberal clamor against the Constitution, the chorus of support raised for the French revolutionists—they came to believe more and more that the mass of the people was not only unfit for self-government but must be rigidly controlled if property was to be safe. By the 1790's such self-made aristocrats were ready to act. Their strenuous campaign against the leveling tendencies of the Revolution and the Enlightenment affected every phase of intellectual life and launched the United States upon a counterreformation which lasted until the age of Jackson.

The jaundiced eyes of this upper-class group could see little good in the program of democracy and humanitarianism advocated by the reformers. Suspicious of the masses and distrustful of the improvability of the common people, it held that a nation's government and intellectual life should be shaped by the gifted few rather than by the talentless many. "The people of all nations," wrote John Adams, "are naturally divided into two sorts, the gentlemen and the simple men. . . . The poor are destined to labor, and the rich, by the advantages of education, independence and leisure, are qualified for superior stations." Adams, unlike his Puritan forefathers, would not go so far as to suggest inequality before the law, but he did insist that differences of birth and wealth exerted a "natural and inevitable influence upon society." He believed, and the majority of the economically elect agreed with him, that the ordinary people were unfit for either governmental or cultural leadership. They must be kept from the ballot box, denied educational opportunities, and hemmed in by social and religious restrictions to keep them in their place. Inequality, stability, and reliance upon authority were the watchwords of conservatives as once they had been in the Middle Ages.

An effective weapon of counterreform was religion, for the reactionaries well knew that orthodoxy would help restore a respect for authority among the masses. They could rely on support from churchmen, who were by this time thoroughly alarmed by the excesses of deism among the common people and the growing strength of rationalism. How beneficial it would be if the economically and religiously orthodox could join forces against the "infamous combination of Jacobism and atheism" that had infected the minds of the lower classes as a result of the French Revolution. Speaking for the whole upper class, Alexander Hamilton, who more than any other man feared the leveling tendencies apparent in postwar society, complained that "a league has at length been cemented between the apostles and disciples of irreligion and anarchy. Religion and government have both been stigmatized as abuses; as unwarrantable restraints upon the freedom of man; as causes of the corruption of his nature, intrinsically good." He proposed a Christian Constitutional Society to uphold orderly government and old-fashioned religion as checks against the liberal ferment.

Hamilton's society was never formed, for by the middle of the 1790's the churchmen had taken matters into their own hands and initiated a powerful drive on deism and rationalism by means of the religious revival. As early as 1792, individual ministers, inspired by their mounting fear of French atheism, found their tongues newly eloquent and capable of emotional pleas that lured increasing numbers of backsliders into the churches. Stimulated by success, they redoubled efforts among their own congregations. Through New England, across the middle states, into the South, isolated one-man revivals spread, leaving a wake of conversion and repentance behind them. The masses alone were affected; the intellectually elite among the Unitarians and Universalists were indifferent to revivalistic emotionalism.

At first the quickening of religious interest was sporadic and local, but by 1800 a full-blown revival fired the nation. Its center was in the trans-Appalachian West, until then a cell of lawlessness and French "atheism," for by this time the Methodist, Baptist, and evangelical Presbyterian clergymen who had long labored there in vain had discovered a device to appeal to frontiersmen—the camp meeting. In the forests or the valleys, open-air arenas for worship would be cleared of brush and trees, rude outdoor pulpits erected, rough benches arranged, and a battery of ministers assembled. Then the crowds would arrive, coming by wagon from far and near, with each family bringing its food, a few neighbors, and perhaps a tent to live in. For five days or more they would listen to almost continuous preaching in a tense atmosphere of swelling hymns, impassioned pleading from the pulpit, shouted prayers, and shrieks of sufferers awaiting salvation. Many of the penitent were carried to heights of emotionalism that found strange expression: one might be seized with the "jerks" and bound about like a football with arms and legs and head all twitching violently, another might run about barking like a dog or dance wildly through the crowds. All, however, emerged ready to accept salvation and renounce their sinful ways.

The camp meeting, starting in Kentucky in 1800, spread rapidly over the remainder of the West, until by 1803 the whole trans-Appalachian country was in the throes of religious rebirth. Nor did this Great Revival burn itself out in the western settlements; instead, its influence spread backward from the frontier as ministers adopted the tactics of western preachers to counteract religious rationalism and win emotional mastery over eastern congregations. During the first decade of the nineteenth century the nation was aflame with religious excitement; deism was dying, conversions increased, and church memberships mounted.

Laudable as were these events in conservative eyes, neither the economically nor the religiously orthodox were content to rest upon their laurels lest there be a return to the godless conditions of the 1790's. To prevent backsliding, the strategists of orthodoxy initiated the second phase of the religious counterreformation, creating new organizations to make more complete their evangelical sway over the minds of the common people. Most prominent among the new organizations were the home missionary societies, which were founded in seaboard states with the avowed purpose of imposing the ideals and standards of the conservative East upon the lawless West. By 1810 their missionaries were everywhere in the over-mountain country, preaching orthodoxy to the "wild frontiersmen," and by 1826 the state societies were sufficiently numerous to unite in a nation-wide organization, the American Home Missionary Society. Supplementing the work of these agents were others who sought to perpetuate old-fashioned religion by placing an approved version of the Scriptures in every American home. The latter activities, directed by local societies at first, were coordinated on a national scale in 1816 with the formation of the American Bible Society. Reaching further down the social scale for converts scarcely literate enough to read the Holy Word directly, the orthodox denominations organized various state tract societies, which by 1825 pooled resources in another national association, the American Tract Society. Its pious little pamphlets—"Advice from a Master to His Apprentice," "To Christian Females on Simplicity of Dress," "An Affectionate Address to a Married Couple," and the like—were soon broadcast wholesale; by 1827 fifty-three million pages of tracts were distributed yearly, indoctrinating myriads in the patterns of conformity.

Closely allied with these religious societies were others formed to stamp out Sabbath breaking, dancing, horse racing, drinking, cardplaying, the use of profanity, and other so-called human frailties. Smacking more of seventeenth-century Puritanism than of the Age of the Enlightenment, these organizations plunged relentlessly into the task of abolishing all practices that displeased the orthodox. Their particular antipathy was the American habit of alcoholic overindulgence, for rare indeed was the property-threatening mob that was not fortified by rum. Taking their cue from doctors' reports on the harm caused by excessive drinking among the Revolutionary troops, they besieged Congress with petitions urging curbs on the liquor traffic or busied themselves forming societies whose members would take the pledge; the Connecticut Society for the Reformation of Morals (1813) was representative. Although this crusade gained little headway before the War of 1812, its mere presence signaled the passing of an enlightened era when liberty and individualism held sway.

The reactionaries who presided over the counterreformation in religion were equally concerned with the educational progress of the United States—but in a negative way. Many of them talked glowingly of the need for public schools, but actions spoke louder than words, and act they would not. Vigorous leadership was needed at this point to establish a state-supported school system, for both the educated classes and the uneducated masses objected to taxes to provide schooling for their neighbors' children; an intensive propaganda campaign was needed to arouse public opinion in favor of free public schools. Few among the economically elect were willing to sponsor such a drive, for whether they admitted it or not, they believed that the common man was unfit for self-government and incapable of improvement. An increase in learning among the masses would only create dissatisfaction and weaken the authoritarian hold of the upper classes.

This attitude alone explains the lag between educational theory and practice in the waning years of the eighteenth century. In the sixteen state constitutions drawn up before 1800, education was mentioned in only seven, and most of these gave publicly supported schools merely a halfhearted word of encouragement. Only Massachusetts, New Hampshire, and Vermont directed the legislatures to establish schools, and even there the educational opportunities were actually poorer than they had been during the colonial period. Thus a Massachusetts statute of 1789 that required elementary instruction in towns of two hundred families or more replaced an earlier law forcing towns of one hundred families to provide a schoolmaster—an obvious step backward. Outside these

New England states even less was accomplished. New York in 1795 promised twenty thousand pounds annually to each county raising half this sum for schools, but such was the state of public lethargy that the fund was never drawn upon. Virginia offered similar inducements a year later, but during the next five years not a single county took advantage of the opportunity. Delaware in 1796 decided that fees from tavern and marriage licenses should be devoted to schooling, but a few months later the legislature suffered a change of heart and diverted the money into a more "practical" channel. Indifference, poverty, and the secret hostility of the upper classes doomed the common people of the United States to another generation of ignorance.

Equally indicative of the conservative trend in education was the emphasis this generation placed on college training, for if the masses were to be kept in check, an educated gentry must be provided to rule them. This was the motive that led many legislatures to establish state universities even though they were unwilling to set up grammar schools. New York authorized a "University of the State of New York" in 1787 although nothing more was done at that time; Georgia opened the doors of its own college in 1785, North Carolina in 1795. At the same time a vigorous attempt was made to transform several older schools into state universities. Dartmouth, Columbia, and Pennsylvania were all brought under partial state control before John Marshall's decision in the famous case of *Dartmouth College v. Woodward* (1819) ended these attempts by holding that a college charter was a contract that could not be legally impaired.

The same trend was evident in education, in religion, in government, and in theory. By the close of the eighteenth century a lusty counter-revolution was under way against the Enlightenment and the leveling tendencies of the Revolution. Alarmed by the "mob action" of the "critical period," horrified by the democratic excesses of the French Revolution, fearful for their newly won property rights, reactionaries were struggling valiantly to reverse the wheel of progress and to inflict their own type of *ancien régime* on the new republic. From both the humanitarian and the intellectual points of view the United States was far more backward in the early years of the nineteenth century than on that glorious day, a generation before, when its leaders promised all men the right to "life, liberty, and the pursuit of happiness."

VI

JEFFERSONIAN REPUBLICANISM

1800–1815

Thomas Jefferson, in his mellower years, liked to refer to the "Revolution of 1800" and dwell on his triumph over the forces of monarchy and conservatism. These boasts had little basis in fact, for John Adams was certainly no monarchist, and Jefferson proved to be little more of a fire-eating radical than Hamilton. He made no frontal attack on property qualifications for voting and officeholding, nor did he open his bountiful heart to the plaints of the common man. Instead, Jefferson was content in the main to leave the Federalist structure intact, substituting an agrarian ruling class for the commercial caste favored by Hamilton. Nor did Jefferson, who subscribed completely to the eighteenth-century concept of a weak national authority as a check on tyranny, succeed in checking the trend toward centralization inaugurated by Hamilton. Actually, he gained his greatest glory through war, which he hated, and diplomacy, which he distrusted.

In justice to Jefferson it must be said that his "Republicanism" was based on reason rather than on prejudice. He sincerely believed that all governments should be entrusted to the people, but only when those people were wise enough to administer their trust properly. Hence universal manhood suffrage must await the education of an intelligent electorate by schools and colleges. In the meantime he would entrust the reins of government to the agrarian upper class—the southern planters and well-to-do northern farmers—who had both the skill to govern and the interests of the masses at heart. This delegation of power, Jefferson reasoned, was just, for 90 per cent of the people were farmers, and a legislative program acceptable to their leaders would please them all. Government for the people, rather than by the people, was a necessary expedient both in the United States and in every newborn republic; his pleas for moderation had amazed the revolutionary radicals of France when he served as American minister to that country just before Washington's inauguration. Jefferson hoped, however, that eventually government by the people would result with the spread of educational facilities, and to this he devoted much of his energy. He was well equipped to do so: as his country's last great universal scholar he had already won Europe's acclaim for his knowledge of classical literature, botany, archaeology, theology, mechanical science, and architecture. A gentleman philosopher with a lively curiosity and a consuming faith in the perfectibility of man, he made his greatest contribution by dangling the democratic ideal before the American people without quite letting them grasp it. But the quest for a broader basis of self-rule was to confront every succeeding generation; and Jefferson in his time was a precursor of democracy.

JEFFERSON VS. MARSHALL

Jefferson entered upon the duties of presidential office in the sprawling new city of Washington, determined to tear down the more obnoxious portions of the Federalists' bulwark. The judicial system irked him most: before they left office his opponents made a desperate attempt to pack this branch of the government with their own appointees in the hope of entrenching their repudiated concepts in the one branch of the government that was beyond popular control. After the election the lameduck Congress passed the Judiciary Act of 1801, reducing the membership of the Supreme Court by one, increasing the number of circuit courts from thirteen to twenty-three and providing these with justices of their own in place of the Supreme Court judges who had "ridden circuit" in the past. During his last hours in office President John Adams solidly filled these new courts with Federalist judges and named his Secretary of State, John Marshall, Chief Justice of the Supreme Court.

The Jeffersonians, whose dislike of an antidemocratic judiciary had been accentuated by flagrantly partisan behavior on the part of some of the justices, first tried to remove obnoxious judicial appointees by impeachment, but when the Senate refused to unseat judges on purely political grounds they were forced to turn their attack against the law rather than the men. A new Judicial Act pushed through Congress restored one justice to the Supreme Court and decreed that the circuit courts be administered not by judges of their own but by one justice from the Supreme Court and one from a district court. The immediate effect of this measure was to sweep away the duties and salaries of numerous court officials just appointed by Adams, including twenty-three circuit court judges. Their refusal to accept dismissal led directly to one of the Supreme Court's most important decisions, the case of *Marbury v. Madison* (1803).

The chain of events leading to this monumental ruling began a few minutes before midnight on March 3, 1801, when President Adams, working feverishly to complete his business before his term expired, signed commissions for dozens of officials whom the Federalists hoped to entrench in the court system. These documents were found the next day by Thomas Jefferson, who, realizing that the law providing for these offices would soon be repealed, ordered his Secretary of State, James Madison, not to deliver them to the Federalist appointees. One of the disappointed office seekers, William Marbury, asked the Supreme Court to issue a writ of mandamus that would force Madison to surrender the important document. The power to issue a court order or mandamus had been granted by Congress in the Judiciary Act of 1789. Chief Justice Marshall, however, refused to exercise the power. By a strict interpretation of the Constitution, Marshall argued that the Court's delegated jurisdiction did not include the right to issue such a writ; therefore the congressional authorization to do so was void. By this invalidation of a section of the law as contrary to the Constitution, the doctrine of judicial review, already recognized in various states, was established nationally by a precedent under which the Supreme Court assumed the important power to declare acts of Congress unconstitutional.

The decision of the Court, denying Marbury a writ of mandamus, was hailed by the Jeffersonians as a victory, but the struggle between the Federalists in the courts and the Jeffersonian Republicans in the other two branches proved at the moment a drawn battle. Although Marshall and Federalist principles continued to dominate the judiciary, the judges became more circumspect and for years to come did not employ judicial review to thwart the will of congressional majorities. Nevertheless, in the long run, judicial review was a triumph for Federalist concepts of protection of property against the legislative power of popular majorities.

Marshall's decision provided one of the possible answers to a question on which the Constitution was not explicit and upon which the framers themselves had disagreed and had never reached formal agreement —the question of where authority was lodged for the determination of what was constitutional. In later evolution after the Civil War, judicial review was to enlarge into a doctrine of judicial supremacy. Long before, in a flash of insight, Jefferson foresaw the danger of such a course. He repudiated any notion of judicial finality as unwarranted by the Constitution, which nowhere stated that the high court possessed a monopoly of decision on constitutional interpretations. Judicial supremacy by such a monopoly on interpretation, contended Jefferson, would give courts the power to "twist and shape" the Constitution like "a mere thing of wax" into "any form they please." Seeking a more democratic concept of constitutional interpretation, Jefferson enunciated a basis for later liberal theory of the proper sphere of courts: under the separation of powers the three branches of the national government had equal and coordinate authority; each branch shared responsibility for interpretations of the Constitution; no single branch was entrusted with finality or the power to compel other branches to bow to its judgment. In Jeffersonian thought, the people had the final power, through the process of elections, to determine the meaning to be given to the Constitution.

ECONOMIC AND COMMERCIAL PROGRAM

Jefferson's attack on Hamilton's financial structure was almost as inconclusive as the struggle with Federalist judges. The President's objective was clear: a program of economy that would rapidly reduce the national debt and relieve the people of the tax burden necessary to pay interest on outstanding obligations. But Hamilton's system was operating so successfully that the Jeffersonians did not dare risk the political consequences of interfering with the funding program or the national bank, and they were forced to vent their rage on the whisky tax, which was repealed soon after the Federalists left office. Although this step won Jefferson the undying support of Westerners, it forced the government to depend for its revenue almost entirely on customs duties. These declined so rapidly when European wars checked importations from the Continent that Jefferson ended his eight years in office with the national debt only slightly reduced.

Less to the liking of Jefferson were the two constructive acts upon which his fame as an administrator rests today, the Barbary War and the purchase of Louisiana. The first was directed against the Barbary pirates who preyed on the ships of small nations from their nests along the southern shore of the Mediterranean. Washington chose to protect American shipping by paying over two million dollars in tribute, but only two months after Jefferson became President he ordered a naval squadron to attack the marauders. For four years the war went on, with the tiny navy hampered by congressional neglect and the long lines of communication, but Tripoli was finally forced to sign a treaty in 1805 that gave the United States better terms than any European power.

THE LOUISIANA PURCHASE

Far more important was Jefferson's diplomatic triumph that added Louisiana to the infant republic. This sprawling Spanish territory, lying between the Mississippi River and the Rocky Mountains and occupied by about forty thousand Creoles and slaves centered around New Orleans, was chiefly valued by Spain as a pawn in her negotiations with the United States. When Pinckney's treaty of 1795 put an end to Spanish designs on the Mississippi Valley, Spain lost interest in her expensive colony; a year later she was more than ever anxious to sell, for a new Anglo-Spanish war placed Louisiana at the mercy of the superior British fleet. France was ready to buy, for her success in Europe conjured up visions of a revived colonial empire. Negotiations went on between 1796 and 1800, when the secret Treaty of San Ildefonso transferred Louisiana to France in return for territorial concessions in Europe. A year later Napoleon ended his European wars with the Treaty of Amiens and turned to the task of developing his American possession.

The United States was horrified by these events. Spain was a satisfactory neighbor, for she could be persuaded to keep the Mississippi open to western trade, but France might revive the Kentucky intrigue and even succeed in separating the trans-Appalachian area from the Union. Jefferson knew that he could save the West only by securing control of the mouth of the Mississippi, and he saw that he could obtain this only if France were threatened with a new war that placed Louisiana at the mercy of the English fleet. He must wait, and prepare himself to take advantage of any opportunity that might arise. To this objective he devoted himself through 1802, hinting to the French and Spanish ministers that the frontiersmen were preparing to seize Louisiana by force, asking Congress to strengthen defenses in the West, and talking covertly of an Anglo-American alliance. "We must," he wrote, "marry ourselves to the British fleet and nation." Fishing in Europe's troubled waters, the President sent James Monroe to Paris with instructions to purchase New Orleans, not because he anticipated success, but only to be prepared if a renewal of war between France and England threw Louisiana on America's doorstep. Jefferson's policy succeeded sooner than he had dared hope. In the spring of 1803 Napoleon abruptly decided to sell, partly because he knew that a new English war was only months away and partly because the twenty thousand fighting men just squandered in crushing a slave insurrection on Santo Domingo made him realize the cost of colonial possessions. Monroe was still on the high seas when Napoleon's foreign minister casually asked Robert Livingston, the American minister in Paris, "What would you give for the whole of Louisiana?" Livingston, slightly deaf, could scarcely believe his ears, but indicated that he was willing to negotiate. Arrangements were concluded on April 30, 1803, when the two commissioners—for Monroe had now arrived—affixed their signatures to a treaty transferring all Louisiana to the United States in return for fifteen million dollars.

When the treaty reached Washington, Jefferson was sorely troubled in mind and conscience. He knew that the United States was little better than the receiver of stolen goods, for Napoleon had wrested Louisiana from Spain, had broken his promise not to resell without Spanish consent, and had, in direct violation of French law, made the sale without consulting the Chamber of Deputies. But more troublesome than these considerations were the President's private scruples. Nowhere did the Constitution give him power to acquire territory. It could be implied from the power to make war and treaties, but Jefferson staunchly opposed the use of implied powers. Characteristically, he wrote an amendment authorizing territorial acquisitions; then, realizing that the opportunity would be lost long before an amendment could be ratified, signed the treaty and hunted for the authority afterward. Few cared whether he found it or not, for the purchase was popular throughout most of the nation.

THE THREAT OF SECESSION

Only a few die-hard Federalists of New England objected. To these high priests of reaction who had shuddered at each democratic step of the Jeffersonians, the Louisiana Purchase was the last straw. This vast region would eventually be carved into agricultural states that would wrest control of Congress from the East and destroy the commerce on which New England's prosperity rested. One Massachusetts representative expressed the fears of his fellows when he told the House:

You have no authority to throw the rights and property of this people into hotch-pot with the wild men on the Missouri, nor with the mixed, though more respectable, race of Anglo-Hispano-Gallo-Americans who bask on the sands in the mouth of the Mississippi. . . . Do you suppose the people of the Northern and Atlantic States will, or ought to, look on with patience and see Representatives and Senators from the Red River and Missouri, pouring themselves upon this and the other floor, managing the concerns of a seaboard fifteen hundred miles, at least, from their residence; and having a preponderancy in councils into which, constitutionally, they could never have been admitted?

Better to leave the Union now than wait for that dread day. Obstinate New England Federalists solemnly contemplated secession from the Union. New York must be included in the new confederacy they were plotting, and they hoped for its delivery into their hands not by a Federalist but by a disgruntled Jeffersonian, Aaron Burr.

The tide of fortune was running out for Burr—and for Jefferson's adversary, Hamilton, too. Burr, who was a brilliant but erratic opportunist, had been Jefferson's running mate in 1800. The framers of the Constitution, not foreseeing the rise of the party system, had simply provided that each elector should vote for two men, with the understanding that the one having the second largest vote should be Vice-President. Hence when the Jeffersonian electors unthinkingly cast their ballots for their party's two candidates, the election resulted in a tie. A more scrupulous man than Burr would have withdrawn at once, but he carried the fight into the House of Representatives, where only the influence of Hamilton, who disliked

Jefferson but distrusted Burr, gave the presidency to Jefferson. It was not surprising that the Jeffersonians cast Burr aside in 1804, or that he was willing to intrigue with the Federalists. According to their schemes, he was to be elected governor of New York with their support, then lead his state out of the Union and into their rebel republic. Only the influence of Hamilton, whose loyalty to his country transcended even his dislike for Jefferson, defeated Burr and caused the collapse of the disgraceful scheme. Boiling with anger, Burr challenged Hamilton to a duel. They met at sunrise on the morning of July 11, 1804, in a tranquil field overlooking the Hudson River not far from New York. Hamilton withheld his fire; Burr shot to kill and his first bullet lodged in his opponent's chest. Two days later the Federalist leader died.

Pursued by an outraged public opinion, Aaron Burr fled west and there launched his infamous conspiracy. Just what he had in mind no one knows, for he told a different story to each confidant: a western uprising that would sever the Mississippi Valley from the Union; an attack on the Spanish southwest and from its conquered remains the creation of a new empire for his daughter Theodosia; an elaborate land-jobbing scheme in Louisiana. Won by his glib tongue and grandiose plans, converts flocked to his standard during the winter of 1805–1806, until his ranks included many prominent Westerners, among them General James Wilkinson, commander of the American army in the West. In the early summer of 1806, Burr, setting out from Blennerhassett Island on the upper Ohio, loaded on boats a company of sixty men ready to follow his command and floated with them down the river toward the Mississippi. Burr had proceeded only a little way before he realized that the Westerners were so well satisfied with their government's purchase of Louisiana that they would have no part in his conspiracy. When he heard that Wilkinson had turned against him and that the President had issued an order for his arrest, Burr left the expedition and fled overland toward Spanish Florida. Before reaching his haven he was arrested and turned over to the custody of the Circuit Court at Richmond to stand trial for treason. Only the partiality of John Marshall, whose hatred of Jefferson blunted his sense of justice, allowed Burr to escape without punishment. The abortive conspiracy demonstrated that the nation was so firmly united that neither the disgruntled New Englanders nor the turbulent Westerners could muster enough force to upset Jefferson's popularity with the people.

THE DANGERS OF NEUTRALITY

This unity owed something to the fact that Europe was at peace, but when Jefferson began his second term in 1805, the dogs of war were loosed once more. Napoleon bestrode Europe like a colossus, supreme on the Continent after the battle of Austerlitz; England's control of the seas was secured by Nelson's victory at Trafalgar, and she looked forward to the day when a new European front could be opened. Neither could strike directly at the other. The war would be protracted, and neutrals were certain to suffer, for each antagonist depended on starving the other out. The next ten years demonstrated once more that the United States could not maintain its neutrality when the leading European powers were locked in a death struggle.

In 1805, an admiralty court held in the Essex case that French West Indian goods were in continuous voyage from the time they left their home ports until they reached Europe, even though they were transshipped in the United States. This ended a thriving trade developed by American shippers: they purchased goods in the French colonies, brought them to their home port, transshipped them to another vessel, and carried them to France under the protection of their neutral flag. Now these goods were subject to confiscation, and one more road to mercantile wealth was closed. France countered in November, 1806, with the Berlin decree, which closed European ports to England's ships and laid a "paper blockade" about the British Isles, followed a year later by the Milan decree, making all neutral vessels bound to or from England subject to confiscation. Not to be outdone, the British answered with two orders in council in 1807, forbidding neutrals to carry goods between the ports of France and her colonies, and throwing a blockade around all European harbors held by Napoleon. These rival decrees and orders closed to American shippers all England and the coast of Europe from Copenhagen to Trieste and placed them at the mercy of English men-of-war on the one hand and French privateers on the other. Losses mounted rapidly as cargoes bound for England were confiscated by France and vessels bound for the Continent were seized by England. Britain's activity was particularly resented by the United States, not because her decrees were harsher, but because her superior navy captured more American ships.

The growing ill feeling between the two nations was brought to a fever pitch by the British practice of impressing American seamen. England resorted to this practice to offset the high wages offered by Yankee shipowners in their frantic search for crews to man the hundreds of new vessels built to replace those that were confiscated; whenever a British man-of-war touched an American port her crew deserted in a body and rushed to find jobs on merchantmen flying the American flag. This steady drain of skilled man power was a real threat to an England that must control the seas to survive, and her warships retaliated by stopping American ships on the high seas, mustering out their crews, and impressing all

British subjects back into the Royal Navy. Unfortunately many of the seamen taken were Americans, for all deserters carried forged papers, and mistakes were easily made. Others were citizens of the United States by adoption, but England's doctrine of "indelible allegiance" refused to recognize the rights of naturalization, and they were impressed with the rest.

As this practice spread, American resentment flamed, for impressment touched the national honor as much as did the confiscation of illegal cargoes. Indignation reached its height in June, 1807, when the United States warship, the *Chesapeake,* sailed out of Chesapeake Bay. Rumors that British deserters were aboard reached the ears of an English commander whose squadron lay near by and he sent one of his ships, the *Leopard,* to investigate under the pretense of delivering dispatches for Europe. As soon as the American commander learned why he had been stopped, he ordered the British searching party from his vessel. The *Leopard* then opened fire, throwing three broadsides into the *Chesapeake* before the unprepared Americans surrendered. Twenty-one sailors were killed or wounded, and an English boarding party carried away four more, only one of whom was a deserter. The Atlantic Ocean, rather than serving as a protective barrier, had been the highway to a crisis that again threatened the country's neutrality.

News of the *Chesapeake-Leopard* affair carried the United States to the brink of war as the whole nation demanded revenge for this insult to its honor. Congress and a united people would have welcomed a chance to fight, but Jefferson, hating bloodshed, determined on a final peaceful effort to bring England to her senses. Under his prodding, Congress in December, 1807, passed an Embargo Act forbidding all American trade with any part of the world. The President, knowing that both France and England depended on American goods, hoped that this rigid boycott would force them to repeal their obnoxious restrictions on neutral trade, much as the British, under the pressure of nonimportation agreements, had been induced to yield prior to the Revolution.

The embargo did hurt England, but it hurt the United States more. Farmers who had planted in anticipation of large foreign markets were unable to sell their grain, consumers were forced to buy inferior native products rather than low-priced English goods, sailors were thrown from employment, and shipowners gloomily watched their ships rot away at the docks. In the Northeast a numbing depression paralyzed economic activity and irate editors demanded either the repeal of the embargo or the secession of the commercial states. Writers transposed the letters of the word "embargo" to read "go-bar-em" or spelled it backward as "o-grab-me." A New Hampshire poet sang:

Our ships all in motion,
Once whiten'd the ocean;
   They sailed and return'd with a Cargo;
Now doom'd to decay
   They are fallen a prey
To Jefferson, worms and EMBARGO.

When every New England state save Vermont cast its electoral vote for
the Federalist candidate in 1808, Jefferson saw that he must back down.
In his last days in office he signed a bill repealing the embargo, sick at
heart that his policy had failed.

In its place Congress passed a Nonintercourse Act designed to continue the boycott in less drastic form. American ships were now free to
trade with any nation except England and France, and those two countries
were told that should either repeal its respective orders or decrees, commercial relations would immediately be resumed. Within a year even the
most prejudiced friends of economic sanctions admitted the Nonintercourse
Act a failure: the law against trade with the belligerents could not be enforced, and nearly every ship that sailed for a neutral port landed instead
in France or in England, where prices were higher. The Jeffersonians were
still not ready to abandon the principle of commercial coercion, however,
and Macon's Bill No. 2[1], which replaced the Nonintercourse Act in May,
1810, boldly attempted to bargain with the European powers. American ships were now free to trade anywhere, but each warring power was
told that if it withdrew its orders and decrees a boycott would be applied
against the other.

Napoleon was in a much more vulnerable position than England.
Since his whole policy aimed at starving the enemy into surrender, he
resorted to subterfuge. He told the United States that the Berlin and
Milan decrees were revoked, "it being understood that, in consequence of
this declaration, the English shall revoke their Orders in Council . . . or
that the United States . . . shall cause their rights to be respected by the
English." Madison, who had succeeded Jefferson as president in March,
1809, paid no attention to these carefully phrased conditional clauses and
fell completely into the trap, despite the fact that every mail from France
brought word of new seizures of American vessels. On November 2, 1810,
he announced that England had three months in which to repeal her
orders in council or accept a boycott, and on February 11, 1811, he issued
a decree forbidding all trade with Britain. This time the English really

---

[1] Macon's Bill No. I, introduced into Congress in December, 1809, by Nathaniel Macon,
chairman of the House Committee on Foreign Affairs, would have excluded both French
and British ships from American ports and admitted French and British merchandise only
when imported directly from their place of origin in American vessels. The bill passed
the House but was defeated in the Senate.

suffered, for European markets were closed by Napoleon's Continental system and the cutting of this last outlet closed factories, jammed warehouses with unsold merchandise, and bred riots among the unemployed. A serious crop failure in 1811 increased popular discontent during the grim winter of 1811–1812 to the point that the ministry was forced to accept defeat. On June 16, 1812, the orders in council were indefinitely suspended. But the concession came too late. On June 18, 1812, the United States formally declared war on Great Britain.

Not the suffering shipowners of New England but the arrogant frontiersmen of the West forced James Madison to recommend war to Congress. By 1812, men of the West held something like a balance of power in the government, for Ohio (1802) and Louisiana (1811) entered the Union on the crest of the wave of population that swept westward over the mountains after the Treaty of Greenville. Only a war with England, they believed, would end the serious depression then prostrating the frontier, open needed new lands to settlement, and check a powerful Indian confederation threatening western security. The desire of the West to solve these practical problems led the nation into the War of 1812.

A depression that gripped the trans-Appalachian region underlay the discontent. Until that time the new settlers who flocked to the frontier in the burst of optimism following the Louisiana Purchase provided a market for the farmers already there, but when this migration slackened after 1808 the Mississippi Valley found itself burdened with a surplus of goods and no buyers. Prices slumped and poverty spread everywhere. Actually, inadequate marketing facilities were responsible. Each spring the farmers made the tortuous journey to New Orleans when floods swept the ice from the rivers, inundating the market with an oversupply that dropped the bottom from under prices. Yet they had no choice but to sell even at a loss, for no storage facilities were available, and most of them were so overawed by the bustling city that they sold hurriedly to get away. Other outlets for produce would have ended the western depression, but the frontiersmen were too unseeing to admit this. They knew that they were prosperous in 1805 when American goods flowed freely to Europe, and that the price of grain fell 20 per cent when England's commercial restrictions closed the Continental markets. Hard times would continue as long as Britain preyed on American ships. Believing this, the West supported the embargo long after the rest of the nation admitted its failure, and demanded war in 1812 as a requisite to the return of prosperity.

War was necessary, moreover, to allow the continual expansion always a part of the frontier dream. The ravenous appetites of the land-hungry Westerners had recently been whetted by the easy conquest of West Florida, when the United States took advantage of Spain's preoccupation with the Napoleonic Wars to seize the region in 1810, using a disputed section in the Louisiana Purchase Treaty as an excuse. East Florida, which remained in Spanish hands, was a no less tempting prize; its occupation would wipe out nests of renegades and Indians who menaced the Georgia planters, as well as open new lands to be exploited by settlers and speculators. A band of southern opportunists who formed their own expedition, and nearly overran East Florida in 1811 before President Madison put an end to this private war against a friendly power, taught the South that Spain's defenses were weak. War with England and her Spanish ally would surely deliver rich Florida into American hands.

While Southerners looked longingly at the Floridas, northern frontiersmen cast covetous glances toward Canada. This vast territory would not only give Westerners limitless room for expansion and open new areas for ambitious fur traders, but would be valuable for two other reasons. Its conquest would allow the United States to strike the one vulnerable spot in England's armor, for the navy protected the British Isles from attack. Once Canada was conquered, a portion of it could be offered back to Britain in return for the repeal of her orders in council. Moreover, the West believed that an immediate attack on Canada would save the frontier from an Indian war that threatened to be more serious than any since the Revolution.

The Indians were on the warpath in 1812, but the Americans themselves were responsible. Since 1802, Governor William Henry Harrison of the Northwest Territory had forced land-grabbing treaties on the red men of the Northwest, buying from fragments of tribes that had no right to sell, bribing chiefs and interpreters, and dangling such attractive presents before conferences that native sales resistance crumpled. Step by step, the Indians were driven west until they met the powerful Sioux and Chippewa tribes pressing into Wisconsin and Illinois from present-day Minnesota in search of furs for Canadian traders. Caught between the aggressive Americans and the bloodthirsty Sioux, the northwestern Indians had no choice but war.

In this emergency a leader appeared. Tecumseh, a fearless Shawnee warrior, was wise enough to see that Indian disunity was the reason for the red man's plight. If all tribes would join in a great confederation whose members were pledged to cede no land without the consent of all, he reasoned, Harrison would be powerless. Tecumseh began forming his confederacy in 1805, aided by his brother, The Prophet, a one-eyed epileptic believed by the Indians to possess supernatural powers. By 1808 the two brothers were influential enough to found the village of Prophetstown at the junction of the Wabash River and Tippecanoe Creek as a headquarters for their confederacy. In the same year Tecumseh first sought aid from the

British agents at Fort Malden, a post on the Canadian side of the Detroit River that served as a western center for England's wilderness intrigue. The English cautioned the Indian leader against hostilities, but he left the fort convinced that should war break out the redcoats and the red men would fight side by side once more.

Harrison, blissfully unaware of this rising threat, went blundering ahead with his land-grabbing treaties. In September, 1809, he convinced tribes not affiliated with the confederacy to cede some three million acres of land on the Wabash River. Tecumseh warned that any attempt to occupy the region would be met with force. Border raids began in 1810, while war belts were passed among the tribes and British agents at Fort Malden worked frantically for peace lest they be charged with responsibility for the conflict. In the face of these threats Harrison dared not act until the summer of 1811, when Tecumseh left to visit the southern tribes. Then he gathered a thousand men, marched them north from the frontier outpost at Vincennes, and on November 6 camped a short distance from Prophetstown. That night the Indians attacked, but the Americans were prepared and beat them off after a bitter struggle. The battle of Tippecanoe was no great victory for Harrison, but he did stand his ground, and the next day the red men abandoned Prophetstown and fled west with their hope of a quick triumph gone. They scattered over the frontier to fall on isolated settlements with tomahawk and faggot. By the spring of 1812 the West was in the midst of a serious Indian war.

Every Westerner was firmly convinced that British agents were responsible. The savages, they believed, were armed at Fort Malden and sent forth to prey on American settlements. Even Harrison wrote: "The whole of the Indians on this frontier have been completely armed and equipped from the British King's stores at Malden." Not a frontiersman but knew that peace could be won only by wiping out this nest and breaking the Anglo-Indian alliance; war with England would not only end a depression, satisfy national honor, and open new lands for expansion but would nip a bloody Indian war in the bud. Westerners expressed their feelings first in the congressional elections of 1811, when they cast aside the older men who had followed Madison's vacillating policy and elected a band of young fire-eaters whose platform called for aggression. These "War Hawks" swooped down on Washington when Congress met in November, 1811, shouting for war with every breath. They elected Henry Clay of Kentucky, then a western state, as Speaker of the House, packed the committees with their own members, and bombarded President Madison with fiery speeches and demands. Only a matter of time was necessary before the President, goaded beyond endurance, sent his war message to

Congress and sat unhappily by while the nation plunged into its second struggle with England.

THE AMERICAN PHASE OF WORLD WAR: 1812

Prospects for an early victory seemed bright when the War of 1812 began. Canada's half million inhabitants, many of them French-Canadians who favored Napoleon rather than England, would certainly prove no match for seven million Americans; and England was too involved in Europe to aid her feeble colony. What matter that the United States was as poorly prepared to fight as any nation in history, its army diminished to seven thousand men, its militia so provincial that they refused to fight beyond the borders of their own states, and its Congress so indifferent that it refused even to authorize a war loan until June, 1812. These obstacles could be overcome, but the War Hawks failed to recognize two other weaknesses that almost proved fatal. One was the opposition of the commercial leaders, who refused to support a war that meant ruin for their shipping. The other was the inability of the antiquated generals cluttering up the army and war office to plan an effective campaign.

These factors spelled disaster for the United States during the first year of the war. Instead of striking northward to take Montreal and cut Canada in two as proper strategy dictated, the incompetent high command divided the weak American force into three parts. One army, sent to invade Canada through Detroit and wipe out Fort Malden, succumbed to superior British strategy and was lost entirely in August, 1812. Another crossed the Niagara River into Canada, but bickerings between officers of militiamen and regular troops over the right of each to issue orders to the other prevented re-enforcements from following, and this army too was destroyed. The third, sent to capture Montreal over the Lake Champlain route, was made up of New York militiamen who refused to cross into Canadian soil; whereupon their commander had no choice but to lead them back to Plattsburg again. Canada was still in British hands when the year closed, and American prestige was lower than when the war began.

Only on the sea did that dark year 1812 provide the United States with any victories. The tiny navy was headed by three heavily armed, fast-sailing vessels, the *Constitution,* the *United States,* and the *President.* Opposing these "fir-built frigates, manned by a handful of bastards and outlaws," as a London journalist contemptuously put it, were the two thousand ships of the Royal Navy, flushed with European victory and confident that no enemy could stand against them. They were rudely awakened by a series of duels in the fall of 1812 where the skillfully built American vessels outsailed and outfired the best that Britain could send against them.

The mighty English frigate, the *Guerrière,* surrendered to the *Constitution* after a brilliant two-hour engagement on August 19; two months later the *Wasp* soundly defeated the *Frolic* in a bloody battle, and the *United States* effectively disposed of the *Macedonian.* Again in December the *Constitution* outlasted the British *Java* in a grueling struggle that won for the American ship its fond title of *Old Ironsides;* in February, 1813, the *Hornet* sank the *Peacock* in a furious fifteen-minute battle. Both American rejoicing and British indignation at these defeats were short-lived. By the spring of 1813, a tight English blockade bottled the American vessels in their harbors, and the navy played no more part in the war on the Atlantic, although four or five frigates, including the *Constitution,* slipped to sea to harass enemy shipping.

The year 1813 promised to be more successful on land, for by this time Washington officials realized that without control of Lake Erie an invasion of Canada was foolhardy. The twenty-seven year old naval captain entrusted with this task, Oliver Hazard Perry, supervised the building of the necessary gunboats at Erie, Pennsylvania, and, after sailing down the lake, defeated the British force at the battle of Lake Erie on September 10, 1813. The way was cleared now for a new attack on Fort Malden. The western army, commanded by William Henry Harrison, was ferried across Lake Erie from Ohio to a point just below its objective, but by the time it was ashore the English had abandoned their stronghold and were fleeing eastward along the Thames River toward Niagara. Harrison, starting out in pursuit, caught up with the enemy on October 5, 1813, and inflicted a decisive defeat at the battle of the Thames. Among the dead were Tecumseh and many of his braves. Harrison's triumph broke Indian resistance in the Northwest and brought peace to the Ohio Valley for the first time since the battle of Tippecanoe. A few months later a force of Tennessee militiamen under Andrew Jackson won an equally important victory over the Creek Indians of the Southwest at Horse Shoe Bend on the Tallapoosa River. These two triumphs assured peace on the frontier for the remainder of the war.

The United States was still not out of danger, for by the spring of 1814 Napoleon's defeat on the Continent allowed England to transfer vast armies of her best fighting men to America. The jubilant British, scenting victory now, planned a four-pronged invasion: one army would push south from Niagara, another would strike along Lake Champlain, a third would invade the middle states through Chesapeake Bay, and the last would capture New Orleans. These well-laid plans went completely astray. The Niagara invasion was blocked by the stubborn resistance of the small American army there, while the Lake Champlain campaign was even less successful. The eleven thousand picked troops who marched against the three thousand Americans defending Plattsburg would doubtless have won, but their commander refused to risk battle until his supply lines were assured by naval control of Lake Champlain. When the fleet of gunboats that he sent ahead was defeated by a flotilla under Captain Thomas Macdonough on September 11, 1814, he dared not go on and returned to Canada.

The fighting in the middle states reflected less credit on either side. A British fleet sailed into Chesapeake Bay in August, 1814, pursued the few American gunboats there up the Patuxent River, and landed a large army only a short distance from Washington. The five thousand militiamen called out to meet the invaders melted away before the steady fire of the regulars, and the English marched unmolested into the city on the night of August 24. After burning the Capitol and the White House they moved on to Baltimore. Here the defenders were better prepared, and when Fort McHenry held out against their bombardment and a landing party was repulsed, they retreated to sea while an exultant young American who witnessed the victory was celebrating the triumph by writing the words of "The Star-Spangled Banner." The fall of Washington was a sore blow to American pride, but did the English little good other than teach them that Americans failed to behave like well-educated Europeans and admit defeat when their capital city was captured.

The campaign against New Orleans met an even more inglorious end. Andrew Jackson, rewarded for his victory at Horse Shoe Bend with a major-generalship and command of the army in the Southwest, first learned of the British plan in November, 1814, when news reached him that an armada of fifty ships and ten thousand men had left Jamaica for the mouth of the Mississippi. With twelve thousand volunteers who answered his call, he hurried to New Orleans and began preparing its defenses. The English hit upon the one route that was poorly guarded and advanced to within a few miles of the city before their presence was detected. An immediate attack would probably have succeeded, but the British missed their opportunity by delay while the Americans threw up earthworks between the Mississippi and a dense cypress swamp. Fighting went on until January 8, 1815, when the English commander ordered a frontal assault. Wave after wave of brave veterans swept against the American earthworks, only to melt away before the withering fire of the Westerners. By nightfall two thousand British dead carpeted the battlefield while Jackson had lost only six men killed and seven wounded. A few days later the attackers sailed away to the West Indies, leaving the Mississippi in American hands and Andrew Jackson the great hero of the War of 1812.

The engagements at New Orleans and Lake Champlain were not

enough to snatch victory from defeat. The United States had failed to secure the objectives for which it declared war; Canada remained formally in British hands, the coast was blockaded, the Capitol burned. To those who sought solace for their national pride, worse than these disasters was the wartime conduct of the New Englanders. Merchants and shipowners there, who should have been most bellicose in a war fought for freedom of the seas, opposed the struggle from the beginning, partly because "Madison's War" was politically unpopular in this Federalist stronghold, partly because they sympathized with England rather than with Napoleon, and partly because the conflict hurt the carrying trade on which their section's prosperity rested. Through the years of fighting, New England men lifted their voices to demand peace, refused to support the war financially, declined to let militiamen leave their own states, and encouraged young men not to enlist in the regular army. They celebrated only two victories during the war—the Russian triumph over the French at Moscow, and the British victory at Waterloo.

Disaffection in commercial states reached a climax during the dark days of 1814, when invading armies were pressing upon the United States, Madison's government was fleeing the capital to escape enemy troops, and defeat seemed near. Instead of rallying to meet this crisis, the New Englanders issued a call for a convention to meet at Hartford and confer on "public grievances and concerns." Fortunately, the moderate Federalists were in control when this Hartford Convention met on December 15, 1814, for the more radical members of the party wanted to separate New England from the Union and make a separate peace with England. The delegates confined themselves to damning Congress for its "deliberate, dangerous, and palpable infractions of the Constitution," vaguely suggested the right of states to nullify unconstitutional laws, and proposed seven amendments to the Constitution that would limit the congressional power to make war, admit new states, lay embargoes, and restrict commerce. More dangerous was a call issued for a second convention at Boston; the Federalists had made their demands and were preparing to act unless their requests were heeded. Only the close of the war ended the threat of secession on the part of New England.

Against this background of defeat and disloyalty, American commissioners in August, 1814, began the negotiations at Ghent that were to lead to eventual peace. The able delegation that Madison appointed was headed by John Quincy Adams of Massachusetts, Henry Clay of Kentucky, and Albert Gallatin of western Pennsylvania. The fact that two of these negotiators represented the western point of view proved to be important, for their first conversations with the British delegates disclosed that either the East or the West would have to modify its demands. The East insisted that the treaty guarantee freedom of trade for neutral ships and contain an admission that England had no right to impress seamen; the West demanded abrogation of the clauses of Jay's Treaty that allowed Canadian traders to cross the border, American naval control of the Great Lakes, and retention of existing boundaries. When these demands were laid before the British commissioners, they countered by insisting that England's interpretation of neutral rights and impressment be accepted, that Canadian traders be assured the continued right to navigate the Mississippi and pass freely over the border, and that the boundary be adjusted to create an Indian buffer state in Maine, the Ohio Valley, and west of Lake Superior. Clearly these claims were irreconcilable and one or the other would have to give way.

The Americans decided upon a strategic concession. They accepted England's contention on neutral rights, largely because they realized that the British would never retreat on this. Their decision placed the question of peace squarely on the English commissioners; would they back down on their western demands or would they continue the war? In England, news of the defeat of Britain's invading army on Lake Champlain, mounting popular resentment against prolonging the war, and realization that the complete conquest of the United States would be a slow and expensive process, helped shape her decision. In the end her government backed down on its western demands as completely as had the Americans on maritime rights. With these mutual concessions the Treaty of Ghent was signed on December 24, 1814.

The treaty was not a happy one for the United States. It provided for the cessation of hostilities on the basis of *status quo ante bellum;* no mention was made of impressment or neutral rights or boundary changes in the West. Technically, the Americans, who had declared war to secure certain ends, suffered defeat when they failed to win their objectives. Actually, they gained a victory. The maritime questions that remained unsettled did not become important again until the twentieth century, while British retreat in the West gave the United States control of the Indians and opened the area to the Mississippi for settlement.

Equally satisfactory from the American point of view were the decisions of several joint commissions established under the treaty to arbitrate the ticklish problems left unsettled. One, which concluded its labors in 1815, did away with trade discrimination and gave American ships free access to British ports except in the West Indies. Another, the famous Rush-Bagot Agreement of 1818, provided that neither nation should build up armaments on the Great Lakes, thus laying the basis for the unfortified border between the United States and Canada that exists today. Still another dealt with the Newfoundland fisheries, for England insisted that the outbreak of war abrogated American rights there guaranteed by the Treaty of 1783. A convention signed in 1818 "acknowledged" the continued right of Yankee fishermen to fish along the Canadian coast and to dry their catch on the shore. In the same year a commission established the forty-ninth parallel as the Canadian-American boundary between the Lake of the Woods and the Rocky Mountains. The peaceful settlement of these problems laid the basis for a new friendliness between England and the United States and encouraged the rapid westward push of the American frontier during the next decades.

VII

THE FLOWERING OF NATIONALISM

1816–1828

When the Treaty of Ghent rang down the curtain on the War of 1812 every American was convinced that his nation had won a glorious victory over the world's greatest military power. Hadn't the "fir-built frigates" blasted the Royal Navy's proudest ships from the seas? Hadn't Harrison trounced the dread Tecumseh and his redcoated allies? Hadn't "Andy" Jackson whipped the British who whipped Napoleon? Little matter that the Capitol was burned, the conduct of New England a disgrace, and the peace a failure. "The Yankee nation could lick all creation," and every heart swelled with honest pride at the might of America and the splendor of its democratic institutions. This was the spirit that sent the United States, intoxicated by its new-found strength, on a giddy nationalistic spree which ended only when a looming sectional conflict brought all the sobering headaches of a dreary "morning-after."

REACTION ABROAD AND AT HOME

This nationalism and its Siamese twin, conservatism, were not based alone on patriotic emotionalism, for something more than this was needed to break down the extreme provincialism of the American people. Two other forces impelled them in this direction. One was the inevitable postwar reaction. Every major conflict in the history of the United States has been followed by periods when reactionary self-interest dominates national thought, and the War of 1812 was no exception. The other, and stronger, force was the world-wide wave of conservatism and reaction that surged across Europe, inundated England, and crossed the Atlantic to spend itself on America's eastern shore. Western Europe, where reactionary monarchs had trembled for a generation before the liberal doctrines of the Enlightenment and the French Revolution, was its place of origin. Here prophets rose to tell the war-sickened people that their salvation lay in obedience, maintenance of the *status quo,* economic isolation, and faithful trust in their betters. For fifteen years after the final defeat of Napoleon

127

they held sway—the last tottering representatives of a doomed regime, trying vainly to stem the flow of change.

Their program varied from nation to nation, but their fundamental objectives were the same everywhere: national self-determination and a return to unenlightened conservatism. In Germany and in Italy they sought to unite the many small states into one independent nation, free of all external control. Italian nationalists accomplished little, for they dissipated their energies by arguing the merits of Pope Pius IX and the King of the Two Sicilies as possible rulers for their dream kingdom, but in Germany some progress was made. A Germanic Confederation, formed in 1815 by the thirty-eight sovereigns of the country's principalities, was only a loose alliance without power; more effective were the efforts of middle-class businessmen who built railroads and extended their trade over all Germany. This trend toward economic unity culminated in 1833 when a *Zollverein,* or customs union, was established to lower tariffs between the states. The strong Teutonic empire of later years was built on this firm foundation.

Among the autocratic countries of Europe the postwar period inspired a movement toward reactionary monarchical control, with Austria's Prince Metternich ruling supreme as the high priest of conservatism. His determination to make the world safe from democracy by restoring class distinctions, favors for the privileged, and archaic absolutism endeared him to the hearts of all Europe's kings, who "crept out again to feel the sun" after the hurricane of revolution. Metternich's influence extended far beyond Austria, for every European monarch was swayed by his constant stress on "no change, no reform." Russia's Czar Alexander I, who had experimented with democratic innovations during the Napoleonic Wars, apologized to Metternich for that sign of weakness and ruthlessly stamped out all men and doctrines not in tune with his autocratic regime. In Spain, Ferdinand VII repudiated a liberal constitution adopted a few years before, abolished the Cortes, and instituted a thoroughly reactionary policy that fostered the Inquisition, suppressed individual liberty, and unwittingly guaranteed success to the revolutions being waged in the more liberal Spanish-American colonies. Portugal's newly revived nationalism was expressed by a violent reaction against all British trade or control, while in France the conservative Charles X rode roughshod over constitutional limitations and established an autocratic government that benefited the clergy and nobility at the expense of the peasants and bourgeoisie.

England's response to the nationalistic tide was less violent but still apparent. The rising middle class was pushed into the background while the reins of government were grasped by reactionary Tory leaders representing the landholding aristocracy and the Anglican clergy. Their whole purpose was to check reform and enact legislation favorable to their own group: enclosure laws that allowed the great estates to expand, high tariffs to benefit agriculture rather than industry, rigid suppression of all protests from the industrialists, merchants, and laborers. The British Tories were just as anxious to stop the wheels of progress as Metternich, even though they worked through parliamentary channels.

In the end they failed, just as did the reactionaries in the rest of the world. The abortive revolutions in France, Belgium, Germany, Italy, and Poland during 1830 and 1831, the middle-class revolt that broadened England's elective franchise between 1829 and 1832, the triumph of Jacksonian Democracy in the United States in 1828—all indicated dissatisfaction with the obsolete rule foisted on mankind during the postwar reaction. Gradually in the 1830's the Age of Nationalism gave way to the Age of the Common Man.

But until that time ruling Americans shared with ruling Europeans the belief that conservatism and nationalism should be enshrined, liberalism and localism relegated to the dead past. The Virginia Jeffersonians who occupied the White House—James Madison and James Monroe—believed that they walked in their master's footsteps, but actually their practices were more nearly akin to Hamilton's than to Jefferson's. This did not mean any stifling of democracy—the current was too strong to check in the United States; during these years a few states liberalized their property qualifications for voting, numerous workingmen's organizations were formed, Massachusetts and Connecticut belatedly caught up with the rest of the nation by severing the last connections between church and state. But the whole spirit of the day was that of Hamilton's mercantile nationalism; unity was stressed rather than localism, the powers of the national government were vastly increased at the expense of the states, unrestrained individual enterprise was fostered, barriers were erected to keep out foreign goods and ideas, and every encouragement was given the few to profit at the expense of the many.

NATIONALISM AND SECTIONAL SPECIALIZATION

This extreme nationalism would not have been acceptable to the provincial Americans had not important economic changes—which both illustrated and strengthened the postwar trend—transformed their mode of life and thought during these years. These stemmed from the new means of making a living made available by the maturing social structure and the changing international role of the United States. No longer able to depend solely on European importations as in the past, the people developed new enterprises best suited to the section of the country in which they lived: manufacturing in the Northeast, cotton growing in the South, and diversified export farming in the West. These changes not only recast the structure of society but made two significant contributions to nationalism: material independence allowed Americans to cut some of the economic ties traditionally binding them to Europe; a mutual interdependence forced on the people by sectional specialization welded the nation into a compact economic unit by breaking down local self-sufficiency and making each section dependent on all the others.

The industrialization of the Northeast was particularly startling. Manufacturing had lagged in the United States, for high production costs, natural in a new country where cheap western lands drained away the labor supply, forced Americans to depend on English goods until just before the War of 1812. Only when Jefferson's embargo and the war closed this source of supply during a wartime period when industrial products were most in demand did they turn to manufacturing. Home industries, scattered along the coast from Maine to New Jersey and financed by capital formerly invested in commerce, supplied the needs at first, and by 1815 the country was producing most of its own textiles, paper, iron, leather goods, and woodenware. These small plants tended to concentrate in the Northeast, largely because the region's excess capital, driven from the sea by war, provided the initial impetus. New England quickly established its supremacy in textile manufacturing, for its swift-flowing streams provided water power, while its stubborn soil, driving farmers' wives and daughters into mills to supplement the meager family income, assured an adequate labor supply. After 1825, when new transportation routes flooded New England with western agricultural products, many of the farmers gave up their unequal struggle with the rock-strewn earth and drifted into the factories. While available workers facilitated the concentration of the textile industry in New England, a happy combination of iron, coal, and limestone centered iron smelting and manufacturing in Pennsylvania, New York, and New Jersey. About these basic industries sprang up numerous small plants that soon absorbed most of the energy and wealth of the Northeast.

The transformation in southern life going on at the same time began in 1793, when a Connecticut Yankee, Eli Whitney, visited Georgia and there turned his inventive mind to producing a machine that would separate the burrlike seeds from the fibers of the cotton plant. His cotton gin gave the decaying agriculture of the South a valuable new crop that could be grown anywhere between Virginia and the Gulf of Mexico. The market was limitless, for Whitney's invention roughly coincided with those of the English inventors whose genius created the mechanical spinning and weaving machinery on which Britain built her industrial revolution. The

British manufacturers and their Yankee imitators who were eagerly re-clothing the world were ready to pay fabulously high prices for all that the South could produce. Until the War of 1812 southern cotton growing remained in the experimental stage, but when Jackson's victory at Horse Shoe Bend broke the power of the Indians, the cotton frontier swept west-ward across Georgia, Alabama, and Mississippi and left the rich-soil areas of all the South dotted with plantations busily engaged in sending an end-less stream of snowy bales to the mills of Old and New England.

The South's growing dependence on this staple crop and the North-east's reliance on manufacturing created a large non-food-producing popu-lation that must be fed. This was the impetus that sent the West into a period of phenomenal growth. Farmers who had been content to fill their own family needs and sell a small surplus to newcomers, or ship it over the unsatisfactory New Orleans route, were suddenly aware of the vast profits that awaited their bulky corn and wheat in these new markets. They expanded their holdings, and demanded more efficient agricultural machinery so insistently that alert inventors developed the iron plow, the reaper, and the thresher between 1825 and 1850. Newcomers who rushed in to share this western prosperity pushed the frontier rapidly westward over Ohio, Indiana, Illinois, southern Michigan and Wisconsin, and across the Mississippi into Missouri and Iowa. From their thriving small farms a swelling stream of foodstuffs flowed to the southern plantations and the northern mill towns.

The sectional specialization that wrought these changes was dependent on the new modes of transportation developed during and after the War of 1812. New roads of gravel and crushed stone came first, to replace the crude mud trails over which Americans traveled until the nineteenth century. By 1825 these improved roads covered the eastern part of the nation, but most were operated as toll roads by private companies whose high charges discouraged the distant shipment of bulky agricultural crops, so that their principal effect was to stimulate local and passenger travel. Only one of these early turnpikes, the Cumberland Road, played an important intersectional role. Built by the national government to con-nect the East with the Ohio Valley, it started at Cumberland, Maryland, in 1811, reached the Ohio River at Wheeling in 1818, and Columbus, Ohio, in 1833. Over it thousands of migrating families plodded toward new homes on the frontier, and long wagon trains bearing wheat or whisky for the eastern markets jostled with herds of cattle bound ultimately for the kitchens of Philadelphia or Baltimore.

This one artery of trade only whetted the national appetite for more. Roads would not do, for privately operated turnpikes were too expensive to use, and constitutional obstacles prevented the federal government from

NEW-YORK
CANAL LANDS
ON SALE.

—◦◦◦◦◦◦◦—

THE unsold part of that extensive tract bounded on the *East end of* *Lake Ontario*, extending North from the mouth of *Salmon River*, to the Towns of *Henderson* and *Adams*, watered by the *Big Sandy* and *Little Sandy* Creeks, and their innumerable tributary streams; every part of the tract being within one day's easy drive of the *Erie Canal*, at the Village of Rome, and at Salt Point or Salina, and will be accessible to it by water, (from the outlets on the Lake) as soon as it shall be united to the Lake at *Oswego*, which it is supposed it will be in two years.

That part of the tract more particularly recommended to the notice of Settlers of industrious and steady habits, includes the Town of *Ellisburgh*, and number one of *Lorraine*, forming the south-west part of the *County of Jefferson;* and the Township *No. 10. of Richland*, north of Salmon River, and *Nos. 6, 7, and 11, of Orwell*, making the north part of the *County of Oswego*.

It contains about two hundred thousand acres, more than one half of which is now under actual improvement, and a great portion of it paid for and deeded; and having been from 10 to 15 years regularly advancing in settlement, has a numerous population, and possesses most of the advantages of old countries, as to schools, public worship, mills, distilleries, mechanics, manufactories, &c

Betterments, or partially cleared farms, may be had reasonably. The price of wild lands has always been held very moderate, and will be continued so until the whole are settled. A reasonable chance as to pay will be afforded, and the same fair and liberal treatment, toward settlers, as has been heretofore practised, will be continued, of which information can be best obtained on the spot.

The present price (the choice *as to quality* allowed to the purchaser) is from two dollars fifty cents, to three, four, and five Dollars per acre, according to situation. The lowest rates are for Lands most distant from the Lake, an' the Villages, which as they recede to the east, beyond the alluvial lands, gradually become more swelly and elevated; every part, however, is susceptible of cultivation, there not being a mountain or considerable hill on the tract.

The soil is strong and durable, adapted to grain, grass, and fruit trees. The more it is cultivated and known, the better it is esteemed. No country can possess a more *healthy* *climate*, or a greater abundance of living springs, and streams of *the purest water*, than this part of the tract; the prevailing Timber is a sufficient indication of the soil, being Sugar Maple, Beach, Ash, Elm, &c. the most profitable kinds for Ashes, which, if carefully saved, will defray the cost of clearing and fencing.

No part of the state of New-York is better adapted for *Cattle;* the air is so dry, and the temperature so uniform, that they do not require to be housed during any part of the winter; and vegetation becomes abundant for their support by the 15th to 25th of April: it is rarely, if ever, necessary to fodder after that date. The prosperous state of the settlement may be inferred from the fact, that more than two thousand head of horned Cattle, and Horses, have been received by the proprietor within the last three years, from settlers on this tract, in payment for Land, and sold in the southern district of this state, and will be continued, as heretofore, to be received in pay, together with Ashes, Grain, Pork, Butter, &c.

The direct route to these Lands, for those who come from the East, is through *Utica* and *Rome*. Settlers, on arrival, will find local agents and others, who will assist them to make selection of their Land, after which they will apply for writings to the *General Land Office*, at *Ellisburgh*, under the superintendance of *William Constable Pierpont*, son of the proprietor, who will also be present at several stated periods, in the course of the year, at which office any information will be afforded, and business transacted, relating to other tracts of Land, owned by the subscriber, also on sale, on moderate terms, and in prosperous course of settlement, in the adjoining *Counties of Lewis, St. Lawrence, and Franklin.*

Apply to Agents in the respective towns—at the Land Office at Ellisburgh—or to the Subscriber, residing on Brooklyn Heights, opposite the City of New-York.

October, 1823.

HEZ. B. PIERPONT.

A circular, typical of hundreds circulated by speculators, which helped lure settlers to the West.

132

further construction. Instead, a new type of transportation—the canal—caught the popular imagination. The canal era opened in 1825 when New York State completed the first extensive artificial waterway in the United States, stretching 363 miles from the Hudson River to Lake Erie. This first all-water route between East and West cut the time between Buffalo and New York from twenty to eight days, lowered the cost of transporting a ton of goods over that route from a hundred to ten dollars, and sent land values in Ohio and western New York skyrocketing. Ohio grain could now be shipped to New York and distributed by water along the coast so cheaply that it undersold eastern cereals. This competition spelled doom to New England agriculture, driving farmers from their sterile farms to the textile mills, but it brought prosperity to the West.

The Erie Canal was principally important because its success inspired imitators; not only did the Erie repay New York's seven million dollar investment but it stimulated trading activities in New York City, which almost doubled its population in the decade after 1825. Private companies sprang up to weave a network of small waterways through the East, and other seaboard states launched gigantic internal improvement schemes in a vain effort to regain their waning prestige. In 1826 Pennsylvania chartered a long canal across the state, broken at one point by a portage railway thirty-six miles long where stationary engines hauled goods up one side of a mountain range and coasted them down to waiting barges on the other. The elaborate "Pennsylvania system" was completed in 1834 but proved less successful than the Erie. Maryland also entered the race for the commerce of the Ohio Valley by defying skeptical engineers and authorizing a canal between the Potomac and the Ohio rivers. Twenty years of intensive labor failed to conquer the mountain fastnesses of western Maryland, but a more fantastic scheme proved successful. The first railroad in America, the Baltimore and Ohio, chartered by the legislature in 1826 in a desperate gamble for western trade, reached the Ohio River in 1853.

In the West the states were ready to squander vast sums on canals that would connect the Ohio-Mississippi River system with the Great Lakes. Ohio chartered two in 1825, the Ohio and Erie from Portsmouth to Cleveland and the Miami and Erie from Cincinnati to Toledo, and pushed them through to completion in 1833 and 1843. Indiana built the Wabash and Erie Canal between 1832 and 1843, running across the state from Evansville to Toledo; in 1848 Illinois opened the Illinois and Michigan Canal, which connected Lake Michigan with the Illinois and Mississippi rivers. Through this maze of waterways horse-drawn barges carried western grains and meat north to Lake Erie for shipment east, or south to the rivers that led to the cotton-belt markets.

The improvement in river transportation that paralleled the canal era also helped draw the sections together. In 1807 Robert Fulton demonstrated his first successful steamboat on the Hudson River; four years later one of his agents launched a similar ship on the western waters, where it was to enjoy its greatest success. This first crude vessel, the *New Orleans,* steamed from Pittsburgh to New Orleans, stopping at each town to convince skeptics by chugging back against the current. Others followed; by 1820 sixty steamships were plying the Mississippi and Ohio rivers, and both the number and the performance of the vessels improved rapidly during the next three decades. Through these years the great floating palaces, with their elaborately carved superstructures and their decks piled high with gleaming cotton bales, steamed in a steady procession down the majestic Mississippi, carrying western goods to southern markets. Others operated on the Great Lakes, where steamboats were introduced in 1819 and rapidly displaced the slower sailing vessels.

These developments in land and water communication wrought a transformation in American life. To the Northwest they spelled prosperity, for now farmers there had a choice of two outlets for their goods—south to New Orleans or east by canal to New York and Philadelphia—and could choose the market where prices were best. The rapid peopling of the western states and the growth of cities at strategic points along the waterways—at Pittsburgh, Buffalo, Detroit, Chicago, and Cleveland for the eastern outlet, at Cincinnati and St. Louis for the southern—were directly traceable to these improvements. The effect on the East was not uniformly good, for while favored urban sections gained, rural regions lost. New York benefited the most, but Philadelphia, Baltimore, and other cities along the routes grew by leaps and bounds, to give the Americans their first sizable cities. On the other hand, the canals doomed large-scale agriculture in the eastern states and forced their people to turn increasingly to manufacturing for a livelihood. Even England felt the impact of the western produce that flowed to market over the Erie and Pennsylvania systems. Industrialists there, foreseeing the day when continued improvements in transportation would decrease the price of American wheat and corn still more, began suggesting that Britain give up hope of competing with the agricultural countries, sweep away the corn laws that protected her farmers, concentrate on manufacturing, and let the Ohio Valley feed England's workers. These men realized, even in a day of intense nationalism, that the principal effect of the better communication systems was to make world-wide specialization and exchange inevitable.

Improvements in transportation also welded the United States into an economic unit. No longer did Americans lean on Europe for many

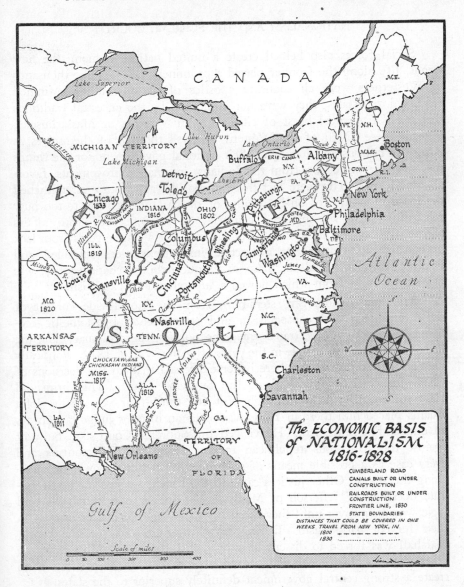

The ECONOMIC BASIS of NATIONALISM 1816-1828

necessities; eastern factories supplied manufactured goods, southern plantations satisfied the ravenous appetites of northern textile mills for cotton, and western farms sent their foodstuffs east and south to feed the city dwellers and the planters. Bound firmly together by efficient transportation systems, each dependent on the others for needed goods, no one section could exist alone. This mutual interdependence laid the material basis for the nationalism that blossomed in the postwar years.

NATIONALISM AND THE SUPREME COURT

Social forces also helped create a united nation. Among the new trends, life along the frontier played a prominent role, for the thousands of Westerners were all coonskin apostles of national unity. Mingled from a dozen states, they were not influenced by the ancestral traditions that made Easterners boast of citizenship in Virginia or Massachusetts; instead, these "Men of the Western Waters" thought of themselves as American citizens and looked to their national government for the things they needed: protection from the Indians, internal improvements, favorable land laws. The mere fact that the world was at peace strengthened the sense of unity, for on both sides of the Atlantic men were too busy rebuilding their war-shattered countries to be concerned with affairs abroad. Although the United States suffered during these years from lack of cultural stimulation, its distinctive institutions were solidified and firmly established. Pride in these, as unique national characteristics, was one of the fonts from which flowed a superabundant patriotism.

The new nationalism, stemming from the world-wide current of self-determinism and conservatism and strengthened by domestic economic and social forces, transformed the politics, the diplomacy, and the life of the American people in the years after the War of 1812. Politically the national spirit was nowhere better expressed than in the decisions of Chief Justice John Marshall of the Supreme Court. This grim old Hamiltonian, who held his high post for thirty-four years after John Adams placed him there in 1801, was often an inferior judge but always an outstanding statesman. He viewed the Supreme Court as a bulwark against the dangerous republican tendencies of the Jeffersonians and every case as a possible means of strengthening national power or weakening the states. Other justices came to the bench, steeped in the strong-state doctrines of Jefferson or Madison, but one by one Marshall's cold logic won them over until they often surpassed the old master himself in their fervent nationalism. During his thirty-four years on the bench, Marshall was forced to dissent in only 8 of 1,106 cases. More than any other man of his generation, Marshall reshaped the Constitution to create a strong central government definitely superior to the states.

One important group of his decisions aimed at strengthening the powers vested in the Supreme Court. Two early cases of this nature indicated the direction of his thinking, but not until the postwar period created a less hostile atmosphere for his Federalist ideas did he give full vent to his prejudices. One of these early cases, *Marbury v. Madison* (1803), by affirming the Court's right to declare congressional legislation unconstitutional, answered the contention of the Virginia and Kentucky resolutions that the states should have this power[1]. The other, *United States v. Peters* (1809), established the Court's right to coerce a state legislature. Pennsylvania was the villain in this controversy, which concerned prize money taken during the Revolution and claimed by both that state and a Connecticut citizen. A federal district court in 1803 ordered the assembly to give up the disputed currency, but was met with a flat refusal. When the question finally reached the Supreme Court, Marshall was forceful: "If the legislatures of the several states may, at will, annul the judgments of the courts of the United States, and destroy the rights acquired under those judgments, the Constitution itself becomes a solemn mockery." Pennsylvania was still defiant; the militia was called out to prevent the federal marshal from attaching the funds, and government troops were summoned to oppose them. Conflict was avoided when the marshal succeeded in serving his writs by a ruse, and Pennsylvania finally backed down. The Chief Justice had made his point, even at the risk of minor civil war.

Important as were these cases in strengthening the Court, they were rivaled by two others handed down amidst the more congenial atmosphere of the postwar years, *Martin v. Hunter's Lessee* (1816), and *Cohens v. Virginia* (1821). The issue in both was the same—could the Supreme Court accept appeals from state courts when rights guaranteed by the Constitution were involved?—but the second allowed Marshall a wider field for his nationalistic logic. The facts were clear: Congress had established a lottery for which Cohens had sold tickets in Virginia in defiance of the state law prohibiting such sales. He had been fined by the Virginia courts, and appealed his fine to the Supreme Court. Marshall swept away the state's two contentions: that Cohens by appealing was actually suing, which was in violation of the Eleventh Amendment; and that the Supreme Court had no right to accept appeals from the highest state tribunals. The first he dismissed by pointing out that the state had originally instituted the suit against Cohens and hence was not being sued itself; the second, by disclosing the absurdity of a system where "the Constitution, laws, and treaties may receive as many constructions as there are States." This was Marshall's finest contribution to nationalism, for he provided a basis for national law affecting all people alike rather than a welter of conflicting laws differing from state to state.

Another group of decisions strengthened the authority of Congress. In *McCulloch v. Maryland* (1819) Marshall not only upheld the right of Congress to establish a national bank but wrote the doctrine of implied powers into the Constitution in classic form. The case arose when Maryland objected to a new bank chartered by the central government in

---

[1] This case is fully discussed above, Chapter VI.

1816 and attempted to tax its Baltimore branch out of existence. When the controversy reached the Supreme Court after the state courts had upheld Maryland, Marshall in a vigorous decision declared that the creation of such an institution was implied by the Constitution and hence within the powers of Congress. "Let the end be legitimate," he wrote, "let it be within the scope of the Constitution, and all means which are appropriate, which are plainly adapted to that end, which are not prohibited, but consist with the letter and spirit of the Constitution, are constitutional." As Congress was within its rights in creating the bank, Maryland's tax was invalid, for "the power to tax is the power to destroy." Marshall supported another broad power of Congress in *Gibbons v. Ogden* (1824), when, on the grounds that congressional control of interstate commerce was absolute and exclusive, he overthrew a steamboat transportation monopoly created by New York. By defining "commerce" not simply as the buying and selling of goods but as "intercourse" of all kinds, he laid the basis for the broad power over the nation's economic life that Congress was later to exercise under the commerce clause of the Constitution.

While Marshall increased the authority of the Supreme Court and upheld Congress, he consistently weakened the power of popular majorities in the states. In *Fletcher v. Peck* (1810), favoring vested interests, he established the principle that state legislative acts were void when they conflicted with the Constitution. Here he declared invalid a Georgia statute that, by rescinding a corrupt land grant made by an earlier legislature, "impaired the obligation of a contract." Closely akin to this was his decision in *Dartmouth College v. Woodward* (1819), which forbade a liberal New Hampshire legislature to meddle with the charter of that venerable college. A corporation charter, he held, was a contract within the meaning of the Constitution and could not be impaired—a judgment that had the detrimental effect of giving corporations for many decades too much immunity from legislative regulation but which had a beneficial effect in encouraging gifts to schools and colleges. An even more rigorous rebuke to the states was *Martin v. Mott* (1827), which denied any state the right to withhold its militia from national service when they were called out by the President.

Marshall's ringing decisions, couched in crystal-clear language and supported by adroit logic, were intended as propaganda documents. They served their purpose admirably. Each new judgment was printed in newspapers throughout the land, accompanied by editorial comment that praised or damned as the editor saw fit. Knowing this, the grim old teacher penned in each passionate appeals for nationalism that no one could ignore. "The government of the Union," he wrote in one of them, "is emphatically and truly a government of the people. In form and substance it emanates from them. Its powers are granted by them, and are to be exercised on them, and for their benefit." And again: "The American people are one; and the government which is alone capable of controlling and managing their interests . . . is the government of the Union. It is their government, and in that character they have no other." Here was an appeal for a strong central government, founded and controlled by the people, with the states acting as administrative units within the broader sphere of national action. Marshall urged his beloved nation not to strip itself of power, and convinced its people that strength and liberty were reconcilable.

THE ERA OF GOOD FEELINGS

The nationalism that inspired these sentiments was reflected even more clearly in Congress, for here its spokesmen were not unreformed Federalists but self-proclaimed believers in Jefferson's liberalism and provincialism. Despite this tradition the Jeffersonians who dominated the first national legislature that assembled after the war cast aside their past beliefs and constitutional scruples to enact three measures that never would have been sanctioned a few years before. One provided that the navy should retain its full war strength, feeble as that was, and authorized a standing army of ten thousand men; another reared the first avowedly protective tariff in the nation's history; and the third established the second Bank of the United States. The latter two laws especially increased national power at the expense of the states, and both depended on a liberal use of implied powers, yet the same men who had branded Hamilton a monarchist when he proposed similar measures now voted enthusiastically for them.

This same nationalistic spirit was well represented in the person of James Monroe who, chosen President in 1816 with almost no opposition, was re-elected four years later by an electoral vote that would have been unanimous had not one stubborn elector cast his ballot for another to preserve for George Washington the honor of being the only President unanimously elected. The Federalist party was dead, discredited by its conduct in the War of 1812 and displaced by the National Republicans, as they called themselves, who had stolen its platform if not its aristocratic concepts. When Monroe toured the New England stronghold of Federalism after his inauguration, a Boston paper coined the phrase that characterized his administration, "The Era of Good Feelings." Party factionalism was dead; a united country apparently faced a tranquil future.

The extent of this unity was shown when the nation survived two major blows during Monroe's presidency, either one serious enough to disrupt a less harmonious people. The first was the panic of 1819. This acute depression caused real suffering in the West, where thousands of frontiersmen, using the credit system authorized by the Land Act of 1800 to buy their farms, found themselves unable to make payments. Looming before these men—almost a third of the inhabitants of the frontier—was the grim prospect of losing their homes and the labor they had lavished upon them. Yet the nationalism of the day was so strong that this panic bred no secession movement, no rebels to match Burr or Wilkinson, no Hartford Convention. The West objected, of course; its papers ranted against the second Bank of the United States, which was painted as a money-grabbing monster solely to blame for the depression, yet these barks contained no hint of disloyalty. When Congress passed the Land Act of 1820, ending credit purchases and lowering prices to $1.25 an acre, and followed this with the Relief Act of 1821, allowing purchasers to return any portion of the lands they had contracted to buy but were now unable to pay for, the Westerners hailed the laws as examples of their country's enlightenment and cheerfully prepared to struggle upward from financial chaos. By 1824 prosperity had once more displaced depression and the crisis was past.

The second blow fell when Missouri applied for admission to the Union as a state. The territory's petition seemed innocent enough when Congress received it in February, 1819, but debate had scarcely begun when Representative James Tallmadge of New York threw a bombshell into the proceedings. He proposed an amendment prohibiting the further introduction of slaves into the state and requiring that all children born of bonded servants already there be freed when twenty-five years of age. Southerners rose to a man against the Tallmadge Amendment, for the spreading cotton culture was elevating slaves to a new position of importance and the South was becoming increasingly sensitive to any attack on its "peculiar institution." Moreover, they saw that a free Missouri would upset the careful balance maintained between states north and south of Mason and Dixon's line[2]. There were at that time eleven slave states and eleven free states, and although the greater population of the North gave that section 105 representatives against 81 from the South, both had 22 senators. The Tallmadge Amendment would give the North a majority in both houses of Congress and open the way to sectional legislation that would harm the South.

Here was an issue to test national unity. Just thirty years later the

---

[2] A line, roughly following the southern border of Pennsylvania, which was surveyed in 1763–1767 by Mason and Dixon, two English surveyors. During the pre-Civil War period the term came to be synonymous with the boundary between slave and free states.

United States split in twain over the same question, but now in all the bitter debate there was no active threat of disunion. Instead, the whole problem was settled peacefully when Massachusetts announced her willingness to give up the territory of Maine, which was ready for statehood. A compromise was quickly arranged on this basis. Missouri was admitted as a slave state and Maine as a free state, thus preserving the balance. At the same time Congress tried to settle the whole problem for the future by barring slavery north of latitude 36° 30′ in the unorganized territory of the Louisiana Purchase. When the Missouri Compromise was passed by Congress in 1820, both sides accepted the solution without question, although the North gained the greatest amount of unsettled territory and the South preserved a balance not justified by its population. The calm acceptance of the compromise was high tribute to the spirit of nationalism abroad in the land; few people had the foresight of John Quincy Adams, who recorded in his diary: "The present question is a mere preamble— a title-page to a great, tragic volume."

The strong sense of national unity that shaped these domestic events played an even larger role in the foreign affairs of these postwar years. The proud American people, thrilled by their new independence and intoxicated by their unaccustomed strength, were no longer content to play a timid role in world matters. Instead, they found it easy to translate their flamboyant nationalism into an international arrogance that sent them forth in quest of new lands, led them to champion the cause of other peoples who were struggling for liberty, and reached a climax when they enunciated a new doctrine that profoundly influenced Latin American history.

Expansion came first. Spanish Florida had long been a plague spot on the southern borderland. Its tangled wilderness provided a mecca for runaway slaves, Indians, and desperadoes who were forever raiding the Georgia plantations, for Spain was so busy with the Napoleonic Wars and insurrections in her Latin-American colonies that her influence scarcely extended beyond the posts of St. Marks, St. Augustine, and Pensacola. The United States finally took matters into its own hands in 1817 when Andrew Jackson was ordered to police the border with a force of Tennessee militiamen. International boundaries meant little to this hot-headed frontiersman, and when a raiding party crossed into Georgia he burst into Florida, chased his quarries to St. Marks, and then in April, 1818, recklessly captured that Spanish city. Taking up the trail from there, he started east after a Seminole chieftain named Billy Bowlegs, only to learn that the renegade had been warned of his coming by two British traders and had escaped into an impenetrable swamp. Jackson was furious, and after a summary court-martial hanged one of the offenders and shot the other. Then, having brought the wrath of Spain and England about his ears, he capped one injury with another by taking Pensacola before returning to the United States to be hailed as a frontier hero. President Monroe was less sure that his general had acted wisely, for this looked like war against a friendly power; only John Quincy Adams' plea in the Cabinet that Jackson was justified by Spain's failure to police its border saved the Tennessean from a public rebuke by the President.

Andrew Jackson's border raid touched off a train of events that added Florida to the United States, secured the final independence of the Latin-American republics, and spread the Monroe Doctrine before an astonished world.

When news of the attack reached Madrid, Spain's ministers realized the danger of the situation. Troubles were pressing in upon the once-mighty nation. Her colonies in Central and South America were struggling for freedom, and Spain's best fighting men were waging a losing war amidst the plains and peaks of Argentina, Chile, and Peru. Defense of Florida was impossible; better to sell before the aggressive Americans used the Spaniards' preoccupation elsewhere as an excuse to seize the colony. In February, 1819, a treaty was concluded with the United States in which Spain ceded all Florida in return for five million dollars, gave up claims to the Oregon country north of the forty-second parallel, and accepted the Sabine River and a line zigzagging northwest from that stream as the western boundary of the Louisiana Purchase, which had not previously been defined. The Senate, delighted with this treaty, which removed the last foreign threat from the eastern part of the country, ratified it without delay.

Spain hung back. So long as she could dangle the uncompleted treaty before the Americans they would not dare recognize the independence of the Latin-American republics, and Spain would have a chance to subdue her rebellious colonies. For two years Spain waited, while her armies absorbed new defeats from the revolutionists. Opinion in the United States divided sharply on the issue. The majority of the people, whose spokesman was the former Kentucky War Hawk, Henry Clay, insisted that the Latin Americans were struggling for their independence and deserved immediate recognition, even though this meant losing Florida. The opposing view was championed by John Quincy Adams, Monroe's able Secretary of State. Favoring the revolting colonies no less than Clay and advocating their eventual recognition, he was unwilling to jeopardize the Florida Treaty or to risk war with Spain by hasty action. Why, he asked, should the United States take such a gamble when the South Americans were so steeped in aristocratic traditions that years must pass before they could set up republican governments? Adams won

Monroe to his view and they waited until 1821, when Spain's armies suffered a series of crushing defeats. Even the Spanish ministers realized that further delay was useless; they ratified the Florida Treaty in 1821 and on March 8, 1822, President Monroe formally recognized the governments of Argentina, Chile, Peru, Colombia, and Mexico.

When Spain sought to delay recognition by the United States she did so partly because she feared that England would immediately imitate the American example, but now the British held back. Opinion there was more evenly divided than in North America. One group, led by George IV and his Tory followers, hated democracy so thoroughly that they were unwilling to encourage liberal revolutions in any form. Another, made up of the business and merchant classes, coveted the Latin-American markets that would be closed if Spain reconquered her rebellious colonies, and favored immediate recognition without regard to idealistic considerations. While these opponents debated England's course, a development abroad stung them into action. In 1823, French armies, led by the reactionary Charles X, invaded Spain, supposedly to rescue the Spanish monarch from a rebellion that had broken out three years before against his autocratic rule, but rumor insisted that their real object was a joint Franco-Spanish expedition against the South American rebels. This venture would be aided, according to these whispered warnings, by the members of the Holy Alliance, a group of reactionary central European powers under Metternich's influence who had bound themselves together to resist the advances of republicanism everywhere, and toward whom the English Tories were by no means hostile.

These developments placed George Canning, the British Foreign Secretary, in a quandary. He shuddered at the thought of the conquest of Latin America by such a traditional rival as France, yet his monarch unalterably opposed recognition. In this dilemma he hit upon a happy solution. Why not join with the United States in warning France and the Holy Alliance to stay out of the Americas? This could be done by a joint declaration in which both nations disavowed any intention of taking any part of the continent for themselves yet made it clear that they would refuse to permit a transfer to anyone else. The solution was brilliant from Canning's point of view: he would protect the independence of the Latin-American republics without committing his nation to the active defense of democracy. The complete plan was laid before the American minister in London during August, 1823, and relayed at once to President Monroe.

The President was delighted. He believed that England was rushing to the aid of republicanism and pictured the two nations as together leading a triumphant attack on monarchy in South America, in Greece, where the people were then struggling for independence from Turkey, and throughout the world. Monroe's attitude reflected the opinion of his countrymen. In their eyes a vast ideological gulf separated the United States from Europe. They pictured the monarchical nationalism of the Continent as an odious system aimed against democracy and freedom everywhere, just as Metternich's puppets viewed America as a constant threat to their royal absolutism. The President, conscious of these irreconcilable differences, was only too glad to welcome England as an ally in the democratic struggle for survival.

John Quincy Adams was less sure, and he was sufficiently accustomed to the hard-driven bargains of his native New Englanders to look a gift horse squarely in the mouth. What, he asked himself, was Canning's real purpose? Certainly not to prevent European intervention in Latin America, for England could stop that at any time through her control of the seas. Adams thought he found the answer in the clause pledging both nations to seek no more territory on the continent. Was this a veiled hint to the United States that it must keep its hands off Cuba or Mexico, should the people of those territories some day wish to cast their lot with the republic? He thought it was. Moreover, Adams, at that time alarmed at another European encroachment on the American continent, was dissatisfied because Canning's proposal applied only to an invasion of South America by the Holy Alliance.

In the Pacific Northwest, Russia, which had long exploited the fur-bearing wealth of Alaska, was creeping steadily down the coast toward the Oregon country. In September, 1821, the czar formally extended the boundaries of his American domain to the fifty-first parallel and announced his intention of confiscating any vessel that intruded on this broad province. Adams was quick to protest, for ship captains from his own New England were trading for furs in the Oregon country and Russia's assertion, if unchallenged, might close a profitable field to commercial exploitation. This was no matter for international cooperation; the national interests of the United States were involved and must be protected. As early as 1822 the Secretary of State concluded that this could best be accomplished by declaring the New World closed to colonization by any European power. This should be done, he believed, through diplomatic correspondence with the nations concerned rather than through any public pronouncement.

These were the two points of view presented to the momentous cabinet meetings from which the Monroe Doctrine emerged: Adams wanted a strong declaration of the noncolonization principle embodied in a sharp note to Russia; Monroe, a broad denunciation of the Holy Alliance and an open statement supporting the Greek revolutionists. By pointing out the possible effects of Canning's proposal on the nation's territorial expansion, Adams easily convinced the cabinet members that the United States should abandon all ideas of cooperating with England. Why not, he insisted, substitute for this a single statement extending the noncolonization principle over all the New World? This would, he said, afford "a very suitable and convenient opportunity for us to take our stand against the Holy Alliance, and at the same time to decline the overture from Great Britain. It would be more candid as well as more dignified to avow our principles explicitly to Russia and France, than to come in as a cock-boat in the wake of the British man-of-war." No amount of persuasion, however, could induce Monroe not to pen a firm statement of the American republican principle as a warning to the Holy Alliance; nor was he to be deterred from making his declaration in a public document rather than in notes to France and Russia.

The famous Monroe Doctrine was accordingly embodied in the presidential message to Congress of December 2, 1823. The Doctrine consisted of two sections widely separated in the President's message. One stated Adams' noncolonization principle: "The American continents, by the free and independent condition which they have assumed and maintain, are henceforth not to be considered as subjects for future colonization by any European powers." The other, written by Monroe, was a ringing declaration of the democratic faith so dear to the heart of every American and a stern denunciation of the monarchism of the Holy Alliance: "We owe it, therefore, to candor and to the amicable relations existing between the United States and those powers to declare that we should consider any attempt on their part to extend their system to any portion of this hemisphere as dangerous to our peace and safety. With the existing colonies or dependencies of any European power we have not interfered and shall not interfere. But with the Governments who have declared their independence and maintained it, and whose independence we have, on great consideration and on just principles, acknowledged, we could not view any interposition for the purpose of oppressing them, or controlling in any other manner their destiny, by any European power in any other light than as the manifestation of an unfriendly disposition toward the United States."

Monroe's courageous distinction between monarchical oppression and republican freedom and his stern warning to the despotic satellites of the Holy Alliance were welcomed with enthusiasm by the American people. Here in their eyes was new evidence of the might of their lusty young nation: the United States stood ready to guard both its hemisphere and its democracy against intrusion—to say "Hands Off!" to all the powers of the world. Once more the welter of European diplomacy had transformed American policy and given birth to a concept that strengthened the independence of the republic. The reaction to Monroe's message was as unfavorable in Europe as it was favorable in the United States. The Continental diplomats realized that it accomplished nothing practical: Russia was ready to back down on her Pacific claims long before December, 1823, and the Holy Alliance had also abandoned all plans to invade Latin America. Hence the President's bold declaration seemed only an ill-timed jibe at European nations which had done nothing to deserve it, and a boastful assertion of defensive power that was actually lacking. Yet Prince Metternich sensed its real meaning when he wrote: "They have distinctly and clearly announced their intention to set not only power against power, but, to express it more exactly, altar against altar. In their indecent declarations they have cast blame and scorn on the institutions of Europe most worthy of respect, on the principles of its greatest sovereigns, on the whole of those measures which a sacred duty no less than an evident necessity has forced our governments to adopt to frustrate plans most criminal." Monroe indeed had set "altar against altar" and dedicated his nation to the support of the republican institutions that were truly worshiped in his native land.

SEEDS OF PARTY DISSENSION

Surveying the American scene when he stepped down from office in 1824, James Monroe could feel a justifiable pride. He left a strong united nation, its factories humming and farms bustling, its world position secure. Yet the situation was not without its perils for the party that had won political supremacy. The National Republicans, with no opposition, were encouraged to magnify internal quarrels. Party factions, all with their eyes on the presidential elections of 1824, disturbed the tranquillity of Monroe's second term and destroyed the old system of presidential nomination.

Growing sectional differences, the lack of an opposition party, and the sectional rivalries of political managers caused the breakdown of the caucus system of nominating that had worked so creditably in elevating to office experienced leaders who generally had the advantage of considerable congressional support. Until 1824 the nomination of presidential and vice-presidential candidates was made by a meeting or "caucus" of the party's senators and congressmen at the nation's capital, much as parliamentary members in England by party caucus developed the custom of selecting a leader who—whenever the party won the elections—would become the Prime Minister. The congressional caucus as employed in the days of Jefferson had the virtue of consolidating party members in Congress behind the legislative program of their President, pledging them to close ranks against the Federalist opposition. By 1824, however, the Federalist party was dead; and for lack of an opposition party to express political differences the triumphant Jeffersonian party was torn by dissension.

The caucus, a political invention devised to enable a party to consolidate against an external foe, lost prestige when challenged from within the party itself. In part the attack on the caucus came from the new states west of the mountains; for party managers in the West were in jealous rebellion against eastern machines that had dominated earlier caucuses and nominated candidates from the powerful seaboard states of Massachusetts and Virginia. But the assault on the caucus came also from eastern party chieftains; a basic factor behind the attack was the growth of local party machinery, producing new pressures to circumvent the centralized control of nominations in Washington. A consequence was that political managers in seaboard states in 1824 divided their strength by supporting several favorite sons; their rivals in the West also divided, offering two candidates whose differing outlook betokened a new cleavage in western society.

Several able men, in and out of the Cabinet, became the leading contenders to succeed Monroe: William H. Crawford of Georgia, Secretary of the Treasury and heir apparent of the "Virginia dynasty"; John Quincy Adams of Massachusetts, the able Secretary of State; John C. Calhoun of South Carolina, Secretary of War, backwoods scholar, and an ardent nationalist; Henry Clay of Kentucky, Speaker of the House, and spokesman for the West; Andrew Jackson of Tennessee, frontiersman and military hero. All of them eager for the presidency and all nationalists and Republicans, these men jockeyed for position for three years, each striving to discredit his opponents and increase his own popularity. Crawford, by seeking nomination from a poorly attended caucus, damaged his own cause. Jackson gained favor with his political sponsors when he spoke against the caucus and urged the decentralized method of nomination by state legislatures. When the race neared the finish, Jackson seemed slightly in the lead, and Calhoun, mending his political fences, arranged a bargain that placed him in the Jackson alignment as vice-presidential candidate and heir apparent to the office.

With only one major party but four candidates in the field, voters were presented with a confusing choice; consequently, the elections of 1824 neither clarified the principles of the party nor registered clearly the popular choice for the presidency. Jackson swept most of the West, Pennsylvania, and the Carolinas to lead with ninety-nine electoral votes; Adams had eighty-four from New England and New York; and Crawford and Clay a smaller number. The fact that no candidate had a majority of all votes cast automatically threw the election into the House of Representatives whose members must decide between the three highest aspirants: Jackson, Adams, and Crawford. This placed Clay in a position at once embarrassing and strategic: as Speaker of the House he must decide which of his three successful opponents to support. He eliminated Crawford immediately, for the Georgian's strict-constructionist views conflicted with Clay's ardent nationalism. Jackson seemed untrustworthy; moreover, Clay aspired to the presidency and he was afraid that Jackson and Calhoun would monopolize that office for sixteen years. Adams, on the other hand, had no successor picked and his nationalism was as violent as Clay's. The Kentuckian threw his support behind the New Englander, and John Quincy Adams entered the presidency so recently vacated by his Federalist grandfather.

Adams' four years in office were far from happy. Although passionately fond of his country, he was a cold man whose backbone had been stiffened by the granite of his native Massachusetts until he was unable to bend to the level of the lesser figures around him. His elaborate plans to bind the nation together by heavy federal expenditures for roads and canals, army and navy, science and scholarship, met the stubborn resistance of a Congress that did not understand, and Adams was helpless when he tried to explain. Even his plans to cement commercial ties with the new republics of South America ended in dismal failure when the Senate defeated his attempt to send delegates to a Panama Congress in 1826, partly because southern congressmen objected to dealing with men of mixed blood. Worst of all, this paragon of New England virtue was forced to listen for four years to a cry of "Bargain and Corruption!" raised by his enemies. Clay, they said, had made Adams President and had been paid with the office of Secretary of State.

Andrew Jackson was behind these charges, which, although untrue, made excellent political fodder. He felt that he had been cheated of the presidency in 1824, and both he and his followers were determined that this should not be repeated in 1828. Their editors and stump speakers so thoroughly convinced the people that Adams was in office only because of a corrupt bargain that in the mid-term elections Jackson's supporters secured control of Congress. For the next two years they carried on absurd investigations of Adams' honesty: he heard himself pilloried as the Federalist author of the Sedition Act; as a corrupt gambler who had filled the White House with gaming devices at public expense (he had purchased at private expense a billiard table and a set of chessmen); and as a relic of aristocracy out of tune with the democratic times. For four years this malicious and degrading campaign went on, until Adams' followers sank to the level of their opponents and filled the land with rumors of Jackson's frontier escapades and tales of his premarital relations with Mrs. Jackson.

The result was decisive. Jackson was carried into office by an overwhelming electoral vote that left Adams the support of only his native New England. The wounds left by that bitter campaign were not to heal for many years. The "Era of Good Feelings" was ended, the din of party strife sounded again through the United States, and these political quarrels were soon to merge into a sectional conflict that culminated in civil war.

VIII

THE CHALLENGE OF SECTIONALISM:
THE JACKSONIAN PERIOD 1829–1840

Andrew Jackson owed his election in 1828 not to campaign cries of "Bargain and Corruption!" but to a growing force which he neither created nor controlled but which was forever to be linked to his name— Jacksonian Democracy. For some years the masses had chafed under the rule of National Republicans, who, for all their lip service to the common man, had no love for true democracy. In Jackson they found a champion who was of, not above, the people—an ordinary rough-and-ready citizen without formal education or training in the wily ways of statesmanship. His school had been the school of life, and his disciples loved to dwell on his rustic experiences: they were proud of his birth amidst the poverty of the Carolina frontier, his struggles as a frontier lawyer in Tennessee, and they admired his shrewd ways and sharp tongue, his military victories at Horse Shoe Bend and New Orleans. If he was crude and impetuous and intolerant, so were the men who flocked to his standard—the leather-clad frontiersmen of the West, the workers in the northern mill towns, the thousands of "one-horse" cotton farmers who lived under the shadows of the southern plantations.

When their hero was elected, their joy was boundless. From all over the countryside his followers came to Washington to gaze reverently on their "Andy"—tall and lean with his white hair bared to the March sun —as he walked through the mud of Pennsylvania Avenue to his inauguration. There was no carriage such as Washington had used, no horse like that ridden by Jefferson, for this common man who had become President. Crowding into the White House afterward, a milling mob stood on the chairs, upset the furniture, and trampled on the glassware. Tubs of whisky and punch hastily placed on the lawn drew them out before the furnishings were a shambles. Washington society was horrified. Conservatives tilted their noses and "walked out on the rabble," muttering about "mobocracy," and talking grimly of a new reign of terror that would probably cost them their estates if this "brawler from Tennessee" were allowed a free hand. But Jackson, even though he had to escape from his own reception by a window, was delighted. These were his people, and he would dedicate his reign to them.

Andrew Jackson did not father the democratic surge that bears his name. Indeed, his own antecedents made him a strange prophet for a popular uprising. Although he had been born in a log cabin, he associated with the aristocratic element in Tennessee politics and had steadfastly combated the people's party in its struggle for laws that would ease the plight of the debtor farmers after the panic of 1819. Nor did his mode of life, amidst the luxurious surroundings of his palatial home, the Hermitage, bear any resemblance to the squalid existence of the thousands who flocked to his standard. Yet his humble origins, his reputation as an Indian fighter, and his frontier distrust of the aristocratic dynasties that had governed the nation in the interest of Virginia planters or New England shipowners made him an ideal figurehead for the American phase of the democratic revolution sweeping the Western world. Andrew Jackson's good fortune was to be in the public eye just as the Age of the Common Man was dawning.

THE LIBERAL UPRISING ABROAD

The common people everywhere were on the march. They had been willing, for a few years, to obey false prophets who told them that the path to security and peace led backward to an archaic world of nationalism and reaction, for they were so numbed by war and so busy with reconstruction that they would listen to any advice. But not even Metternich's frantic efforts could quench the liberal beacon raised by the American and French revolutions or halt the steady progress of the middle class to power. Within fifteen years after the final defeat of Napoleon the commercial and industrial classes of England, the bourgeoisie of France, the peasants of Spain, Germany, and Italy, and the small farmers and laborers of the United States were ready to rise in revolt against the autocrats, Tories, and aristocrats who had tried to turn back the clock.

The violence of this revolution in each country was directly proportional to the repression suffered by the people during the Age of Nationalism, except in the central European nations, where tyrants ruled so absolutely that the uprising was delayed for another generation. France, where the bourgeoisie and workingmen were chafing under the ultraroyalist administration of Charles X, with its legislative program shaped to the needs of the clergy and nobility, again led the way. Discontent reached a climax there in the summer of 1830, when the king, alarmed by the popular protests voiced by the bourgeois members of the lower chamber, dissolved that body, abolished freedom of the press, and disenfranchised three quarters of the voters. Street fighting broke out in Paris in July, and after three days Charles X abdicated, ending for all time in France rule by divine right. The commercial leaders who had engineered the uprising were not ready to bow to the workers' demands for a republic; instead, they took refuge in a constitutional monarchy under the liberal Bourbon, Louis Philippe, who had supported the Revolution in 1789.

The success of the July revolution in France gave heart to liberals everywhere and touched off a storm of protests against tyrannical rulers, particularly in western Europe, where the middle class was most powerful. The Belgians, long resentful of the union that placed them under the rule of the reactionary Dutch monarch, revolted in 1831 and established their own liberal monarchy; the Poles rose against their Russian masters but were cruelly defeated when no foreign power came to their aid; the people of the Papal States in central Italy shook off temporal rule by the Pope; the commercial leaders of several of the German states —Brunswick, Hanover, Saxony, and Hesse-Cassel—staged uprisings that wrung liberal concessions and moderate constitutions from their reluctant rulers. Shaken by this burgeoning popular demand, even autocratic Austria and the other Eastern European nations under Metternich's thumb hurried to protect themselves by giving up reactionary dreams of forcing "legitimacy" on the rest of the Continent. The peasants and workers gained comparatively little from these revolutionary surges—the few that succeeded were middle-class triumphs—but they gave notice that the Age of Nationalism and Reaction was ended.

England needed no violent revolution to liberalize its Tory government, for its parliamentary system allowed reformers to work through legal channels. The English leaders, drawn largely from the middle class created by the industrial revolution, were a group of shrewd, practical men who had been touched only gently by the wand of liberalism. Their objectives were essentially practical: they wanted political power so that they could remove ancient mercantilistic restraints on trade and industry. This could be achieved only by broadening the franchise to allow the newly created mill towns proper representation in Parliament, now dominated by country squires and conservative Tories. Thus the middle class looked on parliamentary reform as a means to economic benefits rather than as a political end; yet neither they nor their reactionary opponents were motivated solely by the hope of personal gain, for they too reacted to the world-wide democratic impulse. The democratic movement alone explains the repeal in 1828 of the Corporation and Test acts, two ancient measures that closed all municipal and civil service posts to Catholics, and the passage a year later of the Catholic Emancipation Act, which restored full political freedom to members of this persecuted sect.

Dearer to the hearts of liberals and their middle-class allies were reforms that would allow England's new industrial and commercial leaders a full voice in Parliament. Agitation for this went on through the late 1820's, aided by the Whig party, which found itself working for change because it was in the opposition rather than because of any conviction. News of the successful French Revolution provided an effective stimulus. Whig pressure grew so intense that the Tories were forced from office, a ministry dominated by Whigs was formed, and three separate reform bills were railroaded through the House of Commons in 1831 and 1832. All were defeated by the Tory-packed House of Lords. By this time the whole land was aflame with excitement; mass meetings in the industrial cities resolved to pay no more taxes until the bill was passed, or talked openly of revolution. Civil war seemed near when the Lords, fearing a proletarian uprising more than a bourgeois reform, backed down. On June 7, 1832, the Reform Bill received royal assent. It was far from a radical measure: seats in Parliament were redistributed to give the new mill towns some representation, and the franchise was extended to landowners worth £10 a year or tenants worth £50. Twenty-one out of every twenty-two adult males in Britain still could not vote, but the bulwark of aristocratic control had proven vulnerable, and during the next years the armies of democracy could widen the breach in its walls.

DEMOCRATIC DISCONTENT

The liberal uprisings in Europe and England differed only in degree from the political revolution that carried Andrew Jackson into the White House. No street rioting, no mass revolts, no congressional battles were necessary in the United States, for there, despite the property qualifications for voting still existing in many of the states, the franchise was sufficiently broad to allow change wherever popular pressure was strong enough. The enduring effects of the panic of 1819 provided that pressure; while politicians talked much of the "Era of Good Feelings," the decade of the 1820's was for the masses an era of bad times. Low wages and cheap farm goods continued to nurture discontent long after the business recovery of 1823, but even worse were the bitter memories of upperclass conduct during the depression years. Not a farmer or laborer but remembered those dark days of 1820 and 1821—the tumbling prices, the mounting debts, the harsh foreclosure laws that threatened their mortgaged homes, the frantic efforts to secure relief from the state legislatures, and the cold indifference of the governing faction to all their pleas. The panic gave the American lower classes a sufficient taste of aristocratic rule; they had waited impatiently ever since for a leader who would bring a more enlightened democracy to their government.

Yet those specific grievances could never have inspired the 1828 revolution had not the American democratic spirit been strengthened by the changed conditions under which the common people were living. Particularly important was the rapid shift of population to the West during these years, for life on the frontier provided a limitless opportunity for self-betterment that inspired a belief in democracy. There each man could go as far as his brawn and his brain would let him. He wanted no aristocratic props for his social structure, for they would only restrain him as he struggled upward. He asked only to be let alone, with no restraining hand upon him, as he engaged in the joyous task of exploiting the rich resources of nature. This equality of opportunity bred a faith in the equality of man; the West believed that all should be given the same chance in politics and in life. In 1828 one third of the American people lived in the trans-Appalachian area under frontier or semifrontier conditions. For them Jackson was the symbol of democracy and they voted solidly for him.

The spawning mill towns of the East were another source of democratic strength, for the thousands of workers who crowded within their borders saw in popular rule an opportunity to better the miserable conditions under which they lived and worked. Hours of labor in these early mills were long, the work was unhealthful, and pay was so low that families could survive only by pressing their tiny children into jobs. At first they endured these conditions, for the New England farm families who entered the factories were accustomed to long hours and low pay, and the tradition of individual freedom was too strong to allow them to join any attempt to dictate to an employer. By the late 1820's, however, they began to realize the difference between endless farm labor and monotonous factory work, and to see that their rights were as important as their employer's freedom. Organization was one answer to their problem, and the local craft unions that sprang up began a valiant battle against hostile public opinion and courts eager to apply ancient common-law conspiracy rules against strikers. They also turned to political action.

As the states slowly broadened their franchise, workingmen's parties began to blossom in the eastern cities during the late 1820's, one in New York throwing conservatives into a panic of fear when it polled 30 per cent of the total vote in 1829. At their head were liberal National Republicans ready to split from their party if necessary to aid the common people. Some were tub-thumping politicians who saw the masses of workers only as prospective voters able to place them in office, but many were sincere men who honestly believed that the promises of the Declaration of Independence should be fulfilled; Martin Van Buren in New York and James Buchanan in Pennsylvania were of this group. By 1828 popular parties existed in all the eastern states. Andrew Jackson's candidacy gave these independent machines a rallying point for national expression and a wave of triumphant democracy swept Jackson into the White House.

THE JACKSONIAN REVOLUTION

The victorious masses were not content with placing their idol in the presidency. Their ire was directed not only against aristocratic politicians but against the whole outworn structure of the society in which they lived. They disliked many things: the property qualifications for voting that still existed in some eastern states, the restriction of officeholding to the wealthy, the lack of popular control over state or federal officials, the inadequate educational opportunities for their children. Jackson's election accelerated an attack on these undemocratic features of government that was already under way and that ended only when most of these relics of aristocracy were swept into the limbo of the past.

The war against voting requirements came first. The battle was carried out state by state, since the Constitution vested in each the right to decide franchise qualifications. Western states took the lead. The eleven trans-Appalachian states that entered the Union before 1828 all boasted manhood suffrage, and their example swept those of the East into line. Maryland, New Hampshire, and Connecticut acted first, Massachusetts followed in 1821, New York in 1826, and Virginia in 1830. The contest was bitter in each case; older conservatives believed "that universal suffrage jeopardizes property and puts it into the power of the poor and profligate to control the affluent," but even this strong opposition crumbled as the movement gained momentum. Rhode Island was the last of the eastern states to give way. In the early 1840's the people of that tiny state, disgusted by the failure of the ruling minority to change the ancient qualifications for voting, marched under the leadership of a reformer named Thomas Dorr and set up their own unauthorized government. Troops had to be called out to suppress Dorr's Rebellion, but even in defeat the people triumphed, for their uprising convinced the rulers that some change was necessary. In 1843 Rhode Island adopted a new constitution that opened the ballot box to all. Only South Carolina retained its archaic laws, and even in that planter-dominated state there were ways whereby the average citizen could cast his ballot.

The democratic surge of Jacksonianism, depending upon workingmen and small farmers for votes, needed more than expansion of the

GROWTH OF MANHOOD SUFFRAGE

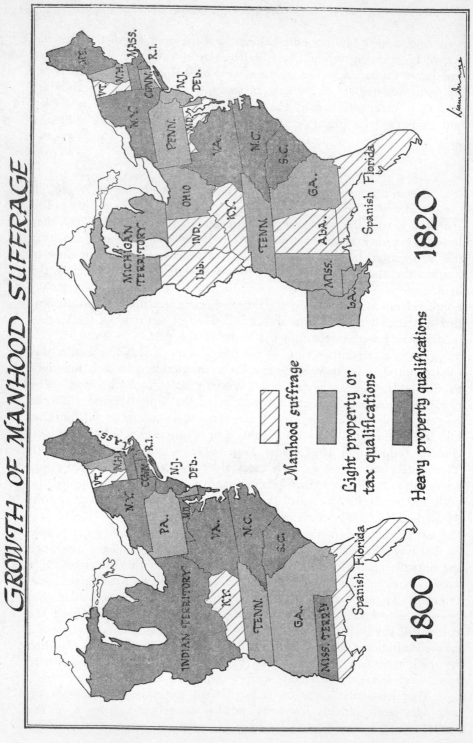

1820

1800

Manhood suffrage

Light property or tax qualifications

Heavy property qualifications

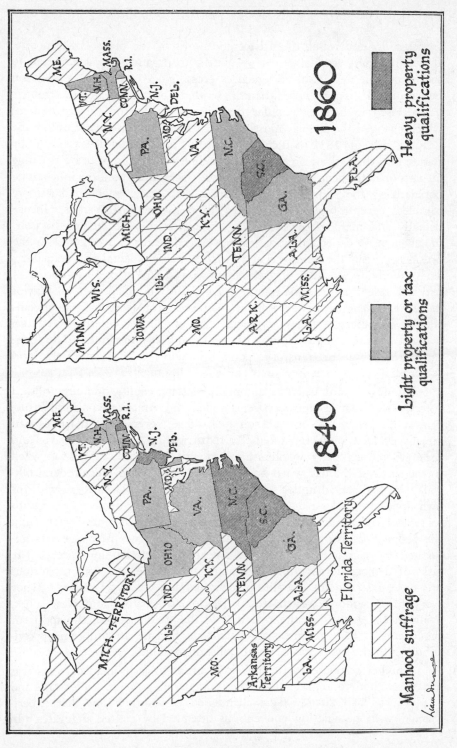

1860

1840

Heavy property qualifications

Light property or tax qualifications

Manhood suffrage

franchise to undermine the aristocratic props of the old social structure. It was necessary to evolve a new politics, to organize the voters, and to set in motion new political practices creating an unwritten constitution better adapted to party needs than the written Constitution that the framers had devised to hamper popular majorities. Unlike the July revolution, which changed the French constitutional structure, and equally unlike the Reform Bill of 1832, which established English middle-class rule by statute law, the Jacksonian movement made its deepest imprint by a change in party management and party behavior. Jacksonian political innovators, popularizing the formula of direct local democracy, established a more complete decentralization of power within the national parties. Inconsistently and momentarily, reflecting the personality of Jackson himself, the movement depended upon strong central leadership centered in the presidency. But the existence of the latter was accidental and transitory. The underlying tendency of Jacksonians was toward a local conception of majority rule that weakened central leadership and made party behavior more discordant and undisciplined than ever, for Jacksonian politicians sought democracy at the grass roots. Striving to get out the vote, they evolved a more complex system of county and city machines. The long-range result was to transform party behavior into a more direct local reflex of heterogeneous sectional and class alignments.

Moving toward a greater autonomy of state, county, and city political forces, Jacksonian Democracy refashioned the American political structure at all levels. Before Jackson took office, several eastern states had already evolved a "spoils system," a redistribution of political loaves and fishes to reward party workers after victory in elections. Jackson acted in the spirit of the day when he dismissed a number of older federal officials who had served under several presidents and replaced them with his own appointees. As a device to assure an upsurging democracy a means to replace conservative old appointees with new incumbents "fresh from the people," redistribution of federal as well as state patronage was advocated by Jacksonians under the slogan of "rotation in office." The tasks of democratic government, thought the people, were not mysterious arts to be reserved for the elite of educated and wealthy families. "They see nothing wrong," vouchsafed a Jacksonian senator from New York, William L. Marcy, "in the rule that to the victors belong the spoils of the enemy." Federal and state patronage became an inducement contributing to the evolution of local political machines.

Another response of the political parties to Jacksonian currents was a new method to replace the older nominating process. The state and local caucus had already been abandoned in several states that experimented with nominating conventions attended by elected delegates. In national politics, too, politicians after 1830 turned to nominating conventions in place of the older congressional caucus and the newer method of nomination of favorite sons by party members in state legislatures. By 1832 parties adopted national conventions as a party arena in which state political leaders who were important enough to "swing" their state delegations began to evolve a new system of bargaining together over platform planks and nominations for the presidency and the vice-presidency.

Political management through national conventions exhibited the new tendencies toward local autonomy in party affairs. Party organizations at the base of the political pyramid, centered in the constituencies rather than in Washington, were evolving techniques for state and local pressure in national affairs and expanding state and local influence over federal appointments and nominations for the presidency and vice-presidency. The new political practices, by the shift to decentralized political management, ostensibly broadened the opportunity of local aspirants for political power. The change did indeed elevate to appointive offices men fresh from the people, and to the presidency itself "favorite sons" and "dark horses" who often had enjoyed little opportunity for formal education and had had little or no experience in the halls of Congress, the federal administration, or presidential Cabinets. More significant still, the Jacksonian tendency toward a more local conception of majority rule accentuated the weakness of the party tie: senators and congressmen became more concerned with the wishes of state and local political managers and powerful local interests than with those of the national party. Sectional voting rather than party voting began to characterize American party behavior. Jacksonian Democracy made politicians in Washington more directly responsive to important constituents at home, but less capable of standing together on national party principles when confronted with national issues.

The new state constitutions adopted under the impact of the new democracy contained other evidence that the old aristocracy was crumbling. By 1832 all states but South Carolina allowed the people to vote directly for presidential electors rather than leaving this important task to the legislatures. At the same time they popularized the methods used in selecting state officials until by the close of Jackson's administration even the judges were elected in thirteen states. Nor did the new laws require these officials to be men of wealth, for property qualifications for officeholding vanished when the franchise was liberalized. As significant as the changes themselves was the fact that they were carried out by democratic means: in nearly every case the new constitutions were drawn up by popularly elected conventions and submitted to the people for ratification.

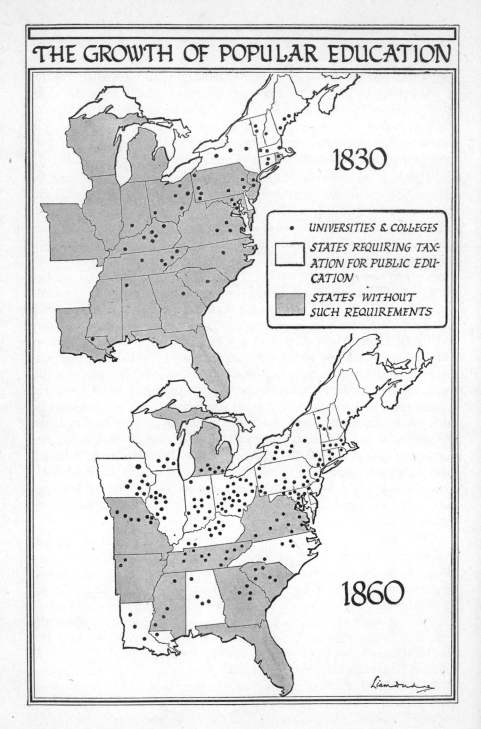

THE GROWTH OF POPULAR EDUCATION

1830

- • UNIVERSITIES & COLLEGES
- ☐ STATES REQUIRING TAX-ATION FOR PUBLIC EDU-CATION
- ▨ STATES WITHOUT SUCH REQUIREMENTS

1860

The movement for universal education, initiated during Jackson's presidency, was intimately connected with political change, for this was the reformer's answer to conservatives who argued that the masses were too ill-trained to control a government. If the people were to vote, they insisted, they must be educated, and at state expense, because the government would benefit most from an intelligent electorate. This was a revolutionary concept—the taking of one man's money to educate another man's child—and the movement for popular education aroused greater resistance than any other reform of the day, just as have all liberal changes that limit individual rights for the benefit of society. Conservatives, the private schools that had carried the educational burden before, the churches that maintained their own schools—all raised a clamor of protest. Undaunted, the reformers worked feverishly for support, operating through trade unions, public officials, and propaganda organizations known as "School Societies" that were formed in every state. Through the 1820's and 1830's this agitation went on, with the cause of popular education slowly gaining adherents.

By the close of Jackson's administration the reformers could reap their initial harvest when Massachusetts in 1837 set up the first board of education in the nation's history. Horace Mann, who forsook a promising political career to become its secretary, made his state a model that others could emulate: he founded normal schools, raised teachers' pay, vastly expanded the number of schools, extended the length of the school year, and popularized educational reform through a series of brilliant annual reports that were nationally read. Other New England states fell into line at once, partly because the concentration of industry there created the wealth needed to support schools. Although the rest of the United States lagged behind until after the Civil War, the principle of state-supported universal education was accepted.

JACKSON AND THE SECTIONAL CHALLENGE

Jackson tried to carry into his administration the spirit that bred these reforms in voting, politics, and education. He ruled with an iron hand—"King Andrew," his enemies called him—because he regarded his voice as the voice of the people, and the people could do no wrong. His predecessors were so reluctant to oppose Congress that the veto power had been used only nine times since Washington's day, but Jackson negated congressional acts with abandon, just as he rode roughshod over the courts or the states when he believed they opposed the popular will. This attitude explains his apparently contradictory course when dealing with two problems that immediately faced him as President: a state that defied the Supreme Court, and another that rebelled against Congress.

The first concerned Georgia and arose when the expanding cotton frontier reached lands occupied by the Creek and Cherokee Indians. Pressure from the Southerners forced the Creeks to move west just before Jackson took office, but the Cherokee, protected by treaties with the United States guaranteeing them their territory, refused to go. Instead, they prepared to defend their possessions by adopting a constitution that asserted their independence of Georgia's control. The irate Georgians countered by ruling that the state's authority extended over all its inhabitants and laid plans to remove the Indians by force. When Jackson showed no inclination to uphold the federal treaties protecting the Cherokee, they turned to the Supreme Court, where Chief Justice Marshall, in the case of *Worcester v. Georgia* (1832), ruled that they formed a "domestic dependent nation" subject only to the jurisdiction of the United States and that Georgia's laws did not extend within their borders. Jackson, furious, was reputed to have made the famous statement: "Marshall has made his decision, now let him enforce it." The President stood aside while Georgia ignored the Court's order and drove the Indians west of the Mississippi. Other tribes, realizing that they could expect no protection from the federal government, reluctantly ceded their lands and prepared to move to a great reservation set up in present Oklahoma; ninety-four treaties were made during Jackson's administration and by 1842 the last of the southern tribes had begun its laborious trek westward.

Jackson supported Georgia against the Supreme Court because his frontier prejudices convinced him that all Indians were wrong and because a majority of the people believed that Georgia was right. Yet when South Carolina defied national authority, he rose to the defense of the federal government so vigorously that no single state in the future dared challenge the nation's power.

The South Carolina controversy centered about the tariff. By 1824, when a new protectionist measure replaced the tariff of 1816, the Southerners who had supported the earlier law realized that the protective policy harmed their section. Their prosperity hinged on the export of cotton to England, and this in turn depended on the ease with which English manufactured goods could be marketed in the United States. Southern opposition to protection was whispered in 1824, but by 1828, when a new tariff was before Congress, the South was ready to shout its objections from the housetops. This boiling resentment was due partly to the honest conviction that free trade was essential to the South's cotton planters, and partly to the nature of the tariff of 1828. Combining high duties on raw materials and manufactured goods, this measure was introduced into Congress by Jackson's supporters as a political maneuver just before the election. They believed it would be defeated by New England's commercial interests who disliked protection because it discouraged shipping, and by manufacturers who would disapprove of the high duties on raw materials. Then Jackson's followers could boast in the West that they had worked for highly protected raw materials; in the East that they had supported the protection desired by manufacturers; and in the South that they had helped defeat an obnoxious law. But to their surprise, this badly drawn tariff, designed only to "manufacture a president of the United States," passed Congress, for industrial New England was by this time so enthusiastic about protection that its representatives would vote for any law, good or bad.

When the chorus of protest against the "Tariff of Abominations" rose from the South, South Carolina's voice was heard above the rest. There declining fortunes left tempers raw. For years the state had grown cotton, but its worn-out fields could no longer compete with the virgin soils of Alabama and Mississippi, and its excess slave population was not large enough to allow wholesale shipments of Negroes to the cotton belt as a means of augmenting declining agricultural incomes. The planters who gathered each winter for the Charleston social season could not understand that these economic forces condemned their state to a prolonged depression; they chiefly blamed the tariff, although higher tariff rates were only one of the factors that aggravated their economic dilemma. Each year, they grumbled, three quarters of their crop was shipped to England. English manufacturers, blocked by the new tariffs from making payment in manufactured goods, gave South Carolinians low cash prices instead. They in turn were forced to buy high-priced protected goods from the northern factories. Why should one part of the country thus pay tribute to another? Why should not South Carolina cotton growers buy the excellent English manufactures at lower prices with no tariff walls to interfere?

The rebellious sentiments of disgruntled planters found a spokesman in Vice-President John C. Calhoun. A War Hawk of 1812, a gifted statesman long experienced in congressional and executive offices, Calhoun loved the Union with an ardor born of his long career as its servant. Until this moment he had been a consistent nationalist, supporting earlier tariffs that promised to lessen American dependence on foreign goods, favoring laws that would combat disunity by binding "the Republic together with a perfect system of roads and canals," fighting the battle for federal aid to the Erie Canal, and as Secretary of War in 1824 drawing up an Internal Improvements Bill that authorized a giant program of canal and turnpike building similar in conception to the nationalist system favored by Henry Clay. Calhoun saw no constitutional obstacles to these plans, for his nationalism made him a firm believer in loose construction with emphasis on expanded federal power. Yet now the plight of his native state and the pressure of local interests forced him into an abrupt about-face. The situation called for a policy that would preserve the republic and protect South Carolina's economic interests; and Calhoun was ready with an expedient rationalization. His solution was embodied in the South Carolina Exposition, a monumental document in the history of federal-state relationships, which was adopted by the state legislature in December, 1828. His purpose was to define the place of the states within the Union in a way that would preserve South Carolina's interests. The Constitution, he maintained, was a compact between sovereign states through which they created a national government endowed with specified powers. Since the states had delegated these powers, they retained the final authority as to their use; should Congress pass any law "so deliberate, palpable, and dangerous, as to justify the interposition of the State to protect its rights" that state should declare the act null and void—or "nullify" the measure. Under this doctrine South Carolina could nullify the tariff of 1828, because this was a protective tariff and the state contended it empowered Congress only to levy duties for revenue purposes.

Having warned the central government by adopting the Exposition, South Carolina was content to wait further developments. She was not kept long in suspense. On Jackson's recommendation, Congress in July, 1832, passed a new protective tariff that retained high duties but did away with some of the worst features of the "Tariff of Abominations." When the final vote was taken, the South Carolina congressmen assembled, issued a protest to the people of their state, and called on them to nullify the obnoxious law. As soon as this protest was received, the state legislature issued a call for a popularly elected convention, which met in November, 1832, and by an overwhelming vote declared the tariffs of 1828 and 1832 "null, void, and no law, nor binding upon this State, its officers or citizens." Federal customs collectors were ordered from the state by February 1, 1833, and any national law that authorized them to collect duties or coerce South Carolina was also declared null and void.

Here was a crisis for Jackson to face; a state had defied federal authority and refused to obey a law of Congress. The President acted at once. He increased the naval strength in Charleston Harbor, issued a proclamation damning nullification as contrary to the spirit and letter of the Constitution, and asked Congress to pass a "Force Bill" authorizing him to use the army and navy to enforce the law throughout the nation. At the same time he recognized that South Carolina had a real grievance and determined to hold the door ajar for some compromise. Under his pressure Congress hurriedly passed a new tariff law in February, 1833, that provided for a gradual reduction of levels until 1842, when they would reach 20 per cent. Jackson signed the Compromise Tariff on the same day that he affixed his signature to the Force Bill. The combination was effective, for South Carolina did not relish war against the United States and saw a face-saving opportunity in the lowered tariff. In March, 1833, the convention reassembled, withdrew the Nullification Ordinance as applied to the tariff, and then nullified the Force Bill. The last futile gesture aroused little interest, for the crisis was past and the Union secure.

The nullification controversy ended a chapter in the history of federal-state relations; never again did a single state defy national authority. Since the days of the Virginia and Kentucky resolutions this had been the usual resort of minorities who objected to what they termed the tyranny of the majority, and time and again the federal government had used force or the threat of force to bring a recalcitrant commonwealth into line with a decision of the Supreme Court or an act of Congress. Jackson's vigorous policy established more securely the supremacy of the central government over the individual states. But in doing so he sacrificed the last remnants of the national unity inherited from the "Era of Good Feelings." The hatreds that flamed amidst this period of strife and turmoil crystallized first into party divisions and then into sectional realignments which finally led to civil war.

THE REALIGNMENT OF PARTIES

The drift of the politicians into two rival camps was well under way even before the forceful handling of rebellious South Carolina brought matters to a head. The "Eaton Malaria" started the process by provoking an open breach between President Jackson and Vice-President Calhoun. John H. Eaton, the Secretary of War, was married to the beauteous daughter of a local Irish tavern keeper. Mrs. Eaton was openly snubbed by Mrs. Calhoun and her following among Washington hostesses. This snobbish conduct pained Jackson, who read the Vice-President long lectures on social equality that Calhoun politely ignored. While Jackson was still pondering whether such an aristocratic couple should occupy the White House, fuel was added to the flames when he learned for the first time that Calhoun, instead of having been his principal cabinet defender as he had previously believed, had advocated censuring him for his Florida raid. The nullification controversy brought the final break between the President and his heir apparent, for Jackson, the ardent nationalist, was shocked and offended by Calhoun's state rights stand. From this time on the two men were avowed enemies, and Jackson openly groomed Martin Van Buren, his Secretary of State, for the presidency.

Calhoun gathered others of the opposition about him, including Daniel Webster of Massachusetts and Henry Clay of Kentucky, and began a systematic attack on the administration program. This conglomeration of strange bedfellows, whose only bond of union seemed to be hatred of Jackson, actually represented a deep-seated division among the American people. The President's supporters were drawn from the ranks of northern workers, farmers, and immigrants, western pioneers and small landowners, and southern yeomen who worked their tiny plantations themselves or with the aid of a few slaves—in other words, from the economically under-privileged in North, West, and South. The members of the new opposition party, who came to be known as Whigs, were from the upper crust of society. They included manufacturers, merchants, and bankers from the northern states, a sprinkling of New England reformers under John Quincy Adams' leadership, the wealthier farmers and commercial aristocracy of the maturing social order in the older sections of the West, the great planters who owned over two thirds of the slaves in the South, and a handful of antique National Republicans from Virginia and North Carolina who rebelled against the "executive tyranny" of "that man" in Washington.

The Jacksonians, political descendants of the "Democratic-Republicans" of Jefferson's day, changed the party label to "Democratic." Meeting in 1832 at the first national nominating convention of the party, the cheering delegates nominated "Old Hickory" for a second term. In 1831, however, the opponents of Jackson, spiritually the descendants of Hamiltonian Federalists, had met in a national nominating convention of their own. Deserting the old Jeffersonian party, they nominated Henry Clay for President.

THE BANK AND FISCAL POLICY

The two rival parties were to dominate the national scene until just before the Civil War. Their first battle was over the recharter of the second Bank of the United States. This institution, which had dominated the nation's financial affairs since its creation by Congress in 1816, was growing increasingly unpopular in the West. The frontiersmen insisted that its many branches formed a "money monopoly" that stifled the enterprise of the state banks; every shortage of credit—and there were many in the expanding prosperity of those years—as well as every failure of a wildcat bank in the western states, was blamed on this "octopus of finance." Jackson expressed the feeling of thousands of his countrymen when he told Nicholas Biddle, the conservative president of the Bank of the United States, that he was "afraid of banks." Yet he probably would not have objected to the recharter if his enemies had not insisted on making political capital of his antibank feelings.

Webster and Clay were to blame. They persuaded Biddle to ask for a new charter during the summer of 1832, hoping thus to force Jackson into either accepting the bank or vetoing a popular measure on the eve of the election. When Congress, reflecting a sentiment that was generally favorable except in the West, passed the bill without serious division, the President did not hesitate. His antagonism had been mounting steadily, aroused by rumors of unsecured loans to congressmen issued by the bank to win supporters, and his veto message was a vigorous plea to the masses. He charged that the Bank of the United States was an instrument used by a few wealthy Americans and foreigners to finance their unprincipled money manipulations, that it concentrated power in a handful of men who felt no responsibility to the people, and that it drained wealth from the West for the benefit of eastern and foreign creditors. Biddle and his friends were delighted. Jackson's message showed such a hazy knowledge of finance that the bank distributed thousands of copies as campaign propaganda, confident that the people would rise against this mountebank in the White House. No maneuver could have been more disastrous. Thousands of Americans now viewed the issue not as the simple recharter of a bank but as a contest between their hero and a cabal of rich aristocrats.

When faced with this question at the polls in 1832—*The Bank v. "Jacksonian Democracy"*—the people rose in their wrath to support the President and his running mate, Martin Van Buren; the Whigs' candidate, Henry Clay, was buried under Jacksonian electoral votes. Jackson's popularity would doubtless have re-elected him regardless of his stand on the bank, but he considered his success a popular mandate against recharter. When the people had spoken so strongly, why should this hated institution be allowed to exist even until 1836? Better to cripple Biddle's "Monster" before it could do more harm. As soon as he began his second term Jackson ordered the withdrawal of the government deposits, amounting to ten or twelve million dollars. This money was deposited in selected state banks—known as "pet banks" by the President's enemies—scattered through the country but concentrated in the West.

The sudden flow of vast sums into irresponsible state banks launched the nation on a period of giddy speculative activity. Despite the care with which they were chosen, many of the bankers were willing to lend government funds to speculators on flimsy security. This encouraged inflation: roads and canals were started or planned, new factories laid out, vast tracts of land purchased in the West to await the day when eager farmers or cotton planters would pay fabulous prices for them. Such unprecedented business activity created a new demand for money, and state banks mushroomed to supply the need—their number swelled from 605 to 788 between 1834 and 1837, and their loans by two hundred million dollars. From their tills a torrent of loans poured into get-rich-quick schemes that would have been laughed out of existence by a people less optimistic than the Americans. Much of the money went to buy government land—sales increased from four million to twenty million acres between 1834 and 1836. The currency that streamed into the land offices was deposited at the "pet banks," only to flow out again in loans to the speculators. This vicious circle seemed innocent enough so long as prices spiraled upward, but it promised grave danger should the speculative bubble be pricked.

To make matters even worse, the government was taking in more money than it could spend. The national debt was paid off in 1835, but still the flow continued: millions from land sales, more millions from tariffs as prosperity increased the purchase of European luxuries. Neither source of government revenue could be scaled down: the East, afraid lest its labor supply be drained away by a cheap public domain, objected to any reduction in land prices; the West opposed any restriction on public land sales; and the whole nation rebelled against any meddling with the Compromise Tariff of 1833. Nor could the money be spent on internal improvements, for Jackson's veto of a bill to help build a turnpike from Maysville to Lexington, Kentucky, in 1830 stamped him as an opponent of this form of federal expenditure. The popular solution was to distribute the surplus among the states; Congress adopted this device in the Distribution Act of June, 1836, which provided that all money in excess of five million dollars in the Treasury on January 1, 1837, should be turned over to the state governments in four installments. This only increased the speculative fever, for many of the states were furiously building roads and canals, and the dazzling promise of federal subsidies tempted them to plunge into reckless new ventures. They borrowed so heavily in anticipation that by 1837 their total indebtedness amounted to $170,000,000, a staggering sum for that day.

By the end of 1836 a few wary individuals saw that this speculative house of cards must topple. Jackson tried to stem the mounting inflation in July, 1836, when he issued his Specie Circular decreeing that henceforth all government lands must be paid for in gold or silver, rather than in the unstable paper currency issued by the state banks. When the upward spiral nevertheless continued, English exporters began to grow alarmed and demanded the payment of overdue bills from their debtors in the United States. This action drained gold from American banks just as they were hard pressed for specie to finance land purchases. When, as a consequence, they were forced to refuse loans to borrowers, faith in the banking system began to weaken. The banks' troubles were multiplied in January, 1837, when the government began withdrawing its deposits to make the first payment under the Distribution Act. A few, unable to stand the strain, closed their doors; panicky depositors started runs on others, and amidst this wave of fear bank after bank suspended specie payments until by May not one remained open. Their frantic attempts to forestall disaster by calling in loans drove many leading mercantile and manufacturing houses in England and America to the wall. The closing of these mills cut off the market for southern cotton planters. They in turn could no longer afford to buy food from the West. Eastern manufacturers, now unable to sell in the South or the West, slid over the line into bankruptcy. A numbing economic paralysis spread over the nation. Overexpansion, fostered by American optimism and inept handling of the financial structure, had plunged the United States into the panic of 1837.

Fortunately for the President, he retired from office with the plaudits of the people ringing in his ears just before the full effects of the depression were felt. His administration was looked upon, with some justice, as one of the most successful in history; he had swept away many relics from the aristocratic past, presided over a period of expanding prosperity, stifled threats of disunion, and ended the career of the unpopular second Bank of the United States. Even his "shirt-sleeved" diplomacy, although ridiculed by Europe's statesmen, solved two rankling problems. One was the right to trade with the British West Indies, closed to American ships since 1795, which Jackson secured when his blustering demands forced England to back down. The other was the settlement of the French "Spoliation Claims" controversy, which involved the claims of American shippers against France for illegal captures under the Berlin and Milan decrees. Jackson finally pinned the French government down to a treaty in 1831, but when the Chamber of Deputies refused to appropriate the money on the grounds that the twenty-five million francs granted the United States was too much, the President threatened reprisals in language which in European diplomacy was virtually tantamount to a declaration of war. When France demanded an apology, the rugged old frontiersman refused, although he did disclaim any intention of insulting the French government. Alarmed French officials were only too glad to start payment on the claims at the end of 1835, while Americans hailed these triumphs with delight as added proofs of their nation's new strength.

DEPRESSION SHARPENS SOCIAL ISSUES

Martin Van Buren, elected as Jackson's successor in 1836 over a divided Whig opposition, achieved neither success nor acclaim. An able and sincere man, he was forced not only to bear the blame for a depression which he had done less to cause than his predecessor, but to struggle fruitlessly for harmony in a nation once more torn asunder. The new divisions, brought to the fore by the depression, were more serious than any in the country's history. During the years after 1837 the United States split into three squabbling sections, each composed of a group of states with similar economic interests. The people of each section, stung to desperation by the panic, were determined to wring laws from Congress that would aid their own distinctive type of enterprise at the expense of their neighbors. Between 1837 and the Civil War every public question was fought out along sectional lines.

The northeastern states—New England, New York, Pennsylvania, New Jersey, and Delaware—formed one section. Manufacturing was firmly rooted there by the 1830's, and they demanded laws that would aid the factory rather than the farm: a protective tariff, a national bank, government-financed internal improvements to tap new markets in the West, high-priced public lands to prevent a rapid drain of labor toward the frontier. The Northwest, comprising the states north of the Ohio River, stood solidly for more liberal land laws, government aid to internal improvements, and a protective tariff, for protection meant higher prices for wool and hemp as well as a large home market for western grain. Most of the Westerners disliked a national bank and preferred the easier credit obtainable from speculative state banks. The two sections stood together for protection and internal improvements, but disagreed on land and banking laws.

The third section was the South. There the legislative program desired by the planters was dictated by the need of marketing the one staple crop on which southern prosperity depended—cotton. Southerners wanted a low tariff most of all. They opposed government aid for internal improvements because this would drain money from the Treasury and bolster the arguments of protectionists for higher duties. Those who lived in the older South traditionally favored a strong banking system, but by the 1830's, under a mounting burden of debt, they were revising their opinions and swinging to the support of state banks that would lend money with fewer restrictions. The Southwest consistently opposed a national bank with all the fervor of the frontier. Southerners supported a liberal land system, although the seaboard states were less enthusiastic over a low-priced public domain than those in the Mississippi Valley. This entire legislative program hinged about the South's principal objective—free trade; the Southerners stood ready to compromise on any other point to obtain it.

SLAVERY AS A DIVISIVE ISSUE

The antagonism between these three sections varied in degree. Mill owners from Massachusetts and wheat farmers from Ohio might quarrel over the land system or the need for a national bank, but they agreed on the tariff and internal improvements, while neither section saw eye to eye with the southern cotton planters on any important issue. These economic forces, which tended to separate the North from the South, were bolstered by strong emotional convictions that developed during the 1830's and were based on the changing attitude of the sections toward slavery. The evolution of southern opinion was rapid under the impact of the expanding plantation system. This created a vast demand for bonded labor, and both the new states in the West that depended on slaves for cotton production and the older states that profited from the slave trade began to see that southern prosperity was built on the labor of black workers. Any blow at slavery was a blow at the whole southern economic system. By 1820 Southerners were apologizing for slavery as a necessary evil, by 1830 they were praising the institution as a positive good, and by 1840 they were searching their Bibles to prove that bonded labor was divinely sanctioned and necessary to the welfare of both whites and blacks.

The transformation in northern opinion was just as rapid. By the 1830's slavery north of Mason and Dixon's line had succumbed to the emancipation processes set in motion during the Revolutionary period, and Northerners, their own skirts clean, were beginning to look askance at bonded labor everywhere. In their eyes the institution was both undemocratic and un-Christian, and hence singularly out of place in a nation founded on democracy and Christianity. This view gained strength through the 1820's as a tidal wave of religious revivalism engulfed the United States, sweeping up a host of reformers who devoted themselves to convincing the North that slavery and all other evils of the social order from intemperance to debtors' prisons were out of place in the emancipated world of the common man.

They were drawn from every level of society, these legions of "high-flying souls filled with the new wine of idealism" who dedicated their lives to the task of freeing their fellow Christians from the chains of bondage. Theodore Dwight Weld, who preached abolitionism through

Ohio and New York with fanatical intensity, was attracted to the cause when he fell under the influence of a revivalistic minister who visited his rural New York home. William Lloyd Garrison, whose violent anti-slavery newspaper, *The Liberator,* became the bible of New England reformers from the day of its first appearance in Boston in January, 1831, was a confirmed agitator motivated by unshakable convictions. "I shall strenuously contend for the immediate enfranchisement of our slave population," he wrote. "On this subject I do not wish to think, or speak, or write, with moderation. . . . I am in earnest—I will not equivocate—I will not excuse—I will not retreat a single inch—AND I WILL BE HEARD." Sarah and Angelina Grimke, two wealthy daughters of an aristocratic South Carolina slaveholding family, joined the Society of Friends, freed their own slaves, and came north to convert Philadelphia to the cause. Wendell Phillips, scion of the New England brahmin class, shocked even the audiences of his own section with his passionate invective, and paid for his enthusiasm by being scorned by his friends and blackballed at clubs. Gerrit Smith, a wealthy New York merchant interested in many reforms, dedicated his life and sizable fortune to his black-skinned fellow Christians. By 1833 these agitators had built up a northern following and united to form the American Antislavery Society; from that time on speakers toured the land, and presses poured forth thousands of books, magazines, and newspapers, all devoted to the evils of slavery.

By the time Martin Van Buren entered the White House the effects of this avalanche of attack were being felt. Southerners were convinced that fanatical Yankee agitators were bent on destroying their property and their lives; southern congressmen writhed in their seats as they listened to the antislavery harangues of abolitionist representatives from the northern states. When they tried to protect themselves in the year of Van Buren's election by persuading Congress to lay all petitions concerning slavery on the table without debate, the North arose in righteous anger to denounce a "gag rule" that violated the sacred American right of petition. On both sides of Mason and Dixon's line a mounting emotional conviction was feeding the fires of sectionalism and leading the nation closer to armed conflict.

It was amidst this clash of sectional interests that Martin Van Buren tried to solve the problems of his administration. When he took office in the spring of 1837, banks were closed throughout the nation, business enterprise was at a standstill, bread lines were clogging the streets of eastern cities, and the federal government was near bankruptcy. A special session of Congress in September repealed the Distribution Act and authorized the issue of treasury notes to meet the country's current expenses, but the fundamental financial problem remained. How could the government keep and administer its funds? State banks were dangerous and Van Buren opposed the Whig solution of a third Bank of the United States, both because he was loyal to Jackson and because his constituents looked with horror on such financial monsters. During these years he was increasingly representative of the liberal northern wing of the Democratic party[1], which reflected the workingmen's distrust of paper money and the credit system. His answer was to propose an Independent Treasury plan to Congress. The government would keep and administer its own funds by setting up subtreasuries in important cities. Money collected from customs duties or taxes would be deposited directly in vaults at each of these institutions, while payments of salaries, pensions, and the like would be made from them on a strictly specie basis. No longer would the United States lose through bank failures, or encourage speculation by throwing its vast resources into the money market.

The first congressional votes on this measure disclosed strong opposition. Westerners foresaw the end of their wild speculative schemes if government funds were withdrawn from state banks; Whigs painted a dismal picture of the business stagnation that would follow the drain of federal money from commercial channels. When the House defeated two efforts to pass the measure in 1837 and 1838, Van Buren realized that it could never succeed without western support. He could win only by backing something desired by the West, and more liberal land laws naturally suggested themselves. Van Buren found this decision easy, for many of his Locofoco constituents were workers who saw that cheap public lands would force wages up by draining away eastern wage earners. He threw his support solidly behind two pre-emption acts then before Congress, each providing that squatters already on the public domain could purchase the land on which they lived for the minimum price of $1.25 an acre. Although this by no means satisfied western demands, Van Buren won enough votes from that section to carry his Independent Treasury plan through Congress in 1840.

His victory was short-lived, for the election of 1840 showed that the people had lost faith in their President. Despite all that the Democrats could do, the illusion persisted that Van Buren was to blame for the hard times, and the Whigs capitalized on this feeling to the utmost. They were so torn by factionalism that they could agree on no program themselves, but they could unite against the "depression Democrats" and devote their campaign to vindictive abuse of the administration. With

---

[1] Known as the Locofocos after they lighted one of their meetings with the new-fangled locofoco matches when conservatives turned out the gas.

this in mind they passed over Henry Clay and nominated William Henry Harrison, a military hero whose views were too little known to offend anyone. Harrison's speeches, and those of his running mate, John Tyler of Virginia, were models of evasiveness on the important questions of the day.

This spiritless campaign was lifted from the level of the ordinary by an ill-natured gibe of a Democratic editor, who remarked that if Harrison were given a barrel of hard cider, a pension, and a log cabin he would be happy for the rest of his life. Whig leaders were wise enough to seize this opportunity; they would represent their candidate as the choice of the common people and capitalize on the democratic sentiment that had grown so remarkably under Jackson. The idea took hold at once, and the "Log Cabin Campaign" swept the nation. Whigs wore log cabin badges, sang log cabin songs, and printed log cabin newspapers; they built log cabins in towns and filled them with barrels of hard cider that were frequently tapped to win thirsty voters; they paraded the streets dragging floats mounting log cabins with real smoke pouring from their chimneys as they chanted songs:

> Let Van from his coolers of silver drink wine,
> And lounge on his cushioned settee,
> Our man on his buckeye bench can recline,
> Content with hard cider is he,
>> The iron-armed soldier, the true-hearted soldier,
>> The gallant old soldier of Tippecanoe.

"Tippecanoe and Tyler too" were the people's choice; Van Buren was an aristocratic lover of wines and silver who ate his meals from gold dishes, scented his whiskers with cologne water, and lolled over a billiard table. Amidst the emotionalism and excitement the voters forgot that the Whigs were really the upper-class party, that they had no platform or program, and that they were so torn by internal disputes that they could do nothing. Harrison was elected by a thumping majority.

SECTIONALISM AND POLITICS

Henry Clay and Daniel Webster were overjoyed. The President was an old man without strong views; they would sit behind the throne and dictate the passage of laws that would give the United States a protective tariff and a national bank. Clay realized that this would appeal only to the Northeast, for the South opposed protection, and the West disliked a strong banking system. To push his plan through Congress he must win votes from one or the other of those sections. Clay decided to entice Westerners by a proposal for federal distribution among the states

The younger Lincoln, opponent of the "Little Giant."
(Bettmann Archive)

Lincoln in the White House, the trials of a nation upon his shoulders.
(Bettmann Archive)

Below —The log cabin of democratic tradition: Lincoln's birthplace. (*Courtesy Historical Pictures Service*)

King Andrew the First, Democrat, whose reign symbolized the new might of the common man. *(Courtesy Chicago Historical Society)*

Statesmen of the Jacksonian era. *Above, left*—The young John Quincy Adams, last of the Jeffersonians (a painting by John Singleton Copley, *courtesy Boston Museum of Fine Arts*); *right*—Henry Clay, who blended western nationalism and Hamiltonian Federalism to become Jackson's most troublesome opponent (portrait by Theodor S. Moïse, *courtesy Metropolitan Museum of Art*) *Below, left*—Martin Van Buren, disciple of Jacksonian democracy and White House spokesman for the workers of the eastern seaboard *(courtesy New York State Historical Association)*; *right*—Noah Webster, who sought to simplify the American language that a literate electorate might assume the burdens of democracy. *(Culver Service)*

New England's new commercial and industrial wealth as symbolized by the classical simplicity of early nineteenth-century homes. *Above*—The home of John Gardner (Pingree House) of Salem, designed by Samuel McIntire in 1804–1805. *(Courtesy Essex Institute)* *Below*—A McIntire interior from "Oak Hill," Peabody, Massachusetts. *(Courtesy Boston Museum of Fine Arts)*

of proceeds from land sales. He believed that this would be so appealing to frontier states left tottering on the verge of bankruptcy by the panic that they would forget their antibank scruples. With these three planks in his platform—protection, a national bank, and distribution—Clay happily awaited the special session of Congress that he persuaded Harrison to call for May, 1841. He was confident that nothing could go wrong, for five of his supporters were in the Cabinet, Webster was Secretary of State, and from his seat in the Senate Clay himself was prepared to lead his measures through Congress.

And then the unexpected happened. Only a month after the inauguration Harrison died, bringing to the presidency John Tyler, whose state rights views were unalterably opposed to such loose-constructionist measures as a protective tariff and a national bank. Clay saw at once that his program could succeed only if he secured enough support to override presidential vetoes, and that the best way to obtain these votes was to bribe the West with a more liberal land policy. The one thing this section wanted was a Pre-emption Act that would allow pioneers to move onto the public domain and, by the act of settling, pre-empt a farm that could then be paid for at the minimum price of $1.25 per acre. Clay was willing to back pre-emption if the West would support his plans for distribution, a bank, and a tariff. A united southern opposition might still defeat his program, for the South disliked both protection and distribution—the latter because the removal of funds from the Treasury opened the way for higher duties. He decided that he must compromise with that section to succeed, and announced his willingness to shelve distribution so long as the tariff was above 20 per cent—or until 1842, when that level would be reached under the Compromise Tariff of 1833.

Although Clay's program was worked out to please every section, its course was far from smooth. The Independent Treasury Act was repealed without difficulty in August, 1841, but Tyler twice vetoed bills for a new national bank, and Congress refused to override the President. A Distribution-Pre-emption Act enjoyed greater success and was signed by Tyler on December 31, 1841. Under its terms 10 per cent of the proceeds of land sales was to be given the states in which the lands lay, and the remainder divided among the states in proportion to their population. Distribution was not to be carried out if customs duties were higher than 20 per cent. The right to pre-empt 160 acres of surveyed land was granted all adult citizens who agreed to clear the plot and erect a dwelling on it. This carefully framed measure left two of the sections more or less satisfied, for the West had its liberal land system and the South its assurance that distribution would not be used as an excuse to raise the tariff. Only the Northeast was doubtful, for many there looked on the bill as a bribe to the West to oppose protection under the threat of losing the federal funds, which would not be distributed if levels were over 20 per cent.

This aspect of the question faced Congress a year later, when the Compromise Tariff of 1833 expired. Northern Whigs favored the restoration of higher duties, but Westerners hesitated to relinquish the largess that distribution promised them. Tyler complicated Clay's problem by letting it be known that he would veto any bill which provided for both distribution and a tariff higher than 20 per cent. Clay was in an unfortunate position. The tendency of a decentralized party of the American type was to place local interest and local principles above the national interest and national party principles. Western Whigs opposed a high tariff without distribution, eastern Whigs a low tariff with distribution, and Tyler a high tariff and distribution. Clay's answer was to push separate bills through Congress, one providing for the restoration of tariffs to the 1832 level, the other for distribution. Tyler signed the higher tariff measure, partly because the depleted condition of the Treasury made additional income necessary, but vetoed the distribution bill. Amidst the outraged cries of the Westerners, the Whig party split wide apart. Tyler's entire Cabinet, with the exception of Webster, resigned at Clay's request and the President was formally read out of the party.

By 1842 sectional divisions and the weakness of decentralized party control had already become disruptive enough to split one of the two major parties. Gone were the days of nationalism and unity: the United States was divided along sectional and class lines into three antagonistic camps, each determined to protect its own local interests; and laws could be passed only by juggling and trading across party lines, with both parties splitting on votes in Congress. During the next decade the increasingly bitter controversy was to be brought to a head by a sudden burst of expansion, by new annexations, by the westward thrust of slavery, and by a growing conflict between agrarian and industrial interests—a combination of combustible ingredients which neither the party system nor the Constitution could peacefully resolve by majority rule and the arbitrament of elections.

IX

THE TRIUMPH OF DEMOCRATIC REFORM

1828–1860

The sectional conflicts dividing the nation during the Age of Jackson mirrored the deep-seated changes reshaping the nature of American life and thought. The common people were the architects of this intellectual revolution; Jacksonian Democracy was at once their inspiration and their goal. For in that day of a broadening franchise, the masses and their sympathizers again caught sight of a vision obscured by the clouds of reaction following the Revolutionary era, the vision of a United States truly self-governing, the one country in the world where a perfect society could be created, free of political and economic inequality. It was a noble vision that promised to secure for all the inhabitants of America the "life, liberty, and happiness" perennially promised. Vigorous action was needed to achieve reality; yet the task was worthy of a free people and they were quick to respond to it. Let the world watch while the self-ruling Americans shaped a modern utopia where the poor would become rich, the weak strong, and the sinners good.

But how could true political and social democracy develop where economic inequality was assuming such dangerous proportions? Those prophets of Jeffersonianism who tried to keep the principles alive after their idol retired from the presidency had failed to find the answer. One of them, John Taylor of Caroline, a planter and an economist, carefully examined the causes of inequality in *An Inquiry into the Principles and Policy of the Government of the United States* (1814) and pronounced a cure. Taylor insisted that an even distribution of wealth was essential to democracy, but his remedy, if not too little, was too late. He proposed to cripple business and banking enterprises, thus forcing all men to engage in farming, which he considered "the guardian of liberty as well as the mother of progress." By the time Jackson became President, the industrial developments that Taylor deplored made such a plan utterly unthinkable. Industry had come to stay, and the problem was how best to further democracy in the new industrial environment. To urge a return to the self-sufficient small farm was futile when employers and large planters reaped the greatest financial rewards.

The passage of time emphasized a growing danger that called for action on the part of friends of democracy. The passive attitude of the past no longer sufficed; then democracy was partially attainable by removing restraints upon the people and allowing self-sufficient small farmers to translate economic equality into political equality—as the struggle for manhood suffrage during the first quarter of the nineteenth century amply demonstrated. But with economic equality threatened by the rise of the planter class in the South and the capitalist class in the North, democratic reformers perceived that inequalities in wealth and opportunity might reverse the democratic trend. One unflinching realist, summing up the situation in 1835, wrote: "It is in vain to talk of Aristocracy and Democracy—these terms are too variable and indeterminate to convey adequate ideas of the present opposing interests; the division is between the rich and the poor—the warfare is between them."

To preserve self-rule, poverty-stricken workers and small farmers required protection from exploitation and assistance for economic and social improvement. The national government alone was powerful enough to challenge the might of capitalists and planters. While Jeffersonians had preached state rights and shuddered at the prospect of a strong central government, Jacksonians understood that aggressive national action was demanded to assure the continuation of popular self-rule in the midst of class divisions inevitable in an industrial society. Democracy, to survive, must become dynamic.

THE DEGRADATION OF THE WORKER

This decision was forced on the progressives in Jackson's camp by the rapidly increasing spread between the earnings of employers and the wages of workers. Industrial profits were fabulously high in that period of expanding economy: countless business concerns reported profits of from 15 to 50 per cent a year, while returns on invested capital were seldom below 10 per cent. Wages, on the other hand, trailed scandalously behind, and after the panic of 1837 they declined almost 50 per cent in a five-year period. New England shoemakers in these impecunious times were able to earn from four to five dollars a week, the weekly take-home pay of weavers was less than three dollars, and other laborers were paid in proportion. Even though prices were then lower, these pittances were far from enough to support a family. Everybody had to work to keep body and soul together; travelers told repeated stories of pitifully small children groping their way to a mill in the predawn darkness, groping their way home again after the sun had set. The usual working day in the factories was eleven to fifteen hours—from sunrise to sunset—and the health conditions were intolerable.

People could live in such poverty only by crowding together in the slum sections of the sprawling cities. A careful survey of housing in New York exposed the fact that one out of every twenty people lived in basement hovels, that the average number per room in the poorer areas was six, that as many as twenty persons permanently occupied some small rooms, that the average number of occupants of every house was sixty, and that in some of the worst districts from two to four families lived together in each room! A city committee in Boston reported conditions in one basement of three floors often flooded by the tide:

One cellar was reported by the police to be occupied nightly as a sleeping-apartment for thirty-nine persons. In another, the tide had risen so high that it was necessary to approach the bedside of a patient by means of a plank which was laid from one stool to another; while the dead body of an infant was actually sailing about the room in its coffin.

Those who could not afford even these dismal habitations frequented disgusting establishments that went under the name of boarding houses, where dinner was served by dumping on the floor, for the guests to fight over, food collected from garbage cans. These were not typical conditions—the bulk of the workers lived more respectable though poverty-pinched lives—but they were too common in a land that boasted of economic opportunity and democratic equality.

The degradation of the American worker was partly the fault of the employers. They were hard men, factory owners who had risen from the ranks themselves, and had no sympathy with those who fell by the wayside. One summed up the philosophy of his kind:

As for myself, I regard my work-people just as I regard my machinery. So long as they can do my work for what I choose to pay them, I keep them, getting out of them all that I can. What they do or how they fare outside my walls I don't know, nor do I consider it my business to know. They must look out for themselves as I do for myself. When my machines get old and useless, I reject them and get new, and these people are part of my machinery.

Another manager, finding that his mill hands grew "languorous" after breakfasting, cut out that meal and produced three thousand more yards of cloth weekly. Such an insensate attitude inevitably meant suffering but so also did the changed relationships between workers and employers that followed the development of the system of corporate ownership. With owners no longer paternally interested in their workers, a clear line of distinction grew up between private and business morality. "As directors of a company," one reformer complained, "men will sanction actions of which they would scorn to be guilty in their private capacity. A crime that would press heavily on the conscience of one man, becomes quite endurable when divided among many."

For Jacksonians this was additional evidence that the chasm between rich and poor imperiled democracy. If the private conscience was no longer sufficient to protect society, if impersonal control bred irresponsibility, the public conscience must intervene through the medium of the government. And if such a step required a sacrifice of private property rights hitherto considered inviolate, it was a small price to pay for democracy. A regulatory program based upon this principle and designed to check the flow of wealth into the hands of a favored few was constructed. Jackson's war on the Bank of the United States was directed partly to this end, for he regarded Biddle's "Monster" not only as a political enemy but as an instrument through which a handful of business leaders controlled an unjustifiable share of the nation's wealth. Inspired by this action, other Jacksonians in the years after the panic of 1837 extended the attack to all manner of banking institutions; some states passed general incorporation laws to prevent banks from securing special concessions through individually granted charters, others provided for careful supervision or for limitations of profits, still others banned banks entirely. These measures did not go far, for the constitutional powers of government over industry were yet to be defined, but they did suggest regulation as a device for checking corporate irresponsibility.

Jacksonians, like contemporary reformers in England and on the Continent, were also active on other social and economic fronts. To aid the workingman, state laws were enacted to equalize the struggle between capital and labor. After a decade of agitation, a vigorous campaign in behalf of a ten-hour day made a vital gain in 1840 when President Van Buren, by executive order, limited government work to this amount without pay reductions. New Hampshire adopted a similar law in 1847, Pennsylvania in 1848, and a few other states took the same step during the next decade. A country-wide struggle for the secret ballot was closely allied with this trend. As long as workingmen could be intimidated by their employers at the polls, they could not freely select candidates of their own choice and representative of their interests. Massachusetts adopted this reform first in the 1840's, and although few others followed its enlightened leadership before the Civil War, the step was a significant one.

Just as indicative of Jacksonian equalitarianism was the consistent effort to strengthen and develop labor organizations. These were vital in achieving economic democracy: it was only a united labor that could wring concessions from unwilling employers in the form of higher wages and better working conditions. Yet strive as the reformers might in behalf of unionization, the results were discouragingly small. Scattered unions, dating from the 1830's, vanished during the panic of 1837, and when in the next decade immigrants from abroad flooded the labor markets, the unions were difficult to revive. The only tangible gains, as a result, came in the form of court decisions that laid the legal basis for later union activity. The Massachusetts case of *Commonwealth v. Hunt* (1842), a legal landmark, held that labor unions were not "conspiracies" against employers and that workers could not be forced to work in the same factories with nonunion laborers.

These two important doctrines—the secret ballot and the decision that labor unions were not conspiracies, which opened the way for unionization and the doctrine of the closed shop—were gradually accepted in the other industrial states during the next years.

IDEALS OF ECONOMIC DEMOCRACY

Creeping progress toward industrial democracy, however, seemed woefully inadequate to many. Alarmed by the increasing social and economic distance between capital and labor, fearful that economic inequality would lead to political inequality, and bewildered by the kaleidoscopic changes wrought by the advancing machine age, sincere democrats set out to secure for the workers everything that the workers had failed to secure for themselves. The number of reformers, drawn from the ranks of labor, from the middle class, and from the intellectual fringes of society, were legion. Their formulas for the salvation of democracy were as numerous as they, but none was too fantastic to arouse enthusiastic support.

One group caught glimpses of social salvation in the broad expanses of the public domain. George Henry Evans, its leader, was a reformer whose passionate devotion to the cause of equality has earned for him a permanent place in the history of democracy. Labor could best be served, he reasoned, by using the magnet of free lands to drain excess workers westward in such numbers that employers would be forced to pay living wages to those who remained. To this end he founded the National Reform Association in 1844 and the newspaper *Young America* a year later. Practical necessity soon forced Evans to abandon his first radical plan for a series of Free Republican Townships in which farmers and mechanics were to labor together in self-sufficient units, and to advocate instead a workable three-point plan: free land for actual settlers, limitation of the amount of land any person could acquire, and exemption of homesteads from seizure for debt. So popular were these suggestions that they induced support from such influential organs as Horace Greeley's New York *Tribune;* in the form of a series of Homestead bills ultimately to triumph in 1862, they became political issues.

Other humanitarians, responding to new international currents of thought, sought to check the trend toward inequality by founding communal colonies where men could live together in self-sufficient harmony. Their prophet was Albert Brisbane, a neurotic enthusiast so concerned for the welfare of society that he journeyed to Europe in the late 1820's in an attempt to "solve the mystery of man's destiny." He found the answer in the teachings of Charles Fourier, a French philosopher who had devoted his life to the planning of a workable social order for the machine age. Brisbane, thoroughly converted, weeded out some of Fourier's more fantastic ideas and summarized the remainder in a book, *The Social Destiny of Men* (1840), intended to reveal the final truth to his own countrymen. "In society as it is now constituted," he asserted, "monotony, uniformity, intellectual inaction, and torpor reign: distrust, isolation, separation, conflict and antagonism are almost universal. . . . Society is spiritually a desert." How could this be improved? By setting up social groups with a full awareness of the passions of mankind yet employing them for social purposes.

Both Fourier and Brisbane advocated the creation of self-sufficient, isolated communal units called phalanxes. Each was to contain one giant building holding sixteen hundred persons, with family apartments at one end, shops and factories at the other, and dining and living quarters in between. All members were to have the right to select the work they wished to do—as farmers, mechanics, or menial laborers—and were to be paid in proportion to the agreeableness of their tasks, those doing the most unpleasant chores receiving greater compensation. The least desirable jobs—caring for garbage and sewage—were to be left to small boys who, Brisbane noticed, seemed to enjoy dirt. Produce from farm and factory was to be used within the phalanx or, if surpluses existed, sold to neighboring communities. A fee from each resident for his apartment and for his meals in the communal dining room was to be charged. There, with peace and plenty seemingly assured, they would live as perpetual examples to the less fortunate mortals in the competitive outside world.

Forty phalanxes were founded within three years after Brisbane's book appeared. Most soon fell victim to poor management, poor personnel, or inadequate financing, but a few survived long enough to arouse conservative alarm. One, at Red Bank, New Jersey—where ninety families lived peacefully together until 1854, when a disastrous fire destroyed their grist mill and dwellings—was the well-known North American

Phalanx. More famous was the collectivist project launched by Concord intellectuals in protest against the evils of industrialism. Their attractive home, Brook Farm, in a pleasant valley near Boston, thrived as long as the members supported themselves by keeping an excellent school, but in 1845 they were converted to Fourierism and their ill-fated industrial enterprises proved their undoing. None of the Brisbane phalanxes survived the 1850's, but their very existence demonstrated a deep-seated disturbance and the reformist dissatisfaction with conditions accompanying the rise of industry.

CRUSADE FOR THE EQUALITY OF WOMEN

The struggle for economic equality that underlay utopian experiments was but a single aspect of Jacksonian humanitarianism. Zealous Jacksonians hoped to extend democratic privileges to sections of society excluded from participation by the aristocratic practices of the past. One huge segment of the population, the women, was disenfranchised and otherwise discriminated against, and the crusade for women's rights was as indicative of the desire for complete equality as the campaign to build a bridge of understanding between the classes.

The subordination of women represented a condition as old as history and as universal as mankind. From time immemorial women had been assigned an inferior role in society, rationalized as suited to their mental and physical endowments. They could not vote, they could own no property, their wages belonged to their husbands or fathers, the professions were closed to them, and they were denied access to decent educational facilities. Nor did most of them object, for many agreed that Man, created in God's own image, was certainly superior to Woman. "Heaven," wrote one subservient female in 1840, "has appointed to one sex the superior, and to the other the subordinate station, and this without any reference to the character or conduct of either. It is therefore as much for the dignity as it is for the interest of females, in all respects to conform to the duties of this relation."

To deny half the people elemental natural rights was a condition no good democrat could endure. The first protest came from Frances Wright, a gifted Scotswoman who emigrated to the United States in 1824, and who immediately raised her eloquent voice in behalf of laborers, public education, abolitionism, and women's rights. Although conservatives gasped with horror to see a frail woman on the lecture platform, her example inspired other bold spirits to invade the sacred masculine world and to speak in behalf of the abolitionist cause that was Fanny Wright's principal interest. When the existing antislavery societies refused to recognize their right to membership, these women formed an organization of their own, the Female Antislavery Society, which grew steadily from 1834 until 1841. Then occurred an event which transferred their interest from the rights of slaves to the rights of women.

In 1841 abolitionists from all over Europe gathered for a World's Antislavery Convention in London. Present were delegates from the American female societies, duly accredited and anxious to lend their weight to the cause. Instead of being welcomed they were forced to cool their feminine heels outside the hall while the lordly males engaged in debate on the propriety of admitting women to the conference. The upshot of the matter was the exclusion of the women purely on the grounds of their sex. Angered by this rebuff, two women—Lucretia Mott of Philadelphia and Elizabeth Cady Stanton of New York—took a solemn vow to dedicate their lives to a crusade for the equality of women. For the next few years they labored at the task of winning converts, and by 1848 they were ready to issue a call for the first Women's Rights Convention in the history of the world, which met at Seneca Falls, New York. "We hold these truths to be self-evident," ran the Declaration of Independence through which they expressed their grievances, "that all men and women are created equal; that they are endowed by their Creator with certain inalienable rights; that among these are life, liberty, and the pursuit of happiness." Then followed a list of grievances to prove that "the history of mankind is a history of repeated injuries and usurpations on the part of man toward woman," and the final insistence on "immediate admission to all the rights and privileges which belong to them as citizens of the United States." This dramatic appeal and the other subsequent conventions strengthened the "women's-righters" and their movement, which gathered momentum in the next decade.

The immediate fruits were few enough. Several states enacted legislation allowing married women to control their own property, some "female seminaries" were founded to introduce selected girls to the mysteries of learning, a few bold colleges, led by Oberlin in 1833, opened their doors to both sexes, some hardy pioneers were admitted to professions long reserved exclusively for men—these were the only results of a generation of reform. Yet feminists could take heart from the knowledge that the supposedly impenetrable barrier of male superiority had been breached. If Oberlin and Antioch and other colleges admitted women now, others were sure to take that step later. If Dr. Elizabeth Blackwell graduated from an approved medical school and opened a women's infirmary in New York, more women doctors could be expected in the future. If Mrs. Antoinette Louisa Brown Blackwell was ordained as a Congregational minister in 1852, even this holy profession might ultimately grant women an equality before God. The United States was far from a land of complete equality—economically or politically—in 1860, but the basis was laid for future improvements.

THE RELIGIOUS SEARCH FOR UTOPIA

Aiding the struggle for democracy was a fanatical religious faith that permeated the activity of this generation and supplied a medium through which the liberal Jacksonian ideas were translated into understandable terms for the common man. Evangelical clergymen were spiritual agents, for the God of their sermons had become the loving Deity whose embracing benevolence endowed every believer with a divine spark. Man, they taught, was not totally depraved or destined to eternal hell-fire; man was good, and needed only to accept salvation as a means of partaking in the infinite powers of the Divine Being. Human beings could accomplish all things with such supernatural aid; continuous progress toward complete perfection was assured for every individual who welcomed God's grace.

The ministers of America in the middle of the nineteenth century borrowed their beliefs from the rationalistic teachings of the eighteenth-century Enlightenment and they copied their methods from the Great Revival of 1800. Stressing the emotional tactics that the people loved, the evangelists of the 1830's prayed for sinners by name, used a "Holy Band" of converts to range through the congregations, encouraged those who felt the call of the spirit to gather on a "mourners' bench," emphasized hymn singing, and strove by every possible means to create an atmosphere of fervid emotionalism calculated to soften the resistance of the hardest heart. The most famous roaming revivalist was the Reverend Charles G. Finney. An upstate New Yorker, himself a convert to the faith, Finney had a passionate conviction, a gift for imagery, a hypnotic voice, a knowledge of psychology, and a knack of making converts into disciples that made him one of the most effective churchmen in America's history. His preaching career, which lasted for a generation and carried him from one end of the country to the other, not only brought the hope of salvation to thousands of individuals but helped initiate a period of revivalism lasting all through the 1830's and 1840's. Everywhere religious interest was high, and everywhere numberless converts eagerly accepted the message stressed by every evangelist: through faith each individual could obtain divine help in improving himself. Thus the doctrine of individual perfectibility took its place beside that of institutional perfectibility as a fundamental concept in American thought.

With the acceptance of such tenets the way was opened for significant changes in the life of the common man. Why should he be content with his status in life? If his material lot was below expectation, he had only to believe and work diligently for the improvement which, with God's help, was not without his reach. If his living conditions were uncomfortable, he need only interest his fellow individuals in securing reforms. If his churches failed to give him the emotional uplift or the spiritual comfort that he desired, he would be justified in attending others where the Creator was more in evidence. Perfection was his goal, and he would be satisfied with nothing less for himself and his countrymen. This was the spirit, born of the Enlightenment and evangelism, that led Americans during the restless thirties and forties to undertake a series of religious and social reforms of far-reaching consequence.

The appearance of new religious cults in the thirty years before the Civil War illustrated the American striving for perfectionism. Thousands upon thousands of Americans, ready to follow any self-proclaimed messiah whose promise of salvation was sufficiently exciting, flocked into their ranks, for here was a means of self-expression, a form of revolt against tradition, an outlet for eccentric individualism bound to appeal to a people who emphasized complete freedom of conscience. Nor was it mere coincidence that most of the prophets and many of their followers were drawn from among the New Englanders settled in western New York. Converts to the new cults—called "come-outers"—were most frequently drawn from groups nurtured upon repressive religious doctrines and stultified by a restrictive social environment.

John Humphrey Noyes was one of the latter-day prophets. A Vermonter by birth, a minister by training, Noyes rejected orthodox Christianity and gathered about him a group willing to accept his belief that divine guidance alone led to perfection. Calling themselves Perfectionists, they established a communal society in Oneida, New York, in 1848, where they could obey the dictates of their consciences without outside meddling. This was not to be, for their unorthodox religious views, the scandalous "Bloomer" trousers and short hair prescribed for women, and the system of complex marriage that made every woman the wife of every man stimulated a number of attacks upon the Perfectionists. Despite this persecution, the members of the sect thrived in their varied occupations as farmers, fruit growers, and makers of silver tableware. For the next generation they increased steadily in wealth and numbers, inspired by the democratic belief that man and God could work together in the everyday tasks of life.

Another "come-outer" was William Miller, a farmer of Low Hampton, New York, who based his prophecies on a diligent study of the Scriptures. As he pored over certain mystical sections of the Bible he discovered a secret message that had escaped the attention of the rest of mankind: in the year 1843 Christ would return to the earth in visible form, gather the faithful about him, raise the dead, and destroy the world and its unbelievers in flames. Father Miller began to reveal this terrifying prophecy in 1831, so convincingly that twelve years later his followers numbered almost a million, all waiting impatiently for the Judgment Day. Twice during that year 1843 they set dates when the end would come, and twice they were disappointed. But a third date, October 21, 1844, was endorsed by Father Miller himself; mistake was impossible. Millerites gave away their property, sold their goods to pay off debts, closed their places of business, and spent the last weeks in tents and tabernacles where they prayed, sang, and prepared to meet their Maker. On the morning of the appointed day they gathered on hills and house-tops, clothed in long white robes, ready to be drawn up to Heaven before the world was consumed. All that day, and through a drizzling rain that fell that night, they stood staring into the skies, awaiting the awful sign. When midnight came, and the morning of October 22 was at hand, they returned to their homes—those who had homes to return to—sick at heart that their vigil was a failure. Father Miller issued a public apology but insisted that his prophecies, although incorrect in detail, were correct in general; the end of the world was coming, and men must live so as to be prepared to meet God.

More influential than Father Miller was a greater seer, Joseph Smith. While still a boy in his farm home near Palmyra, New York, Smith began witnessing visions and communicating with God; finally in 1827 an angelic visitor brought him the thrilling message that he had been chosen to reveal the divine truth to the world. Following instructions of the heavenly messenger, Smith, according to his own testimony, found buried beneath a near-by hill a number of golden plates covered with hieroglyphic signs. With the aid of two transparent stones, also deposited in the same place, Smith was able to translate the strange writing into English. After carrying his find away in its stone casket, and with the help of a succession of assistants who wrote down the divine words as Smith read from behind a screen, he dictated the remarkable volume published in 1830 as the *Book of Mormon*. The new sacred writings revealed the strange adventures of lost European tribes who found their way to America in bygone days, split into factions, and fought a series of wars that ended with the extermination of all of God's chosen people save Mormon and his son Moroni. These two survivors spent their remaining years transcribing the record of the wanderings of their people, together with their prophecies, upon golden plates that were buried until God chose to reveal them to His prophet.

With the publication of the *Book of Mormon,* Joseph Smith organized the Church of Jesus Christ of Latter-Day Saints and set out to gather the faithful. Moving first to Ohio, then to Missouri, then in 1839 to Nauvoo, Illinois, he gradually built up a band of sturdy followers who accepted him as their ruler in matters both religious and secular. At Nauvoo, the Mormon Church experienced a golden era: converts multiplied, a communal economy was organized, and prosperity reigned for four pleasant years. Then came disaster. In 1844 Smith received a final revelation, which commanded polygamy for the Saints. When some refused to accept plural marriage, factional conflicts ensued, weakening them to a point where they could no longer hold back the hostile mobs that had been a constant threat from the very beginning. Before the year was out Joseph Smith died a martyr's death at the hand of a "Gentile" lynching party, and his heartbroken followers prepared to move westward beyond the borders of an intolerant United States. Under their new leader, Brigham Young, they established themselves in 1846 on the shores of the Great Salt Lake, where through highly cooperative social methods they soon turned deserts into fruitful fields in which the harassed Saints for the first time enjoyed the sweetness of peace. Mormonism, like Millerism and Perfectionism, brought religious satisfaction to thousands of rebellious Americans who yearned to express a religious individualism in unorthodox ways.

BLUEPRINTS FOR SOCIAL REFORM

The striving for individual perfection which sired religious experiments likewise expressed itself in social realms. Reform activity was one of the major characteristics of the Jacksonian period. A true age of "isms," scarcely a man or woman was without a pocketful of plans for improving humanity: prohibitionism, abolitionism, feminism, vegetarianism, spiritualism, prison reform, and a hundred other devices designed to stamp out the evils that beset mankind were subjects of constant debate. "It was a day," wrote one zealous reformer, "for ideals in every camp. The general restlessness was as intense among reflecting conservatives as among reflecting liberals. . . . A great wave of humanity, a great wave of social sentiment, poured itself among all who had the faculty for large and disinterested thinking." And Ralph Waldo Emerson, watching this ferment from the aloof heights of his own indifference, observed: "There was an infinite hope, and there was an assurance that all particular mischiefs were speedily coming to an end. . . . What a fertility of projects for the salvation of the world! One apostle thought all men should go to farming; and another that no man should buy or sell; that the use of money was the cardinal evil; another that the mischief was in our diet, that we eat and drink damnation." The heady wine of progress intoxicated intellectual saints and intellectual sinners alike.

Underlying reform were religious, intellectual, and social forces. Ecclesiastical zeal was traceable to the inherent Puritan belief in community responsibility for all sin, and more directly to an acceptance of the doctrine of human brotherhood. Fellow Christians, clergy and laymen alike believed, must be aided by removing the temptation to sin. Moreover, evangelists had shown the need of positive action to save souls, and Jacksonians, too, had demonstrated that aggressive steps would alone preserve democracy. Their success indicated that social evils could also be abolished. Ministers felt this responsibility especially, for they accepted unquestioningly a dictum of the Reverend Charles G. Finney that all clergymen "should set out with determination to aim at being useful in the highest possible degree."

The intellectual stimulus to reform stemmed from the expanding Enlightenment, its emphasis on progress, humanitarianism, and the ultimate improvability of man. These well-known ideas, however, were bolstered by others derived from liberals engaged in social amelioration across the Atlantic. The most important European thinker who contributed to American reform ideology was Jeremy Bentham (1748–1832), an English philosopher whose opus, *Introduction to Principles of Morals and Legislation,* greatly influenced progressive thought. Benthamite utilitarianism, the doctrine that laws should constantly be changed to meet the needs of society and should be judged by the courts on the basis of their ability to assure "the greatest good to the greatest number," struck a responsive chord in a land already committed to the idea of progress. So did the actions of less philosophical Europeans who in their own countries labored for the same reforms that were being advocated in America. English humanitarians, busily engaged in working for abolition, prison reform, the peace crusade, and a galaxy of similar interests, constantly gave inspiration and guidance to Americans.

The most important social factor stimulating the reform movements was the concentration of population that accompanied the industrialization of the Northeast. In the sprawling cities the conditions calling for change appeared in sharpest relief; the mere sight of reeking dram shops and crime-breeding tenements, the pitiful evidence of poverty, spurred reformers into action. And in cities the like-minded interested in stamping out evil were able to cooperate to a degree impossible in isolated rural areas. This unity was essential in the causes of that day where, in the initial stages at least, a minority was faced with the problem of converting an indifferent majority to its point of view. Organization alone offered an answer; the successful reforms were supported by efficient national societies almost invariably rooted in the eastern cities. The speed with which these organizations made headway despite the individualism of the people never ceased to amaze contemporary Americans and foreign travelers alike. William Ellery Channing was astounded by the manner in which "those who have one great object find one another out through a vast extent of country, join their forces, settle their mode of operation, and act together with the uniformity of a disciplined army," while the sage Alexis de Tocqueville marveled that "the power of association has reached its highest development in America." But if the United States was already becoming a nation of "joiners," the newly evolving organizational skill was a product of cities, which made cooperation possible, and of democracy, which bred the habits of organized community endeavor.

The wave of reform of the Jacksonian period touched every phase of American society. Merely to list the causes that enlisted support would fill many pages, but some were so vitally enduring as to deserve at least a passing mention. Such was the cause sponsored by Dorothea Lynde Dix, an angular Massachusetts Quaker, who investigated the barbaric treatment of the insane in state after state, formed societies to publicize her findings, and forced a dozen legislatures to establish asylums where the mentally unbalanced could receive beneficial care rather than cruel punishment. Another was the battle against the ancient custom of imprisoning debtors; this was waged so successfully that by 1860 the inhuman practice had been abolished in the northern states, in Maryland, and in Kentucky. Still another reform was directed against harsh punishments for minor criminals; whipping was abolished in most states, flogging was banned in the navy, and the number of crimes punishable by hanging was greatly reduced. Even more attention was attracted by the societies devoted to the improvement of conditions within jails that prisoners might be rehabilitated rather than degenerated. Although reformers were unable to agree among themselves as to the relative merits of the "Pennsylvania system" of solitary confinement and the "New York system" of individual cells and common workrooms, the very intensity of the debate indicated the depth of humanitarian concern for society's unfortunates.

The concern lavished on criminals and lunatics was far outweighed by the attention riveted on drunkards. Ministers were quick to point out that "gin mills" lured young men from the churches, lessened their social efficiency, and started them on the downward path to poverty and public charity. A self-imposed temperance was regarded as the solution, and during the 1820's several societies made their appearance to preach the need of moderation and to publicize the glories of beer and wine against the iniquities of whisky drinking. These local organizations grew rapidly, and by 1833 the temperance movement was ready to emerge as a national force. In the latter year delegates from twenty-one state societies met at Philadelphia to form the United States Temperance Union —soon renamed the American Temperance Union—which for the next generation carried on a campaign against overindulgence.

Scarcely had this new society been formed than it was faced with a dangerous schism. Some of the more radical members, dissatisfied with the lack of progress, insisted that temperance was not enough; drinking wine and beer, they said, only developed an appetite for stronger beverages. The moderates countered by pointing out that the use of wine could not be considered harmful since it was frequently referred to in the Bible, but this argument was soon demolished by temperance society scholars who demonstrated to their own satisfaction that the Biblical words translated as "wine" really referred to the unfermented juice of the grape. With this obstacle removed, a majority of the American Temperance Union rapidly adopted the radical position and in 1836 went on record as favoring total abstinence.

The ground lost by this division was regained during the early 1840's as a result of aid from an unexpected source. On the night of April 2, 1840, a group of six convivial tipplers accustomed to frequenting the taverns of Baltimore were drinking in a local barroom when they decided to amuse themselves by sending a delegation to a near-by temperance lecture. The members of the committee went to scoff but remained to think, and the arguments they heard enabled them to convert their friends. Before the night was out the six took the pledge and decided then and there to form a society so that others might share in their salvation. Impressed by the fact that they themselves were reformed drunkards, they agreed that this should form the basis of their appeal; they would reform drunkards who would in turn reform other drunkards. The Washington Temperance Society, thereupon organized, grew with amazing rapidity, with branches in city after city and converts by the thousand. For the Washingtonians brought human interest to the temperance crusade: self-proclaimed wretches who stood on upturned whisky barrels and regaled delighted audiences with shocking tales of their sinful past were far more entertaining than the pious pleas of the American Temperance Union.

As effective as the Washingtonians in spreading the gospel of total abstinence was the tide of temperance literature that flooded the nation. For young children there was the *Youth's Temperance Advocate,* poems, songs, and the thrill of joining a "Cold Water Army." For oldsters there were tracts and magazines, novels such as Timothy Shay Arthur's *Ten Nights in a Bar-Room* (1853), and plaintive songs by the score: "The Rumseller's Lament," "Dear Father, Drink No More," "The Drunkard's

Wife's Lament," and one popular number sung to the tune of "Yankee Doodle," which began

> Says Jonathan, says he, today
> I will be independent,
> And so my grog I'll throw away,
> And that shall be the end on't.

and ended

> Kindred spirits, too, shall in-
> To utter darkness go forth
> Whiskey, Toddy, Julep, Gin,
> Brandy, Beer, and so forth.

For adults, too, the propagandists circulated fearsome tales of confirmed drunkards whose spirit-saturated bodies were consumed by flames, and of the diseases that followed the first glass of wine: "dyspepsia, jaundice, emaciation, corpulence, dropsy, ulcers, rheumatism, gout, tremors, palpitation, hysteria, epilepsy, palsy, lethargy, apoplexy, melancholy, madness, delerium-tremens, and premature old age."

On the crest of this deluge of words, temperance reformers eventually reached a state of mind where pleas for self-imposed abstinence no longer seemed sufficient. The worst sinners were clearly too weak to reform themselves; therefore society must save them. In the late 1840's the enemies of liquor advocated state action to stamp out sales of intoxicating drink. This phase was led by Neal Dow, a Maine politician, who persuaded his own legislature in 1851 to adopt the nation's first prohibition law. During the next decade half a dozen other states followed, and although most of these laws were swept away during the freedom of the Civil War period, the basis was laid for a vigorous prohibition movement when peace returned.

Less spectacular than the temperance movement but equally indicative of the spirit of the times was the crusade for universal peace. Churchmen deplored war as contrary to the principle of men's brotherhood, humanitarians condemned it because conflict upset the natural order of society and invited economic chaos. These sentiments influenced popular thought during the 1820's, when the Western world, tired of war after the generation of conflict that ended with Napoleon's overthrow, groped for a formula to end bloodshed for all time. Peace societies blossomed on both sides of the Atlantic, including in the United States state-wide organizations in Massachusetts, New York, Ohio, and elsewhere. By 1828 they were sufficiently numerous to permit one of their leaders, William Ladd of Maine, to issue a call for the national convention that culminated in the American Peace Society. From this time onward the national society developed a vigorous propaganda campaign designed to convince the United States that war was unnecessary.

Its primary object, however, was to secure legislation setting up machinery to settle international disputes by any means short of armed conflict. The magic formula worked out by. William Ladd in his *Essay on a Congress of Nations* provided for an International Court of Ambassadors to codify international law and a Court of Nations to arbitrate disputes on the basis of the code. The American Peace Society's principal efforts were directed toward securing legislative support for its program, and as a result the Massachusetts legislature in 1834 adopted resolutions urging Congress to set up the required machinery. Other states took similar action during the next few years, but not until the 1850's did Washington pay any official attention to the clamor. Then the Senate Committee on Foreign Relations reported favorably, but the rest of the Senate was unwilling to act.

In the meantime peace advocates were extending their efforts in other directions. Some among the more radical New Englanders sought to end war by a universal system of nonresistance. Led by William Lloyd Garrison, Bronson Alcott, and other intellectual left-wingers, they formed the New England Nonresistance Society in 1838 and adopted a declaration of principles based on "the sublime doctrine of acknowledging no government but God's":

Our country is the world, our countrymen are all mankind. We love the land of our nativity only as we love all other lands. The interests, rights, liberties of American citizens are no more dear to us than are those of the whole human race. Hence we allow no appeal to patriotism, to revenge any national insult or injury.

Belief in universal brotherhood was carried even further by Elihu Burritt, the "Learned Blacksmith" of New Britain, Connecticut, a humble man whose self-taught mastery of thirty languages convinced him of their common origin and hence of the common origin of mankind. His efforts led in 1848 to the formation of the League of Universal Brotherhood, a world-wide organization whose members pledged themselves never to take up arms or to fight under any conditions. Burritt was also responsible for a series of world conferences on peace that attracted international attention.

To those who believed so ardently and worked so faithfully, the events of the late 1840's and early 1850's came as a sad blow. Despite their protests, England and the United States resorted to warlike language in settling several minor disputes and—worst of all—their own country plunged gleefully into a war with Mexico. In vain did peace advocates urge men not to enlist and offer prizes for essays proving the immorality of the struggle; converts were few and were recruited largely from abolitionists such as James Russell Lowell, whose *Biglow Papers* summed up their sentiments:

> Ez fer war, I call it murder,
>   There you hev it plain an' flat;
> I don't want to go no furder
>   Than my Testyment fer that;
>
> God hez sed so plump and fairly,
>   It's ez long ez it is broad,
> An' you've gut to git up airly
>   Ef you want to take in God.

These forthright words carried little weight outside New England; nor could the reformers stop England from embarking on the Crimean War a short time later. With the outbreak of the Civil War, the organized peace movement collapsed, not to be revived until the late nineteenth century.

The voices of the peace advocates cried in a world-wide wilderness of cynicism, but their message was nonetheless important. A lusty young America was speaking—for peace, for temperance, for prison reform, for women's rights, for abolition, for free education, for any reform that promised the common man the democracy, the perfected institutions, and the decency he had a right to expect from a benevolent God and an enlightened society. If some who spoke were slightly mad, if others became the laughing stock of their neighbors, and if others sacrificed themselves upon the altar of popular indifference, the mere fact that they spoke was vital. They gathered inspiration from Jeffersonian rationalism and from frontier equality, from the cold reason of the Enlightenment and the fiery emotionalism of the revival, from the faith of their fathers and the perfectionism of the evangelists. Their world was one of ferment and progress, a world plunging headlong along the path to a better day when men would live as brothers—all equal, all free, all sharing in that democracy that was the faith of America. It was the great tragedy of American democracy that the rise of sectional conflict halted the slow and tortuous march toward betterment.

X

SECTIONALISM AND EXPANSION

1840–1850

Territorial expansion provided the spark that touched off the tinder-box of sectional antagonism and carried the nation along the road to civil war. During the 1840's the American people spilled over the boundaries that had hemmed them in for a generation, filled Texas and Oregon with a restless migration, fought a war with Mexico, and emerged as masters of a Union that stretched from sea to sea. When they paused in the midst of this breathless conquest to ask whether their new possessions should be slave or free they found themselves facing one of the most perplexing questions in the history of the republic.

Behind this expansion lay the twin forces of poverty and democracy. The poverty stemmed from the panic of 1837, which drove western prices steadily lower until the early 1840's. By this time many farmers had given up the agricultural ghost: their debts were increasing, their taxes were unbearable in states that had borrowed too heavily, and the prospect of better times was far distant. All about them were mute monuments to their shattered dreams: half-finished canals, abandoned railroads, rough slashes of uncompleted road. They had pinned their hopes for better markets on these internal improvement schemes projected during the booming 1830's; now that work was stopped their last chance for eco-nomical transportation was gone. These were the men who turned their footsteps westward in the search for riches denied them at home. They it was who peopled the rolling plains of Texas, filled the green valleys of Oregon, and elbowed their way among the Spanish ranchers of Cali-fornia—a restless, bumptious crew that immediately set up a clamor to have the authority of their beloved United States extended over the alien territory where they had staked their claims.

A deep national faith in democracy impelled those who remained at home to listen sympathetically to the pleas of these wanderers. They knew that their Constitution, their government, their laws were per-fect. God would never have endowed a few of His children with such perfection had He wished them to be narrowly confined; He manifestly

195

intended them to spread ever onward so that other peoples could enjoy their blessings of liberty and democracy. The manifest destiny of the United States was to expand—north over Canada to bring enlightenment to a timid people who did not dare shake off the shackles of kingship; west to the Pacific; south through Central and South America, where ignorant peons would welcome their saviors; east to rescue the groveling slaves of Europe's despots who were showing their own faith in republicanism by rising against their masters in the liberal revolutions of the 1840's. "What do I consider the boundaries of my country?" asked one editor. "On the east we are bounded by the rising sun, on the north by the aurora borealis, on the west by the precession of the equinoxes and on the south by the Day of Judgment." Expansion to spread the democratic dogma must go on, shedding new light over the world's downtrodden masses. This was the manifest destiny of the United States; opposition was contrary to the will of God and hence futile. Northerners might look askance at the acquisition of more slave territory, or Southerners might shudder at the thought of a free Canada divided into antislavery states, but they accepted these things as inevitable. Even Charles Sumner, who was to lead the abolition crusade within a few years, believed that the capital of the United States would some day be in Mexico City to control a domain stretching from Hudson Bay to the Strait of Magellan. This would mean more slaves, but he was powerless to resist destiny.

The eyes of American expansionists who felt the influence of this spirit of manifest destiny turned first toward Canada. A rebellion that broke out there in 1837 seemed to indicate that the Canadians were at last coming to their senses and needed only a little encouragement to cast off England's despotic rule and join the republic. Thousands of young men in the border states formed Hunters' Lodges, where they drilled in anticipation of the call for aid that must surely come; others rushed to join the rebellious forces. These unneutral acts almost led to war, for the Canadian authorities were finally goaded into destroying an American ship, the *Caroline*, as she lay in the Niagara River loaded with contraband goods for the revolutionists. Scarcely had the two governments weathered this crisis when trouble flared anew, caused by a Canadian named Alexander McLeod, who boasted in a New York saloon that he had taken part in the *Caroline* raid and killed an American. He was arrested and held for murder, while the British minister thundered and threatened, and the State Department, embarrassed by a weakness in the federal system that allowed states to meddle in foreign affairs, worked frantically to maintain peace. Only a change of ministries in England and McLeod's acquittal by a New York court rolled back the clouds of war. Canada's rebellion was crushed, and the Canadians contentedly returned to their place within the empire, well satisfied with the constitutional reforms secured by their protest.

THE EXPANSION WESTWARD

Expansionist enthusiasm now swung toward the West. By the end of the 1830's the eastern half of the United States was settled, and frontiersmen were filling the tier of states lying west of the Mississippi; Louisiana (1811), Missouri (1820), and Arkansas (1836) had been admitted to statehood, and Iowa was in the territorial stage. Farther west lay a vast treeless expanse, covered with grass and sage brush, which reached to the Rocky Mountains. Pioneers accustomed to a forest environment had no use for this plains area—they labeled it the "Great American Desert" on their maps—and were content to leave unmolested the great buffalo herds and Indian tribes that roamed there. But lying south and west of the Great Plains were the fertile lands of Texas, California, and Oregon, where a virgin soil held promise of new wealth. It was of slight consequence that these regions were owned or claimed by foreign powers. Frontiersmen have always been indifferent to international boundaries, and others welcomed a chance to strike a blow at the autocratic nations already established in these regions. Their settlement would not only bring prosperity to the poverty-stricken victims of the collapsed internal improvement schemes of the Mississippi Valley, but would fulfill their nation's manifest destiny by extending its borders to the Pacific.

As in earlier times, word of the riches lying to the west was carried to the Mississippi Valley by explorers, traders, and missionaries. Meriwether Lewis and William Clark, sent by Jefferson to explore the vast Louisiana Territory he had just purchased, had blazed the trail. They started up the Missouri River from St. Louis in 1804, crossed the mountains, and descended the Columbia River to the ocean. When they returned to St. Louis in September, 1806, they reported peaceful Indians, wild country, and abundant furs. The traders were close at their heels. Some went south in the years after 1822, driving their caravans of covered wagons along the trail from Independence, Missouri, to the Mexican outpost of Santa Fe, where they bartered pins and needles and glassware for dollars and furs and mules. Others went north, following the Missouri River into the tangled peaks of the northern Rockies, where they hunted or traded with the Indians and sent a steady stream of shiny pelts down to St. Louis on the spring floods. As these traders extended their operations in their perpetual search for wealth they brought back invaluable information. They discovered the gently sloping Wyoming valley known as South Pass, which crossed the Continental Divide in easy stages; they showed in 1830 that covered wagons could be driven as far west as the Rockies; and they demonstrated six years later that these prairie schooners could not only be taken through South Pass but could safely make the long journey along the Snake and Columbia rivers to the Pacific. Step by step they spied out the trails and passes over which later home-seekers made their westward way.

But the lands to which these trails led were not American. Texas, its boundaries defined by the Florida Treaty of 1821, belonged to the Republic of Mexico. So did the New Mexican country, with its small population clustered about Santa Fe, weakly held to the mother country by hazardous mountain trails fifteen hundred miles long. Mexico held California more securely. Mission stations, where earnest Franciscan friars taught their native charges about God and farming, dotted the coast at such strategic points as San Diego, Santa Barbara, and San Francisco, while the interior valleys were divided among ranchers who hired Indian workers for their cattle-raising and grain-growing enterprises. The Oregon country, embracing the whole region west of the Rockies between the forty-second parallel and the line of 54°40', was jointly claimed by England and the United States.[1] Although the two nations agreed on a treaty of joint occupation in 1818, only England took advantage of this opportunity before the 1840's, and the whole region was controlled by the Hudson's Bay Company's energetic factor, Dr. John McLoughlin. A wild man in a wild country, he was, as one of his contemporaries described him, "such a figure as I should not like to meet in a dark Night in one of the bye lanes in the neighbourhood of London, dressed in Clothes that had once been fashionable, but now covered with a thousand patches of different Colors, his beard would do honor to the chin of a Grizzly Bear, his face and hands evidently Shewing that he had not lost much time at his Toilette, loaded with Arms and his own herculean dimensions forming a tout ensemble that would convey a good idea of the high way men of former days." This was the picturesque despot who ruled supreme over a thriving agricultural community in the Puget Sound Valley and over an army of traders who scoured the wilderness miles for beaver peltry. By the 1830's his agents were clashing with the pioneers of the expanding American fur-trading frontier in the Rocky Mountain country, and both countries were realizing that the time was approaching when the ownership of the disputed region must be settled.

---

[1] Russia gave up all claims to the Oregon country in 1825 when, in treaties with the United States and England, she agreed to surrender all rights to the territory south of 54°40'.

Yet the missionaries rather than the traders precipitated the final clash for the Oregon country. In 1831 a delegation of Flathead Indians from the Pacific Northwest visited St. Louis to ask for instruction in the "white man's Book of Heaven." The novelty of "heathen" actually seeking conversion was sufficient to excite churches just awakening to the religious needs of the Indians. The Methodists, undeterred by the Flathead request that "black-robes" be sent, acted first, and in 1833 established a mission station in the Willamette Valley. Three years later a Presbyterian outpost was founded at the junction of the Columbia and Snake rivers, and before the end of the decade a Catholic mission was erected still farther inland. All were welcomed by Dr. McLoughlin, who gave them supplies and encouragement.

Of the three groups, the Methodists played the most important role in the American settlement of Oregon. Their mission was in one of the continent's richest agricultural areas, a fertile valley where timber was plentiful, rainfall abundant, and a market guaranteed by the large number of ships that loaded with furs along the Oregon coast before sailing westward across the Pacific in the China trade. News of these ideal conditions was carried back to the Mississippi Valley by letters and visits of the missionaries, and by 1841 a mass migration was under way. Settlers gathered each spring at Independence, joined together for mutual protection, and followed the Oregon Trail westward through South Pass and along the Snake and Columbia rivers to the Willamette Valley. Several thousand Americans were established there by the summer of 1844, living under a self-constituted government and growing increasingly dissatisfied with the treaty of joint occupation, which denied them a more stable rule under the American flag with security for their land titles.

Another body of homeseekers, borne along on the current of "manifest destiny," was meanwhile moving into California. Tales of the fertile lands and snug harbors of that Mexican province were carried to the East not by missionaries but by the Yankee shippers who touched there during the 1830's to load with hides and tallow from the cattle ranches. The first Americans in California were deserters from merchantmen and whalers, and not until after 1841 did the mass migrations turn in that direction. In that year a party of forty-eight immigrants branched away from the Oregon Trail, crossed the alkaline deserts of Nevada and the towering peaks of the Sierra Nevadas, and emerged in the Sacramento Valley. Others followed during the next years, building their homes around a fort and grist mill owned by a Swiss pioneer named John A. Sutter. By 1844 nearly seven hundred Americans lived in California, and many were already grumbling against their Mexican rulers and plotting to add California to the United States.

The third area to fall victim to the expansive energy of the Americans was Texas. Since 1819, when the Florida Treaty set the western limits of the Louisiana Purchase at the Sabine and Red rivers, the United States had viewed the vast territory beyond with covetous eyes. Repeated attempts to buy the region from Mexico, made during Adams' and Jackson's administrations, only aroused the suspicion of the Mexican owners, yet at the same time the strangely inconsistent Mexican government encouraged Americans to settle there. This process began in 1823, when the president confirmed a previous Spanish grant to Stephen F. Austin, a Missouri speculator, authorizing him to colonize two hundred families in a fertile part of central Texas. Two years later the concession was extended to other adventurers when Mexico offered each new colonist 177 acres of farm or 4,428 acres of pasture land free of charge, and promised the *empresario* responsible for inducing him to migrate 66,000 acres for every two hundred families brought out. Although this policy was supposed to lure immigrants from many lands, nearly all the *empresario* grants were to Americans. Within a few years their holdings covered the area between the Sabine and Nueces rivers, and they were hurriedly parceling out their domains to pioneers from the United States, attracted by free land and effective advertising. By 1836 nearly twenty thousand Americans lived in Texas.

Some of these settlers, particularly those who arrived in the early 1830's, were swashbuckling adventurers, itching for trouble, and eager to add Texas to the United States (the slave-smuggling Bowie brothers of Louisiana, whose name has been perpetuated in the deadly long knife that they designed, were of this sort), but most were sober citizens who would have been contented with Mexican rule had not a series of irritating incidents made them dissatisfied. Their principal grievance was Mexico's attempt to abolish slavery in its territories, for many of the immigrants were Southerners who felt that bonded labor was necessary for success. They objected, too, to tariffs that prevented them from importing accustomed goods from the United States and they likewise objected to control by Mexican legislators, whose character they made no attempt to understand, and to the uncertainty of life under a government constantly torn by dissent and revolution. These petty irritants were climaxed in 1835, when the Mexican President, General Santa Anna, proclaimed a new constitution that unified the nation and did away with nearly all the rights previously enjoyed by the province of Texas. Alarmed by this threat to the little self-rule that they retained, the Texans drove out the garrison at San Antonio and established a provisional revolutionary government.

The Texan Revolution was brief and decisive. Santa Anna, after leading an army across the Rio Grande and slaughtering the two hundred American defenders of the fortified mission at San Antonio, the Alamo, went down to defeat before an army led by General Sam Houston at the battle of San Jacinto (April 21, 1836). This ended Mexico's hope of reconquering Texas, and the Texans, after drawing up a constitution that established an independent republic, turned hopefully to the United States to ask for annexation. President Jackson was unwilling to receive them, for he feared war with Mexico that would almost certainly follow, but he did extend recognition to the new nation in 1837. Annexation was still the hope of both Texans and Americans, however, and when England showed an inclination to take the "Lone Star Republic" under her protection, the United States was moved to act. A treaty signed on April 12, 1844, added the territory of Texas to the Union. This was overwhelmingly rejected by the Senate, partly because the senators hesitated to commit their nation to a war with Mexico and partly because they were afraid to vote more slave territory into the United States on the eve of the election of 1844.

Expansion was the principal issue in this presidential contest: the people who marched to the polls knew that Texas was eager to be annexed, that Oregon was filled with pioneers clamoring to be added to the Union, and that California was undergoing an Americanization process which would eventually carry the flag to the Pacific. Yet war with Mexico or Britain or perhaps with both would certainly follow any rash step. In this crisis the Whigs were unable to decide on their course; they sensed the popular enthusiasm for new lands but knew that their wealthier constituents—the southern planters, the prosperous farmers and merchants of the West, the eastern businessmen and manufacturers—would suffer most from any conflict. Henry Clay, publicly opposed to adding Texas to the Union, was nominated without serious opposition, and the party launched a campaign intended largely to obscure the principal issue before the people.

The Democrats came out squarely for expansion. They passed over Martin Van Buren because he had spoken against Texan annexation, nominated James K. Polk of Tennessee, who was an ardent expansionist, and adopted a platform that called for the "reoccupation of Oregon and the reannexation of Texas." This plank, they hoped, would appeal to the western farmers who wanted Oregon and the southern planters who longed for Texas, without exposing the party to the charge of favoring one section above another. Before the campaign was well under way the wisdom of their course was clear. "Manifest destiny" was in the air, and great crowds cheered Democratic orators who shouted "All of Oregon or none!" or "Fifty-four-forty or fight!" Clay's evasive straddling fell on deaf ears. When Polk was elected, the people expressed themselves for expansion.

President Tyler stole the thunder of the victorious Democrats. He still had a few months in the White House and saw no reason why he should not receive credit for such a popular move as annexing Texas. A treaty, he knew, would be blocked by northern senators opposed to adding more slave territory, but a joint resolution inviting Texas to become a state needed only a majority vote in both houses of Congress. This was prepared, adopted, and signed by Tyler on March 1, 1845. Texas immediately accepted the invitation and on December 29, 1845, was formally "reannexed" to the United States.

The "reoccupation of Oregon" proved more difficult. Neither Polk nor any other Democrat who shouted so lustily for "Fifty-four-forty or fight!" intended to abide by this slogan: the United States was willing to settle on the extension of the forty-ninth parallel boundary to the Pacific. Nor did England expect to secure the whole disputed area south to the forty-second parallel. Its most extravagant hope was to hold the region as far south as the Columbia River, on which the Hudson's Bay Company depended to carry out its fur from the northern Rocky Mountain country. This triangle between the Columbia and the forty-ninth parallel was the real core of the dispute. Both nations rested their claims on exploration and occupation, but Britain's was far stronger, for McLoughlin's

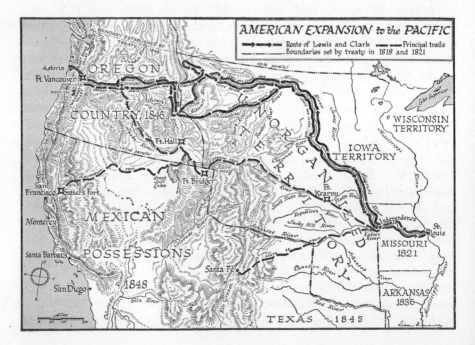

settlers filled the Puget Sound Valley north of the Columbia, while the Americans lived south of the disputed area in the Willamette Valley.

One of President Polk's first actions was to offer England the chance to settle the argument by extending the forty-ninth parallel as the boundary west to the sea. When the English government refused, he adopted a belligerent attitude, asking Congress for permission to terminate the treaty of joint occupation, to erect forts in the Oregon country, and to take other steps seemingly pointed toward war. Although congressmen were unwilling to go this far, they did authorize him to end joint occupation. The situation was critical, for Polk could not back down completely on his campaign pledges and England would not capitulate because the Hudson's Bay Company actually occupied the disputed area. And then, when both sides were squaring away for a seemingly inevitable conflict, the English company suddenly served notice that it was willing to abandon the whole Oregon country by moving its principal post from Fort Vancouver, on the north bank of the Columbia, to Vancouver Island. Its governors took this important step partly because the fur trade was declining in value as the beaver were exterminated, partly because they realized that navigation hazards prevented the Columbia from becoming the "St. Lawrence of the West," and partly because they feared that the boisterous Americans in the Willamette Valley would attack their post and destroy the stores kept there. The British government utilized the chance to establish a peaceful reputation by sacrificing an area no longer valuable to the empire. Word was hurried across the Atlantic that the forty-ninth parallel would be accepted as the boundary, and on June 15, 1846, a treaty with this provision was signed. Within two years, the United States had added two vast domains to its territories.

THE MEXICAN CAMPAIGN

But the period of expansion was not over. That Mexico would refuse to accept the annexation of Texas was almost a foregone conclusion; diplomatic relations were broken off soon after the joint resolution passed Congress in the last days of the Tyler Administration. Both nations girded themselves for war. Polk's territorial ambitions precluded a peaceful settlement, for he was determined not only to keep Texas but to add New Mexico and California to the Union by fair means or foul. In October, 1845, he wrote the American minister at Monterey that if the California people "should desire to unite their destiny with ours, they will be received as brethren." While sewing the seeds of rebellion, Polk held out the olive branch to Mexico by sending an agent named John Slidell with an offer to purchase New Mexico for five million dollars and

California for an additional twenty million. When word reached Washington in January, 1846, that the Mexican government refused to receive Slidell, the President decided that the time for action had arrived.

A boundary dispute provided the excuse. The Texan Republic entered the Union insisting that its southern boundary was the Rio Grande River—an extravagant claim not justified by facts, for as a Mexican province its lower limits never reached beyond the Nueces River and moreover Texas armies had never occupied the territory south of this stream. Polk now pretended to take this claim seriously and ordered General Zachary Taylor, who commanded a detachment of troops in Texas, to cross the Nueces and occupy the northern bank of the Rio Grande. There they camped while tension mounted, each side waiting for the other to strike the first blow. Polk weakened first. On April 25, 1846, he began work on a message to Congress urging war on the basis of Mexico's refusal to receive Slidell, her failure to protect American property during recent revolutions, and her refusal to pay some three million dollars to American citizens for damage done during these uprisings. On May 9 he called the members of his Cabinet together and, after reading them his statement, announced his determination to lay it before Congress three days later. All but one agreed that the grievances were sufficient to justify war; this dissenter held that the United States should wait until Mexico committed a hostile act. That night eagerly awaited dispatches from General Taylor brought welcome news: on April 25 a Mexican force had crossed the Rio Grande, skirmished with the American troops, and retired again.

The President was overjoyed. His message was immediately rewritten to make it seem that this attack was solely responsible for the war. "After reiterated menaces," he told Congress on May 11, "Mexico has passed the boundary of the United States, has invaded our territory and shed American blood upon the American soil. . . . War exists, and, notwithstanding all our efforts to avoid it, exists by the act of Mexico herself." Congress responded to these stirring words two days later, when it agreed that "by the act of the Republic of Mexico, a state of war exists between that Government and the United States." The solid support given this resolution—the vote was 40 to 2 in the Senate and 174 to 14 in the House—correctly mirrored the popular enthusiasm with which the American people entered on a war manifestly destined to extend the beneficial rule of their republic over the misguided Mexicans.

This spirit infused the armies in their triumphant conquest of the enemy. One under General Taylor marched south from Texas and after a bitter three-day fight captured the important city of Monterrey on September 23, 1846. Polk originally intended this force to press on to

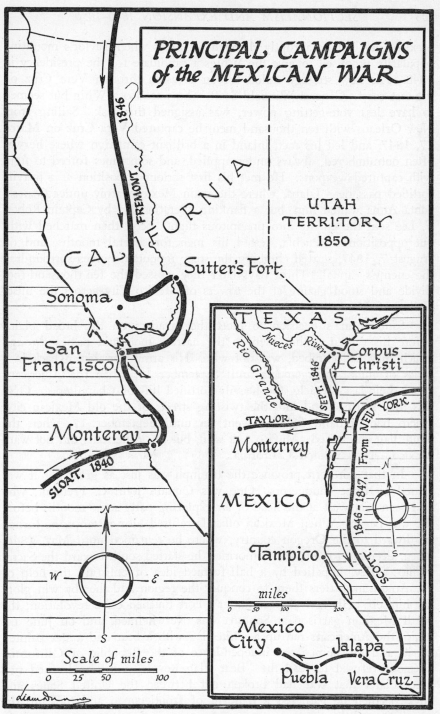

PRINCIPAL CAMPAIGNS
of the MEXICAN WAR

CALIFORNIA

1846

FREMONT,

UTAH
TERRITORY
1850

Sutter's Fort

Sonoma

San
Francisco

Monterey

SLOAT. 1846

N

W   E

S

Scale of miles

0   25   50   100

TEXAS

Nueces River

Rio Grande

Corpus
Christi

SEPT. 1846

TAYLOR.

Monterrey

MEXICO

From NEW YORK

1846 - 1847,

N

S

SCOTT.

Tampico

miles

0   50   100   200

Mexico
City

Jalapa

Puebla   Vera Cruz

Mexico City, but he abruptly changed his plans when Taylor's mounting popularity promised to give the Whigs a candidate for the presidency in 1848. His new strategy called for an invasion through Vera Cruz on the east coast. General Winfield Scott, who was also a Whig but seemed to have less vote-getting power, was assigned this task. Sailing from New Orleans with ten thousand men, he captured Vera Cruz on March 17, 1847, and led his men inland in a brilliant campaign where he was often outnumbered, always undersupplied, and sometimes forced to fight with captured weapons. He met his first serious opposition at a heavily fortified pass near Jalapa, where the main Mexican army under General Santa Anna waited him, but a flanking operation led by Captain Robert E. Lee sent the enemy into precipitous flight. Scott then marched without opposition to Puebla, rested his men for several months, and on August 7, 1847, started climbing the steep mountain ranges surrounding the enemy's capital. Three days later they crossed the ten-thousand-foot divide and stood gazing at the towers of Mexico City across the misty Valley of Mexico.

Santa Anna's decision to meet the invaders on the broad plains before his capital, rather than in the narrow mountain passes through which they had climbed, was not wise. His army was driven back in a series of minor engagements until September 13, when the Americans faced their last obstacle, the heavily fortified hill of Chapultepec. Over this they stormed and into the twisting streets of the old Mexican city, where hand-to-hand fighting went on until September 17, when the white flag was raised. Mexico was won, but the Americans did not want Mexico. They wanted California.

In that northern province the triumph was just as great but it was shared by three conquerors. One was Captain John C. Frémont, who had been sent west at the head of an exploring party some months before the war began. When Mexican officials refused him entrance, he turned northward to the Oregon country, where he remained until May, 1846. Then, deciding to defy the authorities, he started south toward the Sacramento Valley, impelled by a half-formed idea of enlisting the help of the American settlers there to conquer the region and thereby win glory for himself. His arrival near Sutter's Fort touched off a revolution; the small Mexican garrison at Sonoma was overwhelmed, and on June 14, 1846, the Americans ran up a white flag with a bear and a star painted on it, and proclaimed the independence of the Republic of California. Frémont refused to lead the "Bear Flag Revolt" until he learned two weeks later that war had broken out between the United States and Mexico; then he gathered a handful of frontiersmen and took up the march toward the coast.

The people speak. *Above*—The voice of the people in politics portrayed by George C. Bingham, "The Verdict of the People." *(Courtesy The Boatmen's National Bank of St. Louis) Below*—According to A. D. O. Browere's "Mrs. McCormick's General Store," the language of action was often more explicit. *(From the Gallery of the New York State Historical Association, Cooperstown, N. Y.)*

American expansion.

Left—A frontier land office where pioneers and speculators vied for nature's bounties. *Below*—The covered wagon carried eager homeseekers across the Rockies in the restless 1840's.

(Courtesy Library of Congress)

American contraction. While the nation's boundaries were extended to the Pacific, the American people were brought closer to each other and to the world by improved transportation. *Right*—An early Mississippi River steamboat, built before inventors adapted that craft to the needs of western waters *(Brown Brothers);* a scene near Lockport on the Erie Canal, one of the man-made connecting links in the system of interior waterways. *(Bettmann Archive) Below*—A Yankee-built clipper ship, whose billowing sails brought the ports of the world within commercial reach of the United States. *(Courtesy Library of Congress)*

Above—The DeWitt Clinton Railroad, pioneer among the lines that bound the nation together in a network of steel. *(Brown Brothers)* *Below*—The "Progress of the Century." A mid-nineteenth-century Currier & Ives print depicting the inventions of a single generation: steamboat, railroad, telegraph, and automatic printing press. *(Courtesy Library of Congress)*

There another conqueror was already in action. Commodore J. D. Sloat of the Pacific naval squadron, having heard of the declaration of war on July 7, landed a force at Monterey, raised the Stars and Stripes, and proclaimed California a part of the United States. At this very moment still a third conqueror was on his way west. With seventeen hundred troops Colonel Stephen W. Kearny had set out from Fort Leavenworth on the Missouri border early in the summer, captured Santa Fe without a battle, and moved on toward California after detaching some of his men to hold New Mexico. He arrived in time to fight a few skirmishes and to engage in a bitter dispute with Frémont and Commodore R. F. Stockton, who had replaced Sloat, over who should govern the conquered territory.

The occupation of New Mexico and California, which Polk intended to retain as the fruits of victory, strengthened the American hand in the peace negotiations. These were carried on by a State Department subordinate named Nicholas P. Trist, who accompanied Scott's army to dictate the peace terms as soon as the war was won. In the Treaty of Guadalupe Hidalgo, completed on February 2, 1848, Mexico accepted the Rio Grande boundary for Texas, and ceded New Mexico and California to the United States in return for a cash payment of fifteen million dollars and the cancellation of all claims due American citizens. Although a few Americans objected to paying for territory that had already been captured, and a few more shied from adding more slave states to the Union, their lone voices were drowned by the general chorus of approval, for the speedy victory had temporarily solidified public opinion. The treaty was ratified by a vote of thirty-eight to fourteen. The whole nation was proud of its victory—proud, too, that its borders had been extended to the Pacific. Only one step remained to round out the boundaries: in 1853 the Gadsden Purchase secured the Gila River Valley of southern Arizona from Mexico to make possible a railroad route along the southern border.

EXPANSION AND SLAVERY

Yet before the ink was dry on the Treaty of Guadalupe Hidalgo, the United States turned from celebrating its victory to debating a sectional issue that threatened a tragic end to the glorious conquests. Should slavery be permitted in the new territories taken from Mexico, or should they become free states? Once this question was asked, the year of decision had arrived. Gone was the day of conciliation and evasion: the slavery issue was squarely before the American people, never again to be pushed into the background by politicians or parties who feared the disrupting effects of sectional strife. "Manifest destiny" had created a crisis, and from this time the United States drifted steadily toward disunion.

The bombshell that set the nation aflame was thrown by an anti-slavery representative from Pennsylvania named David Wilmot. He, together with many other Northerners, had distrusted the Mexican War from the beginning; they believed that Southerners had annexed Texas and goaded the country into war only to win more territory for their inhuman institution. James Russell Lowell expressed their sentiments in the *Biglow Papers:*

> They just want this Californy
> So's to lug new slave-states in
> To abuse ye, an' scorn ye,
> An' to plunder ye like sin.

David Wilmot saw his chance in August, 1846, when Congress was considering a two million dollar appropriation bill to purchase conquered Mexican lands. He rose in the House and moved that "neither slavery nor involuntary servitude" should ever exist in any territory acquired from Mexico through the war.

The Wilmot Proviso lifted the slavery issue from obscurity into the limelight. The national capital was thrown into a turmoil as northern congressmen rushed to its defense, and Southerners to the attack. From Congress the excited debate spilled over into the states. Throughout the North, Wilmot Proviso Leagues deluged the capital with petitions against slavery, legislatures drafted resolutions urging that the territories be kept free, and street corners rang with the voices of self-appointed orators who denounced the "dark-lantern" conspiracies of the plantation owners. Throughout the South, turbulent mass meetings debated means to end this latest instance of northern aggression, and legislatures passed resolutions demanding the defeat of the Wilmot Proviso. Party lines were forgotten as northern Whigs and Democrats united to support their section and southern Whigs and Democrats, forgetting internal differences, rallied to the defense of slavery. Seldom had tension been so high.

As debate went on—in Congress, in the legislatures, in the cities, villages, and farms—several clearly defined points of view emerged. Northern extremists insisted that Congress had the right to legislate for the territories, and that this power should be used to ban all slavery there. This traditional view, on which the Missouri Compromise was based, rested on the sections of the Constitution that gave Congress the authority to "make all needful rules and regulations respecting the territory . . . of the United States." Extreme Southerners, led by John C. Calhoun, boldly challenged this congressional power. They held that the territories were owned jointly by the states, not by the national government, and that Congress administered them only as an attorney administered affairs for a group of partners. The citizens of each state, as joint owners of the territories, had the right to use their property freely within them. Slaves were property; therefore Congress had no legal right to forbid slavery anywhere.

Between these extremes were advocates of two less dangerous means of settling the controversy. One held that the territories should be thrown open to settlement and that the settlers themselves should then decide whether they should be slave or free. The other similarly brushed aside all constitutional arguments and sought to solve the problem by extending the line of the Missouri Compromise westward to the Pacific. Probably a majority of the people on both sides of Mason and Dixon's line favored one or the other of the last two solutions. President Polk openly advocated an extension of the Compromise line across the continent, while the other method, which was known as "squatter sovereignty," appealed to the democratic instincts of the residents of the Mississippi Valley. Yet this moderation found only a few adherents in Congress, for the heat of battle brought the fire-eaters to the fore. Spokesmen for both North and South insisted that they would be satisfied with no halfway measures.

The election of 1848 took place in the midst of this debate. Neither party dared face the issue; instead, both buried their heads in the sand and let the raging tempest sweep past. The Democrats, whose principal strength was in the South, nominated a colorless Northerner named Lewis Cass and did not even mention slavery in their platform. The Whigs, who were strongest in the North, chose as their candidate General Zachary Taylor, a Louisiana slaveowner, and refused to adopt a platform, depending instead on their standard-bearer's military fame to elect him.

Neither of the nominees satisfied the large group of Northerners who believed that positive action was needed to check the expansion of slavery. Some of these were abolitionists, few in numbers but loud of voice, who would be satisfied with nothing less than the eradication of bonded labor and complete equality for the freed Negroes. Others were free-state Whigs, disgusted with their party's choice and determined to cast no vote for a Louisiana plantation owner. Still more were northern Democrats who looked to Van Buren for leadership. This large faction had inherited the traditions of the earlier Locofocos; the workingmen and liberal intellectuals among them were intense humanitarians who worked steadily for social reforms that would elevate the living standard of the common people. Slavery was repugnant to them, partly because it offended their equalitarian ideals and partly because it was an antagonistic labor system that, if generally extended, would deprive white laborers of jobs. Neither the Whigs nor the Democrats were willing to go as far as the abolitionists. They were content to allow the peculiar institution to continue in states where it already existed, but were determined to prevent its spread into the territories. Yet these three groups, divergent in ideas and background, were thrown together by the common emergency and resolved to form a third party that would represent a northern point of view. The Democratic faction—known as the "Barnburners" because their determination to rid the nation of slaves reminded some wit of the Dutchman who burned down his barn to free it of rats —proved more powerful than the other two and won the nomination for Van Buren. Their advocacy of "Free Soil, Free Speech, Free Labor, and Free Men" fastened the name of Free Soil party upon them, and they were pledged to keep slavery from the western territories.

The results showed that the Free Soilers, while far from successful, held the balance of power. Their three hundred thousand votes, cast largely by northern Democrats, so weakened that party that the Whigs were able to place their latest military hero in office. Moreover, the thirteen Free Soilers elected to Congress were in a strong position, for the other two parties were so evenly divided that neither could muster a majority of the votes. This was the Congress that must finally determine whether the Mexican territories should be opened to slavery or kept free.

Nor could the issue be postponed much longer, since the inhabitants of the conquered lands were clamoring for a civil government to replace military rule. California presented the largest problem, for New Mexico[2] was too sparsely settled to give trouble, and Oregon finally won territorial status in 1848. The discovery of gold near Sutter's Fort in California attracted a stream of immigration that reached mammoth proportions in the Gold Rush of 1849; overnight the sprawling tent city of San Francisco became the center of a turbulent, polyglot population with which the military authorities were unable to cope. A civil government was needed at once, or the situation would become dangerous.

President Taylor was ready to act when he took office in the spring of 1849, for he was a blunt individual who scorned advice and confidently believed that his will was that of the nation. His solution was to urge the Californians and New Mexicans to draw up constitutions, set up state governments, and enter the Union as states with or without slavery as their people decreed. California accepted this hint eagerly and by the end of 1849 was ready for admission with a popularly approved

---

[2] New Mexico included most of the present state of that name, nearly all of Arizona, all of Utah and Nevada, and parts of Colorado and Wyoming.

constitution and a set of officers who were actually governing the state. New Mexico acted more slowly, but by May, 1850, was ready with its constitution. Both proposed to enter the Union as free states, for climate and soil precluded the possibility of slavery within their borders.

Southerners watched these proceedings through 1849 with rapidly rising tempers. Until this time they had managed to maintain a balance of slave and free states in the Senate, and they could count on that body to defeat any legislation hostile to the South. Now no slave territory was awaiting admission to statehood. Instead Minnesota was clamoring to be admitted as a free state, and if California and New Mexico were also brought in as Taylor proposed, the handwriting on the wall would be clear. Southerners could foresee the day when their section would be at the mercy of a government controlled by unsympathetic Northerners. Some talked openly of secession; the wisdom of such a step was debated by the South Carolina legislature, and many a congressman who journeyed to Washington to the opening of the new Congress in December, 1849, expected that he would soon return to help form a confederacy of seceded states. Like the abolitionists who preached separation from the sin-tainted slave states, they had given up hope of settling the sectional differences peacefully.

THE COMPROMISE OF 1850

Fortunately for the United States, the Congress contained wiser and cooler men in addition to these hot-headed extremists. The young fire-eaters were there: Salmon P. Chase of Ohio, William H. Seward of New York, and Charles Sumner of Massachusetts for the North, all urging disunion; Jefferson Davis of Mississippi, Alexander H. Stephens and Robert Toombs of Georgia for the South, the men who were later to dominate the Confederacy. But present too were the giants of an older day of union and harmony—Henry Clay, Daniel Webster, and John C. Calhoun. Calhoun was ready to place his section above the Union and plead for separation, but Clay and Webster were not, and to these aging statesmen all eyes turned in the hope that their wisdom and experience could produce some solution.

Henry Clay found the answer in the welter of minor conflicts that were all but forgotten during the debate over slavery in the Mexican territories. One concerned the boundary between Texas and New Mexico. During the war the federal government had assigned the region around Santa Fe to the latter territory, a fact bitterly resented by Texas and by Southerners, who were afraid that New Mexico might eventually become free. The Texans also believed that the ten million dollar debt they had accumulated as a republic should be assumed by the United States. Another question concerned slavery and the slave trade in the District of Columbia. Abolitionists demanded that both be abolished, while proslavery men were equally insistent that the institution should not be tampered with in a region carved from Maryland territory. Less troublesome, but still of some importance, was the insistence of some rabid Northerners that Congress use its power over commerce to forbid the interstate slave trade.

But the most trying source of friction between North and South, other than the status of the territories, was the question of runaway slaves. As early as 1793 Congress recognized the need of federal aid if escaping Negroes were to be returned to their masters, and the Fugitive Slave Act of that year placed the national government's law-enforcement machinery at the disposal of plantation owners. At first the northern states co-operated with federal officials in this distasteful task, but as abolition sentiment developed, they showed an increased reluctance to give any aid. This was especially the case after 1842, when the Supreme Court, in *Prigg v. Pennsylvania,* decided that the states were not required to help capture fugitives. With this decision many of the northern legislatures refused federal authorities the use of their police forces and courts—a step that virtually ended the effectiveness of the Fugitive Slave Act. Even worse, from the southern point of view, was the open aid given runaway slaves by abolitionists. The "Underground Railroad," with conveniently located "stations" where escaping Negroes could be hidden during their flight northward to free Canada, operated successfully through the 1840's. By the close of the decade Southerners were loudly demanding more rigid fugitive slave laws that would stop this traffic; Northerners, their feelings outraged by the tracking down of the fugitives, were insisting that the existing statutes be made less rigorous.

From this mass of claims and counterclaims, Henry Clay, relying partly on suggestions from a Democratic senator, Stephen A. Douglas of Illinois, forged a legislative program that he laid before the Senate on January 29, 1850. He proposed to admit California as a free state, establish territorial governments in the rest of the conquered Mexican territory without mention of slavery, forbid the slave trade in the District of Columbia but allow slavery to continue there, enact a more stringent fugitive slave law, force Texas to accept the restricted boundaries desired by the North but assume her ten million dollar debt, and guarantee that the slave trade would not be molested. Clay, in a magnificent address urging support for his program, asked the South to accept the inevitability of California's entrance as a free state, and the North to abandon its demands for the Wilmot Proviso because nature had decreed that slavery could not exist in the Mexican territories. Calhoun, so old and feeble that his remarks had to be read for him, asked his colleagues to reject the compromise that upset the equilibrium of the sections. He was answered by Daniel Webster, whose "Seventh of March" speech ranks among the great American orations. Like Clay, he urged Northerners to forget the Wilmot Proviso for lands made free by the "ordinance of nature" and pleaded for the compromise as "one of the strongest and brightest links in that golden chain" of Union binding the nation together. His sincere plea was misunderstood in the North, where abolitionists thought that Webster was deserting his section to win southern votes for the presidency.

> All else is gone; from those great eyes
> The soul has fled:
> When faith is lost, when honor dies
> The man is dead!

So wrote John Greenleaf Whittier, poet laureate of the abolitionists, but among many middle-of-the-roaders Webster's speech had a sobering effect.

Popular sentiment throughout the country rallied behind Clay's program. The people were prosperous, for business was booming under the stimulus of California gold, and neither northern merchants who fattened on trade with the South, nor southern planters whose cotton kept the wheels of New England's mills turning, wished to barter moneymaking for war over a question as academic as the existence of slavery in New Mexico. As this popular sentiment was felt in Congress, more and more representatives fell into line until only a few extremists and President Taylor remained opposed to the program. His sudden death in July, 1850, opened the way to Clay's proposals by elevating to the White House Millard Fillmore, a New York politician to whom compromise was second nature. The new President showed his hand immediately by forming a new Cabinet with Webster at its head. With the opposition of the President removed, Congress was ready to vote. One by one Clay's resolutions were taken up and passed, to form the monumental piece of legislation known as the Compromise of 1850.

Neither the North nor the South was completely satisfied. Southerners disliked the northern majority in both House and Senate that followed California's admission; Northerners were offended by the strengthened fugitive slave act that allowed the status of any Negro accused of being a runaway to be determined by a federal judge, without a jury and without the accused having the right to testify in his own defense. Irate abolitionists insisted that many free Negroes would be railroaded into slavery by this unfair law, but most of the North accepted the fugitive slave act as the South accepted the admission of California: as an irritating but necessary step. Wherever the compromise was debated, prosperity proved the deciding factor, and a majority favored giving it a trial; only South Carolina was opposed and it did not dare secede without the backing of other states. On both sides of Mason and Dixon's line the great mass of peace-loving people gave thanks that the slavery issue was forever laid to rest and that national progress would no longer be haunted by this grim specter.

XI

DRIFTING TOWARD DISUNION

1850–1860

Despite the lulling effects of prosperity, despite the understandable reluctance of the great mass of the people, North and South, to exchange the blessings of peace for the horrors of civil war, Henry Clay's crazy-quilt patchwork of compromise held the nation together in 1850 only because the time was not ripe for division. Two of the sections, the South and the Northeast, were at sword's points, but the Northwest shared its trade with both and hung in the balance. Southerners still hoped to win this unstable region to their side and would never secede until they had either succeeded or lost all hope. Moreover, the economic differences between southern planters and northern businessmen were not yet so great that they would refuse to live under the same roof, even though they considered each other disagreeable neighbors. Both of these conditions changed during the 1850's. The three sections merged into two—North and South—each so dependent on its distinctive type of enterprise that continued compromise was impossible. Underlying these changes was the rapid development of northern industry and southern plantation agriculture, for the Civil War was not only a struggle over slavery and Union but a clash between two antagonistic economic systems.

GROWTH OF NORTHERN INDUSTRY

Northern industry, although well established by 1850, underwent a period of hothouse growth during the next decade. Of the several factors responsible, one was the easy credit made available by the California gold dumped in the money markets; another was the widening market that the higher living standards of the maturing social order created; but more important was the presence of the first adequate labor supply in the country's history. This was provided by a flood of Irish immigration which engulfed the northeastern states in the decade after Ireland's disastrous potato famine of 1845. These people came by the thousands, reaching America on the lumber ships plying between New

Brunswick and their ravaged homeland, and drifting down the coast to seek work in the New England towns, where they could be near their churches and their fellow men.

An even greater stimulus was given northern prosperity by improved methods of transportation that opened new markets at home and abroad. Foreign consumers were brought within easy reach of Yankee merchants by the clipper ships. The billowing sails of these graceful vessels carried them across the Atlantic in thirteen days or around the Horn to San Francisco in ninety, a breath-taking speed that gave New England ship-builders a momentary supremacy in the Atlantic carrying trade. Through the 1850's they slipped in and out of the world's ports, laden with the goods of northern factories and western farms, until the end of the decade, when less romantic British steamships wrested from them the control of the seas. The clipper ships brought fortunes to their owners and builders—the stately mansions with their railed "widows' walks" that still dominate many a New England coastal town testify to that— and they brought to the whole North a taste of the benefits that awaited Americans as the world contracted. Silks and teas from China, casks of claret and magnums of champagne from France, sherry from Spain and Portugal, gin from Holland, spices from the Dutch East Indies, figs from Smyrna, currants from Greece, coffee from Brazil—by the end of the 1850's "Rio coffee" had displaced tea as America's most popular non-alcoholic drink, and 100,000,000 pounds were imported annually—hides and copper from Peru, Sheffield cutlery and Birmingham bar iron from England, fine textiles from the mills of France, Germany, and Great Britain—these were a few of the items regularly brought to American markets by the far-roaming clipper ships. Economic specialization on a world-wide scale, with each area producing the goods to which it was best suited by climate and geography, was at last coming within the grasp of man. And the United States, its supplies of farm produce, cotton, coarse textiles, and manufactured items mounting, was ready to play its part.

While the merchant marine brought the American industrialist in touch with the world's ports, domestic markets were opened by the spreading railroad network. This method of locomotion remained experimental until about 1840, then developed so rapidly that the United States boasted 9,021 miles of track in 1850 and 30,626 in 1860. At first this was concentrated in the most densely settled northeastern regions where way traffic would be greatest; Boston was the center of three thousand miles of road in 1850 that gave it direct contact with northern New England, the Lake Champlain country, Lake Ontario, and the strategic region about Buffalo. During the 1850's, however, expansion proceeded so rapidly that nearly all important coastal cities were placed in touch with a vast hinterland as well as with each other. For the first time, as a result, the bulky products of the interior—coal, iron, wheat, lumber, corn, and the like—could be distributed cheaply through the East. This not only encouraged industry by assuring it raw materials, but tended to diversify manufacturing and concentrate production at points where power, labor, and transportation were available, thus stimulating the growth of eastern cities. More important was the ease with which the industrialist could now market his products in distant areas. All America lay at his door; his textiles and his iron gimcracks could sell in the deepest South or on the remote frontier almost as cheaply as in Boston.

Responding to these opportunities, factories steadily increased their output of cloth, flour, machinery, and leather goods; by 1850 the value of American manufactures passed a billion dollars and in 1860 reached nearly two billion. This expanding volume encouraged consolidation, for cutthroat competition seemed foolish when the economies of large-scale production promised greater profits. The mills of the Northeast combined under joint management and concentrated at strategic points; the number of cotton manufacturing establishments, for example, remained stationary between 1850 and 1860, while the value of their products increased from $65,501,687 to $115,681,774. The concentration of industry allowed workers to unite into local trade unions, which, although comparatively unimportant, paved the way for the national organization of labor after the Civil War. All these developments were evidence of a maturing industrial order.

The social structure reared in the Northeast by this new industrialism reflected that section's prosperity. Cities multiplied and expanded, filled with spreading slums that were shameful reminders of the failure of Americans to cope with the first rudimentary problems of urbanization. To these teeming sections drifted the poorly paid factory workers, especially the immigrants whose unfamiliarity with New World ways and whose position on the lowest rung of the economic ladder condemned them to a continuous struggle with poverty. Little wonder that some of the new arrivals were driven to intemperance in an effort to forget their sorry lot, or even to petty crimes that would supplement their insufficient income. As a result, the native population, shocked by these violations of the strict moral code of that day and by the intrusion of strange alien customs into their solidified social structure, often turned violently against the newcomers. Forgotten were the benefits of this migration—the cultural heritage that enriched American life, the invigorating new blood, the valuable man power so needed by a young nation. Instead, the immigrants, particularly the Irish, were subjected to the abuse and persecution that has since been the lot of all newcomers from Europe; societies demanded laws to close America's gates to Europeans, to bar them from the franchise, and to discriminate against their Catholic religion, which was looked upon as a menace to Yankee Protestantism.

The northern slums hatched this nativistic problem, but beside them in the growing cities were other manifestations of the new class gulf that the industrial revolution was creating—ugly mansions that were monuments to the bad taste of the millowners, and luxurious hotels where members of the nation's leisure class besported themselves. European travelers might poke fun at America's "mushroom aristocracy" and deplore its preoccupation with the "almighty dollar," but it gave the North new leaders to challenge the supremacy of the southern cotton planters in national affairs.

EARLY INDUSTRIAL CULTURE

No better indications of the section's booming prosperity can be found than the host of excellent writers who gave New England its literary Golden Age during the 1840's and 1850's, for wealth begat schools, schools begat a reading public, and a reading public provided the stimulation that inspired authorship. Certainly the correlation between industry and education was clear. Factories concentrated both population and taxable property, making possible better school buildings, better teachers, and better instruction. Under this stimulus the northeastern states forged ahead rapidly, until by the 1850's they alone in the nation boasted a system of free public primary and secondary schools available for all. The colleges of this region were more numerous than those of the South or West and were educationally superior to them as well. Harvard especially was head and shoulders above its sister institutions, largely because the four leading members of its faculty had studied in Germany, where they came under the influence of the intellectual freedom, unflagging scholarship, and limitless erudition of that nation's unrivaled universities. Although the emphasis in colleges in this section and elsewhere was still on training an intellectual aristocracy to guide the common people, rather than on developing a democratic system that would open higher education to all, the Northeast was equipped with a school system that the ambitious could follow from the three R's to the most forbidding advanced degrees. Those with less ambition could use the nation's first public libraries; the Boston Public Library, authorized in 1848, opened its doors in 1854, and others followed to give Northerners a better reading opportunity than was then available to the people of any other section.

The literate public created by these educational advantages inspired the writers of the Golden Age. Ralph Waldo Emerson was their prophet. A Unitarian minister who resigned his pastorate at twenty-nine because he was "no longer interested," traveled abroad to tap the idealistic philosophy of Germany, and settled in placid Concord as "lay preacher to the world," Emerson gave his fellow men a true lesson in democracy. The essence of democratic practice, not the catchwords, was the theme of his essays: tolerance, understanding, freedom from hatred and prejudice. About this high priest of the American faith gathered others who wrote in his spirit: Henry Thoreau, Nathaniel Hawthorne, Theodore Parker. In near-by Boston and Cambridge another literary school flourished during the 1840's and 1850's, with Henry Wadsworth Longfellow, James Russell Lowell, and Oliver Wendell Holmes as its shining lights. Greater than all, because less dependent on English traditions and more typically American, were Herman Melville, whose *Moby Dick* appeared in 1851, and Walt Whitman, the half-Dutch, half-Yankee poet whose "barbaric yawp" in *Leaves of Grass* (1855) set a standard that generations of verse have not obscured. The presence of all these writers in the Northeast indicated a thriving social order, committed to continued progress, and certain to resent any interference with the industry on which its prosperity rested.

PLANTATION CULTURE

The South appeared equally prosperous during this decade. The limitless markets opened to textiles by clipper ships and railroads created a new demand for cotton that could be supplied only by the southern plantations. Under this stimulus the price, which fell after the boom times of the 1830's, began to recover in 1845 and spiraled upward until 1857, when it reached eleven cents a pound. This seemingly spelled prosperity for the planters, although actually the price of slaves was advancing so much more rapidly than the price of cotton that few planters received a large cash return on their investments in land and workers. Under these circumstances there was a natural rush toward the rich-soil regions where fertile fields would offset the exorbitant labor costs; their frantic scramble for new lands carried pioneers westward across Arkansas and Texas and was halted only when they reached the semiarid regions unsuited to cotton culture. Production skyrocketed from about two million bales in 1850 to more than four billion in 1860, when the South supplied seven eighths of the world's cotton. Tobacco production doubled in this golden decade—from 200,000,000 to 430,000,000 pounds— bringing new wealth to the older South and the western states of Kentucky, Tennessee, and Missouri.

The highly stratified social order called into being by the southern plantation system differed markedly from that of the North. The structure was dominated by a few great planters, never numbering more than 2 per cent of the population, who controlled the best land, most of the slaves, and about 75 per cent of the wealth. Their plantations, which monopolized the rich-soil regions, contained a thousand acres each and a hundred or more slaves who worked under hired overseers. The planters lived in great classical mansions, where they read Scott and Thackeray and Goldsmith, and patterned their fox hunts and gay social balls on those of England's country gentlemen. Their lives followed a rigid pattern dictated by the strict code of their set: education along legal or military lines, winters at Charleston or New Orleans, summers at Saratoga or Warm Springs, burial in the hallowed ground of the fashionable Episcopal churches of Mobile, New Orleans, or Montgomery.

Far below them in the social scale were the small planters who supervised their own plantations and labored so mightily beside their slaves that they had no time for learning or amusement. Their influence was out of proportion to their numbers—about a million and a quarter in 1860—because they rubbed elbows with the mass of southern whites and dominated public opinion. All were ardent defenders of slavery, for their dreams of becoming great planters could be realized only if the system were perpetuated and extended. Sharing their views were the six million nonslaveholding whites who lived in the South. Most of these were yeoman farmers who had been pushed onto poor lands not suited to plantation agriculture; they lived in comfortless cabins, dressed in tow shirt and cotton jeans, and labored from morn to night that they might buy a slave and start the slow climb up the social ladder. The remainder, numbering about a million, were the "crackers," "hillbillies," and "sandhillers" who occupied the barrens and piny woods wanted by no one else. They made a pretense of planting a crop, but their energy usually deserted them before the harvest season, and they lived miserably on such little game as they could bring down with their long rifles. These squalid by-products of society were despised by all Southerners, yet they defended slavery aggressively, for only this artificial barrier kept them above the Negroes. Beneath them were the four million slaves who formed the mudsill on which the southern social and economic order was built.

THE SWING OF THE NORTHWEST

The old Northwest, in 1850, was neither completely northern nor completely southern. Its people traced their ancestry to both sections, for Southerners had settled along the Ohio River in Ohio, Indiana, and

Illinois, and Northerners filled the remaining areas. Although its small farms operated by their owners bore little resemblance to the southern plantations, the West shared its agricultural traditions with the South, particularly after the 1840's, when improved transportation facilities encouraged specialization in cash crops for export, and the repeal of England's corn laws (finally secured in 1846 by the middle-class reformers) assured a limitless market for grain. On the other hand, manufacturing was taking root there as industries drifted toward the plentiful raw materials and expanding markets of that section. The iron and coal deposits of western Pennsylvania and eastern Ohio attracted steel mills, particularly during the 1840's and 1850's, when anthracite coal was being substituted for charcoal in the smelting process. Around the Pittsburgh steel plants clustered small producers who turned out stoves, marine engines, agricultural machinery, railroad locomotives and rails, and other finished metal products. Another group of industries settled at strategic points where they could process agricultural goods flowing toward eastern or southern markets. Cincinnati's advantageous situation across the route to New Orleans attracted so many meat packers that the city was long known as Porkopolis, while St. Louis, Buffalo, and Chicago also developed slaughterhouses and flour mills in large numbers. These same cities— Chicago is an outstanding example—also lured manufacturers of items designed for the rural market, particularly farm machinery. Westerners connected with these expanding enterprises naturally preferred the East's high tariffs and sound banking systems to the South's demand for federal laws that would aid farmers at the expense of industrialists. The trade routes of the old Northwest led east and south, for steamboats carried pork and corn down the Mississippi to the southern plantations, while canals and railroads moved grain and flour to New York or Philadelphia. In 1850 70 per cent of its wheat and flour went east, and 70 per cent of its corn was shipped south. The Northwest was firmly bound to both antagonistic sections by strong economic ties.

So long as the Northwest hung in the balance, civil war was impossible. Only its swing to the Northeast during the fateful decade of the 1850's upset the sectional equilibrium and brought the United States to the brink of conflict. By 1860 two sections—North and South—faced each other in the national arena, each suspicious of the other and each determined to dominate American political, economic, and social affairs. Three things convinced the people of the Northeast and the Northwest that their cause was one: their common conviction that slavery was an evil, the influence of German immigrants, and the construction of new transportation routes between East and West.

The hatred of slavery shared by Westerners and Easterners was not new, but it was vastly intensified during these ten years. The steady movement of New Englanders to the West helped cement the bond, for wherever they went they carried the abolitionist views of their homeland. Equally important was the religious excitement culminating in the revival of 1857; the thousands who joined the churches heard slavery denounced as a sin against God. Still more were converted by Harriet Beecher Stowe's *Uncle Tom's Cabin,* a novel inspired by its author's contacts with Kentucky slavery during a long residence in Cincinnati. From the day of its publication in 1852 this powerful indictment was immensely popular through the North, selling three hundred thousand copies a year and passing from hand to hand until nearly every person north of Mason and Dixon's line was familiar with its ringing message and its distorted stereotypes, for Simon Legree was no more typical of the average Southerner than Uncle Tom represented the usual slave. This ideological hatred of slavery was shared by Northeast and Northwest, and tended to bring their peoples together.

The German immigrants also played their part. Driven from their native land by crop failures, they began arriving in the late 1840's to seek farmlands in the Northwest where they could start life anew. Wherever they settled—in Iowa, Wisconsin, Illinois, and Ohio—they fell under the influence of western Yankees and formed a solid phalanx against slavery, which they despised as a competitive economic system and as reminiscent of the tyranny they had left behind. Their leaders were brilliant liberals such as Carl Schurz and Franz Sigel[1], who had fled from Germany with the collapse of the Revolution of 1848; they viewed bonded labor with the horror of all enlightened Europeans and helped hold their countrymen loyal to the cause of freedom. These Germans held the balance of power in many western communities and always threw their influence to the side of the North and antislavery.

More influential than either the abolitionists or the immigrants in uniting the Northeast and the Northwest were the railroads. During the 1850's a number of trunk lines were completed between eastern cities and terminals that stood at the threshold of the West: the Pennsylvania Railroad between Philadelphia and Pittsburgh (1852), the Erie uniting New York and Lake Erie (1851), the Baltimore and Ohio connecting Baltimore with the Ohio River (1853), and the New York Central that ran from New York to Buffalo (1853). These through systems immediately initiated a competition for western trade, lowering their rates each year, buying up end-to-end roads in the West that would carry them

---

[1] Carl Schurz later distinguished himself as an outstanding reformer and politician, while Franz Sigel, as general of a regiment of German-Americans, helped save Missouri for the North during the Civil War.

PRINCIPAL EAST-WEST
& WESTERN RAILROADS
1860

RAILROADS

Scale of miles

0   50   100   200

nearer the centers of agricultural production, and building feeder lines
to tap unexploited areas. This process went on so rapidly that by 1858
Boston, New York, Philadelphia, and Baltimore were all connected with
such important middle-western cities as Chicago, Cincinnati, and St. Louis,
and the two regions were tied firmly together. The southern railroad
network, on the other hand, was built to unite the coastal cities with the
interior cotton country, and had no connection with the east-west lines
of the North. The two independent systems touched at only four places
—Washington, Cincinnati, Louisville, and Cairo—and even here trans-
shipment of goods was necessary.

The close rail connections between Northeast and Northwest broke
the old trade bonds between the South and the West and shifted the bulk
of western trade to eastern markets. The effect of the new transportation
routes was reflected in the figures showing the direction taken by the
exports of the Northwest:

		To the East	To the South
Corn	1850	3,600,000 bushels	2,400,000 bushels
	1860	19,200,000 bushels	4,800,000 bushels
Pork	1850	300,000 barrels	1,200,000 barrels
	1860	930,000 barrels	570,000 barrels
Whisky	1850	66,000 barrels	134,000 barrels
	1860	310,000 barrels	190,000 barrels
Wheat	1850	5,000,000 bushels	500,000 bushels
	1860	28,420,000 bushels	580,000 bushels
Flour	1850	2,070,000 barrels	930,000 barrels
	1860	4,345,000 barrels	1,155,000 barrels

By 1860 the two sections were firmly joined by commercial and ideological ties, their peoples bound together by their hatred of slavery and by the economic dependence of each on the other.

THE SECTIONAL IMPASSE

The emergence of a united North during the 1850's emphasized both the vast gulf separating that section from the South and the position of subservience forced on the southern capitalists because of their refusal to revise their economic ideas and diversify their means of earning a living. Not only were the transportation systems of the two sections distinct: their economics, the mode of life of their people, and their social concepts varied so greatly that further compromise was futile.

The civilization of the North was built on free labor used in industry and diversified small-scale agriculture; that of the South, on slave labor employed on plantations to produce a staple crop. Northerners numbered nineteen million in 1860, they owned eleven billion dollars worth of property and each year sold goods valued at three billion dollars. Southerners numbered only eight million whites, their property was worth five billion dollars, and their annual production less than a billion dollars. The North used its taxable wealth to support a thriving culture; although the South proclaimed itself the modern counterpart of ancient Greece and boasted of a golden civilization built on the labor of black-skinned workers, it could produce no public schools, no libraries, and no writers other than a few unappreciated literary hacks and plodding second-raters. Mason and Dixon's line divided two divergent civilizations—the one bold, prosperous, and progressive; the other stifled by slavery and an aristocratic social structure.

The yawning chasm between the two sections was reflected in their antagonistic social concepts. The thought of the North was crystallized in the writings of Ralph Waldo Emerson, whose transcendental philosophy preached the essential goodness of man, the glories of physical and spiritual freedom, and the inherent right of each individual to shape his own destiny. His fellow Northerners were intense individualists; they were prospering and wanted no interference, they were enthusiastic believers in liberty and democracy, and they were incurable optimists who looked ahead to the day when bountiful fields would yield rich harvests and whirring machines would cascade new wealth. The opinions of the South were voiced by George Fitzhugh, whose *Sociology for the South* (1854) laid down a philosophy of inequality, aristocracy, and absolutism. He argued that all men were not created equal, that the lower classes were incapable of caring for themselves, and that a few gifted leaders should rule for all. These of the elect, Fitzhugh maintained, should see to it that the masses were trained for vocations, then bound out to planters or manufacturers for life in return for support, kindly treatment, and state care for their children. Southerners who accepted these teachings turned their backs on the basic concepts underlying their republic and made it clear that the bond of union was wearing thin.

The impossibility of reconciling the difference between the two sections was shown by the way in which each viewed the other. Southerners realized that they were slipping deeper into a position of political and economic inferiority each year. After 1850 their control of the Senate was gone, never to be regained, even though northern appeasers still voted with the South on most important public questions; moreover, hostile senators would soon be appearing from the new states that were being overrun by swarming antislavery men, while their own westward expansion was stopped by the natural limits beyond which slavery was no longer profitable. Their dependence on a staple crop placed them at the mercy of northern industrialists, for all their needs must be supplied by those hated individuals. They estimated that this "miserable traffic of Northern gimcracks and haberdashery" annually absorbed the total value of the cotton crop, and that the South in addition paid northern merchants to market its crop and northern bankers to finance the transactions. Southerners tried to end this subserviency by starting their own factories—each year after 1845 enthusiastic commercial conventions passed resolutions urging the industrialization of the South—but their efforts came to naught, for southern capital drained steadily into more land and slaves, and none was available for industrial enterprises. As their minority position became clearer they looked upon northern growth and prosperity as a standing aggression; only the fact that the South controlled the presidency until 1860 stopped them from giving up the unequal struggle sooner than they did.

The North, on the other hand, viewed the South as the aggressor in this sectional struggle. Northerners resented especially the succession of Democratic presidents who dominated national affairs after 1844, placed in office by Southerners and by northern appeasers who preferred southern rule to civil war. Why, they asked, should the majority North bow before the minority South? Why should they accept the legislative program that southern Democrats forced on their party and the nation? Behind these anguished wails was the sober realization that both their ideals and their pocketbooks suffered from this leadership. In fact, the combination of aggressive Southerners and compromising Northerners who elected Franklin Pierce in 1852 and James Buchanan in 1856 was prepared to carry out a three-point program that boded only ill for the North. This was designed to check northern industrial growth, to acquire new possessions into which slavery could expand, and to open to bonded labor additional regions within the United States. The struggle of the Democrats to realize these ambitions carried the nation to the brink of war, for their success in curbing northern industry goaded that section beyond endurance, their efforts to secure new lands for slavery embroiled the United States in unpopular diplomatic controversies, and their attempts to open new slave territories within the republic crystallized the whole sectional ill feeling.

The tariff was the principal weapon used to attack northern industry. Northern fear of southern retaliation kept levels low between 1833 and 1842, when the Whigs, in tune with the nationalism of Henry Clay and Daniel Webster, pushed through the only avowedly protective measure in the three decades preceding the Civil War. Their triumph was brief; in 1846 these duties were overthrown in favor of a tariff for revenue only, and another reduction was pushed through Congress in 1857 by Democratic votes over the protests of manufacturers who complained bitterly of foreign competition. Another measure sought by the North was a homestead law that would allow the government to give to each actual settler 160 acres of the public domain. By this time the Irish workers were so plentiful that eastern industrialists no longer feared liberal.land laws; assured now of an adequate labor supply, they favored the homestead measure as a means of expanding their markets. This law, so enthusiastically desired by Northerners and Westerners, was vigorously opposed in the South, because the division of western lands into 160-acre plots would check the expansion of plantations and hasten the development of free commonwealths with antisouthern political views. Through the 1850's the North saw the South frustrate its every effort to liberalize the land system; homestead bills that passed the northern-dominated House were defeated by southern influence in the Senate in 1854 and

1859, and a modified measure squeezed through both was vetoed by the Democratic president, James Buchanan, in 1860. It is no wonder that anger mounted north of Mason and Dixon's line as laws that promised new prosperity were effectively pigeonholed by a persistent southern minority.

Equally objectionable in northern eyes was the revived expansionism of the 1850's, when efforts of Southerners to secure more territory for slavery seriously threatened the national security. Cuba was one of their objectives. When an American ship, the *Black Warrior,* was confiscated by officials of that Spanish colony in February, 1854, for violating port regulations, the Democratic President, Franklin Pierce, seized the excuse to demand an indemnity so stiff that it amounted to an ultimatum. Possibly he intended to carry the country into war for Cuba, but hostile northern opinion and Spain's desire to give satisfaction in any way short of complete surrender forced him to abandon his plans. The *Black Warrior* was given satisfactory compensation and the incident forgotten, but the Democrats had shown their hand. They showed it again a year later, when Pierce, deciding that the time was ripe to secure Cuba, ordered the American ministers at Madrid, London, and Paris to prepare a program for their country to follow. The document that they prepared—known as the Ostend Manifesto—was damning to the southern cause; it recommended an offer of $120,000,000 for Cuba and declared that if this was refused "then, by every law, human and divine, we shall be justified in wresting it from Spain . . . upon the same principle that would justify an individual in tearing down the burning house of his neighbor if there were no other means of preventing the flames from destroying his own home." Again northern protests ended further negotiations, but the North was convinced that the Democratic President was willing to risk war for more slave territory.

President Pierce rose to the expansionist bait again in 1855 when an adventuresome Southerner named William Walker, a shy little "grey-eyed man of destiny," led a motley crew of Americans and Central Americans against the Republic of Nicaragua and established himself as its dictator. The American President immediately extended recognition to this tottering government, and his fellow Democrats wrote a plank into their 1856 platform approving Walker's efforts to "regenerate" Nicaragua. However, treachery and bad liquor ended Walker's brief career before the United States was committed to some foolish course of action.

The sole result of the expansionism of the 1850's was to open Japan to the outside world, a step heartily approved by Yankee manufacturers as well as by southern planters. For some time American ships had traded with China, particularly after 1844 when treaties guaranteed them special privileges in that country's leading ports, but the "Hermit Kingdom" re-mained closed to them as it had to all the world for two centuries. In-dustrialists and planters who dreamed of new markets on the teeming island persuaded their government to send a naval squadron under Com-modore Matthew C. Perry across the Pacific with instructions to secure trading concessions and a coaling station. Perry's fleet entered Tokyo Harbor on July 8, 1853, to the consternation of the Japanese, who had never seen a smoke-belching steamship. When the commander had com-municated his request to the Emperor, he sailed away to wait a decision. However, in the spring of 1854 he was back again, this time with seven black men-of-war. The governors of Japan were so much impressed with this show of power, and so conscious of the need for European weapons to protect their country from the western powers already en-gaged in carving up China, that they consented to a treaty in March, 1854, in which they opened their ports to American trade. Thus did Japan turn from isolation to imitation, and begin the transformation that reached a climax on December 7, 1941, when her planes retraced Perry's path as far as Pearl Harbor.

The North liked the opening of Japan, and Northerners, strong enough to defeat any obnoxious treaty, were never much alarmed by the expansion southward, but when the Democrats turned to their third ob-jective—more slave territory within the United States—the last chance for continued intersectional peace was shattered. The North had sup-posed the whole matter settled. The Missouri Compromise determined the fate of all lands east of the Rockies, the Compromise of 1850 and the forces of nature cared for New Mexico, and California and Oregon were already organized on a basis of freedom. Hence when Democrats pro-posed opening new stretches of the West to slavery and pushed their proposals through Congress, the howl of anguish that rose from the North surpassed any inspired by the whole sectional conflict.

Stephen A. Douglas was responsible for this new crisis. Senior senator from Illinois, idol of the northern Democrats, five feet tall and crammed with shrewdness and swagger that won him the fond nicknames of "the Little Giant" and "the Steam Engine in Britches," Douglas en-tered the slavery controversy because he wished to aid his section and protect real-estate investments he had made in his native Chicago. The occasion was a bill before Congress to charter a railroad to the Pacific. If he could make Chicago the eastern terminus he would not only win the political backing of grateful Illinoisans but would profit handsomely himself. The task would not be easy. The South wanted a railroad across Texas and New Mexico, and argued that this route would run through organized territories where the Indian menace was negligible and where land grants along the right of way would encourage construction companies to build up this area. A road west from Chicago, on the other hand, would pass through unorganized Indian country, where the government owned no land to grant and where savage resistance might be expected. If Douglas were to secure the central route he must first persuade Congress to organize the territory west of Iowa. This move would certainly be opposed by southern congressmen because it opened lands north of the Missouri Compromise line. Political juggling was called for, and Douglas was a master juggler.

He proposed organizing the plains area west of Missouri and Iowa on the basis of what he called popular sovereignty. Settlers could bring in slaves or not as they wished, then vote to decide whether the territory would be slave or free. If a majority were free-staters, they could forbid slavery; if Southerners were in control, they could perpetuate their own labor system. Douglas knew that any scheme which allowed the people to regulate their own affairs would appeal to the democratic West. He knew, too, that the South would gladly barter a southern railroad for more slave territory. There remained only the necessity of bribing the North by dividing the West into the two territories of Kansas and Nebraska. The one lying west of Missouri in all probability would become slave; the other would be settled by Northerners and in all probability would remain free. Douglas had every reason to view his plan with approval: the South would have one slave territory, the North a free territory and the railroad, and the West its cherished democracy. Moreover, his unique means of solving the slavery controversy by popular sovereignty might even charm a grateful people into making him president in 1856.

The Kansas-Nebraska Act was adopted by Congress in May, 1854, after three months of bitter debate. Southern joy was boundless. The gates were down; plantation owners could spread over the whole West, building new slave states as they went until they controlled the nation once more. Only one thing matched the delight of the South, and that was the anger of the North. The cry of rage which rose from that section was greater than any heard since blood was spilled at Lexington and Concord. Horrified Northerners were aghast that their trusted bulwark against slavery, the Missouri Compromise, had crumpled; they had believed it as inviolate as the Constitution and would have been no more shocked if told that Congress had abolished trial by jury or freedom of worship. They would not take such a blow without protest; with the Kansas-Nebraska Act the day of hedging and compromise was past. "It puts freedom and slavery face to face," wrote Charles Sumner, "and bids them grapple."

A HOUSE DIVIDED

The first result was a complete reshuffling of party lines. The Whigs, who had been struggling along with only a semblance of unity since the death of Webster and Clay in 1852, fell completely apart. Southern Whigs drifted into the Democratic ranks, northern Whigs joined one or the other of two new parties that sprang up. One of these was the American party, a secret organization whose members were commonly called Know-Nothings because they parried all questions with "I know nothing about it." The Know-Nothings, who promised their countrymen protection from Catholics and aliens, gained strength steadily through the 1850's, when a large European migration fanned the flames of prejudice, but did not attain national prominence until their ranks were swelled by thousands from the middle states who sought protection from the storm raised by the Kansas-Nebraska Act. People in the border states joined this group all through 1854; knowing that they would suffer most in civil war, they clung desperately to the hope of compromise promised by this nativistic party that placed such emphasis on the glories of union. With their support the Know-Nothings carried six states in the congressional elections of 1854 and 1855, and almost won seven more. Even their enemies conceded them the presidency in 1856, but by this time the party had split over slavery and emerged with only the electoral vote of Maryland.

More important was a new sectional party that emerged to challenge Democratic supremacy. This originated in the West, where irate farmers, troubled lest the further extension of slavery would block their march westward, gathered in indignation meetings through the spring of 1854 and talked of forming a new party that would keep slaves out of the territories. The group who met under the oak trees of Jackson, Michigan, on July 6, 1854, hit on the name of Jefferson's old party and suggested that they "be known as 'Republicans' until the contest be terminated." The idea took hold at once; local Republican organizations springing up through the Northwest were strong enough to challenge Democratic candidates in the fall elections. During 1855 the party spread eastward across New England and the middle states, attracting such leaders as William H. Seward of New York, and by the fall of that year it was firmly entrenched throughout the North. Into its ranks flocked disgruntled "Anti-Nebraska Democrats" who could not support their party's latest proslavery aggression, Whigs, Free-Soilers, Abolitionists, and Know-Nothings who realized that not popery but slavery really threatened the Union. When the Republicans showed their strength in the fall of 1855 by defeating all but seven of the forty-two northern congressmen who voted for the Kansas-Nebraska Act, it was clear that another national tie was broken; now two sectional parties dominated the scene and civil war was nearer.

Yet even then disunion might have been delayed if either side had been willing to abide by the democratic process of free elections. Instead, the Northerners, aflame with indignation, determined to frustrate the southern plot for more slave territory by filling Kansas with free-state men. "Emigrant Aid Societies" sprang up everywhere, money was raised, and parties of immigrants were hurried into the disputed territory. Southerners, horrified at this attempt to usurp a region allocated to slavery, formed their own organizations and sent their own parties of settlers. These two streams poured into Kansas during 1854—the Northerners to the interior, where they founded Lawrence and Topeka; the Southerners to Atchison and Leavenworth along the Missouri River, where they could count on help from the proslavery Missourians, who were always ready to swarm over the border to stuff ballot boxes or "clean out the abolition crowd." By the fall of 1854 the stage was set for a violent struggle.

This began in November, when seventeen hundred Missouri "border ruffians" crossed into Kansas and cast enough votes to elect a proslavery delegate to Congress. They returned in the spring of 1855 and, disregarding the fact that there were only fifteen hundred registered voters in the territory, cast six thousand ballots for the members of the legislature that would decide whether Kansas would be slave or free. When the governor refused to admit these fraudulent returns he was dismissed by President Pierce, and the legislature thus elected assumed control of the territory. Northerners in Kansas refused to recognize this government; instead, they met at Topeka in October, 1855, and drew up a constitution that provided for the admission of a free Kansas to the Union. This was overwhelmingly adopted by the antislavery Kansans, for the Southerners not only refused to vote but went ahead to elect their own legislature and governor. Two governments existed side by side, one slave and one free, and popular sovereignty as an orderly means of settling the slavery question was a demonstrated failure.

But the worst was yet to come. The invasion of Kansas by armed bands of "Missouri ruffians" sent such a thrill of indignation through the North that the antislavery men decided to meet force with force. During the winter and spring of 1856 the Emigrant Aid Societies used their funds to arm prospective settlers with "Beecher's Bibles"—the name applied to the dreaded Sharps rifles after the Reverend Henry Ward Beecher referred to them as a "greater moral force" for Kansas than the Bible —and sent them into the territory. For a time these northern bullies and southern ruffians, all spoiling for a fight and armed to the teeth, sparred cautiously. Then John Brown's Raid provided the spark. Old John Brown was a half-insane abolitionist whose Old Testament God told him that without the spilling of blood there was no remission of sin. On the night of May 24, 1856, he gathered a little band of fanatics about him and at Pottawatomie Creek murdered five Southerners in cold blood, not because they had harmed him or his cause, but because five Northerners had died in the border fighting and blood must be shed for blood. This act of brutality was disavowed by the free-staters, but it touched off warfare all over Kansas. Gangs of armed men from both sides roamed the territory, killing and plundering as they went, until the skies over Kansas were alight with the fires of burning homes. Not until two hundred people were killed did federal troops restore order to the war-torn territory.

"Bleeding Kansas" gave the Republican party a needed stimulus at an opportune time. While Northerners read in their papers a distorted story of how innocent free-state settlers were pillaged and murdered by bloodthirsty southern ruffians, the election of 1856 took place. The slogan of popular sovereignty helped the Democratic candidate, James Buchanan, to win a victory, despite daily evidence from Kansas that the doctrine was unworkable, but more significant was the remarkable Republican showing. With the main plank in its platform pledging the nonextension of slavery into the territories, this party rolled up a popular vote *only half a million less* than that of its opponent. The Democrats won because they retained a semblance of national organization with northern and southern wings, but the Republicans were pressing at their heels, and any split in the former would open the way of the new party to the presidency.

This division began when the Supreme Court, in the spring of 1857, handed down its momentous decision in the case of *Dred Scott v. Sandford*. Dred Scott was a Negro slave who had been taken by his owner into the free state of Illinois, then into the free territory of Minnesota, and finally to the slave state of Missouri, where he was sold to a New York abolitionist named John Sandford. Sandford then arranged for Scott to sue for his freedom on the grounds that his residence in Illinois and Minnesota freed him from slavery. When the case finally reached the Supreme Court the justices needed to answer only one question: Did the Constitution give them jurisdiction? If Dred Scott was a citizen of Missouri it did, for Sandford lived in New York and the Court could settle cases rising between citizens of different states. Hence the justices asked themselves, is Dred Scott a citizen?

They answered, in a decision written by Chief Justice Roger Taney, that he was not, and they advanced two reasons to prove their point. First, they said, he is not a citizen because he is a Negro, and they carefully examined the state laws in force when the Constitution was adopted to show that the framers did not intend to vest citizenship in men of color. Second, they went on, Scott is not a citizen because he is a slave. He is still in bondage because his residence in Illinois did not make him free; his return to Missouri forced the Court to determine his status on the basis of that state's laws and these held that temporary residence in a free state did not release a Negro from servitude. Nor did Scott's residence in Minnesota free him from slavery. For Minnesota was not legally a free territory, the Court decided; the Missouri Compromise forbidding slavery there violated the clause of the Constitution that prevented the national government from depriving any person of his property without due process of law. Slaves were property, and Congress had no right to interfere with their free use. Hence the Missouri Compromise was unconstitutional, and Congress could not prohibit slavery in any territory.

The Dred Scott case profoundly affected both political parties. The Republicans were hard hit, for they had promised the voters to ban slavery from the territories by congressional action, and now the Court said that to do so was illegal. They shouted futilely against the prejudice of the seven Democratic judges on the bench, and insisted in vain that the section of the decision dealing with the Missouri Compromise was mere obiter dictum—the opinion of the Court only—and not legally binding. These protests meant nothing, for a Democratic president sat in the White House, ready to enforce a decision dear to the hearts of his southern constituents. The Republicans could snatch their only solace from the support promised them by the rising tide of northern indignation. Abraham Lincoln expressed the fears of many when he pictured a southern conspiracy under way against the North. He compared this to the building of a log house. Douglas cut one log with popular sovereignty, Taney another with his Dred Scott decision, and when they were brought together they fitted perfectly. Lincoln warned that the next step would be to extend slavery over all the northern states. This made sense to the Northerners, and thousands who had formerly shied from such radicals as the Republicans now flocked into the party's ranks.

The Democrats suffered more than the Republicans, for the Dred Scott case split their party in two. Elated Southerners swung solidly behind a decision that satisfied their wildest hopes, but Northerners were unwilling to follow. They could stay within the party so long as its platform advocated popular sovereignty; their own champion was the author of that solacing doctrine which allowed them to believe they were supporting democracy rather than slavery. But to follow the southern Democrats in accepting the implications of the Dred Scott decision seemed like treason to their section. They hesitated, not knowing which way to turn, while they watched Stephen A. Douglas for their cue. Could he find some means of reconciling the new decision with his older doctrine? If he could, they would still cling to the hope of compromise and vote Democratic. If he could not, their sectional loyalties would transcend their party ties. On the broad shoulders of the Little Giant rested the fate of the northern Democrats, and of the Union as well.

Douglas realized the importance of his decision and delayed as long as possible, but he was finally pinned down by Abraham Lincoln during the summer of 1858. The two men were candidates for the senatorship from Illinois and had agreed to stump the state holding seven debates where they could exchange their views. Lincoln knew that if Douglas publicly supported the Dred Scott decision, he would lose northern support; if he rejected the doctrine and clung to popular sovereignty, the southern Democrats would desert him. His proddings finally forced Douglas to answer the all-important question during their debate at Freeport, and Douglas' solution came to be known as the "Freeport doctrine." Slavery, he said, cannot exist without the protection of local police regulations. A local legislature could keep the institution out of any territory by refusing to enact a black code. Popular sovereignty was still possible, despite the dictum of the Court.

The enunciation of the Freeport doctrine had two important results. It assured Douglas' re-election to the Senate, for northern Democrats welcomed his stand as drowning men would welcome a leaking lifeboat. They could still follow a middle road between the Republicans and the Dred Scott Democrats, still keep their southern trade—for many were merchants who feared blacklisting by planters if they swung completely against the South—still hope to avoid civil war. They threw themselves behind Douglas with the enthusiasm of desperation and returned him triumphantly to Washington. But the second result was more far-reaching, for the Freeport doctrine split the Democratic party in two. Southerners turned as a man against this traitor who would snatch away territory given the South by the Supreme Court; just as the North had done four years before, they compared him with Benedict Arnold and Judas Iscariot. The Little Giant, who had been the Democrats' favored candidate for the presidency, found himself on the eve of the election deserted by one whole wing of the party.

The extent of this division was shown when the Democrats assembled at Charleston in the spring of 1860. Southern fire-eaters made it clear that they would have nothing less than a complete endorsement of the Dred Scott decision, a positive platform assertion that slavery was bene-

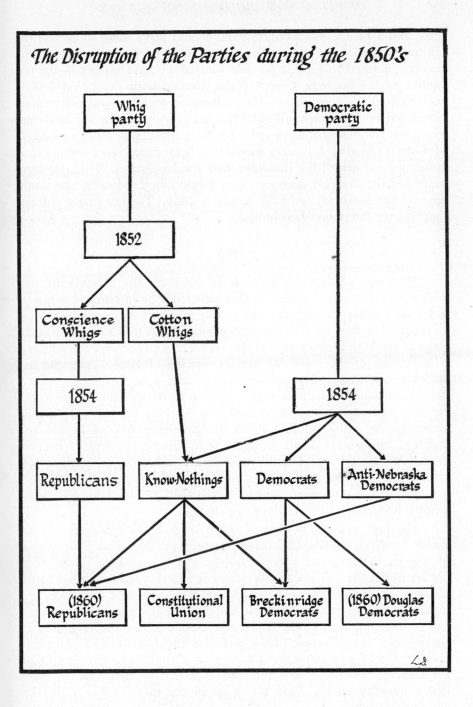

The Disruption of the Parties during the 1850's

ficial, and a pledge that Congress would enact slave codes to protect the institution in the territories. When Douglas' supporters, who were in the majority, refused to go this far and adopted a "leave slavery in the territories to the Supreme Court" plank, the southern delegation stalked angrily from the convention. They adjourned to Richmond, where they nominated John C. Breckinridge of Kentucky on a platform urging slavery extension, congressional slave codes for the territories, and the annexation of Cuba. Douglas' followers meanwhile held their own convention at Baltimore and named the Illinoisan their standard-bearer. Their platform supported the Freeport doctrine. Two Democratic candidates, one southern and one northern, faced the nation in 1860. The last major political link between the sections was broken.

1860

Here was an opportunity made to order for the Republicans, and their enthusiasm was boundless as they gathered at an improvised Wigwam at Chicago in May, 1860. Yet with victory in sight they were wise enough to realize that they must choose a moderate candidate who could win the votes of northern Democrats. For this reason they passed over the acknowledged leader of the party, William H. Seward of New York, who had talked of an "irrepressible conflict" and "a higher law than the Constitution," and nominated the relatively obscure Abraham Lincoln. Lincoln's speeches against slavery were as radical as Seward's but less well known; moreover, he could probably swing the native-son vote of Illinois and Indiana, while his romantic struggle from frontier poverty to national prominence would appeal to the democratic North. Swayed by these considerations, and by cheering galleries carefully packed with Lincoln supporters, the convention named this awkward Illinois lawyer to represent the Republican party in the crucial election.

The party's platform showed the wisdom of its managers and the extent to which the Republicans represented the North and Northwest. No longer did they seek votes simply by pledging to keep slavery from the territories; to this plank they added others that would appeal to the materialistic tendencies of Northerners. The promised the Northeast higher tariffs "to encourage the development of the industrial interests," and a liberal naturalization policy that would attract the migration of cheap labor from Europe. They promised the Northwest a homestead law that would give 160 acres of land to each settler, and government aid for a Pacific railroad. The Republicans were serving notice on the South that a minority section could no longer dictate to the majority on vital economic questions.

The division bred by the slavery controversy did not end even with these three candidates in the field. There remained a group of men who still clung to the hope of union through compromise—older conservative Whigs or Know-Nothings who believed that secession could be avoided only by ignoring the raging political storm and mouthing patriotic platitudes. They met at Baltimore in May, formed a Constitutional Union party, and nominated a Southerner, John Bell of Tennessee, for the presidency, and a Northerner, Edward Everett of Massachusetts, for the vice-presidency. Their platform recognized "no political principle other than the Constitution of the country, the union of the states, and the enforcement of the law"—meaningless phrases designed to attract voters who still lived in a former age of appeasement.

The contest between these four parties in the election of 1860 was exciting, but its outcome was never in doubt, for the people of eighteen populous free states were arrayed against fifteen thinly settled slave states. The extremists in eleven of the southern states, drowning out the considerable unionist minority, voted for Breckinridge; seventeen of the northern states cast their electoral ballots for Lincoln; the border state of Missouri supported Douglas; Virginia, Tennessee, and Kentucky favored Bell; and New Jersey divided its ballots between Douglas and Lincoln. Lincoln's popular vote of 1,666,452 was a million less than that polled by his three rivals—only about 40 per cent of the people voted for the successful candidate—but his majority in the electoral college was 180 to 123. More significant was the fact that both sections spoke against compromise, for the combined vote for the extremists—Lincoln and Breckinridge—was 2,716,233, against 1,965,331 cast for the compromisers, Douglas and Bell. The last political tie was severed and all the nation watched with bated breath the reaction of the South to a "Black Republican" in the White House.

XII

CIVIL WAR 1860–1865

Southern moderates knew in 1860 that Lincoln's election did not justify secession. The President was no fire-eating abolitionist bent on freeing the slaves; instead, he repeatedly promised to protect the southern institutions and even favored a constitutional amendment guaranteeing federal noninterference with slavery in states where it already existed. Thoughtful Southerners were aware, too, that even if he wished to act, his hands were tied. Sixty per cent of the votes cast were against him in 1860; even in the North only five out of every nine men cast their ballots for Lincoln. Democrats controlled the new Congress, with a majority of eight in the Senate and twenty-one in the House, and the Supreme Court was still dominated by the seven justices who penned the decision in the case of Dred Scott. Clearly the people had endorsed no radical program at the polls, and Republicans were not in a position to impose one.

Moreover, these moderates saw that secession would not solve their section's problems. Southerners might complain that abolitionists made unpleasant countrymen, that they flooded the South with antislave propaganda, and that they menaced property by conducting the Underground Railroad. But the Northerners would be equally unpleasant as neighbors, an international boundary could not discourage propaganda as efficiently as the federal postmaster, and slaves could escape to a free United States easier than to a free Canada. Secession would not open the federal territories to slavery, for the Dred Scott decision had already done that; instead, they would be left in the hands of hostile Northerners, who would certainly make them free. Nor would secession forestall interference with slavery in the southern states. So long as the South remained in the Union, her slaves could be freed only by constitutional amendment; by leaving she opened the one door through which her institutions could be attacked: military conquest and emancipation as the aftermath of war. From every point of view, the moderates insisted that the South stood to gain rather than lose by accepting the election returns quietly.

238

THE BREAKDOWN OF THE DEMOCRATIC PROCESS

But the time for sober argument and calm reason had passed. A generation of conflict had left the nation alert and excited; on both sides of Mason and Dixon's line nerves were frayed and patience was short. Each contestant was sustained by a deep emotional conviction. Southerners believed slavery to be a divine institution beneficial to both whites and blacks and argued sincerely through the 1850's that the slave trade should be reopened to bring the blessings of civilization to the African Negroes. Northerners thought of human bondage as a sin against freedom and religion, and formed mobs to rescue runaway slaves from their federal captors or enacted "personal liberty laws" that penalized those who aided government officials in their unpopular task. Each side felt its cause to be just, and thoroughly misunderstood the other. Southerners were told by their papers that every Yankee hated them from birth, that no Northerner would rest easy until they had all been annihilated, and that Lincoln's election predestined the South to Negro rule. "It makes little difference whether we are governed by a gentleman or ruled by a baboon," wrote one editor, "but with Lincoln comes something worse, . . . the daring and reckless leader of the abolitionists." Emotional ranting and strained nerves ruled public opinion, not dispassionate reason.

Yet the South would never have seceded had not its people grown tired of the struggle to maintain their peculiar institution as a minority, for secession held little hope of better times. Certainly their leaders who preached disunion had no solution to the southern problem in mind, nor was one possible. So long as slavery bound the section to a system of staple-crop plantation agriculture, economic nationalism—which was really what the people wanted—could never be attained. Disunion would mean only that they would remain at the mercy of northern capitalists and British traders. Yet to stay within the United States promised little more. For years Southerners had watched the economic scales swing gradually against them. They had seen the North grow steadily in population and industrial might, win the West to its fold, and fatten on foreign immigration, while their own numbers and wealth increased but slowly. True, this economic superiority was not yet translated into politics; the slave states still had low tariffs and other laws designed to aid agriculture. But the election of Lincoln showed them the handwriting on the wall. The majority North would soon control the nation and pass laws to benefit industry: protective tariffs, a homestead act, federal aid to railroads. This the South could not risk, for the slave system was so uneconomical that the plantations could show a profit only when they were protected by the most favorable legislation. A reopened slave trade,

THE YEAR 1860: A COMPARISON

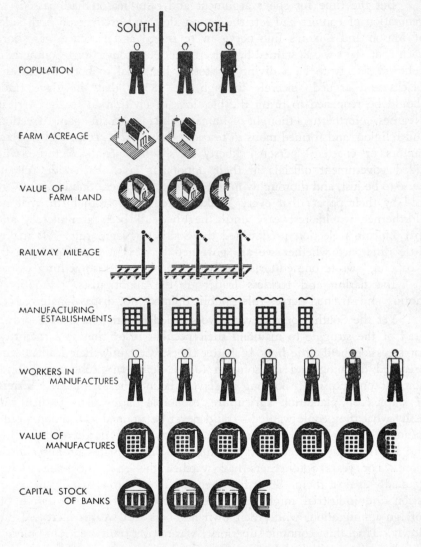

From Hacker, Modley, and Taylor, *The United States: A Graphic History,* Modern Age Books, Inc. PICTOGRAPH CORP.

which would decrease the planters' heavy investment in labor (and many extreme Southerners advocated this in the 1850's), alone held any hope of improvement, and no such step was possible. Better to get out now than wait for the hard times that were bound to come.

South Carolina, where the tradition of rebellion was strong and the aristocracy deeply entrenched (half the planters of the South who owned two hundred or more slaves lived there), acted first. On December 20, 1860, a convention meeting at Charleston unanimously decided that the ties binding the state to the Union were dissolved. Within six weeks the rest of the states bordering the Gulf of Mexico followed, with Texas the last to take the fateful step on February 1, 1861. Their delegates, meeting at Montgomery, Alabama, a few days later to form the Confederate States of America, chose Jefferson Davis of Mississippi president and Alexander H. Stephens of Georgia vice-president, and adopted a constitution strangely reminiscent of the document against which they rebelled. The sectional dispute was reflected in clauses forbidding protective tariffs and appropriations for internal improvements, guaranteeing slavery in the territories, and assuring slaveholders the right to take their property anywhere, while weaknesses in the federal structure were remedied by provisions restricting the president to a single six-year term and allowing cabinet members to sit in congress. This frame of government, adopted by the seven Confederate states, went into effect in April, 1861.

Secession brought Lincoln face to face with the most important problem ever confronting a President of the United States. Should he coerce the recalcitrant states and force their return to the Union? Should he accept the advice of many who believed the South was bluffing and would return home if a few concessions were made? Should he follow the influential New York *Tribune,* which argued that secession was good riddance and allow the "wayward sisters to depart in peace"? The answer must be his own, for Congress was not in session and a divided northern opinion gave him no clue. He summed up the result of long hours of thought in his inaugural address, when he said, "Physically speaking, we cannot separate." Lincoln knew that with the best will in the world a peaceful settlement of the many conflicts between the two governments was impossible—the allocation of the national debt, the division of the territories, the handling of fugitive slaves, the navigation of the Mississippi —and he knew that that good will was lacking. Moreover, he realized the danger of secession: if disgruntled minorities were allowed to leave the Union peacefully, the United States would be reduced to a Balkan-like mass of struggling malcontents. He must restore the nation to save the nation, even though this meant war.

For the President saw that secession was revolution. It was Horace Greeley's confusion on this point that led him to acquiesce in it, and it was Lincoln's clear understanding of majority rule that led him to reject it. Democratic theory had never put forward the right of revolution other than as an extreme resort where a process of free elections had ceased to exist. Secessionists had never been denied the democratic corrective of free elections. They retained within the Union the great fundamental right of the minority—the right to become a majority. Not the Republican party but economic forces and geographic factors made the South a political minority. Any other assumption was a refusal to accept reality. Secessionists confronted a stubborn fact that no political theory could hope to resolve. Independence for the South would not free cotton capitalism from dependence on northern creditors or, alternately, from subservience to English capitalism.

Lincoln's decision was a milepost in federal-state relations. Jackson had established the supremacy of the federal government over a single state; Lincoln was determined to coerce a whole section of the American people, bound together by common economic and ideological interests. Constitutional necessity forced the Southerners to pay lip service to "state rights" and to base secession on the legal right of sovereign states to withdraw peacefully from a compact that no longer pleased them, but what really concerned them was "southern rights," or the freedom of one section of the nation to go its own way when its interests dictated separation. Lincoln must decide whether the United States, or the sections, should be supreme. This was the issue over which the Civil War was fought.

OPENING OF HOSTILITIES

Having made up his mind to use force, Lincoln knew that he must act cautiously to keep the eight slave states still within the Union from joining the Confederacy. Only by goading the South into firing the first shot could the North retain the loyalty of these border states. The opportunity was provided by Fort Sumter, a federal outpost in Charleston Harbor, which needed supplies for its army garrison. The Confederates would certainly attack any relief expedition. Lincoln ordered a small supply fleet south on April 6, and President Davis, knowing that the hour of decision had arrived, countered by commanding the Charleston shore batteries to prevent the re-enforcements from landing. At 4:30 on the morning of April 12, as the Union ships sailed into the harbor, a Confederate battery sent the first shot of the Civil War crashing against the fort's walls. For a day the bombardment went on, as Charleston's elite flocked to the waterfront to watch, but on April 14 Sumter's commander bowed to his superior opponents and surrendered. The war had begun.

The bombardment of Fort Sumter ended indecision on both sides. The Confederacy was already united, for soon after secession the moderates had recognized the futility of opposition and cast their lot with the majority. Indignation now swept the North into line; Pierce and Buchanan announced they would support Lincoln, and Douglas, in a ringing Chicago speech, declared that "there can be no neutrals in this war; only patriots or traitors." From cities and farms, men flocked to recruiting stations to answer the President's call for seventy-five thousand volunteers. The first shot also marvelously cleared the air in the border states, which were forced to choose between defending or attacking the Confederacy. Virginia, North Carolina, Tennessee, and Arkansas joined the South at once; Delaware, Maryland, and Missouri decided to stay within the Union. Only Kentucky hesitated, but when Lincoln maneuvered Confederate troops into invading her soil she swung to the North and within a year was safely in the Union camp. The mountainous regions of northwestern Virginia belatedly followed this same course when in 1863 they split from their native state and entered the United States as a new state of West Virginia. The decision was clear in none of these border states; they gave troops to both sides and fought what was truly a brothers' war.

As North and South squared away for the combat during that spring and summer of 1861 both were confident of victory. The North had the power. Its nineteen million people, plus another two and a half million from the border states, far overbalanced the five and a half million whites in the eleven seceded states. Within its borders were concentrated 92 per cent of the nation's industries and virtually all of the known deposits of iron, coal, copper, and other essential metals; its factories had only to expand to supply the guns and munitions needed for victory. Two thirds of the country's railroad mileage was available for the use of Union troops and supplies. Even the army and navy were safe in northern hands, for the sixteen thousand men in the army, the crews of the ninety ships in the navy, and the commanders of most of the arsenals remained loyal. With this overwhelming strength, and the initial advantage of a well-trained force ready for immediate combat, Northerners believed the result foreordained.

The South was just as confident. The North might have the population, but everyone knew that "any Southerner could lick five Yankees." The North might have the industries, but King Cotton would offset that difference, for all Europe would be the South's arsenal in return for the precious fibers which the Confederacy alone could produce. The North might have the army, but Southerners would be fighting within interior lines, where they could easily shift their forces to meet any attack. But most important of all was the spirit of the Confederacy. They were not fighting for slavery or the right of secession; they were repelling an invader who threatened the sanctity of their homes, the basis of their society, and the supremacy of their race. Few nations in history had quelled rebellions when such motives inspired the rebels; Southerners had only to point to the success of the thirteen American colonies, the Latin-American republics, and the Netherlands. Little wonder that even the European observers who favored the North gloomily predicted the end of the republic.

Yet their reckonings failed to recognize the one thing that finally turned the scales against the Confederacy. This was the steadfast devotion of the American people to the Union. They saw that defeat would end not only their republic but the world's greatest experiment in democracy. Here was a cause worth fighting—or dying—for. Abraham Lincoln felt this as did no other man, and his finest contribution to victory was his unfaltering conviction that government by the people should not perish. His dignified speeches, reaching classical heights in the Gettysburg Address, convinced Americans that the Union and popular rule were inseparable, and that defeat meant the triumph of tyranny over democracy everywhere. Their devotion to this ideal, more than any other thing, sustained them during the four trying years needed for victory.

Overconfidence bred of these sentiments almost cost the North the war. General Winfield Scott, an experienced leader whose keen mind belied his years, was in command, and he urged that the seventy-five thousand green volunteers who responded to Lincoln's call be given some training before they smelled powder. But all the nation was shouting "On to Richmond!" in the belief that the fall of this city, which became the Confederate capital when Virginia entered the Confederacy, would end southern resistance. Lincoln felt this pressure, and on July 16, 1861, he ordered the thirty-two thousand recruits who had reached Washington to march south under General Irvin McDowell. They moved slowly, for the undisciplined soldiers dropped from the ranks to pick berries, and the roads were clogged with Washington socialites on their way to watch the sport; but by July 21 the army reached Bull Run, near Manassas, where an equal number of raw Confederate troops commanded by General Pierre G. T. Beauregard awaited it. The two forces clashed at once, using tactics approved at the time: the Southerners standing in a double line, the Northerners moving forward two thousand at a time in two lines led by their captains and with other officers in the rear to drive on stragglers, until one army or the other gave way or the soldiers met in hand combat with clubbed guns. All day long the battle seesawed back and forth until three o'clock, when the arrival of re-enforcements encouraged the Southerners to charge. Within an hour the Union forces were in panic-stricken retreat. Only the fact that the southern army was, according to one of its commanders, "more disorganized by victory than that of the United States by defeat," saved Washington from capture in the first month of the war.

The battle of Bull Run taught the North that careful preparation, rather than tempestuous action, was necessary. As a result the Union leaders took three important steps: they began their long search for a capable leader, revised the method of raising troops, and planned the strategic moves needed to defeat the Confederacy. The leader selected was General George B. McClellan, a competent but overcautious officer who soon restored order from the chaos left by Bull Run. To provide him with men, Congress in July, 1861, approved an army of half a million volunteers enlisted for three years, rather than for the three-month term required of the first troops. The response was so enthusiastic that by the following spring McClellan was busy whipping into shape six hundred thousand new troops. Geography dictated the plan of campaign, which meant three theaters of war: one on the sea, where northern tactics obviously called for a blockade to keep out supplies and prevent cotton shipments from influencing European diplomacy; one in the east, where the capture of Richmond was the objective; and one west of the Appalachians, where a Union army could cut down the Mississippi to divide the Confederacy, then swing east around the spur of the mountains into Georgia. Three years were needed before men, supplies, and leaders to carry out this campaign were found.

Little was done during the remainder of 1861. McClellan drilled his troops so relentlessly for month after month that "All quiet along the Potomac" became a national jest. Northerners, thirsting for a quick victory, could not realize that delay was the best policy until their superior resources were mobilized for an offensive war. The brilliant Confederate commander, General Robert E. Lee of Virginia, wanted to strike at once before northern power could reach its full strength; he was held back, however, by President Davis, who believed in a defensive policy, and by Southerners who wanted their homes well guarded. So both sides waited, one restrained by proper strategy and a cautious general, the other by a meddling president and a timid public.

Only on the sea were there any significant developments during the winter and spring of 1861–1862. Lincoln proclaimed the entire southern coast under blockade in April, 1861, but for six months this blockade meant little because the ninety federal ships could make only a pretense of guarding a coast line three thousand miles long. The vigorous efforts of Gideon Welles of Connecticut, Secretary of the Navy, gradually improved the situation. Ships of every sort were acquired—steamers, clipper ships, side-wheelers, tugboats, and even ferryboats—and sent out to guard southern ports. At the same time amphibious expeditions captured strategic points that could serve as bases for the blockaders; by November, 1861, Cape Hatteras, which controlled the coastal waters of North Carolina, Ship Island, which commanded the entrance to New Orleans, and Port Royal in South Carolina were occupied by Union forces. During the winter, the capture of Roanoke Island, Newbern, and Beaufort brought the North Carolina coast under control, until the only important Confederate ports left open in that area were Wilmington and Charleston. Yet the coast line was too long to guard effectively and by the spring of 1862 speedy English-built blockade runners were regularly slipping through to Havana or Nassau, where they traded their cargoes of cotton for European armaments. Lee was adequately supplied with military stores in this way, but civilians felt the pinch by the spring of 1862, when medical supplies, tea, coffee, and other essentials first skyrocketed in price and then vanished from tradesmen's shelves.

So desperate was the South's plight that a dramatic attempt to break the blockade was made on March 8, 1862, when the *Merrimac* sailed against the ring of ships besieging Hampton Roads. This awkward-looking vessel, the first of the ironclads, had a low superstructure covered with plating that deflected cannon balls, ten cannon, and a heavy iron ram that could pierce the wooden sides of ordinary warships. Within a few hours the *Merrimac* sank one blockader, forced another to surrender, and was stopped from attacking a third only by darkness. But the southern triumph was brief, for that night another ironclad, the *Monitor,* steamed into Hampton Roads. Built hurriedly by the Union navy after it learned of the *Merrimac's* construction, this "tin can on a shingle" consisted of a flat armored deck surmounted by a revolving iron tower that mounted two heavy guns. The two ships met the next day to fight the first battle of ironclads in naval history, but neither was able to damage the other and the *Merrimac* finally withdrew, never to reappear. The engagement remade naval warfare by proving that wooden warships were obsolete, but the blockade still gripped the South.

This triumph did not satisfy the northern demand for Confederate blood. Rising to prominence in Washington during the winter was a group of "Radical Republicans" whose pointed criticism of Union strategy gained influence as inaction continued. Many were abolitionists who were interested less in preserving the Union than in punishing an insolent slave power; all disliked Lincoln for his calm insistence that slavery was not the principal issue at stake, and all despised McClellan, a Democrat whose delaying tactics seemed treasonable. Their clamor forced the President to name one of his loudest critics, Edwin M. Stanton of Pennsylvania, as Secretary of War in January, 1862, and to inaugurate a more vigorous policy. The resulting campaigns gave the North, if not victories, at least action.

GRANT AND McCLELLAN

The first success was gained in the West, and was due not to the weak and indecisive General Henry W. Halleck who commanded there, but to a comparatively unknown general named Ulysses S. Grant, who had graduated from West Point near the bottom of his class and had resigned from the army rather than face a court-martial for drunkenness. Having drifted through years of poverty which found him a store clerk when war broke out, Grant was now a brigadier general stationed at Cairo, Illinois. He knew that General Albert Sidney Johnston, who skillfully commanded the southern forces in the West, was hurriedly constructing defenses at Columbus on the Mississippi, Fort Henry on the Tennessee, and Fort Donelson on the Cumberland, defenses designed to protect the broad hundred-mile highway toward the heart of the Confederacy where the three rivers ran side by side. Grant wanted to attack before this road was blocked, and in January, 1862, Halleck gave his reluctant consent.

Fort Henry fell first on February 6, after a battering by a river gunboat flotilla, and Grant turned his army against Fort Donelson, fifteen miles away. A frontal assault failed and the Union force settled down to a siege, but the defenders were short of supplies and after losing a bitter woodland battle in which they failed to break the ring surrounding them, surrendered on February 16. The path was cleared for an invasion of the South, but Halleck, already overcautious, was now jealous of Grant, and he refused to allow the pursuit of Johnston's demoralized army. The Confederates had time to reassemble at Corinth before Grant took up the chase. By April 5 he was at Pittsburg Landing, where the Tennessee River turns sharply east just above the Mississippi border. His camp site that night was poorly selected, for the swollen river cut off retreat, and he neglected to throw up earthworks to guard the position. Johnston saw that he had caught Grant napping and attacked at dawn the next day, although the 60,000 Union troops outnumbered his own by 20,000. After twelve hours of bitter hand-to-hand fighting Grant still held his position, but he had lost 13,000 men to a Confederate loss of 11,000. General Johnston, however, had been mortally wounded, and although the Southerners fought valiantly for ten hours more the next day, northern re-enforcements turned the tide and they finally retreated to Corinth. Grant's army was too exhausted to pursue.

Halleck now took over the Union forces, swelled their numbers to 120,000 men, and in May started toward Corinth, where General Beauregard, then in command, waited with less than half of that number. Resistance to the giant Union army would have meant only unnecessary slaughter; hence Beauregard moved his men south and Corinth fell to the North without a struggle on May 30. This was an important victory, for Corinth was a vital railroad junction controlling the main east-west line between Richmond and Memphis, and the north-south route between Ohio and the Gulf. Its fall disrupted Confederate supply lines and seriously weakened resistance.

The eastern army, plagued by an overcautious leader and political meddling, enjoyed less success during 1862. McClellan planned to move his force to the tip of the York Peninsula, land under the protecting guns of the federal Fort Monroe, and march against Richmond, where he would join a smaller army that had come south from Washington. Before he could begin operations, popular pressure forced Lincoln to divide the eastern army into three branches with McClellan commanding the Army of the Potomac, McDowell a force protecting Washington, and John C. Frémont and Nathaniel P. Banks the remainder in western Virginia. Nevertheless, McClellan went ahead and by the end of April his 110,000 men were safely on the York Peninsula, where they faced 65,000 Confederates; McDowell was ready to start south from Washington with 40,000 more, and Frémont and Banks were prepared to move down the Shenandoah Valley with another 30,000. Lee saw that the defense of Richmond depended on checking one of these columns and disrupting the northern schedule. General "Stonewall" Jackson was assigned this task; his 17,000 "foot cavalry" swept up the Shenandoah Valley and fell first on Frémont, then on Banks, to win decisive victories. Panic paralyzed the capital, and McDowell was ordered to protect Washington rather than march south.

When McClellan heard that McDowell's force would not arrive, he was less than five miles from Richmond. Lee knew that the timid Union commander would be shaken by the news and that a sudden blow by an inferior force might dislodge him. He ordered Jackson south, and on June 25 the combined Confederate forces lashed at McClellan. There followed the famous "Seven Days' Battles" in which the outnumbered Southerners forced the Union army slowly back twenty miles to the protection of the gunboats at Fort Monroe. The northern commander was through with frontal attacks, and proposed moving south of the James River to cut off Richmond's railroad communication with the Confederacy, but the amateur strategists at Washington refused to listen to this sensible suggestion. Instead, he was ordered back to the Potomac, a stupid move that allowed Lee to turn swiftly against McDowell's army, now commanded by General John Pope, and soundly defeat it at the second battle of Bull Run on August 30, 1862.

ANTIETAM AND EMANCIPATION

Lee saw that the Union defenses were disorganized and that the time was ripe to strike into enemy territory west of Washington, thus cutting off the capital city. On September 5, 1862, he crossed the Potomac and took Frederick, where he paused to wait for Jackson's army, which was still in Virginia. McClellan saw his chance. Moving with none of his customary caution and ignoring the frantic orders of his Washington superiors to stay and defend the city, he threw his army west in a vain effort to drive between the two Confederate forces. He was just too late, for Jackson crossed the Potomac and joined Lee on September 16, 1862, but McClellan caught the Southerners jammed between the river and Antietam Creek, where Lee had no room to carry out his sweeping maneuvers. The battle of Antietam, which followed on September 17, was not decisive; the valiant Confederates held their ground and fought off a series of crushing attacks, but their losses were heavy. The next day McClellan's timidity reasserted itself, and instead of renewing the attack, which probably would have crushed Lee's army, he allowed it to escape to the safety of Virginia once more.

Although the battle of Antietam could be called a northern victory only by a stretch of the imagination, it gave the North its first glimmer of hope and profoundly affected the international situation. Through the dark summer of 1862 the succession of Union defeats convinced Europe that southern independence was inevitable and the democratic experiment in America at an end. England felt sure enough of this to send out two British-built cruisers, the *Florida* and the *Alabama*, to raid commerce under the Confederate flag. More serious was the fact that both the English and the French governments were on the point of extending recognition to the Confederacy—a step which would have lessened the efficiency of the blockade and probably involved the United States in a war with both these powers. This danger was brought home on September 7, 1862, when the French minister at Washington informed the Secretary of State that Napoleon III only waited England's approval to recognize the Confederate government, and that this would certainly follow the next Union defeat. Lincoln's task during the summer of 1862 was to forestall English action.

He knew that the people there were divided sharply into liberal and conservative factions. The conservatives openly favored the South; they included industrialists who coveted the rich, tariff-free markets of the Confederacy, shipowners who hungered for the carrying trade of the cotton states, and textile manufacturers who depended on southern cotton for their mills. Only a 50 per cent oversupply of cloth and raw materials at the start of the war had kept this group quiet, and its members would certainly demand recognition as soon as they unloaded their surpluses. The liberals were less sure of their own minds. They could not grow enthusiastic about the preservation of a distant union—instead, their humanitarian sympathies inclined them to favor uprisings against established governments—but they would favor the North if the war were transformed into a crusade against slavery. Lincoln knew that a proclamation freeing the southern slaves would pit liberals against conservatives in England, and that the liberals would be powerful enough to block recognition of the Confederacy.

Yet he must also consider domestic opinion. Emancipation would turn the friendly border states against the Union, but would satisfy a growing northern majority which asked, "Why restore the nation if slavery remains?" These were the imponderables that Lincoln had to weigh. His own purpose was clear:

My paramount object in this struggle is to save the Union, and it is not either to save or to destroy slavery. If I could save the Union without freeing any slave, I would do it; and if I could save it by freeing all the slaves I would do it; and if I could save it by freeing some and leaving others alone, I would also do that. What I do about slavery, and the colored race, I do because I believe it helps to save the Union; and what I forbear, I forbear because I do not believe it would help save the Union.

By the summer of 1862 he felt that he must act; northern antislavery sentiment was mounting and cotton shortages were swinging English opinion toward recognition. "The moment has come," he said, "when I feel that slavery must die that the nation might live." On July 22, 1862, he read his Cabinet a draft of a proclamation freeing all slaves in rebel territory. Seward, the Secretary of State, pointed out that this would be interpreted as a gasp of despair and urged silence until after a northern victory. Lincoln decided to wait.

The battle of Antietam gave him his opportunity. Five days later, on September 22, 1862, he issued his Emancipation Proclamation, declaring that all slaves in any territory or state then in rebellion against the United States were to be forever free after January 1, 1863. This marvelously cleared the air at home and abroad. Southerners were probably stirred to greater effort by what seemed an invitation to the slaves to rise against their masters, but Northerners now had a double incentive to fight and warmed to their task. In England the proclamation ended all talk of recognition, and in November the Cabinet firmly rejected a proposal from Napoleon III that France, Russia, and England jointly propose an armistice and the lifting of the blockade. Lincoln's inspired timing of emancipation carried the nation through the most serious diplomatic crisis of the war.

The world looked brighter to the harried President that October, with the foreign danger past, Lee retreating up the Shenandoah Valley, and a Confederate force that had invaded Kentucky hastily retiring after a defeat at Perryville. But more dark days were just ahead. Public pressure forced him to replace the cautious McClellan with the incompetent General Ambrose E. Burnside, who was distinguished more for his flowing side whiskers than for his military ability. Burnside set out after Lee and Jackson, caught them on December 13, 1862, in the wooded heights above Fredericksburg, and rashly threw his forces against the strong Confederate position. Six times the gallant soldiers surged across an open plain to meet a withering fire that left 7,000 of their number dead before Burnside ordered a retreat. That was his last mistake, but General Joseph Hooker, who replaced him, did little better. Late in April, 1863, he led his 130,000 troops against Lee's 62,000 Confederates who still waited at Fredericksburg. Instead of risking a frontal attack, he tried to cross the Rappahannock at Chancellorsville, but Lee, who was waiting there with 10,000 men, for three days thrust and parried so skillfully that the unwieldy Union force was paralyzed. Finally, when "Stonewall" Jackson led his cavalry in a brilliant fourteen-mile sweep across the entire Union front, Hooker accepted defeat and retired across the river. Southern joy was dimmed only by the death of Jackson, who fell mortally wounded.

These two decisive victories at Fredericksburg and Chancellorsville convinced Lee that he should take the offensive again. He moved swiftly, marching his 75,000 men through the Shenandoah Valley, across the Potomac below Harpers Ferry, and by the end of June was safely on Pennsylvania soil. In this new crisis the North tried swapping leaders in the middle of an avalanche once more, and set the reliable General George Meade with 100,000 troops on Lee's trail. Both generals planned to take up defensive positions and await attack, but a chance skirmish between two advance corps at the little town of Gettysburg upset these plans. Meade rushed his main force there at once, taking up a strong position on a curving limestone hill known as Cemetery Ridge; Lee followed and occupied the parallel Seminary Ridge three quarters of a mile away. Fighting began on July 1 and went on for three days, with each army trying to turn the other's flank. On the afternoon of July 3 Lee resolved on a desperate frontal attack. Ten thousand men under General George F. Pickett stormed directly at the Union center, and although the force of their charge carried them to the top of Cemetery Ridge, they were beaten back with appalling losses. When this gamble failed, Lee knew that his chance for victory was gone, and on July 4 he started his retreat to Confederate soil. Forty per cent of his troops were killed or wounded, but Meade had lost 30 per cent of his command and was in no mood to pursue. The battle of Gettysburg saved the North from invasion and ended all fighting in the East until the last year of the war.

THE TIDE TURNS

These spectacular campaigns between Richmond and Gettysburg accomplished little except to divert the attention of both peoples from the more important western theater of war. There unsung Union leaders sensed for the first time the principles of modern warfare and developed a strategy that was far more effective than all Lee's brilliant maneuvering in the East. They wasted no time in useless attempts to capture the enemy capital as European practice dictated. Instead, they struck directly at the enemy's transportation routes, for they knew that modern armies depended on railroads for their supplies and that severed communications would mean confusion and eventual surrender. This was the purpose of the western campaigns that began in 1863 and brought the Confederacy to its knees a year later.

Corinth, commanding the main railroad east from Memphis, was already in Union hands. New Orleans had fallen to a naval force in 1862 and northern gunboats patrolled much of the Mississippi, but two gaps remained. One was at Vicksburg, a powerful fortress on the high banks of the Mississippi, through which western goods could flow toward the Confederate armies. The other was at Chattanooga, where supplies could be sent east to Richmond or south to Atlanta, Charleston, or Savannah. These were the two objectives of the western armies in 1863 and their fall presaged the collapse of the Confederacy.

Grant turned against Vicksburg. In April, 1863, he moved 20,000 men down the Mississippi by water, marched around the Confederate fortress by landing on the west bank of the river, then recrossed and started inland. He captured the railway junction at Jackson, Mississippi, before turning west to engage the defenders of Vicksburg, who had sallied forth to cut his nonexistent communication lines. In a series of bitter engagements they were driven back to their fort and placed under siege, with Grant's army on their east and Union gunboats guarding the river.

From May 22 to July 3 they held on, but when their supplies ran out they had no choice but surrender. A week later a steamboat descended from St. Louis to New Orleans and Lincoln observed with satisfaction that "the Father of Waters again goes unvexed to the sea." The Confederacy was cut in half; no longer could western goods supply Lee's armies.

Chattanooga proved easier to take than to hold. Its capture was entrusted to General William S. Rosecrans, commander of the Army of Eastern Tennessee, who outmaneuvered his outnumbered opponents and marched unmolested into the city on September 9, 1863. The Confederate leader, General Braxton Bragg, refused to give up, and ten days later, after collecting re-enforcements, threw his now numerically superior force against Rosecrans, who elected to defend a steep hill called Missionary Ridge at Chickamauga just south of Chattanooga. The result was decisive; the Union troops were thrown back into Chattanooga and would have suffered a complete rout but for the stubborn resistance of General George H. Thomas, whose refusal to yield the left flank won him the title of "the Rock of Chickamauga." There the troops were penned in by Bragg, with only a single wagon road for supplies and in grave danger of starvation. In this emergency the inept Rosecrans was succeeded by General Thomas, and Grant was given supreme command in the West. A new supply road was immediately cut, new troops were rushed in by rail, and by November 24 Grant was ready to attack. The battle of Chattanooga was a complete Union victory; by nightfall Bragg's men were in full retreat from the wooded ridges across the Tennessee and the road to Savannah lay open to the northern armies.

During that winter of 1863–1864 the North prepared for the kill by sifting out the last of its incompetent commanders. By March, 1864, Grant was in the East in supreme command of all the Union forces, Thomas was in control of Rosecrans' Tennessee army, and Grant's former troops were under General William T. Sherman, who had distinguished himself in the western campaigns. In May they began to move: Thomas, with 75,000 troops, was left to hold the West; Grant undertook to outmatch Lee with the Army of the Potomac; and Sherman was entrusted with the march from Chattanooga to the sea.

Sherman set out in May, 1864, with 100,000 men, following the railroad line to Atlanta and fighting periodic engagements with a smaller Confederate force under General Joe E. Johnston. On September 2, 1864, he entered Atlanta. General John B. Hood, who replaced Johnston as southern commander at this point, decided to strike at Sherman's long communication lines in eastern Tennessee and moved suddenly west. Instead of pursuing, the Union commander decided on an audacious move: to cut loose from his base of supplies and march across Georgia with 62,000 men, living off the country as he went. Thus began the famous "march to the sea" that ended on December 10, 1864, when he emerged at Savannah. Laid bare behind him was a swath three hundred miles long and sixty wide; its crops and livestock destroyed, its cotton gins, mills, and railroads ruined beyond repair. Sherman, who sincerely believed that "war is hell," was trying to convince the South that further resistance was useless. While he was still at Savannah, dispatches from the West brought the cheering news that Hood's army had been beaten and scattered by Thomas at the battle of Nashville on December 15–16. By the dawn of the new year Confederate resistance was confined to the strip of coast where Grant and Lee staged their epic battles.

There the Union forces had been less successful during 1864. Grant started for Richmond in May, confident that his 120,000 troops could crush the 65,000 Confederates opposing him. Lee elected to meet him in a tangled morass south of the Rapidan, where Grant's large army would be handicapped by the dense forest. The battle of the Wilderness lasted two days (May 5–7) and cost the North 18,000 men before Grant decided that Lee could not be dislodged. He then tried to turn the Confederate left flank, but his wily opponent slipped ahead once more and awaited him at Spotsylvania Court House. For five days the two armies fought bitterly (May 8–12), using trenches for the first time in modern warfare and throwing wave after wave of troops into hand-to-hand conflict. Grant's losses were staggering—31,000 men in that one battle—but he knew that his reserves were limitless and on May 11 sent word to Washington, "I propose to fight it out along this line if it takes all summer." Once more he swung to the left, once more Lee slipped in ahead of him, digging hurried trenches and awaiting the waves of Union troops who swarmed forward with names and addresses pinned to their backs so that their corpses could be identified. For a month this slaughter went on. When Grant finally reached the Chickahominy his losses amounted to 55,000 men to Lee's 30,000.

By this time the Union commander saw that this battering at the Confederate "living screen" was too costly and decided to change his tactics. On June 12 he quietly moved his army to a new base on the south side of the James and started west toward Petersburg to cut Richmond's communications. Grant carried out this maneuver so skillfully that for a time Lee did not know where he was; but before Petersburg was taken the Confederates slid smoothly in and threw up entrenchments. Three assaults on their strong position (June 15–18) cost the North 8,000 men and Grant decided to lay siege, knowing that this would bottle up Lee and leave Sherman free to continue his conquest of the lower South. There the two forces camped for nine months.

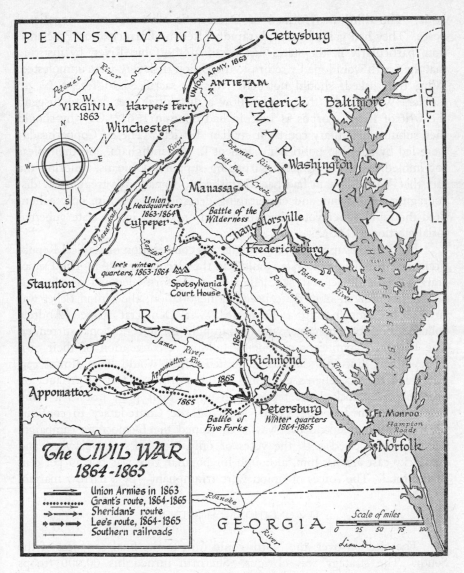

PENNSYLVANIA •Gettysburg

ANTIETAM
W. VIRGINIA Harper's Ferry •Frederick Baltimore
1863
Winchester
Washington
Manassas•
Union
Headquarters Battle of the
1863-1864 Wilderness
Culpeper Chancellorsville
•Fredericksburg
Lee's winter
quarters, 1863-1864
Staunton Spotsylvania
Court House

V   I   R   G   I   N   I   A

Richmond

Appomattox

Petersburg Ft. Monroe
Battle of Winter quarters Hampton
Five Forks 1864-1865 Roads
Norfolk

The CIVIL WAR
1864-1865

Union Armies in 1863
Grant's route, 1864-1865
Sheridan's route
Lee's route, 1864-1865
Southern railroads

GEORGIA Scale of miles
0   25   50   75   100

While they waited, the election of 1864 took place. Three factions, roughly representing northern opinion at this stage of the war, took part. One, headed by Lincoln, was composed of Republicans and War Democrats organized into the Union party. Another, made up of Radical Republicans such as Benjamin Wade and Henry W. Davis, was bent on wresting control of the army and the nation from Lincoln's moderates. Their principal strength was in Congress, where their Committee on the Conduct of the War had mercilessly flayed administration policies since

1862. The third was formed of Democratic advocates of a negotiated peace. They had gained strength rapidly after the Emancipation Proclamation, particularly in the states just north of the Ohio River, by insisting that the South would gladly return to the Union if slavery were unmolested. Why, they asked, should northern lives be sacrificed to free a Negro rabble? Why should the people allow a dictatorial president to suspend the writ of habeas corpus as Lincoln had done in 1861? Or why should they submit to military courts in civilian districts? These "Copperheads" were led by an Ohio politician, Clement L. Vallandigham, and their pleas for immediate peace attracted surprising support. Ohioans, ignoring the fact that Vallandigham had been banished to Canada for treasonably discouraging enlistments and encouraging desertions, gave him only a hundred thousand fewer votes than his Union opponent in the state gubernatorial election of 1863.

For a time it appeared that an amazing combination of Radical Republicans and Pacifist Democrats would win the election of 1864. The Democrats nominated General McClellan on a platform denouncing the war and calling for an immediate peace by negotiation; the Union ticket was headed by Lincoln and a Tennessee War Democrat named Andrew Johnson, both of whom were pledged to fight for unconditional surrender. The Radical Republicans considered holding a convention of their own to repudiate Lincoln's candidacy—a step which would have almost certainly led to McClellan's election—but Sherman's victory at Atlanta on September 2 knocked the props from under their plot, just as a frank statement from Jefferson Davis, pledging the Confederacy to continue the war until independence was won, ruined the Democratic campaign. Lincoln was elected with the votes of only New Jersey, Delaware, and Kentucky cast against him, although his popular vote was but 55 per cent of the total. The forces of union were triumphant—by a narrow margin.

UNCONDITIONAL SURRENDER

The election over, the North could turn to the final conquest of the South. The strategy was obvious. Sherman turned his 60,000 troops northward through the Carolinas to rejoin Grant in Virginia. Again they cut a swath of destruction, burning towns, destroying crops and railroads, and leaving a path of barren desolation behind them. General Joe Johnston, who had been restored to his command by Lee, could offer only slight resistance and fell back steadily before the triumphant juggernaut. By the end of March, 1865, Sherman was at Goldsboro, North Carolina, only 150 miles from Grant's besieging army.

Lee's time was also running out. Outnumbered almost three to one, he could keep up his resistance only so long as supplies reached him from the rich Shenandoah farmlands or by rail from the West. The first source was closed by General Phil Sheridan, whose dashing cavalry had swept through the valley from Winchester to Staunton, wiping out all forage and foodstuffs. By the end of March, 1865, Grant was ready to close the last gap; he pushed his lines westward to cut the railroads entering the stricken cities of Petersburg and Richmond. When he failed to stop Grant at the battle of Five Forks on April 1, Lee knew his cause was lost and slipped his army out of Petersburg in an effort to join Johnston. Both Sheridan and Grant took up the pursuit once more, Sheridan charging ahead with his cavalry to head off the Confederates, and Grant following at their heels. By April 9 they were surrounded, and Lee, knowing that further resistance would be suicidal, ordered a white flag shown. That day the two commanders met in the little courthouse at Appomattox, Lee splendid in full dress uniform and sword, Grant in a bedraggled private's blouse. Small talk first, then the terms of surrender: officers and men to be paroled and officers to keep their side arms, all arms and material to be given up, all cavalrymen to take their horses home with them "to work their little farms." A few days later Johnston turned over his dwindling force to Sherman on similar terms. Jefferson Davis was captured on May 10 and on May 26 the last Confederate resistance ended. The war was over.

The reasons for northern victory were made clear by the condition of the two antagonists in 1865. The North was booming. Farm prices were high and the agricultural frontier, swept along by unprecedented military demands, by free lands offered under the Homestead Act of 1862, and by recently invented laborsaving machinery, was pushing into the plains area where Kansas (1861) and Nebraska (1864) had already won statehood. Manufacturing reflected an even giddier prosperity. New plants and methods developed to meet Gargantuan military needs proved so economical that by 1865 the entire civilian population was using factory-made clothing and shoes and eating prepared foods, rather than the locally manufactured items traditional to the nation. This trend not only assured producers a steady future market, but strained production facilities until manufacturers could keep pace with demand only by consolidating their plants to achieve the economies of large-scale operations. By the end of the war the movement was well under way that was to transform the small, independently owned and operated mills of the past into the giant industrial monopolies of the later nineteenth century. All this spelled prosperity, not to the workers, who were not well enough organized to force wages up as rapidly as prices, but to a "shoddy aristocracy" which fattened on government contracts and lived so lavishly that patriots wondered if they knew whether a war was being fought.

The southern picture in 1865 was chaotic. Invading armies left scorched fields in their wake, factories built at the start of the war were decaying monuments to inadequate materials or to managerial inefficiency, the transportation system was so collapsed that people were starving when barns only a few miles away were choked with grain. The confusion was compounded by the toppling financial structure. Southern wealth was insufficient to permit the Confederacy to follow the northern methods of raising money: excise taxes on industry, protective customs duties, heavy borrowing through sales, and the issue of a limited number of "greenbacks," or paper dollars, which stimulated prices without unduly inflating the currency. Instead, the South by 1865 had printed a billion dollars worth of paper money which had slumped until it was worth only two cents on the dollar. The soaring price levels and lowered standard of living that followed this wildcat inflation contributed to the discontent that spelled defeat. The Confederacy was already physically beaten when Lee's surrender at Appomattox ended the unequal struggle.

Even this burden might have been borne had the South remained united, but by 1865 its people were wasting their energies in needless squabbles that weakened their military efficiency. Their traditions of localism and provincialism, bolstered now by their state rights philosophy, were too deep rooted to accept the strongly nationalistic policy of their government. They resented the suspension of the writ of habeas corpus by President Davis and applauded when state courts refused to recognize his act. They denounced conscription, adopted by the South in 1862 and by the North a year later, as a despotic encroachment on their rights; North Carolina refused to enforce the law and South Carolina grumbled threateningly of nullification. Lincoln had been prophetic when he warned that secession would breed secession; northern victory was a triumph not only for Union but for nationalism against localism. The modern nation that emerged from the Civil War was to be reunited on a firmer foundation, with the provincialism of state sovereignty relegated forever to the limbo of the past.

XIII

THE ROAD TO REUNION 1865–1876

The dramatic rush of events that brought General Robert E. Lee face to face with the victorious Grant at Appomattox finally ended the war between the states. But while the unconditional surrender of General Lee marked the cessation of armed conflict, it failed to bring peace either to the North or to the South. Gigantic though the war was in the scope of its operations and in its savage destruction of half-spent lives, the social tolls of the postwar years were no less great. Wars are times which try the souls of the men who live them, but the years which follow try the souls of generations of men who live after them; for the problems of peace are as stupendous as of war.

The American people were as unprepared for peace in 1865 as they had been unprepared for war in 1861. Social attitudes, nurtured by conflict and suicidal to peace, could not be stripped of motivating force by the mere flourish of a pen on a solemn agreement any more than the passions heated by four years of bloody battle could be cooled by the irenic prose of presidential proclamations. The issues of reconstruction were psychological as well as constitutional, social as well as political, and human as well as economic. One of the strangest observations on human experience is the fact that cooperative energy which the threat of military defeat induces disappears almost before the ink on the agreement that ends the threat is dry. Differences are momentarily fused in the common social purpose, but when the military struggle has ended, the fissures of society are exposed to the chaos of postwar readjustment, deepened by the changes wrought by the conflict itself and the experiences of those forced to endure it. Debts can somehow be paid, the physical ravages of war repaired, but suspicion and hate can be banished only if the human spirit is not permanently crushed and the human heart hardened by fear and insecurity. The issues of reconstruction absorbed the energies of Americans for years, but the reconstructionists created more problems than they solved.

America endured despite reconstruction rather than because of it. The aftermath of conflict was an episode in the drama of social struggle just as the war itself was an interlude in American development. Peace was not made by oratorical grandiloquence or by congressional edicts. Neither the makers of the peace nor the creators of subsequent reconstruction plans actually healed the breach between North and South, though the first halted the carnage and the second fashioned the environment in which peace had somehow to be secured. The long struggle for American nationality reached a bloody climax at Gettysburg, and thereafter southern independence became a lost cause as hopeless as Pickett's futile charge, but the basic question whether the United States was truly a nation of indissolubly united peoples was not finally decided by the failures of Lee or the successes of Grant.

Actually, in the making of the peace, defeated Southerners upheld a constitutional theory clearly at variance with the political faith for which they allegedly fought, while their northern brethren espoused doctrines no less irreconcilable with their earlier professions. The northern view in 1861 was premised upon the illegality of secession; the southern view, upon its validity as a final instrument of redress. Each was the correlate of a larger constitutional faith. To the North, the American nation was an indestructible union of indestructible states; to the South, it was a voluntary confederacy of individually sovereign states. The northern position implied that once the war was won, the states were to resume their normal functions with all the rights they had previously possessed. Secession being invalid, the conflict was less a civil war than a rebellion.

In 1865 political expediency caused northern Republicans and their southern opponents to reverse themselves completely. Southerners took the northern view, holding that seceded states had never been out of the Union in a constitutional sense and were entitled to resume their normal functions with the rights of home rule like any northern state. Northern proponents of radical reform of the old southern regime after 1865 were impelled toward the finespun theories that secessionists had advocated in 1861. Thus reconstructionists in the North virtually accepted the secession premise that the Union had been dissolved and that the war had really been a war between two confederacies of states. Northern Republicans accordingly sought to legalize the postwar military occupation of the South on the grounds that seceded states had lost by conquest their constitutional status and their rights as states.

Nothing reveals the futility of the reconstruction years more clearly than the southern longing for peace. Loyalty to the Union, which had existed before hostilities and had expressed itself in votes for Douglas and Bell in the election of 1860, was still actively present. Robert E. Lee, who, even when the dust of battle was still in his nostrils, had no rancor in his heart, wished only for the return of peace and believed that if the authorities truly wanted peace they could achieve it in thirty days. Although General Grant substantially endorsed this view after making a southern tour, it was more than thirty years rather than thirty days before Congress in 1898 removed the last political disabilities from ex-Confederates. Moreover, Federal troops remained in the South for seven long years after Lee's death in 1870.

Most Southerners were ready to accept as well as to admit defeat. To be sure, the men who had so recently been devout Confederates had not yet learned to love the North, but they were prepared to learn to love the Union. For those to whom the pain of wounded pride and splintered hopes was too great to be borne, flight offered the only release, and they fled with their dreams to Mexico, to England, and to Canada to rebuild their shattered lives. But the majority of those who lived in Dixie wanted only the chance to rebuild them on their own beloved soil. Common men—black as well as white—cared less for political, constitutional, and anthropological theories than for tobacco, cotton, and rice. They were eager to exchange the right of secession for the right to live. If they had fought hard to destroy the Union, they were anxious to work hard in helping indirectly to rebuild it. The South was not humbled, it was weary; it was not yet hopeless, it was simply crushed.

STAGES OF RECONSTRUCTION

The history of reconstruction passed through four stages. Dominated by the towering personality of Abraham Lincoln, a policy tempered by understanding made considerable progress in restoring the southern states to their former position. Extending from the beginnings of federal control over Confederate territory in 1862 until President Lincoln's assassination on April 14, 1865, it was followed by a troubled interlude in which Andrew Johnson was to sit in the White House and bear the brunt of the rising tide of congressional wrath. Although the storm was already brewing in Lincoln's day, Johnson could not withstand it, and by the fall of 1866, the congressional opponents of the President were firmly in control. While the conflict between the executive and legislative branches continued without abatement throughout Johnson's term, Congress ruled the nation, and a minority ruled the Congress. The third phase, from 1866 to 1870, marks the transition from the presidential plans of reconstruction to the congressional plan, which was put into effect during these years. Finally, from 1870 to 1877 Union soldiers stationed in the South attempted to enforce congressional edicts, but gradually—beginning with North Carolina in the former year and ending with South Carolina in the latter—conservative southern whites recaptured both political dominion and social control.

These temporal stages clarify only partially the maze of legislation that goes under the name of reconstruction. The key to the labyrinth of conflicting purposes and fluctuating opinion lies not in the dissection of its static parts but in the analysis of the dynamic whole. It is not, in other words, the anatomy of a specific stage or of a specific law that yields insight, but the physiology of the process of changing events, personalities, and motivations. Otherwise it is impossible to understand why reconstruction, virtually completed by December, 1865, was then completely undone, why Lincoln was successful and Johnson failed, why the divided South became the Solid South, why a determined minority succeeded in convincing the North of southern recalcitrance, why a minority in the South recaptured domination, and why, finally, after eleven years of congressional supremacy, the main objectives of congressional reconstruction utterly failed.

Society was divided North as well as South. To represent the conflict as a clash between the Union and the former Confederate states is misleading; to represent opinion as divided between conservative and radical groups, one seeking the restoration of peace, the other revenge, is an oversimplification. While there were Southerners who took their stand with the South and Northerners who were for the Union right or wrong, the struggle was really a multiple struggle: for power, for principle, and for security. Parallel to the constant struggle for power was the continuing struggle for democracy; parallel to the struggle for privilege was the struggle for ideals; and parallel to the struggle for peace and revenge was the struggle for personal and social stability.

Representatives of northern industry comprised a nucleus of attitudes and desires. Men of business interested chiefly in manufacture and finance —the conservative wing of the Republican party—recalled earlier restrictions imposed upon industrial aims by political combinations of the agrarian South and West. Anxious to order the life of the nation to suit their own advantage, to insure maintenance of the tariff, to protect credit, and to enlist the aid of the government on the side of business expansion without restraint, they knew exactly what they wanted. To transform the Republican party from a minority to a majority party was a condition precedent to power, a condition realizable only by prevention of the historic alignment of southern and western agrarians that premised the political disqualification of former Confederates and the political emancipation of the Negroes. The political disqualification of Confederates precluded a return of the prewar political situation; the political emancipation of Negroes planted political seeds in the South certain to yield a rich Republican fruitage. Conservative northern industrialists were the natural exponents of a reconstruction program weighted with

penalties for Confederates and privileges for the Negro. Northern businessmen favored severity, but revenge was not their goal. Vengeance was
an item in a scale of larger values, for the logic of industrialism drove its
protagonists to identify opposition with rebellion in the South and disloyalty in the North. Conscious of their minority status, they saw everywhere the imminent union of divergent elements that threatened their
tenuous control.

Merging with the goals of industrialists were the aspirations of
democrats. Humanitarians, former leaders of the abolition crusade, and
friends of the Negro hoped to improve the opportunity provided by the
aftermath of war to expand democracy, to liberate the Negro in both sections of the country, and to emancipate the poor white North and South.
Like northern industrialists, they favored a harsh program in which four
elements predominated: disenfranchisement of former Confederates, enfranchisement of Negroes, protection of Negro political and social rights,
and an economic program to guarantee the political and social equality of
depressed classes regardless of color or section. Radical humanitarians
and conservative industrialists thus stood together. The logic of the democratic position coerced its leaders into an advocacy of stern retribution for
the planting class; thus a soft peace would not only be treason to the
Union, but treason to the democratic principles for which liberals contended the war had been fought.

While northern industrialists and humanitarians were in general accord, southern businessmen were in disagreement with both. To the ruling southern gentry who became absentee landlords of farmlands tilled
by renters or who moved into the towns at the birth of southern industry,
the labor supply was paramount. Southern landlords and businessmen—
a highly conservative class soon labeled "Bourbons"—viewed federal policy
that looked toward the emancipation of the Negro and the economic liberation of the poor white as a threat to the South's traditional reliance upon
cheap labor. The Negroes had supplied the labor for agriculture since
the eighteenth century; the poor white, in the opinion of Bourbons, should
supply labor for industry. National policies that wiped out the color distinction between Negro and poor white made political unity between the
two groups inevitable. And political dominance of the business group,
always a minority, depended upon the continued division of the races.
The logic of the southern Bourbon position made for unrelenting opposition to rigorous reconstruction. The elite white minority of the South resented their own disqualification just as adamantly as they objected to the
emancipation of the southern common man of whatever pigmentation.
They denounced strict federal regulation as antidemocratic, and punitive
devices as sadistic malice. Strict measures threatened their control; mild

measures assured it. They became the detractors of the black man and blocked efforts to ensure his economic welfare, they demeaned his potentialities and denounced social equality. They became the upholders of white supremacy as much because they disbelieved in the Negro as a reliable worker and as a responsible citizen as because racism kept poor white and poor Negro politically apart. They marshaled the white population against the blacks, made white cooperation with social uplift equate with treason to race, and northern effort to improve the lot of the oppressed an odious intrusion. Reconstruction became harsher as their recalcitrance mounted, but success was finally theirs.

Between such extremes of opinion were moderates of all shades of confusion. Certain northern humanitarians urged expansion of democracy, but felt former slaves were fitted neither by nature nor by experience to assume the obligations of citizenship. Others in the North, democrats on a white level, opposed liberty for the blacks in the South if such a change meant liberty for blacks in the North. Temperate men, men without deep democratic convictions, confused men, and men who could not see beyond immediate, selfish, and sectional advantage wished for peace, for an end to debate, for a smooth plan that would speedily restore the South to the Union and permit a return to the serenities of a past already grown sublime in memory.

A number of relatively fixed quantities affected the social situation. Advocates of severity were the beneficiaries of four years of hate which made their plans appear more reasonable than harsh. And each instance of southern resentment, real or fictionalized, enhanced their prestige and augmented their cause. But the logic of the proponents for Negro freedom was seemingly irrefragable. Slavery was a wrong, the war had been fought in part because of it, and it had been won with the aid of colored troops, colored workers, and colored loyalty. The Thirteenth Amendment, which became a part of the Constitution in 1865, made the slaves free in law; the slavery system had been destroyed, and justice, reason, and democracy stood on the side of the defenders of Negro liberty. Yet in the South, the tradition of generations re-enforced racial antagonism, misunderstanding, and fear. For a determined minority to channel ancient hates into political and social grooves was not difficult. The more Congress was coerced into the use of force, the easier it was for the South to insist upon elemental democratic rights and to enlist northern compassion. A welter of self-contradictions was reflected in reconstruction. Democracy, as exemplified by humanitarianism, was served by hate, by vengeance, and by the use of military coercion. Reaction, as exemplified by southern Bourbonism, the suppression of minorities, the return of an oligarchy to power, was served by the verbal profession of democratic ideas—justice instead of malice, freedom of governmental processes for home rule instead of military dictatorship, liberty instead of tyranny.

As soon as Confederate territory came under the control of Federal arms, restoration of statehood became an immediate issue. Impatient of fine constitutional distinctions, Lincoln sought a practical method for re-establishing the Union as swiftly and as painlessly as possible. Accordingly, he devised a simple procedure as considerate of the feelings of the South as it was mindful of the safety of the North. Excluding only former Confederate civil and diplomatic officials, high-ranking officers in the armed forces, and those who had resigned Federal office to serve the South, he offered pardon to those who would take an oath to support the Constitution and agree to accept the Thirteenth Amendment abolishing slavery. To these the franchise was to be restored and when as many as one tenth of the number who had voted in the election of 1860 had done so—hence the 10 per cent plan—they could constitute a government which the executive would recognize. Lincoln was not merely putting words together when he said feelingly, "No bloody work after the war is over. No one need expect me to take part in hanging or killing. . . . We must extinguish our resentments if we expect harmony and union."

Lincoln's mildness was rewarded by swift cooperation. Tennessee, Louisiana, and Arkansas accepted his generous terms, framed constitutions abolishing slavery, and were thereby returned to the Union fold. Although the President was generally applauded in the North, there was an immediate adverse reaction. Congressional critics, long resentful of the wartime expansion of executive power, sharply denounced what they considered encroachments on legislative authority and demanded sterner conditions as the price of northern forgiveness. The Wade-Davis bill of July 2, 1864, outlining a harsher formula, reflected the feeling that malice there had to be at least toward some and that Lincoln's clemency would do little to discourage future treason. Its true import, however, must be sought elsewhere. The Wade-Davis bill marked the first articulate breach between two opposing attitudes, a breach that was continuously to widen until there was no possibility of bridging it.

Five notable provisions were contained in the bill. States not in the Union were to be regarded as territories. Reconstruction was to be considered a congressional rather than an executive function. After each state was completely subdued, a full census was to be taken, and no convention was to be held until such time as a majority of all the male white population had taken an oath of allegiance. Membership in the convention or the right to vote in selecting it was to be restricted to those who had not voluntarily borne arms against the Union. Finally, Confederate officials, excluding only officers of administration and army men below the rank of colonel, were to be disfranchised, slavery was to be abolished, and Confederate debts were to be repudiated.

A sharp manifesto followed Lincoln's disposal of the bill by a pocket veto. "The President," this congressional document announced, "must confine himself to his executive duties . . . and leave political reorganization to Congress." Lincoln was too much a master of statecraft to blunder in the face of an incipient split in his party. Instead of condemning the insurgent Republicans, he offered conciliation. Realizing, of course, that none would choose the rough road while the smooth one was still open, he acknowledged the Wade-Davis plan and agreed to recognize any state that wished to come in under its provisions. In a Washington speech on April 11, 1865, he answered his adversaries in a typical homespun analogy that has made his prose so famous. "Concede that the new government of Louisiana is only . . . as the egg is to the fowl, we shall sooner have the fowl by hatching the egg than by smashing it," but there was already some indication that the opposition was less concerned with the fowl than with the egg. Certainly moderates could find little comfort in the comment of Congressman Thaddeus Stevens of Pennsylvania that the late Confederate states "ought never to be recognized as capable of acting in the Union . . . until the Constitution shall have been so amended . . . as to secure perpetual ascendency to the party of the Union."

As yet there was no impasse, and Abraham Lincoln might have avoided one. But it is by no means certain that even his great prestige with the masses of the people, his political adroitness, and the quality of his character could have prevented the catastrophe that followed. Two unforeseen events conspired to turn an age of tragedy into an age of hate. One was the assassination of Lincoln; the other was the succession of Andrew Johnson to the presidency. The death of Abraham Lincoln was a national disaster, but to the South it was a fateful calamity. By a strange irony the black Republican who had been the symbol of southern fear in 1860 had become the symbol of its hope in 1865.

Lincoln's removal changed the immediate situation and basically altered the course of reconstruction. Abraham Lincoln and Andrew Johnson shared much in common, but they were separated by even greater differences. Both came of poor stock, Lincoln from the pioneer West, Johnson from the frontier of Tennessee. Lincoln graduated from rail splitting into law; Johnson from tailoring into politics. Each possessed unusually fine intellectual endowments, a feeling for words, and limitless stores of courage, and both absorbed their passionate democracy from identical sources. Yet where Lincoln was a master craftsman at the art of politics, Johnson was a mere apprentice, tactless, dogged, and blunt. Johnson was no less honest than Lincoln, but he lacked both his tolerance and his sagacity. Few could long withstand the rigor of Lincoln's logic mellowed as it always was by disarming humor, but Johnson's logic, no less rigorous, was as cold as his humor was grim.

Nevertheless, the Radicals in Congress had every reason to hope when Johnson became President on April 15, 1865. A native poor white and a Jacksonian Democrat, he had scant cause to love the planting aristocracy of the South; a militant opponent of secession, he had been appointed by Lincoln military governor of Tennessee following Federal occupation. On the strength of this record the Republicans honored him with the vice-presidential nomination in 1864 as much to reward his fidelity as to strengthen a ticket that appealed to "War Democrats" and Republicans on a platform of Union. But Johnson's background as a southern poor white mortgaged his thinking. He was indubitably the enemy of entrenched wealth, but he shared the prejudices of his class regarding the Negro. He might have wished to free the slave to humble the planting aristocracy, but he was less militant about the potentialities of the black man. While he offered to serve as the Moses of former bondsmen, he envisaged a long hard pilgrimage before he could lead them to the Canaan of political and social equality. Late abolitionists and unequivocal democrats, who saw disaster in delay and who supported the Republican party only as the instrument of democratization, were certain to clash with such principles. Republican leaders of industry who wished only to assure their power by establishing the Negro in southern politics were likewise certain to founder on the rock of Johnsonian conviction. But Radicals saw no reason to abandon their faith in Johnson when, soon after his induction as chief executive, he told a New Hampshire delegation in the best Radical manner that treason was "a crime before which all other crimes sink into insignificance. . . ."

Johnson, however, turned out to be the bitter adversary of congressional extremism, which he fought doggedly, if somewhat ineptly, to the end of his presidential days. The war had been fought to save the Union, not to destroy the South; to reconstruct the Union was the main goal of peace as it had been the main goal of war. As President, he was charged with the solution of other problems, economic, social, diplomatic, and he was naturally anxious to dispose of the southern question with the greatest possible dispatch. Congress was in recess when Johnson took office in mid-April and he seized the opportunity to hasten the process of reconstruction.

Johnson's method was a compromise between the Wade-Davis bill and the Lincoln plan. All except Confederate leaders were granted a general amnesty. Also exempted from pardon were those who owned property amounting to $20,000, a reflection of Johnson's animus toward wealthy Bourbons. These and Confederate officials were required to sue for pardon individually, but since pardons were freely granted, Radicals and humanitarians were by no means reassured. Lincoln's governments —Virginia, Tennessee, Arkansas, Louisiana—were recognized, and temporary governors were appointed in other states. In the latter instances, the governors were to call conventions, to qualify for which voters were to take the oath of allegiance. Like Lincoln, Johnson suggested the possibility of permitting certain Negroes, able to read and write and who possessed a minimum of property, to vote. Like Lincoln, too, Johnson accepted the constitutional power of Congress to determine suffrage. Each state was required to invalidate the acts of secession, repudiate its debts, abolish slavery, and ratify the Thirteenth Amendment. When Congress reconvened on December 4, 1865, all save Texas, Delaware, and Kentucky had fulfilled every presidential condition including repeal of the ordinances of secession and acceptance of the Thirteenth Amendment. Superficially, they were now ready to take their places in the halls of Congress and in the life of the nation. But what were the realities behind these formal events?

With whom was the government of the United States to deal? Which groups in the South were loyal? What did loyalty mean? Which elements of the defeated population represented the majority will of the community? Whatever the President was seeking to accomplish, Radical Republicans could no more sanction an appeasement policy that restored the former leaders of the South than the humanitarians could sanction a policy that excluded the Negro. Under either the Lincoln or the Johnson plan a minority of the white population without full Negro participation formed the basis of the reconstructed governments. Neither could satisfy the congressional coalition of industrialists and democrats. If to this was added the struggle between the executive and legislative branches for mastery, it was apparent that Johnson would fail.

Inherent in the structure of the American government, the struggle between Johnson and Congress represented more than the irritation of legislators following the emergency expansion of presidential power. It was a perennial conflict, aggravated by crisis, which stemmed from the American system of separation of powers. Separation of powers diffused responsibility and eliminated the prospect of joint executive-legislative leadership under national party controls. Without a coordinated party leadership, in which all branches worked in concert, the division between the President and Congress was unavoidable. Johnson lacked a popular mandate, he was the advocate of a policy that threatened to revive the Democrats and unseat the Republican party. Republicans in Congress, fearful of executive plans and suspicious of presidential integrity in executing congressional acts, were the natural opponents of the titular leader of their own party. In consequence of the absence of national parties with national programs between which the electorate could choose, the policy of a faction—in this case the Radical reconstruction faction—precipitated a confused division with the President and the Democratic elements on the one hand and humanitarians, democrats, and industrialists in the Republican group on the other. Combinations of factions, each with conflicting purposes, took the place of party government. Andrew Johnson was President of the United States, but he was a President without a party; Congress ruled the nation, but, having stripped the President of power, it ruled without executive leadership.

The Radical minority in Congress at once perceived the threat to their position in the Johnsonian program, but the majority of the people in December, 1865, were closer to Johnson than to the Radicals. Yet under the leadership of Charles Sumner of Massachusetts in the Senate and Thaddeus Stevens of Pennsylvania in the House, the Radicals "secured a mandate" from the people in the congressional elections during the fall of the following year. Strengthened by the verdict at the polls, they undid the work of Lincoln and Johnson and launched their own program, with results which have influenced American life from that day to this. Such a reversal of policy was accomplished by a combination of skillful propaganda, political manipulation, and the inevitable reaction of the South. How and why it was done is the story of the final stages of the reconstruction conflict.

Refusing to seat the elected representatives from the reconstructed South, the Radicals had already challenged the legality of everything thus far done by creating a joint committee of both houses to investigate their right to be seated. Under the acknowledged leadership of Thaddeus Stevens, this famous Committee of Fifteen was ultimately responsible for the formulation of the congressional alternative to the presidential reconstruction program. Accepting Sumner's theory that the states had committed suicide by secession, Congress insisted that they had reverted to a territorial status and were completely under the jurisdiction of that body. If Congress was determined to wrest control from the executive, it was because of fear of agrarian predominance should Johnson's plan succeed. And the fear was not without foundation, for the Democratic party, still in control of the Middle West, could easily have wiped out Radical strength with the help of Southern agrarian votes. Hence Radical leaders attempted to identify Johnson in the public mind with the Democratic party and the Democratic party with treason.

An important part of reconstruction legislation was a bill, passed in February, 1866, extending the life of the Freedmen's Bureau and broadening its powers to employ military aid in protecting Negro rights. The original act of March, 1865, was a wartime expedient designed to take over the task of postwar relief. Johnson vetoed the bill on the ground that it was a war measure that the return of peace made unnecessary, but Congress jubilantly overrode his veto in July. More than the object of a legislative scuffle, the Freedmen's Bureau, the only federal attempt at economic rehabilitation, was the crux of the reconstruction issue. Although the bureau was a relief agency that succored many from want, illness, and abuse, it was at best but a half measure, for no provisions were made for land distribution and the extension of long-time credits. And the major defect of the Radical reconstruction program was economic, the failure to build a foundation for social and political change. Political equality for the Negro could not be achieved by legislative fiat unless coupled with measures that gave the Negro economic opportunity. The race problem was less cultural than economic. Cultural equality leading to a visible equality in intellectual stature was the long-term answer, but it was rooted in the economic emancipation of the southern poor white and the southern poor black. However inadequate, the Freedmen's Bureau was the beginning, but it was permitted to die before it really developed. After the industrial factions in the Republican party had secured their objectives, they were no more concerned with the southern problem than with the southern Negro vote.

THE FOURTEENTH AMENDMENT

As vital as the Freedmen's Bureau bill was the Civil Rights Act of April, 1866, which guaranteed to Negroes the equal protection of the laws, and vested in the federal courts jurisdiction in cases arising under the act. But its provisions were far less important than its results, for out of this enactment grew the Fourteenth Amendment, one of the most consequential in the history of American law. Vetoed by the President as unconstitutional, it was passed nevertheless, for the severity of state codes defining Negro status, together with Radical insistence upon southern infidelity, drove all but the most partisan of Democrats from the presidential standard. Radical leaders, filled with legal doubts themselves because the Bill of Rights expressly prohibited Congress from enacting legislation that would impair civil liberties, submitted a constitutional amendment instead.

Remarkable for its inclusiveness, the Fourteenth Amendment covered every aspect of the southern question. Unlike earlier enactments, however, it was divided into five separate parts that stood or fell together, a strategic device to enforce acceptance of all its provisions even if there were opposition to some of them. The first section declared the Negro a citizen with full citizen rights, exactly the opposite of what the Supreme Court had ruled in the celebrated Dred Scott case of 1857. Granting the Negro the franchise, the second section gave the southern states the option of according the Negro the right to vote or suffering a proportionate reduction in their congressional delegation. Third, former Confederates were made ineligible for public office until pardoned by a two-thirds vote of Congress. The pardoning power was thus transferred from the President to Congress, and the rapidity with which the leaders of the rebellion could be returned to politics was halted. In the fourth place, the amendment repudiated the southern war debt, validated the northern debt, and stipulated that former slaveowners were never to be reimbursed. Finally, the amendment specified that the legislative branch—not the judiciary or the executive—had charge of the enforcement of its provisions.[1]

Nothing better indicates the scope of Radical purpose than the Fourteenth Amendment. Thus, only a few years after the slaves had been freed by a similar legal enactment, Congress handed down a new decision. By this dictate, the South was required to send its leaders into political banishment and to agree that only Congress could lift the ban. The South was asked further to consent to Negro equality and, notwithstanding the shattering losses in personal property, land, and equipment, Confederate bonds and paper were to be dishonored and the owners of slaves bereft of their property without financial recourse. Could the South accept so stunning a second defeat? Could it stand the cumulative effect of all three, even if it could have withstood them singly? If the South rejected these newest demands, few would be able to refute the Radical charge that the South, for all Lincoln's and Johnson's efforts, was still unreconstructed.

THE CRITICAL YEAR

Such was the state of affairs on the eve of the congressional campaign of 1866. To complicate a situation already tense, a fierce race riot took place in New Orleans during late July, fanning the smoldering ashes of suspicion that the Radicals sought to stir into a consuming blaze. President Johnson, on behalf of the moderates, undertook a speaking tour in eastern and midwestern cities, but conducted himself so immoderately, making intemperate speeches and assailing his adversaries, that he probably alienated more votes than he gained. The Radicals, on the other

---

[1] This final section of the Fourteenth Amendment is generally overlooked. Forgetful of the fifth section, Congress in the 1880's was glad to hand over the responsibility of nonenforcement to the courts in the Civil Rights cases. A constitutional revolution is possible whenever Congress decides to resume its powers under section 5.

hand, were as astute as Johnson was unwise. They carefully ignored the
issues and appealed to patriotic emotion, for the stakes in this election
were high. Johnson and his colleagues attempted to convince the electorate
that the presidential program was adequate; the Radicals, forswearing
restraint, sought to identify wisdom with party fidelity and to confound
retribution with justice. Typical was the oratorical bombast of New
York's Roscoe Conkling:

> Shall one white man have as much share in the government as three other
> white men merely because he lives where blacks outnumber whites two to one?
> . . . Shall such be the reward of those who did the foulest and guiltiest act
> which crimsons the annals of recorded time?

Reason was inundated in torrents of such emotion, and the election resulted in a Radical Republican triumph.

The mid-term election of 1866 was critical and its consequences were
momentous. Andrew Johnson was still unbowed, but his conciliatory
hopes and his plans for a national party of moderation encompassing both
North and South were buried under an avalanche of Republican votes.
When all southern states save Tennessee speedily rejected the Fourteenth
Amendment, such obstacles as remained in the Radical path were completely removed. Lincoln was dead and Johnson had been defeated.
Opinion in the North, apparently convinced of southern perfidy, had entrusted the tasks of peace to the opponents of Lincoln's successor. It was
as though the two Presidents had never undertaken reconstruction at all.
Except in terms of southern distress, the situation was the same as it had
been before 1865. Peace existed only in name, for blue-clad soldiers
were soon to be stationed below Mason and Dixon's line. This time,
however, they did not face a rebel army full of pride and determination,
but a defeated population full of weariness and despair. They also faced
a grim minority determined to recapture control of the South.

Congress, acting as if the election were a command from the people,
commenced to translate the verdict into action. On March 2, 1867, it
declared that no legal government, except in Tennessee, existed anywhere in the South. Consequently, the South was divided into five military
districts, each under the command of a general whose function was to
preserve order and to superintend the process of congressional reconstruction. Two other laws passed the same day completed the program.
By the Army Appropriations Act, Congress instructed that military orders
were to be issued only through the general of the army; by the Tenure of
Office Act, the President was prohibited from removing his own appointees without the consent of the Senate. The one curtailed the President's constitutional power as commander in chief; the other limited

his powers by restricting the right of dismissal even with respect to members of the Cabinet.

Radical propagandists convinced posterity as well as the postwar generation that there was justice in their cause. And there was much to condone it. Both Johnson and his critics wished for reconstruction, but were not Johnson's plans premature? The Radicals insisted that the South was still unregenerate and pointed to certain categories of evidence to substantiate their assertion. One was the return of former Confederates to governmental posts, local and national; the other concerned the so-called "black codes" drafted by Johnson's reconstructed governments to regulate life between white folk and the newly emancipated Negroes. For the South to have chosen men who had been Confederates was natural, but to the Radical mind it indicated nothing but treason all over again. Yet it appeared strange to ask men who had so recently fired upon Federal troops to take an active part in preparing legislation for those who remained. And more important, they were elected by a minority of the people from which the freedmen were normally excluded. Even if majority opinion in the North was still dubious about Negro equality, there existed an uncomfortable anomaly between the Thirteenth and Fourteenth Amendments and the social and political situation in the South that negated them in letter and in spirit. And it was certainly difficult to reconcile the presence of Confederate generals in Congress so short a time after Lee's surrender.

More convincing still were the black codes, which seemed like nothing more than an artful device to undo one of the great results of the war. States reconstructed under Johnson passed laws regulating the conduct of Negroes and governing their social and economic relations with whites. While they varied in different states, the tenor of all was similar. Idle Negroes were vagrants. Such individuals might be brought before a justice of the peace, fined fifty dollars, and apprenticed for six months if unable to pay. It needed little argument to convince even moderates that with the breakup of the plantations there must necessarily be many "vagrants," that for an unemployed person fifty dollars was a fortune, and that to be hired out for failure to pay such a fine was enslavement rather than justice. Children, separated from their parents and without funds, could also be apprenticed. The black codes contributed to Radical success and to the embarrassment of moderates; outstanding were the Mississippi laws, which denied the Negro the right to own land, to intermarry, to testify in court actions in which whites were parties, or to make contracts except in writing. The South had abolished slavery in law but continued to enslave Negroes in fact. The election of former

Confederates to national office argued for further disbarment of southern whites; the black codes, for an eternal vigilance over Negro rights.

Proscription of Confederates and protection of Negroes remained the bases of the Radical contention. Once the outlines of Radical demands took shape, it became apparent that the militant southern leadership would not accept them. The more the South rebelled, the more Radical insistence mounted, and the easier it was to convince the North of southern duplicity. Moderation disappeared just when moderation was needed most. If there were just grounds for the belief that the Negro was maltreated in the reconstruction years, the Radical program is partly responsible, for by barring seasoned judgment from active social participation, it brought to the fore a new, intemperate, and violent vigilante leadership. Nowhere were wisdom and patience more seriously needed than in the delicate field of race relations. Laws, however well-intentioned, could not erase more than two centuries of cultural conditioning, and the greater the zeal of injudicious reformers, the greater the social chaos in the South.

But if Southerners rebelled at increasing disenfranchisement of whites and heightened concern for the Negro, Northerners became easy converts to both. The former made it possible for Radical propagandists to tap the mainsprings of northern patriotism; the latter, the deeper reservoir of American humanitarianism. If the contest had ever been simply a clash between moderates and Radicals over the method of southern restoration, it had now become a conflict in which the destiny of the South became an incident in a raw struggle for power, and the Negro a pawn in the quest for political control. The controversy between the White House and the legislature, though acrid and constant, was but an echo of the larger struggle for the economic and political domination of the country, and in the South for the economic and political domination of the section.

The severity of the Radical program was dictated by partisan expediency as well as by sectional vengeance. There were still men in Congress who vividly recalled the solidarity of the southern delegation in the years when an "aggressive slavocracy" ruled the cotton kingdom. Nor could they fail to remember the ease with which southern planters and western farmers frequently allied to further agricultural interests, an alliance that effectively blocked northern commercial and industrial ambitions. To invite the southern gentry back to Washington was simply to ask history to repeat itself, and that the gentry would return was a hard fact and not a tenuous theory. Even the erstwhile Vice-President of the Confederacy, Alexander H. Stephens of Georgia, had been returned to his congressional seat by a constituency created under Johnson's dispensation. It was clearly one thing to forgive Southerners for the crime of treason; it was quite another to err in rebuilding a reunited southern and northern phalanx of Democrats in Congress. Many a moderate, divine enough to be forgiving, was still human enough to be self-interested, for "unreconstructed" Southerners allied with Democrats of the agrarian West would be as certain to vote against measures of stern retribution as against economic legislation favorable to northern industrial interests. The immediate threat could be avoided only by the disqualification of Southerners tainted with the heresy of rebellion; the permanent threat, by the entrenchment of the Negro in southern politics whose advantage and loyalty would then ensure Republican domination. There is also evidence that the Radicals purposely contrived to debar the South from legislative participation until a program conducive to the economic welfare of the North was formulated, but their activity in this direction during the absence of southern congressmen speaks more eloquently than their plans.

Many in the North were heartily in favor of Negro suffrage as much because they were sincere believers in equality as because they were genuinely concerned with the welfare of the emancipated slaves. Others, however, were motivated by additional considerations less specifically humanitarian. Even Charles Sumner, as ardent as Thaddeus Stevens in the crusade for Negro rights and the broadening of American democracy, admitted that it was necessary "to acquire the voting force . . . for the protection of unionists, whether white or black . . .," while Stevens, almost always as politically astute as he was zealous, stated frankly that his purpose was to "insure the ascendency of the Union party." "I believe," he confessed, that "if impartial suffrage is excluded in the rebel States then every one of them is sure to send a solid rebel . . . delegation to Congress, and cast a solid rebel electoral vote."

Under the impact of Radical triumph the nature of the American government momentarily changed. Congress alone was supreme. The President of the United States, outmaneuvered in the game of politics, was soon to be further humbled by a conspiracy of partisanship resulting in impeachment. Nor could the Supreme Court, when finally it raised its judicial hand, stay the congressional course. Johnson, still certain of the illegality of congressional plans, yet considered it his duty to execute them, a duty he performed with a fine sense of administrative integrity. But the position was hardly one to mellow a man of Johnson's caliber. As the defender of the Constitution against Radical onslaughts, he became increasingly bitter, stubborn, and relentless.

Congressional disdain of the Supreme Court reflected a growing certainty of power. While those who sought to escape from the rule of the major generals were heartened by the Court's decision in *Ex parte*

Milligan (1866)—that trial by military courts was unconstitutional as long as civil courts were open—Congress disregarded it. When a Mississippi editor, tried and convicted by a military tribunal, appealed the decision and the Supreme Court accepted jurisdiction in *Ex parte McCardle* (1868), Congress passed an act, March 7, 1868, that denied jurisdiction to the Supreme Court in cases involving the reconstruction acts.

Contempt for the Court was more than matched by contempt for the President. Johnson's consistent record of opposition, his forthright vetoes, and his ill-concealed opinion of various leaders had long fathered the wish for his removal. To extremists, his vetoes were no less treasonable than southern efforts to circumvent congressional acts. Although the temperature of opinion permitted reference to the President as a foreigner from an alien state on the floor of Congress, the House was loath to indict him without good legal grounds. Johnson himself provided the pretext when, goaded far beyond political caution, he dismissed Edwin M. Stanton, Secretary of War, who had served the President's enemies with irritating fidelity. Alleging violation of the Tenure of Office Act, the House, on February 24, 1868, voted to impeach Andrew Johnson, President of the United States, for "high crimes and misdemeanors."

The episode is memorable in American annals less because it is unparalleled than because it represents the apex of Radical partisanship. After it was apparent that the charges were without legal foundation, the effort was continued on political grounds alone. The Radicals failed to achieve success, but they were only a single vote short of the necessary two thirds. Every known device of party pressure was employed, and the seven Republicans who resisted were never able to recoup their political fortunes.[2] One of them, Senator Lyman Trumbull of Illinois, made the interesting observation that had the impeachment succeeded no subsequent President who disagreed "with a majority of the House and two-thirds of the Senate on any measure deemed by them important" could be certain of serving out a full term. Election of Grant, errand boy for the next Republican Congress, reduced the attraction of impeachment as a device to ensure the responsibility of the executive to his party in Congress.

MAKING THE SOUTH SOLID

While the Radicals were attempting to unseat a President of the United States, their representatives were seeking to reorganize a culture. On the whole, the rule of the major generals was moderate, honest, and

---

[2] Senators Trumbull, Fessenden, Fowler, Grimes, Henderson, Ross, and Van Winkle voted against impeachment.

reasonably efficient, but it was nonetheless thoroughly military. Military government replaced civil government, and as elections could not be held until after the congressional mechanism was in operation, appointments and removals were made through headquarters instead of through the polls. Opposition to Radical intentions caused many whites to resign, and so many whites were disqualified by the ironclad regulations that there was actually a dearth of available men for office. New appointees came directly from the army personnel or were recruited from the ranks of northern migrants—the Carpetbaggers—and native southern Radicals— the Scalawags. Since part of the plan was to ensure the creation of a southern wing of the Republican party, the former slaves were swiftly elevated to public office.

Southern Bourbons disliked military rule, which they were quick to brand as a usurpation, but they lost little time in branding Carpetbaggers, Scalawags, and Negroes as desecrators of white culture in league with a vengeful North. If average southern whites were apathetic and refrained from political activity, the Bourbon minority immediately organized a campaign to convince them that without concerted white activity the culture of the South was doomed. And by June, 1868, seven of the ten southern states were reconstructed in the congressional sense and firmly under Republican control.

To white irreconcilables the presence of the Negro in politics seemed a reversal of the laws of nature, but in actuality the illiterate Negro, so long the butt of southern scorn, was learning the art of self-government as scores of colonial illiterates who had signed the hallowed charters of liberty with the tell-tale "X" had learned it before. Formal learning was not the equivalent of intelligence and good character in colonial Boston any more than in the Charleston of reconstruction. If some of the mixed legislatures were found to have indulged in shady deals, they were deals in which southern white families took their princely cuts when, indeed, white Southerners did not actually initiate them. Nor were such practices any better or worse than the graft and bribery in northern states and cities engineered by political gangs composed of individuals whose color, at least, was not in question.

The reconstruction record, written under the tutelage of scholars of Bourbon lineage seeking a gentlemanly road to reunion, has long demanded reappraisal. As a social record, the legislation of the so-called black and tan governments for education, sanitation, and public works was much more significant than the legislative deportment of former slaves in the sacred chambers of government. South Carolina, for example, enshrined in historical memory as an instance of the "prostrate South," mapped out, under joint black and white leadership, a system of

free compulsory education still capable of serving as a contemporary
ideal. Roads were constructed, public buildings repaired, and new ones
projected. That such social progress cost a great deal was doubtless true,
but the increase in state debt was not as important as the revival of
southern liberalism premised in the legislation, the resurgence of Jacksonian Democracy challenging southern Bourbonism. If the new state
governments were undemocratic because Federal bayonets repressed a
southern minority, the later Bourbon governments were equally undemocratic because the Negro and the poor white majority were coerced, intimidated, and illegally suppressed.

Disdain for Negroes was easily equaled by disdain for Carpetbaggers,
whom Bourbons described as northern fortune seekers who invaded the
South with all their worldly possessions in a carpetbag although they
needed considerably more luggage when they returned. This cartoonist
description served political ends alone. Interstate migration was the
American norm and the American right. Native sons of Massachusetts
who migrated to Ohio represented as normal a shift in population as
the ante-bellum movement of Virginians to Louisiana. Northerners who
went South after the Civil War were no different. Many were inspired
by the same high motives, however mixed with the desire for economic
advancement, that had sent earlier missionaries to Oregon or New England
abolitionists to Kansas. Nor was it unusual for native Easterners to become governors of western states any more than it was extraordinary for
Southerners to become legislative officers of states in the Southwest.
Pride in native sons was a provincialism then as now, save that in the
post-bellum South, provincialism was purposefully associated with native
sons who were "sound" on the race question. Certain Northerners were
indubitably corrupt, but to emphasize corruption rather than social contributions and the free right of movement obscured the cleavage within
southern society and the veiled political intentions of the southern
minority.

Deepest Bourbon scorn, however, was reserved for the Scalawags,
native whites who cooperated with Northerners and Negroes alike.
Scalawags, like Carpetbaggers, were often missionaries for freedom, but
this point was obscured by artful propagandists who succeeded in splitting
the natural alliance between poor whites and the other half of their economic class, the poor blacks. If "Scalawag" was a term that meant race
treason, it was used in a deliberate attempt to ensure white Bourbon
supremacy. Failure of the Federal government to produce an economic
program to begin the elimination of southern poverty made the poor
white the ally of the Bourbon minority, a psychological escape from

frustration in which "race solidarity" supplied the compensation for economic uncertainty.

While the southern states were being reconstructed and Johnson's trial was in progress, the presidential campaign of 1868 began to receive the attention of professional politicians. Alarming to the Republicans were recent Democratic gains in Ohio, Pennsylvania, and New York, but these were more than offset by Republican domination in the reconstructed states. In truth, the assiduous activity of the registrants in the South and the speed with which the states were readmitted could not have been unrelated to the forthcoming election.

There were many aspirants for the Republican presidential crown, but once the name of Ulysses Simpson Grant was placed in nomination, the contest was all but over. General Grant was the most popular man in the North. As the great hero of a great war, he was almost universally admired as a strong, silent man who inevitably got things done. The choice of Grant indicated a naïve though popular faith that military talents were adequate in almost any exigency. But the unity that prevailed in the Republican camp was understandably absent in the Democratic wigwam. Sharply divided by economic differences, Democrats were embarrassed by the personal unpopularity of Johnson. Horatio Seymour, New York's war governor, was chosen as the standard-bearer, and a Union man from the South, General Francis P. Blair of Missouri, a close supporter of Johnson who advocated undoing the work of Congress in the South by force if necessary, was given second place on the ticket. The Republicans warmly endorsed the handiwork of Congress and just as warmly condemned Johnson. The Democrats, on the other hand, approved the Johnsonian technique and roundly scored the system then in operation as "unconstitutional, revolutionary, and void."

Grant won the election handsomely in the electoral college. He carried twenty-six out of thirty-four states with an electoral majority of 214 to 80. But analysis of the vote showed his victory to have been something less than complete and gave Republican politicos pause. Although Grant was close to being a sectional idol, 2,700,000 Americans voted for Seymour as against 3,000,000 for Grant. The general's margin was a scant 300,000, and his total included approximately 450,000 newly created Negro votes. In addition, the race in several states was so uncomfortably close that a swing to Seymour might have altered the result. The implications of the election returns were abundantly clear. Accordingly, when Congress reconvened in December, 1868, the Fifteenth Amendment, providing that the right of suffrage was "not to be denied . . . on account of race, color, or previous condition of servitude" was quickly passed and made a condition of readmission for those states still out of the Union.

The amendment made Negro suffrage mandatory not only for the South but for those northern states in which the Negroes were denied the ballott. The Republicans thus attained momentary security, for the grateful Negro could be counted upon to follow the Republican party line.

But the southern Bourbons were not satisfied with the outcome of the election. If Grant spoke for most Americans when he said, "Let us have peace," he did not speak for the discontented whites in the South. Although Southerners had had enough of war and the strife of reconstruction earnestly to wish it, the Bourbons were just as earnestly determined not to have it at any price. The final chapter of reconstruction is not only a story of Negro and Carpetbag rule, but the story of the return of the Bourbon minority to power. Southern Bourbons were driven to revolt against the reign of the Radicals by rage and by fear, but neither emotion was inspired solely by their erstwhile slaves. Illiterate Negroes in responsible government posts disgusted them, swaggering black troops in uniforms of blue outraged them, but their anger was kindled to its whitest heat by the loss of social status and political dominion. They could accept poverty instead of wealth because fortunes could be remade, but only if political power, centered in their hands, allowed them to re-order southern society. They could not fail to rise against their virtual banishment from the social world they had so recently ruled. Anger was their response to what they considered chaos—the "perfidy" of Scalawags, the "pillage" of Carpetbaggers, and the entrenchment of the Negro in politics. Force was their response to what they denominated dictatorship— the bayonets of Federal soldiers who made possible the degradation of their class. They could hardly acquiesce in the election of a black man to the seat of Jefferson Davis, one-time president of the South, in the Senate of the United States. The exhibition of Carpetbaggers, Scalawags, and Negroes stirred Bourbon fury and melted northern suspicion into sympathy. Moreover, northern reformers, weary of failure and doubtful of the Negro experiment, sought new outlets for humanitarian benevolence.

While northern ardor for the politics of reconstruction gradually waned, the Bourbon South responded to Radical organization with the resistance of violence. The Ku Klux Klan, founded in 1866 and typical of similar organizations, sent nocturnal bands of horsemen robed in sepulchral white to intimidate the credulous Negro and his white allies. An even more dangerous use of force than the military governments of Congress, the Klan quickly got beyond the control of its founders, who formally disbanded their "Invisible Empire" in 1869; in the hands of the unscrupulous, it remained to whip, to maim, and to kill long after the southern white minority was socially and politically entrenched. The temperate may take their choice between the evidence presented by modern historians revealing the atrocities of the Klansmen and the evidence of southern historians revealing the atrocities of the Federal military authorities. But the sagacious will perceive at once that the Klan more closely resembled Nazi stormtroopers than the Union army resembled marauding conquerors.

Far more effective, if less spectacular, in aiding militant whites was the growing antipathy to Radical measures outside the former Confederacy. The fantastic night riders of the notorious Klan, successful in keeping the Negroes from the polls, seriously weakened the Carpetbag governments. But when, in 1872, Congress passed a general amnesty restoring most whites to citizenship, Southerners were able to accomplish their purposes with greater efficiency. By 1875 seven states, recently safely Republican, were already "redeemed." The Supreme Court likewise began to interpret the acts enforcing the great amendments in a manner that made it easier for whites to circumvent their apparent intent. The states, the Court held, could make no laws depriving the Negroes of political or social rights guaranteed by the amendments, but Congress was powerless to prevent individual citizens from depriving Negroes of these rights. In such cases, recourse was to the state legislatures, not to the Congress.

Only the power of Federal arms kept those states still unredeemed in Radical hands, and the evils of this situation were made clear enough during the election of 1876. Samuel J. Tilden, governor of New York, the Democratic contender for the presidency against Rutherford B. Hayes, Republican governor of Ohio, was apparently elected when the votes were first counted. Tilden had a clear popular majority of a quarter of a million, and had carried every doubtful state. But in three southern states, Louisiana, Florida, and South Carolina, there were disputes, each party submitting contested returns. Striving to oust the Carpetbaggers, the whites had conspired to keep the Negroes from voting, but the political mechanisms that certified the returns were controlled by Carpetbaggers. Hayes could win only by carrying all three states. Tilden needed only one electoral vote from any of the three to win. An impasse was unavoidable, and when finally a special commission was appointed to weigh the evidence, Hayes was declared elected by a strictly partisan vote of the Republican majority. The Democrats, bitterly disappointed and convinced that the presidency had been "stolen," nevertheless acquiesced, but the elections marked the last stand of the Radical governments in the South. With the withdrawal of Federal troops after the final count, the Republican regimes crumbled, leaving the native whites in undisputed control.

THE LEGACY OF RECONSTRUCTION

The Radical plan to revise southern society had little immediate chance of success. Negroes were elevated to a position of social eminence, while their former masters were made socially subordinate. Legal enactments raised the Negro to man's free estate, guaranteed his right to vote, and safeguarded his social, economic, and political relations with hostile whites. But constitutional amendments and the laws drafted to enforce them were without economic substance. Bourbon militancy drove the Radicals to employ force as a last resort. Yet it was the reliance upon force and the rapid rise of the Negro to political power in conjunction with poor whites that led to the undoing of both. If the Republican party was an instrument of "Black Republican" oppression, the Negro's association with it made him an accomplice of tyranny in astigmatic Bourbon eyes. If the Scalawag and the Carpetbagger were the enemies of the southern white minority, the Negro's alliance with them made him party to the conspiracy. What good there was in the Radical program—and there was much good in it—was forfeited by the means employed to achieve Radical objectives.

But neither the Negroes nor the Scalawags and Carpetbaggers were primarily responsible for the reconstruction fiasco. Even the Bourbons did not bear the major burden of guilt. Failure must be traced to that part of congressional policy which excluded a large body of southern whites from political participation. The Radical Republicans answered southern white resentment with force to keep the ex-Confederates in their place as the Bourbons later resorted to force to keep the Negroes in their place. The alternative was more democracy in both instances: economic democracy, security for the southern poor; political democracy—the two-party system—so that both parties, locally and nationally, would have been able to compete for the support of all groups, black as well as white, with divergent social programs.

The lot of the South, when contrasted with the usual treatment accorded the vanquished, was not unduly harsh. Confederate leaders were not executed, but their quiet descent into oblivion was a personal tragedy, pathetic, futile, and grim. Few were as fortunate as General Lee, who lived out his years in fruitful service; most, like Jefferson Davis, spent the remainder of their spectral lives parrying the thrusts of the righteous or vainly seeking justification. But no less pathetic and equally grim was the social tragedy of the descent of Negroes and poor whites, the basis of southern liberalism, into political oblivion. No territory was taken by right of conquest, but the North continued to occupy the South long after its adversaries had lain down their arms. The victors took no hostages, but they used the Negro as a political hostage against a revival of southern nationalism. All but a handful of the former rebels were pardoned by 1872, but after the reconstructionists had had their day it was a new South in which former Confederates had to live.

If the war had been a trial of American nationality, the events following the peace created one of the perennial trials of American democracy. The substitution of military government for civil government in the South resulted in the suppression of democratic institutions. Upheaval of southern society made violence on both sides unavoidable, and the use of force by the white minority resulted in an even more complete perversion of democratic institutions. In the first instance, force was temporary; in the second, it continued for generations. Millions of colored men and women became the victims of the lust for party power or of unreasoned, often sentimental, benevolence. Hundreds of thousands of whites were robbed of elemental political rights, while their pride was pulverized by the loss of social status.

The war and reconstruction ended the sectional dominance of the South and forever destroyed the threat of the "slave power" to American democracy. But the war and reconstruction accelerated the growth of the "money power," which constituted an even greater threat. Twenty years after the conflict, corporate interests in the United States measured their assets in terms that made cotton capitalism seem puny by comparison. And they wielded a power commensurate with their wealth and in contrast with which the influence of the southern oligarchy of ante-bellum days was insignificant.

The sins of reconstruction were manifold and far reaching. An emotional dike of prejudice was erected against the Negro, and the "race question" became dominant in southern thought. Coloring regional life with the stain of hate and suspicion, the affinity between Negroes and Republicans drove whites into the Democratic ranks, where they have since remained. Since the Republican party continued to be an "alien" and a "nigger" party, a Democratic allegiance was alone respectable. A solid political South blunted the impact of national issues and made it virtually impossible for southern agrarians to combine with their natural agrarian and labor allies in the West and the Northeast. The disproportionate influence of the industrial Northeast, therefore, in shaping the destinies of the nation, was weighted by the inability of the southern masses to give political effect to their grievances. As a result, consideration of remedial social and economic legislation was postponed, and the liberal and oppressed elements of the Democratic party in the South, anchored to dominant conservative blocks, had little hope of extracting the social issues from the deeply encrusted layers of the southern past.

While a Solid South has been an asset to Democratic fortunes in national contests, it has been a constant liability to progressive Democratic leaders who have attempted to make their party the instrument of reform.

Although the Civil War marks a revolutionary stage in American history, certain seeds in the social pod failed to mature. The collapse of the Confederacy brought about the collapse of the planting aristocracy that had dominated southern life since the time of Thomas Jefferson. With the decline of the planter class, the small upcountry farmers, once championed by the great democrat of Monticello, took over the lands of their former overlords. But as the small farmers and poor whites acquired a share of the divided plantations, the southern gentry moved into the cities. Allied with the industrialists of the new South, they captured the Democratic party, which, because of the reconstruction tradition, spoke, not for the poor farmer or sharecropper, but for the new aristocracy of industry and trade. Likewise revolutionary was the emancipation of the slaves, who, potentially at least, became active members of society with a stroke of Lincoln's pen. But here again the aftermath of reconstruction intruded to blight the possibility of a development that would have enriched the life of the Negro as well as the life of the nation.

The peacemakers of 1865 failed. Instead of making peace they made war; instead of paving the road to reunion with the cement of tolerance, they obstructed it with the wreckage of ill-conceived plans. Not only did they fail as peacemakers; they failed as abjectly to achieve their avowed aims. Every hope of the Radical reconstructionists was finally crushed, every Radical principle ultimately destroyed. The Negro was freed only to be economically and spiritually enslaved again. If the bonds that once held him were legal, they have since become economic. Laws framed to protect him have been ignored, devices to ensure his political existence circumvented. Poor, ignored, without status in the community as a whole, he became neither the free man for whom Charles Sumner longed nor the cornerstone of the Republican bastion that Thaddeus Stevens believed he had erected. So desperate has his plight become that many have questioned whether the Negro was not better off during the age of slavery in the ante-bellum South than during the age of poverty in the post-bellum South. The difference between black slaves and black sharecroppers seemed to many to constitute a difference in words alone. The southern Republican party, the darling of Radical desire, after 1876 possessed little power in national campaigns and almost no local prestige. Useful to leaders of the party in nominating conventions, it permits political strategists to control blocs of southern delegates by effective use of the patronage. The Democratic party, the special object of Radical displeasure, is the ruling southern party, which has reared a political barrier to joint action between oppressed southern groups and the disaffected in other sections of the country.

The Civil War, like all wars, created an age of hate, but Radical reconstruction and militant southern Bourbonism prolonged it. While the reconstruction period was indubitably a tragic era, it was also a futile one. If the American people have outlived its immediate effects, they have not yet survived its fundamental consequences. Few veterans from either side remain to fondle the golden hours of past memories. The sons and grandsons of both have marched together in three later wars, but there is still a "Negro problem." There is also a southern problem. Both may be traced to reconstruction.

Historical tradition has made "reconstruction" the conventional term for this period. Actually, it is a misnomer, for the bonds of a stronger American union were welded in the crucible of contemporaneous revolutions in economics. The representative from Pennsylvania who led the battle for congressional policies, Thaddeus Stevens, had far less to do with forging American nationality than another gentleman, also associated with Pennsylvania, whose name was Andrew Carnegie. The Civil War did not end on the battlefield in Pennsylvania but later in its steel mills. The final blows were not struck by youths in blue or in grey in lush Virginia fields before Richmond; they were struck by Irish laborers, Chinese coolies, and native workers who hammered the spikes into transcontinental railroad tracks and dug coal from the mines in Alabama.

XIV

THE REVOLUTIONS IN ECONOMICS

1865–1900

While northern political forces entrenched in Congress were rallying their battalions for the reconstruction of the South and the creation of a system of Republican supremacy, economic changes quietly at work strengthened the hands of conservative Republicans in the North and conservative Democrats in the South. The Civil War marked a turning point in man's American adventure. When General Robert E. Lee met General Ulysses S. Grant at Appomattox he came to surrender an army and relinquish a cause, but he also surrendered a civilization and relinquished a culture. A whole world died with the martyred Lincoln, for a series of economic revolutions changed not only the face of America but altered the American spirit and the American mind.

American history since the Civil War is the story of a new world. It is the story of a world of cities and a world of machines, of millions of men and women living beneath the ever-lengthening shadows of city buildings and of millions of other men and women living on open plain and in prairie village whose lives were nevertheless affected by the activities in offices, factories, and shops crowded together in urban America. It is the chronicle of agricultural workers laboring in the fields and of industrial workers laboring at the forge, of shining steel rails spanning a continent, of falling timber in primeval forests, of cavernous mines explored and exploited, and of acres upon acres of fertile land furrowed and sown. American life after 1865 is the amazing record of cities that grew out of the wilderness and of prairie towns that grew into metropolitan communities, of scores of lusty business buccaneers in quest of fortune and thousands of human beings in quest of life, of breath-taking inventions that startled civilization and finally remade it. It is a record of triumph and of failure, of aspiration and despair, a chapter in the epic of man's constant striving to conquer his environment and to master his destiny. In the process, Americans, like Germans, Japanese, and Frenchmen in the same decades, created a new culture more universal than national.

It was an age of revolutions. In four separable but interrelated areas the upthrust and direction of change are clearly apparent: in industry, in transportation and communication, in agriculture, and in the growth of cities. Life in the United States underwent a fundamental reorientation, for these epoch-making transformations in turn revolutionized each other. The basic human import, however, was not merely economic change but social change—the shrinking world and the interdependence of society, mechanization and the increasing complexity of existence, the rise of the city and the growing impersonality of social relationships, and the terrifying rate at which these transformations took place. Less easily discerned, these proximate consequences were equally shattering. In brief, a whole culture was silently passing when reveille sounded in Lincoln's Washington; another, still maturing, was just beginning to take shape.

The revolutions in industry, transportation, communication, agriculture, and urbanization were simply the most spectacular parts of a series of multiple, interacting changes. The industrial revolution, for example, was more than coal, iron, steel, and oil; it was a revolution in the organization of business, the conduct of politics, and the interpretation of law as well. Ships, locomotives, and dynamos did not by themselves sum up the transportation revolution since they produced a revolution in human relationships from one end of the globe to the other. And telephones, cables, and telegraph wires did not exhaust the final scope of the revolution in communication, for new communication techniques presaged a revolution in ideas. In scarcely half a century the human adaptation of steam and electricity shrank a world which the natural forces of geology had taken milleniums to fashion. The globe in the geographer's study retained its spherical shape, but the powers of science applied to the needs of man completely altered its social contours. If an intellectual revolution was implicit in geographical change, a cultural revolution was implicit in the transportation change that initiated one of the greatest population movements in the history of man. Similarly, plows, harvesters, and crops signified more than a shift in the balance sheet of production and export, for the agricultural revolution shifted the course of social evolution. An old civilization, the cotton South, perished, and an ancient culture as old as civilization itself, the rural way of life, was for the first time seriously threatened by the swift process of urbanization.

THE QUADRUPLE REVOLUTIONS

The purpose of the chapters which follow is a triple one: to delineate the nature of the economic revolutions and the forces that produced them; to trace the impact of the new social environment; and to describe the efforts of succeeding generations of Americans to cope with the challenge of a new society. The revolutions in economics, one of the keys to an analysis of American development, produced the machine age. They are the dynamic social and economic forces that give meaning to the triumph of business enterprise and the bankruptcy of politics; the conquest of rural America and the rise of the city; the mingling of peoples, the sins of society, and the shrinking world.

The emergence of industrial America is definable only by contrast with the America from which it evolved. When Jefferson Davis resigned his seat in the United States Senate to become President of the South, America was only a small country of 31,000,000 people, less than three times the present population of the state of New York. The United States, merely seventy-seven years old, was but a junior member of the international family. America was young. Abraham Lincoln, whose majestic personality towered over his contemporaries, was born in the very year that James Madison entered the executive mansion. And Madison, who had helped to write the Constitution, was himself alive when Andrew Jackson surrendered the presidential crown to Martin Van Buren in 1836. By that year the steam locomotive was developed, but not until the 1850's were the first East-West railroads in the United States even begun. Not until the dynamo was perfected in 1877 did electricity become a commercial as well as a scientific reality.

America in 1860 was still youthful economically and innocently rural. A magnificent empire, as vast as the most glamorous dynasties of ancient times, had still to be carved out of the fabulous West, and fifteen states had yet to take their places in the republic. Between the Mississippi River and the Rocky Mountains stretched endless virgin prairies, and even to the east of the great river, just as west of the great mountains, much unoccupied land awaited the settler and the trader. Society east of the frontier was still predominantly rural. Not only did the vast majority of people live on farms, but they were motivated by a rural psychology and conditioned by a rural set of attitudes and values. The heart of America was in its soil, and as against more than 2,000,000 farm enterprises in 1860 there were only 140,433 industrial plants of all types and descriptions. Farm implements and farm property alone represented a value in excess of $8,000,000,000, whereas the entire investment in domestic manufactures was well under $2,000,000,000.

More conclusive than mere statistics was the testimony of American practice. Americans still looked to Europe for goods of better quality, and even such industrial staples as coal and copper were imported from abroad in considerable quantities. Before the Civil War, some two hundred companies were engaged in the manufacture of farm implements, particularly reapers and mowers, but they had a restricted market, as expensive farm machinery was commonly used only on better farms. The existence of two hundred such concerns indicated the extent to which industry was decentralized, and what was true of farm machinery was also true of boots, shoes, textiles, and meat packing. Almost every community had at least one slaughterhouse and the city of New York had more than two hundred. Transportation, invention, urbanization, and capital had many stages to go before Chicago could become "hog butcher to the world and meat packer to the nation."

Cities and industries there were; indeed, in the ten years before the Civil War the economic roots planted in the early days of the republic began to bear an abundant fruit, but the extent of earlier industrial growth, while impressive, paled in comparison with the scope of the later revolution. During the decade from 1880 to 1890 manufacturing for the first time took primacy in the economic life of the people. Already in 1870 there were fewer farmers than others listed as gainfully employed, the proportion being 5,920,000 to 6,586,000. And in 1899 the value of manufactured products reached a total of $11,407,000,000 as against $4,717,000,000 for agriculture. Infant industry had approached maturity and a milestone in the life of the republic was passed. It was also a milestone in the life of the Western world, but that was not apparent until later.

The physical landscape in 1860 accurately reflected the economic order. Transcontinental railroads were but dreams in the minds of promoters or at best roughly sketched plans on the blueprints of industrial engineers. Asthmatic locomotives jogged along iron rails, pulling drafty, uncomfortable coaches. No Pullman cars, block signals, Westinghouse air brakes, or electric power existed to make travel safer and more pleasant. There were no palatial terminals or commodious stations and few luxurious hotels. Urban transit was hardly better than interstate travel, as the buggy and the horsecar were not yet superseded by the trolley. American cities were without good sewage facilities, decent sources of water supply, adequate lighting, or paving. Public health systems were still in their infancy, and it was not unusual to see herds of cattle milling and bellowing as they were driven down Fifth Avenue in New York City, where fashionable shops and residences were shortly to be erected. The idea of the telephone had still to enter the brain of Alexander Graham Bell, and the wireless and the cable had not yet begun effectively to weld the American people into a nation and the world into an interdependent society. When, in 1855, Moses Yale Beach, proprietor of the New York *Sun,* published *Wealthy Men of New York,* he listed only nineteen millionaires. Land was still the measure of status, and the great fortunes he catalogued were made in real estate, commerce, and trade. But the merchant princes of his time were soon to be replaced by lumber barons, railway kings, and emperors of business new to the industrial purple.

The decades from 1860 to 1900 witnessed an astounding series of changes. An industrial Johnny Appleseed had been let loose on the American earth to perform unbelievable feats of growth. Each ten years the tables of population faithfully indexed American industrial expansion. In those forty years the population of the country more than doubled, reaching almost 76,000,000 at the turn of the century. Mechanization of farm as well as factory explained the over-all economic growth, but alterations in the structure of population and two great migratory movements of the period likewise figured in the logbook of momentous change. Ships, railways, and factories lured the immigrant horde to America just as the city lured both natives and immigrants to the economic hubs of the nation. Rural decline in New England and the Ohio Valley followed the industrialization of the East and Middle West, and the lands further west were opened to settlement under the impetus of the machine and the applications of science to agriculture.

Industry moved southward and westward and by 1900 was no longer confined to the northeastern segment of the United States. Alabama's Birmingham became the Pittsburgh of Dixie, although cotton fields still covered the site of the city as late as 1870. By 1878 Birmingham had a population of 3,000 in large measure dependent upon iron. Not long afterward lumber mills were operating in Georgia and Tennessee, sugar refineries multiplied in Louisiana, and North Carolina could boast of 118 plants making tobacco products. Most spectacular was the movement of cotton mills from New England to the new South. Because of proximity to the source of supply and an abundance of cheap labor, the textile interests gradually deserted the region that had given birth to American manufacturing. By 1880 there were 44 textile factories in Georgia, 33 in North Carolina, 18 in Alabama, 14 in South Carolina, and 9 in Mississippi.

The nationalization of industry was evidenced by a westward penetration of manufacturing. Cyrus H. McCormick had already moved his reaper plant to Chicago before the Civil War, and by 1865 other concerns were producing mowing machines in Akron and Canton, Ohio. There were pottery works in the prairie city of Peoria as well as in New Jersey towns; and Illinois, like Connecticut, was becoming famous for recording the march of time after the erection of the American Watch Factory at Elgin in 1865. Meat packing gradually moved westward from New England to Ohio and by the seventies was already settled in Chicago, where George Pullman had centered his Pullman Palace Car Company some years before. Beer began to make Milwaukee and St. Louis famous at the same time, and the milling of flour gave Minneapolis international repute. The hoary sectionalism of North and South, East and West, changed its geographical and political base. Factories no longer solely distinguished the Northeast any more than cotton solely distinguished the South. Slums, labor unions, and the urban environment, far from being peculiar to a single region, became common to all. Each section of the United States now possessed common problems that emerged finally as national rather than local issues.

All along the economic line there was a corresponding development. Manufacturing plants, which numbered slightly more than 140,000 when destiny grasped Abraham Lincoln's roughened hand, had grown to 355,415 when destiny beckoned to William Jennings Bryan at the outset of the nineties. The value of domestic manufactures, which did not reach $2,000,000,000 in Lincoln's day, was over $9,000,000,000 in Bryan's. Over 4,000,000 people were classified as wage earners in the ninth decade of the century as against 1,300,000 in the sixth decade, and the amount of manufactured goods exported to foreign lands rose from $48,000,000 to almost $179,000,000. When Lincoln, bidding his Illinois neighbors farewell, spoke from the rear of his railway car at Springfield in 1861, but 30,626 miles of track comprised the railway net. When, in 1900, William McKinley was for the second time elected to the presidency, the railway mileage was 192,556. Even the stark statistics of the output of coal, petroleum, pig iron, steel, and copper from 1860 to 1890 are arresting. The amount of coal mined soared from 13,000,000 tons to over 140,000,000, petroleum production from 21,000,000 gallons to almost 2,000,000,000, copper from 7,200 tons to 115,966, pig iron from 821,000 tons to 9,202,000, and steel from an infinitesimal figure to 4,277,071 tons.

The industrial revolution was reforged in the caldron of the Civil War. Two persistent factors in American experience stimulated social effort to substitute mechanical power for human energy. One was the problem of physical space; the other, the shortage of labor. Both were constantly present in American life, but the Civil War created social pressures that accelerated the drive toward mechanization. Wartime needs demanded economy of man power and spurred the development of mechanical processes then in operation. The war exposed the military dangers of physical space and speeded railroad building just as problems of supply made for improvements in transportation. The war also accentuated the labor shortage, thereby fashioning an atmosphere favorable to invention.

Consequently, the struggle served to accelerate economic expansion. Textiles, food processing, and the heavy industry necessary to combat mushroomed under the influence of sectional conflict. Motive power, applied to Elias Howe's recent invention of the sewing machine and Gordon McKay's device for sewing shoe uppers to soles, turned the boot and shoe marts of New England into thriving centers of activity. "Buildings for shoe factories," wrote one enthusiastic contributor to a Lynn paper, "are going up in every direction. . . . " What was true of leather goods was likewise true of cotton and wool. New mills were busy turning out uniforms and blankets for the soldiers as well as articles for civilian consumption. If the finished product contained a high percentage of "shoddy" and soldiers at the front picked chicken feathers from their coats, it did little to diminish the profits that swelled the stream of business prosperity. Military demands for coal, iron, and steel gave fresh impetus to those industries, and by the end of the war America was already exporting light guns to Europe, which was just beginning another war of its own. In the Quaker City alone 180 industrial plants appeared in the years from 1862 to 1864.

Once the industrial process was begun it proceeded on its own momentum. Agriculture, responding to the task of feeding armies of fighters and armies of labor, enormously expanded. After 1862, the government gave 160 acres to any actual settler, and 2,500,000 acres were taken up while the war was still in progress. The dearth of labor on farm and in factory produced a flowering of inventive genius in agricultural tools and mechanical devices for plants and mills. Hands that had held plows, hoes, and sickles now held swords, guns, and pistols; but laborsaving machinery solved the shortage of farm laborers. The output of agricultural machinery trebled and in turn widened the market for those who dealt in coal, iron, and steel. Every year additional reapers and mowers were to be found in the West, giving to each worker in the field the power to accomplish what five workers had done before. One bumper crop succeeded another. American corn and American wheat fed not only the army of the United States and northern civilian workers, but the teeming populations of English industrial centers. At least in England King Cotton was dethroned and American wheat and corn were bidding for his crown. In the single year 1862 England purchased fifty times as much flour and wheat from the United States as she had imported four years previously. "Within five years," an official American document recorded in 1869, "more cotton spindles had been put in operation, more iron furnaces erected, more iron smelted, more bars rolled, more steel made, more coal and copper mined, more lumber sawn and hewn, more houses and shops constructed, more manufactories of different kinds started, and more petroleum collected, refined, and exported, than during any equal period in the history of the country."

Symptomatic of the age of enterprise was the development of the American railway net. The colossal size of the United States, forever a threat to political stability and a bar to the economics of distribution, was finally mastered by the national transportation system. When completed, the trans-Mississippi roads supplied a constantly widening market so essential for the success of mass production of goods. As a by-product, uncharted roads to wealth were discovered in the realms of finance and interesting side tours in the manipulation of railway stock were explored, forecasting the advent of a financial age of capitalism after industrial capitalism had had its first heyday.

Steel rails and the iron horse united the United States. When America was finally to come of age, the basic design of American life, though shot through and through with local colors and deeply dyed with historical strands, was yet a closely knit fabric with a traceable design. If uniformity was the price of cultural unity, it was the machines of communication and transportation that counteracted cultural sectionalism and gave America and the world joint social boundaries.

The railroad builders expressed America's youthfulness by the grandeur of projected transcontinentals, her optimism by the recklessness with which they laid out track far in advance of settlement or freight. But they justified America's faith in herself, for they overcame the insuperable. Where streamliners would one day rush across the continent, the first chugging locomotives had to invade a country alive with herds of buffalo and tribes of hostile natives. Hardly less disturbing were ideological barriers. When railways first began to stir the American imagination, Senator Thomas H. Benton of Missouri predicted in 1830 that rail transport could never compete with internal transport over western rivers. The Mississippi, the senator declared, the great inland sea of the West, its steamboats, and the cities built along its shore would suffer by the introduction of railroads. Anyway, he concluded, the railroads would be so costly that Westerners could never afford to use them. To accomplish the impossible in the face of such obstacles took courage, resourcefulness, and genius. But it was a courage in which thousands of workers along every mile of track shared, a resourcefulness which laid the whole store of human knowledge under contribution, and a genius in which unnumbered scientists and inventors were in silent partnership with forceful architects of business and administration.

The influence of the railroads was ubiquitous. As the vehicles of internal population movement they had no rival. They served not only as carriers of immigration, but were one of the prime inspirations of it. They changed time and space, if not mileage. Industry became mobile, and synchronized; distances that separated raw materials from manufac-

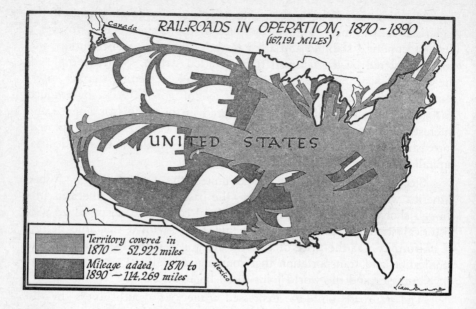

RAILROADS IN OPERATION, 1870–1890
(167,191 MILES)

Canada

UNITED STATES

Mexico

Territory covered in
1870 — 52,922 miles
Mileage added, 1870 to
1890 — 114,269 miles

turing plants and processed goods from markets shrank in terms of time
if not in space with each additional mile. Almost every sphere of economic
activity reacted to the development of transportation, which transformed
self-sufficiency into interdependence. Iron, coal, and steel were molded
into the heart of freight cars and locomotives, but it was the engines that
brought Lake Superior to Pittsburgh and Pittsburgh to the nation. Alabama's mines at Selby, its furnaces at Birmingham, and the coal pits of
West Virginia were as near to Detroit, Duluth, or Chicago as the nearest
freight yard that fringed the city's limits. The cattle industry and meat
packing took a new direction following the expansion of transport, which,
by peopling the western plains, changed lumbering and the milling of
flour as well. And it was the railroads that finally won the West and
altered the nature of American agriculture. The locomotive, leaving horse
power behind and leashed to the mercurial power of steam, was the talis-
man of the economic revolutions. Space and time, literally in the palm
of the engineer's hand, shrank perceptibly as he touched the miraculous
throttle. The locomotive, hauling the mounting production of field and
factory, carried 15,000 gallons of water and 18 tons of coal for its own
use while it performed a degree of labor equivalent to the work of 65,630
pairs of muscles behind the wheelbarrow.

Bringing agriculture within the sweep of the new economic transition, the railroads influenced the career of modern man as profoundly
as the discovery of fire influenced the career of his primitive ancestors.

While the natural importance of food remained the same, the social importance of food altered markedly. Biologically, food was as vital as ever before, but its social significance decreased as machines created potential abundance. Factors of economics rather than soil, climate, and geography controlled the degrees of plenty and scarcity as transport increasingly tied together nonproducing areas and surplus-producing areas. Production of food so vastly increased and the price of food so greatly decreased that foodstuffs alone no longer determined the margin between survival and death. Food, clothing, and shelter were once the prime economic goals, but the raw materials that incited industrial cupidity were minerals and petroleum rather than fibers and grains. The revolutions in economics dethroned the primary wants of man from their ruling place, and at the same time made it possible to carry the mounting accumulation of materials and machines all over the nation and the world.

The magical transformations in agriculture were dwarfed by the mechanization of industry. Although agriculture declined in national import and the city rather than the village became the American cultural norm, agriculture experienced its greatest growth between 1860 and 1900. When the nineteenth century merged into the twentieth, more people were living on farms than lived in the whole country when Abraham Lincoln took over the trials of a divided nation. As a result of government land policy, the reclamation of arid regions, scientific farming, and invention, the number of acres under cultivation more than doubled while the value of land, livestock, buildings, and equipment increased from $8,000,000,000 to $20,000,000,000. In one single decade, 1870 to 1880, an area as large as Great Britain and Sweden combined was put to agricultural work by the rush of farmers into the apparently endless West.

If agriculture was demoted to a subservient place in American economy, the agricultural regions were nonetheless central to the great business expansion. Eastern mills and factories, pulsating with new energy, were busily engaged in converting the products of farms, ranches, and mines into marketable goods. Minerals from western mines were forged into the machines of factories as well as the products they manufactured. The very railroads that carried agricultural fruits to eastern destinations were the materializations of western coal, iron, lumber, and lime. Cows and pigs from western farms and ranches were themselves the foundations of the meat-packing industry, while plows, harvesters, binders, and reapers were industrial ventures which, however far removed in distance or thought, stemmed from the agricultural soil. The harvest of crops, made into bread and meat, fed the ever-increasing urban populations who manned the machines, drove the railroads, and kept the books in which the triumphs of man in America were recorded. Europeans who invested in American enterprise, in mines, ranches, railroads, and manufacturing establishments, created an unfavorable balance in international finance. Agricultural surpluses, exported abroad, helped to balance the accounts of international trade, gradually canceling American indebtedness to foreign investors, while American industry was itself developing. The agricultural revolutions were parts of the revolutions in economics. Without the revolutions in agriculture, the industrial edifice could not have been built.

Four controlling features characterized the eventful shift from the older agriculture. The destruction of slavery and the plantation system was chronologically first, but no less revolutionary was the application of machine processes to agricultural operations. Swelling the totals of farm output to figures as unbelievable as the extent of territorial expansion, the march of population westward rounded out the agricultural domain and put an end to the frontier stage of American existence though not to the existence of free land. Finally, agriculture became almost as mechanized as industry; but the increase in farm acreage, the widening use of laborsaving tools, and the attendant increase in production did not prevent agriculture from becoming subordinate to manufacturing.

The rise of the city accompanied the decline of the farm, for everywhere urbanism was the counterpart of industrialism. The factories, the forges, the mills, and the shops became the flesh and blood of modern American civilization, and the cities its living heart. As the processes of manufacturing in the decades after the Civil War deserted the home and moved to the city, the people followed. And by a process of interaction, the city pumped new energies, new ideas, new conflicts into the arteries of rural life. Only on the remotest frontiers, where old and new Americans were for the first time opening up territory to civilization, was the influence of the city momentarily checked. To the generation that inherited America in 1900, the city was the dominating economic and cultural force. What the small farm had been to Thomas Jefferson and Abraham Lincoln, the plantation to John C. Calhoun and Jefferson Davis, the city was to Grover Cleveland and J. Pierpont Morgan.

The transition from the comparatively simple society in which Abraham Lincoln grew to manhood was aggravated by unsolved problems bequeathed to society by the urban revolution. Substitution of machinecraft for handicraft freed man from one set of burdens only to present him with a combination of different ones. Machines, shifting the weight of labor from muscle to motor, cut the time of operation in the factory, in the home, and on the farm. The farmer, worker, and housewife were slowly emancipated from slavish toil, but the substitution presented them with other difficulties that weighed no less heavily upon their minds and hearts. The martyrdom of man is the quest for security that constantly eludes him. After countless centuries, man, having painfully learned something of nature's way, had battled his way to a compromise with her forces. But no sooner had he done so when he came into conflict with other forces of his own creation. The most profound meaning of America's prairie years, the rural society of Lincoln's boyhood, is to be found in the cleavage between man and nature. The most profound meaning of America's urban years, the period of the revolutions in economics, is to be found in the cleavage of man and society. Man did not make nature, but he made the city, and the conflicts he was destined later to wage were conditioned by the urban worlds he built and the machines he created to build them.

The series of economic revolutions, therefore, constitute the skeleton of American life; the constant and continuous struggle to accommodate a democratic social heritage to the changing American scene constitutes its flesh and blood. American energies were challenged by a novel social environment that ruthless men and humane men alike strove to change and to master, to bring into correspondence with their needs, their ideals, and their aspirations. And as they sought to reforge their instruments of work, to remold their habits, and to refine their ideas, they were themselves transformed. New conditions demanded new techniques; new problems called for new solutions, and new experiences initiated new trends of speculation. Scholars have long had names for the social responses to the impact of an altering environment, but adaptation, maladjustment, and "culture lag"—descriptive rather than explanatory terms—are far too anemic to portray the red-blooded activities of life. Americans since the Civil War were not simply confronted with the task of adapting older ideas and institutions to newer circumstances; they were living in the midst of a conflict of cultures.

NATURAL RESOURCES

In all countries the release of economic energies was based upon the exploitation of natural resources; but to describe the riches that awaited adventurers in the United States requires comparison not with another country but with another continent. Almost as breath-taking as the speed of accomplishment was the vastness of the theater of economic operations. All of Greece if not its glory could have found place on the western prairie. The whole extent of the Roman Empire and much of its grandeur could have been comfortably set down in the tremendous area west of the Mississippi. Omnipotent Egyptian Pharaohs and arrogant Assyrian kings whose imperial caravans met at the crossroads of the world were

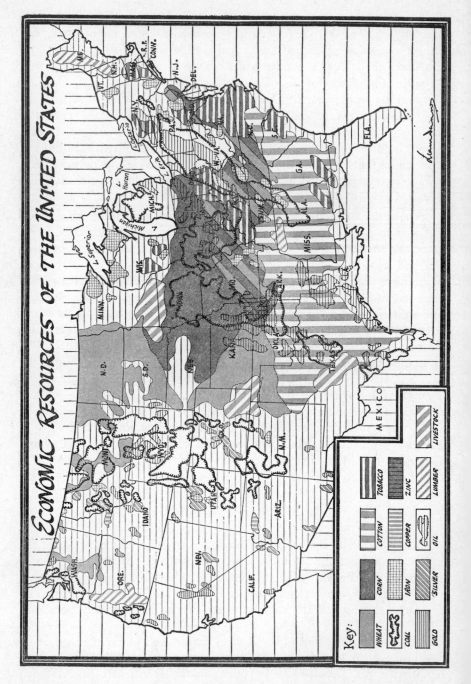

ECONOMIC RESOURCES OF THE UNITED STATES

Key:

WHEAT	CORN	TOBACCO	LIVESTOCK
COAL	IRON	COTTON	ZINC	LUMBER
GOLD	SILVER	COPPER	OIL

298

almost paupers compared to American lords of steel whose wealth was based upon native deposits of iron, coal, and lime. Proud caliphs of fabled Bagdad with bursting coffers of precious stones could not match the treasure of the copper, gold, and silver mines of the American West. All the sparkling jewels of the most powerful Indian princes could not begin to buy the virgin forests that spread over the territory of Wisconsin, Michigan, and California. The natural resources of the United States, its soil, mines, forests, and rivers, were greater by far than those of any single state in previous world history. Relatively untouched for centuries, the natural wealth accruing to the American people proved easier to exploit in the years after 1865 than to bring into efficient social relation with legitimate human wants.

With more than half the coal reserves of the world, America possessed an abundance of fuel and potential power for manufacture and transport. Nowhere are the scope and meaning of the innovations in economics more suggestively revealed than in the domain of coal. In eastern Pennsylvania the anthracite deposits provided the United States with a virtual world monopoly, and only eighteen of all the forty-eight states were without native coal. The black kingdom of bituminous extended for almost half a million square miles, covering a territory greater than England, Scotland, Ireland, and Wales combined, and larger than either Germany, France, or the old Dual Monarchy of the Austrian Hapsburgs.

Coal furnished the sinews of the economic transition. Notwithstanding the inroads later made by oil, it remained the chief source of industrial energy, particularly in the field of transport. Coal in the form of power drove the railroads that crisscrossed the land in all directions, gave speed to the ships of steam that traversed the seas, and supplied the energy that propelled the wheels, pistons, and gears in manufacturing plants. Coal in the form of coke made steel, and steel in turn made the drills, undercutters, and loaders with which the coal was mined. And King Coal also ruled the engines it had helped to create, for the bulk of both rail and shipping freight was made up of ton upon ton of these dusky jewels in the industrial diadem.

Liberal, too, were other resources which Americans had not created but which the caprice of nature had bestowed upon them. Iron ore lay hidden in the Adirondack Mountains, in the eastern states of New Jersey and Pennsylvania; southward in Virginia and Alabama; and westward in the Ohio Valley region, in Minnesota, and the Michigan shores of Lake Superior. Close to the Pennsylvania mines of iron and coal—which made steel only a matter of time—and deep beneath them lay the murky wells of oil just beginning to spout when the war between the states closed, and westward to the mid-continent and beyond were other great pools. Buried also in the prolific American earth were ores of copper and gold, of silver, and of lead. Copper came from the Michigan peninsula until 1887, when Montana, followed by Arizona in 1900, took first place in providing the essential material for the electrical industry, the telephone, the telegraph, and the cable. On the industrial altar Colorado and Nevada offered up their silver, which, whatever its influence on American finance and politics, helped to extend the American mind through photography and American life through medicine and dentistry. Gold from California and South Dakota, lead from Illinois, Missouri, and Colorado contributed their part to the building of industrial America, and throughout more than a third of the continent, forest land of almost every variety merely awaited the development of human enterprise. Added to these were the great systems of internal waterways providing easy paths to internal commerce and the boundless potentialities of the rich and diversified American earth.

Modern ingenuity, by bringing world resources into new relationships, revolutionized the economic opportunity of modern man; but the impact of such rapid change inevitably produced human maladjustment and waste of opportunity on an equally large scale. The economic upheaval, accordingly, accounted for America's major problems as well as for America's major triumphs. Machines annihilated distance and conquered time. Machines, transmuting materials in ever new combinations, made capacity to produce abundance an industrial fact of vast social significance. Steam engines and dynamos, turbines, and Diesel engines were the greatest tributes to man's continuing victory over his physical environment. But while the economic revolutions testified to man's greatest achievement, they presented society with its greatest trials. They gave the more comfortable classes a leisure the like of which the world had never known, but they did not always relieve the drabness and long hours of toil in the lives of multitudes of men and women—and children —on isolated farms and in huge impersonal factories. Potential abundance by itself did not banish poverty or equalize opportunity.

Natural resources alone did not account for the economic metamorphosis, for to ascribe the mammoth changes to natural wealth simply posed the problem in different terms. The American continent, teeming with undeveloped riches, existed long before the advent of Leif Erickson and his Viking band. Prior to the coming of Europeans, slightly over half a million Indians lived in the New World on a primitive economic level. They struggled among themselves for subsistence, although the wealth of geological ages lay within easy reach. Social forces must join with physical forces to produce discovery and inventive activity. Early societies without coal deposits never developed iron implements any more than cultures in the pastoral stage of existence discovered steel despite the proximity of coal, iron, and lime. Indian culture had no need for fire-arms until it came in contact with Western culture, nor did the Chinese have use for oil before they were introduced to Western lamps.

SOCIAL CORRELATES

While the treasures of the American earth supplied the physical basis for revolutionary developments, it was the combination of social as well as physical change that explained them. Resources were relative to a given social context, and mines, forests, or rivers divorced from man had no cultural significance whatever. Natural resources, therefore, were dynamic rather than static, relative rather than absolute, and functional rather than sterile. They were relative because they were meaningful only in terms of human needs, dynamic because their relationship to man altered in response to constantly changing needs, and functional because they operated only in response to human ends. They were themselves variables in a changing scheme of human relations. Expanding wants stimulated the creation of new techniques in order to supply them, new techniques created new environments, and new environments in turn created a series of new wants. But the social interrelations of the industrial, agricultural, urban, and transportation upheavals—interdependence, impersonality, and the rate of transformation—were equally potent factors that conditioned the wants and needs of man in the America after the Civil War.

Of all the social consequences that followed in the wake of the economic revolutions, interdependence—of industry, of trade, of existence—was the greatest. The industrial whole became utterly dependent upon its economic parts. Trade was dependent upon transportation, and industrial activity was dependent upon both. The city exemplified the interdependence of existence, for urban living was communal and cooperative, resting upon an infinite division of labor into manifold specialties with no one self-sufficient. The life of modern man was inextricably linked with the lives of others, with the work of remote, unseen hands and brains. He was utterly dependent upon highly specialized arts, skills, goods, and services that once had been completely unnecessary for either food or clothing or shelter during an earlier and more primitive time. And the new relationships were symbolized by the massive structures reared with steel.

If coal was king in the new America, steel soon became a powerful contender for the industrial throne. An infant industry in the seventies, it grew beyond man's estate into gianthood in a scant thirty years. By 1900 twice as much steel was produced in the United States as in Britain, its nearest competitor, and America became steelmaker to the world. Built upon the trinity of coked coal, iron, and limestone, the romance of steel was the romance of industry. Once remote from common experience, touching life only in the knives on kitchen tables and in expensive precision tools, steel touched life everywhere. Steel rode with man in railway cars and crossed the ocean with him in steel ships. Reared into bridges and elevated lines, it enabled him to connect sprawling cities and to reach with new speed and comfort the more spacious suburbs of an overgrown New York, Boston, or San Francisco. His homes, his offices, his farms, and the mills, factories, and forges where he worked were all intimately related to steel. Nails of steel drove out iron nails, and barbed wire fences, based upon steel, revolutionized the packing industry and changed the history of cattle. The same barbed wire hastened the settlement of the trans-Mississippi West with far-reaching results upon agriculture, politics, and social philosophy. Skeletons of steel in the shape of giant factories and giant skyscrapers became the pyramids of modern America and the symbols of her towering strength.

The process involved in steel manufacture telescoped modern industrial history. Iron ore, coal, and limestone, the primary requisites, had first to be mined and then transported to smelting furnaces, where the iron was separated from the ore. When smelted, the iron was then refined into steel, after which the subsequent manufacturing stages only began. Once iron, coal, and limestone were altered to make steel, steel was made into finished products: rails, pipes, wire, and nails. Semifinished products, bars, steel plates, and steel sheets, were in turn metamorphosed into railway cars, ships, and machines.

Long before steel emerged from the blast furnace ready for conversion, a series of prior operations, literally industries in themselves, were necessary. Mining, quarrying, and transportation by rail and by water had first to be planned, organized, and administered. Before a single bar of steel could be made, ships had to be built, canals dug, locks constructed, tracks laid, cars manufactured, and mining implements devised. Before iron could be made into steel, coal and iron must be mined, limestone quarried, coke made from coal, iron smelted from its ore. Nor was this all, for the sciences of chemistry, physics, and engineering had to be translated into the technology of locomotives, steam shovels, ships, converters, and blast furnaces. Even with all these factors amazingly intertwined, the record was still not exhausted. Mines depended upon the miners as much as miners depended upon the mines, rails were laid by workers, and ships had crews. Stevedores, firemen, smelters, bookkeepers, accountants, lawyers, administrators, brokers, and Wall Street speculators were as much a part of steel as of coal, iron, meat, and oil.

Although steel was basic to American industry, it was the common store of knowledge that was basic to steel. Interdependence was the

Typical of the age of enterprise were Jay Gould *(upper left)*, a sick little man, who successfully pursued power but died before his time; Cornelius Vanderbilt *(upper right)*, pioneer in monopoly, who left over ninety millions to his son; James J. Hill *(lower left)*, the great rival of Henry Villard for the railroads of the Northwest; and Andrew Carnegie *(lower right)*, ironmonger, steel master, dispenser of largesse, who personified the contradictions of an era. *(Culver Service)*

The age of invention.

A prima donna records for Edison's "talking machine."
(Bettmann Archive)

A new means of locomotion, Edison's electric railway, 1880. *(Bettmann Archive)*

Inventive genius and trained capacity, exemplified by Henry Bessemer *(lower left)* and William Kelly *(lower center)*, inventors of the oxidizing process for steel, and John A. Roebling *(lower right)*, bridge builder, were responsible for such construction marvels as the Brooklyn Bridge *(right)*. They gave modern civilization a new physical framework and modern thought a new dimension. (All photos *Bettmann Archive* except Roebling, *Culver Service*)

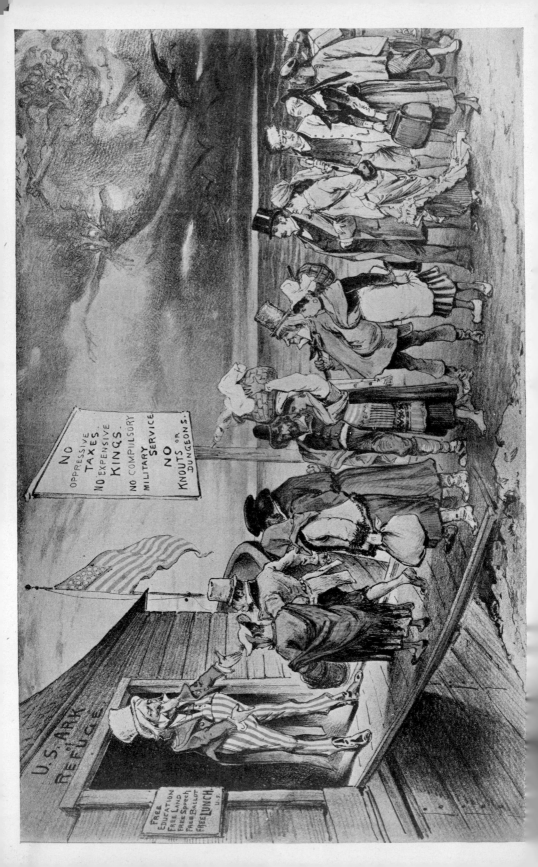

essence of ideas as of industry, and men of many nations contributed to the technological and economic advancement of this prime metal. An Englishman, Henry Bessemer, and a Kentucky Irishman, William Kelly, invented the oxidizing method for the making of steel. Two Germans, Charles and Ernest Siemens, and two Frenchmen, Pierre and Emil Martin, added other discoveries that speeded production and lowered price by allowing commercial use of lower-grade ores. No less global were commercial ties. Steel ships of peace and war began to appear in the eighties; steel reached out to cross the ocean lanes of commerce. There was steel for the railways of China, and the iron brew from American furnaces found its way to the land of the Mikado and to the lands of the Dutch in Java. Steel was needed in the immense Argentinian wheat fields and in the mines of Bolivia and Peru. Railways that converged in far-off Tokyo ran on rails made in Pittsburgh, made with coal mined in West Virginia and Pennsylvania by erstwhile peasants from Slovenia from whose labors came the coke that enabled the furnaces in Illinois and Ohio, worked by Bohemians and Slavs, to pour out their product so that the occupants of the rail carriages might reach the Japanese capital.

Every year the web of the economy spun tighter and tighter. Pittsburgh, once the gateway to the West, became a huge industrial artery pumping life into the economic tissues of the nation and fed in turn by other veins of pulsating human enterprise. A thousand miles away men dug in the Lake Superior mines to provide iron ore for Pittsburgh steel, just as thousands of miles farther away Malayans slaved in Dutch mines to provide tin for Pittsburgh tin plate. Other men in West Virginia and in Pennsylvania, stooping in dark caverns, hacked away at walls of coal formed during remote ages of geological time. Barges on the Great Lakes and on the Ohio and hundreds of freight cars brought cargoes of iron and coal to the city that had once been Fort Pitt, while masses of workers all over the country produced tools, dies, and materials, that the forges, furnaces, cars, and ships might play their parts in the making of steel. When something happened to steel, puddlers in Pittsburgh as well as miners in the Kanawha Valley, workers in Youngstown, Gary, and Scranton were affected. Clerks in factories, railway yardsmen, river bargemen, who never saw each other, and hosts of others were similarly interconnected.

Impersonality was the concomitant of the subdivision of human activity, for who actually made the locomotive, the ship, or the machine? Was it the scientist in the laboratory, the engineer at the drafting board, the broker on Wall Street, or was it the miner, the puddler, the Ohio River boatman? The emotional satisfactions that derived from independent craftsmanship were likewise gone forever, for whose ego was reflected in a gleaming bar of steel? Was it the worker who withdrew it from the steaming furnace, the manager who directed the operations in a single plant, or the administrative colossus who presided over the destinies of a combination of related corporations? The law gave a terse answer to the question of ownership, but who was truly·identified psychologically with the turbine as Paul Revere was once identified with his precious silver plate?

When industry turned to volume production and the corporate technique, a fateful change in human relations took place. Owners rarely operated their own enterprises or worked together with their employees. Ownership was divided among hundreds and thousands of holders of stock who did not know the workers and felt no responsibility for their fate. The intimacy that had governed industrial relations in Jackson's day was gone forever. The machine became central to manufacturing and entailed a heavy outlay of capital, but labor had to adjust to the machine, not the machine to labor. Whatever the economic justification of this reversal of the obvious, it made little sense in human or moral terms. Workers tended more and more to become the auxiliaries of machines. They ceased largely to be craftsmen. Instead of their skill and their livelihood being creatively one, their work became a job—a means to the end of life rather than a creative satisfaction of life itself.

Instead of the intimate relations that had once obtained between owners and workers, both of whom labored together under one industrial roof, the corporation became the employer. Ownership, like responsibility, was distributed by shares of stock and the manager stood in the place of the onetime co-worker who had also been the boss. The gap widened between employer and employee. Business was geared to profit, and labor to existence, nor did absence from the scene of activity make the stockholder's heart grow softer. Corporate managers were responsible only to boards of directors; they, to holders of stock. The former were charged with making money; the latter, with the duty of seeing that money was made.

If workers had to be laid off, if pay had to be cut, if hours had to be lengthened, these were problems of corporate finance and business management, not social or human problems. Rare indeed were the instances when layoffs were weighed against insecurity, decreases in wages against want, or increases in hours against health or safety. Machines could operate continuously even if men could not; it was economical to run furnaces day and night even if it meant a staggered twelve-hour day. Machines were impervious, and so indeed were the distant stockholders, the equally distant managers, and the austere gentlemen who sat on the dignified board. While machines in the long run created work, they did not provide employment for particular men displaced by new machines. Wholesale destitution in periodic depression was the child of the machine; want was the child of social irresponsibility; and social irresponsibility was the child of the impersonality of industrial society.

Individual workers could not effectively bargain with widely dispersed employers. Individual men of business, philanthropic, undeviatingly loyal to particular Christian creeds, lived private lives beyond reproach. Yet labor's battle for elemental decency, for adequate compensation, humane hours, and healthful surroundings was stubbornly and consistently opposed. The conservation of energy by use of machines testified to the brilliance of inventors, to the multiplication of laborsaving devices, but labor's campaign for shorter hours was blocked at every turn. The social wealth of the nation was exploited with a speed that shocked the provident, but the share of labor was in no sense commensurate with its contribution. Monopolies made millions, thousands of stockowners increased their fortunes, but the worker at the bench and the assembly line earned a meager return.

While the material rewards of labor were few, the social rewards were even fewer. The workers toiled, but to the masters of capital went the credit—except on the Fourth of July and other memorial occasions. The man in overalls, on farms and in factories, was a glittering verbal symbol often on the lips of tariff orators, but less commonly weighing upon the hearts of those who voted in the halls of Congress or who controlled the organs of public opinion. Millions of men in overalls lived in urban tenements, in company towns, or in shoddy houses on American farms. They worked in unsanitary shops and dangerous factories, they sweated under the broiling western suns, they struggled against debt, and were relentlessly pursued by the specter of insecurity. If the man on the street was slow to feel the direct consequences of urban impersonality, the man in the shop, the mill, and the mine could not escape it. Business and society as a whole, clinging to the old concepts of individualism, failed to perceive it. The extent to which business in particular and society in general failed to appreciate the moral and human aspects of the "labor problem" is an accurate index of the growth of impersonal relations in the age of the city and the machine. Wherever and whatever the guilt, the effect on the common man was the same.

The rapidity of social change complicated existence and intensified the gravity of adjustment. If time measured in human life was swift, time gauged in terms of the life of society was winged. The span of history from 1492 to date is infinitely shorter than the period between the so-called beginnings of civilization five thousand years before the Christian Era and the Columbian voyages. Compared with the time between the appearance of man and the rise of Egypt and Babylonia, the history of society becomes microscopic. The passage of time from 1860 to the present is brief indeed contrasted with the whole period of American development, briefer when compared to the evolution of the Western world, and almost infinitesimal in the light of the history of man. But there are few instances in the whole record of human achievement comparable to the years following the Civil War in the range of transformation, and still fewer instances in which the tempo of the transformation can be matched, for in little more than an average lifetime America passed from one stage of evolution to another.

To one who had lived two generations earlier—even if he were equipped to grasp a modern vocabulary—it would be hard successfully to describe the sorceries of chemistry, physics, and mechanics as they materialized from the assembly lines of gleaming factories; and still harder to explain our habits of living or the altered values and social relationships that they united to produce. Even the wisest of the earlier philosophers would be baffled by modern concepts of space, time, and deity, of evolution, thermodynamics, and relativity.

The meaning of speed, impersonality, and interdependence in everyday life cannot be elicited from the cold beauty of statistical compilations. The human impact of the new economy cannot be measured by the mathematics of railway mileage any more than it can be gauged by bushels of wheat, bales of cotton, or tankers brimming with oil. The staggering totals of acres subdued by wistful people in search of peace or absorbed by eager adventurers in search of wealth were by themselves empty of significance. Even the arithmetic of the census returns, denoting the growth and density of population, was inconsequential divorced from the vibrant dreams of living men and women. The trim statistical edifice of the census and government reports made it possible to describe the economic transition, not to understand it. Agricultural expansion was not the record of acres under cultivation alone, but the trials, yearnings, and failures of men who planted seeds of life on the plains as well as seeds of oats and corn. Stately columns of numbers did not tell the epic of ocean liners docked in European ports awaiting their cargoes of human freight, of the desires and prayers of the millions of human beings they so neatly catalogued. The economic revolutions, throbbing in the engines of trans-Atlantic vessels and in the hearts of bold business promoters with imperial plans, throbbed as well in the hearts of clerks and miners, stevedores and inventors. They hummed in the locomotives of half a hundred railway lines which carried thousands to American farms and American cities, to homes and to happiness, to sorrow and to defeat.

The series of revolutions in economic life represent the apex of human control over natural forces up to that point in chronological and cultural time; but they did not of themselves necessarily foster a sounder democracy. Formidable problems and widespread unrest, besetting industrial Europe and industrial America, posed a fundamental question—whether man, having learned to control the creations of nature, could learn to control the creations of man. During the age of power and the age of the machine, the goal of consumption was gradually succeeded by the goal of production. The politics of industry stressed producer economics, to the neglect and detriment of consumer economics. The end of industrial activity was still fabricated or converted goods, but industrial statecraft came more and more to be centered upon the mechanisms of production and finance—machines, motive power, and control of resources, large-scale organization, large-scale dividends, and control of markets—rather than upon a plentitude of goods or the problem of their distribution for maximum satisfaction of human wants. But in this the history of the United States recapitulated the history of the Europeanized world.

From 1492 to 1865 American development was evolutionary; after 1865 it was revolutionary. Before the Civil War the United States followed a course clearly marked out in the existing experience of mankind; after the war, Americans, as did their fellow citizens of the globe elsewhere, embarked upon a new adventure. Following the introduction of the machine age, the United States emerged as a modern industrial nation. American history from 1865 to 1900 is the history of that transformation, a history which cannot be told in the conventional chronological pattern of political developments and legislative acts alone. Accordingly, the following chapters deal with the various phases of American life as they were altered by the new economics, the new industry, and new social relationships. They describe the manner in which government and political parties disintegrated in contact with machine civilization. They recount the story of the conquest of rural society and the rise of the city, the saga of the immigrants, and the social evils that followed the victory of business and the machine. Finally, they analyze the constant efforts of man to eradicate the sins of society, and the shrinking world which ushered in the global stage of human society.

XV

THE POLITICAL TRIUMPH OF BUSINESS

1865–1900

Every fiber of American life responded to the revolutions in economic life taking place between 1865 and 1900. A business civilization of railways, ships, and corporations was its social outcome; a business government of tariffs, franchises, and special legislation was its political outcome. Three basic elements transcended all others: the overthrow of the southern plantation aristocracy; the transfer of power from agrarians to industrialists; and the altered economic organization of society that outmoded political institutions, thwarted reform, and deflected democratic processes. The first presaged the end of the political alliance between agrarians—farmers and planters—who had built a sectional barricade against commercial and industrial encroachments; the second marked the ascendancy of manufacturing and finance in politics as well as economics; the third exposed the disparity in politics between older rural and agricultural techniques and newer industrial-urban needs and gave modern form to the continuing democratic challenge.

The Civil War demolished the political and economic power of the planters. At one legislative blow, the Thirteenth Amendment, emancipating the Negroes, confiscated private property worth almost three billion dollars and destroyed the planting class. If the war was truly a clash between a rural civilization represented by the South and an urban civilization represented by the North, the defeat of cotton assured the final victory of industrialism. But there were other factors far less speculative. Whatever the veiled motives of northern business leaders and their congressional henchmen, one of the political effects of reconstruction was the temporary exclusion of southern agrarian representatives from participation in the Federal government. When the Southerners finally returned, they were confronted with a body of accomplished legislative facts. So completely were the designs of law translated into economic operation that it was thereafter impossible to turn back the industrial clock.

Politically, the Civil War subordinated the agrarian opposition to commercial, financial, and industrial enterprise. Not only a change in the balance between the two rival parties resulted, but a change in the balance of forces within the parties. In consequence, the agrarian phalanx, never fully united, was more completely split. When farmers of the northeastern section of the Mississippi Valley deserted the Democratic party for the Republican in the fifties, the liberal strength of the Democratic combination was fatally weakened. The Civil War left Democratic groups in the South under the wing of conservatives—big landlords and financial-industrial groups, both of whom owed allegiance to northern financiers and industrialists with southern investments or business connections. Conservative Democrats, therefore, both North and South, were in control of the party machinery until the campaign of 1896. Republicans, increasingly under the domination of business leaders, similarly were unresponsive to the needs of common folk. Small farmers, who with eastern workers had made Andrew Jackson the leader of the people, were divided between the parties and ousted from the control in both. In the inner councils of party organization, Democratic and Republican alike, the break in agrarian unity upset the traditional two-party alignment and made it impossible to revert to the Jacksonian technique of combining small farmers and small workers in one party. All attempts between 1865 and 1894 to accomplish this unity were frustrated, although such a combination would at all times have spelled out victory for the majority will. As a residue of reconstruction, the political and emotional blockage between the agricultural South and the agrarian West was intensified, making cooperation between the solid Democratic South and the normally Republican West difficult of attainment. The industrialists, devoted to protective tariffs, sound currency, subsidies for business, and the protection of property, were all but assured of congressional dominion.

THE PROGRAM OF BUSINESS

The legislative program adopted while the war was still in progress certified the triumph of business enterprise. Yet it was as much a victory for Alexander Hamilton, long since gathered to his fathers, as it was for the Hamiltonian Republicans of the Lincoln era. The economic blueprint put into action after the election of 1860 initiated a Hamiltonian conquest, for it heralded the final triumph of business, the dominance of industrialism, the rise of the city, the advent, in short, of a new civilization under the auspices of men of large affairs.

High on the list of industrial objectives was the tariff. When manufacturers had earlier sought protective immunity from foreign competition, the representatives of staple-producing planters, small farmers, and traders on the high seas had joined their congressional votes to prevent it.

Western farmers were more concerned with the disposition of lands and internal improvements, and southern planters had already come to view the tariff as a symbol of northern industrial aggression. Despite all that eastern manufacturers, southern hempgrowers, and Pennsylvania iron-mongers could accomplish, the tariff sank to a discouraging low by 1857. But unrestrained by southern opposition and under the impress of the war, the Morrill Act of 1861, the highest tariff up to that time, established protection as a national policy. Attempts to lower the tariff thereafter, especially in 1872 and 1894, failed dismally. Instead, the rates rose consistently, for the tariff, as a device for shutting out foreign competition and maintaining rewarding profits for industry, became a business credo for manufacturers as sacred as contract and as divine as property. Passage of the Morrill Act itself suggests a revolutionary shift in power; maintenance of protection in spite of constant opposition signifies the emergence of a new economic order and a new political regimen.

If the upward swing of the tariff pointed to a change in the political center of gravity, the development of centralized banking confirmed it. Jefferson and his colleagues were no less opposed to a national bank than Jacksonians, since it was the financial arch of the Hamiltonian edifice, whether in the eighteenth century or the nineteenth. After Andrew Jackson had driven the second Bank of the United States to the wall in the 1830's, all the efforts of businessmen were unable to restore it until the Civil War paved the way for a new federal banking system. The National Banking Act of 1862 curbed the uninhibited flow of currency stemming from almost fifteen hundred state banks and bolstered business confidence. The altered arrangement required banks desirous of issuing currency to purchase federal bonds against which the Treasury issued national-bank notes up to 90 per cent of the market value of the bonds. Bankers now looked to Washington for the protection of their investments as well as of their business, and a volume of sound credit through bonds and notes was established. When Federal contracts for food, clothing, and the articles of war multiplied, business, equipped with credit, confidence, and government aids, was more than eager to share in the rewards. Fluctuating local currencies were taxed out of existence in 1865 and though the Union was forced to issue paper money—the greenbacks—to finance the war, ten years later in the Resumption Act the government provided for their redemption in good, hard coin of the industrial realm. Creditors, persistent agitators for the resumption of specie payments, welcomed this development, since their holdings increased in value as money increased in worth. Debtors, on the other hand, believing that more money in circulation would relieve their economic difficulties, were distressed by the turn in events, since they had hoped to discharge their obligations in a depreciated medium. Inflation of the currency was often the weapon of social dissent, but after the Civil War the proponents of "sound money," regardless of party labels, were always in command.

As crucial to business dominance as tariffs and banking was government aid to corporations, and none received more ample assistance than the railroads. Pioneers in large-scale business, the railway builders amassed the first truly great American fortunes and opened up a major area of speculation in the period after the Civil War. By control of transportation and hence of markets—the economic nucleus in a nation of continental proportions—the railroad magnates captured the base of the industrial pyramid while it was still in the process of construction. Railroad legislation, typical of government beneficence to private capital, loomed large on the program of big business on the eve of the peace between the states.

Unhampered by southern jealousy of a northern transcontinental route, the Pacific Railroad Act was passed in 1862. With a lavishness that betokened more than the need for adequate transport, several companies were granted a right of way through the great American West with the privilege of taking construction materials from the public domain wherever they might be found. Ten sections of government land for each mile of track built were granted outright, and to ease the strain of construction cost, the United States agreed to lend $16,000 for each mile traversing level country, $32,000 for each mile in the mountain foothills, and $48,000 for each mile running over the mountains. So zealous indeed was the government in aiding the struggling railways that imaginary mountains were reared up over hundreds of miles of level territory by congressional decree in order to increase the size of federal loans. Should the road fail of completion by 1876, all the rights and the part finished up to that time were to revert to the government, but if completed on schedule, the loans were to be repaid out of earnings. Two years after the passage of the original act, Congress doubled the land gift and granted the roads the special privilege of selling first-mortgage bonds in the open market.

More than the railroad net came out of the fabulous generosity of the Congress of the United States. The dull bills that granted franchises, lands, and rights of way and provided for loans, bonds, and subsoil ownership were the levers wrenching a world from its moorings. As the rails fanned out across the continent, the mines of Colorado, Nevada, Montana, and Idaho became dependencies of a growing industrial empire, and the mighty forests of California, Oregon, Washington, and Minnesota were leveled in reckless haste by a generation of fortune hunters. Wealth poured into the private holds of the masters of American capital as public lands were transferred to private ownership and wantonly squandered without regard to public policy of conservation and control. As the iron horse puffed across the prairies and up the valleys of the virgin West, the incantations of Indian medicine men drowned out by the engine's roar were as ineffective as the arrows, unloosed from angry bows, that glanced harmlessly off the locomotive's iron sides. The steam locomotive drove the Indian and his horse from plain and plateau, for behind the locomotive in drab coaches came masses of men and women in search of happiness and security who built yet more miles of track, dug into mines, struck down the primitive forest of the Pacific, plowed up the fertile soil, and fenced in the open range. The men who sat in committee rooms at the nation's capital or in directors' rooms in every city of the land, who framed laws and changed their amorphous dreams into the hard realities of railroads, mines, lumber mills, cattle ranches, and oil wells, had scant time to speculate on the consequences of their ceaseless activity. They saw only power in the coal that they ordered from the mines, their own wills superimposed upon the rivers, mountains, and trackless wastes that they bent to their hopes and their plans. If they paused to consider the millions of men and women, from Europe, from Asia, from the United States, whose lives were uprooted and changed in the wake of their successes, they did not contemplate their roles as destroyers of an old culture and builders of a new.

Intimately related to railway promotion and the settlement of the West was the disposition of the public domain. Long the dream of western agrarians and labor reformers, legislation for free land before the Civil War was blocked by sectional diversities. Industrialists feared the effect of such a policy upon the labor market, land speculators despaired of their investments should homesteads become a social fact, and Southerners dreaded the rapid settlement of the West by free-soil immigrants and northern farmers. When finally a homestead law was passed by Congress in 1860, it was vetoed by a Democratic President, James Buchanan, who feared for the safety of the Union as well as for the safety of the South. But the emerging Republican party, seeking to catch votes wherever it could find them, made free homesteads a part of its program, for free land was as alluring to western farmers as to eastern workingmen. It also had a charming and unmistakably metallic sound to the promoters of transcontinental railways.

Although the Homestead Act of 1862 has long been considered a charter of economic independence for the landless, it was a greater boon to the propertied than to the poor. Under the provisions of the act any citizen or person who had declared his intention of becoming a citizen was eligible to receive 160 acres of the public domain by payment of a nominal fee and residence on the land for a five-year period. The terms

of the law read well, but congressional conduct indicated that other objectives, inconsistent with the homestead principle, took priority. Granting
land to railways, however justifiable as a means of speeding construction,
negated the spirit of Homestead. Five times as much land was given to
the railroads in the eight years after its passage than during the twelve
years before. For example, 127,628,000 acres were given outright to railways between 1862 and 1871. As land was withdrawn from sale pending
the final determination of the railway route, 100,000,000 additional acres
were placed outside the reach of the landless as late as 1883. In addition, more than 146,000,000 acres of federal lands were given to the
states in which they lay, and about 175,000,000 acres of Indian lands acquired by government treaty were allowed to pass into the private hands
of capitalists and corporations. Land given to private corporations had
later to be purchased by the landless. When the figures were finally computed, it was found that the Illinois Central more than paid for the cost
of construction with the proceeds of the sale of its lands; and the Northern
Pacific, completed in 1883 at a cost of $70,000,000, acquired more than
$136,000,000 from the disposition of its government gift. Nevertheless,
scores of farmers obtained farms under the provisions of Homestead and
continued to look upon the Republican party as their benefactor. There
were other important political consequences. Land in the form of railroad grants and as speculative investments was a vital source of power, a
benefaction that political managers could dispense, a prize that men of
business sought. This was the stuff out of which political history behind
the scenes of party conflict was made.

If government solicitude for the indigent farmer was belied by the
facts, government solicitude for employers seeking a cheap industrial labor
supply was apparent. Lest the Homestead Act interfere with the labor
market, Congress passed the Immigration Act of 1864, which authorized
the importation of contract labor. Twenty years later the practice of importing labor gangs by contract was officially banned, but continued illegally notwithstanding. Meanwhile, with or without contracts, immigration from Europe—14,000,000 strong from the Civil War to 1900—
guaranteed a cheap and plentiful labor supply and weakened the power
of organized labor to bargain collectively.

The triumph of American capitalism was made certain by a dual
struggle for power. Leaders of business, striving to capture the economic
resources of the nation, sought aid and protection from those who held
the reins of political control. With the vision of industrial empire already
clear, they looked to those who had rights to grant, bounties to give, and
land to dispense. Leaders of politics, bent upon the capture of the institutions of government, sought the support and assistance of those who

held the reins of economic control. The politicians had organizations to weld, elections to win, and power to seize. The one had things to buy; the other had things to sell. Railroad promoters, for example, wished not only for charters and government mail contracts; they wished to strangle water transportation rivals, to prevent the passage of bills for the improvement of rivers and harbors. If the emissaries of business sought privileges, the leaders of politics sought support.

Beauty and the Buzzard: Cleveland chooses economic virtue. *(Courtesy Collection of Regional History, Cornell University.)*

Differences of detail sometimes distinguished Republicans from Democrats, but they were not in basic disagreement. Both were devoted to business, to the exploitation of the natural resources of the nation with government aid and without government interference. Such divisions as existed were greater between the liberal and conservative wings of either party than between the two parties themselves. In both parties conservatives were dominant. If President Benjamin Harrison, the Republican, was a corporation lawyer, so, too, was Samuel J. Tilden, a leading Democratic contender. Rutherford B. Hayes was a Republican President bitterly opposed to currency inflation, but Grover Cleveland was a Democratic President just as adamantly in favor of "sound money."

Northern Democratic strength was recruited from the great cities of the industrial belt in the Northeast and the Middle West. Republican strength was greatest in the rural districts of the North and West and the smaller cities. Republicans in New England mill towns, in mining towns of Pennsylvania, and in the rural Northeast could not muster a national majority, but when joined by voters in the mining camps of the mountain slopes, by prairie farmers in the corn belt, and by ranchers and fruit-growers of the Pacific coast, they could compete on equal terms with the manipulators of Democratic landslides in the big cities and the solid South. This alignment of Republican voters, moreover, made it difficult for the party of Jefferson and Jackson ever again to consolidate a for-midable majority of small farmers and workers in all sections of the nation. So long as both parties thus kept liaison with Wall Street and Main Street, no very fundamental ferment could find political outlet, and no realignment of voters could threaten to check the triumph of business.

When Lord Bryce, the most astute observer of the American com-monwealth in the late nineteenth century, remarked that "there was no politics in politics," he meant that there were no national policies, plat-forms, or issues. Neither party, continued Bryce, "has any clean-cut prin-ciples, any distinctive tenets. Both have traditions. Both claim to have tendencies. Both have certainly war cries, organizations, interests, en-listed in their support. But those interests are in the main the interests of getting and keeping the patronage of government. Tenets and policies, points of political doctrine and points of political practice have all but vanished. . . . The American parties now continue to exist, because they have existed. The mill has been constructed, and its machinery goes on turning, even if there is no grist to grind. . . ."[1]

THE AGE OF ENTERPRISE

The alliance of business and government was the consequence of an identity of interest, but it rested also upon more solid foundations. Busi-ness dominated society. Acquisitive zeal had captured the world and taken hostage the ideals of mankind. Men in America were bewitched by the glitter of wealth, and in an era of rapid acquisition the successful believed that the ascent from poverty to wealth was easy. And the un-successful in large measure shared this creed. So great was the faith in

---

[1] James Bryce, *The American Commonwealth.* New York: Macmillan, 1910, II, 21, 24, 29. By permission of The Macmillan Company, publishers.

America—in its railways, its bridges, its cities and in the notes, bonds, and stocks which helped to build them—that greatness was confounded with bigness and bigness with material gain. America had not completely elevated crass materialism to the place of the liberal conception of a good society, but material accomplishment was the symbol of achievement and material gain the object of pursuit. Successful men were the living embodiment of what was soon to be called the "gospel of wealth," and they were the most active proponents of the philosophy of acquisition. And the gospel of wealth was not only the process of acquisition, but its justification; not only conspicuous consumption itself, but its social sanction. There was, as Thorstein Veblen, keenest economist of his generation, observed, "a naïve, unquestioning persuasion abroad among . . . the people . . . that, in some occult way, the material interests of the populace coincide with the pecuniary interests of business men." The American people were fascinated by success, applauded and envied those who succeeded, and fervently wished themselves to succeed.

And well they might, for industrial America was taking shape before their eyes. The United States was young not only in years of statehood; it was a country built by young men. The work of settling a continent and building an economic empire was work for men at the height of their physical and intellectual powers. It was a giant task for giant men whose vision matched the continental expanse and whose energy resembled the potential power of American resources. What some could accomplish others could emulate, and all could dream. Indeed, for most only the gossamer of dreams remained. But if optimism waned in the years after 1880, it was the victims of the economic revolutions and their spokesmen who were embittered by pessimism; not the masters of capital who seemed ever more masterful as the power derived from capital increased.

Cornelius Vanderbilt, the great commodore, was over seventy when he gave up his maritime interests and began to make his railroad fortune, but he was almost an exception. It was youth that grasped the throttle of business power. In 1889, when the Homestead Steel Works and seven other plants were consolidated into the Carnegie Steel Company, Andrew Carnegie was only fifty and about to translate his wealth into a gospel of getting and giving. Henry Clay Frick, Carnegie's associate, became chairman of the board at forty, and Charles Michael Schwab, chief engineer of a Carnegie plant at nineteen, became the company's president at thirty-five. Nelson Morris, famed packer of meat, founded Morris and Company at forty-one, while Philip Armour, after having made millions in pork speculations before the end of the Civil War, was still but thirty-eight in 1870, when Plankington, Armour and Company became Armour and moved to Chicago. Life in America did not begin at forty, but the masters of capital were in their prime when they set out to try their fortunes in the great land of plenty.

A deeply rooted optimism permeated the national community. Nor was it simply a wishful hope based upon the promise of the future; it was the full-bodied glow of confidence reared on the solidity of accomplishment. The impressive achievements of the age of enterprise as they appeared in the sticks and stones of city buildings and in the technics of civilization, in the tools of factories and the millions of everyday things with which life was lived, gave Americans boundless assurance. Men of high as well as low degree were stirred to dreams of conquest and were persuaded that America was in truth the best of all possible worlds. Indeed, for many it was, and for countless more it held out the prospect of becoming so. No rigid stratification of mass and class existed to block the aspirations of ability, for at both poles of American society there was a fluid mobility. Most Americans would have scoffed at the patient thrift characteristic of middle-class Europeans, for their own observation taught them that the palaces of American nabobs were the rewards of boldness, speculation, and the wooing of luck as well as plodding thrift. No Horatio Alger was needed to tell this generation that a poor Scottish immigrant, Andrew Carnegie, could become the president of one of the greatest corporations in the world, or that a small businessman, John D. Rockefeller, could become the Genghis Khan of oil. Americans, already converts to the gospel of work, became its missionaries and never were there fairer vineyards ripe for cultivation or greater numbers ready to answer the evangelical call.

The congressional program of the years following the Civil War successfully launched the great age of industrial enterprise. Thereafter, high tariffs shut out effective foreign competition, and currency and credit policies provided special advantages to accumulators of capital. Subsidies were lavishly granted to business corporations long after they passed the infant stage. National laws supplied a growing market for native steel in the construction of railways and the building of ships, while outright gifts of public lands so huge as to stagger the imagination were given the entrepreneurs of transport. Forest lands, mineral and oil reserves, and fertile agricultural soil were supplemented by loans and donations of money. In addition to such direct beneficences, there were other indirect aids to sustain the privileges won by the drives of special interests. Efforts to control the untrammeled activities of business concerns were long impeded, even when a vast popular demand had arisen for legislation to regulate railways, trusts, and monopolies. After 1887 and 1890, when such laws were finally enacted, ways were found to render them innocuous.[2]

The triumph of business in its political phase represented an elaboration of the gospel of wealth into a system of special privileges. Legislative enactments and court decisions were shaped to this end under the now dominant formula of aid-to-industry. The decline in the influence of agriculture and labor was attested by the slight attention paid by either party to the cry of farmers and workers for equal privileges. Political managers were not neutral as between conflicting interests in American society; aid to agriculture and aid to labor were not included in the political applications of the gospel of wealth. The governments of the states, for example, were no more impartial as between capital and labor than the government of the nation. Coal and iron police were sanctioned by the commonwealth of Pennsylvania, and state governments generally permitted the militia to be used to restrict picketing and to aid employers when they began the practice of hiring professional strikebreakers. Property and property rights enjoyed a privileged position. In 1877 President Hayes, far from neutral, expressed the hope that the strikes of that year would be broken. Cleveland's early faith in the impartiality of government (1886) was belied in his second term when his administration sanctioned the use of the federal injunction to prevent collective bargaining.[3]

THE GOSPEL OF WEALTH AND THE SUPREME COURT

A powerful auxiliary to the expansion of business was the Supreme Court. Its decisions based on precedent, the Court was by nature conservative and slow to change. Moreover, for years after the Civil War all the justices were men who had been born before 1820—long before the social maladjustments stemming from industrialization darkened the scenes of modern life—and three dated their birth from the eighteenth century. Justices ordinarily served for life or until senescence compelled their retirement. Appointments to the Court were made by the President with the consent of the Senate—and men whose social and economic views were suspect were not likely to be chosen. In almost every case only those well past the prime of life were considered; nearly all were lawyers whose active professional careers had been spent in lucrative corporate practice. They tended to enhance rather than to detract from the conservative character of the supreme judicial body; and none of them gained fame and public esteem as a "Tribune of the People."

---

[2] See Chapter XVI for the record of the parties and Chapter XXI for the struggle for public controls.

[3] For the advantages of employers see Chapter XXI.

In the conversion of the Court to the gospel of wealth the Republican party played a decisive role. During the period from 1861 to 1886, fourteen new justices were named to the Supreme Court. Of these one was a Democrat appointed by Lincoln, one was without political record in either party, and the remaining twelve were Republicans. Four were nominated by Lincoln, four by Grant, two by Hayes, and two by Arthur, Republican Presidents all. Nor were members of the Supreme Court oblivious of the connection between economic changes, political appointments, and judicial decisions. Justice Samuel F. Miller, in the case of *Davidson v. New Orleans* (1876), remarked:

It is in vain to contend with judges who have been, at the bar, the advocates of railroad companies, and all the forms of associated capital, when they are called upon to decide cases where such interests are in contest. All their training, all their feelings are from the start in favor of those who need no such influence.

With such a personnel on the Supreme Court and a legal implement such as the Fourteenth Amendment, property rights unencumbered by responsibility acquired a judicial protection hard to breach. Adopted during reconstruction, the Fourteenth Amendment was ostensibly a protective safeguard for the Negro. "No state," ran the wording of the amendment, "shall make or enforce any law which shall abridge the privileges or immunities of citizens of the United States; nor shall any state deprive any person of life, liberty or property without due process of law; nor deny to any person within its jurisdiction the equal protection of the laws." The all-important phrases—"life, liberty or property," "privileges or immunities," "equal protection of the laws," and "person"—were left undefined and it remained for the Court to give them meaning. Regardless of the purpose of the framers, the amendment exerted little effect upon the Negro; its social function became instead the protection of property rights.

The judicial career of the Fourteenth Amendment passed from a liberal phase of respect for legislative majorities to a laissez-faire concern for vested interests. As a result the power of legislative majorities was sharply constricted. At first the Court did not assume a sweeping judicial veto upon state action. Negroes were left to the mercy of local legislatures in such matters as civil rights and elections, and business organizations were likewise left subject to state regulation. In 1873 (the Slaughterhouse cases), the Court held that the amendment was framed as an insurance for the Negro and that a state law designed to promote public health, even if it affected unfavorably certain business interests, was legitimately within state police power. Again in 1876 (the Granger cases), majority judicial opinion, still on the side of the states, refused to invalidate a state statute regulating a corporation sought on the ground that it was a deprivation of property without due process. "Property," declared Chief Justice Waite in *Munn v. Illinois* (1876), "does become clothed with public interest when used in a manner to make it of public consequence. When, therefore, one devotes his property to a use in which the public has an interest, he, in effect, grants to the public an interest in that use, and must submit to be controlled by the public for the common good." And, said the Chief Justice, "For protection against abuses by legislatures the people must resort to the polls, not to the courts."

New appointments to the bench after 1881 stimulated a judicial reaction against liberality toward state regulation. By a decision of 1886 *(Wabash, St. Louis and Pacific Railway vs. Illinois),* the high tribunal insisted that state regulation of railways with interstate connections was a variety of regulation which "cannot be . . . remitted to local rules. . . ." Within six years the Court had determined that a rate fixed by a local legislature might be so unreasonable as to deprive a corporation of property without due process of law *(Chicago, Milwaukee and St. Paul Railway Co. vs. Minnesota* [1889]). Fixing of rates, therefore, became a matter for judicial review, a position reaffirmed by other decisions, notably *Smyth vs. Ames* in 1898. The reasoning upon which rates were reviewed was elaborated by Justice David Brewer in the case of *Regan vs. Farmers' Loan and Trust Company* (1894). "The courts are not authorized," said Justice Brewer, delivering the majority opinion, "to revise or change the body of rates imposed by a legislature. . . ." It was not, he continued, the function of the Court to "determine whether one rate is preferable to another, or what under all circumstances would be fair and reasonable . . . , but still there can be no doubt of their power and duty to inquire whether a body of rates prescribed by a legislature or a commission is unjust or unreasonable, and such as to work a practical destruction to rights of property, and if found to be so, to restrain its operation." Under the prevailing philosophy of laissez faire, the Fourteenth Amendment was later employed to block social legislation affecting wages, hours, and conditions of labor. But the Court was not only active in protecting the rights of property from interference by the states; it was just as vigilant in restraining the federal Congress.

THE REPUBLICAN PARTY

It was largely under the aegis of the Republican party that this program was enacted. Striving to re-establish Hamiltonian ideas, its leaders, no longer supplicants in 1861, were ready to make the most of the opportunities that the withdrawal of the South provided. Republican politicians won favor with business czars, for they had consistently advocated what industrialists considered sound currency, sound banking, and sound tariff policies. Orthodox Republican policy was under attack by agrarians, consumers, debtors, reformers, and social ideologists, but businessmen were interested in business facts rather than in theories of party government and the economics of social welfare. If property was under threat of regulation in federal, state, or local spheres, it was to the appropriate governmental agencies that men of business turned for relief. The Republican party was in the saddle, and it changed from a minority to a majority party because it best served the ends of business as it was itself best served by business collaboration.

Agricultural legions as well as industrial chieftains rallied to the Republican standard. Notwithstanding a historical tradition that aligned agrarians against industrialists, scores of western farmers faithfully supported the Republican cause. Republican measures worked to the interest of corporate wealth, but numberless farm owners traced their title to Homestead and the Grand Old Party. But the husbandman was not always the same as of old. The farmers of the old Northwest waxed wealthy from rising land values and real-estate subdivisions as the frontier line moved westward. As manufacturing and the city invaded the former bailiwicks of Jacksonian Democracy in the Middle West, farmers with a financial surplus enlarged their holdings, invested in urban developments, purchased stocks of industrial enterprises, and drew politically closer to the industrial chiefs than to the legions of agrarian dissent. Nor did the big commercial farmers—kin of agrarians in name only—desert the Republican ranks when agricultural distress engulfed the West, for their interests led them to trust Republican business leadership to exorcise depression and to re-create prosperity. And the directors of the party machinery were not unmindful of the obvious. All but one of the Republican candidates for the presidency between 1868 and 1900 came from the Middle West. In fact, all but one were born in Ohio, a state that remained west geographically but came politically within the orbit of the industrial East.

To the uneasy Republican alliance of western farmers and eastern industrialists must be added the veterans of the Union army, almost a million strong. Banded together in the Grand Army of the Republic, they constituted a formidable pressure group. If they were ever permitted to forget that Abraham Lincoln—their own "Father Abraham"—was a Republican, they could scarcely forget the liberality with which his Republican successors distributed pensions. Between 1879 and 1899, almost two billion dollars were dispensed to former Federal soldiers, who certainly took note when the first Democrat in the White House since James

Buchanan—Grover Cleveland—was as active in vetoing pension bills as his opponents were in sponsoring them.

With like Republican fidelity, Negroes voted their undying thanks to the "Great Emancipator" in the North in repeated elections, and in the South as long as they could. And local party organization, nourished by over thirty years of control, had the advantage of an army of officeholders well trained in campaign leg work and in the implications of strings attached to campaign contributions. The bankruptcy of parties ensured the dominance of business; the dominance of business perpetuated the bankruptcy of politics.

Such was the transformation wrought in American government between 1865 and 1900. Gone was the day when a Thomas Jefferson, an Andrew Jackson, or an Abraham Lincoln could rule the American people with resolute insistence that the will of the majority must prevail. Gone, too, was the time when a rail splitter might dream of sitting in the White House. Proud parents, thinking of the future that might await their favorite offspring, were likely to dream of him as the possessor of wealth rather than of office. Quite understandably, the ambition of imperious men of affairs was the presidency of a corporation rather than the presidency of the United States. By 1900 true governmental power rested in the hands of business, not the people. Railroad leaders and financiers like Commodore Vanderbilt and J. P. Morgan regarded political henchmen as servitors, not equals.

XVI

THE BANKRUPTCY OF POLITICS

1876–1900

American political history between 1876 and 1900 left a record as dreary as it was barren. "One might," said the historian Henry Adams in a famous statement, "search the whole list of Congress, judiciary, and executive during the twenty-five years 1870–1895, and find little but damaged reputations." Damaged reputations there were in profusion. Reputations were sullied by corruption and noble talents squandered in the pursuit of ignoble ends. Toward the shattering urban and rural dislocations accompanying the birth of an industrial universe, the vision of politicians was dim. The impact of economics altered the course of history and in so doing altered the direction of life, but to the political parties the revolutions meant only greater opportunities for political plunder and political power. By 1900 the political parties had squandered their birthright as instruments in the American struggle for democracy.

Railway land grants and subsidies for ships awakened business cupidity and avarice in Congress, but railroads united the nation, and ships the world. As the basis of historic isolationism receded in the wake of the internationalism of trade, historic sectionalism receded in the wake of the nationalism of business. But the manipulators of votes kept the sectional bitterness between North and South alive as long as an ember of hatred smoldered. Republican orators, distracting popular attention from the real issues, "waved the bloody shirt" of patriotism and vengeance in election after election until rabble rousers no longer could excite an audience by associating Democrats with secession and rebellion. Union war heroes, under the circumstances, were a cheap and favorite political commodity. Beginning with General Grant and ending with Major McKinley, every successful Republican aspirant for the presidency in the forty years after the Civil War had a war record. If the Republicans identified themselves with the abolition of slavery and the preservation of the Union, they posed also as the conservators of rural virtue, of the America of the pioneer West, and of the log cabin. All the successful presidential candidates were from the West, although their resemblance to the rail splitter grew less and less discernible. From 1860 to 1884 the only unsuccessful Republican was James G. Blaine: he came from Maine and had no war record.

Such Republican pretensions were political myths perpetuating disregard of economic realities. The economic revolutions not only moved westward; the center of industrial capitalism moved into the heart of the Jacksonian West. Of the ten states with the highest annual value of manufactured products in 1910, only four were in the East—New York, Pennsylvania, New Jersey, Massachusetts; all the others were western states—Illinois, Ohio, Michigan, Wisconsin, Indiana, Missouri. Grant, successful Republican candidate in 1868 and 1872, was indubitably the hero of Appomattox just as Garfield, victorious Republican in 1880, was unquestionably born in a log cabin, but neither the glory of a peace nor the coincidence of humble ancestry equipped men for leadership. They were political stratagems with which to win campaigns and devices to cloak the issues.

Just as indifferent to the waning of isolationism as to the waning of sectionalism, the men in the foreground of American politics had little understanding of America's new role in a shrinking world. Politicians catered to Old World prejudices to ensnare the immigrant vote: twisted the British lion's tail for the satisfaction of the Irish; outraged the Chinese by excluding her nationals to placate nativism on the Pacific coast; and made political capital out of a feeble gesture in the direction of hemispheric accord. So little did American lawmakers comprehend the facts of economic life that rural congressmen demanded foreign markets for agricultural products and urban congressmen demanded higher tariff walls for the industrial home market. Agricultural exports were the basis of industrial credit from abroad; yet the representatives of industrialism were deaf to the pleas of the depressed farmers.

If foreign insights were lacking, domestic vision was also blurred. In sharp contrast to the record in European states, scarcely a notable item of social legislation was placed on United States statute books between the end of the Civil War and the beginning of the war with Spain. Business zeal caused mines to be tunneled and proud ships to sail on every ocean; in response, sprawling tenements and unsightly factories changed the lives of millions. But to the human implications of these activities politicians were blind, for they still continued to follow the precepts of laissez faire, as feudal a vestige in legal and economic theory as in the practical spheres of merchandising and technology. Pompously they talked of the sanctity of the individual, his freedom of economic action, and the unabridged equality of opportunity while they ignored the mounting disgrace of American poverty and the threat of coordinated wealth that they did little to rectify. They crowned the farmer with the individualist's halo, but they turned a stony ear to the persistent rumble of agrarian revolt and were loath to admit the existence of an argicultural problem until an incipient political revolution threatened the party system. The political history of the United States from 1865 to 1900 was a travesty on democracy and rewards investigation only for what it reveals of the dynamics of politics and the inadequacy of governmental institutions.

NATIONAL POLITICS: 1880–1900

While the Republican party was strong by 1880, it was by no means unified. In the national convention of that year the Republican incumbent, President Hayes, cold, reserved, elected only by a partisan decision of Congress, and suspected by the professional politicians, was forgotten in the clamor for General Grant. Hero of the masses and politicians alike, Grant would have yielded to a third-term draft, but his eight-year record as chief executive was more likely to bolster Democratic strength than to ensure Republican victory. After a deadlock between James G. Blaine of Maine and John Sherman of Ohio, James A. Garfield received the nomination. Convention managers were scarcely chastened by their party's narrow escape from defeat in 1876. As a concession to the boss-ridden delegations from New York, Pennsylvania, and Illinois, which had boomed Grant for a third term, Chester A. Arthur, nationally discredited as a spoilsman of the New York machine, was given the vice-presidential place.

James A. Garfield was the Galahad of the American political legend. Handsome, dignified, and an orator in an era when oratory was prized, Garfield was born in an Ohio log cabin in 1831. As a barefoot, hardworking boy, he obtained an education in a manner almost Lincolnesque, taught school, and at twenty-six became principal of Hiram Eclectic Institute, of which he was himself an alumnus. So typical of the American homespun saga was he that the indefatigable Horatio Alger celebrated his career in the familiar sterotype, *From Canal Boy to President.* When the war broke out after his admission to the bar, he had volunteered for service and was mustered out as a model major general in 1863. Shortly thereafter his election to the House of Representatives marked the beginning of his political rise.

If the Republicans could capitalize on war records, the Democrats could at least try. Like Garfield, General Winfield S. Hancock, his opponent, had a distinguished military career. Described as "a good man weighing two hundred and fifty pounds," Hancock had much politically to recommend him. He came from industrial Pennsylvania and was favorably known to Southerners because of his temperate rule as military commander of Louisiana and Texas. That economic theory did not differentiate the parties is indicated by the choice of William H. English for vice-president, a wealthy banker who came from Indiana, a state both doubtful and pivotal.

Republicans stood staunchly on their record in the late war; Democrats thundered about the "Great Fraud" in the disputed election of 1876. But the campaign was without issue: Garfield's cohorts took credit for prosperity; Hancock's lieutenants endowed their party and their candidate with all the virtues in the decalogue. When the votes were counted, Garfield had won conclusively in the electoral college, but his popular plurality was less than 10,000. The popular vote stood 4,454,416 for Garfield and 4,444,952 for Hancock; the Democratic party was well organized too.

Garfield did not live long enough to try his talents. On July 2, 1881, he was assassinated by a demented office seeker, and "Chet" Arthur became President of the United States. A man of marked abilities, he had been quartermaster general of New York during the civil conflict, but all his charm and tact were devoted to professional politics. However well he accounted himself as aide-de-camp to Roscoe Conkling, unscrupulous boss of the New York Republican machine, he forswore his former masters and tried to expand into presidential stature. After four years, the *Nation,* stern critic of politicos, remarked that his administration was "above the average of post bellum respectability." If this comment appears to damn him with the faintest of praise, it should be remembered that none hoped his term would rise to Lincolnian heights while most feared it would sink to Grantian depths.

But civic virtue is not its own political reward, and Arthur was given scant consideration in 1884. Instead, the Republican convention, dominated by professionals, nominated James G. Blaine of Maine, an irresistible leader without a cause, for the high office he had so long coveted. Blaine's nomination gave the Democrats their cue, for Blaine was a name that taunted the righteous. Suspected of using his influence while Speaker of the House in behalf of a land-grant railway and of receiving favors from another, his selection as Republican standard-bearer made reform the battle cry of the election.

The Democrats, having a mission, needed only a prophet, and Grover Cleveland was his name. Elected mayor of Buffalo, his honest and efficient conduct in office inspired the Democratic leaders of New York to groom him for the governorship, less because they loved him and the reforms for which he stood than because popular disgust with the depravity of party politics made him a likely winner. As governor he thrilled the reformers and chilled the politicians, but he was just as promising a candidate for president as he had been for governor, and managers of machines seldom permit personal predilections to interfere with political realities.

That the Democratic managers interpreted the situation accurately was clear at once. A number of younger Republicans—Charles W. Eliot, president of Harvard, Henry Ward Beecher, a leading liberal minister, and George W. Curtis and Carl Schurz, two active reformers—captivated by Cleveland's virtues and appalled by Blaine's vices, gave the Democratic candidate their active support. The deserters were called "Mugwumps," a term later defined by a comedian as "a bird who sits on a fence with his mug on one side and his wump on the other." Aside from the verbal conflict between the upholders of civic righteousness and the alleged perpetrators of political evil, the great campaign of 1884 was devoid of real issues. Only the tariff planks of the two parties echoed a measure of difference; otherwise the platform could have been interchanged, for such was the divided nature of the rival parties that neither could face the actual problems and still hope to win. Cleveland won a narrow victory—the vote for Blaine being 4,848,000, for Cleveland, 4,911,000. The electoral college stood 219 to 182. Further analysis illustrated how narrow the victory really was. Cleveland won only by carrying New York by the infinitesimal margin of 1,149 out of a total of 1,167,169 votes cast. Significantly the protest vote, the combined showing of the minor parties, effectively prevented either party from obtaining a clear-cut majority.

Cleveland's victory was a rebuke to reaction rather than a triumph of reform. Republican indifference to popular wants, its relationship to big business, and fear of the money power of which it had become the symbol explained its first defeat since the presidency of Lincoln. Yet Republican disaster did not result in the satisfaction of popular desires. Whatever advantages Cleveland possessed over Blaine in integrity, courage, and devotion to duty made only the slightest of difference with regard to the framework in which he had to operate. If Cleveland stood for reform, his party did not. Democrats were as hungry for the spoils of office and the taste of power as the Republicans they had ousted. The mills of politics did not stop grinding, and they continued to grind exceeding small. No change in the structure of parties took place as a consequence of Cleveland, who in reality had little understanding of the mighty forces so swiftly changing America and the world.

Whatever hopes reformers still entertained were dissipated by the Cleveland record. For nearly thirty years farmers had agitated for relief, but Cleveland gave no executive attention to agriculture. Although the Interstate Commerce Act to regulate the railroads was passed in 1887,[1]

---

[1] For the struggle for government regulation see Chapter XXI.

culminating a quarter of a century of western effort to regulate monopoly, it remained to be seen whether the machinery of enforcement was adequate to the task. If western disaffection was stilled by the statute, nothing had yet been done about the currency problem, which was just as much the emblem of eastern aggression as the railway octopus. And labor had as yet received hardly more than a passing official notice, although its praises were sung to the tune of every campaign. Yet it was from the masses of common men that Cleveland drew his greatest support. Sated by inefficiency and indifference to the public weal, the common man respected Cleveland for the enemies he had made. By his systematic vetoes of pension bills, he angered the veterans of the Grand Army of the Republic but demonstrated his defiance of legislation for special interests. As an opponent of extreme protectionism, he aroused the fury of industry by his courageous stand on the tariff in 1887,[2] which seemed to some an attack upon privilege, however oblique. The protectionist members of his own party blocked him at every legislative step, but the revisionary Mills tariff bill was passed by the House in 1888 only to be blocked by a Republican Senate.

The tariff appeared as the issue in 1888, but not far beneath the surface were the real issues that the tariff controversy mirrored. To harassed workers in labor and agriculture to whom the trusts and special privilege were meaningful words, the Cleveland assault on the tariff was a ray of new hope. To reformers it promised a measure of control over predatory interests. But to the recipients of tariff blessings in industry, Republican and Democratic alike, it inspired the wish to defeat him.

Cleveland was renominated by acclamation in 1888. However party bosses disliked him, they clung to him as the only candidate in thirty years who had carried them through to the spoils. In opposition, the Republicans presented Benjamin Harrison of Indiana. Descendant of the hero of Tippecanoe, Harrison was a general like his better-known ancestor. But if Harrison was a son of the West, it was not the West of Indians and of cabins built of logs. As a lawyer, he had amassed wealth representing powerful corporations, among them the railroads, while his single term in the Senate would not have been recalled had it not been for this turn in political events. Nor did the Republican choice for vice-president soothe the disaffected, as Levi P. Morton, a New York banker, better known to his contemporaries than to posterity, was cited for this honor.

The campaign was drab, but its implications were profound. Party orators warned workers that Republican success and the tariff alone could stay the competitive threat of European labor. A Republican slush fund of over four million dollars helped immeasurably to defeat Cleveland.

---

[2] For the tariff issue see Chapter XXI.

Chief among the fund raisers was John Wanamaker, known as the merchant prince of Philadelphia, who asked his big business colleagues: "How much would you pay for insurance upon your business? If you were confronted by from one to three years of general depression by a change in our revenue and protective measures affecting our manufactures, wages, and good times, what would you pay to be insured for a better year?" Big business paid, and big politics used the proceeds where it would do the most good. Cleveland was defeated by an electoral vote of 233 to 168, but Harrison's popular vote was less than Cleveland's by more than 100,000. Again, as in 1884, the election turned on the vote of New York, but this time Harrison carried it largely because Tammany deserted the Democratic leader. There was no popular mandate, for the people had not been presented with broad alternatives from which to choose. Four hundred thousand voters cast ballots for minor candidates. In 1888, for the fourth consecutive presidential election—1876, 1880, 1884, 1888—the president represented the minority choice.

Little in the Harrison administration served to increase his popularity with the people or to enlarge his historical stature. Indubitably honest and unquestionably sincere, he simply did not comprehend the problems of modern industrial society. He offered no executive leadership, and his four years in the presidential office suggest the extent of America's political insolvency. Both Senate and House were in Republican hands, and Thomas B. Reed, czar of the House, changed the rules so that nothing stood in the way of remedial legislation, but there was none. Actually Reed created a system of centralized control of committees and of congressional procedure whereby conservative domination of the speakership could prevent the introduction of reform bills or facilitate their emasculation in committee or on the floor. Right of way, however, was given to a pension bill in 1890 that drained the Treasury of more than sixty million a year; some of the appointments to office in return for political favors were a mockery of such civil service advances as had been made; there was a tariff bill—the McKinley tariff of 1890—which wiped out everything that Cleveland had attempted. Business received whatever it asked. Special legislation, the product of pressure groups, was the result of the failure of the parties to operate as parties. And even the parties, decentralized though they were, could not forever ignore the mounting totals of dissident votes. The Sherman Antitrust Act of 1890, the most notable legislative aspect of the Harrison years, was an indication of the awareness of party managers. Like the Interstate Commerce Act three years before, it was calculated to appease the prevailing fear of the money power, but since group pressures still operated through the sectional decentralization of the parties, the antitrust law had almost no effect upon the concentration of wealth.[3]

The addiction of the Republican party to a program of lavish government spending, reversing Cleveland's insistence on economy, bore a visible relation to the politics of special interests. On the one hand, local machines were gratified; for the surplus was spent by joyful "logrollers" who teamed up to vote river and harbor improvements for districts of other congressmen and senators in return for votes for "pork barrel" appropriations to be spent in their own constituencies. On the other hand, great merchants were gratified by government spending: under the new authorization for nineteen more warships the position of American venturers into overseas business was considerably enhanced. But the public was not elated by beneficence to the few at the expense of the many. A sharp increase in commodity prices following the passage of the McKinley tariff was reflected in the congressional elections of 1890. Republican candidates were defeated by scores, with the result that the Republican majority in the upper house was reduced from 14 to 6; in the lower house, from 166 to 88.

A popular storm was brewing, and the election of 1892 registered it accurately. Agrarian resentment centering on the unsolved problems of railway monopoly, credit monopoly, and industrial monopoly responded to the renominations of Harrison and Cleveland with flaming hostility. Following the Republican and Democratic conventions, the Populist party, political and psychological heir of agricultural disaffection, met in Omaha on the Fourth of July, 1892, and adopted an explosive program generally regarded as subversive. The ensuing campaign was prosaic, but the results were electrifying. More than a million voters expressed their preference for Populism, a figure too large not to register on the political mind. Harrison went down to defeat, and Cleveland received a popular plurality for the third successive time, but as in the four preceding elections the President was a minority choice. More impressive still were the twenty-two electoral votes of Populist dissent, a political reality within the comprehension of party managers. Between Harrison, Cleveland, and their platforms there were no distinctions worthy of mention. If Republicans endorsed the McKinley tariff, the Democrats and Republicans agreed on sound money. The success of Cleveland was a tribute to the efficiency of the Democratic machine just as the success of Harrison in 1888 was a tribute to the efficiency of the Republican machine. Democrats in Congress violated campaign pledges that the party would rid the country of the scandal of Republican surrender to tariff lobbyists in the Mc-

---

[3] For the McKinley tariff and Sherman Act see Chapter XXI.

Kinley Act of 1890. The Wilson-Gorman Act of 1894[4] merely changed the label but not the substance. Aside from this sham battle, no important party measure was fought through in Cleveland's Congress. And yet the country, caught by the panic of 1893, clamored for remedial action. Unassuaged dissatisfaction led to the Populist awakening of 1892; the encouragement of 1892 led to the exciting campaign of 1896, the last luckless assault by the forces of nineteenth-century liberalism.

The campaign of 1896 was the most memorable since 1860. While silver vied with gold in the party platforms, and the economics of bimetallism was debated over cracker barrels and on street corners, the deeper clash was between government by the interests and government by the people. Governor William McKinley of Ohio, guided by the fine political hand of Mark Hanna, one of the neatest players of the political game, upheld the Republican standard, which was also the gold standard, the standard of protection, of business, and of economic laissez faire. William Jennings Bryan of Nebraska led the Democrats in whom he infused a crusading spirit, and the Populists whose cause he made his own. He raised anew the standard of revolt that in 1896 was the standard of silver, of depressed agriculture, of labor, and of American protest. To eastern men of business the effort to make silver the equal of gold constituted a "dishonest" attempt to foist "unsound money" upon the nation, a move that would discredit the government and cripple the country's commercial structure. Freely coined silver would filch from the wealthy the gold they had earned. Genuine anxiety was transformed into hysteria by artful propaganda. With an expanded currency, urged the opponents of silver, debts contracted in gold would be paid in a depreciated medium, the purchasing power of incomes reduced as prices soared, and the financial mechanisms controlled by eastern interests—bonds, notes, mortgages backed by gold—would be destroyed. In other words, the free and unlimited coinage of silver, instead of the legalized rate of 16 ounces of silver to 1 ounce of gold, would, to conservative minds, amount to repudiation—repudiation of solid gold for ephemeral silver. But to debtors, on the other hand, particularly in the West and South, whose farms were mortgaged to the chimneys, whose machinery was owned by urban banks, whose crops—as much a part of their bodies as their arms and backs—brought depression prices, who paid interest rates beyond human endurance and prices for manufactured goods that placed every heart's desire beyond reach—to these men silver promised release from debt, from sinking prices, and from the stringency of credit. The election was not decided by economic abstractions relating to gold versus silver; it was decided by the artful politics of gold and placed a tarnish upon silver as

---

[4] On the Democratic tariff see Chapter XXI.

the bright symbol of American dissent. Bryan was defeated 271 to 176 in the electoral college; but he polled 6,533,000 votes to 7,107,000 for McKinley. No industrial state was to be found in the Bryan column and McKinley was weakest in the South and the West.

However memorable the campaign, its consequences were far reaching. As a result of the merger between Populists and Democrats, the Democratic party acquired a potent left wing but was weakened internally. For the time being the day was postponed when Republicans in political self-defense would have to make concessions in order to attract reformist support. In the long run, Populist demands were to be incorporated under conservative twentieth-century auspices in the quiet manner by which the political radicalism of yesterday becomes the political orthodoxy of tomorrow. In the interim, however, new issues and new dangers had emerged, while the old, unsolved problems became more difficult of solution.

The extent to which political institutions were outmoded and parties ill adapted to public serviceability was illustrated again in the election of 1900. The candidates were the same, McKinley and Bryan, but the issues were not. Between 1896 and 1900 a war with Spain was fought and won, an empire acquired, and the trend toward consolidation of business and concentration of wealth quickened. The new issues were imperialism abroad and progressive reform at home. But the old problems, even if pushed into the background, were not removed; they were only aggravated. In political history the election of 1900 is important less because McKinley won and Bryan lost than because Republicanism was substantially unchanged. It is also important because Theodore Roosevelt, marooned in the vice-presidency by the Republican bosses of New York, emerged as a national political leader.

THE SUPREMACY OF MEDIOCRITY

American Presidents from Grant to McKinley were all honorable men who took the responsibilities of high office seriously, but save for Grover Cleveland they were undistinguished. If they made any notable contribution to America, it is nowhere revealed. Rutherford B. Hayes had little but respectability to recommend him, and his conscientiousness was hardly a substitute for ingenuity and leadership. James A. Garfield had little time to display his mettle before he was assassinated, but his earlier political record demonstrated that his abilities were more frequently used for partisan than for social purposes. Chester A. Arthur represented the worst elements of a party that had already lost the confidence of the masses, although he acquitted himself better than anyone had reason to expect. Benjamin Harrison was known less for his single uneventful term in the Senate than for his presidential grandfather and the dull propriety of White House parties. William McKinley, genial, tactful, and sincere, never rose above his concern for the Republican party, which, like his crafty mentor, Mark Hanna, he equated with the welfare of the United States. Grover Cleveland alone saves the presidential pageant from mediocrity. Solid, courageous, and honest, he made a valiant fight against corruption, but he rarely saw beyond the tariff which, though grossly in need of revision, was something less than a means of social salvation. His election in 1884 was hailed as a liberal victory, yet Cleveland was a thoroughgoing conservative, and a spectacular assault upon the tariff for which his first administration is noted was a complete failure.

The men on Capitol Hill who played stellar parts in the great political spectacle during the last twenty-four years of the century differed sharply from the occupants of the White House. They were brilliant and colorful. If few of them were wise, many were worldly and urbane. They squandered great abilities in trivial efforts and transitory causes. They rang the changes on political dogma without reference to issue, and when party loyalty did not replace loyalty to national ideals, sectional and group interests did. American farmers were on the verge of peonage, but American "statesmen" affected to believe that there was no "agricultural problem," and none seemed to have been aware that dejection was as abundant in rural America as wheat, cotton, and corn. Revolutionary economic change shattered the past, but party chieftains outdid each other in repeating social and economic platitudes as if grandiloquence made them true. If they believed them, they were lacking in wisdom; if not, they were lacking in candor. Although the evidence of poverty was inescapable, the lawmakers apparently believed that destitution was caused by conditions which could not be unmade. And if their words are to be credited, they were convinced that unemployment was ordained by a higher law with which they were powerless to interfere. Cities introduced problems the like of which men had never known, but members of Congress seemed to be concerned with cities only in relation to political machines, votes, and public-utility franchises. Concentrated wealth imperiled every principle which political orators fervently extolled on public occasions, but they never abandoned the hoary dictum that business made wealth and wealth made prosperity. They paid as little attention to the protest of labor as to the protest of agriculture, dismissing both with an epithet, while they filched the ideals of the Declaration of Independence to still the angry voice of dissent. Labor leaders were "agitators"; agricultural leaders "radicals"; and reform leaders "cranks."

Nowhere is the futility of competence better indicated than in the life of James G. Blaine. Although Blaine captured the popular imagination as few Americans save Bryan, he never espoused the people's cause. Gifted with a powerful mind and a scintillating personality, he served in the House and the Senate, and as Secretary of State under Garfield and Harrison. He was, in the words of a famous orator, the "plumed knight," but he preferred to tilt with the windmills of politics than to lift his lance in behalf of the people. Expert in the committee room and the party caucus, he failed in his greatest effort—Pan-Americanism—in large part because the Latin republics doubted American probity, a reaction to which the conduct of public officials, typified by Blaine, contributed. The brilliance of his oratory was placed at the disposal of business when it was not enlisted in behalf of personal aggrandizement. Aside from Pan-Americanism, he grappled with no compelling problem, endorsed no significant program, and left his imprint on no vital movement. Reform was frustrated because the servants of the American people served other masters.

Greater and lesser Blaines took part in the political game, but historians alone recall them. Republican Senator Chauncey Depew's reputation rests upon feats of after-dinner oratory rather than upon feats of statesmanship, and few remember that Mark Hanna, who personified the influence of business in government, possessed a senatorial chair. The name of Nelson W. Aldrich, long Republican senator from Rhode Island, suggested textiles then as now. He maneuvered a high tariff bloc with an astuteness often recalled by parliamentarians, but no consequential social act attaches to his memory. Arthur P. Gorman, Democratic senator from Maryland, was also coupled with the tariff and opposition to the mildest kind of civil service improvement. The New York Republican state bosses, Senators Thomas C. "Me Too" Platt and Roscoe Conkling, were associated only with patronage, machines, and local chicanery; neither contributed a jot to social advancement. And Republican Senator Henry Cabot Lodge, a gentleman and a scholar, of Boston, Harvard, and New England, bartered his agile mind for a mess of political pottage. When David Graham Phillips, a second-rate novelist but a first-rate journalist, investigated the Senate at the opening of the twentieth century, he adjudged its membership guilty of treason to the public, but the inquiry revealed statistically what all already knew. Seventy-five senatorial gentlemen were directly connected with big business; the service of oil, steel, sugar, and beef had a higher claim on their loyalties than the people whose welfare they were there sworn to serve. Although they rationalized that the interests of business and the interest of the people were one, their record belied it. The Senate was a "rich man's club"; it was certainly

A noted cartoonist views the movement for restrictive immigration. "Holding off the New," by J. Keppler. (*Puck*, 1893)

Millions of brave men and women like these new arrivals *(above)* fled from the blight of oppression and the curse of poverty in the Old World. But a tenement in one of America's big cities *(below)* meant an exchange of one kind of oppression for another —and poverty was the same everywhere.

(Bettmann Archive)

From humble cottage to resplendent palace. In the light of the modest origins of Carnegie *(inset, above)* and Vanderbilt *(inset, below)*, the munificence of their later homes made many Americans believe in the Horatio Alger myth. (All photos *Culver Service* except Vanderbilt mansion, *Wurts Brothers)*

Above—In the slum areas the advent of the water wagon was an exciting adventure. *Below*—The race track, equally exciting, was a more costly form of amusement. Society, incidentally, was not so neatly divided as the phrase "the other half" implied. *(Bettmann Archive)*

composed of men of wealth, and its atmosphere more closely resembled a society for mutual advancement than a forum for the analysis and solution of questions affecting the welfare of the republic.

This dismal record of squandered talents and perversion of duty was not unrelieved by the activity of politicians who made social justice the criterion of public conduct. Carl Schurz, Republican liberal of Missouri, served in the Cabinet of Hayes and represented his state in the Senate; George F. Hoar, Massachusetts Republican, also graced that body, where he spoke out against imperialism; Lucius Q. C. Lamar went to the upper house as a Democrat from Mississippi and while Secretary of the Interior in the Cleveland administration strove to preserve the public lands from rapacious buccaneers; and Abraham Hewitt, a New York congressman and Democratic party leader, pierced through the political maze to recognize some of the issues that beset the nation. The list could be extended, but the most distinguished public service was supplied by men outside national politics, by the artists and writers, and by hosts of men and women who were vitally active in the cause of reform.

Behind the scenes of formal government were the masters of politics, the bosses of state, city, and county machines. They were the men whose business was selecting men for office, getting out the vote, and turning the results of these labors into the rewards of favorable legislation, lucrative contracts, patronage, the feel of power, and the satisfactions of prestige. For them there were no issues, there were only areas marked on political maps which could or could not be delivered on election day. And behind the bosses were the masters of capital who bribed state legislatures and federal officials and who made deals with the bosses. And it was not cynicism which prompted a noted observer to comment that the Standard Oil Company had refined everything in Pennsylvania but the state legislature. This was the invisible government, and in the years from Grant to McKinley it was the real government of the United States.

DEMOCRACY AND PARTY THEORY

Americans were aware of the disparity between the ideals of democracy and the realities of life. Passionately devoted to the goal of a "government of the people, by the people, and for the people," they were just as passionately devoted to precepts that made this goal unattainable. They piously repeated the ritual of majority rule, but they espoused political dogmas that defeated it. They flouted the plainest lessons of their experience, for Americans misunderstood the function of parties, confounded direct and representative democracy, and confused the role of social institutions with the drives of individual men. They respected Woodrow Wilson and read his *Congressional Government,* which by 1900 had already run through fifteen editions. They praised Lord Bryce and his *American Commonwealth;* but they did not take to heart either Wilson's or Bryce's analysis of the problem. Herein lay the bankruptcy of political thinking and of this frustration was born, for Americans, having formulated the philosophy of democracy, failed to develop competent mechanisms for its operation.

The question was not whether democratic ideals were valid, but whether they were realizable; not the efficacy of majority rule, but how to determine the general will and how ceaselessly to reformulate it into public policy. Failure was not inevitable. Woodrow Wilson had learned a method of mobilizing the general will by the study of English politics in which he found parties that were strong and majorities possessed of the capacity to govern. There the general will could be elicited only through the medium of parties, parties with programs, accountable to the electorate, and cohesively organized so that they could act as parties. Even if a country were blessed with an efficient two-party system, the people could speak only monosyllabically; they could answer only yes or no. But they could speak and be heeded, as they could not in the American system. Nor was it reasonable to cling to Jacksonian party theory in which the deliberative processes of frontier communities, town meetings, or corporate directorates were likened to the voice of millions who spoke through representatives in sectional dialects, in local idioms, in the thousand different varieties created by individual differences of personality, geography, and economics. There was, however, an alternative to Jacksonian decentralization.

Only a strongly knit party could really effectuate the popular will; only in this way was representation of the people conceivable in a world of cities and machines in which differences were multiplied and individual participation was curtailed. If responsible party theory was alien to popular American thought, it was not alien to democracy. If a policy was inadequate or improperly administered, the people could register their disapproval by turning the party responsible out of office. Thus the party was accountable for its acts, for only by devising a formula embracing the needs of the whole community rather than a particular segment of it could a party escape defeat or censure. Existence of an opposition party, equally well organized, administered, and equipped with a program designed to win popular support was implied in this process. By criticizing the party in power, by causing it to define its motives and to defend its methods, and finally by offering a rival program so that it might supplant the party in power, the opposition gave the electorate an opportunity of choice. This was the method of mobilizing a majority; this the manner in which the people could speak. But a party had to be a party with the attributes of a party; national not local, united not divided, with principles and a program.

Parties in the United States after the Civil War were not parties at all. They were loose confederations of sectional units and local machines whose prime object was the seizure of power. Well organized locally, they possessed neither programs nor principles. Vagueness was deliberate rather than accidental, for instead of being announcements of clear-cut policies, platforms were adroit compromises between conflicting economic and sectional desires. Accordingly, the parties failed to register the majority will, and party lines broke on major social and economic issues.

Bipartisan behavior betrayed a lack of national purpose and evidenced decentralization. Virtually every issue cut across sectional and group lines. Particularly was this true of the tariff, allegedly a major bone of party contention. Whatever the formal Democratic pronouncements, Democratic performance reflected the prevalent attitude of local constituencies. If Republicans were protectionists, it did not follow that Democrats wanted a low tariff or free trade. When in 1884 and 1886, Democrats were in congressional control, bills looking toward tariff reduction met a fate that might have been expected from a Republican majority. Pennsylvania Democrats were as avid for protection of iron, coal, and steel as New England Republicans were the special guardians of textiles. Ohio Democrats responded to the pleas of iron manufacturers just as New Jersey Democrats responded to the needs of native pottery works. Even southern Democrats—Virginians interested in coal, and Louisianians interested in sugar—sometimes found it convenient to sing the industrial praises of the tariff. Congressmen and senators, local rather than national representatives, were themselves lobbyists as active in exerting pressures for local advantage as were organized minorities outside government.

What was true of the tariff was true of all social and economic legislation. Laws relating to land, to agriculture, to regulation of monopolies were weighed with reference to local or group interest rather than to the public interest. Victories went to organized minorities—pressure groups like the veterans who traded support for pensions, sectional blocs like New England textiles that traded support for tariff protection, special interest lobbies like railroad, oil, and other business organizations that traded support for advantageous legislation—rather than to organized majorities. Majorities were organized into parties, but they had no way of expressing their demands. There were, in other words, national parties but not national programs. And sectional or group goals, when realized, meant the inevitable suppression of larger social goals; particular ends could not be served without sacrificing the general welfare.

Although the parties were basically alike, they were competing organizations in the political market. The struggle between Democrats and Republicans was real, but it was a raw struggle for power and the spoils, not a rivalry of principles. Both existed to capture the institutions of government for purposes of their own. Under the aegis of the Republicans, a congressional Campaign Committee was set up in 1866, composed of one man from each state, to serve as a link between Congress and the party. In the years that followed, the state bosses, either in person or through their agents, dominated the national committees of both parties; but the national committees did not formulate party programs or clarify principles. They functioned only to control national conventions and select safe standard-bearers who would not neglect the hunger of machines for federal patronage. More directly, through liaison between legislators in Congress and machines back home, local interests were assured of a share in the distribution of "pork" and protected against the passage of reform bills. Local interests were thereby satisfied and adequate patronage kept the machines running smoothly with effective delivery of local votes on election day.

If party organization in Congress had any notable cohesion, it was for private party ends rather than for public ends. Seniority of service on a committee and not ability was the avenue to key positions as committee chairmen, a system which, while not to the public interest, was decidedly to the interest of a powerful local machine in "safe" districts that continuously returned the same man to Senate or House. The Committee on Rules, composed of the Speaker of the House and two other members, controlled appointment to all committees. By determining the order in which bills were considered, the committee controlled the fate of all legislation, an arrangement that made it simple to protect special interests and to prevent the enactment of laws inimical to business politics or political business. Congressional committees, staffed with representatives of local communities dependent upon local support for political existence, were the easy prey of lobbyists. Few congressmen, even when moved by the loftiest motives, were able to defy the Committee on Rules. To do so was futile; it was also political suicide.

The results of this system are clarified in the words of a noted student of politics: "The national policy of the Democratic party, as defined by the national conventions, was determined by the Northern Democrats. But when the party got into power, the execution of the policy, so far as it was dependent on Acts of Congress, was largely in the hands of the Senators and Representatives from the South who under the rule of seniority generally dominated the important committees and controlled the course of business. The Democrats who wrote the party platforms were not the ones who would carry them into effect. Moreover, since the electoral votes of sixteen states were almost certain to be cast for the Democratic presidential candidate it was not necessary to give much consideration to the aspirations of Democratic leaders from that part of the country."[5]

The very organization of the parties made for localism rather than nationalism. Nowhere was this better illustrated than in the function of the "steering committee" of the Senate, counterpart of the House Committee on Rules. By the practice known as "senatorial courtesy," the Senate would confirm no appointment by a President if it was not approved by the senators from the appointee's state. While this was a device to maintain and expand congressional control of administrative personnel, it was local control, for the practice exploited patronage to tighten the bonds between local machines and local politicians. As senators from 1789 until almost World War I were elected by state legislatures, and since legislatures worked in concert with the machines, the machines were thus represented in the Senate, whose members perpetuated machine power from reciprocal need to perpetuate their own. And the machines, existing only for power and the perquisites thereof, were the best customers of organized minorities and wealthy contributors whose prime wish was to benefit themselves.

That the system was effective is certified by the record. Civil service reform, accomplished with far greater efficiency in England and Germany many years before, was stifled until the Pendleton Act of 1883; federal regulation of railways impeded until the Interstate Commerce Act of 1887; antitrust legislation delayed until the Sherman Act of 1890; and the direct election of senators postponed until 1913. Popular indignation did not halt the rise of the tariff, wealth remained uncontrolled, and remedial social legislation slumbered in congressional committees or, if enacted in state laws, was outlawed by the courts. Nor did the passage of statutes actually mean the achievement of reform. Richard Olney, Attorney General to Cleveland and corporation lawyer of Massachusetts, cautioning a railway magnate against an attempt to repeal the Interstate Commerce Act, wrote, "It satisfies the popular clamor for government supervision of railroads at the same time that supervision is almost entirely nominal."

Partly the result of the swift flow of change, lags in government

---

[5] A. N. Holcombe, *Political Parties of Today*. New York: Harper & Brothers, 1924, p. 195.

institutions also derived from an outmoded political theory. Americans attempted to nourish democracy with ideas that predated parties. Identifying power with corruption, they wished to avoid the lodgment of power in government and sought instead to distribute power to the people. Anxious to avoid centralization, they tended to revert to direct democratic forms and were loath to experiment with representative forms. Political reform revealed a nostalgia for "grass-roots" democracy of which the Populist demand for the direct election of senators was an outstanding example. Since government was regarded as a passive arbiter between competing forces and democracy an idyllic condition in which conflicting motives canceled out in a mythical equilibrium like that of classical economics, parties could hardly be conceived as creative implements of democratic evolution. But if Americans viewed parties and politicians as inherently evil, they elaborated neither a theory nor a method to wield the sovereign power of the people. Liberal reformers, fearful of organized minorities, and conservative standpatters, fearful of the power of organized majorities, demanded a legislative independence that would violate fidelity to party principles, but they forgot that independence of legislators was fashioned to safeguard parliamentary bodies from dependence upon an absolute monarch. The doctrine of the separation of powers under a system of checks and balances that made it difficult for a party to function was historically a predemocratic stratagem to prevent a king from interfering with the deliberations of the people.

American critics demanded national programs while supporting institutions perpetuating localisms and encouraging bipartisan behavior. They condemned legislators as representatives of groups, sections, and moneyed interests, but they endorsed feudal ideas of representation and of representatives as delegates of a particular community or as the spokesmen of a special-interest point of view. They remained unimpressed by the anomaly of congressmen, chosen by an infinitesimal minority from a geographical segment, who defied the President elected by a majority of the whole nation. They saw nothing incongruous in the crossing of party lines at each legislative crisis and the frequency with which Presidents vetoed legislation bearing the stamp of their own party.

Well before 1900 direct democratic processes were outmoded by industry and the city; representative processes alone remained. But representative democracy was inconceivable without power; power without social accountability was socially dangerous, and power with accountability was possible only through parties. Americans did not yet understand the political implications of the revolutions in economics, but in the next century they were slowly to learn their meaning in the school of the city and the university of the shrinking world.

XVII

THE CONQUEST OF RURAL AMERICA

1865–1900

While business triumphed over government and blunted the effectiveness of political parties, the manner in which the American people lived underwent an equally disturbing transformation. Traditionally Americans, like people everywhere, were farm dwellers. As late as 1868 an elementary geography described agriculture as "the principal business of the people in nearly all the states." But the age of dominant agriculture was swiftly terminated by the economic revolutions. In a portentous shift of populations, new Americans from abroad and old Americans from rural villages and farmlands drifted into cities, impelled by the profits awaiting those willing to sweat over forges, to guide whirring factory wheels, or to work in new office buildings of a rising metropolis. The city and city folkways became the distinguishing marks of modern America. Urban culture and an urban outlook gained preponderance throughout the United States; the farmer, long "the bone and sinew of the nation," found himself demeaned in the land he had fathered a "hayseed" and a "rube." So rapid was the change that after the turn of the century Congress was one day to feel called upon to create a Federal Farm Board for the purpose of placing the "industry" of agriculture "on a basis of economic equality with other industries." The conquest of rural America in a few brief decades was all but complete.

On the farms and in the villages of the United States, an era drew to a close. Heading the inventory of rural changes was an incomparable agricultural expansion and the largest population movement in American history. The settlement of the West brought about the end of the frontier, though not the end of free land, and completed an evolutionary cycle begun in 1607 at Virginia's Jamestown. Rapidity of settlement quickened social development so that primitive societies were succeeded by settled societies with breathless haste. Accordingly, the march of statehood almost paralleled the march of settlement, in the process of which the proud Indian was humbled and despoiled, a cattle kingdom rose and declined, and a mineral empire glittered and died. If, in less than half a century, the workaday farmer with hoe and pitchfork vanquished his storied rivals—the feather-bedecked red man, the lone pioneer, the coon-capped trapper, the hard-riding cowboy, the lordly rancher, and the grizzled miner—he was himself about to be vanquished by a prosaic urban army equipped with pens, account books, and adding machines. The farmers won the battle of the plains, but the corporations won the battle of agriculture.

EXPANSION OF AGRICULTURE

But the conquest of rural America was more than a catalogue of the startling innovations that took place in the golden land of the West. Science and technology wrought the agricultural miracles just as they called the industrial wonders into being. Wheat was still rooted in the timeless soil, but the endless bushels pouring out of granaries evidenced a partnership with harvesters, binders, and the chilled steel plow. White flour ground in Minneapolis mills was the product of experimental research with grains and soils, the technological triumph of methods and machines. Men behind the plow still planted and reaped, but the railroads, prodigious offspring of steel and steam, brought the farmers from Europe and eastern United States to the land, and their products to Europe, Asia, and all America. The mechanization of agricultural processes, the application of biological research to the problems of cultivation, and the coming of the transcontinental railroads were the causal links of the agricultural revolutions.

Dramatic though the revolutions were, their social consequences were even more arresting. The employment of mechanized equipment and the speed of transportation substituted commercialized farming for self-sufficient farming. Tillers of the soil were thereafter dependent; dependent upon credit, markets, prices, and machinery. Operations, streamlined by tools, constantly augmented agricultural surpluses, but the actual laborers on the nation's farms received diminishing compensation both in dollars and in emotional satisfactions. Machines, on farms as in factories, created abundance, but economic and spiritual poverty constituted one of the venal sins of society. And agricultural discontent, the political manifestation of the subordination of agriculture to industry, demonstrated the bankruptcy of American politics.

Portentous in its implications for the future of America, political, economic, and social, was the end of the westward movement. Less than thirty years after the Homestead Act (1862) and only twenty-one years after the completion of the first transcontinental railroad (1869), the frontier ceased to exist. Two hundred and five years elapsed from the

GROWTH OF THE CONTINENTAL U.S.

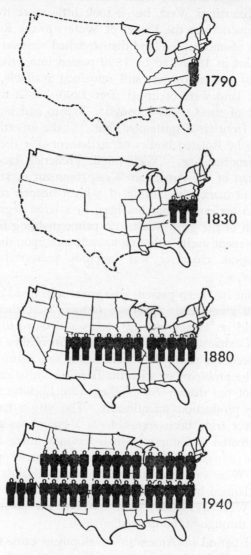

1790

1830

1880

1940

PICTOGRAPH CORPORATION

From Hacker, Modley, and Taylor, *The United States: A Graphic History,* Modern Age Books, Inc. PICTOGRAPH CORP. (Each man represents 4 million people. Dotted areas indicate territories.)

settlement of Virginia to the admission of Louisiana (1812), first state in the trans-Mississippi West, but it took little more than fifty years to colonize the region from the Father of Waters to the Rockies. Almost a thousand miles of unoccupied land that stretched westward from Nebraska to the mountains in 1865 had by 1890 passed into private hands. Land in the hands of private owners still remained available, and huge tracts of government land were occupied after 1890, but at the latter date the Superintendent of the Census reported: "Up to and including 1880 the country had a frontier of settlement, but . . . the unsettled area has been so broken into by isolated bodies of settlement that there can hardly be said to be a frontier line." Well might Frederick Jackson Turner, the greatest historian of the American West, comment in 1893: "This brief official statement marks the closing of a great historic movement Up to our own day American history has been in a large degree the history of the colonization of the great West." A prime molding force of American life had finally spent itself, although its influence upon the American mind and the American character was indelibly preserved in the national psychology.

A milestone had been passed—the government had given all the good lands it had to give away. American farmers were thenceforth on their own; they could no longer pick up stakes and move to fresh areas once their land was exhausted. Like European farmers they were soon to experience the need for using their land again and again. They were confronted with the problems of scientific farming and scientific distribution. And in the not too distant future they were likewise to be confronted with planning production scientifically. The virgin land of the West, which had never truly been accessible as a bounteous source of security for the discontented and impoverished, was now more than ever a plundered preserve of absentee owners and commercial proprietors. The mirage of the West vanished as the last available lands, formerly passed over, were reclaimed by scientific methods of irrigation and dry farming. The frontier West was gone; gone too was the prospect of economic independence through a homestead.

If a great period of American development came to an end, it was the consequence of the increasing pace of western settlement. The speed at which the pioneer West disappeared is faithfully clocked by the progress of statehood. Arizona, Colorado, Dakota, Idaho, Montana, Nevada, and Wyoming already possessed territorial status in the sixties, but full membership in the Union, denoting the end of the primitive period, soon followed. Nevada became a state in 1864, Nebraska in 1867, Colorado in 1876, and in 1889–1890 North Dakota, South Dakota, Montana, Washington, Idaho, and Wyoming were also admitted. Utah, having

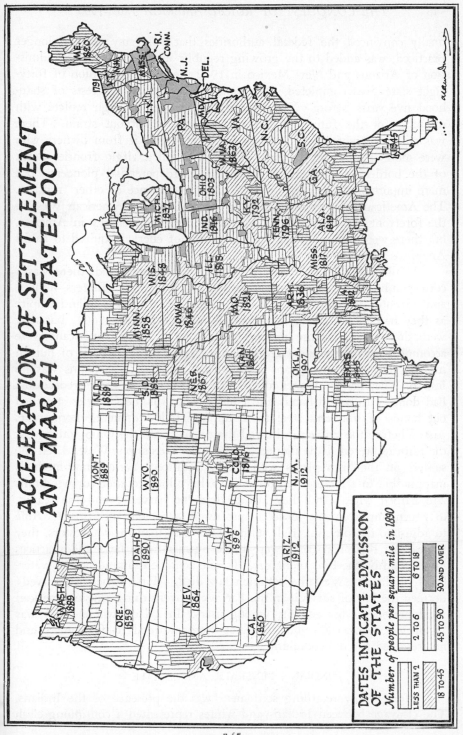

ACCELERATION OF SETTLEMENT
AND MARCH OF STATEHOOD

DATES INDICATE ADMISSION
OF THE STATES
Number of people per square mile in 1890

LESS THAN 2	2 TO 6	6 TO 18
18 TO 45	45 TO 90	90 AND OVER

finally convinced the federal authorities that polygamy was no longer practiced, was added to the growing republic in 1896. With the admission of Arizona and New Mexico in 1912 the American Union of forty-eight states was completed, Oklahoma having passed the tests of statehood five years before. Yet the end of the West, though replete with meaning for the future of the nation, arrived without strain. There was still plenty of land if one had money to buy it from owners who were more than willing to sell. There was still a virgin frontier north of the border in Canada for those who were perennial pioneers. But more important than either of these was the existence of other frontiers. The American city was ready to take the place of the American West in the forefront of adventure. There was no dearth of energy in America, but there were also no limits to the amount of energy required to fulfill America's destiny.

While the rate of westward advance was phenomenal, there was a corresponding increase in the tempo of social evolution. Hunters, miners, and adventurers followed the lone pioneer into the great inland empire as they had in the earlier westward movement (1607–1860), but they were dispossessed by the farmer much sooner. What Americans were accomplishing in city and factory was a graphic demonstration of human mastery, but what Americans accomplished on the great plains was no less so. They had no longer to make their own way, as their predecessors had done, with naked hands and clumsy tools, for the factories stretched out hands of iron and steel to hasten social development. Long years passed before the railway followed the pioneer into the Ohio Valley, but the railway preceded the pioneer in the trans-Mississippi West. Even the settlers on the high plains who found traditional agricultural methods inapplicable to a strange terrain did not have long to wait for windmills and barbed wire. And they already had the harvester and the reaper, to which improvements in costly profusion were constantly made. Able to adjust to the physical trials with greater ease than their ancestors, they found that their real trials were made by man-made laws and practices rather than by the laws of nature. To cite a single example: at the water-holes of the dry West the common law died. "First come, first served" decreed the law of survival in the Far West, overturning Anglo-American legal precedents for equality among users. In a land where water was insufficient, property rights to water were awarded to firstcomers and not reserved for the community.

INDIANS, MINERALS, AND CATTLE

Momentarily retarding settlement was the presence of the Indians. The cleavage between Indians and whites represented a continuing clash between two civilizations dating from the discovery of America by Europeans. Battles on the western plains were the final episodes in a long series of encounters, but Indian-American dissonance was part of a larger cultural clash. Diverse cultures were in conflict on many American fronts. Reds and whites warred in the West; whites clashed with blacks in the South; and in every American city European whites contended with American whites of a different cultural hue. Each encounter was motivated by special and specific considerations, but all three were basically one. They were conflicts between differing ways of life, between older cultures and a swiftly developing new culture, between primitive and relatively static cultures and a restless, acquisitive, and dynamic one.

Indian-American relations between 1862 and 1886 were marked by almost continuous warfare. Unrestrained generalization alleging that Americans have been pacific in nature must be tempered by the record of Indian wars, for during the years from 1868 to 1882 alone the engagements require over a hundred pages simply to list. It was an irreconcilable conflict. To the average frontiersman, the only good Indian was a dead one. To the average Indian, on the other hand, only dead whites could be fully trusted. The whites were the despoilers of Indian civilization and the robbers of Indian land. Pushed farther and farther westward as the frontier line receded, the Indian was precipitated into a last stand against the invaders by the staking out of homesteads and the penetration of the railroads into the remaining Indian country. Government efforts, however sincere, were not strong enough to control the earth hunger and the metal hunger of acquisitive whites. Nor had government learned to control the glowing passions of a proud but humbled race, and once the Indian arose in his own defense, the whites found justification for retaliation in kind. And the red man had no monopoly on brutality and savagery. After the floodgates of emotion were opened, the issues were lost in torrents of blinding hate.

Attempts to alleviate the growing tension were made in 1869. The Board of Indian Commissioners, appointed to advise the Indian Bureau, effected some changes in the grosser aspects of government policy, but no planned management was conceived until 1887. The destruction of the buffalo herds, which began to disappear in the wake of the railroads, caused animosity to flare forth anew, for elimination of the buffalo deprived the Indians of subsistence and they fought back for life. Yet Indians were no match for railway builders any more than their tribal chiefs were a match for the Confederate and Union veterans who commanded regular troops on the plains.

While the rise of the mining empire finally impelled a revision of

Indian policy, it hastened the disintegration of Indian civilization.[1] Prospectors were the precursors of farmers in the well-grooved sequence of western settlement. Mining camps were followed by the establishment of territories, territories by states. The emergence of the cattle kingdom was the prologue to its decline, for the railroad, bringing the people to the soil, shortened the life cycle of Indian, miner, and cattle king alike.

The temporal span of the mineral empire was short, but its results were by no means unimportant. Fifty-niners followed forty-niners, this time to Colorado's Pikes Peak and Nevada's Comstock Lode. Boom proportions were reached in the sixties, but by the eighties the bearded prospector with his hardware-store pan had given way to absentee combines employing former prospectors and mechanized techniques. Whatever the wealth accruing to rugged miners and great corporations, the mining advance into the interior advertised its opportunities, real or fictional, and contributed to filling in the continent and completing the Union. Gold was discovered in Carson Valley of Utah Territory in 1859, and Nevada, where Mark Twain roughed it in 1861, imperishably recording its territorial stage, became a state three years later. Idaho, Montana, New Mexico, and South Dakota also attracted the acquisitive in search of precious metals. When gold was found in the hills of what came to be South Dakota, and prospectors rushed into the Black Hills Reservation, Sitting Bull, leader of the Sioux, took council with his warriors. The result was Custer's Last Stand (June, 1876), where, in southern Montana, the colonel and his 250 men were ambushed and annihilated.

The mining frontier and the cattle frontier preceded the agricultural frontier. Union of the three, abetted by the railroad, was more than the Indian could withstand. The Indian barrier to white settlement was thereby removed, but the Indian problem remained. Also remaining was the history of Indian-American relations. Early mining towns have been made to seem romantic in certain types of literature, yet they represented an evanescent stage in the building of civilization. In amorphous societies without the pale of law, populated by smooth adventurers and rough miners, life was lonely because it was artificial and artificial because it was lonely. The miners pursued gold or other metal wealth; the rest of the population was in pursuit of whatever the miners chanced to find. Colorful and exciting they indubitably were, but they succumbed to the onrushing farmer as did the Indian and the cowboy.

The cattle kingdom, developing simultaneously, was as much an interlude in the history of the later West as in the history of expanding

---

[1] For the crusade for justice for the Indians see Chapter XXI.

industrialism. While the range cattle industry dated from the colonial days of New Spain when great herds were bred in Texas, the long drive of cattle from the Southwest to the northern plains was economically futile until the advent of the railroad. Thereafter a huge area—almost a quarter of the entire United States—from the Missouri River west to the Rocky Mountains and from Canada's Saskatchewan province southward to the Red River—provided a mammoth stage for cowboys, cattle, and ranch owners, with rustlers operating from the wings.

To produce the kingdom of cattle a number of factors happily combined. Elimination of wild buffalo herds and the removal of the Indians opened up enormous stretches of land. Because of the growth of urban centers in Europe and America the demand for meat increased, while at the same time eastern and midwestern cattle production declined in sections where farming and industry overtook it. Texas was an ideal breeding ground for cattle, the public domain rich in grasses for feed. All that remained was to connect the well-fed cattle from Texas with the potential markets of the East.

This joinder was effected by the railroads. When, in 1867, the Kansas and Pacific Railroad reached Abilene, Kansas, the first cow town took its place on the economic map and the ranchers had found a market. Fattened by the long drive from the Southwest without charge to their owners, the cattle were ready for sale to slaughterers and packers whose representatives awaited them at the cow towns. With transportation assured, packers were eager to buy, and by 1875 the refrigerator car solved the final technical problem, for dressed meat could then be safely sent anywhere. As settlement followed close upon the receding range, the cow towns moved westward. The Atchison, Topeka and Santa Fe had its Dodge City, the Union Pacific its Ogallala, and the Northern Pacific its Miles City. Without transportation difficulties, the packing industry remained close to the sources of supply at Chicago, St. Louis, Kansas City, and Omaha.

With land and grass both free, together with an assured market, initial investment in the cattle business was low and financial returns were high. Large companies were quickly formed to take advantage of the opportunities in which capital from Europe and the East was more than ready to invest. Up to 1882 profits remained seductively great, but five years later overexpansion had caught up with the cattle industry and the cattle frontier was closed. Thereafter the number of cattle did not decline, but corporate methods and business enterprise had changed the nature of the range, the ranch, and the cowboy. For a brief time stampeding herds of cattle on the great plains took the place of stampeding herds of buffalo; the cowboy, innocent victim of romantic ardor, took the place of the Indian. But the Indian and the cowboy, the herds of buffalo and of cattle, enjoyed brief careers. The buffalo fell as a victim to the railroad; the cowboy to barbed wire. Cattle and the Indian alone remained, but each thereafter lived in a restricted demesne.

The railroads, which had helped to create the cattle kingdom, helped to destroy it. With the railroads came settlers just as hostile to cattle as to buffalos and Indians. Against the Indian and the buffalo the Colt revolver was the weapon; against the cattleman, barbed wire, although the gun was sometimes brought into play. As railway and covered wagon brought an increasing number of homesteaders to the plains, the farmers employed barbed wire to fence in their holdings against the cattle; and the cattlemen used barbed wire to fence in their herds against depredation from any source. The wide expanse of the cattle kingdom, its millions of animals, its picturesque cow punchers, had a heyday of less than thirty years, for by the late eighties the workaday farmer replaced the glamorous cattleman and the acres over which hard-riding cowboys and stampeding cattle had once roamed were thereafter put to the plow. Institutions of the range and the ranch were succeeded by the institutions of the farm and the village, but they were rural institutions in a growing urban industrial world that had already overshadowed them.

Cowboys and Indians, cattlemen, and gold seekers continued to lend a vivid pioneer note to American life, but the plains and valleys of the great West belonged to the farmer. The cow town and the mining camp were succeeded by the church and the school; the Indian in resplendent dress was replaced by the farmer in unromantic overalls. The West was not yet gone, but those with penetrating vision could already foresee its end. While John Quincy Adams was still President, and before the Mexican conquest was incorporated in the American public domain, a government official predicted that five hundred years would be required to settle the West. Yet in little more than half a century the incredible had actually occurred.

BUILDING THE RAILROADS

The speed of the transition from the pastoral life of the Indian and the isolated life of the frontiersman to the community life of the village is not difficult to explain. First on the inventory of social causation were the railroads. Making all sections of the country easily accessible, their construction furnished a powerful incentive for inducing settlement, and their managers became active agents of colonization. By promising security to the adventurous and the disaffected in the United States and in Europe, they inspired thousands with hopes of social and economic betterment. A generous government provided land to speculators and settlers almost for the asking, while the advertising of interested landowners and the experience of actual farm workers forever dispelled the illusion that the great plains of the American West were the great American desert. Inventive response to social need, particularly the discovery and perfection of barbed wire in 1874–1875, enabled eager farmers to fence in their land against the cattleman's zeal for profit. But highest on the list of factors hastening the agricultural advance were the masses from eastern farms and eastern cities and the equally willing masses from across the sea whose bodies built America and whose hopes nourished the American dream.

The great inspiration of early railroad enthusiasts, once called visionaries, was finally realized on May 10, 1869, when the Union Pacific met the Central Pacific at Promontory Point in Utah. The "wedding of the rails" ended a dramatic chapter in American annals fittingly celebrated by silver sledges and golden spikes. But the sturdy rails that tied the Atlantic and the Pacific together were the real dramatic elements. Delayed because of sectional antipathies before the Civil War, the new central route cut the time of travel by twenty-one days. California was thereafter only a week away from New York, but the Central Pacific promoters—Leland Stanford, Collis P. Huntington, Charles Crocker, and Mark Hopkins—did not accomplish this tremendous feat alone.

The success of the Central Pacific stimulated the zeal and the cupidity of other railway promoters. Only fifteen years after the "wedding of the rails," four principal roads connected the Valley of the Mississippi with the Pacific. The new lines provided for transcontinental traffic by the Northern Pacific, the Union Pacific, the Atchison, Topeka and Santa Fe, and the Southern Pacific were supplemented by the Canadian Pacific, which followed the same direction from east to west. Government generosity, public enthusiasm, and the possibility of profit both in the business of transport and in the gymnastics of stock, made railway building an industry of top rank. During 1872 alone, the banner year of construction until 1893, 7,439 miles of track were laid. By 1900 there were just under 200,000 miles, more than in all of Europe put together.

In general, railroads built east of the Mississippi followed settlement, while those built west of the river preceded it. Trunk lines were formed in the East by consolidating existing lines in order to connect inland centers, such as Chicago and St. Louis, with the Atlantic seaboard, an ante-bellum development that played a considerable part in Union victory. Western lines, built to connect the cities along the Mississippi with the Pacific, covered unpopulated regions instead of traversing regions where population was dense. Since capital was loath to invest in a long-time venture which awaited the maturity of the country between the Mississippi and the west coast, government was forced to step in with loans and land grants. The difference in the nature of the problem between eastern and western roads partially explains federal subsidies; it also explains the colonizing activities of the major railroads. Their holdings could appreciate only if the country was swiftly settled, for the railroads were worth only as much as the territory through which they ran.

Building the railway net was an accomplishment of the first magnitude, but the social consequences of the railways far outweighed the importance of the men who are said to have built them. While the great promoters were motivated by profit, the execution of their plans involved a major encounter between human objectives and natural obstacles, an encounter won by man. Potentates of finance were concerned with power as well as with bonds, but the great triumph of the railways was the peopling of the valleys of the West, the building of cities, and the release of America's natural resources. Not to the unmistakable genius of a James J. Hill of the Great Northern, who built an empire, or a Collis P. Huntington, who with his associates envisaged the Central Pacific, belongs the credit for the work of legions.

Huntington and Hill were not exceptional in an age in which Rockefellers, Carnegies, Schwabs, and Fricks were making history. There was no scarcity of men of colossal stature in the colossal land that bred them and shaped the contours of their plans. Place must be found on the agenda of appraisal for the bitter struggle of pigtailed Chinese coolies, of Irish "paddies," of thousands of ex-soldiers alternately freezing in mountain cold and sweltering in desert heat who realized the schemes of the railway builders. They it was who stood in constant readiness to drop their shovels and pick up their guns to beat off Indian attacks; they dug the road beds and hammered the steel spikes into thousands of miles of rail. Behind them were the inventors of tools, the chemists and engineers who devised processes for mining coal and iron for making steel, the discoverers of lighting methods, air brakes, and automatic couplers that made communication swifter, safer, and more comfortable. We have long since learned that the majestic pyramids of Egypt testify to the greatness of her mathematicians and engineers and to the humble hewers of stone rather than to the half-forgotten Pharaohs whose proud inscriptions they bear. The American railways, like the Egyptian pyramids, are monuments to cooperative social effort. Both were reared on the common foundation of the cultural heritage of civilization which it has been their major social purpose to serve. Archaeologists, laboriously engaged in deciphering the hieroglyphics on imperial Egyptian tombs, seek to unravel the threads of a civilization rather than a royal personality. Burial remains become units of time and the mausoleum furniture delineates not the life of arrogant monarchs but the subjects over whom they ruled.

The epic of the railroads is the epic of humanity. The significance of the railway net is the conquest of nature and the building of civilization, not the conquest of fortunes and the building of careers. The triumph of capitalism was the building of the railroad net, but the function of the railroads was less to line the pockets of its builders with gold than to populate a continent. That James G. Hill's beguiling agents and Henry Villard's scouts, who swarmed over Europe in search of men and women to populate their lands, were unconcerned with the welfare of immigrants and concerned with figures in the company books matters less than the salient fact that they came, and coming, built America. These newer Americans with their faces to the wind subdued the farmlands of the West with plow and pitchfork. They cut down the forests of Minnesota, Oregon, and Washington, fed the blazing steel furnaces in Pittsburgh and Duluth, and caused half a hundred towns to rise where once "the plumed hereditary lord of all America" had hunted his buffalo and struck terror into the hearts of earlier migrants who traveled by caravan instead of by train. With their battered trunks and homely baggage, they also brought their folkways, their skills, and above all their ideals, their yearning to walk upright in the New World as men. No seventeenth-century Englishman who left the *Susan Constant* or the *Mayflower* to tread for the first time on American soil was a more vital contributor to America than the later Europeans of the nineteenth century who left the trains of the Great Northern or the Northern Pacific to tread for the first time on the soil of the American West.

Railroads were science in motion, for as science supplied the techniques for city and factory, it forged the tools for farm and country. The nineteenth century, the age of Charles Darwin, like the seventeenth century, the age of Isaac Newton, was a scientific era. It was not only the science of great speculators who worked at laboratory bench and dissecting table, but the science of great technologists who applied speculative discoveries to human wants and human needs. Science in the form of steel for tools, coal for fuel, cream separators, and milk containers conditioned farm life, however little individual farmers knew about research and scholarship. Scientists at the nation's capital, in the laboratories of the agricultural colleges, and experimenters on the scene discovered new fertilizers, hardier and more fertile breeds of stock and grain, methods of irrigation, reclamation, and scientific farming that made barren ground productive.

Nowhere was the influence of science more apparent than in the multiplication of tools that eased the physical strain of farm work, reduced hours of labor, and again increased production. Although great agricultural inventions were made before 1860, agriculture was far from mechanized when the Civil War closed. It was not until 1869 that James Oliver presented agriculture with the chilled steel plow. The reaper of Cyrus H. McCormick, though patented in the thirties, was not used extensively after its introduction until the Civil War made the mechanization of the farm imperative. Thereafter, implements that reduced harvesting time—the bottleneck of grain producing—developed rapidly. John F. Appleby, in 1878, perfected the binding technique, an improvement over the harvesting methods devised by the Marsh brothers in 1858. The results of such inventions appeared at once. By 1880 almost four fifths of the wheat grown in the United States was cut by machine; it had required 183 minutes to harvest one bushel of wheat in 1830, but seventy years later the amount of time needed to harvest a similar quantity had been reduced to 10 minutes.

The lightning speed of machines pushed the frontier line ever farther westward, and contributed to swell the volume of agricultural surpluses. Between 1860 and 1880 the production of wheat and corn doubled, and in the next twenty years it doubled again. By 1880 the United States had become the greatest wheat-exporting nation in the

PRODUCTIVITY IN AGRICULTURE (PER MAN HOUR)

1830 'HAND METHODS)

1896 (EARLY MACHINES)

1942 (MODERN MACHINES)

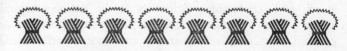

Each symbol represents 40 lbs. of wheat produced   PICTOGRAPH CORPORATION

From Hacker, Modley, and Taylor, *The United States: A Graphic History,* Modern Age Books, Inc. PICTOGRAPH CORP.

world. Such fantastic increases could not fail to have far-reaching results, and Europe as well as America was affected. Dr. Alexander Peez, an Austrian legislator, compared the influx of American farm produce to Europe in the years following the Civil War to the influx of precious metals following the Spanish conquests in the New World. In both cases European economy experienced a serious shock from which it was not quick to recover. With transportation by sea and by rail a commonplace, American wheat was shipped to far-off Bohemia and was reexported from Fiume and Trieste, long the disbursing points for Austrian, Hungarian, and Italian produce. European agricultural journals, legislative committees, and publicists exhibited grave alarm because of the competition of the American farmer to whom the machines of science had granted a new productive potency. Produce of the farmers by 1900 made up nearly 70 per cent of the total exports from the United States.

Productive potency, however, did not produce contentment, for all was not well with the American farmer. Rapid expansion and mechanization had transformed agriculture—and therefore rural life—from self-sufficiency to dependence. The farmer produced surpluses to be sold on the market, national and international, in return for cash with which he purchased requirements for home and farm. American agriculture became a dependency of the capitalistic estate, and the farmers, guided by precepts dating from an anachronistic self-sufficient age, found themselves in an interdependent, industrialized world in which those ancient precepts failed to apply.

CAPITALISM CAPTURES THE FARMER

The new economy brought about new economic and social relationships. Agricultural peace and prosperity were no longer the certain rewards of sinewy hands and honest sweat. Individual men could no longer build towers of security out of 160 acres of land simply by dint of hard labor and persistent effort, for the farmer had become as much the ward of capital as the industrialist. Forever gone were the days when he could make his own clothes and tools. He was dependent upon the outside world for almost everything he used and sometimes even for his food. The altered economic circumstances made him a producer of surpluses for a world market, and the world price of his product determined his income. Tools that his ancestors had used since the time of Cincinnatus, long-lived and inexpensive and often bequeathed to his grandchildren, were replaced by intricate and expensive machines that required an outlay of cash and frequently needed repairs during their brief period of usefulness. Whether he liked it or not, however, he had to buy tools, for his margin of profit was determined by the cost of production on mechanically operated farms. Either he acquired the machines or he was forced to hire himself out as a laborer to those who could afford to purchase them. Once the harvester, the reaper, the binder, and the plow were perfected, the old-fashioned farmer, the stereotype of rural life, was outmoded in the realm of economic fact, if not in the realm of romantic fiction.

Likewise binding the husbandman to the web of capitalism were rising land values. The farther westward the frontier line receded, the more land appreciated in price. Since to operate in a competitive economy the farmer needed more and more capital for land, tools, interest, and charges paid to middlemen, he had no choice but to use his land as an instrument of credit. By mortgaging his farm, the farmer acquired the cash or credit necessary to continue in business, but the necessity brought him into ever closer contact with banks and the holders of notes and bonds. Eastern mortgage companies loaned money at rates between 8 and 15 per cent or more. Although Civil War prosperity lasted until 1868, from 1870 to 1897 these interest charges plus taxes created a crushing economic burden aggravated by the falling prices of crops. Instead of striving to produce for home consumption or in terms of the local market, as was more or less the practice before the Civil War, the farmers attempted to grow as much as could be grown at the lowest possible production cost and to obtain as high an increment from the yield as the market would bear. Farm machinery was pivotal in this economic cycle, hence farmers mortgaged their land to buy machines so as to attain the maximum yield and thus pay off their indebtedness. By 1900 the farmers had a stake of $750,000,000 in farm implements and modern machines.

But the farmer produced neither in national nor in international isolation. Consequently, the greater the surplus, the lower the price. Although the farmer became capitalistic and competitive, he had none of the capitalistic devices to control his market or the price of his product. The steel used in his chilled plow, his harvester, or his binder was protected by a tariff, but the price of wheat was not. Protective tariffs, operative consistently throughout the period, permitted industry to evade foreign competition. Big business was completely commanded by manufacturers with the power to fix the price of their products. The situation in agriculture was exactly the reverse, and this was the crux of the agricultural problem. Farmers sold in a cheap and uncontrolled market; they bought in a dear and protected one. And revolutionary economic changes made the dilemma catastrophic. The more land placed under cultivation, the more the total agriculture yield; the railroad swelled the output while mechanized equipment multiplied the capacity to produce. Application of scientific methods—to fertilizer, seed, and the reclamation of barren soil—contributed to overexpansion which, with the rivalry of virgin wheatlands, had a disastrous effect upon agricultural prices.

Agricultural workers came to be dependent upon machines; without them the soil could not be tilled nor the crop harvested and sent to market. And the thousand and one things that the machine produced—machine parts, tools, clothes—became as essential to the farmer's existence as the soil itself. The legendary figure of the sun-tanned farmer, rugged, free, and self-sufficient, beholden only to his God, was the by-product of a fertile political imagination. The farmer was the master neither of his present nor of his future. If the laws of nature—droughts, agricultural pests, floods—did not control his life, the laws of man did. The independent western farmer died in an eastern factory. He was tied to banks, to railroads, and to middlemen who dominated his existence. Agriculture had become a part of industrial capitalism: as much dependent on bank credit as on climate, as dependent on manufactures as on rainfall. And in this new arrangement the farmer failed to derive a reasonable share of the national income or a fair reward for his labor.

FARMER'S SHARE OF NATIONAL INCOME, 1859-1944

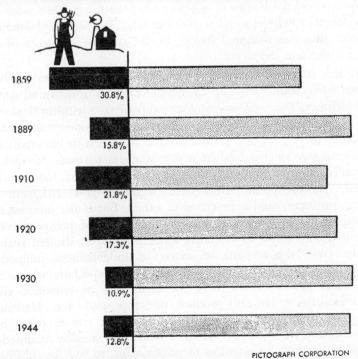

1859   30.8%

1889   15.8%

1910   21.8%

1920   17.3%

1930   10.9%

1944   12.8%

PICTOGRAPH CORPORATION

With brief flashes of golden prosperity, sufficient only to dazzle hope and allay despair, prices for agricultural goods pursued a downward trend. Wheat, which brought a dollar a bushel in the seventies, was worth only half as much in the nineties, while in the same decades cotton dropped from 17 cents a pound to 9 cents. The average price of cotton from 1886 to 1895 was less than 8 cents, a cent and a half less than the average between 1876 and 1885. Because prices dropped and debts mounted with more foreclosures, additional farmers were faced with the choice of becoming tenants on the land they had previously owned or joining the eastward movement to the industrial centers.

Statistics of falling prices are even more conclusive when converted into figures of purchasing power. One bushel of wheat was worth a dollar on a mortgage note in 1870; twenty years later two bushels, double the amount, were needed to accomplish the same financial result. A farmer who owed $3,000 in the former year could repay his obligation with 3,000 bushels; in 1890 he required 6,000 bushels. While the increase meant greater work and less return, it also meant less for elementary comforts to relieve the drabness and monotony of farm life, less for the newest gadget in the kitchen of the farm wife, and less to send the children to the state university. If they were able to go at all, they went on a restricted budget, but, more often than not, they were needed on the farm to help raise the 6,000 bushels. In the placid language of economics this was marginal living; in the realistic language of life, it meant futility and desperation.

At the same time another series of difficulties plagued native husbandmen. Everything went up except the price of agricultural commodities. Machines, the weapons in the competitive agricultural race, were expensive, thus raising the cost of operations. Money was dearer and ever harder to get. As the farmer became beholden to his creditors who held a mortgage on his land or a note for the payment of agricultural implements, interest rates mounted and credit became more and more stringent. As the public lands were engrossed and settlement spread over the continent, land appreciated in value. But if the increase in land values aided larger owners, it damned the future of prospective owners and invited all owners to capitalize more heavily; in the ten years from 1880 to 1890 the amount of mortgage indebtedness jumped from $343,000,000 to $586,000,000. The railways, especially where no collateral water routes existed, held the farmer in an economic vise, for without facilities to ship his produce, the crop would rot. He could not hold agricultural raw material against a possible rise in price, but the processor could. In addition, state and local taxes steadily mounted: taxes to support the growing activities of government, to pay for subsidies and bounties, to offset legislative favors to special groups that took money out of the Treasury—not to mention the cost of wholesale graft and corruption. No imagination is required to see why the farmer accounted himself the enemy of middlemen and bankers, bondholders and corporations, railroads and warehouse owners; still less to understand why he ardently desired to see the government "restored to the people."

RURAL LIFE IN AN URBAN WORLD

Agriculture presented the farmer with a dilemma and the nation with a paradox. Grain elevators were filled to bursting, the number of laborsaving machines in use was statistically impressive, and more land was under cultivation than ever before. Yet prices continued to drop. The farmer had never worked harder. Although he had many comforts that his forefathers had never thought necessary, his spirit failed to soar. When the sun smiled and the rain fell, the fields brought forth a bountiful harvest and the farmer was usually in distress. Only when grim misfortune overtook farmers in other parts of the world—a famine, a war, a flood—did fortune seem to favor the American agricultural worker. When drought or insect pests ravaged the American farmer, the margin between profit and loss was always so thin he could not meet his obligations and sank deeper into debt.

The triumph of American capitalism was to create abundance. Machinery that made man free may be accounted one of the greatest achievements of business enterprise. Railroads that diminished time and space and made the nation and the world a unit were but one of the many marvels of a marvelous age. To have eliminated scarcity, the mammoth achievement of science and the machine, was the signal contribution of the agricultural revolutions. But abundance, instead of eliminating want, created it. By a strange irony, abundance produced poverty, misery, and broken lives. When in 1880 the United States census first recorded tenancy, 25 per cent of all the farms in America were found to be tilled by renters. Twenty years later the number had grown to 35 per cent. One of the historic functions of the West was the creation of optimism; one of the historic functions of agricultural experience after the Civil War was the creation of the raw materials of pessimism. Hamlin Garland's dedication in *Main-Travelled Roads* (1891) to "my father and mother, whose half century of pilgrimage on the main travelled road of life has brought them only pain and weariness" was no isolated chronicle. "No splendor of cloud, no grace of sunset," he wrote in another place, "could conceal the poverty . . . the gracelessness . . . and the sordid quality of the mechanical daily routine. . . ." What had blighted the magnificent

FARM OWNERS AND TENANT FARMERS, 1880–1940

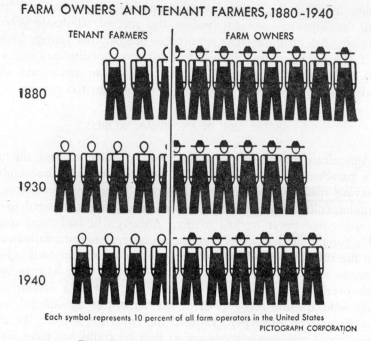

Each symbol represents 10 percent of all farm operators in the United States

PICTOGRAPH CORPORATION

PICTOGRAPH CORP. for Ginn and Company.

hopes of Thomas Jefferson, who once supposed that an agricultural exist-ence meant earthly felicity? Whatever the answer, to have endured what Garland and others reported demanded a stoicism that only the gods pos-sess. The farmers did not possess it and they retorted, as had their west-ern predecessors, with a series of mighty protests. That there should have been an "agricultural problem" was itself a paradox of the first magni-tude. Machine technology affected labor adversely in the factory as well as on the farm; the revolutions in economics made America rich but left Americans poor.

Yet agricultural irritation did not proceed entirely from economics, for the tiller of the soil was as culturally poor as he was financially im-poverished. While the material advantages of modern urban-industrial civilization largely passed him by, the cultural advantages did likewise. American farming communities reaped few satisfactions from the mechani-cal contrivances that made the city seem more attractive, stimulating, and convenient. The telephone, the electric light, and educational and cul-tural opportunities had not yet reached the farming hinterland. Without possibilities for frequent commingling of personalities and without theaters, libraries, and music, the farmer's outlook tended to shrink rather than to broaden. But although the farmer was deprived of urban amenities, he was not unaware of their existence, and grew to resent his rural isolation. Farmers' wives flocked into the Grange, a social and fraternal order that arose in the sixties, and farmers' sons and daughters migrated to the city—the former to satisfy a yearning for companionship, the latter to satisfy a craving for a larger life. Opportunities in rural America, especially when compared with those in urban America, seemed limited and confining, and however long the hours in the factory, the hours of labor in the field were longer. In the city were careers and fortunes to be made, on the farm was only drudgery with frustration at the end. Time and time again in fable and in story—as well as in the historical documents—farm parents urged their offspring to achieve what they themselves had missed, the satisfaction of normal ambitions, contentment, and emotional peace. Inevitably, the road to what was conceived to be a richer life led through teeming urban highways; almost never along twisting country lanes.

When compared with urban splendor, agricultural drabness nurtured a feeling of inferiority that furnished the driving emotional force of agrarian upheavals. Sometimes it expressed itself in violent political protests; other times it took the form of a compensatory superiority that romanticized the farmer as the guardian of the American way of life. The antitobacco league was a thrust at urban vice. Prohibition sentiment first raised its dry voice in the Maine of the fifties and later found its greatest support among the inhabitants of the countryside. It was in Hillsboro, Ohio, during the seventies that a praying crusade to save the souls and bodies of the intemperate began, which led in turn to a convention of women at Chautauqua, New York, and the birth of the Woman's Christian Temperance Union at Cleveland in 1874. And from the W.C.T.U. in 1893 stemmed the Anti-Saloon League, parent of prohibition. Nativistic organizations had more rural adherents than urban ones. The Ku Klux Klan arose in Pulaski, Tennessee; the American Protective Association, descendant of the Klan and as violently "native American," anti-Catholic, and "Protestant," in Clinton, Iowa (1887). If the country set itself up as the conservator of the home, it was the city where women were first emancipated by the economic opportunities of shop, store, and professional careers. The Bible belt was as rural as the corn belt. Venerable theological standards were most zealously upheld in the pulpits of the rural church, but it was in the city that secularism and what passed for infidelity abounded. The city was the center of apartment-house living, of divorce, of juvenile delinquency, of organized vice. The city was the locus of the "godless" university and the "agnostic" lecture hall. Agrarian America was the home of "100 per cent Americanism" for the city was the home of "foreigners" where men with Irish, Jewish, and eastern European names sat in municipal administrative bodies.

Already challenged by the advance of urban-industrialism after 1850, rural modes of life and thought were threatened with a cumulative insistence after the sixties. Easy as it was to shift from one kind of tool to another in the performance of daily tasks, the shift brought about social alterations and finally conceptual ones. To use a Dover egg beater instead of the old manual method, for example, involved no complex adjustment in itself, but this device together with other mechanical changes spelled out an institutional revolution. With increasing leisure and the improvement in communication, the status of women underwent a marked transformation with repercussions upon the home, the family, and the church. The ultimate effect on politics, marriage, courtship, and economic relationships brought a whole set of cultural innovations in its train.

The farm and the homestead were the classic rural institutions. In preindustrial America the home was a relatively self-sufficient unit, largely independent of other groups. A spirit of close cooperation among its members and a corresponding spirit of individual self-reliance developed. The family was the center of production—of crops, of food, and of clothes, in the fabrication of which every member had a prescribed function. Literal dependence of each member upon the other tightened the bonds of kinship, created an emotional cohesiveness, and made the family the dominant institution of the rural world.

The home served as the agency for the transmission of the cultural legacy. It taught its members their primary occupational techniques, gave them the elemental precepts of the rural world view, and supplemented the formal education of the schoolhouse. The family was the adjunct of the rural church; the church the coadjutor of the family. Each underwrote the same moral code, an identical ethic for marriage, parenthood, and secular conduct. While the church taught in elaborate theological detail, the family learned in homely metaphors and the vernacular of experience. Marriage was stable, divorce rare, promiscuity in morals savagely condemned. The paterfamilias, armed with shotgun on the nuptial eve, was a behavior pattern associated with the head of the rural clan. Urban influences infected the home with the virus of change, but the rural church stubbornly guarded its immutable sanctity. Country moralists feared that the chastity of womanhood was imperiled by urban vices and woman's proper place in social life threatened by economic temptations. Nor were deviations to be countenanced in matters of parental governance. The way had long since been pointed out, and transgressions whether in creed or deed received no support from those who lifted protesting voices in village churches throughout the land.

Life was by no means grim, but neither was it urbane. Absence of recreational facilities made the church and the home the centers of relaxation, and on the Sabbath the church was the principal recreational focus. The gaiety of the church picnic was not the gaiety of the dance hall; the hilarity of the village barbecue not the hilarity of the saloon. Social status was determined by family prestige and reputation rather than by occupational calling or wealth. The neighborhood enforced the prevailing moral code, and transgressions meant ostracism, the more terrifying when relations were mostly face to face. From birth to death, in sickness and in health, members of the family served as counselors and protectors; the home was the haven of refuge and shelter. The immutable ways of nature, fixed seasons and facts of climate, accentuated conventional religious attitudes and the tendency to look to God rather than to society for assistance, release, and reassurance. Beneath rural political discontent from 1865 to 1900 lay rural virtue, which aggravated rural animosity toward the city, accentuated rural suspicion of urban ways, and compensated in some measure for the glaring inadequacies of rural life.

The influence of the agricultural way of life went further and deeper. The farmer was a generalist rather than a specialist. Agriculture, a many-sided activity, required in addition to conventional operations that the farmer become a carpenter, a veterinary, a hunter, and a smith. The machine demanded a further diversification of his abilities. He had to become a machinist as well. If the farmer acquired many techniques to accomplish his daily rounds, the farmer's wife had likewise to become a Jacqueline of all trades. She was a field hand as well as homemaker, canner as well as cook and seamstress; teacher, nurse, and maker of soap, polish, clothes, and dye. Although communication and invention lessened her burdens, she remained, compared to her urban sister, the possessor of a much wider range of proficiencies. The farmer's work, moreover, like the chores of his female partner, was almost never done, and labor from dawn to dusk was no mere poetic license. And the farmer's work was not only harder but more unremitting than the work of his urban neighbor, a condition reflected in his moral values, his outlook on labor's struggle for shorter hours, his sentiments toward the activities of the urban "idle rich," and his scornful reaction to unearned increment derived from stocks, bonds, and speculation.

Yet wealth was seldom the reward of agricultural toil, for the round of debt and solvency was rarely relieved by opulence. Debt and subsistence were the certainties, and opulence, however general a wish, was scarcely ever the normal condition. If the spread between great wealth and abject poverty was less wide in the country than in the city, rural standards, when not frugal, were extremely modest. While the ordinary farmer was not much richer than his neighbor, he was also not much higher or lower in the rural social scale. He did not work at a specialized job under the eye of an overseer. Regardless of his position, legal, economic, or social, he performed his tasks at the command of nature instead of at the command of a master, superior, or employer. Even when the farmer hired a helper, both did the same manual chores.

All this the new economic forces changed. As the revolutions in economics expanded, the functions of the home were curtailed. Self-sufficiency gave way to dependence and dependence to interdependence. Intimate, personal relations yielded to remote, anonymous relations, and those to impersonality. The farmer and his stalwart sons still went out into the fields, but more and more his offspring, male and female alike, looked to the city as a fairer arena in which to joust with fortune. Their places were taken by the hired man, the migratory laborer, and by numerous laborsaving tools that enabled his sons and daughters to leave. Most of the things he used were made in the urban factory rather than on the farm. Farmers' wives and daughters still canned, preserved, and pickled, but they competed with huge corporate rivals who provided cheaper if not better results. Their wives and daughters used sewing machines, egg beaters, and cream separators at the same time that their urban sisters were becoming accustomed to relief from household cares.

But the voices that spoke from American country pulpits spoke in a universal social idiom. Similar discourses in French, German, and Italian, as well as in many other tongues including the Scandinavian, were heard wherever these languages were spoken. Although there was a babel of tongues, the message was everywhere the same, for geographical size, density of population, and diversity do not alone account for the urban habit of mind. The city is distinguished from the country by the character of its social relationships. Whatever the differences in custom, in language, or in cultural traits, the urban impact was virtually the same in Berlin as it was in London, in Minneapolis as in Stockholm. Urban issues were no different for Swedes, Americans, Englishmen, or Germans, and the cleavage between urban center and rural hinterland was also substantially the same. Pomerania stood in the same cultural relation to Berlin as Hampshire did to London and agricultural Minnesota to Minneapolis.

Not the machine alone but the city also conquered rural America. Penetrating the one-time frontiers of western settlement, machines substituted economic and social interdependence for economic and social self-sufficiency. The science of transport and the science of communication contracted the globe at the same time that they shrank the American world. America was not yet a world of cities, but the influence of urban ways of living and the influence of urban attractions were making themselves felt in every aspect of rural existence. Estimable village patriarchs could not stay the urban trend, nor could pious hopes arrest the collision between two ways of life. The urban-rural clash colored American experience in all its phases, but if technology made the farmer dependent upon urban commerce and trade, the technology of the machine had actually made each dependent upon the other. The old rural America of Thomas Jefferson and Andrew Jackson was gone, but a new rural America was in formation. The expansion of rural life developed under the aegis of the city, of urban institutions and urban thought. In 1900 more than 60 per cent of the people still lived in an agrarian or small-town environment. But if rural vestiges everywhere abounded, the culture of the United States was to be a culture of cities.

XVIII

THE RISE OF THE CITY 1865–1900

If rural America was subjugated by the revolutions in economics between 1865 and 1900, the hubs of the revolutions were in the cities of the United States. Like the advance of industrialism, the movement of population cityward had been in evolution since earlier American times, but no mass shift developed until the last three decades of the nineteenth century. Parents to the city were not the machine and industrial capitalism, for the city was born long before capitalism and long before the machine. Modern economy and modern industry adopted the city, accelerated its growth, and were responsible for its adult nurture. By 1900, urban America dominated rural America: the United States had become a civilization of cities.

The ancient traveler reined in his horse and gazed at the stately spires of a medieval town with their promise of the society of man and the society of God. Relaxing as his journey came to a close, he thought of his appointment in the tavern for business or pleasure, his errand in the monastery, or his meeting at the fair or the marketplace. The fair, the tavern, and the monastery have given way to other institutions that serve similar human needs. As the modern traveler, leaving the green of the countryside behind him, steams into the gray city in cars of iron and steel, he sees the converging lines of track leading to the railway shed, which is buttressed on both sides by factories, warehouses, and shops. He, too, relaxes as the trip nears its end and thinks of his appointment at the hotel, his errand at the library or the museum, or his directors' meeting in a large company plant. The spires of the majestic cathedrals have been succeeded by the towering cathedrals of business and finance, taverns by palatial hotels, monasteries by art galleries, bookstores, and schools, but the city remains the nerve cell of intellectual and economic life.

Within the walls of the city were housed the social and economic institutions of the new America. Here the lines of transport and communication had their source, the lines of credit tightened into a financial maze, both winding their way to and from the factories, stores, and industrial plants that dotted the principal thoroughfares or sprawled out toward the rural countryside. Here, too, the toilers gathered, laboring and

366

The Grant administrations invariably suggested political corruption, of which patronage was an obvious symptom. *(Courtesy Collection of Regional History, Cornell University) Below, left*—James G. Blaine, perennial presidential aspirant, was an irresistible leader without a cause; *right*—Chester A. Arthur, notorious spoilsman, became president after the assassination of Garfield. *(Culver Service)*

Rutherford B. Hayes *(upper left)*, James A. Garfield *(upper right)*, Grover Cleveland *(center left)*, and William McKinley *(lower right)*, Presidents of the United States. None save Cleveland was identified with the people's cause. William Jennings Bryan *(lower left)* led the common man in political revolt.

(Culver Service)

THE FIGHT FOR THE STANDARD.

The fine art of huckstering. Here the symbol of liberty was pressed into the service of "astral oil"; beauty became the handmaiden of balm; and courage was identified with pills. *(Courtesy Collection of Regional History, Cornell University)*

An early Woolworth store in the age of the dime.

(Bettmann Archive)

The machine and the city created a new woman's world.

Mary Lyon *(upper left)*, founder of Mt. Holyoke College, helped to free society from the double standard in education; Amelia Bloomer *(center left)* strove to emancipate womankind from the entanglements of archaic dress.

Jane Addams *(center right)* and Lillian D. Wald *(lower right)* sought to aid both men and women suffering from the double standard in economic life.

(All photos *Culver Service* except Lillian Wald, *courtesy Visiting Nurse Service of New York*)

living in the shadow of the mill and the factory, while workers of the middle class performed the countless services that the urban subdivision of labor demanded. In banks, in corporation directors' rooms, the capital accumulated by business enterprise was reforged into plans for further economic conquest, with results that changed the relationships of all classes of society.

THE URBAN IMPACT

Intellectually as socially, the city became the driving center of stimulation. Physically, it was the home of the largest and best libraries, the oldest and most elaborately equipped schools and colleges, the bookstores, the publishing houses, and the centers of journalism. The arts found their patrons in urban masters of capital, and their audiences from among residents of the towns. Music, painting, and such sculpture as there was gravitated around the opera houses, art galleries, and museums in the metropolis. Recreation in the form of the theater, the dance, the music hall, and organized sport throve in the bracing atmosphere of the city. Hospitalization, medical and scholarly research, social settlements, and other reforms were urban rather than rural interests largely because they were inspired by urban needs and urban problems.

The intellectual ascendancy of the city resulted from specific social factors. Density of population offered opportunity for the widest spread of individual differences, which is the lifeblood of change. Not only did the city afford the opportunity for minds of equal quality and temper to merge in scholarly or artistic production, but it provided the maximum degree of clashing mental traits which made for variety. Diversity is as vital as like-mindedness for the intellectual stimulation of mankind; the city afforded both. The modern city, however, was no innovator in this respect, for ancient cities performed the same function. The English tongue, delicate barometer of attitudes and viewpoints, offers a measure of urban intellectual dominance in historical times. The very word "urban" is rooted in the Latin word for city, *urbs,* and its derivative, "urbane," reveals the extent to which the city dweller regarded himself the superior of his country cousin. Equally suggestive is the Latin *civis,* from which the words "civic" and "civil" descend, but "civilization" itself, the word as well as the thing, is rooted in the concept of urban citizenship.

Yet urbanization was no more confined to the United States than the revolutions in economics that conditioned its rise. Cities on the Seine and on the Rhine grew in response to the same conditions that stimulated their development on the Dnieper and the Tyne. The competition of commerce and industry with agriculture was a conflict universal in scope and manifesting similar traits in America as in Europe. Everywhere the rural world was contracting and the urban world expanding. Abandonment of farms in rural New England for mill towns and factories in the decades immediately succeeding the Civil War was paralleled by a rural exodus in England, Belgium, France, and Prussia and a corresponding expansion of the towns. Conditions that account for the growth of Boston and New York account also for the growth of London and Berlin, of Brussels, Berne, and Bratislava.

Unprecedented urban growth, almost entirely unplanned, presented issues of such magnitude and gravity that the resourcefulness of man was sorely tried. Americans had to learn to cope with densely populated communities. For certain problems there was a reservoir of experience upon which they could draw, but some were so new that experimentation was the only remaining method. Most insistent were the physical problems that could not brook delay. Prosaic as they may seem, the solutions devised for traffic, sewerage, and paving testify not only to the genius of American inventiveness but to the dependence of America upon the collective ingenuity of the world.

Nowhere were streets adequate for the increased pedestrian and vehicular traffic that crowded city roads and city lanes. Conventional cobblestones and granite blocks in the East and wooden blocks in the West quickly deteriorated under the heavy strain of added busses, drays, and service vans. Americans went to the island of Trinidad to obtain pitch, copying the asphalt pavements of London and Paris, which soon made their appearance in Washington, Buffalo, and Philadelphia. Native brick continued to rival asphalt, but by 1900 the major American cities, with the exception of Chicago, had adopted the more durable and more satisfactory foreign substitute.

As cities expanded under the pressure of growing numbers, internal transport became as critical as paving. When it became necessary to convey large numbers of people from home to work at approximately the same time, the horse was seen to have run its course. Other means of locomotion, more rapid, more dependable, and more economical, had to be found to supplement the horse-drawn bus, cab, or streetcar. A Scotch immigrant, Andrew S. Hallidie, brought out the cable car for the steeply pitched streets of San Francisco in 1873, which other cities soon adopted. But the electric trolley based upon the dynamo ousted the cable car more quickly than the cable car had ousted the horse.

The first practicable dynamo in America was the joint work of Moses G. Farmer, an American, and William Wallace, an Englishman residing in Connecticut. Patented in 1875, the dynamo was reared upon foundations laid by the great British scientist, Michael Faraday, a French experimenter with the exotic name of Hippolyte Pixii who improved it, and the famed American physicist, Joseph Henry, who, after Benjamin Franklin, was the first American to make important contributions to the field of electricity. Once the cheapness and operative ease of the electric trolley were demonstrated, the age of the cable car and the horsecar was ended. As early as 1867 an electric trolley was operated in Berlin, and by the eighties Boston, Cleveland, Kansas City, and Denver were experimenting with this type of transportation. Frank Julian Sprague, often called the "Father of Electrical Traction," installed an electric railway in 1887–1888 in Richmond, Virginia, the first actually to run through a city's streets. America far outdistanced Europe in taking advantage of the new electrical devices. Two years after Sprague's trolley appeared in Richmond, over half a hundred cities had similar installations, and by 1900 America had more electric trolleys in operation than all Europe together.

Overhead and underground expedients were also attempted. The opening of New York's Sixth Avenue Elevated in 1878 marked the second effort in that city to solve the problems of congestion and rapid transit, but the expense of construction deferred large-scale building of elevated tracks and stations until the twentieth century. The subway was more successful. Following the lead of Hungary and Britain, which had begun to explore the possibilities of underground travel in Budapest and London, Boston undertook to build the first American subway in the final years of the nineties. As spectacular as elevateds and subways were bridges, for man had to span urban as well as continental space. Urban transit was complicated by the presence of rivers, the great natural arteries of intercourse, where pioneers ancient and modern sought first to build communities. To connect Manhattan and Brooklyn, John A. Roebling, an American of German birth, planned the Brooklyn Bridge, which was executed by his son and successor, Colonel Washington A. Roebling, born with singular appropriateness in Saxonburg, Pennsylvania. When finished after thirteen years of labor in 1883, the longest suspension bridge yet built, it was one of the many wonders of an age still not calloused to the marvels of technology.

If horse and buggy days were numbered in the city after the introduction of the dynamo, the life span of the lamplighter was also to be curtailed. The feeble light of gas jets was as inadequate for urban illumination as the old mare, gray or otherwise, was too slow for urban rapid transit. Once the dynamo had appeared, the power of electricity lay coiled within it. In the nonnational and nonracial realms of science and inventive genius, interdependence was a proud tribute to man's concern for man. The city, if it was anything, was cosmopolitan—and so was its science. Americans in collaboration with Europeans made gleaming contributions to electricity. The internationalism of electrical discovery is permanently imbedded in the language of all nations—amperes for Ampère of France, ohms for Ohm of Germany, and volts for Volta of Italy—for labors in many lands enabled man to turn night into day and apply electricity to transportation and manufacturing. The sparkling genius of Joseph Henry and Thomas Alva Edison was not dimmed by the fact that the light shed by the incandescent bulb was no more native American than the bamboo strips procured from the tropical palm fans essential to make it. Credit for lighting city streets must be accorded Charles F. Brush of Ohio, who improved upon the arc lamp of the Russian engineer, Paul Jablochkoff, in 1879. The following year, Edison perfected and patented his incandescent lamp, and the basic problems of home lighting were thus solved. In spite of Edison and Brush, gas was yet to enjoy a final spurt because of the invention of the Welsbach mantle, designed by Auer von Welsbach of Vienna in 1885. But the displacement of gas lighting was only a matter of time.

Less competent was the American response in the matter of sewerage and garbage disposal. A great Boston divine once remarked that sewerage bore an intimate relation to morals, and if the relation of both to ethics was not immediately apparent, their connection with public health could not be escaped. The welfare of densely populated areas, always an invitation to disease, was imperiled by the practice of dumping refuse into the most convenient body of water along seaways and riverways or the rural expedient of feeding garbage to swine. The one polluted supplies of drinking water; the other provided material for modern scientific dissertations on roast pig. The consequences could be read in the statistics of infectious diseases and the mortality tables of urban centers. Considerable attention was given to the question of disposal, but a complete solution was retarded less by lack of good will than by ignorance. It was not until the maturing in the eighties of the germ theory of disease, the result of a triple alliance between German, French, and English scientists— Robert Koch, Louis Pasteur, and Joseph Lister—that intelligent controls could be effected. With this new knowledge and the enlargement of European experience in preventing urban plagues, American boards of health and socially minded practitioners attacked water supplies, garbage, sewerage, and contagious maladies with increasing success.

Ingenious and rapid readjustment on physical levels contrasted with the slowness with which the impact of urbanism created a more perfect intellectual readjustment. For the greater part of the time during which man has been a resident of the globe, he has lived in a rural world. His habits, his attitudes, and his views of life were conditioned by his rural surroundings, his agricultural occupations, and the impress which the struggle with nature made upon his soul. An astute analyst of man's history, Graham Wallas, sagely observed that after centuries of attunement to the soil, to the values nurtured by generations of agricultural experience, man was suddenly transferred to a new and unfamiliar environment. And the transition was sudden, even if the beginning of cities is placed in the valley of the Nile or in the valley of the Tigris-Euphrates. To this strange social situation man has been forced to adjust the norms of rural life and conduct developed over a span of centuries roughly coincident with the evolution of society itself. The wonder, from this temporal point of view, is not that man has done so poorly in accommodating himself to the culture of cities, but that he has done so astoundingly well. Nor is the wonder that comparatively he has done so little and that infinitely more still remains to be done.

The changed environment of the city altered the basis that had once led intelligent men to assume a philosophy of life based upon individualism. The urban citizen was torn between two worlds: the one, older and rural in its genesis, personal, relatively static, and self-contained; the other urban, impersonal, interdependent, and highly dynamic. The city demanded, even if it did not compel at once, a revolution in ideas and social values. Electric light made night life as well as creative life at night a reality, with broad effects upon scholarship, art, crime, courtship, and recreation. A change to a collective society meant that one rode with strangers in an electrically propelled trolley instead of hitching old Dobbin to the shay. The trolley was symptomatic of the passing of the individualistic age; and the personal relationship between man and man, as between horse and man, passed with it. The trolley, displacing the family horse, was operated by a dynamo, obeyed the laws of physics, and was as indifferent to human personality as to rain or sleet.

The social structure of urban communities had comparatively little to do with national cultures; urban sociology was the same for people everywhere. As the physical size of the city was enlarged by the widening arc of economic expansion, more. individuals became dependent upon other individuals in every category of daily living. For intimate, personal relationships were substituted impersonal, casual contacts in cities all over the globe, regardless of the cultural antecedents of their inhabitants.

Whether city dwellers spoke Japanese, Chinese, or Dutch, their dependence, instead of being positive and charged with the emotionalism of acquaintance, was based instead upon utility. Contacts in agricultural regions were face to face and personal; in the city, while still physically face to face, they were socially distant. The urbanite, for example, came into close proximity with the driver of the trolley and placed his fate in the driver's hands, but the highest degree of impersonality characterized the relationship. The city wife came in close contact with sales-people in department store and chain grocery, but the relationship ended almost where it began—with the consummation of the sale. The man behind the counter in the rural country store, on the other hand, might also be a church deacon or a village official, and his ancestors were prob-ably known by the ancestors of the purchaser.

As the home and the family gave way to the school, the factory, and a multiplicity of city institutions, the neighborhood, the village, and the community lost their primacy in American life. The physical distinctive-ness of local neighborhoods disappeared when merged with a great me-tropolis; with them disappeared also the values and the attitudes that the local community had so long nurtured. Weakening of kinship bonds was a result of the exchange of primary contacts for secondary ones. Reliance had perforce to be placed upon strangers rather than upon kinfolk or old friends as areas expanded geographically and populations multiplied. And the weakening of the ties of kin was the counterpart of the decline of the family. The social significance of the home, following the natural subdivision of urban labor, was dwarfed by other agencies that gradually encroached upon the home's pristine duties. The social responsibility and the group solidarity that the environment of the rural village fostered were undermined, and with them the ancient bases of social cohesiveness. This, in addition to mere size, density, and heterogeneity, was the impact of urbanism, and Americans no less than other peoples confronted with the social changes of the economic revolutions were forced to come to terms with it.

A NEW DESIGN FOR WOMEN

Urban civilization accordingly fashioned a new women's world. In-ventions released the American woman from domestic enslavement and made it possible for female hands and brains to take advantage of the increasing opportunities presented by the revolution in economic life. First on the list of housewife's aids was the prolific increase of processed foods after the Civil War. Breakfast concoctions made their appearance, saving hurried mothers precious morning time and promising unimagined nutritive benefits to young and old alike. Illustrating the trend in American economics, the early processors of cereals advertised little, but when the American Cereal Company, a combine of the nineties, made its corpo-rate entrance, all the devices known to the advertising art were employed. In 1890 the company sent a train loaded with its products from Cedar Rapids, Iowa, to the Golden Gate, which left samples of its wares at every crossroad. Billboards heralded the value of cereal in terms of irresistible economic appeal, for one pound of Quaker Oats was said to make as much muscle as three pounds of beef. Bread, long the crowning achievement of the homemaker, was available at the store, and its price and quality quickly overcame its plebeian associations. As a result of refrigerated cars and canning, fruits and vegetables were taken out of their socially exclusive categories and made available to urban women with the price to pay for them. Milk could now be shipped in cans from farm to bottling station and thence to distributing points, while synthetic foods like oleomargarine and bottled drinks took their places in the family icebox and on the dining-room table.

Such things as remained to be done in the kitchen were lightened by the introduction of the gas toaster, the egg beater, the double boiler, and —marvel of marvels—cake tins with removable bottoms. In the nineties, sparkling aluminum began to replace the drab granite and drabber iron on the shelves, and before long washing machines promised, as advertisers later averred, to make every washday a holiday. Ironing was simplified by the discovery of removable handles, laundries for those who could afford them eliminated consideration of washing and ironing, but dishes still had to be piled up in the kitchen sink, washed, dried, and put away.

Few developments testify so convincingly to the transformation of the status of women as the appearance of cooking schools. Culinary dexterity was by no means a lost art, but more and more women found it necessary to acquire proficiency by way of formal study, a need supplied by the New York Cooking School in 1874 and the Boston Cooking-School in 1877. The inclusion of cooking in the public school curriculum and the advent of Mrs. Fannie Merritt Farmer's *The Boston Cooking-School Cook Book,* first published in 1896, suggested that the kitchen had ceased to be the training ground for all homemakers.

With mounting hours of leisure, women were given a chance for fuller social participation. Education for women, though not without a struggle, became almost a commonplace, and the collegiate female student population increased from under 3,000 in 1880 to over 25,000 eighteen years later. While fainthearted critics described "identical education of the two sexes" as "a crime before God and humanity . . .," coeducation became the rule in state universities. With but three southern exceptions, state institutions appearing in response to the Morrill Act of 1862, designed to stimulate agricultural education by grants of federal land, were all coeducational, while private institutions soon saw the advisability of admitting "serious females." Harvard's sacred portals remained securely locked to aspirants of the fairer sex, but certain assiduous individuals were permitted to study with Harvard professors in 1879. What was known as the "Harvard Annex" became Radcliffe College in 1894, and many another proud masculine intellectual reservation was forced to adopt a like expedient. Meanwhile, new colleges designed exclusively for women were established, and older "female seminaries" were academically reconditioned. Vassar led the feminine way in 1865 and Smith and Wellesley followed in 1875. Bryn Mawr was founded ten years later, and in 1888 the Mount Holyoke Seminary was empowered to grant degrees. The dominion of the superior male, already challenged by the female breadwinner, was threatened in every field, for women emerged from the colleges fully equipped to take active parts in public life and the professions.

For poorer womenfolk, the store and factory took the place of college. Each year greater numbers were engaged in the multifarious activities created by the division of labor in the expanding commercial world. Already in 1880 2,500,000 women were gainfully employed; in the next twenty years the number was more than doubled. The figures alone suggested the great change overtaking the American family, for in the lower income brackets leisure to work, not leisure, was the great problem. The poor could not avail themselves of all the mechanical devices, but they had just enough of the elemental things without which the double slavery of drudgery in the home and drudgery in mill or factory would have been too great to bear.

Increasing equality of opportunity between the sexes in industry and education opened the way to economic independence. Women had still to await the day of liberation, but masculine lords of creation were truly embattled. From the point of view of conservatives, male and female alike, the home and the family were imperiled, and even the republic itself, not to mention all civil society, was gravely endangered. If the economic revolutions had taken women from the kitchen, they had also taken them from the home. Economic independence began to effect changes in courtship and marriage, for many women now commenced to choose their mates as partners in a joint venture rather than to exchange a promise of obedience for a promise of support. The retiring female— the clinging vine of romantic fiction—was, at long last, changed into a personality, a transformation that struck terror into the hearts of traditionalists, who feared that the essence of femininity would vanish with the horsecar and the fall of the bustle. Even the majesty of the law relented its rigorous code and admitted that women had some rights in a man's world. By 1900 all but six states—five of them rural ones—had made a partial acquiescence to the new status the city and industry had granted to women. In all other sections of the country, women were accorded the right to own property, to make valid contracts, and to sue and be sued in courts of law.

While the expanding role of women in public affairs met with continuous opposition, the campaign for political equality was a veritable battle. The fight for the ballot was hotly waged on both sides, with many women joining forces against militant suffragettes. A leading eastern divine characterized the efforts of those who sought votes for women as "an attempt to make trumpets out of flutes, and sun-flowers out of violets," but Wendell Phillips, with greater logic as well as greater forensic astuteness, countered, "One of two things is true; either woman is like man— and if she is, then a ballot based on brains belongs to her as well as to him; or she is different, and then man does not know how to vote for her as well as she does." Progress was made, as in Britain and the Scandinavian countries, permitting women to exercise the franchise in local contests and on particular issues. Beginning with Kansas in 1861, sixteen states allowed women to vote in school elections by 1895, but successful action in the direction of complete equality was to be deferred until the present century. Despite the failure to obtain the full objective, four western states—Wyoming, Colorado, Utah, and Idaho—granted political equality to women before 1900, evidence that it was easier to write reform into a new constitution than to amend an old one. But the organized core of the movement was in the city.

The alarm of traditionalists, while unfounded, cannot be dismissed. Girls did not deteriorate morally or physically from intellectual exposure. Women who worked in stores and factories did not succumb morally, nor did the right of women to own property, to make contracts, and to vote on specified occasions detract from feminine allure. Even the reforms in female costume, including the invention of Mrs. Amelia Bloomer, whose fame, somewhat dimmed in later diaphanous days, did not render women any less attractive. There was no evidence that marriage was on the decline, although there was an astounding increase in divorce. Rising appreciably every decade, one divorce was granted for every sixteen weddings performed in 1890. Urban alarmists had grounds for anxiety, but rural castigators of the city as the den of wickedness found additional cause for righteousness in the statistical facts. It was in the cities that the tempo of increase was greatest, and the marriage tie was more frequently unloosed in larger cities than in smaller ones. There could be little doubt that apartment-house living, the economic independence of women, the tenuousness of urban relationships, and the bitter frustrations of urban living were vital in explaining it.[1]

More distressing than divorce was the fate of children in the environment of the city. Although other influences far more powerful than the emancipation of women contributed to juvenile delinquency, in 1880 one

---

[1] For maladjustments in urban life see Chapter XX.

of every twenty inmates of American prisons was below twenty-one. While some critics decried the inroads of women into business life and the professions as a factor causing the decline of the home, reformers pointed to the census of child labor. While advocates of male dominion over the vote argued that women in politics would destroy the family and throw innocent children upon the streets, reformers called attention to the slum. In 1880 a million children from ten to fifteen years of age were sweating in shops and working in factories, and by 1900 there were three quarters more. Children of the slums escaped from the squalor of the tenement into the squalor of the street. It was not so much the lack of recreation as the economic and social disorganization of poverty-stricken homes that caused them to slip into the underworld bordering the alleys in which they were forced to play.

NEW WAYS OF LIFE AND THOUGHT

The declining influence of the home was matched by the dislodgment of religious institutions from their former primacy in social life. The American church was as profoundly stirred by altering social conditions as its individual members were dismayed by coeducation and divorce. Actually the issues confronting the changing church were the same issues confronting the changing home. Not only was organized religion the custodian of morals; the churches were exposed to the same forces that undermined the rural foundations of society. Competing urban institutions encroached upon the older rural functions of the church in the same way that they encroached upon the functions of the home. It was no longer possible to separate the home from the larger community, and it was equally impossible to separate the kingdom of Caesar from the kingdom of God. Social interdependence perforated the immunity of the church as it broke down the isolation of the home. As the center of production, the home was succeeded by the factory; as the center of education, the church was succeeded by the school. In providing recreation, the church and the home yielded to the countless distractions of the city, for social life no longer revolved about the old homestead and the village church. News and gossip were purveyed by the newspaper; entertainment was afforded by sport, restaurant, theater, and music hall; stimulation, by clubs, learned societies, books, and periodicals. And the weak in body and the troubled in mind now had access to social-service agencies, for private philanthropy alone could not cope with the burdens of social disorganization.

The church and the home suffered a curtailment of function, and both were forced to devise new methods of serving their time-honored social roles. Unprepared for the coming of the industrial-urban kingdom, the church was apparently robbed of its primeval duties. Its ultimate philosophy, originally inspired by the requirements of an agrarian society, was not attuned to the needs of urban living, just as its specific injunctions, couched in rural simile, seemed inappropriate to contemporary life. As a source of stimulation, emotional and intellectual, it competed with secular distractions; as a guide to conduct, its doctrines failed to elicit the expected responses; and as a haven for spiritual and physical regeneration, it had many urban rivals. It was no longer rooted in congenial soil, for instead of being the instrument of a homogeneous population that followed its leadership and underwrote its precepts, it found itself in the midst of a polyglot population with different allegiances and conflicting interests.

As city employment and recreation drew the family outside the home, the secularization of life lured the family away from church. Organized religion was imperiled as never before, but it was not simply organized religion in America or the modifications in the structure of economics that were responsible for its plight. An intellectual revolution challenged older ways of thinking; the transformed physical environment challenged older ways of living. Both reflected the perennial clash between an old and a new order, but while the physical revolutions jarred attitudes and institutions, the intellectual revolution attacked the entire Judaic-Christian point of view. The initial point of impact of the intellectual revolution was the city, however, where older attitudes and institutions were already most vulnerable.

The trials of Christianity in the years after Lincoln were cumulative, simultaneous, and global. Because the revolutions in economics and the revolutions in science came precisely at the same time, upholders of conventional religion were forced to review basic assumptions just when economic and social problems demanded immediate solution. Awareness of the merger of social and intellectual forces alone makes it possible to appreciate the full force of the theological dilemma under urban pressure. The primitive home, the ancient family, and the rural mode of existence were attitudes steeped in religious tradition and grounded in the theological ways of an agricultural folk. The institutional arrangements and the social attitudes upset by economic change were as rural as the religious traditions upset by conceptual change. Economic and conceptual change, moreover, combined in so many ways that they were really one in thought. Intellectual and social thrusts both emanated from the city, were disseminated from urban centers, and purveyed by urban instrumentalities. The urban-rural clash was intensified because the implications of speculation struck at the core of revealed religion.

The publication of the *Origin of Species* by Charles Darwin in 1859 initiated a debate in science, philosophy, and religion as intense and fundamental in London, Paris, and Capetown as in Boston, Philadelphia, and New York. Suggesting that all life developed from pre-existing life and that the normal increase of any one species, if unchecked, exceeded the physical capacity of the earth to sustain it, Darwin concluded that animals and plants were gradually evolved in the course of untold years. Living things had not been specifically created; instead, a process of selection and adaptation in terms of a given environment accounted for the forms of life at specific periods of the earth's history. Contradicting the account in Genesis, Darwin destroyed the creation myth believed by millions in every corner of the world; and the theory that became identified with his name placed the Bible, the only documentary source of Protestantism in America as elsewhere, under the shadow of skeptical doubt.

Not only the Bible, but ideas of God, the sanction of morals, and the very nature of knowledge were called in serious question. If species were not permanent, to what could continuous mutation in forms of life be referred? And if a species was itself a mere category of thought, what became of other thought categories such as God, evil, the good, and the beautiful? How was any knowledge permanent and therefore certain if change and not immutability was the changeless rule of the universe? No wonder the clergy was embattled. In the world of conventional theology there was no place for universal and continuous change any more than there was place in theological ethics for the relativity of morals. Good was good as evil was evil, and the twain could never blend.

When Darwin in 1871 published the *Descent of Man,* the human species was expressly included in the evolutionary chain. With this pronouncement science seemed to have severed the umbilical cord of theology, for in general theological understanding man's kinship with God derived from his special creation. That the divinity of man was to be found in his humanity was soon discovered, but that was small consolation to the harassed defenders of a waning faith. Man was thus twice debased. He ceased to be the lord of all creation at the same time that the male ceased to be the ruler of the domestic roost.

While the warfare between science and theology raged with bitterness throughout the remainder of the century, by the eighties the scientific struggle for the acceptance of the theory of evolution was over in centers of urban knowledge. With the death of Darwin's most resolute scientific opponent in America, Professor Louis Agassiz of Harvard in 1873, opposition progressively declined. Conversion was speeded by the cogency of expert interpreters: Asa Gray, Harvard's famed botanist; Edward L. Youmans, editor of the *Popular Science Monthly,* which began publication in 1873; and John Fiske, lecturer and popularizer extraordinary. Pressed by a solid scientific phalanx and a dual attack of skeptical foes emboldened by science and potent critics concerned with social ills, orthodoxy gradually capitulated by incorporating the findings of science. But the conversion of orthodoxy was almost completely an urban one, for the proud flag of what came to be known as fundamentalism waved from redoubtable battlements in the American hinterland. Rural United States became the conservative section of the nation, striving for a return to a primitive code of theology as it agitated for a return to primitive standards in economics, social attitudes, and folkways.

Darwinism was in many respects an urban phenomenon. Darwin borrowed a hint from the Malthusian doctrine of population, itself a generalization of urban experience in early industrial England, and Darwinism came to American cities from Continental ones. Transported on ships of steam, popularized by power-driven presses here and abroad, it was first debated in urban centers, in the lecture halls of urban universities, in urban forums and urban seminaries. Urban pulpits, particularly Henry Ward Beecher's, in Plymouth Congregational Church, Brooklyn, pioneered in accommodating Darwinian evolution to the old faith, while urban newspapers spread scientific information to the remotest frontier.

Darwinism was urban in still another and more subtle sense. While the countryman tended to associate Darwinism with other aspects of urban infidelity, the urbanite, accustomed to machines and the impersonal relations they helped to create, found scientific speculation less forbidding. Change, a major Darwinian premise, was a mere generalization of daily experience, and the struggle of quadrupeds for survival in a callous, changing environment was no less bitter or casual than the struggle of human bipeds. And it was easy to identify, erroneously to be sure, the struggle for survival in urban life with the Darwinian doctrine of adaptation. The urban dweller, already alienated from rural standards, was less attached to a theological tradition that had ceased to serve his daily needs; but the country dweller, outside the immediate range of secular influences, was the natural adversary of tendencies attacking his culture. Not only did the rural culture pattern still operate, but it was subjected to the strain of rearrangement by industrialism.

The implications of science were buttressed by the revival of Biblical criticism—the scientific study of Testament authorship and meaning—and a renewed interest in the faiths of the past, the scientific study of comparative religions. Like biological theories, they too were imported from abroad, vital links between the culture of the. Old World and the New. Each served as aides to Darwin, for the criticism of the Bible impugned its literal correctness as Darwinism impugned its philosophical approach. The study of ancient religions suggested the impropriety of monopolies in truth, while Darwinism sanctified the scientific methodology employed by both and induced a widespread skepticism of all theoretical certainties.

But the social demands of the city were infinitely more pressing and could not be postponed. The intellectual crisis presented by science, philosophy, and criticism, never quite resolved, remained to be further analyzed in the cloistered atmosphere of the seminar after the heat of the controversy had cooled. While leaving wide gaps in the chain of thought, science accepted Darwinian evolution, but failed to make all the logical adjustments to which it was committed by acceptance. Religious compromise was in no better position, and the general public, holding to vestiges of the old faith without fully perceiving the new light of science, neither appreciated the one nor understood the other. However, infidelity and nonconformity were not products of science and scholarship alone.

The failure of American Christianity to concern itself with social issues drew acrid fire from ecclesiastical critics, while the indifference of organized religion to the inequities of the industrial order alienated the common man from the church. Markedly disturbed by large-scale Catholic and Jewish immigration, American Protestantism, like all major institutions, was ill prepared to cope with the city. Since the dominant theological tradition was rural, the institutional mechanisms were keyed to the middle class, to a social situation in which inequalities were not marked. Protestantism, historically more interested in the spirit than in the flesh, was slow to learn that bodies had some claim to salvation. Jews and Catholics, on the contrary, charged with the heavy responsibility of caring for the lowly who crowded American ports of entry, established city missions and other institutions to minister to the needs of their respective flocks. Such energy was in part dedicated to help the immigrant keep the faith, but it was also dedicated to keep faith with the humanitarian principles that underlay all religions.

Protestant apathy to the social application of Christian precepts stemmed partly from a division of function. Historically, Protestantism had cast off many of the social, educational, and charitable functions of the medieval church. The office of the church was to preach spiritual truth; it was the duty of individual Christians to apply it. Yet the sins of society were so shockingly exposed in American cities that individual Protestants, whatever the attitude of the church, could no longer condone them. No social sin was more apparent than the immorality of business; none more distressing than poverty. To save the people from desperation was as pressing as the teaching of ethics. The church could not forever ignore the plight of the poor or continue hostile to labor organization while giving at the same time its blessing to those who blocked labor's aim. Were it to retain the devotion of the urban masses, it had to understand the grievances of the urban poor. If the common man could not be brought within the range of the pulpit, the pulpit would have to be brought within range of the common man. Leaders of religious opinion accordingly sought to combine realism with the humane spirit, to study industrial chaos and human suffering directly and in their entirety, and, in spite of vigorous sectarianism, to unite all Protestant effort in a crusade for justice and equality.

To this noble, albeit somewhat belated, goal, the most forward-looking and the ablest thinkers of American Protestantism gave of their strength and their minds. Washington Gladden, Congregational minister of Columbus, Ohio, was the acknowledged leader of the hundreds of progressive clergymen and laymen in this movement. With a broad experience gleaned from service in industrial centers, Gladden was well informed, astute, and courageous. Workingmen, he knew, were losing faith in the church. He knew also that while wealth was accumulating with pathological speed, "poverty, even pauperism" was "increasing still more rapidly." Gladden valiantly insisted that rugged economic individualism and humane Christian cooperation were incompatible. Christianity, he stoutly maintained, must be applied.

While Gladden firmly believed in state intervention and the socialization of certain monopolies, he tried to avoid an endorsement of socialism. Others, however, were undismayed by socialist principles, for an active and articulate group of Christian Socialists soon made their unorthodox bow. Led by the Reverends Jesse H. Jones and W. D. P. Bliss, they averred that "the teachings of Jesus Christ lead directly to some specific form or forms of Socialism."

Yet most exponents of applied Christianity were content to help where they could without regard to fundamental causes or fundamental cures. For those, the Salvation Army, imported from England in 1879, was an adequate instrument of social improvement. Originally geared to the uplift of "rumdom, slumdom, and bumdom," it broadened its field of service in 1889 by maintaining employment agencies, cheap lodging houses, and other similar forms of assistance. More significant was the institutional church, actually a Christian social settlement, equipped with recreation facilities, guidance centers, and what today would be called occupational therapy clinics. So rapidly did the movement spread that by 1894 the number of such churches was sufficient to warrant the formation of a national league.

Social Christianity helped to revitalize American Protestantism imperiled by science and the city, but its salient contribution lay in another direction. With persistent eloquence, its leaders from pulpit, seminary, and the popular rostrum called public attention to the vices of society, to poverty, injustice, and the effects of degeneration created by economic inequality. Leaders of this great movement adopted the evolutionists' belief in the kinship of all mankind and did much to infuse a needed optimism and a faith in humanism—notwithstanding the bitterness life had brought to so many toilers in the green valleys and fertile plains of the countryside and the dark, gray towns spread all over the land.

An irresistible array of facts supported the Christian protest. Earnest preachers of the social gospel like Washington Gladden aimed their arrows of criticism at the heart of economic injustice, but they shot telling barbs at every species of social sin as well. And theirs were not voices crying in a wilderness. From every segment of society—from farmers, laborers, reporters of the social scene—came a vociferous chorus of protest. They dissented politically, rebelled emotionally, and censured intellectually. For if the city was the glory of modern man, it was also the precipitator of many of the ills that harassed him.

Whatever the cause, it was the city that fostered the slum from which crime, vice, and delinquency emanated. Nor was it solely in the centers of poverty that social evils were bred. Crime flourished in high places in the well-known form of political graft and in the less well-known form of lust for profit regardless of social cost. Vice thrived in an unconscionable irresponsibility for poverty no less than in gangs of city hoodlums; delinquency flowered in individual ignorance of civic duty no less than in the petty thievery of boys bereft of homes and in the waywardness of girls deprived of adolescence. The city had a seamy side, but the slums of Prague differed from the slums of Boston only in degree; the vice of London from the vice of New York only in detail. If the glitter of the city was universal, the drabness of urban life was no less so.

URBAN COSMOPOLITANISM

Cosmopolitan as its sociology and its science, the city was an international highway of intellectual crosscurrents. Main Streets throughout the United States and the world were great because of the mute partnership of human beings from all ages and places whose creative energies glowed from numberless street lamps and took form in the iron, tin, and steel of millions of home appliances. Their spirit emerged daily in the techniques of urban organization; in the smooth roads that fanned out from city squares, village greens, and town commons and in the speeding traffic that traversed them. They lived forever in the freight yards at the city limits that linked town and country, nations, and the world;

in the food packed high in the cars; in the myriad activities of school, factory, and office. They belied every provincialism ever uttered, for the Zeniths of the world—the Berlins, the Bostons, and the Viennas—were truly great only when their differences fathered creative social change.

Peoples and ideas from everywhere commingled in the cities. If the river Shannon was left behind in old Ireland, Irishmen planted new homes where the East River flowed along the shores of Brooklyn. From the Celestial Empire, Chinese exchanged one shore of the Pacific for the other to build new lives in American communities bearing proud old Spanish names, while Jews with names of every extraction exchanged all the cities of Europe for all the cities of the United States. Nor was this all. Each wheel that revolved in the American land, in whirring machines, in farm implements, and in locomotives, omnibuses, and carriages harked back to the Egypt of the Pharaohs. Each day as men of business checked their calendars, periodically glanced at their watches, computed their profits, traded mortgages, notes, and negotiable instruments, they were beholden to long-forgotten innovators of Sumer and Akkad, the progenitors of Babylonia. Engines of transport, tools, appliances bore an invisible hallmark, the crest of mankind, for every nation contributed vitally to each major technical and speculative advance. Physical science in the speculations of a Darwin or in the applications of an Edison were prime exemplifications; the first brought the universe within range of learned men, the second lit up the world for all. The scientific investigation of Biblical origins conveyed the learning of Holland, France, and Britain to American students, who in turn fertilized the thinking of scholars in Africa's Natal and Germany's Heidelberg. Receptive minds were steeped in scientific method broadened by a knowledge of comparative religions that brought a breath of Persia, India, and China into Boston, Chicago, and other American cities.

In American universities—at Harvard, Johns Hopkins, Michigan, and Yale—graduate students fresh from German seminars spread the burning message of scholarship. Whatever revisions later scholars found it needful to make in method, emphasis, and ideology, they nevertheless communicated a zeal for learning and a faith in the capacity of man to understand. But if Simon Newcomb, an American scientist born in Nova Scotia, became one of the foremost astronomers in the world, the field of his interest was the heavens, which no more belonged to America than thermodynamics was the sole possession of Willard Gibbs, the American genius in the science of physics. And the light that Albert A. Michelson for the first time measured in 1887 redounded to the glory of man rather than to the Germany where he was born or to the United States where he worked and lived.

Universality was as characteristic of the creative arts as of creative scholarship. Henry Hobson Richardson, the most promising architect after the Civil War, imported the Romanesque of France and Spain to American cities, notably in Boston's Trinity Church and Harvard's Sever Hall. Charles Follen McKim and Stanford White, his students, later added a touch of the Renaissance to Boston in its Public Library and to New York in the buildings of Columbia University. In symphonic music as in opera, the performers and conductors were mostly European by birth and training, but the music performed in New York City in the Metropolitan Opera House, built in 1883, and by symphonic orchestras elsewhere was written in a spiritual esperanto. As in music so in the theater; foreign actors—Sarah Bernhardt, Henry Irving, Helena Modjeska, and Eleonora Duse—played the American boards, but their art was dedicated to the portrayal of roles that, whatever the local color, scenic effects, or temporal backdrops, were perennial to the life, the trials, and the conflicts of man.

Nor were the mainsprings of literary creation dissimilar. Émile Zola, Honoré de Balzac, and Leo Tolstoy provided technical models and mental modes for American writers, but William Dean Howells, Mark Twain, and Walt Whitman stimulated literary circles in Europe as Ralph Waldo Emerson, Nathaniel Hawthorne, and James Fenimore Cooper had done before. If Henry James, master of the psychological novel, and Bret Harte, prime recorder of the novel in the experience of the primitive Far West, found America too provincial and sought maturity in Europe, Walter Hines Page, later editor of the *Atlantic Monthly,* and George Washington Cable, preservator of the Louisiana Creole in literature, left the rural South for the urban North. Hamlin Garland abandoned his midwestern farm for the literary citadel of Boston, but the ideas that caused his "mental diaphragm" to expand were the pulsating ideas of the Western world, science, evolution, and the philosophy of realism that were simultaneously expanding the intellectual diaphragms of Howells, John Burroughs, and Mark Twain.

The vanishing civilizations of the Indian, the frontier West, the plantation South, and New England farming communities found their literary chroniclers. Helen Hunt Jackson recorded the Spanish phase of California in *Ramona* (1884); F. Hopkinson Smith and Thomas Nelson Page wrote of Virginian rulers in the old cotton kingdom; *In the Tennessee Mountains* (1884) Charles Craddock described those who were ruled by a system to which they had to conform but in which they had no voice. Joel Chandler Harris immortalized the Negro in his Uncle Remus series, while Sarah Orne Jewett and Rose Terry Cooke investigated the character of New England folk with insight, understanding, and

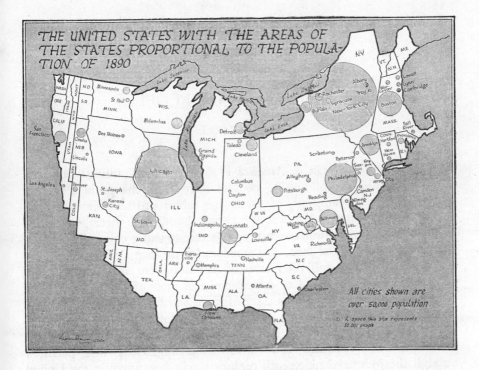

THE UNITED STATES WITH THE AREAS OF THE STATES PROPORTIONAL TO THE POPULATION OF 1890

All cities shown are over 50,000 population

A space this size represents 50,000 people

literary skill. Mark Twain wrote *Huckleberry Finn*, perhaps his greatest characterization, in 1884, employing as social background Mississippi River scenes known to an increasing number of Americans in the pages of literature alone. American writers stood on native grounds—in the geography of space and the episodes of time, in the American variants of the timeless human urge for freedom, peace, and security—but the moral problems they transferred to prose and verse transcended local geography or limited chronology. Howells delved into the basic problems of human beings in the changed environment of the machine and the city, and Garland was concerned with human frustration that was not confined to western farms. Cities, European and American, differed from each other, but their differences in 1900 were dwarfed by their community of origin, the identity of their problems, and the unity of their cultural impact.

XIX

THE MINGLING OF PEOPLES

1860–1900

The history of man in America is the history of uniting states, but it is also the history of uniting peoples. Economic change in a century of railroads and steamships, of submarine cables and telephones, shrank the world physically, but it was the people huddled in steerage quarters and crammed into railway coaches who tied it together culturally. Ambitious men, discontented men, and freedom-loving men again were on the march. On a global scale the masses of mankind were moving to Canada, to Brazil, to Australia, and to Argentina. But most of all they moved to the United States. For economic transformations fostered social mobility, and the new opportunities and the new unrest of the world's industrial age uprooted millions from their fathers' homes and sent them abroad in search of betterment. The world-wide migrations that persisted through the industrial nineteenth century reached a climax in the United States between 1860 and 1900. In 1880 the foreign born in an American population of 50,000,000 were nearing a total of 7,000,000. By 1900 some 8,000,000 more newcomers had mingled among the varied 76,000,000 who peopled the United States at the end of the century. As the twentieth century opened, children whose parents came from China, from the Ukraine, from the Black Sea, and from the Mediterranean sat in the schoolroom beside the children of earlier American families. Human invention contracted the world physically during those years; the dispersion of mankind brought an end to cultural isolation.

The movement of peoples united the American states into the American republic. The agricultural frontier, following the rays of the setting sun, added acres, crops, and states in their appropriate columns, but "waves of settlement" were people, people from Europe, Asia, and the older sections of the United States. As eastern men moved westward to the farm and western men moved eastward to the factory, northern men moved southward to take part in the economic revolutions of the cotton lands. Southern men, black and white, moved northward to industry, labor, and agriculture, for the road to reunion between North and South merged into the highroad of freight traffic and interlocking business. Europeans from all nations and Americans from all sections supplied the man power and the brain power that turned the natural products of field, forest, and stream into the products of life. They conquered primitive America. At the same time others planned and manned the machines in urban factories that in turn conquered rural America. It was this many-sided movement, propelled by the engines of transport and communication, that brought forth a new nation. As economic unity and interdependence produced national problems, the political importance of economic sections declined. If newer sections in the American nation or elsewhere took shape, they defied the facts of cultural diffusion and the shrinking world, and were fathered by men who directed the machines rather than by the machines that gave new power to men.

Immigration, therefore, was one of the dominant themes of American history, but it was likewise a dominant theme of the history of the world. Small viking ships with prows pointing bravely westward crossed the perilous Atlantic and their crews, mingling briefly with the native "Skraellings," were the first Europeans to see the sun shining through northern mists. The hardy Scandinavians of the tenth century were a part of the same movement that had earlier pushed the lusty tribesmen of the Danubian valleys across the northern frontiers of Roman Italy and later sent adventurous mariners from Genoa, Cadiz, Lisbon, and Bristol to American shores. "Earth hunger," as William Graham Sumner called it, drove the Mongolians over the Russian steppes and the Teutons into the lush fields of imperial Gaul as it later drove Spaniards, Frenchmen, Englishmen, and Germans to seek fame and fortune in the fabulous lands of the West. And the Russians, Poles, Austrians, and Italians who came later were likewise inspired by a longing for peace and security that are the perennial goals of man.

GLOBAL MIGRATION

Culturally the New World was the Old World writ large. If Western civilization was the heritage of the ancient Near East, as diffused through Greece and Rome, American civilization was the heritage of Europe. The United States was the cultural consequence of the impact of European civilization at different stages of American growth just as the developing culture of Europe reflected the continuing influence of American experience. America and Europe were interactive parts of a larger whole. They were bound together by the exchange of goods and a mutual interdependence in terms of markets and raw materials. They were united not only by the golden threads of commerce, the throbbing engines of transport, and the invisible bonds of communication, but by the subtle interchange of ideas. They were also tied together by human links forged by millions of men and women who stemmed from every corner of the world. Immigrants created American culture by contributing their own—their aspirations, their ideals, and their everlasting belief in the symbol that America became.

Time and sentiment alone distinguished the seventeenth-century colonist from the nineteenth-century immigrant. The Cohens were colonists and the Endicotts were immigrants, for all Americans are of foreign descent. The settlement of the United States was the result of a world movement of peoples; the making of America, the result of the fusion of the people of the world. "These States," sang Walt Whitman, who was the great poet of democracy because he was the great poet of humanity, "are the amplest poem. Here is not merely a nation, but a teeming nation of nations." Whether the immigrants put out from England's Plymouth in the days of the Stuart kings or whether they started from a sleepy village in the realms of the Romanoff czars, they acted in response to similar urges and were confronted with problems that were much the same. The Bradfords and the Winthrops, the Roosevelts and the Schuylers, the Zengers and the Schurzes, as the Kelleys and the Levines who followed them, were alike uprooted from the old familiar soil of the homeland and thrust into a strange new world. If the earlier arrivals had first to subdue the physical environment, the later arrivals had first to subdue the social environment. Which exacted the higher toll as the price of survival posed a neat question that no one has yet answered.

The history of immigration cannot be evaluated in simple national terms. There was a European as well as an American phase in the mingling of peoples, for immigration to America recorded Europe's reaction to the changing social and economic order as it reflected the changing social and economic order in the United States. Each stream of immigration had its source in different levels of European change, and each stream flowed into America at different levels of American development. The movement of peoples in the United States during the latter half of the nineteenth century was a triple one. The settlement of the American West, the rise of the American city, and the colonization of America by foreigners were all aspects of one mighty process.

But the settling of unexploited agricultural regions and the building of cities were no more confined to the United States than were migrations from one country to another. Shifts in population encompassed the world. Englishmen, dissatisfied with conditions in the homeland, resolved to try again in America, but others, no less dissatisfied, chose the British dominions beyond the seas. While southern Italians, adversely affected by the industrialization of northern Italy, hitched their hopes to the rising American star, other Italians saw brighter stars twinkling in the Latin-American firmament. Polish peasants staked out new claims to life in American cities, but other Poles dreamed out their dreams in Argentina. Migration brought strangers to the open portals of America as well as to Canada, New Zealand, Australia, and the South American republics whose gates were also ajar. What was true of migration in general and of agricultural migration in particular was no less true of the urban trend. The lure of the city worked its charm on Europeans and Americans alike. Germans who forsook Rhineland villages for Milwaukee were followed by others who went to Cologne. Englishmen who set out for Melbourne were matched by Englishmen who went to Leeds, and many a brother, cousin, or friend of eastern Europeans who came to the Pennsylvania mines migrated to Budapest, Warsaw, or Prague.

The figures of immigration can be stated briefly. In the forty years between 1860 and 1900 nearly fourteen million foreigners came to the United States. When compared with the estimated quarter of a million who sought to realize their goals in America between 1776 and 1820, the extent of the later immigration takes on added significance, but no array of numbers in the tranquillity of print can ever adequately translate the human meaning of one of the greatest wanderings of peoples in history. Something of its scope may be glimpsed from the fact that enough aliens arrived in every decade following the election of Abraham Lincoln to replace completely the total population—some two million persons in the thirteen colonies on the eve of the Revolution. More important than numbers was the ethnic composition of the new American population and their geographic and occupational distribution, for within these quiet columns of figures lies a living part of the social and intellectual history of modern America.

The stupendous volume of the immigrant invasion does not by itself reveal its significance. Immigration to America represents a blending of cultures that gives American civilization its cosmopolitan quality, but it also reflects broad epochal changes in the parallel evolution of great culture areas. The vikings, heralds of the commercial revolution that transformed the Middle Ages, mark the beginnings of North American settlement; the later vikings, offspring of the economic revolutions that transformed the modern age, mark the completion of the North American settlement. Although begun before colonial days and completed in the era of the recent past, both were stages in a larger evolution that reached tidal proportions after the Civil War. Particular and memorable events have obscured the relation of these population shifts, which were parts

IMMIGRATION TO THE U.S.

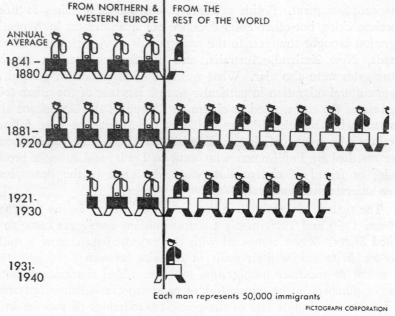

Each man represents 50,000 immigrants

PICTOGRAPH CORPORATION

PICTOGRAPH CORP. for *Story of America*, copyrighted 1937
by Henry Holt and Company.

of a unitary development. In the largest sense, they reflect the changing character of the world from a feudal, pastoral, static civilization to an urban, industrial, dynamic one. The viking ships with sails spread to the Atlantic wind are symbols of man's never-ending adventure on the uncharted seas of tempestuous change. Beginning what others were destined to finish, they touched the coast of the New World. Other ships, following the horizon of the western sea, shattered the isolation of Europe, bringing forth a new Europe as well as a new world from which America grew. The history of the United States is thus the history of the Western world in transition, for the development of America is bounded by the commercial revolution of the age of Columbus on the one hand and by the economic revolutions of the modern era on the other. The United States is the history of the world in miniature in another and even deeper sense. Immigration brought the world to America. From the landing of the Pilgrims in Provincetown Harbor to the landing of the Slovaks in the harbor of New York, a steady flow of Europeans created a civilization, while their minds and hearts created the American spirit and fashioned the American dream.

Immigration after the Civil War differs from the earlier movement of peoples in several respects. Like the earlier rush of Europeans to the North American continent, it was primarily a movement of agricultural folk, but unlike those who preceded them, these immigrants did not migrate to an agricultural environment. Instead, they found themselves in a strange society as well as in a strange home. Millions of Europeans, accustomed to the rhythm of rural life and conditioned by ancient rural standards, were thrust into the turbulent vortex of expanding American industrialism. Others, continuing their stormy Atlantic passage in jolting emigrant cars of enterprising railroads, set out for the farmlands and prairies, only to find that they, too, had new techniques to learn. Strange though the America of an earlier age must have been, it was never as bewildering as it appeared to the anxious hearts of Europeans in the years following the sixties. The first immigrants, it is true, had to cope with a wild and untamed world, but it was literally an open country upon which in part they could exert the force of their wills. Their followers of the later eighteenth and early nineteenth centuries had a difficult adjustment to make, yet it was a world with which they had some acquaintance. But the colonists of industrial America had to make peace with a world that was almost as novel to them as the world of Massasoit was to William Bradford.

PERSPECTIVES: EUROPEAN AND AMERICAN

If the seventeenth-century pioneers had first to wrest control from the forces of nature, the eighteenth- and nineteenth-century pioneers did likewise. The task of the Bradfords in Plymouth was not essentially different from the tasks of thousands of unknown Olsens who sweated under a broiling Dakota sun more than two hundred and fifty years later. Nor was the burden of Slavs, Magyars, and Jews appreciably lighter because they had to adjust themselves to tenements instead of log cabins or sod houses, and were forced to learn to live with savage prejudice instead of savage beasts. Nor was it any simpler for English farmers and shopkeepers to find a spiritual home in the naked forest than it was for German, Polish, and Hungarian farmers to find emotional tranquillity in the midst of looms, pistons, and forges to which they were equally unaccustomed. Not only were they confronted with the need for psychological adjustment, but they came at precisely the time when the nation was passing through the most rapid change in its history. While America was faced with the mammoth issues of internal rearrangements, immigration reached its highest peak. The insistent demands of the new civilization of cities and machines were thereby intensified, and the plight of the foreign groups was in no way eased.

Western and northern Europe continued to be the prime source of emigration in the decade after the Civil War, but in the eighties a change in the points of origin was already noticeable. Before 1860 subjects of the British crown had supplied the greatest number of Americans, but of this group a heavy proportion looked to Dublin rather than to London as their spiritual home. Next to the English and the Irish in numerical strength were the Germans and their kinsmen from the Scandinavian north.

Although Danes, Norwegians, and Swedes continued to pour into the country until the end of the century and British and German migration began to falter markedly only ten years earlier, there was a steady increase in the volume of immigration from southern and eastern Europe. So swift was the current of the new tide that by the 1890's New York City had become the ethnic hub of the universe. The island of Manhattan became a new Emerald Isle, for there were more sons of Erin in New York than in Dublin. On the banks of the East River colonies of Jews, more numerous than the colonies that had once settled on the banks of the Jordan, began to worry the scions of modern Canaan, for there were twice as many Jews in Gotham as in Warsaw. Half as many Italians as lived in Naples and almost as many Germans as in Hamburg had already found work, and homes, and life in America's greatest city.

From Austria-Hungary, land of the proud Hapsburgs, came a conglomerate variety of peoples of whom the great majority of Americans had seldom heard. Hungarian peasants from the Transylvanian plains, Austrians from the hinterland of Vienna, Bohemians from the banks of the Moldau, and Jews from Galicia as well as from other provinces of the Hapsburg monarchy became items in the ledger books of competing navigation lines. The vaster lands of the Romanoffs were no less generous in providing America with scores of citizens. At European ports of embarkation, Ukrainians, Poles, and Russians joined with Austrian Serbs who hated the imperial Hapsburgs and with Russian Jews who hated the imperial Romanoffs. Italian mingled with Magyar and Slav. Eager Sicilians from the Mediterranean shores and former inhabitants of historic Campania willingly abandoned the hearths of their forefathers in exchange for the promise of American life.

It is easy to imagine the mingling of these people as they assembled on the dock of some European port. Far from their homes, separated from their families, depressed by a longing they tried not to show, apprehensive yet confident, stricken by an undefinable terror and striving to be brave, they could sense little in common with the loud-speaking, wildly gesticulating groups who stood outside their own inner circle. They were divided by a thousand hates. Austrians were suspicious of Russians, and Italians had scant cause to trust the Austrians. Greater than the misunderstandings between nationals of different countries were older animosities between national minorities and their conquerors. Poles seldom forgot the cooperation of Austrians and Russians in the partitions of their beloved nation, and prideful Hungarians despised the arrogant Austro-Germans who had formed the ruling class in the homeland they had left. Bohemians vainly remembered that there were sovereigns in Prague when the first Hapsburgs were petty nobles in a remote Swiss canton, while Serbs and Slovenes from Austria's restless southeastern domains were never certain whether St. Petersburg, Vienna, or Rome offered the greatest threat to their safety. And the Jews, who had been everywhere, could not erase from their hearts the horrors of persecution, ever the same in any place and in any language.

In the steerage during passage, and ashore as they were disgorged from Castle Garden, immigrants could exchange their vague fears only with their compatriots, for most of them spoke dialects rather than the formal tongues of their native countries. Jews from Russia built a bridge of words between themselves and Polish Jews, but German-speaking Austrians could not converse with Hungarians, Serbs, or Bohemian Czechs unless they had somehow been able to obey their former monarch's edict making German the official language of the realm. But if there were no linguistic bonds to unite them, there were others. Poverty, visible in the shabbiness of their dress and the extent of their worldly possessions, was no less apparent than the despair of loneliness that a desperate fraternity with their fellows only served to expose. Yet they were partners in a joint venture that, however little they may have realized it then or thereafter, was to bind them forever together.

Reasons for the shift in the areas of emigration are to be found both in Europe and in America. Particular factors that had stimulated the exodus from northern and western Europe were no longer operative. In Germany, for example, political and religious intolerance were less potent than before the advent of Bismarck and the unification of the empire, and the conditions following the Irish famine of 1845 never precisely recurred. But Bismarck's system of compulsory military service, copied all over Europe, made the nonmilitarism of the United States attractive. A new set of specific causes motivated the inhabitants of the southern and eastern sections of the European continent. The Russian persecutions of 1881 to 1883, to cite but a single instance, made life so hazardous for the Jews that they were willing to attempt anything that

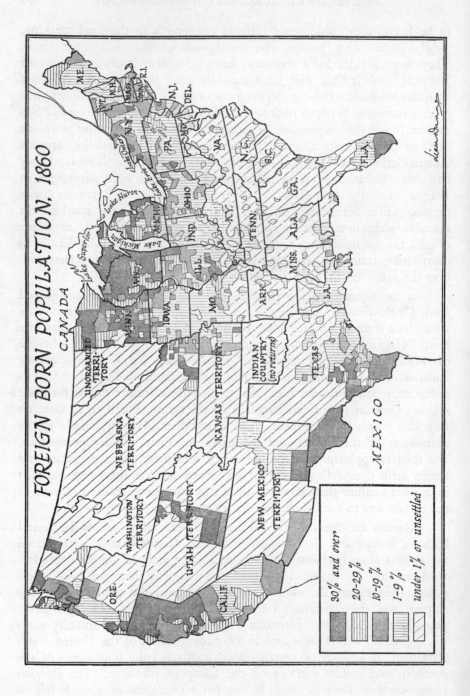

FOREIGN BORN POPULATION, 1860

30% and over
20–29%
10–19%
1–9%
under 1% or unsettled

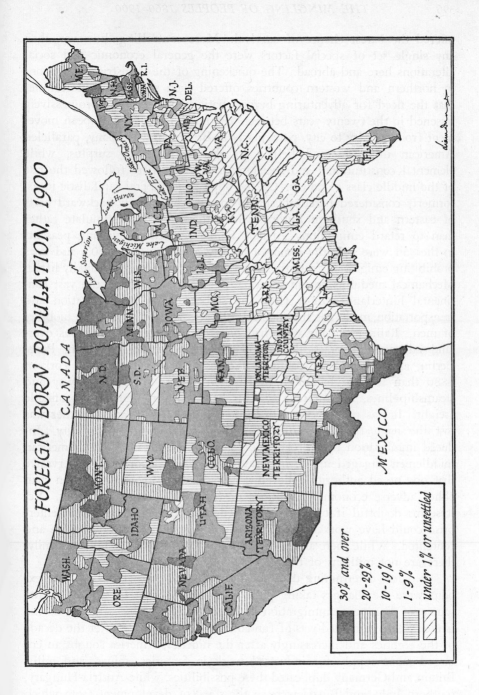

FOREIGN BORN POPULATION, 1900

Legend:
- 30% and over
- 20-29%
- 10-19%
- 1-9%
- under 1% or unsettled

offered the barest chance of survival. More controlling, however, than any single set of special factors were the general economic and social alterations here and abroad. The quickening of the industrial revolutions in northern and western countries offered such seductive opportunities that the need for adventuring beyond national borders was progressively lessened in the twenty years between 1880 and 1900. A European movement from country to city, particularly in Britain and Germany, paralleled American urbanism and helped to absorb the labor surplus, while elemental constitutional and social reforms everywhere followed the rise of the middle class to power. On the other hand, liberal capitalistic ideas, formerly considered heretical, spread to the economically backward parts of eastern and southern Europe, where they served to stimulate rather than to retard emigration. Archaic feudal restrictions binding peasants to the soil were partially removed in Russia during the 1860's and laws prohibiting emigration from the Hapsburg territories were gradually lifted. Mechanical mediums spread information about America in the vast continental hinterland remote from the seaboard, for communication and transportation made for the mobility of ideas as well as for the mobility of men. Railroads made what had once been a long and perilous overland adventure a practical and relatively easy matter. London, Paris, Berlin, and other major continental cities were closer to New York in 1880 than London had been to Paris in 1800. For both railway and steamship lines, the migrant and his baggage were the most profitable freight. It was not necessary to load or unload them, and if either was lost the navigation companies bore only a dubious responsibility. Induced immigration by railroad lines, steamship companies, and American middlemen engaged in the importation of cheap labor was so pervasive that one noted authority believed it accounted for more emigration than either adverse economic conditions or restricted social possibilities. Yet it seems doubtful if even the most seductive agents of American enterprise could have worked their charm upon people who were secure and contented. While there are many daring adventurers in the human family, there are not millions of them.

No less determining than the European forces that directed the exodus were the changes taking place in America. That the change in the source of European immigration and the change in the structure of the United States coincided was of fundamental significance. After the decade of the eighties and increasingly after the nineties, America sought an enlarged labor supply for industrial work in factories, mines, and mills. Britain and Germany duplicated these possibilities, while Austria-Hungary, southern Italy, and Russia were in the stage of development from which Britain and Germany had already emerged. It was the city and the factory rather than the farm and the country which now enticed Europeans to America. Russian peasants, for example, not members of persecuted or suppressed minorities, pioneered on their own eastern frontiers toward Siberia rather than on the western frontier of the United States.

As earlier, migratory peoples continued to be recruited from agricultural communities, but while the agricultural folk of the first period reverted to the soil, the ruralists of the second period remained in the cities. Of the three largest non-English stocks before the Civil War—the Scandinavian, the Irish, and the Germans—only the. Irish congregated in the large urban centers. Despite their rural origin, they were schooled in a special kind of agricultural technique, the breeding of cattle and the culture of the exotic potato, which proved far less attractive to them than the demand for their labor in the towns. Since the Catholic Church was opposed to wide dispersion of the immigrant flock, economic desire and religious influence combined to make the Irish the first important ethnic group in American political and social life. The Scandinavians, on the contrary, left the Atlantic coastal cities as the population of Wisconsin, Minnesota, and the Dakotas abundantly reveals, while the Germans, notwithstanding the once famous German-American centers, Milwaukee, Cincinnati, and St. Louis, elected to continue the age-old battle against the giants of the earth.

Exactly the opposite was true of the more recent arrivals from the south and the southeast of Europe. For them the purchase price of farms and machinery was too great and the need of immediate employment too insistent. The social situation, moreover, was not only different from what it had been for their Scandinavian and German precursors but more difficult. Poverty, social ostracism, and loneliness propelled them in the direction of their kinsmen or "landfolk" from whom they sought aid, comfort, and encouragement. In obedience to another urge equally deep, they avoided the isolation of rural life, for they were attracted to the city for the same reasons that Americans left the farms. In a very real sense, the invasion of American cities by Hungarians, Austrians, and Italians was a response to the same drives that sent other Italians, Hungarians, and Austrians to Milan, Budapest, and Vienna.

THE IMMIGRANT AND AMERICAN LIFE

The occupational distribution of the recent migrants was as conclusive as their geographical distribution, and faithfully mirrored the changing American scene. Classic is the example of the New England cotton mills. When about 1830 the spindles in cities like Lowell began to whirl faster, the prim daughters of New England farmers were glad to exchange

the monotony of pastoral life for the excitement of a novel experience—
not without a Yankee eye to cash, with which good farm girls had only
a limited acquaintance. Scarcely ten years later many of the native workers, both male and female, were supplanted by the Irish, then on top of
the immigrant heap. But the sway of the Irish over spindle and loom
was challenged in a scant decade and a half by the infiltration of the
provident French-Canadians, who seemed firmly in possession between
1865 and 1875. Yet from that time onward until 1900 they, too, were
dislodged by hordes of Greeks, Poles, Russians, and Italians, who were
forced to take jobs at poverty wages. Shortly after the end of the century the ethnic composition of New England mill operatives, once almost
exclusively "native American," was 70 per cent foreign born and 20 per
cent native born of alien parentage. The remainder, an illuminating figure in American social history, a mere 10 per cent, was of native
parentage.

In the Pennsylvania coal fields the same transformation was repeated,
save that the ethnic groups were different. Ninety-three per cent of all
the miners were English-speaking in 1880, but by 1900 the percentage
had dropped to 44. Leading the army of the unskilled laborers were the
Slovaks, who came in the eighties followed by heavy re-enforcements of
Poles, Italians, Croatians, and Russians. Hard as it seems now to believe,
the needle and tailoring trades were monopolized by Americans, Scots-
men, and Englishmen, until Jews and Italians, or others from southern
Europe, took over these occupations. Occupational mobility still con-
tinues, for the garment industry, long supposed a bailiwick of Jewish
labor, eventually acquired its heavy non-Jewish, southern European complexion. Similarly, the Irishman was lord of the construction gang until
the Italian took his place. Lads from Killarney and County Cork likewise made most of the rope manufactured in the United States, until
other brawny lads who spoke Swedish better than English began to pre-
dominate, but here, too, the hard-working sons of Italy came finally to
reign.

Hardly a sector of American life remained isolated from the surging
immigrant tide. Rural placidity was often rudely shocked, as earlier, by
the introduction of a different code of morals, secular and religious.
German clubs, beer gardens, and Sabbath hilarity seemed just as odd to
the sons of New Englanders transplanted in the West as they had seemed
to their fathers. Lutheran churches with sermon and ritual in Scandinavian tongues were no less strange to American Protestants than the
theological folkways of Bohemians in Nebraska or Hollanders in Michigan. But if the national fate of agriculture hinged finally upon mounting

"Bubble blowing" was a fashionable parlor game, but an increasing number of "serious females" sought careers.

Below—The science laboratory at M.I.T.

(Bettmann Archive)

The "shotgun wedding" was a behavior pattern associated with rural life.

"Demon Rum" was an index of urban maladjustment.

(Courtesy Collection of Regional History, Cornell University)

Changing folkways. Guardians of individual and social virtue were only slightly more alarmed by urban distractions that competed with the Church than by new modes of behavior associated with what was called "sand spooning." *(Courtesy Collection of Regional History, Cornell University)*

To the harassed male of the old school, woman's proficiency in the housewifely arts, as exemplified in the cooking class above *(Bettmann Archive),* was more important than her emancipation, caricatured in "The Age of Brass" below *(courtesy Library of Congress).*

THE AGE OF BRASS.

production, it was alien as well as native sweat that brought abundance out of the plains.

Urban social tensions far outweighed rural ones. If the cities were smirched with the oil of political machines, immigrant cogs helped to assure their smooth operation. If urban communities were branded with the scarlet letters of slum, vice, and delinquency, tottering rows of tenements, packed with immigrants, in all the metropolitan areas and in countless shantytowns fringing factory and mill, were well-known entries in the ledgers of shame. If the power of wealth was truly pitted against the ideals of commonwealth, the immigrants played living parts in the struggle. The fact that immigration solved the problem of the labor supply both quantitatively and qualitatively eased the path to wealth, but immigration complicated the social problems blocking the path to commonwealth. Crusaders for public health were all but worsted in the battle of the slum, for wretched housing was not their only enemy. The crime, corruption, and vice lurking in tenement alleys could be alleviated but not cured by the playground and the settlement house. The sin of society was poverty, and the city exposed it most glaringly. And it was poverty that was most intimately related to housing, disease, and social frustration.

The story of immigration has too often been told in purely American terms. Accent has been on the United States rather than upon the areas of dispersion, and what was once called Americanization has almost completely dwarfed the interactive function of Europeanization. American critics have laid angry stress upon the need for unity in realms of action, economic, political, and social; they have ignored the need for diversity in realms of thought and feeling, in attitudes, aspirations, and ideas. The rapid social effects of the injection of alien masses into the current of American society have received swift and often bitter analysis, but the slower merging of cultural patterns has rarely been understandingly appraised. Accordingly, attention has been focused upon the American problems created by the immigrant instead of upon the problems created for the immigrant by America. Zeal for assimilation has been so steadfast that consideration for cultural adjustment has sometimes been wholly verbal. Foreign enclaves in great American cities have been celebrated for their charm and color, the piquancy of their folkways, and the excellence of their cuisine. They have just as frequently been savagely ridiculed as barbarian, or heedlessly condemned as the breeding grounds for the most shocking social evils, but little has been said of urban ghettos and little Italies as havens of refuge in the hurricane of a bewildering world. Heroes of immigrant sagas have been the exceptions—the inventor, the scholar, the artist, the entrepreneur—not the thousands of unsung Polish peasants in the maze of Chicago or the thousands of singing Italians on the sidewalks of New York. The immigrant depression of the wage standard, the alien pollution of native stocks, the foreign threat to democratic institutions, and the danger of divided national loyalties have been closely examined, but the psychology of despair, the psychiatry of loneliness, and the sociology of cultural disintegration are factors that need to be balanced with them if the social equation of immigration is to be redressed.

Peasants and farm laborers, ignorant of the mechanical arts, swarmed into the mining, manufacturing, and industrial trades. Jobs there were aplenty, but unskilled workers without knowledge of the language and the ways of the New World commanded the lowest wage. Generations of submarginal living had inured them to penury, but poverty restricted their opportunities just as the frugality it demanded hardly endeared them to their fellow workers whom they so often displaced. The immigrant was the inhabitant of tenements, but it was not because he preferred squalor; it was because he was poor. He was not necessarily clannish although he loved his kinsfolk, but his search for status and security led him to the foreign sections where he could, perhaps, repair the shattered temple of his spirit. He depressed wages, but not because he chose to work for little or even because he was not accustomed to much, but because he could normally find work only where conditions were worst, where the pay was lowest, and where the hours were longest. Inhibited by language and pressed by the urgency of need, he became the easy victim of unscrupulous employers, or their agents, who underpaid and overworked him. If he accepted these conditions stoically it was because long, hard, back-breaking hours in a Pennsylvania coal mine were as heaven compared to life in a regiment of the imperial Russian army. If work in a New York sweatshop brought headaches from eye strain and heartaches from purse strain, the pain was as nothing compared to the sting of a brutal Cossack's whip in a squalid Ukrainian town. Man has learned to bear the cross of labor; it is the crucifixion of life against which he rebels.

Often immigrant children, driven to work in their teens to add their pitiful pay to the meager earnings of the breadwinner, sought release from emotional bondage in saloons, dance halls, and gangs. It was not because they were congenitally vicious that they succumbed to crime, but because they were tired, discouraged, and poor. Polish, Lithuanian, and Slovakian girls, huddled in shabby rooming houses, who became mothers before their time, were not natively immoral, but were full of the weariness of solitude and oppressed by the fright of despair. If father and son both admired the genial henchmen of the great ward boss and loyally voted the "straight ticket," it was not simply because of election foodbaskets, but because the political machines were made up of human beings who were warm and friendly. From the cool heights of criticism political rings could be labeled machines, but in the seething valleys of the slum, they seemed for all the world to be made up of men. The immigrant no more stopped to ask who made the slum than he queried the machine; for him it was enough that a warm hand grasped his own and that a native voice called him friend. The furious critic, liberal or reactionary, might well have sought the connection between economic and spiritual poverty. The immigrant in this respect, however, learned more quickly than the native. As one of them quaintly remarked, the servant of the machine appeared as a prince until he was recognized as a politician, for the machine was but a pale shadow of the full-bodied challenge to democracy.

PRIDE AND PREJUDICE

So enormous an increase in immigration coupled with so radical a change in its character could not fail to accentuate the trials of a society striking out on a new and uncharted course. But the trials were not created by the foreign invasion, however much it may have aggravated them. Fears inspired by what was called the alien threat were real enough at the time, but the bill of indictment with which the immigrant was charged was largely without valid foundation. Even those strictures which seemed contemporaneously to possess the substance of reason have since been dissipated by the material of fact. When the final balance is cast up, the United States appears as the debtor of the immigrant and the immigrant as the debtor of America. Yet the arithmetic is not quite so simple, for the American price paid for the immigrant contribution, even after deductions are made for the fears that time dispelled, was cheap indeed when compared with the toll exacted of the immigrant.

High on the list of alien crimes was the allegation that immigrants lowered the American standard of living. Cheap, unskilled masses of European workers not merely depressed the wage scale, but seriously complicated the organization of labor. It would be idle to deny either charge, but that the general standard of living, despite the abject poverty of America's immigrants, kept well to the fore of Europe's is a significant comparative item. But differences in living standards, however vital, are not exactly correlated with ethnic differences. Today Slavic industrial workers in Detroit light their flats with electricity, drive their own cars down Woodward Avenue, and possess radios that bring the world into their homes, while native workers on southern farms cannot afford any of these onetime luxuries. The Polish truck farmers in the Connecticut Valley are financially better off than the southern mill hands of indubitably native origin. Moreover, the arrival of hordes of ready labor, willing to work for little, sometimes bettered the economic position of workers already here who, even if at first displaced, later rose in the wage scale. Lack of training has not been the primary factor. Increase in technological innovation, though doubtless inhibited by the abundance of labor, generally followed the increase in the immigration of the unskilled. It was the unfamiliarity with language and custom added to need that forced the newcomer into the lowest ranks of labor, from which his offspring sometimes graduated as long as a freshman class of immigrants remained to do the hardest and dirtiest work.

Union organization was unquestionably handicapped by the immigrant. American business was enthusiastic about foreigners for labor power and purchasing power, and actively cooperated with transportation companies in seducing them from their native lands. While immigrants were good for work, they were also good as a means of controlling unions. As long as there were large blocs of unorganized workers, effective collective bargaining except in restricted trades was difficult and the closed shop almost impossible. Long hours and low wages were not unusual, but immigrants were forced to pay the price of ignorance and want by exposure to conditions that the native worker would not tolerate. Not infrequently employers lighted the fires of animosity that smoldered beneath ancient grudges, thus pitting one ethnic group against another and preventing union in a common cause. Organized labor itself was placed in a most embarrassing position. Even when labor was organized on an industrial rather than a craft basis, union leadership found itself in opposition to immigration on grounds of self-preservation. Those who endorsed the principle of a united labor front were in the anomalous position of themselves discriminating against other workers on class and national lines. During this period, however, labor was in a transitional stage, and the unions finally learned, belatedly to be sure, that the way to cope with immigration was to organize the immigrants.

The impulse to preserve cultural purity from the threat of alien contamination is as ancient as the mingling of peoples. Even in the old colony days there was grave alarm. The dominance of English Protestant culture was supposedly imperiled by French Catholicism after the peace of 1763. Nor had certain colonial patriarchs been less worried about Judaic influence from Spain, Portugal, and Holland, or the suspect Protestant varieties that stemmed from the Delaware Swedes and the New Amsterdam Dutch. Later Celtic inroads into the heart of New England and the Germanic invasion of the West in the 1840's inspired a Protestant crusade designed to dam the flood of Catholic immigration. Nativism has consistently recurred in America partly because immigration has been a constant factor in American social life. Belief in cultural superiority is a universal trait of mankind.

The "new" immigration of the latter nineteenth century was likewise viewed with dark foreboding. Those who envisaged a barbarian invasion on the traditional imperial model forgot that the barbarian invasions of Rome were neither barbarian nor invasions and that the very culture they so ardently wished to preserve was itself a composite in which among many others the Roman and Teuton merged. Theories of "racial" superiority are entirely without scientific foundation. The "Aryan myth" is only a recent expression of the cultural arrogance that all groups share, for history testifies that only the advocates of "racial" superiority vary. To equate American culture with specific temporal stages of its development is to defy the hypotheses of science. Cultural traits are as subject to change as the composition of ethnic groups. The original inhabitants of the American continent were Indians. The primitive culture of America represented a mixture of differing Indian cultures; the culture of the United States represents a mixture of differing European cultures. While the so-called Anglo-Saxons sank their roots deep in the soil of what was to become America, they were even then in close partnership with so-called Latins from the Spanish borderlands and the French-Canadian frontier. Nor were these Spaniards, Frenchmen, and Englishmen any purer racially than their remote forebears. The process of racial admixture began long before Celts and Danes, Jutes and Angles, Normans and Teutons became Englishmen, and before Gauls, Romans, and Germans became Frenchmen. Merrie England and beautiful France were the melting pots of nations centuries before a sensitive Englishman of Jewish lineage applied that misused term to America.

Older Americans have always regarded newer Americans with suspicion. As early as 1755 the colonial assembly of Pennsylvania complained to its governor that the "importations of Germans have been composed of a great Mixture of the Refuse of their People, and that their very Jails have contributed. . . ." The American Protective Association, popularly known as the A.P.A., appeared in the final decades of the nineteenth century to warn Americans of the Catholic menace from southern and eastern Europe. Kin to the revived Ku Klux Klan, which later added Negroes and Jews to the lists of the proscribed, it incited the same antipathies that earlier nativism had stirred against the Catholic Irish and Germans. And the unknown Irishman who, after Poles, Slovaks, and Italians began to march down the gangplanks, allegedly insisted that something be done about "these foreigners," expressed a social attitude substantially the same. "America for the Americans!" was the cry of superpatriots who lived in a shrinking world but did not comprehend it. While they were never certain of what constituted an American, they were certain of what an American was not. They saw the frontiers of sections crumble under the impact of the railroad, and the boundaries of nations contract under the impact of steam and electricity, but they drew new boundaries of the mind to divide men. Social causes made for opposition to immigration, but economic causes were more fundamental. Labor and industry joined to curtail immigration and together with superpatriots created a public attitude favorable to restriction.

In the view of the managers of business, there was a palpable connection between immigration and radicalism. Propagandists of big business extolled the American industrial way, but they were not blind to the fact that the lot of labor was hard. Otherwise they would have been less worried about radical European ex-patriots who, expelled from the Continent by German chancellor, Russian czar, and French emperor, sought justice, equality, and happiness in the land of the free. Business executives, moreover, well knew that desperate social solutions could be sold only to desperate men, that the urge for radical social change does not stem from contentment. Yet it was indisputable that German emigrées first preached socialism in America, that anarchism came over in the steerage to bolster a native American strain, and that labor unrest in Pittsburgh, Homestead, and Haymarket had its radical participants. Willing to import contract labor and to employ aliens as strikebreakers, businessmen wished to restrict the influx of foreigners with radical ideas. The Immigration Restriction League, founded in Boston in 1894, hoped to convince the government that legislation was needful because radical ideologies were responsible for labor strife, because immigrants lowered the wage scale, became public charges, and increased American poverty, and because they came not to adopt American institutions but to change them.

Organized workers were not unmoved by such argumentation. Unrestricted immigration prejudiced immediate job security and long-term labor progress. Foreigners crowded the labor markets with cheap and willing hands. They were difficult to organize, for their unfamiliarity with language and custom made them resistant to union techniques, while their need made them accept almost any conditions at almost any price. American workers met the problem when they first came into competition with the "heathen" Chinese of California. Not an important minority until after 1849, the Chinese continued thereafter to migrate in ever larger numbers until they composed 9 per cent of the California population. Attracted like the southern Europeans by larger economic opportunities, they were also forced into the lowest wage brackets. Violence was the answer to the flooded labor market in San Francisco. Led by Dennis Kearney, whose name in this case reveals his lineage, gangs of irate workers in 1877 fell upon the Chinese, drove them from their humble laundries, snipped off their precious pigtails, and murdered some of them. The Irish followers of Kearney, who are said to have chorused "Immeriky for the Immerikans, bejabbers" as they rushed into the fray, have been suggestively characterized by Bret Harte as "a mob of half grown boys and Christian school children." Some insight into the basic motivation of the opposition to the Chinese may be gleaned from the following interchange between a French visitor and a Californian of that period.

> "The Chinese are unproductive."
> "Why?"
> "They make a lot of money and take it back to China."
> "What else is the matter with them?"
> "They won't become citizens."
> "Why?"
> "Because we won't let them."
> "What else?"
> "They are corrupt."
> "How so?"
> "They tried to influence the state legislature not to pass the exclusion bill."

Economic causation is something less than half the answer; but there is some foundation to the story of the Chinese who, after enactment of both state and federal exclusion bills, asked an American missionary in China why, if he could go to the same heaven as Americans, he could not go to America. The missionary is said to have replied, "There's no labor vote in heaven." Pressure of the labor vote and organized political exploitation of the "race" issue brought about the restriction and ultimately the exclusion of Chinese immigration. Under the provisions of the Burlingame Treaty, signed by the United States and China in 1868, the Chinese were accorded the same privileges as others and permitted to come and go as they chose. A subsequent treaty of 1880 gave the United States the right "to regulate, limit, or suspend" immigration, and two years later Congress suspended Chinese immigration for ten years. A decade later this act was extended for an additional ten years.

Restrictive legislation, however, was by no means confined to the Chinese. As a result of the effective insistence of the Knights of Labor, the contract labor law was repealed in 1885. Three years earlier, the "undesirables"—paupers, criminals, convicts, and the insane—had been placed under legal ban, and in 1891 the category was extended to include prostitutes, polygamists, and those suffering from incurable or loathesome diseases. A tax of fifty cents was put upon each immigrant head, immigration was placed under federal supervision, the office of Supervisor of Immigration established, inspection introduced, and government control of entry and selection made possible. During the same year Henry Cabot Lodge introduced a literacy bill into the House that was finally passed by Congress in 1897, only to be vetoed by Cleveland. Nevertheless, the objectives of the restrictionists were now well formed. They wished to impose a head tax, a literacy test, an examination not only to prove physical fitness but social desirability, and to require the possession of property upon admission.

But American culture could be threatened with impairment only if foreigners were of an inferior breed. Untutored laborers admittedly raised the total number of illiterates in the country, but illiteracy is scarcely the same as a low intelligence quotient. Full information is still lacking, but scores of competent studies show that recent immigrant groups produced as many great leaders in every walk of life in proportion to the whole population as older immigrant groups. Crime, disease, and pauperism mounted, and on the rolls of prisons, the rosters of reformatories, and the dockets of the courts, later immigrant names are heavily represented. The alleged criminal record of the foreign born, when analyzed carefully, reveals that it was not the European-born immigrant but his American-born and American-conditioned offspring who forsook the narrow path of civic virtue. The ultimate causes for poor health, delinquency, and poverty among immigrant families seem, on the basis of modern research, to be social and environmental rather than physical and hereditary. Even the staggering statistics of institutional hospitalization for the insane, the feeble-minded, and the incurable were by no means to be attributed to congenital affliction. Immigrant children were children of the slum, of child labor, of families in the heartbreaking throes of adjustment. And the general urban rate of crime suggests that the city rather than the germ plasm bears an intimate relation to the figures.

"WE WHO BUILT AMERICA"

To Europe's "huddled masses yearning to breathe free," America has been a shining hope in a dark, bleak world—hope not alone for riches in a land where streets were paved with gold, but hope for living in a land whose gold was the promise of life. For millions of men and women who came to America and for millions who never went beyond the borders of their native towns, America provided a haven of sustaining faith. In countless Russian villages broken Jews who survived the measured torture of a fiendish pogram took courage from the assurance of some local sage that there was an America where men walked upright in the sight of their God. Polish patriots exiled in Siberian wastes were heartened by the knowledge that American Poles spoke their own tongue and sang their own songs openly and unafraid. Toil in the salt mines was not made the lighter on that account, but it was good to know that somewhere men could laugh in Polish and that no arrogant minister of a Russian czar could blot out a culture with an imperial ukase. In market places all over Lithuania and Hungary and Bohemia, peasants gathered to listen to the news from America as some learned villager painfully pieced out the words in letters from fellow townsmen. The listeners marveled that no American laws enforced service in the hated army of a hated king and that no flashing uniforms were to be seen on the streets of American cities except the drab blue of the policemen, who often belonged to the same political club as the immigrant. They were amazed that one who had so lately been among them had an important job in a mine or factory and earned a king's ransom weekly, for the small portion that found its way back to the purses of envious kinsfolk often made the difference between want and plenty.

The gift of America to Europe was no less priceless than the gift of Europe to America. Names all over the American land silently proclaim the continuing affinity of the states of Europe and the United States. There is a Florence in Alabama, a Stuttgart in Arkansas, a Rome in Georgia, and a Moscow in Idaho. Illinois has a Batavia, a Venice, a Paris, and a West Frankfort; Indiana, a Warsaw; Kentucky, a Glasgow, and Michigan, a Holland and a Norway as well. New Ulm and New Prague are found in Minnesota, Berlin in New Hampshire, Guttenberg in New Jersey, and Carlsbad in New Mexico. North Dakota has its Bismarck, Pennsylvania its Manheim, while New York fittingly possesses Amsterdam, Rome, Dunkirk, Frankfort, and Hamburg.

Each immigrant group from the oldest and most numerous to the most recent and least populous pridefully presents a roster of great names whose hands and hearts helped to build America. The Danes are mindful of the career of Jacob A. Riis, who migrated to New York in 1870 and who, after serving an apprenticeship as police reporter for the New York *Evening Sun,* exposed the frightful living conditions of the other half with such quiet realism that Governor Theodore Roosevelt and others were shamed into action. Belgian-Americans point with satisfaction to their great compatriot, Leo Hendrik Baekeland, chemist, the inventor of Bakelite and innovator with plastic materials, and to Eugene Ysaye, the violinist. Germans claim John A. Roebling, builder of bridges; Charles P. Steinmetz, "wizard of Schenectady"; the reformer

Carl Schurz; and Steinway, Knabe, Weber, and Wurlitzer, whose names have become almost synonymous with pianos. When Czechs in America or in their homeland sing the songs of Rudolph Friml or listen to Anton Dvořák's *Symphony from a New World,* all men sing and listen with them.

But the contributions of immigrants to America lie not in the deeds of great individuals, but in the elements that made their achievements great. The American immigrant inventors, Michael Pupin and Nikola Tesla, were born in Yugoslavia, but their contributions to electrical discovery were of human rather than national import and increased mastery over nature in England and France as well as in Croatia and Montenegro. Danes give to Niels Poulson abundant credit for the iron ornaments in New York's Grand Central and Pennsylvania stations and for his support of the American-Scandinavian Foundation for international accord, but fireproof stairs and library bookstacks, which are also associated with his name, serve all mankind. And if Baekeland belongs in part to Belgium and in part to the United States, plastics belong to the world.

But immigrants made America. They made it literally by cutting down its primitive forests and laying out its broad highways. They built its railways and operated them, planned and reared its buildings and its bridges. They tilled its good earth and made it better, and they burrowed deep beneath it to bring its buried treasures to the surface. Not only did they supply the muscle that built America but they supplied the mind that made America culturally rich. Scholars, scientists, inventors, and artists crowded into Castle Garden with the humblest tillers of the soil and with them gazed rapturously at the Goddess of Liberty who held "the lamp beside the golden door." Pious students from Vilna's wretched ghetto read dog-eared old books written in the holy language of the prophets as the steamer pushed its nose into the harbor of New York, while the pockets of their gabardine caftans were stuffed with medieval commentaries on Talmudic law. Eager young men filled with ideas and equipped with the fervor of ambition hoped to accomplish in such schools as the factories afforded what the universities of St. Petersburg, Dorpat, Budapest, or Vienna denied them. Others already trained as doctors, lawyers, scientists, and artists sought only the chance to give their knowledge to mankind. And Czechs, Italians, and Poles, who at long last set foot on the promised land, not only had strong sinewy hands for holding a pneumatic drill, but deft, agile hands for converting materials into the folkcraft of their people. They had their hands, their brains, and their hearts. To America they gave the greatness of unity that derives from diversity, for they were the living agents in the highest human experiment, the experiment by which out of the diversity of mankind the unity of mankind is reached.

By 1900 the new immigrant, like the old, was proving his human worth as well as his economic value in the land of his adoption; and the land he had left was benefiting likewise from cultural interchange. Yet in the era of the rise of the city and the triumph of the machine, the immigrant family, like the more depressed strata of older American families, was all too often a victim of the darker phases in the changing life of industrial America. But directly or indirectly, every person in the nation had a share in the sins of society.

THE SINS OF SOCIETY 1865–1900

The revolutions in economics took on different guises at different levels of observation and appraisement. Through the telescope of wealth they appeared in forms that the microscope of poverty did not confirm. There were files in the offices of the Standard Oil Company with data on gushers, pipe lines, and marketing agreements, and there were files in the offices of social settlements with data on human wreckage. Wanderers of the world, checked in at Castle Garden or at Ellis Island, appeared as silent figures in the pages of the Immigration Bureau Reports, but they were neither silent nor tranquil in the crowded loneliness of American cities. Statistics on immigration reappeared in minutes of directors' meetings concerned with labor, strikes, and the correlation between wages and prices, in the monographs of scholars who hailed the advent of plural cultures as the promise of human fulfillment, and in the admonitory strictures of bigots who made out the strident case for nativism. There were precise blueprints on the drafting boards of architects who supervised the building of town houses and country estates, and there were designless slums in every city in the nation. There were the breath-taking triumphs of society, but there were also the breath-taking sins of society.

THE CHALLENGE OF WEALTH

Triumphant Andrew Carnegie, foreign born but as full of pride in the United States as his money bags were full of American gold, wrote of his adopted country in the 1880's:

The United States, the growth of a single century, has already reached the foremost rank among nations, and is destined soon to out-distance all others in the race. In population, in wealth, in annual savings, and in public credit; in freedom from debt, in agriculture, and in manufactures, America already leads the civilized world.

No less enthusiastic was the opinion of Edward Atkinson, a contemporary economist, who regarded the changes that had taken place since the peace between the states as the greatest in the history of civilization, while in 1889 David A. Wells, a brother economist, wrote, "To one whose present memory . . ." does not extend back over a longer period than one generation, "the economic experiences . . . of the generation next preceding is very much akin to . . . ancient history."

The judgment of the redoubtable Carnegie few would venture to deny. His optimism was attested by the incontrovertible pages of the census and the clipped reports of the United States Treasury as well as by private banks and steel corporations. But at what cost had this phenomenal greatness been achieved? And was greatness truly measured by the rate of population increase, the amount of money on deposit in the nation's savings banks, and the fiscal balances of the federal Treasury? If these criteria were satisfactory to hard-headed men of business and to the learned economists of the academies, they failed to satisfy others. For what was the price measured in living values; what toll did this unprecedented transformation exact from the men and women who added the endless columns of figures in banks, government bureaus, and business offices, or who turned molten iron into bars of steel?

Greater men than Andrew Carnegie were neither so complacent nor so confident. Almost two decades before Carnegie wrote his paean to American business, Walt Whitman expressed serious misgivings about the direction of American life. "The great cities reek with respectable robbery and scoundrelism," he wrote. "In business (this all-devouring modern word, business,) the one sole object is, by any means, pecuniary gain. In vain do we march with unprecedented strides to empire so colossal, outvying the antique, beyond Alexander's, beyond the way of Rome. In vain do we annex Texas, California, Alaska, and reach north for Canada and south for Cuba. It is as if we were somehow being endowed with a vast and more thoroughly-appointed body, and then left with little or no soul." If Whitman feared that Americans consumed by the spirit of life had lost touch with the life of the spirit, George Santayana, a great philosopher, was later to speak out even more forthrightly:

> My heart rebels against my generation,
> That talks of freedom and is slave to riches
> And, toiling 'neath each day's ignoble burden,
> Boasts of the morrow.[1]

And another of this generation, Woodrow Wilson, spiritually a poet before he was a scholar and by nature a philosopher before he was a statesman, was also one day to make an equally blunt indictment:

---

[1] Ode II, "My heart rebels against my generation," *Poems*. New York: Scribner, 1923, p. 73.

We have been proud of our industrial achievements, but we have not . . . stopped . . . to count the cost, the cost of lives snuffed out, of energies over-taxed and broken, the fearful physical and spiritual cost to the men and women and children upon whom the dead weight and burden of it all had fallen pitilessly. . . .[2]

There was another side to the triumphs of American capitalism that found no place in Carnegie's lusty portrayal. Not all American lives followed the Carnegie course from penniless immigrant to magnate of steel. America was a land of millionaires, but few Americans were rich. And to draw American lineaments in the physical terms of bustling fac-tories, thriving cities, and the abundant life of rural villages presented a picture of the United States that was totally out of perspective. Steel mills were not segregated items in social cartography. They did not stand alone in splendid isolation as sparkling testaments to the glory and genius of man. Nor did they simply connote blazing furnaces, managerial bank balances, and fat dividends to stockholders. They also connoted the weary faces of men who worked in the mills, the human lives that neither be-gan nor ended with the shriek of the factory whistle, and the human strivings that transcended the lunch box and the pay envelope. They con-noted homes and hearths and hopes. They suggested slums and steel towns; good times and bad; strikes and privation; want and fear. Social good must be balanced against social evil; the sins of society against the virtues of civilization.

When the balance was cast up were men as well as machines tri-umphant? Was democracy as triumphant as business? The economic revolutions ushered in a strange new world, but whether they had made men's lives richer and fuller was a question all were not prepared to answer affirmatively. Machine technology had shamed the incredulous, but machines had given neither peace nor plenty to the common man. Machines had enabled a virile citizenry to create more food than could be consumed, yet men and women starved and children grew to adult-hood with twisted bodies and adolescent minds because there was not enough to sustain them. Manufacturing, geared to motive power, yielded enormous wealth, but poverty, insecurity, and death were no less appar-ent than in the leanest years of scarcity. Want was a stark commonplace in American cities, and even the husbandman, hero of the Jeffersonian idyll, drank deep of the cup of despair, although reapers, harvesters, and binders made millions of busy farms out of a wooded frontier and a trackless prairie. Other machines possessed the capacity of fabricating

---

[2] Inaugural Address.

untold numbers of shoes and garments, but cold was the companion of hunger in the crowded tenements of urban America.

Wealth and comfort were evident in every town and hamlet. Fifth Avenue in New York boasted fine brownstone mansions, and everywhere there were snug homes of wood and brick, but the slums in northern cities were only scarcely less disgraceful than the miserable huts of southern sharecroppers, black and white. America was truly the land of plenty; but America was just as truly a land of poverty. Foreigners joined with natives in praise of the machine, its speed, its perfection, and its Aladdin-like capacity for answering the wants of mankind. But behind the façade of iron, steel, and electricity were the fathers, mothers, and children whose lives were at the mercy of the men who controlled the machines from remote offices in the financial districts.

Not only were workers scandalously exploited in the development of industry, but no place was found for the employment of the old, the weak, and the incapacitated. Humanitarianism was the formal creed of most Americans, but there was no humanitarianism in the hours, wages, and conditions of labor. Unemployment, partial in seasonal industries and wholesale in lean economic years, added the curse of insecurity to the misery of subsistence living. Unemployment fluctuations blighted the lives of millions of Americans in the period from 1865 to 1900. In 1865 the figure for unemployment reached 1,000,000 for the North alone, and one authority estimated that almost 1,300,000 workers and professional men were out of work. In Massachusetts 29.9 per cent of the total employables in that state for the year 1884–1885—241,589 of 816,470—were either completely out of work or occupied only partially.

Public health, too, failed to keep pace with the great strides made by science. The nineteenth century was the golden age of biology, the century of Charles Darwin, of Thomas Huxley, of Louis Pasteur, of Robert Koch, and of Joseph Lister. Scholars were electrified by the scientific results published in stately monographs and the journals of research, and the general public could perceive corresponding advances in medicine, sanitation, and public health as they appeared in hospitals, preventive techniques, and the vigilance of boards of health. Yet disease was still in active partnership with death, a combine that did little credit to a culture boasting of scientific accomplishments. Even more shocking was the sordid story suggested by the statistics, for the grim hand of the reaper might often have been stayed by a minimum of knowledge and a modicum of cash. But poverty and ignorance centered in urban slums, and marginal farms invited hookworm, tuberculosis, pellagra, and syphilis.

The depressed areas in town and country contributed to vice and crime no less than to disease. Prostitution, juvenile delinquency, and major criminality flourished, and crime was a symptom of American health. But crime was no less distressing than punishment that was a travesty on American humanitarianism if not on justice. Nor was the treatment accorded offenders against the law any better than the social attitude reflected in the treatment of the poor, the unfortunate, and the weak in body and spirit. And from the pulpits of American churches the message of Jesus was preached on successive Sundays, but there was nothing of the Sermon on the Mount in American conduct toward the Negro, the Indian, and the immigrant whose rights were shamelessly flouted in the piratical search for gold. It was not only the slow who lost in this race in which the swift were always victors, but the deaf, the dumb, and the blind. If they had always been handicapped, the uncertainties of employment in a machine age made them more helpless misfits.

Poverty was a social sin long before the prophet Amos called down the wrath of his Hebrew God upon the oppressors of the lowly, but the revolutions in economics made poverty a social crime. Who was responsible for poverty, for the grinding torture of the sweatshop, for the mean streets of the slum that crucified millions of individual lives? Social responsibility was no longer personal; economic and institutional rearrangements had fashioned a civilization so complex and so interdependent that the old codes of social morality were no longer pertinent. Social evil was the consequence of proximate rather than direct causes, intangible rather than concrete, but the consequences of social change were nonetheless venal and their results were nonetheless calamitous. Above all they were impersonal, and impersonality created a new variety of social sin unknown to the ancient decalogues. Impersonality was the industrial counterpart of the rural-urban clash in the realm of conduct, for interdependence diffused responsibility and altered personal and group relationships. A complex institutionalized society was substituted for a simple individualized society; an intimately personal society for an impersonal one. The integration of the economic process, typified by the corporation, became the modern vehicle for the perpetuation of evil. But a child who died as a result of drinking infected milk was nonetheless murdered despite the fact that the stockholders in the milk company, the bottle makers, the carriers, and the delivery men were innocent. Workers in factories who perished in consequence of faulty or unprotected machinery were slain even if no one was apparently guilty in terms of the law. The new criminal, wrote the sociologist Edward A. Ross, was quite unlike the villain made famous by the contemporary dime novel. His character was not stamped on his face nor was he dressed to fit the part. Instead, "the modern high-power dealer of woe wears immaculate linen, carries a silk hat and a lighted cigar, sins with calm countenance and a serene soul, leagues or months from the evil he causes. Upon his gentlemanly presence the eventual blood and tears do not obtrude themselves."[3] It was impersonality and the diffusion of social responsibility that embattled the spirit and the institutions of democracy. Together with great, uncontrolled wealth and great, unrelieved poverty they were the cardinal sins of modern society, but although the generation after the Civil War in part perceived them and sought valiantly to combat them, it was left for posterity to continue the struggle. Freedom and democracy are goals not easily won.

THE CHALLENGE OF POVERTY

That America was unbelievably rich none could gainsay, but a glittering place in society did not evoke a concern for the myriads who comosed society. People who lived their lives in fine houses could scarcely even in imagination appreciate the experience of people who did not. Munificence was the word for the masters of American capital. Vast and expensive mausoleums of brownstone served them as homes. Well-paid agents ransacked half of Europe for remnants of bygone cultures to furnish their mansions and to satisfy a deeper urge for association with what was considered a noble past. Norman castles and the palaces of Venetian princes yielded up their proud treasures and found new, though often incongruous, abodes in New York, Boston, and Chicago. So avid was the craving for *objêts d'art* that a brisk trade in paintings and sculpture resulted which, it was said, made it possible to rid Europe of most of the works that merit had relegated to a well-deserved obscurity. Nor was conspicuous consumption confined to homes and furnishings. Clothes, food, and pleasures revealed the same extravagance and gilded opulence. Entertainments and parties were sometimes so bizarre that on one occasion chorus girls popped out of huge pies to the amazement of the guests, and at another the men were afforded the sordid thrill of smoking cigars rolled in hundred dollar bills.

The figures of national wealth told the same story less colorfully. When Abraham Lincoln became President in the fatal year 1860, the national wealth was in excess of 16 billion dollars. Thirty years later it had grown to over four times that amount, 65 billion; and in 1900 it rose to the unprecedented total of 88.5 billion. Estimates of the per capita wealth of the nation indicate a corresponding increase—in 1860, $514; in 1890, $1,036; and in 1900, $1,165. But that the ownership

---

[3] E. A. Ross, *Sin and Society*. Boston: Houghton Mifflin, 1907, pp. 10–11.

of the riches of the country was disproportionately concentrated was as certain as the existence of wealth itself. Regardless of the differences in various estimates, the tendency was clear. Wealth increasingly concentrated in the pockets of the few, with the result that wealth was more unevenly distributed in 1900 than before the Civil War. A study of income made by a census bureau official in 1893 revealed that an estimated 71 per cent of all the wealth in America was owned by 9 per cent of its families. Even more suggestive were the findings of Charles B. Spahr, a careful student, made three years later, indicating that more than half the wealth of the nation, 51 per cent, was owned by 1 per cent of the families, while the total possessions of 88 per cent of American families amounted to only 14 per cent of the wealth. Poverty lurked everywhere in the background. If some chose to doubt that the poor were getting poorer by absolute standards of comparison, none could doubt that the rich were getting richer both relatively and absolutely. Also beyond the possibility of statistical doubt was the fact that the poor were not receiving either an adequate or a just share of the total increase in social wealth. Nor did these unwholesome tendencies show any signs of reversal in the next century.

Tables representing the unequal distribution of wealth and income cannot possibly convey the meaning of want to those who experienced it. Carnegie rightly signalized the growth of cities as a "stupendous change" which marked "the development of the Republic from the first stage of homogeneity of pastoral pursuits into the heterogeneous occupations of a more highly civilized state." "Its mechanical and inventive genius," he continued, "has full scope in the thousand and one diversified pursuits which a civilized community necessarily creates, and which necessitate the gathering of men together in masses." But Carnegie, in his zeal to justify the evils of this epochal stage in social evolution, forgot to dwell upon the plight of the masses that the economic and social changes of the modern world had gathered together in cities. The Sanitary Census of New York City of 1891 was poignantly, if dispassionately, precise. In that year 276,565 families were housed in tenements in New York, and within this unholy section of the city lived 160,708 children under the age of five. The whole tenement population at that time was slightly under a million and a quarter.

Although New York City, largest of American urban centers and immigrant port of entry, held the slum record, Hartford, Cincinnati, Boston, and Jersey City did not lag far behind. Approximately 10 per cent of the whole population of America lived in slums that resembled nothing so much as the oldest cities of the Old World. Only proud Prague, capital of ancient Bohemia, rivaled New York in the degree of congestion, but the American Gotham was typical of the slum evil everywhere. Varying in height from five to six stories and about ninety feet wide, the tenement was entered by a dark passageway that served as a hall. Few rooms were provided with direct ventilation, but were lighted and aired by a shaft, certain to act as a draft in case of fire. Families were forced to make one room their home without regard to age, sex, infirmity, or physical condition. In such surroundings children learned to accept ugliness before they had a chance to recognize beauty.

But the slum had consequences that extended far beyond its shoddy boundaries. Disease, vice, and juvenile delinquency hardly begin to exhaust the list of evils to which the slum was heir or to which it in great measure contributed. To its unfortunate inhabitants democracy could hardly have been more than a meaningless dogma further degraded by political manipulators who turned human misery into votes on election day. The institutions of democracy were imperiled by destitution, which at the same time made a mockery of the home. Love did not bloom in an atmosphere of despair, and mortals could not forever relight the lamp of hope. There was no escape from squalor. If enraptured youth were able to look beyond it and live momentarily in the haze of unreality, they awakened later to the stark bitterness of wives enslaved to the sweatshop, of depressing, unremitting jobs, of children sacrificed to labor, and the mounting, omnipresent filth to which they daily returned. The struggle with the slum was a losing battle as long as low wages forced workers to live in the most inadequate places. After a long career with dependent children and delinquent girls, Josephine Shaw Lowell, founder of the New York Charity Organization Society, found herself somewhat dubious of the principles that had guided the better part of her life. When she determined to resign from the State Board of Charities, she wrote, "If the working people had all they had to have, we should not have the paupers and criminals. It is better to save them before they go under than to spend your life fishing them out when they're half drowned and taking care of them afterwards."[4]

But economics, ethics, and sociological principles were seldom merged into a unified program. The factory system created a brisk demand for cheap labor. As operations became more and more mechanized, the tasks of manufacture could be entrusted to the unskilled hands of women, children, Negroes, and immigrants. Workers—male and female, young and old, black and white—were driven into mill, factory, and sweatshop by the employers' demand for low-priced labor and greater

[4] W. R. Stewart, *The Philanthropic Work of Josephine Shaw Lowell*. New York: 1911, pp. 358–359.

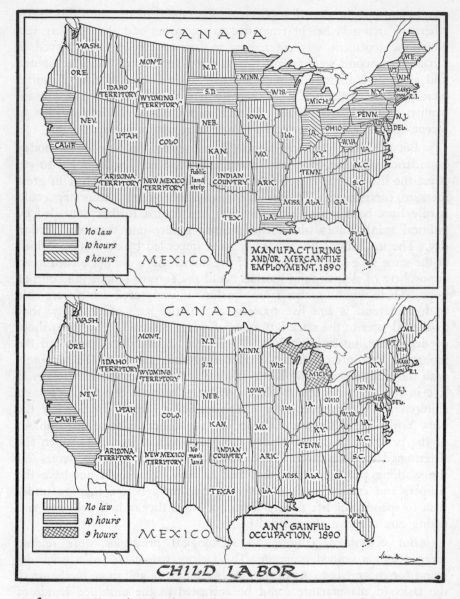

CHILD LABOR

profits as well as by the irresistible economic pressure of making both ends meet.

Man exhibited an inhumanity not only to his fellow men, but to children and the women who bore them. Jane Addams, a leading humanitarian and guiding spirit of a center for social work among the underprivileged, famed Hull-House in Chicago, graphically documented the statistics of poverty as they affected the women who worked and the children who, with them, figured in the social cost. Early in her Chicago career she encountered three crippled children, left to fend for themselves while their mothers—as the phrase euphemistically had it—were gainfully employed. One had fallen from a third-story window; the second was severely burned; and the third had an injured spine as a result of having been tied to the leg of a table from which he was released at noon by an older brother who stole time from his lunch hour to give the infant food.

Although accurate data are not available, there were almost three quarters of a million children engaged in labor in 1870. By 1880 the figure had swelled to a million, and twenty years thereafter had increased by almost a quarter of a million more. The official census figures are doubtless far below the mark, and a careful student estimated that shortly after 1900 "the number of children workers under fifteen is at least 2,500,000." Children were mostly employed in the textile industries, particularly in the towns of the new South where whole families worked as units in the local mills. Also important as exploiters of the young were the glass works, the Chicago stockyards, the mines of Pennsylvania, the canning industry, and the sweated trades of eastern cities. Some state legislatures forbade the labor of children under twelve or fourteen years of age, but such laws were lacking in most of the southern states and were rarely effectively enforced anywhere. In addition, the universal need of the poverty-stricken led to the falsification of age certificates, in which officials and employers frequently connived.

The existence of child labor in mid-century America can be explained, but not condoned. A disgraceful commentary on the state of public morals, it was relieved only by the courageous efforts of those who strove to abolish it. In the glass factories of Pennsylvania, New Jersey, Ohio, and Indiana, boys under sixteen worked regularly on the night shift from half past five in the afternoon until half past three in the morning. After eight hours of benumbing work in hot, unhealthful surroundings (during which by actual computation the average boy covered twenty-two miles, eleven of them with hot loads of glass), they went out in the early morning air, thinly clad, perspiring, and exhausted. Being normal boys, they preferred play to sleep during the day, with effects upon their health all too readily imagined. For this labor the lowest reward was 40 cents a night; the highest, $1.10. Boys from reformatories and orphanages, often employed in this industry particularly in New Jersey, were boarded out with laborers' families and the charges deducted from their pay. The results of this system were as corruptive socially as they were economically vicious. And in New York City alone there were

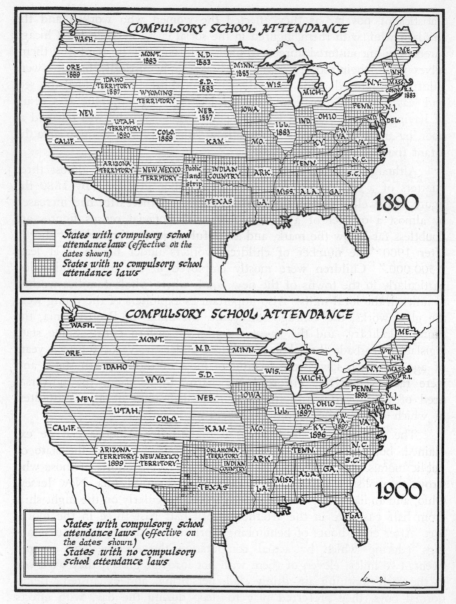

23,000 licensed home factories of one type or another where children not compelled to go to school until eight years of age were customarily employed.

No more pardonable was the plight of children in Pennsylvania mines. Although the law expressly prohibited employment of children under fourteen, a competent investigation made in 1905 revealed that in one small community of 7,000, 35 nine-year-olds, 40 ten-year-olds, 45 eleven-year-olds, and 45 twelve-year-olds were actually on the pay roll of the mining companies. John Spargo, a noted reformer who studied the conditions minutely, reported:

The coal is hard, and accidents to the hands, such as a cut, broken, or crushed fingers, are common among the boys. Sometimes there is a worse accident: a terrified shriek is heard and a boy is mangled and torn in the machinery, or disappears in the chute to be picked out later smothered and dead.

Little can be added to the reputed comment of a foreman in one of "the kindergarten" industries, so called because of the number of children employed, that it was "enough for one man to do just to keep the kids awake."

Even the most dexterous sophistry could not justify the exploitation of women and children. Least significant was the economic complication which, by displacing adult male workers, lowered the general wage scale. Either the employment of children and of women at degrading wages was essential for the productive needs of the nation or it was not. If not, the question answered itself, and the motives that induced the practice and the theories that rationalized them furnish a commentary upon contemporary morals as sordid as the conditions were reprehensible.

The tragedy of waste was not simply economic, but moral, psychological, and cultural. Child labor contracted childhood. Under the conditions of existence in the factory, of life in a crowded flat, and of play in a mean alley, children became adults before they had time to be adolescents. Poverty deprived them of proper nourishment, physical, mental, and spiritual. With weakened bodies they were destined for the human scrap heap, with undeveloped minds they were unfitted for the economic struggle; with both they became the unwitting victims of vice and corruption. With approximately two million children of school age forced to earn what passed for a living, the oft-heralded advantages of a free public school system sounded hollow in the ears of the socially minded engaged in front-line warfare with the slum. "When we exploit the immature strength of little children," concluded John Spargo, whose *Bitter Cry of the Children* was a fact-crammed expose of the callousness of society, "we prepare recruits for the miserable army of the unfit and the unemployable, whose lot is a shameful and debasing poverty."

Child labor, women in industry, and the slum were interrelated aspects of the problem of inadequate income. At the root of all three was poverty, and the ramifications of poverty were as wide as society. Poverty was the correlate of death just as it was the correlate of crime. Though children succumbed more easily to disease, their mothers and fathers were by no means exempt. The slums represented the worst environment in America, and conditions in mines, mills, and factories were hardly better. Unhealthful conditions at home and at work, standards of living that demeaned humanity by making the limited goal of common decency unattainable, made the city gang a vehicle of self-justification, the saloon an avenue of escape, and the political machine a psychological means of identification with power.

Inadequate food, clothing, and shelter and the lack of wholesome family life influenced parent and child alike. When a great reformer condemned poverty as "the Herod of modern civilization," he was not indulging in idle rhetoric. The facts spoke no less convincingly, if less passionately, for the statistics indicated that death was greatest where poverty was greatest. It was in the city slum that the death rate was highest; there was, in addition, an ugly coincidence between the lowest wage scale and the highest proportion of deaths.

Lack of sanitation, bad housing, and limited emotional compensations do not alone account for the high mortality among the poor. The science of health and the science of economics were intimately related. There were diseases of poverty and diseases of ignorance in America, the existence of which in a civilization devoted to democracy was a sickening anomaly. A social worker of impeccable standing reported as late as 1900 that the 14,288 infant deaths from convulsions and the 8,645 infant deaths from measles which occurred in that year were for the most part directly traceable to poverty. And when Jacob Riis made a tour of the reformatories as part of his study of the children of the poor, he found that of over 5,000 juvenile inmates of Elmira only slightly more than 1 per cent had lived in a wholesome environment prior to conviction.

The ledger of American accomplishment had to be debited on two counts. To snuff out the hopes and sometimes the lives of men, women, and children was clearly a wanton process of which the social toll was, as Spargo phrased it, "the silent atrophy of potential genius, the brutalization of potential love, the corruption of potential purity." But society paid an even higher price in the debasement of ideals and the corrosion of the spirit. For thousands for whom the dream of America was blasted by poverty and the slum, Anzia Yezierska, herself a Russian immigrant whose love for America was great enough to enable her to see its crimes, asked: "Had the starved villagers of Sukovoly lifted above their sorrows a mere rainbow vision that led them—where? Where? To the stifling submission of the sweat-shop? or the depression of the streets! . . . God! God! . . . Where—where is America?"[5]

---

[5] Anzia Yezierska, *How I Found America.*

And where in all truth was it? To this all-important question many attempted an answer. But the nature of the answer depended, after all, upon the source from which it emanated, whether from the professorial study in the ivy-towered halls of the university, from the comfortable security of the board room of the modern corporation, from the political pulpit, or from the "depression of the streets." When in 1898 Edwin Markham, inspired by Millet's famous painting, wrote the concluding stanza of "The Man with the Hoe," he may have been thinking only of the landless peasant:

> O masters, lords and rulers in all lands,
> How will the future reckon with this Man?
> How answer his brute question in that hour
> When whirlwinds of rebellion shake all shores?
> How will it be with kingdoms and with kings—
> With these who shaped him to the thing he is—
> When this dumb Terror shall rise to judge the world,
> After the silence of centuries?[6]

But many thought also of the man at the assembly line and at the flaming forge, of the woman who tended the whirring bobbins in textile factories, and of those who made buttonholes for shirts in the dank cellars of New York City.

THE POVERTY OF PROGRESS

But the sins of society did not pass unnoticed nor did the sinners escape unscathed, for if society was indifferent to suffering, scores of individuals were not. American prophets, like Jacob Riis, Jane Addams, and Henry George, rose up to call a sin a sin and to enlist small armies of ardent apostles whose goal was justice and whose creed was democracy. They dedicated their lives to the extirpation of evil, giving aid and comfort to its victims along the seemingly endless way. Writers heaped literary scorn upon contemporary inequities and pierced the armor of many a modern Croesus with sharp and acrid words. If weapons made of metered rhyme did not inflict mortal wounds, they prodded many along the rough road to awareness if not to understanding. Religious denominations, having gradually come to the conclusion that good and not evil was their spiritual calling, girded themselves to meet the new Gargantuan Lucifer who gathered up men's bodies before they could develop souls. Organized anew in what was called social Christianity and social Judaism, they centered their efforts upon the earthly kingdom. With the aid of new and revitalized institutions—the Y.M.C.A. (1851), the Salvation

---

[6] Edwin Markham, *The Man with the Hoe and Other Poems,* 1899.

Army (1879), and the city mission after 1887—they strove to touch off the divine spark in human hearts as a preliminary step toward the creation of the brotherhood of man. And charity, with a supreme faith in the power of money and an abiding hope in social regeneration, spent millions of dollars derived from public and private sources in the attempt to cure the surface consequences of evil.

Yet then, as now, thoughtful minds were sorely troubled. Could wealth amassed by reprehensible methods, but poured back directly through organized philanthropy (foundations, endowments, hospitals) or indirectly through public, tax-supported agencies (boards of health, schools, relief) ever atone for the privations, miseries, and frustrations incident to the mode of its acquisition? It was not merely that the money was "tainted," as the Reverend Washington Gladden of Columbus, Ohio, said, but it set up a painful paradox that exposed a cultural malady: antisocial conduct productive of evil instigated social conduct to assuage the evil thus caused. It produced the paradox of estimable gentlemen, moral, honest, and charitable in their private lives, but with no civic responsibility in their professional lives: men who felt no compunction in drawing their wealth from corporations whose managers sweated labor and crucified children; men who built armored plate for battleships and contributed financially to world peace; men who owned real estate in wretched slums and endowed universities to build healthy minds in sound bodies; men who employed immature children in the factory district and supported social settlements in the slum district; and men who caused temples to be erected to the glory of their God and the ennoblement of their fellow man but who traduced commandments sacred to both.

Nevertheless, American humanitarians were not deterred, and the record of their striving is impressive. Not only did each particular vice have its particular band of shining crusaders, but their activity reveals a deep moral earnestness, a high degree of social responsibility, and an irrepressible faith in the capacities of man. Protest came both from those who suffered and from those who were witness to suffering they could not abide. They rightly diagnosed inequality and destitution as symptoms of democracy's decline. Whatever their political allegiance, they were active exponents of the Jeffersonian maxim "to go forward, instead of backward," to refuse to believe "that nothing can ever be devised more perfect than was established by our forefathers."

In this spirit reformers like Jacob Riis, a Danish immigrant, took up the challenge of the slum. When in 1890 he called attention to Murderers' Alley, Hell's Kitchen, Poverty Gap, and Penitentiary Row, notorious names for notorious places in New York, the public finally became sensitive to the dangers of the tenement block. If they did not always recognize the social causes, they were at least made to see the social consequences and the moral obligation of rectifying them. Of similar purport was John Spargo's fully documented account of the prevalence of child labor and the social disasters accompanying it. Social workers, borrowing a leaf from the English notebook, migrated into the slum areas of great cities to establish frontier settlements for a new type of social pioneering. Originally Jane Addams' Hull-House in Chicago and Lillian D. Wald's Henry Street Settlement in the East Side of New York were conceived as laboratories for social workers, but they came to be infinitely more. "Social-service agency" is a tepid name for a flesh-and-blood institution that so frequently spelled out the difference between nourishment and starvation, between survival and death.

Although reformers labored with Jeffersonian fervor, they labored in a world that the sage of Monticello would not have recognized. The battle with the slum was merely begun when the century closed, and it was not until 1901 that improper housing was even mildly checked under a tenement law passed in New York following the report of a commission appointed by Governor Theodore Roosevelt. Braving the objections of the lords of the slum, other states followed the lead of New York during the next ten years, but it remained for another Roosevelt to tackle the problem anew. Some of the foulest aspects of slumdom were eliminated after 1890, but poverty remained. And as long as poverty existed, the slums were bound to endure. The reformers were concerned with surface features rather than with basic causes, for slums were less the result of the petty avarice of callous real-estate owners than of the poverty that permitted avarice to flourish. And modern poverty was a condition rooted in the new sociology of the urban-industrial world of which slums were an integral part. Periodically to prune the twigs was something less than a cure.

Society's response to the most devastating inequities was as ineffective basically as it was genuinely inspired. The settlement houses were remedial agencies devoted to the salvage of wrecked lives, but they gave scarcely any attention to the economic whirlpools that produced social catastrophe. The existence of half a hundred settlement houses by 1895 is more an eloquent reminder of human want than a testament of victory in the mammoth task of social engineering. Five years later there were almost a hundred, irrefutable evidence that the problems of poverty had increased but had not been solved. Jane Addams herself wrote that the neighborhood settlement resembles a "big brother whose mere presence on the playground protects the little one from bullies," but the settlement did little about the environment that produced the bullies in the neighborhood and less about the environment that produced the bullies on the battleground of American life.

American discontent generated a mighty protest, but American dissent was also recorded by the gentler barometer of the protest of fantasy. Distressed by the harshness of the life about them, many Americans sought deliverance from the struggle in a perfection that existed in their minds alone. With facile pens they built new mansions of the mind to shelter their wounded spirits and to furnish living space for their broken dreams. The quest for a literary utopia was constant from the eighties until 1900, and in the gay nineties alone the appearance of almost half a hundred such romances suggests the extent to which the famed nineties were not really gay. Lewis Mumford, leading analyst of urban culture, remarked that the true explanation of the fantastic popularity of the little men and little women of Louisa May Alcott resided in the fact that in youth and youth alone was there any semblance of the golden day.

Edward Bellamy's *Looking Backward, 2000–1887* portrayed an "ideal humanity" peopled by heroic Americans who had outgrown acquisitiveness. With the elimination of profit, the latent capacities of society were released for creative activities that produced a veritable renaissance in the arts and crafts. The extraordinary extent to which Bellamy touched a responsive chord among Americans who yearned to look forward as well as backward is evidenced by the four hundred thousand persons who bought his book between 1887 and 1897 and by the more than 150 "Nationalist Clubs" organized to further his version of the scientific industrial millenium.

To the searchers for a panacea, the internationally famous book of Henry George, *Progress and Poverty* (1880), was second in popularity to Bellamy's. "Unpleasant as it may be to admit it," wrote George, "the enormous increase in productive power . . . has no power to extirpate poverty or to lighten the burdens of those compelled to toil. This association of poverty with progress is the greatest enigma of our times. It is the riddle which the Sphinx of Fate puts to our civilization and which," George solemnly warned, "not to answer is to be destroyed." For this riddle George had his own solution: he believed men had as inalienable a right to land as to sun and air; to deny it was to deny the principles of democracy. Ironically, George's insistence on the crucial import of land came just when the tangible assets of land were already becoming subordinated to the intangible asserts of finance. Nevertheless, George's proposal for a single tax on land (which would deprive owners of real estate of unearned profits stemming from the natural increase in value) elicited enthusiastic support, and the devastating term "unearned increment" was thereafter incorporated into every language. By 1905 more than two million copies of *Progress and Poverty* were sold, and in 1886 Henry George himself received the thumping vote of 68,110 citizens as a candidate for mayor of New York, nosing out Theodore Roosevelt, the poor third, while the Democratic winner, Abram S. Hewitt, polled 90,552.

But though America furnished the stuff out of which dreams were made, dreams were incapable of curing the ills that afflicted America. Thoughtful Americans were aware of the extent to which unsound economic changes imperiled democracy. Other Americans—farmers, workers, reformers, and writers—not fully aware of the causes but conscious that democracy was threatened, resolved, if they could, to save it and themselves as well. If in their brilliant analyses of social decay, Henry Adams and his brother Brooks succumbed to pessimism, most of their compatriots revealed an optimistic faith in their tireless efforts to assuage, to cure, and to build.

Reformers grappled with evil wherever they found it; and they found it in the pattern of "race consciousness" that so often dishonored democratic thought. The conduct of Americans toward their colored population, black and red, was thoroughly illiberal if not inhumane. American whites imposed upon the Indians by seizing their lands, upon the Negroes by denying their rights. The Indians became the neglected stepchildren of Uncle Sam, dependent, victimized, and subdued. The Negroes, bereft of whatever security slavery afforded, were left to the mercy of an embittered South or shared the fate of all the lowly in the urban, industrialized North.

General concern for the Negro abated after reconstruction, and the "freedman" was left to work out his own redemption. Although many colored folk migrated northward, the greater proportion remained in the South, where the four million of 1860 grew to eight million in 1900. It remained for Booker T. Washington to try to lead his own people out of the jungle of ignorance and the morass of poverty. Avoiding conflict on the field of racial equality, Washington chose education as his battleground. Once a slave himself, he felt the Negro could not attain social equality until after he became an effective contributor to the work of society. With this purpose Washington founded the Normal and Industrial Institute (1881) in Tuskegee, Alabama, to give the Negro specialized training and to develop the occupational skills acquired during serfdom.

Although northern money was freely spent to aid the Negro, Americans and their national government chose to regard the problem as a southern one. Most Southerners were not willing to regard it otherwise, and laws forbidding intermarriage between the two groups and providing for separate educational facilities were quickly passed. Tennessee in 1881 pioneered in discriminatory legislation requiring "citizens of color" to ride in specially provided sections of trains and cars, and soon other communities extended the ban to include amusements, hotels, and restaurants. And the Supreme Court in the Civil Rights cases (1883) denied that the Fourteenth Amendment, designed to protect Negro rights, gave power to the federal government to interfere in the state's control of the private lives of its citizens.

Thus native whites succeeded in relegating Negroes to an inferior social position; they also succeeded in depriving them of political rights. The rough-and-ready physical methods of reconstruction days gave way to formal legalistic methods no less effective. By manipulation of representative districts, the number of Negroes in the state legislatures was systematically reduced. Other expedients that undermined the core of representation—the franchise—ensured "white supremacy." Mississippi (1890) required that all voters be taxpayers—with taxes paid—who could read and interpret a part of the local constitution. If the first requirement failed to disqualify, the second, manipulated by members of the dominant class, was certain to do so. Other devices, particularly the infamous "grandfather clause"—by which Louisiana (1898) excluded from the voting lists those men whose fathers or grandfathers had not been eligible to vote before 1867—worked with predictable efficiency. The Negro was reduced to political impotence.

While black citizens of the United States were stripped of their rights, Indian wards of the United States were stripped of their manhood. Although in the eighties there were scarcely 260,000 Indians remaining, they comprised a serious problem. Herded on reservations, living their ancestral tribal life, they were dependent upon the bounty of Washington. Their reservations were threatened by the greed of the land-hungry; their impotence made them the victims of avaricious traders and dishonest officials. The congressional answer to the plight of the Indian was education, and by 1887 the government was spending a million and a quarter dollars for that purpose. This policy rested on the belief that the young, trained in the ways of a new world, would gradually substitute the white man's system for the red man's civilization. But the environment of the tribal home was too strong to be sapped by a few brief years of teaching, and generally incompetent teaching at that. Yet Congress, far more interested in other matters, remained unperturbed by the mounting evidence advanced by those who knew the facts.

Not until eastern reformers, horrified by conditions, organized to correct them, was it possible to breach the dike of public ignorance and official indifference toward the plight of the Indian. In this campaign

Helen Hunt Jackson's *A Century of Dishonor* (1881) performed an important function, and six years later the Dawes Act, providing citizenship and ownership of land to all Indians who renounced tribal loyalties, was passed. Undivided land was to be opened to white settlement, and Indian titles were limited by a restriction of sale to safeguard them from white encroachment. Tribal patriarchs were rarely converted, but members of the younger generation gradually adapted themselves to the life of a small farmer. It was a notable beginning, but the task was barely begun.

Indians and Negroes were victims of rural disorder, but urban maladjustments supplied ample outlets for reformist zeal. Increase in city population exposed ever larger numbers to contagious infection, which, even without ignorance and poverty, was a prelude to epidemic. Yet no one seriously questioned that, although occurring in individual bodies, disease was a social responsibility. Bacteria were indifferent to the philosophy of individualism, and few people insisted that one must be protected in the right to die as one saw fit. Personal liberties were invaded by the activities of state boards of health just as they had long been invaded by the system of compulsory education. Beginning with Louisiana in 1867 and Massachusetts in 1869, the total number of state boards of health increased to thirteen in 1878. When in 1878–1879, yellow fever, especially disastrous in Memphis and throughout the South, taught a grisly lesson in the language of death, suffering, and community danger, the laggards were converted to a minimum of forethought, and twelve more states acquired boards of health by 1882. As knowledge of the germ theory of disease, sanitation, and preventive medicine expanded, social safety grew in exact proportion to interference with personal liberties in matters of health, but the victory of knowledge over ignorance was severely limited by the victory of economic vice over social responsibility. Boards of health were impeded by slums, medical skills were blunted by long hours and lack of recreation, and improvement in preventive techniques was inhibited by low wages of those who most needed and could least afford medical care.

Added to the unfortunates who languished from bodily illness were others who were rendered helpless by what the lawyers called "acts of God." People caught in fires, floods, earthquakes, and similar catastrophes became the beneficiaries of organized aid after the heroic struggle of Clara Barton of Massachusetts was rewarded by the formation of the American Red Cross in 1881. In the next year the United States tardily ratified the Geneva International Pact, which provided such comfort as humanity could offer to mitigate the inhumanity of war. But the American peace movement in this era, flanked on one side by the Civil War and by the war with Spain on the other, made little headway. People whose hearts overflowed with righteousness supported a variety of peace societies, but for the most part they expended their energies upon the external rather than upon the basic causes of wars.

While the effort to eliminate war faltered, considerable advancement was made in softening the unforgiving vengeance meted out by society to the maladjusted victims of social strife. Those to whom injustice was a challenge could not but view the criminal code with horror. Penological methods were archaic, officials often corrupt and vicious, and the physical surroundings of prisoners more conducive to the increase of criminality than to its elimination. The practice, especially in the South, of leasing out penal gangs for manual labor was hardly better than slavery, while something of the shocking reality may be gleaned from the comment of a Kentucky governor that the state penitentiary resembled the "Black Hole of Calcutta." The National Prison Reform Association, under the impressive leadership of Franklin B. Sanborn, Z. R. Brockway, Dr. Theodore Dwight, and the Reverend E. C. Wines, succeeded in breaching the antiquated penal doctrine of retribution and substituting the principle of regeneration. And society, by accepting the change, accepted the implied premise that it was partly responsible for the transgressions of its members.

Inspired by the novelist Kate Douglas Wiggin, who insisted that children had rights, more attention was given to the influence of urban life upon the young. In 1874 the Society for the Prevention of Cruelty to Children was founded, while creditable progress was made in the treatment of juvenile delinquents. Under the old common law a child above seven was capable of crime; above fourteen he was subject to adult responsibility. As late as 1893 convicted children in New York were jailed together with adults—a nursery of crime—and not until 1899 did Illinois lead the way in establishing a special children's court. Nevertheless, inspired by prison reforms adopted in Ireland, Z. R. Brockway set a higher American standard by superintending the establishment of the New York State Reformatory at Elmira in 1877. There the young were separated from the old and given an indefinite sentence depending upon conduct and development while in prison. Together with the parole system adopted by Massachusetts during the same period, the Elmira system signalized an important social gain, but the social consequences of economic inequality made these gains seem slight indeed. Even the playground movement, dating from 1885 when a recreation center was first founded in Boston, could not begin to wipe out the social forces that accounted for the waywardness of the young. In the nineties New York City had thirty-one playgrounds, but they hardly controlled the factors

The spelling bee *(Frank Leslie's Illustrated Newspaper)* and the Sunday meeting *(courtesy Collection of Regional History, Cornell University)* were recreational as well as cultural institutions in rural America.

Town and country. *Above*—New York City in 1895: Madison Avenue at 42nd Street. *Below*—A typical village center. *(Culver Service)*

Buildings of social significance. *Above*—One of the buildings of Howard University, famous Negro center of learning, Washington, D. C. *(Scurlock Studio)* *Below*—Hull-House, South Halsted Street, Chicago, pioneer social settlement in urban America. *(Courtesy Hull-House)*

The common man did not want for champions. *Upper left*—Samuel Gompers helped to organize labor; *right*—Jacob Riis exposed the evils of the slums; *center*—Edward Bellamy created a literary utopia that pointed a moral; *lower left*—Henry D. Lloyd unflinchingly attacked monopoly; and, *right*—Henry George excoriated economic vice as it applied to unearned increment in land. (All photos *Culver Service* except Henry George, *courtesy Henry George School of Social Science*)

that forced the parents of the children who played there to live in the slums.

Concern for the underprivileged was matched by concern for the public interest. Reformers, dismayed by corruption in politics so obvious in prisons and in the slums, thought they could cure it without allaying the corruption of business, which was politics under a different name. But neither responded to the ministrations of the well intentioned, for the structure of American parties was decentralized, and the local machine, organized for plunder, constituted their cohesive power. The attempt to reform the civil service manifests the virility of the democratic spirit, but it was basically insignificant. The flagrant political immorality of the Grant administrations initiated the attack on the political manipulations of office in 1868 and was carried on by all the public-spirited throughout the century. Resulting in the Pendleton Act of 1883, the merit system for federal employment was extended and gradually enlarged by succeeding presidents. But the merit system did not abolish the spoils system, which was forever immune from flanking maneuver as long as the national parties were national simply in name, and the political boss remained to dominate the country, city, and state fiefs of a political organization essentially feudal in character.

THREATS TO DEMOCRACY

Yet the task to which liberal humanists and militant reformers dedicated themselves was a task for the stouthearted. America had become an urban civilization and an industrial culture. Old institutions, social attitudes, and ideas had become as ineffective as old ways of doing things. To attempt to solve the problems of society with the intellectual weapons of an outworn age was as hopeless as an attempt to operate a factory with the ancient instruments of manufacture. Americans were in the process of acquiring a new set of attitudes, a new moral code, a new pattern of life. These were transitional years, and transitional years are always difficult and perilous, for they become transitory only after they are passed. The rugged individualism that sufficed for the era of agrarian simplicity would not serve America in an age of urban complexity. Americans had to learn the social meaning of interdependence by experience. They had to cope with the changed nature of social relationships that had become impersonal and that made the time-honored sanctions of human conduct woefully inadequate. They had to redefine social responsibility in terms of the anonymity of urban-industrial living. The issues, moreover, had to be solved in a world in which big business, through the instrumentalities of trusts and monopolies, had mortgaged the natural resources of the nation to private profit and had taken labor into bondage. Exploitation of social resources, physical and human, had resulted in an unequal distribution of wealth that stultified opportunity and made the legend of a classless society in America a palpable fiction. If the practices that served the America of George Washington were outmoded in the America of Grover Cleveland, the instrumentalities that served the England of Edmund Burke were inoperative in the Britain of Benjamin Disraeli. The technology of urban life had antiquated the sociology of Western culture. While the machine made the major problems of society national, a shrinking world made the deeper problems international. As localisms pitted against the general welfare inhibited the solution of national problems, larger localisms in the form of political nationalisms made the basic problems of peace and plenty impossible of solution. Philosophies—social, political, economic—inherited from the rural age of relative independence and self-sufficiency, blocked the road to reform.

Only a philosophy of government dedicated to the general welfare could span the abyss of impersonality, the sociological and psychological counterpart of the city and the machine. But the existing philosophy of government was based upon the doctrine of nonintervention, correlate of optimistic early agrarian belief that progress marched inexorably to a preordained goal. Accordingly, to Jefferson's generation the less government the better, but laissez faire was no longer rooted in an agricultural age, which the machine annihilated in fact as well as in theory long before the majority of thinkers were aware of it. And the right of self-determination, whether of individuals or of nations, was a principle that stemmed from the seventeenth-century environment of Grotius and was annihilated by clippers, steamboats, and locomotives long before statesmen and industrialists came intellectually abreast of it. Only a government endowed with power adequate to the problems with which it had to cope and a reconditioned political machinery geared to the tasks that modern society imposed could meet issues transcending county and state lines just as they were soon to transcend national lines. The rise of the city with its anonymity raised social havoc with a culture whose moral code was the outgrowth of a primitive rural life—simple, homogeneous, and personal. A new type of social responsibility had to develop, and it could mature only in experience.

The years from 1865 to 1900 witnessed the appearance of great maladjustments stemming from the folkways of industrialization; and democracy called for a sound social answer. New men must find new measures to eliminate or reduce the social causes and human costs of disease, frustration, and poverty. How might the generation that lived in the great city, or on the farm in the era of subservience to industry, strive to meet democracy's challenge? Could the institutions of government, molded by earlier rural conditions, be remolded by urban influences to serve those Americans who longed for security and peace? Could the people recapture their government? One thing was certain: in the years after the Civil War the growth of dissent was a paramount reality. Not forever could frustration be countenanced without inviting an extremist preference for something other than a democratic answer.

XXI

DISSENT AND FRUSTRATION

1865–1900

The history of man in America reveals that every social evil called forth a social retort, every ill a plan for reform. Americans, in the years preceding 1900, as Mark Sullivan wrote, were afflicted by a "prevailing mood." "It was a mood of irritation. The average American in great numbers had the feeling that he was being 'put upon' by something he couldn't quite see or get his fingers on; that somebody was 'riding him.' . . . Vaguely he felt that his freedom of action, his opportunity to do as he pleased, was being frustrated in ways mysterious in their origin and operation, and in their effects most uncomfortable; that his economic freedom as well as his freedom of action, and his capacity to direct his political liberty toward results he desired, was being circumscribed in a tightening ring, the drawing strings of which . . . were being pulled by the hands of some invisible power which he ardently desired to see and get at, but could not. This unseen enemy he tried to personify. He called it the Invisible Government, the Money Interests, the Gold Bugs, Wall Street, the Trusts."[1] Deeply conscious of the sins of society, Americans dissented, and from the hard years following the Civil War to the end of the century their irritation echoed in a hundred-voiced protest, long, angry, and constant.

The American protest possessed a unified design. Historical practice has canonized the custom of dividing the dissent after the Civil War into particular categories: the greenback movement, the agrarian crusade, the labor movement, the war against political corruption, and the campaign against the trusts. But the agrarian movements, Greenbackism and Populism, were rural only in part; antimonopoly and the renovation of the civil service were only partly urban. Farmers knew that agricultural prices, railway rates, and mortgage notes had urban roots. If trusts seemed to be located in urban areas, their activities were not confined to the city. And urban reformers well knew that there was no difference between

---

[1] Mark Sullivan, *Our Times*. New York: Scribner, 1928, I, 137.

price fixing by railroad pools engaged in transporting wheat and price fixing by packing combines whose products fed the nation.

Discontent in American cities coincided with discontent on American farms; agricultural upheavals paralleled industrial upheavals in time as well as in social aims. Industrial workers organized in unions; agricultural workers in the Grange and the Farmers' Alliance. While unions resorted to the strike, farmers' organizations struck with the ballot in local and national politics. American laborers protested against the conditions that denied them a fair share of the profits of industry; American farmers protested against the system that denied them an adequate share of the profits of agriculture. Concentration of wealth was monopoly, whether of wheat, reapers, or railroads; whether of oil, steel, or jobs. The symbols of agrarian discontent were greenbacks, gold, and the corporation; the symbols of industrial discontent, the corporation, stocks, and bonds. Farmers and workers alike dissented from the constriction of opportunity and the narrowing scope of life. They rebelled against poverty and economic uncertainty, for concentration of economic power had corrupted democratic government and the unequal distribution of wealth had destroyed opportunity.

Reformers fought social injustices relentlessly. They failed, however, fully to reckon with the dynamics of industrialism and the sociology of urban change that made society interdependent. They upheld a moral code of venerable lineage, but they failed to recognize that by subdividing activity the machine and the city had depersonalized human relations and diffused responsibility.

THE PROTEST OF LABOR

The modern labor movement is in large part a case study in the history of the machine. Workers not only anticipated public awareness of the altered social relationships between men, but they also anticipated public realization of the menace of the corporate monster and uncontrolled wealth. Yet the efforts of labor to adjust itself to the machine were not crowned with spectacular success. Labor activity from 1865 to 1900, although continuous and often violent, reflected a constant indecision as to purposes and methods. Labor failed, for the most part, to re-evaluate its earlier philosophy; big business, on the other hand, had a philosophy adequate to its goals. Business was completely dependent upon labor, but it was business, not labor, that dictated the terms of economic life. And economic life in an age of monopolies and trusts had become synonymous with life itself. Labor organized—and for the first time on a wider national scale—but after forty years of agitation, of one group succeeding another, the masses of labor still remained outside union ranks. No effective political liaison was established between country workers and city workers; the principle of collective bargaining, the strike, the boycott, and better conditions of work and wages were either nullified by the courts or vitiated by a hostile public opinion.

Agricultural agitation was equally barren. Minor agricultural parties were proofs of social distress; they were also proofs of political failure. Blocked by major party ignorance or unconcern, agricultural dissidents attempted to work out their own political salvation. Without any real prospect of capturing power, they could only hope to batter down major party indifference, but only after protest votes mounted to such proportions that political managers were forced to take notice could they expect legislative attention. Even such small gains were tinged with frustration. The major parties did not reflect the popular will nor were they accountable to it. Local interests were paramount in legislative committees; pressure groups were the instruments of combines of capital, not of the common man. Reform measures were drafted and often enacted, but they were either emasculated before passage or subsequently by judicial review. If they escaped legal and congressional barriers, they frequently met with administrative laxity in performance.

The nationalization of industry, however, opened a new chapter in the history of organized labor, for workers learned that only national solidarity promised release from their difficulties. Instead of broadly diffusing the benefits of modern production, economic change often caused a deterioration in personal welfare. The machines challenged the importance of skills; the corporate device depersonalized industrial relations; and both deprived the most proficient workers of their livelihood and the fruits of their special competence, and deprived workers of the human concern that the interdependence of human beings had always evoked in any society worthy of the name. With the increase in living costs during the boom years of the Civil War and the consolidation of business, labor began slowly to learn that in union alone was there strength.

The National Labor Union appeared in 1866 as an effort to consolidate all existing labor groups. Although it reached a membership of 600,000, its platform indicated indecision rather than labor solidarity. General reform, cooperative shops, currency revision, and trade unionism were advocated, but arbitration rather than the strike was urged as the instrument of conflict. After six years of existence, the National Labor Union secured two important pieces of legislation—repeal of the Contract Labor Law of 1864 and an eight-hour day for workers on government projects.

Far more consequential was the Noble Order of the Knights of

Labor, established in 1869. Founded by Uriah S. Stevens, a garment cutter of Philadelphia, the Knights of Labor dominated the industrial scene until 1886, when the American Federation of Labor moved to the fore. Unlike their immediate predecessor, the National Labor Union, the Knights perceived the value of solidarity and made their appeal to the whole working world regardless of sex, color, or trade. With an insight into the general situation which few then possessed, their leaders argued that the machine had doomed the craft. All wage earners were in the same economic quandary, and only the unity of labor could successfully compete with the unity of capital. On the other hand, the Knights of Labor were violently opposed to political action and frowned upon the strike. Although arbitration and producers' cooperatives were preferred to the strike as solutions of economic ills, the preamble of the constitution declared:

The alarming development and aggressiveness of great capitalists and corporations, unless checked, will inevitably lead to the pauperization and hopeless degradation of the toiling masses. It is imperative, if we desire to enjoy the full blessings of life, that a check be placed upon unjust accumulation and the power for evil of aggregated wealth.

Grandiose was their purpose: "To secure for the workers the full enjoyment of the wealth they create; sufficient leisure in which to develop their intellectual, moral, and social faculties . . ." but this amalgam of radical goals and idealistic methods failed to accomplish much until after 1885, when even among the Knights the strike became a recognized procedure. Though the strike helped to swell the order's membership and increased its prestige with realistic adversaries, it was in large part the failure of strikes that hastened the Knights' decline.

Contributing to the demise of the Knights was a new labor group committed to different principles. The American Federation of Labor, which ruled the labor roost in this country almost until the present, represented the working elite rather than the working democracy. Instead of being based on the unity of labor, it was based on the unity of crafts and first emerged in 1881 fathered by a group of disaffected Knights. Many skilled workers affiliated with the Knights of Labor had never been wholly converted to the ideal of a united labor front, for it was the trained worker who felt the immediate effect of the employer's wrath. The unskilled, protected by anonymity, could move from hostile territory but the skilled worker often enrolled himself on the employer's black list. When the later unsuccessful strike activity of the Knights imperiled the security of the crafts, the skilled workmen began to desert the old organization for the new.

Under the leadership of Samuel Gompers, an immigrant of English-

Jewish background, the American Federation of Labor was reconstituted in 1886. It parted company with theorists and doctrinaires, abandoned the idealistic program of its precursors, and devoted itself solely to immediate objectives—objectives, as one of its leaders said, "that can be realized in a few years." Among these were the recognition of unions, the passage of favorable labor legislation, and the use of collective bargaining in industrial disputes. To achieve these purposes, the Federation abjured political methods and pinned its hopes to the strike and the boycott. Unlike the Knights, who carried a banner flecked with unorthodox red, the Federation went into industrial battle with the white flag of capitalism, for it was resolved to effect reform within the scope of the economic *status quo*. While recognized as the official spokesman of organized labor until 1936, the Federation was no more fully representative than were its forebears. Most workers still remained outside unionism and even large segments of the skilled, notably the four Railway Brotherhoods—the Engineers (organized in 1864), Conductors (1868), Firemen (1873), and Trainmen (1883)—refused to affiliate. The American Federation of Labor was a minority, but until the establishment of the Committee for Industrial Organization it spoke with an authoritative voice.

Men of industry and men of labor spoke of industrial peace, but there was no peace. Peace was an interlude between periods of warfare, for the relations of capital and labor from the seventies to 1900 were marked by strikes, by violence, by bloodshed, and by destruction. In the nineteen years from 1881 to 1900 the Bureau of Labor recorded 23,798 strikes that involved the lives of 6,610,000 workers, the property of 132,-442 plants, and the well-being of the entire nation. When labor forswore the ultimate end of reform for the end of immediate improvement —hours, wages, and conditions of work—the strike and the boycott were the inevitable results. And employers retorted as in the past with the weapons of organized business: the strikebreaker, the lockout, the black list, and the injunction.

Labor unrest was a part of the American pattern of dissent. Strikes were waged to obtain recognition of unions as bargaining agents, to raise wages, to lower hours, and to better working conditions. But these were simply surface grievances. Beneath the dissatisfaction with the job, there was a dissatisfaction with life. Americans who worked were in spiritual as well as in economic revolt. They wanted not only better wages and better hours: they wanted an opportunity to live as men. They wanted to put the slum behind them, to escape from the incubus of the company town, to free their children from the menace of the streets, or to deliver them from the bondage of the mill. They wanted shorter hours to sweeten and prolong their lives, and many wanted leisure to give wings to their imprisoned dreams. They rebelled against the feeling of constriction that came from their helplessness in the face of the monopoly of goods, of natural resources, of lands, and of jobs. They wanted their share, as their leaders constantly memorialized, in "the wealth they had helped to create." To employers, to directors of corporations, and to company managers, labor was a collective noun, an ingredient, together with others, that went to make up the triumph of American capitalism. It did not loom as large as executive genius or capital investment on the pages of the company books, in which there was nothing to read save long rows of impersonal figures.

While concentration of wealth was the emblem of material success, it was also the emblem of material failure. Financial domination by a small element meant not only control of fluid wealth, but control of the instruments of production. And if notes, bonds, dollars, and cents were simply another side of tools, factories, and patents, they had to be ripped from the steel and concrete moorings of impressive bank buildings and set in a foundation of human values. Otherwise it was easy to forget that tools were wielded by human hands, that factories were places in which battalions of men and women struggled for life, and that every patent growing out of the social experience of mankind was more than a blueprint to improve a process or initiate a new industrial way: it revised the conditions of life and work without any conscious planning to better those conditions for the generality of the toilers. The spearhead of protest was variously currency, tariff, or business in politics, but the nature of the protest was an attack upon the social and political implications of concentrated wealth united in corporate monopolies.

The campaign against monopoly began early. In 1879 Henry George leveled his single-tax thunder against the monopoly of land. Utopian writers held up monopoly to perfectionist scorn by delineating the beauty of societies from which it was absent. Nor did any fail to see the relations between the consolidation of business and freedom, opportunity, and liberty. The evidence of popular apprehension was later written into a famous decision by a Supreme Court Judge: "All who recall the condition of the country in 1890," remarked Justice John M. Harlan in the Standard Oil case of 1911, "will remember that there was everywhere among the people generally a deep feeling of unrest. The nation had been rid of human slavery . . . but the conviction was universal that the country was in danger from another kind of slavery . . . that would result from the aggregation of capital in the hands of a few . . . controlling, for their own advantage exclusively, the entire business of the country, including the production and sale of the necessities of life." And Henry

Demarest Lloyd in *Wealth against Commonwealth* (1894), a book that had a wide influence and a wide circulation, stated the matter even more pointedly:

A small number of men are obtaining the power to forbid any but them-selves to supply the people with fire in every form known to modern life and industry, from matches to locomotives and electricity. They control our hard coal and much of the soft, and stoves, furnaces, and steam and hot-water heaters: the governors on steam boilers and the boilers; gas and gas-fixtures; natural gas and gas-pipes; electric lighting and all the appurtenances. You cannot free yourself by changing from electricity to gas, or from the gas of the city to the gas of the fields. If you fly from kerosene to candles, you are still under the ban.

But monopoly was not the concern of labor or of agriculture alone. It was the concern of all Americans, and no inventory of goods, mapped by curves of production and distribution, made social sense if computed solely in digits of profit and loss. Food that flowed from factories in an endless stream of improvement and variety, neatly packed on ware-house shelves or coursing through the arteries of traffic in freight cars, river boats, and bulky wagons rumbling across urban streets, could not be clocked by business machines and then transferred to waving lines on business charts without violating the facts of life. Food was blood and bone, health and disease, poverty and plenty, labor and agriculture. The Beef Trust, for example, had its center in Chicago, but its heart was not in the money marts of the East. The grasp of the Beef Trust extended from the cattle range in the West to the kitchen range in the East.

These complaints were buttressed by others. Labor's earnings lagged far behind the cost of living. In 1866, 15,000 wage earners in New York City were receiving between $2.50 and $4.00 a week, and some ten years later the average compensation of workers on the New York Central Railroad System was $41.08 a month. From the decade of the eighties until well after 1900, unskilled labor was usually paid $10.00 a week; pay for skilled workers was roughly double. Wages for women were even lower, and even by 1900 the fight for equal pay for equal work had scarcely begun. And children of nine in New Jersey received $2.00 a week as late as 1886. The average yearly earnings of American industrial workers, skilled and unskilled, were about $600.00, inadequate to main-tain the body and utterly inadequate to sustain the spirit. And the test of the adequacy of wages was not the difference between American wages and European wages, but the relation of earnings of American labor to the earnings of American business. Crucial, of course, was the purchas-ing power of the American dollar, and $600.00 was at no time sufficient to ensure decent living. To this must be added unemployment not only in depressions, but even in boom years. The seasonal character of many industries made part-time rather than full employment the rule.

Hours were as high as wages were low. Ten hours or more comprised the customary working span in 1900, even though the eight-hour day without pay cuts had been a labor objective for four decades. Steel workers were riveted to a twelve-hour day; mill operators, trainmen, and sweatshop employees worked even longer. Such conditions make the strike seem the mildest kind of retort; even violence becomes less incomprehensible.

Although the strike was a commonplace during the thirty years after 1870, four were uncommonly spectacular: the railroad strike of 1877, the first serious explosion of labor dynamite in America; the incident at the McCormick Harvester plant in 1886, which climaxed in the Haymarket affair; the Homestead strike of 1892, which began in a bloody battle and ended in a labor rout; and the Pullman strike of 1894, in which the possibilities of the injunction as an antilabor weapon were unfolded.

The railway strike of 1877 was the result of a 10 per cent wage cut on the Pennsylvania System. When the Gould lines slashed wages, other roads, as anxious as the Pennsylvania to eliminate unions, followed suit. A number of strikes and riots in July at Baltimore, Chicago, St. Louis, and Pittsburgh brought out the militia of the several states, whose mission it was to break the strike and the union as well. Where the state militia failed, the governors applied to President Hayes to replace the local soldiery by federal troops. Pittsburgh was the scene of the greatest violence. The local national guard was in sympathy with the strikers, but when the Philadelphia militia arrived and killed twenty-five workers the mob besieged the soldiers for twelve hours. Except for loss of life and property, nothing was accomplished, for the men finally went back to work without having gained their point. But the strike marks an era in the history of American labor as well as in the history of American life. At the behest of capital, the state and national governments had intervened with coercive force to break strikes. If the public did not fully realize that a struggle "between the orders" existed in the United States, such was nevertheless the case.

A national strike in behalf of the eight-hour day took place in 1886. Almost at its very beginning on May 3, pickets at the McCormick Harvester works in Chicago became the targets of police guns, which, according to newspaper reports, killed six men and wounded many others. The Harvester incident, the climax of ten years of police terrorism against labor groups in Chicago, did not go unanswered, and the following day a protest mass meeting was held at Haymarket Square. Tempers ran high, but the crowd was orderly and peaceful. After the meeting was virtually over, a police squad appeared. Somebody threw a bomb, and eight policemen were killed, twenty-seven more injured. Americans everywhere were shocked, and since anarchists had been active in the Chicago region, they adopted the comfortable theory that foreign anarchistic agitators rather than native workmen were responsible. The frenzy of the local citizenry and the alarm of the nation were transferred to the court, whose decision condemned seven anarchists to death though none was found guilty of murder. One committed suicide, four were hanged, and two were given terms of life imprisonment. The latter were pardoned by Governor John P. Altgeld of Illinois in 1893, by which time it had become clear that anarchism and not seven hapless men had been on trial.

Six years after Haymarket a conflict broke out between the Amalgamated Association of Iron and Steel Workers and the Carnegie Steel operators at Homestead, Pennsylvania. The introduction of laborsaving devices that threatened a general wage cut and the refusal of the company to recognize the union were the main issues involved. Although Andrew Carnegie was far away in his Scottish retreat, he had given his blessing to Henry Clay Frick, the manager, to smash the union if he could. While negotiations were still in progress, Frick hired three hundred Pinkerton agents to protect the property of the corporation. As the Pinkertons—mercenary thugs who, with a fine carelessness for words, were called detectives—began to arrive, the strikers fired upon them. When the fire was returned, a battle ensued in which sixty were wounded and ten were killed. Eight thousand state militiamen, who made it possible for the plant to resume operations with "scab" workers, finally broke the strike that broke the Homestead union. Carnegie's success stimulated other steel companies to violate their agreements with the workers. Some of the Carnegie dollars, later poured into a fund for world peace, came from money saved in wages as a result of victory in industrial war.

Pennsylvania had its Pittsburgh and its Homestead, but Illinois had its Haymarket and its Pullman. Again it was wages that produced the rift between the Pullman Palace Car Company and its employees. When the company announced a severe reduction in 1894, the workers protested. Their case seemed particularly strong, as the salary reductions applied neither to officials nor to managers, and the corporation's huge surplus was common knowledge. George Pullman's arbitrary conduct in dismissing some of the protestants enlisted the support of the American Railway Union. Created by Eugene V. Debs, the union was reared upon his conviction that the only salvation for railroad workers lay in the industrial organization of all workers rather than in the organization of a few crafts. After pleas for arbitration failed to move Pullman, the 150,000 members of the American Railway Union were instructed to leave the Pullman

Palaces severely alone. While the union members scrupulously followed Debs' order to abstain from all acts of violence, irresponsible groups— criminals, gangs, some of them allegedly *agents provocateurs* hired by the company to furnish a good atrocity story—seized the opportunity to loot and to plunder. One such mob halted a mail train and damaged the engine. The General Managers' Association, on the part of the railways, appealed to the federal government for troops, although John P. Altgeld, governor of Illinois, consistently opposed the use of the army since no conditions beyond the control of the local authorities had arisen. But Grover Cleveland listened to the advice of his Attorney General, Richard Olney, a former railroad lawyer, who promptly instigated the procurement of a blanket injunction enjoining Debs and his fellows from interfering in the operation of the railways. Over Altgeld's opposition, on July 3, 1894, 2,000 federal soldiers entered Chicago. Olney maintained that it was a federal function to protect the mails—but, nevertheless, Pullman cars were attached to every mail train. Eugene V. Debs was jailed for violating the federal injunction as well as the Sherman Antitrust Act restraining him from normal strike activities. The injunction smashed the strike but made Eugene V. Debs. He used his jail term for reading and study, became an ardent Socialist, and as the leader of the Social Democratic party (which later became the Socialist party) founded in 1898, he infused it with life, strength, and high moral purpose.

Organized labor had won no significant battles and had still to win the war. The most serious encounters lay in the future, and the rights to organize, to bargain, and to strike were not genuinely recognized by 1900 or for three decades thereafter. The wages of labor were still a social scandal and the hours a public disgrace. Some years were to elapse before the condition of women and children in industry began to be alleviated, and in matters of social security legislation—unemployment insurance, workmen's compensation, and old-age pensions—the United States was considerably more than a step behind the advanced states of western Europe. A few forward-looking men of business and a small segment of public opinion had learned the lesson of industrial negotiation in the hard school of strikes, but the greater proportion of Americans remained to be educated. To them strikes were wanton, "un-American" interferences with the sacred rights of property. They had not yet begun to understand that labor was a commodity which perished during a strike, with calamitous effects upon wives and children and the serenity of the home. They had a long way to go if they were to understand that when hope died in a human heart society was the loser. They had been trained to regard the manipulations of business as legitimate and to think of labor as of raw materials, regulated by the "iron law" of supply and demand. And until the public learned, society would pay the piper—in rising prices, in the cost of philanthropy and relief, in the social regression implied by destruction. There was another bill for misunderstanding, a cumulative toll of bitterness, of suspicion, and distrust that bred violent cleavage in society instead of social coherence.

THE AGRARIAN CRUSADE

The dissent of labor was amplified by the protest of agriculture. While there was no political unity between rebels in town and country, the most astute spokesmen of both understood the unity of their woes. But in the new universe of political and economic discourse, the monopoly of economic combines and the misrepresentation of parties were the twined cords that tied factory worker and farm worker together.

Agricultural unrest was constant. Following the painful rhythm of debt and falling prices, one outburst succeeded another with insistent regularity. Like labor, agriculture organized, and like labor, agriculture experimented with political pressures to break the vicious round of depression, diminishing returns, and uncertainty. Railways served as the first target for the farmers' wrath, for without transportation facilities agricultural toil brought no economic reward. Grain elevators were coupled with railroads in this initial assault upon public utilities, for their charges, based upon what abject dependence would bear, shrank small profits even smaller. In the classic agricultural tradition, true of the agricultural West as of all rural economies, the farmers struck at the monopoly of finance manifested in credit stringency, farm mortgages, and debts for machinery, tools, and other necessities. Inflation of the currency was the agricultural expedient, first of paper greenbacks, then of silver as the equal of gold. To circumscribe the dominance of combinations that purveyed goods and services the farmer could not do without, agricultural groups also tried cooperative marketing and purchasing, but with small immediate gains.

The stages of the agrarian crusade are easily distinguishable. Founded in 1867, the Patrons of Husbandry, better known as the Grange, was the original movement after the Civil War and was followed in the middle seventies by Greenbackism. Greenback parties, though not the greenback principle, disintegrated by 1884 to make way for the Farmers' Alliance, a combination of many organizations that arose in various sections in response to the agricultural depression after 1880. Populism was the fruit of this merger, and the People's party, because of its astounding political performance in the election of 1892, gave political leaders and conservative businessmen a much-belated jolt. Four years later, in conjunction with

Bryan Democrats, protesting groups in America reached the peak of their strength in the contest of 1896, a landmark in the record of American politics. Their failure then, however, stilled reform until progressivism later sought to alleviate the frustrations of nineteenth-century dissent.

The Patrons of Husbandry, officially a society without political purpose, was not, however, without political results. Its ego-satisfying rituals and festive social occasions answered the craving for larger contacts that rural isolation made difficult, and its membership expanded to a million and a half by 1874. By the later seventies it had already dropped out of political sight, but not before it had placed the granger laws, regulating railway and warehouse rates, in the law codes of several western states. In collaboration with independent protest parties and the Democratic minority, especially in Illinois, Wisconsin, Iowa, and Minnesota, the farmers acquired executive offices, control of the legislatures, and momentary political power.

Enraged farmers were at first successful in combating the monopoly of transportation. Originally sought with a wistfulness almost pathetic, competing railways were welcomed as a protection against high freight rates, but the farmers bargained without the host of great consolidators. Corporate consolidation of the means of transport symbolized the grievances of the farmer in the same way that personification of the Wall Street bondholder later served as an outlet for his frustration in the continuing years of falling prices, high freight rates, and exorbitant interest charges. When irate farmers burned their corn instead of transporting it, rates were clearly beyond all reason. The financial difficulties of the railways in depressions were no excuse for stock watering and the manipulation of construction charges. In addition, the unfair and discriminatory practices in which the management indulged hardly improved public relations—at least with the humbled farmer. Two practices were especially galling: preferential rebates, giving large shippers enormous cuts in charges, and the long and short haul, making it cheaper to send goods over long distances than over short ones wherever the traffic would bear it. Politicians received free passes, important clients were accorded favored treatment, and the unsavory conduct of railroad lobbyists at state capitals raised the resentment of farmers to a discordant pitch.

Agricultural disquiet was constantly intensified by the alarming rate of consolidation. The history of the Vanderbilt line was typical. In 1865 Cornelius Vanderbilt, dubbed "the great Commodore" by an indulgent generation, forsook the waterways for the railways. First he gained control of a route from New York City to Albany, and by 1867, having come into possession of the New York Central, he connected his lines with Buffalo. By 1873 the Vanderbilt road had cleared to Chicago. Vanderbilt's feat was repeated by others—the Pennsylvania, the Baltimore and Ohio, the Erie—but the consolidation of short lines to make trunk lines was only the prelude to the consolidation of trunk lines into traffic pools, agreements, and other forms of managerial cooperation to control rates, profits, and traffic territory. Competition, instead of assuring a fair price, resulted in an exorbitant price; competition became "cutthroat," forcing combination for the sake of protection, with monopoly as the outcome. Figures succinctly tell the tale. Mile after mile of track was laid down from 1880 to 1900, but whereas there were fifteen hundred separate roads in the former year, there were only about eight hundred in the latter.

MONOPOLY, CURRENCY, TARIFF

The purport of the granger laws was crystal clear. "All chartered monopolies," resolved the farmers of Springfield, Illinois, "not regulated and controlled by law, have proved detrimental to the public prosperity, corrupting in their management, and dangerous to republican institutions." And they were just as convinced "that the railways of the world, except in those countries where they have been held under . . . strict regulation . . . have proved . . . arbitrary, extortionate and as opposed to free institutions and free commerce between states as were the feudal barons of the middle ages." Therefore, they resolved that "this despotism, which defies our laws, plunders our shippers, impoverishes our people, and corrupts our government, shall be subdued and made to subserve the public interest at whatever cost. . . ."

Railroad companies, however, refused to accept regulatory laws without a legal fight. They countered that regulation of rates was an unjust deprivation of property, and for the states to regulate rates transgressed the federal power to regulate commerce. But the Supreme Court in *Munn v. Illinois* (1876) held that regulation was a legitimate use of state power on the classic doctrine that "when private property is devoted to a public use, it is subject to public regulation." In *Peik v. Chicago and Northwestern Railway* (1876) the Court further declared that a state might act to fix the rate of a public carrier engaged in interstate operations if the federal government had not yet acted. These principles were reversed in the famous Wabash case (1886), which prohibited state interference with federal commerce, but the Court concluded, "regulation can only appropriately exist by general rules . . . which demand that it should be done by the Congress of the United States under the commerce clause. . . ." If granger laws achieved relief for farmers, it was of short duration. Federal remedies rather than local remedies were required, but here agricultural demands were frustrated by political institutions inadequate to the task.

Agrarian insistence combined with judicial directive in the Wabash case led to the passage of the Interstate Commerce Act on February 4, 1887. But a large part of congressional concern is explained by granger success in state elections, which a contemporary doggerel illumines:

> The railroads and the old party bosses
> Together did sweetly agree;
> And thought there would be little trouble
> In working a hayseed like me
>
>   . . . . . .
>
> But now I've roused up a little
> And their greed and corruption I see
>
>   . . . . .
>
> And the ticket we vote next November
> Will be made up of hayseeds like me.

The act responded specifically to the farmers' grievances, outlawing the most baneful abuses of the railroad monopoly: extortionate rates, discriminatory charges between large and small shippers, rebates to preferred clients, and pools of operators to control traffic charges. Among its more important provisions was the creation of the Interstate Commerce Commission, composed of five members. Although a notable precedent in behalf of federal regulation, the commission was not only weak and ineffective but signally failed to reach its goal. Without power to establish freight rates or to enforce its decrees, it was more a fact-finding body than an instrument of government. Railways usually dissented from the findings of the commission, whose only recourse thereafter was to bring suit in the federal courts, where the laissez-faire tradition of the judges operated in favor of the roads rather than the public. And the interstate commerce clause upon which the act was based naturally precluded control over intrastate railway lines. That the American railways remained a virtual monopoly long after the first attempt at regulation is suggested by the Populist avowal of 1892 "that the time has come when the railroad corporations will either own the people or the people must own the railroads. . . ."

Fixing of freight rates and elevator charges by state laws neither raised the price of crops nor relieved the agricultural debt burden. To achieve both, the Greenback party in 1876 advocated the expansion of the currency. Whatever the economics of federal banking policy, it was of greater advantage to industrialists, bankers, and creditors than to farmers, workers, and debtors. The National Banking Acts of 1863 and 1864 were designed to centralize the banking system and to eliminate the independent banks by which Jacksonians had tried to control the "money power." Under the pressure of war needs, several hundred million dollars of paper money, backed only by government credit, were issued. These "greenbacks" almost at once commenced a dizzy downward course, which induced the government to stop the printing presses, to retrieve as many of the bills in circulation as possible, and to stabilize the value of the notes remaining. But contraction of the currency, or deflation, aided the well to do, prejudiced the position of the marginal economic groups, and brewed a frenzy of excitement in rural America. A fluctuating currency invited speculation, especially as long as the greenbacks were by law acceptable as payment for government bonds. Until 1864, therefore, those with ready cash could buy notes at forty cents on the dollar with which they could buy bonds redeemable at par. The angry irritation expressed in the phrase "bloated bondholder" was no idle bombast. Union soldiers, farmers, and workers were paid in a medium that had a low and indeterminate purchasing power, while the government paid the interest and principal on its bonds, often bought with greenbacks, in gold. The contraction of the currency, moreover, contracted credit and made money high—just at the time when the farmer, after the collapse of prosperity in the seventies, and the worker, in the bleak years after the panic of 1873, needed it most. The currency problem sharpened class lines and intensified the bitterness of the agricultural and laboring groups, but though the currency was a consistent problem from the Civil War onward, no solution was achieved until the Wilson administration.

Resentment against the tariff burned just as fiercely as resentment against control of money, credit, and transportation. If the tariff was not itself a monopoly, it was a means of business consolidation and a weapon of business control. But while the tariff was something of a public issue from 1870 to 1897, it had ceased to divide the parties. The tariff inspired a loyalty greater than party loyalty among manufacturers. While it was no longer rational to speak of infant industries after the eighties, protectionism had become a part of the politician's faith and a powerful word with which to tyrannize unthinking sections of the electorate. The Populists, however, were not wholly inaccurate when they warned in 1892 that it was not forever possible to "drown the outcries of a plundered people with the uproar of a sham battle over the tariff."

The course of tariff legislation between 1862 and 1897 might easily be graphed in an upward swinging curve. The Morrill Act of 1862, while designed for war purposes, was too lucrative for certain industries to be abandoned lightly. In spite of the Liberal Republican movement of 1872, which waged an unsuccessful campaign against the tariff and corruption, faint-hearted gestures toward revision between 1867 and 1875 are memorable less for reduction than for increases in the textile and iron schedules. By 1881 the situation began to take a new turn as the accumulation of a treasury surplus inevitably linked the tariff with the mounting balance. Federal affluence, a temptation to reckless spending, quickly assumed the shape of a "pork barrel," a legislative vehicle in which only the public goes for a ride, as special interests traded votes for special bills. Republicans, consistently the majority among protectionists, were under the urge to spend lest the necessity of reducing the tariff in the face of a surplus made the need for revenue a hollow argument. Money in the Treasury, moreover, suggested that the people were burdened with needless taxes and that the flow of capital was clogged by stored-up funds, a relationship which agricultural spokesmen were quick to point out and aggrieved farmers quick to perceive.

A congressional committee in 1882, dominated by protectionists, recommended significant reductions. No sooner were their findings made public than the first well-established lobbies descended upon Washington. When the revised bill of 1883 emerged from committee, the special interests had won. President Cleveland, worried by the surplus, called public and legislative attention to the tariff in his annual message of 1887. Mincing few words, he explained that the tariff gave special benefits to a special class and raised the cost of living for all the people. He recommended immediate relief, not, however, without cautioning that "the existence of our manufacturing interests" was not to be impaired.

In the Harrison-Cleveland presidential campaign of 1888 the Republicans coupled the tariff with God and country, while the Democrats, far from advocating the "heresy" of free trade, urged mild reform; but big business made lavish contribution to the Republican fund as a sound insurance investment. Business and Republicans, long affianced to the tariff, became wedded to it after their precarious victory in the elections, and in 1890 the tariff soared to unprecedented heights. Although the act of 1890 was officially a collaboration between William McKinley of Ohio and Nelson Aldrich of Rhode Island, senators of the United States, the real authors were the National Association of Wool Manufacturers, the Louisiana sugar planters, and other groups anxious to protect their special economic preserves. Retail prices rose skyward following the McKinley tariff, which in part accounts for the Democratic victory at the polls in the congressional elections of 1890.

Again in 1892 Cleveland and Harrison competed for the presidency with the tariff in the forefront of campaign verbalism. But the striking workers at Homestead belied the Republican contention of the coincidence of a high tariff and high wages. Andrew Carnegie, then in his Scottish shooting box, knew with certainty that the tariff had fathered fortunes in steel, a knowledge that behooved him and his partners to speak less glibly of self-made men. There were other men, certainly as self-made, as thrifty and hard-working, upon whom the tariff had not bestowed fortunes. Farmers were beginning finally to see that while railroads, warehousemen, and bankers were real and visible, there was something about the less apparent tariff that affected their prices. Republican political strategists were commencing to have difficulty with angry rural voters who complained bitterly about the soaring cost of all they had to buy and the declining price of all they had to sell. And the public in general, as they heard more of the cloakroom activities in Congress, of the pressure boys who flocked to the Capitol to threaten, to cajole, and to bribe, began to wonder who sat in the seats of the representatives of the people. Were they the representatives of the trusts or of the American voters? And who governed the nation? Was it the trusts, through their lobbies, or was it the Congress of the United States?

But the tariff, jealously guarded by the manufacturers and congressional protectionists, never veered from its ascending course. Beginning as a sincere effort at revision, the Wilson-Gorman Act of 1894 was so mangled in joint committee that it emerged with no less than 634 changes, generally upward rather than downward. The year 1893 was a black year of depression, with thousands upon thousands out of work, and want, suffering, and hopelessness to be seen everywhere. Bands of unemployed, of which "General" Jacob S. Coxey's "army" is the best known, descended upon Washington seeking redress and relief. If the congressional answer was the Wilson-Gorman tariff, the future of the common man in America looked dark indeed. A memorable portion of the bill provided for a tax of 2 per cent on incomes over $4,000, but its judicial fate served only to increase popular displeasure, for the income tax was declared unconstitutional in 1895 *(Pollack v. Farmers' Loan and Trust Co.)*. And as apprehension mounted, so did the tariff. Even after the great campaign of 1896, when class lines were drawn as tightly as ever before in American history, Congress saw fit to enact the Dingley tariff (1897), the apex of protection up to that point. But there were peaks yet to be scaled.

The dangers of consolidation were not lost upon the American people. Powerful as were the analyses of George, Bellamy, and Lloyd, the public had more direct contact with business associations, trusts, and pools than the flaming words of social critics. To the farmers, bills of lading, mortgage notes, and promises to pay for reapers, harvesters, and binders were the economic thorns that pricked the flesh of life rather than the sharp points of the single tax, just as pay envelopes, layoffs, and strikes were more potent in prodding the minds of urban workers than the merciless logic set forth by Lloyd in the pages of *Wealth against Commonwealth*. Few were ignorant of the ruthlessness of business buccaneers whose only idols were power and gold. None but knew of John D. Rockefeller and his depredations in oil, and the story of oil was the story of meat, steel, tin, and sugar.

But if the social perils—the engrossment in private hands of the resources of the nation, the barter and sale of public office and public trust, the desecration of American ideals—were not always immediately apparent, various groups charged themselves with the responsibility of fostering awareness. Thus, in 1874, the National Grange of the Patrons of Husbandry wrote into its declaratory principles: "We are opposed to . . . any corporation or enterprise as tends to oppress the people and rob them of their just profits. We are not enemies to capital, but we oppose the tyranny of monopolies." The action of farmers spoke more loudly than their words. Labor parties consistently avowed themselves the enemies of "trustification," and in 1884 the Anti-Monopoly party appeared on the political stage, if only for a brief and unspectacular performance. If urban workers and rural workers failed politically to unite in what was obviously a common cause, they were on this vital subject united in thought. Finally in 1887, President Cleveland in his famous tariff message confessed that "the people can hardly hope for any consideration in the operation of these selfish schemes."

Goaded by local pressures, the several states, with the exception only of the three most notorious corporation chartermongers—New Jersey Delaware, and West Virginia—passed antitrust laws. And the same influences forced the major parties to bow to the gale of reform. In the campaign of 1888, Democrats and Republicans alike wrote reformist words into their respective platforms; in 1890 Congress passed the Sherman Antitrust Act. Twelve years thereafter, a distinguished theologian, Walter Rauschenbusch, was still able truthfully to write:

We have allowed private persons to put their thumb where they can constrict the life blood of the nation at will. The common people have financed the industry of the country with their savings, but the control of industry has passed out of their hands. . . . The profits of our common work are absorbed by a limited group; the mass of the people are permanently reduced to wage-earning positions. The cost of living has been raised by unseen hands until several million of our nation are unable to earn even the bare minimum. . . .[2]

The Sherman Antitrust Act had the enthusiastic support of the nation. Only one member of Congress cast his vote in opposition, and the

---

[2] Walter Rauschenbusch, *Christianizing the Social Order*. New York: Macmillan, 1912. By permission of The Macmillan Company, publishers.

lawmakers required but a day for discussion; it was the culmination of a popular fear, and bespoke on the part of the people a wistful faith in the power of government as then constituted to preserve democratic institutions. "Every contract, combination in the form of trust or otherwise, or conspiracy, in restraint of trade or commerce among the several states," read the first section of the act, "is hereby declared to be illegal. . . ." Whether its purpose, as Republican Senator Orville H. Platt of Connecticut averred, was less to curb the trusts than to curb discontent, its avowed purpose was certainly not realized. More trusts were organized from 1890 to 1900 than in the three decades before, and the 157 combinations of the first period were capped in 1901 by the formation of the United States Steel Corporation, the first billion dollar trust.

Whatever the intent, Congress had passed an inadequate law and little attempt was made to rectify it. Up to the time of the billion dollar corporate debut of steel, but eighteen suits to break up corporate aggregates were instituted, few of moment. When the sugar trust succeeded in gaining control of 95 per cent of all the sugar refining in the country, the Supreme Court declared that the simple purchase of stock (by which control was established) was not an act of interstate commerce and hence did not come within the purview of the law *(United States v. E. C. Knight Co.* [1895]). Although the phraseology of the act was simple, to the people the ways of the Court were past finding out. Ineffective for the protection of the public against the trust, the Sherman Act was highly effective in blocking the labor movement, for which the words "or otherwise" supplied the judicial warrant. Used in breaking the Pullman strike of 1894, it was subsequently employed to kill a union boycott which, crossing state lines, was interpreted as a conspiracy in restraint of trade.

Perversion of the Sherman Act and dissatisfaction with the McKinley tariff heightened the animosity of those who felt themselves oppressed. Farmers rose in revolt in the nineties and gained an astounding success at the polls, while in the election of 1892, James B. Weaver, presidential candidate of the People's party, received over a million dissident votes. Old-line politicos were quick to note that for the first time since the Civil War a minor party had captured an electoral vote—in this case twenty-two. They likewise noted the implacable bitterness in the charge of an indignant Kansas woman: "Wall Street owns the country. It is no longer a government of the people, by the people, for the people, but a government of Wall Street, by Wall Street, and for Wall Street. Our laws are the output of a system that clothes rascals in robes and honesty in rags." And the Populist platform, stretching out the farmer's hand to the city toiler, referred to Pinkerton agents as "a large standing army of mercenaries," "the hired assassins of plutocracy, assisted by Federal officers."

The Democrats were successful, Glover Cleveland was inaugurated for a second term in 1892, but the *Review of Reviews* commented:

The Republican party was condemned because the voters believed that its policies had come to be too favorable towards the concentration of wealth. It was felt to be growing plutocratic. . . . There are plenty of millionaire Democrats . . . but . . . this campaign involved to some extent a movement of the poor against the rich, and the Republican party was more generally thought to stand for the rich.

1896

If the election of 1892 was a revolt, the election of 1896 was a crusade. Uniting with Populists, the Democrats waged the most spectacular political battle since 1860. But although the currency was their weapon, it was not their cause. More than the free and unlimited coinage of silver was at issue; the fundamental issue was the free and unlimited development of man. Three decades of broken political hopes, three decades of frustrated reform, and three decades of disillusionment smashed the barriers of restraint. The cry of the silverites echoed the cry of the Greenbackers, the plea of farmers to their government to supply a currency to serve their needs. Barbed shafts aimed at monopoly and the concentration of wealth came from the same quiver from which the Grange, the Anti-Monopolists, and labor had earlier released arrows of outraged justice against railroads, banks, and corporate pyramids. The campaign of 1896 was not an academic forum in the economics of bimetallism; it was a campaign for social justice. Not since Abraham Lincoln had personalized the aspirations of Americans had the common man possessed such a cause and such a leader. William Jennings Bryan appeared as the tribune of the people. His opponent, William McKinley, wore the senatorial toga, and behind him stood the entrenched wealth of America. Bryan, to the cheering millions who supported him, was the Great Commoner, and McKinley the tool of the Gold Bugs and the Trusts.

The avalanche of popular dissent was swelled by the grievances of the immediate present as well as by those of the recent past. Hardly had the Populists been defeated in 1892 when the furies of depression were unleashed once again. The panic of 1873 was trivial compared to the devastation of 1893. And in every business crisis the same pattern of horror was repeated. Economists are wont to speak of financial crashes in economic metaphors—bank failures, insolvencies, receiverships, and credit stringency. But depressions are real. They mean bread lines and hunger, fear and death. Let severely alone by Cleveland, conditions grew steadily worse; 1894 was a year to curse with, and recovery was not in sight until three years later. Nor is 1894 memorable for the depths of depression alone; 1894 was the year of Pullman, of the "armies" of unemployed. And it was followed by the year of the Knight case and what appeared to be the nadir of the Sherman Act; the year of the income tax case, which plotted a new low in popular esteem for the Supreme Court. These were the items on the roster of public wrath, and 6,467,946 Americans who voted for Bryan voted their resentment. Silver was a shining symbol —and so was gold.

The violence of the campaign remained a legend until recent times, when contemporary bitterness exceeded it. In a famous speech that helped to win him the Democratic nomination, Bryan cut the issues sharply. "I come to speak to you," he said deliberately, "in defense of a cause as holy as the cause of liberty—the cause of humanity." Gold was the chief enemy, but the platform also attacked banks and credit, the tariff, and the failure to equalize the distribution of wealth through an income tax. The real fight, however, was fought between the masses and the classes. "Upon which side," asked the "Boy Orator of the Platte," "will the Democratic party fight; upon the side of the 'idle holders of idle capital' or upon the side of the 'struggling masses'?" And in a grand peroration that has become a part of American folklore, Bryan answered:

Having behind us the producing masses of the nation and the world . . . we will answer their demand for a gold standard by saying to them: you shall not press down upon the brow of labor this crown of thorns; you shall not crucify mankind upon a cross of gold.

But the cross of gold signified much more than bars of metal bolstering government obligations. It meant what it has meant in all times and places even before the glamorous Jezebel inspired the wise men of Judah to pious wrath: wealth, privilege, and evil. Bryan referred to the sins of society and his impassioned followers were determined to bring the sinners to justice.

To Republicans, Bryan was the incarnation of Satan. The platform was not only "anarchistic" but "seditious," while one eastern clergyman assured his parishioners that it had been "made in Hell." Mark Hanna, mentor of McKinley and guiding genius of the Republican party, wheedled millions from corporations to forestall the Bryan threat. Workers were intimidated by being told that they would lose their jobs or be paid in inflated currency should McKinley be defeated, and businessmen entered into commercial agreements that depended for their operation on Republican success. So effective was Republican propaganda that the Democratic party bore the stigma of "unsound money" for fourteen years. From 1896 to 1910, Democratic political virility was sapped by an identification with free silver. The white-collar and professional groups were converted to the Hanna gospel; if other countries had abandoned silver, the United States could not alone uphold bimetallism in a gold-standard commercial world. Even labor, frightened by dire prophecies of economic ruin, deserted the Democratic standard for the promise of Republican security. When the votes were counted McKinley had won, but Bryan had not lost; he polled almost a million votes more than Cleveland in his successful campaign four years earlier. Bryan called the campaign the "first battle," but it was neither the first nor the last. Before William Jennings Bryan came Thomas Jefferson, Andrew Jackson, and Abraham Lincoln; after Bryan, Woodrow Wilson and Franklin Delano Roosevelt.

Bryan's defeat was not only the defeat of agriculture but the defeat of the people; McKinley's victory was the victory of big business. No disquisition on laissez faire could bare its meaning more brazenly than Republican action. The very year after the campaign came the Dingley tariff, and, under the bland McKinley sun, more combinations were spawned than ever before. To let things alone in the interdependent, impersonal, rapidly changing society of the machine and the city was a certain guarantee of human disorder and social disaster. Laissez faire, however, continued to frustrate reform. Although in some spheres—education, public health, penology, and in such governmental activity as the Interstate Commerce Act and the Sherman Act—it seemed to be crumbling, it still stood up stoutly in the American courts, where it served for many years as a barrier to social change.

Yet the social theory of dissent was almost universally conservative. Reformers looked backward rather than forward, were optimistic rather than pessimistic, conservative rather than radical. For the reformist spirit, rooted in native soil, spurred by the ideals of the Declaration of Independence, spoke in language neither new nor alien—the dignity of man and his inalienable right to economic opportunity as the basis of the continuing pursuit of happiness. Democracy was the universal dogma, degraded but not destroyed. Government was to be cleansed, retrieved from those who used it for selfish purposes, and returned to the sovereign people. While the writings of Karl Marx and Friedrich Engels were known, American proponents of socialism made little headway until the twentieth century. Reformers sounded dangerously radical to alarmed conservatives, but actually their economic assumptions were not divergent. "Wealth belongs to him who creates it," insisted the Populists, who were viewed with the same horror by conservative businessmen as their spiritual descendants regarded later left-wing critics, "and every dollar taken from industry without an equivalent is robbery." The reformers rested their case on the uneven distribution of wealth, which deprived large portions of the population of its benefits. Social critics believed modern changes had interfered with the operation of natural laws. If, for example, better administrative practices were devised for the civil service, better government would follow. If corporate and concentrated wealth were regulated by law, competition would restore freedom for enterprise and social justice for freedom. If the total amount of money in circulation were increased by greenbacks or silver, a more democratic distribution of income and opportunity would result for the laboring and agricultural classes.

Rural reformers were even less radical than those who hailed from the city. Behind the acrid controversy between rural and urban areas respecting money, credit, and monopoly was a social, psychological, and emotional conflict. There was not only a discrepancy in wealth, a difference in social advantage, but a disparity in moral values. The country remained the citadel of conservatism. When the agricultural regions espoused what was considered a radical political cause, it was a radicalism that advocated a return to primitive virtues which urban industrial experience had corrupted. If they attacked the "money power," it was because the intricacies of finance prevented the operation of "natural" economic laws. If they attacked corporate structures, it was because monopolies interfered with the "normal" flow of trade and discounted "free individual enterprise." And if they castigated a corrupt and inefficient government, it was because they wished the government "returned to the people" through direct democratic forms.

The record of reform between 1865 and 1900 was one of achievement and futility. That the reformers failed to root out social evil is not as important as that they tried; that they were unable permanently to secure social justice was not nearly so important as their crusade against social injustice. American reformers were faithful to the great American tradition: rebellion against oppression, refusal to surrender to obstacles blocking the path of human achievement. Being mortals, the reformers failed to capture perfection, but being uncompromising democrats, they contributed to human betterment. Public-spirited efforts and organized philanthropy alone, however, were powerless to right the wrongs of the new social order. To resolve the paradox of wholesale poverty in the midst of immeasurable plenty, political theory and the federal structure of government required revision. The revolutions in economics, which produced both plenty and poverty, propelled the country toward an institutional crisis. But if the changing world of the machine and the city presented Americans with internal crises, the shrinking world was to present Americans and all mankind with a series of global crises no less trying to the body of man than to his spirit.

XXII

THE SHRINKING WORLD 1865–1900

While the integrating impulse of economic forces united America between 1865 and 1900, they likewise united the world. To the aged concept of the unity of mankind, a speculation now grounded in biology by Darwinian evolution, the revolutions in economics gave a new structure: a structure of steel, of steam, of interdependent economic parts, of commercial exchange, of dissemination of ideas. Interdependence made the well-being of every community implicit in the well-being of its neighbor. What the iron ore of Michigan was to the steel of Pittsburgh and the steel of Pittsburgh to the girders of New York buildings, the wheat fields of Minnesota and the corn of Nebraska were to the industrial markets of Europe. Every acre of farmland planted in America, every processed article that emerged from German factories or English forges, reduced in each nation the feasibility of economic independence. Man's collective genius and effort created a bridge of interdependence. And just as domestic social relations responded to the contraction of the national community, external social relations responded to the shrinking of the global world.

END OF GEOGRAPHICAL ISOLATION

From time to time, man celebrated the shrinkage, without, however, realizing what shrinkage entailed. On the tenth of May, 1869, the streets of Philadelphia resounded to the peal of the Liberty Bell in old Independence Hall, New York's Trinity Church bells chimed in response, and Americans in the heart of the West watched a triumphant parade in Chicago. It was a date to celebrate, for five miles west of the town of Ogden, in far-off Utah, the rails of the Union Pacific joined the rails of the Central Pacific. The East had met the West, and the states of the American Union were finally united. The Atlantic and the Pacific oceans were thus for the first time brought together by the power of steam, and another event united three of the remaining seven seas. In November of the same year the Suez Canal was completed and opened to traffic. Again East met West, and the Indian Ocean, the Red Sea, and the Medi-

terranean merged with the broad Atlantic to form a new link in the highways of the world.

    Even as then measured, the distance between the American West and
the northern shore of Africa was great, but the first American transcontinental railroad and the canal at Suez were not unrelated. The canal
and the railroad were milestones in the march of humanity. Each represented the culmination of a long evolutionary series of mechanical in-

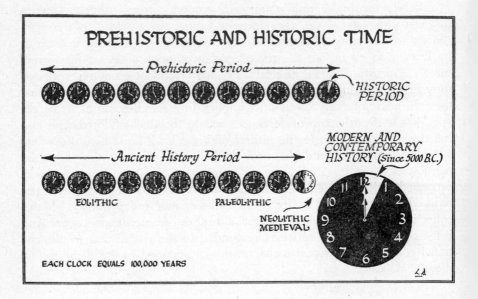

PREHISTORIC AND HISTORIC TIME

← Prehistoric Period →

HISTORIC PERIOD

MODERN AND CONTEMPORARY HISTORY (Since 5000 B.C.)

← Ancient History Period →

EOLITHIC   PALEOLITHIC

NEOLITHIC MEDIEVAL

EACH CLOCK EQUALS 100,000 YEARS

vention just as each was a forecast of triumphs yet to come. The sacred
Liberty Bell in Pennsylvania's most famous city rang to honor the men
who put the final steel touch on locomotive power, but it also honored the
half-forgotten Egyptians who discovered the wheel and the Chaldean
seers who laid the foundations of mathematics. Owners of proud ships
that steamed through the hundred-mile ditch at Suez were as much in
debt to ancient mariners, who made the Mediterranean their own long
before the glory of Crete gave way to the glory of Greece, as they were
indebted to James Watt and his forerunners who translated the mysteries
of steam into the commonplaces of daily use. With few periods of exception, the world has been in the process of contraction since earliest
times; but the contracting world was the consequence of the perfection
of human artifacts, the tools and inventions of man. And these, as in
the past, rested upon the common store of human experience and human
knowledge.

    The wedding of the rails and the wedding of the seas linked the common store of knowledge as well as continents. Since the dawn of modern times, search for a route to the riches of the Indies had fired the imagination of Europeans and encouraged them to tempt fate in the effort to find it. Once having crossed the Atlantic, they did not give up hope of a northwest passage to the eastern lands ruled by the descendants of the Grand Khan. But the path to the Orient, whether ships sailed westward across the ocean or followed the western course of internal rivers, was blocked by the American hemisphere until trancontinental railroads gave the United States windows on the Pacific. And the prayers of Prince Henry of Portugal and the bold Vasco da Gama were answered by the Suez. No longer forced to plow through troubled Atlantic waters around the great bulge of Africa to the Cape of Good Hope, ships could now reach the Indian Ocean by traveling from Gibraltar to Suez and from Suez to the East. Articles of trade and commerce which thereafter sped on wings of steam from Occident to Orient, from America to Europe and to Asia, not only swelled the money bags of merchant princes, but swelled the streams of culture which, with natural resources and fabricated goods, were diffused throughout the world.

At the close of the Civil War the American people, weary of conflict, turned their energies inward. Dedicating their strength to building the West and to creating an industrial empire, they planted virgin fields with wheat and virgin cities with the seeds of life. To many, America was not only the new world but the world itself. The Far East was far away indeed. Pigtailed Chinese were familiar on the Pacific coast as were the saturnine Japanese, but to most Americans the legendary lands of the Orient were farther away than Zipangu and Cathay had once been to Richard Hakluyt. Except in periods of crisis, Europe, though closer in time, hardly ruffled the minds of most Americans. More consciously aware of Europe than in the earlier stages of their national career, Americans were nevertheless absorbed by their own tremendous tasks. In addition to a preoccupation with internal affairs, the myth of historical isolation erected a powerful emotional barrier between America and Europe.

Nevertheless, American life was touched by European influences in a hundred different ways, just as European life was deeply affected by American experience. But the ruling force of intercontinental contact was the shrinking world. The physical factors that contracted time and space in America simultaneously contracted time and space everywhere. Railroads were not built in America alone. Great Britain continuously expanded her railway net, and in a single generation after 1875 Germany more than doubled her trackage. The 16,000 miles of internal rail communication in Russia in 1885 grew to more than 40,000 twenty years later, while French mileage expanded to over 31,000 during a like period. Not only were Paris and Lyons brought closer together, but St. Petersburg was nearer to Berlin, Hamburg, and Bremen. All lines converged at the great seaports, the outermost edge of national boundaries, where the lanes of import and export traffic met.

Keeping pace with international developments in the sphere of internal transport, improvements in ocean travel were universal and everywhere manifested the same characteristics: speed, the use of motive power, and a growing interdependence. Winds from the heavens propelled the great merchant fleets of the commercial powers in the seventies as they had formerly driven the miniature fleet of Christopher Columbus, but in the next decade the power of wind was replaced by the power of steam. Limitations of the marine engine retarded the change, but newer improvements gave steam a dominance over the ocean that it already exercised on land. The compound engine lowered the consumption of coal by half, and a new condenser made water in the boilers last for two months. The additional cargo space acquired by freeing some of the room formerly reserved for coal and water decreased the cost of operation as well as increased the possibilities of freight profits. Quickly following these innovations in the eighties was the substitution of lighter steel hulls for the older iron ones. Cheaper and safer, they displaced less water, again adding to available space.

Despite progress in transportation by rail and by sea, methods of communication were no better or swifter than the means of transport. Messages still had to be carried by ship, horse, or train. Although the telegraph, perfected in 1832 by Samuel F. B. Morse, had connected the principal cities of the East and the Midwest by 1847, it was not until 1861 that San Francisco was reached by wire. At that date, eight years before the first transcontinental railroad, 50,000 miles of telegraph line in operation had succeeded the pony express and spanned the continent. Supplementing the telegraph was the post office, which grew correspondingly. Free delivery was established in large cities by 1863, and in 1883 the ease of transport made it possible to lower the postal rates appreciably. As the expansion of the postal system served the common man, the Atlantic cable served the needs of expanding commerce. Business enterprise, as heedless of national boundaries as inventors were undeterred by physical distance, sought quicker means of contact with wide-flung markets and channels of trade. After many unsuccessful attempts, Cyrus W. Field and Peter F. Cooper, aided by British capital, laid a permanent submarine cable on the Atlantic floor. Four years later, in 1866, there were two more, and the ocean bed came to be crisscrossed with the wires of world communication as land areas were crisscrossed with the wires of the telephone.

The telephone did for local American communication what the cable did for world society. Although ultimately it was to affect Europe and Asia, it remained up to 1900 essentially a native device. Alexander Graham Bell, a Scottish immigrant interested in education for the deaf, used his knowledge of the physiology of the human ear to invent the telephone in 1876. A sensation at the Philadelphia Centennial Exposition, its imperfections were speedily corrected, so that between 1880 and 1890 the number of commercial subscribers increased from 50,000 to 1,700,000. During the nineties it was possible to talk with Chicago and Milwaukee from Boston or New York, but even when the century turned there were twice as many telephones in the United States as in all Europe.

Perfection of transportation and communication devices stimulated the spread of information. Steam was already applied to drive American newspaper presses, but new inventions to mechanize typesetting were required to equate the speed of printing with news gathering and dissemination. As late as the eighties, printers were still setting up type as Benjamin Franklin had done for *The Pennsylvania Gazette.* Ottmar Mergenthaler, a German immigrant working in a Baltimore machine shop, invented a typesetting machine that bore some resemblance to the typewriter. Christened "Linotype" by Whitelaw Reid of the New York *Tribune,* it was first operated in the *Tribune* building in 1886. The tedious, painstaking work of the compositor was at an end, and the speed of printing introduced a new era in the field of journalism.

If the spirit of man failed to keep pace with the rapidity of social change, the spirit of the world moved in a new social orbit. Continents were to shrink to islands; oceans, to lanes of traffic. Internal transportation routes contracted land masses as external transportation routes contracted the surface of the seas. Cities separated by rivers, mountains, and national frontiers were brought into closer contact by ships, steam, and steel. Town merged into countryside, hinterlands became geographical areas between commercial entrepôts, and nations merged with the world. Provincialisms—local, sectional, national—began to lose their primordial security. While they still remained, forces other than physical anchored them to the past. Escape from the world became increasingly difficult, for, if avenues still existed, they were charted on the map of the human mind alone.

DIPLOMACY: 1861–1867

Even in the field of diplomacy where the dogma of isolationism had its longest day, the United States was far from free of European entanglement. Americans could not fight a private civil war without regard to their European neighbors. The North, no less anxious to prevent Confederate successes in foreign chancelleries than the South was anxious to attain them, was powerless to check the favor that the southern cause found in the heart of the Emperor of the French or the enthusiasm with which northern reverses were acclaimed by the ruling British classes. Southerners in Richmond believed the lack of raw cotton in English mills would bring John Bull to the support of Jefferson Davis; Northerners in Washington hoped that the lack of wheat would enlist British aid behind Abraham Lincoln.

The conduct of England and France during these perilous years of combat threatened the preservation of the Union, but the designs of France and Spain threatened its future. Spain ignored the Monroe Doctrine; France challenged it. The Dominican Republic, torn by revolution in 1861, petitioned for readmission into the Spanish empire. Protests of William H. Seward, American Secretary of State, availed nothing, for warm Spanish hearts in Madrid responded to the solicitations of longing Latin hearts in the New World. But the ministers of royal Spain had learned nothing from the experience of two hundred years, and restrictive colonial measures brought about another Dominican revolt. Coercive economic policies together with yellow fever made even the native advocates of a return to Spain somewhat dubious of the wisdom of their course. When, in 1865, victorious Union armies ready to fight were added to the ravages of disease and Dominican discontent, the Spanish themselves withdrew.

While the Spanish defied the American eagle, the French attempted to clip its wings. The Spanish sought to annex former territory; the French sought to curb the growth of the American republic and to establish monarchy in the Western Hemisphere. Since the treaty of Guadalupe Hidalgo (1848), Mexican conditions, rendered unstable by periodic revolutions, had resulted in loss of life and property to American and other nationals. Reaching a formidable crisis in 1861, a bankrupt Mexican government declared a two-year moratorium on foreign debts, a move that alarmed investors in Britain, France, and Spain. By the convention of London, the powers determined upon joint military steps to collect the debts. In December, the Spanish and British withdrew from the proposal, leaving the field clear for Louis Napoleon, who inherited the imperial ambitions as well as the name of the first Bonaparte.

The precise designs of the French emperor remain unknown, but the broad outlines were discernible. If the French supported a claim generally regarded as illegitimate, no better time for Napoleon's schemes could have been chosen. Holding power insecurely, Napoleon could not

Wall Street symbolized the apex of financial achievement for many Americans. *(Ewing Galloway)* Scientific progress was attained in modern medicine, as symbolized by Eakins' painting, "Dr. Agnew's Clinic." *(Courtesy University of Pennsylvania School of Medicine)* Money made in trade supported medical research, but those who needed help often could not afford it.

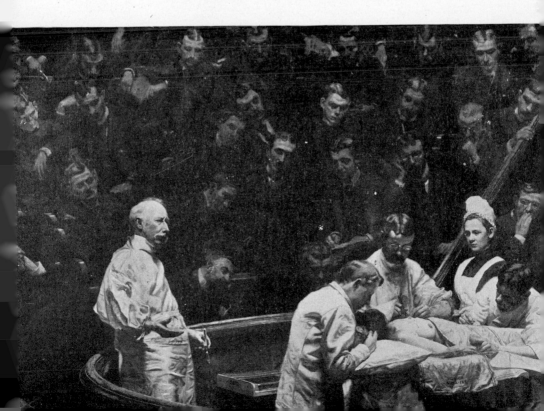

World trends in scholarship were reflected in American learning. *Upper left*—William James was an exponent of the pragmatic technique and one of the founders of modern psychology; *right*—John Fiske expounded Herbert Spencer's philosophy to eager Americans; *lower left*—Louis Agassiz, world-famous naturalist, was one of Darwin's leading adversaries; while, *right*—Asa Gray, a renowned botanist, became an early convert to Darwinian ideas. *(Culver Service)*

Creative artists were deeply concerned with man and society. *Upper left*—Walt Whitman, poet of democracy; *right*—Henry James, master of prose and master of psychology; *lower left*—Mark Twain, a philosophical pessimist who became famous as a humorist; and, *right*—William Dean Howells, exponent of literary realism. *(Culver Service)*

THE WHITTLER FOR THE WORLD.

have been blind to the need for popular support, which the restoration of colonial power might secure. Nor could he have been unaware of the advantages which would accrue to French industry if freed from dependence upon southern cotton or the dramatic role he could play with French Catholics if he came to the aid of the Mexican devout, long badgered by republican anticlericals. Not the least important of his objectives was the dream of a Catholic, Latin bloc in the Western Hemisphere as a barrier to the "Anglo-Saxon," Protestant republic of the north.

The Civil War provided a golden hour of opportunity, for a severed Union alone rendered these hopes possible. Hence Napoleon's sympathy for the South and his apparent willingness to recognize the Confederacy in return for a promise of hands off in Mexico. The convergence of events, outside the control of the United States, brought about an invasion of Mexico. The same events made an unhappy Austrian archduke a Mexican emperor who, despite the aid of French regulars, sat insecurely upon his throne and who, without them, was unable to retain either his crown or his head.

In the spring of 1867 Napoleon took French leave, consigning Mexico to a republican fate and the Austrian Maximilian to an inglorious death. Many factors induced the last Bonaparte to abandon his Mexican project. French public opinion was hostile, and the drain on the exchequer did nothing to heighten its enthusiasm. Persistent guerilla warfare of republican bands under the indefatigable leadership of President Benito Juárez, combined with the ominous state of Franco-Prussian relations, cooled the ardor of Napoleon and his subjects alike. But not the least of the factors that permitted the United States to escape unscathed was the masterly diplomacy of Secretary William H. Seward. Cautious while the Civil War was not yet won, he steadfastly refused to recognize French intervention or to acknowledge Maximilian. As victory turned in favor of the North, Seward's tone grew bolder. Without mentioning the Monroe Doctrine, always unpopular in Europe, he took advantage of every twist in the complex situation. Finally, he made it possible for Napoleon to withdraw, saving enough of his face for Bismarck to crush a few years later.

The intrusion of the French in the affairs of Mexico suggested that America was not foreign to the interests of Europe; but neither was Europe foreign to the interests of the United States. The Civil War momentarily abated the American expansionist impulse, but even during the war itself the course of American empire continued to move beyond the nation's frontiers. Long before the territorial limits of the United States were reached, Americans sought and found new worlds to conquer that inevitably linked their destiny with that of other peoples. Under the guidance of Secretary Seward, who took to heart the lessons learned from Confederate blockade-runners, the United States sought a naval and coaling station in the Caribbean. Failing to convince Congress of the wisdom of purchasing a naval station from the Dominican Republic in 1869, Seward tried to buy the Virgin Islands from Denmark, but the treaty, ratified by the Danes, met a quiet death in the Senate.

Seward was more successful in the Arctic than in the tropics. Where he failed to further expansion in Hawaii, Cuba, Puerto Rico, and the West Indies, he won his point with reference to Alaska. To the Russians, Alaska had not only become a "sucked orange," but something of an international lemon as well. With the Russian American Company—a colonial trading enterprise—on the brink of insolvency in the sixties, the ministers of the Russian czar were loath to continue that decrepit venture. But there were other considerations. Fearful of the British sea arm, the Russians were fully aware that in case of hostilities with England, ever their enemy, they could not hold their Arctic possession. To sell to America would accomplish a dual purpose: it would rid them of a liability and checkmate their adversary, for to that extent British ambitions in the Pacific would be thwarted. Careful planners in diplomacy, the Russians could not discount the possibility that Alaska might eventually cause difficulty with the United States. They were sufficiently acquainted with the American past to know that American manifest destiny meant the absorption of contiguous territory. To sell was the better part of strategy as it was the best part of economics. When news of the Russian disposition blew across the diplomatic winds, Seward did not hesitate to broach the subject to the Russian ambassador. On March 13, 1867, the fate of Alaska was sealed for the sum of slightly more than seven million dollars. If this was "Seward's Folly," as most contemporaries ignorant of Alaska seemed to agree, it repaid America many times the purchase price in natural resources alone. But it began an expansion that made the United States a Pacific power and brought Uncle Sam within the rays of the rising Japanese sun.

ACQUISITIVE NATIONALISM

The acquisitive nationalism that stirred Seward also coursed through average American veins. Stimulated by victory, opportunist Americans looked upon Canada with the same longing as of old. In distant British Columbia there was sentiment in favor of incorporation and a petition for annexation to the American Union was actually dispatched, not without some effect in London, where attempts to cure disaffection were speedily made. American correctness could not restrain the animosity of Irish separatists, the Fenians, who hoped to get at England through Canada. Two of their attempts to invade the Dominion in 1866 and 1870 solidified Canadian feeling, but though these were efficiently handled by the American government, Anglo-American relations were not improved.

Far more vexatious were the misunderstandings that grew out of British violations of American neutrality during the war between the states. An ominous turn in the negotiations for the settlement of the "Alabama Claims" as the matter came to be called—occurred on April 13, 1869, when Senator Charles Sumner, chairman of the Senate Foreign Relations Committee, made a bombastic speech asserting that the raids of the *Alabama* and her sister ships, built in Great Britain, had prolonged the war for two years. The United States was entitled to compensation for the direct as well as the indirect damage. Since the total amount was huge, many inferred, and with cause, that Sumner was suggesting the cession of Canada as a happy solution. But Hamilton Fish, worthy successor to Seward, handled the delicate diplomacy so astutely that the Alabama Claims, together with other pending matters, were settled by the Treaty of Washington in 1871, which provided for arbitration. The United States received compensation of $15,000,000 for damages caused by the Confederate raiders, the boundary dispute between Canada and the United States over the northwest waterway was submitted to the German emperor as arbitrator, and the dispute concerning fishing privileges in the North Atlantic was amicably settled. The Treaty of Washington, one of the few bright spots in Grant's eight dark years, represented the greatest triumph for the principle of arbitration and removed all obstacles to Anglo-American peace.

While the American Civil War created difficulties between the United States and Britain, the outbreak of a Cuban civil war in 1868 created difficulties between the United States and Spain. Isolationist tradition could not restrain American sympathy for the Cubans, whose cause was identified with liberty. Cubans in the United States organized themselves into juntas and took every advantage of American prejudice. They engaged in extensive propaganda and even offered gifts of money to congressmen and publishers. Filibustering expeditions set out from American harbors with arms and supplies for the insurrectionists, but government officials were largely successful in preventing such expeditions from leaving American ports. Influential papers, such as the New York *Sun* and the *Herald,* clamored for intervention or at least a grant of belligerency for the rebels. President Grant favored such a move, and a belligerency resolution was voted down in Congress by a scant vote of 101 to 88. The ruling order in Spain, desperately trying to preserve the remnants of its

A young, but ever-righteous, Uncle Sam defies a decrepit Spain, too
weak and degenerate to prevent chaos in Cuba. *(Courtesy Collection
of Regional History, Cornell University.)*

colonial estate, escaped the grasp of rival American imperialists for
twenty years longer.

Following the Cuban civil war, diplomatic issues were less dramatic.
Superficially, from 1877 to 1889, the United States, secure in its external
position and devoted to the multiplication of wealth, appeared to have
forsaken the world. In the latter year, the budding imperialist, Senator
Henry Cabot Lodge of Massachusetts, wrote: "We have separated ourselves so completely from the affairs of other people that it is difficult
to realize how large a place they occupied when the government was
founded." But the nationalistic senator missed the significant fact that

many Americans were interested in the affairs of others and that, from the tip of Cape Horn to the shores of China's Yellow River, the fate of other people and the fate of Americans were one.

Ostensibly, there was ground for Lodge's comment on the country's withdrawal. Whatever the zeal of those who wished to badger Britain, an Anglo-American accord had been reached by arbitration. The Cuban danger spot in the Caribbean had been stamped out by Spain, and after the Franco-Prussian War (1870), Bismarck contrived in the main to keep the European peace until the Kaiser dismissed him in the nineties. On the other hand, the United States, unprepared for great diplomatic or imperialistic ventures, had no effective army or navy; not until 1883 did Congress grudgingly appropriate funds for four new men-of-war to be made of steel. Americans appeared to be self-centered because they were building cities and railways, constructing factories and the machinery to run them. Yet it was exactly because Americans had made the West yield its natural wealth of forest, mine, and farm, and had filled its docks and warehouses with the products of the machine that the years of seeming isolation from the world were actually preparatory for a greater participation in it. The United States emerged at the end of the century bursting with a power undreamed of by the founding fathers, and set out on a course whose end is not yet in sight. Even while the American people were busily engrossed in the problems of daily life, they were no more immune to the affairs of the world than they had been when the government was founded. Contacts were closer, whether with China or Chile on either side of the Pacific or with Mexico, Panama, and Spain on both oceans. Border difficulties with Mexico in June, 1877, induced the United States to dispatch troops to pursue irresponsible elements across the international line. A mere incident, the order was withdrawn in February, 1880, when Porfirio Diaz, former plotter against the democracy of Juárez and now dictator nineteenth-century style, was able to do with his own iron hand what the mailed American fist had intended. If such policies diminished intercontinental friendship, Oriental good will likewise was not increased in Peking by American exclusion of Chinese immigrants. Americans as a whole were indifferent to China, but politicians whose ears were never off the ground were sensitive to the complaints of constituents about Chinese infiltration. The Burlingame Treaty of 1868 granted Chinese the unrestricted right to immigrate, but congressmen from the Far West, supported by organized labor and in spite of employers, railways, steamship lines, and missionaries, succeeded in passing discriminatory legislation. A new treaty with China, concluded in 1880, permitted the United States to limit or suspend Chinese immigration. Restrictive measures passed in 1882, 1884, and 1892 failed to prevent local outbursts against the Chinese and filled the cup of Oriental displeasure to overflowing.

The Chinese incident built up a store of ill will in the memory of the Far East, but Latin America was of more pressing concern to statesmen than Asia. James G. Blaine, Garfield's Secretary of State, initiated a policy that eventually became Pan-Americanism. Blaine was stimulated more by economics than by sentiment, for the character of trade with Latin America was not satisfactory to rising American manufacturers and ambitious exporters. South Americans, while exporting huge amounts of raw materials to the United States, purchased most finished products in Europe. To dislodge Europe from the markets of the Western Hemisphere was Blaine's great desire. Since trade presumably followed peace in Latin America, Blaine sought continental friendship as a prelude to commercial solidarity. While the plan was not unreasonable, each succeeding event conspired to prevent its realization. Nor was Blaine quite free of blame himself, for his good intentions were rarely marked by good diplomacy. During a boundary dispute between Mexico and Guatemala, Blaine favored the smaller country and urged Mexico to arbitrate. Mexico firmly refused, with the result that Guatemala was not protected against its stronger disputant and Mexico was enraged. In another boundary disagreement, Colombia and Costa Rica referred their problem to a European power for settlement. Resentful that an American territorial matter should be decided abroad, Blaine again interceded, but nothing save animosity was achieved. Finally, in the war of the Pacific between Chile on one side and Peru and Bolivia on the other, victorious Chile, in 1884, coveted the nitrate mines of Peru as a prize. Blaine, ever distrustful of continental territorial changes, interposed his good offices. Chile, however, had the power to enforce her demands, while Blaine earned nothing for his pains save suspicion that the passage of years did not dispel.

Undeterred by rebuffs, Blaine presented President Arthur with a plan for an inter-American conference in 1881. Before much progress could be made, Blaine, having fallen out with Arthur's wing of the Republican party, resigned. His successor, Frederick Frelinghuysen, devotee of the dubious maxim that well enough should be let alone, recalled the invitations although some of them had already been cheerfully accepted. By fitting coincidence Blaine, again Secretary of State in 1889, presided over the first Pan-American Conference.

Delegates from seventeen American nations gathered in Washington on October 2, 1889. After an exhausting tour of American industrial centers during which businessmen, mindful of possible sales, played host, the weary representatives finally returned to the capital to discuss the subjects on the planned agenda. Blaine made a noble effort to attain two objectives, but it was his destiny to fail. Large in his thinking was the strategy of a customs union to break down inter-American commercial barriers and to bring about a decline of European trade. Closer to his heart was the erection of machinery to arbitrate disputes between American countries. Blaine made a brilliant oratorical effort, but fear of the United States and mutual hostility between the nations prevented the adoption of either plan. Behind the scenes European powers with large commercial stakes south of the Rio Grande stoked the fires of distrust against the United States. Although the conference failed to attain its specific aims, the Pan American Union was established, together with a precedent for future international meetings.

But the reaction of businessmen and diplomats to industrial expansion altered the relations of the Americas and Europe. Stacks of wheat on the prairies and carloads of processed goods piled high at the loading stations suggested the extent to which natural resources and human toil had made the United States a titan in the world. What made abundance an industrial reality also created the logic of a new series of events in international relations. Regardless of the pronouncements of newspaper editors or politicians, which were heightened by patriotic enthusiasm or the heat of international crises, the logic of events had changed America and the world.

Imports exceeded exports in the balance of trade from the Civil War to 1880, when the relationship was reversed. Thereafter the opposite was the normal situation, and the total volume of goods exported increased with every decade. Even more important was the fact that not only a flood of agricultural goods but larger consignments of manufactured products were to be found on the docks, in the warehouses, and in the holds of ocean-going ships. In 1860, exports were valued at $333,576,000; in 1880, the amount increased to $835,639,000; in 1900, the total, passing the billion mark, reached $1,394,483,000. Industrialism was maturing and with it came a sense of power.

REVIVAL OF "MANIFEST DESTINY"

Internal economic consolidation, feeding upon tariffs and strengthening the trend toward economic nationalism, bred not only a sense of power but revived the spirit of "manifest destiny." Already in 1885, the Reverend Josiah Strong, a leading Protestant churchman, in an influential volume entitled *Our Country,* acclaimed the so-called Anglo-Saxons as a "race of unequaled energy . . . of the largest liberty, the purest Christianity, the highest civilization . . . ." which "will move down upon Mexico,

The sickle mightier than the sword: a cartoonist explains the difference between America and Europe. *(Courtesy Collection of Regional History, Cornell University.)*

down upon Central and South America, out upon the islands of the sea." With imperial prevision, Senator Albert J. Beveridge of Indiana told an approving audience in 1898 that "American factories are making more than the American people can use; American soil is producing more than they can consume. Fate has written our policy for us; the trade of the world must and shall be ours. And we will get it as our mother has told us how. We will establish trading-posts throughout the world as distributing points for American products. We will cover the ocean with our merchant marine. We will build a navy to the measure of our greatness. . . . Our institutions will follow our flag on the wings of our commerce. And American law, American order, American civilization, and the American flag will plant themselves on shores hitherto bloody and benighted, but by those agencies of God henceforth to be made beautiful and bright." Well might the head of the Bureau of Foreign Commerce write the year before: "The 'international isolation' of the United States so far as industry and commerce are concerned has . . . been made a thing of the past by . . . the change in our economic requirements . . .," for the United States had become a "competitor in the world-wide struggle for trade."

Global competition for special privileges among powerful nations in the markets of the world was itself the culmination of world-wide forces that engulfed America in their sweep. Yet the very factors that solidified national societies overran the national boundaries they had helped to erect. Trade, commerce, and industry ultimately made civilization interdependent. While national self-interest during the latter half of the nineteenth century cut across the internationalism of trade, industrial technology shrank the world, revealing that the only self-sufficient unit was the world itself.

The shrinking world decreased the time and cost of travel for individuals and goods, but increased the national urge for conquest. Those who had already acquired places in the sun wished for an ever-larger share of its wealth-giving rays; those whose tardy appearance on the industrial scene had deprived them of the most favored localities strove to capture such places as remained. National states sought to establish protected markets, national and international, under the formula of prosperity for one country rather than the formula of prosperity for the world. If modern technology brought countries closer together in fact, the desire for national gain, as in the commercial revolution of the age of Columbus, further separated them in spirit. In a society in which private gain was the premise of action, international rivalry was the consequent in thought. Provincialisms and cultural isolation were threatened with extinction as nations moved closer together in space and time, but political nationalism took on parochial vigor. As the extent of the world dwindled under the irresistible pressure of telephones, telegraphs, and turbines, bringing peoples from everywhere into community relations, political nationalisms continued further to divide humanity.

After 1870 the changes that remade Europe likewise remade the United States. Thereafter Europe forsook the Continental theater for the international stage, while the United States, no longer solely concerned

WE NEED THE PRODUCTS OF OTHER LANDS

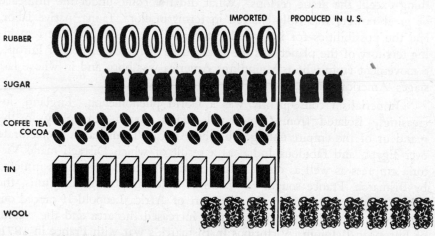

Each symbol represents 10 per cent of apparent U S. consumption

PICTOGRAPH CORPORATION

with the Western Hemisphere, became increasingly concerned with the world. The Continent of Europe, swiftly industrialized, began first in the 1870's to compete seriously with Britain. The United States after 1880, no less swiftly industrialized, began to compete with England and the Continent. Machines in England, in Germany, in Italy, in the United States turned out mountains of goods with scant regard either to wants or to needs. Growing surpluses induced a search for markets and for raw materials to make more surpluses. It was not that there was an insufficiency of steel, or oil, or copper, but for a civilization organized on the basis of competition, local and global, there was never quite enough. The greater the proficiency of machines, the greater the need became, and the more success attended the owners of machines, the more fluid capital was accumulated which, like the goods that the machines produced, sought outlets for expansion. Wealth from banks and factories, from appreciated landholdings, from the building of roads, canals, railways, and public utilities that serviced the cities of the world, was attracted to the undeveloped territories of Africa, Asia, South America, and the innumerable islands of the great seaways.

Following the Franco-Prussian War, all Europe felt the imperialistic impulse. The political and economic unification of Germany and Italy as well as the unification of the United States and the nationalizing of American industry gave new impetus to nationalism. Blending patriotic fervor, naked greed, and religious ardor—the noblest human motives and the basest—modern imperialism swept over all the remaining unexplored and unexploited regions. From darkest Africa to the yellow Yangtze in China, the new expansion of Western society covered everything except the arctic regions. What did not come under the influence of great powers was fully charted in terms of flora, fauna, native labor, and the possibilities for industrial enterprise. Acquisition of the remaining territory of the planet was the final phase of the expansion of Europe, a movement from whose beginnings America was born and in whose last stages America shared.

Imperialism consequently was a world phenomenon. England, increasingly isolated from Continental affairs, found new glory in the grandeur of the empire enlarged by the African Transvaal, a protectorate over Egypt, and fabulous India, as a result of which Disraeli made Victoria empress as well as queen. To heal the Continental wounds inflicted by Bismarck, France sought the balm of colonial prestige in Tunis, the Sahara, and French Congo. In the heart of Africa Leopold II carved out a golden principality that many times increased the area and the wealth of European Belgium. Victorious in Bismarck's war with France in 1871, Germany entered the race late, acquiring shares in Africa, and in the crumbling empire of a China worsted in battle by Japan in 1895 and thereafter the prey of European and Japanese imperialists alike.

No immunity protected American democracy against the impulses of American nationalism. Prospective markets and untapped riches in distant lands glittered as brightly for Americans as for Europeans. Nor were Americans less conscious than Germans of their duties to civilization or less sensitive than Englishmen to their patriotic obligations. What Rudyard Kipling and his burden of the white man was to the England of Victoria, Albert J. Beveridge and his destiny manifested in growing surpluses from field, forest, and factory was to the United States of William McKinley. Nor was it accidental that American readiness to embark upon ventures outside its continental domain coincided with the end of the frontier and the triumph of manufacturing over agriculture.

The American people were only remotely interested in the Asiatic mainlands and less so in Africa, but they were vitally interested in Latin America and in Pacific trade. In European relations the United States clashed with Old World tariffs that injured the export of American farm products to European markets, and European exporters in turn were injured by American tariffs. American interests also clashed with European interests in both South America and the Orient. Hawaii, between the Far East and California, once an island heaven for missionaries, a halfway station for whalers, and a stopping place for China traders, acquired newer meanings in a society concerned with naval bases, coaling stations, and cable landings. Pearl Harbor, a magnificent port near Honolulu, was leased as a naval base in 1884. Sugar was mixed with the grand designs of national strategy, for the economics of sugar represented an American investment in Hawaiian plantations totaling $25,000,000 by 1890. Preferential treatment was accorded all Hawaiian products by treaty in 1875, but the tariff of 1890 reversed this arrangement, and Hawaiian planters were placed in the same position as other exporters. The law further provided bounties for American sugar growers that gave them the advantage over all foreign competitors.

But tariffs, however domestic in intent, were economic foreign policies with international consequences. The deliberations of the American Congress in Washington, affecting sugar, produced a crisis in remote Hawaii. In 1893 a revolution, inspired by American residents, deposed Queen Liliuokalani, and the insurrectionists created a new government recognized by the United States minister at Honolulu with unseemly haste. Unfortunately for the annexationists, who yearned for a tunnel under the American tariff wall, their treaty, although rushed to Washington, arrived too late for action at the close of Benjamin Harrison's Republican administration. Returning to office in March, 1893, for a second term, Grover Cleveland, certain that American residents in Hawaii had been unfair to Queen Lil, withdrew the treaty, sent an investigating commission to the islands, and hauled down the American flag. The commission later reported that the United States minister had allowed acquisitive zeal to color his judgment and that a majority of the inhabitants did not want annexation. Nevertheless, many Americans agreed with the sentiments expressed by the New York *Commercial Advertiser:*

In ordering "Old Glory" pulled down at Honolulu President Cleveland turned back the hands on the dial of civilization. Native rule, ignorant, naked, heathen, is re-established; and the dream of an American republic at the crossroads of the Pacific . . . which the more enlightened of our 65,000,000 people awaited with glad anticipation, has been shattered by Grover Cleveland, the Buffalo Lilliputian.

More pressing to contemporaries was the question of an isthmian canal. Long within the vision of Americans, the matter was given dramatic primacy by the appearance of the captivating Ferdinand de Lesseps, famed builder of Suez, with plans for a Panamanian link between the Atlantic and the Pacific. Contemplated as an undertaking with French capital, it failed to coincide with basic American objectives. On March 8, 1880, President Hayes announced that Panama was "virtually a part of the coast line of the United States," a declaration that sounded better in Boston and Washington than in Lima and Rio de Janeiro. That Americans were beginning to link American expansion with the isthmian project is evidenced by Hayes' remark that American policy envisaged "a canal under American control." The following year, James G. Blaine, then Secretary of State, attempted to convince Downing Street that the Clayton-Bulwer Treaty of 1850, restraining American initiative in building a canal, had been outmoded by thirty years of change. Although Blaine's note was defiant, the British kept their tempers with admirable restraint, but politely rejected the American argument. British opinion, however, in 1901 was not prepared to thwart American power, and the Hay-Pauncefote Treaty abrogated the Clayton-Bulwer Treaty. But that was after the United States had defeated Spain and had come to be recognized as a naval power of international consequence.

If the United States was drawn into contact with the great powers by the advance into the Pacific, she entered the labyrinth of European affairs of her own accord. American officials considered events in North Africa of sufficient moment to warrant joining various European powers in a conference relating to Morocco in 1880, the settlement of which the Senate formally ratified. The Berlin Conference four years later, convened to discuss trading rights in the Congo, was attended by an American representative, but Cleveland advised the Senate not to ratify its conclusions. At a second Berlin assembly America was represented only by observers who witnessed the deliberations, and the Senate ratified merely the tariff and slavery provisions, but in 1889 the United States, Great Britain, and Germany entered into an "entangling alliance" that established a protectorate over Samoa.

The Samoan archipelago was as much a prize for Germany and England as for the United States. At Pago Pago, a harbor splendid enough to dazzle Neptune himself, an American naval officer had secured coaling privileges in 1872. Six years thereafter the United States, in return for a naval base, agreed to use its good offices in differences arising between Samoa and any foreign nation. Although this agreement did not constitute a legal protectorate, the United States bound itself to protect Samoa. Britain and Germany, actuated by the same motives as the Americans, soon acquired rights in Samoa by solemn treaty. Commercial agents vied with consuls and naval officers with frank seekers after tropical booty —all of whom carried on private wars in which the natives were the habitual losers.

At last the full weight of imperial Germany was brought to bear on the unhappy native king, against whom the mighty Iron Chancellor declared war. While emissaries of President Harrison were sent to Berlin in an effort to stave off disaster, British, German, and American warships rode at anchor in the Samoan harbor at Apia. In spite of German and British unwillingness, a three-power protectorate was arranged at Berlin. In 1899, after the war with Spain, the protectorate, never entirely satisfactory to any of the signatories, was abrogated and the archipelago divided between the United States and Britain. Germany received compensation elsewhere in the Pacific; America received Samoa. But American activity was not confined to Hawaii and Samoa. During the eighties and nineties alone the United States came into possession of half a hundred Pacific islets. Although the advantages were not immediately apparent, they loomed larger in the next century, when the airways became avenues of transport and communication.

The changing course of events was likewise indicated by relations with Latin-American republics. Confidence in the United States was not increased as a result of American conduct during the Chilean civil war in 1890–1891. The American minister, Patrick Egan, a professional Irish partisan, looked with disfavor upon the rebels, largely, it would appear, because the English in Chile favored them, and President Harrison, mindful of the Irish vote on the eve of a national election, did not say him nay. Still more provocative was the official reaction to a barroom brawl that occurred in Valparaiso in October, 1891, between American sailors from the *Baltimore* and certain Chileans. Since seventeen Americans were killed, a righteously indignant government insisted upon satisfactions that Chile refused to grant. War seemed imminent until a new Chilean government, conciliatory and reasonable as the United States was not, made acceptable amends.

The Chilean episode brought the United States close to war, but the Venezuelan dispute produced an international crisis. An age-old boundary disagreement between Venezuela and British Guinea, vital to the South American nation but of secondary importance to a great world empire, nearly brought about a war between England and the United States. Venezuela demanded that the dispute be settled; Great Britain refused. Virtually certain of American diplomatic support, the Venezuelans took a firm tone, and the State Department strongly seconded the plea for arbitration. While Britain continued to reject Venezuelan insistence even when coupled by American endorsement, opinion in the United States became more and more hostile to what seemed to be indefensible British obstinacy. President Cleveland was no imperialist, but he was too astute a Democrat to permit Republican jingoes to make capital out of British stubbornness. Accordingly, Richard Olney, formerly Attorney General and now Secretary of State, drafted a note, less diplomatic than belligerent. First and last a corporation lawyer, Olney wrote with the positive assertion of the pleader rather than with the circuitous dissemblance of the diplomat. "The United States," declaimed Olney, insisting that Britain's failure to arbitrate called the Monroe Doctrine into operation, "is practically sovereign on this continent, and its fiat is law upon the subjects to which it confines its interposition."

While Olney's undiplomatic note was by no means a barometer of American opinion, it reflected a militant consciousness of power. The American republic was practically sovereign, not because "wisdom and justice and equity are the invariable characteristics of the dealings of the United States" but rather because "in addition to all other grounds, its infinite resources combined with its isolated position render it master of the situation and practically invulnerable as against any or all other powers." In less royal tones, Olney addressed part of his note to Americans, warning them that European imperialisms then rampant in Africa might be transported to the American continent: "thus far . . . we have been spared the burdens and evils of immense standing armies. . . . But with the powers of Europe permanently encamped on American soil, . . . ideal conditions . . . cannot be expected to continue. We too must be armed to the teeth, we too must convert the flower of our male population into soldiers and sailors, and by withdrawing them from . . . pursuits of peaceful industry we too must practically annihilate a large share of the production energy of the nation." Despite the contracting world, Olney was confident that "distance and three thousand miles of intervening ocean make any permanent political union between a European and an American state unnatural and inexpedient. . . ."

When Lord Salisbury, then in command of British policy, tardily responded, he firmly rejected Olney's contention. Without violating diplomatic etiquette, his lordship found the Monroe Doctrine inapplicable and suggested that the United States leave the dispute to the disputants. The question, he reminded, involved the frontier of a British possession "which belonged to the Throne of England long before the Republic of Venezuela came into existence," a time, it was unnecessary for Salisbury to add, that also antedated the advent of President Monroe and the doctrine bearing his name.

"Mad clear through," President Cleveland took the matter directly to the Congress. He rejected the British analysis of the Monroe Doctrine and urged that the United States itself determine the boundary line, although he was duly regretful that the English government had spurned American offers to assist. To accomplish this end, he recommended an American investigation committee and implied that once the boundary line was determined, the United States would fight to maintain it. Cleveland's proposal met with almost hysterical approbation. The House unanimously voted the funds for a boundary commission. Republican critics of the President warmly seconded his stand, and the New York *Sun* appeared with the headline, "WAR IF NECESSARY."

If war did not result, it was not because America had been unprovocative. Cleveland had spoken and it was for Britain to make answer. And British officials were truly in a dilemma grave to diplomats. If they conceded, their stock in trade, national prestige, might be diminished; if they refused, war would unquestionably follow. Help came neither from the keen in mind, who perceived the stupidity of conflict, nor from the pure in heart, who viewed the prospect of war with understandable horror. Aid came rather from the European situation. Britain, stronger both on land and on sea, was not intimidated by the United States. Guns from its men-of-war were capable of spreading destruction and panic all along the American coast, and Canada was a convenient base for operations. British leaders might have undertaken a war with America with reasonable confidence. But democratic peoples do not relish war with one another; and diplomats have their own less obvious considerations.

To fight an American war left Britain at the mercy of Europe, where she had few friends and fewer allies. Germany, Austria, and Italy were leagued in the Triple Alliance after 1882; Russia and France, long arch foes, concluded the Dual Alliance in 1891. To cap the diplomatic climax, England was embroiled in South Africa, where the Boers, descendants of the Dutch, had just withstood a raid led by an overly enthusiastic Englishman. On January 3, 1896, Kaiser William II, the bad boy among European monarchs, sent a telegram to the Boer leader, congratulating him on thwarting an invasion. Resentment against America was swiftly transferred to the Germans, and English imperialists were compelled to remember that if they moved forward against the United States, Europe remained at their rear.

Once again America profited from the strife in Europe. Britain acceded to arbitration after the commission had already begun to operate, and on October 3, 1899, the arbitral decision gave British Guinea the lion's share of the disputed region. The Olney note and the Cleveland message were roundly condemned by Europeans and met with less than enthusiasm in Latin America; but the capitulation of Britain bolstered the jingo spirit of those who wished to see the United States dominant in the Western Hemisphere. And the response to Olney's blustering reference to the Monroe Doctrine revealed the force of a rising nationalism.

The Spanish-American War three years after the Venezuela crisis was less an innovation than a culmination of the new national tendencies. But the events that followed in the wake of war were finally to shift the center of international gravity from East to West and ultimately dispelled the great American illusion that the United States lived apart from the world.

THE GLITTER OF EMPIRE

While the remote causes of the war with Spain date back to the presidency of Grant, the immediate causes arose out of the second Cuban insurrection begun on February 24, 1895. Long-standing grievances between Spain and her island colony were aggravated by the growing protectionism of American industry, which hurt Cuba's vital market by removing sugar from the free list in 1894. Anxious to draw the United States into war with the mother country, the Cuban insurrectionists set up propaganda bureaus in American cities and, flouting official neutrality, sought military supplies from American sources. Unable to meet Spain in open encounter, they adopted a policy of thoroughly devastating the land, at the same time financing the revolt with the payments extracted from American sugar planters for special dispensation. Since the Spanish authorities were unable to distinguish friends from foes, they rounded up the rural populace—where the plantations were located—into concentration camps, in which disease and pestilence soon became rife. Brutal as were the warriors of Spain, Cuban patriots were never loath to employ the barbarisms that are the commonplaces of war.

Americans could not remain spectators in Olympian detachment, for Cuba possessed a fateful geographical location, commanding entrance to the Gulf of Mexico and the Caribbean. No naval strategist was needed to tell a people contemplating an interoceanic canal and economic advantages in Latin America that the United States had a deep interest in Cuba's future. Strife on the island imperiled a trade that had reached the proportions of a hundred million dollars, and American investors had sunk half as much in Cuban sugar plantations, railroads, and mines. Nor could a revolution take place anywhere without eliciting American solicitude, for was not this revolution another instance of a people striving to be free? With access to only one side of the story, American sentiments were outraged by accounts of Spanish atrocities and inhuman concentration camps. Cuban masters of the propagandist's art were quick to turn such natural advantages to account, and the New York *World* and the New York *Journal*, the first piloted by Joseph Pulitzer and the second by William Randolph Hearst, gave them a maximum of journalistic aid and comfort. Whether Hearst and Pulitzer were as interested in Cuban freedom as in the circulation of the *Journal* and the *World* respectively may still be debated, but by 1898 each was selling 800,000 copies daily, and after Manila Hearst was counting the profits on the sale of 1,500,000.

As chief executive, Grover Cleveland did what little he could. He tried to prevent illicit shipment of goods to Cuba and otherwise to preserve strict neutrality, but Spain, deafened by American shouts of "Free Cuba!" heard only the echoes of American encouragement, which alone seemed to infuse the revolution with life. So irresistible was the cyclone of popular sentiment that even Cleveland told Congress in December, 1896, that if Spain should lose Cuba—an outcome that the yellow press had led Americans to expect—the United States because of its "higher obligations" might feel constrained to intervene. William McKinley took office in March, 1897, and in the following October, Spain indicated a willingness to grant Cubans a larger part in the management of their affairs and to rectify the evils of the concentration camps.

Spain was now more than ready to make the best of a bad situation, but a dramatic occurrence made peace seem vain. On February 15, 1898, the *Maine,* an American battleship in Havana Harbor, exploded with the loss of 260 men. Who was responsible for blowing up the *Maine* will always remain a mystery, but the tragedy made a peaceful solution of difficulties unlikely. Unbridled emotionalism gripped the nation, which an irresponsible press stirred into frenzy. "Remember the Maine! To hell with Spain!" became the war cry. Congress was as belligerent as the people, and the church, formerly the anchor of the peace movement, was wrenched from its moorings by a torrential sweep of popular resentment.

Hearst's *Journal,* this time accurately, reported in a screeching headline "THE WHOLE COUNTRY THRILLS WITH WAR FEVER," and pictured McKinley as an old woman vainly trying to sweep back giant waves of public opinion. Undergraduates at Princeton held a demonstration, and in Youngstown, Ohio, the chamber of commerce solemnly resolved to boycott onions of Spanish origin.

But the President, convinced that peace was preferable to war, sought to avert the impending catastrophe. Commercial interests, well aware that war was bad for business, rallied to his side, for only those few directly tied to Cuba financially were favorably disposed to war. McKinley therefore suggested on March 27, 1898, that Spain enter into an armistice with the rebels while peace was negotiated. Spain, as heartily sick of the rebellion as she was eager to avoid war with the United States, agreed to give up the concentration camp policy as McKinley requested. But the wheels of diplomacy in Madrid moved slowly.

By April 10, Spain was ready, but McKinley was not. William Jennings Bryan, apostle of the Democrats, was making speeches for a free Cuba, and the rank and file of the Republican party was no less war-minded than the Democratic opposition. On April 11, two days after the Spanish had agreed to the terms that McKinley had himself proposed, the President sent a message to Congress advocating armed intervention. He averred that the "commerce, trade, and business" of the United States was endangered and that the Cuban situation constituted "a constant menace to our peace." Congress quickly authorized intervention with armed forces. At the same time it pledged the United States not to maintain "sovereignty, jurisdiction, or control" over Cuba.

The Spanish-American War, allegedly fought to liberate Cuba, began after the Cuban war for independence was three years old. The "splendid little war," as John Hay called it, lasted but four months and is noteworthy in a military sense for the dominant role played by the fleet. Theodore Roosevelt, Assistant Secretary of the Navy and one of the few Americans who knew the location of the Philippine Islands, ordered Admiral George Dewey, then stationed at Hong Kong, to attack the Spanish armada in the islands' waters. On May 1 Dewey destroyed the Spanish fleet without a single American loss. The record of the army was less distinguished. Behind the lines, politics and incompetence made the task of mobilizing, equipping, and transporting men doubly difficult. Soldiers appeared at ports of embarkation clothed in winter uniforms for service in a tropical country. Equally distressing was the indifference to diet and hospital care, with the shocking result that for every 289 men killed or badly wounded, 13 perished of disease. The general confusion is suggested by the fact that Dewey, having sunk the Spanish fleet, awaited re-enforcements for several weeks before he could capture Manila. Dash and glamour, inevitable accompaniment of all wars, was furnished in this instance by Theodore Roosevelt, advocate of the strenuous life, who resigned from the Navy Department to recruit a volunteer cavalry band, the "Rough Riders," of which he served as colonel.

As her naval and military power disintegrated, Spain sued for an armistice and on August 12 agreed to preliminary terms. Cuba was handed over to the victor pending the establishment of independence; Puerto Rico and the island of Guam were ceded outright to compensate for the expense of the war; and the Philippines were purchased for the sum of $20,000,000. It was reserved to the United States to determine the social and civil status of the inhabitants of the former Spanish colonies.

The treaty of peace expelled Spain from the world at whose beginnings her navigators, colonists, and conquistadores had presided; but if the treaty of peace signaled the death of an ancient empire, it heralded the birth of a new one. Already a world power, the United States became a colonial power as well. As heirs of the Spanish legacy, particularly in the Philippines, the American people became partners in the future of the Orient as they had always been partners in the future of Europe. With the territories of the Pacific came their populations, black and brown, civilized and uncivilized, European and Asiatic. If colonies supplied the key to imperial status, America had achieved it.

Yet Americans were by no means unanimous in their enthusiasm. To take over Puerto Rico and Guam accorded with the practice that nations had ever respected—losers pay the costs of war. And the spectacular exploits of the American navy underlined the advantages of the island of Guam as a coaling station. But against acquisition of the Philippines, bought outright by the United States, populated by groups alien in culture and tradition, opposition stiffened. Anxious Americans protested that the Constitution did not permit the United States "to acquire territory to be held and governed permanently as colonies" and that the inhabitants of the islands, having declared their independence, could not be annexed without "the consent of the governed." They further charged that sordid motives of trade rather than ideal motives of humanity prompted American desire; that Wall Street strove to convince Main Street of the moral duty of Americans toward their "little brown brothers," while actually their concern for the natives was no less exploitive than their concern for the natives' land. But big business could hardly initiate the forces that had created big business itself. The opponents of annexation also alleged that to add noncontiguous territory raised problems of administration too great for the machinery of democracy to bear. And the cost in plain, unvarnished dollars, it was insisted, amounted to more than the islands could ever be expected to yield.

The question, to annex the Philippines or not to annex, transcended territorial acquisitions in general or the Philippines in particular. It plumbed to the bottom the fundamentals of the democratic social tradition. Since the Filipinos were patently anxious for independence and their leader, Emilio Aguinaldo, was scarcely less hostile to American domination than to Spanish control, how could the United States flout the will of the Filipino people? Americans who believed that the United States had interceded to aid the Cuban fight for freedom found it somewhat ironical to approve steps that would enslave the Filipinos. Even if doubt as to the real attitude of the islanders existed, was democratic government at home compatible with colonial administration abroad? Was the American political structure appropriate for dependent territories far removed from the governmental source? Democratic processes, already strained by corporate business and the growth of the city, could not further be taxed by an expansion of executive administration and an augmented bureaucracy. That American democratic processes had failed to cope with internal evils suggested the ineptitude of assuming external obligations. Nor was it overlooked that such a geographical extension placed America in the midst of the international scramble for territory and prestige, involving military and naval commitments that the most farsighted could not possibly foresee. Many an ardent anti-imperialist felt moved to warn his fellow countrymen that the decay of the Roman Republic commenced with the beginning of Roman conquest.

Protagonists of the anti-imperialist case were as distinguished as their arguments were weighty. Leaders of the two major parties momentarily forgot political differences in the face of what they considered a threat to national security. The magical voice of William Jennings Bryan, titular Democratic leader, blended with that of George F. Hoar, the respected Republican senator from Massachusetts. Briefs against annexation were weighted by the opinion of William James, Harvard's noted philosopher, and William Graham Sumner, eminent sociologist of Yale. Mark Twain aimed a barbed shaft at President McKinley—"To the Person Sitting in Darkness"—which stung only slightly less than the pointed accusations of David Starr Jordan, president of Leland Stanford University, who named international bankers as makers of the wars to which clashing imperialisms led. Samuel Gompers spoke for labor against imperialism, and Charles William Eliot, scholarly mentor of Harvard, added his counsel to the growing opposition. William Vaughn Moody admonished those in high places:

Tempt not our weakness, our cupidity!
For save we let the island men go free,
Those baffled and dislaureled ghosts
Will curse us from the lamentable coasts
Where walk the frustrate dead . . .
O ye who lead,
Take heed!
Blindness we may forgive, but baseness we will smite.[1]

But if Moody and his comrades in spirit felt that this was a time of hesitation, their adversaries were not inclined to hesitate at all. They endeavored to impress their contemporaries with diverse arguments, economic, political, and strategic. They spoke of national interests, national honor, and national prestige, all of which would be seriously jeopardized should the Stars and Stripes come down from Manila's mastheads. Yet when they abandoned emotionalism for argument, they made their viewpoint unmistakably clear. "If it is commercialism," argued Mark Hanna, who was as fervent a believer in American expansion as the Reverend Josiah Strong, "to want the possession of a strategic point giving the American people an opportunity . . . in the markets of that great Eastern country, China, for God's sake let us have commercialism." And little doubt could be attached to the statement of Senator Beveridge of Indiana, who, answering the objection that the Philippines were far removed from the United States, answered: "The ocean does not separate us . . . the ocean joins us. . . . Steam joins us, electricity joins us—the very elements are in league with our destiny." So strong was the army of the opposition, however, that ratification of the peace treaty in the Senate was attained by a margin of a mere two votes.

Meanwhile, in the former island kingdom of Queen Lil, the forces of Christianity and sugar finally had their way. After Dewey's victory at Manila Bay, Hawaii still retained its fixed position on the map, but when Americans were fighting in the Philippines its international position was radically altered. And the voice of Japan, powerful after her victorious war against the Chinese Empire in 1895, and now raised in staccato protest against American control of Hawaii, sharpened national motives. In July, 1898, Hawaii was annexed by joint resolution of both houses of Congress. No longer simply a rendezvous for traders en route to the Orient, Hawaii was portrayed as the pivot of the Pacific, essential to American destiny. An independent Hawaii seemed as dangerous in 1898 as the Spanish outpost in Florida had seemed in 1819. The expression "coast line" had a specific meaning for geography, but in terms of social dynamics,

---

[1] "An Ode in Time of Hesitation," *The Poems and Plays of William Vaughn Moody.* Boston and New York: Houghton Mifflin Company, I, 25.

its meaning shifted in relation to world shrinkage and expanding national power.

The American war with Spain closed an old era and opened a new epoch. When the guns had boomed at Fort Sumter, thirty-seven years before, many Europeans, doubtful of the success of the democratic experiment, looked for its imminent collapse. Thereafter, the world's statesmen, industrialists, and thinkers learned not to leave America out of their considerations. And Americans, whatever their inclinations, were irresistibly drawn into the vortex of the world. Not that they had ever been separated from it, but a kind of egotism, typical of adolescence, induced the fiction that the culture of the United States was a rare variety that developed virginally without benefit of intercrossing.

Internationalism, for the United States as for others by 1900, was an established physical fact. Men could no longer get along without each other. Cranes in Hamburg lifted packing crates of machines and finished products into the deep holds of merchantmen, while cranes in Southampton, New York, and Havre lifted textiles, cotton bales, and the wines of France from the crowded wharves. And in Berlin, London, and New York, men dispatched telegrams concerning prices, orders, and credits. A word dashed off in a Wall Street office, and ships moved out of England's ports laden with goods; a figure chalked up on a blackboard in the Chicago pit, and the wheels of Minneapolis flour mills stopped grinding and the price of bread went up in scores of European cities. Men's needs constantly transcended the conventional boundaries of nations. More than 250 international meetings were held from 1880 to 1889, covering the whole range of human intercourse, and the number steadily increased. Meteorologists, mathematicians, nurses, educators, social workers, theologians had global ties no less than bankers, shippers, and the advocates of peace.

But the shrinking world exposed a glaring incongruity. Interdependence united men, but interdependence also tended to keep men apart. Indeed, the contracting world was paralleled by expanding nationalism, for the process of mechanization after 1865 was followed by world discord rather than by world concord. And if war was one of the sins of society, it was the consequence of irresponsible political nationalisms that cut athwart the unity of man. Yet nationalisms were prolonged less by the overt commission of antisocial acts than by the absence of adequate social and political institutions appropriate to the altered universe. The issue was the same on the home front as on the world front, for individual men were as irresponsible for the crimes of local communities as for the sins of the great society. Man's cooperative wisdom and energy made the world, but men failed to employ their cooperative wisdom and energy to match their physical creation with an institutional and moral renovation. Interdependence had formed an empire of business and a world republic of letters; the Republic of Man remained an iridescent dream.

Yet what was once Venetia, Florence, and Piedmont became Italy. Normandy, Burgundy, and Gascony became France; Swabia, Franconia, and Brandenburg became Germany; and New Spain, New France, New

The UNITED STATES IN GLOBAL PERSPECTIVE

Sweden, New Netherland, and New England became the United States. New France still lives in Canada's Quebec as in Louisiana; New Spain south of the border from Mexico to the Strait of Magellan, as in California and New Mexico. New Netherland lives in Michigan, and New Sweden in Minnesota. But if these developments occurred only yesterday in the arithmetic of social time, all men live in times of their own with which they must come to grips. The machine and the city remade America and Americans; the machine and the city remade the world and man. Continuing American experience was to yield an insight into the pervasive problems of Western civilization, for after the frustration of reform, new energies were kindled; after the world's illusion, new hopes were born. No sooner had martial ardor cooled after war with Spain, than social ardor flamed; America marched anew, under the banner of progress, in massive assault on the bankruptcy of politics and the sins of society.

XXIII

MIDDLE-CLASS PROGRESSIVISM

1900–1917

The expanding role of the United States in world affairs after 1900 by no means engaged the primary attention of the American people. The Spanish-American War, although satisfying to the pride of nationalists who looked to a future in which the United States would grow in power and wealth by aggressive intervention in world affairs, did not satisfy the more democratic aspirations of middle-class idealists or answer the longings of toiling masses. Against the forces working for imperialism were arrayed other forces. Earlier currents of social criticism broadened, after the turn of the century, into a national outburst. A new onward march of democracy known as the Progressive Movement gained ascendancy in the years from 1901 to 1917, for the first time since the days of Lincoln seriously disturbing the concentration of power that had accompanied the triumph of modern capitalism. But a literature of exposure and protest had recurrently revealed social evils in each of the preceding two decades. What lifted the scales from middle-class eyes? What gave new potency to the demand for reform?

THE UNIVERSAL PROGRESSIVE IMPULSE

Progressivism was not a national phenomenon to be explained wholly in terms of unsavory American conditions or wholly in terms of the first two decades of the twentieth century. Beneath the surface of protest and reform was a maturing stage in modern industrial society, generating in country after country a new climate of opinion presaging international political change. Progressivism was the American phase of a general movement of reform which in Europe produced various forms of "Social Democracy" and which in England was known as the "New Liberalism." Divergent tendencies were sundering the two great nineteenth-century forces, industrial capitalism and democracy. Maladjustment and unrest characterized all nations seriously affected by industrialization; and in each country democratic intellectual and ethical forces rose to protest

487

and struggled for reform. Not only in western Europe from Scandinavia to France, but in "backward" monarchies, Austria-Hungary, Italy, Russia, the Balkans, reform was in progress.

Unsavory American conditions described in sensational new exposures were neither invariably worse nor essentially unlike those in other countries at the same stage of development. But there were differences in degree. The reform spirit in the late nineteenth century had been frustrated to a much greater extent in the United States than in western Europe. Twentieth-century progressivism went less far in the United States than in many other countries. When progressivism reached full tide in the United States, finance capitalism had already developed a greater aggregation of wealth in consolidated monopolies and achieved more pervasive political power, both secretly and openly, than in older and less avowedly democratic countries. Moreover, in the United States, progressivism was stronger as a local movement than as a national movement—reflecting in part the decentralized character of national parties.

There was little that was unique in the progressive awakening in the United States, either in the ethical sources of the movement or in its conception of the modern need for social control. The ultimate ethical basis of the new liberalism was a reflection of a change taking place through centuries, a religious and philosophical shift from preoccupation with personal salvation to growing concern for the welfare of society. This old but accelerating shift toward increasing social idealism and toward a social conception of the political responsibilities of democracy was speeded and intensified by economic revolution and resultant maladjustments. Progressivism took to heart the sobering fact that man had evolved techniques for control of vast economic concerns, but had lagged in evolving techniques for humane control of the vast social concerns of modern life.

On the plane of action the organized pressure of the middle class outweighed the masses in the United States as elsewhere, but the industrial population, labor unions, and mass unrest were essential elements in accounting for the trend toward "social politics." The middle class was dominant in the reform movement, since it was better organized than the masses and more politically conscious. Middle-class spokesmen were not only more vocal by habit but had readier access to the public platform, the pulpit, newspapers, and agencies for the molding of public opinion. The attitude of labor, as well as its inferior position in society, limited the scope of working-class contribution. American labor unions, conservative in the main and restricted to the better-paid workers, not only avoided politics but constantly sought to purge their ranks of those who flirted with socialist ideas of the kind embraced by European workmen and Continental Social Democrats. Nevertheless mass unrest, the rise of socialism, the pressure of unions, and the struggle for broader rights of collective bargaining were important ingredients in American social politics. The wavering line of reform reflected an uneasy dual alliance: the conjuncture of moderate middle-class progressivism with a warmer social democratic endeavor to emancipate the masses. But it was more than that. The spiritual guilt and physical pinch of the sins of society accounted for the contemporaneous rise of social reform in all free countries at the outset of the twentieth century.

An evaluation of ends and means in the American movement would be provincial if it disregarded international diffusion of the political inventions and standards of progress adopted elsewhere. Something of a social lag is apparent in the Progressive Movement in America if it is viewed in terms of the chronology and intensity of similar movements elsewhere. In England, laissez faire triumphed in the adoption of free trade (1846), but laissez faire even then was losing ground in respect to governmental intervention in the internal conduct of private business. Unlike American major parties and Congresses, English Parliaments and parties recognized that maladjustments engendered by the economic revolutions were national problems requiring national legislation. Parliament regulated hours and conditions of work of women and children in the laws of 1819 and 1842 and introduced national standards of managerial responsibility in the factory acts of 1833 and 1847. France, though less extensively industrialized than the United States, followed England in recognizing that machine age maladjustments, conflicts of capital and labor, the fleecing of investors, and the disregard of the public interest were national problems requiring national regulation. American national parties voiced similar words—but did not accept their substance. American state governments separately continued to develop their power to promote health, safety, and welfare by regulation of business, only to discover that revolutions in the economy had nationalized industry and removed it from their jurisdiction—with the assistance of the courts.

It remained for a foreign country that was anything but a constitutional democracy to delineate earliest and most successfully the embryonic features of the modern welfare state. In the fourth quarter of the nineteenth century the economic revolutions hit home in Germany. Socialist unrest and an aggressive labor movement nourished on Marx and Engels impelled a political opportunist who was a stranger to the spirit of democracy to inaugurate the first radical challenge to the brutality of early laissez-faire capitalism. Assure the workingman "care when he is sick and maintenance when he is old," said Prince Bismarck to the Reichstag; then in vain would Marxian socialists "sing their swan song" of capitalism, for the workingman then would have none of them. So, beginning in 1883, the aristocratic German monarchy pressed on ahead of the English, French, and American democracies in a momentous experiment. Unemployment insurance was deferred until the days of the Weimar Republic in the 1920's, but well before 1890 Germany's Iron Chancellor launched a broad national program of social security, including compulsory workmen's compensation for accidents and sickness, old-age pensions, and compulsory government care for the tubercular.

German success stimulated social legislation throughout Europe: a general movement by 1900 was signalized by "emergence of the socially conscious state." While socialism in England as in the United States had an educational influence, it did not develop into a powerful political force. Nevertheless, the Disraeli party of landed aristocracy and the Gladstone party of middle-class industrialists found it necessary to compete for the workingman's vote. The basic reorientation in the English outlook became visible in the 1880's. Gradually appeared the New Liberalism, compounded of middle-class humanitarianism, the driving force of trade unions, and the deepening appeal of "social politics" to England's recently enfranchised masses, who had won the right to vote in 1884. By 1906 the maturing of the labor movement was heralded by the entrance of "labor" into politics—employing the very tactic most execrated by Samuel Gompers and the American Federation of Labor. With a scattering of seats in Parliament, the new Labor party formed a liaison with Lloyd George's Liberals that was to prove the kiss of death for the latter. Between the two world wars the Laborites replaced the Liberals as a major party. Political action in England quickly disproved the American contention that labor weakened its energies if it went into politics. By 1914 English unions had enrolled over four million members, while American unions, with a much larger working population to draw upon, had organized less than two and three quarters millions.

In England, progressivism reached full tide in precisely the same years as in the United States, but it began earlier, penetrated further, and reflected a more sensitive and responsible system of party government. Cabinet leadership of disciplined majorities gave effective expression to campaign pledges. National public health acts, national·housing legislation, and national protection of the right of collective bargaining antedated the twentieth century, whereas in the United States the same problems remained the largely neglected subjects of local and state concern until the administration of Franklin D. Roosevelt. After 1906 the liaison of England's Liberals and Laborites produced a record of achievement never seriously envisioned by the party of McKinley, Hanna, and Theodore Roosevelt, and only thinly imitated by the Democrats during the presidency of Woodrow Wilson. Lloyd George made stirring issues of

"The People's Budget" and then of "The People's Insurance." The English program of tax justice through progressively steeper rates on big incomes (1909)—in part inspired by the writings of Henry George—was supplemented by a broad program for social security, providing for workmen's accident compensation (1906), government employment offices and unemployment insurance (1909), old-age pensions (1908), and minimum wages in "sweated industries" and coal fields (1909 and 1912). These impressive advances toward a welfare state were rounded out by the National Insurance Acts of 1911 and 1913, which provided sickness insurance, free medical care, and maternity benefits; and by the trade-union acts of 1906 and 1909, which extended far more substantial legal protection in regard to picketing, union finances, and damage suits than American unions were able to obtain for a generation.

The emergence of the socially conscious state, foreshadowed in Germany, exemplified in England, and emulated in a well-integrated social security program in twentieth-century France, stimulated the establishment of higher standards elsewhere in Europe and around the world. In the far South Pacific the progressive British commonwealths launched their own significant social experiments with a boldness that marked anew the sweep of modern forces in a shrinking world. Westward across the Atlantic came ideas as well as immigrants. Cultural isolation from time to time had narrowed the horizon of the American people, but never in the true sense had the people been isolated from alien "isms" or the stream of world thought. Just as Henry George's paradox of "progress and poverty" stimulated English Fabians and European reformers, so by circular action American social pioneers began to glimpse abroad the specifications for new attacks on the dislocations of industrial urbanism. Many an American social worker, sleuthing at the immediate scene of the crime, supposed that he detected only an evil genius native to his country. But constructive theorists, recognizing in the American scene a reflection of evolving world conditions, familiarized themselves with the contemporary evaluations of a noted group of English thinkers—Toynbee, Hobson, Tawney, Hobhouse, the Webbs—and with the great works of the liberal social scientists of the Continent.

The trend toward social politics in the modern world was everywhere accompanied by reforms to give the people greater control over the government. The spread of universal manhood suffrage in limited monarchies like Italy (1912), the victory of woman suffrage in England (1918), efforts to democratize methods of voting, the Australian secret ballot, the czar's gesture toward a national Russian legislature (1906), and the Chinese democratic revolution (1911) attested that the political principle of progressive democracy was a universal phenomenon. Sun Yat-sen, father of the Chinese Republic, imbibed democratic formulations in the Hawaiian Islands under the flag of the United States; social democracy in revolutionary China derived inspiration from the socialist writings of a New York dentist. Behind new devices to protect and extend the ballot was an agitation in each country to undermine the supremacy of older, elite minorities by introducing new machinery to give added force to the will of the majority. From the United States, Joseph Chamberlain and the Birmingham reformers in the British Liberal party borrowed an American idea of direct democracy—national party conventions—only to discard the experiment after 1894 because its decentralizing tendencies undermined the priceless advantage of responsible party leadership. Similarly moved to experiment by lessons learned abroad, Americans imported and domesticated several kinds of direct democracy, including the Australian secret ballot and, with less ultimate success, the Swiss devices of the initiative and referendum.

THE INTELLECTUAL PREPARATION FOR PROGRESSIVISM

No explanation of domestic changes solely in terms of international inspiration and irreversible world trends would be sound. Why did progressivism find a favorable reception in American thought? Did American conditions demand such sweeping reforms as those adopted in Europe? What were the immediate catalysts of American social action? Answers to these questions lie in the contributions of three groups most responsible for the intellectual and emotional preparation that galvanized public opinion and produced organization and leadership.

Social science, developing rapidly in the United States after 1880, enriched American thought on the problems of social politics and progress, drawing on the world's common store of civilized knowledge in a search for "scientific" means to achieve social ends. No previous American social movement was bolstered by such a brilliant galaxy of intellectual leaders with such wide knowledge of world thought. Instructed by findings in anthropology, sociology, psychology, and other new fields of fruitful investigation, Thorstein Veblen, Lester F. Ward, John R. Commons, J. Allen Smith, Charles A. Beard, John Dewey, and other social scientists discovered that society was overburdened with ill-assorted survivals of a rural environment and a predemocratic age, and that outmoded ideas and behavior patterns held society enchained, preventing rational adjustment to altered conditions of modern life. The constitutional fictions of defenders of special interests and the laissez-faire folkways of industrialists were examined and identified as obsolete concepts in accord neither with the professions of democracy nor with the facts of reality. Great changes in modern life, observed the specialists, belied the supposedly democratic implications of nineteenth-century theories. A rail splitter or even a taxi driver might still go to the White House—although none did—and the opportunity of a son of poor people to rise from the industrial assembly line to company president still remained a theoretical possibility. But the data of social science disclosed little mathematical probability of any fluid social mobility whereby the economically depressed could escape from their lowly status, acquire the comforts of middle-class families, and win for their children an equality of opportunity.

A basic characteristic of the new intellectual currents was the inspiration of science, stimulating a search for accurate techniques for the investigation of concrete human problems. But experimentation with methods for analysis of society bore the imprint of two other basic characteristics of the progressive intellectual outlook. One was a growing belief in the principle that the government should employ experimental measures, of a more positive kind than in the past, to provide a channel for social progress toward sounder democratic goals. This principle overthrew the nineteenth-century idea of progress in which individualistic liberty was presumed to bring progress automatically. The other basic characteristic was the discovery that political democracy was inseparable from economic democracy; and that if political democracy had faltered and failed, it was largely because economic democracy had not even been tried. Rising young intellectual leaders, such as Ward, Veblen, and Dewey, inspired by these new concepts, rejected individualistic self-assertion as a panacea either for individual freedom or for social security.

Lester F. Ward, an Aristotle from the frontier West, reared among impoverished pioneer families, was not a young man when his country began to recognize him as a foremost sociologist. His *Dynamic Sociology,* first published in 1883, did not begin to sell until after 1897, when a second edition was printed. Attacking the "social statics" of individualism as blind social evolution by an unplanned process, Ward proposed planning by experts; and upon the hesitant and complacent he urged the dynamic principle responsible for progress, the "efficacy of effort." No socialist but a prophet of a coming era of social planning, he looked forward to a great role for governments in the making of legislation to equalize opportunity. Individualism had relied upon governments for the creation and protection of special privileges; and therewith democracy had failed in its logical purpose of elimination of man-made inequalities. Ward attacked untrammeled individualism as based on "the fundamental error that the favors of this world are distributed entirely according to merit." Any idea of progress worthy of a democracy must evolve better planning; the new generation must undertake "the improvement of society by cold calculation."

More shocking to middle-class complacency was the unconventional social scientist Thorstein Veblen. This midwestern son of Scandinavian farmer stock contributed mordant analyses of undemocratic features of the American class structure. Inspecting the theory of the leisure class, he riddled the favorite pseudo-Darwinian assumption of the well to do that material success equated with superior biological fitness. Studying what he called the instinct of workmanship, he concluded that predatory and "pecuniary" traits tending toward aggression were most pronounced among the upper classes, and that workmanship—industrious and peaceable traits —was more common among classes directly and personally engaged in work with modern mechanical processes.

Evolving a theory of business enterprise based on existing practices of going concerns, Veblen pointed out that learned laissez-faire abstractions about a "frictionless and beneficent economic system" were naïve. He sought understanding of economic behavior "in terms of the process itself." Evaluating absentee ownership, restriction of production, and price fixing, he classified the existing order as "a pecuniary culture" and its "economic laws" as folklore peculiar to that culture and not absolute laws of eternal validity. Influencing the next generation of sociologists and economists both at home and abroad, Veblen in ironic prose dissected the hidden tissues of monopoly and inefficiencies of capitalism that retarded maximum employment of men and machines. Modern business organization with its emphasis on profits rather than on maximum production, he concluded, had altered the economy into a contest between consumers, representing the public, and salesmen, representing the producers. In 1918, war turned Veblen's attention to the neglected problem of the economics of peace. Veblen was more responsible than most of his compeers for new perspectives on irrational behavior among practical men who directed the affairs of the world's economy.

The work of sociologists like Ward and economists like Veblen was buttressed by the findings of social-service investigators and allied experts on the problems of public health and the growing question of relief for the sick, the aged, and the impoverished classes. Dr. John A. Ryan, pioneering in methods for accurate measurement of standards of living, amassed data for a sober volume, A Living Wage (1906). His study revealed that the average wage earner had a yearly income certainly below the minimum necessary for maintenance of a family at the bare level of health and decency. Dr. Edward T. Devine in a moving analysis, Misery and Its Causes (1909), similarly exposed the encrustations of age-old prejudices about the extent and sources of poverty. He called attention to the effect of low wages in impairing mental health as well as physical health. A welter of such studies began to appear.

From the findings of the specialists came a portentous challenge to preconceived ideas of orthodox churchmen and other conservative defenders of economic inequality. Public health experts like Dr. Devine and social economists like John R. Commons made a frontal attack on the nineteenth-century gospel of wealth. Early in his career Commons criticized orthodox Christianity as concerned too much with charity and much too little with justice. The younger generation of intellectual pioneers rejected the orthodox preachment that poverty was inevitable, that poverty reflected in fact the working of divine and natural law.

New investigations threw light on the history of the idea of poverty. Orthodox religious thought, it was pointed out, had given impoverishment a supernatural significance, as a "trial" or "punishment" visited upon those who were undeserving or who needed the pressure of poverty to force them to useful labor. Conservative theologians still perpetuated a fear of abundance and disseminated a confused idea that higher standards of living would signify materialism and cause a decline in the appeal of orthodoxy. Equally pervasive among men of affluence had been the traditional ridicule of ideas of economic abundance as utopian nonsense. New historical investigations of the conservative reaction in the era of Hamilton and the Federalists, of the social philosophy of big slaveowners, and of other economic elites revealed the persistence of an aristocratic belief that poverty was inevitable as well as beneficent from a business standpoint. The prod of necessity not only compelled lazy masses to useful labor but fired the select few among the poor to rise from rags to riches. As for the rest, low wages were fixed by the impersonal determination of economic law, the value of labor in terms of the labor market. Collective bargaining by unions, minimum-wage laws, and regulation by governments were unintelligent interferences with natural economic processes.

Having dissected such patterns of conservative thought, twentieth-century investigators condemned them as class sophistry. The gospel of wealth and the "economic laws" of unrestrained individualism presupposed an idea of progress, but it was progress for the few at the expense of the many. Mankind could do better if it abandoned drift and asserted mastery; if the individuals composing society were to shape their own destiny, they could do so in the twentieth century only by collective action and public planning.

No one more perfectly characterized the new range of social thought than John Dewey, and none rivaled him in leadership of the intellectual assault upon the old absolutes, supposed eternal laws, and fixed dogmas.

Nor was any one more emphatic in making a distinction between a selfish materialism and an economy designed for social efficiency, for fullest development of the individual capacities of all and not of only the few. Born in Vermont and trained in philosophy and psychology at two eastern universities, he first gained prominence in the West teaching at the universities of Minnesota, Michigan, and finally Chicago. As a young man he concluded that political democracy was without any solid foundation—and therefore meaningless—unless accompanied by economic democracy. When in 1894 he went to the University of Chicago, he quickly became impressed with Hull-House and Jane Addams, to whom he owed much for the clarification of his ideas and for a concrete knowledge of evil inequalities in industrial life. He was also profoundly influenced by the theories of William James, who believed that philosophy should be pragmatic—that is, concerned with practical applications and tested by actual consequences, much as scientific hypotheses were tested by experience in the laboratory.

Dewey taught that ideas were instruments; the object of social thought was not to understand or defend the existing order but to control and shape the world to human betterment. The educational system, economic institutions, the governmental process, and other instrumentalities of society should be remolded to change the environment of man and thus by social planning change man's behavior. Dewey's psychological studies convinced him that individual thought and behavior were so profoundly influenced by the environment that it was vain to think of creating a good society by merely seeking to reform the individual. For conscious social planning the old code of individualism was not only inadequate; it was a positive foe of experimental attempts at improvement of the environment. As such, the gospel of wealth, while boasting of progress, was opposed to any scientific idea of progress, for it insisted instead upon an unplanned process of social evolution.

Dewey's insistence that ideas were instruments occasioned the name given his philosophy, "instrumentalism." Like William James, he repudiated notions of eternal verities or fixed goals. Truth was not absolute. The needs of future generations were unknown. Morality itself must be relative, for social morals must be related to actual conditions and problems of changing life. Practical morality should be evolved by a trial-and-error process of testing and observing consequences, as a scientist would seek to do. "Not perfection as a final goal, but the ever enduring process of perfecting, maturing, refining, is the aim in living," declared Dewey. Social speculation should be concerned with the here and now, with practical wants, with what the next steps should be. Believing that moral values were relative to time and place and changing conditions, he was critical of the ethical values of those who upheld absolute property rights and an authoritarian system of private enterprise. There was no fixed, eternal line between what was public and what was private; the public was that which had consequences.

When John Dewey returned to the East in 1904 to train successive college generations at Columbia he had already taken national leadership in revitalizing the social ideas of American educators. Injecting new meaning into educational enterprise, he rejected ideas of an unchangeable heredity. Human nature could be and had been changed; and the school system should deliberately be devoted to modifying human conduct by training in social attitudes. Dewey's followers, rebelling against authoritarian instruction, taught students to examine the consequences of ideas. Traditional preconceived doctrines must be tested by analysis of actual problems of life and judged by the concrete results. "Learning by doing" became a slogan of the progressive movement in education. Dewey's influence was visible in a deeper concern of teachers for development of the individual interests and capacities of students, and in an equally warm concern for social attitudes necessary in a complex democratic society. Although personally nothing but a stout believer in education for democracy, Dewey found himself attacked by manufacturers' associations over the kind of education needed for an industrial society. During his long experience, abundant evidence accumulated of subtle pressures from groups seeking to make schools an agency for perpetuating the aristocracy of the machine age.

The expanding influence of progressive social philosophy received dynamic re-enforcement through aggressive leadership and organized action in religious and humanitarian fields. Though scholars soberly diagnosed the ills of society, they did not necessarily prescribe remedies or reach popular audiences. Religious and humanitarian forces, drawing on the findings of the specialists, contributed both intellectual preparation for the Progressive Movement and emotional impetus on a popular plane. Clergymen, civic-minded business and professional men, women's organizations, and other liberal elements of the middle class were not impressed by the Marxian intimation that capitalism was doomed by its own ineradicable economic inefficiency. Like the bulk of middle-class scholars, they were aroused primarily by social inefficiency and the searing effect of social maladjustment upon human life. Seeking correction through ethical endeavors, religious and social leaders posed the Judaic-Christian tradition against the profit drive and the practice of private plunder at public expense. Responding to the same moral idealism that converted English bishops from high Tories into pink Liberals or red Laborites, American Protestant churchgoers after 1890 gradually went through a soul-searching process occasioned by the rise of the new "social gospel." By 1900 a widening group of clergymen, educators, and leaders of reform condemned the fundamental ethics of any economy based upon competition, and some became converts to Christian Socialism. Weighing capitalism in the moral scale, they objected that realities did not conform to capitalist theory. The gospel of wealth, dear to conservatives, assumed that the bold and enterprising would survive and prosper, and that the weak and unfortunate would benefit from the stewardship of the strong and the bold. The realities, contended liberal churchmen, were indeed that the strong had prospered, but veneration of profit became veneration of greed: it debased the human spirit into callous acceptance of misery and exploitation.

The ferment of the social gospel among Protestants produced in 1908 a vigorous new reform organization, the Federal Council of the Churches of Christ in America. Developing into an energetic national association, the council urged applied Christianity and engaged in the tactics of agitation and political pressure to induce the state and national governments to match European standards of social legislation. Meanwhile among American Catholics, a liberal movement, younger and relatively weaker and less well organized than in European Catholic countries, drew inspiration from Leo XIII's encyclical on social justice. The famous papal pronouncement, "Rerum novarum" (1891), identified moderate socialist ideals with Christianity and dissociated the ethical values preached by the church from the materialistic values associated with capitalism. The social gospel could not be dismissed as irresponsible agitation, for it came from respectable quarters and was voiced by national figures like Washington Gladden and Walter Rauschenbusch. Re-enforcing the middle-class intellectual preparation for progressivism, it added emotional dynamite because it spoke to the moral conscience on the basis of values at least as sacred as those of capitalism.

A small but able group of liberal magazine editors and publicists, breaking away from the conventional conservatism of middle-class journalism, re-enforced social science and religious humanitarianism and galvanized public opinion by focusing attention on shocking revelations. Popular magazines, produced at lower costs with modern machinery and sold to a widening audience, gave space to exposures of the railroads, the trusts, the fleecing of investors and consumers, the evils of prostitution, child labor, fake medical cures, harmful foods, and all the old and new devices for extorting profit from human weakness or human need.

From Finley Peter Dunne, favorite humorist and known to the nation as "Mr. Dooley," came sly approval:

Now whin I pick me fav'rite magazine off the flure, what do I find? Ivrything has gone wrong. Th' wurruld is little betther thin a convict's camp. . . . All th' pomes be th' lady authoressesses that used to begin: 'Oh, moon, how fair!' now begin: 'Oh, Ogden Armour, how awful!' . . . Here ye ar-re. Last edition. Just out. Full account iv th' Crimes iv Incalculated. . . . Graft ivry-where. 'Graft in th' Insurance Comp'nies,' 'Graft in Congress,' 'Graft in th' Supreem Coort,' 'Graft be an Old Grafter.' . . .[1]

Liberal journalists, some of whom frankly resorted to sensationalism to attract popular attention, were stigmatized as "muckrakers"; but it was their prudent habit to keep in reserve carefully prepared documentary proof in case of a suit for libel. Their charges were true in the main, and irate men whose deeds they condemned dared not take a case to court.

Toward the end of the muckraking era, hostile business interests began to exploit a form of boycott—withdrawal of important advertising contracts upon which periodicals depended to pay operating costs—to bludgeon publishers to drop articles of social criticism. But beginning in 1902 and for the next half dozen years, Lincoln Steffens and other leading journalists succeeded in exposing "the shame of the cities" and evils in the life of the underpaid masses. Ida M. Tarbell, able editor on the staff of *McClure's Magazine*, in 1903 began to run as a serial her celebrated "History of the Standard Oil Company." Combining the sincerity and scrupulous documentation of a careful historian with the popular flair of a skilled journalist, when she laid bare many infamies of the most notorious of American trusts, she touched a responsive public chord. "Read Idarem on Jawn D.," said Mr. Dooley; "she's a lady, but she's got th' punch." Ray Stannard Baker, also in *McClure's*, shocked the middle class with a graphic description of the brutalizing life of child laborers in the coal mines. Exposures in *Leslie's, Everybody's,* and other middle-class periodicals disclosed unpleasant facts of race discrimination, exploitation of labor, unhealthful housing and sewage, and other social blemishes which, though large in the microscope of an investigator, were normally invisible from the remote vantage point of "residential districts" and comfortable suburbs.

Although middle-class hearts were touched, no very deep appreciation of the life and labor of the working multitudes accompanied the ethical awakening. The moral conscience was indeed deeply stirred when aroused to the fact that in 1910, for example, nearly two million children under sixteen and nearly half of them girls were among America's workers. The moral conscience equally condemned the immoral filth, vermin, and disease that was the shame of the cities. *The Jungle* (1906), an accurate novel by Upton Sinclair, centered attention upon criminous conditions in the Chicago orbit of the meat-packing trusts; yet the public grasped, not the

---

[1] *Dissertations by Mr. Dooley*. New York: Harpers, 1906, pp. 257–258.

Heyday of the Muckrakers

(From *Collier's,* March 25, 1905.)

author's intention, but the lurid details on the manufacture of food. A sensational best seller, the book facilitated passage of the Pure Food and Drug Act of 1906. The author declared that he had appealed to the heart of the public but had reached its stomach. What Sinclair intended in his novel was a description of human realities in industrial life—a peasant, lured to the land of plenty by glowing advertising circulated by steamship companies in his native Lithuania; then his slow awakening—an immigrant in "Packingtown" who had to pay graft before he could get a job, who was worked beyond his strength and yet forced by poverty to live in filth, where his family succumbed to physical and moral infection; a new American, with faith in his adopted country, who trusted a bank with his slender savings and was fleeced of the product of his thrift when reckless financial mismanagement caused the bank's failure; a loyal worker who trusted the great packing company until he was repeatedly laid off with no means of achieving security for his family; a striker in a strike that failed, defeated and exiled from his occupation by the company "blacklist," and ultimately driven to degradation; an immigrant, an American, an American failure.

SOCIAL LEGISLATION

Symptomatic of the American failure, the movement to establish higher minimum standards of social and economic security was not as far reaching in the United States as abroad; nor was it formulated into a national program as in other countries. Social legislation sought by progressives included state laws for limitation or abolition of child labor, school attendance requirements, health and safety standards to protect workers in dangerous occupations, limitations on hours for women workers, and some of the various forms of social insurance that other countries had adopted. Three quarters of the states had provisions against the cruder exploitations of child labor in 1913 when Woodrow Wilson became President; but these laws proved inadequate, and the chief advance was made in a smaller number of progressive states by the indirect method of raising the age of compulsory school attendance to eighteen years. When Wilson's first term ended, employers' liability laws, although enacted in many states, remained seriously defective; and virtual lack of law in eighteen states still denied the elementary justice of compensation from business establishments for loss of a hand, arm, eyesight, or life, incurred by men, women, and child laborers in the line of ordinary duty.

Despite the vitalizing progressive impulse, social and economic insecurity for the masses remained the existing reality. In addition to accident insurance under the less defective employers' liability laws, some states began in 1911 to provide mothers' pensions. But the comprehensive European national programs to provide security against unemployment, sickness, and old age were still foreign to the United States. Nor did American progressives find solution for the paradox of mass poverty in the great land of plenty. Attempts to reduce maldistribution of wealth and hereditary great fortunes by the devices of progressive state and national income taxes were not far reaching. Even the moderate European measures to maintain at least better-than-starvation standards of living by a minimum wage in "sweated" industries, while occasionally emulated, made little headway in American states.

In view of the intensity and depth of popular ferment in the United States and the extent of progress in other lands, what accounts for the limited achievement of American progressivism? The American quest for social welfare and economic security was not a broad national movement; its organized political expression did not come primarily through either major party. On the contrary, battles for higher standards were a series of local actions in progressive states induced by the leadership of the reformers, the support of labor unions and humanitarian associations, and the pressure of public opinion. Each gain, state by state, was won in the teeth of opposition from legislators who owed office to the alliance between the managers of politics and the managers of business. Failure of the major parties to make social security a new national issue and to broaden constitutional functions embracing economic welfare compelled reformers to place a dubious reliance on local regulation by the agency of the states. The impressive volume of social legislation, exceeding numerically the previous total in the whole period of American history, was eloquent testimony to the fortitude and perseverance of the forces of enlightenment. But quantity production by state legislative mills still did not bring the nation abreast of the far fewer laws but far higher and more inclusive standards in other liberal countries. "America is lagging far behind England," lamented a writer for *Collier's* in 1913. "Lloyd George might well have given up as impossible the task of securing the adoption of his program, if it had involved the passage, through forty-eight legislatures, of forty-eight separate acts for each of the great ameliorative measures he has forced through the British Parliament!"[2]

The primary deterrents to success were neither public apathy nor lack of capable leaders. Among American obstacles was the unbalanced relation of power-groups that accompanied the splitting of northern and southern agrarian forces during and after the Civil War, ensuring a more complete dominance by the forces of transportation, industry, and finance. A second obstacle arose from the unrepresentative character of national parties, retarding reform by compromises of expediency engineered by vested interests and elected representatives, both of whom were intent on private objects rather than public good. Finally there were the assorted impediments of the constitutional structure. Under the federal system, progressives were forced to fight each battle not once but forty-eight times. States controlled by local industrial elites became islands of rampant individualism, subjecting progressive states and enlightened employers to

---

[2] R. M. McClintock, "The New Politics," *Collier's* LI, 19 (July 26, 1913), p. 24.

unfair competition from employers who exploited lower standards and lower costs. In progressive states, because of the survival of the system of machine politics, progressives had to attempt the virtually impossible; to make reform stick, they must stand on the alert and repeatedly whip up public pressure to save the laws from repeal or from sly, circuitous non-enforcement. Equally baffling was the constitutional hurdle: under a constitutional system of judicial finality, American progressivism encountered a legal structure which, scarcely in accord with majority rule, struck down countless liberal laws or so extracted their teeth as to make them unenforceable.

SOCIAL REFORM AND THE LEGAL BARRICADE

Gradually it dawned on outstanding progressive thinkers that they were face to face with a dual institutionalized check to social changes. One of these checks, federalism—dividing authority between state and national governments—gave strategic advantages to resourceful opponents of reform. A federal structure facilitated resistance, sometimes sectional in character, by blocs of states in which the machines of both major parties were under conservative management. Federalism equally facilitated resistance in those states where one party was so dominant that it was not compelled to compete actively against the other party for votes and offices. A second important institutional basis of resistance to change was separation of powers in the national government, which had led to a slow growth of the power of judicial review. The enlarging judicial prerogative facilitated resistance by the predominance of conservative judges—many of them onetime corporation lawyers—who limited the exercise of the legislative power of the majority in progressive states, and who at the same time frowned upon any alternative national remedy through congressional action.

Progressive political theorists moved hesitantly toward a critical contention that judicial finality and majority rule were incompatible. Theodore Roosevelt denounced the "twilight zone" in which, under current rulings, neither the state nor the national government could act. A noted political scientist who became president of Johns Hopkins University emphasized this weakness in a solid book, *Social Reform and the Constitution* (1911). Marshaling the evidence of countless court rulings, President F. J. Goodnow contended that the American form of government had become an inherent barrier to democratic change. Complaint became common that the judicial arm of the government in Washington did not allow to the state governments a wide local freedom as laboratories for experiment. The residual authority of the states—the "police power" for regulation of property and business under legislation to promote "health, safety, welfare, and public morals"—was so seriously restricted as to prevent intelligent expansion of a flexible power to legislate for the general welfare.

Examples of the persistence of the judicial barricade were the struggles to provide for accident compensation and to regulate working hours and wages for women. Liability of employers for accident compensation was not recognized by legislation in a single state until 1902, when Maryland took feeble action. The third state to act, New York, passed a better law in 1910. But this law and the previous ones were declared unconstitutional. On the whole, judges in American courts were as dogmatic as corporation lawyers in stretching the economic doctrines of laissez faire into constitutional doctrines affording immunity for owners of property. Not until the second decade of the twentieth century were even the most moderate laws for accident compensation upheld in the courts. The same frustration dogged the movement for protection of women workers. In 1895 a court decision on Illinois legislation outlawed liberal programs to reduce the working hours of women. Not for thirteen years, when a new ruling gave sanction to an Oregon law, did the courts permit the states to regulate hours. To win the Oregon case of 1908, the nation's greatest labor lawyer, Louis D. Brandeis, prepared the epochal "Brandeis brief"—filled not with constitutional abstractions but with sociological analyses of actual conditions, justifying the law on the basis of hard facts that only the blindest or most prejudiced of laissez-faire judges could dismiss as irrelevant. Encouraged by sanction of regulation of hours, Massachusetts in 1912 enacted the first minimum-wage law for women. But in the 1920's a reaction toward extreme conservatism terminated judicial liberality for half a generation. In 1923 the Supreme Court decided that minimum-wage laws were unconstitutional.

THE ROLE OF LABOR

A noted progressive economist, after conducting a monumental study of the history of American labor in 1918, concluded that constitutional federalism and the threefold separation of authority in the national government had been obstacles to progress not duplicated in other nations. These were among the forces molding the character of the American labor movement. "By vetoing the laws which labour in its political struggles has been able to secure," wrote John R. Commons, "the courts, joined to divergent state policies, have excluded or delayed labour from legislative influences." The consequence of "our Federal and judicial system of government," he observed, was to force labor "to acquire by trade union action what in other countries has been granted by legislation."[3] Any

---

[3] John R. Commons and Associates, *History of Labour in the United States*. New York: Macmillan, 1918, I, 9. By permission of The Macmillan Company, publishers.

final evaluation of progressivism in the United States must consider this contention.

The deterrents to reform peculiar to the United States and the lag in effective application of international standards in social legislation were conditioning factors unfavorable to the development of labor statesmanship and industrial tranquillity. Reform did not instill—or deserve—unfaltering trust from American workers. One of the consequences of stretching the immunity of property into a constitutional blockade was a mounting volume of criticism of the judiciary by labor organizations, denoting a loss of confidence in the justice dispensed in American courts. More ominous was the growth of radicalism indicated by the rise of the violent revolutionary philosophy and strong-arm activities of disaffected unions which, flouting the American Federation of Labor, conducted sensational struggles under the banner of the Industrial Workers of the World. Another tendency appeared in the conservative leadership of the bulk of the unions that still clung to the Federation. This, the result of disillusionment toward the end of the progressive era, was the tendency to place greater hope in economic bargaining than in political reform.

Undoubtedly on the all-important matter of hours and conditions of work, on wage bargaining as a technique to deal with maldistribution of the nation's income, the gains made by the economic action of unions had been as substantial as those made by the strenuous endeavors of reformers for social legislation. In some respects the unions had extended these gains over a wider area of the whole nation. By 1915 Federation champions of "pure and simple unionism" began to assert that they could win higher minimum standards through strikes and bargaining than through state labor legislation. They had been defeated in the long struggle to get laws to prevent arbitrary governmental alliance with employers, an alliance cemented by court orders—labor injunctions—used as political weapons to break strikes. The favorite legal fiction, "freedom of contract," was still a virulent judicial fetish menacing state authority to regulate in the interests of health and welfare. In legal theory, freedom of contract meant a worker's right to agree to work under substandard conditions; in actual practice, it meant an employer's right to hire and fire on his own terms.

In sum total, legislation for social security and fair employment practices had made only the most rudimentary progress. In 1916 in a standard work on labor economics, George G. Groat concluded that no "definite program" for social security could be anticipated. Employers' liability "in case of accidents," he noted, had "quite completely broken down," and had never been extended on the inclusive European basis to make provisions for sickness, occupational diseases, health tests, and the like. The crusading labor lawyer, Louis D. Brandeis, had converted Massachusetts to a state plan of low-cost insurance offered by mutual savings banks; but while this was a genuine gain for many individuals, it was not a substitute for the national compulsory savings plans in Europe, where the government and the employers both made contributions. Frustrated in countless battles for legislation, suspicious of politicians, rigid minimum wages, and legislative norms, various Federation leaders opposed wage and hour laws. Collective bargaining, they contended, was more flexible and more reliable; it was more in accord with a democratic process of free contracts made by "free men and free women." Collective bargains on wages and hours, it was observed, could not be carried to the courts and declared unconstitutional.

DIRECT DEMOCRACY VS. PARTY GOVERNMENT

Labor leaders were not alone in their dissatisfaction with the process of government. Middle-class leaders of the Progressive Movement shared the fear voiced by Bryan in his contention that "the great issue" was "Democracy against Plutocracy." The issue was whether "property shall be the servant and not the master in the commonwealth," declared Theodore Roosevelt. "The great issue before the American people today is the control of their own government," thundered Wisconsin's leader, Robert M. La Follette.

Long-growing dissatisfaction with the major parties had been attested by party splits, the Liberal Republicans, the procession of third parties, and farmer and labor combinations from grangers and Greenbackers to Populists. Dissatisfaction culminated at the outset of the twentieth century in a deepening distrust of legislatures, politicians, conniving bipartisan political "rings," and corrupt alliances between political spoilsmen and "predatory wealth." The poet Whitman had given authentic voice to public revulsion against the ill-famed breeds that exploited urban citizens:

bawling office-holders . . . kept editors . . . bribers, compromisers, lobbyers, spongers . . . pimpled men, scarr'd inside with vile disease, gaudy outside with gold chains made from the people's money and harlots' money . . . the lousy combings and born freedom-sellers of the earth.

Lord Bryce's friendly and widely read estimate, *The American Commonwealth* (1888), had pointed to American city life and machine politics as outstanding failures. Traveled Americans were well aware of the significant absence of spoilsmen and corruption in English municipalities. American scholars who studied abroad were familiar with the corresponding achievement in Germany where, despite monarchy, the cities had become centers of democratic local government conducted on a plane immeasurably above the practice in the United States. Now the progressive ferment broke through older apathy, boiling over in attack upon "the shame of the cities."

It was natural that public indignation should first find outlet in civic reform in individual communities and in "good government" movements in progressive states. A remarkable group of reform mayors and governors won election in spite of the superior organization of local and state machines. Among the new governors, Charles Evans Hughes of New York, Robert M. La Follette of Wisconsin, Hiram W. Johnson of California, and Woodrow Wilson of New Jersey were eventually to go on to high office in the inner temples of national politics.

New discoveries about the relation between economics and politics led to demands for something more fundamental than the movement for good government. The democratic program, contended leading progressive spokesmen, had somehow failed. Social scientists set themselves to discover how and why democratic aspiration had been thwarted; why the state had been captured by the political spoilsman and economic overlord; and why the government was so largely given over to selfish private advantage. Historians and political scientists went back to the masterful forces that had molded American politics and the structure of government. Corrosive investigation dissipated the nationalistic romanticism and "arid constitutionalism" of nineteenth-century accounts of politics and government. The distinguished historian Frederick Jackson Turner instructed a generation in the influence of a frontier environment. Turner and his followers focused attention upon the westward movement of common men, upon the democratic quest for open land and equality of opportunity, and upon historic struggles of common folk of the back country against the privileged upper classes of the Atlantic seaboard. New economic realism was stimulated by concrete studies of conflicts of interest between economic classes as a primary factor in sectional politics.

From sober scholars came the shocking pronouncement that the Constitution was "not a democratic instrument" and "was not intended to be." Most provocative among such studies, Charles Beard's sensational volume, *An Economic Interpretation of the Constitution* (1913), documented the discovery that the Constitution had been framed—in Madison's phrase—to serve the purpose of the "minority of the opulent." The framers had created checks and balances to thwart popular majorities. The constitutional structure was not designed as a democratic instrument for government by the people. On a higher plane of analysis a political scientist, J. Allen Smith, had already anticipated Beard. His small but incisive volume, *The Spirit of American Government* (1907), placed under the microscope the crucial features of the Constitution—separation of powers, federalism, the amending process—which handicapped twentieth-century democracy in its struggle to devise more adequate institutions for majority rule. Less well known was a pioneer study of political misrepresentation. Arthur Bentley, in *The Process of Government* (1908), investigated the connivance between elected representatives and the anonymous lobbyists of powerful special interests. Piercing through the shams of party war cries, Bentley analyzed pressure-group techniques by which organized minorities acting for private interests masqueraded as the majority and persistently defeated the public interest.

Such writings injected the data of reality into political science. The astigmatism of nationalistic romanticism was corrected by a growing appreciation of the power ambitions of organized economic groups and the advantages that accrued to them from predemocratic checks and balances inherited from the eighteenth century. Those who, like Bentley, studied the behavior of political spoilsmen as legislators contributed the discovery that usages and customs of the "unwritten constitution," grafted upon the governing process by political parties, likewise weighed heavily against the forces of modern democracy.

Conservative spokesmen deplored critical analysis as unpatriotic, but in so doing they missed the significance of the new history and the new political science. The progressive intention was not shallow "debunking." If famous national heroes shrank to smaller stature, that result was incidental to a major constructive purpose. Critical analysis had as its object a realistic understanding of creaking, antique machinery of government and accompanying fetishes and constitutional symbolism that, surviving too long from a predemocratic age, now impeded a sound and reliable procedure to give force to majority rule.

Fired by new insight into the realities of political manipulation, militant progressives enlarged the movement for good government into a crusade to democratize the political process. If the power of property was to be subjected to the will of the commonwealth, the power of democracy must somehow be strengthened. If the constitutional system enfeebled democracy, then the Constitution itself was in need of reform. The majority must rule. "Direct Democracy" became a slogan; and progressive politicians and reformers hopefully advocated new devices intended to democratize the machinery of government.

Because of the bankruptcy of party leadership in Congress, reform began at the bottom rather than at the top, in local communities and civic organizations rather than in congressional debates or national conventions. Accordingly the movement for direct democracy was restricted to devices aimed primarily at state and local abuses. Federal machinery and political abuses in the national parties went largely unscathed. There were three exceptions: the sanction of income taxes (Sixteenth Amendment, 1913), correcting the obduracy of the federal judicial branch; direct popular election of senators (Seventeenth Amendment, 1913), correcting the undemocratic provision of the Constitution; and woman suffrage (Nineteenth Amendment, 1921). In the last two cases, local progressive pressure for action in separate states, rather than national leadership by major parties, forced through the reforms.

Four favorite formulas of direct democracy, designed as state and local devices to unseat the corrupt alliance of bosses and vested interests, were the initiative, referendum, recall, and the direct primary. Reflecting the lack of confidence in parties as democratic instruments, the initiative was intended to allow an aroused citizenry to propose and vote on reform measures that misrepresentative legislative bodies refused to enact. By giving the voters power to force a referendum on unpopular laws, the electorate was ostensibly protected against the machinations of politicians and private interests. The recall, adopted in a few states and some municipalities, sought to empower the voters to remove bad judges, legislators, city councilors, and other elected officers. These devices of direct democracy, carrying further the localism of Jacksonian Democracy, sought to place responsibility on private citizens and not on party leaders. On this formula, the direct primary was intended as a means to displace the

Direct Democracy: the Initiative and Referendum

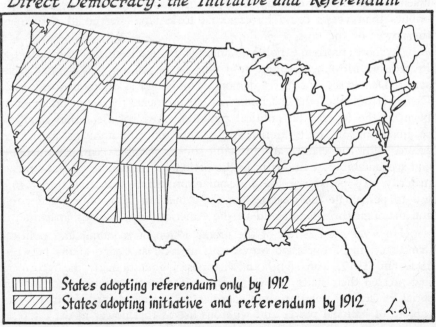

|||||||| States adopting referendum only by 1912
///// States adopting initiative and referendum by 1912   *L.d.*

nefarious machine caucus or nominating convention whereby bosses and ward heelers controlled the drafting of the state and local party "ticket."

The direct primary embodied the concept of nominating "good men" for office. But as a device to place good parties in power, it did not repair an age-old neglect. Parties, since their birth, had been orphans unknown to the Constitution. Necessary to the very existence of a majority choice, parties were products of the unwritten constitution, extra legal associations virtually subject to no regulation under federal law. Local law and custom regulating parties varied widely from state to state but were rigged universally to entrench the power of local political managers. To eradicate this "government by intrigue, concealment, and bribery," the direct primary replaced the machine caucus with an open voting system in which any citizen who was a party member could compete for popular election to the ticket as nominee of the party. By 1913 most of the forty-eight states had adopted primary laws, but longer experience brought disillusion. Direct primaries struck at a crucial point—the nominating process—the point at which local party organizations most flagrantly disregarded consideration of national party principles. The primary was not, however, aimed at this problem; nor did it prove adequate even for its ostensible object of nominating "good men." "Leg work" by the machine, lack of organization behind "good government" candidates, and the confusing array of names on the "long ballot"—the mistaken overburdening of busy citizens with more responsibility for party politics than voters could be expected to assume—served to perpetuate the power of the boss.

A more profound political analysis by intellectual leaders of the Progressive Movement suggested from the beginning that neither Jacksonian Democracy nor direct democracy provided a key to majority rule. Democratization of the machinery of government, they concluded, must begin at the top of the political pyramid. Any basic solution required readjustment of constitutional forms and reorganization of parties to accord with the elementary principle of responsible central leadership and accountability of the party to the nation-wide mandate of the national majority. To perpetuate the Jacksonian principle of local majority rule was to perpetuate the weakness of the American form of national party and maintain the stranglehold of the American type of local machine.

However short it fell of the grand design of economic and political democracy, the Progressive Movement, in local and state affairs between 1900 and 1917, won significant victories. Unquestionably the reformers had pressed their states and communities forward to higher standards of social efficiency. But the same energies and ideals demanded more—recapture of national power and vigorous use of that power in the interests of the whole people. No movement so explosive could fail as completely as Populists and Bryan Democrats had in 1896; and well before 1917, when American energies began to be consumed in war against Germany, strong political leaders and ardent advocates of equalized opportunity were to contribute measurably to the theory and practice of modern democracy on the national stage.

XXIV

PROGRESSIVISM AND THE G.O.P.

1901–1909

Middle-class progressivism, despite its great strength in local communities and states, was easily deflected and often defeated in party battles over national affairs. Yet, surging upward in the first two decades of the twentieth century, the "ferment of progress" challenged the system of rule by the few, discredited the "stand patters" in Congress, placed at least one strong liberal in the White House, then spent its force in the aftermath of World War I. Through direct election of senators, woman suffrage, and income taxes, the movement left an indelible mark on national government. Progressives contributed also to two constructive tendencies: reliance upon experts in the work of government, notably in the executive branch and administrative agencies; and increasing reliance upon presidential leadership in an effort to remedy the recurrent impotence of an elected majority in the legislative branch. But it was precisely here, in its search for a principle of leadership, that progressivism faltered. Only a few among the intellectual leaders of the progressive generation carried rigorous democratic analysis to the point of proposing a functional theory of responsible party management.

The Republican and Democratic parties, said Lord Bryce in one of the twentieth-century editions of *The American Commonwealth,* were "like two bottles. Each bore a label denoting the kind of liquor it contained, but each was empty." Great and growing dislocations called for action, but Republicans and Democrats alike failed to alleviate them. Neither of the two major reform measures, the Interstate Commerce Act (1887) and the Sherman Antitrust Act (1890), had allayed public apprehension of the corrupt power of railroads and trusts; these laws had not been distinctively party measures, nor had they been enforced either by a Republican administration or by a Democratic administration. Parties of the American type had, in fact, achieved so little utility as sensitive instruments to register majority will that a vast and indignant literature excoriated politicians, fumed at the deliberate technique of vagueness in party platforms, and bitterly lampooned the contradictory campaign pledges of differing candidates, all of whom professed to speak for the same party. What accounted for the widespread loss of public confidence in national parties? Why did democracy fail? Was failure caused by misrepresentation through an undemocratic legislative procedure controlled by machines in alliance with pressure groups? Was it caused by defective institutions that perpetuated a system of loose party manage- ment denying effective authority to able leaders who sought to serve the public interest? Soberly the experts sought an answer.

Devotees of an economic interpretation, such as Charles A. Beard, refurbished the old seventeenth-century law of Harrington—that concentration of economic power produces concentration of political power in the same social class. Disproportionate power was undoubtedly a fact. It was so recognized, by congressional investigations of lobbies, corrupt practices acts to restrain the power of money in elections, popular election of senators, and direct primaries; but progressives who resorted to these new forms of surgery failed to remove the cancer of "invisible government." For if misrepresentation was at the heart of the problem, the question of leadership was inseparable from it. The most incisive diagnoses revealed functional disorders in the organs of government, frustrating leadership and confusing the public mind.

LEADERSHIP IN A DEMOCRATIC PROCESS

Leading political scientists, men of the stature of Walter Bagehot and his fellow Englishman, James Bryce, and outstanding Americans— Woodrow Wilson, Frank Goodnow, Henry Jones Ford, J. Allen Smith, and Abbott Lawrence Lowell—reached a portentous common conclusion on the American problem of government. Leadership did not automatically emerge when the voters elected representatives. The organizational principle of a majority was as crucial as the principle of representation itself. The will of the people could find actual expression only through a party organization that could command a working majority among its members in Congress. Outworn political forms and anomalous customs of party management, imbedded in the usages of the unwritten constitution and to some extent in the Constitution itself, made the problem of democracy and leadership in the United States difficult of solution. Forcing a new breach in the walls of old provincialism, Wilson and leading American authorities drew on the world's political science then emerging from the vast parliamentary upheavals of the nineteenth century. Deriving new perspectives from the international scene, they discovered in the comparative study of existing governments and systems of party manage ment a more reliable key to democracy's problems than the mechanics described in the eighteenth-century *Federalist Papers*.

In the minds of such experts, party government under a cabinet system, notably the English model, exemplified the most workable procedure for efficiency and stability, at the same time giving reality to checks and balances to assure accountability to public opinion. They pointed to a cardinal difference between American and English government. The English Parliament and executive were not "independent" under a separation of powers but were united under the central leadership of the dominant party. The executive was composed of the legislative leaders of the majority party. As administrators, these cabinet officers and ministers served as heads of all the great executive departments; as legislators, they took the lead in parliamentary debates as official spokesmen. Technically, the legislature alone was supreme; actually, the party that had won in the elections was the supreme governing power.

Such complete party integration of the power to govern converted all hotly contested public issues into party issues; government became party government; responsibility became party responsibility; opposition became a party opposition. Initiation of all major measures fell to the joint executive-legislative leadership, the Cabinet-Ministry, which acted as a single great committee to formulate government policy. Since this committee was drawn from the majority party, the opposition party had no direct share in drafting major bills. But far more effectively than in American party practice, the minority filled the great democratic role of "responsible opposition," questioning and criticizing the ministers, compelling the government to make a continuous public defense of every major action, holding the majority party accountable. The consequence was to make legislative debate a significant and enlightening medium for instructing the average voter and arousing public opinion.

A crowning democratic device—dissolution of Parliament and the holding of new elections whenever conflict developed between the Cabinet and the legislative majority—assured respect for a mandate from the voters. The cabinet members, composed of the dominant party leaders, were held responsible to the rank and file in the legislature by the understanding that the Cabinet held office only so long as it had the support of a majority of the elected representatives. Whenever the majority defeated a cabinet bill or voted a resolution of want of "confidence," the Cabinet either resigned or dissolved Parliament. Dissolution of the legislature meant that in less than a month new national elections would return a new Parliament. If the voters sustained the Cabinet by re-electing a parliamentary majority of that party, the cabinet leaders continued in office and the Parliament accepted its bills. If the opposition party had a majority, its legislative leaders thereupon became the "Government," forming their own Cabinet and taking command of the executive branch. Thus, on the immediate issues between the parties, a clear mandate was made and respected; the will of the people was decisive.

Party leadership, party unity, party discipline, and party responsibility were all achieved through the great power to force dissolution of Parliament and call a new election. The dominant party leaders were held responsible to the legislative majority by the power to compel resignation of the Government at any time. The customary dissolution of the legislature following a defeat of the Government gave voters an opportunity to repudiate a party for failure to introduce a bill, or for bringing in an unpopular one, or for blunders or malfeasance in office. Party unity was strengthened by the consciousness of majority representatives at all times that reckless voting against their own Cabinet might vote their own party out of power. Party discipline inhered in the power of the Cabinet to call new elections, forcing insurgent party members to consider the risks of losing their seats; or, if their recalcitrance against their own party warranted, of being barred from the party ticket by an understanding between the local constituency and the national committee of the party, the Central Office. In the latter extreme case, a candidate of national reputation, loyal to party principles, would receive the party nomination and campaign against the recalcitrant insurgent.

Rising American interest in European government suggested a loss of the braggart Jacksonian faith. We had lost our "wonted tone of confident hope," noted a Princeton senior in 1879; we had exchanged it for "anxiety about the future of our institutions . . . we hail an adjournment of congress as a temporary immunity from danger." They were the words of young Woodrow Wilson in an article suggesting cabinet government in the United States. New need brought a new amalgam of old contradictions. Men like Wilson brought back the Hamiltonian ideal of strong government but sought to convert it to Jeffersonian ends. The structure of American parties, they contended, frittered away the power to govern; and neither party could be held accountable.

Wilson's classic, *Congressional Government* (1884), demonstrated that American parties were loose rival confederations highly organized in local districts to win office and spoils, but so weakly organized in Congress as to be incapable of carrying out a coordinated party program. The United States had no joint committee like a Cabinet to give the Senate and House the advantage of unified leadership or to give Congress the power to control or remove the executive. Congress, Wilson disclosed, operated not under a party government but under a multitudinous "committee government." Because of the chaos of competing committees in

Senate and House, the nation was ruled by a score and a half of "little legislatures." In fact,

to be exactly accurate, the House has as many leaders as there are subjects of legislation. . . . The chairmen of the standing committees do not constitute a cooperative body like a ministry. They do not consult and concur in the adoption of homogeneous and mutually helpful measures; there is no thought of acting in concert.

The performance in Congress was "unsystematic, confused, and desultory"; legislation was "conglomerate, not homogeneous"; and it was "impossible to discover any unity" or "common purpose."

"The more power is divided the more irresponsible it becomes." The two parties, Republicans and Democrats, divided responsibility in appointments to committees and selected their weaker men as well as their stronger men to serve on them. A Cabinet-Ministry, on the contrary, was composed of the strong men; and all of them were members of the majority party. Since a Senate or House committee was bipartisan, the minority party had "a share in law-making"; committee votes were, therefore, not party votes, and bills were not party bills. Congressional debate, by the same token, was not party debate. No member could speak with authority for the "Government"; no party member could take the floor as official spokesman of the "Opposition." "The great need is, not to get rid of parties," but to organize Congress so that parties acted as parties, each responsible for its party record. Unless "punishment can be extended to the party," no triumph can be "gained by public opinion."

The irresponsible character of congressional government, Wilson observed, reappeared in the American executive under the separation of powers. "Congress does not deal so directly with our executive as do the French and English parliaments . . . and cannot, therefore, control" an administration "so effectually." "The anomaly which has resulted" was seen in the frequency with which a President vetoed "legislation passed by the party whom he represents." Related to this was the question why congressmen felt free to lash at a President and why a President took his political life in his hands if he dared to reply to Congress in kind. Responsible party government was impeded by the "separation of the Cabinet from real party influence, and from the party leadership which would seem properly to belong to its official station." Because of this lack of joint executive-legislative leadership, "Congress looks upon advice offered to it by anybody but its own members as gratuitous impertinence." At the same time the absence of direct party control over the President and Cabinet made the resources of the legislature in dealing with bureaucracy "limited and defective. . . . Congress stands almost helplessly outside the departments."

Wilson trusted to "practical common sense" to overcome the obstacles of divided power and "leaderless government." The fertility of the unwritten constitution had never been exhausted. The existing governing process, Wilson noted, had evolved through changing party practice, "practically amending the Constitution" without formally amending it. "If the character and opinions of legislators and administrators change from time to time, the nature of the government changes with them." The lucid pages of *Congressional Government* did not dwell specifically upon such constitutional obstacles as staggered fixed terms of senators, representatives, and Presidents, or the prohibition against a member of Congress simultaneously holding office in the executive branch, or the absence of an express power for the dissolution of Congress and the calling of special elections. In 1884 Wilson expected congressional parties to take the lead in establishing "responsible" legislative supremacy. Resignation upon defeat, he asserted, was the essence of responsible government. Although Wilson never pursued the point, speculation might suggest that the Constitution did not necessarily prohibit resignation or the holding of special elections.

Wilson's crucial contention dealt with the world trend toward centralization. Democracy would be in danger if it continued to tolerate increasing centralization without increasing responsibility. In an oft-quoted passage he summed up experience in modern organization:

If there be one principle clearer than another, it is this: that in any business, whether of government or of mere merchandising, *somebody must be trusted,* in order that when things go wrong it may be quite plain who should be punished. . . . *Power and strict accountability for its use* are the essential constituents of good government.

But the chaos of leaderless committee government continued. In 1908 Wilson wrote on the enlarging role of the executive and presidential initiative as a tendency resulting from the internal confusion of Congress and parties.

In a now forgotten debate between progressive publicists like Herbert Croly and leading specialists on political science, the issue was "direct democracy" versus "representative party government." Proponents of the latter, Bryce, Goodnow, Ford, Smith, and Lowell, shared the conviction that responsible party government under a cabinet system was the greatest democratic invention of the nineteenth century. The American problem of government was traceable to political machinery of an earlier age in which people who knew little of political parties supposed there was a virtue in distributing powers into many hands. American government, concluded Bryce, suffered from the weakness that "no one acts under the full sense of direct accountability." The party system did not enable voters to know "how or where to fix responsibility for misfeasance or neglect." Goodnow's pioneer work, *Politics and Administration* (1900), remarked that the cabinet system of concentrating leadership had the great advantage of giving "the people as a whole the power to say nay to a policy of which they do not approve" and the power to replace unpopular leaders with those "more in accord with the popular mind"; whereas the American system made it possible for differences between the executive and the legislature "to exist immediately after the election." In *The Spirit of American Government* (1907), J. Allen Smith traced "the misrepresentative character of the American political party" to the multiple division of powers that frustrated majorities and prevented party accountability. Advocates of reform were mistaken when they "directed their attention mainly to the party machine." "Where the party which has carried the election is powerless to enforce its policy . . . there can be no responsible party government."

Lowell's classic, *The Government of England* (1908), began to open the eyes of American students to the extraordinary achievements of representative government under a disciplined party system. Centralized English parties had provided the courage and will to abolish the spoils system and eradicate "boss" politics at the same time that they developed the strength and integrity to resist pressure groups. Direct democracy, trusting in eternal vigilance and arduous agitation by public-spirited citizenry in a thousand communities, was not an effective substitute for "responsible party government." Comparing "the strength of parties" in England and America, Lowell instructed a generation of students in the significance of the cardinal fact, still amazing, that American parties had a vast, multitudinous, and labyrinthian organization in local constituencies, while England, with nothing more than a skeleton party organization, was free of local machines. American parties were organized at the bottom, outside Congress, to prey on city governments and extract spoils from state and national authorities. English parties were organized at the top, inside Parliament, and were strong enough to resist sectionalism, local pressures, and spoilsmen.

Implicit in Lowell's analysis was the contradiction between direct democracy and representative government. In the American theory, inherited from the pre-party days of feudalism and monarchy, legislators were either one of two things: delegates pledged to obey the dictates of their local constituencies; or local representatives professing to obey personal conviction regardless of national party ties. In English theory, Lowell observed, parties were presumed to represent the national interest. Representatives were presumed to represent the national principles of their party, not local special interests or private personal preferences. Any other theory of representation would entrench pressure groups and bosses and would defeat party responsibility.

POLITICAL MANAGERS AND THE STEWARDS OF WEALTH

In the twentieth century as in the nineteenth, American parties exemplified the analysis of the experts. President McKinley, elected for a second term in 1900 with Theodore Roosevelt as his Vice-President, was the favorite of Mark Hanna and other big businessmen. Friendly to imperialism abroad, in home affairs McKinley was equally hospitable to his friends in great enterprises. He made no effort to curb trusts and special privilege. His opponent in the campaign, Bryan, on a platform denouncing imperialism, monopolies, and "trust-breeding" tariffs, fought a lost battle with a badly divided party. Progressives who looked back at the record of Democrats in Congress under Cleveland could read confirmation of Bryce's contention that both parties were like empty bottles. But if, at the opening of the twentieth century, reformers seeking a welfare state gained nothing by electing representatives to Congress, fate suddenly gave them a spokesman in the White House by the bullet of an assassin. The shooting of McKinley by a demented person elevated Theodore Roosevelt to an office for which party chieftains would never have nominated him.

The ensuing hectic years were to prove that no democratic upsurge as powerful as the Progressive Movement could wholly fail to stamp its impress upon national laws betokening the stirring of the social conscience. But the same years gave proof also of a changed organization of forces that made more difficult the battle for the people against the established system of rule for the few.

The key to national politics in the twentieth century was to be found in two interacting sets of institutions: one, the new structure of supercorporations and trade associations evolving as the base of a business system of power; the other, the constitutional and party base as described by the major political analysts. The interaction of these two sets of institutions was all too neatly symbolized in the exact coincidence of the consolidation of irresponsible power of the Speaker of the House under "Czar" Reed in 1890, the sham of the passage of the Sherman Antitrust Act in the same year, the camouflaged negation of the law by the executive and the judiciary, and the discovery of the holding company in 1889, soon used as a legal disguise for the outlawed trust. Consolidated economic power did not seek to uproot democratic forms but the drive of big enterprise for political authority resulted in infiltration of both major parties. The managers of capital not merely accepted but applauded the old antiparty idea of representation of local interests; for under a decentralized local system of party organization, political potentates and business barons could work together.

At the time when Roosevelt succeeded McKinley, it was precisely this interaction of business managers and political managers which most acutely alarmed the champions of democracy. In the twenty-five years from the Civil War to the Sherman Antitrust Act, only twenty-four new trusts were organized. Lax judges and administrators applied the Sherman Act against loose market agreements and pools but not against the newer and strong types of trusts created by holding companies and mergers. In the ten years after the Sherman Act, 1890 to 1900, 157 new trusts were formed. At the end of Roosevelt's first term, John Moody's celebrated *Truth about the Trusts* (1904) listed 318 monsters created by interlocking directorates, mergers, and holding companies. The last were "combines" incorporated to dominate other corporations by the purchase of a sufficient fraction of the latter's stock to assure "control." Such huge constellations of finance startled the nation. The greatest holding company, the United States Steel Corporation, first of the billion dollar trusts, was formed in 1901, when the firm of J. Pierpont Morgan paid Carnegie $447,000,000 and capitalized the new corporation at $1,402,847,000.

The public admired constructive enterprise that built industry and spanned the continent with a network of rails, but democracy feared concentration of economic might in a small circle of persons beyond the reach of public control. A new American aristocracy, based on economic power, had entrenched itself, employing wealth and often corruption to retain command of political power. Of such substance was compounded the fears of those who cheered Roosevelt when he fulminated against the trusts; and the fears of those who read the crusading journalists or sober economists who investigated watered stock, markups of the value of intangible or fictitious assets as "good will," and other forms of excessive capitalization based on prospects of monopoly profit behind excessive tariff protection. The fleecing of investors shook middle-class complacency as much or more than the fleecing of consumers.

More fearful in the public mind was the gradual growth of a "money power." Consolidations of railroads and of industrial organizations were now being paralleled in banking and investment. Economic power was passing from captains of industry to great emperors of finance. The consolidation of capital was heralded by the rise in New York of one of the world's largest financial institutions, the National City Bank, eventually a symbol of Wall Street imperialism in Latin America; and by the spreading web of Morgan control over insurance as well as industry and rails and over other of the world's greatest banks, the First National and the Chase National, both of New York. The "dominating influences in the trusts," Moody admonished, were composed of "an intricate network of large and small capitalists" who were dependents and allies of the two "mammoth" Rockefeller and Morgan banking groups. These two mammoth combines jointly constituted "the heart of the business and the commercial life of the nation." Subsequent experience in the United States, England, and elsewhere was to confirm Moody's conclusion that concentration by means of the banking business constituted the natural and easy route to destruction of the competitive system.

THE STANDARD OIL AND MORGAN INDUSTRIAL EMPIRES, 1904[1]

Standard Oil	*Morgan*
Standard Oil Co.	United States Steel Corp.
Colorado Fuel and Iron Co.	American Steel Foundries Co.
Lackawanna Steel Co. (Vanderbilt affiliation)	Crucible Steel Co.
Republic Iron and Steel Co. (community of interest)	Cambria Steel Co. (Pennsylvania Railroad domination)
Tennessee Coal, Iron and Railroad Co.	International Mercantile Marine Co.
Amalgamated Copper Co.	Allis-Chalmers Co. (machinery trust)
American Smelting and Refining Co.	United Shoe Machinery Co.
National Lead Co.	International Harvester Co.
United Lead Co.	
American Telephone and Telegraph Co. (with Gould)	
Western Union (with Gould)	
United Gas Improvement Co. (Elkins-Dolin-Rockefeller)	
Consolidated Gas Co.	
Consolidated Tobacco Co. (Ryan affiliation)	
American Linseed Oil Co.	

If McKinley's successor could reorient his party to keep pace with "progress" in the world at large, there were alternatives to the past record of political surrender to special interests. One was the nineteenth-century program of humanitarian reform and governmental intervention to revive the classical system of free competition. Another, suggested by world thought and contemporary example, was a more positive governmental intervention, to establish "welfare capitalism" and social democracy. Whereas Germany, England, and progressive industrial countries, small and large, moved appreciably along the second route—toward a welfare state—the more limited concept of free competition was America's traditional choice. The competitive ideal had been deeply imbedded in the whole American agricultural and industrial development until challenged by big business. The Interstate Commerce and Antitrust acts theoretically protected consumers through a free market. If the govern-

---

[1] From *The Truth about the Trusts*, by John Moody. Used by permission of Moody's Investors Service.

ment destroyed monopoly, it would free enterprise; prices would become truly competitive, and efficient producers would achieve lower costs and undersell their rivals.

Confusing the issue, American proponents of "laissez faire" likewise professed to believe in free enterprise. Yet there was a profound difference between the individualistic competition condoned by the classical economists and the laissez-faire symbols invoked by big business. The great businessmen were not concerned over the survival either of the competitive system or of the little businessmen whose fortunes depended on it. Big business, if anything, was neomercantilist in its approach to the economic function of the government. For years it had availed itself of bounteous aid and protection, ranging from public land grants to tariffs and special privileges in franchises and charters of incorporation. For years, contradictorily, its spokesmen in Congress had invoked the symbols of a free market and no governmental intervention. Stalwart Republicans and Democrats, professing allegiance to the venerable concept of competition, sharply limited the government to a perfunctory police duty. They verbally condemned "unfair" competition, but they left concrete definition of the policy to equally Stalwart courts.

Republicans and Democrats alike dodged the question of concrete statutory definition of unfair methods of competition and the problem of administrative machinery adequate to meet the ingenious complexities of corporation finance, monopoly through patent rights, and the "secret diplomacy" of mergers and price fixing to snuff out competitors. In the debate of 1890 Senator O. H. Platt exposed the strategy of congressional abnegation of the function of defining policy. The truth was, he stated, that "the whole effort has been to get some bill headed: 'A Bill to Punish Trusts,' with which to go to the country." This maneuver was bipartisan, and the nugatory results of the bill were precisely what Platt anticipated. The Cleveland administration in the Sugar Trust case (1895) was halfhearted in its presentation of evidence, while the Supreme Court majority was wholehearted in ignoring the evidence. Through extraordinary legal legerdemain, the Court held that a monopoly in "manufacture" did not constitute monopoly restraint of "commerce." In subsequent "trust busting," the government was to lose many a court battle through the lack of precise congressional definition of unfair methods of competition and the lack of democratic controls over the judiciary.

INTERNATIONAL EXPERIMENTS WITH GOVERNMENT CONTROLS

Contrasts between American and foreign handling of the same fundamental problem lay not merely in simplified unitary national regulation, but in concrete statutory provisions governing the structure and obligations of economic enterprise. Beginning with a German law of 1884, all countries affected by industrial combinations began to establish specific national restrictions. Great corporations in Germany dominated economic life even more than in the United States. Yet, indicative of the difference in political power of organized interests, stockholders had a security not available in American statutes. Germany outlawed stock watering; capitalization and stock issue must bear a sound relation to actual assets. Irresponsible finance, exploitation of investors by unscrupulous promoters and underwriters, and looting of bankrupt corporations through reorganization proceedings were effectively restrained. Investors had the protection of compulsory publicity of corporate transactions. Directors incurred personal liability for misleading balance sheets; and for falsification in annual reports even a prominent businessman could be lodged in jail. The issue of no-par stock and similar loose practices were illegal. The German law of 1884, which went much further than any act of Congress prior to 1933, was so effective that there was little revision until after World War I, when the Weimar Republic added the requirement that employee representatives sit on boards of directors.

Similar laws regulating corporations appeared in other countries at the beginning of the twentieth century. In England the Consolidation or Companies Act (1908) likewise stressed publicity and personal liability of directors and promoters. Long operating without a protective tariff, England feared giant monopolies less and relied on the common law for trust busting more. Canada established restrictive legislation one year before the Sherman Antitrust Act and amplified it in 1906 with criminal penalties for corporation officials guilty of monopoly practices. In 1910 additional Canadian legislation set up machinery and definitions of unfair practices, antedating a somewhat comparable experiment initiated in the United States four years later. Canada provided for the revocation of a patent when it protected a monopoly and for reduction of tariffs on commodities that fell under control of monopolies. Australia in 1906 and New Zealand in 1910 likewise adopted antitrust legislation and went beyond American regulation in placing the burden of proof on business combinations accused of monopoly practice.

ROOSEVELT AND THE TRUSTS

In the United States, the man who captured public imagination in the struggle to assert the public interest rode a storm that had been brewing long before. Theodore Roosevelt's attack on the trusts sprang from a sense of ominous changes. Widespread response to his war on the trusts may be understood in the light of world trends toward social controls, the unusual degree of corporate centralization in American business, the apparent invulnerability of corporations to public control, and the counterthrust of a great democratic tradition that survived and exploded in an intense popular demand for defense of the public welfare. The party of Populism was dying, but the Populist demand for energy in government had never abated, and the nation was prepared for something more positive than nineteenth-century humanitarianism and the formula of individualistic self-assertion.

McKinley's death elevated a man to the presidency who was not the Republican party's choice. Youngest President in American history, ambitious for a second term, alert to public opinion as few of his predecessors had been, Theodore Roosevelt was torn between the desire to get on with the nation's business and his cautious inclination to keep on good terms with ruling party cliques. A talent for sensing and expressing the moral sentiments of the middle class made him famed in later memory for pungent phrases: "malefactors of great wealth," "muckrakers," "corporation cunning," and "the wealthy criminal class." Although he was known as a good-government reformer, he had never been an unfaltering advocate of liberal causes. In 1884 he supported the rebellious Republican reformers known as Mugwumps, but when the bosses in the convention nominated Blaine, he turned "regular" and endorsed the ticket. He succumbed to the hysteria over the Haymarket bombing in 1886, assuming the anarchists were guilty despite lack of evidence. Those episodes, as much as his work on the Civil Service Commission, were a measure of the man. Nevertheless, as head of New York City's police board from 1895 to 1897, he learned how "the other half" lived; by the time he entered the White House he was acquiring an appreciation of social abuses.

Notwithstanding White House recommendations to Congress and popular pressure, legislative acts in Roosevelt's first term were no different from what would have been expected had McKinley survived. Roosevelt's first message to Congress sounded the keynote of civil service reform, a down-to-brass-tacks regulation of trusts and railroad corporations, conservation of natural resources, and public irrigation works, a series of items that made him popular with liberal elements. Roosevelt's accompanying proposals were equally appealing to conservative elements—a bigger navy and army, an Atlantic-Pacific canal, a modern imperial system for colonies, the maintenance of the Monroe Doctrine. When making public speeches in 1902, the President discovered a growing source of popularity in his demands for a vigorous antitrust policy and publicity on the hidden activities of business managers. Except for the Newlands Act (1902), a conservation measure for western irrigation projects, Congress took no action on any Roosevelt proposal. The next year Congress similarly ignored public demand and remained deaf to Roosevelt's second message, which requested comprehensive revision of the Sherman Act. The only statutory responses to White House leadership were two minor reforms.

While Congress remained adamantly supine, a Wall Street financial combination, affiliated with the Morgan group and in command of the anthracite resources of the nation, presented Theodore Roosevelt with an opportunity for antitrust action. The hard-coal monopoly was based not only on its control of a natural resource, but on its financial domination of coal-carrying railroads. Labor conditions in the anthracite fields of Pennsylvania were eloquent of unregulated industrial feudalism. When the facts were bared, the nation was shocked, for wages were low, hours excessively long, foremen brutal, and seasonal unemployment was chronic. Workers were regimented in "company towns" at prescribed rents; they bought in company stores at company-dictated prices. In 1902 the United Mine Workers went on strike. The basic issue was "recognition" of the union—basic because it meant acceptance of the principle of peaceful collective bargaining and of the union as negotiating agent. Subsidiary demands concerned abolition of the "pluck-me stores" and the feudal exploitation of the company town. There was no question that the union, under the able and temperate leadership of John Mitchell, represented the workers, 150,000 of whom struck in May and endured five months' privation on the picket line. Nor was there any serious question of labor violence or unwillingness on the part of the union to discuss reasonable terms. But the owners rejected negotiation, since a contract would lead toward recognition of the union. When the strikers offered arbitration, the owners took the position that there was nothing to arbitrate. George F. Baer, president of the Reading Railroad and leader of the coal interests, gave unblushing absolutist expression to the traditional dogma of managerial omnipotence: "The rights and interests of the laboring man will be protected and cared for—not by the labor agitators, but by the Christian men to whom God in His infinite wisdom has given the control of the property interests of the country." Baer, notorious overnight, was soon forgotten; but his words became classic.

As winter neared and coal scarcity threatened householders, Roosevelt asserted the power of the government against the assertion of the divine right of property. At a White House conference, operators' spokesmen yielded nothing and used language offensive both to the miners and to the President of the United States. Disregarding the owners, Roosevelt privately determined to send troops to police the mines and start government operations, on the ground that a public emergency existed. The threatened precedent of commandeering private property in public emergency was decisive. Secretary of War Elihu Root, Mark Hanna, and other patrons of property rights privately warned the J. P. Morgan group of Wall Street overlords. Command from the financial sovereigns brought the owners to arbitrate; and the crisis ended. The award raised wages and reduced the ten-hour day to nine; but the owners succeeded in defeating the basic demand for recognition of the union and acceptance of bargaining.

Realms of finance were disturbed by another unexpected action by the government. J. P. Morgan, hurriedly called to the telephone in February, 1902, was indignant to hear that his latest merger would be prosecuted for violation of the Sherman Antitrust Act. The combine in question, known as Northern Securities, tied together under a Morgan holding company three great transcontinental railroads. The massive sovereign of the financial world descended upon Washington to settle with the President. "Send your man to my man," Morgan told Roosevelt, "and they can fix it up." The President expressed a differing view of the duties of office; the case went to the Supreme Court. "Wall Street," reported a midwestern paper, "is paralyzed at the thought that a President of the United States would sink so low as to try to enforce the law." The Court's decision in 1904, going against the holding company, pointed out that "no scheme could more effectively and certainly suppress free competition."

By this victory, presidential leadership achieved reversal of the inane precedent of the Sugar Trust case (1895), and Roosevelt achieved greater personal popularity as the "trust buster." In 1902 his Attorney General, Philander C. Knox, moved against another monopoly, a holding company of former competitors among the big meat-packing corporations, Swift, Morris, and Armour. Again there was an ostensible victory for the public. But as Justice Holmes pointed out in his opinion, the government's case failed to set forth specific facts. While housewives rejoiced at newspaper reports of victory over the Beef Trust, Roosevelt's administration was quietly accepting a court decree that failed to order dissolution of the holding company, thus permitting the Swift, Armour, and Morris companies to continue operation as partners instead of competitors. Other suits in Roosevelt's two terms similarly dazzled the public into the belief that the President was going through with his pledge that "the biggest corporation, like the humblest private citizen" would be "held to the law of the land." The Gargantuan Rockefeller interests appeared no more sacrosanct than the Morgan group. In 1907 prosecution of the Standard Oil was launched. Du Pont interests were challenged in the prosecution of the Powder Trust. Before the end of Roosevelt's second term the Morgan group and associated railroad interests were confronted anew with prosecu-

Right — President Woodrow Wilson. *(Underwood-Stratton)*

Below — Presidential leadership. Breaking century-old precedent, Wilson returns to example of the first president, reading messages to Congress in person. *(Brown Brothers)*

Crusaders for liberal enlightenment. *Above*—Robert M. La Follette and George W. Norris. *Below*—Oliver Wendell Holmes and Louis D. Brandeis. (All photos *Brown Brothers* except Norris, *Harris & Ewing)*

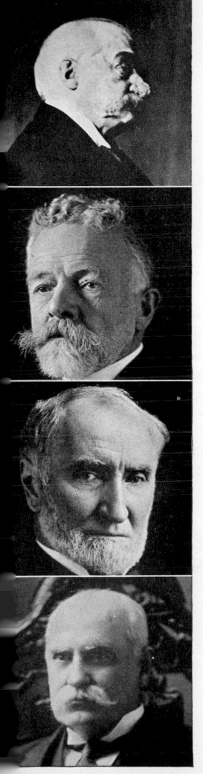

"Teddy" and the Old Order. *Above*—Roosevelt as President. *Left, top to bottom*—The elder J. P. Morgan, Henry Cabot Lodge, "Uncle Joe" Cannon, Nelson W. Aldrich. *Below*—Pennsylvania boss, Senator Boies Penrose.

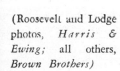

(Roosevelt and Lodge photos, *Harris & Ewing;* all others, *Brown Brothers)*

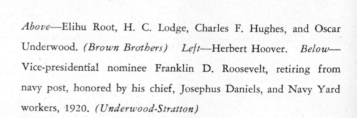

Above—Elihu Root, H. C. Lodge, Charles F. Hughes, and Oscar Underwood. *(Brown Brothers)* *Left*—Herbert Hoover. *Below*—Vice-presidential nominee Franklin D. Roosevelt, retiring from navy post, honored by his chief, Josephus Daniels, and Navy Yard workers, 1920. *(Underwood-Stratton)*

tions of the Reading, the Union Pacific, and the New York, New Haven, and Hartford networks.

Whatever the public supposed, Roosevelt had no great love for trust busting. He ordered his Attorney General not to file suits against Morgan's Harvester Trust unless given "further instructions." In his first message to Congress, Roosevelt renounced much of the Sherman Act by making a distinction between large-scale business and monopoly. "Combinations and concentration should be, not prohibited," he declared, but "supervised, and within reasonable limits controlled." He asserted that the government must be given "full power," by a constitutional amendment if necessary, but he reassured big business by adding that once the power was granted, "it would be most unwise to exercise it too much." He paid tribute to "the great captain of industry" who built large-scale enterprise. "Good, not harm, normally comes from the upbuilding of such wealth." Thus echoing the old apologetics of the gospel of wealth, Roosevelt decided to enforce the antitrust policy only in selected cases. His straddle of the trust question did not escape ironic paraphrase by a contemporary humorist, the inimitable "Mr. Dooley":

"Th' thrusts," says he [Roosevelt], "are heejous monsthers built up be th' inlightened intherprise iv th' men that have done so much to advance pro-gress in our beloved counthry," he says. "On wan hand I wud stamp thim undher fut; on th' other hand, not so fast. What I want more thin th' bustin' iv th' thrusts is to see me fellow counthrymen happy an' continted. I wudden't have thim hate th' thrusts. Th' haggard face, th' droopin' eye, th' pallid complexion that marks th' inimy iv thrusts is not to me taste."[2]

On railroad regulation the President was more forthright and single-minded, and in 1903 Congress made a gesture of response to his demand to confer power on the Interstate Commerce Commission. But the Elkins Act, although establishing new penalties for violating the provision of 1887 outlawing secret rebates, was a substantial victory for railroad senators. It did not grant the President's request for enlarged authority for the Interstate Commerce Commission. After two years of delay, the law-makers grudgingly acceded to one presidential request. Establishing a joint Department of Commerce and Labor, Congress accepted the Roosevelt proposal for publicity on corporate transactions by means of a Bureau of Corporations, which was authorized to make investigations and recommend legislation. The conservative Republican machine of Senator Nelson Aldrich, czar of the Senate, and Speaker "Joe" Cannon, czar of the House, little suspected that a decade later this infant bureau would be transformed into an important regulatory agency, the Federal Trade Commission.

---

[2] Finley Peter Dunne, *Mr. Dooley at His Best,* ed. Elmer Ellis. New York: Charles Scribner's Sons, 1938, pp. 104–105.

"WHAT ARE YOU DOING HERE?"

A cartoon on Democratic affiliations with Wall Street in 1904. *(Bettmann Archive)*

As the presidential campaign of 1904 drew near, bosses of the Grand Old Party anxiously considered means to "stop Roosevelt." When Senator Hanna, trusted member and favorite candidate of the Aldrich machine, died a few months before the Republican convention, public clamor frightened the bosses into acceptance of the beloved "trust buster." Plati-

tudinous and ambiguous verbalisms in the party platform and the choice
for Vice-President, Charles W. Fairbanks, one of the rich men in the
Aldrich clique in the Senate, a corporation lawyer and servitor of trusts,
reassured special interests that the party leadership in Congress would
resist the policies of the party's candidate for President. The performance
in the Democratic convention was likewise meant to reassure conservatives;
eastern bosses wrested control from the Bryan Populist elements and
nominated Alton B. Parker, a "safe and sane" New York judge, with an
eighty-year-old millionaire ex-senator as running mate on a platform as
meaningless as the Republican document. Old Guard Democratic bosses,
hoping to make the party "respectable" by repudiation of Bryan, so ineptly
judged the popular temper that they met their worst defeat in more than
a century. And Roosevelt, chosen with unconcealed reluctance by the
Republican party managers, proved to be their salvation.

"Teddy" himself was the issue in the campaign. The election, first
of the great landslides, was a sensational mandate for the progressivism
that "T. R." symbolized. Roosevelt polled 50 per cent more votes than his
Democratic rival, a plurality breaking all records. Significantly, four
states that went for Roosevelt—Massachusetts, Minnesota, Missouri, and
Colorado—elected progressive governors on the Democratic ticket.

EXECUTIVE LEADERSHIP AND CONGRESSIONAL OBSTRUCTION

Though Roosevelt now had a resounding vote of confidence from the
voters, the machine-selected Republicans in Congress remained party horses
of a different color. The Aldrich and Cannon organization understood the
national mood even if unwilling to do anything about it. The old lameduck Congress that lingered after elections, faithful to the system of rule
for the few, ignored the President's call for a child labor law, workmen's
compensation, and prohibition of the practice of corporations subsidizing
political bosses by lavish contributions of money to help win elections.
Roosevelt sidetracked the great and growing issue of tariff reform—on the
advice of Speaker Joe Cannon and the Republican machine. Instead, the
President made revitalization of the ICC (Interstate Commerce Commission) his chief goal. Though opposed to a general grant of rate-making
power, he demanded that the commission be given limited power to set
a fair rate in notorious cases when shippers complained. The House, impressed by the elections, passed the administration's bill in February, 1905,
but the Aldrich phalanx pigeonholed it in the Senate. Roosevelt's first
administration closed with nothing on the statute book to distinguish it
from McKinley's.

When the new Congress assembled for its first session, the Republican machine was still unrepentant. The President, on the contrary,

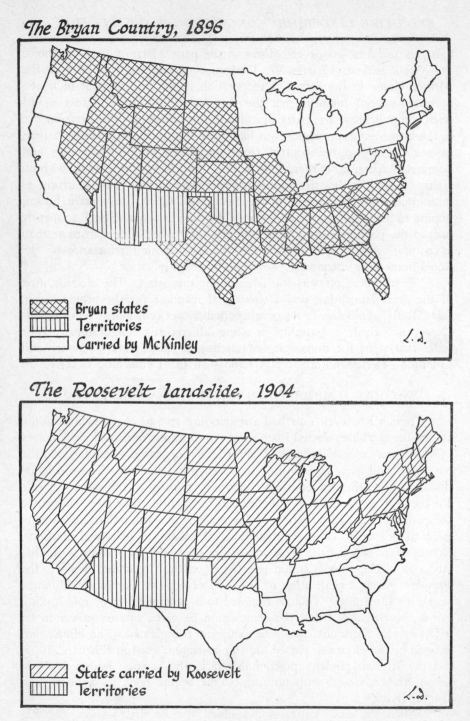

The Bryan Country, 1896

Bryan states
Territories
Carried by McKinley

L. d.

The Roosevelt landslide, 1904

States carried by Roosevelt
Territories

L. d.

was moving ahead, accepting the Bryan and La Follette formula for the ICC—a general rate-making power and full publicity of railroad accounts. Congress dallied, and subsequent passage of a railroad bill in 1906 was not the result of a regenerate Congress, but of a new dynamic type of presidential politics and a vociferous public outcry aroused by brilliant journalists who made a savage onslaught on Congress.

Roosevelt had no patience with what he called the "legalistic" tradition that regarded a President as the passive "servant of Congress." When the legislative branch was obstructionist, he said later in his *Autobiography,* "I achieved results only by appealing over the heads of the Senate and House leaders to the people." He attempted to establish a new role for the presidential office. The chief executive, he contended, as "the steward of the people," should formulate legislation and even "manage Congress." Local Democratic bosses, fearing a rival central management, inserted in the platform of 1904 an attack on Roosevelt for attempting to be a dictator. Republicans like Senator Boies Penrose, boss of Pennsylvania, shared the sentiment but dared not express it. Neither Republicans nor Democrats relished an executive who stirred up their sleeping constituencies by use of publicity. Conservatives were indignant in 1903 when Roosevelt made congressional defiance risky by exposing the activity of the hated Standard Oil lobby against the bill for the Bureau of Corporations.

Roosevelt followed up his request for railroad legislation, in December, 1905, instructing his Attorney General to institute prosecutions of railroad abuses. It was shrewd timing. Within a few days grand jury indictments of a number of great railroad corporations were issued; and on December 15, the "Big Four" of the Beef Trust—Cudahy, Armour, Swift, and Morris—were likewise indicted for violation of the law against rebates. Meanwhile the President relied on an understanding with Speaker Cannon based on spoils and a secret bargain: Roosevelt would suppress the tariff question, Cannon in payment would deliver a railroad bill. Four days after introduction of the administration measure, under a congressional disguise as the "Hepburn Bill," Cannon delivered; the House steamroller flattened opposition with 346 yeas to 7 nays.

When the bill reached the Senate in February of the following year, the Aldrich machine attempted to kill it. The archconservative of Massachusetts, Senator Henry Cabot Lodge, undeterred either by close friendship with Roosevelt or by the stark fact of the noncompetitive character of the great railways, blandly declared that there was no need for rate regulation. "Natural economic forces" prevented abuses in rates, said the senator, "by the competition of the market." To build up popular pressure against the Senate Republicans, Roosevelt publicized the report of the Bureau of Corporations on abuses in rates and used its figures to denounce the Standard

Oil's secret rebates of "at least three quarters of a million a year." The report exposed similar violations by the Sugar Trust—the American Sugar Refining Company. The public was treated to a curious spectacle in the Senate: a West Virginia industrialist, Stephen B. Elkins, Republican chairman of the commerce committee in charge of the bill, refused to sponsor it; in consequence the steerage of Roosevelt's bill fell to a Bryan Democrat, "Pitchfork" Ben Tillman of South Carolina.

While the Hepburn Bill was stalled in the Senate, the electorate was presented with two devastating journalistic investigations of national politics. Early in 1906 Lincoln Steffens, fresh from investigations of state and city machines, went to Washington to inspect the terminus of the "system." He found Roosevelt reluctant to discuss the inside story of presidential relations with the Senate and House. Since the President was anxious for congressional action, he felt obliged to make concessions that would not stand public scrutiny. Steffens, as the price of information, had to refrain from naming names, but his syndicated articles were nevertheless shrewd demonstrations that Congress did not represent majority will, that the President was forced to employ the traditional corruption of "senatorial courtesy" in order to "bribe" congressmen to vote for bills that the electorate demanded. Under senatorial courtesy, Presidents placed the appointment power of the executive at the secret disposal of senators and congressmen, who distributed the spoils at the behest of state and local bosses to whom they owed office.

Another investigation threw additional light on the uncoordinated system of separation of power and the irresponsibility of parties after elections. In March, 1906, the crusading novelist, David Graham Phillips, began his magazine series on "The Treason of the Senate." He not only named names, but exposed the upper chamber as the "indefatigable agent" of private interests dedicated to blocking the majority will. Since senators were not popularly elected, the result was the dominance of agents of plutocracy like Senator Chauncey Depew of New York, whose membership on seventy boards of directors yielded him $50,000 a year from corporations for attendance fees alone. Roosevelt's friend, Henry Cabot Lodge, was characterized as the usual "familiar coarse type of machine politician disguised by the name of the 'Gentleman Scholar.'" The right arm of "the Interests" was Senator Aldrich, Republican floor leader, and Elkins was their "second lieutenant." Elkins and the newcomer, Knox, former Attorney General, were rich men. Joseph B. Foraker, Republican boss of Ohio after Hanna's death, and Aldrich were particularly close to the mammoth financial interests represented by the Rockefeller-National City Bank group; Aldrich, himself weathy, had married into the Rockefeller family. More significant was Phillips' exposure of the bipartisan sham whereby the Democratic organization led by Senator Arthur P. Gorman of Maryland worked hand in glove with Aldrich's Republican machine. Instead of constituting the fundamental democratic check and balance of an honest party opposition, machine senators of both parties did business together in a secret "merger"; debates on bills were "sham battles" over trivial details. No one but the electorate was deceived.

To the surprise of Steffens and Phillips, their exposures of bipartisan shams roused indignation in the White House. In a public denunciation, Roosevelt attached an undying odium to writers of the school of social protest. He compared them to Bunyan's Man with the Muck Rake "who could look no way but downward" and who raked "the filth of the floor." The stigma stuck. Crusading liberal publicists were thereafter damned as "muckrakers." Steffens called on Roosevelt next day and told him "you have put an end" to the journalistic investigations "that have made you."

In the face of public exposure, the Aldrich machine finally accepted a compromise on the Hepburn Bill. For three months Robert La Follette, newcomer from Wisconsin and greatest Senate expert on railroad regulation, had fought for an amendment to give the ICC authority to determine the real value of the common carrier; his purpose was to establish a basis for computing a fair rate that would stand up in hostile courts. Roosevelt privately admitted the soundness of the amendment but withheld his support. Knowing the disposition of the judicial branch to favor the railroads on rates, the President had strongly urged administrative finality in rate making, but to placate the Republican machine he broke an understanding with the Tillman Democrats and accepted a Knox amendment that in effect invited court injunctions setting aside rates made by the ICC. Experience proved La Follette right in his contention that the limited rate-making power in the Hepburn Act was a pallid victory. But the penalties against free passes, rebates, and overnight shifts in rates, the new jurisdiction over pipe-line, sleeping car, express, and terminal companies, and the power to regulate accounting enabled the ICC within five years to cut thousands of rates approximately in half.

The same pressures that forced Congress to pass the Hepburn Bill produced two other enactments of 1906 dealing with the trust problem. For a generation an agitation for consumer protection had harped on the unwholesome effects of reckless business practices upon the American kitchen and dinner table. Patent-medicine manufacturers, as well as the great canning and packing corporations, were under fire from muckrakers and crusading women's organizations. The legislative strategists of the "System" had defeated every attempt to enact an American counterpart of the English Pharmacy Act. Between 1889 and 1906 no less than 140 bills for pure food and drug standards had died in Congress. Scientific demonstration of fraudulent adulteration and injurious and even deadly ingredients in various products by some of Roosevelt's able bureaucrats, Dr. Harvey Wiley and his "poison squad" of the Department of Agriculture, and Upton Sinclair's shocking novel, *The Jungle*, induced the President to voice the national demand that something be done to curb the Beef Trust and the medicine fakers. The Meat Inspection Act and the Pure Food and Drug Act, fought by the lobbies of the packers and drug concerns, who ingenuously predicted that passage would kill their business, became law; in the sequel, consumers bought with greater confidence, and the industries profited as never before. Yet nothing more than the most superficial kind of protection for consumer welfare appeared in the legislation of 1906 or for a whole generation thereafter. Frauds in labeling and vicious deceit in advertising were committed with impunity; pricing and grading on the basis of quality were forms of regulation not even considered.

Political spoilsmen and pressure groups, standing pat on their obstructionist control of Congress, defeated virtually all the remaining important legislation requested by the President. Congress disregarded Roosevelt's call for income and inheritance taxes to reduce the growing inequality in wealth and income, and rejected his reiterated pleas to limit the arbitrary tactics of the judicial branch in sanctioning labor injunctions that restricted civil liberties of workers and deliberately helped employers break strikes. The President's plea for regulation of child labor was also rejected, as was a recommendation for clarification of the Sherman Antitrust Act, which had just been interpreted as applying to unions, so that an employer was allowed to collect triple damages from a hatters' union in Danbury, Connecticut. The sole congressional response to Roosevelt's famous pledge of a "square deal" for labor was an employers' liability law providing accident compensation for interstate railroad employees. Subsequently, the Supreme Court, in a 5-4 decision, held the law unconstitutional, but in 1908 the law was re-enacted in more limited form and survived the encounter with conservative justices.

If Roosevelt failed to achieve his professed aims, his failure did not pass unnoticed. La Follette in his *Autobiography* excoriated Roosevelt for executive nullification of the antitrust act. The conservative Taft administration, in a single term, prosecuted twice as many trusts as Roosevelt did in two terms. La Follette's figures told with sufficient accuracy the story of opportunity missed for crushing monopoly in its crucial days of incubation: there were 149 trusts capitalized at less than $4,000,000,-000 when Roosevelt took office; there were 10,020 "monster" combinations capitalized at $31,672,000,000—"more than seventy per cent water" —when the "trust buster" left the White House.

Nevertheless, Roosevelt did have a trust program. Never reconciled to the Bryan and La Follette concept of extermination of big business, belatedly in 1907 he became specific. Roosevelt urged governmental regulation in place of trust busting, under national standards regulating corporate conduct as in the consolidation or companies laws of other nations. The proposal called for federal charters of incorporation or a simpler alternative, national regulation of the existing state-chartered corporations under federal licenses to do interstate business, with supervision by an administrative agency. The movement for federal incorporation or licensing of corporations reached its height in the years from 1904 to 1914. First broached in 1885, the proposal was elaborated by the Bureau of Corporations, which reported it favorably in 1904. Within the next few years a body of stringent and conflicting regulations enacted in progressive states and called "blue-sky laws" induced a president of the National Association of Manufacturers and business leaders like John D. Archbold of Standard Oil to endorse voluntary federal licenses or incorporation.

The program appealed to Roosevelt ideologically because it distinguished between "good" and "bad" corporations and administratively because it depended only slightly on slow-moving litigation and dilatory judicial regulation. Relegating antitrust decisions to a secondary role, it would substitute regulation by an agency of administrative experts. Definitions and norms to distinguish between good and bad trusts would not be written and applied in court decisions; instead, they would be written by Congress and applied by the administrative agency. Roosevelt had become increasingly critical of the assumption of lawmaking functions by federal courts and of judicial laxity in enforcing laws made by Congress. Under the American separation of powers, the normal corrective was the slow and uncertain process of new judicial appointments. Roosevelt used the presidential weapon of publicity. Declaring in 1907 that courts were not exempt from public criticism, he attacked interpretations that made the Constitution a "strait jacket" and accused judges of being too disdainful of public opinion. As the government met reverses in antitrust suits, often on technicalities, his dissatisfaction grew. After a circuit court set aside a $29,000,000 fine laid against Standard Oil for violation of the Elkins Antirebate Act, Roosevelt in 1908 announced he would start suit anew and, in defiance of the court, asserted there was "absolutely no question as to the guilt of the defendant." Privately he denounced two of the judges as the usual type, prone to "improper subserviency to corporations."

Congress was as subservient as the judges; it made no legislative answer to Roosevelt's repeated request for antitrust revision. Bills for federal chartering of railroads and voluntary federal incorporation of industrial firms were introduced in 1907 and subsequent years, but the Aldrich-Cannon organization employed the old strategy of pigeonholing such measures so that they never reached the floor.

The last major battle of the administration—over conservation—was indicative of the same degradation of the democratic doctrine. Once again the President defended the public interest; and once again the divergence between the action and policy of the Republican President and the action and policy of the Republican Congress was self-confession of failure to organize a party as an instrument of the majority. Congress, heeding the lobby of lumber corporations, in 1907 made it illegal for the President to set aside additional forest reserves in lumbering areas in the Far West. By executive action Roosevelt had already withdrawn about 150,000,000 acres of public forest land from private exploitation. He had popularized the principle of conservation of natural resources by expanding and calling attention to the significant work of Gifford Pinchot's forestry bureau and kindred activities of the Departments of Agriculture and Interior. In an era of cumulative social anger against corporations, the public took to its heart the belated attempt to protect what remained of its domain from reckless waste in private exploitation. Congress yielded to Roosevelt's proposal for an Inland Waterways Commission to study the interconnected problems of forests, floods, and navigable streams. And in 1908 an epoch-making conference of scientists and governors at Washington, summoned by the President, outlined broad planning for flood control and conservation of soil, forest, and subsoil resources. The recommendations, including regulation of commercial exploitation of resources, aroused the ire of vested interests and their congressional supporters. Roosevelt instituted a National Conservation Commission that began valuable work, but at the end of his term Congress cut off its appropriations.

As the election of 1908 approached, rival Republican bosses boomed candidates who believed in the rule of the few: Senator Foraker, Senator Knox, and Speaker Joe Cannon; but Republican voters demanded a third term for "Teddy." Intending to retire but determined to have a successor who would carry on his policies, Roosevelt used his own "machine" —presidential appointees to federal office who commanded Republican delegations from the South—to swing the nomination to his genial Secretary of War, William Howard Taft of Ohio. The candidate and the platform promised the electorate a sound, continuing progressivism, including "scientific revision" of the tariff downward to a point where fair competition would be restored between goods produced at home and abroad. Western progressives prevailed in the Democratic convention, nominating Bryan on a platform specifying abolition of tariff duties on "trust-made" products, prohibition of the labor injunction, and enactment of a progressive program including an income tax. Bryan made the federal license plan for prohibiting holding companies and watered stock a leading issue, only to find the Republican candidate in firm agreement with him. A contest in which both parties seemed committed to progressivism obscured the persistent power of their reactionary machines. The electorate did not yet understand the lack of internal cohesion and irresponsible character of American parties. Seeking re-election in Indiana, Senator Albert J. Beveridge, who had dared to migrate from Old Guard conservatism toward La Follette liberalism, found his own party knifing him and privately began to admit that party professions were a sham. Bryan, always formidable in midwestern and mountain states as well as in the South, received 1,323,000 more votes than were cast for the conservative Parker in 1904. But the magic of Roosevelt's mantle, draped on Taft's ponderous shoulders, once more swung the election to the Republicans.

Taft's election was another referendum endorsing Roosevelt policies. But the country was promptly treated to an extraordinary spectacle by the lameduck Congress in the last three months before the beloved President retired. Released at last from respectful consideration of the man who controlled patronage, reactionary members of Congress seized the closing hours of the old administration to take the floor and voice contempt for Roosevelt and all his works. The election returns were in and the gloves were off. Roosevelt's "friends" and fellow Republicans, including Lodge, sat mute while one by one machine spokesmen released their spleen. Only Senator Beveridge rose to rebuke the narrow and timeserving senators who had fought the President in his every attempt to defend the public interest.

Ere long, under President Taft, the "hate-Roosevelt" politicians congratulated themselves upon a safe return to the nineteenth-century system of representation of special local interests. Taft was a party man who deferred to the "organization" rather than to public opinion. He, like congressional bosses, clung to the old attitude expressed by the Washington *Post* in criticizing Roosevelt for his assertion of leadership over his party: "It is better that Congress pass a bad law as a result of its own free and independent deliberation than to enact a good law at the dictation of the Executive." But the politicians and newspaper editors who rejoiced with Taft were to have a rude awakening. Republicans who berated "T. R." were to discover that he had cast a reflected glory of progressivism upon the Grand Old Party; and that an irresponsible party that repudiated the glory was committing the three crimes that seared the souls of politicians—the loss of the White House, the Congress, the patronage.

XXV

THE RISE OF WILSONIAN DEMOCRACY

1909–1916

No democratic impact as powerful as the Progressive Movement could fail to explode the political dynamite that had been accumulating for the forty and more years since the death of Lincoln. Degradation of the democratic doctrine under irresponsible parties was swiftly bringing a day of atonement. The decadence of both parties in years of misrule prepared the way for Republican insurgency, party schism, and abysmal defeat; and for a resurgence among the Democrats of the Jeffersonian tradition, taking twentieth-century form in Wilsonian Democracy.

The rude awakening that lay in wait for Republican machines was traceable only superficially to such personal factors as the failings of Taft as President and party leader. Progressive revolt, it is true, personalized the issue and condemned the President, but the deeper causes of public anger were underlying conditions that no man in the White House personally could correct. For the underlying, molding forces that frustrated capable leadership were the same two interacting sets of institutions that robbed even strong presidents like Roosevelt of the fruits of their labors. The strength of obtuse and cynical defense of private plunder at public expense sprang from the interaction of the old political system of weak major parties, which exposed individual legislators to the full pressure of machines and powerful interests, and the new economic system, which consolidated the power of corporations and concentrated the pressures of managers of capital.

Congressional management in the twentieth century, as in the nineteenth, perpetuated an incongruous institution contradicting the principle of democratic representation of the popular majority. The "System," as Lincoln Steffens called it, had made Congress seemingly impregnable as the inner citadel for rule by the few. A party devoted to a privileged order had won every election in the fourteen years between 1896 and 1910. For a longer period spanning six presidential terms, from Harrison to Taft, only one of the presidents, Roosevelt after his mandate of 1904, had boldly battled for the interests of the public. In the whole first decade of the twentieth century there was sponsored in Congress only a single far-reaching measure to deal with trusts. It never reached the floor. No great laws like those of other lands in the same ten years graced the United States statute books of the twentieth century. Despite direct primaries, "the people's choice" generally continued to be a secondary ratification of a party ticket nominated by bosses. The Republican Senator Beveridge coined in 1910 the famous phrase "invisible government." He knew whereof he spoke—and knew, too, the risks of dissent; for the machine of his own Indiana Republicans in 1910 covertly aided the Democrats to retire him from the Senate. But—for Republicans—1910 was the end of an era.

DOWNFALL OF THE "SYSTEM"

William Howard Taft, taking office on March 4, 1909, proved himself not the man to measure up to new responsibilities demanding a strong executive. The times called for progressive measures that would increase the scope of the government. Profound analyses by specialists like Woodrow Wilson and J. Allen Smith clearly pointed to the danger of increasing centralization without increasing responsibility. The multiplying functions of a welfare state required a more genuine over-all party control to give meaning to elections and to harmonize the work of the three branches of the government. President Taft, conservative at heart but honest in endorsing progressive concessions to public opinion, had small conception of the disparity between his avowed public objectives and the private special interests cherished in Congress by his own party majority. A decidedly conservative judge before he became a cabinet officer and favorite trouble shooter for Roosevelt, Taft was amiable, honest, but legalistic. Lacking political flair, he clung to a lawyer's abstractions regarding checks and balances and assumed the competence of party cliques in Congress to devise general policy in the public interest. In this, he repudiated one of the cardinal discoveries of progressives in their search for an adequate principle of leadership.

A principle of party leadership inescapably entailed the winning of the initiative in legislative affairs; and the example of Theodore Roosevelt in the presidential office corresponded to the practice of progressive governors in the various states. A centralization of party leadership was necessary because of "the difficulty of maintaining party coherence"; so announced Charles Evans Hughes, New York's progressive governor, in a cogent address of 1910. In his new responsibility as party leader, declared Hughes, the executive "emerges as the representative of the people as a whole"; elected by the voters of all the constituencies, the executive was concerned with broad policies in the public interest, whereas the legislator thought of special interests and political favors in his local district. The public interest must have a voice; "the people have come to look to the Chief Executive for that voice."

Taft did formulate policies and was not wholly unsuccessful in winning legislative action, even though he was unwilling to risk battle with congressional bosses. The recommendations of the new President included centralization of government finance through reform of the loose congressional budget system; more efficient control of currency and finance through central banking; and even a small amount of governmental competition with business in fields hitherto monopolized by banks and express companies. The last proposal culminated in postal savings banks (1910) and the parcel-post system (1912), in both cases a laggard American imitation of measures widely adopted in other nations. Tax reduction was good business gospel, and Congress approved Taft's request for an economy commission, which reported in favor of the more efficient and coordinated national budget systems employed in Europe. Financial interests, shaken by the panic of 1907, supported Taft's return to Hamiltonian conceptions of central banking, and Senator Aldrich headed another commission that went abroad to study the Bank of England and Continental central banks, reporting favorably on a "National Reserve" system in 1911. But the much-divided Congress under Taft took no action either on the budget or on currency and banking.

Taft's attempt to carry out the commitments of his party revealed the incongruity of a progressive platform sponsored by political machines that in turn depended upon campaign contributions from big corporations. Tariff reduction, an income tax, antitrust controls under federal incorporation, and stronger railroad regulation were major administration objectives, but the Aldrich-Cannon organization wooed the conservative in Taft and deflected him and the party from carrying out campaign pledges.

Voters who had cast Republican ballots in expectation of reform received their first shock with the framing of the Payne-Aldrich tariff (1909). Congressional irresponsibility was never more clearly demonstrated. Cannon's blocking of Roosevelt's desire for tariff revision permitted the notorious Dingley Act of 1897 to survive longer than any tariff since 1846. The prodigious growth of trusts since 1897 coincided too neatly with the Dingley tariff to escape association in the public mind. Rising price levels and complaints against the high cost of living strengthened criticism of protectionism. Farmers in the Middle West, though Republicans for two generations, began to support the "Iowa idea" of assault through the tariff on extortionate prices charged by monopolies. Belief in economic nationalism did not die, but reformers of the La Follette-Brandeis-Bryan school urged as an irreducible minimum the abolition of duties protecting trust-controlled products. Senator Beveridge, after study of the German system of tariff making by administrative experts, advocated a "scientific" tariff commission to determine rates that would equalize the costs of production at home and abroad. Taft and his party platform pledged such a program, but Aldrich's Senate finance committee, in co-operation with lobbyists of the National Association of Manufacturers, scuttled the Beveridge bill. Instead, they substituted an advisory tariff board to be composed predominantly of representatives of industrial corporations. Beveridge subsequently discovered that Cannon opposed his tariff commission because a President might appoint to it professional economists from the universities!

Meanwhile the Payne-Aldrich tariff, born in the murky secrecy of machine-picked committees, was rushed through the House under rules that prevented effective public discussion. A perturbed midwestern Republican, Congressman George W. Norris, mindful of election pledges and inflamed public opinion regarding Standard Oil, fought for abolition of duties protecting oil. A committee member confessed to Norris that Rockefeller interests had provided a slush fund to swing elections, and Cannon insisted that it was a requirement of good faith to preserve the oil tariff. In the Senate, Aldrich's committee rewrote the tariff, opening committee chambers to the lobbyists of special interests and ignoring the party's pledge of an "honest" tariff that would balance the production costs of foreign and home manufacturers. As an Alabama Democrat, Senator Oscar Underwood, later phrased it, Congress once more devised a tariff with the object of "damming back competition at the custom-houses." Senator Aldrich, a much better parliamentarian than statesman, misjudged the ability and popularity of the small bloc of western Republicans. La Follette led a brilliantly organized attack on separate schedules of the tariff. Iowa's sterling senator, Albert C. Cummins, father of the "Iowa idea" of tariff reform, made an onslaught on iron and steel duties, pertinently asking why supercorporations like United States Steel needed protection. Similarly the progressive Republicans, Joseph L. Bristow (Kansas) and Jonathan P. Dolliver (Iowa), joined La Follette in tearing apart the sugar, wool, and cotton rates, asking why the big sugar and textile corporations should be favored at the expense of the vast majority of American consumers.

The Aldrich stratagem of escaping public outcry by rushing the tariff through without adequate debate had failed. The Old Guard thereupon resorted to one of its most effective minority-rule tactics: packing the Senate-House conference committee. Aldrich appointed himself, Boies Penrose, nationally known as the boss of Pennsylvania, and other venal northern protectionists, while Cannon named Sereno E. Payne (New York), Joseph W. Fordney (Michigan), and similar high priests of the same earthly temple. With this committee as final arbiter, many obnoxious provisions that the two houses had voted down were restored. As the bill passed, a leading southern Democrat made the barbed prediction that the opulent who had fattened upon Republican tariffs had won their last license "to rob and plunder industrious consumers." Taft furnished no leadership, and in August, 1909, he disillusioned the country by signing the bill.

"The House and Senate Confer"

A cartoon on the tariff. (From the Denver *News*,
reproduced in *Collier's,* December 4, 1909.)

Democrats and progressive Republicans led by Cummins made a valiant effort to write an income tax into the tariff bill. Senator William E. Borah (Idaho), a new insurgent Republican, presented a long line of English and American precedents to show that the Supreme Court decision of 1895, ruling out income taxes as unconstitutional "direct taxes," was an interpretation that squared more neatly with economic prejudice than with legal authority. In the hope that the justices of 1909 would reverse the extraordinary and unpopular 5–4 decision of 1895, he urged Congress to challenge the Court to rule anew on income taxes. Taft and the Republican regulars won over a hesitant Senate with the archconservative dogma that the other two branches must not question the infallibility and finality of the judiciary. Borah was soon telling his constituents that there were 53 Senate votes for the income tax, but strategists of the Old Guard hypocritically prevented action by proposing a constitutional amendment. Another four years were to elapse before income taxes were to be levied by Congress.

Trusts, the burning issue in the public eye for the past ten years, likewise escaped congressional intervention for another four years. In 1910 Taft urged Congress to enact the federal incorporation program that both parties had endorsed in the campaign of 1908. The Taft-Wickersham bill was introduced in both houses as a re-enforcement of the Antitrust Act. Incorporation was voluntary, but trusts that refused would be subject to prosecution as monopolies. Taft and his Attorney General, George W. Wickersham, believed that federal chartering of corporations would centralize trust supervision in Washington, correct lax state control in regulating stock issues, prohibit watered stock and holding companies, and compel publicity on corporate practices by requiring full reports to the Department of Commerce and Labor. The administration's bill never came to debate, nor did similar bills sponsored by Cummins of Iowa and by the Democratic leader, Senator John Sharp Williams of Mississippi. In 1911 Taft renewed his appeal for federal charters, urging a Federal Corporation Commission as the regulatory agency. His party again ignored its campaign pledge. No trust legislation was enacted. But the idea of an administrative approach toward government regulation had been planted; it germinated in the Federal Trade Commission three years later and reappeared long afterward in the Securities and Exchange Commission.

The decade from 1900 to 1910 was the high point of congressional defense of governmental laxity in the interests of the new aristocracy born of the machine age. Never had there been so audacious an inversion, so great a volume of public protest, so massive a structure of corporate power, and so astonishingly small and so inferior a product from the legislative and judicial mills. But the year 1910 marked the breakdown of a system. The forces of reform began to assert themselves; minority interests were placed on the defensive and a breach was opened for a politics of public interest. The irresponsible dictatorship of the Speaker of the House of Representatives was attacked in March; a reactionary railroad bill was rewritten by insurgent Republicans in collaboration with Bryan Democrats in June; and Democratic victory for the first time in sixteen years was registered at the polls in November. A turning point in American progress was reached at last.

The combined force of public indignation and congressional progressivism struck at the old system, which had failed so dismally to give the country an intelligible choice between parties and party principles. The smooth-working congressional organization, winner in every contest since 1896, had made the fatal error of exposing itself nakedly as an instrument to win elections and not to serve the public. And it was the progressive Republicans who had accomplished this unmasking. The opposition party needed similar critical inspection. Behind the thin façade of party unity, an inner conflict had long divided the Democrats. Bryan's wing, predominant in the West and popular in the South but with only limp support from some southern leaders, was always strongest with the mass of Democratic voters. Southern forces, often Bourbon Democrats, by the rule of seniority held strategic posts in congressional committees. Bryan liberals, in rebellion against Bourbon Southerners and northern city machines like Tammany, captured presidential nominations and wrote the platforms in three out of the four contests from 1896 to 1908. But the swing in the 1910 elections reflected a vote against Old Guard Republicans, not confidence in the Democrats. The condition in the parties, enfeebling them for a twentieth-century struggle to advance the public interest, explains the rise of insurgency, the Republican debacle, and the limitations of Wilsonian Democracy.

INSURGENCY AND THE DEMOCRATS

"Insurgency," a new word in the American political vocabulary, signified an experiment in the bloc politics of a multiparty system, in default of an effective major party system. A small band of fighting progressive Republicans had begun to coalesce into the Senate bloc led by La Follette and the House bloc led by George W. Norris of Nebraska, but they had been "read out of the party," denied patronage by the Republican machine, and relegated to obscure committees where their talents could find little scope at the decisive stage of drafting major bills. Among these men, La Follette, Borah, and Norris became leaders in the battles for an income tax and direct election of senators; Beveridge, the gallant champion of federal child labor legislation; and Cummins of Iowa, the advocate of La Follette's earlier idea of a national presidential primary to destroy boss control of presidential nominations. Fiery, ambitious, resourceful, uncompromising, La Follette was the master strategist and unrivaled expert on economic legislation, an arsenal of unanswerable facts and figures on trusts, conservation, railroads, utility rates, and tariff schedules. Soft-spoken, unassuming, but adroit and persistent, George Norris, the soul of homespun integrity, became leader in the reform of government, meditating ways to achieve a universal civil service without patronage, a democratic House procedure that would establish majority rule, and an election process that would make the government truly representative. The insurgents had the brains but not the votes. They numbered too few to bid for outright control of party organization, but they had a strength not matched by Aldrich, Cannon, and the numerical majority. They, and they alone among Republicans, spoke with the power of public opinion. When Taft openly took sides with his congressional leaders against the insurgents, he lost the confidence of thousands of earnest men who had cast their ballots for him. They would have taken the President to their hearts had he turned his wrath the other way and belabored Aldrich, Cannon, and notorious big bosses like Senator Boies Penrose.

The insurgent attack was necessarily oblique. Under the undemocratic method of appointment of senators, Aldrich's control was unshakable, but the hold of Cannon's machine in the House was not. When Taft's first Congress assembled in 1909, the insurgent bloc united with the Democrats and voted down the old customary rules of the House. But John Joseph Fitzgerald, Tammany wheel horse affiliated with Judge Parker's Wall Street Democrats, a cooperative member of Cannon's reactionary Rules Committee, subsequently swung enough Tammany votes to retain the old rules. Rumor had it that Cannon and Tammany had made a deal: New York Republicans were to help Tammany defeat election reforms pending in the state legislature. The incident and the rumor bespoke the looseness of party lines and the ill fame of machines as unprincipled seekers of local advantage.

Nevertheless, the Norris bloc won a sensational victory in March, 1910. House rules had been designed to prevent debate and to muzzle opposition. To be debated, a resolution must be placed on the calendar, but it could not be put on the calendar without a rule. The Rules Committee was composed of cooperating Republicans and Democrats appointed by the Speaker, who dominated them. Accordingly, since 1908 Norris had been blocked in all efforts to introduce a resolution to amend the rules. But on March 17 a chance ruling by the Speaker allowed Norris an opening to disregard the calendar and get the floor. He rose, drew from his pocket an old crumpled paper that he had carried for two years, and read his resolution for the reform of the House. After a record-breaking all-night debate, the Speaker ruled Norris out of order. By a close vote the Democrats and the insurgents reversed Cannon's ruling. Then the House adopted the Norris resolution removing the Speaker from the Rules Committee, stripping him of his power to appoint its members, and making them elective by the House. Overnight Norris became a beloved national figure.

Yet the victory was more apparent than real. A top organization with authority to control procedure of the House was necessary for party control over a body that contained several hundred members who introduced thirty thousand bills in a single Congress. Norris, however, pierced through the sham of Cannon's contention that the Speaker was the agent of the majority and derived his power from them. Cannon's inner organization derived power not from the confidence of the party, but from coercive power to deny patronage and thereby turn the local machine at home against an individual member. As a substitution for the Speaker's discipline, the Democrats revived the unifying device of a party caucus.

Soon afterward the Old Guard suffered a second great defeat. As one of his primary objectives, Taft was pressing for railroad legislation. Led by La Follette and Cummins, the insurgents turned in rage on the Mann-Elkins Bill, an administration measure drafted by Attorney General Wickersham. They attacked the retention of the old privilege whereby railroad corporations could obtain court orders to block the ICC (Interstate Commerce Commission). Particularly infuriating to the insurgents was Taft's proposal to give the commission power to suspend the antitrust law to permit collusion between railroads in making rates. To require competition and to save the ICC from conversion into a tool of special interests, they proceeded to rewrite the bill. They forced an amendment denying a proposed Court of Commerce the power to set aside orders of the ICC. They modified a provision that might have legalized an inflated capitalization as the basis upon which the ICC would be forced to fix rates. Even the unamended Taft measure was much too progressive to please business allies of the Republican organization. The National Association of Manufacturers began an active lobby against it, and but for the growing power of the coalition of Democrats and insurgents, the bill would have suffered the same emasculation encountered in Roosevelt's struggle for the Hepburn Act. Passed by Congress three months after the successful attack on Cannonism, the Mann-Elkins Act marked a significant climax of La Follette's struggle for a fair rate base. The new law authorized a survey of the actual physical value of railroads. This, said La Follette, was the only basis for fixing a rate that would not enrich speculators and defraud the public by legalizing profits on watered stock. But in a rear-guard action, the retainers of the railroad baronage blocked appropriations. Not until the Physical Evaluation Act of March, 1913, signed just before Taft left office, was the ICC launched on the great survey, a work not completed until 1921.

The mild progressivism of the President did not divert his party from arrant obstructionism even on smaller issues. In June an ill-assorted alliance of Taft, the insurgents, and the Democrats won two minor victories, the Postal Savings Act and a corrupt practices law that attempted to counteract the power of money in elections by requiring publicity of the sources of congressional campaign funds. Meanwhile Republican voters had been learning harsh lessons from the La Follette technique of reading the record. A Republican Congress, heeding the lobby of the National Association of Manufacturers, had disregarded Taft's plea to carry out the campaign pledge for restriction of labor injunctions. Congress had rejected Taft's recommendation for sweeping extension of civil service, including abolition of spoils in the post-office budget. Congress had dodged the issues of direct election of senators and an income tax. Finally and decisively, the unsavory Payne-Aldrich tariff had alienated not only angry forces of labor and disillusioned advocates of progressive reform but farmers of the Middle West. The elections of November, 1910, were an autopsy revealing the fatal senescence of a system of special privilege that had lived too long on borrowed time.

The Democrats made inroads in the Senate and won control of the House. The Democratic floor leader, Champ Clark, superseded Cannon in the Speaker's chair, and the rules were liberalized to give committees more freedom to present bills and the House more freedom to get a bill out on the floor if a committee pigeonholed an important measure. Destruction of the misrepresentative leadership under the Speaker system left a vacuum that had to be filled. Within a few years a Continental critic of political parties, Robert Michels, was formulating the famous "iron law of oligarchy," revealing the inevitability of open or secret control by a small, top organization in any legislative body. The Democrats, to the chagrin of Norris, revived the congressional caucus and set up a Committee on Committees. The result was to give a strategic position to the inner group of moderately conservative southern leaders, who thereby acquired power to discipline the rank and file by control of committee assignments or by denial of patronage.

Democrats like Champ Clark (Missouri), Oscar Underwood (Alabama), Cordell Hull (Tennessee), John Sharp Williams (Mississippi), and Carter Glass (Virginia) were progressive mainly on the tariff issue, but otherwise disposed to go little further than President Taft had gone. On the old issue of direct election of senators, southern conservatives lined up with Old Guard Republicans. For years public clamor had been growing, and the House several times had voted in favor of amending the Constitution, only to be frustrated by misrepresentative senators keen to avert their personal political demise. With southern Bourbons it was partly an issue of class rule and partly a question of white domination. The biographers of Senator Glass credit their hero with writing the clause into the Virginia constitution disfranchising the Negro and poor white by the system of literacy tests and poll taxes.

Despite the clause in the Constitution that authorized federal control of the election of representatives and the sweeping but unused grant of congressional power in the Fourteenth Amendment, Congress deferred to state control of the federal suffrage and national elections. By 1900 Jacksonian manhood suffrage no longer existed in various states, a situation attesting the decentralized character of parties and the locus of power in local machines. Two northern and seven southern states had established taxpaying or other barriers to free elections; and by 1910 Texas and Virginia had also been brought into the poll tax system. But the progressive swing in the elections of 1910 was unmistakable. The popular nomination of senators through the direct primary in half of the forty-eight states was beginning to tell. In June, 1911, the Bryan Democrats and the insurgent Republicans at last won their long battle, mustering a two-thirds majority for the Seventeenth Amendment for popular election of United States senators. Delaying tactics by southern Bourbons prolonged the struggle another year before the House approved the amendment. In spite of opposition by local bosses, it was ratified quickly by northern and western states, becoming effective in May, 1913—without ratification by ten southern states, where local machines resisted to the end.

1912

Meanwhile the unthinkable was happening. The Republican party, split on the rocks of progressivism, was suffering the fate that had befallen the Democrats in the crusade of 1896. Assured by events that they reflected the swing of Republican voters, the insurgents met at La Follette's house in Washington and in January, 1911, formed the National Progressive Republican League. Insurgency had come of age. From an attempt by minority bloc tactics to sway votes in Congress, it now changed into a movement to capture the Republican organization. La Follette became a leading contender for the Republican nomination for the presidency. Suddenly Theodore Roosevelt announced that his hat was in the ring and slowly wooed the Progressive League away from La Follette. In states that had adopted primaries, Roosevelt supporters won place as delegates to the Republican convention, far outdistancing both Taft and La Follette. But once again patronage and local machines played a decisive role in producing a nomination contrary to the overwhelming demand of party voters. The skeleton Republican organization in the South, linked with the chief executive through the network of federal patronage, supported Taft and threw control of the Republican National Committee into the hands of big eastern bosses, William Barnes of New York, Senator Murray Crane of Massachusetts, and Senator Boies Penrose of Pennsylvania. The National Committee used its control of convention machinery to refuse seats to numerous Roosevelt delegates. This, with the 278 southern "spoils" delegates, gave the bosses more than the 590 delegates required to nominate. Taft chose a hack politician from his own state, Warren G. Harding, to place his name in nomination. Boss Penrose was cynically disdainful of the fact that his own Pennsylvania primary had turned out a delegation for Roosevelt.

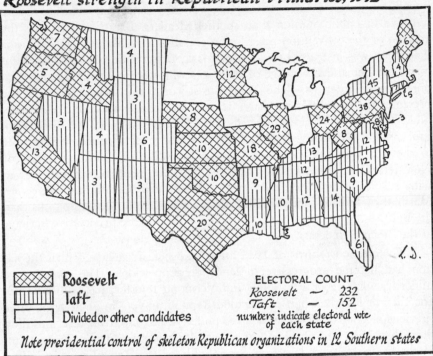

Roosevelt strength in Republican Primaries, 1912

	ELECTORAL COUNT
▨ Roosevelt	Roosevelt — 232
▥ Taft	Taft — 152
☐ Divided or other candidates	numbers indicate electoral vote of each state

Note presidential control of skeleton Republican organizations in 12 Southern states

The nomination of Taft broke the Republican party. The conservative forces had dominated for years not through public confidence but through control of inner party machinery. No right was more fundamental in democratic belief than the right of a minority to become a majority. Roosevelt accused Taft and the bosses of violating the commandment "Thou shalt not steal." The liberal forces held a separate convention and organized a new Progressive party. They made the bull moose their emblem and placed Roosevelt and Governor Hiram Johnson of California on a national Progressive ticket. The organization included such redoubtable leaders of American thought as Jane Addams, John R. Commons, and Louis D. Brandeis. The Progressive platform endorsed Roosevelt's

New Nationalism, embracing an impressive program of social reform on the new concept that regardless of outworn state rights, wherever there was a national evil there must be found a national remedy.

The Democratic convention was nearly as stormy as the Republican battle over the nomination of Taft. The same forces contended in both parties. Champ Clark was first choice of machine delegates and the leader in the primaries. But for the intervention of Bryan and the obstacle of the party's rule requiring two thirds to nominate, the Democrats, like the Republicans, would have offered the voters a conservative ticket. More sensitive to public opinion than southern leaders, Bryan insisted that the keynote of the convention must be progressivism. Although his Nebraska delegation was instructed to vote for Clark, Bryan suddenly attacked Tammany and demanded a purge of delegates who were in secret alliance with big business interests. The Wall Street connection was visible in the presence of the utilities magnate, Thomas Fortune Ryan of Fifth Avenue, New York, as a Virginia delegate, and August Belmont, the New York banker, as a Tammany delegate. Bryan's maneuver produced a stampede to the next leading contender, Woodrow Wilson, reform governor of New Jersey, who was bitterly opposed by New Jersey bosses and viewed with suspicion by other machines. Wilson and Governor Thomas R. Marshall of Indiana were nominated on a platform far less ambitious than the Bull Moose program but nevertheless reflecting the progressive heritage of the Bryan Democrats.

The election returns of 1912 afforded conclusive evidence that the nation had become progressive in landslide proportions. The conservative minority, winning only in Utah and Vermont, registered 3,483,922 votes for Taft, or less than half of the total Republican vote in each of the three previous elections. The Progressives polled 4,126,020, over half a million more than Taft, winning Pennsylvania and five western states. Triumphant in the midwestern and eastern strongholds of the Republicans including New England, Wilson swept forty states in an election that gave Democrats a working majority in both houses of Congress. Wilson was a minority President, leading Roosevelt by little more than 2,000,000 votes; but more significant of the division of the country was the small vote, less than 3,500,000, for Taft and the Old Guard Republicans as compared with the prodigious combined total of more than 11,000,000 votes for the progressive candidates, Wilson, Roosevelt, and the Socialist, Eugene Debs. Prior to the election a poll conducted by the National Association of Manufacturers among its members showed that 90 per cent of the leading businessmen favored Taft, 8 per cent Roosevelt, and 2 per cent Wilson; the poll was another confirmation of the popular taunt that the Republican organization was primarily an instrument for minority interests.

THE PROGRESSIVISM OF THE DEMOCRATS

In their new choice for the White House, the people had acquired a President of more penetrating insight than any since Lincoln, and the first in a hundred years to match Jefferson and Madison in intellectual range. So different in character from the magnetic Theodore Roosevelt, Woodrow Wilson was to triumph where Roosevelt had failed. Except for Wilson's enfeebled last months in office, when he lost touch with the people and unsuccessfully defied the opposition in Congress, he acquitted himself as one of the most masterly of American party leaders. Previously a college president at Princeton, he had fought against academic reproduction of the existing class snobberies of wealthy society. A progressive governor, he had fought against bosses and business organizations in New Jersey, a state that had led all others in the laxity with which it chartered holding companies. A progressive President, he quickly acquired stature as a persuasive leader in the battle of the Democrats against rule by the few. The magic of his words was not impetuosity as with "Teddy" or oratorical charm as with Bryan; it was the magic of classic simplicity and honesty of intellect addressed to common folk by a man whose imagination impelled him to identify himself with the people. For Wilsonian Democracy recognized the necessity of a principle of leadership, but it was a principle solidly based upon faith in the people.

Bred to the Jeffersonian tradition of Virginia liberalism, himself Virginia born, President Wilson promptly drafted the experienced southern leadership in Congress and spurred it forward by adroit appeal to the driving force of popular opinion. Summoning a special session of Congress in April, 1913, a few weeks after his inauguration, the new President dramatically indicated the qualities of vigorous leadership necessary to enact a party program. Reviving a custom that had fallen into disuse since the presidency of John Adams, Wilson electrified the country by reading his message in person before a joint assembly of the two houses. He urged fulfillment of the party pledge to enact a low tariff. This was the first in a series of special messages delivered in person and usually focused on a single major issue. The new technique revealed in Wilson a mastery of timing and legislative management. Unlike Theodore Roosevelt, whose long and frequent messages laid down a barrage in all directions, Wilson pushed one policy at a time, assuming a degree of executive control over the congressional order of business. American presidents lacked European cabinet power to control the "time" of a legislature, but Wilson succeeded in his announced purpose of coordinating the first two branches of the government through executive leadership of the party. William Randolph Hearst, more of a demagogue than a Democrat, was soon attacking Wilson for introducing the English system of government. But a merit was quickly demonstrated. For two years—perhaps the first time in American political experience—a congressional majority worked on a coordinated party program in substantial fulfillment of election pledges.

Wilson's tariff message, reviving Cleveland's contention that the tariff was the mother of trusts, denounced the Payne-Aldrich Act as "a set of privileges and exemptions from competition" behind which even rudimentary forms of combinations could "organize monopoly." The President urged return to a tariff for revenue only. Under Taft, the Democrats controlling the Ways and Means Committee had already worked on new tariff schedules. It was not normal, however, for unity in committee to be duplicated by party unity in debates on the floor and votes for enactment. Democrats, observed Underwood, ranged "all the way from those who believe in absolute free trade to those who favored protection for their own constituents and were willing to reduce the taxes on the other fellow." Wall Street, a few days after Wilson's message, was stunned when Underwood, as chairman of the Ways and Means Committee, introduced a House bill that reversed the fifty-year trend toward high protectionism. Republican tariffs, Underwood contended, had eliminated desirable foreign competition, and this protection had perpetuated backward technology and business inefficiency, as in the textile industry. The misleading Republican proposal of a tariff to equalize costs at home and abroad, Underwood regarded as a protectionist "excuse rather than a method" of tariff reform. His own bill called for 958 reductions, striking particularly against protection of inflated prices on food, clothing, and the primary necessities for American families.

Party unity in committee had resisted the normal surrender to tariff specifications demanded by powerful pressure groups that packed committee hearings; but only presidential leadership supported by disciplined party behavior saved the Underwood Bill when it came to debate. Underwood himself, able and incorruptible Alabama congressman, became the President's lieutenant, guiding debate like an English finance minister, aided by his strategic position as floor leader of the party and chairman of the tax committee. Backed by the authority of the party caucus, he held Democrats in line despite pressures from the lobbies. The Underwood tariff passed the House in May, 1913, intact.

Frustrated in their attempts to continue to dictate tariff rates in the secrecy of committee or through amendments in the House, interest groups transferred their pressures to the Senate, buttonholing timorous and lukewarm Democrats. In the more "independent" Senate, the Democratic majority was slight and less well organized. A switch of a few votes would open the floodgate of amendment. To stiffen party morale, Wilson wrote personal letters to hard-pressed senators and made effective use of the presidential advantage in publicity. Newspapers all over the nation carried the President's arresting statement that "Washington has seldom seen so numerous, so industrious, or so insidious a lobby." The dreaded pressure groups, confronted by a unified party, displayed surprising weakness, verifying earlier conclusions of experts who considered that party discipline under a central leadership and not the "independence" of Congress was the secret of resistance to powerful interests. Pleading for special interests, the New York *Times* charged that the President had "mistaken for lobbying" the "usual" and "legitimate" efforts of industry to present its case. But telegrams and letters pouring in from the voters revealed a social anger not to be deceived by pious rationalizations. Old Guard Republicans professed outrage at the intimation that they would make "deals," but the Progressive Republican, Senator Cummins, furthered the Wilsonian strategy of forcing pressure groups into the open by instigating an investigation of lobbies. In June the investigation began to take testimony that laid naked the realities of the legislative process.

In July Wilson's supporters won another victory for party discipline. The caucus, virtually extinct as a Senate procedure, was revived and succeeded in binding Democrats to support the tariff as "a party measure." Party lines did not hold against amendments, but the bill passed. Only the sugar Democrats from Louisiana supported the Republicans. In the conference committee La Follette helped avert the notorious practice of introducing "jokers" at the behest of special interests. Signed by Wilson in October, 1913, the Underwood-Simmons tariff fell short of the Wilson and Underwood goal of abolishing protection of monopoly profits or of encouraging a substantial amount of importation, but it reversed the long trend toward excessive economic nationalism.

On this measure as on others following, most of the Progressives opposed the administration. A Republican from Washington, Miles Poindexter, stood with La Follette in voting for the Underwood tariff, but Norris, Borah, and most western Progressives clung to the isolationist economics that Charles Beard later eulogized as an "open door at home." Scornful of free trade, they favored a restricted tariff-tinkering to hit at monopolies. They attacked Underwood's tariff as they had Aldrich's on the ground that it failed to authorize a commission of administrative experts to recommend rates. They won a partial victory in 1916, when Congress created a Tariff Commission.

The Underwood Bill afforded an opportunity to apply the progressive social theory of taxation as an instrument to provide a more democratic distribution of wealth. With the exception of the brief experiment of Alexander Hamilton and the structure of war taxes after 1812 and 1861, the United States, unlike European nations, had never established a genuine internal revenue system. Taft had defeated inclusion of an inheritance tax in the Aldrich tariff, but the Progressives had succeeded in tacking on an internal revenue tax on corporation profits. Now the Democrats in the Underwood tariff re-established at long last the income tax system that the Supreme Court had made unconstitutional in 1895. In 1916 a new law rounded out the internal revenue system by making an inheritance or estates tax a permanent part of federal taxation. The institution of the income tax in 1913 was initially a triumph for southern Democrats and their principle of a tariff for revenue. Cordell Hull of Tennessee, rising tax expert on the Ways and Means Committee, wrote the income tax not as a social policy but as a straight revenue measure to compensate for losses from tariff reductions. Progressives were disappointed. Family net incomes between $4,000 and $20,000 were taxed at a normal rate of 1 per cent, with only slight increases on upper brackets; for example, on incomes between $20,000 and $50,000 the tax was only 2 per cent. Not until 1918 was the principle of progressively steeper taxes on higher incomes seriously attempted, and even then Hull and his associates sought revenue for war purposes, rather than for "social ends" or redistribution of wealth.

Wall Street, at the time of the Underwood tariff, charged the administration with destroying business confidence. A depression did not result, although business confidence was insulted anew by a succession of regulatory enactments. Wilson, employing his dramatic tactic of delivering his message personally in Congress, next urged currency and banking reform. Three days later, on June 26, the Federal Reserve Bill was introduced in the House. Its main object was to make the national-bank system more flexible and the currency more elastic and at the same time to check the gigantic aggregation of financial power popularly denounced as the Money Trust. In the six years since the panic of 1907, lack of co-ordinated leadership in Congress had prevented effective action despite careful study by a monetary commission and urgent calls for action first by Roosevelt, then by Taft.

Sponsored in the upper house by Robert L. Owen, a Democratic reformer from Oklahoma, and by Carter Glass in the House, the Federal Reserve Bill became law in December, 1913. In essence it was a system of banks-to-serve-banks, with a degree of power either to contract or to inflate the currency. The difference between the Wall Street scheme of Aldrich's monetary commission and the Democratic measure was superficially in the amount of centralized control; more fundamentally, in who would control—government officials or representatives of private banking institutions. The Aldrich commission, after months abroad studying European central banks, reported in favor of a Hamiltonian system with centralized private control, eminently satisfactory to creditor interests. Glass and Owen rejected private management but converted the Democratic party to a bill that departed radically from the old Jacksonian tradition, for it established a nominally decentralized system of regional reserve banks actually subordinate to a Federal Reserve Board in Washington. Board members were to be chosen by the President and Senate with "due regard to a fair representation of the financial, agricultural, industrial, and commercial interests and geographical divisions of the country." Banking interests eventually sang praise of the Federal Reserve Act. The stigma they had fixed on Democrats as a reckless party of Bryanism and inflation was dissipated by the Wilsonian achievement of "sound" monetary reform. But liberal Democrats and progressive Republicans had reservations. Norris, one of the three Republican senators voting for the Federal Reserve Act, attacked Democratic domination through the caucus, charging that Glass and Owen had put over "bank ownership and bank control" in place of an outright democratic central bank under government ownership and government control. Soon afterward, when Wilson appointed to the Reserve Board a man from Morgan's Harvester Trust and another from the Money Trust, Norris considered that his worst fears had been confirmed.

Revision of the antitrust laws was next on Wilson's agenda. The preceding Republican Congresses—with Democratic votes—had legislated on corporations only in the field of railroads. The new Wilsonian tax laws, by striking at monopoly profits and hereditary great fortunes, had obliquely touched the trust problem through the customs house and the internal revenue system. Similarly the Federal Reserve System sought to fence in the "money power" by erecting public safeguards against the power of private banking institutions to contract or expand currency and credit and thereby facilitate speculative profit for creditor interests at the expense of farmers and debtors. But these were flank attacks. Wilson, in campaign speeches, had pledged a "New Freedom" for business, labor, and the public—a freedom from monopoly and from an "economic system which is heartless." His administration was committed to a much wider use of governmental power to strip concentrated corporate wealth of undemocratic political and economic privilege.

THE "NEW FREEDOM" AND THE "RULE OF REASON"

Republican failure in the crucial years of the trust movement, 1897 to 1912, saddled the Democratic administration with a problem far more formidable than when Congress passed the Sherman Act. Vigorous enforcement by cooperating executive and judicial branches in the era from

McKinley to Taft theoretically could have prevented incubation of the "supermonopolies." Until 1904 the government side-stepped the responsibility of bringing trust managers to justice under the criminal penalties of the antitrust statute. In that year the Northern Securities decision was a doubtful victory. A corporation was forbidden to continue practices that amounted to criminal conspiracy, but the "person" held guilty was the fictitious legal person, the corporation itself. The famous dissenter, Justice Oliver Wendell Holmes, scorned the "artificial" interpretation of the Court majority which, on a technical ruling that the suit was civil rather than criminal, saved J. P. Morgan and James J. Hill from personal liability. This distinction became normal judicial policy, and thereby men responsible for violations were shielded from the Sherman Act penalty of a $5,000 fine or a year's imprisonment.

Executive and judicial failure in antitrust suits stemmed also from disinclination to develop precise general definitions to be applied universally. Neither the Supreme Court nor the Department of Justice attempted an organic approach or an over-all policy through basic rulings to compel universal adherence to approved methods of competition. Judicial regulation was confined to particular injuries in particular cases, on the complaint of individuals. For example, the Northern Securities holding company was dissolved, but holding companies as a monopolistic form of organization were not universally sentenced to death. Economists, on the contrary, taking an organic approach in describing the actual structure of American business, defined trusts very differently from the Supreme Court's definition. In addition to the outlawed form of "trust," economists gave the same designation to "gentlemen's agreements" between ostensible competitors; to pools between corporations to control output, markets, earnings, or patents; to consolidations or mergers of big competitors; and, above all, to holding companies. The holding company was a disguised form of trust to establish control over supposedly competing corporations by acquiring ownership or a controlling interest in their business and properties.

The famous "rule of reason" adopted by the Supreme Court in 1911 was a crucial departure from judicial antitrust policy. The rule was not precisely defined in court decisions, but it meant that monopolistic practices and combinations to restrain trade were not contrary to the judicial interpretation of antitrust laws unless such monopoly behavior constituted an *unreasonable* restraint of trade. This rule frankly sanctioned an uncertain judicial discretion in place of any, settled general organic policy. Long afterward it was remarked that the Sherman Act was written in language so plain that only lawyers or judges could misunderstand it.

Wavering antitrust policy in administrative pleadings before the courts and wavering court decisions in trust litigation, like congressional disagreement over a proper trust policy, were normal accompaniments of conflicting interests and sympathies in the unrelenting struggle for power. When the rule of reason was adopted, great business magnates were frightened by the antitrust activity of Roosevelt and Taft. The great masters of capital feared that a growing public demand would place administrations and judges in power who would give full face value to the Sherman Act, possibly condemn all holding companies, or actually enforce the criminal penalties against big businessmen. Not a few Wall Street men were favorable to Taft's proposal of federal licensing or incorporation; they saw a refuge in the Taft and Roosevelt principle of an administrative discretion in distinguishing between good and bad trusts. Most particularly they pressed Taft for governmental approval in advance of specific plans of a corporation, thereby to escape subsequent liability to prosecution. Nor did Wall Street lack respectable support among American economists for the saving distinction between good and bad trusts. The more friendly economists, impressed by the giant strides of American corporations, had helped to undermine the old belief in the principle of the Sherman Act. Expounding theories of the efficiency of large-scale organization, they departed from the classical economics of Adam Smith, which had explained efficiency as a consequent of continuous competition among smaller enterprises. Attacking the brilliant analysis by Brandeis of inefficiency and bureaucracy in large-scale business and of irresponsible finance in the pyramids of holding companies, these economists frankly defended big consolidations—provided they were operated in the public interest. The public interest was to be ensured by governmental regulation.

Less favorable to government regulation, conservative justices similarily sought escape from the unpalatable law of enforced competition. To a jurist, unless he had been a "people's lawyer," like Brandeis, it was an affront to sit on a case where conviction could send to jail a personage of the magnitude of J. P. Morgan. Searching for a loophole, legal writers began to look abroad, pointing to other countries where such a painful duty had been evaded by a decorous judiciary. President Taft expressed the fear in 1909 that the high court might adopt a rule of reason. But such discretion to distinguish between righteous and wicked trusts, he contended, would give judges "a power which it would be dangerous and impossible for them to exercise." The sensational suits launched under Roosevelt against the American Tobacco Company and against the ever-unpopular Standard Oil trust were then pending. Two years later, 1911, both trusts were dissolved by the Supreme Court into their smaller components, the operating companies, but Taft's premonition was fulfilled. The Supreme Court in the Standard Oil case, distinguishing between the direct and indirect effects of "restraint of trade," declared that under its new judicial criterion, "of course the rule of reason becomes the guide." In the Tobacco case the Court added that exercise of judicial reason was necessary because Congress had not "defined" the words "restraint of trade." The discretionary reason of the Court majority, remarked Justice John M. Harlan in his separate opinion, "does not justify the perversion of the plain words of an act in order to defeat the will of Congress."

Adoption of the rule of reason, six months after the Democratic victory of 1910 and at a time when Progressives were mobilizing for capture of the Republican party, came at a strategic moment. Storm clouds were obscuring the upthrust of the rugged and mountainous trusts. But however timely the adoption of the rule of reason, the new judicial policy reflected a general world trend and not simply a strategic countermeasure at a critical stage in American politics.

All the industrial nations of the world relied upon corporation law and the process of litigation to restrain irresponsible financial practices or illegal monopolies; and as in the United States, country after country experienced disillusionment with regulation by litigation. The rule of reason did not originate in the United States; the only surprising fact is the lag of American courts in following the general trend. English courts, in common-law prosecutions for conspiracy in restraint of trade, adopted a "rule of reason" as early as the eighteen nineties. Attempts in Australia and New Zealand to put the burden of proof on the accused did not prevent their courts from also taking a lenient view favoring the defendants. Canada, which had the sharp weapons of tariff reductions on monopoly products and revocation of patents protecting monopolies, likewise encountered difficulties with a judiciary that resisted a vigorous enforcement of antitrust legislation. In all countries, litigation and judicial rulings as a governmental procedure to deal with trusts exhibited the same weakness. Despite popular pressure through representatives who made the laws, the courts, taking an amiable view of the compatibility of monopoly with the public interest, countered with the loose and discretionary judicial doctrine of the rule of reason.

In the United States a minority on the Supreme Court was converted to the doctrine of "reason" as early as the eighteen nineties. In the Trans-Missouri Freight Association case (1897) the conservative dissenters protested the majority refusal to write the rule of reason into American constitutional law. A basic case, *Smyth v. Ames* (1898), however, did in effect write the rule of reason into railroad rate litigation. But in 1911, when the majority corrected the social lag and the Supreme Court imitated foreign judicial practice in its acceptance of the rule for cases involving monopoly, the action in an institutional sense was far more significant than

Above—Company houses for families of coal miners in Pennsylvania "captive mines." *Below*—New York bread line for unemployed during postwar business recession, 1920. *(Brown Brothers)*

Before the closing of the door to immigrants.

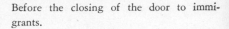

Top—Polish *émigrés* crowding the rail before debarkation.

Center—Immigrant girls ashore from Ellis Island.

Below—Barge Office near Battery Park about 1900. Here carts met immigrant families and transported them and their belongings to cheap lodging places later known as flophouses.
(Brown Brothers)

Right—Suffragette parade up Fifth Avenue, New York, 1915—a monster procession of over 100,000 women continuing all day and into the night. *(Brown Brothers)*

Below—The Big Four at the Versailles Peace Conference—Lloyd George, Orlando, Clemenceau, and Wilson.

(Underwood-Stratton)

Postwar reaction. *Above*—Nightshirted nobles of the K.K.K. in patriotic conclave at Ohio steel city about 1920. *(Brown Brothers)* *Below*—The Devil in the guise of Science unmasked by antievolution books at the "monkey trial," Dayton, Tennessee, 1925. *(Press Association)*

in other nations. Under the unique American conditions of judicial finality, the discretion of courts could not readily be reversed by representatives elected by the people. To this extent in the United States the rule of reason substituted the rule of the Court for the rule of Congress.

The judicial impasse heightened American interest in a stronger technique than litigation. By the second quarter of the twentieth century, industrialized societies began to rely more heavily on expert regulation by administrative process. In attempting to regulate business by this method, the United States set the fashion for other countries. Disappointment in the empty victories in the Standard Oil, American Tobacco, Du Pont, and Beef Trust prosecutions crystallized sentiment. Upholders of legislative power and majority rule were driven to statutory and administrative regulation as alternatives to a process of litigation that resulted in judicial formulation of antitrust policy. After a two-year investigation of Court decisions, a congressional committee reported in February, 1913, that the rule of reason made it "imperative to enact additional legislation." Subsequent Wilsonian legislation reflected a struggle of Republican and Democratic liberals, acting through the first two branches of the government, to defeat the industrial and financial forces entrenched in the third branch and still powerful in Congress.

Judicial interpretation convinced Wilson of two things: court treatment of corporations as "persons" had robbed the Sherman Act of its most effective penalties; second, the rule of reason required the antidote of statutory definition of unfair competitive practices combined with an administrative process of regulation. "Corporations do not do wrong," said Wilson in 1910. "Individuals do wrong. . . . Society cannot afford to have individuals wield the power of thousands without personal responsibility." He urged modification of the "demoralizing fiction that a corporation is an indivisible person." Under the theory that a corporation was a person, nobody, "no matter how intimate his use and control, may be brought into the suit by any genteel lawyer bred in the orthodox schools of law." He remarked that if a few conspicuous dummy directors or managers were put in the penitentiary, there would soon "be no more dummies for hire." In the campaign of 1912, Wilson maintained that competition must be revived "by changing the laws and forbidding the practices that killed it."

Against the advice of party leaders to "go slow," Wilson made reform of big business the main concern of Congress in 1914. In January, again delivering his message in person, the President presented an organic formula based on the expert advice of Louis D. Brandeis. Wilson urged that the "processes and methods of monopoly . . . be explicitly and item by item forbidden by statute in such terms as will practically eliminate uncertainty. . . . We are agreed, I take it, that holding companies should be prohibited." He added his own principle that penalties and punishments should be visited directly on the guilty individuals and not on the corporation and its stockholders. In response, Congress in September, 1914, created a Federal Trade Commission and in October passed the Clayton Antitrust Act. These measures were not so comprehensive as Wilson's program or so rigorous as earlier proposals for a federal incorporation or license system.

The FTC, created by the Federal Trade Commission Act of 1914, was calculated to give force to a new general definition that "unfair methods of competition" were unlawful. Under this authority, the commission subsequently, in modest foreshadowing of the later NRA (National Recovery Administration), worked out codes of fair practices in consultation with concerns in a particular industry and issued orders to "cease and desist" in case of violation. The commission's second great power was that of investigating and making public report on the management, finances, and structure of corporations. This principle was hailed as important because it theoretically brought the practices of industrial and commercial firms under governmental scrutiny, but the commission never had funds, staff, or political support requisite for any broad inspection or regulation. Contrary to Wilson's earlier classic theory of complete responsibility of the majority party in policy-forming administrative posts, Congress modeled the FTC on the earlier ICC, making it an "independent" agency composed of members of both parties with staggered terms of service.

The legislative history of Wilson's antitrust measures betrayed the limitations of the twentieth-century role of the President as party leader. Wilson suffered his first substantial defeat by virtue of the very party weaknesses that he had once so cogently analyzed. Southern Democrats, led by administration wheel horses like Senator John Sharp Williams of Mississippi and Congressman Underwood, had little actual relish for centralized national regulation. Underwood, although he strongly supported the Wilson proposal to revive competition by enforcement of criminal penalties against individual corporation managers, looked with mistrust on the Federal Trade Commission. Liberal southern thought, in the austere spirit of John Taylor and Jeffersonian agrarianism, favored a root-and-branch destruction of the legal privileges that gave life to the aristocracy of finance. To reassure such supporters, Wilson stated that the proposed trade commission would have no power to make terms with monopoly. Senator Williams, who had once urged federal incorporation and favored extirpation of financial "pyramids" and holding companies, unsuccessfully urged an absolute prohibition of the practice legalized by state charters whereby a corporation purchased stock in other corporations. Such views represented the last stand made on the simon-pure Sherman Act principle. Wilson himself had assailed Theodore Roosevelt's acceptance of a distinction between good and bad trusts. The outcome was a partial conservative victory. Congress rewrote the administration measures and opened the door to tolerance of good trusts.

In the House, opponents of centralized regulation stripped the Trade Commission of its power. The Senate substituted the original bill. The final form of the law was decided, as so often, by a small joint conference committee of senators and representatives—a bipartisan anomaly not elected by the majority but composed of appointees named by the chair in each house and representing neither the administration nor the congressional caucus of the majority party. Since Congress had never invented any responsible party control to iron out disagreement between the Senate and the House, the Democratic majority in each house, perforce, ratified the compromise bill of the conference committee. The crucial change made by the conference committee gave business firms recourse to the courts against acts of the FTC. The Iowa Progressive on the conference committee, Senator Cummins, fought against authorizing the courts "to review the discretion and the judgment exercised or the facts passed upon by the Trade Commission," since this would substitute litigation and judicial regulation for the administrative process. His point was soon demonstrated when the Supreme Court took the position that the meaning of "unfair methods of competition" was a matter for final determination by the judicial branch.

The Clayton Act, as a supplement both to the Trade Commission and the Sherman acts, passed the House in a form that antitrust champions attacked as surrender and that conservatives criticized as so vague that honest businessmen could not tell what would constitute violation. The bill defined as illegal several specific practices, chiefly interlocking directorates, intercorporate stockholding, and monopolistic contracts binding customers not to accept goods from competitors. Responding to the pressure of interest, the Senate leaped to the defense of the holding company and diluted the prohibitions against interlocking directorates and intercorporate stockholding by removing the criminal penalties. The conference committee destroyed the force of the law by making none of these prohibitions universal; they were illegal only when the government could prove in a particular instance their tendency to lessen competition or create monopoly. Responsibility for administration of the Clayton Act was parceled out among the three major agencies, the Federal Reserve Board, the Interstate Commerce Commission, and the Federal Trade Commission. But enforcement in the last analysis was left to the judicial branch.

Progressives like Norris favored the Trade Commission but voted against the Clayton Act. Borah called the latter a "political makeshift." Norris denounced it as "a shield for big business" and a "fraud" that retained effective criminal penalties only "for the little man." The public believed that Wilson had won a substantial victory. In actuality, the continuing loose organization of the parties once more had facilitated an anonymous combination of conservative Republicans and Democrats who whittled away much of Wilson's program. As Norris realized, the President had been defeated on his cardinal principle of making individual businessmen personally responsible. He was likewise defeated on the principle that no administrative or judicial body should have any discretionary powers to make terms with monopoly.

In the first two years of the Wilson administration the movement for social reform reached its peak. Gradually foreign affairs divided American thought between progress in home affairs and security in external relations. At the end of summer in 1914, when Wilson had been in office scarcely more than a year and a half, war broke out in Europe and threatened to engulf the world. Wilsonian Democracy was nonetheless to gain new ground in continuing battles against the old policies of protection and aid to business at public expense but without public safeguards. Before the end of Wilson's first term, the struggle for economic democracy was to supplement older policies by governmental concern for the nation's farmers; and to shake the authoritarian structure of private enterprise by friendliness toward labor. Manufacturers' associations, which had never doubted the virtue of aid to industry, were to be shocked by yet another Wilsonian conception—that aid to agriculture and aid to labor might likewise be in the public interest.

Not clearly visible on the horizon, but no less real, was the restless flow of modern life that for decades had been sweeping agriculture and labor into the grip of world forces. Suddenly war tightened the grip of these forces, and at war's end farmers and workers were left with twentieth-century problems to which the era of progress provided no answer.

XXVI

THE ENIGMA OF LABOR
AND AGRICULTURE 1900–1920

The history of agriculture and labor during the years when Theodore Roosevelt and William Howard Taft occupied the presidency can hardly be gleaned by consulting statutes infrequently passed by a dilatory Congress. Nor can the weakness and strength of the Wilsonian search for economic democracy be adequately appraised without consideration of the weakness and strength of organized labor and organized agriculture. More than that, the human problems involved and the slow change in American social attitudes cannot be gauged solely in American terms. The Iowa farmer whose produce crossed to Europe in the holds of sluggish freighters was linked to a destiny larger than that of his own beloved nation. The union organizer in San Francisco, the steelworker in Pennsylvania forced to sign a contract specifying that he would not join a union looked to the creation of labor standards that were less national than international.

The position of labor after the Homestead and Pullman strikes and of agriculture after the defeat of Bryan constituted a riddle. Not from the Populism of the 1890's, the Progressivism of the next decade, or from Wilsonian Democracy did a majority of the people achieve assurance of the progress they sought. For the majority of the people beyond any dispute were farmers and workers; and the progress they sought must comprise beyond all doubt a dependable answer to the persisting enigma of labor and agriculture.

The nation was not conscious of the dilemma of industrial workers and workers of the farms until the golden glow of the twenties was obscured by the black days of the early thirties. Few Americans asked the vital questions to resolve the enigma. What mysterious forces, amid the prosperous years after 1900, explain the inability of the farmer to recover from his previous loss in economic status and political weight? Why the declining volume of farm protest in radical third parties? What were the ominous unresolved contradictions in agriculture and what conditions in the world obscured their meaning in American thought? Why by 1920

TRADE UNION MEMBERSHIP

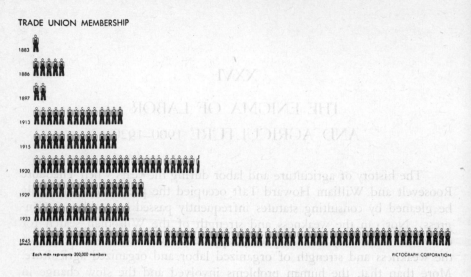

Each man represents 200,000 members   PICTOGRAPH CORPORATION

did the organized farm protest abandon third parties and turn to pressure politics and the extreme panaceas of economic nationalism? Why, during a period of such democratic ferment, did labor union membership creep so slowly upward from 868,500 in 1900 to only 2,716,900 in 1914? Why, in such a vast laboring population, was the greatest peak of union enrollment, slightly more than 5,000,000 in 1920, so far short of the percentage abroad? And why did collective bargaining decline, and unions, in the third decade of the century, lose more than a million members? How explain violence in the warfare of capital and labor in an America that prided itself on achieving a global role as one of the great progressive democracies?

WORLD TENDENCIES AND AMERICAN LABOR

Before Wilson's administration, national policies toward labor and the position of unions under American law exhibited a lag as marked as that in the failure to enact national laws for social security. As compared with various countries, this condition indicated the relative weakness of the American labor movement. But failure to unionize the great masses of workmen in a country that had already become the world's most prodigious workshop, setting the pace in technical skill, scale of enterprise, and number employed, was paradoxical.

Success of the managers of American corporations in ordering back the tide of a world labor movement would be unintelligible without a consideration of public confusion, party behavior, and the privileged position of employers derived from a long command of political power. The difference between the United States and Great Britain, the contrast most frequently noted in expert studies during the Wilson era, indicated the extent of American variation from prevailing progressive standards. In the fifty-year period from 1870 to 1920, the law of labor relations in England underwent a rapid liberalization. Quite in keeping with American legal lore, an English act of 1871 regarded picketing, "watching," or "threatening" as criminal. Deliberate national policy of reducing inequality in bargaining power dated from 1875. In that year the conservative Disraeli Cabinet accepted a striking departure from the common-law "conspiracy" doctrine that restricted union activities as illegal restraints of trade. The new act accorded collective bargaining substantial legal recognition. Group activities of unions no longer were held criminal. In 1906, the Trade Disputes Act, passed by the Liberal party, abolished the vestiges of the conspiracy doctrine. Both unions and employer associations were exempted from civil liability for damages due to strikes. Only a guilty individual, whether belonging to the union or to the employer association, was liable for unlawful coercion or acts of violence. These and subsequent laws strengthened the protection of bargaining devices, including picketing, on the principle of reducing violence and protecting the public by fostering a relative equality between capital and labor.

Thus both English major parties and their government were committed to a national policy of promoting collective bargaining as an orderly, normal, and desirable process for settling industrial disputes. Troops, deputized guards, and other modes of governmental intervention to break strikes were irrelevant, and arbitrary court injunctions did not in England become a burning issue. Moreover, legal recognition was followed by economic recognition. Employers, acceding to the law and the climate of opinion, gradually "recognized" unions and accepted collective bargaining. As early as the famous English strikes of 1889—three years after the Haymarket bomb frenzy in the United States—a sympathetic public initiated the period of gradual approval of collective bargaining as a democratic system of representation and compromise, viewing company officials as accredited representatives of the owners or stockholders and union officials as elected representatives of the workers.

American attitudes were in sharp contrast with English repudiation of industrial authoritarianism and inequality in the bargaining relationships of employers and workers. As late as World War I a large and vocal part of the American public opposed even a mild policy of requiring employers to negotiate with representatives of their workers. Prejudices on the labor question persisted among many of the middle class in the United States, and dictatorial authority wielded by the successful upper classes had long been tolerated and often supported by public officials. That such enjoyment of power by wealth was not democratic did not deter conservatives who admired the self-made aristocrats of the industrial age, for in their heart of hearts they believed not in the movement of modern democracy toward social idealism and elimination of inequality but in the old formula of class interest, individualistic liberty, and legal privileges for persons of property.

If, under prevailing conditions, there was no genuine equality under the law nor equality in bargaining power between capital and labor, a primary explanation was to be found in the lawmaking process and the unrepresentative character of American political parties. There were other fundamental conditioning factors: the rapidity of technological change and the maturing stage in economic organization; the labor supply and its effect on the labor market; the psychological environment and the prevalent middle-class identification of its own interests with those of employers; and the court decisions, laws, and administrative policies as they affected the bargaining advantages of employee and employer. While these factors operated in all countries with varying force, they were so combined in the American environment that the result was far less favorable to labor than in most of the socially advanced areas where modern capitalism had come of age.

The pressure of changing technology and economic organization in conjunction with an abundant labor supply had a profoundly disruptive effect. The American Federation of Labor adopted the program of organizing skilled trades at precisely the time when a broader, more inclusive type of industrial union was necessary if labor were to keep pace with economic changes. By 1900, laborsaving machinery and mass-production techniques were being introduced in the United States at a rate faster than in most countries, accentuating "technological displacement" and accelerating the decline in the bargaining power of skilled workmen. New methods facilitated reliance upon the unskilled and unorganized masses of native Americans and immigrants. The growth of hungry urban masses dependent on jobs and the cheap "competitive labor" of the ever-increasing horde of immigrants combined with technological displacement to create a labor market increasingly favorable to employers. In the infancy of industry a century earlier, labor had been scarce and bargaining power more equal. Since 1840, the American labor market had progressively become a "buyer's" rather than a "seller's" market. Buttressed by this advantage, employers of 1900 not only believed in but were able to practice the old capitalist concept that labor was a commodity to be bought and sold in the cheapest market. And a buyer's market kept wages from advancing. For half a generation prior to

Wilson's election, despite the normally booming prosperity, there were only a few years in which the "real wages" of labor showed even a slight gain.

A labor mart favoring employers, together with the maturing stage of American economic organization, encouraged the disposition of prominent businessmen to mobilize a concerted opposition against bargaining with unions. An obdurate spirit of managerial omnipotence gained strength with America's pronounced addiction to huge corporate enterprises, and it hardened into a readiness to use Gatling guns and armed guards to intimidate a picket line and to hire professional strikebreakers, job-hungry immigrants, and Negroes to operate the plant until the union was beaten. The pattern of employer ideas handed down by the age of the "iron buccaneers" and "robber barons" of oil, railways, and mines depicted a harsher, less democratic ethic and a colder, more impersonal relationship than in the early local face-to-face relations of the preceding age of competitive small business. The spirit of exploitation that swept railroad lands, timber, oil, and mineral riches into corporate grasp, with so little moral squeamishness at corruption, permeated employer policies toward workmen. It was no accident that Rockefeller corporations, controlling pipe lines, oil refineries, and mines, broke strikes and rejected the legitimacy of collective bargaining; or that the Pullman Company in 1894 spurned mediation with the truculent assertion that there was "nothing to arbitrate." Similarly the managers for the Morgan financial dynasty, acquiring the bitter heritage of the Homestead strike when launching United States Steel, repudiated bargaining and broke the back of the old ironworkers' union. In the early years at Dearborn, workmen looked on Henry Ford as a friendly small employer, but by 1920, Ford, expanding a family proprietorship into a great basic industry, had set the approved pattern for automobile corporations: to purge the business of unions.

The growth and consolidation of big business widened the disparity in the resources and bargaining power of capital and labor. It was precisely in the new basic industries of the machine age, where technology reduced the reliance on skilled hands and increased the reliance on a host of the unskilled, that collective bargaining became virtually extinct. In the rush to adopt the corporate type of enterprise, railroad, industrial, and mining interests organized capital on a national scale much more quickly and compactly than labor was organized. As the loose combination of the Knights of Labor disintegrated and while the American Federation of Labor was still in its swaddling clothes, capital organized for bargaining advantages on a still larger scale through employer associations. Attorney General Richard Olney, who intervened in the Pullman strike, had been a former member of the railroads' General Managers'

Association. Employer organizations, seeking to mobilize whole industries to present a united front on the labor question, included a formidable list: the American Newspaper Publishers' Association (1887), the National Association of Manufacturers (1895) known popularly as the N.A.M., the National Metal Trades Association (1899), the League for Industrial Rights (1902), the Association of Manufacturers and Erectors of Structural Steel and Iron (1903), and many others. The results were soon visible. The metal trades organization took the lead in 1901 when the corporation managers forming it, rejecting collective bargaining *in toto,* agreed to refuse trade agreements with any union. By 1906 every union that had had such an agreement had lost it; and by 1910 the N.A.M.'s *Open Shop Review* boasted that "no strikes of any moment have been won by the machinists' union since the organization of the National Metal Trades Association."

The National Association of Manufacturers, largest, most pervasive, most famous of the associations, and similarly adamant in defense of the anti-union, open-shop system, distributed tons of propaganda, lobbied against labor legislation, defended the courts against accusations of partiality, and sought to prevent the re-election of progressive legislators. Necessarily the manufacturers' association was constrained to use propaganda to discredit advances in liberal labor standards in other countries. To combat the contagion from Henry D. Lloyd's study of favorable labor conditions in New Zealand, *A Country without Strikes,* for example, the association made an "investigation," and early in Wilson's administration publicized a stinging indictment of the protection afforded collective bargaining methods by the laws of Australia and New Zealand. Spearhead of a concerted drive on Wilsonian labor policies, the N.A.M., with affiliated employer associations, brazenly proclaimed the open shop as the "American principle."

As compared with the advance of labor legislation abroad, American legislative inaction stood out starkly. Roosevelt, Taft, and Wilson successively sought to restrain judicial intervention under labor injunctions, but the legislators refused to take decisive action. The confused bipartisan organization of Congress allowed exaggerated weight to pressure groups representing employers. The chronic lack of an over-all responsibility, imposed squarely upon the dominant party, eased the way to bipartisan maneuvers that killed labor bills in committee or defaced them on the floor. To dissipate this anonymous responsibility, the American Federation of Labor began to issue lists of members of Congress, both Republican and Democratic, who were hostile to labor, together with a "white list" of labor's friends. The National Association of Manufacturers retaliated with a "black list" of the latter, urging their defeat at elections. Spokesmen of the N.A.M. repeatedly assured their more numerous congressional supporters that there was no "labor vote" in the United States. In 1908 the American Federation of Labor began its practice of endorsing the presidential nominee most favorable to labor; but the Federation's unsuccessful opposition to Taft in that year seemed only to prove the N.A.M.'s contention. The labor vote remained divided between Republicans and Democrats, with a small scattering for Socialists, and in Congress neither major party committed itself to broadening the legal recognition of union methods or to fostering a more equal bargaining power between capital and labor.

The first mild conversion of the administrative branch of the government toward liberal international labor standards dates from the coal strike of 1902. Thereafter, in the struggle for enactments to correct the disparity in the legal privileges of capital and labor, political leadership passed from the congressional party organizations to progressive executives like Roosevelt and Wilson. But presidential labor policies were seldom supported in Congress by more than a handful of liberals who coalesced from the two parties. In default of action by either party in Congress, the real formulation of public policy on labor fell into the hands of the state and national judiciary.

COLLECTIVE BARGAINING AND THE COURTS

In the fifty-year period in which English political parties and employers accepted collective bargaining as a democratic representative process, American law regressed to the point of denying the fundamentals of legal recognition of unions. Employer organization was strong, unions were weak, and political parties were neither unified nor as directly responsible as in England; moreover, the superior independence of the Supreme Court and its unique power of judicial review led to an elaboration of common-law barriers to collective bargaining as a new "higher-law" constitutionalism contrasting sharply with growing liberality abroad.

Thomas Reed Powell, witty expert of the Harvard Law School, published in 1918 a biting survey of the leading cases on "Collective Bargaining before the Supreme Court." In *Adair v. U. S.* (1908) a ten-year-old regulation by Congress forbidding railroads to fire men because of membership or activities in unions was held unconstitutional. "Justice Harlan," concluded Powell, "maintained its unconstitutionality by asserting it." In his dissent from the Court majority, Justice Holmes, a liberal appointed by President Roosevelt, declared that he did not suppose it "unwarranted if Congress should decide that to foster a strong union was for the best interest" of the men, the railroads, and the country; "but for the decision of my brethren, I should have felt pretty clear about it." The effect of the decision was judicial amendment of the Constitution, transforming a common-law doctrine into a new constitutional right of employers. "An immunity against an individual," observed Powell, "has been enlarged into an immunity against the government." In other words, a common-law right against interference by an individual had been added to the Constitution and stretched into meaning the right of employers against regulation by the government.

The Supreme Court swung into line with state courts, intimating that neither Congress nor state legislatures would be permitted to pass laws to restrain employers from coercing their workers into surrender of their right to form unions and bargain collectively. One of the issues was the attempt of liberals and labor forces to outlaw yellow-dog contracts. Such contracts, compelling workmen to bind themselves not to join a union, were devices to ensure a nonunion open shop. The contracts were defended in courts on the pretense that each applicant had his opportunity to bargain individually with the employer—the old, unreal legal fiction known as "liberty of contract"—and that if he did not want the job he did not have to take it.

In *Coppage v. Kansas* (1915), the Supreme Court held unconstitutional a state law that prohibited yellow-dog contracts. Justice Holmes, in a dissenting opinion, defended the law on the grounds that it sought to establish a genuine "equality of position" between the bargaining parties, without which "liberty of contract" on the part of the workmen was imaginary. But the Court majority decided that though a laborer had a right to join a union, "he has no inherent right to do this and still remain in the employ of one who is unwilling to employ a union man." Two years later, when Wilson had avowed the intention of the administration to extend "the right hand to labor," the Supreme Court decision in *Hitchman Coal & Coke Company v. Mitchell* (1917) was equally prejudicial. The company employed yellow-dog contracts, and a lower federal court issued an injunction making it illegal for the United Mine Workers to persuade company employees to form a union. The Supreme Court upheld the injunction on the grounds that where workmen had been hired on the condition that they would not join a union, organizing for collective bargaining was illegal.

The famous collective bargaining cases between 1908 and 1917 became the basis for the truculent assurance of corporation lawyers in the New Deal era that the Wagner Act and the National Labor Relations Board were unconstitutional. On several forms of social legislation, the Progressive Movement made a breach in judicial conservatism; but on the law as it sought to promote an equality of bargaining power between capital and labor, the trend of the judiciary was regressive. Most judges, including those on the Supreme Court, were adamant in the opinion that when an employer was unwilling to recognize a union and bargain with it, it was unlawful to carry on union activities. The Supreme Court had accepted the open shop or "American principle" of the National Association of Manufacturers.

Middle-class attitudes made the triumph of employers more difficult to attack. When Wilson took office, the sovereign sway of American business magnates over vast corporate domains was recognized; but the general public little realized that in no other country had such great businessmen been legally vested with such powers of industrial autocracy and with so large an immunity from bargaining with unions and so little a restraint by a public that was becoming more socially minded. By contrast, in the smaller and more stable English labor market, public pressure aided labor leaders to turn from craft unions to "industrial unions" as early as 1889, thus creating a pattern of labor relations that rapidly extended the benefits of collective bargaining to the hitherto unorganized mass of workers.

THE I.W.W.

The growing irrelevancy of older attitudes in the face of contradictory reality set the stage for explosion. The danger lay in the clash between the American belief in opportunity for self-betterment and a situation in which labor found its rights given and taken away by the same hand. For repression, too overt, and privilege, too presumptuous, could not exist in a modern democracy without revealing class exploitation and inciting class war. The Western Federation of Miners, which was provoked into "direct action" in 1903, took the law into its own hands with something of the old frontier spirit and with something of the bellicose new radical spirit of European syndicalism. Soon its members combined with other unions dissatisfied with the cautious higgling of the American Federation of Labor for limited immediate gains in wages and hours. Calling themselves Industrial Workers of the World and led not by foreigners but by native Americans, these men intended nothing less than the abolition of capitalism by an international class war. Like English labor, they favored industrial organization, "one big union" of all workers in a plant. Scorning craft unions as complacent middle-class combinations of the skilled "aristocracy of labor," men of the I.W.W. were radically class-conscious and advocated sabotage and violence as the only realistic way of dealing with hard-boiled employers, who themselves were resorting to all the weapons of violent industrial warfare.

As this red dawn appeared on the industrial horizon, a large part of the American public became increasingly subject to a psychosis of panic and looked with fear and hatred upon the radical wing of labor. Naïve in its understanding of the forces at work, the middle class was still prone to attribute violence to unions alone, overlooking the resort to violence by employers. But a growing sympathy was ushered in by the Progressive Movement. Although in 1907 Borah won national fame and election to Congress by prosecuting Big Bill Haywood, leader of the I.W.W., in 1912 public sympathy swung to the I.W.W. in the famous strike of the workers against the great American Woolen Company at Lawrence, Massachusetts. Copying the thrifty technique of French unions, to prevent depletion of the strike fund, the I.W.W. sent the children of workers to other cities to be fed by union sympathizers. Brutal interference by local authorities to force the children to remain in Lawrence aroused public protest and the strikers won.

Gradually the public was learning that violence was precipitated by agents of the employers as well as by strikers. On the eve of a strike in 1914, John D. Rockefeller, Jr., announced that he would make no compromise on the open-shop policy in the mines of the Colorado Fuel and Iron Company. His corporation hired armed gunmen as "deputized" company guards and induced Colorado to send out militia when several thousand miners struck. On April 20 occurred the Ludlow Massacre. Trapped in their colony of tents, some of the strikers and their families were mowed down by machine guns or caught by the flames that swept through their camp. In this battle and those that followed, thirty-three persons were shot or burned to death. Other such incidents shocked the public conscience. In 1915, during a strike at New Jersey fertilizer factories, deputized professional strikebreakers fired on the strikers and wounded twenty-eight, six of whom died.

The brutal force which money can exert in America in the workshop, the corrupt force it can exert on the bench and in the capital of every State, make it the most natural thing imaginable for labor to contemplate a resort to such force as it can command—dynamite, sabotage, bad work, the revolutionary strike.[1]

So, in 1912, wrote a parliamentary leader of English labor and future prime minister, Ramsay MacDonald.

WILSONIAN VISIONS OF INDUSTRIAL DEMOCRACY

To investigate the conditions that made the relations of American capital and labor among the most violent in the world, the Wilson administration sponsored extensive hearings before a Commission on Industrial

---

[1] J. Ramsay MacDonald in the London *Daily Chronicle;* quoted in L. Adamic, *Dynamite.* New York: Viking Press, 1931, p. 99.

Relations. This was not the ordinary congressional investigation like that following the Pullman strike. It was a commission of experts. Wilson appointed Frank P. Walsh, prominent labor lawyer, as chairman, with associates including the nation's leading labor economist, John R. Commons, B. M. Manly of the Department of Labor, and also Mrs. J. Borden Harriman and William M. Leiserson—all of whom had distinguished careers as experts on labor relations and social problems.

Broadening the horizon of Wilsonian Democracy, the Commission on Industrial Relations laid bare a complex of outworn, traditional ideas that permeated public attitudes regarding the position and rights of capital and labor. Public enlightenment, concluded the commissioners, could proceed only from a realization that something more than improvement of conditions of work was necessary to cure industrial unrest. Pointing to this conclusion, in hearings before the commission, Louis D. Brandeis contended that workingmen "must have the opportunity of deciding, in part, what shall be their condition and how the business shall be run." Seeking "industrial democracy" as a process for resolving disputes, the commission recommended legislation to prohibit unfair labor practices, specifically employer behavior that deliberately condoned arbitrament by brute economic force and that precipitated industrial warfare by rejection of the very principle of bargaining by unions.

The hearings held by the Commission on Industrial Relations revealed that since the shooting down of workers at Homestead in 1893 there had not been a single important strike in which plant managers had not employed labor spies, "detective" agencies, and accompanying tactics of violence such as the use of armed strikebreakers. Moderate language in unimpeachable testimony contrasted with the heated charge of the Populists in the nineties that Pinkertons were "the hired assassins" of the plutocracy; but the facts were the same. Espionage by professional "detective" agencies was discovered to be a frequent cause of violence; "secret agents of employers, working as members of labor unions," sometimes instigated and frequently encouraged acts of violence with the malicious intent of bringing the public to the side of the employer and at the same time persuading employers to divert more of the company's funds to "detective services." "The union spy is not in the business to protect the community. He has little respect for law, civil or moral." Confirming these findings, a contemporary Scotland Yard report on American methods informed the British government that strikebreakers furnished by detective agencies were frequently ex-criminals; but not till twenty years afterward did a more famous investigation by the Senate Civil Liberties Committee make all the unsavory facts familiar to an unsuspecting American public.

In its final report the Commission on Industrial Relations recommended governmental encouragement of the organization of labor and "recognition" of unions by employers as a cure for violence. Denial of the elementary right to organize was stressed as one of the major causes of industrial unrest. Since 1890, strikes had been caused less by demand for better conditions than by a deep-seated rebellion against oppression. Mob violence was a natural consequence of the weakness of unions in a situation where the essential element, free collective bargaining, was unequivocally rejected by employers. There could at best be "only a benevolent despotism where collective action on the part of the employees does not exist." Citing its investigation of the notorious Colorado Fuel and Iron Company strike, the commission pointed out that mere "recognition of the union" was the basic issue.

It cannot be said that Wilsonian findings accomplished the purpose of educating the middle-class public or of formulating a program acceptable to the major parties. Congress did not act on the commission's recommendations for a more basic legal recognition of the rights of labor. Even the administration failed to press the recommendations to prohibit interstate transportation of armed guards, Gatling guns, and other instruments of intimidation. Nor for nearly a generation was there any response to the urgent plea for national regulation or prohibition of espionage and strikebreaking activities by "detective" agencies, or to the plea for state regulation to prevent abuses of privilege through such practices as "deputizing" vigilantes to help employers break strikes. Nothing more eloquently revealed defective understanding and immaturity in public policy than the continuing legal tolerance of ruthlessness in strikebreaking for another generation in the United States, despite the fact that such managerial practices had never grown to such proportions in other industrial countries nor had long remained acceptable there.

Only one national act designed to equalize conditions under which labor was forced to bargain with capital came out of the whole two decades of the era of progress. This was the Clayton Antitrust Act of 1914, passed more than a year before the Commission on Industrial Relations completed its work. Ostensibly, the Clayton Act exempted unions from prosecutions under the antitrust laws; but it provided no such group exemption from civil and criminal liability as the earlier English acts. Hailed as labor's Magna Carta, the measure placed limitations on arbitrary judicial discretion in issuing labor injunctions, marking the first congressional notice of urgent pleas from the executive during four successive presidential terms. Seemingly, the act ended the use of injunctions as a denial of the legal right to organize unions. Labor supposed that there would be an end of conditions under which temporary injunctions could be granted by prejudiced judges in a few minutes, requiring no hearing of the accused union men and no jury trial. Strikes, boycotts, picketing, and peaceful assembly were declared lawful by the Clayton Act, but most of the Republicans in Congress and conservative Democrats joined forces to defeat the purpose of the law by qualifying language that invited the judiciary to continue old practices. Wilson was gratified because jury trial was prescribed in some contempt cases; but labor soon awakened to the realization that strikers arrested under injunctions could still be sentenced to jail for contempt of court, without jury trial, by the judge who had issued the injunction. The state judiciary was still largely unrestrained, and virtual amendment of the Clayton Act by the Supreme Court permitted federal courts to make widespread use of injunctions and contempt proceedings in order to suppress strikes.

The Clayton Act was important chiefly as an ethical recognition in national law of current world standards. It declared expressly that labor was not a dehumanized commodity to be bought and sold in the cheapest market. This affirmation was symbolic recognition of the growing irrelevancy of traditional middle-class doctrines of individualism and individual" "liberty of contract" that had regarded tolerantly the American managerial practice of treating labor as a marketable commodity. But the act was not enforceable as a measure to promote equal freedom in collective bargaining.

Three subsequent developments in labor policy delineated at once the humanism of Wilsonian Democracy and the middle-class reluctance to break boldly away from anomalous social attitudes. One involved regulation of labor relations in seaborne commerce; another, their regulation in railroad commerce. The third, more portentous but less enduring, comprised the experimental gropings of the administration in wartime toward general governmental regulation for industrial peace. The La Follette Seamen's Act of 1915, applying to toilers of the sea whether on the Great Lakes or on the ocean highways, made tardy reparation for long American delinquency. Pushed through Congress by the doughty leader of the insurgents with administration support, the law struck at brutal working conditions in the merchant marine, required better quarters, food, and wages, and reformed the servile vestiges of the old law of the sea in matters like desertion. Regulation of railroad labor conditions a year later proved far more complex; for the presidential elections of 1916 impended, and the issue of national labor policy was colored by the struggle to restore supremacy to the forces that sought destruction of Wilsonian Democracy.

The four great Railway Brotherhoods, not affiliated with the American Federation of Labor, demanded an eight-hour day at the same wages as for the prevailing ten hours. Three months before election, presidential initiative, taking a quite different form from that in the coal strike of 1902, averted the danger of a walkout that might tie up the nation's transportation system. Wilson spoke before Congress, urging legislation substantially answering the complaints of the brotherhoods. Republican campaign oratory appealed to prejudice by denouncing Wilson's "surrender" of the government to "labor." But the government was not surrendered. Implicit was the principle that the people were a third party in any disastrous industrial dispute. To Wilson's mind, the nature of railroads as public utilities subject to federal regulation justified intervention by a government responsible for the public interest. Moreover, by general world standards, the demands of the workers were fair. "The eight-hour day," Wilson told Congress, "now undoubtedly has the sanction of the judgment of society." With elections only a few weeks away, Congress promptly gave its own sanction by passage of the Adamson Bill.

But Congress did not support the President's concept of the public interest in two important respects. Wilson urged strengthening of an existing governmental mediation and conciliation board by a provision that a strike or lockout was unlawful until the government had made "a full public investigation of the merits of every such dispute." Going much beyond precedents of the Cleveland and Roosevelt administrations, Wilson urged Congress, again with no success, to authorize the executive not only to take over the properties temporarily but to draft train crews and company officials to operate the railroads if military necessity warranted. Years later, during World War II, Franklin Roosevelt made a partial return to Wilsonian policy, encountering in his Congress similar criticism for overriding property rights in "surrender" to labor.

In Wilson's second term the administration brought American government closer to an approximation of international labor standards than at any time before the New Deal. The President announced that the time had come when the government should "extend the right hand to labor." What he had tried to do, he remarked, was "to get rid of any class division" and "any class consciousness and feeling." To achieve this, justice must not be cold and forbidding but "warm and welcome." When, a few months after the elections, the great production crisis of the war came, union leaders strongly supported the war effort, endorsing Wilson's principle that nobody had a right to stop the productive process until all methods of negotiation and conciliation had been exhausted. In 1918 the President opposed a congressional drive for a compulsory "draft labor" bill. Meanwhile, the President's Mediation Commission, appointed in 1917, reported that "direct dealing with employees' organizations is still the minority rule in the United States." It stated that recognition of unions by employers was indispensable to industrial peace. Wilson then appointed a War Labor Board actively headed by Frank P. Walsh and B. M. Manly, former members of the Commission on Industrial Relations, and a War Labor Policies Board with Felix Frankfurter as chairman. In language closely paralleled in the later Wagner Act, these agencies affirmed "the right of workers to organize in trade unions and to deal collectively with their employers through their chosen representatives." The War Labor Board intervened in numerous disputes and, in cooperation with union leaders, succeeded in greatly reducing the number of strikes. To protect workers from discharge because of union activities, the board found it necessary to take over one of the oldest and best established plants in the United States.

Progressive world standards for labor, sanctioned in the peace settlement by the creation of the International Labor Office, seemed to informed American opinion an auspice of constructive advance in industrial life. War experience and European example indicated to Wilson and liberals in Congress a way to industrial peace. Ingredients that were later combined in labor policies of the New Deal were already at hand. Emulating English practice, the War Labor Board induced employers to recognize unions where they were already organized, or, where there were no unions, to deal with local shop committees like the contemporary Whitly councils in England. Where employers had hitherto kept out unions and feared even the "entering wedge" of shop committees, the board intervened, particularly in the great steel and munitions plants, to ensure election of shop committees by secret ballot. The success of this new agency in winning wartime agreement of employers to abstain from lockouts marked the first breach in the hitherto unrestricted right of American employers to discharge en masse employees who went on strike.

As war ended, the war labor agencies and the President urged constructive utilization of the fruits of experience. Frankfurter, speaking for the War Labor Policies Board, declared American business needed "a substitution of the processes of law and order for the present oscillation between anarchy and autocracy by which it is too largely governed." Closer understanding between capital and labor would not come "until in industry we introduce those principles of representative constitutional government which have been worked out in England and America for three hundred years." In such views, Wilsonian Democracy evidenced the growth of progressive thought beyond the humanitarian sympathy of 1900 to a more advanced definition of social justice in terms of "industrial democracy." Wilson, in his annual message of 1919, urged Congress to provide some such "organic" process for settlement of industrial disputes. "The seed of revolution is repression," he warned. Congress should seek a formula for a more "genuine democratization of industry," recognizing the right of those who work "to participate in some organic way in every decision which directly affects their welfare." At Versailles, he reminded Congress, the world's statesmen had recognized the justice of labor's demand for freedom from "the fear of poverty" and "want" in old age. The President urged the legislators to create a permanent board to settle industrial disputes.

But the lawmakers decreed otherwise; for a decade and a half the United States was to make no progress toward industrial democracy. No action was taken to promote honest bargaining in place of strikes by unions and lockouts by employers. The English Cabinet, which was at this very time promoting a similar *rapprochement* between capital and labor, had the party discipline and the public approval necessary to speak with authority; but in America the tide was turning against the Wilson administration. The national conference of employers and unions sponsored by the English government in 1919 endorsed the twin principles of universal organization of labor and "recognition" of unions by employers. But in the United States the fruitful concept of peaceful industrial settlement on the principle of representation and bargaining, with governmental supervision, went into eclipse for half a generation. Congress took no action to perpetuate the policies of the War Labor Board.

Employers, more skillful in the new dimensions of "public relations" and "personnel management" in the twenties, were not less obdurate on basic issues. Public criticism in the progressive era had induced some corporation managers to confess that they had neglected the responsibilities of "stewardship." In a campaign to win public confidence, John D. Rockefeller, Jr., found it expedient to employ a skilled propagandist, Ivy Lee, as publicity chief and took his advice to modify business practices. The Colorado Fuel and Iron Company and the Standard Oil concerns adopted the Rockefeller creed, which endorsed a system of company unions, eliminating a part of the medievalism of previous practice only to substitute another. The prevailing views of employers were expressed in 1919 by the president of the National Association of Manufacturers, who demanded no compromise on the open shop and who declared that a workman's right to cease work "does not carry with it the right to conspire with or influence fellow workers to quit simultaneously with him." In the same year in a commencement speech at Trinity College, Judge Elbert H. Gary, leading American business figure entrusted by the Morgan partners with management of United States Steel, alluded with disparagement to the ethical principle of the Clayton Act. "Necessarily," he asserted, "and properly, the question of supply and demand is, and always will be a factor in determining prices of labor, as it is in dealing with commodities." The rapid development of company unions in the 1920's was merely a postponement of the real issues, but it signified employer determination to continue rejection of collective bargaining nonetheless.

The enigma of labor—a great liberal ferment and movement of reform that touched so little the basic realities of democratic well-being— was the enigma of agriculture. For workers of the farms as for workers of the mills and mines, after years of rejoicing with a "trust buster" in the White House, after other years of friendly assistance from a government committed to Wilsonian Democracy, the future closed down. For the man with the hoe and the man with the machine, wartime sweat won a modicum of prosperity. Thereafter, in the postwar decades, first the farmer, then the laborer, looked into the darkest future he had known.

FARMERS IN A CHANGING WORLD

Although neither farmers, Congress, nor the Department of Agriculture were particularly aware of it, American agriculture in the first two decades of the twentieth century was rapidly progressing into a new stage. Farmers were trapped by impersonal economic and international forces that drove them inexorably to a status similar in some respects to the position of labor. International developments too often ignored were bringing American farmers into a world economy and an economic position of chronic insecurity. Major problems of American agriculture, reflexes of world insecurity, were inadequate income, the lag of rural standards of living behind advancing standards of urban property classes, and the trend toward a land system of tenant farmers instead of the Jeffersonian ideal of small landowning farmers. The radically changed position of the farmer called for equally radical solutions. Forbidding in their enormity were other interconnected problems. Rural overpopulation and misdirected migration demanded a policy for resettlement and improvement in terms of rational development of human and natural resources. Psychological and cultural lags that helped perpetuate maladjustments called for new attitudes, re-education, and a new social integration. And for this, not the sharecropper or the "hard-scrabble" farmer on submarginal land, but society had the major responsibility.

Still more formidable, and inclusive of all the others, was the intertwined national and international problem of reconciling special interests in agriculture and industry with the commonweal of nations. For these were not simply America's problems: they affected Europe as well as America and they sprang from a common source. All were related to world developments; each was complicated by universal pressures demanding new adjustments of agriculture to capitalism as well as to an onrush of nationalism that first curtailed world markets and then shattered them by the mechanisms of war.

Even before World War I, the prospective shape of American agricultural destiny might be guessed from the varying patterns of social tension and farm policy in hard-pressed Europe. Simultaneously in the Old World and the New, came a deep ground swell of adjustment of agriculture to capitalism. The expansion of commercial farming for burgeoning urban markets, technology that spurred global interchange of giant competitive surpluses and compelled transformation of farming into a more heavily capitalized enterprise, and a profound shift in the economic position of farmers vis-à-vis the new centralized metropolitan industry and finance, produced alternations of long-term crises and eras of spotty prosperity.

The profitable inflationary rise in world prices accompanying the fabulous gold rushes in California and Australia was reversed in 1873 by the dismal onset of a long-term fall in prices as injurious to European farmers as to their American brothers. On both sides of the Atlantic the panic of 1873 began an agricultural depression lasting until 1896. Farmers in England, Denmark, Germany, France, Spain, and elsewhere could not compete with the flood of cheap staples from abroad. Technology, sweeping agriculture into a world economy, deepened the effect of the fluctuating relation of world currencies and price structures. Steel rails opening the interior American farm belts were also opening the vast hinterlands of countries like Russia and Canada. Technology's contribution to the sea—the tramp steamer equipped with refrigeration—was as important as the McCormick reaper and the railroad refrigerator car. The reduced cost of global ocean transport made Australia, South America, India, and the United States all competitors in a world economy. European farmers were buried under an avalanche of Russian and Canadian wheat, Australian wool and mutton, South American beef, and Mississippi Valley hogs and wheat. Europe's flight from the land, overseas migration, shrinkage in cultivated acreage, and difficult adjustment to intensive husbandry with new products—all reflected the deepening drives of world economy.

Much earlier and more extensively than in the United States, European countries sought solutions through national policy. Government subsidy for agriculture through bounties or protectionist tariffs was adopted by Germany, France, Italy, and most of Europe by the 1880's, and inspired Joseph Chamberlain's abortive campaign to convert free-trade England. Nationalistic tariffs and subsidies— though restrictive and improvident, as Adam Smith had pointed out a century before—seemed a plausible way out for the food-importing countries, for they kept national prices of home produce above the world price. The trend toward subsidized agriculture abroad increased the difficulties of the United States as a great agricultural exporter; and the American tariff was useless as a device to aid Mississippi Valley farmers whose surplus went to Europe. The inherent global problem was indicated in an international agreement at Brussels in 1902, in which governments representing sugar-beet producers agreed to drop nationalistic bounties and retaliate against nonconforming nations.

In other ways besides protectionism, European farmers and governments, driven by growing social tensions and economic maladjustment, reacted against the nineteenth-century belief in free competition, turning instead to public controls as a check to excessive individualism. National policy to promote conservation, forest care, and better land use was accompanied by a trend toward social controls and government aid affecting land tenure and agricultural credit. Completing the long movement toward competitive individualism, the termination of servile tenure by the freeing of serfs in Russia and the Balkans was followed by agitations in Hungary, Italy, Spain, and other great landlord countries for changes in tenure to establish a more democratic system of family-size farms. New enactments, affecting Irish, Scots, German, and farmers of other countries, introduced government financing, extending capital to help tenants to become owners or to resettle small farmers on the land where economic conditions had diminished their ranks. Much as in belated English policy toward the Irish or in still more belated New Deal policy toward colored and white sharecroppers, czarist Russia paid for peasant lands through long-term credits allowing the farmer forty-nine years to repay the government.

Other European enactments and new organizations of farmers for collective action betokened retreat from individualism and an unregulated economy. Intervening to adjust financial capitalism to the needs of agriculture, the governments of Germany, England, and other countries regulated interest rates by revival of usury laws. Meanwhile, employing the principle of self-help, farmers banded together to better their position as a debtor class. *Landschaft* banks, first organized by great Junker landlords of Prussia, suggested a variation on credit unions. In 1862 appeared the Raiffeisen system of German peasant cooperative banks, which cut interest on loans to 4 or 5 per cent; by 1895 a government central cooperative bank aided the movement. The *Landschaft* and Raiffeisen systems or varying forms of public land banks spread through Europe. Underlying social tensions induced other projections toward collective self-help. Producers' cooperatives, modeled on the Danish creamery or bacon factory, were rapidly organized in Baltic lands and in western Europe, and extended east and south to Russia and Greece. Agrarian collective bargaining, in emulation of organized labor, appeared in Italy, where unions of impoverished sharecroppers sought to fight off demands of greedy landlords to increase to two thirds the customary owner's share of one half of the farm's yield. Equally significant, in various countries where owners of great estates employed ragtag battalions of migratory farm workers on a seasonal basis at degrading wages, foundations began to be laid for the organization of this landless proletariat into farm labor unions.

In the United States radical agricultural alliances and farmer parties were swallowed up in the surge of progressivism. Better prices produced an interval of seeming security. Agricultural discontent was not dead; it was channeled into the major parties and pressure groups in the great movement supporting trust busting and social control of the "money power." The more fortunate farmers began to have both tractors and telephones; their sons and daughters received specialized training at agricultural colleges and state universities. Rural movies began to enliven Saturday night. But hundreds of thousands of farm families were still passed by in the peripheral extension of urban advantages. As late as 1920, 90 per cent lacked modern plumbing and sanitary facilities; scarcely a third had automobiles or trucks. Quite unlike farmers in western Europe, only a small minority of American farm families were reached by the power lines of public utilities; and perforce the great market opened up in the 1920's for electric refrigerators and washing machines was primarily limited to metropolitan purchasers. The poor light of oil lamps on the farm still symbolized a disparity in leisure and health that accounted for the silent rebellion of countless younger members of country families who escaped to the city. The old round of chores—cleaning lamp chimneys, leaning over washtubs, and getting meals in poorly equipped kitchens—told how little of the contemporary gains in comfort and welfare had fallen to the lot of the country girl who stayed as wife of a farmer.

Romantic songs about the "cabin in the cotton" masked the grimness of the debased life later dramatized in *Tobacco Road*. To degradation springing from maladjustments in rural economy was added the backwardness resulting from malnutrition and parasitic infestation. For a brief time public attention was drawn to the undeserved plight of "hillbillies" and "clay eaters" by the report on hookworm of Charles W. Stiles in 1903 and the medical discoveries of the immortal Joseph Goldberger, notably on pellagra, a decade later. The United States Public

Health Service, of which both men were members, was inadequately staffed, but its work revealed the prevalence and degrading effects of hookworm, pellagra, and improper nourishment. At the time that Wilson became President, 60 per cent of the children examined in southern schools were found to have hookworm. The country doctor was often a beloved and overworked benefactor, but any map of endemic disease in the United States revealed the spread of human blight through the poverty belts of American agriculture.

DEMOCRATIC FERMENT AND FARM POLICY

The government's response evinced a democratic concern, in marked contrast to the bankrupt statesmanship of the preceding quarter century. English commissions to deal with rural social lag were emulated in 1908 when Roosevelt sponsored a Country Life Commission. The old policy of stimulating "production at all cost," leaving farmers at the mercy of periodic gluts or depressed prices made by the Tobacco Trust and other great processors working in collusion, began to be modified by the time of the Wilson administration. American policy, paralleling the reaction overseas against competitive individualism, was tinctured with a dawning conception of the problem of credit and marketing. The Department of Agriculture acquired a Bureau of Marketing; and, to protect farmers and consumers against middlemen, Congress by the 1920's regulated grain standards, warehouses, and speculation on the Cotton Futures Exchange.

Social controls went beyond regulation to more direct government aid. The legitimate function of government aid had formerly been debased by the greed of operators who fattened on lavish railroad grants and fraudulent titles to government timber and mineral lands; but Wilsonian Democracy socialized the function for the advancement of rural welfare. The Smith-Lever Act of 1914 inaugurated federal grants-in-aid to match state appropriations for extension work through the state agricultural colleges, teaching farmers on their own land the latest techniques. Similarly in a new public works policy, federal "dollar matching" under the Road Aid Act of 1916 benefited the rural population by adopting the century-old policy of internal improvements to meet the needs of mechanized highway transport. But the Congresses that enlarged Wilsonian Democracy by the federal grants-in-aid system little suspected that they had set a constitutional precedent of spending for the general welfare that could be enlarged again under the later New Deal, not to revive agriculture alone but to rescue the industrial population and the whole economy.

For the most part, rural statesmen at the national capital believed in encouraging organized self-help among farmers in place of blind competitive production. A few who knew "dirt farmers" as neighbors and friends sought more positive public encouragement of collective action by farmers. By 1911, Senator Norris was reading intensively the literature on foreign cooperative societies and credit unions; and his agriculture committee soon reported in fat government documents on German *Landschaften* and European public land banks which, as Norris put it, had "driven money-lenders off the earth." In 1913 a Norris bill to provide farm loans through the Department of Agriculture at 4 per cent interest was killed in committee. But the Clayton Act declared farmer cooperatives, as well as labor unions, immune from antitrust prosecution, and in 1916 a Farm Loan Act partially imitated European systems of public land banks. The practice reduced overhead costs by lowering existing interest rates and providing much-needed long-term credits, alleviating the evils of dependence on the banks and insurance and mortgage companies that had maintained an ill-devised and costly system of short-term mortgages. Norris, urging direct governmental loans, objected to predominant control by private interests and felt that interest running up to 6 per cent was still too high.

The increasing governmental response to agriculture did not mature in a broad program taking full account of long-range developments. Farm statesmen like Norris were disturbed by a series of changes menacing the old democratic ideal of family-size farms under the free tenure of individual owners. A tendency toward huge capitalistic corporate farms was paralleled by a trend toward undersize farms, subdivided by inheritance, the exigencies of sharecropping, or land prices beyond the means of young newcomers. Flight from the land, rural migration to urban opportunity, continued—a slow and defective individual quest for a better relation of resources and labor, leaving behind great islands of population on farms incapable of supporting a family at the level of well-being. Poor whites took jobs in southern mill towns and Negroes filtered north to run city elevators, but the sharecropping population remained as large as ever. Under an expanding system of great landlords in Texas, California, the mountain states, and some sections of the Midwest and East, tenants, seasonal hired hands, and dispossessed migrants—native white, Mexican, or Oriental—worked the land with small return and less security.

The assimilation of agriculture to capitalism, the requirement of a heavier investment for modern farming, and the mounting proportion of mortgage indebtedness made ownership of the land more precarious. A glut in world markets, crop failure, a break in the wheat pit or the cotton exchange—any one of these spelled foreclosure. Continuation until 1920 of the long era of unearned increment from rising land values encouraged heavier investment to modernize the farm but merely postponed many a reckoning. Census figures and agricultural statistics had long flashed warnings of the dwindling of onetime social security. That security had been derived from the nineteenth-century form of aid to agriculture—access to government land—and from several other factors. One was the fertility of virgin soil, not yet wasted by heedless competitive methods. Another was the marginal profit due to rising land values. A third was the comparative advantage of cheap American produce in world markets. These favorable factors now no longer existed. The average equity, or value of the farmer's property above his liability for debts, had steadily declined. In the thirty years from 1880 to 1910, it dropped from 62 to 50 per cent; and then, despite war prosperity, moved downward to 46 per cent by 1920. Increasing insecurity was similarly registered in the figures on tenancy. Farms rented by tenants rose from 25 per cent in 1880 to 31 per cent by 1900, and thereafter crept upward, foreshadowing the great depression, when well on toward 50 per cent of America's farm families no longer owned their farms. The none too enigmatic future of the farmer was glimpsed, too, in agricultural export figures, which after 1900, except for the war years, showed spotty declines symptomatic of imminent baneful dislocation. Governmental figures of 1920 accurately indicated the need of more drastic social planning: 25 per cent of all farms of the United States were in dismal areas where soil fertility and local economic opportunities had radically retrogressed. In these areas of human blight, rural families on the antiquated basis of self-sufficiency struggled for a grim marginal subsistence.

ORGANIZED AGRICULTURE

Meanwhile, the impact of war had postponed any likelihood of long-range planning. The government spurred farmers onward in a patriotic expansion to sustain the Allies; but neither farmers nor government conceived a plan to meet the problem of overproduction when the war should end. There were farmers, however, who recognized that the existing pattern of rural livelihood did not permit a rational readjustment to modern conditions. As in Europe, organization of farmers for collective action evolved in reaction to the changed economic and political position of agriculture in relation to industry. As a family enterprise, farming was the old type of proprietary small business. Lower prices could not be countered by discharging workers and reducing output; when income fell, the family worked harder, produced more, and consumed less. Nor had the farmer found any recourse as the city worker had, through strikes or collective contracts, in dickers with business firms on the prices of their wares or the value of his own labor. Yet the twentieth century evoked challenge to the older psychology and class presuppositions of rural life. To offset the dilemma of fixed costs, fluctuating prices, and lack of bargaining power, impoverished Texans in 1902 organized the Farmers' Union. Gradually spreading through the Mississippi Valley and western states, the Farmers' Union and other associations followed the English and European example in establishing credit unions and cooperatives to escape loan sharks, middlemen, and price fixing by Pillsbury, Swift, American Tobacco, and other great millers, packers, and canners.

With the demise of Populism, agricultural political organization turned from third parties to pressure groups. Organizations like the Farmers' Union lobbied for the farm loan banks. The National Grange remained the largest organization and was strongest in the Northeast. The Nonpartisan League, emerging in North Dakota in 1915, spread through the Midwest to the Pacific. Heralding a "green rising" of businessmen-farmers to win legal advantages as other business interests had done, it began to support candidates in either party if they agreed to back the league's program. As Republicans took office in 1921, organized agriculture was a force to be reckoned with. Federal aid for agricultural education had produced a vast network of county farm bureaus, linked together in state federations. A professional corps of businesslike, state agricultural politicians was in the making. In 1919 they launched the American Farm Bureau Federation, mobilizing farmers in a powerful national pressure group. In 1921 the federation successfully organized the bipartisan farm bloc in Congress.

As America turned its back on the era of progress, the enigma of agriculture was receiving in one respect a disturbing clarification. The more prominent commercial farmers, led by their strongly entrenched local political allies, the state agricultural agents, were moving backward with the nation. The large conservative organizations speaking for big farmers, the Farm Bureau Federation and the Grange—but not the aggressively democratic Farmers' Union—embraced the regressive philosophy of powerful business organizations. Industrial instigators of higher protective tariffs were wooed by agricultural sponsors of self-defeating panaceas of economic nationalism. Prominent among advisors of the federation and the farm bloc in Congress were eminent midwest businessmen associated with the manufacture and sale of farm machinery. And big commercial agriculture followed big business in the dangerous pathway of economic nationalism.

Nor was the enigma of labor clarified in ways fulfilling the promise of American life. Industry and its political allies rose to command, turning away from Wilsonian Democracy, coupling national advantages with internal repression, damming the tide of international labor standards. The position of labor in a system of nationalism, like the position of agriculture, was to bring human disorder and social disaster But nationalism and drives for special interests, and their culmination in economic constriction and the outbreak of war, were not scourges of American democracy only but problems of world society—indelibly so revealed in World War I.

XXVII

THE WORLD'S ILLUSION

1900–1917

Although the momentum of world change at the outset of the twentieth century threatened the peace of mankind all over the earth, Americans were as little prepared as Europeans to seek an orderly world and international justice by concerted measures and prudent limitations on national sovereignty. National salvation, by government aid to agriculture, was the fond desire of friends of American farmers who turned in bafflement from the overseas marketing difficulties of American agriculture or who shrugged helplessly when studying the depressed world prices that made rural incomes inadequate on the farms of the United States. National salvation was the mirage pursued also in many walks of life by people who were indoctrinated by the orators of the full dinner pail and by the aging oracles of infant industries. And if an American workingman, apprehensive of disaster from the competition of cheap foreign labor abroad and immigrant labor at home, found comfort in the dream of national salvation, he but shared the illusion of his country, which in turn was an illusion shared among all nations. Nor did twentieth-century progressivism, in its first decade and a half, challenge the illusion: national planning for welfare in one country stops short all too easily at national salvation. Yet a challenge was on the way; and so was war.

Although the American people looked inward, to themselves, for redemption, their relation to other peoples was fundamentally altered during the era from 1900 to 1917. The change, mirrored by a new and not reassuring diplomatic behavior, possessed a variety of interrelated facets: a tendency to seek hemispheric predominance by giving an aggressive twist to the Monroe Doctrine; a greatly enlarged exertion of national power in world affairs in the Far East and Europe as well; and finally, foredoomed to failure, an erratic recoil into neutrality and isolation from European entanglements. Readjusting to a new position in the shrinking world, American policy exhibited a wavering course betokening the clash of old and new attitudes. While the American government was taking on the habiliments of a world power, the American people were divided between those who believed that security on the basis of isolationist nationalism was an illusion and those equally convinced that security through participation in world politics was an illusion. To a later generation, three elements underlying these transitional conflicts loom large: the onset of world wars, the reasons for their appearance, and the disastrous contradictions in American behavior toward international organization.

THE FALL OF LIBERAL NATIONALISM

The new phase in American history after 1898 has been described as the rise of the United States as a world power. What this meant is understandable only by a knowledge of what world powers were and what they were doing in that era. A world power was a giant state with sufficient industrial and financial resources to maintain such a degree of sea power, land power, and money power that its voice and pressure could counter or give pause to other great nations in diplomatic exchanges, military rivalries, and international competition for economic preponderance. The emergence of "world powers" signified an era of world-wide empires and world-wide diplomacy. To give concise identification of trends underlying the changing behavior of these powers, historians employ special terms: liberal nationalism, open door; integral nationalism, imperialism. Historians also speak of international anarchy, balance of power, and militarism, terms which likewise require definition.

The term "liberal nationalism" referred to the earlier form of nationalism resting on a democratic formula dating from the American and French revolutions, the idea of self-government and self-determination. It was a "live-and-let-live nationalism," which stressed the equality and independent sovereignty of all nations. Generally its spirit was against intervention in the affairs of other peoples, although movements, even revolutions, to establish liberal government based on the consent of the governed were heartily applauded and sometimes assisted. In practice, it was often isolationist, although for reasons of expediency and defense it could lead to erratic attempts of liberal national states to establish a "balance of power" against undemocratic aggressors, chiefly national monarchies or dictators like Napoleon. Bolstered by British control of the seas and the friendly liberal nationalism of England, the Monroe Doctrine in the nineteenth century represented in fact, if not in theory, a tacit Anglo-American balance of power against aggression in the American hemisphere.

Another basic concept historically associated with liberal nationalism also calls for definition: the economic law of comparative advantage. Applied to economic foreign policy, it is generally known in American tradition as the "open door." Stemming from Adam Smith's famous conception of abundance for all nations through an internationalist economics, the law of comparative advantage meant that the producers and workers of each nation would prosper most if they made and sold abroad those goods that the nation could produce at low cost. By inseparable corollary of the same law, the nation's consumers would benefit because the nation would find a comparative advantage in importing from abroad those goods that other nations could produce better and at lower costs. Great economists in the classical tradition of Adam Smith rested their case on the superior efficiency of an international division of labor. Economic interdependence in a world economy was the most efficient means of providing more jobs, lowering costs, and increasing the world's purchasing power; inefficient, on the contrary, was mercantilism, or economic nationalism, the expensive and restrictive system of self-sufficiency maintained behind a "closed door." The economic success of an open door, however, depended upon governments; they must foster a system of free enterprise protected not against competitors at home or abroad, but against monopolies at home and cartels abroad. Reciprocity treaties negotiated in the McKinley era partially recognized the law of comparative advantage, but the Senate's refusal to ratify these treaties in 1899 led to abandonment of the reciprocity technique until it was revived by the New Deal.

Between 1870 and 1914, governments, under new pressures in a shrinking world, reversed their earlier tendency toward a live-and-let-live nationalism and reverted instead to a dog-eat-dog psychology. The spirit of the age changed in the century since Jeremy Bentham, finding no English word to express his meaning, had coined a new one, "international." The workaday world was moving away from the century-old economic liberalism of *The Wealth of Nations* (1776), in which Adam Smith stressed an international open door to assure international abundance. A nationalistic world was moving away from the vision of Tom Paine and the French revolutionists who conceived of a world at peace under the protection of an international political organization. Instead of global *liberté, égalité,* and *fraternité* through liberal nationalism, instead of economic cooperation through a free international division of labor, instead of a growing spirit of tolerant cosmopolitanism through cultural interchange, the world after 1870 began to be plagued by three malignant forces of reaction: international anarchy, economic imperialism, and integral nationalism.

"Imperialism"—a term added to the world's vocabulary after 1870 —denoted overseas extension of great nations for world power and profitable exploitation through economic penetration into regions that had not reached a high level of economic development, and through conquest or partial political control of the governments and peoples of such regions.

Liberal nationalists like Gladstone in England opposed imperialism; but England was soon extinguishing the Boer republic, seeking a Cape to Cairo railroad, and taking "the road to Mandalay," extending the British Raj eastward from India to Burma and Singapore. Similarly, Cleveland, Schurz, Bryan, and Wilson, ardent advocates of the liberal national principles of the Declaration of Independence, feared the corrosive effect of weakening the tradition against the rule of one people by another. But economic penetration, proceeding apace, gave Americans control of the economic, if not the political, destinies of Cuba, Haiti, Santo Domingo, Nicaragua, Colombia, and other Latin-American states. Meanwhile the peoples of Puerto Rico, the Canal Zone, Hawaii, Samoa, and the Philippines came not as citizens but as subjects under direct American rule. Between 1870 and 1914 approximately half of the world passed under the domination of a small number of imperialistic nations. With the economic conquest of the non-European world came the reincarnation of the exclusivist mercantilism that Americans had actively resented in the era of the Revolution. "I believe the whole theory of free trade to be wrong," announced Bismarck, the German apostle of blood and iron. A distinguishing mark of economic imperialism became the closed door. Ambitious businessmen and diplomats cultivated the illusion among their people that it would not suffice simply to buy or sell abroad; it was supposedly necessary to own or control sources of raw materials outside the mother country, to obtain spheres of influence whereby competitors could be excluded by imperial tariff systems and franchises for monopolies.

"Integral nationalism" was an emotional force or group psychology that led people into a national egotism exalting their national culture and national ambitions above nearly all other values. That the unifying force of national patriotism generally proved stronger than the divisive force of internal class conflict attested its pervasive emotional power. It accentuated patriotic love of country into a hypersensitive national pride and will to power, justified aggression, imperialism, or even war on the grounds of defending a beneficent superior civilization or spreading it to peoples regarded as less fortunate. Psychologically it produced an emotional blockage inhibiting appreciation of parallel values in the cultural heritage of others. It emphasized national differences; it turned the mind of man away from basic common denominators in human nature, biological inheritance, and general culture. Integral nationalism was compounded in part of the centralizing impulse of the economic revolutions and the strengthening of governments as they assumed greater responsibilities for the national well-being.

The emotional force of nationalism, stimulated by conscious and unconscious propaganda, pressed inward toward integration of the national culture. Through the school, the church, the press, literature, political oratory, and even art and music, masses previously inert were indoctrinated with an emotional devotion to the national image and a hazy sense of sharing its attributes. This integration of society within the national boundaries pressed toward standardization or nationalization of a particular cultural pattern and insisted on "assimilation" of divergent cultural elements. Such psychic identification led to a mystical and unscientific belief in a unique "national character." As a constructive force, integral nationalism expressed a genuine human need for a greater social coherence; but it was an internal coherence that stopped short of a unity and psychic identification more inclusive than that of a single nation. It bred superiority notions, magnified differences between cultures, created a vicious and unscientific mythology of differences between "races" and nationalities, and raised formidable barriers to free migration and travel—exclusion laws, immigrant quotas, naturalization restrictions, passports, visas. Integral nationalism, containing within itself a malignant growth that was to burgeon into totalitarianism, weakened the religious and democratic concept of common brotherhood and made the pathway to enduring good will between nations grow rank and impenetrable. At home, integral nationalism demanded conformity, harrying minorities with a new persecution: assimilation or suppression.

"International anarchy" sprang from the excessive nationalism that substituted the nation for mankind. This substitution was the final outcome of the tribal spirit which, as the historian A. J. Toynbee has remarked, made people "feel and act and think about a part of any given society as though it were the whole of that society." The political and economic core of international anarchy was the sovereign insistence on national freedom from all transcendent or superior claims. Nations clung to a basic legal illusion, embedded in international law: the fiction that each nation had absolute sovereignty, that no nation was answerable to a larger social responsibility or an international authority. In practice, small nations had no such sovereignty, and strong nations could not exercise it without the risk of a war in which others would seek to strip them of their sovereign might. International anarchy did not mean that nations or statesmen were not peace-loving, but the pattern of ideas and practices thus stimulated barred the way to collective security. Even men of peace were under the illusion that the family of nations had no right to limit the sovereign power of any country to establish an authoritarian political structure for itself and expand its army and navy. Similarly, peace-loving people innocently cherished the illusion that no other nation had a right to object when their own homeland exercised its sovereign power to wall itself in behind high tariffs. International anarchy sprang from internal contradictions in the existing order. Great powers sought security, through rival alliances and control over smaller nations and "backward peoples." Small powers sought an equally uncertain security by alternating "friendships" with rival great powers. National minorities sought escape through further splintering of the world into more and more nations, multiplying world frictions from overlapping national claims. In the absence of universal controls to maintain peace with justice, not even peace-loving countries surrendered the belief that clashes of sovereign nations must be settled by force. Despite religious pacifists like Leo Tolstoi, war was an accepted social institution, and no responsible statesman proposed to outlaw war as an instrument of national policy.

Militarism was the natural consequence of international anarchy. Nations sought the great goals of freedom from fear and freedom from want, but they sought them separately and not by cooperation. Historians later assessed the motives of alliances, militarism, and imperialism in terms of national "fear and greed." Instead of working jointly to remove the causes of fear and want, nations great and small sought security and prosperity for themselves by methods both costly and self-defeating. National budgets doubled and tripled, burdening the people with taxes to cover huge deficits, as even democracies sanctioned armaments races under the slogan of "preparedness." An English naval armament program of 1889 adopted the principle of a "two-power" navy. Before the end of the 1890's, the United States, Japan, and Germany began to lay keels in a naval race to wrest supremacy from England. Meanwhile Bismarck spread militarism by setting the fashion of national service acts—compulsory military training conscripting the citizenry for the modern mass army. Under Bismarck's program, army indoctrination courses ridiculed the aspirations of liberal Social Democrats, and each yearly levy of draftees was inculcated in "the 'Germanic' virtues of Duty, Obedience, Sacrifice of Self for the State, and . . . Loyalty and Devotion to the Emperor." England and the United States were content with huge navies. Other nations resorted to compulsory military service and indoctrination. The world became an armed camp.

Despite the reaction against liberal nationalism and international economics, economic interdependence was and remained a fact no matter how deplored by propagandists of self-sufficiency. The great achievement in the "long peace" between 1815 and 1914 was the growth of interdependence. A world economy had come into being. Economists remarked the significance of shipping costs in 1900—two cents to get a bushel of wheat from New York to Liverpool, or a cent and a quarter a pound for wool from Australia to Europe. Half of Europe's food came from other continents when war broke out. Exchange of goods between nations had by 1914 mounted to the fabulous yearly value of $20,000,000,000. Aside from iron and coal, nearly all Europe's indispensable minerals like copper and alloy metals came from abroad, as did cotton, rubber, and huge percentages of her requirements for oil, lumber, leather, and countless other basic commodities. In 1914 the United States, with its agriculture long geared to world economy, was on the eve of transition from a debtor to a creditor nation when a great surplus of its manufactures and investment capital must—by the law of profits—find foreign markets and when, dismal to nationalistic contemplation, America's import of goods must willy-nilly grow larger than the export.

The molding forces of industrialism and nationalism facilitated physical interdependence on a world-wide plane, but achieved it through a national behavior at once caused by, and a cause of, profound domestic and international dislocations. All nations were "have-not" nations; all required materials from abroad and trade with their neighbors; and all benefited from the fruitful interchange of cultural ideas, science, art, medicine, and valuable social discoveries. Some were "have" nations in the sense that they possessed more than others, but all were "hungry" powers bent on the normal human pursuit of greater well-being, security, and progress.

The stresses and strains of capitalism and nationalism amid growing interdependence compelled American involvement in world affairs. After 1898 nothing but a dire plan for controlled isolation through a dangerously centralized government could have prevented the outward extension of American economic energies. Traditional isolation policy had never frowned upon American citizens and property abroad. This negative policy was now to prove insufficient. The United States could not continue its growth as an industrial giant in an interdependent world without concern for the stability of that world.

AMERICAN EXPANSION AND POWER POLITICS

Among the more positive policies favored by world powers, the United States had a choice of three techniques: preponderance, a balance of power, or international cooperation. Preponderance, an extreme form of excessive nationalism, meant that a nation sought security by outright preponderance in regions where the nation had a more advantageous position than rival world powers. The second formula, balance of power, was based on the idea that nations should align themselves in such a way that no particular power would get so strong as to threaten weaker nations. Shifting alignments among nations were theoretically presumed to reduce international anarchy by forestalling aggressions that would unsettle the balance and establish preponderance. All too easily, balance of power diplomacy, responding to expediency and a will to power, degenerated into a jockeying for position that induced antagonism rather than cooperation and ended in war rather than in peace. At best it seldom long succeeded in maintaining more than an unstable equilibrium liable to dangerous fluctuations. The third alternative, international cooperation, also sought national security predicated upon a larger scheme of world security through international conferences and organizations to assure a general peace. This formula of collective security, sometimes called a concert of power, was least favored of the three types of diplomacy. As a practical matter, it was seldom more than a convenient mask at international conferences in which nationalistic considerations concerning a balance of power actually held sway.

After 1898 the American government experimented with these formulas somewhat hesitantly and inconsistently in three primary zones. Preponderance began to mark American policy toward Latin America as far south as Colombia, resulting in that zone in a destruction of the international balance. The open-door policy toward China on the other hand, was the concert of power technique provoked by an upset of the balance of power; but since it never achieved genuine international cooperation, it became primarily a defensive policy, seeking to prevent further instability in the balance of power. Toward the European zone, the United States still largely continued a policy of isolation, yet this essentially was a tacit recognition of the supremacy in that region of balance of power politics, coupled with a refusal to have any concrete American policy in regard to the existing instability. Theodore Roosevelt's inclination to exert American influence toward stabilizing the European balance and Wilson's more far-reaching but equally unsuccessful attempt to substitute international cooperation for a European balance of power marked the first major challenges to the traditional American policy of escape from responsibility.

Revival of American expansion was one of the first evidences of the degree to which the United States shared in the world's regressive tendency toward economic imperialism and integral nationalism. This was no longer expansion into contiguous continental territory for the purpose of homesteads and settlements to re-create America by the making of new states. By 1899, American business was outward bound, and American power had acquired without bloodshed Alaska and the small Pacific islands like Howland, Baker, Jarvis, Wake, Midway, and Samoa (Tutuila); the strategic Hawaiian Islands, won by the devious course of revolution; and the Spanish-American conquests, the Philippines, Guam, and Puerto Rico. The American flag was also soon to fly over the Canal Zone (1903) and over the Virgin Islands (1917).

Strategic expansion outward through the mid-Pacific to Samoa and Guam and acquisition of the Philippines in a drive for commercial advantages in the Far East were merely American reactions to the rising competitive clash of world powers around the globe. The Chinese Empire was disintegrating, and Japan, quick to seize the advantage in 1895, attacked China and took Formosa, expanding southward to a point scarcely more than 200 miles from the Philippines—first step in a revival of the sixteenth-century Japanese vision of world domination. Following the Japanese example, other world powers immediately began a "scramble for concessions" in China. Much as in subsequent Latin-American penetration by the United States, but on a more ambitious scale, Germany, Russia, Italy, and France, competing with Japan, carved out spheres of influence, extracted naval bases, leased ports, and demanded monopoly control of railroads, banks, resources, and trade. England, although she had also sought concessions, favored an open door to place businessmen of all nations on an equal footing. The United States rejected an English suggestion of outright alliance to support this policy, but McKinley's Secretary of State, John Hay, induced the powers to pledge maintenance of an open door in China. Chinese antiforeign sentiment culminated in the Boxer Rebellion (1900), and American troops joined an international police force to suppress the Boxers. Hay circulated notes and obtained adherence to a new open-door pledge to which he added a principle that became fixed American policy: a pledge of the territorial integrity and political independence of China. The open-door pledges, however, covered only discriminatory railway rates, tariffs, and harbor dues. The door remained partly closed. Concessions for banks, railroads, mines, and similar monopolies were not disturbed.

Theodore Roosevelt, sensitive to interconnected shifts of the balance of power in Europe and the Far East, enlarged on Hay's diplomacy by exerting American influence in both European and Far Eastern crises. When Japan in 1905, after an unheralded attack that sent the Russian fleet to the bottom, emerged victorious in her second war of expansion, Roosevelt played the role of peacemaker. By treaty negotiated at Portsmouth, New Hampshire, Japan acquired half of the Russian island of Sakhalin and the concessions Russia had extorted from China, which included a leased port in Manchuria and the South Manchurian railroad. Spectacular victories had whetted the Japanese appetite. Japanese diplomats home from Portsmouth allowed their people to blame the intervention of President Roosevelt for Japanese failure to obtain a money indemnity and greater territory from Russia.

Russia's demonstrated weakness upset the tenuous balance in the Far East; and the ill will of Japan and her new position of strategic power in the far Pacific induced Roosevelt to seek means to appease Japan and at the same time to delimit the rival Japanese and American spheres so as to re-establish equilibrium. Through his Secretary of War, William Howard Taft, Roosevelt in 1905 negotiated an agreement in which the United States recognized Japan's sphere of influence in Korea, with Japan in return pledging nonaggression regarding the Philippines. But frictions inevitably multiplied. American businessmen in Manchuria found their progress blocked by the privileged position of Japanese businessmen. Meanwhile, the spirit of integral nationalism in California, which a generation earlier had induced the anti-Chinese movement, was duplicated in an anti-Japanese agitation culminating in the segregation of Japanese school children in San Francisco. And Congress was considering immigration barriers against Japanese. Japan protested with Oriental courtesy but with diplomatic firmness. Unveiled hostility would disturb relations between America and Japan if Congress enlarged Chinese exclusion into a general exclusion of Far Eastern peoples. Roosevelt prevailed on California authorities to end the insulting segregation of Japanese in Oriental "Jim Crow" schools and in return for this restoration of "face," the proud Japanese made a "Gentlemen's Agreement" (1907) to shut off the flow of unwanted immigrants.

In 1908 Roosevelt took another fling at balance of power diplomacy, making a sea-power adaptation of the militarist device of "rattling the saber." He sent the American navy from the Atlantic to the Pacific, where it made ostentatious calls at Australia, China, and finally Japan, affording Japanese eyes the unwonted spectacle of America's great new fleet of battleships in Japanese home waters. Japan soon afterward sought an extension of the nonaggression understanding of 1905. The Root-Takahira agreement of 1908 appeased Japan again by sanctioning her new aggression in openly annexing the ancient country of Korea and temporarily checked instability by pledging both countries to maintenance of the status quo. The agreement theoretically extended the open-door principle by pledging an equal footing for all in regard to investments and industrial development.

With or without acquisition of the Philippines, the United States could not have avoided rubbing elbows with Japan; but another problem could have been avoided. The new type of American expansion into already populated overseas regions posed a new problem for democracy. Americans, long imbued with the ideals of liberal nationalism, had a constitutional aversion to the rule of one people by another. Liberal Democrats like Cleveland and Bryan and liberal Republicans like Carl Schurz were strenuously opposed to the spirit of Kipling's famous invocation to "Anglo-Saxons" to establish dominion over "the lesser breeds without the law." Experience with the Filipinos dramatized the issue. The Philippine forces had revolted against Spain in 1898 and aided the American conquest in the cherished hope of winning self-government for themselves. In 1899, upon news that the American Senate had voted against Philippine independence, the islanders took up arms. The election of McKinley and Roosevelt a year later, while neither a landslide nor a clear mandate for imperialism, was interpreted as both and settled the respective positions of the major parties. Democrats were officially pledged to independence for the seven million Filipinos and to withdrawal from imperialism. If Republicans remained in power, the American flag was to stay; rebellious Filipinos would have to be subjugated.

There was still another question for democracy. Did the Constitution follow the flag? Were new overseas acquisitions to be allowed the home rule that Arizona and other western territories enjoyed? Must Hawaii, the Philippines, and Puerto Rico eventually be admitted as states? Republican Congresses under Presidents McKinley and Roosevelt and the Republican-controlled Supreme Court decided in the negative.

The Republican Congress in the Foraker Act of 1900 established an imperialistic policy not altered until the administration of Franklin D. Roosevelt. This policy offered no promise of eventual independence and did not even provide for advance toward statehood. Instead, the Puerto Rican government followed the model of English royal government in the early American colonies. Congress gave the President a position like that of George III, with power to appoint the governor and a council of eleven of which only five were to be Puerto Ricans. An assembly was elected by the people. Similarly, in the Philippine Act of 1902, Congress established an American governor and council appointed by the President and a popularly elected lower house. The first elections to the lower house, however, were delayed until nine years after the American flag was raised over the islands.

Meanwhile in the Insular cases, the Supreme Court gave a new reversible stretch to the Constitution. The Constitution, it was decided, did not automatically extend to territories, but only when Congress so provided. On the other hand, the Constitution did follow the flag, even in imperial territories, to the extent necessary to entitle the Court to assume jurisdiction when it chose to do so. In the somewhat diffused light of the Court's decisions, the new territories were unincorporated dependencies, under the rule of the United States government but not a part of the United States. Like a foreign country, Puerto Rico was to remain outside American tariff walls unless Congress declared otherwise. The Insular cases gave Congress and the Court a free hand. It was apparently constitu-

tional to disregard the long line of democratic precedents for rapid territorial advance to full civil rights, representation in Congress, and statehood.

EMPIRE IN THE AMERICAS

First step in a series of actions to create a zone of American predominance was the removal of Spanish power from the Caribbean by the
treaty of 1899. Subsequent phases in the extension of the world power of
the United States southward have been described separately as America's
"Panama policy," America's "Caribbean policy," American "Navalism,"
the "Theodore Roosevelt Corollary to the Monroe Doctrine," and "Dollar
Diplomacy." However variously expressed, the underlying stimulus was
the world trend toward competitive nationalism, armaments, and imperialism. Under Theodore Roosevelt, Taft, and Wilson, separate factors differed in importance, but the assorted policies were basically one. Strategic
control and political influence, as in the case of other world powers, were
indissolubly connected with aid to American property and citizens in foreign fields of exploitation. Whatever the name given the over-all Latin-
American policy, its economic importance soon far exceeded the economic
stake in Pacific policy, including the maintenance of the flag in the Philippines and the open door in China. American capital in China by 1930
amounted to $130,000,000, as compared with the huge Caribbean stake
of $2,200,000,000.

The second step in creating the new sphere of American predominance was the metamorphosis from the Teller Resolution to the Platt
Amendment. At the outset of the Spanish-American War, Congress, by
the Teller Resolution, pledged itself against the sinister imperialism of
European powers. The United States, it declared unequivocally, "hereby
disclaims any disposition or intention" of exercising "sovereignty, jurisdiction, or control" over Cuba, except for its "pacification"; after which
the United States would "leave the government and control of the island
to its people." But after the elections of 1900, McKinley's new Congress
stipulated by the Platt Amendment (1901) that Cuba must not surrender
any of her territory to foreign powers or run up a large debt to foreign
creditors who might induce their governments to intervene. On the other
hand, Cuba must make it legal for the United States to intervene and must
allow the United States to set up naval bases. Acceptance of the Platt
Amendment by Cubans subordinated the sovereignty of their country to the
sovereignty of the United States. Occupation of Cuba by the American
military made it somewhat difficult for the Cubans to refuse. Cuba accepted; the Platt Amendment was ratified by treaty. Under its terms the
United States resorted to armed intervention under Roosevelt, under Taft,

and again during World War I. Meanwhile the American navy extended its strategic predominance by erecting a naval base on Cuban soil—Guantánamo, a Pearl Harbor for the Caribbean. The father of the Platt Amendment was the Secretary of War, Elihu Root, not yet distinguished by an interest in the World Court. For more than thirty years the Teller Resolution was forgotten until, under the second Roosevelt, the Platt Amendment was finally abrogated.

The third step in the series that was to swing Central America into the new sphere of influence and convert the Caribbean into an American lake was taken in 1903. This was the Panama policy of Theodore Roosevelt. The Clayton-Bulwer Treaty of 1850 had called for a joint Anglo-American canal, but the ambition for world power induced nationalists, dazzled by Captain Alfred T. Mahan's vision of a big navy and power politics, to prefer a less international canal. Even before Mahan, Roosevelt, and Lodge started to popularize "sea power," the United States in 1880 stood twelfth among world naval powers; twenty years later, American participation in the armaments race had given the country the third largest navy in the world. And the champions of strategic nationalism and command of the sea triumphed in the second Hay-Pauncefote Treaty (1901). John Hay's new treaty allowed the United States to build an all-American canal and fortify it. Within the next two years, lobbyists for American speculators who had acquired the Panama rights of a defunct French canal company got the ear of Washington. President Roosevelt decided on the Panama route in preference to Nicaragua, and Congress authorized payment of $40,000,000 for the French canal property. When Colombia rejected the terms of a treaty, Roosevelt used "the big stick"—the American naval equivalent of "rattling the saber." The "proper way of handling international relations," declared Roosevelt, was by *"speaking softly and carrying a big stick* . . . the American fleet represented the big stick."

Americans hoping to sell the French canal property stirred up a revolution in Colombia with the knowledge, if not connivance, of the American government. The navy dispatched the *Nashville* to the scene in expectation of trouble. Several hours before the uprising, a blunder resulted in a premature telegram from the State Department to the American consul at Panama: UPRISING OF ISTHMUS REPORTED. KEEP DEPARTMENT PROMPTLY AND FULLY INFORMED. The reply came: NO UPRISING YET. REPORTED WILL BE IN THE NIGHT. Several hours later Panama became independent of Colombia, without bloodshed. American naval forces prevented Colombian troops from crossing the isthmus to deal with the rebels. Two days later the United States recognized the new republic with indecent haste. The United States acquired a small but valuable strip of land ten miles wide, the Canal Zone, which it ruled under

U.S. COLONIAL EMPIRE in the CARIBBEAN

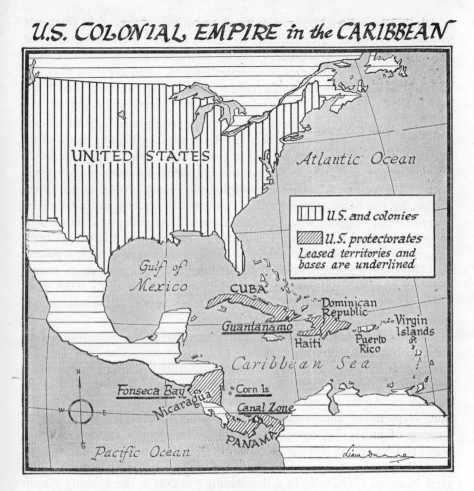

military government. It is said that when Roosevelt inquired about legal propriety in the Panama episode, Attorney General Philander C. Knox urbanely expressed sorrow that the President asked, since American proceedings were "without the taint of law." The "big ditch," however, commenced in 1906, was completed in 1914.

The fourth step in the evolving policy of predominance was the Theodore Roosevelt Corollary to the Monroe Doctrine. In 1902, in response to the pleas of European bondholders and corporations, Germany, England, and Italy blockaded Venezuela because that country defaulted on its debt. Roosevelt brought the countries to arbitration. When a similar financial instability developed in Santo Domingo, Roosevelt established a protectorate and the American government took over the Dominican customs. The precedent of the Platt Amendment suggested a general American policy to stabilize the national budgets of small countries and their debt payments to foreign creditors. Accordingly, in 1904, Roosevelt attached the "big stick" to the Monroe Doctrine. "Chronic wrongdoing," he informed Congress, ultimately led to forcible intervention "by some civilized nation"; in the American hemisphere adherence to the Monroe Doctrine "may force the United States . . . to the exercise of an international police power."

This departure from the live-and-let-live principles of liberal nationalism was soon known as the Theodore Roosevelt Corollary to the Monroe Doctrine. Not an international police power but a strictly national policy of intervention, it reflected a competitive but shrinking world in which investments abroad were bolstered by diplomatic protection and armed intervention by the home governments. Undoubtedly orderly exploitation of underdeveloped regions would proceed more rapidly under an international police power; and conceivably Pan-American conferences might have been converted into a regional international agency for exercise of such a power. But Theodore Roosevelt favored isolated national action more in accord with the economic nationalism of world powers. Like giant states elsewhere, the United States was simply claiming preponderance in a vast sphere of influence.

Under President Roosevelt, American intervention was justified in order to forestall intervention of other world powers. The State Department under President Taft and Secretary Philander C. Knox expanded this "preventive" formula into "Dollar Diplomacy." A policy for colonial expansion of American dollars on new external frontiers, it consisted of State Department encouragement of American economic penetration as a means of preventing economic penetration by business interests of other world powers. Knox laid the groundwork for intervention in Haiti in 1910 by diplomatic pressure, which put New York banks, particularly the great National City Bank, in a dominating position in the banking system of Haiti, displacing the older supremacy of French and other outside capital. In 1915 marines were landed. A new constitution, giving the United States a veiled political control of Haiti, was forced on the people. After the intervention, as in the case of Panama, a treaty legalized the proceedings.

Economic imperialism similarly swept Nicaragua into the American orbit. The State Department under Taft and Knox promoted contracts permitting Wall Street banking interests to acquire security for loans in the form of a 51 per cent control of the Nicaraguan banking and railroad systems. Control of Nicaraguan customs also passed into American hands. To bolster an acquiescent but tottering Nicaraguan government, American marines landed in 1912 without pretext of treaty right. The marines were withdrawn thirteen years later by the Coolidge administration, but returned the next year, 1926, to remain until the New Deal began finally to implement the Good Neighbor policy.

WILSONIAN DEMOCRACY AND INTEGRAL NATIONALISM

Under pressure of entrenched interests and a diplomatic corps trained in the new techniques, even a change in administration did not check these tendencies. Wilson renounced the theory of imperialism, but found his administration entangled in its practice. During World War I, American military forces dominated Haiti, Santo Domingo, and Cuba in addition to Nicaragua and Panama, and there, as elsewhere, economic penetration by American banks and corporations gathered speed. In subsequent years American influence in various countries forced repeal of laws that formerly prevented absentee foreign landlords or corporations from displacing small farmers and consolidating huge plantations.

The liberal intentions of Wilsonian Democracy, frustrated in the Caribbean by the different nationalist intentions of the diplomatic and consular corps, were best exemplified in the President's own policy toward Mexican revolutions. In population and natural wealth a leading American country, Mexico, under the corrupt dictatorship of Diaz, had been the prey of Mexican upper classes in partnership with foreign corporations, chiefly American and English. The American stake in 1910 reached the imperial proportions of a billion dollar investment and included predominance over Mexican railroad, mining, and oil properties. Expropriation of land and resources and backward social development had left 85 per cent of the people in the impoverished condition of landless peons. A wise and gentle leader, Francisco Madero, launched a new and progressive government in 1911. British and American interests, aided by the American minister in Mexico, a dollar diplomat appointed by Taft, opposed Madero; and possibly with some connivance in the American embassy, Madero was assassinated, and a crude new dictator, General Victoriano Huerta, took power. Wilson, resisting the pressure of American interests, developed a "moral diplomacy" that he called "watchful waiting." He refused to recognize a government created by assassination and force. On the other hand, he followed the liberal national aversion against intervening in Mexican affairs. His policy was ridiculed by conservative elements, who clamored for armed protection of American interests. Twice Wilson temporarily intervened with American forces: in 1914, when two American marines were arrested at Tampico; and a year later, when General Pershing pursued the bandit-revolutionist, Francisco Villa, who had raided American border towns. To strengthen the slender thread of Pan-American good will, already seriously weakened by dollar diplomacy and the big stick, Wilson spurned American demands for war and accepted the offer of mediation by Argentina, Brazil, and Chile. Meanwhile Wilson aided the Madero party by lifting an embargo on arms shipments. Huerta fled, and the United States recognized the government of President Venustiano Carranza. In 1917 a new Mexican constitution further infuriated foreign exploiters by providing for the recovery and use of Mexico's land and resources for the benefit of the people.

Nationalistic spirit in the twentieth century permeated all vital American policies, but as in Mexican relations it was by no means uncontested. If in Latin-American and Far Eastern policies, imperialistic tendencies existed side by side with nonimperialistic tendencies, the same internal struggle between liberalism and excessive nationalism appeared in battles over the tariff, Panama Canal tolls, immigration, and international organization. In the Far East, where the United States was weak, American influence was directed against a closed door. But Nipponese nationalists favoring a Japanese Monroe Doctrine in East Asia pointedly observed that the Roosevelt Corollary sought a closed door in the American zone. Dollar diplomacy itself was simply an outward expression of deeply rooted drives toward a closed door at home, internally expressed in the protective tariff and the growing opposition to immigration from abroad. But so wagged the world. The Dingley and Payne-Aldrich tariffs of 1897 and 1909, respectively, were counterparts of the economic foreign policy of imperial Germany and the integral nationalism of imperial France.

Against the tide of integral nationalism and imperialism, Woodrow Wilson, alone of the seven presidents between 1897 and 1933, fought for the economic policy associated with old-style liberal nationalism—a lower tariff more in accord with the economic law of comparative advantage. The Underwood Tariff of 1913 sought an open door both at home and abroad. In the same spirit in 1914 Wilson induced Congress to repeal the enactment of the Taft administration that had given American vessels in the coastwise trade a privileged exemption from Panama Canal tolls. But the forces of exclusive nationalism remained strong. The Webb-Pomerene Act (1918), passed by Democratic and Republican nationalists with inconsistent Wilsonian sanction, fostered cartels by its exemption of American export combines from the Sherman Antitrust Act—with the proviso that inside American boundaries they must not violate the trust law. Meanwhile, the old mercantilist policy of excluding foreign vessels from the coastwise trade of the United States was enlarged into an imperial system, beginning with the act of 1902, which excluded foreigners from the "coastwise" traffic between Puerto Rico and the United States. Wilson refused to act on congressional authorization to extend the coastwise system across the Pacific to the Philippines in 1920. But he was no more successful in resisting the anti-immigrant movement than in checking the tide of imperialism in the Caribbean.

American nativists were not satisfied with the exclusion of Chinese immigrants in 1882 and of Japanese in 1907. Re-enforcing the nativists, labor spokesmen urged restriction of immigration from Europe. Unless the nations turned to international regulation of immigration, coupled with action to establish equitable international labor standards, labor in a melting-pot country was bound to protect itself against unorganized cheap labor that destroyed collective bargaining gains. But it was less this motive than the irrational patriotism and superiority notions of integral nationalism which led nativists and leaders of polite society to demand a Chinese wall against the barbarians. A literacy test designed to discriminate against the common people who sought asylum in America was successively defeated by the vetoes of Cleveland, Taft, and Wilson. But there was no doubt of the nativist sentiment of a majority of Congress. When World War I came, Senator Norris was mortified by defeat of his bill to admit refugees from distracted Europe. In 1917, war-bred nationalism swept Congress, and the literacy test became law in spite of the President.

A change had come over the American spirit since the famous lines were written, to be carved at the base of the Statue of Liberty:

> Give me your tired, your poor,
> Your huddled masses yearning to breathe free,
> The wretched refuse of your teeming shore,
> Send these, the homeless, tempest-tossed, to me: . . .

The United States had once stood in the forefront of the world movement to accord the right to change citizenship by immigration and naturalization. Under Theodore Roosevelt, anti-alien controls by the passport system had begun to be tightened, and naturalization was made more difficult. By the end of the Wilson administration, federal law as interpreted in the courts was moving away from liberalism toward the rule laid down by the Supreme Court in 1922 that no alien except a white or a person of African extraction could be made an American citizen.

WORLD CRISIS: CLASH OF NATIONALISMS

Excessive nationalism, immigration restriction, imperialism, and military preparedness were attempted adjustments to the new age of industrialism, global interchange, and closer cultural contacts. But the crisis of 1914 shattered the nations' illusion of achieving security by drives for preponderance or by jockeying for position in the balance of power. The irrationality of such attempted adjustments to the problems of a shrinking world was epitomized in the difficulty of making the average citizen understand why most of the peoples around the globe should be drawn into war because an inconspicuous archduke was assassinated in an Austro-Hungarian city nestling in the mountains of what is now Yugoslavia.

Behind 1914 lay a series of earlier near-catastrophes. The old balance of power device, a coalition of nations as a check to a would-be aggressor, had become unworkable in a contracting world. Once national rivalry became world-wide, with all nations engaged in scrambles for strategic points, closed spheres, and protected markets, the outcome was the division of nations into two competing systems of alliances—with potential "friends" warming up on the side lines. From time to time, nations swapped sides; former "enemies" suddenly became partners; and each of the great powers, in its turn, made threats of war. Germany, before 1890 an ally of Russia, after 1890 relied upon a Triple Alliance with Austria-Hungary and Italy; and when war came, German rulers found their onetime allies, Russia and Italy, fighting against them. England, long avoiding alliances, in 1898 collided with her old enemy, France, at Fashoda in the African Sudan and threatened war over rival ambitions for control of the upper Nile. France, smarting from Bismarck's victory in the Franco-Prussian War, had meanwhile picked up Russia as an ally when Germany terminated her Russian flirtation. By 1904 England and France also struck a bargain, forming an entente by secretly agreeing to support French predominance in Morocco and English predominance over Egypt and the Suez Canal zone. In 1907 France promoted an entente between Russia and her traditional enemy, England, facilitated by Anglo-Russian bargains involving Persian oil.

In successive crises up to 1914 the governments of each of the major partners menaced the world's peace by a deliberate threat of war. The German rulers, moved by designs on Morocco rivaling those of the French, nearly precipitated war in 1905. When the Hapsburg monarchy of Austria-Hungary defied Russia and Serbia in 1908 by annexation of Bosnian territory inhabited by Serbs, Germany defended her Austrian ally by threatening war. The designs of the French on North Africa again nearly caused war in the crisis of 1911. The equally covetous German overlords, furious when the French occupied the Moroccan capital, landed forces at the Moroccan port of Agadir. England, partner of the French, this time promised war: Germany must not challenge France's sphere of influence. Again in 1912 Balkan wars stirred national rivalries, and Germany and Austria-Hungary threatened war against little Serbia and the big partner of England and France—Russia. In 1914 Austria threatened war on Serbia, and Russia threatened war in return; and war came.

Assassination of the Austrian archduke in 1914 was the work of

Serbs who wanted independence for all Yugoslavs under an expanded Serbia. Austria sent an ultimatum to Serbia. Serbia, counting on Russia, refused to abandon entirely her aspirations for Yugoslav independence. Austria declared war. Russia protested and mobilized her army. Germany declared war on Russia. France refused to promise neutrality; whereupon Germany declared war on France. When Germany struck at the vulnerable French front by invasion through Belgium, England declared war. Japan declared war. The United States declared its neutrality. In 1915 Italy abandoned her German alliance and attacked Austria, Turkey attacked Russia and the English Suez, and Bulgaria made war on Serbia. In 1916 Rumania attacked Austria. Then the United States entered, drawing in Panama, Cuba, Nicaragua, Haiti, Guatemala, and Honduras. China, Siam, Liberia, and Brazil likewise joined the Allies. As war proceeded, 65,000,000 armed men were locked in combat.

INVOLVEMENT IN WORLD WAR

Like American presidents during the Napoleonic era, Woodrow Wilson—no believer in imperialist wars—placed faith in neutrality, a policy not seriously tested since America's involvement in the last great world war in 1812. A program for national security rather than for international security, isolation was now again to prove no solution in a balance-of-power world. Proponents of power politics were quick to make capital of the successive shocks that attended Wilson's effort to avoid entanglement. A campaign of detraction of administration foreign policy, shrewdly appealing to emotional nationalism, coincided with a movement to reunite the G.O.P. and the Bull Moose Progressives. Conservatives, to dim the luster of Wilsonian domestic reforms, diverted attention by attacking Wilson's weakling "surrender" to lawless Mexico. Nationalists like the Bull Moose, Theodore Roosevelt, and the Republican, Lodge, recemented their divided forces by ridiculing Wilson's neutrality policy.

But the eventual breakdown of neutrality and repudiation of isolation arose from a greater and more significant complex of aspirations, pressures, and changed world conditions. Underwater technology brought European war to the American coast line; American ships only three miles from their home shores came within the orbit of submarine blockade. There began an arid diplomatic debate over international law and submarine warfare—arid, because in a world of international anarchy, international law was "law without force." Germany warned neutrals in February, 1915, to beware of entering the waters around Britain. Americans could not isolate their emotions when on May 7 the British liner *Lusitania* was callously sunk with a loss of 1153 men, women, and children, including more than 100 Americans. Wilson's stiff notes induced Germany to be more scrupulous regarding destruction of American commerce and lives. Again, after violating her pledge in the sinking of the steamer *Sussex* early in 1916, Germany paid heed for nine months to Wilson's threat of severing relations. But on February 1, 1917, Germany returned to unrestricted sinkings and relations were broken.

Secretary of State Bryan resigned in 1915 because he took the extreme neutrality position that American citizens and property should not enter war zones except at their own risk. The American public, however, was incapable of such a doctrinaire conviction. Ideals and interests drew the public steadily toward the side of England and the Allies. Allied propaganda and atrocity stories were more readily believed in America than German propaganda, partly because of the unprovoked invasion of Belgium, the sinking of the *Lusitania,* and the unreliability of German pledges against unrestricted submarine warfare, and partly because of ideological sympathy for the democracies, France and England, and distrust of the militaristic aristocracies and monarchs of Germany and Austria-Hungary. The psychological illusion upon which the neutrality concept depended was dissipated by wartime economic interdependence that drew American producers and investors into collaboration with the Allied war effort. Before America went to war, J. Pierpont Morgan, as general purchasing agent for the Allies, was placing war orders in the United States at the rate of $10,000,000 a day.

Americans could remain neutral neither in heart nor in deed. The sinking of eight American vessels in February and March, 1917, and the disclosure of German negotiations with Mexico crystallized sentiment. The Zimmermann note, a secret communication from Germany's foreign secretary, offered Mexico the recovery of her "lost territory of New Mexico, Texas and Arizona" in case the United States entered the war; in return Mexico must attack the United States and urge Japan to shift sides and join the attack. American eyes were startled by the specter of international anarchy stalking south of the border as well as rampant in the Far Eastern and European zones. On April 6, 1917, the United States entered the war.

While known as World War I, this was the eighth international conflict in the American record. It differed, however, from the four wars under the English flag and the conflicts of 1776, 1798, and 1812. Nationalists, to be sure, even before the Zimmermann note, had asserted that the United States should join the Allies to protect American interests in the three zones, Latin America, East Asia, and Europe. The same nationalistic critics pressed Wilson onward to his great preparedness program of 1916; and while still at peace the United States made the largest single appropriation in world history, prior to World War II, for naval armaments. Yet the significant difference between earlier involvement in great conflicts and the involvement in 1917 was the nature of popular war aims. The vast majority, repudiating the tradition of no entanglements and the nationalist concept of a balance of power system, followed Wilson in embracing war aims that went beyond mere self-preservation or national advantage. Americans tended to view the war in ideological terms, as a conflict between democracy and autocracy and between exploitive power politics and peaceful internationalism. "The world must be made safe for democracy," ran Wilson's famous appeal for a declaration of war:

> Its peace must be planted upon the tested foundations of political liberty. . . . We desire no conquest, no dominion. We seek no indemnities for ourselves, no material compensation for the sacrifices we shall freely make. . . . we shall fight for the things we have always carried nearest our hearts, for democracy, . . . for a universal dominion of right by such a concert of free peoples as shall bring peace and safety to all nations. . . .

NATIONALIST CHAOS AND THE SEARCH FOR SANITY

Behind Wilson's appeal lay a rapidly spreading movement to foster internationalism. Both public and private action had registered the growing power of a noble vision of an organized structure for peace and justice among the family of peoples. Myriad associations of citizens to promote peace multiplied in the twentieth century on both sides of the Atlantic. Registering a deepening reaction against militarism and a growing recognition of world interdependence, these societies urged governments to abandon imperialistic drives for preponderance and to abate nationalistic clashes over the balance of power. New social thinking was beginning to demand an international concept of common welfare.

Although governments made only gestures of limited character toward international cooperation, even Theodore Roosevelt, always a contradiction, eschewed the big stick long enough to push America's traditional policy of fostering international arbitration. In 1905, Roosevelt and Hay negotiated arbitration treaties with Great Britain, France, Germany, and four other European nations, only to see them cut to pieces by Senate obstructionists who jealously guarded American sovereignty by insisting on reservations protecting special interests. In 1907 Secretary Root nevertheless accepted the treaties with their crippling Senate amendments. Additional treaties were ratified during the Taft administration, and under Wilson the State Department supplemented them with Secretary Bryan's "cooling off" treaties. "Justiciable" questions covered by treaties did not reach to the core of the problem, sovereignty. The outbreak of the European conflict dissipated the illusion of a structure of peace based on flimsy foundations of "law without force." In 1907 the second Hague Conference had been called on the initiative of the United States, meeting in the Hague Peace Palace built in Holland by Andrew Carnegie. The American delegates met a stone wall when they urged establishment of an international court and a limitation on naval building designed to check the competitive armaments race. Lip-service agreement was reached in acceptance of a Latin-American proposal, the Drago Doctrine, disavowing the imperialistic practice of forcible intervention in a small country to collect debts owed to the business firms and citizens of strong countries.

The war crisis intensified the popular demand for international organization. Ex-President Taft, by 1916, was actively associated with a new and portentous organization, the League to Enforce Peace. Jane Addams of famed Hull-House, turning from domestic social evils to the problem of war, was similarly active as leader of the Woman's International League for Peace. Wilson, sympathetic with the global aspirations of peace organizations, shared the suspicions of Senators La Follette and Norris of the "preparedness" pressure groups such as the National Security League organized by New York businessmen at the start of the war. But, although he discarded belief in neutrality for belief in international organization to maintain peace, the President became increasingly certain of the imminence of armed clash. By the spring of 1916 Wilson supported the armaments demand and obtained the then unparalleled appropriation of half a billion dollars for naval building. Within a few months the presidential campaign of 1916 was under way, and Republican exponents of the big stick were attacking Wilson's anti-imperialist Mexican policy and his struggle to maintain neutrality in the face of submarine warfare. The Democratic slogan, "He Kept Us Out of War," and the progressive reforms of the administration won Bryan's old strongholds, including the trans-Mississippi West and the South. Charles Evans Hughes, the Republican candidate, calling for belligerent defense of national interests, swept all but two of the industrial states from Illinois to Maine, and came within a handful of the electoral votes necessary to re-establish Republican supremacy.

Immediately after the election Wilson exerted the full power of the American government in an effort to bring the warring nations to an agreement on a just basis for negotiating a peace. Power politics on both sides frustrated the attempt; and the renewed submarine warfare and the Zimmermann note ruled out any second one. Within four months the United States was in the war. But Wilson spoke not alone for America but for masses of humble people in other lands when he proclaimed it a war "to make the world safe for democracy." In January, 1917, Wilson began to define war aims on the basis of principles that were to give the struggle the character of a crusade. The peace settlement should recognize fully the rights and needs of small nations and oppressed minorities, he told the Senate, and the great nations should make a peace that ruled out militarism, secret alliances, and the nationalistic policies of preponderance and balance of power. Through the magic of his words and the authority of his great office, Wilson, more than any other statesman, stirred the world's multitudes. The lofty ideal took root—the vision of a postwar world dedicated to recognition of interdependence by international cooperation for the general welfare of man.

But there were differing war aims, too: those of nationalists who could see an advantage in stripping Germany of imperial power but who were prepared to abandon neither the drives of special interests nor the pattern of conservative ideas that had propelled the world toward integral nationalism, economic imperialism, and international anarchy. And these men were determined that the postwar world should rely upon practical men; in the United States, unconvinced of a world illusion, they were determined to turn from Wilsonian Democracy to practical vision, the older certainties, nationalism and normalcy.

XXVIII

NATIONALISM AND NORMALCY

1917–1929

Since the rise of modern nationalism and the succession of great economic revolutions, two portentous struggles have confronted all mankind: to distribute more equally a greater abundance of the material and other satisfactions of life; and to make political power responsible by displacing self-interested upper-class government both within nations and within the over-all international community. The necessities of war obscured but did not diminish the intensity of the struggle for democracy and a greater common welfare. In the postwar decade, however, the United States lagged behind many other countries in striving for both the national and the international objectives of democracy.

WORLD WAR I

In nation after nation, mobilization for war induced tendencies that continued far into the future and posed a crucial question of how the collectivist requirements of modern technology and planning could be assimilated for the purposes of democracy, international cooperation, and the general well-being. After 1918 the heritage of new engines of war—tanks, bombing planes, machine guns, mobile artillery, and modern mechanized units—diminished the democratic power of resistance in every country in which the dominant orders held or usurped military power. Meanwhile, during the war, immense demands for the new weapons and equipment made the battle of production on the home fronts as fundamental as the battle of extermination on the war fronts. World War I revealed that in a technological age only giant industrial states could engage in giant mechanized wars. Toward the end of the military campaigns American industrial power and the high productive capacity of American labor provided a decisive additional counterweight to the industrial might of Germany. But the battle of production was won only by a high centralization of control over production and labor relations. Some failures were recorded. The Navy and War Departments, industrialists serving in

Washington as dollar-a-year men in hastily improvised war agencies, and business firms under government contract shared responsibility for several bad fiascoes: heavy artillery, machine guns, and airplanes. America's allies had to meet the crisis in producing this material.

Another failure, growing out of the reluctance associated with the industrial tradition of exemption from public controls, was the refusal to use the full power of the American government in dealing with shortages and in controlling wartime inflation. The English parties in Parliament, better organized and disciplined than their American counterparts in Congress, authorized a more comprehensive and successful structure of controls. In the United States, chiefly food, fuels, and railroads felt the impact of governmental supervision. Herbert Hoover, a mining engineer who had spent years overseas in the promotion of concessions in the Far East and elsewhere, became a national figure as food czar. The breakdown in transportation of troops and war supplies led to exertion of the full power of the government to coordinate and operate the whole national network of railroads. In agricultural production the handling of the wheat problem provided an example of successful wartime government planning. Wheat farmers were stimulated under a direct subsidy with guaranteed government purchase of the whole national crop at an attractive minimum price of $2.20 a bushel. Though successful, this system of incentive controls was sparingly used because the congressional majority and business leaders in charge of the programs shared a distaste for the precedent and the principle. Controls of profits and prices by Bernard Baruch of the War Industries Board and Herbert Hoover of the Food Administration did not prevent padded costs on government contracts in war industries and failed to ward off the general price inflation.

To ordinary grumbling against wartime regulations were added far more justified complaints against profiteers and protests against the "H. C. of L."—the high cost of living. World War I produced nothing comparable to the antiprofiteering and anti-inflation drive under the wage and salary freeze, renegotiation law, excess profits tax, and price control of the second Roosevelt during World War II. After the armistice of 1918, the congressional Republican majority, in combination with conservative Democrats, rejected Wilson's leadership and made no genuine provision for reconversion to peacetime production. This bipartisan combination committed Congress to the mistake of forcing immediate abandonment of price controls, with the result that postwar inflation for several years spiraled upward even more seriously than during the war itself. Labor and the salaried middle-class were caught in the squeeze of reconversion, reduced employment, cuts in wages, and higher prices. Labor

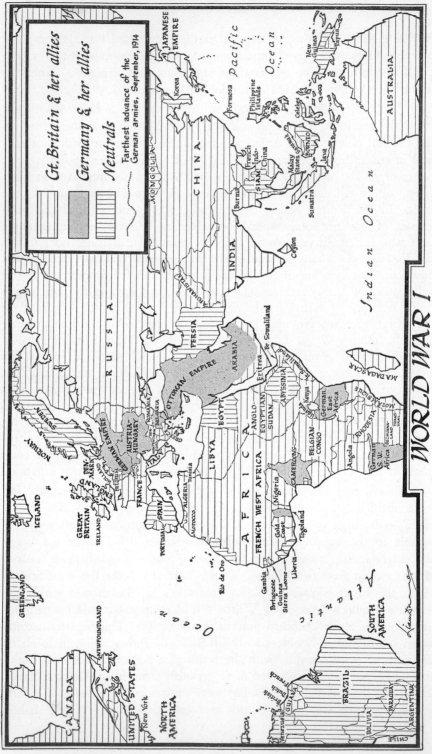

WORLD WAR I

Gt. Britain & her allies
Germany & her allies
Neutrals
Farthest advance of the
German armies, September, 1914

unrest and great strikes made 1919 and 1922 bitter years in the history of trade unions.

Meanwhile, during and after the war, the congressional attitude on financial aid to America's allies led to still another unfortunate postwar economic snarl. On advice of the Allies, the original American reenforcement was to consist more of war goods than of troops. However, goods were recorded in government ledger books in money values, technically as debts, although contributions of men in the American armed forces were not. It was freely said in Congress and out that these American "loans" were really outright contributions to aid the veteran armies of the Allies, which were doing the bulk of the fighting. Neither the State Department nor Congress settled the point that government loans in the form of goods were simply part of the American war effort. Subsequently, although the debts were originally incurred by shipping American goods to Europe, the Allies were not permitted to repay them in the form of European goods shipped to the United States. In consequence, world economy in the 1920's struggled under the handicap of a colossal snarl of tariffs, war debts, refunding negotiations, and gold shipments.

The blunder of American civil authorities in appraising long-range results of wartime decisions was matched by mistakes of the military. Miscalculations by the professional soldiers soon had to be corrected by upward revision of the Allies' estimate of the American military reenforcement required for the knockout. Plans eventually called for 5,000,-000 Americans at the western front. But only in the last campaign prior to the armistice was the nation able to put more than a million fighting men in the field. The military crisis requiring greater American reenforcement arose from Germany's successful escape from her nightmare of a two-front war. By 1918, German arms had crippled Italian forces and forced Russia and Rumania out of the war. In March, 1918, came Germany's big push, made possible by concentration on a single front. Meanwhile, Germany came near to winning the battle of supply lines. Submarines blockading England struck fear into the Allies over the imminent danger that England would be starved out. With effective teamwork the British and American navies developed counterweapons: the convoy system, camouflaged vessels, the zigzag course, and Q-boats to prey on subs. The supplies went through, and the United States and the Allies combined in a supreme effort to ward off the big push into France. After years of squabbling, the Allies for the first time agreed upon unified command. Marshal Ferdinand Foch, as supreme commander over all the western front, met the oncoming Germans with a well-timed counteroffensive. The British attacked on the left flank of the German bulge in August, the French held the center, and half a million Americans went into action on the right flank at Saint-Mihiel. Subsequently, the main American action took place in the Meuse-Argonne sector, with over a million men slogging it out for nearly two months in the slow motion of trench warfare. After one of the most savage and bloody campaigns in the entire American record, the Germans were pushed back to the line of battle of the armistice, roughly the same line reached twenty-six years later by the American Third Army after its incredibly rapid "blitz" across Normandy and France.

INTERNATIONAL PEACE OR BALANCE OF POWER?

As peace neared, Wilson became the leading spokesman for myriads who recoiled from a world of national aggrandizement and aggression. On January 8, 1918, the American President laid down the Fourteen Points, a document as famous throughout the world as the later Atlantic Charter. The Fourteen Points were based upon three principles: economic liberalism, liberal nationalism, and international organization. The economic settlement was to look toward a world open door in the spirit of the international economics of Adam Smith: "The removal, so far as possible, of all economic barriers and the establishment of an equality of trade conditions among all the nations." The live-and-let-live principles of liberal nationalism were to be applied in recognizing new governments and boundaries. Such a political and territorial settlement on the basis of self-determination opened the way to an accentuated nationalism, but this was intended to be corrected by the Fourteenth Point, looking toward a permanent structure to establish international cooperation. To promote such cooperation, colonial claims were to be settled on a basis giving the interests of colonial populations as much "weight" as the claims of outside governments. Militarism as a nationalistic force was to be attacked through a reduction of armaments. Old-style power politics, secret alliances, and furtive Machiavellian diplomacy were to be attacked by insistence on publicity and accountability to world opinion through "open covenants . . . openly arrived at." The famous Fourteenth Point looked toward the diminution of policies of preponderance or balance of power by permanently establishing an international concert of power through a "general association of nations."

Allied governments had inspired their people with the slogan "A war to end war," but "realists," entrenched in the foreign offices of the same governments, made treaties secretly during the war to cement alliances by mutual aggrandizement. A secret treaty between Japan and England, for example, divided German spoils in the Pacific, Japan taking islands north of the equator. Just before the United States entered the war, the Allies hastily agreed to Japan's claim to the imperial concessions in the province of Shantung that Germany had once extorted from China. The Fourteen Points placed the imperialists on the defensive by condemning aggrandizement and secret diplomacy. Wilson's statements on war aims won astonishing support from the people of Europe and from Allied leaders like Lord Robert Cecil, noted English champion of a league of peaceful nations. But the undercover battle continued. During negotiation of armistice terms, Allied foreign offices demurred at full acceptance of Wilsonian war aims. Wilson's hint that he might carry the matter to Congress and raise the question of a separate peace forced an armistice on the basis of the Fourteen Points. The Allies, however, insisted on German reparations.

Historical revision, Nazi propaganda, and American isolationist oratory in later years combined to blacken the peace settlement made at Versailles in 1919. The Germans were compelled to accept more severe conditions than the armistice terms had led them to expect. Subsequently, in Nazi propaganda, Wilson was portrayed as betraying Germany. Americans eventually imagined something like the unforgettable picture of the "Big Three" set down by John Dos Passos in his powerful trilogy, *U.S.A.:* Lloyd George and Clemenceau sitting down with Wilson at a fateful game of international poker; Lloyd George and Clemenceau "taking Wilson to the cleaners"; the American President exalted by his great honors, isolated in royal splendor, no longer hearing the cries of the people for a constructive peace. Idealists, too readily tracing postwar problems to a single hero and a single document and not to contradictions within society as a whole, ended by pillorying their greatest friend. Later studies restored a more balanced perspective. Wilson lacked the leverage to dislodge the Allies from excessive demands for German reparations, and he was forced to compromise at Versailles on other political, territorial, and economic questions. But Wilson's own country similarly would not permit a writing off of the war debts due from the Allies. Wilson did not compromise on basic international theory; Lloyd George and Clemenceau made the concessions. Forgoing vengeful plans to cripple Germany forever, the Allied statesmen, in return for Wilson's pledge of American military and diplomatic support of collective security, heeded the cries of the people by acceptance of a league of nations.

Germany signed the Versailles Treaty, not without protest, in June, 1919. A so-called German "war guilt" clause was later called false to history inasmuch as all countries, not Germany alone, had contributed to the nationalism and imperialism that brought on the war. In actuality, the clause merely sanctioned reparations by compelling Germany to admit "aggression" and therefore "responsibility" for loss and damage.

The post-treaty reparations terms were harsh and weakened the struggle of German democrats to resist the Hitler nationalists. Nevertheless, it was not what Nazis later claimed—a "Carthaginian peace in Wilsonian disguise." Bismarck's unification of Germany was preserved by the Versailles Treaty in accordance with the self-determination principle of the Fourteen Points. German territorial aggrandizements were stripped away on the same principle: Alsace-Lorraine was ceded to France, and other border territories went to Poland and smaller German neighbors. German colonies came under the administration of England, France, Japan, and Belgium, not as permanent spoils but as international mandates under the League. Provisions for the destruction of German militarism were essential to the success of Wilsonian internationalism. Hence the vast German armaments industry was placed under international control. German manufacture of tanks, big guns, and bombers was prohibited. German fortifications and garrisons in the Rhineland were abolished forever. The United States and the Allies agreed on a fifteen-year military occupation of a large section of the industrial heart of Germany, the Saar Valley, and the whole strategic zone west of the Rhine. A fifteen-year French control of coal resources in the Saar basin was combined with political administration of the Saar by the League of Nations. To make disarmament a reality, Germany was allowed only a skeleton navy and army. The Bismarck system of compulsory military training was prohibited.

The League of Nations embodied Wilson's Fourteenth Point. The League Covenant, incorporated as an inseparable part of the Versailles Treaty, sought to meet the recurring objection to older treaties that time and again had set nation against nation and had ever failed to provide for peaceful world change. The Covenant afforded means for an international remedy of inequalities or maladjustments resulting from the peace settlement itself or from subsequent alterations in world conditions. In place of nationalist drives for advantages by force and fraud, the plan substituted international cooperation through auxiliary agencies of the League: the World Court, the International Institute of Intellectual Cooperation, the International Labor Office, and similar bodies. These agencies dealt with social problems, child welfare, international health, and world economic and financial questions such as the problem of equalizing labor standards among competing countries like Japan and the United States. In subsequent years the exploratory work of agencies like the International Labor Office made an impressive contribution.

Central in subsequent American debate were the thorny political and economic issues of national power and international authority. In the new structure the Assembly of the League was a sort of lower house composed of delegates from all the member nations equally represented with one vote apiece. Self-governing British dominions were given a vote. The more important Council, or upper house of the League, was composed of one delegate each from the five great powers including the United States, and four delegates representing four lesser powers, the latter delegates to be elected by the Assembly. The League was entrusted with two primary powers for preserving peace: authority to apply an economic boycott (sanctions) against aggressors; and, second, the advisory power of the Council to recommend to national governments the quotas of military, naval, or air forces that the League hoped they would contribute to check an aggressor. The power of the League to act was handicapped by the requirement that decisions of the Council should be unanimous; yet even so, obstructionists in the United States objected to these extremely limited powers.

The provision most violently criticized and grossly misrepresented in the United States was Article X of the Covenant. This article merely pledged the League to respect and preserve the territorial integrity and political independence of the members and did no more than authorize the Council to "advise" the sovereign member-nations regarding the means to fulfill the pledge. The League was not what is now regarded as a strong international organization. Unlike the federal system under the American Constitution, the central world authority acted upon the governments rather than upon the people. In practice, League delegates were directly responsible not to the people, but to national governments and their state departments.

THE SENATE: SOVEREIGNTY TRIUMPHANT

As the Peace Conference neared its end, American nationalists in the Senate were dismayed by the country-wide swing to internationalism. A small Republican clique of "irreconcilable" isolationist senators, led by Hiram Johnson (California), William E. Borah (Idaho), and Robert La Follette (Wisconsin), fought for rejection of the Versailles settlement in its entirety. More significant, since it commanded the margin of votes decisive in encompassing ultimate defeat of the League, was the large phalanx of conservative regular Republicans. Spurred on by aging servitors of the greater national industries—Henry Cabot Lodge of the Brahmins of Massachusetts, Boies Penrose, Pennsylvania boss, Philander C. Knox of Pittsburgh's golden triangle, former promulgator of dollar diplomacy as Secretary of State, Reed Smoot, the Utah high priest of high tariffs, and Albert B. Fall, New Mexico's spokesman for western mining, timberland, and railway interests—the Republican regulars, far from sharing the anti-imperialism of La Follette, retained their nationalist sentiments. But, on an immediate straight vote, not even Old Guard senators would have dared to defy public opinion by repudiating the League. The Ohio Republican, Senator Warren G. Harding, told the isolationist Borah he would like to join him in the fight against "this League of Nations, but the people of my state are all for it." Lodge also said it was "hopeless"; all the newspapers in Massachusetts "are for it." Thirty-two state legislatures endorsed the League.

The Republican Senate majority, however, found a strategy more effective than the die-hard opposition of Borah and the irreconcilables. In May, 1919, the Republicans, having gained a majority on the Foreign Relations Committee of the Senate, made Lodge chairman and adopted the tactics of delay and obstruction. Toward the end of the Versailles negotiations the Republican member of Wilson's Peace Commission asked Lodge to propose modifications that would remove Senate objections to the League. Henry Lodge, however, rejected the role of Henry Clay and refused to suggest compromises. When the treaty went to the Lodge committee in July, the strategy of delay was combined with a campaign of public detraction. In committee hearings and in anti-League demonstrations organized around the country, appeals were made to Irish-Americans, who were led to suppose that the votes of British dominions in the Assembly would be more significant than the limitation of the British Empire to one vote on the all-important Council. Criticisms of the treatment of defeated countries were made with the purpose of inducing Americans of German extraction to think of themselves more as Germans than as Americans. England and France were presented not as America's allies in the great struggle for international cooperation, but as though they were enemies of the United States. Andrew Mellon, a Pittsburgh financier of coal, steel, aluminum, and oil, in company with other grateful beneficiaries of high tariffs, contributed funds to the campaign to discredit the League. Wilson toured the country in September, carrying to the people a counteroffensive against the obstructionists. In Colorado he suddenly collapsed. A broken man, he never again had the physical vigor and keenness for mastery of the tactics of presidential leadership.

The Republican majority on the Senate committee made the most of the stratagem of delay. The Versailles Treaty, bottled up in committee for three months, was undergoing a striking change. On September 10 the committee brought out the treaty with forty-five amendments. Lodge's collaborators on the committee, determined to insist upon national sovereignty, had carefully framed the amendments so that they seemed to cling to the advice of the founding fathers on the subject of entanglements in European politics. But the century-old language of Jeffersonian liberal nationalism was a masquerade. The Lodge amendments were framed for a different world in which the United States, as a great country, was inextricably entangled. The spirit of the amendments was not liberal nationalism, but the later and quite opposite type of regressive nationalism that sought special privileges while evading responsibilities. The committee's report opposed any American obligation to administer a League mandate and repudiated any obligation to apply sanctions against an aggressor. In short, the amendments were a skilled form of Senate surgery, cutting into the Versailles Treaty to remove the connective tissues that united the American people with others in joint responsibility for administering and enforcing the political and economic agreements of the Peace Conference. After a parade of obstructionists in the ensuing Senate debate, the amendments were rejected on grounds clear from the first: Senate amendments would necessitate a second peace conference and new negotiations. But delay and detraction had succeeded in dividing the newspapers and arousing national bias by diverting attention from the general interests of mankind to the supposed special interests of the United States.

In the face of public clamor for the League, the Republican majority, defeated on the amendments, resorted to reservations. "The best we can do," Lodge once confided to Borah, "is to get changes that will emasculate it as much as possible." The fourteen Lodge reservations were a covert assertion of nationalism. One proclaimed the Monroe Doctrine "wholly outside the jurisdiction of the League." Another struck at the Assembly vote of British dominions. One emphasized the right to secede from the League. A vital reservation, ignoring the precedents of executive initiative against the Barbary pirates and the Boxers, asserted the sole power of Congress to decide on employment of American forces in upholding international order. Another excluded "domestic" American legislation from League consideration. During the Versailles conference, ex-President Taft, as spokesman for the League to Enforce Peace, had cabled Wilson that the ground could be "cut from under" Senate nationalists only by such an amendment; congressional sovereignty on domestic legislation would "answer objections as to Japanese immigration, as well as tariffs." Wilson opposed concessions that would render the League powerless to consider domestic policies standing in the way of peaceful world progress. But on the Senate objections, Wilson followed the advice of Taft, Elihu Root, and other leaders of the League to Enforce Peace. By final amendments of the Covenant, the nations at the Peace Conference made substantial concessions to American nationalists, recognizing the Monroe Doctrine and the right of secession from the League and restricting League power over matters that by international law were "solely within" domestic jurisdiction.

Although these were crucial concessions, they did not appease either the La Follette insurgents or the Old Guard nationalists, none of whom had ever been genuinely critical of the old diplomacy of balance of power. The Republican majority, voting as a compact unit, carried the Lodge reservations one by one. Not a single reservation would have obtained a majority but for the fifteen votes of irreconcilables. The isolationist strategy to defeat the treaty was to strengthen the reservations until Democrats could not accept them. The Democrats, seeing no sign of compromise in the White House, voted against the reservations. Wilson, by urging Democrats to defeat reservations, erred in tactics rather than in principle. It was idle to join the League on a basis of special exemptions. Unless the United States entered the League "scorning privileges," he believed there was little hope of transforming balance of power diplomacy into genuine international techniques.

On the crucial day of November 19, 1919, the vote of 42 Democrats defeated the Lodge sabotage of the treaty. The Democratic floor leader could not woo Republican votes for a substitute set of reservations. On a vote for the treaty without reservations, Wilsonian internationalism failed by 38 yeas to 53 nays, Republicans almost solidly opposing. The country was shocked. Although nationalism and the breakdown of responsible leadership in Congress defeated ratification, during the whole time in the Senate and in the country only a small minority dared take a die-hard position against the League of Nations. Under public pressure the Senate resumed debate and, four months later, March, 1920, voted again. This time with the Lodge reservations, the treaty received a decisive majority, 49 yeas against 35 nays, but not a two-thirds majority.

Behind the successive rejections lay something other than the two-thirds rule—a reaction of nationalists and conservatives against a presidential leadership exerted for the goals of Wilsonian Democracy. Exploitive individualism and dollar diplomacy went hand in hand, and its postwar strategy was a reassertion of congressional power. The oil magnate Edward L. Doheny spoke for his kind when ridiculing Wilson as "a college professor gone Bolshevik." Defeat of the treaty was a repetition of the disastrous cross-purposes that produced the tragic era of Lincoln and Johnson in which congressional Republicans rose up against presidential peacemaking. Discussing the Constitution and world organization long afterward, Edward S. Corwin pointed out that it had been "generally overlooked" that the struggle between Wilson and Lodge "was the natural, if not inevitable, outcome of 120 years of institutional development." Ironically Wilson, who had contributed to diagnosis of the cancer of party irresponsibility, himself fell a victim to its evil effect in frustrating the only kind of leadership that could give unity to the branches of government.

The legislative branch of the government made its own peace with Germany in 1921. Again, as after 1865, the administration's peace was defeated and discarded, but more was at stake. The peace made by the nations of the world was crippled as well. "Without us," declared the report of the Lodge committee, "their league is a wreck." Peace without strong international organization, as events subsequently proved, was merely an armed interlude between wars.

CONSERVATIVE SUPREMACY

Like Senate proceedings on the League, the campaign of 1920 was by no means conducted on the high plane of a great debate. The blackening of administration policies reached reckless proportions under the leadership of Lodge assisted by a vitriolic press and industrial leaders equally vitriolic in their opposition to the Clayton Act and Wilson's support of collective bargaining. Alarmed liberals launched a savage indictment: reactionary forces were more concerned with putting an end to progressivism in the United States than with putting an end to war and aggrandizement among civilized nations.

The Republican nomination for the campaign of 1920 reflected the imperious determination of congressional stalwarts to have a president who valued American interests above international cooperation; who was "safe" on the issue of reversing progressive reforms and eliminating the "socialist" precedents of wartime government controls over business; and who would ensure the triumph of conservatives by surrendering party leadership to Congress and abandoning the Wilsonian practice of presidential initiative in the formulation of legislation. A Lodge reservationist, Senator Warren G. Harding, an undistingushed party hack of the old Mark Hanna "Ohio gang," became the Republican candidate with the equally "safe" Calvin Coolidge, the Governor of Massachusetts, as his running mate. The platform attacked Wilsonian presidential leadership as "executive autocracy." The record of the party in Congress showed an obvious leaning toward nationalism, but the platform shrewdly deferred to public opinion by a pious straddle endorsing a vague internationalism. The restoration of special immunities for the propertied classes was espoused openly in demands for less government regulation and covertly in promises of economy and reduction of progressive income taxes and war profits levies, which had fallen heavily on those in the larger brackets. The keynote of the campaign was a demand for practical men and practical vision; or, as Harding expressed it, "not nostrums but normalcy," not "internationality" but "triumphant nationality."

The Democratic convention nominated candidates who were internationalists in foreign policy and progressives in domestic policy, Governor James M. Cox of Ohio for president and the Assistant Secretary of the Navy, Franklin D. Roosevelt of New York, for vice-president. Facing the issues of progressivism and internationalism squarely, the Democratic platform strongly endorsed both and demanded prompt entrance into the League without America-first reservations.

The campaign of 1920 was not the "solemn referendum" on the League that Wilson had desired. The realities of the struggle for power were artfully obscured. Well-meaning Republicans helped befuddle the voters. Thirty-one of the most eminent Republicans in the country, including former cabinet members of the Theodore Roosevelt and Taft administrations, issued a "round-robin" letter affirming that election of Harding would guarantee American participation in an "effective" League of Nations. "The Republican party is bound by every consideration of good faith to pursue such a course," declared the statement of the thirty-one Republicans. Elihu Root, father of the World Court, signed the letter. Taft, Stimson, Hughes, Hoover, and the presidents of Harvard, Columbia, and Princeton also signed. Internationally minded Republicans believed them, and millions of honest citizens voted for Harding, convinced that they were voting for strong international organization. Harding himself in different speeches spoke with like sincerity on both sides of the League issue. The bulk of Republican candidates for Congress individually campaigned on the basis of vague generalities concealing nationalist preferences. A landslide victory gave Harding the presidency with a total of 16,152,000, or about 60 per cent of the popular vote. After the election, in retort to the triumphant cries of Senate leaders, the new Vice-President, Coolidge, quietly declared the election was not a mandate against the League of Nations. But gradually the election was so interpreted. A combination of nationalists and isolationists dominated the Senate Foreign Relations Committee for years to come. The struggle for power had been resolved. The elections of 1920 initiated a Republican supremacy that controlled the Congress till 1930 and the administration till 1932. Republican selection of eight new appointees to the Supreme Court in this period ensured continuance of a judicial conservatism that the previous liberal appointees named by Theodore Roosevelt and Wilson had never succeeded in reversing.

The Republican party narrowly escaped disaster in the elections of 1924 because of Harding's weakness for cabinet members of a type whose backstage activities conformed to Mussolini's cynical propaganda that the democratic process was a device for deceiving voters and exploiting

Oscillations in the presidential vote, 1916-1928

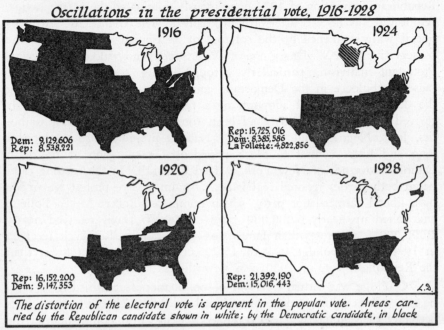

1916

1924

Dem: 9,129,606
Rep: 8,538,221

Rep: 15,725,016
Dem: 8,385,586
La Follette: 4,822,856

1920

1928

Rep: 16,152,200
Dem: 9,147,353

Rep: 21,392,190
Dem: 15,016,443

The distortion of the electoral vote is apparent in the popular vote. Areas carried by the Republican candidate shown in white; by the Democratic candidate, in black

Note: In 1924 LaFollette won Wisconsin.

a country for the corrupt profit of greedy business classes. The Department of Justice was smirched when Harding's Attorney General, Harry M. Daugherty, was connected with frauds in the office of the Alien Property Custodian. A "hung" jury enabled the Attorney General to escape imprisonment, but the Alien Property Custodian was given a jail sentence. Likewise, for dishonest use of government funds, Charles R. Forbes, Director of the Veterans Bureau, received a federal sentence. Harding died before the country learned the full story of corruption in the notorious Teapot Dome oil scandals. Nationally known businessmen bribed Secretary of Interior Albert B. Fall to make fraudulent leases of government oil reserves. Harding and Secretary of the Navy Edwin Denby approved the leases. The oil executive Edward L. Doheny advanced Fall a "loan" of $100,000; from Harry F. Sinclair he accepted a gratuity of $260,000 in Liberty bonds. Fall received a year in jail for accepting bribes, but the oil executives escaped conviction. The Secretary of the Navy was forced to resign. A congressional investigation revealed that Sinclair's Liberty bonds came from profits mulcted from stockholders by oil executives.

The death of Harding in August, 1923, and the inauguration of the mild, quiet Vermonter, "Cal" Coolidge, stilled whatever doubts the Republican voters and the conservative press entertained. Gratefully the

Republican convention of 1924 unanimously nominated the party's savior, "Saint Cal" as he was afterward nicknamed. The Democratic party, its liberal wing weakened by the collapse of Wilsonianism, nominated the conservative John W. Davis, one of Wall Street's most successful lawyers. Protestant nativism, particularly strong among southern politicians, caused turbulence in the Democratic convention. Sharp division among the delegates prevented adoption of a resolution condemning a newly revived Ku Klux Klan that had been fomenting hatred against Catholics, Jews, Negroes, and foreigners. Nativist prejudice also produced a long and bitter contest to block presidential nomination of the Irish Catholic Governor of New York, Alfred E. Smith. In the ensuing campaign both parties ignored real issues. An impressive protest was made by a liberal farmer-labor party, which nominated Robert M. La Follette and rolled up nearly 5,000,000 votes. John W. Davis received nearly 1,000,000 fewer votes than James Cox and Franklin Roosevelt received in 1920. The Coolidge total of 15,725,000, also somewhat lower than the Republican vote of 1920, was nevertheless a landslide.

Coolidge was virtually certain of nomination for a third term until he issued his cryptic announcement that he did not "choose to run." His Secretary of Commerce, Herbert Hoover, easily won nomination in the 1928 Republican convention, while Governor Smith, this time without bitter opposition, won the Democratic nomination. The evasive platforms, as in 1924, showed little difference between the dominant conservative wings of both parties. Smith, backed by prominent businessmen who financed his campaign, abandoned the Cleveland-Wilson tradition of assault on protective tariffs and differed little from Hoover except in opposing prohibition and private monopoly of power sites by utilities. Opponents of Smith brazenly made demagogic capital of Protestant prejudices against a "Catholic in the White House." Unfortunately it proved, as politicians had long contended, political suicide to nominate a Catholic. Appeals to nativist prejudice gave the Republicans a margin sufficient to capture even half of the Solid South and to win by another great landslide with 21,392,000 for Hoover. Though Smith polled 15,016,000, he carried only eight states.

A WORLD DIVIDED: DEMOCRACY AND REACTION

The decade of Republican rule bore out the Harding slogan of "back to normalcy"; but normalcy in the United States was darkened by events around a world that was something other than normal. The war victors had liberated many peoples, and the peacemakers, for the moment at least, had underwritten constitutional governments that allowed a freedom of speech, press, and economic bargaining, a freedom of political opposition by radical as well as conservative parties, unknown under previous rulers. Geographically, more people lived under representative government than ever before. But for ordinary mortals freedom from fear and from want had yet to be won; and peace appalled many a member of the world's upper classes more than war. As the armistice came, kings fled their thrones and privileged orders everywhere feared social overturn. Adopting the slogan, "From each according to his ability; to each according to his need," Russia became communist under Lenin in 1917, sending a shudder throughout all parts of the world wherever monied and clerical classes felt insecure. Russia but dramatized an older struggle in sharper terms, now accentuated everywhere by the postwar heritage of devastation, debts, impoverishment, and disease, and by the problems of dislocated markets, inflation, and business uncertainty that attended reconversion. Normalcy, Harding's slogan for control of government by practical men of the propertied class, expressed a determination common to men of the business world in all countries—a determination to resist change and suppress unrest.

Thus, though one war had been won, the peace could still be lost, for two tendencies in conflict with each other disturbed the postwar world. One was the persisting tendency toward gradual social democracy, in some countries swiftly driven by a battle for survival into a more extreme movement toward social revolution. The other tendency was the conservative reaction. After 1929 the conservative reaction took an extreme form in more and more countries, moving from mere addiction to national advantages and national security by tariffs, armies, alliances, and power politics to outright nationalist revolutions, setting up the fascist form of dictatorship.

And yet for a decade after World War I, the men who professed practical vision seemed merely to have slowed the march of democracy but not to have imperiled it. Conservative parties or coalitions, ultranationalists, ruled France until 1924; but thereafter liberal and conservative combinations alternated in the French fashion. Conservatives in England ruled most of the time from the first of the world wars to the second, and in one election stampeded the voters against Laborites by demagogic faking of a "red menace"; but the Labor party twice had its own Prime Minister before 1930. Even under conservatives, social legislation was enacted in England and France. The continuing democratic upsurge was manifest less in the United States than in older European democracies and in new republics like Germany's new Weimar Republic and Czechoslovakia. The most notable strides in social legislation were concurrently made in Austria, Switzerland, the liberal Scandi-

navian countries, and the British Dominions of New Zealand and Australia; whereas in the United States progressive social reform suddenly
ceased. Until struck down by the cataclysmic depression of 1929, Latin
Americans continued on the whole to make gains in stability, civil liberty,
and social legislation. In Mexico, Yugoslavia, Greece, Turkey, India,
China, democracy struggled for newborn life against the internal resistance of old, entrenched classes and the external pressure of imperial
interests.

But conservative resistance to change in lands of capitalism and
representative government slowed domestic progress; abroad, it endangered democracy itself. Conservative governments, cartel promoters,
and world traders were more fearful of social democracy, regulation of
business, and radicalism in other countries than of "strong men" who
rose to dictatorship. What later won ill fame as "appeasement" was
first evolved in the twenties by practical men who usually gave tolerance
and sometimes aid to dictatorial regimes engaged in overthrowing or
repressing democrats and radicals whose ideas threatened the old order
among privileged classes. For the communist revolution in Russia made
conservatives more extreme in resistance to change and sharpened social
tensions around the world—in Italy, England, and all Europe; in China,
Mexico, and the United States. All over the world those who were fearful for capitalism and property rights sought to bolster ecclesiastical
structures and the social order against agrarian and labor unrest. Accordingly, the conservative dilution of democracy in progressive countries expressed itself externally in refusal to intervene or employ international remedies against outright reaction and suppression in the more
backward countries. In Italy—Fascist after Mussolini's march on Rome
in 1922—and in Spain, Portugal, and the Balkans, tottering European
monarchies, supported by entrenched clerical, business, and landlord
classes strengthened by control of arms, police, and the military, frustrated the upswell of agrarian and labor democracy. Small Baltic countries taken from Russia lapsed from republics into dictatorships in 1934.
Poland had lapsed as early as 1926, and Hungary almost immediately
after the armistice fell under a dictator who served later as a willing
Nazi ally. Yugoslavia succumbed in 1929 under a dictator-king; Portugal,
in 1932; Germany, in 1933; Austria, in 1934; Greece, in 1935. Yet
practical men clung to the convictions of nationalism and conservatism;
the maintenance of representative government was a local question, not
an international one.

NATIONALISM AND NORMALCY

Normalcy exhibited in America as in Europe the tendency among conservators of the established order to make more extreme resistance to new democratic challenges. The United States after 1917 preserved its democratic forms but lost something of its democratic spirit. The American reaction drew strength from the powerful force of integral nationalism. As in Europe, immoderate emotional patriotism manifested itself in a suppressive tendency ill according with democracy. Propaganda wooed the naïve and the cynical to extremist notions of rooting out ideas and activities that reactionaries and nationalists chose to stigmatize as "un-American." Frequently linked with suppression were aristocratic suppositions of a superior class, often unacknowledged but implicit in defenses of a return to the past. Normalcy spelled revival of the privileged system of rule by the few as stewards for the many. Neither American democracy nor democracy elsewhere had ever been free from bigots addicted to gross ideas of inferior and superior; nor free of organized propaganda by nativists and ultraconservatives who sought to give respectability to discriminations against members of a creed or nationality and people from a lowly walk of life. War psychology had given strategic opportunity to purveyors of assorted prejudices against immigrants, labor groups, Negroes, Catholics, Jews, reformers, and radicals. In the disguised struggle to defeat internationalism and progressivism, as war ended, these old prejudices were capable under shrewd manipulation of diverting patriotism into something other than a crusade to make the world safe for democracy.

Suppressive and class tendencies were sanctified by shrewd proponents in the name of "100 per cent Americanism," much as in Germany, where Hitler's infant party, organized in 1920, sought to sanctify reaction in the name of German nationalism. For there was more than met the eye in the proliferation of integral nationalism. An interchurch organization, investigating the nation-wide steel strike of 1919, chanced upon secret company instructions: "Stir up as much bad feeling as you possibly can between the Serbians and Italians." The Serbs and Italians, imported by United States Steel years before as cheap unorganized labor to break unions, had rebelled at last against feudal regimentation, a twelve-hour day, and even a seven-day working week. Raise "every question you can," ran the company instructions, to incite "racial hatred between these two nationalities." The Serbs were to be told that the Italians would get their jobs. Judge Elbert Gary, ruler of the United States Steel Corporation, spoke in another vein to the public: If unionism triumphed, the result would be a communist division of property. Thus unthinking patriots and their manipulators condoned violation of ordinary civil liberty, won support in editorials for ruthless tactics in suppressing the great strikes of 1919, aided the breaking of unions in a

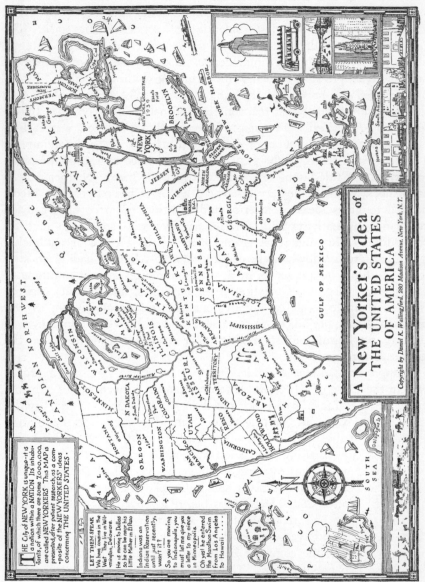

A New Yorker's Idea of THE UNITED STATES OF AMERICA

Copyright by Daniel K. Wallingford, 280 Madison Avenue, New York, N.Y.

THE City of NEW YORK is unique—it is a nation within a NATION. Its inhabitants, of which there are some 7,000,000, are called NEW YORKERS. This MAP is presented, after patient research, as a composite of the NEW YORKERS' ideas concerning THE UNITED STATES.

LET THEM SPEAK
We have cousins in the West. They live in Wilmington, Delaware.

He is moving to Dallas. So he can meet his little Mother in Elkins

Indiana was an Indian Reservation until just recently, wasn't it?

So you are moving to Indianapolis, you must let me give you a letter to my niece in Minneapolis.

Oh yes! he entered the Marathon Swim from Los Angeles to Hawaii.

powerful revival of the open-shop drive, and made gullible converts to "red hunting," deportation of aliens, "racism," and barriers to immigration.

In part, the obscurantist spirit of integral nationalism reflected a rural and urban anti-intellectual reaction. The fiery cross of the Ku Klux Klan, which revived in 1915 and suddenly spread in 1920, summoned nightshirted nobles to anti-Catholic, anti-Semitic, anti-Negro, and anti-birth-control crusades in the North and West as well as the South, winning adherents in the city as well as in the country. Active throughout the early 1920's, the Klan leaders, mystical worshipers of a superior national breed, spoke approvingly of America's rejection of the League and the World Court. In a sleepy, poverty-ridden town in rural Tennessee a schoolteacher won sudden fame in the Scopes case of 1926 by defying an unscientific state law that prohibited the scientific teaching of evolution. In the dry years of Prohibition, zealous organizations, disregarding nineteenth-century ideals of temperance and individual responsibility, returned to the medieval idea of sumptuary legislation governing private conduct by the fiat of law. By the compulsions of the Eighteenth Amendment and the Volstead Act outlawing the sale of "hard likker," they sought to mold a nation in an evangelical pattern of superior national purity.

Similarly, the attack on birth control exhibited racial and class prejudices associated with the spirit of integral nationalism. Rural moralists and ecclesiastical stewards of national purity invoked censorship to impede biological enlightenment and sought legislation against birth control clinics. Such roundsmen of the Lord were re-enforced by one hundred per cent patriots who, echoing Theodore Roosevelt's earlier cries for big families, shuddered at the Asiatic "yellow peril," urged the nation to repent of its declining population rate, and enlisted the compulsion of state laws to prevent family self-government from lowering the multiplication rate of the American "race." Older native stocks, self-blighted by overenthusiastic birth control, sought to preserve their dominance by shutting off the influx of big-familied immigrants. Meanwhile well-bred persons, fearful of the rise of the masses, gullible upon the subject of the depravity of the mass mind, and ignorant of rapidly advancing discoveries concerning heredity in the great science of genetics, drew unscientific but comforting aristocratic conclusions about class differences from the new findings of intelligence testers, and became converts to the eugenics movement. Eugenists solemnly urged a high rate of breeding for genteel classes, but advocated birth control for working-class "morons." Extremists quite unscientifically advocated compulsory sterilization of the "gaping primates" at the lower end of the intelligence scale.

But the obscurantist spirit of integral nationalism more distinctly revealed the urban-industrial struggle for power. Certainly not all employers, company officials, and corporation lawyers, but an ominous segment of the business community—favoring company towns, execrating unions, and habituated to the use of armed guards, tear gas, professional strikebreakers, and labor spies—had a strong-arm idea of democracy, equating it with rule by the powerful through coercions of law or direct intimidation. Reactionaries in urban centers were the more dangerous because persuasive among the more literate and dynamic social classes. To urban proponents of normalcy, intellectual freedom was not a sacred cow like freedom of enterprise. In a world which had seen the rise of red Bolshevism in Russia, many a businessman was fearful of criticism of the existing order and far from anxious that American children be broadly trained in a world view of social theories and historic trends. It was not in rural Tennessee but in metropolitan New York that a business-minded Lusk Committee won the front page at the close of the war. This committee investigated teachers and schools, employing suppressive legislative enactments and a conservative press to intimidate educators whose teaching sought to cultivate daring and independent minds. Moreover, the business community in many states defended distortion of criminal syndicalist laws into antilabor weapons, urged government deportation of "agitators," and defended the world-famous execution in 1927 of the Massachusetts anarchists Sacco and Vanzetti on flimsy circumstantial evidence. The "red smear" evolved into a recognized technique for disrupting unions, inflaming local community prejudices, breaking strikes, and jailing labor leaders.

Mechanical checks and balances of the Constitution afforded little protection against the reaction. Political leadership in all three branches made no serious attempt to counteract illiberal manifestations. The main policies of the postwar era were laid down by Congress. The transfer of power from liberal forces under presidential leadership to the forces of nationalism and normalcy under the leadership of shifting congressional combinations allowed the primary issues in home affairs and international relations to be seen but dimly. Congressional debate proved, as Wilson had observed in his book of 1885, a dubious medium for public enlightenment.

Congress, responding to the spirit of integral nationalism, made a basic decision on immigration policy. The immigrant tide, long a factor in expanding the American home market and in redistributing the world's population in terms of better utilization of developed resources, was temporarily dammed up in 1921 by congressional action. This emergency enactment limited the flow of immigrants to 3 per cent of the total of each nationality represented in the United States as estimated in the census of 1910. President Coolidge urged higher immigration walls, declaring "America must be kept American." Making the policy permanent in the Johnson Act of 1924, Congress limited immigration to still smaller national quotas and discriminated against the predominantly Catholic immigration from southern and eastern Europe. As first applied, the new "national origins" quotas discriminated against Slavs, Greeks, Jews, and Latins. Under the Johnson Act, a bustling and intrepid nation of about 120,000,000 put Americanism on an invalid's diet, cutting immigration mastication from a yearly average of 1,000,000 or more down to a nibble of 150,000. Spokesmen in Congress and in the press little supposed that economists would later conclude that the United States had established another barrier both to world economy and to American prosperity.

Again retreating from broader international perspectives, Congress rejected expert advice on the wisdom of cancellation of war debts. In an act of 1922 the lawmakers insisted on bonding the debt at an interest rate which, in conjunction with America's new creditor position and congressional return to the old protectionist tariff, made repayment of interest and principal an economic impossibility. Since such political leadership popularized the mercantile idea of taking European gold but not European goods, international commissions under the Dawes plan and subsequent agreements were unable to cancel the debts or scale them down to workable levels. Nationalistic astigmatism obscured the rudimentary economic law that a creditor must accept more imports. Welcoming the pressure groups of powerful special interests, Congress instead passed the Fordney-McCumber tariff in 1922, setting European nations a discouraging example in economic nationalism. Congress further strengthened the tendency in 1930 when under Hoover the Hawley-Smoot tariff reached the high point of high tariffs in American history.[1] Against such impediments it was difficult for European nations to repay the debts in normal course by exporting goods to American markets in order to obtain American dollars.

Meanwhile, economic nationalism caught the American farmer in a double squeeze. As a consumer he was caught by American tariffs protecting monopolistic prices in the American market; as a producer he was caught by European tariffs blocking the ready outlet of the huge American agricultural surplus that sought to enter the great European markets. Not even the golden glow of zooming stocks in boom years

---

[1] For Hoover and the tariff see Chapter XXIX.

could conceal the disparity between industrial profits and declining agricultural income. The American Farm Bureau Federation—powerful new national pressure group of big commercial farmers, state and county farm officials, and business-minded local bankers and politicians—pressed strenuously for farm relief. Angered by economic nationalism in Europe that curtailed marketing of American farm products, but supporting economic nationalism by and for the United States, these forces exerted pressure through the farm bloc in Congress toward a revival of mercantilist commercial warfare. In the name of farm relief, Republican and Democratic nationalists broke party lines and twice passed the McNary-Haugen bills. · Essentially old-style mercantilism reminiscent of the English rebate and bounty devices that precipitated the Boston Tea Party, the bills were to require the government to dump American farm products on world markets, undersell Canadians, Argentineans, and other competitors, but assure American farmers a good price in the home market by indirect government subsidy. The Fordney-McCumber tariff and the McNary-Haugen bills were to fortify each other. Farmers were to support a high tariff because it would prevent reimportation of the cheap American produce dumped abroad. Presidents Coolidge and Hoover successively vetoed or blocked such farm relief—not so much because the congressional enactments would accentuate economic nationalism around the world, but because industrial proponents of normalcy required the government to stay out of business and lower taxes. Fixing of prices lay within the domain of free enterprisers and not of politicians.

Against nationalism and normalcy congressional liberals were unable to muster effective resistance. The insurgent Republican bloc was small and seldom in position to exploit a balance of power between the two parties. The Democrats, as a party, did not constitute what was known in English politics as "the Opposition." Democrats nearly won control in the elections of 1922, but party unity had been broken since 1916. Southern conservatives, traditionally fearful of centralization of national power, welcomed Republican defense of state rights and tended to acquiesce in the Harding-Coolidge-Hoover formula of "less government in business and more business in government." Democratic Senate leaders like Henry F. Ashurst (Arizona) and Atlee Pomerene (Ohio) applauded the call for normalcy in Harding's inaugural address. With the executive and judicial branches in safe hands, congressional strategists did not invite public anger by outright repeal of the Clayton Act and all Wilsonian vestiges. Business-minded appointees to the Federal Trade Commission and the federal courts exemplified the strategy of neutralizing government regulation by putting it in the hands of friends. To the business world the Federal Trade Commission ceased to be a dread ogre; instead, Senators Norris and Borah began to demand its abolition. Nonenforcement of surviving Wilsonian legislation became one of the real but neglected major issues.

The legislative branch supported the administration policy of non-enforcement of antitrust laws and the tactics of the judiciary, which extracted the teeth of the labor protections in the Clayton Act. Complacent legislators sanctioned perversion of labor's "charter of liberties" by refusal to strengthen the act. Even after such flagrant distortions as the blanket injunction of 1922, obtained from the federal judiciary by the corrupt Attorney General Daugherty, there was no congressional action. Because of wage reductions, 400,000 railroad shopmen were on strike. The court injunction, most sweeping in history, inverted the Clayton Act's provision against use of injunctions to break strikes: it forbade strike meetings, picketing, use of union funds, and even went so far as to enjoin union officials from using telephones or the telegraph for communicating with each other in conducting the strike. The National Association of Manufacturers, marshaling the postwar open-shop drive, hailed the injunction as putting an end to the "labor menace"; but Attorney General Daugherty justified it under the old patriotic rubric that the United States mails must go through. The Department of Justice, aided by the judiciary and unopposed by the legislative branch, suppressed the strike. To conservative Democrats and Republicans, the nation-wide open-shop drive backed by governmental might appeared less "un-American" than the Wilson policies of supporting collective bargaining through the War Labor Board. Just prior to the depression in 1929 only one out of every twelve of those gainfully employed was a union member. Neither the incumbent administrations nor their congressional majorities saw a disturbing sign of suppressive tendencies in the shrinkage of union membership from the 1920 figure of over five million to about half that total by 1932.

Despite congressional jealousy of strong executive leadership, Republican administrators contributed to the formulation of legislative policy. Andrew W. Mellon led the drive for fiscal policies favoring special interests. Multimillionaire financier from Pittsburgh's "golden triangle," Mellon was appointed Secretary of the Treasury in 1921 and served under Harding, Coolidge, and Hoover. Congress endorsed part of Mellon's theory in 1922, repealing Wilsonian taxes on excess profits. Democrats and insurgent Republicans, however, for several years staved off complete congressional acquiescence to the Wall Street theory of "incentive" taxes, which called for reductions on corporation taxes and on surtaxes hitting big incomes. Such reductions, it was argued, would enlarge the pool of big capital and stimulate investment. This repudiation of the social principle of taxation scaled in accordance with capacity to pay was advocated on the "trickle down" theory: lower taxes on the rich would produce prosperity for all. On this theory Congress gradually cut the surtax on big incomes until it was 12 per cent lower than the slash Mellon originally had proposed. At the same time, Congress cut the rate on corporation incomes. Meanwhile insurgent Republicans and Democrats failed to muster enough votes to plug loopholes in the tax laws that made tax evasion a notorious practice. Mellon stiffened the nationalist position of Congress on war debts by his agreeable theory that payments by the Allies afforded a "sound" basis for reversal of Wilsonian fiscal policy, at one stroke enabling reduction of American taxes and reduction of the national debt. Ironically, the policy of Mellon and Congress, by reducing potential government income in years of prosperity, prevented reduction of more than one third of the national debt, which had shot up to $24,000,000,000 as a result of war. The Hoover administration caught by the depression of 1929, fell heir to the dilemma of a deficit in tax revenues, mounting charges for interest on the national debt, and cessation of income from war debts.

Other administrative architects of the politics of special interests were Herbert Hoover as Secretary of Commerce under Harding and Coolidge, Attorney General Daugherty, and Coolidge's Attorney General J. G. Sargent. Daugherty and Sargent relaxed antitrust prosecution. Hoover led a drive for "self-government by industry." Dollar-a-year men on wartime boards had encouraged the formation of business associations to organize wartime production and control prices. The natural tendency of such associations was not only to increase the disparity between large and small business but to cripple business as a whole by baneful growth of what economists defined as "monopoly rigidities." Secretary Hoover frankly utilized the Department of Commerce to organize trade associations, fostering countless conferences of businessmen in various industrial fields. Though even the diluted Federal Trade Commission protested against the resultant stimulus of price fixing and the elimination of competition, the Department of Commerce continued the erection of a gigantic phalanx of industrial associations. Under the "self-government" formula, they regulated competition among themselves through their own codes of acceptable practices. Although Hoover declared he did not believe in monopoly, he desired amendment of the Sherman Act to sanction the program of self-government by industry. It was cosmic irony that in 1933 the Roosevelt administration temporarily adopted the Hoover policy in the NRA.

Under the smiling sun of normalcy, pyramids of supertrusts lifted their corporate heads beyond the old-time "blue-sky limits." The country scarcely noticed the repeal in New Jersey of the last of Governor Woodrow Wilson's famous Seven Sisters—blue-sky laws to prevent laxity in chartering the giants of industry and finance. Political machines, having sloughed off reformers for the nonce, fattened on revenue from charter-mongering; New Jersey was herself again, mother of corporations. The new trust-building movement reduced the over-all number of American power companies through mergers and the holding device. Mail-order houses like Montgomery Ward and grocery and other retail amalgamations spanned the country with chain stores. Financial syndicates tied together the food processors of various national brands in mammoth holding companies. Banks and newspapers diminished in total numbers as independents went to the wall or were taken in by great corporations. The Scripps-Howard, Gannett, and McCormick interests joined Hearst in a spreading control over urban newspaper chains and syndicated news features. Two corporations began to consolidate huge national networks in the new field of radio. The antitrust faith, as an over-all formula to deal with big business, finally died in the chambers of the Supreme Court in the 1920's, after an unequal contest with conservative forces in the committee rooms of Congress and behind polished desks in the departments of Commerce and Justice. And men of practical vision cashed in: stock prices soared on the wings of Wall Street speculation and watered stocks, for the moment at least, spouted fortunes.

The judicial branch of the government supplemented the policies of Mellon, Daugherty, and Hoover. The decision in the United States Steel case (1920), applying the judicial "rule of reason," denied the government's charge of monopoly price fixing and refused to bust the trust. Every economist in the country knew that under the basing-point system, generally called the "Pittsburgh plus," the Morgan properties established price understandings that the handful of other steel corporations dared not disregard. Basing points for rates had once been exploited by southern railroads as an internal system of protective tariffs. Steelmakers evolved their own basing point to maintain uniform non-competitive prices, regardless of differences in transportation costs of steel shipments from rival firms whether ordered from Pittsburgh or the Great Lakes belt. Defended by steelmen as "equalizing opportunity," the Pittsburgh plus was a private internal tariff system to stabilize monopoly prices under the parasitic formula of "keeping everybody in business." Steel prices remained rigid for years, and steel companies became the favorite examples of economists who wished to illustrate inefficient but profitable operation of plants at an excessively low percentage of total productive capacity. The Federal Trade Commission in 1924 condemned the Pittsburgh plus. Without bothering to seek aid from the Supreme Court, the Steel Trust simply adopted a new multiple basing-point system.

The Supreme Court in the twenties nullified Wilsonian antitrust provisions. By 1926, judicial decisions had made meaningless the Clayton Act's prohibitions of consolidation of competitors through inter-corporate stockholding. By 1934, the future Chief Justice, Harlan Stone, was protesting in a strong dissent that "however gross the violation of the Clayton Act" or "however flagrant the flouting" of the Federal Trade Commission, Court sanction of the loophole of mergers "leaves the Commission powerless to act." But the lenient majority of the Court, judicially echoing the prevailing attitudes in Congress and the administration, encouraged the new trust movement and led ranking economists like William Z. Ripley of Harvard and Frank Fetter of Princeton to excoriate governmental laxity. Ripley's famous *Main Street and Wall Street* (1927) revived the theme of Brandeis' earlier and equally famous *Other People's Money*. Ripley revealed anew the failure to democratize the management of capital, exposing the technique for inside control by small oligarchies of a few stockholders. Fetter, in *The Masquerade of Monopoly* (1931), scrutinized with care the quick-change artistry by which trusts paraded before the Supreme Court without being recognized.

Nostalgic for normalcy, the justices took an illiberal view of economic democracy and even civil liberties. The repressive decisions of the preceding period opposing collective bargaining continued with unabated force after 1920; Court approval of yellow-dog contracts and labor injunctions whittled away the provisions of the Clayton Act. The Supreme Court in fact reversed the law's intention of limiting the scope of labor injunctions and making them difficult to obtain; and employers under new precedents had even easier access to court orders with sweeping restrictions on picketing, boycotts, and normal strike tactics. On civil liberties the Court agreed with the Congress which, enacting the Sedition Act in the war hysteria of 1918, carried the country back to the authoritarian spirit of the first Alien and Sedition acts. A famous woman pacifist was solemnly denied citizenship because she refused to take oath that she would bear arms in defense of the United States!

Conservatism on civil liberties and social legislation was not unchallenged. In *Freedom of Speech* (1920), Zechariah Chafee of the Harvard Law School compiled the first of his celebrated and powerful criticisms of suppressive tendencies. The public at large took particular offense at the child labor decisions of 1918 and 1922, which ruled out two successive acts of Congress to abolish child labor. The public was even more disturbed by the decision in the Minimum Wage case (1923). Justice Sutherland, a lameduck Republican senator appointed by Harding, wrote the majority opinion. The decision was a classic example of narrowing the concept of common welfare by reading into the Constitution the higher law of laissez faire. Sutherland's language betrayed the animus of a congressional wheel horse against administrative agencies. A minimum living standard he described as a wage question to be settled by the individual wage earner, "not by a general formula prescribed by a statutory bureau." Workers, the Court admitted, had an "ethical right" to a living wage, but not a constitutional right. The "fallacy" of the law was the notion that an employer was "bound" to furnish a minimum living standard. Ignoring the fact that the justices were split 5–4, the Court set aside the act of Congress with the bombastic assertion that unconstitutionality was "no longer open to question." Justice Holmes, dissenting, remarked that conservatives had read the "dogma, Liberty of Contract," into the "vague contours" of the due process clause; yet freedom of contract was not even mentioned in the Constitution, which, after all, was the real "text" the Court was presumed to construe.

THE APPEAL OF INTERNATIONALISM

Although in their cavalier view of democracy's problem the three branches of the government suffered from myopia, Presidents and the State Department made concessions to public demands for international cooperation. Charles Evans Hughes, Secretary of State under Harding, was stigmatized as an imperialist because of his efforts to force the Mexican government to abrogate reform policies that struck at the exploitation of Mexico by American corporations. Hughes, though as conservative as Taft in domestic and imperial affairs, in 1921 called the Washington Conference on armaments and Far Eastern disputes. As a result, Japan backed out of Shantung and by the Four-Power Treaty (1921) joined Great Britain, France, and the United States in pledging nonaggression in the Orient and settlement of disputes by international arbitration. By the Nine-Power Treaty (1922) the United States, Japan, and other nations agreed to preserve the independence and territorial integrity of China and renewed the open-door pledges. President Harding assured the country that "nothing in any of these treaties" committed the United States to any kind of "alliance" or "entanglement." The Washington Conference did nothing to limit competitive armaments in regard to land and air forces, but the great naval powers established limitations on capital ships. Treaty agreements scaled down the naval strength of the United States, England, Japan, France, and Italy, respectively, according to the ratio of 5–5–3–1.7–1.7.

The principle of cooperation to decrease competitive armaments was significant, but nationalist motives were of equal import. It had become the national policy to make the United States a sea power second to none, ensuring parity with Great Britain and superiority over Japan. Naval preponderance was coupled with continuing rejection of any program of world security enforced by an organized, permanent international authority. Dominance on the sea went hand in hand with a balance of power concept of individual national security, but the security obtained proved a miscalculation; the Washington Conference, unaccompanied by organized world cooperation, amounted to the greatest sea victory of the Axis. At later disarmament conferences in 1927 and 1930 the United States continued its effort to shrink naval expenditures, an effort that was self-defeating without a parallel attack on the virus of sovereignty. The failure of the whole program in 1936 dissipated the illusion of achieving disarmament without combining it with effective international power to correct general world maladjustments.

Toward the end of the 1920's the United States followed Europe in asserting the moral principle of international responsibility for elimination of war. At the Locarno Conference of 1925 leading European nations signed nonaggression pacts in which they accepted existing boundaries and agreed never to go to war with one another. In 1928 Coolidge's Secretary of State, Frank B. Kellogg, stirred tremendous popular enthusiasm by shepherding the United States into the movement to outlaw war. Under the Kellogg-Briand Pact, sixty-two nations promised to "renounce war as an instrument of national policy," but no provision was made for effective international enforcement. Senator Borah described the pact as "an international kiss." Reservations in the report of the Senate committee stated that the treaty did not interfere with the Monroe Doctrine or impair the sovereign power of the United States to see to its own security. Thus reassured, Senate nationalists ratified the pact. But no Congress, despite successive pleas by Harding, Coolidge, and Hoover, was willing to commit itself to American participation in the World Court. Nor did Hughes' successors as Secretary of State abandon efforts to force upon Mexico an immunity for American oil and mining companies from Mexican laws that sought the development of natural resources as a national heritage of the Mexican people.

The superficiality of American approaches to the great problems of world economy and international government was to be apparent by the end of the decade, when world order collapsed. The wavering course of American foreign policy in the twenties reflected both the weakness and the strength of world aspirations. Continuance of imperialism and boycott of the League of Nations, in contrast with disarmament conferences and the Kellogg-Briand Pact, were indicative of internal contradictions and absence of a central party leadership with power to speak for genuine party principles. In the Republican era, as later, the administration was generally more internationalist than Congress. But the reassertion of congressional power destroyed the possibility of any effective international cooperation under executive leadership. Nationalistic dominance in Congress sprang from the fluctuating alliance of Republican insurgents, who were isolationist, with the conservative nationalists of both parties. Despite the trend in Congress, public pressure for international cooperation remained potent. Millions of thoughtful citizens made a serious study of world affairs. The activities of the newly organized Foreign Policy Association, the League of Women Voters, and countless college and church groups and peace societies reflected sober recognition that the United States lagged in striving toward a civilized world.

In America as elsewhere the hopeful drew comfort from the new star rising above the horizon; internationalism moved toward the ascendant. While the United States, now nicknamed Uncle Shylock, remained something of a pariah among the nations, fifty-six countries were League members by 1926. Hostile to the Monroe Doctrine and disillusioned by violation of the Pan-American ideals of reciprocal friendship, virtually every Latin-American nation joined the League. Canada likewise joined. North and south of the boundaries of the United States, the other Americans concluded that twentieth-century conditions refuted the hundred-year-old implication of the Monroe Doctrine: that the American hemisphere had its own ideals and interests and that they had little or remote connection with the ideals and affairs of Europe and other continents. After Italy's success in blackmailing the League by temporary occupation of the Greek Isle of Corfu in 1923, even the aggressive nationalism of Mussolini was tempered by the exigency of international cooperation. After 1924 the spirit of Locarno began to give life and meaning to international consultations in the fine new buildings at Geneva. Until the world's economic crash at the end of the decade, one of the great aspirations of mankind seemed at long last to be moving toward fulfillment. But the United States was not in the van; stout statesmen of practical vision, incapable of foreseeing the economic catastrophe ahead of them, still swore allegiance to the industrial arcanum, the nostrums of normalcy.

XXIX

THE ROOSEVELT REVOLUTION

1929–1934

In the years following the armistice, the world sowed the dragon's teeth, and the harvest came when a host of armed men sprang from the earth. In the fateful decade, 1919 to 1929, the United States in common with, but more completely than, other countries turned its back on the responsibilities of a sound world order; and in the next and not less fateful decade nemesis overtook all the strong countries together with the small. For a peace had been lost, and security frittered away, and prosperity with it. In the perilous decade, 1929 to 1939, the world drifted down into the clutch of a violent economic maelstrom, to be dragged under into the vortex of war.

THE NEW ERA

To isolated America of the gilded twenties so stark a destiny was inconceivable, as inconceivable as a revival of witchcraft, as unimaginable as conquest of the world by avid fascists. People who moved decorously in the promenade of patriotism, people who shared in the lush proceeds of prosperity, glibly assumed that progressivism was a dangerous disturber of the public safety; internationalism, an impractical sentimentality. Men of affairs, hardheaded and efficient, had eliminated the weaknesses of capitalism, and the American way would conquer the world.

A rigid dogma of the sanctity of property and an ungenerous mood of immediate self-interest narrowed the horizon of isolated America. The failure of foresight was produced by parsimony of spirit and class pretension, for a conservative pattern of mind isolated the eminent from the plain people within the nation and from struggling humanity in the world at large.

"Stabilize America first, prosper America first, think of America first, exalt America first"; such was approved Harding doctrine. Practical government was epitomized by Calvin Coolidge in terse statement: "The business of America is business." There were forward-looking men in industry and the professions who were concerned for a world more meaningful than a blind competition of human bipeds resembling the brute struggle of quadrupeds for survival. But in towering office buildings and behind imposing desks the conservative mind was moved by the process of natural selection toward aristocratic suppositions of survival of the fittest. To men of practical outlook it was axiomatic that a free hand for the United States was a sound policy for a country so rich and self-sustaining, no matter how idealists might descant on moral and material interdependence in the modern world. It was axiomatic that moral and material advantages accruing to the moneyed class were diffused to the rest of the people, no matter what reformers or agitators might say about predatory business and inequality. And in the spacious twenties it also began to be an axiom that the directive genius of industrialists and financiers, given full scope under the sound policy of more business in government and less government in business, assured so much business confidence and so much prosperity that it augured a New Era, a permanent boom, no matter what crackpots might spout about limitations of capitalism.

Oracles of the New Era were heard with respect; and never was the prestige of industrialists higher. There were protests—against the

DISTRIBUTION OF OCCUPATIONAL INCOMES, 1929

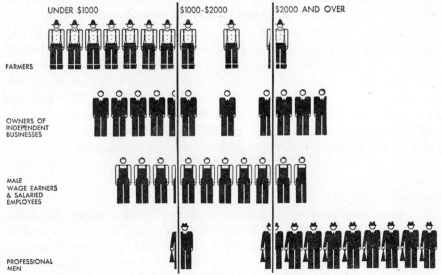

Each symbol represents 10 percent of total in specified occupational group

NOTE: Groups are composed mostly of men

PICTORIAL STATISTICS, INC

PICTOGRAPH CORP. for *Your Income and Mine*, published by Public Affairs Committee, Inc.

supposition that the good things of life were widely diffused, against the arrogance of class, against repression, against a more rigid status for the many in a position of permanent inferiority; and protests by experts against an unsound organization of business and an unsound direction of major public policies. But to outward appearances the formulations of nationalism and normalcy were not impractical or unrewarding; and the prestige of business statesmanship rose as prices on the ticker tape of the stock market rose. For in the middle of the twenties commenced the Coolidge boom—the wildest the country had yet had. American business seemed suddenly to move upward upon a high plateau whence men could look down pityingly upon struggling humanity in a less orderly outside world, the poverty and distractions of which surged and buffeted about the base of the American plateau but could not reach the high elevations where Americans lived and worked.

League of Nations figures in 1927, with crisp and monotonous repetition, listed American output in basic products as "First in the world": first in wheat, first in tobacco, first in copper, first in aluminum, first in artificial silk; and first with 75 per cent of the total world supply of corn. America produced more than half the world's cotton, 44 per cent of the total coal output, 52 per cent of the steel, 48 per cent of the pig iron and alloys, 60 per cent of the copper smelter output, and 70 per cent of the petroleum. Outmoded protective tariffs and political isolation, however much they inhibited optimum economic welfare, did not subtract from the magnitude of American resources. America was first.

But if America was first, events proved again as in previous decades that prosperity in one country could not be fenced in; neither could it be stored up against the disruption of a global economic world. Curiously, economic disruption struck first and remained most critical in the richest country, isolated America. For the world depression of 1931 followed the American crash of 1929. Wild and unstable fluctuations appeared in the very country where men of affairs were most confident, most certain of the soundness of policy and the stability of business.

BOOM AND BUST

From the dream of permanent prosperity in one country, Americans awoke in the winter of 1930 to find themselves in the coils of a mysterious benumbing force. It was the business cycle, the economists said. But as a world slowed down to a full economic stop with heaped up surpluses of goods, idle machines, and impersonal frozen assets, human rebellion welled up against senseless economic slackening when food was urgent and jobs were necessary for life. The falling off of work and income, the capacity to produce but inability to buy, the intensification of insecurity, the intolerable strain of the business cycle, posed a question of survival. Could democracy itself survive within the old framework of concentrated and privately controlled economic enterprise? Against the challenge of insecurity and the goad of exploitation, Russia in 1917 had already made one answer. After 1923, Italian Fascists averred they had the true answer; and after 1933, Hitler's National Socialists, trampling on the prostrate German Republic and erecting a fascist state-capitalism into the greatest engine of tyranny the Western World had ever seen, proclaimed theirs the answer revealed to a little Austrian corporal. By 1932 men who were not foolish somberly perceived combustible elements for social crisis gathering in the United States. Competent observers in the next two years hazarded the belief that the "Roosevelt revolution" headed off a drift toward an American fascism.

To men trained in the workings of the economy, the instabilities and rigidities that blasted the dream of prosperity in one country were neither astounding nor mysterious. Noted economists like Wesley C. Mitchell had pioneered in the study of the erratic character of capitalism and the prodigious problem of the business cycle. America's golden twenties had been neither very golden nor very stable. Nor in any fundamental sense had the architects of isolated America been successful: at no time had the country evaded economic interdependence and the impact of political conditions abroad. World fluctuations were also American fluctuations. World War I immensely stimulated American business activity. As war ended, business contraction began. A small boom accompanied the Peace Conference, then petered out as the Senate chose the path of isolation. Following a crash in Japan, depression began in 1920 and became severe in 1921. Fifteen per cent of American workers, over four million, were unemployed. Recovery came in 1922, but increasing business activity did not prevent continued fluctuations. After a slump of over a year dating from 1923, business picked up for three tantalizing years, became sluggish in the fall of 1926, boomed again in 1928, only to become spotty by February, 1929.

Although national income increased, the proportion going to big investors also increased and played a part in stimulating the great bull market on Wall Street, which roared into high speed in 1927 and plunged the country into the most extraordinary and dangerous speculation in history. The velocity of stock exchange transactions until September 3, 1929, continued to break new records as a prelude to the breaking of lives. Symptoms of unstable conditions were disregarded by the business community and the investing public. The great boom in home building came to an end in 1928, steel and oil activity lagged, and the cycle in automobile production passed its peak. Agriculture, to the detriment not only of farmers but of industries producing machinery and farm equipment, had been languishing for eight years. However, business confidence reigned, Republican tax policies had released additional money for investment, and individuals and corporations poured capital into towering pyramids of inflated stocks. A typical index of common stock prices showed a rise from an average of 99 in 1922 to the fantastic level of 469 at the height of the inflation. Fortunes came easily—if the fortune makers got out in time. Attracted by the bull market at home, American capital flowed less extensively abroad, where it was needed for support of the tottering structure of international finance. Meanwhile, American tariff and war debt policy, coupled with foreign investment, drained gold from European debtors and undermined the financial foundations of foreign nations. In September, 1929, with English uncertainty accentuated by a recent failure, the Bank of England raised its discount rate. American stock prices wavered, and business activity continued to decline. Then on October 24 the great crash began.

Financial instability and panic, centering first in the United States, spread outward in the next two years and dragged the world down into global depression. On Wall Street, thousands of paper fortunes vanished as margin accounts were closed out. Retrenchment by American creditors weakened the props of American capital abroad. Loans to Europe abruptly ceased. In the five weeks after the crash of October 24, 1929, an aggregate of capital approximating the total American outlay for World War I—$30,000,000,000—vanished in the collapse of the stock market. The shattering of the American bull market led to the European collapse of 1931. Successive crashes in country after country in turn dragged the United States into deeper depression. The foremost English economist, John Maynard Keynes, concluded that the American boom had gambled away capital created and required by legitimate business enterprises all around the world.

Conservative American business leaders and their political spokesmen, so long accustomed to plaudits—and votes—as the architects of prosperity, exhibited an unsuspected lack of competence and understanding in the presence of the great and accelerating crisis of capitalism. There was little recognition in the nation's business communities or in high governmental circles that the international situation, always important in gyrations of the business cycle, had become still more important than in any other great depression. Several months after the crash, Secretary of the Treasury Mellon, one of the half dozen notable American multimillionaires, told the country that he saw "nothing" in the "present situation" that was "menacing." He had "confidence."

The country could expect a "revival" in the spring. There "may be some slackness or unemployment" in the winter, he added, but "hardly more" than usual "at this season of each year." Advocates of normalcy had never been disturbed by seasonal unemployment; but the Secretary exhibited strange lack of economic understanding in failing to recognize an unemployment rise that was cyclical and not seasonal. In spite of successive declines, business spokesmen tended to analyze the problem in terms of temporary isolated American conditions—chiefly "bearish" sentiment on the stock market, "selling short," and lack of "business confidence." President Hoover in public statements likewise relied upon verbalism to exorcise the evil spirit that had destroyed business confidence. As months passed and unemployment rose, the country was told that "prosperity was just around the corner." Instead, more and more unemployed men and women appeared on the streets selling apples—a new form of cyclical beggary—and growing throngs of demoralized workingmen, clerks, stenographers, and former executives, turned away by each successive employment agency, formed in the bread lines of local charities.

In contrast to the optimism or wishful thinking of those on top, desperation grew among the great body of people dragged down into economic purgatory. The public was losing confidence in business. Bewildered victims of the economic catastrophe began to ask why people without food stood in the city bread lines, while farmers produced foodstuffs in abundance that they could not sell. The American people, together with millions all over the world, were discovering that the economic revolutions and world financial complexities had eliminated individual self-sufficiency root and branch. Huge monoliths of large-scale enterprise and great "tycoons" of business ceased to impress hungry Americans, who once had believed in normalcy and had looked upon these men as philosopher-kings. Unparalleled plant capacity, the great technology of mass production, and abounding natural resources provided neither self-sufficiency for the nation's business nor even a bare minimum security for the private citizen. Dire, universal uncertainty dissipated social buoyancy and national optimism. The American people had never known such desperate want and individual helplessness, and the numbing reality chilled the old faith in the sanctity of laissez faire and rugged individualism. Demands became insistent that something be done to restore a reasonable certainty of livelihood. People must be freed from fear and want which they had done nothing to deserve.

Leaders in Congress, the administration, and Wall Street were not prepared to cope with issues that now at long last had to be faced. "Men who live differently think differently." The insulation of established position, unfamiliarity with the life and problems of millions, and en-

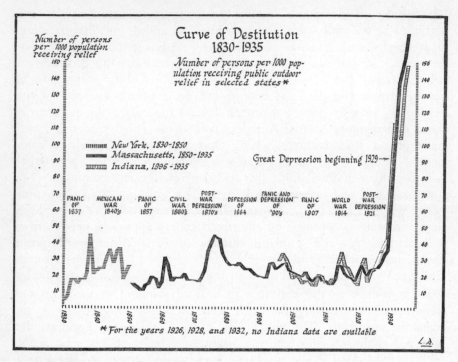

Curve of Destitution
1830-1935

Number of persons per 1000 population receiving public outdoor relief in selected states*

From K. D. Lumpkin and D. S. Douglas, *Child Workers in America,* 1937. New York: Robert M. McBride & Company.

crustations of social prejudices lead insensibly to loss of the common touch. Persons so insulated had no program adequate to human need. Leaders like Herbert Hoover had not, by their personal life, been attuned to the wants of inconspicuous people, nor were such leaders suddenly made sensitive to the remote voices of the unseen myriads. As a mining promoter, Hoover had spent years abroad, preoccupied with concessions in the Orient, mining contracts, and financial dickerings. As a member of the managerial class, his point of view was influenced by past experience, by concern for ore shipments, control of markets and prices, and cheap labor. His service as head of American relief missions did not change his basic outlook. As engineer, as Secretary of Commerce, and as President, his experience made him more familiar with problems of finance and management than with the daily yearnings of ordinary humankind. Hoover's supporters in Congress likewise looked for counsel from prominent business magnates whose minds were confined by the same insulation. Cut off from the mass of humanity by their experience and habits of thought, they had no program. They could only resort to the old inadequate panacea of friendly governmental encouragement of big corporate interests. They were hesitant about exercising the power to govern even when millions on the verge of desperation looked to them for action.

Confronted with something terribly wrong in the old system of production and distribution, business leaders and political stalwarts saw no need for social legislation and forthright reform. Bread lines and malnutrition, the eviction of unemployed laborers, the uprooting of thousands of farm families by foreclosure on mortgages, the loss of home and job by hundreds of thousands of salaried middle-class workers imperiled capitalism, and democracy, but the administration and its supporters were oblivious, or forgetful, or bewildered. They were unwilling to sponsor reform or even federal relief that would stay starvation and check the loss of homes and goods.

DISRUPTION OF WORLD ECONOMY

A conservative leadership that had turned its back on progressivism and the League of Nations, preferring nationalism and normalcy, was unprepared to cope with the aggravated problems it had sought to evade. Nevertheless, though clinging to the antiquated dogma of economic individualism with prosperity trickling down, Hoover and Congress were not so inclined to "masterly inactivity" as their less hard-pressed predecessors. The government acted in four primary fields: in connection with farm relief; international economic relations; relief and recovery for industry; and, to a very minor extent, reform of abuses in labor relations. But the conservative approach in each of these four fields was so timid and ineffective as to mark the end of an era and discredit the system of business rule.

The Agricultural Marketing Act of June, 1929, indicated a partial recognition of the seriousness of agricultural inequalities. Aimed not at the production but at the distribution sector of farming enterprise, the enactment struck at a crucial point too long neglected in the calculations of business statecraft. Instead of farm bloc projects for government aid in fixing prices, Hoover relied on government funds to purchase agricultural surpluses and withhold them from the market until prices increased. The Marketing Act entrusted a board with half a billion dollars for use as a revolving fund. In accordance with Hoover's addiction to the business formula of self-liquidating undertakings, the fund would supposedly be replenished by eventual sale of surpluses. But surpluses continued to pile up, prices continued to fall, warehouses bulged with the governmental purchases, and the revolving fund disappeared. The spread of the world depression completed the collapse of agricultural policy. Farm families, now needing relief or credit still more imperatively, were exposed to the dismal laissez-faire "solution": elimination of the insolvent by eviction, and their disappearance into the ranks of the dispossessed and unemployed.

Failure in agriculture was connected with a laggard and inept use of the power of the United States to promote recovery in the world economy. Standpatters rejected once again any realistic program for reform of economic nationalism. The old system of business rule, basing governmental action upon the politics of special interests, stood in the way of energetic cooperation with other nations to stimulate recovery in the world economy. It also frustrated internal reform to check America's own economic nationalism. In its two major aspects, tariff revision and a moratorium on war debts, the economic foreign policy of the Hoover administration did not meet the emergency.

In April, 1929, Hoover called Congress in special session to revise the Fordney-McCumber tariff and to pass the Agricultural Marketing Act. Increased tariff protection was recommended as a method of aiding the farmers and reviving sick industries. The House promptly voted a bill, but in the Senate a battery of predatory pressure groups in month after month of protracted proceedings, aided by arch-conservatives under the leadership of Senator Reed Smoot of Utah, increased the protection of special interests to even greater heights in schedule after schedule. Cordell Hull of Tennessee, outstanding Democratic tariff expert in the House, urged the opposite policy of reducing barriers to international trade—but to no avail. Meanwhile, the crash came, but Hoover did not urge reform of the tariff. In March, 1930, after a ten months' free-for-all of pressure politics, the Hawley-Smoot tariff, known throughout the world but by other less respectable names, went to the White House. One thousand economists joined in public protest. They stated unequivocally that tariff protection was of no real aid to farmers, and actually a bar to economic recovery. For the Hawley-Smoot tariff would invite retaliation and result in a further limitation on the sale abroad of surplus farm commodities and American manufactures. Nevertheless, like the majority in Congress, the President disregarded the view of trained economists and signed the measure. The tariff system, Hoover contended, "protects the farmer" and "stimulates him . . . to grow products that he could not otherwise produce, and thus lessen his dependence upon foreign markets." Economists, less theoretical, knew better the solid facts of interdependence, including the fact that 85 per cent of American farmers were world producers for world markets at world prices. In the years following, the Hawley-Smoot tariff produced precisely the evil results the economists predicted.

The failure of agricultural policy and of the tariff accentuated the laissez-faire "solution" of the farm problem. Foreign trade shrank to scarcely more than one third its former level. As foreign markets contracted or were completely closed to American farm commodities, the cash income of the nation's farmers plummeted down from the inadequate 1929 total of seven billion dollars to the ruinous figure of two billion dollars in 1932. Behind these cold figures was an uprooting process repeated in thousands of communities as families lost their stake in the land. Meanwhile, however, the disruption of world economy forced reluctant intervention to check collapse abroad. By 1931, Hoover, to the dismay of various supporters, advanced toward a straddle between an international position and the traditional isolationist position on war debts and reparations.

Under the blight of depression, the huge intergovernmental debts and reparations were an intolerable barrier to recovery. The discontinuance of American loans and investments in Europe cut off one of the methods by which for a decade the international ledger book had been balanced. The forbidding ramparts of the Hawley-Smoot tariff and the decline of American purchasing from Europe made payment in goods out of the question. The greatest bank in Vienna, the Kredit Anstalt, went to the wall in May, 1931. Collapse in central Europe was followed by a rapid breakdown of the whole structure of international currency exchange, loans, debts, and foreign trade. In June, 1931, Hoover called for an international moratorium to postpone—for one year—Germany's payments to the Allies and the Allies' payments to the United States. Though immediate action was urgent, jealous nationalism caused a six months' delay before Congress reluctantly approved. As a measure for world recovery the moratorium was both too little and too late. The Darmstädter, one of the great banks of Germany, defaulted in July while Congress still dallied. Foreign credits were frozen, and stringency in England halted her loans to buttress European business. Supposedly giltedged bonds began to fall everywhere, as stocks had earlier. American banks, carrying bonds in their portfolios, began to crash like the great banks abroad. In September, 1931, England went off the gold standard. When the Hoover moratorium expired in 1932, the debtor countries defaulted, yet a measure calling for an international tariff conference was vetoed by Hoover in the same year. Simultaneously, in retaliation against the Hawley-Smoot and other tariffs, England abandoned free trade (1932) and swung back toward an eighteenth-century empire-tariff system. A world of desperate men moved toward currency and tariff wars, nationalistic exchange controls, import quotas, and the devices that fascists appropriated as techniques to prey on the economy of their neighbors.

"RECOVERY WITHOUT REFORM"

Outmoded ideas in the American government, exhibited by the absence of any international policy for reform of economic nationalism, were also revealed in the domestic policies of government and business. Nothing more discredited the system of business rule and traditional shams of the tariff and a "full dinner pail" than the Republican attitude toward relief and recovery for labor and industry. After more than two years of ruinous deflation, the Hoover administration in 1932 proposed a limited program for relief and recovery designed to aid business firms. Congress responded by creating the RFC (Reconstruction Finance Corporation), a governmental loan agency that bolstered tottering railroads, banks, insurance companies, and industrial corporations. The RFC was a belated recognition of the dangerous and disastrous consequence of following the classic dogma of laissez faire—letting a depression cure itself. The new policy of placing a "cushion" under tottering firms was, however, a pale imitation of extensive activities abroad, where governmental credit, mildly inflationary currency policies to stimulate recovery, and governmental funds to provide relief for the jobless were widely utilized.

For many months liberals had been calling for a broader program of relief and public works. Current estimates of unemployment climbed to over 8,000,000 in 1931, and as the figures rose upward toward 14,000,000, rebellion grew in the country. After Republican reverses in the 1930 elections, Democrats for the first time since the Wilson administration placed their own Speaker, John Nance Garner of Texas, in the Chair of the House. The liberal wing of the Democrats, gaining strength, coalesced under new leaders who introduced a series of relief measures. Most of these were killed by congressional conservatives, but one for federal aid to state employment agencies—sponsored in February, 1931, by Senator Robert F. Wagner, liberal Democrat from New York City—passed on to the White House. The President, with unemployment figures before him, vetoed the bill.

Relief for corporations under the RFC precipitated a long, bitter debate in 1932 over relief for human beings whose need of food was at least as pressing as the need of dollars for the maintenance of banks and railroads. The liberal phalanx of Democrats, with a handful of insurgent Republicans, revolted. They assailed a limited program of governmental resuscitation of big corporations as a reflection of callous upper-class ideas, a cure of poverty by permitting prosperity to trickle down in rivulets from the mountain top of wealth. But a Wagner-Garner relief bill of 1932, extending RFC relief to small businesses and distressed citizens, failed to receive the President's signature, and liberals lacked the votes to override the veto. Just before the party conventions, Hoover yielded half a loaf to the liberals, acceding to an increase of RFC funds in order to allow it to loan limited amounts to farm organizations and to bankrupt states for relief purposes and self-liquidating public works. A second concession, establishing home loan banks, primarily buttressed banks, building and loan associations, and insurance companies. On a small scale it afforded indirect benefits of government credit to a limited number of homeowners.

As contrasted with previous Republican policies, the administration's total exertion of governmental energy broke new ground; but governmental intervention was still narrowly conceived in the interests of big property. The public was incensed when it was discovered that whereas only $300,000,000 was allotted for relief, the RFC had extended $80,-000,000 to a single bank, the Chicago institution of Coolidge's vice-president, Charles G. Dawes. As compared with loans to corporations, the cushion placed under farmers, workers, and homeowners was infinitesimal. And on the question of direct relief for the people as distinct from the gentry of property, Hoover was adamant; relief for distressed families was a state and local function and a matter for private charity. In this the President merely registered the conventional insensitivity of the conservative mind. Business leaders generally endorsed Hoover's opposition to federal relief or anything comparable to the English "dole." They applauded Hoover's insistence that any program of public works and government hiring of the unemployed must be "self-liquidating"—that such relief projects should not be undertaken unless they would pay back their cost. Hoover finally sanctioned government spending, ultimately exceeding $600,000,000 a year, for federal public works, roads, river and harbor improvements, and one big project, Boulder Dam. But any wide-scale work relief and internal improvements program was resisted until, with depression sweeping everything before it, the New Deal took command.

The fourth and greatest failure of the Republican leadership was the rejection of reform. Instead of responding to the nation-wide feeling that something was glaringly wrong, the old leaders, like their predecessors of McKinley's generation, stood pat. Clinging to a rigid, narrow interpretation of the Constitution in conformity with laissez-faire strategy of limited governmental power, the sponsors of business rule were unready to accept public national responsibility for a full-scale attack on depression. Neither the Republican organization nor powerful business groups like the National Association of Manufacturers recognized that unemployment was now a permanent problem requiring a permanent national policy. While Secretary of Commerce, Hoover had initiated an investigation of the technological revolution, but even when statistics of the departments of Labor and Commerce revealed an actual decrease in the number of factory workers employed during the boom years, the government did not concern itself with long-range questions of technological displacement and permanent joblessness. Neither Hoover nor Republican congressional leaders conceived of any broad social security reforms like those in the national systems already provided in England, France, and other comparable countries. Conservatives, rejecting the modern concept of the welfare state, clung to the callous laissez-faire sentiment once expressed by President Coolidge, who condemned unemployment insurance on the grounds that workers would receive money that they didn't "earn."

Social anger, in conjunction with party competition for votes in an election year, accounted for a labor reform that the Old Guard dared not resist. Sponsored by Nebraska's sage George Norris and New York's fiery Fiorello La Guardia, the Anti-Injunction Act (1932) passed the Senate 75–5 and the House 362–14. The language of the law, breathing the cleansing spirit of freedom, sought to dispel noxious vapors of a decade of repression. Without unions a worker "is commonly helpless to exercise actual liberty of contract and to protect his freedom of labor"; for equality in bargaining he must have full freedom to organize and designate "representatives of his own choosing, to negotiate the terms and conditions of his employment." First significant measure for collective bargaining to be enacted in the fourteen years since the Republican resurgence in the elections of 1918, the law attempted in part to regain the statutory ground lost since the Congress of 1914 wrote anti-injunction provisions into the Clayton Act. Equally significant, the enactment was the first in fourteen years to seek to correct abuses in the exercise of high prerogative by the judicial branch. Directed against crass inequality in bargaining, the new reform struck at the reactionary ruling in the Hitchman case (1917) whereby the antilabor majority on the Supreme Court not only sanctified yellow-dog contracts but enforced them with injunctions that virtually prohibited unions. Limiting the power of federal courts to issue injunctions, the Norris-La Guardia Act outlawed yellow-dog contracts and stipulated a fair trial before a jury for workmen accused of disobeying a court order. The forty-year agitation against arbitrary fines and imprisonment for contempt of court without a fair trial had at last been recognized in American law.

In other respects the Hoover administration stoutly resisted the clamor for reform. Current congressional investigations of abuses in banking evoked no administrative support of public demand for correctives. Other investigations, and the crash of unsound holding company pyramids like Samuel Insull's vast utilities empire—the latter at a cost of nearly $700,000,000 to American investors—revealed widespread financial

Secretary Hull and Canada's Prime Minister King sign trade reciprocity agreement, 1935.

New York's Governor Franklin D. Roosevelt, accompanied by "Al" Smith, inaugurating public works program as depression deepens.

Below, left—President of the Philippine Senate Manuel Quezon witnesses F.D.R.'s signing of bill for freedom of Filipinos.

Right—New medium of presidential leadership: a "fireside chat" by F.D.R., 1937.

(Underwood-Stratton)

Above, left—Wendell Willkie, prophet of a Republican New Deal and exponent of One World; *right*—Sidney Hillman of C.I.O. after White House conference on the wage and hour law, 1938.

Below, left—Ohio's isolationist, Senator Robert Taft, peers at the past; *right*—Chester Bowles, wartime price control chief.

(All photos *Harris & Ewing* except Willkie, *Brown Brothers*)

above—Florida estate of wealthy mid-western farm-machinery family, where President-Elect Hoover in 1928 laid plans for his administration. *(Miami News Service)*

right—Several hundred war veterans in bonus army march, escorted to Indiana line by Illinois sheriff and state police, May, 1932. *(Brown Brothers)*

J. P. Morgan and T. W. Lamont, with John W. Davis *(center)* as counsel, cross-examined in Senate investigation of private banking practices, 1933. *(Harris & Ewing)*

Hearings on bill to regulate paid lobbyists, 1935, conducted by Senators Norris, Black, Neeley, and Hatch.

(Underwood-Stratton)

Regional planning for the land and people of seven states. Hiwassee Dam, higher than Niagara Falls, built for flood control, public power, and navigation. *(TVA Photo)*

malpractice. But Republican leaders offered neither antitrust reform nor a program to prevent repetition of the frenzied finance of the Coolidge boom. Republican orthodoxy was perduring, and Hoover gave it rigid expression in the view that regulation of the stock exchange was not the nation's business but a local matter for the state of New York. Tax battles by Hoover Republicans betrayed the same animus against reform; only a congressional rebellion defeated an administration drive in 1932 for a general sales tax to shift tax burdens more heavily on those least able to pay. Under pressure of the liberals, Hoover accepted a reversal of the Mellon policy of repealing estate taxes and gift taxes, but the Old Guard successfully resisted attempts to employ taxation as an instrument of thoroughgoing reform to prevent tax evasion and the excessive concentration of wealth in a small number of families.

Despite the infamy of Insulls in American public utilities, Republican regulars stoutly defended private monopoly of power sites and the policy of lax federal regulation. Monumental reports by the Federal Trade Commission, after exhausting investigation of financial jugglery and dishonest propaganda by power companies, did not induce Hoover Republicans to waver. Although ever since the war year 1918 the government owned power sites at Muscle Shoals on the Tennessee River, every liberal bill to continue a government power program in peacetime had been defeated. Senator Norris, who had become the champion of public power as early as the Wilson administration, in 1928 won passage of his Muscle Shoals bill, only to see it vetoed by Coolidge. Once more it passed in 1931, this time to be vetoed by Hoover. The latter veto was a deathbed act in a dying age: a day was fast approaching when the Norris project for the Tennessee River would be enlarged into the mighty plan of the TVA (Tennessee Valley Authority). Still unseeing as the campaign of 1932 unfolded, the elder statesmen of business rule opposed reform with the old slogan, "Free private enterprise," and invoked the constitutional fetish of state rights and narrow construction of federal power.

1932

The election of 1932 was one of the great turning points in American history, for it ushered in the Roosevelt Revolution. The Republican program, recovery without reform, evoked less enthusiasm than disdain. The record of the nominee, Hoover, and the barren Republican record in Congress exposed the emptiness of old catchwords and the futility of old expedients. An angry conviction that conservative politicians and business leaders were incompetent in the face of a crisis because they were the prisoners of ideas that incapacitated them was entertained by high and low.

The liberal wing of the Democrats captured the organization in the party convention for the first time since 1920, relegated the conservative contender, John Nance Garner, to the vice-presidential place, and for party standard-bearer nominated Franklin D. Roosevelt, Governor of New York, a lifelong spokesman of the best in the Wilson tradition. Gifted with the precious quality of leadership, Roosevelt campaigned for a "new deal" and for the "forgotten man." He pledged governmental intervention on a scale commensurate with the magnitude of social danger. Outstanding liberal Republican leaders crossed party lines and endorsed Roosevelt. A noted farm spokesman, Henry A. Wallace, son of a former Republican Secretary of Agriculture; Senator Norris; the young Robert La Follette, succeeding his father as senator from Wisconsin; Senator Borah; and various Republicans like Harold L. Ickes, soon to be conspicuous in the next administration, were among the scores who manifested their primary allegiance to democracy by their desertion of a bankrupt leadership.

As the elections drew near, Republicans imitated Mark Hanna's strategy in the depression year of 1896 and attempted to stampede voters by pitching the campaign on the note of fear. If Roosevelt was elected, asserted Hoover, "grass will grow in the streets of a hundred cities." The "so-called new deals" of the Democrats, declaimed hundreds of Republican spellbinders, would "destroy" the American system. After the election, Senator Borah, commenting on the magnitude of the Democratic victory, remarked that the people were hungry and the Republicans offered them the Constitution. But Borah might have added that the people were courageous as well as hungry, and that Franklin Roosevelt offered them a program and leadership instead of fear and submission. Roosevelt polled 22,800,000 votes as compared with the crushing decline of the Republican vote to 15,700,000. The amazing increase of nearly 8,000,-000 in the Democratic column, as compared with the vote in 1928, came not only from discontented Republicans and "independent voters," but from inconspicuous people, former nonvoters to whom national politics had become suddenly meaningful in their direct personal life. The Republican ticket carried only six states.

The heritage from the Republican era grew more gnarled and bitter in the immediate period prior to the inauguration. The country was threatened by disruptive severance of the connective tissues of settled society. In the years from 1929 to 1932 the national income had fallen more than half, from almost $83,000,000,000 to less than $40,000,000,-000. Feeding upon misery and need, unrest produced strange ideas and agitations: a Bonus Army composed of uprooted war veterans; Technocracy, an anticapitalist movement for rule by engineers; a Farm Holiday amounting to a sit-down strike in agriculture; and various organized assaults on disproportionate wealth, including a nation-wide drive for fabulous old-age pensions (the Townsend plan), and Share-Our-Wealth clubs organized by Louisiana's boss and virtual dictator, the demagogic United States Senator Huey Long.

The dangerous increase in social tensions was exhibited in the march of the Bonus Army in 1932 and its expulsion from Washington. Thousands of unemployed veterans converged on the capital from as far as the Pacific coast. On July 28 Hoover dispatched troops, under command of General Douglas MacArthur, with tanks, machine guns, and tear gas to disperse them. And dispersed they were with complete military efficiency. Two were shot and killed and a thousand, including women and children, gassed. Just before elections, Technocracy became a national catchword, attracting many who began to believe that democratic government must be abandoned. The Technocrats outlined an engineer's utopia in glowing terms that won the attention of numerous business leaders and a public harried enough to be gullible. Those who knew something about Fascism saw in Technocracy the seeds of a revolutionary movement that might lead to undemocratic domination by engineers and the managerial class and were alarmed by its vogue in urban society. The no less menacing Farm Holiday organization, rising to its peak after the elections, betokened an equally profound dislocation in rural America. As in the days of Daniel Shays, bands of angry farmers, this time in the Mississippi Valley, sought to intimidate local authorities and prevent foreclosures. Farm Holiday organizations in the West and East joined together in "strikes," overturning trucks carrying produce, seeking to dam the flow of milk and food cityward until dealers offered better prices. The constabulary was called out in New York State and elsewhere to patrol the highways and break up the strikes. Meanwhile, as Hoover was about to leave office, financial chaos brought the country to the stage of calamitous emergency. The American credit mechanism ceased to function; the banking system of the nation collapsed. One by one, state governors proclaimed a bank holiday, and banks closed their doors.

Franklin Delano Roosevelt took the oath of office on March 4, 1933. His inaugural address was a reaffirmation of the democratic faith. His courageous voice, firm, confident, and reassuring, reached out to the millions. "We have nothing to fear," he told them, "except fear itself." Americans, ears glued to their radios, took heart as the President called for broad use of governmental power. "This nation asks for action, and action now." The popular mandate for "undelayed action" was necessarily a mandate for "discipline" and "leadership." The crisis was like a foreign invasion. If necessary, the executive would seek from Congress a broad delegation of emergency power. Democracy must be equal to the enormity of its task.

THE HUNDRED DAYS

The President went into action. Unprecedented demand for central leadership transferred the initiative from the legislative branch to the executive. Roosevelt called Congress immediately into emergency session. In the ensuing period, now famous as the Hundred Days, the Congress in special session cooperated as no other Congress has ever cooperated with an American President. The problems of speed and expert services in drafting bills establishing a vast program of great public policies were resolved by reliance on executive initiative. The President's inner corps of advisors, cabinet officers, economists, and administrative experts were soon symbolized in the popular mind by the nickname "the Brain Trust."

On March 4 the bank panic had already closed two thirds of the banks. Prompt and resolute action headed off the still more paralyzing force of general psychological panic. Roosevelt declared a moratorium for banks on March 6 and closed every bank in the country by executive proclamation. Insolvent banks were closed permanently; others reopened after the brief respite. Within the next three days the first of the administration's long series of bills came from the executive to Congress. This was the Emergency Banking Act, which authorized executive regulation of credit and currency and the appointment of federal conservators over banks in shaky condition. "The house is burning down," declared the Republican floor leader, "and the President of the United States says this is the way to put out the fire." The bill passed House and Senate the day it was submitted.

On March the tenth the legislative mill began to grind, and this time it did not grind small. The President proposed an Economy Act, slashing governmental salaries and veterans' pensions; three days later came a beer bill marking the end of Prohibition. An emergency agricultural relief bill was submitted on the sixteenth—the first "Triple A" (Agricultural Adjustment Act)—and on the twenty-first two unemployment relief bills were submitted providing nation-wide work relief for young unmarried men under the CCC (Civilian Conservation Corps), including forestry improvement, drainage, and erosion control, and federal grants for immediate state and local relief under FERA (Federal Emergency Relief Administration) with an initial fund of half a billion dollars. But Franklin Roosevelt had only begun to fight the depression. On March 29 he proposed a Truth-in-Securities Act—first significant attempt to prevent speculative abuses and defrauding of investors since

Wilson's Trade Commission. Then, on April 10, he threw the magic of his influence behind the Muscle Shoals dream of Senator Norris. After a total of six hours of debate, Congress authorized the famous TVA (Tennessee Valley Authority) in May. For the relief of small homeowners, the administration on April 13 proposed the HOLC (Home Owners' Loan Corporation) providing governmental aid for refinancing home mortgages. A manifold recovery plan, including a huge program of public works, regulation of competition under codes of fair practices, and a guarantee to labor of rights to organize and bargain collectively, was sponsored on May 17 in a National Industrial Recovery Act.

Never had Congress acted with such dispatch, for by June 16 these and other executive proposals were enacted into law. Never had a democracy in an economic crisis projected so prodigious a program of relief, recovery, and reform. The American people had given Roosevelt and the Democratic party a mandate; the achievement of the Hundred Days was a revolution by consent. The vast output of far-reaching legislation and the administration's mobilization of governmental and private energies gave hope and courage. For an indefinite future, party leadership successfully departed from the old politics of heterogeneous policies in behalf of special interests. American democracy at long last was on the march, with bold leadership and a bold vision of a welfare state. Collectively, the great and expanding program and the leadership of the new administration won the attachment of millions as "The New Deal."

The Roosevelt Revolution fundamentally altered traditional public policy for recovery from depressions. The New Deal went into action on seven major sectors of the economic battlefront: money and credit; farm relief and readjustment; government credit for relief of private enterprise; efforts to stimulate business recovery, to promote higher labor standards, and to reform business by government regulation; labor rights; federal social security; and international cooperation to lift economic paralysis from the world as a whole as well as from its several parts.

THE ROOSEVELT REVOLUTION

The first sector in the war on depression was concerned with money and the collapse of credit. Emergency banking legislation permitted the use of governmental credit to bolster solvent banks. The ruined banks were liquidated. The bank moratorium was followed by the Banking Act of June 16, 1933, which provided greater control of banks under the Federal Reserve System and created FDIC (Federal Deposit Insurance Corporation) to protect the money of depositors. This and other legislation established longer-range public controls over credit and money under a policy of mastering the disastrous fluctuations of the business cycle. The United States followed England and other nations in abandoning the old laissez-faire principle of the self-regulating gold standard. Reform, based on rapidly developing economic theories of a "managed currency," led to rejection of the "sound money" school of older economists and creditor interests. Deliberately the administration sought, by a mildly inflationary policy, to raise prices to aid agriculture and stimulate industrial production.

Farm relief and readjustment was the second item on the Roosevelt prospectus. The government was committed to the formula of "parity" between prices for farm products and prices for industry. The giant surplus in the great crops now at last induced national planning to put an end to the desperate unregulated competition between farms under the old policy of "production at all costs." In the Coolidge-Hoover era, the new business-minded pressure group of big commercial farm interests, the American Farm Bureau Federation, had moved toward isolationist economic nationalism. McNary-Haugen bills had envisioned disposal of the agricultural surplus through governmental financial aid, ultimately reducing American "overproduction" by competitive dumping of the surplus abroad. But Roosevelt's Secretary of Agriculture, Henry A. Wallace, sought a sane and cooperative world. The Agricultural Adjustment Act of 1933 applied normal business theory: attack overproduction by agreement on restriction of output, an idea as universally acclaimed by business as it was universally practiced. Enlarging on Hoover's precedent in organizing trade associations through the Department of Commerce, the AAA employed the Department of Agriculture to organize farmers in a concerted national plan to control production. Rental or benefit payments provided farmers who accepted the plan with a governmental subsidy commensurate with the reduction of acreage. Our surplus here and the resulting alternatives of reducing acreage or widening foreign markets, said Secretary Wallace, "is really part of a world surplus problem." To place surplus control on an international basis, the administration in August, 1933, sought an agreement between wheat-consuming and wheat-producing countries, but the dissatisfaction of Argentina frustrated the program. Meanwhile in a famous pamphlet, *America Must Choose,* Secretary Wallace outlined national planning for long-range reform of agriculture, contributing the concept of an "ever-normal granary" whereby supply would be adjusted to the realities of demand and neither agriculture nor industry sacrificed to the interests of the one or the other.

The third thrust to alleviate the depression involved an enormous extension of government credit for the relief of private enterprise, distressed property owners, and bankrupt communities. Although remaining under the conservative stewardship of Jesse Jones, Hoover's appointee, the RFC was expanded into a giant lending agency. Loans to banks, railroads, insurance companies, and various corporations under the Insurance Company Loan Act (1933) and the Loans-to-Industry Act (1934) continued the Hoover approach, but RFC acquired additional responsibilities for the welfare of small businessmen, farmers, and inconspicuous people. Under the new dispensation, it was authorized to bolster state insurance systems for workmen's compensation; to loan up to $75,000,000 to bankrupt communities to pay schoolteachers their back salaries; and to provide $500,-000,000 for relief under FERA. The HOLC was expanded as a loan agency, with credit up to $3,000,000,000 for the aid of homeowners threatened with foreclosures or unable to make improvements and repairs. Similarly, under the Farm Mortgage Foreclosure Act (1934), credit was extended to dispossessed farmers so that they could buy back their lands. A moratorium, similar to the "stay laws" demanded in the days of Daniel Shays, was extended under the Frazier-Lemke Farm Bankruptcy Act (1934), giving farmers needed time on mortgage debts.

Combined measures to stimulate business recovery, to promote higher labor standards, and to reform business by government regulation constituted a fourth phase of the New Deal. By extension of an unprecedented volume of government credit to banks and corporations, Roosevelt "bailed out Wall Street." This was merely an enlargement on the Hoover policy of governmental aid as a cushion to stop deflation and promote recovery. The NRA (National Recovery Administration) also expanded the Hoover trade-association policy, but the Republican formula of "self-government in industry" was coupled with federal regulation intended to eliminate unfair competition rather than competition itself.

To concert measures for greater production and fair competition, the NRA, in partnership with the business leaders of separate industries, devised codes that were intended to expand into a national system the earlier code experiments of the Federal Trade Commission. Through the various "code authorities," private enterprise enjoyed a supervised but unblushing power of a kind long frowned upon by antitrust laws—including a limited authority to restrict production so as to raise prices and to set noncompetitive "administered" prices by agreement among competitors. The avowed purpose was to stimulate business confidence and create favorable conditions to offset the specter of unsold surplus, cutthroat competition, continued deflation, curtailment of production, and layoffs of labor. The NRA continued only two years, but before the end of Roosevelt's first term, Congress was engaged in enacting a more far-reaching body of reforms for regulation of corporation finance, stock markets, utilities, and labor relations.

Recognition of the rights of labor and heroic efforts to provide jobs and relief gained under the New Deal an importance as great as had ever been accorded earlier policies of aid to industry. The emergency FERA and better contrived subsequent agencies provided immediate relief on the basis of temporary work projects. The forestry projects of the Civilian Conservation Corps and the long-range public works projects of the Public Works Administration began a huge internal improvements program that at once provided jobs and left enduring monuments of constructive public enterprise. Coupled with NRA was a new and portentous bill of rights for labor. Under the famous Clause 7-A, employees were to have "the right to organize and bargain collectively through representatives of their own choosing"; in bargaining, labor was to be "free from the interference, restraint, or coercion" of employers or their agents, and no employee as a condition of employment should be required "to join any company union" or refrain from joining a union "of his own choosing." With millions out of work desperately seeking jobs, labor standards disappeared with living standards, and collective bargaining ceased. In January, 1933, just before the Republican era ended, *Business Week* estimated unemployment at about 15,250,000. Only in Germany was there anything like a comparable percentage of people without a livelihood. Men do not strike when other men will take their jobs. But Clause 7-A, reviving the Wilsonian ideal of a democratic equality in bargaining power, was not a mere policy of attack on depression. It initiated a program of dredging out a broad legal channel for the flow of the long dammed-up energies of the labor movement. With the termination of NRA in 1935, the New Deal experiment with governmental protection of collective bargaining was extended and amplified in the Wagner Labor Relations Act. American labor practices began to catch up with the most advanced labor standards in other countries.

Perhaps the most widely revered achievement in the great attack on depression was the long overdue initiation of federal social security comparable to the national systems of social insurance existing in other countries. In 1935, Roosevelt proposed and Congress passed the Social Security Act.[1] This was designed to protect the helpless in times of seasonal or technological unemployment; and in time of baneful downsweep of the business cycle, to provide a cushion by a limited amount of automatic relief for the unemployed. Old age was a growing national problem. A larger proportion of the population survived to old age, and managerial policies tended to displace older people at an earlier age. The Social Security Act constituted the first American adaptation of well-tried European provisions of social insurance for aged dependents. To a limited extent other provisions also began to eliminate the long American lag in making

[1] For the political history of the Wagner and Social Security acts, see Chapter XXX.

available national aid for impoverished widows with dependent children, and for the blind, sick, maimed, and others afflicted by misfortune.

A gradually evolving international policy, hopefully directed toward a cooperative world attack upon the creeping economic paralysis and numbing nationalistic fear and greed, rounded out the Roosevelt program. But the international policies of the New Deal were slowest to take form. Isolationism was strengthened by the depression. In Congress isolationism hardened into a body of doctrinaire neutrality legislation that seriously checked cooperation for collective security. Though the administration fought against isolationism, economic nationalism was deepened by the depression and for a time led several administration advisors to conceive of planning as primarily national, to the end that one's own house be put in order before joining with one's neighbor to tackle common problems. More significant in the long run, Roosevelt named as Secretary of State the man in Congress who talked sense in debate against the Hawley-Smoot tariff and who recognized the chaos wrought by economic nationalism—Cordell Hull. During the Hundred Days, Hull went to the World Economic Conference at London, where representatives of the nations sat down to consider ways to end currency wars and to demolish barriers to trade. Roosevelt abruptly withdrew American support by cable.[2] Nevertheless, although the New Deal seemed temporarily to place trust in national planning for recovery, it did not sanction greater nationalistic excesses along the pathway of the Hawley-Smoot tariff. Wallace's ever-normal granary plan, unlike the McNary-Haugen subsidy proposals, did not countenance blind nationalistic competition and the ruin of foreign agriculture by dumping the American farm surplus on world markets. When Congress authorized executive negotiation of reciprocal trade agreements in 1934, Cordell Hull began to make headway in a constructive attack on the tariff. High-tariff pressure groups were short-circuited because Congress did not have to act on separate trade agreements. Under this celebrated reciprocity policy, the United States lowered specified rates of the Hawley-Smoot tariff by means of bargains with countries that reciprocated by likewise lowering specified tariff rates. Surplus American corn, cotton, and manufactured goods began to move abroad more freely, and in return, European, Latin-American, and other nations began to find more buyers in the United States. The promise of internationalism appeared also in a policy of liquidation of imperialism in the Philippines, Puerto Rico, and Latin America, in the proclamation of the Good Neighbor policy, and in an unsuccessful attempt by Roosevelt to win Senate ratification for the World Court.

---

[2] For the conference and later foreign relations, see Chapter XXXI.

THE NEW LIBERALISM

Until what is sometimes called "the second New Deal" began to emerge in 1934, the administration's program was not composed of broadly coordinated or wholly self-consistent policies. The Hundred Days were dominated by unremitting pressure for emergency legislation. Contradictions between sound national objects and sound international objects reflected in part a divergence within the administration and more particularly a divergence between New Dealers and conservative nationalists in Congress. Few of the initial emergency acts were to stand up as basic instruments for long-range reform. Nevertheless, in general conception and in specific content, the vast total of important enactments between 1933 and 1936 constituted a prodigious break with the conservatism of outworn tradition. Whether temporary and not particularly successful measures, like NRA, or whether permanent measures, like TVA, the Wagner Labor Relations Act, Social Security, reciprocal trade agreements, and reform of the banks, corporation finance, stock exchanges, and power companies, the bulk of New Deal legislation represented a distinctly modern, virile, twentieth-century form of liberalism. The New Deal was democracy in action.

The character of the new liberalism suggested an impressive dissolution of the old fetish of limited powers. Roosevelt's inaugural address challenged the conservative formula. Stressing the necessity of the power to govern, rejecting the eighteenth-century attitude of fear of government, and ignoring old undemocratic sophisms of checks and balances, the twentieth century moved away from theories of the schoolmen that there were different "powers" inherently belonging to separated branches of government. In the Hundred Days and in the subsequent years of the New Deal, popular thought approached the functional view that there was only one power in government: the power to govern.

In accordance with popular need and overwhelming demand, the government asserted the power to govern in fields where, under Republican leadership, the United States had signally failed to develop a policy. Never before in any forthright program had the United States taken the position that it was the responsibility of the government to see that none should starve, that the right to work was also inalienable. Uniting with the President in this tremendous affirmation, the Congress of the Hundred Days underwrote the modern liberal principle that "the right to work is the right to live." In later years Roosevelt was to win popular esteem for two fundamental liberties, freedom from want and freedom from fear. These he proclaimed as two of the four basic freedoms, sacred and unchallengeable extensions of the Bill of Rights, as basic as freedom of speech and freedom of religion.

To give reality to the basic freedoms, the New Deal undertook to establish public responsibility in vital economic empires formerly not governed by any positive public policy. The New Deal was in essence the creation of a public policy toward all economic enterprise affected with a public interest. In agriculture, in labor relations, in industry, in the utilities field, the government intervened to establish a public policy in full repudiation of nineteenth-century individualism, which had sanctified the immunity of property interests from governmental intervention as a magical solvent of the ills of society. Behind this new liberalism was a thoroughly modern assumption—self-evidenced by the depression— that old-style capitalism, left to itself, was demonstrably inefficient. The basic ethical defense of the old economics, the supposition of an efficiency that resulted in the promotion of maximum production, full employment, and maximum satisfaction of wants, was finally challenged and overthrown.

The year 1933 was a watershed in history. Congress and the President, supported by an extraordinary public unity, had subscribed to the enormous proposition that none should go hungry, lack for a livable habitation, or go indecently clad. The nation became inspired by a new ideal, "jobs for all" or what the new economists were soon to call "full employment." The goal was an "American standard of living." That standard was to represent a minimum sufficient to promote the independence, integrity, and basic human values that Thomas Jefferson had envisioned in the life and westward march of hardy yeomen, tillers of the soil. In the new dimensions of a complex, modern urban-industrial world, the United States was keeping alive the best of the American spirit, applying new methods to the old, snarled problem of a just distribution of wealth, equality of opportunity, and enrichment of human life. Much legislation remained to round out the enlarged conception of a general welfare state. But the sleeping giant of the Western Hemisphere was aroused at last. With Gargantuan strides, the United States had moved into the vanguard of nations in the march toward social democracy. But the liberal quest of democracy and world security was not to escape bitter challenge at home and cataclysmic warfare abroad.

XXX

THE CHALLENGE OF SOCIAL DEMOCRACY

1934–1939

If the Roosevelt Revolution made the United States an advanced battleground of hard-beset modern democracy, it did not automatically arm warriors of the people with modern legislative procedures or coordinate their actions by close party organization and unified command. No crusade for social democracy so powerful as the New Deal could fail to strengthen the inspired band who battled against Bourbon and Stalwart in the perennial challenge to the rule by the few. But if countless enemy countermeasures to "stop Roosevelt" met with repeated defeat, Roosevelt himself on as many occasions had to withhold fire because of disunity within his own camp. The Roosevelt Revolution, although it was commanded by a great president, did not leave as a heritage for the future a solution of the problem that America had too long dismissed: democracy and leadership.

The most perplexing problem of majority rule is the translation of a party mandate into governmental action. As Woodrow Wilson had contended in 1885, the American problem was essentially one of effective party organization under a combined leadership to control and harmonize the primary branches, legislative and executive. Franklin D. Roosevelt, following Wilson's precedent of reading his message in person, opened the 1934 session by emphasizing the need of "a strong and permanent tie" between the two branches. The Constitution had "declared a separation, but the impulse of a common purpose declares a union."

Nevertheless, before the end of Franklin Roosevelt's first term, party unity began seriously to disintegrate. Conservative resistance to further reform was only superficially ascribable to the fact that legislators were almost solidly representative of the middle class; the key to democratic politics was not a mathematical computation of class alignments. Actually the middle class was divided as always; and public opinion polls, instituted in 1935, showed that a preponderant majority of all class groupings, except the large-income group, supported the President. Nevertheless, party lines split. Sometimes northern Democrats deserted their party leaders, but gradually a loose bloc of conservative southern Democrats and a sprinkling of northern and western Democrats joined conservative Republicans seeking to extract the teeth from administration measures. The local base of the American party organization, more compatible with the politics of patronage and special interests than with strong party leadership and national party principles, accounted for the difficulties of the New Deal. Since, under the theory and practice peculiar to the United States, parties were normally expected to divide, individual congressmen thought of future election chances in local terms rather than in party terms, and thereby succumbed more easily and abjectly to the drives of pressure groups for privileges and exemptions. In the absence of a strong-party theory of majority rule, it was, and remained, the practice for bipartisan blocs to override the official party leadership.

THE NEW DEAL AND CONGRESSIONAL INDEPENDENCE

Factious Democrats frequently held important committee posts by virtue of seniority. Conspicuous among conservatives was Senator Carter Glass, opponent of federal relief and aged father of Virginia's poll tax. The notorious Long machine was represented by the Louisiana senators, John H. Overton and Huey Long himself. Boss Crump of Memphis for a short time represented himself in the House. Senators like Bennett Champ Clark (Missouri) and House members like Howard Smith (Virginia) and Martin Dies (Texas) were not spokesmen for the forgotten man, the impoverished sharecropper, the underpaid southern workman. The new southern Bourbon looked to the special interests of southern employers and northern capitalists who exploited the southern "advantage" of low wages.

If the old southern tradition of Jeffersonian liberalism was poorly represented by politicos of Virginia, the progressive spirit had not yet perished. No northern president had ever held so closely to heart the welfare of southern people. Below Mason and Dixon's line, contended the President, lay the nation's number one economic problem. The more enlightened sons of Dixie responded gallantly to their gallant leader. Liberals won abolition of poll tax restrictions in two of the nine poll tax states. Progressive Governor Ellis G. Arnall fought for the remaking of Georgia. By 1945, leading Bourbons—Bennett Champ Clark, Robert R. Reynolds, "Cotton Ed" Smith, and Martin Dies—had been defeated by aroused constituents. Northern beneficiaries of the New Deal owed much to southern administration wheel horses in Congress, James F. Byrnes (South Carolina), later named by F.D.R. to the Supreme Court and

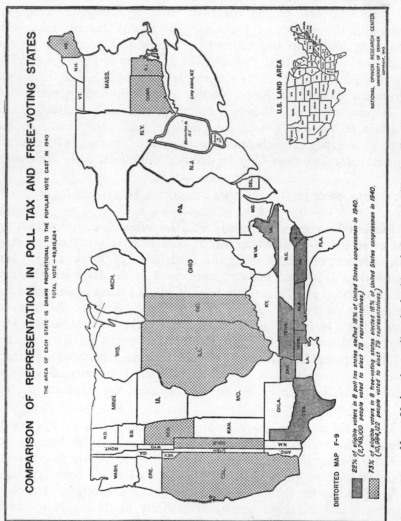

COMPARISON OF REPRESENTATION IN POLL TAX AND FREE-VOTING STATES

THE AREA OF EACH STATE IS DRAWN PROPORTIONAL TO THE POPULAR VOTE CAST IN 1940
TOTAL VOTE — 49,815,624

U.S. LAND AREA

NATIONAL OPINION RESEARCH CENTER
UNIVERSITY OF DENVER
COPYRIGHT, 1943

DISTORTED MAP F-9

22% of eligible voters in 8 poll tax states elected 18% of United States congressmen in 1940.
(2,749,000 people voted to elect 78 representatives)

73% of eligible voters in 8 free-voting states elected 18% of United States congressmen in 1940.
(10,984,122 people voted to elect 79 representatives)

Note: Under the sterling leadership of Governor Ellis Arnall, Georgia was subsequently liberated from the poll tax.

Truman's choice as Secretary of State, Hugo Black (Alabama), Roosevelt's first choice for the Supreme Court, and Alben W. Barkley (Kentucky), Senate majority leader. Others who spoke for an awakened South were Harry S. Truman (Missouri), Claude Pepper (Florida), Harvey M. Kilgore (West Virginia), and Fred M. Vinson (Kentucky).

In general, the party leadership in Congress, almost exclusively southern, held the line for the President and beat back the persistent drives of various blocs. Southern Bourbons in 1934 assailed Rexford Guy Tugwell, well-known economist attached to the Department of Agriculture, and, supported by the farm bloc pressures of big producers of commercial crops, halted the Tugwell program to improve the lot of tenant farmers and sharecroppers. On the other hand, in June, 1934, northern Democrats deserted the party, voting against the Frazier-Lemke Farm Bankruptcy Act in response to the pressures of insurance and banking lobbies against provisions allowing a five-year moratorium on mortgage foreclosures. The South and West passed the bill. No senator from New England, New York, New Jersey, Delaware, Maryland, or Ohio voted for its final enactment. Less sectional in its support, a bipartisan isolationist bloc also passed the Johnson Act, prohibiting loans to nations in default on their war debts. Counterbalancing this defeat for Roosevelt's policy of international cooperation, however, was the passage of the Reciprocal Trade Agreements Act in the same year, 1934.

Blocs representing pressures of special interests began to win other battles over the administration. One was the victory of the silver and inflationary money group in the Silver Purchase Act of 1934. A second was the triumph of the American Legion in the $2,200,000,000 soldiers' bonus bill in 1935. A third was the usual victory of local machines in preventing extension of the merit system of civil service. Patronage became an open issue in the debate over the Housing Authority Act of 1934. Avid for the vast spoils of enlarged or new governmental services, leaders as diverse as Carter Glass and the Tennessee spoilsman Kenneth McKellar began to press for expansion of "senatorial courtesy" to require Senate confirmation of executive appointments to various better jobs paying $4,000 or $5,000 or more. Meanwhile, in his first year and a half, Roosevelt vetoed as many bills as Hoover had rejected in four years. In 1934, Congress, over the President's veto, forced repeal of part of an economy act. In the next two years, Roosevelt, like Harding, Coolidge, and Hoover, was also defeated in attempting to veto the soldiers' bonus. Once more, as in the Congresses of 1922, 1924, and 1931, bonus legislation passed over the President's veto—in the House by the lopsided vote of 318 to 90.

Special interests, aided by the Senate veto on treaties under the two-thirds rule, also defeated in 1934 the treaty with Canada for a vast, joint internal improvement known as the St. Lawrence Seaway and Power Development. For Mississippi Valley farmers, the project offered a better market by freight rate reduction. For the entire population of the region it promised cheap and abundant power output from the international rapids potentially as great as the entire TVA, but because of this as well as the cheap water transportation by the shorter great-circle route to western Europe, which would compete with New Orleans, New York, and Atlantic seaboard ports, it roused the lobbies of utility companies, railroads, and shipping interests to strenuous political action. Sponsored both by Coolidge and Hoover, the treaty had been negotiated before Roosevelt took office. Despite Republican presidential sanction, 20 Republican senators voted against the seaway, while 14 Republicans joined 31 Democrats in favor. Even with Roosevelt's prestige and the effort of the Democratic floor leadership to hold the party in line, 22 Democrats deserted the administration. Huey Long and his Louisiana henchman, John H. Overton, responding with revealing alacrity to New Orleans shipping interests, and all Atlantic seaboard senators, regardless of party, fought the treaty. In both parties the vote testified to a revival of the normal politics of special interests. Once again local economic pressures and local machine considerations were more potent than national party leadership striving to formulate national party principles on the basis of national interest. Less significant was the fact that under the two-thirds rule, a minority frustrated majority rule. By a narrow majority the senators favored the seaway, but another treaty was defeated.

Against mounting conservative resistance, Congress in 1934 made occasional response to presidential leadership. In 1934, long-belated governmental regulation in two important areas was initiated over the communications industry and the stock exchanges. Congress created the FCC (Federal Communications Commission), modeled on the ICC, to license radio and to regulate telegraph and telephone companies with power to investigate abuses and fix reasonable rates. A more cosmic disturbance to special interests was congressional assent to the administration bill creating the SEC (Securities and Exchange Commission). The SEC, like the ICC, was a bipartisan agency empowered to regulate stock exchanges, compel full and truthful information for investors, and restrain the reckless practices of gullible investors, unscrupulous brokers, promoters, and corporation managers whose fraudulent speculations had contributed so much to the crash of 1929. Financial interests launched a tremendous counterattack through newspapers and Washington lobbies. The bill marked time in Congress. Roosevelt, back from fishing in deep-sea waters, greeted congressional leaders with the remark that he would have to apply the "tough guy" tactics he had learned in battling the "barracuda and the shark." Not party organization in Congress but administrative pressure and public demand beat back special interests and forced enactment.

THE WILL OF THE MAJORITY

Ostensibly, the mid-term elections of 1934 augured public confidence in and democratic sanction of the great social forces that were pushing America toward social democracy. When elections to Congress were tabulated, the power and popularity of the Roosevelt Revolution was manifest: no party had ever had such an overwhelming numerical majority. Republicans retained less than 25 per cent of the seats of the House. Of the 96 senators, only 26 were Republican. The nation by the election process had unmistakably registered approval of greater economic controls.

The Roosevelt landslide of 1934, when contrasted with party divisions in Congress after election and with growing success of pressure groups and demagogues, revealed anew the peculiar American problem of majority rule. The history of emasculated and defeated legislation is often as significant in the history of American politics as the statute book itself. Although Roosevelt by 1935 was already under the hot fire of conservatives as a "dictator," the simple facts of the record showed that the President and party leaders needed greater control over their followers in Congress if the party program was to be carried through. The anomaly was presented of Democrats from the North as well as South periodically swept into office "on Roosevelt's coattails," only to drop away from their leader when the election was won. The sharpening contrast between a clear popular mandate and a political structure that crippled the majority's power to govern led within a decade to a new literature on "streamlining Congress" and added to the ferment of political theory seeking answer to the question, "Can representative government do the job?"

Slowly Americans confronted the question of a new political theory of party unity as requisite to national majority rule. Such was the issue in a decade of debate on the question whether it was democratic or undemocratic for a party member in Congress to be "independent," or contrariwise, "a rubber stamp" for the party leadership. History revealed the deception of artful words; instead of honoring a man who was "independent," the founding fathers, George Washington and James Madison, called such a legislator "factious" or "leader of a faction." The independent—in the days of the New Deal as in the days of slavery and sectionalism—was generally a man who was greedy in behalf of local interests. He took his stand on localism, the wishes of the powerful among his local constituents, rather than on the majority will of his party as expressed by the national electorate. Modern analysis of pressure politics suggested that "subservient" might be more appropriate than "independent," since no members of Congress were more assiduous servitors of predatory special interests than those Democrats who repudiated party principles and battled against reform. Supporters of the New Deal, indignantly rejecting "rubber stamp" as weasel words, substituted the English concept, party loyalty.

Twentieth-century social democracy was groping toward the democratic axiom of party responsibility, the belief that the local interests of a constituency (or the local will of a local machine) had less sanctity than the national will of a national majority. Gradually in the literature of liberal social theory the conviction emerged that executive and legislative teamwork under a strong centralized party leadership was an elementary need, if responsibility of the legislator was to conform in practice to the general theory of party accountability and popular mandates. Unless responsibility was so centralized that busy citizens could know what party and what leaders to hold accountable for results, national majorities in elections were as meaningless as the votes in annual meetings of absentee company stockholders.

In the 1935 session of Congress, party leaders suffered a succession of defeats. For the moment, if not for good, wrote the historian Charles Beard, "President Roosevelt's spell of leadership has been definitely broken." The first stunning defeat was the Senate's rejection of American participation in the World Court. This was no novelty, for six similar attempts by Harding, Coolidge, and Hoover had met with an identical fate. Roosevelt had an outright majority for the World Court, but a White House conference failed by seven votes to get the necessary two thirds. Sixty thousand isolationist telegrams, inspired by the Hearst papers and the Michigan radio priest Father Charles E. Coughlin, and attacks on Rooseveltian internationalism by Huey Long, Hiram Johnson, and the "irreconcilables," bolstered the opposition. "To hell with Europe and the rest of those nations!" cried a Republican senator from Minnesota. Twenty Democrats bolted to join fourteen Republicans to defeat adherence to the World Court.

On a "must" bill, a $4,880,000,000 relief and public works appropriation, House leaders were forced to resort to a Democratic caucus and to yield to congressional demands for patronage involved in the bill. Carter Glass, anti-Roosevelt chairman of the vital Senate Appropriations Committee, fought the very principle of federal relief. Although the need was immediate and urgent, conservatives on the Glass committee nearly succeeded in forcing a drastic reduction of relief by changing it to a simple dole. The vote was a tie—10–10. Amendments on the floor further imperiled the bill. Ultimately, the appropriation passed in a form constituting a victory for the New Deal; but it had taken the new Congress over three months to pass a single major bill.

To utilize the huge appropriation, Roosevelt reorganized federal relief to meet earlier objections against direct relief and hasty temporary projects like "raking leaves." The less efficient and decentralized system of primary control by state and local officials, which had prevailed under the previous FERA, was now corrected by central responsibility under the new WPA (Works Progress Administration) directed by Harry Hopkins, long trained in the field of social welfare. Projects of lasting value or of broad immediate social benefit were organized and developed. Where feasible, WPA sought to implement recommendations of the new National Resources Board for integrated, planned development of land and water resources. Under the Rural Electrification Administration, power lines were run by WPA workers to farm districts never reached by power companies. Illustrative of the many and varied social benefits were 1,654 medical and dental clinics, 2,000,000 calls at homes by visiting nurses, the transcription for the blind of over a million pages in Braille, and the erection of several thousand buildings for schools, tuberculosis sanatoriums, and other social institutions of lasting benefit. Meanwhile, the NYA (National Youth Administration) sought through work relief to forestall the devitalizing psychology of the dole and at the same time help students from bankrupt families to continue in school or college.

Under dilatory congressional procedure the famous Social Security Act of 1935 required seven months for passage. New Dealers in the administration and outside experts, after a year of thorough study, presented a specific plan that Roosevelt recommended on January 17 in a strong special message. Three months later, Robert L. Doughton, conservative North Carolina stock raiser and chairman of the House Ways and Means Committee, reported that the bill "has been entirely rewritten" with "important modifications." Long delay in enacting the bill was due in part to congressional fondness for protracted hearings. Assorted agitations accompanied the hearings; a rising clamor of organizations demanding varying forms of redistribution of the wealth of the nation, frightening legislators with the specter of massive unrest springing from the insecurities that had made precarious the livelihood of millions. In view of intense demand for social security legislation, the House bill, once submitted, readily passed, 371–33, amid a flood of sentimental oratory. In August the Senate concurred, although conservatives like Senator Arthur H. Vandenberg were disposed to say more than nay. Meanwhile the National Association of Manufacturers and spokesmen for illiberal employers denounced social security pay-roll taxes, raised the cry of "bureaucracy," bewailed governmental "handouts" as tokens of "the decline of the American backbone." They promptly instigated a campaign to convince the country—and the Supreme Court—that social security, like the rest of the New Deal, was unconstitutional. Others, including Townsendites, demanded more generous security allotments. Roosevelt, in signing the bill, called it a cushion against depressions but admitted its coverage was "by no means complete." Liberal critics regarded some of the provisions as more limited than the national social insurance adopted by Germany half a century before.

The Social Security Act, while national in intention, relied upon federal financial support of the social insurance programs of the separate states. The weakness of variable federal grants-in-aid, the amount dependent upon the amount appropriated by the individual state, became apparent when an impoverished commonwealth like Mississippi allowed an old-age pension of only $4.79 a month. Farm laborers, house servants, salaried workers, and others were excluded from benefits of the act. Conservative leaders of the medical association helped block provision for public health insurance. A decade later, indicative of new ferment inspired by England's famous Beveridge Plan, Senator Robert Wagner, sponsor of the administration bill in 1935, was leading the fight for a new social security law.

"Organizations promoting fantastic schemes," Roosevelt warned, "have aroused hopes which cannot possibly be fulfilled." The Social Security Act was one of several policies deflating the Townsend Planners, who claimed 6,000,000 adherents; Father Coughlin's Union for Social Justice, with an alleged following of 8,000,000 who endorsed money inflation and government ownership of banks; and Huey Long's Share-Our-Wealth Society, with a reputed membership of 3,000,000. An irrefutable if frightening evidence of mass unrest, the Townsendites demanded that Congress make America a Shangri-La for the aged. The cost of the Townsend panacea, $200 a month old-age pensions with a requirement that it be spent within 60 days, was estimated at twenty billions or more a year. Most hard-boiled and successful of would-be American fuehrers, Huey Long adopted the slogan "Every Man a King," promised a government guarantee of $5,000 income to every family, and copied the original Nazis of the early 1920's in spreading anti-big-business propaganda. The "Louisiana Kingfish" also copied the Nazi secret police system and ruled his state by graft, strong-arm men, and "reform," aided by ballot box manipulation that astonished the experts of Tammany and even the Pennsylvania Republicans of Allegheny County.

HOUSING AND NEGRO DEATH RATES

(FROM TUBERCULOSIS IN CINCINNATI)

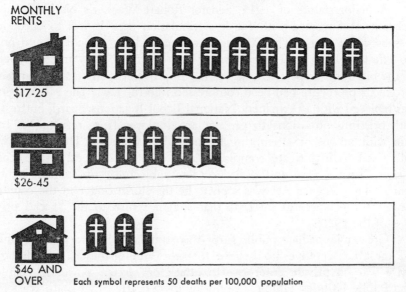

MONTHLY
RENTS

$17-25

$26-45

$46 AND
OVER

Each symbol represents 50 deaths per 100,000 population

PICTOGRAPH CORP.

Always Huey Long was a "100 per cent American." When fascism came in this country, he remarked privately, it would come in the name of antifascism. Such phenomena were symptomatic of unresolved social tensions. Among others, the Texas Congressman Martin Dies resorted to every-man-a-king language to win an election, and when Long was assassinated, aspired to the role of the nation's leading "100 per cent American."

Aware of radical pressure inspired by glaring inequalities and concentrated wealth, Roosevelt in June, 1935, urged enactment of social welfare taxation to uproot Secretary Mellon's system of favoritism to upper income groups. "Social unrest and a deepening sense of unfairness," warned the President in his message to Congress, "are dangers to our national life which we must minimize by rigorous methods." The response of Congress was the Revenue Act of 1935. While it was not "rigorous" in applying Roosevelt's principle of widening the diffusion of wealth, it nevertheless increased taxes on inherited estates, big incomes, excess profits, big corporate incomes, and decreased taxes on smaller business incomes. The press bitterly denounced the bill as a "soak-the-rich" measure. Aiding its passage was a lingering national indignation aroused by an earlier revelation on the part of a Senate investigation: under Republican enactments of the 1920's, J. P. Morgan and partners had managed to escape payment of income taxes in 1932.

A major statute of 1935, Senator Robert Wagner's National Labor Relations Act, passed with far less tribulation than it was to encounter in subsequent years. The Wagner Act replaced the temporary and none too effective labor experiment under the defunct NRA, and opponents of the bill little suspected how vast an improvement in structure and enforcement procedure had been compressed into the law. The NRA agency was replaced with a permanent National Labor Relations Board, buttressed with bristling provisions to prevent an employer from refusing to bargain with unions or attempting to intimidate workers. The NLRB was authorized to investigate complaints and, like the Federal Trade Commission, issue "cease and desist" orders subject to enforcement by the courts. The Wagner Act was soon to be the storm center in the counter-thrust of the powerful interests that sought return to the special privileges of the 1920's.

Greater immediate public furor was stimulated by propaganda which led most conservatives to believe that the administration had declared active war on private enterprise by attack on electric power companies. The Public Utilities Holding Company Act, drafted by "brain trusters," was sponsored in the Senate by Burton K. Wheeler (Montana) and in the House by Sam Rayburn (Texas). The utilities bill passed at the end of the 1935 session after a seven months' struggle in which factious party members rebelled against administration leaders and seriously impaired New Deal prestige. Party splits, sectional votes, opposition by northern members in response to local interests, gigantic lobby activity, nonrecord votes, and deadlock between the two houses—all exhibited the abysmal breakdown of party responsibility. More than in any other battle in Roosevelt's first term, the cherished "independence" of Congress was revealed to be not so much a defense of the public interest as a screen for response to the pressures of powerful special interests.

The utilities bill was by no means as rigorous as Wilsonian antitrust proposals to abolish all holding companies. Years of investigations had conclusively demonstrated that the financial jugglers of the utility empires had made indefensible use of the holding company device to water stocks, mulct investors, conceal monopoly profits, and bleed consumers by extortionate rates. For such purposes rather than for efficiency, holding company had been pyramided on top of holding company to as many as seven tiers. Samuel Insull had not been forgotten—erstwhile Chicago millionaire who enriched himself by pyramiding utilities upward toward a three billion dollar structure, only to flee the country when he crashed, leaving investors to pocket a loss approximating two thirds of a billion dollars. Though the facts were common knowledge, the crucial section of the bill, a so-called "death sentence" on nonessential holding companies, squeezed through the Senate by a margin of only one vote. Senate amendments to mitigate the death sentence were sponsored by northern Democrats, and on the crucial vote twenty-nine Democrats joined the opposition. Senate Republicans split 15–8 against the death sentence. In the House, conservative Democrats controlling the Commerce Committee reported a bill shorn of power to deal with pyramids. The Democratic majority split—166–130—rejecting the Senate bill and preferring the weak House bill without the death sentence. Votes showed the South and West most united for utility regulation, with bipartisan support of laissez faire mainly centered in the industrial East and Midwest.

Such disregard of the need for an effective public policy revealed that the New Deal had found no remedy for the weakness of the party tie and the caprices of divided responsibility. The party tie once again proved easy to sever when powerful pressure groups mobilized full strength. Six hundred utilities lobbyists descended on hapless congressmen, nearly one for every legislator. "Inspired" telegrams, stacks of them identical, poured in on Congress at a peak rate of four thousand an hour. Roosevelt demanded a lobby investigation and pointed the moral for public view: "I have watched the use of investors' money to make the investor believe that the efforts of Government to protect him are designed to defraud him." Instead of investigating the telegrams, "independent" Democrats such as Howard Smith of Virginia, Eugene Cox of Georgia, and John J. O'Connor of New York City, who was chairman of the powerful Committee on Rules, converted the House investigation into a whitewash of the utilities and an assault against "administration lobbying" to get the bill passed! But the Senate investigation, ably led by Hugo Black, revealed scandal in all its fullness, the barrage of fake telegrams fraudulently signed with names taken from telephone directories, and a colossal lobby expenditure of some four million dollars taken out of the pockets of stockholders to defend pyramiding. William Randolph Hearst, who had been in direct communication with heads of the great Associated Gas and Electric system, vainly sought to prevent the Black committee from exposing telegrams in which he instructed his Washington staff to slant the news against the bill. Publicity strengthened party responsibility sufficiently to break the deadlock over the denatured House bill and the Senate death sentence. The law passed in a compromise form permitting two tiers of holding companies. The compromise proved largely ineffective in the ensuing decade; for the death sentence had changed into a reprieve. Nevertheless, the utilities act signalized the first important reversal of long federal neglect by authorizing utility regulation through the Federal Power Commission and the SEC.

There were other administration defeats in the 1935 session. A government contract bill, a shipping bill, and pure food and drug legislation failed. A new banking act was restricted under amendments sponsored by Carter Glass. Congress rejected Roosevelt's proposal of a constitutional amendment to correct a long series of court decisions that had provided an escape from income taxes by ruling that government securities were tax exempt. Through a drive of the isolationist bloc, splitting party lines, the legislature also defeated the administration by threatening a filibuster and thus forcing acceptance of a compromise Neutrality Act. But time and the rising menace of war were to prove Roosevelt right in his criticism that the neutrality law's mandatory feature endangered defense.

When in the 1936 session the pressure of the American Legion was rewarded by prompt passage of the bonus over the President's veto, this drain and others on the Treasury led Roosevelt to ask additional taxes. Once again Wall Street cried out against New Deal tax reforms. Nevertheless, the equalitarian social policy of the "Wealth Tax Act" of 1935 was extended by a new graduated tax on undistributed profits. Hitherto, many corporations, by saving up profits instead of paying larger dividends, had contributed to the economic evil of "oversaving" and at the same time had provided a loophole for tax avoidance. A ship subsidy bill, defeated in the 1935 session but to prove of great value when war broke, now passed, creating a National Maritime Commission and providing authority to build a government-owned merchant fleet. Senator Black's antilobby bill, emanating from the utilities investigation and requiring lobbyists to register and reveal the sources of their income, passed the Senate, only to be defeated in the House by the wily amendments of Howard Smith, arch-conservative of Virginia Democrats.

WEAPONS OF OPPOSITION

Despite the popularity of the New Deal, victories were won by the Old Deal. Pressure groups capitalized on the weakness of majority leadership under the system of separated powers and on two other strategic advantages: a one-sided interpretation of public opinion in most of the great newspapers; and a drastic process of nullification of New Deal laws by the ostensibly impartial operation of the judicial veto. The bulk of the press, although favorable in Roosevelt's first year, rapidly swung to vehement hostility. The Supreme Court, likewise cooperative in the "emergency" period, began to levy harsh indictments against the chief executive and his party program.

Unregenerate protagonists of normalcy, columnists, commentators, and congressional die-hards, seeking to revive the faith of the twenties in "practical" statesmanship, attacked Henry A. Wallace's world view of the agricultural problem as visionary and flayed Secretary of Interior Harold L. Ickes as a reformer. An anti-intellectual campaign evoked ridicule of the drafting of "the brain trusters" and trained experts into governmental service. Artful conservatives well knew that the mind of a trained expert, a government engineer, an economist, or a social scien tist was no respecter of special privileges and exemptions that stood in the way of rational democracy. Economists associated with the administration like Rexford G. Tugwell and brilliant lawyers like Benjamin Cohen were scurrilously attacked as enemies of capitalism and impractical visionaries, although they were neither. The increasing clamor in the press and radio against the New Deal was hailed by wishful conservatives as an indication that, despite the mid-term landslide, growing divergence had appeared between the government and the people. From 1935 through 1945 a foreign visitor who based his judgment of public opinion by what he read in the papers would have supposed the Roosevelt administration the most unpopular in American history. But public opinion polls and Roosevelt's successive triumphs in elections belied such appearances.

The ineffective opposition of the Republican party and its candidate, Governor Alfred Landon of Kansas, in the presidential campaign of 1936 was actually less significant than the larger and more effective opposition engineered by great leaders of America's financial and industrial corporations. Not merely for the few months preceding elections but continuously over the years, powerful special interests, marshaled by potent organizations like the National Association of Manufacturers, mounted an offensive against reform. Its magnitude even exceeded Mark Hanna's spectacular organization of business against Bryan in 1896. Its psychological intensity was gradually canalized into an irrational, emotional "hate-Roosevelt" stereotype in which the New Deal leader came to personify or explain away great social forces beyond the comprehension of "economic royalists" of the bygone age of normalcy. Of more permanent significance was the organized character of the opposition, which indicated a profound change in economic institutions. Business leadership was becoming institutionalized all over the world. Cartels in international trade and trusts and trade associations within nations were creating greater solidarity in the inner councils of business leaders. "Peak associations" like the N.A.M. in the United States and similar central organizations abroad confirmed a tendency toward an institutionalized leadership long in evolution. Possessing tremendous prestige as the semiofficial voice of the businessmen of a given country, such associations became an international counterweight to social democracy. These nuclear business associations took on a political complexion, serving as central organs for the molding of business opinion and for organized exertion of pressure to sway government policies. The N.A.M., declared its president in a masterpiece of understatement, "has been forced to enter the political arena."

Less permanently significant than "peak associations" was a succession of transitory "front" organizations financed by wealthy families to wage propaganda war for "recovery without reform." Most famous was the American Liberty League. Others masqueraded as farmers', or economists', or lawyers' committees to preserve "the American Way." Among such were the Farmers' Independence Council, the Southern Committee to Uphold the Constitution, and the Economists' National Committee on Monetary Policy. To the Liberty League and associations of its kind the Du Ponts—uncles, aunts, and retainers with varying names but identical views—contributed well over $350,000. The Mellons, the Morgans, the Pews, the Rockefellers and their widely ramifying connections were similarly generous. Nevertheless, for "public relations" publicity, pamphlets, speaking engagements, and advertising, N.A.M.'s total expenditure, when magnified by the estimated value of contributed space and free publication of "news" items, exceeded the outlay of all of the front organizations and the combined reported campaign expenditure of the Democratic and Republican parties. Testimony of N.A.M. officials revealed a cash expenditure of over $4,000,000, and contributed aid which N.A.M. valued at some additional $30,000,000. Features of the N.A.M. campaign were the daily comic, "Uncle Abner Says," and the radio program, "The American Family Robinson." Columnists like George Sokolsky and radio commentators like Fulton Lewis, Jr., received material benefits or encouragement from N.A.M. and affiliated interests. By 1939 the Senate Committee on Education and Labor, after celebrated investigations under leadership of "Young Bob" La Follette, reported on the vast extension of N.A.M. activity since 1934.

The National Association of Manufacturers has blanketed the country with a propaganda which in technique has relied upon indirection of meaning, and in presentation upon secrecy and deception. Radio speeches, public meetings, news cartoons, editorials, advertising, motion pictures and many other artifices of propaganda have not in most instances disclosed to the public their origin with the association.

Even with the institutionalized leadership to elicit a more unified response from the business community, business forces were as divided as other social groups. Peak associations flagrantly misrepresented business solidarity. The N.A.M. and the American Medical Association, for example, concealed divergence within their own ranks. Institutionalized leadership drowned out lesser voices of small dissenters and diverted attention from conflicts between small enterprise and monopolistic interests. In 1936 only slightly more than half of the nation's businessmen, as tabulated by public opinion polls, favored Republican victory. All the other groups polled distinctly favored the New Deal. Kinship to N.A.M. was exhibited by great newspaper enterprises, where opposition to social democracy was staggering. Over 70 per cent of the big metropolitan press fulminated for Landon and Republican normalcy. The Hearst press, various other Democratic papers, and all but one of the great chains echoed N.A.M. and the Liberty League.

But propagandist fury and news distortion in the campaign of 1936 had a boomerang effect. Nonvoters, and people who seldom voted, indignantly cast ballots to vindicate Franklin Roosevelt. The Democrats, in the largest vote that had ever been polled, carried every state except Maine and Vermont for the most complete sweep of the electoral vote in over a hundred years. In the popular vote, Roosevelt rolled up the all-time record total of 27,751,000 to 16,682,000 for luckless Landon. The six greatest industrial states gave the Republicans scarcely more than 40 per cent of the vote. In 1936, as later in 1940 and 1944, the President would have had a majority even had he lost every state of the Democratic South. The unparalleled landslide owed more to the size of the total vote than to a switch of Republican voters and independents to the Democrats. The tremendous magnetism of Roosevelt's leadership and the popularity of the New Deal among the plain people induced millions of nonvoters and new young voters to turn out on election day. A momentous democratic expansion of the electorate, as in the Jeffersonian and Jacksonian revolutions, was an important social consequence of the Roosevelt Revolution.

THE TWILIGHT OF THE SUPREME COURT

Yet at the moment of its greatest victory, the New Deal seemed on the verge of its greatest defeat. What Old Guard forces were unable to accomplish through pressure groups in Washington, through the barrage in the newspapers, and through the ballot box on election day, they nevertheless were accomplishing through conservative predominance in the judiciary. By 1935, the uncompromising minority, like the great slavery interests before them, widened their massive assault on advancing democracy, hiring a distinguished battery of legal talent to fight an enormous body of litigation through state and federal courts. What the Liberty League and the N.A.M. had failed to achieve began to appear possible by judicial veto. In 1935 successive blows of the Supreme Court struck down NRA, the Railroad Retirement Act, and the Frazier-Lemke Farm Mortgage Act. In 1936 the Court nullified AAA, the Bituminous Coal Stabilization Act—"the little NRA"—the New York Minimum Wage Act, the Municipal Bankruptcy Act, and left the constitutionality of TVA in jeopardy by an oblique decision. Two other decisions indicated judicial hostility to regulatory agencies. In the Humphrey case (1935) the Supreme Court accused the President of unconstitutional action in dismissing a Republican who had been appointed by Coolidge and reappointed by Hoover to the Federal Trade Commission, where he had contrived to convert that agency to his genial disbelief in taking -seriously the duty of enforcing antitrust laws. In the Jones case (1936), involving the new SEC, a 6–3 decision against the administration indicated repetition of the historic judicial process of whittling down the powers of a government agency as the Supreme Court had previously done with the ICC and the FTC. Justice Benjamin Cardozo pointedly remarked in a dissenting opinion that the decision made the SEC "the sport of clever knaves."

At the moment when the people sought strong governmental action to attain social democracy, the Supreme Court boldly insisted on strict construction, denying to popular majorities the power to govern. By the new doctrine of "dual federalism," the Court twisted the Tenth Amendment into a novel state rights device to narrow traditional powers of Congress. Similarly, assumption of judicial prerogative to forbid delegation of authority to administrative agencies withered legislative and executive power. The same doctrines stretched the Court's own power, allowing it wider incursions into the fields of political policy. When judicial strict construction stifled congressional power over commerce, blocking social reform, Roosevelt reacted strongly. Like the first Roosevelt, the President accused the Court of creating a zone in which neither federal nor state government had the power to govern. Narrow interpretation of the commerce clause, he declared, turned the country back to "the horse-and-buggy age."

The American mind was ill prepared for re-evaluation of the place of a judiciary in a democratic system. In no other country had constitutional mechanics won such uncritical attachment. Schoolbooks emphasized the formal constitutional structure rather than the functional realities of majority rule by political parties. Constitutional symbols made the Court a "lighthouse" or the "balance wheel" of government, as

Thomas Reed Powell urbanely noted, so that "you see the Supreme Court shining and balancing in a very wonderful way." Comfortable housewives, people who worked in office buildings, and the fortunate who clipped coupons or cashed stockholders' checks had fervent faith in the austere impartiality of judicial review. True, some millions in the trade unions, from bitter experience with labor injunctions and court bias for the open shop, had a diminished reverence for the majesty of the law. But the public was conditioned to believe that if the Court whittled down the powers of an administrative agency, or outlawed a state statute, or struck down an act of Congress, the Court spoke with impartial finality. That the Constitution did not explicitly assign finality to the Court, few realized.

It had not always been so. The Jeffersonian challenge to the judiciary had been based on the early theory of power divided between the three branches. Instead of accepting judicial finality in constitutional interpretation, Jefferson held that the Court was merely a coordinate branch equal to but not superior to the chief executive and the Congress. By the twentieth century a whole generation of erudite justices like the beloved Oliver Wendell Holmes, scholars like the learned Edward S. Corwin of Princeton, and rapier-wits of the law schools like Thomas Reed Powell of Harvard had demonstrated that under the "unwritten constitution" the unique institution of judicial review had enlarged judicial power beyond anything conceived by the framers. Older democratic traditions had never assumed it legitimate for the judiciary to determine political policy. Yet the Court was encroaching on the lawmaking function. The Court majority, frequently in split decisions, determined public policy as truly as votes in Congress. Among constitutional experts it was no secret that in annulling or sustaining a law, conservative and liberal justices necessarily satisfied their consciences not by immutable legal principles but by personal political philosophy. How otherwise explain the conservative consistency of the Republican justices, Pierce Butler, George Sutherland, Willis Van Devanter, and the Bourbon Democrat, Justice James C. McReynolds? Or famous dissenting opinions of liberals, Louis D. Brandeis, Harlan Stone, and Benjamin Cardozo?

Split decisions became significant when they turned not so much on plain language of the Constitution as on political questions of public policy. Few decisions were unanimous. New Deal currency devaluation escaped nullification by hairline 5–4 decisions in three Gold Clause cases. The justices split 6–3 in the AAA tax case of January, 1936. In Justice Owen J. Roberts' decision, personal philosophy was visible: by the broad constitutional construction of Congress in AAA there was danger that the Constitution would be "subverted" and the independent states "obliterated," leaving to the central government "uncontrolled" power over every state and community. The liberals, Stone, Brandeis, and Cardozo, dissented. The Securities Act of 1933 was upheld 6–3. In ruling against old-age pensions by voiding the Railroad Retirement Act of 1934 the Court split 5–4; Chief Justice Charles Evans Hughes joined the dissenting liberals. The same split, 5–4, with the same dissenters, reappeared in outlawing the Municipal Bankruptcy Act of 1934. The Guffey Bituminous Coal Conservation Act of 1935 was held unconstitutional in a multisplit decision, 5–1–3, with Hughes writing a separate opinion, and Brandeis, Stone, and Cardozo dissenting.

By 1934, prior to the adverse New Deal decisions, Edward S. Corwin, America's leading scholar on constitutional history, concluded that the judiciary had slowly been moving to an untenable position. In *The Twilight of the Supreme Court,* a volume as prophetic as it was profound, Corwin observed that Court precedents had multiplied on both sides of crucial questions. Accordingly the Supreme Court was vested with virtually "complete freedom of choice whether to sustain or to overturn the New Deal." Industrialism and technology, making state lines and old legal clichés increasingly anomalous, doomed any attempt to keep the Constitution in "cold storage." Twilight was approaching unless the Court retreated from attempts "to supervise national legislative policies" on a basis which, "in the name of the Constitution, repeals and destroys that historic document."

Abandonment of what Justice Stone called judicial "self-restraint" set the stage for a movement to reform the Supreme Court. The swing of the judicial scythe against the New Deal enactments coincided with the rising opposition whereby great city newspapers and pressure groups sought defeat of the utilities holding company bill and similar pending legislation. Whether or not encouraged by outside opposition to the New Deal, the Court departed drastically from the century-old principle of judicial respect for the constitutional views of the other two branches of government. "Presumption of constitutionality" was a long-revered axiom. "This Court," said Justice Sutherland in an opinion, "by an unbroken line of decisions from Chief Justice Marshall to the present day, has steadily adhered to the rule that every possible presumption is in favor of the validity of an act of Congress. . . ." Nonetheless, by the end of 1936 eight New Deal acts had been voided. Organizations like N.A.M. and the Liberty League confidently proclaimed that the Wagner Labor Relations Act would be next. TVA, the Public Utilities Holding Company Act, and even the Social Security Act were in jeopardy. The issue was again much as it had been eighty years before, when Abraham Lincoln had spoken:

. . . if the policy of the Government upon vital questions affecting the whole people is to be irrevocably fixed by decisions of the Supreme Court the instant they are made in ordinary litigation between parties in personal actions, the people will have ceased to be their own rulers. . . .

At other great historic changes in party supremacy, after 1800, 1828, and 1900, the people had encountered the problem of judicial nullification that threatened to frustrate majority rule. So again in 1935, institutional drives revived the unresolved conflict, this time in the setting of social democracy. Once more the conflict sprang from the incongruity of the mechanics of separation of powers and the dynamics of a party system of majority rule. More reverent toward the dynamics of majority rule than toward eighteenth-century mechanics, Roosevelt boldly made issue of judicial nullification. The elections had given him an imposing mandate and amassed a Democratic majority of 328 to 107 in the House and 77 to 19 in the Senate. On February 5, 1937, he submitted a Court reform bill to the new Congress. It would empower him to appoint an additional new justice for each of the justices aged 70 or older who had held office for ten years or longer. There followed the bitter struggle of "The 168 Days" during which Congress balked. The proposal to reform the Court involved the undeniably constitutional power of Congress to enlarge the Court and the President's right to appoint progressive justices to fill vacancies. In his "fireside chat" of March 9 Roosevelt candidly declared his intention of infusing new blood into the judicial branch by appointing "justices who will not undertake to override the judgment of the Congress on legislative policies."

Conservative Republicans and Democrats in Congress defeated the original reform bill, but Roosevelt remarked that this seemed merely a battle that was lost in a campaign that was won. The Supreme Court beat a strategic retreat; Hughes' and Roberts' desertion of the die-hard conservatives gave currency to the witticism, "A switch in time saves nine." A series of decisions, delivered during the 168 days, reversed the industrial strict construction that had often frustrated legislative majorities in the fifty years since 1886. The Wagner Labor Relations Act, already confidently ruled unconstitutional by distinguished lawyers of the Liberty League, was suddenly christened constitutional by a somewhat chastened Court; but even so, its NLRB escaped nullification only by a 5–4 decision, McReynolds, Butler, Sutherland, and Van Devanter dissenting. The four dissenters became a permanent minority. Soon Van Devanter, aged 78, announced he would resign. Meanwhile conservative Republicans and Democrats killed the original reform bill. But Congress enacted piecemeal parts of the bill, including the provision to stimulate voluntary resignation of superannuated justices by offering to those who had reached 70 a retirement pension at full salary. Roosevelt's purpose was achieved.

Both the public and the Court gained in understanding of the incongruity of judicial finality and majority rule. The new line of decisions overturned the Coppage case (1915) and other precedents upholding the open shop and stifling collective bargaining. The Social Security Act passed the judicial gamut by a scant margin of 5–4 on the unemployment compensation provision. Nevertheless, social security was now constitutional. Following the example of Congress, the Court majority adopted a modern broad construction that liberated the Constitution as an instrument of social democracy. State minimum-wage laws and unemployment compensation acts, a new federal railroad act covering even intrastate "shop" employees, and a new federal Farm Mortgage Moratorium Act, all were held constitutional before the end of the 168 days. Roosevelt's eventual appointment of seven new justices speeded the Court's extrication of itself from the coils of the past.

Basic in the constitutional revolution wrought by the Supreme Court bill was the broad construction typified in the case validating the Wagner Act, *NLRB v. Jones & Laughlin Steel Corporation* (1937). The decision expressed horror of a constitutional construction that "would effectually obliterate the distinction between what is national and what is local"; but the decision itself in effect obliterated the distinction. The Court recognized, as Presidents and Congresses had decades earlier, that virtually all manufacturers had long ago ceased to produce for local markets; and that legal abstractions, conjuring up a difference between manufacturing and commerce, bore no relation to reality. The decision rejected the Jones & Laughlin argument that commerce was limited to "movements of commerce"; that "manufacturing is not commerce"; and that wages, hours, and union affiliations of "production employees" had no "legal connection" with commercial shipments of the steel corporation. Congress, by the Wagner Act, had made a legal connection; and the act was constitutional. The rulings against labor unions in the Adair and Coppage decisions of 1908 and 1915 were "inapplicable"; and the exemption of manufacturing from regulation by the ruling in the Knight case of 1895 had been "necessarily and expressly decided to be unsound." The Standard Oil and American Tobacco decisions of 1911 had already applied the commerce power to "productive industry." The "reach of federal power" could extend to activities connected with "productive industry although the industry when separately viewed is local." The Court, indignantly declining the steel corporation's persuasions to operate "in an intellectual vacuum," observed that 75 per cent of Jones & Laughlin production was destined for interstate and foreign trade.

A. P. Sloane, W. P. Chrysler, C. W. Nash, and other auto makers leaving White House, 1934, after rejecting advice to accept the inevitable, and recognize unions. *(Acme Photo)*

R. T. Frankensteen (second from right) and other organizers at company gates peacefully distributing union literature in 1937, just before beatings by "loyal workers."

(Press Association)

ne of 1937 beatings. andcuffs dangling from cket led *Time* to infer at at least one "worker" s a company guard.

(Press Association)

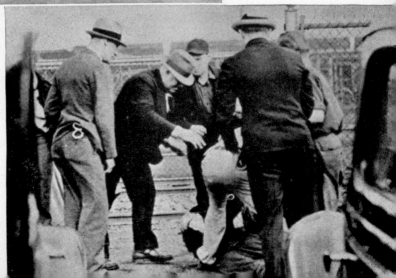

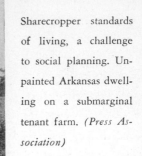

Sharecropper standards of living, a challenge to social planning. Unpainted Arkansas dwelling on a submarginal tenant farm. *(Press Association)*

The Dust Bowl, 1934–1936, another challenge to planning. Misuse of land, the dry cycle, and drifted soil desolate this Kansas farm. *(Brown Brothers)*

Upon the ashes of an antiquated firetrap hospital, the people of a small Pennsylvania community erected a well-equipped, modern structure with WPA funds.

(Underwood-Stratton)

Top—Large-scale housing. Parkchester, in New York City, built with private funds (Metropolitan Life Insurance Company) to provide modern housing for families of moderate income. Accommodates 35,000 people; has its own shops and recreation facilities.

(Fairchild Aerial Survey, Inc.)

Center — Arsenal of Democracy. Production miracle of workers, officials, and government financing in a California war plant, 1943.

(Acme Photo)

Below—Big Government in wartime. Huge Pentagon Building, War Department Headquarters, virtually a city itself, employing 22,000 men and women workers.

(Signal Corps Photo)

Above—Prime Minister Churchill in Washington addressing a joint session of Senate and House, 1943. *(Press Association)*

Below—A quarantine on aggressors. Opening session in New York of United Nations Security Council, 1946. *(Acme Photo)*

We are asked to shut our eyes to the plainest facts of our national life and to deal with the question . . . in an intellectual vacuum. . . . When industries organize themselves on a national scale, making their relation to interstate commerce the dominant factor in their activities, how can it be maintained that their industrial labor relations constitute a forbidden field into which Congress may not enter . . .?

The decision, flashing a green light to broader congressional controls over production, was likely to bulk large in the future. Had the Court switched to this position earlier, it would not have made some of its previous decisions.

UNIONS OF THEIR OWN CHOOSING

The Supreme Court in the Jones & Laughlin decision expressed the belief that if employers recognized the "right of their employees to their own organizations and their unrestricted right of representation," controversy between capital and labor would become less grave. But employers who had never negotiated with unions were less philosophical about compliance with the law; and labor unrest, long brewing, resulted in another great battle running through the furious days of Roosevelt's second term. Reaching peak proportions in the months of the Supreme Court controversy, industrial conflict gave hostile newspapers and members of Congress wider opportunity to blacken the experiment in social democracy. For 1937 was the violent year of the "Little Steel" strike, the "Chicago Massacre," and the amazing "sit-down" in the plants of the automobile makers.

The international force of social democracy was older than the crash of 1929, but its dynamic expression in American labor law and labor organization was born of depression and coincident with the New Deal. Strikes—risking the loss of one's job—fell to a fraction in the hopeless years of economic collapse. Submission, enforced by depression, was replaced by hope inspired by the New Deal. If strikes are acts of anger and frustration, they are also symbols of hope. By 1934 a yearly total of over a million workers were striking against automobile manufacturers, textile firms, Pacific coast shipping interests, and other employers who refused to bargain. The strikes were broken. In cities around San Francisco Bay the waterfront strike of longshoremen was smashed by "vigilantes"—citizens beguiled into thinking they were upholding "law and order" by patrolling the streets armed with pick handles, in reality victimized by employers for the lawless end of denying workers their democratic right to picket and bargain. Vigilantes, antiunion authorities in state and local governments, police and state constabularies contributed to the defeat of a nation-wide textile strike. Labor and the government would have to exert their strength if workers were to enjoy their legal rights.

In law, if not immediately in fact, Senator Wagner's improvements on Clause 7-A of the NRA broadened the protection of the rights of labor in 1935. The Wagner Act re-established the NRA principle of free elections enabling plant workers to select representatives of their own choosing. Its new agency for industrial peace, NLRB, empowered to conduct shop elections and to prevent employer interference or domination, began to intervene when requested by workers and energetically applied new procedures to prevent notoriously bad employers from using unfair means to prevent equality in bargaining. The immediate result of the Wagner Act was exacerbation of relations between unions and that segment of the managerial class which still glorified the open shop as the American way. Many leading corporations in the 1920's, finding blunt insistence on a nonunion shop no longer tenable, had adopted the device of a company union. Welfare programs coupled with company unions had been successfully utilized in Rockefeller mines, Morgan steel plants, and the American Telephone and Telegraph Company. Welfare programs betokened a more humane attitude on the part of scattered employers, but most company unions were devices to prevent collective bargaining. As such, they were sanctioned by the National Association of Manufacturers, which had never abandoned cherished belief in the managerial omnipotence of the open shop. The Wagner Act challenged the N.A.M. program: it outlawed "yellow-dog contracts," required employers to bargain collectively, and restrained the common practice of firing employees who were attempting to bargain. The Jones & Laughlin decision in 1937 left no grounds for questioning the law's constitutionality; but enforcement depended on the strength of the NLRB and the unions and the attitude of the public and the courts.

A new phenomenon in America, a government seeking to meet the challenge of social democracy, gave mighty stimulus to the self-help process whereby workers united to struggle for higher standards of employer responsibility. But another stimulus made for dissension within labor's ranks. The semiaristocratic form of union favored by the American Federation of Labor, craft unions composed of the better-paid and more easily organized skilled workers, did not truly answer the objectives of social democracy. Industrial unions on a mass base had successfully made headway in England forty years before. The "one big union" principle had captured American imagination in the early days of the Knights of Labor, only to be snuffed out in the black reaction of the Haymarket frenzy. As Wilsonian Democracy faded out in war years, the government had been stampeded into destroying the industrial unions of the flamboyant but poorly consolidated Industrial Workers of the World. Thereafter the Federation itself, though cherishing respectability under conservative leaders, had shrunk from a membership of over four million to little more than two million in 1933.

Aggressive younger leaders urged the creation of large-scale "vertical" unions to organize an entire industry. They contended that division of workers into scattered separate workers' craft unions left large numbers unorganized, and weakened potential bargaining powers in mass production industries. By 1935 secession loomed in the Federation. A movement to organize a vertical union in steel, to repair the damage of 1919 when the open-shop drive had broken the union, was blocked by President William Green, Matthew Woll, and other old-line labor leaders. Various vertical unions that had already emerged within the Federation formed a Committee for Industrial Organization in 1936—the original C.I.O. The leading sponsors were level-headed Philip Murray of the United Mine Workers; the Midwesterner, John L. Lewis, smart, beetle-browed, square-jawed, avid for power, the messiah of the United Mine Workers, leading their struggle against dismal poverty and annual seasonal unemployment in the coal fields; David Dubinsky, Polish immigrant who had recoiled against American sweatshops and who was leader of the International Ladies' Garment Workers, an organization dedicated to economic democracy and a broad union program of medical care, recreation, and standards of living worthy of America; and the Lithuanian-born leader of the Amalgamated Clothing Workers, Sidney Hillman, who as a young immigrant in Chicago living at Hull House had imbibed a liberal understanding of the good life and who thereafter sponsored a broad union welfare program and became a statesman of labor by insisting that unions must acquire understanding of the problems of management.

The first sensational victory of the C.I.O. was won in March, 1937, when negotiations between Myron Taylor and Lewis produced a contract between the Steel Workers Organizing Committee and "Big Steel"— the famous Morgan holding company, U. S. Steel. But dangerous days had come. Encouraged by N.A.M. and Liberty League pronouncements that NLRB was unconstitutional, anti-union employers had refused to bargain for two years. "Little Steel," led by Tom Girdler, intractable president of the Republic Steel Corporation, revived the tactics of violence, tear gas, and weapons. Soon the La Follette Civil Liberties Committee of the Senate investigated a barbarous "massacre" at the Chicago plant of Republic Steel. The strikers had not provoked violence. Yet, reported the committee, "with callous indifference to human life" the guards had fired on a parade of workers and their families, killing ten and wounding forty. Eventually NLRB and the process of law forced Little Steel to accept peaceful bargaining.

Although industrial violence was antediluvian, the public was still divided. Aside from those prejudiced by identification with the employer class, there was a sober public that did not comprehend. Shocked and alarmed, it was led by newspapers to view with apprehension and hate the growing strength of organized labor. But a part of the public was gaining in liberal understanding. Many were awakened—somewhat rudely to be sure—by the sordid record uncovered by the La Follette committee; by discovery, for example, that the National Association of Manufacturers sponsored a strange method for nullifying an act of Congress. The Mohawk Valley Formula had been publicized by the N.A.M. in 1936 as a "constructive" way to break strikes and "a real contribution to civic dignity." The very next year Bethlehem Steel, Republic, Youngstown, and Inland Steel applied the formula under the new label "The Johnstown Plan." First employed by Remington-Rand, the "plan" envisaged furtive and brutal violation not alone of the Wagner Act but the Byrnes Act, which made it illegal to import strikebreaking gangs for the purpose of defeating collective bargaining. The N.A.M. technique countenanced employment of professional "tough guys" and ex-convicts furnished by industrial "detective agencies" as strikebreakers and *agents provocateurs* to stir up violence for which the union would then be blamed. Two other features—alien to democracy—rounded out the N.A.M. contribution to civic dignity: heavy expenditures by corporations for tear gas, machine guns, barbed wire, armed guards, and bribed workers employed as company spies; and finally a cynical and elaborate semifascist technique for poisoning local public opinion and mobilizing deluded citizens in vigilante organizations using mob methods to preserve "law and order."

As Little Steel applied the Johnstown plan, the C.I.O. successfully invaded the empire' of the automobile makers. Leading corporations, General Motors, Hudson, Chrysler, rejected the obligations of law and fought NLRB. In 1936 the I.W.W. tactic of the strike-on-the-job began to be revived in the United States, encouraged by contemporary stay-in-strikes that won successes in France under the administration of Léon Blum. The sensational French "sit-down" was widely publicized in American papers and motion-picture newsreels. Automobile workers, struggling for recognition of the Wagner Act by recalcitrant midwest employers, spontaneously copied the French tactics. In a sit-down, workers simply stayed in the plant, remained idle, prevented scabs' coming in to break the strike, and refused to leave until employers began to bargain in good faith. In other countries where the managerial class was in the habit of negotiating and averse to the violence accompanying the hiring of scab labor and professional strikebreakers, a sit-down might not have been so shocking. But to property-conscious members of society conditioned by class identifications to think of ownership of the machine rather than of the human concerns of the man who operated it, the virulent attack by great papers on the sit-down as "un-American" proved convincing. When state and local governments threatened use of armed force against sit-down strikers, sober labor leaders realized that the French stay-in, at least in the American social environment, had taken on the semblance of a revolutionary tactic. The sit-down was quietly abandoned. Meanwhile Congress condemned it, and two years later the Supreme Court labeled it an unlawful seizure of property.

C.I.O.'s new union, the United Automobile Workers, organized General Motors under a contract negotiated with William S. Knudsen. Contracts with other companies followed, but not with the world's largest automobile manufacturer. The Ford Motor Company exercised local option on compliance with the law; and the Ford staff of industrial spies and strong-arm men under the captaincy of Harry Bennett gained notoriety in labor circles as an "un-American" company Gestapo. Not until 1941 did the Ford dynasty bow to the sovereignty of the American people. In 1941 the Wagner Act of 1935 became law in the empire of Ford. The company signed a union contract.

Although the Wagner Act reduced the menace of violent industrial warfare, the law remained a bone of contention in the press and in Congress. Antilabor Democrats and Republicans, led by a red-baiting corporation lawyer, the Virginia Congressman Howard Smith, impugned the integrity of administrators of the Wagner Act and from time to time seemed on the verge of winning passage of ingenious amendments to make the Wagner Act ineffectual. On the other hand, progressive leaders of enterprise like Henry J. Kaiser gradually rediscovered the almost forgotten idea of a harmony of interest between capital and labor, and forward-looking businessmen learned to deal with unions on a basis of give and take. Others continued to battle with the NLRB to the bitter end; but a slow death was overtaking the employers' squatter sovereignty whereby vested interests and local authorities undertook to exercise local option and nullify a national law. Before the end of the New Deal era the Federation and the C.I.O. each claimed a membership of five million workers. C.I.O., excommunicated by the Federation, had taken permanent form in 1938 under the new title of Congress of Industrial Organizations. But John L. Lewis left its ranks; bitter against Roosevelt, he encountered resistance within the C.I.O. and resigned from the presidency. His United Mine Workers subsequently joined the A.F. of L.

Rivalry between the two great labor organizations both impeded tranquil organization of new unions and weakened labor solidarity in political action.

THE DECLINE OF PARTY LOYALTY

While labor organized in its great drive of 1937, the New Deal was engaged in a running battle with a strengthening coalition of congressional conservatives. Immediately following the landslide election in which 27,000,000 votes were cast for Roosevelt, and coincident with the judicial controversy, the President sponsored three major bills. He submitted a Reorganization bill to answer criticism of overlapping bureaus and agencies; a Wages and Hours bill to provide national standards and prevent long hours of work and excessively low wages; and legislation to repeal mandatory neutrality provisions, particularly the automatic arms embargo whereby Congress prevented the executive branch from free use of American resources to discourage and check aggressors. The President in January, 1937, sent the Reorganization bill to Congress, where it speedily passed the House only to be killed for the session by conservatives in control of the Senate committee. Introduced in May, the Wages and Hours bill suffered a like fate in the House, where strategically placed conservatives successfully pigeonholed it. Thus despite unprecedented Democratic majorities in both chambers, the new Congress elected in 1936 had defeated every major bill emanating from the White House. No president had ever been so overwhelmingly the choice of party voters for leadership of an American party, and at the same time, never had party representatives more flagrantly repudiated the party leadership which their party platform, national convention, and pre-election oratory had pledged them to follow.

Roosevelt called a special session in October, 1937, in an attempt to re-establish executive leadership. Besides seeking enactment of the Wages and Hours and Reorganization bills, he proposed new legislation to establish six more TVA's in various great valley regions in different parts of the country and recommended a new AAA to re-establish crop controls in place of those outlawed by the Supreme Court. But Congress gave constructive consideration only to the AAA problem. A renewed newspaper war broke out against Reorganization, and a virtual congressional blockade was organized against the "enemy" measures of the President of the United States. Though the White House remained only a mile from Capitol Hill, the sappers and miners in the Democratic delegation of Congress, fraternizing with their Republican opponents, successively set up hidden defenses and committee earthworks to prevent restoration of peaceful collaboration between New Deal administrators and the legislative branch of the party. As in the preceding session, Congress produced nothing. The split in the party defeated the broad plan for additional TVA's to integrate the land, water, and human resources of the nation's great valleys. Conservatives controlling the House Rules Committee led by the chairman, the Tammany reactionary John J. O'Connor, blocked action on the Wages and Hours bill, and the same Republican and Democratic coalition again achieved a stalemate on the Reorganization measure.

Democrats had overwhelming predominance in Congress; yet as the party tie weakened, politics degenerated to the level of 1880. The irresponsible politics of special interests was once more rampant on Capitol Hill. Republicans and factious Democrats who attacked the administrative structure as a bureaucratic hodgepodge were now in the curious position of using legislative power to prevent the executive branch from establishing better order in its own house. "Congress," observed a well-known commentator, "has almost quit legislating." In an ominous flight from reason, a bipartisan coalition, oblivious to the real question of the actual merits of specific bills, was united in emotional opposition to everything proposed by the administration. "They call this making the nation's laws," remarked the commentator. "What they are really trying to do is to unmake the nation's President." Yet the ultimate verdict of voters, again giving Roosevelt a 27,000,000 total in the next presidential election, revealed anew that from lack of strong party organization Congress misrepresented the national majority.

Congress responded to presidential leadership by reviving AAA in 1938. The Agricultural Adjustment Act was a comprehensive improvement on the laws outlawed by the Supreme Court. Applying Secretary Wallace's "ever-normal granary" principle, it employed acreage allotments to check the production of unsalable surplus. If despite this, unexpected overproduction threatened the farmer's prices, the law authorized marketing "quotas" to prevent flooding the market. Quotas could be applied only if a referendum won a favorable two-thirds vote from farmers. To foster a sounder equilibrium or "parity" between agricultural and industrial prices, provision was made for a government subsidy to farmers called parity payments. Opportunity for voluntary crop insurance, a modern protection against the hazards of nature, offered greater security to farmers. The ever-normal granary policy included commodity loans whereby farmers could store the surplus during good years as a protection to society against poor years. Congress, however, was still niggardly in carrying out the New Deal in agriculture as it applied to small farmers. The administration won victory in principle for a policy successfully employed by England a half century before to

relieve the distress of Irish tenants. Congress at Roosevelt's
urging accepted the Bankhead-
Jones Farm Tenant Act
(1937) authorizing long-term
government loans to enable
farm tenants, hired hands, migrants, and sharecroppers to
acquire family-size homesteads
of their own. By cutting appropriations, the Republican
and Democratic coalition ham-
strung the program, compelling the rejection of thousands
of applications from tenant
farmers and dispossessed migrants.

In June, 1938, the two
years' blockade by the House
Committee on Rules against
the Wages and Hours bill was
broken. Soon revered as a
major New Deal achievement,
the act resurrected the substance of Wilsonian child labor laws, which had been
struck down by judicial veto
twenty years before. It also
revived the minimum-wage
and maximum-hour regulation
that the Court had interdicted
only three years earlier. The
objective, said Roosevelt, was
"a floor under wages and a
ceiling over hours." Hours
were to be reduced gradually
to forty a week, with overtime
work paid at a time-and-a-half
wage. The low initial minimum wage, 25 cents an hour,
was a concession forced by
congressional spokesmen for

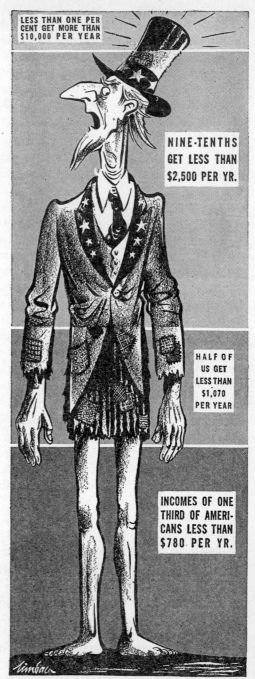

Our National Wealth!

Cartoon by R. T. Limbach on the report
of national income in 1937.

southern employers and by lobbyists for northern financial interests with southern investments, who still fought for the "advantage" of low southern wages. Gradually the minimum was to rise to 40 cents. Liberals like Senator Claude Pepper of Florida spoke for southern people in fighting for the bill.

Reorganization was still blocked, partly because spoils were involved. Roosevelt's proposal to extend the merit system of civil service to all except top policy-making officials struck at local machines, for it meant abolition of patronage. Not until a year later, 1939, would Congress sanction even a limited reorganization. The mutilated enactment, omitting Roosevelt's civil service reform, was a triumph for machine politicians. Meanwhile, terminating a five-year struggle against the lobbies, the Food and Drug Act of 1938 marked the first advance beyond the thirty-two-year-old law of 1906; but the law was a fleshless skeleton compared to the original Tugwell proposal for broad protection of consumers. Shifts in the burden of taxes in the Revenue Act of 1938 were likewise an achievement of the Old Deal, traceable to the weakness of party organization whereby the Democratic leadership was compelled to accept a drift back toward tax policies of Coolidge and Hoover.

House conservatives struck another blow in 1938 by creating the Dies committee. Its investigation of subversive and "un-American" activities became a front-page performance. The newspapers made Martin Dies a national figure. The Dies pronunciamentos prevented a fair hearing and used the smear technique to identify labor unions and Roosevelt supporters with foreign "isms." Secretary of Interior Harold Ickes was surprised to discover himself a Communist. Dies' evidence of his un-American activities consisted of Ickes' friendliness toward a noted group of defenders of individual freedom, the American Civil Liberties Union. Judicious observers soon realized that Democrat Dies was more interested in aiding notorious reactionary interests than in ferreting out fascist festers in America. Nevertheless, Dies and the front page did much to mislead millions by the implication that liberalism in the United States was rather more serious than Nazi aggression.

The realization by Democratic leaders of the necessity of a stronger party tie produced a portentous experiment in the mid-term elections of 1938. A disciplinary force was essential to modern liberal theory of responsible party government; and to supply it, New Deal supporters in several states combined with the central party leaders in an effort to retire a handful of the more factious Democrats. This small-scale party "purge" had one noteworthy success: it defeated John J. O'Connor, Tammany Democrat who had fought the party leadership through his powerful post as chairman of the House Committee on Rules. But in

spite of being listed for purge, quite a number of the others won renomination. Since the purge was endorsed by Roosevelt, its results were hailed
by the hostile press as a resounding rebuff to "dictatorship." Yet the
President's underlying theory was a significant reflection of the need of
party discipline to reorganize parties on the basis of party principles.
The purge presented a straight issue between the national will and the
local will. As readers of public opinion polls well knew, the principles
of social democracy advocated by the national party leadership reflected
the general will of the national majority and quite decisively represented
the national will of Democratic voters. Against the purge in the half-
dozen contested nominations and elections, the local will ostensibly prevailed. But small inner organizations of local party members, the machine, in actuality prevailed. Party ferment was to continue, and in 1944
a secondary reverberation of the purge was to have more success. Local
"political action" committees began to challenge the political monopolies
of local machines. A significant attempt to destroy the hoary sham of
lip service to national party principles was under way.

The greater immediate importance of the elections of 1938 was the
weakening of the administration's hand at a moment of world crisis.
The loss of prestige stemming from Democratic irresponsibility in Congress enabled Republicans to purge their opponents. The normal American behavior of mid-term victory for the opposition, hitherto inoperative
during the New Deal, nearly reasserted itself. Democrats lost their seats;
Republican gains left the Democrats with only a slender majority. The
great battles over isolation and national defense were to be fought by
Roosevelt and Hull and an aroused public in the face of an obstructionist conservative predominance in Congress. And time was running short.

NEANDERTHAL NATIONALISM

1933–1942

The march of social democracy under the New Deal alleviated depression and averted the danger of internal revolution; but social democracy limited to a few peace-loving countries was no panacea in an interdependent world. If it alleviated certain internal maladjustments in the United States and some other lands, it neither extended to all peoples nor answered every need in a disunited world. National planning in one country in an isolationist pattern would serve no better than imperialist nationalism in the crisis following 1929. And the climax of nationalism was approaching. Fascism stalked through the years of the world's economic crash, presaging an onrush of greater crisis—the march of brute nationalism in a spirit that harked back to primitive man.

RECESSION FROM NATIONALISM

Much worthy and sober social thought illumined the concern of democratic peoples in the face of world depression; but much of the new social knowledge served as a measure of failure rather than as guideposts heeded by governments. Nevertheless, American policy after 1929 made significant advances beyond the ostrich policies of the 1920's. A congressional bipartisan majority to be sure, winning strong popular support, adopted a more extreme isolationism in the 1930's. But the Hoover administration countenanced a reconsideration of policies of preponderance in Latin America, and Franklin Roosevelt and Secretary of State Cordell Hull extricated the government from political imperialism. Even more significant, the New Deal, after a faltering start with contradictory policies, began the abrogation of deeply embedded policies of economic nationalism.

Initial indecision was shown when Roosevelt rejected an immediate stabilization of the leading world currencies at the World Economic Conference held in London in 1933. For the moment it appeared that the desperate improvisation of New Deal relief and recovery measures during the Hundred Days made it politically inexpedient to broaden national planning into international agreement for economic stabilization. But other nations were under the same desperate pressure from their unemployed and suffering millions. National policies everywhere reflected the prodigious internal contradiction of objectives of security and national well-being in an interdependent but disunited world. Matching American refusal to embark on currency agreements was the refusal of the World Economic Conference to accept Secretary Hull's proposal to eradicate "extreme nationalism" by multilateral reciprocity agreements and other devices to revive the world's trade. Conservative American bankers blamed the failure of the conference on Roosevelt's refusal to join with Continental nations who insisted on the gold standard. Like England, the United States left the gold standard. But following the initial currency devaluation, the United States by the end of Roosevelt's first term became a leading factor in the stabilization of the world's currencies. The exchange value of the dollar, franc, pound, and other national currencies was regulated under international agreements. Slowly the United States progressed on the course of cooperative action that laid the basis for future international currency and banking institutions.

Rapidly assuming world leadership in a drive toward liquidation of economic nationalism, Roosevelt and Secretary Hull advanced beyond Wilsonian internationalism. In April, 1933, Roosevelt intimated that he would ask Congress to authorize reciprocal tariff reductions "to break through trade barriers." A few days later Hull castigated economic isolation as a "broken-down and discredited policy." Undeterred by international rejection of comprehensive multilateral reciprocity at the World Economic Conference, Hull turned to bilateral agreements as a second-best medium for the emancipation of international business. The imports and exports of the United States had dropped as much as 68 per cent during the depression as businessmen of all nations became voluntary prisoners behind their own "closed doors." Under the leadership of Hull and Roosevelt, despite the outcry of by-passed pressure groups, Congress enacted the Reciprocal Trade Agreements Act of 1934. The law gave the President power to reopen the closed doors through bilateral trade agreements negotiated by the executive directly with other countries. Trade agreements circumvented lobbyists for high tariffs by avoiding the old process of legislative tariff making by blocs of senators and congressmen devoted to special local interests. The law repealed the spirit but not the letter of the tariff inherited from the Hoover administration. Hull's reciprocity bargains could lower the rates of the Hawley-Smoot tariff by as much as 50 per cent. Under "most-favored-nation" clauses, American reductions for a given country were automatically extended to other nations having reciprocal trade agreements with it. Similarly, reductions between two foreign signers automatically were extended to the United States. The strength of economic nationalism in Congress, expressing the power of pressure groups, limited the reciprocity law to three years and compelled its periodic renewal. Indicative of party differences was the House vote for renewal in 1937: Democrats, 278 yea, 11 nay; Republicans, 3 yea, 81 nay. In later successive re-enactments, Republicans, joined by an increased scattering of Democrats, mustered a strong opposition vote that threatened revival of the discredited system of economic nationalism.

Recession from economic nationalism reflected a growing recognition of the international role of the United States as a creditor nation; but Congress was not prepared to go as far or as fast as expert opinion advised. Isolationist and nationalist attitudes made the problem of the uncanceled but defaulted war debts of Russia, England, and others impossible to resolve. The Senate acquiesced in 1935 to membership in the International Labor Office; but the Labor Office under the League structure lacked power to remedy nationalistic competition exploiting cheap labor. After sixteen years of "nonrecognition" of the Soviet government, Roosevelt made a contribution to international amity and trade between future United Nations partners by resumption in 1933 of formal diplomatic and commercial relations with Russia. But the United States was not yet ready to go as far as Russia in the development of a strong international organization for collective security. World economic pacts on wheat, rubber, sugar, and raw materials, to control prices and prevent overproduction, pointed a way to international economic cooperation. The United States participated in a silver pact, and Secretary Wallace nearly succeeded in reducing wheat acreage to the American quota under a wheat pact; but economic agreements without international regulatory power to sustain them inevitably failed, one by one. Meanwhile the onrush of economic fascism, an ill-concealed form of commercial warfare on a world-wide scale, blotted out international economic freedom and put a full stop to the liquidation of the economic nationalism of democracies.

The Roosevelt administration coupled its reversal of nationalistic economic policies with a retreat from political imperialism. Liberals in the world's democracies were winning support for the "liberal national" principles of the American and French revolutions. Social democrats in Léon Blum's France inaugurated a movement, later embraced by the Free French, looking toward termination of French imperialism in the Near East. English policy in Iraq, Egypt, and more confusedly in India, moved in the same direction. But world leadership in the liquidation of imperialism was assumed by the United States.

At the time of the Pan-American Conference of 1928, Latin Americans publicly condemned the United States for political domination and economic imperialism in small neighbors such as Cuba, Haiti, and Nicaragua. Subsequently Hoover's State Department disavowed the aggressive imperialism sanctioned by the Theodore Roosevelt Corollary to the Monroe Doctrine. Political control symbolized by American troops in Caribbean countries slowly ended. The Platt Amendment, however, and financial receiverships remained; and in 1932 Hoover vetoed an act of Congress providing for Philippine independence in 1946. The Roosevelt Revolution, reviving the anti-imperialism of Bryan and Wilson, scorned halfway measures. "I would dedicate this nation," announced Roosevelt in his first inaugural, "to the policy of the good neighbor." Subsequent action broke sharply with the nationalistic principle of imperialism. The original independence act for the Philippines, passed over Hoover's veto, had been rejected by the Filipinos, since American troops were slated to remain, but a new act in 1934 satisfied them. In the following decade, in the year after American and Philippine forces liberated Manila from the Japanese, 1946, independence at last became a fact.

Retreat from aggressive preponderance in countries south of the American border gave substance to the Good Neighbor policy. At the Montevideo Conference (1933) Secretary Hull proposed to change the Monroe Doctrine from a national or unilateral policy of the United States to an international, multilateral policy. The new principle meant joint inter-American application of the old Doctrine's principles of independence and defense against imperialism and aggression. The new policy, the Franklin Roosevelt Corollary to the Monroe Doctrine, required renunciation of treaties authorizing intervention and other vested rights that American imperialists had extorted by the big stick and dollar diplomacy. In 1934, the United States, by abrogating the Platt Amendment, freed Cuba from political and financial subordination. In the same year the last of the imperialistic occupations ended when Roosevelt ordered the marines out of Haiti. A treaty of 1936 relinquished legal devices permitting intervention in the Panama Republic.

Mexican relations also exhibited the new spirit. When Mexico renewed the attempt to redistribute land to impoverished peasants and landless farmers, oil properties controlled by American and British corporations were nationalized. English oil operators, supported by the diplomatic pressure of the Tory home government, talked of intervention, but in the new spirit of social democracy the American administration turned instead to amicable negotiation without pressure. A joint commission settled the oil claims as war broke; and Mexico became an active partner in the battle against Nazi submarines in Gulf waters.

To South Americans, so often disillusioned in earlier decades, North American actions spoke more dependably than North American words. Hull's reciprocity reductions partially answered Latin-American protests against Hawley-Smoot rates. The Roosevelt administration in 1934 launched the Export-Import Bank to promote international trade, particularly to facilitate a two-way exchange within the Americas. In 1941, the financial receiverships that the United States maintained over Haiti and Santo Domingo, dating from the early years of dollar diplomacy, were abolished. But American interests, doing large business in small countries as "foreign corporations," were too powerfully connected with native ruling cliques to be subjected to the reform legislation sought by the local forces of social democracy. American corporations abroad, operating oil and mining properties and sugar and fruit plantations, and international cartels in which American corporations were partners, were not subject in any effective sense to antitrust controls of the United States or the restraints of American labor law. The final liquidation of economic imperialism and monopolistic world trade awaited the development of global regulation of the international twilight zone created by the cartels and big corporations that controlled prices and markets, resources and labor policies, in regions beyond the reach of separate liberal governments.

NEANDERTHAL NATIONALISM: THE FASCIST MENACE

As the spirit of the Good Neighbor rose, so also the evil star of totalitarianism was rising, beckoning to the frustrated and ambitious, debauching its victims with malignant obsessions that drove for preponderance and magnified the contradictions of a disunited world. Austrian-born Adolf Hitler, onetime unsuccessful student of art, then an inconspicuous corporal in the defeated army of the German Kaiser, but now the master demagogue of the Nazi party, became dictator by playing on internal conflicts and hatreds within society, capitalizing on party chaos in a poorly organized parliament, and whetting the fires of German patriotism with diabolical oratory. The label, Nazi, stood for National Socialist party; but Nazi leaders were nationalists, not socialists. After the March elections in 1933, Hitler, with a plurality over the numerous other parties but not a majority, formed a cabinet; but he consolidated power only by means of the collaboration of another party, the German Nationalists. Nationalist parties gained adherents because of depression, insecurity, and discontent, particularly among lower middle classes. Glorification of the German "race," propaganda attacks on the Versailles Treaty, blame for depression on foreign bankers, monopolists, and their diplomats—all capitalized on the emotional power of nationalism as a unifying force—and as a means to get into office. It was significant that German conservatives were less fearful of the nationalist parties than were liberals and radicals. The German multiparty system, like the French, was ill suited to majority rule and the strain of crisis government. German democracy had a fatal weakness in its failure to evolve major parties with effective leadership and disciplined working majorities in the national legislature. The democratic appeal of liberal parties for moderate reform was drowned out by bawling Nazi orators or brutally stifled by Nazi strong-arm men in the days preceding the elections.

Once in power, the Nazis outlawed all other parties, liberal, conservative, Catholic, Communist. "Private armies" of uniformed Nazis, storm troopers, were fastened on the German army, just as the Nazi terrorist secret police, the Gestapo, was fastened on the regular police and administrative bureaus. So also Nazi gospel was grafted on or drowned out the gospel of the chuches. The internal economy, like the church, was "coordinated." The conglomerate "Aryan race" was purified—by the robbery and enslavement of Germanic families of Jewish faith. Meanwhile the new masters of the "pure race" looked outward, evolving a national robber economy: magnifying the old contradictions of world interdependence by exploiting the parasitic techniques of nationalism to capture world trade, and on the other hand seeking to exorcise destitution at home by economic self-sufficiency.

"The German nation must export or die," cried Hitler. Yet a nation that must export was dependent upon its neighbors. There must be no "dependence" upon outside nations, declaimed Hitler's second-in-command, Field Marshal Hermann Goering; "for a self-conscious people" —endowed with the "desire to live"—dependence was "simply intolerable." The contradiction of self-sufficiency and dependence could be resolved only by expansion—by war.

In economic foreign policy, seeking strategic self-sufficiency, the totalitarians of Germany, Italy, and Japan went beyond the normal nationalist fallacy, the belief in "sheltered markets" protected against cheaper goods from outside and similar disturbances from international business fluctuations. Nazi and Japanese zealots, planning on war, rightly anticipated blockade. The peacetime Fascist "Battle of Wheat" in Italy was both economic nationalism and military strategy, national planning in anticipation of war with its specter of starvation. Under similar Nazi planning, German cartels developed artificial Buna rubber and, by patents and secret agreements with American oil interests and world businessmen, restrained Buna production outside Germany. Yet even totalitarians could not, and did not, attempt to seal their nation off as a self-sufficient unit. Insufficient resources in many categories and surplus production in others demanded world interchange. By the eve of war, Germany, Japan, and Italy had monopolized much of Latin-American trade. Hull's reciprocity program was countered by Axis exploitation of every hoary nationalistic device of commercial warfare to aggrandize a single country. Ruthless Nazi practices included currency and trade controls, blocked marks, barter quotas, closed trade agreements, contracts to take the exports of others on a fraudulent basis of deferred repayment in German goods—in some cases never paid or repaid in goods that the receiving nations did not want.

The initial success of this aggressive program, coupled with destitution and social tension at home, converted Latin America's ruling orders to an intense nationalism. The aristocracy of the military, the big feudal landowners, and the investors supported by foreign business interests repressed the liberal or revolutionary forces of small businessmen, middle classes, workers, and peasants. Military dictatorships began to destroy twentieth-century democratic gains. In the Americas as in Europe and Asia, nationalism, high tariffs, immigration restrictions, in an ever-widening arc of social negations, sought to evade the problems of democracy.

Economic nationalism in all countries expressed world failure to solve the modern paradox: unutilized capacity to produce and consume, and a human desire for abundance contrasting with fear of "overproduction" and dread of downswings of the business cycle. Behind the nationalistic idea of self-sufficiency was imperious insistence on the sovereignty and power of a chosen people. Sovereignty and self-sufficiency were but means whereby superior peoples exercised their "right" to control their own destiny. Thereby nationalism repudiated democracy; the sovereignty of a destined people rose ascendant over democratic belief in humankind. Nationalists in democracies succumbed to a corruption of the democratic faith; nationalists in totalitarian revolutions extinguished democracy itself.

National self-sufficiency was an escape neither from the problem of the business cycle nor from the problem of war. Solution of world economic insecurity lay in analysis and reform of the existing economic and political order. Although Nazis, just prior to their aggression on Poland, boasted that their six years in power had given them immunity from business cycle fluctuations abroad, their propaganda about the absence of unemployment in Germany was a palpable deception. Poverty and insecurity not only remained but existed in tyrannical forms unknown under the Weimar Republic. Self-sufficiency sacrificed economic efficiency and limited the purchases of German consumers. The vaunted Spade Army and Labor Front provided work at utter sacrifice of personal freedom and security. Germans were subject to sudden transfer, by compulsion, to different parts of the country and to different occupations for which they had neither training nor liking. The struggle for security of the nation resulted in sacrifice of the security of the citizen. Human and democratic values vanished; rise of the terrorist Gestapo was a symbol of security for the nation, insecurity for the individual. A government despotic enough to break labor unions was despotic enough to prey on the profits of businessmen, to fix arbitrary prices as well as arbitrary wages, to tell the investor precisely when and where his capital must be invested. When workers were stripped of the right to unions of their own choosing, employers lost the right to a business of their own choosing.

THE REBIRTH OF ECONOMIC THOUGHT

Social democracy, however, was groping toward a democratic denationalized solution of the conditions that bred totalitarian man. It was no accident that the Labor party in England was more sincerely devoted to the League than the Conservative party; that the New Deal in America, appearing after the League was atrophied, sought collective security and international cooperation to put a stop to war and to economic piracy by cartels and governments. Liberal democrats rejected closed-door propaganda because they recoiled from the antidemocratic philosophy on which it was based. Social democracy was recognizable by three things it rejected: economic nationalism with its undemocratic and tragic insistence on special advantages; ethnic or racial nationalism, the undemocratic myth of a chosen people and its unscientific aristocratic biology purporting to prove certain races and families superior, the rest of mankind inferior; and suppressive nationalism, with its monopoly of governmental power, its abrogation of the democratic process of social change, its repression of internal tensions by enthronement of the elite.

Social democracy coupled its rejections with a constructive policy to reduce the tensions that fostered nationalism. Democratic analysis of the economic structure produced nothing less than a veritable revolution in social understanding. After 1936 the international impact of a new economics struck the areas of democracy with vitalizing force. The rebirth of economic thought reversed the political bias of classical economics that had prevailed for 160 years. Adam Smith's economic declaration of independence in 1776 protested against selfish nationalism, against monopoly and monarchy. It represented a proper liberal fear of irresponsible government under the numbing control of a ruling class. In the fourth decade of the twentieth century the economics of John Maynard Keynes protested against selfish private monopoly of economic power and represented a proper modern belief in governmental energy and authority in the liberating hands of a democratic people. Fear of government by economists in the decadent age of monarchy was metamorphosed into belief in government by the economists of social democracy.

The eighteenth-century defense of laissez-faire economics by Adam Smith was based upon an honest conviction that self-interest and economic individualism acted like an "invisible hand," so directing energies as to maximize production and consumption through free competition. Twentieth-century economics broke away from a mistaken trust in the regulative force of competition alone. Even Adam Smith, patron saint of laissez faire, foreseeing the danger, warned that whenever two or more businessmen got together, "conspiracy" was afoot. A noted American analysis of the modern corporation and private property revealed in 1932 that 2,000 men composed the top leadership of America's 200 largest corporations and exercised the directive power over more than 50 per cent of the nation's economy. This consolidated structure of control was praised in conservative quarters as "the American economy." By the end of Roosevelt's second term, the elaborate joint administrative and congressional investigation by TNEC (Temporary National Economic Committee) disclosed a spreading web of control rivaling the regimentation of economic enterprise and suppression of competition under the cartel giants of the German Reich.

The rebirth of economic thought placed the problem of monopoly in new perspective. Corporate consolidation and collusive price fixing were only examples of many structural rigidities and maladjustments requiring public reform to clear the way for an expansion of the national income. The new emphasis in economics grew out of a world disillusioned by depression and inspired by social democracy. New investigation, centering on the over-all problem of the business cycle, led to a new synthesis concerned not with an atomic economic individualism but with the economy as a functioning whole. The revolution in economic thought, heralded by the fertile analysis of Keynes in his General Theory of Employment, Interest and Money published in 1936, expressed the modern drive of great thinkers toward reintegration of accumulated knowledge. The new approach was comparable in its revolutionary social significance to relativity and the new field theory of modern physics. Like Gestalt psychology, Keynesian economics centered upon the functional relationships of the whole. It recognized the key position of government as historical agency for creation and control of credit and the need of cooperation of government and industry for the attainment of full employment. Herein lay a portentous intellectual impetus toward coordinated domestic and international social planning, offering dazzling prospects for the progress of man.

The revolution in economic thought tended to correct nationalistic preoccupation with producer interests. A better balance between producer economics and consumer economics became visible in a growing recognition that reform of the economic system should be directed toward the sound democratic goal of raising the standard of consumption throughout the world. For planning against depressions, Keynesian economics envisioned much more far-reaching recovery measures than the early "pump-priming" devices of the New Deal. Sweden, famed among progressive countries as the land of the "middle way," adopted a cyclical budget relying in large part on governmental fiscal policy for mastery of the business cycle. Not until the spring of 1938, following a business recession, did Franklin Roosevelt accept the larger implications of the new economics. In that year, the administration endorsed large-scale deficit spending under an unbalanced budget as a major weapon against depressions, and in 1940 Roosevelt's budget message openly incorporated the revolutionary new concepts. Under the cyclical budget policy, governments would counter an economic downswing by heavy expenditures for relief, welfare, and public works. Instead of balancing the budget by taxes, they would cover deficits by governmental borrowing, deliberately, because avoidance of increased tax burdens would not simply foster a maximum purchasing power among consumers but would also encourage business expansion and private investment. In time of economic upswing, governmental policy would be reversed, taxes increased, the budget balanced, the debt reduced, and emergency spending for relief and public works abandoned as fast as rising national income permitted.

THE ROAD TO WAR

Democracy, while finding in Keynesian economics a new strength for war on depressions, was weakened internally in its war against war. Weakness of the French multiparty structure facilitated the drive of organized special interests toward appeasement of Hitler and, eventually, collaboration. Leaders of the dominant Conservative party in England, wooed by Nazi, Japanese, and Italian propaganda urging a common front against Russia and all Communists, abandoned the principles of the League of Nations for the the blind folly of appeasement of the Axis. There were two Englands, two Frances, and two Americas, and through each country the cleavage between the forces of special interest and the forces of the common man was clear. The forces of special interest were always more concerned with the perquisites of nationalism than with the broadening of democracy; the forces of the common man more concerned with peaceful world change and broadening distribution of potential abundance. In the United States appeasement had its parallel in neutrality legislation; and its apogee in the supposition of the complacent that American interests could do business with Hitler.

The United States and all the world unwittingly turned down the road to war when Japan in 1931 was permitted to dismember disunited China by seizure of Manchuria. Western people, lulled into the self-deception that human nature in Japan was an unfathomed mystery, seldom recognized in Nippon a three-hundred-year-old anticipation of totalitarianism. The "great sword hunt," disarming the Japanese common people in the same period when Elizabeth ruled in England, paralleled the tactics of Mussolini and Hitler in disarming their people. An interrelated group of rich families ruled Japan from the sixteenth century to V-J Day, 1945. Purges by assassination, "thought control" of amorphous masses (under the Hoko system of "hostages" or Gestapo spies), Bushido (indoctrination in the way of the warrior), Shinto worship of the Japanese emperor (a fuehrer or "leader" principle), and similar totalitarian stratagems were the masks of militarism and political monopoly by a combined business and military ruling class, presenting the face of Hitlerism in Oriental pigmentation. Japanese industrialization, followed by imperialism in wars with China (1895) and Russia (1905), made Oriental ways less enigmatic. Japanese adoption of parliamentary cabinet government by political parties in 1918 seemed again to bridge the gap between East and West. The mysterious gap was to prove deceptive. Human nature in both East and West could express itself in either undemocratic or democratic ways; but parliamentary Nippon was merely a front for totalitarianism like the Reichstag of Hitler; under emperor worship the leader principle ensured power to militarists; the citizen was nothing, the state was all.

APPEASERS AND ISOLATIONISTS

Seeking power like its kin the Nazis, the militarist Seiyukai party—spawned from the fascist cells of the Black Dragon—projected a New Order as Nippon's solution of the great depression. Tanaka, leader of the party, gave secret circulation to a vast plan of conquest in which even America was subordinated to the Son of Heaven, the Emperor Hirohito. In 1930 the militarist party won; in 1931 occurred the "incident." The march of Supermen began; Manchuria was occupied; and then, in

1935, North China. American isolationism and the appeasement policy of European imperialists tied the hands of Hoover's Secretary, Henry L. Stimson. Collective security in Asia, pledged in the international guarantees of the Washington Conference (1921), was weakly asserted on the escapist plane of international law lacking the force of law. The United States and the League agreed on "nonrecognition" of totalitarian aggression. Simultaneously, a delegation of England's "peak" trade association, the Federation of British Industries, negotiated in Manchukuo without extracting the fruits of appeasement. Japanese cartels replaced American and British cartel interests; and by Japanese law in 1934 the open door was closed. Japan's aggression sounded the death knell of the League of Nations, and with it died the Kellogg Pact, the sanctity of treaties, and disarmament agreements. Japan repudiated naval limitation in 1934 and quit the League—but was permitted to retain her League mandates, strategic islands in the far-flung Pacific.

As international order disintegrated, the isolationist United States buried its head in congressional investigations and pious neutrality laws. Congress passed the Johnson Act in April, 1934, partly from a nationalistic desire to wring the old war debts from Europe, partly from an isolationist desire to preserve neutrality by escaping any economic entanglement like that with England prior to 1917. The act prohibited loans to governments in default on debts to the United States. The same month witnessed the birth of the Nye committee of the Senate. Southern and western Democrats, Bennett Champ Clark and Burton K. Wheeler, joined the Mississippi Valley Republicans, Arthur Vandenberg and Gerald P. Nye, in a front-page Senate investigation of the "merchants of death" in a vain attempt to prove that munitions makers were responsible for wars and that America's entry into World War I had been a mistake. Isolationist and anti-British sentiments were strengthened by western suspicion of Wall Street power. Sensational disclosures of World War I profiteering and arms lobbying rapidly popularized the belief that J. P. Morgan, Wall Street bankers, U. S. Steel, Du Pont, and the arms manufacturers, together with British propaganda, had drawn the country into a futile war in 1917 and would do so again unless neutrality were erected into a "permanent" system.

The height of isolation was reached not in 1920 but in the neutrality laws of 1935 and 1937. Roosevelt and Hull, impressed by cartels and international ramifications of the armaments question, believed in international control of the munitions business; but a bipartisan coalition, favoring isolated national action, overrode the administration. The law of 1935 prevented arms shipments to victims of aggression by ordering the President to proclaim an embargo against both belligerents in any future wars. The administration's countermeasure, to apply an embargo only against aggressors, was sidetracked. Congress added a prohibition on loans to belligerents in 1936 and in 1937 consolidated the new laws in a "permanent" isolation statute. Americans were barred from ordinary travel on ships of belligerents; the American flag in effect was not to be seen in dangerous war trade; American exports to war zones were to be in foreign ships on a "cash-and-carry" basis. Thus Congress contributed to appeasement. Democratic "independents," joining national-minded Republicans, legislated congressional foreign policy that repudiated the party leadership and contradicted the world policy of Roosevelt and Hull.

The blustering march of aggressors contrasted strangely with the indifference of isolationists and appeasers. In June, 1933, Hitler's new Reich blocked payment to businessmen of the United States and other outsiders to whom Germany and her businessmen owed money. Foreign business firms in Germany began to be coordinated. German cartels were meanwhile subsidized for economic warfare. In October, 1933, Germany quit the League. The Versailles peace settlement, which limited German armament, was boldly disregarded; the Reich rearmed. In March, 1935, Hitler repudiated the peace treaty, brazenly announcing violation of provisions against a mass army and compulsory military service. Fast new "unsinkable" German battleships outclassed the slow American and English "fat boys." In March, 1936, came the derisive march of Nazi warriors into the strategic Rhine Valley—which Wilson and the peacemakers had committed a negligent world to demilitarize forever. The Versailles Treaty was dead—crippled at birth in 1919 by brawlers in the United States Senate, purged in 1936 by Hitler's storm troopers, and buried in England by Tory appeasers. Two months later saw the end of the seven months' campaign in which Italian Fascists overran Ethiopia. Meanwhile, in July, 1936, the three years' Spanish war broke, instigated by Spanish fascists in alliance with the military, the big landowners, and the financiers. Europe's conservative orders, under their appeasement formula of "non-intervention," permitted aid to reach the rebel general and future dictator, Francisco Franco, sent by the newly formed Rome-Berlin Axis. Units of German and Italian armed forces provided the military punch to overthrow the Spanish Republic and impose totalitarianism. On the convenient Spanish proving ground, Hitler tried out new weapons and tactics—German dive bombers, flak guns, and mechanized deployment.

Russia, throughout the prewar years the only powerful proponent of collective security, was virtually alone as an arsenal for defense of Spanish democracy. The American Congress in the Spanish Munitions

Act of January, 1936, outlawed the Roosevelt technique of aiding the democracies. In the summer of 1937 Japan took Shanghai; totalitarian hands were reaching for all China. Against Italy, Roosevelt had been quick to apply the arms embargo; slight though the benefit, it aided Ethiopia. He hedged on Japan's undeclared war: poorly armed China would gain most by refusal to proclaim an American embargo. Presidential opponents, in strange flight from reality, flayed Roosevelt in and out of Congress as an unscrupulous dictator who circumvented national law.

The foreign policy of the executive branch, as in Wilson's time and to some extent under Coolidge and Hoover, was as internationalist as the foreign policy of Congress was isolationist. Nowhere was the weakness of the American system of party control so apparent as in the unresolved contradiction that consistently prevented a sound foreign policy. Amid totalitarian rearmament, aggression in Spain, aggression in China, aggression in Ethiopia and the Rhineland, Roosevelt in October, five months after passage of the 1937 Neutrality Act, called for a "quarantine" on aggressors. The "epidemic of world lawlessness" was spreading. "When an epidemic of physical disease starts to spread, the community approves and joins in a quarantine of the patients in order to protect the health of the community against the spread of the disease." Isolationism could not "insure" us against the contagion. "There must be positive endeavors to preserve peace."

The nation refused to take heed, although one quarter of the world's peoples were already at war in 1937. Isolation and nationalism still rendered the United States blind to democracy's stake in the outcome of the conflicts in China and in Spain. The munitions investigators had so ridiculed the Wilsonian faith in a world made safe for democracy that only Roosevelt and a few other members of the government still reasserted the democratic ideal. Like Wilson, Roosevelt recognized the organic unity of the world: the essential fact that the internal structure and ideals of nations were inseparably connected with their external behavior. Such had been the basis of the Good Neighbor policy; and so Roosevelt had declared it in retracting "intervention" under the Monroe Doctrine. Maintenance of constitutional government, he held, was primarily the duty of the nation concerned; but when failure to maintain it threatened general order, internal government became "the joint concern" of both American continents.

In 1938 Nazi aggression engulfed Austria, and Hitler demanded the "Nordic" fringe—the Sudeten area—of Czechoslovakia. Conservative leaders of the great European democracies, neglecting Russian cooperation for collective security, desperately trusted to the last and greatest appeasement. At Munich, the Czech republic was forced to cede the Sudeten to Hitler; Prime Minister Neville Chamberlain, leader of the Conservative party, returned to England with the promise of "peace in our time." Six months later, in the spring of 1939, the Reich seized the whole Czech republic, under the soon notorious strategy of "one at a time." On August 23, Russia, having found no partners for collective security, turned to nationalism; Germany and Russia signed a nonaggression pact; nine days later—September 1, 1939—the Nazi blitzkrieg was loosed on Poland. England and France, unequipped to withstand modern warfare, entered the conflict. Japan became a partner in the Axis; Franco's Spain, a silent partner. The Nazi fifth column was preparing the way in Norway, Holland, Belgium, France, the Balkans, and the Americas. The German *Bund,* Nazi agents, and Nazi funds won isolationist cooperation in the United States from nationally prominent newspaper owners. World war, declared and undeclared, gripped Europe, Asia, Africa, and the Americas.

"THE ARSENAL OF DEMOCRACY"

The elections of 1938 left anti-administration Democrats and the Republicans, generally isolationist, in a commanding position in debates on defense. In his first term Roosevelt had begun the rebuilding of the navy and the merchant marine. In his second term, although the peril was closer, the President had greater difficulty in winning support from a majority of Democrats and Republicans. Public opinion polls by January, 1939, revealed that the congressional opposition was increasingly less representative of the desires of the people. To win broader support for national defense, Roosevelt brought Republicans into his Cabinet—Henry L. Stimson as Secretary of War, and Frank Knox, Republican candidate for Vice-President in 1936, as Secretary of the Navy. The extent to which parties split and rebelled against leadership in Congress was nevertheless extraordinary. Roosevelt's call for a billion dollar naval expansion in 1938 met with angry opposition. Senator Vandenberg opposed it as a "super-super Navy bill" for which there was no clearly demonstrated "national necessity." Keels of new capital ships were laid; but throughout 1938 Congress heeded neither Hull nor Roosevelt despite their strong pleas for repeal of the arms embargo. Although Roosevelt in January, 1939, warned that there was "a new range and speed to offense," Congress rejected appropriations to strengthen the defenses of Guam and opposed the President's policy of supporting democracy abroad by measures "short of war." The administration won additional military and naval appropriations; yet when war broke, the neutrality laws were not repealed; their immediate automatic effect was to forbid delivery to the Allies of 5,000 planes already ordered before the war. Not until weeks after the blitzkrieg on Poland could the administration win even a partial victory for aid to England and France; on November 3 the mandatory embargo was modified by opening the flow of American munitions to belligerents on a cash-and-carry basis. As a "permanent" national policy, Congress still retained the basic neutrality laws. England and France could now buy American munitions, but the American merchant marine could not aid in their shipment.

Dominant Democratic and Republican forces in Congress continued obstruction long after the outbreak of war; yet public opinion tabulations for many months had shown that they did not speak for the national majority. As totalitarianism spread, it became ominously clear that obstructionists in Congress, wittingly or not, served the purposes of a weird minority—William Randolph Hearst, Robert R. McCormick of the Chicago *Tribune,* and kindred "America First" propagandists, the German-American *Bund,* the "nightshirt nobles," Crusaders, Silver Shirts, Father Coughlin's Christian Front, and the fascist underground spawn of would-be American gauleiters.

Not for the first time was a President wiser and more representative than a coalition in Congress. Common sense of the people gradually asserted the strength of democracy. The Roosevelt Revolution by the end of the decade was winning a majority to internationalism. That the people be neutral in thought, declared the President, "I cannot ask." Time was running out for minds isolated from conscience. A "Committee to Defend America by Aiding the Allies" and a militant "Fight for Freedom" movement won widespread support in a counterattack on the clamorous network of "America First." With public support but against bitter congressional resistance, Roosevelt made the United States the "Arsenal of Democracy." Neutrality remained a law but ceased to be a fact.

The hour of decision was fatefully near. The long blockade against release of democratic energies exacted a price. In April and May of 1940 the Nazi fifth column rose up successively in country after country, paralyzing resistance to a simultaneous invasion by crack German armies; and one by one, areas of democracy, Norway, Denmark, Holland, Belgium, France, were engulfed in the New Order. The resources of western Europe were at Hitler's disposal.

In January, 1940, before the blow descended, Roosevelt asked immediate increase of the defense appropriation by well over a billion dollars. For months—until France fell—the bipartisan opposition stalled defense appropriations. On May 16, four days after the Nazis struck at Holland, Roosevelt asked for an additional billion. His proposal that

America assume responsibility as the Arsenal of Democracy startled the world: the United States would attain the amazing production of 50,000 planes a year. A few weeks later the mechanized might of the Nazis fell upon the French and English in the battle of France. The fate of Europe, cried Hitler, would be decided for a thousand years. The disorganized French Republic fell as quickly as Poland. The R.A.F. and the British navy covered the bloody evacuation at Dunkirk. Italy scurried into the war, the fascist jackal savoring the prospect of African spoils from the empire of France. The Free French raised their standard in England under General Charles de Gaulle. But England stood alone. Chamberlain was superseded. Prime Minister Winston Churchill, with a prose as majestic as the courage of his fellow citizens, rallied his people to fight to the end:

. . . we shall fight on the seas and oceans, we shall fight with growing confidence and growing strength in the air, we shall defend our island, whatever the cost may be, we shall fight on the beaches, we shall fight on the landing grounds, we shall fight in the fields and in the streets, we shall fight in the hills; we shall never surrender. . . .

Even if England were to fall, then the navy and the empire would continue to fight, "until, in God's good time, the new world, with all its power and might, steps forth to the rescue and liberation of the old."

Roosevelt recognized as clearly as Churchill the indispensable role of the New World. Great Britain had become a more vital strategic outpost than any base in American possession. When France fell the President asked a total of nearly five billion dollars for the army and navy. Meanwhile the Selective Service bill, introduced on June 20, had been roundly denounced as administration warmongering. "We should not exaggerate the emergency," objected Senator Robert Taft of Ohio. For three months, obstructionists held up the draft. In the Senate, fully a fourth of the Democrats voted against the bill; in the House, the Republicans voted two to one against it. Passed on September 16, the law was immediately utilized to register 16,000,000 men between twenty-one and thirty-six, and overnight the army expanded to more than five times its former size. Meanwhile, Pan-American solidarity in the Act of Havana warned Dutch and Vichy collaborationists against transfer of Martinique or of French and Dutch Guiana as Caribbean bases for undersea wolf packs and the Nazis' famed Messerschmitts and Heinkels.

In September, 1940, the "air blitz" raised the menacing prospect of invasion of England. The United States Government, by circuitous sale, was buttressing Great Britain with World War I equipment, old rifles, machine guns, field guns. On September 3, Roosevelt made a sensational announcement of aid to England—transfer to the English flag of fifty overage destroyers of the United States Navy in exchange for 99-year leases on air strips and naval bases rimming the American coast from Newfoundland to Bermuda and south to Trinidad. The bases were opened to cooperating Latin-American countries. The "destroyer deal" was attacked as "unconstitutional," and Hamilton Fish of New York, Republican leader of the House Foreign Affairs Committee, denounced it as "an act of war." In October, when Japan became a full-fledged member of the Rome-Berlin Axis, the administration clapped an embargo on scrap-iron shipments to Japan. By the time of the national elections in November administration forces had fought through Congress total defense appropriations of eighteen billion dollars.

In the elections of 1940 the Republican party for the first time since 1904 put forward a candidate who was a born leader of men with qualities auguring growth into a statesman. Republican voters were aroused by Wendell Willkie as they had not been since the first Roosevelt thundered from the White House. Engineered by an adroit preconvention drive of prominent Republicans not associated with party machines, the Willkie boom stole party voters to such a degree that the professional politicians were stampeded in the convention. Leading rival contenders for the nomination, all tinctured with nationalist preferences—Senator Vandenberg of Michigan, Senator Taft of Ohio, and Thomas A. Dewey, who had made headlines as New York District Attorney—were more acceptable to the Old Guard. Willkie was a Midwesterner, albeit Wall Street; a corporation lawyer who had risen to the presidency of a great utilities system; an ex-Democrat who shifted his party when leading the battle against TVA. In his subsequent career, Willkie revealed himself as the leader of a mildly progressive Republican minority urging an injection of social democracy to halt the decline of Republican appeal. On foreign affairs Willkie endorsed Roosevelt's policy of aid to England.

Willkie Republicans, running on the same ticket with the unrelenting Old Dealers still dominant in Congress and in local machines, presented party voters with the same dilemma that frustrated New Dealers who voted for Roosevelt and at the same time found themselves forced to vote for Old Deal Democrats. But Willkie revived Republican enthusiasm. To many Republicans, unfamiliar with discords within the party, Willkie symbolized belief that younger men with liberal ideas had reformed their party. John L. Lewis of the United Mine Workers, now a bitter opponent of the administration, was enlisted by Republicans and went on the air to attack the Democrats. Roosevelt, renominated, smashed the third-term tradition with 27,243,466 votes—nearly the same record-breaking total as in 1936. But Willkie brought the Republican vote up to 22,304,755— better than Dewey's four years later. In the 1940 elections a new factor in New York politics—420,000 votes of the American Labor party, cast for the Democratic candidate who was placed also on the Labor ticket—accounted for the margin that defeated Dewey in his race for governor. Willkie voters and Roosevelt voters were to be disappointed in the new Congress. Neither party could depend upon loyalty to party principles.

A crucial battle of the war, fought not over London but in Washington, marked the next six months. The President warned the new Congress of imminent peril. The aggressors had the offensive; "they—not we—will choose the time and the place and the method of their attack." Roosevelt's address to Congress on January 6, 1941, called for lend-lease legislation. The enactment, bitterly contested though speed was urgent, required three months for passage. It answered a desperate need. Neither China nor the British Empire could continue to obtain the dollars necessary to buy lifesaving arms under cash-and-carry provisions. Under the isolationist Johnson Act, American loans were barred. In essence, lend-lease was a brilliant device to escape the strait jacket of isolationist legislation and to avoid the postwar folly of economic derangement by war debts. In the Senate, lend-lease was opposed by Burton K. Wheeler, supported by 20 per cent of his Democratic colleagues. Willkie openly endorsed the bill. In the House a fraction of his party, 24 Republicans, voted for lend-lease; 135 Republicans voted against it.

Lend-lease truly converted the United States into an arsenal of democracy. Quickly England placed orders for hundreds more of the desperately needed 7,000-ton merchant ships. By the spring of 1941 more than 1,000 airplane engines a month were going to countries opposing aggressors. By July the administration had won protracted battles for additional funds; by that date the total United States defense outlay and requested armaments expansion were more than twice the Greater Reich's comparable war expenditure. That these defense policies were needed was shown on June 22, when the Nazis, postponing plans for invasion of England, suddenly struck for the industries, wheat, and oil of Russia. As breakthroughs swept the Nazis north toward Leningrad and eastward through the Ukraine in August, congressional obstructionists so little understood the world they lived in that they strove for and almost succeeded in a substantial abolition of the United States Army. The situation "looks infinitely safer," was the solemn verdict of Senator Taft. By a one-vote margin in the House, 203–202, administration leaders prevented defeat of the bill to retain the army draftees beyond their year of service. By a vote almost as close two months later the administration barely succeeded in modifying the neutrality laws to permit the arming of merchant ships. Nazi forces were then swiftly converging on Moscow.

A few weeks later, on December 7, 1941, the Japanese struck at Pearl Harbor.

WAR – FOR SURVIVAL

The American people, in the black months that followed, endured a period of uncomprehended defeat. No strategy was feasible except a costly defensive—sacrificing the "expendables," planes, ships, men. Defeats of English and Russian forces in the European theater, cruel attrition in the Battle of the Atlantic, and almost uninterrupted reverses in the Far East brought depletion that could mean the loss of freedom. The loss of advanced bases in the Pacific theater—Guam, Manila, Hongkong, Singapore, Rangoon, and Rabaul—was more critical than the crippling of the eight battleships at Pearl Harbor; nearly all of these were one day to pour deadly broadsides in the second battle of the Philippines. The surprise attacks on the Philippines, Hawaii, and British Asiatic bases were designed to give Nippon command of the sea. Nazi and Japanese army warlords demanded attack on Russia, not America; but Japanese naval strategists insisted on striking the United States as the only sea power still in a position to challenge their expansion to India and the East Indies. The strategy succeeded. With air and naval forces paralyzed temporarily, the United States could not check Japanese seizure of advanced bases and of the oil, tin, rubber, and other resources marked out by Japanese totalitarians for their "East-Asia Co-Prosperity Sphere."

Over immense distances Japan launched the greatest seaborne invasion the world had yet seen. The fall of Malaya, Burma, and Sumatra closed the Burma Road and placed Japan upon the Indian Ocean and the borders of India. The fall of Guam and the Philippines, and the seizure of the East Indies from Java to northern New Guinea and the Solomons, completed the control of the South and Central Pacific, threatening the life lines of New Zealand and Australia. The inadequacy of Allied defense revealed the hollowness of the age-old policy of imperialists from Holland and England who had refused to supplement their small colonial armies by training and equipping the peoples of the East Indies. While liquidating imperialism in the Philippines the United States had embraced the opposite principle; but the sturdy contingents of armed Filipinos matched the enemy in bravery but not in numbers and equipment. From Bataan and other points of heroic last stand, Japanese forces herded survivors to the totalitarian hells of prison-camp beatings and deliberate starvation. But again East and West had met: when American troops tore the Nazi roof off Germany they found the same camps, the same brutality and starvation, and the final horror and stench of cremation plants to burn the thousands of anti-Nazis rounded up for "liquidation."

As 1942 wore on, depletion of the Allies brought defeat near in the European theater, producing what the American Chief of Staff, General George C. Marshall, soberly pronounced a "terrifying" situation. "Had the U.S.S.R. and the British Army of the Nile been defeated in 1942," declared Marshall, "as they well might if the Germans, Japanese, and Italians had better coordinated their plans and resources," the United States would have fought "in the western hemisphere confronted by enemies who controlled a greater part of the world." To the loss of resources to Nazi conquerors and the sacrifice of Russians under their gallant scorched earth policy were added the appalling casualties of the Red Army. The winter offensive had given Russia precious time but in the summer of 1942 Russia's hour was dark indeed. Successive breakthroughs threatened encirclement as the Russians withdrew their armies to the area of the Black Sea, southeast into the wall of the Caucasus, and eastward to Stalingrad and the Volga. Russia's oil fields were falling to the Nazis and the Caspian Sea beckoned; for there and up the Volga and behind the Urals lay the "heartland," with the vulnerable economic vitals that kept alive the Russian resistance.

Russian reverses were paralleled by deterioration of the Allied position in the Atlantic, Africa, and the Mediterranean. When war broke, England had only fifteen battleships, mostly old, as compared with forty-two modern dreadnoughts in 1916 at the time of Jutland. Vichy control of the French fleet held the balance of naval power. At one stroke Italy's entrance into war placed the Nazis under General Erwin Rommel in Libya on the Egyptian border threatening Suez. Land-based Axis aircraft in Italy, Greece, Crete, and North Africa deprived England of priceless Mediterranean sea lanes, the short route through Suez to the Far East. The English navy no longer could command the Mediterranean Sea; neither R.A.F. raids from Malta nor old-style blockade by warships could cut the supply lines of Rommel's panzers.

The crucial Battle of the Atlantic also favored the Nazis, preventing a second front to bring relief to the gallant Red Army. The World War I minefields and blockade of exits from the North Sea would not suffice to pen up the Nazis. Axis land-based air power from Norway to the Spanish border and the deadly modern torpedo from crash-diving submarines outmoded classic forms of naval containment. The Allied embargo, tightened by the expanding coalition of United Nations, gradually achieved a more stringent commercial blockade on a grander scale than any in history. But meanwhile the Battle of the Atlantic remained one of the two crucial battles—as crucial as the vast and bloody 1,500 miles of battlefront in Russia. On the North Atlantic convoy, on the Murmansk run, in the Caribbean, in the South Atlantic, the deadly wolf packs struck. Allied and neutral losses totaled over 1,000 ships and nearly 4,500,000 tons by the end of 1940. In 1941 the losses mounted; and in 1942 the Allies were losing 1,000,000 tons of shipping a month —faster than ships could be built. The air blitzkrieg in 1940 did not come as close to defeating England as the underwater wolf packs that ranged unchecked in 1942.

The war had become in good earnest what Roosevelt described it— a "war of survival."

XXXII

CENTURY OF THE COMMON MAN?

1942–1946

Total war required total mobilization of men and resources. Democracies were forced to resort to drastic powers inadmissible in times of peace, to preserve freedom itself from its direst threat in modern history. The American government, like embattled England, harnessed the scattered energies of the people in a supreme effort to stem the forces of brute nationalism that threatened to trample over the earth.

THE BATTLE OF PRODUCTION

Slowly, as the war months lengthened, the majesty of liberty-loving peoples aroused to sacrifice was revealed in the crucial battle of the unarmed forces—the Battle of Production. To overcome shortages, to build the bridge of ships across the seven seas, to arm and provision more than ten million Americans and millions of Allied fighting men, to build up supplies and mount an offensive and ultimately the "second front" that desperate Russia asked for and that the Allies pledged, required centralization and energy that totalitarians claimed only their New Order was capable of achieving. But free labor was proving the master of slave labor. The United States and the British commonwealths were casting off democratic sloth, expending their fat, and flexing unused muscles as they drew to the full upon their huge strength in labor efficiency, technology, and productive resources, and upon the strength of free men who had never known defeat. Blood, sweat, and tears had their counterparts in human strain in Washington bureaus, in business offices, on undermanned farms, on production lines of war workers.

When war began, the productive resources of Britain, her commonwealths, and the United States approximated 55 per cent of the world's total; but peacetime potential was not war potential. In her critical hours England drafted labor and management, rationed food and materials, wiped out profiteering, and imposed taxes and inflation controls more extensive than the American political structure ever permitted. Roosevelt, following English example, sought "equality of sacrifice," only to

719

meet resistance in Congress. Conversion to war work brought complaints of administrative confusion and bureaucracy and complaints from administrators of the resistance of corporate managers who wanted "business as usual." A struggle for power was involved. An investigator for the government, reporting in a TNEC monograph on political pressures, spoke bluntly: "Business refuses to work, except on terms which it dictates." But Pearl Harbor was then a year away, and Congress had not given administrative authority to organize production.

The President's answer to congressional indifference was to create executive boards, which utilized the power of persuasion. A year before Pearl Harbor, Roosevelt drafted business and labor leaders, including William S. Knudsen of General Motors and Sidney Hillman of the C.I.O., to streamline production. To prevent the disastrous inflation of World War I, the President in April, 1941, created the OPA (Office of Price Administration). After Pearl Harbor, Roosevelt centralized control of war materials and conversion to war work under an able Chicago executive, Donald Nelson. His agency, WPB (the War Production Board), brought a rapid improvement in efficiency. Strict priorities and allocations put an end to "business as usual." Under a War Labor Board wages were pegged. Cooperation between labor and management became better than at any time since the rise of big business. Good relations facilitated such achievements as the miracles wrought by Henry J. Kaiser in huge new shipyards. Judicious Senate investigations by the Truman-Mead committee helped correct faulty administration in Washington. The committee traced serious "bottlenecks," as in rubber, aluminum, chemicals, to American trusts, international cartels, and patent monopolies. Government funds were poured out to tap aluminum resources and build plants for rubber and other vital war materials. The public works of depression years, great dams and water power, now proved a vital necessity, averting what would have been acute shortage in electric power.

The Battle of Production was won by the democracies. The sudden spurt in 1942 gave the country the world's most magnificent air force and equipped an immense military establishment. In less than a year after Pearl Harbor, the army had grown to be more than three times as large as it had been at the same point in World War I; and the merchant marine, navy, coast guard, and marines were expanding at a rate without parallel in the previous war.

DEFEAT AND RESURGENCE

Global offensive must wait for the ships—convoys and escorts; but the turn toward victory in the Battle of Production came in time for a general turning of the fortunes of war late in 1942. Depletion of Allied power in the Mediterranean, Atlantic, and Pacific continued unchecked until the summer of 1942. Peacetime Allied Asiatic squadrons could not stay Japanese sea power. In February, 1942, a force of five cruisers and nine destroyers—Australian, English, Dutch, and American—was overwhelmed in the Battle of Java Sea, not a ship escaping. A synchronized Axis offensive brought stunning new blows in May as Corregidor fell and the Burma Road was cut in the East, while Nazi desert panzers carried Rommel's great drive from Libya across Egypt in June to El Alamein, only sixty-five miles from Britain's main base at Alexandria. In July the Japanese occupied Guadalcanal, and the last Russian defenders of the Crimean Peninsula fell as the Nazi tide rolled on toward the Volga and the oil fields.

Simultaneously in June a Japanese seaborne invasion struck across the Pacific for the Aleutians and the Hawaiian Islands. Attu and Kiska fell, but the invasion of Hawaii was checked at the Battle of Midway, where the Japanese navy suffered its first defeat in the three hundred and fifty years since the victory of the Koreans in 1592. Carrier forces and land-based planes won control of the air, and the invasion force of perhaps eighty Japanese transports was put to flight. The United States lost a veteran carrier, the *Yorktown;* and of one of the air groups launched from the *Hornet,* not a plane returned and only a single pilot survived. Enemy losses were even more staggering. All of the Japanese carriers were either badly damaged or sunk, the first line of Nippon's pilots was decimated, and enemy naval air power was crippled, not to recover for more than a year. But Japan retained command of the sea and land-based air supremacy in the Central and South Pacific.

Naval war in the Pacific had no parallel for intensity except in the seventeenth-century struggles between Dutch and English and the later British triumphs over Napoleon's Grand Fleets. American and Nipponese commanders revived the fierce and headlong yet well-calculated style of sea fighting made famous by Nelson when defeating Bonaparte's invasion of Egypt and later when destroying the naval power of the French and Spanish at Trafalgar. In a daring Allied offensive-defensive, a combined operation landed marines on Guadalcanal on August 7, 1942. Then began the four months' battle to maintain the perilous toe hold around Henderson Field against superior naval and air concentrations and Japanese jungle fighters. On August 9 came a repetition of the Java Sea disaster; a screening force of heavy cruisers, three American and one Australian, was surprised and sunk in a night action off Savo Island by an enemy squadron that suffered no losses. Guarding Guadalcanal, an Amer-

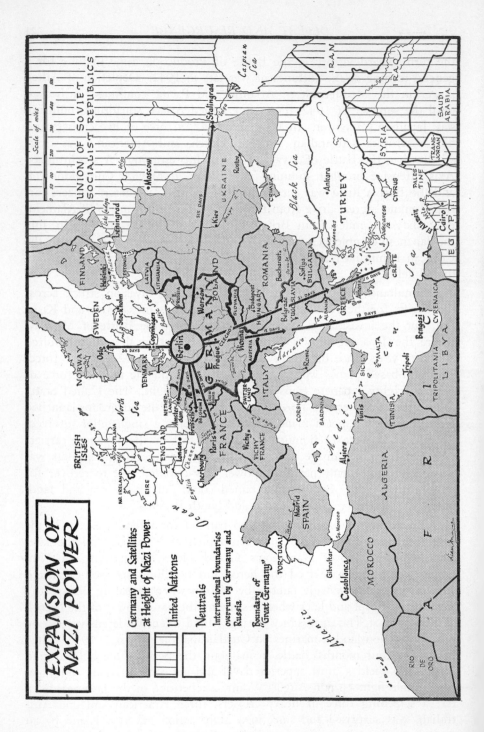

EXPANSION OF NAZI POWER

Germany and Satellites at Height of Nazi Power

United Nations

Neutrals

International boundaries overrun by Germany and Russia

Boundary of "Great Germany"

722

ican force on October 12 intercepted a superior enemy force and sank virtually every ship—four Japanese cruisers and five destroyers. Meanwhile the marines hung on at Henderson Field amid bitter fighting. The badly needed carrier, *Hornet,* went down later in October in another naval battle off Guadalcanal. Marines and army troops made counterattacks to restore their lines, and on November 6 re-enforcements began to come. On November 12, in Admiral Ernest J. King's words, began "one of the most furious sea battles ever fought," the three-day battle of Guadalcanal, which was decisive in the Solomons campaign. Heavy toll was taken of American squadrons, but unendurable depletion caused enemy withdrawal. Other actions in the air and on the sea reduced the threat of the "Tokyo Express" and within three months the Japanese evacuated the southern Solomon Islands.

The critical period of Allied defeat ended in November, 1942. Within a few days of the Guadalcanal victory the tide turned in Russia, in the Mediterranean, and in the Atlantic. General Bernard L. Montgomery's revitalized and magnificently mixed Eighth Army broke through Rommel's defenses at El Alamein on November 6. On November 7 a great armada, some 850 ships, brought American and English landings over a thousand-mile stretch of French North Africa. On November 27 the scuttling of the French fleet to keep it from Hitler decided the balance of naval power. On November 19 began the Russian miracle at Stalingrad. Surprise concentrations outflanked and encircled the enemy, weeks later lifting the siege, destroying the Nazi legend of invincible supermen.

By 1943 the United Nations held the initiative, winning victories on the outer circle, containing and constricting the enemy. "For three years," had run the heartening words of Montgomery to the troops about to assault Rommel at El Alamein, "we have been trying to plug holes all over the world. Now, thank God, that period is over." Before the new year Rommel was routed again at El Agheila, seven hundred miles beyond El Alamein, and a month later the "Desert Fox" had been pursued across Tripoli and run to earth at the Mareth line in southern Tunis. Command of the sea and soon command of the air cut Nazi and Italian communications; for the vaunted Africa Corps and Mussolini's Fascists there was no Dunkirk. In May, 1943, Rommel, like Napoleon before him, left his forces to their fate. The North African campaigns cost Italy and Germany nearly a million men killed or captured. Meanwhile nearly a third as many were killed or captured by the defenders of Stalingrad; and the Red Army raced westward to liberate Kharkov.

Three main drives in 1943 gradually pressed inward, from the outer rim of the war toward the strategic inner circle. By November, 1943, the now mighty Russian surge was drawing closer to Germany, driving to Kiev, mounting a great winter offensive through the Ukraine. The Anglo-American drive, following Churchill's strategy, struck at "the soft underbelly of Europe." Sicily was taken in the summer of 1943 and the southern tip of Italy in the fall; but despite the collapse of Mussolini and unconditional surrender, the "soft" approach proved a miscalculation. Nazis took over; no campaign proved more bitter than the slow advance from Salerno and Naples, from bloody Anzio beachhead and Cassino to Rome, and then the final year of rugged fighting in the mountains northward from Florence. In contrast, both in the immense scale of operations and in the sensational leaps forward, was the triple drive in the South, Central, and Northern Pacific. By February, 1944, amphibious forces, landings, and jungle fighting with sea and air action by prowling task forces, screening warships, carriers, and air forces, carried northward in the Solomons, neutralized Rabaul, and moved west up the long coast of New Guinea. The Aleutian drive recovered Kiska and Attu. In the Central Pacific the costly assault on Tarawa in the Gilberts opened the great naval offensive to take advanced bases. Early in 1944 Kwajalein and other bases in the Marshalls were stormed and captured.

VICTORY IN THE WAR EFFORT

Production by 1944 paved the way for the final offensive. The spurt from 1941 through 1943 produced 153,061 planes, 23,867 landing craft, and 746 fighting ships, including a new battle line of superbattleships and carriers. Five ocean-going ships were sliding down the ways every twenty-four hours. By September, 1943, General Marshall reported extensive lend-lease shipment to Russia: for example, 16,000 jeeps, 80,000 trucks, 109,000 submachine guns, 130,000 field telephones. Average losses on the Murmansk run fell from 12 out of every 100 ships to 1 out of 100.

Wartime public works far outmatched earlier New Deal battles against depression. The Budget Director in 1944 reported that new war plants financed by the government were worth about $20,000,000,-000. Over $9,000,000,000 worth of plants were directly owned by the government. The country was applying Keynesian economics, for government spending bridged the gap between private investment and expenditure and the total new investment and spending required for full employment. As the government's Defense Plant Corporation built plants and leased them to companies, economists drew hopeful conclusions from the self-evident potential of the new "mixed economy." Swiftly unemployment shrank—from over 8,000,000 in 1939 to the rock bottom of "frictional unemployment," 842,000 in 1944. Full employment and a stupendous rise of the income of the nation gave laboratory demonstration to economic hypothesis. From the 1939 record peacetime production, a gross output valued at $88,600,000,000, the national output rose steadily in wartime, by 1944 reaching the fabulous magnitude of $198,700,000,-000. Correspondingly, national income doubled, reaching the ultimate prodigious war peak of $165,000,000,000 a year.

Wartime rivalry of management and labor for public esteem resulted in gains for the business community. Great managerial skills, required for the scale of production needed to defend democracy, called for and received their full meed of praise. The "tycoon" and dollar-a-year man in Washington, made glamorous in *Life, Time,* and *Fortune,* gained favor for proponents of government by businessmen. Labor lost ground in the hidden struggle for political prestige; and yet WLB held wages down by the Little Steel formula and settled thousands of industrial disputes, assisted by the no-strike pledge and cooperative spirit of the two leading labor organizations. No longer associated with either of these, John L. Lewis and the miners were not subject to the no-strike pledge, and several times the miners struck. In extreme cases not yielding to WLB controls, the government seized war plants. Employer incompetence was sometimes the occasion. Spokesmen for employer interests capitalized on the war psychosis, coupling strikes with treason. Cold facts of statistical curves and figures showed that labor, management, and the government as a whole had never before achieved teamwork on such a vast scale—under frozen wages—with so little interruption. Yet the purposive drone of strike news in press and radio encouraged employer spokesmen in Congress, led by Howard Smith, factious Democrat more representative of a poll-tax machine than of the people of Virginia, to pass the Smith-Connally Act. Legalizing seizure of strike-bound plants, Congress incorporated in the law the old antilabor formula of criminal liability, sanctioning imprisonment of instigators of strikes. The Smith-Connally Act, passed over Roosevelt's veto, proved ambiguous and during the war years accomplished nothing.

Estimates in *The New Republic* in September, 1943, showed a heartening loyalty and teamwork of labor and management: the total man-hours lost amounted to only .5 per cent of the total working time of the nation. Despite wage freezes, the no-strike pledge was overwhelmingly observed. Subsequent Bureau of Labor figures, covering 30,000,000 workers for the three years after 1941, showed that loss from strikes was less than 1 day's work per worker for the whole three years. As the labor force expanded upward to a total employed man power of nearly 60,000,000 persons, the Truman committee reported nearly 45 per cent more man-days of work in mines, farms, and factories in 1943 than in

1939, and more than 89 per cent in the single field of manufacturing.

The nation gave of its brain, its brawn, and its bullion. In the last year of war, government expenditure moved upward toward $100,000,-000,000; and bond drives pushed the public debt to upward of $250,-000,000,000. The armed services became the best-equipped striking force in a world that totalitarians had mapped for their own under the fantastic notion that despised democracies would not and could not fight. The "output of American farms and factories," reported General Marshall proudly, "exceeding any similar effort of man," enabled a vital lend-lease re-enforcement of the gallant British and Russian peoples whose refusal "to accept what appeared to be inevitable defeat was the great factor in the salvage of our civilization." Giving their utmost, England and her commonwealths mobilized 12,000,000, while the U.S.S.R., ex-hausted but rallying, put, all told, some 22,000,000 men and women into the fight. By V-J day over 12,000,000 Americans, men and women, were under arms—8,050,000 in the army, 3,400,000 in the navy, and 600,000 in the marines and coast guard—with over 200,000 more in the merchant fleets that helped defeat Hitler and Hirohito.

VICTORY IN ARMS

Equipped for the knockout, the Allies prepared for Continental en-velopment of Hitler's Europe and for the closing of the gigantic Pacific pincers on Nippon's captive Asia. At the Teheran meeting in December, 1943, Roosevelt, Stalin, Churchill, and military experts planned the "scope and timing" of a Russian offensive and an Anglo-American second front. The only direct British and American blows at Germany's inner circle had so far been limited to strategic bombing. As invasion of France neared, the global offensive prepared simultaneously for liberation of the Philippines. The great drive through the Central Pacific began in June, 1944. Task force raids and air strikes all around the circle pitted the fields and wiped out land-based air power on Japan's strategic chains of islands. Under cover of bombardment by the old Pearl Harbor battle-ships and planes from the fleet of baby carriers, landing craft swept first upon Saipan and then upon Guam. A new weapon, rocket fire, covered the final dangerous dash over the reefs to seize the beachheads.

Concentrating near the Philippines, the Japanese navy launched a carrier force larger than the flights at Pearl Harbor and Midway, strik-ing far over the sea toward Saipan. America's fast battleships and big carriers—all but one built since war began—were not taken by surprise. In the "great turkey shoot," initial action of the First Battle of the Philip-pines, 404 planes were downed—more than the best day's bag of the

R.A.F. in the blitz over London—with almost no American loss. The battle was concluded the next day by an appalling air assault launched from big new American carriers at extreme range, taking heavy toll on the fleeing Japanese fleet. The new first line of enemy naval air power, carefully rebuilt since Midway, had been destroyed like its predecessor. Saipan and Guam fell, and then Peleliu. On October 20 combined operations brought converging forces from the Solomons-New Guinea theater and from the captured Central Pacific bases to the beachhead at Leyte. For the last time the Japanese fleet came out. In the four days of the Second Battle of the Philippines, the reconditioned Pearl Harbor battleships slaughtered the southern Japanese squadron; air power sank or routed the battleships and cruisers of the central enemy force; and Halsey's big carriers wiped out the northern enemy force—Japan's last carrier group. A surprise descent upon American baby carriers covering Leyte nearly cost the United States heavily. But the four-day battle proved "a Trafalgar, not a Jutland." In its most decisive naval action, the United States had won mastery of the sea. The way was open to the inner circle.

On June 6, 1944, as Pacific forces concentrated for the Saipan landing, Supreme Allied Commander Dwight D. Eisenhower set in motion Operation OVERLORD. A roaring canopy of planes from England and some 4,000 ships converged on Normandy, and landing craft disgorged mighty forces on "Omaha Beach." D day and the second front had come. Strategic and tactical bombing reduced German oil supplies and deprived the Nazis of rapid mobile concentration. "Terrific air power," confessed the Prussian commander, Marshal Karl von Rundstedt, "broke up all bridges and pinned me down completely and the terrific power of the naval guns made it absolutely impossible for reserves to come up." Nine days after D day, deadly buzz bombs from the "robot coast" began to rain destruction on England. By early August the breakthrough at Saint-Lô swept Allied forces into Brittany, and eastward and north, trapping the Nazi center in the Falaise pocket. On August 15 Allied armies from Italy and Africa invaded southern France and struck northward up the Rhône Valley. Plunging onward from Normandy, Montgomery's British and Canadians turned the enemy flank on the Channel coast, captured robot-bomb launching platforms, and struck across the Somme; in the center the United States First Army raced to other World War I battlefields, Belleau Wood and Château-Thierry; while Patton's heavily armored Third Army, deep in France, fanned out to protect the French underground, which had risen to liberate Paris, and then lunged onward through Verdun to Saint-Mihiel, laying siege to the fortress of Metz in the Maginot line. At the end of six months the rampaging Allied armies under Eisenhower had carried to the approaches of Germany's vaunted Westwall.

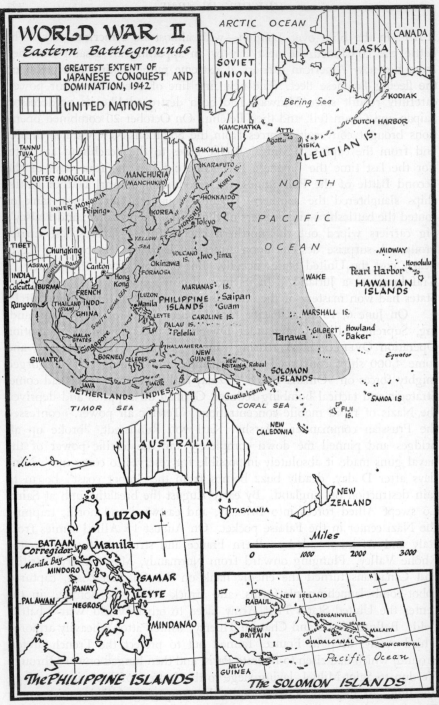

WORLD WAR II
Eastern Battlegrounds

GREATEST EXTENT OF JAPANESE CONQUEST AND DOMINATION, 1942

UNITED NATIONS

ARCTIC OCEAN

CANADA

ALASKA

SOVIET UNION

KODIAK

Bering Sea

KAMCHATKA

DUTCH HARBOR

ATTU

Agattu   KISKA

ALEUTIAN IS.

TANNU TUVA

OUTER MONGOLIA

SAKHALIN

KARAFUTO

KURIL IS.

NORTH

INNER MONGOLIA

Peiping

MANCHURIA (MANCHUKUO)

KOREA

HOKKAIDO

SEA OF JAPAN

PACIFIC

CHINA

TIBET

Chungking

YELLOW SEA

HONSHU

Tokyo

JAPAN

OCEAN

MIDWAY

Honolulu

ASSAM   BURMA ROAD

Canton

VOLCANO IS.   Iwo Jima

Okinawa

FORMOSA

Hong Kong

WAKE

Pearl Harbor

HAWAIIAN ISLANDS

INDIA
Calcutta BURMA

FRENCH

LUZON
Manila

MARIANAS IS.

Saipan
Guam

Rangoon

THAILAND (SIAM) INDO-CHINA

PHILIPPINE ISLANDS

LEYTE

CAROLINE IS.

MARSHALL IS.

MALAY STATES

Singapore

PALAU IS.
Peleliu

GILBERT IS.   Howland
Baker

SUMATRA

BORNEO

CELEBES

HALMAHERA

NEW GUINEA

Tarawa

Equator

JAVA

TIMOR

NETHERLANDS INDIES

NEW BRITAIN Rabaul

SOLOMON ISLANDS

TIMOR SEA

Guadalcanal

CORAL SEA

SAMOA IS

FIJI IS.

NEW CALEDONIA

AUSTRALIA

Liam Dunne

Miles

0   1000   2000   3000

TASMANIA

NEW ZEALAND

The PHILIPPINE ISLANDS

LUZON

BATAAN
Corregidor   Manila

Manila Bay

MINDORO

SAMAR

PANAY   LEYTE

PALAWAN   NEGROS

MINDANAO

The SOLOMON ISLANDS

RABAUL   NEW IRELAND

BOUGAINVILLE

CHOISEUL ISABEL MALAITA
THE SLOT

NEW BRITAIN   GUADALCANAL
SAN CRISTOVAL

NEW GUINEA   Pacific Ocean

WORLD WAR II
Western Battlegrounds

GREATEST EXTENT OF AXIS CONQUEST AND DOMINATION, 1942

UNITED NATIONS

UNITED NATIONS SUPPLY LINES

NEUTRALS

THE NORMANDY CAMPAIGN

Between January, 1943, and January, 1944, the power drives of the triumphant Russians had swept from the Volga to the gates of Warsaw deep into Poland; into Finland, where Nazi collaborators fell and where Russian policy did not dictate unconditional surrender; through Rumania to Bulgaria, which likewise escaped with lenient terms; and up the Danube to knock out the fascists of Hungary and assist the Yugoslav Partisans of Marshal Tito. On the western front in December, 1944, the Nazis made their last offensive; but the sudden lunge of the panzers in the battle of the Ardennes Bulge was contained before New Year's Eve. By the end of winter, Russian offensives captured Warsaw, drove across Poland and East Prussia to the approaches of Berlin, and stormed up the Danube to Budapest; while on the Flanders sector the Allies broke through to Cologne and the Rhine, on March 7, 1945, dashing across the Remagen bridgehead. On March 16, with the Fighting French covering the flank southward to Switzerland, the American Third and Seventh armies in lightning thrusts broke the Westwall and overran the rich Saar Basin in a one-week blitzkrieg carrying to the Rhine.

By the end of March, Götterdämmerung for Hitler's Reich was sounding. An immense amphibious smash across the Rhine won bridgeheads. In two weeks the industrial Ruhr was severed from the Reich. A week later Austria was liberated as Russian armor clanked through Vienna; and eight days later Russians began to storm Berlin. The shattering Allied air pounding destroyed communications and broke the coordination of enemy armies. Bewildered Nazi commanders could no longer shift reserves, establish new lines, or draw on vast stores of hoarded munitions. Eisenhower announced on March 27 that orderly resistance on the west was broken. Holland was liberated by Montgomery's men. Americans raced south of Berlin to link up with the Russians and again into Czechoslovakia and the Danube country to make another link. In rugged mountain fighting the April offensive in Italy broke vicious Nazi resistance, took Bologna, and fanned out on the northern plains. Mussolini lay dead in a Milan square, executed by Italian Partisans. On May 2 Berlin was in Russian hands. Adolf Hitler went underground, one way or the other. His "hangman" Himmler poisoned himself. V-E day, May 5, brought Germany's unconditional surrender.

The war against totalitarians in the Far East moved rapidly to a climactic finish under command of General of the Army Douglas MacArthur and Fleet Admiral Chester W. Nimitz. D day in the Philippines at Leyte was followed in January, 1945, by landings on Luzon and the smash into Manila on February 13. Six days later opened the bloody campaign for an advanced base on Iwo Jima. Exactly a month later the largest amphibious force in Pacific history began assault at Japan's doorstep, Okinawa, 325 miles from the enemy homeland. Nippon's naval remnants were slaughtered, and land-based air strikes from Guam, Iwo Jima, and Okinawa, and gigantic air blows from prowling carriers blockaded Japan, destroying shipping, and bombing and burning out Nipponese industrial cities. Meanwhile the navy, suffering serious damage, fought off and downed several thousand of the dreaded suicide planes in the Kamikaze raids. On August 5, 1945, the city of Hiroshima dissolved in the disintegrating explosion of uranium atoms. Three days later the second bomb fell on Nagasaki. Russia, declaring war, began to roll back the crack Japanese armies in Korea and Manchuria. On August 14, four years after Roosevelt and Churchill proposed the Atlantic Charter, the emperor of the Eastern totalitarians bowed in unconditional surrender. Early in September Tokyo was occupied by Allied forces.

Sketchy preliminary estimates set Axis battle casualties in Europe at 15,000,000, with equal casualties for the United Nations. Beyond this, totalitarian liberation of the evil in man had exacted a toll of incalculable proportions in civilian suffering and damage to the human spirit. Under the Nazi heel the "inferior" peoples of occupied countries had been robbed, uprooted, and enslaved; and antifascists and stigmatized "races" had been exterminated. Untold numbers perished in concentration camps and in Nazi death camps. In Poland alone, some 10,000,000 people—Russian, Jew, Pole—had "disappeared."

To the United States the money cost of the war was more than six times as great as World War I. Casualties were nearly four times as great, about 1,075,000—over three fourths of them incurred against Italy and Germany. The death toll among American forces in the Pacific was over 100,000; in the European theater, about 150,000.

As the blackout lifted in ruined streets, what did peace promise to the stouthearted who had stayed the black tide of totalitarians? Politics during war had already forecast the pattern of the postwar struggle for power. Abroad, the movement was toward a people's peace. The Labor party after V-E day won a smashing victory in England, displacing the politically bankrupt Tory party, which had ruled without a general election for ten years. In the liberated western Europe of France, Belgium, and Italy, the forces of social democracy were also making a stronger challenge than they had made after World War I.

POLITICS IN WARTIME

A trend toward conservatism in the American Congress, setting in during the war years, contrasted with the trend in European democracies. The Republican party won no mandate, nor even a mid-term election, during Roosevelt's years in office. The elections of 1942 nevertheless encouraged the financial and commercial interests that had dominated politics in the boom years of Calvin Coolidge. An apathetic campaign and a light vote proved advantageous to the Republicans. Although Democrats held nominal command of the Senate with 57 seats, Republican gains cut the Democratic majority in the House to 5. Repudiation of the Democratic party leadership by Democrats in the new Congress of 1943-1944 on occasion gave the actual power of legislation to the Republican party. Making party principles and election mandates still more deceptive, splits in both parties impeded intelligent action.

The decline of party discipline among nominal Democrats and the assertiveness of G.O.P. leaders, who hailed the "conservative trend," weakened legislative resistance to the drives of powerful lobbies. Responding to the organized pressure of the big farmers and industrialists, the farm bloc and special-interest spokesmen opposed price controls, ceilings on salaries, and other items in the Roosevelt program to check inflation and meet the burdens of war with an "equality of sacrifice." Heavier taxes—essential for mastery of the inflationary swing of the business cycle—were resisted by the majority of Republicans, now joined by a considerable segment of Democrats. Willkie as well as the nation's leading economists called for heavier taxes to reduce consumer competition for goods and help close the "inflationary gap." On November 30, 1943, Walter Lippmann, observing the underlying struggle for power, commented upon ludicrous double talk in Congress: on Tuesday the House outlawed certain farm price controls, "arguing that the people have lots of money and can afford to pay higher prices for food"; a day later, Wednesday, the House defeated large tax increases, "arguing that the people now have so little money left that they cannot pay more taxes."

Early in 1944 Roosevelt urged Congress not to pass a revenue law that revived tax theories of Mellon and the 1920's. Republicans aided by Democratic insurgents passed the bill. Roosevelt vetoed it as "relief for the greedy and not for the needy." The Senate took the veto message as an affront; the administration floor leader, Alben W. Barkley, resigned; Congress passed the bill over the veto. American parties had evolved no means like an English general election for carrying such an issue immediately to the voters for a popular mandate. The Democrats needed the President's leadership, and the Barkley rebellion proved abortive. The Senator was renamed as administration leader. The incident betrayed not only the Democratic split but Republican strategy. Unable to win a national mandate by defeating Roosevelt at the polls, his opponents asserted the "independence" of the legislative branch as a means of achieving mastery over the executive.

Within a few months the presidential elections once more were to reaffirm that the executive represented the will of the national majority. The campaign of 1944 made the public conscious that the split in 'the Republican party on foreign affairs was as serious as the split of the Democratic party on domestic affairs. When the Republican national convention met, Willkie, who had taken his stand in *One World* (1943), had already been counted out by the opposition in his own party. The Old Guard could not follow a man who, opposed to economic nationalism, favored abandonment of the protective tariff and who committed heresy again by accepting parts of the Roosevelt domestic program. Thomas E. Dewey, critical of New Deal reforms but hospitable to international organization, was nominated for the presidency, with an isolationist governor of Ohio, John W. Bricker, as his running mate. Roosevelt was nominated for a fourth term, but conservative Democrats, blocking renomination of Vice-President Henry A. Wallace, ostensibly won a victory by naming Senator Harry S. Truman of Missouri.

The real issues in the election—except on reciprocal trade agreements—were visible less in the platforms and campaign oratory than in the voting records in Congress. Compilations of votes were widely circulated by P.A.C., labor's new Political Action Committee, and by the C.I.O., the League of Women Voters, and liberal organizations. Congressional voting records revealed the dominance of nationalists among Republicans. Despite the international stand of Senators Joseph Ball and Harold H. Burton and the wavering of Arthur H. Vandenberg, the majority of Republicans in Congress still followed the isolationist leadership of Nye and Taft. Four fifths of the opposition to the first and second lend-lease appropriations had come from Republicans. The same men had been the backbone of opposition to various Senate and House proposals for mild resolutions endorsing international organization. The great battle over isolation appeared to have turned into a rout in September, 1943, when only twenty-nine representatives voted against the Fulbright Resolution. To the unforgettable twenty-nine "whose dim, aloof spirit walks by its wild lone," *The New Yorker* awarded "a special ribbon for unusual density above and beyond the call of duty." But appearances were misleading. In the vote in June, 1943, on extending trade agreements, Republicans remained divided; fifty-two of the sixty-five tariff isolationists in the House were Republicans; in the Senate the split among Republicans was exemplified in the Ohio vote, Burton for, Taft against, as likewise in the vote of Minnesota Republicans, Ball for, Shipstead against.

During the campaign of 1944, the Roosevelt-Hull program for peace posed a clean-cut issue through the medium of international conferences in the United States—the Bretton Woods meeting of United Nations experts, who drafted a plan for an international bank and international regulation of currencies; and the Dumbarton Oaks meeting, which drafted a preliminary plan for an international political structure. Citizen organizations in every constituency asked the embarrassing question of congressional nationalists: were they for or against Bretton Woods and Dumbarton Oaks? Among the significant results of the elections was retirement from office of Nye, Fish, and several other die-hards. Three more—Wheeler, La Follette, and Shipstead—were to succumb two years later.

Roosevelt victories had sprung from the increase in the number of voters who regularly went to the polls. Discovery of this fact led to active competition by both parties and by P.A.C. to register the millions of nonvoters. An act of Congress for a "state rights" soldiers' vote—a defeat for Roosevelt, who sought a simplified federal ballot by which the twelve million servicemen could vote—was engineered by the coalition of Republicans and Bourbon Democrats of the South who hoped to restrict the size of the vote. Public opinion polls had indicated a still heavier New Deal preference among soldiers and young voters than among the people as a whole. Soldier-vote impediments and civilian migration to centers of war industry, disqualifying voters by registration and residence requirements, contributed to reduce the size of the vote. Dewey had a smaller total than Willkie, 22,018,000, but carried twelve states. Roosevelt received 25,611,000 votes. The Democrats, increasing their majority in the House with a gain of twenty-one seats and retaining three fifths of the seats in the Senate, once again had a national mandate.

UNITED NATIONS—OR SOVEREIGN NATIONS?

Three months after the elections and just before the final push into Germany, Roosevelt attended the Yalta Conference in the Crimea. Russia's chief objection to the Dumbarton Oaks plan was resolved by a veto arrangement whereby each Big Power could block international intervention directed against itself. Churchill, Stalin, and Roosevelt also called for a general conference in April at San Francisco, where the United Nations would consider the Dumbarton Oaks proposals and draft the charter of the United Nations. To facilitate bipartisan agreement in Senate action on the charter, the President named as delegates leading Republican and Democratic senators from the foreign relations committee—Tom Connally of Texas and the ex-isolationist of Michigan, Arthur Vandenberg. Roosevelt did not live to see fulfillment of the twelve years in which he and Hull had labored to liquidate the excesses of nationalism.

On April 12, two weeks before the San Francisco Conference, radio networks flashed the shocking words, "Roosevelt is dead." From friend and foe came tribute. Franklin Delano Roosevelt, beloved not alone by America's millions, had enriched man's faith in democratic ways among other millions in a war-torn world. The time called for greatness and he gave it. By strong courage and superb leadership in the Hundred Days, Roosevelt carried the people out of panic through the most severe economic crash ever to confront the nation. In the hazardous years that ensued he met and countered the world crisis. As war loomed, Roosevelt led the country wisely to gather its strength and make itself an arsenal for the defenders of freedom. When the international explosion of fascism let loose the primitive evil in man and engulfed democracies one by one, he rose in stature as a great war leader. As victory neared, the President's statesmanship helped to win as great a victory in the minds of people—turning them from the narrowness of nationalism toward united enterprise for the welfare of man. After his death there was no compelling voice that could simplify issues and unite popular elements on a course of constructive action.

Upon unassuming Harry S. Truman fell the momentous responsibilities that Franklin D. Roosevelt had shouldered for twelve years. Scarcely had the new President been sworn into office than the architects of the United Nations met in San Francisco. Reported in sensational dispatches, the conference jolted the high expectations of war-weary peoples. Criticism of the great powers by the small and differences between the Big Three bogged down proceedings. Russia's participation, instead of reassuring, became the occasion for a bitter outcry in the American press. The more responsible papers as well as the Hearst chain, the Chicago *Tribune,* and habitual Red-baiters joined the chorus. Although isolationism was appreciably strengthened thereby, the United States, as in 1919, was experiencing the early stages of a "Red scare." The conference dragged on from April 25 to June; but amid conflicting national purposes the delegates found compromises. Suggestion of a war with Russia for the moment lost force as the conferees completed drafting of the Charter of the United Nations.

President Truman, in a gradual reshuffle of cabinet posts, chose a Secretary of State who had the confidence of Congress, James F. Byrnes of South Carolina. As former senator, Supreme Court justice, and wartime administrator, Byrnes had generally been sympathetic with the Roosevelt program; as Secretary of State he carried on the Hull policies, avowing his country's belief in advancing "social and economic democracy at home and abroad." His colleagues at various international meetings, Senators Vandenberg and Connally, like their respective Republican and Democratic followers in Congress, while endorsing American leadership in international affairs, were less concerned with economic democracy. Indeed, Congress, despite the mandate on internationalism in the 1944 elections and in spite of the bipartisan team of Connally and Vandenberg, was not easily led to underwrite the global policies that came before it.

An important victory on reciprocity agreements was won in June, 1945, by congressional assent to an additional lowering of the Hawley-Smoot tariff by as much as a 50 per cent cut. A majority hearkened sympathetically to testimony of the administration spokesmen, Fred M. Vinson, soon to be Chief Justice, who underlined the point that tariffs and other barricades against imports would "impede exports as well, by making it difficult for our would-be customers to get the dollars with which they buy our goods." Though authority to reduce the tariff by the reciprocity method had been renewed repeatedly since 1934, opposition remained strong. Attempts to outlaw trade agreements failed; but congressional votes were even more perilously close than in 1943. The House divided 212–181. Democrats, North and South, united to support the bill. Republicans split, 140 opposing, 33 supporting. In the Senate the vote of 37 Democrats and 9 Republicans sustained the power to make additional 50 per cent reductions, overriding 25 Republicans led by the official party leaders, Taft, White, and Wherry. Eight Democrats bolted to aid the Taft Republicans.

When the Bretton Woods pact came to the floor a month later, endorsed by overwhelming public opinion, unrepentant nationalists prudently practiced the maxim of "he who fights and runs away." The issue involved not only a restraint upon sovereignty through exchange controls exercised by an International Bank. It entailed also a heavy contribution of American dollars to an International Monetary Fund. The bank and the fund offered facilities to improve the relationships of debtor and creditor nations. They likewise provided fiscal instruments to battle against world depressions and international currency wars. When the House passed the bill in July, 1945, the only opposition votes were cast by 18 bitter-end Republicans. In the upper house, Senators Ball and Burton stood with the almost solid Republican phalanx, voting to postpone action until the Allies "laid their cards on the table." The maneuver was defeated, and Senator Wagner steered the bill through to a 61–16 triumph against die-hards led by Taft and urged on by lobbyists of bankers who reflected Main Street more than Wall Street. The United States was first of the 44 signers to approve the Bretton Woods pact.

Russia withheld acceptance but other nations joined. The bank and the fund, formally established in December, 1945, became a new force for international progress.

Hard on the heels of the Bretton Woods victory in Congress, the long campaign for Dumbarton Oaks was won. It had become political suicide to oppose the United Nations Charter. In August, 1945, when the charter was ratified, only two of the nationalist senators, both Republicans from the Midwest, voted nay. Burton K. Wheeler, voting yea, grimly promised that the "real fight" would come later when appropriations and legislation to implement the United Nations program reached Congress. Old opponent of imperialism, "Young Bob" La Follette, voting yea, criticized the Big Power supremacy and the veto provisions as "gross violations of the democratic principles which can alone provide a political climate for enduring peace." A month earlier, reporting the work of the San Francisco Conference, the ex-isolationist, Senator Vandenberg, had defended the Big Power domination of the Security Council: "The world is at the mercy of Russia, Britain and the United States regardless of whether we form this league or not. Those happen to be the facts of life. . . ."

The discrediting of the isolationist brand of nationalism compelled an epochal reversal of the "betrayal" of 1920, but there was wide room for both conservative nationalists and international social democrats in the airy structure of the United Nations. Quarantine on aggression was the function of the Security Council composed of the United States, Russia, Britain, China, France, and six other members elected by the Assembly. The function of the Assembly, where all nations were equally represented, was to focus world opinion by discussion and to make recommendations for peaceful readjustments. The Assembly controlled the Economic and Social Council, which in turn was empowered to call international conferences that might seek international agreements on tariffs, labor standards, and deleterious nationalistic competition. A reorganized World Court and an international Bill of Rights expressed a hope rather than a fact; the power of enforcement was limited by the legal entrenchment of national sovereignty. Nationalists who objected in 1919 might not have objected to the Charter of the United Nations. The charter itself made reservations nearly as sweeping in preserving sovereignty as the 1919 reservations of the Lodge Republicans. The charter prohibited intervention in matters within the "domestic jurisdiction" of a member nation—unless the Big Powers agreed that the domestic policies or behavior of a country endangered peace.

By August 9 Truman's signature was affixed to the United Nations Charter, making the United States one of the first to ratify. Within two weeks Russia likewise assented and others followed. On October 24, 1945, Secretary Byrnes proclaimed the United Nations formally established.

The working majority of Republicans and southern Democrats, a coalition that held firm on domestic affairs, broke apart on international issues. The split in the Republican party on foreign policy weakened the official leadership of Taft, Wherry, and White in the Senate and of Minority Leader Joseph Martin in the House. The Taft Republicans clung to party tradition on high tariffs, war debts, and repayment of loans made by the United States. Favoring economy and lower taxes, they shied away from large government spending for international relief and international agencies. Opposing them was a Republican minority less inclined to place national interests first. The Democratic party, more unified than Republicans on external issues, generally provided the congressional votes necessary to sustain international measures. In November, when the United Nations Organization Bill reached the Senate, Taft with the Republican whip, Kenneth S. Wherry of Nebraska, and fifteen Republican colleagues emulated the amendment tactics of the Lodge Republicans; but 1945 was not 1919. Their amendments defeated, Taft and Wherry, resisting to the last, voted against the bill. Similarly until the same November, obstructionism delayed—when devastated countries most needed assistance—the essential American contributions to the United Nations Relief and Rehabilitation organization. The UNRRA Participation Act, passing both houses belatedly, permitted the world agency to speed its tragic work of feeding the dying.

Sanction of the United Nations, the International Bank, the International Monetary Fund, UNRRA, and renewal of the Reciprocal Trade Agreements Act in 1945 did not necessarily mean that the American Congress had permanently determined not again to prefer the road of economic nationalism down which it had wandered in the 1920's. The near-defeat of the postwar lend-lease policy and the British loan, essential for an international open door to replace closed economies, revealed resurgent motives of nationalism swaying southern extremists and recently reformed Republican isolationists. Administration policy grew out of the economic constriction attendant upon the suspension of lend-lease. On August 31, 1945, President Truman declared himself opposed to collection of war debts on the formula prevailing after World War I: it might contribute to another depression and to war. Subsequently the State Department began negotiations with England, completing them on December 6. The President in the following January urged Congress to sanction a loan to Britain of $3,750,000,000. The loan was coupled with an agreement to write off lend-lease aid in such a way as to avoid the economic evils of a snarl of war debts. The spirit of "America First" produced endless delay on the

British loan and flared in debate six months later, when popular support and administration urging finally dislodged the measure from committee. The more undiscriminating exponents of "free enterprise" inveighed against aid to an England in which a Labor Government had won the elections. American advocates of lower taxes, a balanced budget, and government economy, gagging at an outlay of over three billion and the "unbusinesslike" arrangement in respect to deferred repayment and interest on the loan, voiced nationalist sentiments in their opposition to the "Santa Claus" policy of lend-lease settlement. Two thirds of the Republicans in the House—155 in all—on July 13, 1946, voted against the Anglo-American agreement, disregarding the fact that England was to purchase American goods and that both countries agreed to use the loan as an instrument to break down economic barriers that had grown up as wartime expedients among British commonwealths and various small countries in the "sterling bloc." A scattering of Democrats, 11 from the South and 21 others, voted with the Republican opposition. Despite outbursts of assorted nationalist phobias, the bill passed the House by a vote of 219 to 155 and survived its ordeal in the Senate.

The same parade of nationalist argument preceded and interposed delays to the passage of the McMahon bill for control of atomic energy. The bill provided for control by a civilian board and for government patents and licensing in respect to research by scientists and utilization of atomic energy by industrial firms. Contrary to historic American practice, opponents favored military rather than civilian control. Zealots on the subject of private enterprise hearkened to persuasions of the N.A.M. and industry lobbyists and demanded that commercial atomic development be more sharply divorced from governmental supervision. The McMahon bill passed the Senate in a form that permitted and invited ultimate international controls. The House maneuver to substitute a bill more pleasing to the military clique and readers of the Chicago *Tribune* was substantially defeated in July, 1946, by compromises effected in the conference committee of the two houses. By a narrow margin Congress chose the course of enlightenment that public opinion on the issue had steadily endorsed.

The first year of peace did not quiet fears that the seeds of war had already been sown within the United Nations by a new alignment of nations trusting to older techniques of a balance of power. A head-on collision over Iran and oil brought hot charges in the American and British press and countercharges from Russia, each side accusing the other of "imperialism." The Security Council found a superficial solution for the dispute, but in Korea and Japan, Greece and the Balkans, Poland and Germany underlying conflicts remained. Commentators spoke of the gulf between East and West: the East following the Russian concept of what constituted "economic democracy"; the West, divided on questions of economic democracy, placing primary stress on political democracy. Nine times in the first year of the United Nations, outvoted, the Soviet exercised the veto. In September, 1946, the national policy of the American government had hardened into one described by Byrnes as "patience and firmness" toward the Soviet.

Cross-purposes stemming from the survival of nationalism blocked disarmament and slowed agreement on peace treaties. Byrnes in 1945 had initiated a successful negotiation with England on atomic bombs, declaring it a first step to "rescue the world from a desperate armaments race." The foreign ministers' conference at Moscow in December, 1945, decided upon creation of the United Nations Atomic Energy Commission. Secretary Byrnes in June, 1946, strove for the sharing of atomic secrets under international control and inspection. The commission divided, 10–2; Russia and Poland, favoring sovereign immunity from outside controls under an "honor system," urged international agreement to outlaw atomic war. When the United Nations Assembly met in November, 1946, Russia proposed universal disarmament with no provision for inspection. Meanwhile successive meetings of foreign ministers to draft five peace treaties seemed to bear no fruit but headlines. Stalemates moved the French minister to echo the wry phrase of the peacemakers of 1815: "We are striving here for an equality of dissatisfaction." The intransigence of sovereignty intruded even into the Economic and Social Council of the United Nations. Eleanor Roosevelt, American representative, declared that experts on special commissions should speak their own minds. The Council, by a vote of 11 to 5, sustained the Russian view that experts, hewing to the lines of national policy, should speak with the voice of their governments; otherwise agreements would not subsequently be accepted by governments.

Progress was somehow made, albeit Russia got a bad press in the United States and the "Western bloc" an inadequate portrayal in the Soviet orbit. By December, 1946, compromises were ironing out differences on atomic inspection and peace treaties. Slowly, in fear and want, the world was moving—India and the Philippines experiencing the distractions of newborn self-government amid internal strife, Java and the Dutch East Indies approaching a semi-independent status, Japan astir, with aristocratic capitalism and nationalist emperor worship clashing against free elections, free labor unions, and international tutelage.

Although Russia did not participate in the International Bank or the Monetary Fund and did not evince interest in American proposals for release of the sovereign controls whereby governments hemmed in national economies all over the world, supporters of economic internationalism were cheered by an evolving American policy that sought to make more of the Atlantic Charter's pledge to remove trade barriers than the United States had been disposed to make of the same pledge by Woodrow Wilson in the Fourteen Points. Far-reaching propositions drafted by economic experts serving under Byrnes, issued by the State Department in December, 1945, called for an International Trade Organization and regulations covering "trade barriers, restrictive business practices, intergovernmental commodity arrangements, and the internal aspects of domestic employment practices." The United Nations Economic and Social Council the following February gave its sanction, and in October, 1946, a London meeting prepared for the creation of the new ITO, using American proposals as the basis for its charter. Meanwhile, the United States, as a member of the FAO (the United Nations Food and Agriculture Organization), in the same October was considering a plan submitted by an English delegate for an agency to protect both producers and consumers by a global ever-normal granary and regulation of agricultural output, prices, and exports—an "AAA on a world scale."

The unquenchable idealism that never surrenders to the defeatist view that practical difficulties are insurmountable found outlet in other broad propositions. The United Nations Economic and Social Council in its first year fostered some eleven international agencies. UNESCO (the Educational, Scientific, and Cultural Organization) met in November, 1946, to consider the intellectual dilemma of nationalist mentality in an interdependent world. Conscious that ideas are weapons, good or bad, UNESCO began the search for means to knock down national impediments to the spirit of globalism. From the United States came suggestions for rewriting the world's textbooks to denationalize histories and counteract cultural arrogance and insular thinking. Various proposals—for an untrammeled world radio network for objective news dissemination, for international agreements to end censorship—raised the question whether sovereign members would assent, and whether the Eastern bloc would comply, should the Soviet Union join UNESCO. Other practical difficulties did not deter the emanation of prodigious visions from an International Health Conference in New York where in June, 1946, all fifty-one of the United Nations and thirteen nonmembers were represented. With the U. S. Surgeon General, Dr. Thomas Parran, presiding, and the Soviet Deputy Minister of Health giving able assistance, experts worked upon American, French, and Yugoslav suggestions for the charter of a World Health Organization. "For the first time," reported *Science,* "emphasis was laid not upon quarantine and checking epidemics . . . but upon positive aggressive action toward health in its broadest sense." The final agreement defined health as "complete physical, mental, and social well-being and not merely the absence of disease or infirmity." Health, declared the new charter, was "one of the fundamental rights of every human being."

INTERNAL CLEAVAGE: THE STRUGGLE FOR CONTROL

If Democratic unity on foreign issues enabled the administration to maintain steerageway amid international shoals, in domestic waters Congress circled like a rudderless ship. After September 5, 1945, when the first postwar session began, legislation urged by the President was pointedly ignored. "Congress on Strike" ran. the headline in liberal weeklies. Though the President's party had nominal command of both houses, only three of the eleven chairmen of important Senate committees and four of the twelve similarly placed House chairmen shared Truman's loyalty to official party principles. Democratic "control" of Congress made election pledges meaningless because bipartisan coalition made the numerical majority an illusion. The Democratic split gave Republicans the decisive legislative role on domestic affairs. A transfer of power was already on the way.

Defeats of sensible legislation were attributable to the tendency in Congress to return to the politics of special interests in the spirit of the 1920's. A Full Employment bill, based on experience since 1929 with governmental attack on disastrous fluctuations of the business cycle, was not to the liking of the followers of Senator Taft. For months the bill remained bottled up in committee until outside pressure made action expedient. In 1946 a watered-down Full Employment Act, authorizing an expert board, without power, to "advise" the government, was accepted by the Republican-Democratic coalition. A temporary Emergency Housing bill was passed, but a long-range measure for a ten-year program to further private and public home-building emerged from the Senate after onslaughts by real-estate lobbies, manufacturers of building materials, and the construction trades, only to be stifled in House committee with the aid of Minority Leader Martin.

Throttled in committee or killed on the floor were other long-pending bills for internal improvements and broad social purposes. Valley planning inspired by TVA, proposed as an MVA for the great watershed of the Missouri, was defeated; as also was an old perennial, the St. Lawrence Seaway. Preferring logrolling of the type prevailing when "Chet" Arthur was President, congressmen rushed for a share in a gigantic pork barrel, authorizing expenditures of some hundreds of millions in a River and Harbor Improvements catchall. In sharp contrast was the defeat of a desirable bill for medical research, seeking $100,000,000 for a modest assault upon one of the great scourges, cancer. American men of science were rebuffed by congressional defeat of a bill for a national research foundation, whose benefits reached much further than river and harbor improvements, and whose cost was much less. Defeated likewise were provisions for extending Social Security to millions of people not covered, including old-age benefits for farmers, domestic servants, and the self-employed; for increasing federal aid to poor states and establishing a genuine national system of social security with uniform benefits; and legislation to provide disability and health insurance as contemplated or adopted in current European exemplifications of the Beveridge plan. A measure to raise the minimum wage standard from 40¢ an hour to 65¢, though passing the Senate, was successfully blockaded in House committee. The desire for social security did, however, move congressmen to provide a pension system for themselves—as well as a salary increase to $12,500 and a tax-exempt expense account of $2,500.

President Truman, faced by hostile obstructionism, addressed the nation on January 3, 1946, calling public attention to the issue in Congress. The President's address was a confession of the weakness of the system of party management traditionally favored in American politics. "I seek no conflict with Congress," declared the President, but he pointedly remarked that orderly legislative procedure did not mean "endless delay." Like Wilson, who had once denounced a small group of "willful men," Truman placed the onus on a handful of men who had abused committee prerogatives to "hold up action on bills." Often, the President noted, "a bare majority of a committee—a handful of men—can prevent a vote by the whole Congress on these measures of majority policy." Directing attention also to the massed ranks of professional lobbyists who thronged the Capitol, the President's appeal went over the radio to the people, urging them to counteract misrepresentation of public opinion.

Another official confession of the ineptitude of the American form of parties was eloquently documented by Congress itself in a bill to "streamline" the national legislature. A Congressional Reorganization Act, hailed as badly needed to modernize eighteenth-century machinery, became law in the summer of 1946. Even in voting a measure to strengthen itself, Congress proved incapable of passing a bill without devitalizing deletions that substituted interest for principle. The original bill sought improvement of party responsibility under recognized leadership through a central committee for each party intended to serve as a unifying force in the formulation of party policy. Most constructive feature of the bill, it was stricken out at the behest of the Speaker and the ruling clique of the House, who feared loss of personal prestige and power. Deleted also was a liaison committee to seek better relations between the executive and legislative branches. Obscure provisions to compel the registration of paid lobbyists survived, but with such loopholes that few lobbyists registered. The residue of value in the law was its authorization to reorganize and merge the creaking and cumbersome apparatus of congressional committees. Otherwise the bill failed at critical points. The decrepit seniority system, which conferred command of committees on other grounds than brains or statesmanship, went unscathed; as also the Senate vice of filibustering and the undemocratic dominance of the House Rules Committee. Nor was there a provision modeled after that of Massachusetts, which prevents the pigeonholing of a bill in committee. The bill was sweetened by providing for the increase of congressional salaries and the establishment of congressional pensions.

Three other congressional performances in 1946 did not reassure those who feared relapse into the Lilliputian politics of nationalism and normalcy. One, the FEPC fiasco presenting the issue of racial intolerance, exhibited the incapacity of a majority in Congress to mobilize itself against a minority. The second, involving a rupture between capital and labor, high-lighted the incapacity to govern when a stalemate separated the executive and legislative branches. The third, involving OPA, was another illustration that a leaderless Congress was incapable of grappling with problems of the business cycle.

The issue of racial intolerance arose from President Roosevelt's executive order, establishing in 1941 a Fair Employment Practices Committee. The FEPC undertook to protect government employees and workers engaged upon war work under government contracts against discriminations based upon creed, color, race, or ancestry. The new agency was a landmark in history; for the first time since reconstruction days, the social tensions and inequalities associated with discriminations against minorities were recognized as a national problem. Experience under the FEPC underlined the fact that the problem was nation wide rather than only southern. Not more than a quarter of the complaints to the FEPC involved discriminations against Negroes in southern states. The shortage of man power strengthened the FEPC by combining patriotic need with practical idealism. Though "Jim Crowism" and race tension afflicted the armed services and took serious form in Detroit and other congested centers, great strides were made. In a war-induced migration from the South, 600,000 colored folk, benefiting by conditions of full employment, found long-sought-for green pastures. In industrial centers and on Yankee farms the demand for labor leveled old barriers. Negroes as well as

THE NEGRO MOVES NORTH

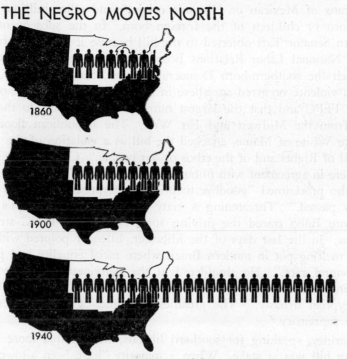

1860

1900

1940

Each negro represents 1 per cent of all negroes in U. S.

PICTOGRAPH CORPORATION

refugees and the foreign born escaped for the nonce the discriminations which made them "last to be hired and first to be fired."

During World War II the Ku Klux spirit, so militant in the era of the previous war, was forced on the defensive. In June, 1945, an anti-poll tax bill passed the House for the third time with a small scattering of southern members courageously supporting it. Moreover, in the campaign of 1944 the Republican party as well as Roosevelt and Truman was formally pledged to make FEPC permanent, and bills for this object were introduced in both houses. After elections and throughout the following year the bipartisan coalition dominating the House Rules Committee prevented the FEPC bill from reaching the floor. In the Senate, after reposing eight months on the calendar, the bill came up for debate in January, 1946—to be killed by filibuster.

The FEPC bill applied equally to employers and unions, reported Senator Dennis Chavez of New Mexico. He cited the committee findings that "the fear of discriminatory discharges weighs heavily upon all who have ever known the bitterness of job discrimination, notably 22,000,000 Catholics, 13,000,000 Negroes, 5,000,000 Jews, 3,000,000

Americans of Mexican or Hispanic origin," and other millions of foreign born or children of the foreign born. In the subsequent debate northern Senator Taft objected to the bill because it used the procedures of the National Labor Relations Board instead of voluntary persuasion; to which the southern-born Democratic leader, Senator Barkley, replied that no violence occurred anywhere in the South because of the operation of the FEPC and that the largest number of complaints to the agency came from the Midwest and Far West. The Republican floor leader, Wallace White of Maine, attacked the bill as a violation of the "American Bill of Rights and of the ethos of our people." Conservative Republicans were in agreement with filibustering Senator A. J. Ellender of Louisiana, who proclaimed "goodbye to private enterprise if a law of this nature is passed." Threatening a sixty-day speech, Mississippi's Senator Theodore Bilbo traced the driving force behind the FEPC straight to Moscow. In the last days of the filibuster, Ellender pointed with horror to the melting pot in modern Brazil where racial equality had produced "a mongrel race." He shuddered at the deterioration of the "Aryan race" in ancient Egypt to a point where a "mulatto was at the head of the Egyptian dynasty." The greatness of America would depend upon "white supremacy."

Barkley, speaking for southern liberals, warned that more than the pending bill was at stake. When a minority "have been allowed to express their views," they were bound by the democratic principle "to accept the will of the majority." Earlier in the course of the filibuster, Maryland's Senator Millard Tydings had already given the answer of Bourbon extremists to the question of rule of the majority:

The rule of the majority. The rule of votes. Majority to Hades. . . . The rule of the majority. The rule that has brought more bloodshed and turmoil and cruelty on this earth than any other thing I know of.

On February 9, 1946, the twenty-four-day filibuster for the time being won the battle. Well over a majority of the Senate by a vote of 48 to 36 attempted to close debate and force a vote on the bill itself. Archaic rules of procedure required a two-thirds majority. Party honors were even. At no time could the filibustering Democratic minority have defeated the FEPC had it not been for the silent support of Senator Taft and conservative Republican leaders who were unwilling to muster the necessary additional votes to close debate and allow a straight test on the bill—to the substance of which both parties were solemnly pledged. After the victory of the bipartisan coalition, Bilbo presented to the Senate an article emanating from the Southern States Industrial Council and proclaiming that the South held "the Balance of Power," that it was the last "stronghold of true Americanism," and that it should put nation above party by using its balance of power to block the FEPC and similar bills that established "State socialism."

Congressional abnegation on the FEPC was matched by an antediluvian muddle on the question of industrial unrest. A wave of postwar strikes strengthened the hand of congressional opponents of laws on collective bargaining. The Case bill, a curb on labor sponsored by a South Dakota Republican, was voted through the House in February, 1946. The President proposed impartial fact-finding committees to investigate and make public report when a strike was in the offing; and improved machinery for peaceful mediation. Critics of existing legal rights of collective bargaining, rejecting the presidential proposal, urged legislation to favor employers. Stalemate, continuing in Congress as great strikes succeeded one another, prevented constructive action to get at the roots of industrial unrest.

Inflation—the dollar had shrunk to 76¢ when war ended—and union ambitions to maintain wartime gains in "take-home pay" were merely the more obvious symptoms of deep-seated human maladjustments. Experts on labor problems and enlightened employers recognized that what was needed for economic peace was not fundamentally a "curb" on labor by resort to older coercions such as injunctions, but an improvement in the total human equation between management and workers. Labor unrest, as the Industrial Relations Commission long ago reported in President Wilson's day, was increased, not diminished, by sitting on the lid and ignoring the real causes of intransigence of employers and unions. What was needed, declared the trained specialists and wise employers, was more economic democracy, not less; teamwork and better incentives, not raw struggles for power. More imaginative employers experimented successfully with honest acceptance of bargaining, incentive plans, impartial arbitration, and, most significantly, with face-to-face discussion of difficulties the instant they arose. Favorable results were reported of a system of conferences between labor and management committees in a "goldfish bowl" where company and union spectators could witness negotiations unclouded by secrecy. The experience of "advanced" employers who broke down impersonality and enjoyed the confidence of the men in the shop sustained the none-too-recent discovery that American economic life in the corporate age lacked a sound democratic relationship between workers and managers.

Seeking immediate economic gains at the risk of losing political influence, auto workers, steelworkers, coal miners, railroad brotherhoods, truckmen, and seamen struck. Likewise seeking immediate economic gains but more shrewdly calculating the prospects of increased political influence, the employers concerned refused union terms until government labor boards induced acceptance of cost-of-living raises after weeks of strikes. More conciliatory employers like the younger Henry Ford dealt with unions without serious conflicts. Many, however, who took their cue from national industrial associations, looked forward to a day when New Deal labor laws could be abolished. Many an employer organization still held to the position illustrated in the 1946 convention of the belligerent National Metal Trades Association, where the 600 members by unanimous vote demanded repeal of the Wagner Act.

Strikes of such magnitude strengthened the political allies of management. Although ordinary consumers, crying for an end of shortages, were not deprived of immediate necessities, food and clothing, by strikes in steel and heavy industry, the coal strike called by John L. Lewis, causing a shortage in fuel, and the menace of a railroad tie-up provoked a political crisis in May, 1946. President Truman on May 25, still opposing a permanent antistrike law, urged a temporary enactment to expire after the emergency. The administration bill would authorize government seizure of basic industry, the drafting of strikers into the army so that they could be ordered to work, and a penalty on management by accrual to the government of any profits during the period of seizure. The initial Old Guard reaction exhibited extreme distaste for the nonprofit provision, but subsequent debate turned on the drafting of workers. The Senate substituted the Case bill with amendments, reviving the weapons of suits under antitrust law and of court injunctions, negating many of the constructive features of the Wagner and Norris-La Guardia labor laws. Truman vetoed the Case bill but accepted another, the Hobbs Anti-Racketeering Act. A plea by the President for a long-range congressional investigation of causes of industrial unrest, to afford a sound basis for permanent labor legislation, was scorned.

The administration was in the unhappy predicament of seeking industrial harmony and full production to alleviate shortages and to close the inflationary gap; and of seeking some recognition of the workers' case for cost-of-living increases in pay, which in turn exerted strains on the administration's anti-inflation controls and increased the opposition of employers to unions and OPA. Those company managers and politicians who favored the clamping of government controls on labor but a "free enterprise" system for industry, relaxing government controls on business, found it easy to capitalize on the situation. Their activities less publicized in the press than strikes by unions, businessmen and big commercial farmers bucked price controls, seeking ends and employing means analogous to those which they criticized so caustically when employed by workingmen. Occasionally a forthright admission that "capital was on strike" appeared in sober periodicals circulating in business communities. A Republican congressman defended the black market as free enterprise. Textile manufacturers and many others found ways to upgrade cheaper wares and raise prices despite OPA. The law itself survived by a precarious margin in 1945 and was administered slow poison by Congress in 1946.

For one year following the end of the war the battles of Chester Bowles to hold the line against inflation were so successful as to inspire popular approval. There was no answering enthusiasm amidst the free enterprise coalition in Congress. The hostile House majority in the frenzied night session of April 17, 1946, passed a fraudulent bill ostensibly continuing the Price Control Act to June, 1947. The original bill, urged by Bowles and the President, succumbed to the onslaught of 171 Republicans and 88 Democratic allies, the latter mainly of the South. A steadfast majority of 130 Democrats and 6 Republicans fought helplessly to protect consumers. A series of "ripper amendments" designed to satisfy the appetites of hungry pressure groups slashed the powers of the OPA. In the small hours of the night a northern Democrat who had defended consumers moved insertion of the words, "We sympathize with the American people." Scarcely awake to the irony, the weary majority voted against expressing sympathy for the people. Weeks later, on the eve of the expiration of OPA, the Senate agreed to extend its life—though amendments fathered by Taft and Wherry ordained relaxation of price controls to such a degree as to mock hopes of the people for an avoidance of the skyrocketing prices that cursed the country after World War I.

President Truman courageously vetoed the bill, demanding a law that could be enforced. A month of rent gouges and soaring prices followed as OPA lay moribund and Congress angrily debated. Not daring to kill OPA outright, the Old Guard led by Taft and Wherry again breathed unhealthy life into OPA and the President was forced to accept. The end was in sight—the "Meat Strike." Cattle and hogs had jammed the stockyards in the month when OPA had been suspended. After the restoration of controls, the meat supply fell to virtually nothing. Bellicose associations of cattlemen, the American Farm Bureau Federation, and political allies of the farm bloc demanded the abandonment of inflation controls. On October 14, after the country had had weeks of meatless meals, the President gave up the fruitless struggle with an unenforceable law. Meat was decontrolled and OPA was liquidated, with little surviving but controls over rent and a few items still critically short.

After the collapse of OPA the responsibility for prices and wages, shortages and fluctuations of employment rested squarely upon private interests. Cattle once more jammed the stockyards; but hamburger shot up to $1.00 a pound. Food prices, already advanced in wartime by 50 per cent, suddenly zoomed upward between July and October, 1946, about 60 per cent more. The decline of wartime unity and the disappearance of willingness to abide by the principle of "equality of sacrifice" had encompassed the death of OPA. It died unpopular. It remained to be seen whether the restoration of the "free enterprise" system had been postponed long enough to avoid the worst excesses of 1920 and the subsequent slump.

The off-term elections in November, following soon after the meat shortage and the strikes, slurred over issues of international policy and turned on reactions closely associated with the stomach and pocketbook. The Republican slogan, "HAD ENOUGH?" shrewdly appealed to jangled nerves and middle-class dissatisfactions. Secretary Byrnes' anxiety for bipartisan support on external matters led Democratic candidates to muffle critcisms of the congressional record of those Republicans who were lukewarm or less in their affection for internationalism. Of the Republican press, editors who opposed isolationism widely advertised the bipartisan teamwork of Senator Vandenberg. Opinion polls before elections intimated that OPA was a leading grievance and that commercial agriculture and business interests were heavily on the Republican side with considerable support from the urban middle class. Wage earners were reported as more evenly divided between parties than at any time in the past fifteen years.

Election results followed forecasts. The Republicans won control of Congress. Promptly preparing for the 1947 session, the congressional organization of the victorious party assigned posts of leadership to men who for the most part had teamed up with Taft in support of what the Ohio Senator described as "the party line." Senator Fulbright, Arkansas Democrat, without intending to embarrass Truman, created a sensation by a postelection statement that responsible party government required a President with a working majority in Congress. Declaring that it would be sound democracy for a President rebuffed in mid-term elections to resign in favor of the leader of the opposite party, the Arkansas luminary announced his intention of introducing a constitutional amendment not only for such emergencies but to permit the settlement of any sharp dispute between President and Congress by means of special elections.

Reverberations of the American elections, extending abroad, revealed uncertainty among friends of the international policy of Secretary Byrnes. From the respectable pages of the London *Economist* gloom emanated. The "high tariff party" had won. The "liberal minority" among Republicans had been "weakened by the death of Mr. Willkie." "Proposals like that for maintenance of full employment by international agreement" were likely to obtain no more than "nominal obeisance."

The world had moved. The United Nations were in being. An overwhelming desire of the common man around the world was a peace that would endure. Yet the patchwork system of sovereign national governments still held mankind in psychological toils; and global war had enmeshed nations more deeply than ever in economic toils national in character. Closed economies amid postwar shortages clogged the interchange of the world's goods and services. Other democracies, moving away from America's choice, were accepting economic planning with state control of the national bank and of selected fields of economic activity. "Enterprise," averred England's chief of economic planning, "does not have to be private to be enterprise."

Profound problems awaited answer as Europeans in the East sought security through the five-year plans of Communism, as Europeans of the West sought economic democracy through national plans of their own, and as Americans, preferring normalcy, sought to leave the function of planning to the play of the free market. For those within the Russian fold and for the family of nations with whom Russia and her friends must live and cooperate, riddles persisted. The deepest of questions stirred mankind. Could economic democracy on a one-party model move toward the basic civil freedom, the right to oppose? Was national planning, Soviet model or English model, compatible with the give-and-take required for the elimination of economic nationalism and commercial imperialism? Could domestic conservatism in the United States, nurtured by the renascent spirit of normalcy, continue without reviving also the pressure of great organized interests for special advantages at the expense of other nations? Was a return to the politics of special interests at home compatible with a diplomacy and economic foreign policy identifying the public interest of the United States with the public interest of the world? Was this to be the century of the common man?

EPILOGUE

We, the peoples of the United Nations,
[ran the Preamble of the Charter of the United Nations]
determined
To save succeeding generations from the scourge of war . . .
Do hereby establish an international organization . . .

Delegates, speaking as "We, the peoples," were accredited to the Conference at San Francisco with diplomatic credentials and full powers— "in good and due form." The preamble of the Great Charter was written in the language of democracy; the credentials were framed in the archaic tongue of national monarchies and diplomatic usage current before the birth of modern democracy. "Due form" recalled national power politics, which survived long after democracy had come of age. So like the League Covenant of 1919—albeit so unlike it—the charter looked backward. But it likewise looked forward; for it was recognized that the issues pressing for solution were global in scope, too enormous for a single nation or for any group of them. The World Conference at San Francisco formally ushered in the Global Age, and globalism and political nationalism were incongruous.

The world's problem prior to the outbreak of World War II—the first truly global war—was similar to the problem before World War I. On the plane of economics, it involved a solution of the paradox between potential plenty and universal poverty; and such a solution implied a degree of prosperity sufficiently diffused among all peoples everywhere so that insecurity, social tensions, and frustrated ambitions could not lead again to nationalistic "solutions"—to rearmament, to militarism, to conquest, to imperialism—and, ultimately, to totalitarian revolution. As global conflict ended in 1945, the basic economic and social requirements were defined in democratic thought as full employment within the nations and—between the nations—a liberation of the world's productive capacities through an international economy. Old nationalist policies for a full dinner pail in one country—never actually achieved—had proved catastrophic. The national objective of full employment at home was utterly inseparable from the international objective of a general world diffusion of the fruits of prosperity. But nationalistic forces were still

753

powerful in every nation. Each country had its superpatriots, its sappers of social democracy, its fifth columnists working for selfish private interests. Each country had its prototype of an American celebrity who, scoffing at the Century of the Common Man and all "globaloney," heralded the "American Century," slogan of an unregenerate and heedless nationalism.

In 1945, the world was still accustomed to three traditional diplomatic techniques: a drive for regional spheres of influence or world preponderance; balance of power diplomacy, more common and moderate, but essentially negative; and the less common policy of mild international understanding. Even the third policy indicated an enormous lag in adapting political institutions to produce economic and social security for mankind as a whole. Even the most hopeful international cooperation was enfeebled by the elements inherent in sovereignty which made a national government the fulcrum for dynamic groups possessing the balance of power within a given nation. A solution of world economic and social tensions depended upon internal and international changes to transform national monopoly of sovereign power; and to limit the exercise of sovereignty by and for the special interests of separate peoples.

Economic internationalization and full employment—the democratic formula for peaceful economic progress at home and abroad—depended internally upon a form of political organization that would give genuine representation and responsible leadership to the submerged forces of the common man. No easy solution was likely to be found. Even within the United States the power of nationalistic pressure groups, reflected in the perennial dissension between Presidents and Congress, exemplified the difficulty of developing party discipline to strengthen majority rule and to beat back special interests. Beyond this was the undefined question of the residual rights of national governments and the delegated powers of international authorities.

In the international sphere the problem of sovereignty of the people under an accountable leadership was far more forbidding. The vast dimensions of the world of diplomacy and power politics constituted a twilight zone, never democratized: an area of human affairs in which the motives and practices of diplomatic exchange as of economic foreign policy were either a direct heritage from or a throwback to the nationalistic institutions of monarchs, mercantilists, and monopolists. People who live differently think differently; there was an aristocratic drive, an undemocratic lag behind public opinion, in every department of commerce, foreign office, embassy, or consulate. But it was not simply because offices for foreign relations were manned by well-born gentry and nationalistic bureaucrats far removed from the plain people; it was because they dealt in an area and through a medium which national government had never assimilated to the democratic goal of the welfare of mankind. Passports, visas, and immigration quotas, tariffs and import quotas, national currencies and national patents, like national armaments and national compulsory military training, bespoke *national* institutions designed as instrumentalities of *national* sovereignty and *national* interests.

Neither the League of Nations after World War I nor the United Nations after World War II institutionalized the peaceful force of majority rule. Historical experience records that with the rise of civil liberty and freedom of opposition, democratic peoples had seldom or never gone to war against one another. Yet experience with democracy as a medium for open debate and peaceful change had not yet been projected into international institutions. Suave diplomats made reference to an international law; but no man had ever seen an international law enacted by a legislative body elected by and responsible to the common man. Delegates were diplomats; they acted under a unit rule, speaking with one voice for a given country. Inevitably, they misrepresented the internal division of opinion among their own people. Sovereign governments were a cause of war. Sovereign national political institutions contradicted interdependence and inhibited international democracy. National governments had a monopoly of decisions; they permitted in world councils no official participation and dissenting votes by a "loyal opposition" composed of their own citizens. They perpetuated vertical divisions along national lines; and they blocked horizontal international divisions allowing democratic representation in world decisions. Open covenants openly arrived at, the ameliorating force of world public opinion, awaited the invention of social institutions by means of which businessmen in all countries could coalesce to speak for international economic interests, and liberals in all countries could coalesce to promote international reform and social democracy. National parties, observed Frederick Jackson Turner, great historian of the American West, had been a constructive unifying force, tending to create a national majority of like-minded people, disregarding state boundaries and counteracting a divisive sectionalism. Why, he suggested to President Wilson, might not international parties be utilized for the same purpose in the institutions for international government?[1]

When, nearly three decades later, the gentlemen talked of peace at the San Francisco Conference, the time had not yet come for a Parliament of Man to speak for the peoples without the intermediary of sovereign national government. Symbolic—just prior to the Senate debate on the

---

[1] Frederick J. Turner, "American Sectionalism and World Organization," *American Historical Review*, XLVII, No. 3 (April, 1942), 545–551.

Charter of the United Nations—was the demand of nationalist forces for annexation of conquered bases as permanent American soil. On the contrary, responded President Truman, the United States wanted "not one piece of territory": the country had fought for the "welfare of mankind" and "peace and prosperity for the world as a whole." Democratic nationalists, led by Senator Walter F. George, joined Taft and Republican nationalists in immediate dissent.

Contradictory tendencies were apparent at the San Francisco Conference. Yet horizontal lines of division had ever run through all societies and must so run through world society. Democracies assimilated or reconciled such cleavages through the political solvent of alternating majorities. Could man apply the lesson in international politics? Nationalism assuredly was no more the highest end of humankind than tribalism or feudalism. Somewhere in the almost limitless scope of the great concepts—justice, peace, progress, security, interdependence, social integration, and democracy—lay the key to the goals of modern man.

Lilliputian plans in the aftermath of global catastrophe—plans for laissez faire in the United States and an American Century abroad—contrasted strangely with the liberating forces of the revolutions in economics and the Gargantuan forces constantly released by technology and science. A new epoch in the history of man had burst upon a world unprepared for its coming. The two-dimensional world of the flat maps of land masses and oceans had given place to a three-dimensional world. By the great circle, the Empire State Building was closer to Mt. Fujiyama than the Golden Gate Bridge; Washington, D. C., only a day's flight from Tokyo.

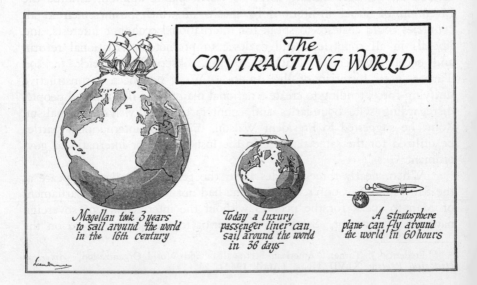

The CONTRACTING WORLD

Magellan took 3 years to sail around the world in the 16th century

Today a luxury passenger liner can sail around the world in 36 days

A stratosphere plane can fly around the world in 60 hours

The meaning of the new age was writ large in the revolution in geography; transportation companies and businessmen reckoned space not in miles and national boundaries but in time and cost. With the same integrating compulsion that created One World, interdependent although disunited, new technical "know-how," new science, and new social knowledge were shattering antiquated folkways of labor and production, making available to man from the secret sinews of nature an "energy equivalent" of fabulous millions of wild horses.

Dimly, without wholly comprehending it, mankind knew that the year from the breakthrough in Normandy to the victory in the Pacific in August, 1945, spanned the greatest events in modern times. New issues and new leaders emerged with the peace. An older generation passed from the scene: war criminals of the Axis; the Quislings and the Darlans of betrayed and defiled democracies; the war cabinet of England; in the United States, the national leaders, Willkie, Hull, Roosevelt. And on August 6, 1945, Hiram Johnson died; with his passing the old-style isolation also died. Survivor of the bloc that had fought and defeated Woodrow Wilson, Johnson voted against the charter from a hospital bed, unconvinced to the last. But the passing of the last of the irreconcilable isolationists of 1919 did not mark the terminus of nationalistic drives by businessmen, farmers, and workers for protected markets, protected prices, and protected jobs; nor the terminus of drives by conservative diplomats and politicians for protection of national sovereignties as the postwar base for the policies of pressure groups and special interests. It still remained to be seen whether the structure of the United Nations could gradually provide a substitute power-base to give legitimate international expression to the interplay of varying interests. Yet time was pressing onward, for August 6 was more than the end of an era; it also opened a new epoch, for on that day occurred the greatest event since man wrested the secret of fire from nature.

On August 6, 1945, the first atomic bomb fell on Japan. With shattering clarity the cosmic bomb confronted mankind with the necessity of an organized world liberated from war. For two generations pioneers of modern thought had been searching for international techniques to gauge the will of the peoples and to ensure its sobering impact upon the statesmen who directed international affairs. The people of the world, stunned by atomic destruction, faced the urgency of rethinking the diplomatic significance of the great principle of liberty, that sovereignty lies in the people. To the thoughtful, who knew now as never before that the institutions of nationality were hopelessly inadequate for modern life, was driven home the conviction that a sane future in its distant perspective must in some way be compounded of cultural autonomy within a spiritual globalism and representative institutions for international democracy. If the United Nations' structure was to have the international popular sovereignty requisite for its task, its officers must represent and be answerable to the peaceful force of the world public opinion in which Woodrow Wilson and Franklin Delano Roosevelt had placed their trust. And indeed if the people willed it, United Nations politics might be transformed by the international political parties envisioned by Turner in his prophetic recommendations for a democratic union of peaceful peoples. Man's fate and man's hope lay in perilous balance, but man was never more the master of his fate, never more the hope of his kind.

APPENDIX

SUGGESTED READINGS

CHAPTER I

THE TRANSIT OF EUROPEAN CIVILIZATION

The rise of European capitalism and the effect of this new economic system on the voyages of discovery are described in L. M. Hacker, *Triumph of American Capitalism* (1940), 16–62. S. E. Morison, *Admiral of the Ocean Sea* (1942), 197–235, pictures the last stages of the Columbus voyage and the thrill of discovery.

J. T. Adams, *Founding of New England* (1921), 64–85, provides an interpretive, although somewhat hostile, background for the New England settlements, while the first English invasion of the South is the theme of W. E. Dodd, *The Old South* (1937), 16–52, and T. J. Wertenbaker, *The Old South* (1942), 1–18. The birth of a liberal tradition in Rhode Island is emphasized in S. H. Brockunier, *The Irrepressible Democrat: Roger Williams* (1940), 101–128. T. J. Wertenbaker, *The Founding of American Civilization: The Middle Colonies* (1938), 1–28, stresses the mingling of races in the middle colonies.

The role of the European born in the eighteenth-century expansion and the molding influence of the frontier receive adequate treatment in F. J. Turner, *The Frontier in American History* (1920), 67–125, while A. M. Schlesinger, *New Viewpoints in American History* (1922), 1–21, deals with the immigrant contribution in this period and later ones.

CHAPTER II

THE COLONIAL MIND

T. J. Wertenbaker, *First Americans* (1927), 87–114 and 139–163, describes the narrow intolerance of seventeenth-century New England and the witchcraft epidemic in all the colonies. This pessimistic account of Puritan bigotry should be offset by S. E. Morison, *The Puritan Pronaos* (1936), 172–263, a telling defense of the New Englanders that emphasizes their literary and scientific contributions.

The standard brief account of colonial intellectual progress and the impact of the Enlightenment on eighteenth-century thought is in Merle Curti, *Growth of American Thought* (1943), 79–126. V. L. Parrington, *The Colonial Mind* (1927), 164–178, vividly pictures the mental activities of one American disciple of the Enlightenment, Benjamin Franklin. Carl Bridenbaugh, *Cities in the Wilderness* (1938), 467–481, shows the influence of urban forces on American thought and society.

CHAPTER III
THE AGE OF REVOLUTION

J. C. Miller, *Origins of the American Revolution* (1943), 1–78, and C. H. Van Tyne, *Causes of the War of Independence* (1922), 1–54, describe the social and intellectual conditions in both England and the colonies which led to revolt, while Schlesinger, cited above, pictures the whole revolutionary process in the light of modern scholarship. C. L. Becker, *The Eve of the Revolution* (1918), 50–97, deals with the rise of the lower classes to power during the early phases of agitation, and Merrill Jensen, *The Articles of Confederation* (1940), 16–53, emphasizes the conflict over who should rule at home as a major factor leading to independence. C. L. Becker's delightful essay, "The Spirit of '76," in his *Everyman His Own Historian* (1935), 47–80, catches the spirit of this class struggle as do few other works, while the same author develops the philosophical aspects of the Declaration of Independence in *The Declaration of Independence* (1922), 224–279. The liberal and humanitarian reforms that accompanied the Revolution are the theme of Allan Nevins, *American States during and after the Revolution* (1925), 420–469. The democratic stirrings of the "critical period" and the conservative forces arrayed against them are briefly described in E. B. Greene, *The Revolutionary Generation* (1943), 306–360.

CHAPTER IV
THE CONSTITUTION AND CONSERVATISM

R. L. Schuyler, *The Constitution of the United States* (1923), 85–127, describes the drafting of the Constitution, but should be supplemented by the important study of C. A. Beard, *An Economic Interpretation of the Constitution of the United States* (1913), 149–188, which emphasizes the economic connections of the framers and assesses their work in terms of their class interests. A briefer summary of Beard's interpretation is in A. M. Schlesinger, *New Viewpoints in American History* (1922), 184–199.

V. L. Parrington, *The Colonial Mind* (1927), 279–320, brilliantly analyzes the conservative forces operating during the Federalist period. A delightful contemporary description of Federalist efforts to inflict their will on the nation during Washington's first administration is in *The Journal of William Maclay* (1890 and later editions), 1–42.

CHAPTER V
ENLIGHTENMENT AND REACTION

Merle Curti, *The Roots of American Loyalty* (1946), 3–29, explores the Revolutionary origins of American nationalism. Equally interpretive and valuable is Hans Kohn, *The Idea of Nationalism* (1944), 263–325, while A. M. Schlesinger, "Patriotism Names the Baby," *New England Quarterly,* XIV (1941), pleasantly emphasizes one little-known aspect of the period's patriotism.

A thorough analysis of the expanding Enlightenment and the Conservative reaction during these years is in Merle Curti, *Growth of American Thought* (1943), 155–210; a discussion of the literary developments that took place against this background will be found in V. L. Parrington, *The Colonial Mind* (1927), 357–395. The effect of the conservatism of this period on American thought is the theme of J. A. Krout and D. R. Fox, *Completion of Independence* (1944), 247–278, while religious aspects of the reaction are treated in D. R. Fox, "The Protestant Counter-Reformation," *New York History,* XVI (1935).

CHAPTER VI
JEFFERSONIAN REPUBLICANISM

A brief but adequate description of Jefferson's presidential career is in S. K. Padover, *Thomas Jefferson* (1942), 287–360, but this should be supplemented by the thoughtful interpretive essay on Jefferson's role in the developing American democracy in Avery Craven, *Democracy in American Life* (1941), 1–37. Merle Curti, *Growth of American Thought* (1943), 213–258, shows that American intellectual life remained fundamentally conservative during this period. Jefferson's attempt to democratize the judiciary is described in E. S. Corwin, *John Marshall and the Constitution* (1919), 53–85, and in C. G. Bowers, *Jefferson in Power* (1936), 268–293. A brief appraisal of Jefferson's foreign policy in relation to its world setting is in T. C. Smith, *The United States as a Factor in World History* (1941), 1–45.

CHAPTER VII
THE FLOWERING OF NATIONALISM

Chief Justice John Marshall's role in the developing nationalism of this period is explained in Louis Boudin, *Government by Judiciary* (1932), 267–316, and in E. S. Corwin, *John Marshall and the Constitution* (1919), 121–146 and 173–197. The revolution in transportation, which contributed to the nationalistic spirit, is described in H. J. Carman, *Social and Economic History of the United States* (1930–1934), II, 94–157. Merle Curti, *Roots of American Loyalty* (1946), 92–121, thoughtfully appraises the effect of these economic forces on American nationalism. Any understanding of the part played by the frontier in this process must begin with Frederick Jackson Turner's important essay, "The Significance of the Frontier in American History," in his *Frontier in American History* (1920), 1–38, while Avery Craven, *Democracy in American Life* (1941), 38–67, deals with the contributions of the West to democracy. The impact of the new national spirit on foreign policy is summarized in Dexter Perkins, *Hands Off; A History of the Monroe Doctrine* (1941), 27–64.

CHAPTER VIII
THE CHALLENGE OF SECTIONALISM

Any study of the Jacksonian period must begin with A. M. Schlesinger, Jr., *Age of Jackson* (1945), 132–209, which traces the roots of Jacksonian Democracy to the ferment among eastern workers. The impact of this mighty force on education is the theme of Merle Curti, *Social Ideas of American Educators* (1935), 50–125, and A. F. Tyler, *Freedom's Ferment* (1944), 227–264, while M. Ostrogorski, *Democracy and the Origin of Political Parties* (1910) deals with its political effects.

A broadly interpretive study of sectionalism in this period and later ones is in F. J. Turner, *The Significance of Sections in American History* (1922), 22–51. The rise of the South as a distinct section is the theme of U. B. Phillips, *Life and Labor in the Old South* (1929), 91–111; R. S. Cottrill, *The Old South* (1936), 261–279; and W. E. Dodd, *The Cotton Kingdom* (1919), 24–47. A brief history of the shift of northern opinion under the influence of abolitionism is in D. L. Dumond, *Anti-Slavery Origins of the Civil War* (1939), 1–50. F. J. Turner, *The United States, 1830–1850* (1935), 575–591, deals with the impact of sectionalism on politics during the period.

CHAPTER IX
THE TRIUMPH OF DEMOCRATIC REFORM

Merle Curti, *Growth of American Thought* (1943), 344–396, is a stimulating and thoughtful analysis of the equalitarian forces operating during the Jackson era. The social and spiritual basis for these forces is assessed in A. F. Tyler, *Freedom's Ferment* (1944), 5–45, while the remainder of this helpful book deals with the resulting reforms, which are also summarized in C. R. Fish, *Rise of the Common Man* (1927), 256–390. A. M. Schlesinger, *New Viewpoints in American History* (1922), 200–219, deals broadly with the impact of Jacksonian Democracy on American life. Democracy as a faith and as a militant intellectual force is appraised in R. H. Gabriel, *Course of American Democratic Thought* (1940), 13–37, and in V. L. Parrington, *Romantic Revolution in America* (1927), 317–378. A. M. Schlesinger, Jr., *Age of Jackson* (1945), 306–390, shows the manner in which various phases of American thought responded to the stimulus of Jacksonian Democracy.

CHAPTER X

SECTIONALISM AND EXPANSION

J. C. Parish, *The Persistence of the Westward Movement* (1943), 1–45, is a thoughtful interpretation of the frontier process during this period and earlier ones, while A. K. Weinberg, *Manifest Destiny; A Study in Nationalist Expansionism in American History* (1935), 100–129, describes the idealistic factors underlying the wave of expansion during the 1840's. The expansion itself is briefly described in W. J. Ghent, *The Early Far West* (1931), 313–387. On the westward movement into Texas, E. C. Barker, *Life of Stephen F. Austin* (1925), 135–167, is brief but sound; F. L. Paxson, *Last American Frontier* (1910), 70–118, deals with the peopling of the Great Basin and California, while Frederick Merk, "Oregon Pioneers and the Boundary," *American Historical Review*, XXIX (1924), shows the effect of the American migration on the international settlement that secured the Northwest for the United States.

CHAPTER XI

DRIFTING TOWARD DISUNION

A. C. Cole, *The Irrepressible Conflict* (1934), 58–100, views generally the economic gulf between the sections during the 1850's. A classic work on immigration during this period is M. L. Hansen, *Atlantic Migration* (1940), 242–306, while the same author describes the movement of European peoples to New England in *Immigration in American History* (1940), 155–174. Nativistic objections to the new arrivals are treated in R. A. Billington, *The Protestant Crusade* (1938), 53–117, and in A. F. Tyler, *Freedom's Ferment* (1943), 358–395.

Important in understanding the forces underlying the passage of the Kansas-Nebraska Act is F. H. Hodder, "The Railroad Background of the Kansas-Nebraska Act," *Mississippi Valley Historical Review*, XII (1925). A study of the peopling of Kansas that embodies the findings of modern scholarship is R. V. Harlow, "Rise and Fall of the Kansas Aid Movement," *American Historical Review*, XLI (1935), while the still unexplored economic factors underlying the Kansas warfare are briefly assessed in J. C. Malin, *John Brown and the Legend of Fifty-Six* (1942), 498–508. F. H. Hodder, "Some Aspects of the Dred Scott Case," *Mississippi Valley Historical Review*, XVI (1939), presents the latest findings of scholars on this important decision.

CHAPTER XII

CIVIL WAR

The economic causes of the Civil War are admirably summarized in Charles and Mary Beard, *Rise of American Civilization* (1927), II, 3–51, but the idealistic factors described in A. C. Cole, *The Irrepressible Conflict* (1934),

262–284, cannot be neglected. C. R. Fish, *The American Civil War* (1937), 153–177, pictures the contestants on the eve of conflict. The international aspects of the struggle are summarized in F. L. Owsley, *King Cotton Diplomacy* (1931), 562–578. The impact of the Civil War on the growth of American democracy is considered in Avery Craven, *Democracy in American Life* (1941), 68–102, and R. H. Gabriel, *Course of American Democratic Thought* (1940), 111–122.

CHAPTER XIII

THE ROAD TO REUNION

The course of reconstruction is set forth in J. G. Randall, *Civil War and Reconstruction* (1937), 689–879, and interpreted in Charles and Mary Beard, *Rise of American Civilization* (1927), II, 52–121. Paul H. Buck, *The Road to Reunion* (1937), from which this chapter takes its name, esp. pp. 263–307, is a provocative discussion. Howard K. Beale, *The Critical Year* (1930), 149–195, is a special study of the election of 1866 and an arresting interpretation. His article "Reconstruction," *Encyclopedia of the Social Sciences,* is a summary statement. No student should miss the story of reconstruction as seen through the penetrating eyes of Henry Adams, *The Education of Henry Adams* (1927), 237–254, 255–267; W. E. B. DuBois, *Black Reconstruction* (1935), written "to prove a thesis," contains more of vision than of bias, esp. pp. 237–379, 711–728. R. W. Winston, *Andrew Johnson, Plebeian and Patriot* (1928) and L. P. Stryker, *Andrew Johnson: A Study in Courage* (1929) are two fairly recent biographies of Lincoln's successor. P. S. Pierce, *The Freedmen's Bureau* (1904) is standard, but should be supplemented by L. J. Webster, *The Operation of the Freedmen's Bureau in South Carolina,* Smith College Studies in History (1916), I, nos. 2, 3.

P. L. Haworth, *The Hayes-Tilden Election* (1927) is a revised edition of a work long standard on the disputed election of 1876. Two studies of Grant are W. E. Woodward, *Meet General Grant* (1927) and W. B. Hesseltine, *Ulysses S. Grant Politician* (1935). C. R. Williams is the author of *The Life of Rutherford B. Hayes* (1914); *Samuel J. Tilden* (1895) is by John Bigelow.

CHAPTER XIV

THE REVOLUTIONS IN ECONOMICS

No complete study of the revolutions in economics has yet been made. By all odds the best introduction is A. M. Schlesinger, "The Foundations of the Modern Era," *New Viewpoints in American History* (1922), 245–264. Suggestive comments abound in Stuart Chase, *Men and Machines* (1929), 1–41, 64–107, 318–348; and in Charles and Mary Beard, *Rise of American Civilization* (1927), II, 166–210. T. C. Cochran and W. Miller, *The Age of Enterprise* (1942), 129–153, is a neat summary. H. S. Commager, "Henry Adams," W. T.

Hutchinson, ed., *The Marcus W. Jernegan Essays in American Historiography* (1937), 191–206, contains the most penetrating observations on the meaning of the whole period. David A. Wells, a contemporary economist, makes a number of interesting observations in *Recent Economic Changes and Their Effect on the Production and Distribution of Wealth and the Well-Being of Society* (1891), especially pp. 1–69. Although the phrase "economic revolution" was first used by C. A. Beard, *American Government and Politics* (1910), it has not yet superseded the less satisfactory term "industrial revolution," as Schlesinger noted in 1922. The plural form is employed here for reasons cited in the Schlesinger essay and in the present text. For background, students are urged to consult L. Mumford, *Technics and Civilization* (1934), 9–211. The elemental facts are traced in F. A. Shannon, *America's Economic Growth* (1940), 339–355, 412–432, 433–449, 450–466, 467–483; and in E. C. Kirkland, *A History of American Economic Life* (1939), 409–464, a volume equipped with excellent bibliographies. Equally helpful is H. U. Faulkner, *American Economic History* (1924), 453–489, 514–582.

The social interrelations of the revolutions are intimated in A. M. Schlesinger, *New Viewpoints in American History* (1922), 256 ff.; and in A. W. Calhoun, *A Social History of the American Family* (1917–1919), III, 85–224. J. M. Williams, *Our Rural Heritage* (1925), a volume much neglected by historians, esp. pp. 25–31, 50–55, 111–120, merits the most careful study. T. Veblen, *The Theory of Business Enterprise* (1927), 5–91, and the same author's *Absentee Ownership* (1923), 82–100, 119–201, 205–250, are incomparable. Merle Curti, *Growth of American Thought* (1943), 507–525, is a stimulating commentary. V. L. Parrington, *Main Currents in American Thought* (1927, 1930), III, 7–10, 23–33 ff., cannot be omitted by the serious student.

CHAPTER XV
THE POLITICAL TRIUMPH OF BUSINESS

T. C. Cochran and W. Miller, *Age of Enterprise* (1942), 181–210, provides an excellent introduction. Civil War consequences are specifically treated in J. G. Randall, *Civil War and Reconstruction* (1937), 625–645. For the tariff, see F. W. Taussig, *Tariff History of the United States* (1900), 155–283, and E. Stanwood, *American Tariff Controversies in the Nineteenth Century* (1903), II, 109–394; for banking and currency, W. C. Mitchell, *A History of the Greenbacks* (1903), D. R. Dewey, *Financial History of the United States* (1903), 271–462.

R. H. Gabriel, *The Course of American Democratic Thought* (1940), 143–172, is the best recent analysis of the gospel of wealth, but no account can be compared to T. Veblen, *The Theory of Business Enterprise* (1927), chs. 2–3, 7–10. Cochran and Miller, cited above, 121–128, have written the most cogent statement of the relation of evolutionary doctrines, particularly Herbert

Spencer's, to business expansion, and since amplified by R. Hofstadter, *Social Darwinism in American Thought, 1860–1915* (1944), 68–85, 121–145. The over-all implications of evolutionary thought in America are suggested in B. J. Loewenberg, "Darwinism Comes to America, 1859–1900," *Mississippi Valley Historical Review*, XXVIII (1941), 339–368.

CHAPTER XVI

THE BANKRUPTCY OF POLITICS

Despite scholarly preoccupation with political history, there is no synthesis of politics since 1876. There is no comprehensive analysis of democracy and party government or of political theory and the revolution in power relations. The most consequential work of recent scholarship is E. E. Schattschneider, *Party Government* (1942), written in the tradition of W. Bagehot's *British Constitution* (1867), of J. Bryce, *The American Commonwealth* (1910), and of W. Wilson, *Congressional Government* (1885). These last three works are fundamental to an understanding of democratic government and majority rule. H. J. Ford, *The Rise and Growth of American Politics* (1898) is a much neglected study by an astute political scientist who early stressed the significance of parties in relation to democracy. P. D. Hasbrouck, *Party Government in the House of Representatives* (1927) describes how the party system functions in that body. K. H. Porter, *National Party Platforms* (1924) contains the essential source material under that heading. H. F. Gosnell, *Boss Platt and His New York Machine* (1924) is a scholarly introduction to a typical political phenomenon. K. G. Crawford, *The Pressure Boys* (1939) is excellent. M. Josephson, *The Politicos, 1865–1900* (1938) is a vivid narrative that contains the raw material for a dynamic analysis. Students should refer to Henry Adams, *The Education of Henry Adams* (1927), 255–267, 268–298, which contains the most incisive comments by an alert witness of contemporary events.

CHAPTER XVII

THE CONQUEST OF RURAL AMERICA

The best single-volume account of the topics treated in this chapter is F. A. Shannon, *The Farmer's Last Frontier* (1945), but every student should read Charles and Mary Beard, *Rise of American Civilization* (1927), II, ch. 22, "The Triple Revolution in Agriculture," one of the most suggestive accounts to be found anywhere. Nor is it possible to omit F. J. Turner's masterly essay, "The Significance of the Frontier in American History," in his *The Frontier in American History* (1920), 11–38.

Agricultural changes are surveyed by E. E. Edwards, "American Agriculture—The First 300 Years," *Farmers in a Changing World*, in *Yearbook of Agriculture, 1940* (1940), 221–266. The same author has compiled the most exhaustive bibliography of the subject, *A Bibliography of the History of Agriculture in the United States* (1930), helpful at every point. P. W. Gates has written studies indispensable for an understanding of land policy and the disposition of the public domain. "The Homestead Act in an Incongruous Land System," *American Historical Review,* XLI (1936), 637–651, places the subject on a new level of comprehension. His *The Illinois Central and Its Colonization Work* (1934) illumines the interrelated problems of railway development and acceleration of western settlement, as does J. B. Hedges, *Henry Villard and the Railways of the Northwest* (1930). For later stages of the westward movement, W. P. Webb, *The Great Plains* (1931), chs. 5–8, 11, arc essential.

L. B. Priest, *Uncle Sam's Stepchildren* (1942) covers the whole field of Indian relations for this period. For mining, Mark Twain, *Roughing It* (1873) tells of the Comstock Lode in the inimitable Twain style. Webb, *Great Plains,* 205–268, and Shannon, *Farmer's Last Frontier,* 197–220, cited above, survey the cattle kingdom.

CHAPTER XVIII
THE RISE OF THE CITY

The most fundamental volume on the city is A. M. Schlesinger, *The Rise of the City, 1878–1898* (1933), which has given a new direction to the study of American life. Schlesinger's method and viewpoint, however, should be supplemented by L. Wirth, "Urbanism as a Way of Life," *The American Journal of Sociology,* XLIV (1938), 1–24.

Technological changes and particular inventions which transformed urban life are treated in E. W. Byrn, *Progress of Invention in the Nineteenth Century* (1900), W. Kaempffert, ed., *A Popular History of American Invention* (1924), Holland Thompson, *Age of Invention,* chs. 6–9, George Iles, *Leading American Inventors* (1912), T. C. Martin and S. L. Coles, eds., *The Story of Electricity* (1919), F. L. Dyer and T. C. Martin, *Edison; His Life and Inventions* (1910).

The emergence of a new women's world is traced in Schlesinger's *Rise of the City,* ch. 5, cited above. The earlier phases of the struggle for equal suffrage may be followed in E. A. Hecker, *A Short History of Women's Rights* (1911). Marriage, the family, and changing values are all discussed in A. W. Calhoun, *A Social History of the American Family* (1919), III. T. Woody, *A History of Women's Education in the United States* (1929) covers its subject thoroughly.

Social Christianity, the institutional church, and related topics are fully explored in A. I. Abell, *The Urban Impact on American Protestantism, 1865–1900* (1943), 3–26, 57–87, 137–165. See also J. Dombrowski, *The Early Days of Christian Socialism in America* (1936) and C. H. Hopkins, *The Rise of the*

Social Gospel in American Protestantism, 1865–1915 (1940), 24–49, 54–66, 149–183.

For science, comparative religion, and Biblical criticism, see B. J. Loewenberg, "Darwinism Comes to America," *Mississippi Valley Historical Review,* XXVIII (1941), 339–368.

CHAPTER XIX
THE MINGLING OF PEOPLES

Immigration has been a persistent factor in American life, but American historians became aware of its meanings belatedly. Awareness of scholars was stimulated by A. M. Schlesinger's pioneering essay, "The Influence of Immigration," *New Viewpoints in American History* (1922), 1–21. The accounts of immigration and the histories of immigrant groups have usually been marred by a narrow, nationalistic emphasis. Indeed, the whole field requires re-evaluation in terms of cultural diversity and political unity. There is no good analysis of the relationship of democracy and immigration. M. R. Davie, *World Immigration* (1936), as the title suggests, is the closest approximation to the thesis outlined in this chapter. E. Abbott, *Historical Aspects of the Immigration Problem: Select Documents* (1926) is an excellent collection. In the title cited above, Davie has compiled an extremely helpful list of immigrant biographies and literary material dealing with the immigrants and immigration, pp. 563–571. M. L. Hansen, *The Immigrant in American History* (1940) is an important volume in which special attention should be called to chs. 1, 4, 7, 9. A recent cooperative volume is D. F. Bowers, ed., *Foreign Influences in American Life* (1944). Other general accounts are C. Wittke, *We Who Built America* (1939) and G. M. Stephenson, *A History of American Immigration, 1820–1924* (1926).

CHAPTER XX
THE SINS OF SOCIETY

E. A. Ross, *Sin and Society* (1907) is a provocative analysis by a leading sociologist. J. A. Riis, *How the Other Half Lives* (1890), *The Battle with the Slum* (1902), and *The Children of the Poor* (1892) are vital historical documents as well as expert analyses. The same may be said of the works of John Spargo and Jane Addams: Addams, *Democracy and Social Ethics* (1902), *The Spirit of Youth and City Streets* (1909) ; Spargo, *The Bitter Cry of the Children* (1906).

The "facts and figures" of the distribution of wealth and standards of living are set forth in the following studies: L. B. More, *Wage-Earners' Budgets* (1907), R. C. Chapin, *The Standard of Living among Workingmen's Families in New York City* (1909), P. Roberts, *The Anthracite Coal Communities*

(1904) ; *Hull-House Maps and Papers* (1895), P. U. Kellogg, ed., *The Pitts-burgh Survey* (1910). S. Ratner, *American Taxation: Its History as a Social Force in Democracy* (1942), 219–222, summarizes the evidence. C. B. Spahr, *The Present Distribution of Wealth in the United States* (1896) is a con-temporary account. F. H. Streightoff, *The Standard of Living among the In-dustrial People of America* (1911) is a brief but factual statement. R. Hunter, *Poverty* (1904), J. A. Ryan, *A Living Wage* (1906), E. T. Devine, *Misery and Its Causes* (1909), and J. S. Lowell, *Public Relief and Private Charity* (1884) are even more specific. On the social settlement consult F. C. Montague, *Arnold Toynbee of London* (1889), A. J. Kennedy, *The Settlement Horizon* (1922), J. Addams, *Twenty Years at Hull-House* (1910), L. Wald, *The House on Henry Street* (1915).

CHAPTER XXI

DISSENT AND FRUSTRATION

There are numerous accounts of the history and problems of organized labor. R. T. Ely, *The Labor Movement in America* (1886), the work of a dis-tinguished, socially minded economist, and F. T. Carlton, *The History and Problems of Organized Labor* (1920) are especially useful. The Knights of Labor are given special attention in N. J. Ware, *The Labor Movement in the United States, 1860–1895* (1929), and the Federation is discussed in L. L. Lor-win, *The American Federation of Labor* (1933). The latter is amplified with dramatic richness by S. Gompers, *Seventy Years of Life and Labor* (1925).

On the general issue of monopoly, see W. Z. Ripley, ed., *Trusts, Pools, and Corporations* (1905) and J. W. Jenks, *The Trust Problem* (1902). I. M. Tarbell, *History of the Standard Oil Company* (1904) is a classic account. H. D. Lloyd, *Wealth against Commonwealth* (1894) is one of the most notable books of the era.

On wages, *History of Wages in the United States from Colonial Times to 1928* (1929), compiled by the Bureau of Labor Statistics, is indispensable. Data on hours and general working conditions will be found under "The Sins of Society." L. Adamic, *Dynamite* (1931) discusses violence in labor disputes, and H. David, *The History of the Haymarket Affair* (1936) is one of the best studies of its kind.

The agrarian protest is treated in N. Fine, *Labor and Farmer Parties in the United States, 1828–1928* (1928), and the whole subject is luminously set forth in S. J. Buck, *The Agrarian Crusade* (1921). On the Populists, J. D. Hicks, *The Populist Revolt* (1931) is definitive, but special importance at-taches to H. Farmer, "The Economic Background of Frontier Populism," *Mississippi Valley Historical Review*, X (1924), 406–427.

CHAPTER XXII

THE SHRINKING WORLD

The best over-all coverage of the specific events described in this chapter is to be found in T. A. Bailey, *A Diplomatic History of the American People* (1940), 340–531, and in S. F. Bemis, *Diplomatic History of the United States* (1936). Two vital studies are A. K. Weinberg, *Manifest Destiny: A Study in Nationalist Expansionism in American History* (1935), 224–323, and B. M. Williams, *Economic Foreign Policy of the United States* (1929), 1–7, 11–56. On the French crisis and Napoleon, D. Perkins, *The Monroe Doctrine, 1826–1867* (1933), 318–548, covers the episode in scholarly detail. For the Dominican affair, see Bailey, 377–378, cited above, where expansion after the Civil War is also treated, 392–404. The purchase of Alaska is fully explored by T. A. Bailey, "Why the United States Purchased Alaska," *Pacific Historical Review,* III (1934), 39–49, which evaluates public opinion in the United States. The Alabama Claims and related matters form an important part of the exhaustive treatment in A. Nevins, *Hamilton Fish* (1936), 423–566. Cuban relations are handled in Nevins, *Fish,* 239 ff., and Bailey, 413. One of the best accounts of the resurgence of imperialism is J. W. Pratt, *Expansionists of 1898* (1936), especially ch. I. F. R. Dulles, *America in the Pacific* (1932), 98–198, provides the essential material on both Hawaii and Samoa, and most students will be interested in R. L. Stevenson, *A Footnote to History: Eight Years of Trouble in Samoa* (1891). A Nevins, *Grover Cleveland* (1934), ch. XXIV, is comprehensive on the Venezuela crisis; its repercussions on the Monroe Doctrine are expertly handled in D. Perkins, *Hands Off: A History of the Monroe Doctrine* (1941), 171–191.

In Bailey's work cited above, ch. XXX is excellent on the coming of the war with Spain; Walter Millis, *The Martial Spirit* (1931) is a full-dress study. Pratt, *Expansionists,* cited above, discusses the attitude of business in ch. VII. F. H. Harrington has contributed a significant article entitled "The Anti-Imperialist Movement in the United States, 1898–1900," *Mississippi Valley Historical Review,* XXII (1935), 211. The struggle for ratification in the Senate may be followed in W. S. Holt, *Treaties Defeated by the Senate* (1933), ch. VIII.

CHAPTER XXIII

MIDDLE-CLASS PROGRESSIVISM

A competent recent survey of the Progressive movement appears in T. C. Cochran and W. Miller, *The Age of Enterprise* (1942), 273–297. Early twentieth-century social conditions are described in H. U. Faulkner, *The Quest for Social Justice* (1931), 1–51. Progressive ferment in social science and religious thought is treated in R. H. Gabriel, *The Course of American Democratic Thought* (1940), 293–338; and in Merle Curti, *The Growth of Ameri-*

can Thought (1943), 555–579, 629–632. Various Progressive contributions to political and social theory are discussed in E. R. Lewis, *American Political Thought* (1937), 361–367, 470–482, 493–496; and in R. Hofstadter, *Social Darwinism in American Thought* (1944), 121–145. For a critical estimate of Lippmann, Brandeis, and other contributors to progressive ferment, see J. Chamberlain, *Farewell to Reform* (1932), 222–233, 302–305; and for John Dewey see Merle Curti, *The Social Ideas of American Educators* (1935), 499–541. International standards in social legislation are traced historically and critically in J. R. Commons and J. B. Andrews, *Principles of Labor Legislation* (1920), 182–198 (minimum wage), 260–262 (eight-hour day), 392–397 and 415–448 (social security laws). Resistance of American courts to progressive legislation receives lively treatment in E. S. Bates, *The Story of the Supreme Court* (1936), 229–252. Laissez faire in the courts and contemporary protests are traced in G. G. Haines, *The American Doctrine of Judicial Supremacy* (1932), 421–466. The power of state and local machines to resist reform is analyzed in E. E. Schattschneider, *Party Government* (1942), 99–123.

CHAPTER XXIV

PROGRESSIVISM AND THE G.O.P.

Contributions of Woodrow Wilson to the theory of party responsibility may best be gleaned from his *Congressional Government* (1885), 58–103, 108–123, 294–332; or in shorter compass in *The Public Papers of Woodrow Wilson* (1927), I *(College and State)*, 19–42, 336–359. The party system is evaluated in J. Allen Smith, *The Spirit of American Government* (1907), ch. 8. The "truth about the trusts" is summarized in T. C. Cochran and W. Miller, *The Age of Enterprise* (1942), 181–202, 238–243. Antitrust prosecutions and court decisions from 1900 to the 1911 rule of reason are analyzed by economists in H. R. Seager and C. A. Gulick, *Trust and Corporation Problems* (1929), 386–415. A stimulating, brief historical analysis of presidential leadership under Roosevelt, Taft, and Wilson appears in T. K. Finletter, *Can Representative Government Do the Job?* (1945), 14–21, 25–28, 32–45. Insurgent criticism of Republican politics may best be inspected in R. M. La Follette, *Autobiography* (1913), chs. 9–11. The struggle for pure food laws is recounted in M. Sullivan, *Our Times* (1927), II, 501–552; the Hepburn battle is treated in (1930), III, 191–275. The conversion of George Norris from Old Guard Republican to insurgent progressive is traced in R. L. Neuberger and S. B. Kahn, *Integrity, Life of George Norris* (1937), 24–65. For D. G. Phillips' articles on "The Treason of the Senate," one must go to *Cosmopolitan Magazine*, XL (1905–1906), 487–502, 628–638, and subsequent issues in XLI (1906). Roosevelt's trust and labor policies are discussed in H. Pringle, *Theodore Roosevelt* (1931), 251–278, 413–431, 476–485.

CHAPTER XXV
THE RISE OF WILSONIAN DEMOCRACY

The battle against the speaker system is described in A. Lief, *Democracy's Norris* (1939), 85–128. The Payne-Aldrich tariff battle is traced in C. G. Bowers, *Beveridge and the Progressive Era* (1932), 313–365. Battles over tariffs and tax reform under Taft and Wilson are covered in S. Ratner, *American Taxation* (1942), 265–309, 321–340, 345–361. Taft's tariff and trust policies are presented in H. Pringle, *William Howard Taft* (1939), I, 411–457, and II, 654–677. The Brandeis-Wilson thesis on the social and economic inefficiency of big business appears in L. D. Brandeis, *Other People's Money* (1933), 51–68, 189–207. Wilsonian Democracy and presidential leadership are treated in F. L. Paxson, *Pre-War Years* (1936), 1–30, 68–100. The best recent biographical study is H. C. F. Bell, *Woodrow Wilson and the People* (1945).

CHAPTER XXVI
THE ENIGMA OF LABOR AND AGRICULTURE

Traditional attitudes and institutions complicating the American farm problem and various European approaches to questions of land tenure and conservation are discussed in L. C. Gray *et al., Soils and Men* (U. S. Department of Agriculture, 1938), 111–136. History and economics are integrated in a significant article by A. P. Chew, "The Meaning of Foreign Trade for Agriculture," in *Farmers in a Changing World* in *Yearbook of Agriculture, 1940* (1940), 566–584. A suggestive article by R. Turner, "The Cultural Setting of American Agricultural Problems," appears in the same agricultural yearbook (1940), 1003–1031. A useful, brief analysis of the changed position of agriculture appears in W. E. Atkins *et al., Economic Behavior* (1939), 700–736. A standard treatment of agricultural history, running from 1900 to 1930, is in F. A. Shannon, *Economic History of the People of the United States* (1934), 825–850. Industrial disputes are graphically related in S. Yellen, *American Labor Struggles* (1936), 136–250; and in L. Adamic, *Dynamite* (1934), 124–196, 257–263. A standard general account is given in L. L. Lorwin, *The American Federation of Labor* (1933), 41–145. Liberal ferment and the radical fringe of the labor movement are treated in L. Symes and T. Clement, *Rebel America* (1934), 244–285, 320–334.

CHAPTER XXVII
THE WORLD'S ILLUSION

Intellectual rebellion against power politics and the movement for international organization are discussed in Merle Curti, *Peace or War* (1936), 166–261. The evolution of the aggressive twist of the Theodore Roosevelt Corollary to the Monroe Doctrine is traced in D. Perkins, *Hands Off* (1941), 228-275. The evolution of twentieth-century American ideas of racism, national superiority, and imperialism are surveyed in Merle Curti, *The Growth of American Thought* (1943), 659–685; in R. Hofstadter, *Social Darwinism in American Thought* (1944), 146–173; and in R. H. Gabriel, *The Course of American Democratic Thought* (1940), 339–356. J. W. Pratt studies the historical roots of the ideology of American expansion in A. Craven, ed., *Essays in Honor of William E. Dodd* (1935), 335–355. American imperialism and foreign policies are covered in T. A. Bailey, *A Diplomatic History of the American People* (1942), 533–609; and in S. F. Bemis, *A Diplomatic History of the United States* (1936), 479–564.

CHAPTER XXVIII
NATIONALISM AND NORMALCY

A good, incisive treatment of the battle of democratic internationalism against nationalism and aristocracy between 1917 and 1920 is W. E. Dodd, *Woodrow Wilson and His Work* (1927), 354–434. The war and the problems of peace are broadly treated in S. Neumann, *The Future in Perspective* (1946), 39–88. Analysis by F. J. Turner of requisites for democratic international organization, written at Wilson's request, is printed in the *American Historical Review*, XLVII (1942), 545–551. Wilson, Versailles, and the Senate are discussed in J. C. Malin, *The United States after the World War* (1930), 5–69. Nationalistic repression and the postwar reaction are covered in P. W. Slosson, *The Great Crusade and After* (1931), 287–303, 307–317; and in F. L. Allen, *Only Yesterday* (1931), 45–75, 84–87, 136 158, 195–206. Scattered materials on suppressive tendencies in employer policies toward labor appear in S. Howard, *The Labor Spy* (1924), 167–199. Postwar cleavages in education are studied in Merle Curti, *The Social Ideas of American Educators* (1935), 542–580. The same author treats postwar peace organizations in *Peace or War* (1936), 262–300. The clash between Wilsonian internationalism and nationalist champions of the Monroe Doctrine in the years 1919–1932 is traced in D. Perkins, *Hands Off* (1941), 276–313. Economic foreign policy and the interdependence of isolated America and the outside world are succinctly treated in A. Nevins and L. M. Hacker, eds., *The United States and Its Place in World Affairs* (1943), 166–199. Wartime liberalism in taxation and the postwar normalcy policies of Mellon are studied in S. Ratner, *American Taxation* (1942), 364–433.

CHAPTER XXIX
THE ROOSEVELT REVOLUTION

The stock market inflation, crash, and aftermath are pictured in F. L. Allen, *Only Yesterday* (1931), 290–347. The economic foreign policy of

Hoover is discussed in T. A. Bailey, *A Diplomatic History of the American People* (1942), 716–731. Domestic affairs and the Hoover administration are treated in Charles and Mary Beard, *America in Midpassage* (1939), 24–45, 55–77, 86–112. The early history of the New Deal is covered in B. Rauch, *History of the New Deal* (1944), chs. 8–10; in D. L. Dumond, *Roosevelt to Roosevelt* (1937), 401–463, 488–502; and in the Beards' *America in Midpassage,* 150–255. TVA is popularly treated in D. Lilienthal, *TVA—An Experiment in Democracy* (1944). Important is the pamphlet by H. A. Wallace, *America Must Choose* (1934). The most luminous survey of the New Deal printed in pamphlet length is by A. M. Schlesinger, *The New Deal in Action* (1940). A useful longer account of the first two years is L. M. Hacker, *A Short History of the New Deal* (1934), 29–128.

CHAPTER XXX

THE CHALLENGE OF SOCIAL DEMOCRACY

The political course of the New Deal is treated in B. Rauch, *History of the New Deal* (1944) ; and in Charles and Mary Beard, *America in Midpassage* (1939), 256–298, 320–380. A popular account of the trend in Supreme Court decisions to 1936 is contained in E. S. Bates, *The Story of the Supreme Court* (1936), 284–317. The problem of parties and political leadership under the New Deal is discussed in R. Young, *This Is Congress* (1943), 3–22, 28–79, 87–98, 241–267. See also T. K. Finletter, *Can Representative Government Do the Job?* (1945), 1–21, 73–147; and E. E. Schattschneider, *Party Government* (1942), 53–61, 99–115.

Two valuable short appraisals of the economic and political problems of the South are R. B. Vance, *The South's Place in the Nation* (Public Affairs Pamphlet, 1936), 1–31; and W. G. Carleton, "The Conservative South—A Political Myth," *Virginia Quarterly Review* (Spring, 1946), reprinted in the appendix of the *Congressional Record,* XCII, no. 66 (April 11, 1946), A 2197– A 2200. Conflicts between small farmers and the farm bloc conservatives of big agriculture are examined in C. McWilliams, *Small Farm and Big Farm* (Public Affairs Pamphlet, 1945), 1–31. Rural and urban labor struggles are traced in the Beards' *Midpassage,* 501–576, cited above. Democratic advantages of a sound system of collective bargaining are discussed in T. R. Carskadon, *Workers and Bosses Are Human* (Public Affairs Pamphlet, 1943), 1–31. A cogent analysis of persisting confusions in middle-class attitudes toward industrial disputes is M. J. Barloon, "Violence and Collective Bargaining," *Harper's* (May, 1940), 625–634.

CHAPTER XXXI

NEANDERTHAL NATIONALISM

The illusions of economic nationalism are conveniently dissected and international alternatives indicated in M. S. Stewart, *Colonies, Trade, and Prosperity* (Public Affairs Pamphlet, 1937), 1–31. New Deal diplomacy is summarized in T. A. Bailey, *A Diplomatic History of the American People* (1942), 732–754. Transformation of the Monroe Doctrine under the Good Neighbor policy is traced in D. Perkins, *Hands Off* (1941), 314–361. The isolationist response to world perils is treated in A. Nevins and L. M. Hacker, eds., *The United States and Its Place in World Affairs* (1943), 388–409; and the breakdown of neutrality, in the same volume, 453–474, 496–532. The march of the dictators is luminously traced in S. Neumann, *The Future in Perspective* (1946), 210–318. An appraisal of conflicts between the administration, Congress, and pressure groups in the critical years, 1939–1942, may be found in E. Stein, J. D. Magee, and W. J. Ronan, *Our War Economy* (1943), 3–50.

CHAPTER XXXII
CENTURY OF THE COMMON MAN?

A convenient brief introduction to the revolution in economic thought and the new role of government is J. H. G. Pierson, *Fiscal Policy for Full Employment* (National Planning Association, Pamphlet, 1945), 1–22, 40–45. See also "The Road to Freedom: Full Employment," *New Republic, Supplement* (September 24, 1945), 395–415; K. Boulding, *The Economics of Peace* (1945), 96–101, 124–140, 179–220; and see also the inexpensive pocket-size revision of A. H. Hansen, *America's Role in the World Economy* (1946), 1–28, 34–40, 72–155. Significant criticism from liberal business, farm, and labor groups urging correction of irresponsible legislative practices is summarized in R. Heller, *Strengthening the Congress* (National Planning Association, 1944), 1–35. A major item in the unfinished business of democracy—race relations— is cogently explored in terms of antidiscrimination legislation in C. McWilliams, *Race Discrimination—and the Law* (National Federation for Constitutional Liberties, 1945), 1–24; reprinted from *Science and Society,* IX, no. 1 (Winter, 1945). The same author treats the Nisei problem in *What About Our Japanese Americans?* (Public Affairs Pamphlet, 1944), 1–29. An interpretation of the war and the relation of the United States to evolving international organization appears in S. Neumann, *The Future in Perspective* (1946), 318–384. Alternatives confronting atomic man are argued in N. Cousins, *Modern Man Is Obsolete* (1945), 10–49.

DECLARATION OF INDEPENDENCE

In Congress, July 4, 1776,

THE UNANIMOUS DECLARATION OF THE THIRTEEN UNITED STATES

OF AMERICA

When in the Course of human events, it becomes necessary for one people to dissolve the political bands, which have connected them with another, and to assume among the powers of the earth, the separate and equal station to which the Laws of Nature and of Nature's God entitle them, a decent respect to the opinions of mankind requires that they should declare the causes which impel them to the separation.

We hold these truths to be self-evident, that all men are created equal, that they are endowed by their Creator with certain unalienable Rights, that among these are Life, Liberty and the pursuit of Happiness. That to secure these rights, Governments are instituted among Men, deriving their just powers from the consent of the governed. That whenever any Form of Government becomes destructive of these ends, it is the Right of the People to alter or to abolish it, and to institute new Government, laying its foundation on such principles and organizing its powers in such form, as to them shall seem most likely to effect their Safety and Happiness. Prudence, indeed, will dictate that Governments long established should not be changed for light and transient causes; and accordingly all experience hath shewn, that mankind are more disposed to suffer, while evils are sufferable, than to right themselves by abolishing the forms to which they are accustomed. But when a long train of abuses and usurpations, pursuing invariably the same Object evinces a design to reduce them under absolute Despotism, it is their right, it is their duty, to throw off such Government, and to provide new Guards for their future security. Such has been the patient sufferance of these Colonies; and such is now the necessity which constrains them to alter their former Systems of Government. The history of the present King of Great Britain is a history of repeated injuries and usurpations, all having in direct object the establishment of an absolute Tyranny over these States. To prove this, let Facts be submitted to a candid world.

He has refused his Assent to Laws, the most wholesome and necessary for the public good.

He has forbidden his Governors to pass Laws of immediate and pressing importance, unless suspended in their operation till his Assent should be obtained; and when so suspended, he has utterly neglected to attend to them.

He has refused to pass other Laws for the accommodation of large districts of people, unless those people would relinquish the right of Representation in the Legislature, a right inestimable to them and formidable to tyrants only.

He has called together legislative bodies at places unusual, uncomfortable, and distant from the depository of their public Records, for the sole purpose of fatiguing them into compliance with his measures.

He has dissolved Representative Houses repeatedly, for opposing with manly firmness his invasions on the rights of the people.

He has refused for a long time, after such dissolutions, to cause others to be elected; whereby the Legislative Powers, incapable of Annihilation, have returned to the People at large for their exercise; the State remaining in the mean time exposed to all the dangers of invasion from without, and convulsions within.

He has endeavoured to prevent the population of these States; for that purpose obstructing the Laws for Naturalization of Foreigners; refusing to pass others to encourage their migrations hither, and raising the conditions of new Appropriations of Lands.

He has obstructed the Administration of Justice, by refusing his Assent to Laws for establishing Judiciary powers.

He has made Judges dependent on his Will alone, for the tenure of their offices, and the amount and payment of their salaries.

He has erected a multitude of New Offices, and sent hither swarms of Officers to harass our people, and eat out their substance.

He has kept among us, in times of peace, Standing Armies without the Consent of our legislatures.

He has affected to render the Military independent of and superior to the Civil power.

He has combined with others to subject us to a jurisdiction foreign to our constitution, and unacknowledged by our laws; giving his Assent to their Acts of pretended Legislation:

For quartering large bodies of armed troops among us:

For protecting them, by a mock Trial, from punishment for any Murders which they should commit on the Inhabitants of these States:

For cutting off our trade with all parts of the world:

For imposing Taxes on us without our Consent:

For depriving us in many cases, of the benefits of Trial by Jury:

For transporting us beyond Seas to be tried for pretended offences:

For abolishing the free System of English Laws in a neighbouring Province, establishing therein an Arbitrary government, and enlarging its Boundaries so as to render it at once an example and fit instrument for introducing the same absolute rule into these Colonies:

For taking away our Charters, abolishing our most valuable Laws, and altering fundamentally the Forms of our Governments:

For suspending our own Legislatures, and declaring themselves invested with power to legislate for us in all cases whatsoever.

He has abdicated Government here, by declaring us out of his Protection and waging War against us.

He has plundered our seas, ravaged our Coasts, burnt our towns, and destroyed the lives of our people.

He is at this time transporting large Armies of foreign Mercenaries to compleat the works of death, desolation and tyranny, already begun with circumstances of Cruelty & perfidy scarcely paralleled in the most barbarous ages, and totally unworthy the Head of a civilized nation.

He has constrained our fellow Citizens taken Captive on the high Seas to bear Arms against their Country, to become the executioners of their friends and Brethren, or to fall themselves by their Hands.

He has excited domestic insurrections amongst us, and has endeavoured to bring on the inhabitants of our frontiers, the merciless Indian Savages, whose known rule of warfare, is an undistinguished destruction of all ages, sexes and conditions.

In every stage of these Oppressions We have Petitioned for Redress in the most humble terms: Our repeated Petitions have been answered only by repeated injury. A Prince, whose character is thus marked by every act which may define a Tyrant, is unfit to be the ruler of a free People.

Nor have We been wanting in attentions to our British brethren. We have warned them from time to time of attempts by their legislature to extend an unwarrantable jurisdiction over us. We have reminded them of the circumstances of our emigration and settlement here. We have appealed to their native justice and magnanimity, and we have conjured them by the ties of our common kindred to disavow these usurpations, which would inevitably interrupt our connections and correspondence. They too have been deaf to the voice of justice and of consanguinity. We must, therefore, acquiesce in the necessity, which denounces our Separation, and hold them, as we hold the rest of mankind, Enemies in War, in Peace Friends.

We, therefore, the Representatives of the united States of America, in General Congress, Assembled, appealing to the Supreme Judge of the world for the rectitude of our intentions do, in the Name, and by Authority of the good People of these Colonies, solemnly publish and declare, That these United Colonies are, and of Right ought to be Free and Independent States; that they are Absolved from all Allegiance to the British Crown, and that all political connection between them and the State of Great Britain, is and ought to be totally dissolved; and that as Free and Independent States, they have full Power to levy War, conclude Peace, contract Alliances, establish Commerce, and to do all other Acts and Things which Independent States may of right do. And for the support of this Declaration, with a firm reliance on the Protection of Divine Providence, we mutually pledge to each other our Lives, our Fortunes and our sacred Honor.

CONSTITUTION OF THE UNITED STATES[1]

WE the people of the United States in order to form a more perfect union, establish justice, insure domestic tranquillity, provide for the common defence, promote the general welfare and secure the blessings of liberty to ourselves and our posterity, do ordain and establish this CONSTITUTION for the United States of America.

ARTICLE I

Section 1. All legislative powers herein granted shall be vested in a Congress of the United States, which shall consist of a Senate and House of Representatives.

Section 2. The House of Representatives shall be composed of members chosen every second year by the people of the several States, and the electors in each State shall have the qualifications requisite for electors of the most numerous branch of the State Legislature.

No person shall be a Representative who shall not have attained to the age of twenty-five years, and been seven years a citizen of the United States, and who shall not when elected, be an inhabitant of that State in which he shall be chosen.

Representatives and direct taxes shall be apportioned among the several States which may be included within this Union, according to their respective numbers, which shall be determined by adding to the whole number of free persons, including those bound to service for a term of years, and excluding Indians not taxed, three fifths of all other persons. The actual enumeration shall be made within three years after the first meeting of the Congress of the United States, and within every subsequent term of ten years, in such manner as they shall by law direct. The number of Representatives shall not exceed one for every thirty thousand, but each State shall have at least one Representative; and until such enumeration shall be made, the State of *New Hampshire* shall be entitled to choose three, *Massachusetts* eight, *Rhode Island* and *Providence Plantations* one, *Connecticut* five, *New York* six, *New Jersey* four, *Pennsylvania* eight, *Delaware* one, *Maryland* six, *Virginia* ten, *North Carolina* five, *South Carolina* five, and *Georgia* three.

When vacancies happen in the representation from any State, the Executive authority thereof shall issue writs of election to fill such vacancies.

---

[1] Jonathan Elliot, *The Debates in the Several Conventions on the Adoption of the Federal Constitution* (1836), 1–21, "copied and carefully compared with the original in the Department of State. Punctuation, paragraphs, and capital letters, same as said original," p. 1.

The House of Representatives shall choose their Speaker and other officers; and shall have the sole power of impeachment.

Section 3. The Senate of the United States shall be composed of two Senators from each State, chosen by the Legislature thereof, for six years; and each Senator shall have one vote.

Immediately after they shall be assembled in consequence of the first election, they shall be divided as equally as may be, into three classes. The seats of the Senators of the first class shall be vacated at the expiration of the second year, of the second class at the expiration of the fourth year, and of the third class at the expiration of the sixth year, so that one third may be chosen every second year; and if vacancies happen by resignation or otherwise, during the recess of the Legislature of any State, the executive thereof may make temporary appointments, until the next meeting of the Legislature, which shall then fill such vacancies.

No person shall be a Senator who shall not have attained to the age of thirty years, and been nine years a citizen of the United States, and who shall not, when elected, be an inhabitant of that State for which he shall be chosen.

The Vice President of the United States shall be President of the Senate, but shall have no vote unless they be equally divided.

The Senate shall choose their other officers, and also a President protempore, in the absence of the Vice President or when he shall exercise the office of President of the United States.

The Senate shall have the sole power to try all impeachments: when sitting for that purpose, they shall be on oath or affirmation. When the President of the United States is tried the Chief Justice shall preside: and no person shall be convicted without the concurrence of two-thirds of the members present.

Judgment in cases of impeachment shall not extend farther than to removal from office, and disqualification to hold and enjoy any office of honor, trust, or profit under the United States: but the party convicted shall nevertheless be liable and subject to indictment, trial, judgment and punishment, according to law.

Section 4. The times, places and manner of holding elections for Senators and Representatives, shall be prescribed in each State by the legislature thereof; but the Congress may at any time by law make or alter such regulations, except as to the places of choosing Senators.

The Congress shall assemble at least once in every year, and such meeting shall be on the first Monday in December unless they shall by law appoint a different day.

Section 5. Each House shall be the judge of the elections, returns and qualifications of its own members, and a majority of each shall constitute a quorum to do business; but a smaller number may adjourn from day to day, and may be authorized to compel the attendance of absent members, in such manner, and under such penalties as each House may provide.

Each House may determine the rules of its proceedings, punish its members for disorderly behavior, and, with the concurrence of two thirds, expel a member.

Each House shall keep a journal of its proceedings, and from time to time publish the same, excepting such parts as may in their judgment require Secrecy; and the yeas and nays of the members of either House on any question shall, at the desire of one-fifth of those present, be entered on the journal.

Neither House, during the Session of Congress, shall, without the consent of the other, adjourn for more than three days, nor to any other place than that in which the two Houses shall be sitting.

Section 6. The Senators and Representatives shall receive a compensation for their services, to be ascertained by law, and paid out of the Treasury of the United States. They shall in all cases except treason, felony and breach of the peace, be privileged from arrest during their attendance at the session of their respective Houses, and in going to and returning from the same; and for any speech or debate in either House, they shall not be questioned in any other place.

No Senator or Representative shall, during the time for which he was elected, be appointed to any civil office under the authority of the United States, which shall have been created, or the emoluments whereof shall have been increased during such time: and no person holding any office under the United States shall be a member of either House during his continuance in office.

Section 7. All bills for raising revenue shall originate in the House of Representatives; but the Senate may propose, or concur with, amendments, as on other bills.

Every bill which shall have passed the House of Representatives, and the Senate, shall, before it become a law, be presented to the President of the United States; if he approve he shall sign it, but if not he shall return it, with his objections to that House in which it shall have originated, who shall enter the objections at large on their journal, and proceed to reconsider it. If after such reconsideration two thirds of that House shall agree to pass the bill, it shall be sent, together with the objections, to the other House, by which it shall likewise be reconsidered, and if approved by two thirds of that House, it shall become a law. But in all such cases the votes of both Houses shall be determined by yeas and nays, and the names of the persons voting for and against the bill shall be entered on the journal of each House respectively. If any bill shall not be returned by the President within ten days (Sundays excepted,) after it shall have been presented to him, the same shall be a law, in like manner as if he had signed it, unless the Congress by their adjournment prevent its return, in which case it shall not be a law.

Every order, resolution, or vote to which the concurrence of the Senate and House of Representatives may be necessary (except on a question of adjournment) shall be presented to the President of the United States; and before the same shall take effect, shall be approved by him, or, being disapproved by him, shall be repassed by two-thirds of the Senate and House of Representatives, according to the rules and limitations prescribed in the case of a bill.

Section 8. The Congress shall have power To lay and collect taxes, duties, imposts and excises, to pay the debts and provide for the common defence and general welfare of the United States; but all duties, imposts and excises shall be uniform throughout the United States;

To borrow money on the credit of the United States;

To regulate commerce with foreign nations, and among the several States, and with the Indian tribes;

To establish an uniform rule of naturalization, and uniform laws on the subject of bankruptcies throughout the United States;

To coin money, regulate the value thereof, and of foreign coin, and fix the standard of weights and measures;

To provide for the punishment of counterfeiting the securities and current coin of the United States;

To establish post offices and post roads;

To promote the progress of science and useful arts, by securing for limited times to authors and inventors the exclusive right to their respective writings and discoveries;

To constitute tribunals inferior to the supreme court;

To define and punish piracies and felonies committed on the high seas and offences against the law of nations;

To declare war, grant letters of marque and reprisal, and make rules concerning captures on land and water;

To raise and support armies, but no appropriation of money to that use shall be for a longer term than two years;

To provide and maintain a navy;

To make rules for the government and regulation of the land and naval forces;

To provide for calling forth the militia to execute the laws of the Union, suppress insurrections and repel invasions;

To provide for organizing, arming and disciplining, the militia, and for governing such part of them as may be employed in the service of the United States, reserving to the States respectively, the appointment of the officers, and the authority of training the militia according to the discipline prescribed by Congress;

To exercise exclusive legislation in all cases whatsoever over such district (not exceeding ten miles square) as may, by cession of particular States, and the acceptance of Congress, become the seat of the government of the United States, and to exercise like authority over all places purchased by the consent of the Legislature of the State in which the same shall be, for the erection of forts, magazines, arsenals, dock-yards, and other needful buildings;—And

To make all laws which shall be necessary and proper for carrying into execution the foregoing powers, and all other powers vested by this constitution in the government of the United States, or in any department or officer thereof.

Section 9. The migration or importation of such persons as any of the States now existing shall think proper to admit, shall not be prohibited by the Congress prior to the year eighteen hundred and eight, but a tax or duty may be imposed on such importation, not exceeding ten dollars for each person.

The privilege of the writ of *Habeas Corpus* shall not be suspended, unless when in cases of rebellion or invasion the public safety may require it.

No bill of attainder or ex post facto law shall be passed.

No capitation, or other direct, tax shall be laid, unless in proportion to the census or enumeration herein before directed to be taken.

No tax or duty shall be laid on articles exported from any State.

No preference shall be given by any regulation of commerce or revenue to the ports of one State over those of another: nor shall vessels bound to, or from, one State, be obliged to enter, clear, or pay duties in another.

No money shall be drawn from the Treasury, but in consequence of appropriations made by law; and a regular statement and account of the receipts and expenditures of all public money shall be published from time to time.

No title of nobility shall be granted by the United States and no person holding any office of profit or trust under them, shall, without the consent of the Congress, accept of any present, emolument, office, or title, of any kind whatever, from any king, prince, or foreign State.

Section 10. No State shall enter into any treaty, alliance, or confederation; grant letters of marque and reprisal; coin money, emit bills of credit; make any thing but gold and silver coin a tender in payment of debts; pass any bill of attainder, ex post facto law; or law impairing the obligation of contracts; or grant any title of nobility.

No State shall, without the consent of the Congress, lay any imposts or duties on imports or exports, except what may be absolutely necessary for executing its inspection laws: and the net produce of all duties and imposts, laid by any State on imports or exports, shall be for the use of the Treasury of the United States; and all such laws shall be subject to the revision and control of the Congress.

No State shall, without the consent of Congress, lay any duty of tonnage, keep troops, or ships of war in time of peace, enter into any agreement or compact with another State, or with a foreign power, or engage in war, unless actually invaded, or in such imminent danger as will not admit of delay.

ARTICLE II

Section 1. The executive power shall be vested in a President of the United States of America. He shall hold his office during the term of four years, and, together with the Vice-President, chosen for the same term, be elected as follows:

Each State shall appoint, in such manner as the Legislature thereof may direct, a number of electors equal to the whole number of Senators and Representatives to which the State may be entitled in the Congress; but no Senator or Representative, or person holding an office of trust or profit under the United States, shall be appointed an elector.

The electors shall meet in their respective States, and vote by ballot for two persons, of whom one at least shall not be an inhabitant of the same State with themselves. And they shall make a list of all the persons voted for, and of the number of votes for each; which list they shall sign and certify, and transmit sealed to the seat of the government of the United States, directed to the President of the Senate. The President of the Senate shall, in the presence of the Senate and House of Representatives, open all the certificates, and the votes shall then be counted. The person having the greatest number of votes shall be the President, if such number be a majority of the whole number of electors appointed; and if there be more than one who have such majority, and have an equal number of votes, then the House of Representatives shall immediately choose by ballot one of them for President; and if no person have a majority, then from the five highest on the list the said House shall, in like manner, choose the President. But in choosing the President, the votes shall be taken by States, the representation from each State having one vote; a quorum for this purpose shall consist of a member or members from two-thirds of the States, and a majority of all the States shall be necessary to a choice. In every case, after the choice of the President, the person having the greatest number of votes of the electors shall be the Vice-President. But if there should remain two or more who have equal votes, the Senate shall choose from them by ballot the Vice-President.

The Congress may determine the time of choosing the electors, and the day on which they shall give their votes; which day shall be the same throughout the United States.

No person except a natural born citizen, or a citizen of the United States, at the time of the adoption of this constitution, shall be eligible to the office of President; neither shall any person be eligible to that office who shall not have attained to the age of thirty-five years, and been fourteen years a resident within the United States.

In case of the removal of the President from office, or of his death, resignation or inability to discharge the powers and duties of the said office, the same shall devolve on the Vice-President, and the Congress may by law provide for the case of removal, death, resignation or inability, both of the President and Vice-President, declaring what officer shall then act as President, and such officer shall act accordingly, until the disability be removed, or a President shall be elected.

The President shall, at stated times, receive for his services, a compensation, which shall neither be increased nor diminished during the period for which he shall have been elected, and he shall not receive within that period any other emolument from the United States, or any of them.

Before he enter on the execution of his office, he shall take the following oath or affirmation: *"I do solemnly swear (or affirm) that I will faithfully execute the office of President of the United States, and will, to the best of my ability, preserve, protect, and defend the Constitution of the United States."*

Section 2. The President shall be commander in chief of the army and navy of the United States, and of the militia of the several States, when called into the actual service of the United States; he may require the opinion, in writing, of the principal officer in each of the executive departments, upon any subject relating to the duties of their respective offices; and he shall have power to grant reprieves and pardons for offences against the United States, except in cases of impeachment.

He shall have power, by and with the advice and consent of the Senate, to make treaties, provided two-thirds of the Senators present concur; and he shall nominate, and by and with the advice and consent of the Senate, shall appoint ambassadors, other public ministers and consuls, judges of the supreme court, and all other officers of the United States, whose appointments are not herein otherwise provided for, and which shall be established by law: But the Congress may by law vest the appointment of such inferior officers as they think proper, in the President alone, in the courts of law, or in the heads of departments.

The President shall have power to fill up all vacancies that may happen during the recess of the Senate, by granting commissions which shall expire at the end of their next session.

Section 3. He shall from time to time give to the Congress information of the state of the Union, and recommend to their consideration such measures as he shall judge necessary and expedient; he may, on extraordinary occasions, convene both Houses, or either of them, and, in case of disagreement between them, with respect to the time of adjournment, he may adjourn them to such time as he shall think proper; he shall receive ambassadors and other public ministers; he shall take care that the laws be faithfully executed, and shall commission all the officers of the United States.

Section 4. The President, Vice-President and all civil officers of the United States, shall be removed from office on impeachment for, and conviction of, treason, bribery, or other high crimes and misdemeanors.

ARTICLE III

Section 1. The judicial power of the United States shall be vested in one Supreme Court, and in such inferior courts as the Congress may from time to time ordain and establish. The judges, both of the supreme and inferior courts, shall hold their offices during good behaviour, and shall, at stated times, receive for their services, a compensation, which shall not be diminished during their continuance in office.

Section 2. The judicial power shall extend to all cases in law and equity, arising under this constitution, the laws of the United States, and the treaties made, or which shall be made, under their authority; to all cases—affecting ambassadors, other public ministers, and consuls;—to all cases of admiralty and maritime jurisdiction;—to controversies to which the United States shall be a party;—to controversies between two or more States;—between a State and citizens of another State;—between citizens of different States;—between citizens of the same State, claiming lands under grants of different States, and between a State or the citizens thereof, and foreign States, citizens or subjects.

In all cases affecting ambassadors, other public ministers and consuls, and those in which a State shall be party, the supreme court shall have original jurisdiction. In all the other cases before-mentioned, the supreme court shall have appellate jurisdiction, both as to law and fact, with such exceptions, and under such regulations, as the Congress shall make.

The trial of all crimes, except in cases of impeachment, shall be by jury; and such trial shall be held in the State where the said crimes shall have been committed; but when not committed within any State, the trial shall be at such place or places as the Congress may by law have directed.

Section 3. Treason against the United States, shall consist only in levying war against them, or in adhering to their enemies, giving them aid and comfort. No person shall be convicted of treason, unless on the testimony of two witnesses to the same overt act, or on confession in open court.

The Congress shall have power to declare the punishment of treason, but no attainder of treason shall work corruption of blood, or forfeiture except during the life of the person attainted.

ARTICLE IV

Section 1. Full faith and credit shall be given in each State to the public acts, records, and judicial proceedings of every other State. And the Congress may by general laws prescribe the manner in which such acts, records, and proceedings shall be proved, and the effect thereof.

Section 2. The citizens of each State shall be entitled to all the privileges and immunities of citizens in the several States.

A person charged in any State with treason, felony, or other crime, who shall flee from justice, and be found in another State, shall on demand of the executive authority of the State from which he fled, be delivered up, to be removed to the State having jurisdiction of the crime.

No person held to service or labor in one State, under the laws thereof, escaping into another, shall, in consequence of any law or regulation therein, be discharged from such service or labor, but shall be delivered up on claim of the party to whom such service or labor may be due.

Section 3. New States may be admitted by the Congress into this Union; but no new State shall be formed or erected within the jurisdiction of any other State; nor any State be formed by the junction of two or more States, or parts of States, without the consent of the Legislature of the States concerned as well as of the Congress.

The Congress shall have power to dispose of and make all needful rules and regulations respecting the territory or other property belonging to the United States; and nothing in this constitution shall be so construed as to prejudice any claims of the United States, or of any particular State.

Section 4. The United States shall guaranty to every State in this Union a republican form of government, and shall protect each of them against invasion; and on application of the legislature, or of the executive (when the legislature cannot be convened) against domestic violence.

ARTICLE V

The Congress, whenever two-thirds of both Houses shall deem it necessary, shall propose amendments to this constitution, or, on the application of the legislatures of two-thirds of the several States, shall call a convention for proposing amendments, which in either case, shall be valid to all intents and purposes, as part of this constitution, when ratified by the legislatures of three-fourths of the several States, or by conventions in three-fourths thereof, as the one or the other mode of ratification may be proposed by the Congress; provided, that no amendment, which may be made prior to the year one thousand eight hundred and eight, shall in any manner affect the first and fourth clauses in the ninth section of the first article; and that no State, without its consent, shall be deprived of its equal suffrage in the Senate.

ARTICLE VI

All debts contracted and engagements entered into, before the adoption of this constitution, shall be as valid against the United States under this constitution as under the confederation.

This constitution, and the laws of the United States which shall be made in pursuance thereof; and all treaties made, or which shall be made, under the authority of the United States, shall be the supreme law of the land; and the judges in every state shall be bound thereby, any thing in the constitution or laws of any State to the contrary notwithstanding.

The Senators and Representatives before mentioned, and the members of the several State legislatures, and all executive and judicial officers, both of the United States and of the several States shall be bound by oath or affirmation, to support this constitution: but no religious test shall ever be required as a qualification to any office or public trust under the United States.

ARTICLE VII

The ratification of the conventions of nine states, shall be sufficient for the establishment of this constitution between the States so ratifying the same.

Done in convention by the unanimous consent of the States present the seventeenth day of September in the year of our Lord one thousand seven hundred and eighty-seven and of the independence of the United States of America the twelfth.

THE BILL OF RIGHTS: 1791

AMENDMENTS[2]

ARTICLE I

Congress shall make no law respecting an establishment of religion, or prohibiting the free exercise thereof; or abridging the freedom of speech, or of the press; or the right of the people peaceably to assemble, and to petition the government for a redress of grievances.

ARTICLE II

A well-regulated militia being necessary to the security of a free State, the right of the people to keep and bear arms shall not be infringed.

ARTICLE III

No soldier shall, in time of peace, be quartered in any house without the consent of the owner, nor in time of war but in a manner to be prescribed by law.

ARTICLE IV

The right of the people to be secure in their persons, houses, papers, and effects, against unreasonable searches and seizures, shall not be violated; and no warrants shall issue but upon probable cause, supported by oath or affirmation, and particularly describing the place to be searched and the persons or things to be seized.

ARTICLE V

No person shall be held to answer for a capital or otherwise infamous crime, unless on a presentment or indictment of a grand jury, except in cases arising in the land or naval forces, or in the militia when in actual service, in time of war or public danger; nor shall any person be subject, for the same offence, to be twice put in jeopardy of life or limb, nor shall be compelled in any criminal case to be a witness against himself; nor be deprived of life, liberty, or property, without due process of law; nor shall private property be taken for public use without just compensation.

---

[2] The first ten Articles declared in force December 15, 1791.

ARTICLE VI

In all criminal prosecutions the accused shall enjoy the right to a speedy and public trial, by an impartial jury of the State and district wherein the crime shall have been committed, which district shall have been previously ascertained by law; and to be informed of the nature and cause of the accusation; to be confronted with the witnesses against him; to have compulsory process for obtaining witnesses in his favor; and to have the assistance of counsel for his defence.

ARTICLE VII

In suits at common law, where the value in controversy shall exceed twenty dollars, the right of trial by jury shall be preserved; and no fact tried by a jury shall be otherwise reëxamined in any court of the United States, than according to the rules of the common law.

ARTICLE VIII

Excessive bail shall not be required, nor excessive fines imposed, nor cruel and unusual punishments inflicted.

ARTICLE IX

The enumeration in the Constitution of certain rights shall not be construed to deny or disparage others retained by the people.

ARTICLE X

The powers not delegated to the United States by the Constitution, nor prohibited by it to the States, are reserved to the States respectively, or to the people.

LATER CONSTITUTIONAL AMENDMENTS

ARTICLE XI[3]

The judicial power of the United States shall not be construed to extend to any suit in law or equity commenced or prosecuted against any one of the United States by citizens of another state, or by citizens or subjects of any foreign State.

ARTICLE XII[4]

The electors shall meet in their respective States, and vote by ballot for President and Vice-President, one of whom, at least, shall not be an inhabitant of the same State with themselves; they shall name in their ballots the person voted for as President, and in distinct ballots the person voted for as Vice-President; and they shall make distinct lists of all persons voted for as President, and of all persons voted for as Vice-President, and of the number of votes for each; which lists they shall sign and certify, and transmit sealed to the seat of the government of the United States, directed to the President of the Senate; the President of the Senate shall, in the presence of the Senate and House of Representatives, open all the certificates, and the votes shall then be counted: the person having the greatest number of votes for President shall be the President, if such number be a majority of the whole number of electors appointed; and if no person have such majority, then, from the persons having the highest numbers, not exceeding three, on the list of those voted for as President, the House of Representatives shall choose, immediately, by ballot, the President. But, in choosing the President, the votes shall be taken by States, the representation from each State having one vote; a quorum for this purpose shall consist of a member or members from two-thirds of the States, and a majority of all the States shall be necessary to a choice. And if the House of Representatives shall not choose a President whenever the right of choice shall devolve upon them, before the fourth day of March next following, then the Vice-President shall act as President, as in the case of the death or other constitutional disability of the President. The person having the greatest number of votes as Vice-President shall be the Vice-President, if such number be a majority of the whole number of electors appointed; and if no person have a majority, then, from the two highest numbers on the list, the Senate shall choose the Vice-President: a quorum for the purpose shall consist of two-thirds of the whole number of Senators, and a majority of the whole number shall be necessary to a choice. But no person constitutionally ineligible to the office of President, shall be eligible to that of Vice-President of the United States.

[3] January 8, 1798.
[4] September 25, 1804.

ARTICLE XIII[5]

Section 1. Neither slavery nor involuntary servitude, except as a punishment for crime whereof the party shall have been duly convicted, shall exist within the United States, or any place subject to their jurisdiction.

Section 2. Congress shall have power to enforce this article by appropriate legislation.

ARTICLE XIV[6]

Section 1. All persons born or naturalized in the United States, and subject to the jurisdiction thereof, are citizens of the United States and of the State wherein they reside. No State shall make or enforce any law which shall abridge the privileges or immunities of citizens of the United States; nor shall any State deprive any person of life, liberty, or property, without due process of law; nor deny to any person within its jurisdiction the equal protection of the laws.

Section 2. Representatives shall be apportioned among the several States according to their respective numbers, counting the whole number of persons in each State, excluding Indians not taxed. But when the right to vote at any election for the choice of electors for President and Vice President of the United States, Representatives in Congress, the Executive and Judicial officers of a State, or the members of the Legislature thereof, is denied to any of the male inhabitants of such State, being twenty-one years of age, and citizens of the United States, or in any way abridged, except for participation in rebellion, or other crime, the basis of representation therein shall be reduced in the proportion which the number of such male citizens shall bear to the whole number of male citizens twenty-one years of age in such State.

Section 3. No person shall be a Senator or Representative in Congress, or elector of President and Vice President, or hold any office, civil or military, under the United States, or under any State, who, having previously taken an oath, as a member of Congress, or as an officer of the United States, or as a member of any State legislature, or as an executive or judicial officer of any State, to support the Constitution of the United States, shall have engaged in insurrection or rebellion against the same, or given aid or comfort to the enemies thereof. But Congress may by a vote of two-thirds of each House, remove such disability.

Section 4. The validity of the public debt of the United States, authorized by law, including debts incurred for payment of pensions and bounties for services in suppressing insurrection or rebellion, shall not be questioned. But neither the United States nor any State shall assume or pay any debt or obligation incurred in aid of insurrection or rebellion against the United States, or any claim for the loss or emancipation of any slave; but all such debts, obligations and claims shall be held illegal and void.

Section 5. The Congress shall have power to enforce, by appropriate legislation, the provisions of this article.

[5] December 18, 1865.
[6] July 23, 1868.

ARTICLE XV[7]

Section 1. The right of citizens of the United States to vote shall not be denied or abridged by the United States or by any State on account of race, color, or previous condition of servitude.

Section 2. The Congress shall have power to enforce this article by appropriate legislation.

ARTICLE XVI[8]

The Congress shall have power to lay and collect taxes on incomes, from whatever source derived, without apportionment among the several States, and without regard to any census or enumeration.

ARTICLE XVII[9]

The Senate of the United States shall be composed of two senators from each State, elected by the people thereof, for six years; and each Senator shall have one vote. The electors in each State shall have the qualifications requisite for electors of the most numerous branch of the State legislature.

When vacancies happen in the representation of any State in the Senate, the executive authority of such State shall issue writs of election to fill such vacancies: *Provided,* That the legislature of any State may empower the executive thereof to make temporary appointments until the people fill the vacancies by election as the legislature may direct.

This amendment shall not be so construed as to affect the election or term of any Senator chosen before it becomes valid as part of the Constitution.

ARTICLE XVIII[10]

Section 1. After one year from the ratification of this article the manufacture, sale, or transportation of intoxicating liquors within, the importation thereof into, or the exportation thereof from the United States and all territory subject to the jurisdiction thereof for beverage purposes is hereby prohibited.

Section 2. The Congress and the several States shall have concurrent power to enforce this article by appropriate legislation.

This article shall be inoperative unless it shall have been ratified as an amendment to the Constitution by the legislatures of the several States, as provided in the Constitution, within seven years from the date of the submission hereof to the States by the Congress.

ARTICLE XIX[11]

The right of citizens of the United States to vote shall not be denied or abridged by the United States or by any State on account of sex.

Congress shall have power to enforce this article by appropriate legislation.

---

[7] March 30, 1870.
[8] February 25, 1913.
[9] May 31, 1913.
[10] January 29, 1919.
[11] August 26, 1920.

ARTICLE XX[12]

Section 1. The terms of the President and Vice-President shall end at noon on the 20th day of January, and the terms of Senators and Representatives at noon on the 3d day of January, of the years in which such terms would have ended if this article had not been ratified; and the terms of their successors shall then begin.

Section 2. The Congress shall assemble at least once in every year, and such meeting shall begin at noon on the 3d day of January, unless they shall by law appoint a different day.

Section 3. If, at the time fixed for the beginning of the term of the President, the President elect shall have died, the Vice-President elect shall become President. If a President shall not have been chosen before the time fixed for the beginning of his term, or if the President elect shall have failed to qualify, then the Vice-President elect shall act as President until a President shall have qualified; and the Congress may by law provide for the case wherein neither a President elect nor a Vice-President elect shall have qualified, declaring who shall then act as President, or the manner in which one who is to act shall be selected, and such person shall act accordingly until a President or Vice-President shall have qualified.

Section 4. The Congress may by law provide for the case of the death of any of the persons from whom the House of Representatives may choose a President whenever the right of choice shall have devolved upon them, and for the case of the death of any of the persons from whom the Senate may choose a Vice-President whenever the right of choice shall have devolved upon them.

Section 5. Sections 1 and 2 shall take effect on the 15th day of October following the ratification of this article.

Section 6. This article shall be inoperative unless it shall have been ratified as an amendment to the Constitution by the legislatures of three-fourths of the several States within seven years from the date of its submission.

ARTICLE XXI[13]

Section 1. The eighteenth article of amendment to the Constitution of the United States is hereby repealed.

Section 2. The transportation or importation into any State, Territory or possession of the United States for delivery or use therein of intoxicating liquors, in violation of the laws thereof, is hereby prohibited.

Section 3. This article shall be inoperative unless it shall have been ratified as an amendment to the Constitution by conventions in the several States, as provided in the Constitution, within seven years from the date of the submission hereof to the States by the Congress.

---

[12] February 6, 1933.
[13] December 5, 1933.

PRESIDENTIAL RECORD, WITH VOTE

Election	Candidates	Parties	Popular Vote	Electoral Vote
1789	GEORGE WASHINGTON John Adams	Federalist Federalist		69 34[1]
1792	GEORGE WASHINGTON John Adams George Clinton	Federalist Federalist Jeffersonian		132 77[1] 50[1]
1796	JOHN ADAMS Thomas Jefferson Thomas Pinckney Aaron Burr	Federalist Jeffersonian Federalist Jeffersonian		71 68 59[1] 30[1]
1800[2]	THOMAS JEFFERSON Aaron Burr John Adams C. C. Pinckney	Jeffersonian Jeffersonian Federalist Federalist		73 73[1] 65 64[1]
1804	THOMAS JEFFERSON C. C. Pinckney	Jeffersonian Federalist		162 14
1808	JAMES MADISON C. C. Pinckney George Clinton	Jeffersonian Federalist Jeffersonian		122 47 6
1812	JAMES MADISON De Witt Clinton	Jeffersonian Federalist		128 89
1816	JAMES MONROE Rufus King	Jeffersonian Federalist		183 34
1820	JAMES MONROE John Quincy Adams	Jeffersonian Jeffersonian		231 1

[1] Candidates for the vice-presidency.
[2] Final election in House of Representatives.

SECRETARIES OF STATE AND SUPREME COURT JUSTICES

Secretaries of State	Supreme Court Justices[3]	Party Affiliation of Justices
Thomas Jefferson, 1789–1794	JOHN JAY, 1789–1795 John Rutledge, 1789–1791 William Cushing, 1789–1810 James Wilson, 1789–1798 John Blair, 1789–1796 Robert Harrison, 1789–1790 James Iredell, 1790–1799 Thomas Johnson, 1791–1793	Federalist Federalist Federalist Federalist Federalist ? Federalist Federalist
Edmund Randolph, 1794–1795 Thomas Pickering, 1795–1797	William Paterson, 1793–1806 JOHN RUTLEDGE, 1795–1795 Samuel Chase, 1796–1811 OLIVER ELLSWORTH, 1796–1799	Federalist Federalist Federalist Federalist
Thomas Pickering, 1797–1800 John Marshall, 1800–1801	Bushrod Washington, 1798–1829 Alfred Moore, 1799–1804 JOHN MARSHALL, 1801–1835	Federalist Federalist Federalist
James Madison, 1801–1809	William Johnson, 1804–1834	Jeffersonian
James Madison, 1801–1809	Brockholst Livingston 1806–1823 Thomas Todd, 1807–1826	? Federalist
Robert Smith, 1809–1811 James Monroe, 1811–1817	Joseph Story, 1811–1845 Gabriel Duval, 1811–1836	Federalist ?
James Monroe, 1811–1817		
John Quincy Adams, 1817–1825		
John Quincy Adams, 1817–1825	Smith Thompson, 1823–1843	Jeffersonian

[3] Justices are listed in order of appointment. Capitalized names indicate Chief Justices.

Election	Candidates	Parties	Popular Vote	Electoral Vote
1824[2]	JOHN QUINCY ADAMS	Nat. Republican	108,740	84
	Andrew Jackson	Nat. Republican	153,544	99
	William H. Crawford	Nat. Republican	46,618	41
	Henry Clay	Nat. Republican	47,136	37
1828	ANDREW JACKSON	Democrat	647,231	178
	John Quincy Adams	Nat. Republican	509,097	83
1832	ANDREW JACKSON	Democrat	687,502	219
	Henry Clay	Whig	530,189	49
	John Floyd	Whig	} 33,108	11
	William Wirt	Anti-Mason		7
1836	MARTIN VAN BUREN	Democrat	761,549	170
	W. H. Harrison	Whig		73
	Hugh L. White	Whig	} 736,656	26
	Daniel Webster	Whig		14
	W. P. Mangum	Whig		11
1840	WILLIAM H. HARRISON	Whig	1,275,016	234
	Martin Van Buren	Democrat	1,129,102	60
	J. G. Birney	Liberty	7,069	—
1841	JOHN TYLER	Whig		
1844	JAMES K. POLK	Democrat	1,337,243	170
	Henry Clay	Whig	1,299,062	105
	J. G. Birney	Liberty	62,300	—
1848	ZACHARY TAYLOR	Whig	1,360,099	163
	Lewis Cass	Democrat	1,220,544	127
	Martin Van Buren	Free Soil	291,263	—
1849	MILLARD FILLMORE	Whig		
1852	FRANKLIN PIERCE	Democrat	1,601,274	254
	Winfield Scott	Whig	1,386,580	42
	John P. Hale	Free Soil	155,825	—
1856	JAMES BUCHANAN	Democrat	1,838,169	174
	John C. Frémont	Republican	1,341,264	114
	Millard Fillmore	American	874,534	8

Secretaries of State	Supreme Court Justices	Party Affiliation of Justices
Henry Clay, 1825–1829	Robert Trimble, 1826–1828	Federalist
Martin Van Buren, 1829–1831 Edward Livingston, 1831–1833	John McLean, 1829–1861 Henry Baldwin, 1830–1844	Democrat Democrat
Louis McLane, 1833–1834 John Forsyth, 1834–1837	James M. Wayne, 1835–1867 ROGER B. TANEY, 1836–1864 Philip P. Barbour, 1836–1841 John Catron, 1837–1865	Democrat Whig Democrat Democrat
John Forsyth, 1837–1841	John McKinley, 1837–1852 Peter V. Daniel, 1841–1860	Democrat Democrat
Daniel Webster, 1841–1843 Hugh S. Legare, 1843 Abel P. Upshur, 1843–1844 John C. Calhoun, 1844–1845	Samuel Nelson, 1845–1872	Democrat
James Buchanan, 1845–1849	Levi Woodbury, 1845–1851 Robert Grier, 1846–1870	Democrat ?
John M. Clayton, 1849–1850 Daniel Webster, 1850-1852 Edward Everett, 1852–1853	Benjamin Curtis, 1851–1857	Whig
W. L. Marcy, 1853–1857	John A. Campbell, 1853–1861	Democrat
Lewis Cass, 1857–1860 J. S. Black, 1860–1861	Nathan Clifford, 1858–1881	Democrat

Election	Candidates	Parties	Popular Vote	Electoral Vote
1860	ABRAHAM LINCOLN	Republican	1,866,452	180
	Stephen A. Douglas	Democrat	1,375,157	12
	John C. Breckinridge	Democrat	847,953	72
	John Bell	Union	590,631	39
1864	ABRAHAM LINCOLN	Republican	2,213,665	212
	George McClellan	Democrat	1,802,237	21
1865	ANDREW JOHNSON	Republican		
1868	ULYSSES S. GRANT	Republican	3,012,833	214
	Horatio Seymour	Democrat	2,703,249	80
1872	ULYSSES S. GRANT	Republican	3,597,132	286
	Horace Greeley	Democrat	2,834,125	66
	Charles O'Conor	Ind. Democrat	29,489	—
	James Black	Prohibition	5,608	—
1876	RUTHERFORD B. HAYES	Republican	4,033,768	185
	Samuel J. Tilden	Democrat	4,300,590	184
	Peter Cooper	Greenback	81,740	—
	Green C. Smith	Prohibition	9,522	—
1880	JAMES A. GARFIELD	Republican	4,449,053	214
	William Hancock	Democrat	4,442,035	155
	James B. Weaver	Greenback	307,306	—
	Neal Dow	Prohibition	10,487	—
1881	CHESTER ARTHUR	Republican		
1884	GROVER CLEVELAND	Democrat	4,911,017	219
	James G. Blaine	Republican	4,848,334	182
	Benjamin F. Butler	Greenback	133,825	—
	John St. John	Prohibition	151,809	—
1888	BENJAMIN HARRISON	Republican	5,444,337	233
	Grover Cleveland	Democrat	5,540,050	168
	Alson J. Streeter	Union Labor	146,897	—
	Clinton B. Fisk	Prohibition	250,125	—
1892	GROVER CLEVELAND	Democrat	5,554,414	277
	Benjamin Harrison	Republican	5,190,802	145
	James B. Weaver	People's	1,027,329	22
	John Bidwell	Prohibition	271,058	—
1896	WILLIAM MCKINLEY	Republican	7,035,638	271
	William J. Bryan	Democrat	6,467,946	176
	Joshua Levering	Prohibition	141,676	—

SECRETARIES OF STATE AND SUPREME COURT
JUSTICES *(Cont.)*

Secretaries of State	Supreme Court Justices	Party Affiliation of Justices
William H. Seward, 1861–1869	Noah H. Swayne, 1862–1881 Samuel F. Miller, 1862–1890 David Davis, 1862–1877 Stephen J. Field, 1863–1897 SALMON P. CHASE, 1864–1873	Democrat Republican Republican Republican Republican
William H. Seward, 1861–1869		
E. B. Washburne, 1869 Hamilton Fish, 1869–1877	William Strong, 1870–1880 Joseph P. Bradley, 1870–1892 Ward Hunt, 1872–1882	Republican Republican Republican
Hamilton Fish, 1869–1877	MORRISON R. WAITE, 1874–1888	Republican
W. M. Evarts, 1877–1881	John M. Harlan, 1877–1911 William B. Woods, 1880–1887 Stanley Matthews, 1881–1889	Republican Republican Republican
James G. Blaine, 1881 F. T. Frelinghuysen, 1881–1885	Horace Gray, 1881–1902 Samuel Blatchford, 1882–1893	Republican ?
Thomas F. Bayard, 1885–1889	Lucius Lamar, 1888–1893 MELVILLE W. FULLER, 1888–1910	Democrat Democrat
James G. Blaine, 1889–1892 John W. Foster, 1892–1893	David J. Brewer, 1889–1910 Henry B. Brown, 1890–1906 George Shiras, Jr. 1892–1903 Howell Jackson, 1893–1895	Republican ? Republican Democrat
W. Q. Gresham, 1893–1895 Richard Olney, 1895–1897	Edward D. White, 1894–1910 Rufus Peckham, 1895–1910	Democrat Democrat
John Sherman, 1897 William R. Day, 1897–1898 John Hay, 1898–1901	Joseph McKenna, 1898–1925	Republican

803

Election	Candidates	Parties	Popular Vote	Electoral Vote
1900	WILLIAM MCKINLEY	Republican	7,219,530	292
	William J. Bryan	Democrat	6,358,071	155
	Eugene V. Debs	Socialist	94,768	—
	Wharton Barker	People's	50,232	—
	Joseph Malloney	Socialist-Labor	32,751	—
	Seth Ellis	Union-Reform	5,098	—
1901	THEODORE ROOSEVELT	Republican		
1904	THEODORE ROOSEVELT	Republican	7,628,834	336
	Alton B. Parker	Democrat	5,084,401	140
	Eugene V. Debs	Socialist	402,460	—
	Thomas E. Watson	People's	114,753	—
	Silas C. Swallow	Prohibition	259,257	—
	Charles E. Corregan	Socialist-Labor	33,724	—
	Austin Holcomb	Continental	830	—
1908	WILLIAM H. TAFT	Republican	7,679,006	321
	William J. Bryan	Democrat	6,409,106	162
	Eugene V. Debs	Socialist	420,820	—
	Eugene Chafin	Prohibition	259,683	—
	Thomas Hisgen	Independence	83,562	—
	Thomas E. Watson	People's	28,131	—
	August Gilhaus	Socialist-Labor	13,825	—
	Daniel Turney	United-Christian	461	
1912	WOODROW WILSON	Democrat	6,286,214	435
	Theodore Roosevelt	Progressive	4,126,020	88
	William H. Taft	Republican	3,483,922	8
	Eugene V. Debs	Socialist	897,011	—
	Eugene Chafin	Prohibition	208,923	—
	Arthur Reimer	Socialist-Labor	29,079	—
1916	WOODROW WILSON	Democrat	9,129,606	277
	Charles E. Hughes	Republican	8,538,221	254
	Allan Bensen	Socialist	585,113	—
	J. Frank Hanly	Prohibition	220,506	—
	Arthur Reimer	Socialist-Labor	13,403	—
1920	WARREN G. HARDING	Republican	16,152,200	404
	James M. Cox	Democrat	9,147,353	127
	Eugene V. Debs	Socialist	919,799	—
	Aaron S. Watkins	Prohibition	189,408	—
	William W. Cox	Socialist-Labor	31,175	—
	Parley Christensen	Farmer-Labor	26,541	—
	Robert Macauley	Single Tax	5,837	—
1923	CALVIN COOLIDGE	Republican		

SECRETARIES OF STATE AND SUPREME COURT
JUSTICES *(Cont.)*

Secretaries of State	Supreme Court Justices	Party Affiliation of Justices
John Hay, 1901–1905	Oliver W. Holmes, 1902–1932 William R. Day, 1903–1922	Independent Republican
Elihu Root, 1905–1909 Robert Bacon, 1909	William H. Moody, 1906 1910	Republican
P. C. Knox, 1909–1913	EDWARD D. WHITE, 1910–1921 Horace Lurton, 1910–1914 Charles E. Hughes, 1910–1916 W. Van Devanter, 1911–1937 Joseph Lamar, 1911–1916 Mahlon Pitney, 1912–1922	Democrat Democrat Republican Republican Democrat Republican
William J. Bryan, 1913–1915 Robert Lansing, 1915–1920	J. C. McReynolds, 1914–1941 Louis D. Brandeis, 1916–1939 John H. Clarke, 1916–1922	Democrat Independent ?
Robert Lansing, 1915–1920 Bainbridge Colby, 1920–1921		
Charles E. Hughes, 1921–1925	WILLIAM H. TAFT, 1921–1930 George Sutherland, 1922–1938 Pierce Butler, 1922–1939 Edward T. Sanford, 1923–1930 Harlan F. Stone, 1925–1941	Republican Republican Republican Republican Republican

Election	Candidates	Parties	Popular Vote	Electoral Vote
1924	CALVIN COOLIDGE	Republican	15,725,016	382
	John W. Davis	Democrat	8,385,586	136
	Robert La Follette	Prog. Socialist	4,822,856	13
	H. P. Faris	Prohibition	57,551	—
	Frank T. Johns	Socialist-Labor	38,958	—
	William Z. Foster	Workers'	33,361	—
	Gilbert O. Nations	American	23,867	—
	William Wallace	Commonwealth-Land	2,778	—
1928	HERBERT HOOVER	Republican	21,392,190	444
	Alfred E. Smith	Democrat	15,016,443	87
	Norman Thomas	Socialist	267,420	—
	William Z. Foster	Workers'	48,770	—
	Verne L. Reynolds	Socialist-Labor	21,603	—
	William Varney	Prohibition	20,106	—
1932	FRANKLIN D. ROOSEVELT	Democrat	22,821,857	472
	Herbert Hoover	Republican	15,761,841	59
	Norman Thomas	Socialist	884,781	—
	William Z. Foster	Communist	102,991	—
	William Upshaw	Prohibition	81,869	—
	W. H. Harvey	Liberty	53,425	—
	Verne L. Reynolds	Socialist-Labor	33,276	—
	Jacob Coxey	Farmer-Labor	7,309	—
1936	FRANKLIN D. ROOSEVELT	Democrat	27,751,612	532
	Alfred M. Landon	Republican	16,681,913	8
	William Lemke	Union	891,858	—
	Norman Thomas	Socialist	187,342	—
	Earl Browder	Communist	80,181	—
	D. Leigh Colvin	Prohibition	37,609	—
	J. W. Aiken	Socialist-Labor	12,729	
1940	FRANKLIN D. ROOSEVELT	Democrat	27,243,466	449
	Wendell Willkie	Republican	22,304,755	82
	Norman Thomas	Socialist	112,274	—
	Roger Babson	Prohibition	57,812	—
	Earl Browder	Communist	46,251	—
	John W. Aiken	Socialist-Labor	18,677	—
1944	FRANKLIN D. ROOSEVELT	Democrat	25,602,505	432
	Thomas E. Dewey	Republican	22,006,278	99
	Norman Thomas	Socialist	80,518	—
	Claud A. Watson	Prohibition	74,758	—
	Earl Browder	Communist	—	—
	Edward A. Teichart	Socialist-Labor	45,336	—
1945	HARRY S. TRUMAN	Democrat		

SECRETARIES OF STATE AND SUPREME COURT
JUSTICES *(Concl.)*

Secretaries of State	Supreme Court Justices	Party Affiliation of Justices
Frank B. Kellogg, 1925–1929		
Henry L. Stimson, 1929–1933	CHARLES E. HUGHES, 1930–1941 Owen Roberts, 1930–1945 Benjamin Cardozo, 1932–1938	Republican Republican ?
Cordell Hull, 1933–1937		
Cordell Hull, 1937–1944	Hugo L. Black, 1937— Stanley Reed, 1938— Felix Frankfurter, 1939— William O. Douglas, 1939— Frank Murphy, 1940—	Democrat Democrat ? Democrat Democrat
Edward Stettinius, Jr., 1944–1945	HARLAN F. STONE, 1941–1946 James F. Byrnes, 1941–1945 Robert H. Jackson, 1941— Wiley B. Rutledge, 1943—	Republican Democrat Democrat Democrat
James F. Byrnes, 1945–1947 George C. Marshall, 1947—	Harold H. Burton, 1945— FREDERICK M. VINSON, 1946—	Republican Democrat

POPULATION GROWTH BY DECADES

Year	Immigration during Decade	Total Population
1790		3,929,214
1800		5,308,483
1810		7,239,881
1820		9,638,453
1830	143,439	12,866,020
1840	599,125	17,069,453
1850	1,713,251	23,191,876
1860	2,598,214	31,443,321
1870	2,314,824	38,558,371
1880	2,812,191	50,155,783
1890	5,246,613	62,947,714
1900	3,687,564	75,994,575
1910	8,795,386	91,972,266
1920	5,735,811	105,710,620
1930	4,107,209	122,775,046
1940	529,131	131,669,275

ADMISSION OF STATES TO THE UNION

State	Entered Union	State	Entered Union
Delaware	1787	Arkansas	1836
New Jersey	1787	Michigan	1837
Pennsylvania	1787	Florida	1845
Connecticut	1788	Texas	1845
Georgia	1788	Iowa	1846
Maryland	1788	Wisconsin	1848
Massachusetts	1788	California	1850
New Hampshire	1788	Minnesota	1858
New York	1788	Oregon	1859
South Carolina	1788	Kansas	1861
Virginia	1788	West Virginia	1863
North Carolina	1789	Nevada	1864
Rhode Island	1790	Nebraska	1867
Vermont	1791	Colorado	1876
Kentucky	1792	Montana	1889
Tennessee	1796	North Dakota	1889
Ohio	1803	South Dakota	1889
Louisiana	1812	Washington	1889
Indiana	1816	Idaho	1890
Mississippi	1817	Wyoming	1890
Illinois	1818	Utah	1896
Alabama	1819	Oklahoma	1907
Maine	1820	Arizona	1912
Missouri	1821	New Mexico	1912

FISCAL RECORD OF THE UNITED STATES

Year	Receipts		Expenditures		Public Debt	
	Total	Per Capita	Total	Per Capita	Total	Per Capita
1800	$10,848,749	$2.04	$10,786,075	$2.03	$82,976,204	$15.63
1810	9,384,215	1.30	8,156,510	1.13	53,173,217	7.34
1820	17,880,670	1.86	18,260,627	1.89	91,015,566	9.44
1830	24,844,116	1.93	15,143,066	1.18	48,565,406	3.77
1840	19,480,115	1.14	24,317,579	1.42	3,573,343	.21
1850	43,603,439	1.87	39,543,492	1.70	63,452,773	2.74
1860	56,064,608	1.78	63,130,598	2.00	59,964,402	1.91
1870	411,255,477	10.64	309,653,561	8.01	2,436,453,269	63.19
1880	333,526,611	6.64	267,642,958	5.32	2,090,908,872	41.69
1890	403,080,984	6.39	318,040,711	5.04	1,122,396,584	17.92
1900	567,240,852	7.45	520,860,847	6.84	1,263,416,913	16.56
1910	675,511,715	7.32	693,617,065	7.52	1,146,939,969	12.69
1915	697,910,827	7.03	760,586,802	7.66	1,191,264,068	11.83
1920	6,694,565,389	62.83	6,482,090,191	60.84	24,297,918,412	228.32
1925	3,780,148,685	32.91	3,529,643,446	30.73	20,516,272,174	177.82
1930	4,177,941,702	33.91	3,994,152,487	32.42	16,185,308,299	131.38
1931	3,189,638,632	25.70	4,091,597,712	32.99	16,801,485,143	135.42
1932	2,005,725,437	16.06	5,153,644,895	41.28	19,487,009,766	156.12
1933	2,079,696,742	16.54	5,142,953,627	40.91	22,538,672,164	179.32
1934	3,115,554,050	24.64	7,105,050,085	56.19	27,053,141,414	213.75
1935	3,790,045,732	29.88	7,375,825,166	58.00	28,700,892,624	225.71
1936	4,115,956,615	32.17	8,879,798,258	69.41	33,778,543,494	263.01
1937	5,293,840,237	40.93	8,105,158,547	62.69	36,424,613,732	281.63
1938	6,241,661,227	47.89	7,691,278,108	59.70	37,164,740,315	285.41
1939	5,667,823,625	43.21	9,268,338,030	70.65	40,439,532,411	308.29
1940	5,924,836,402	44.09	9,665,085,539	73.16	42,967,531,037	325.19
1941	7,607,211,852	57.29	12,774,890,324	96.21	48,961,443,536	368.74
1942	12,799,060,621	95.25	32,471,307,398	241.80	72,422,445,116	538.56
1943	22,281,642,709	163.25	73,182,348,641	572.83	136,696,090,330	1008.34
1944	44,148,926,968	319.92	93,743,514,864	679.29	201,003,387,221	1448.56
1945	46,456,554,580	332.78	100,404,594,685	719.25	258,682,187,410	1853.01

Political	Social	Intellectual & Technological
1066—William the Conqueror invades England		
	1081 — Commercial privileges in Eastern Europe granted by Pope to Venetian traders	1079–1142—Peter Abelard
	1086—Compilation of English Domesday Book, an inventory of landed property	
1096–1270—The Crusades, leading to sacking of Jerusalem, 1099, and capture of Constantinople, 1204		
	1163–1304 — Notre Dame, Paris, built	
	1167–1168 — Oxford University	
		1176–1209—London Bridge built; stood until 1832
		1200–1300—Introduction of compass
1215 — King John seals Magna Carta at Runnymede		
		1225–1274—Thomas Aquinas
	1245–1300 — Development of jury trial in England	
	1255–1295 — Journeys of Polo brothers of Venice to Asia	
1258—English barons extort provisions of Oxford, promising three parliaments yearly, Committee for Political Affairs		
1265—Summoning of first Commons		1265–1321—Dante
1268—Kublai Khan establishes reign		
	1270—Beginnings of Portuguese exploration of west coast of Africa	
		1280—Glass mirror invented
	1290-1340—Opening of trade between Europe and eastern Asia	

Political	Social	Intellectual & Technological
		1300–1400—Development of balance clock
1302—First Meeting of French Estates-General		
		1304–1374—Petrarch
		1313—Berthold Schwarz of Germany invents gunpowder
		1314–1321—Dante writes *Divina Commedia*
1322—Parliament enacts legislation requiring consent of King and Parliament		
1337—Outbreak of Hundred Years' War		
1339–1349 — Division of Parliament and emergence of Commons as separate house		
1344—Formation of Hanseatic League		
	1347–1351—Black Death devastates Europe	
		1348–1353—Boccaccio writes *Decameron*
1368—Overthrow of Mongol Dominion in China and establishment of Ming Dynasty		
1376—English Commons claims right of impeachment		
1385—Portugal established as national kingdom		
	1387—Milan Cathedral begun	1387–1400—Geoffrey Chaucer's *Canterbury Tales*
		1400–1492—Development of round-hulled sailing ships revolutionizes water transport
	1407—Charter granted Merchant Adventurers by Henry IV of England	
	St. George's Bank, Genoa, founded	
1409–1449—Conciliar Movement		
	1418—Prince Henry the Navigator establishes navigation school	

Political	Social	Intellectual & Technological
	1430–1460—Prince Henry seaches for all-water route to East	
	1445—Portuguese round Cape Verde and begin trade with West Africa	
	Charles VII creates standing army for France	
	1450—John Gutenberg of Mainz employs movable type for printing	1450—Pope Nicholas V establishes Vatican Library
	1450–1700—Commercial Revolution	
1453—Capture of Constantinople by Turks		1452–1519—Leonardo da Vinci
1455–1485—Wars of the Roses		
1469—Unity of Spain through marriage of Ferdinand of Aragon and Isabella, heir to Castilian throne		
	1476—Caxton's printing press set up in England	
1485—Beginning of Tudor reign	1485—First license to operate printing press	1483–1546—Martin Luther
1488 — Bartholomew Diaz passes Cape of Good Hope on southern tip of Africa		
1492—Expulsion of Moors from Spain		
First voyage of Columbus		
1493—Spain and Portugal divide the world by papal Line of Demarcation	1493—First permanent settlement on island of Hispaniola (Haiti)	1493–1541—Paracelsus, "Father" of modern chemistry
1497—John Cabot discovers Newfoundland in England's name		
1498—Vasco da Gama sails around Africa and reaches India		
1499—Amerigo Vespucci describes expedition of which he is a member		
	1504—Henry VII places guilds under state supervision	

Political	Social	Intellectual & Technological
1507—A geographer gives Amerigo Vespucci immortality		
		1508–1512—Michelangelo paints roof of Sistine Chapel in Rome
1509—Henry Tudor (VIII) becomes England's king		1509–1564—John Calvin
1513—Ponce de León explores Florida		
Balboa crosses Panama; discovers the Pacific	1517–1528—Coffee, chocolate, and cocoa beans first introduced into Europe from New World	1517—Martin Luther nails his theses to Wittenberg church door
1519—Charles V, King of Spain, becomes Emperor of Germany		
1519–1521 — Cortez conquers Aztecs of Mexico	1519–1522 — Magellan circumnavigates the globe	
	1521—Manufacture of silk begins in France	1521–1523—Luther translates Bible into German
1524–1536 — Pizarro conquers Peru	1524—Peasants revolt in Germany	
Spain occupies Central America		
1527—Beginning of English revolt against Catholic Church		
		1531—First complete edition of Aristotle by Erasmus
1534—Jacques Cartier enters Gulf of St. Lawrence	1534—Papal power in England abolished	1534—Rabelais writes *Gargantua*
	1535—First printing press in New World in Mexico	
	1538—Jesuit Order founded	
1539 — Hernando de Soto reaches Florida		
1540–1541—Coronado explores continental interior as far as eastern Kansas	1540–1600—Catholic Counter Reformation	1540—Michael Servetus believed to have discovered that blood circulates
		1543—*On the Revolutions of the Heavenly Orbs* by Copernicus appears
1545—Council of Trent		
	1546–1601—Tycho Brahe, astronomer, who kept accurate astronomical records of calculations	

Political	Social	Intellectual & Technological
1547—First Russian czar crowned		
	1549—Enclosures legalized in England	
	1549–1551—St. Francis Xavier introduced Christianity in Japan	
		1551—University of Mexico; San Marcos de Lima University
1553–1554—Willoughby and Chancellor expedition to northern Russia		
1555—Peace of Augsburg	1555—Muscovy Company chartered	
1556—Philip II becomes ruler of Spain		
1558—Elizabeth becomes England's queen		
	1560—Protestant revolt in Scotland	
		1561–1626—Francis Bacon
		1564–1616—William Shakespeare
		1564–1642—Galileo
1565—St. Augustine, Fla., becomes first permanent European settlement in future United States	1565–1571—Spanish occupy Philippines	1565—Manufacture of pencils begins in England
	1568–1598 — Wars of religion in France	
		1569—Mercator's map of world founds modern cartography
	1571—Royal Exchange opened in London	1571–1630—John Kepler
		1576 — Jean Bodin, De la République, urges religious toleration
		François Viète introduces decimal fractions
	1577–1580—Francis Drake sails around the world	
	1581—Levant Company chartered	
	1582—Publication of Hakluyt's Voyages	1582—Gregorian calendar introduced
		First waterworks in London
		1584—Potatoes imported into Europe

Political	Social	Intellectual & Technological
		1584—William Gilbert discovers terrestrial magnetism
1588—Defeat of Spanish Armada		
	1593–1630—Spanish missionary expansion on South Atlantic coast	
		1596–1650—René Descartes
		1597—Galileo invents thermometer
1598—Edict of Nantes		
	1600—East India Company formed	
	1602 — Dutch East India Company formed	
1603—Death of Elizabeth; James Stuart of Scotland becomes King James I of England		
		1604—First English dictionary published
	1605—First important French settlement at Port Royal, Acadia	1605—Bacon's *Advancement of Learning*
		1606—Galileo invents proportional compass
	1607—Settlement of Jamestown, Virginia	
	1608—Champlain settles Quebec	1608–1674—John Milton
	Spanish establish town of Santa Fe	
1610–1611—Henry Hudson explores river and bay which bear his name		1610—Galileo's *Sidereal Messenger* completes revolution of Copernicus; presents world as mechanical order
1611—Dutch occupy Java		1611—King James version of Bible
		Kepler develops telescope
	1612—English occupation of Bermuda	
	John Rolfe cultivates tobacco	
1614–1616—Captain John Smith explores and charts New England coast		1614—First logarithmic table appears
	1616—Dutch-Japanese commercial treaty	1616—Law of refraction of light discovered by Snellius
		1618–1621—Kepler's researches in astronomy

Political	Social	Intellectual & Technological
1619—House of Burgesses in Virginia	1619—Hamburg and Venice banks founded	
	Dutch bring slaves to Virginia	
1620—Pilgrims land		
Mayflower Compact		
	1621 — Dutch West India company founded	
	1622 — First weekly newspaper in England	
		1624—Jan van Helmont introduces the term "gas"
	1625–1664 — French settle Guadeloupe, Martinique, and other West Indian islands	1625—Hugo Grotius, *The Law of War and Peace*
	1627 — Swedes and Finns settle on Delaware	1627—Bacon's *New Atlantis* urges social value of science
1628—Passage of Petition of Right by Parliament securing popular liberties and Parliament's control of taxation		1628—William Harvey discovers that blood circulates
1629—Charter of Massachusetts Bay Company		
1632—Maryland charter granted		1632—Galileo's *Dialogue*
		1632–1677—Spinoza
		1632–1704—John Locke
		1633—Galileo forced to recant by Inquisition
1634—Beginning of representative government in Massachusetts	1634—Mistress Anne Hutchinson defies Massachusetts elders	
	1635—Boston Latin School	
	1636—Rhode Island settled by Roger Williams	
	Harvard College	
1637—Pequot War in New England		1637—Descartes's *Discourse on Method*
	1638—John Davenport founds New Haven	1638—Descartes establishes the science of analytical geometry
1639—"Fundamental Orders" of Connecticut	1639—Stephen Daye's printing press, Cambridge, Mass.	
1640—Long Parliament		1640—*Bay Psalm Book*, first book printed in New England

Political	Social	Intellectual & Technological
1642—Beginning of English political parties		1642–1727—Isaac Newton
1643—New England Confederation established		1643—Evangelista Torricelli invents barometer
1644–1912—Manchu Dynasty in China		1644—Descartes, *Principles of Philosophy*
		Milton, *Areopagitica*
		Roger Williams, *Bloudy Tenent of Persecution*
	1645—Roxbury Latin School	
	1646 — John Eliot begins missionary work among Indians	
	1647—Massachusetts enacts world's first law for state-supported schools	
	First "witch" executed in America	
1648—Peace of Westphalia; end of Thirty Years' War		
1649—Charles I loses his head	1649—Maryland Act of Toleration	
1649–1660—English Commonwealth		
		1651—Thomas Hobbes, *Leviathan*
1652–1654—English-Dutch War		1652—Boston's first bookstore
		Air pump invented by Otto von Guericke
1653–1658—Cromwell Lord Protector of Commonwealth		
	1655—First newspaper in Berlin	1655—First pendulum clock built by Christian Huyghens
	1656—Beginning of Quaker persecution in New England	1656—James Harrington, *Oceana*
	1657—Halfway Covenant	
1660—Restoration; Charles II King of England	1660—First enduring Navigation Act	
		1661—Robert Boyle, *Sceptical Chemist,* begins modern chemistry
		John Eliot translates Bible into Algonquin

Political	Social	Intellectual & Technological
	1662 — Colbert begins installation of mercantile system in France	1662—Royal Society incorporated
		Michael Wigglesworth, *Day of Doom*
1664—English end Dutch rule in New York		
		1665—Robert Hooke, *Micrographia*
	1666—London fire	1667—Milton, *Paradise Lost*
	1668—Hudson's Bay Company formed	1668—Red blood corpuscles discovered
		1669—Phosphorus discovered
1671 — French proclaim ownership of interior of North America		1671—Newton constructs reflecting telescope
1672–1674—Anglo-Dutch War		1672 — Samuel Pufendorf, *Law of Nature and Nations*
		Newton propounds law of gravitation
	1673—Père Marquette and Louis Jolliet explore upper Mississippi	
1675–1676—King Philip's War	1675—Stock exchange emerges as financial institution	1675—Royal Observatory established at Greenwich
	1676—Bacon's Rebellion in Virginia	1676—Gottfried Leibnitz establishes the science of differential calculus
		Olaus Römer's observations on velocity of light
		1678—Anne Bradstreet, *Poems*
		John Bunyan, *Pilgrim's Progress*
1679–1689—La Salle explores Mississippi Valley and attempts to occupy mouth of Mississippi		
1681—William Penn's charter for Pennsylvania		
		1683—Anton van Leeuwenhoek discovers the existence of bacteria
1684—Revocation of Massachusetts charter		
1684–1689 — Dominion of New England		
1685—Revocation of Edict of Nantes		

Political	Social	Intellectual & Technological
1685–1688—Reign of James II		
	1687—James II issues Declaration of Liberty of Conscience, granting liberty to all denominations	1687—*The Principia* of Newton appears with analysis of law of gravitation
1688—Glorious Revolution; James II (Stuart) overthrown		1688—First plate glass cast
		1688–1744—Alexander Pope
1689—William and Mary sovereigns of England	1689—English Toleration Act	
English Bill of Rights establishes supremacy of Parliament		
King William's War begins		
		1690—Locke, *Essay Concerning Human Understanding*
	1691—Massachusetts charter abolishes church membership as qualification for voting	
	1692—Salem witchcraft trials	
	1693—College of William and Mary	1693—First scientific astronomical tables by Edmund Halley
	1694—English laws of censorship lapse	1694–1778—Voltaire
	Bank of England established	
1697—Treaty of Ryswick closes King William's War		
	1699—French occupy Louisiana and Illinois	
	Massachusetts legislates to avoid spread of infectious diseases	
	1701—Detroit founded by French	
	Yale College	
1702—Queen Anne's War breaks out		
1702–1714—Queen Anne's reign		
1704—Gibraltar taken by English	1704—First successful newspaper in English colonies, Boston *News-Letter*	

Political	Social	Intellectual & Technological
		1705—Thomas Newcomen invents steam engine
		1706—Carriage springs invented
1707—Last veto of a law by an English king		
	1709—Beginning of large German migration to America; Scotch-Irish soon followed	1709—Coke used for iron smelting in England
		1711—Tuning fork invented
		1711–1776—David Hume
		1712–1778—Jean Jacques Rousseau, one of the great contributors to the theory of democracy
1713—Treaty of Utrecht ends Queen Anne's War		
1714–1727 — Reign of George I, first of the Hanoverians		1714—Gabriel Fahrenheit constructs mercury thermometer
	1717 — Compulsory school attendance in Prussia	
1721–1742 — Robert Walpole, first English prime minister		
		1731—Quadrant for use at sea invented
		1732—Hermann Boerhaave founds organic chemistry
1733—Sugar Act forbids colonies to trade with French West Indies		1733—John Kay invents fly shuttle
	1735—Zenger trial aids freedom of press	1735—Linnaeus publishes *System of Nature*
		1737–1809—Thomas Paine
		1738 — First spinning machines patented in England
1740–1748—King George's War		1740—Crucible steel produced in Sheffield
		1743–1794—Condorcet, philosopher of progress and liberation
		1745—Leyden jar invented
	1746—Princeton University (College of New Jersey)	
		1748—Montesquieu, *On the Spirit of Laws*

Political	Social	Intellectual & Technological
	1749—University of Pennsylvania	
		1751–1752—French *Encyclopédie*
		1753—British Museum founded
		Franklin invents lightning rod
1754–1763 — Seven Years' War	1754—Columbia University (King's College)	1754—Jonathan Edwards, *Freedom of the Will*
1759—Fall of Quebec to Wolfe		
1760–1820—Reign of George III		
		1762—Rousseau, *Social Contract*
1763—Treaty of Paris, ending French hold on continental North America		1763—Voltaire, *Treatise on Tolerance*
Pontiac's War		
1764—Sugar Act inaugurates "New Imperial System" and arouses first colonial opposition	1764—Brown University	
1765 — Stamp Act and Quartering Act passed		
Nonimportation agreements		
Oct. 7 Stamp Act Congress		
1766 — Repeal of Stamp Act and passage of Declaratory Act		1766—Henry Cavendish discovers hydrogen
1767—Townshend Acts; renewed colonial opposition		
	1769–1776—Spanish occupy southern California	1769 — Richard Arkwright patents cotton-spinning frame
		James Watt patents steam engine
1770 — Boston Massacre; repeal of Townshend Acts	1770—First public restaurant in Paris	1770—Spinning jenny invented by James Hargreaves
		1770–1827—Ludwig van Beethoven

Political	Social	Intellectual & Technological
		1770–1831 — Georg W. F. Hegel
		1770–1850—William Wordsworth
1771—Batttle of Alamance		1771—First edition of *Encyclopedia Britannica*
		1772–1834—Samuel T. Coleridge
1773—Tea Act *Dec. 16* Boston Tea Party		1772–1837—Charles Fourier
1774—Passage of Coercive Acts and Quebec Act *Sept. 5* Meeting of first Continental Congress at Philadelphia	1774—Attempt by Turgot in France to carry out economic reforms aimed at laissez faire Pestalozzi begins using modern educational methods in Switzerland	1774—Discovery of oxygen by Joseph Priestley
1775—*April 19* Battles of Lexington and Concord		
1776—*July 4* Declaration of Independence	1776 — Jefferson's Virginia abolishes entails, beginning democratic reform in land system of all states Spanish settle San Francisco Delaware first state to abolish slave trade Adam Smith's *The Wealth of Nations,* classical formulation of doctrines of laissez faire 1776–1781—Exodus of Loyalists	1776—First iron rails constructed in England Phi Beta Kappa literary society established at College of William and Mary Thomas Paine, *Common Sense*
1777—*Oct. 17* Surrender of Burgoyne *Nov. 15* Articles of Confederation adopted by Congress 1778—*Feb. 6* French Treaty of Alliance	1777—Publication of John Howard's *State of the Prisons in England and Wales* Vermont abolishes slavery	
1779—Spain enters war	1779 — First Universalist congregation in America meets Jefferson's Bill for Religious Freedom introduced in Virginia Legislature	1779—Samuel Crompton invents spinning mule

Political	Social	Intellectual & Technological
	1780 — Pennsylvania begins gradual emancipation of slaves	1780—Luigi Galvani's discoveries in electricity
1781—Surrender of Cornwallis		
Articles of Confederation ratified		
		1782—First air balloon
1783—Peace treaty signed at Paris		1783—Noah Webster writes *Spelling Book*
	1784—United States begins trade with China	1784—Ethan Allen's deistic work, *Reason the Only Oracle of Man*
	1785 — American Unitarian Church formed	1785—Edmund Cartwright invents the power loom
	Georgia first to charter state university	
	Land ordinance adopted	
	Primogeniture abolished in Virginia	
	1785–1787—Depression	
1786 — Annapolis Convention to consider amending Articles of Confederation	1786—Shays' Rebellion	1786—Philip Freneau, *Poems*
	Statute of Religious Liberty adopted by Virginia	Coal gas used for lighting
1787—*May 25* Constitutional Convention assembles at Philadelphia	1787—First American prison reform society	1787—Jefferson produces scientific treatise, *Notes on Virginia*
	Northwest Ordinance	
Sept. 17 Constitution signed		
	1787–1788—*The Federalist* defends Constitution	
	1788 — Serfdom abolished in Denmark	1788–1824—George Gordon (Lord) Byron
	British convicts colonize Australia at Botany Bay	Publication of Kant, *Critique of Pure Reason*
1789—French Revolution; meeting of the Estates-General at Versailles	1789—*Aug. 27* French Declaration of Rights of Man	1789—Noah Webster, *Dissertation on the English Language*
Mar. 4 First U.S. Congress meets in New York		Jeremy Bentham, *Introduction to Principles of Morals and Legislation*
April 30 George Washington inaugurated as first President of the U.S.		
June 17 French National Assembly		
July 14 Destruction of Bastille; rise of peasants against feudal lords		

Political	Social	Intellectual & Technological
	1790—John Carroll named first Catholic bishop in United States	1790—Goethe, *Faust*
1791—Bill of Rights added to Constitution Vermont first state admitted after establishment of U.S.	1791 — Alexander Hamilton's *Report on Manufactures* 1791–1814 — Beginning of Industrial Revolution in America	1791—Publication of Thomas Paine, *Rights of Man* 1791–1814 — Samuel Slater and Moses Brown use power-driven machinery to spin cotton yarn, Pawtucket, R. I. 1791–1867—Michael Faraday
1792 — Political parties (Federalist and Jeffersonian Republican) take shape George Vancouver explores Pacific Northwest for England War of First Coalition against France French National Convention elected by manhood suffrage Abolition of monarchy in France 1792–1815 — French revolutionary and Napoleonic Wars		1792—Eli Whitney introduces cotton gin
1793—*Jan. 21* Execution of Louis XVI, King of France *Apr. 22* Washington proclaims neutrality of U.S.	1793 — Alexander MacKenzie first to cross continent overland French introduce military conscription Fugitive Slave Act adopted 1793–1794—Reign of Terror in France Abolition of worship of God; establishment of Cult of Reason in France	
1794—Congress passes Neutrality Act Whiskey Rebellion Jay Treaty with England		

Political	Social	Intellectual & Technological
1795—*Oct. 27* Pinckney Treaty (Treaty of San Lorenzo)		1795–1881—Thomas Carlyle
1795–1799—Creation of the Directory in France		
1796—Paul I Emperor of Russia after death of Catherine II	1796 — Virginia humanizes its criminal code, launching movement later imitated by all states	1796–1798—Charles Bulfinch designs classical state house for Massachusetts
Sept. 18 Washington's Farewell Address	First successful use of vaccination, in England	
1797 — Frederick William III becomes King of Prussia		1797 — Charles Newbold patents iron plow
1798—Alien and Sedition Acts		1798 — Charles B. Brown, *Wieland,* first nationalistic novel
1798–1799 — Virginia and Kentucky Resolutions		Eli Whitney manufactures guns on standardized principle of interchangeable parts
Second coalition of European powers against Napoleonic France		T. R. Malthus, *Essay on Population*
		1798–1857—Auguste Comte, philosopher of positivism
1799—Napoleon overthrows Directory		1799–1850—Honoré de Balzac
Russia lays claim to Alaska		
		1800—Alessandro Volta invents electric battery
		Beethoven's *First Symphony*
		Mason Weems, *Life of Washington*
		1801 — A locomotive built by Richard Trevithick first to use steam carriage on railway
1802—Ohio admitted to American union, first state from Old Northwest	1802 — First law against child labor in England	1802 — John Dalton introduces atomic theory into chemistry
		1802–1885—Victor Hugo
	1803—Louisiana Purchase	1803–1882—Ralph Waldo Emerson
1804–1815 — Napoleon I, Emperor of the French	1804—Prussia adopts Pestalozzian educational methods	

Political	Social	Intellectual & Technological
	1804–1806 — Lewis and Clark Expedition	1804–1807—John Marshall, *Life of Washington*
		1804–1864—Nathaniel Hawthorne
1805—Third European coalition against France		
English naval victory at Trafalgar		
1806—British declare blockade of Europe from Brest to Elbe River		1806–1873—John Stuart Mill
End of old Holy Roman Empire		
Berlin Decree of Napoleon blockades British Isles		
1806–1812 — War between Russia and Turkey		
1807 — British Order in Council blockades European coast from Copenhagen to Trieste	1807 — Abolition of slave trade in British Empire	1807—Gas begins to light London
Milan Decree of Napoleon declares neutrals belligerent if they obey English order		Robert Fulton and Robert R. Livingston travel from New York to Albany in the *Clermont*, first successful steamboat
Jefferson's Embargo Acts		
	1808—African slave trade abolished by U.S. law	
1809—Repeal of Embargo Acts		1809—Humphry Davy invents arc lamp
Non-Intercourse Act, commerce with all save England and France		Washington Irving, *History of New York*
		1809–1849—Edgar Allan Poe
		1809–1865 — Pierre Joseph Proudhon, modern exponent of anarchism
		1809–1882—Charles Darwin
		1809–1892 — Alfred Tennyson
	1810—University of Heidelberg	1810—Founding of Krupp Works at Essen
		1810–1849—Frédéric Chopin
1811—Paraguay, Venezuela, Colombia proclaim independence from Spain		1811—Steam power used in England to convey coal on railway
		First steamboat on Mississippi River

Political	Social	Intellectual & Technological
1812—*June 18* U.S. declares war on England		1812–1889—Robert Browning
Napoleon invades Russia		
Napoleon retreats from Moscow		1813–1883—Richard Wagner
1814—Armies of Coalition enter Paris		1814—George Stephenson adapts steam engine to railroad
Napoleon abdicates		Francis C. Lowell opens factory at Waltham, Mass., combining all processes of cotton manufacture under one roof
Congress of Vienna		
Treaty of Ghent ends war between England and U.S.		
1814–1824—Louis XVIII King of France		
Ferdinand VII restored to throne of Spain after English victory over Napoleon		
1815—Napoleon returns from Elba	1815—English Corn Law virtually excludes importation of foreign grain to protect agriculture in interest of landlords	1815—First American literary magazine, *North American Review*
June 18 Waterloo		
Napoleon abdicates; prisoner on Island of St. Helena		
Dominance of "Metternich System"		
	1816—Second Bank of the United States	1816—Black Ball Line begins regular service between New York and Liverpool with fast sailing ships
	American Bible Society	
	American Colonization Society	
1817—Rush-Bagot Agreement; U.S. and Great Britain limit naval forces on Great Lakes		1817 — David Ricardo, *On the Principles of Political Economy*, propounds thesis that wages seek subsistence level
1818—Chile proclaims independence from Spain		1818—Use of iron in ship building
England and U.S. agree on 49th parallel boundary		1818–1883—Karl Marx
		1818–1883—Ivan Turgenev

Political	Social	Intellectual & Technological
1819—Treaty with Spain (*Feb. 22*) cedes Florida and defines western boundary of Louisiana Purchase	1819—Depression and panic in U.S. Twelve-hour day in England for young workers Jefferson establishes University of Virginia Carlsbad decrees bind sovereigns under Metternich system to control universities	1819—René Laënnec invents stethoscope *Savanna* crosses to Liverpool partly under steam Steamboats introduced on Great Lakes 1819–1820—Washington Irving, *Sketch Book* 1819–1892—Walt Whitman
1820—Missouri Compromise George IV England's king	1820—Beginning of revolutions in Spain First American missionaries in Hawaii Revolution in Portugal Neapolitan revolution	1820–1895—Friedrich Engels
1821—Russia claims Pacific coast north of 51st parallel Peru issues Declaration of Independence from Spain 1821–1831—Greek War for Independence	1821—Uprising in Piedmont	1821—Scott, *Kenilworth;* Cooper, *The Spy* Jean François Champollion deciphers Egyptian hieroglyphics 1821–1831—Faraday develops electric motor and generator 1821–1867—Charles Baudelaire 1821–1880—Gustave Flaubert 1821–1881—Feodor Dostoyevsky
1822—Brazil declares its independence of Portugal U.S. recognizes Latin-American republics Congress of Verona		1822—William Church designs first typesetting machine
1823—Central America declares independence *Dec. 2* Monroe Doctrine French troops invade Spain to support monarchy of Ferdinand VII		
1824—Charles X becomes King of France Last caucus to nominate a U.S. president	1824—Repeal of anticombination laws allows English workmen to organize New Harmony, Indiana, founded by Robert Owen, first of many communistic experiments in the U.S.	1824—Henri J. Paixhans invents shell gun

829

Political	Social	Intellectual & Technological
1825—Bolivia proclaims independence	1825—Trade unions recognized as legal in England American Tract Society	1825—Erie Canal finished First railway, Stockton to Darlington, in England
1826—First Parliament in Brazil	1826—American Home Missionary Society	1826—Dutch steamer *Curaçao* first to cross Atlantic entirely under steam Cooper, *Last of the Mohicans*
		1826–1864—Stephen C. Foster
		1827—First horse-drawn railway at Quincy, Mass. First of Edgar Allan Poe's verse published Noah Webster's two-volume *An American Dictionary of the English Language*
	1828—William Ladd founds American Peace Society in New York Workingmen's party formed in Philadelphia	1828—Baltimore & Ohio Railroad begun 1828–1910—Leo Tolstoi
1829—Greeks secure independence from Turkey	1829—Catholic Emancipation Bill passes British Parliament: suffrage and right to sit in Parliament granted Catholics White manhood suffrage established in most of the states in the U.S.	1829—James Mill, *Analysis of the Phenomena of the Human Mind,* pioneer work in psychology First U.S. railroad from Carbondale to Honesdale, Pa. 1829–1833—*Encyclopaedia Americana*
1830—*July 25* Revolution breaks out in France Revolutions in Brunswick, Saxony, Hesse-Cassell; rulers abdicate	1830—Mormon Church organized by Joseph Smith in Fayette, N. Y.	1830—Liverpool-Manchester railroad opens, first to use locomotive for traction *Godey's Lady's Book* founded 1830–1833 — Sir Charles Lyell, *The Principles of Geology,* ushers in evolutionary view of earth's development
	1831—William Lloyd Garrison establishes *Liberator* at Boston; urges unconditional emancipation of slaves	1831—Faraday demonstrates electromagnetic induction

Political	Social	Intellectual & Technological
	1831—Uprisings in Modena and Parma; suppressed with aid of Austrian troops; rebellion in Poland Italian Giuseppe Mazzini organizes new revolutionary society	
1832—Use of national nominating conventions Jackson's war on second Bank of the United States 1832–1833—South Carolina nullification episode	1832—New England Anti-Slavery Society founded	1832—Samuel F. B. Morse perfects electrical telegraph
1833—German *Zollverein* established	1833—American Anti-Slavery Society and American Temperance Union formed English Reform Bill enacts democratic reforms and extends franchise Oberlin College, Ohio, admits Negroes and women Trade unionism begins to take place of workingmen's parties Revolution in Hanover; more liberal constitution provided Britain abolishes slavery in her colonies Factory Act to investigate English labor conditions First grant for public education in England Massachusetts last American state to separate church and state	1833–1897—Johannes Brahms
	1834—The Grand National Consolidated Trades Union organizes in England	1834—Cyrus Hall McCormick patents reaping machine 1835—First German railway 1835–1881—Modest Moussorgsky 1835–1910—Samuel L. Clemens (Mark Twain)
1836—Texans declare independence from Mexico		1836—Samuel Colt invents revolver

Political	Social	Intellectual & Technological
		1836–1883—Edouard Manet
1837—Victoria becomes Queen of England	1837—Massachusetts creates nation's first State Board of Education with Horace Mann as secretary	1837—Emerson, *The American Scholar,* "American intellectual declaration of independence"
	Mary Lyon opens Mt. Holyoke, first women's college	John Deere begins manufacturing steel plows
	Depression and panic in U.S.	
	1838—Organization of Underground Railroad	1838—Cell theory of physiology developed by Matthias Jakob Schleiden
	1839—First normal school in United States opened at Lexington, Mass.	1839—Louis Blanc, *Organization of Labor,* urges elimination of capitalism
	Chartist Movement in England reflects labor's dissatisfaction	Regular steamship connections between England and Alexandria, Peninsula and Oriental Line
		D. S. Rockwell invents double-row corn-planter
		Kirkpatrick MacMillan produces first bicycle
		Charles Goodyear discovers method for vulcanizing rubber
		1839–1906—Paul Cézanne
	1840—Uniform postage established in United Kingdom	1840—Richard Henry Dana, *Two Years before the Mast*
	Ten-hour day established for United States government workers	First incandescent light, William R. Grove, inventor
		Samuel Cunard establishes steamship line which bears his name
		1840–1917—Auguste Rodin
		1840–1926—Claude Monet
		1840–1928—Thomas Hardy
	1841—First law for protection of workmen in France	1841—Publication of Emerson's first *Essays,* and Longfellow's *Ballads*
	World Anti-Slavery Convention in London	1841–1919—Auguste Renoir
1842—Webster-Ashburton Treaty between U.S. and Great Britain	1842—England forbids child or female labor underground in mines	1842–1910—William James

Political	Social	Intellectual & Technological
	1842—Second National Convention of Chartists in London	
	Massachusetts legalizes formation of trade unions	
	1843—Workingmen's cooperatives founded in England	1843–1916—Henry James
	Dorothea Dix's Memorial to Legislature of Massachusetts on treatment of insane	
	1844—Factory Act in England regulates hours of labor for women and children	1844 — Dr. Horace Wells, dentist of Hartford, Conn., discovers that nitrous oxide might be used as an anesthetic
	First unions in Germany	
	George Henry Evans forms National Reform Association	Samuel F. B. Morse transmits first telegraph message between Baltimore and Washington
		1844–1924—Anatole France
1845—U.S. annexes Texas by joint resolution	1845—National Association of the United Trades for the Protection of Labor forms in England	1845—First submarine cable, between England and France
1845–1847—Famine in Ireland and Irish immigration to U.S.		Poe, *Tales of Mystery*
1846—Oregon Treaty between U.S. and Great Britain	1846—Repeal of British Corn Laws	1846—Elias Howe patents the sewing machine
Wilmot Proviso		Richard Hoe builds first rotary printing press
1846–1848—War between Mexico and U.S.		Dr. W. T. G. Morton, dentist of Boston, Mass., employs ether as anesthetic
	1847—Severe depression in France; great unemployment	1847—H. L. F. von Helmholtz propounds theory of the conservation of energy
	New Hampshire establishes ten-hour day for workers	Hamburg-American Line founded
		1847–1931—Thomas A. Edison
1848—Treaty of Guadalupe Hidalgo ends war between Mexico and U.S.	1848—*The Communist Manifesto* by Marx and Engels	1848—J. R. Lowell, *Biglow Papers*
Feb. 24 Louis Philippe abdicates; Second French Republic	*Jan. 24* Gold at Sutter's Fort, Calif.	1848–1903—Paul Gauguin

Political	Social	Intellectual & Technological
1848—Milan starts independence movement against Austria	1848—Ten-hour day in English textile mills for youths and women	
Venetian Republic; Piedmont declares war on Austria	England adopts first Public Health Act	
Louis Napoleon becomes President of France	Kossuth demands responsible government for Hungary in defiance of Vienna	
	Serfdom abolished in Austria	
	J. S. Mill's *Principles of Political Economy* published; sets forth classical economic theory	
	Slavery abolished in French colonies	
	Revolution in Prussia	
	Croats seek autonomy from Hungary	
	Revolutionary beginnings in Austrian provinces of Moravia, Transylvania, Dalmatia, Galicia	
	Frankfurt National Assembly, middle-class efforts to unite Germany	
	Revolutionary outbreak in Sicily	
	Outbreak of revolution in France	
	Formation of national workshops to provide work relief for French unemployed	
	1848–1854—Large German immigration to United States	
1850—*Jan. 29* Compromise of 1850	1850—Old age insurance introduced in France	1850—Bunsen burner invented
Clayton-Bulwer Treaty between Great Britain and U.S. regarding future interoceanic canal	Congress begins policy of land grants to railroads	*Harper's Magazine* established
	Oxford Movement effort to prove Anglican and Roman Catholic doctrines	Hawthorne, *Scarlet Letter*
	Papacy sets up hierarchy of Catholic bishops in England	1850–1860—Golden Era of clipper ships
		1850–1893—Guy de Maupassant

Political	Social	Intellectual & Technological
	1851—Neal Dow sponsors prohibition law in Maine	1851—Herman Melville, *Moby Dick*
	New York *Times* established	Hawthorne, *House of the Seven Gables*
	Harriet Beecher Stowe, *Uncle Tom's Cabin*	
	Joseph Arthur de Gobineau, *Inequality of Human Races*	
1852—Cavour becomes Premier of Piedmont		
Second Empire of France established, Napoleon III as emperor		
	1853—Prussia prohibits labor of children under twelve	1853–1890—Vincent van Gogh
	New York and Chicago connected by rail	
1854—Kansas-Nebraska Act	1854 — Boston Public Library opened	1854 — Abram Gessner patents kerosene
Birth of Republican party	Commodore Perry negotiates trade treaty with Japan	Henry David Thoreau's *Walden* published
	First railroads in India and Brazil	George Fitzhugh, *Sociology for the South*
	Dogma of the Immaculate Conception of the Virgin	Electric bulbs invented by Heinrich Goebel
	1855 — Paris International Exposition	1855—Whitman, *Leaves of Grass*
	1856 — Peace Congress at Paris	1856 — Henry Bessemer develops the Bessemer process for steelmaking
		George Bernard Shaw born
		Production of aniline dyes begins
		1856–1925—Louis Sullivan
		1856–1939—Sigmund Freud
	1857—Dred Scott decision	1857—*Atlantic Monthly* established
	Depression and panic in U.S.	1857–1924 — Joseph Conrad
1858 — Hungarian Republic; Kossuth president	1858 — Gold near Pikes Peak, Colorado	
Russian czar offers to help Francis Joseph to put down Hungarian revolt	Removal of disabilities on Jews in England	

Political	Social	Intellectual & Technological
1859—War of France and Piedmont against Austria	1859 — John Brown's raid on Harpers Ferry	1859 — Beginning of Suez Canal John Dewey, renowned philosopher, born Charles Darwin, *Origin of Species* First ironclad frigate Opening of Drake's oil well in Titusville, Pa.
1860 — South Carolina adopts Ordinance of Secession	1860—England's first pure food law	
1861 — Confederate States of America formed *April 12* Firing on Fort Sumter begins Civil War Morrill tariff, beginning of protection Louis Napoleon sends army to Mexico	1861—Serfs emancipated in Russia	1861—Wagner's *Tannhäuser*
1862—Otto von Bismarck becomes Prussian minister	1862—World Exhibition in London Homestead Act	1862—Hugo, *Les Misérables* Nobel patents mixture for dynamite Introduction of the machine gun by Richard J. Gatling 1862–1918—Claude Debussy
1863—Archduke Maximilian proclaimed Emperor of Mexico West Virginia (loyal section of Virginia) becomes 35th American state	1863—Lincoln's Gettysburg Address Emancipation Proclamation Poles revolt against Russian rule	1863—First subway built in London Clerk Maxwell describes the electromagnetic theory of light T. H. Huxley, *Man's Place in Nature* Charles Lyell, *The Geological Evidence of the Antiquity of Man* Ernest Renan, *Life of Jesus*
1864—Austria and Prussia make war on Denmark to incorporate Schleswig and Holstein into German confederation	1864 — Right to organize granted workers in France Geneva Convention for Protection of Wounded launches International Red Cross New liberal constitution in Sweden	1864 — George Pullman builds sleeping cars for railroads Richard Strauss born

Political	*Social*	*Intellectual &* *Technological*
1865—Lee surrenders to Grant at Appomattox Russia begins imperialistic advance into Central Asia *April* 14 Abraham Lincoln assassinated	1865—Vassar College Congress adopts Thirteenth Amendment	1865—William Bullock invents continuous roll press Joseph Lister begins practice of antiseptic surgery Mendel's laws of heredity first published Open-hearth process for making steel, joint contribution of William Siemens and Pierre Martin Jean Sibelius born 1865–1936 — Rudyard Kipling
1866—Prussia defeats Austria at Sadowa, ending Austro-Prussian War	1866—Municipal Board of Health created in New York National Labor Union organized American Society for the Prevention of Cruelty to Animals chartered in New York	1866 — Laying of Atlantic cable First oil pipeline in U.S.
1867—U.S. purchases Alaska from Russia Creation of North German Confederation under leadership of Prussia and Bismarck Emperor Maximilian of Mexico executed	1867 — Peabody Fund for education and development of Negroes established Ku Klux Klan organizes Patrons of Husbandry (The Grange)	1867—Walter Bagehot, *The English Constitution* 1867–1933—John Galsworthy 1867–1934—Marie S. Curie
1868 — Impeachment trial of President Andrew Johnson Cuba revolts against Spain	1868—Liberal press law in France *July* 28 Fourteenth Amendment ratified Liberal revolution in Spain	1868—L. M. Alcott, *Little Women* C. L. Sholes invents the typewriter
	1869—State Board of Health created by Massachusetts American Woman Suffrage Association organized at Chicago Knights of Labor Wisconsin grants women full suffrage	1869—Francis Galton, *Hereditary Genius* Westinghouse air brakes James Oliver invents chilled steel plow Refrigeration used in rail transportation Unofficial opening of Suez Canal

Political	Social	Intellectual & Technological
		1869—Union Pacific and Central Pacific railroads meet in Utah
		Ducos du Haroun succeeds with color photography
		Henri Matisse born
		Mark Twain, *Innocents Abroad*
1870—France declares war on Prussia	1870 — Organization of Standard Oil Company	1870 — *Scribner's Monthly Magazine* begins publication
Prussian victory over Louis Napoleon at Sedan; collapse of second empire		
1871 — German Empire founded	1871—Chicago fire	1871 — Darwin, *Descent of Man*
Treaty of Frankfurt ends Franco-Prussian War		Whitman, *Democratic Vistas*
		1871–1922 — Marcel Proust
	1872 — English Ballot Act provides for secret vote	1872—E. Muybridge applies moving-picture principle
	1873 — Discovery of silver in Nevada	1873—Walter Bagehot, *Physics and Politics*
	Panic and depression	Mark Twain and C. D. Warner, *The Gilded Age*
		1873–1934 — Jacob Wassermann
	1874—Women's Christian Temperance Union founded	1874—Pillsbury and Washburn discover process of reducing wheat to flour with chilled steel rollers
		Arnold Schönberg born
	1875—English Public Health Act codifies earlier legislation, remains basis of English sanitation	1875—Carl Jung born
	Growing opposition to czar by Russian middle-class liberals	Thomas Mann born
	Socialist Congress at Gotha, Germany; formation of Socialist Workingmen's party	Robert Frost born
	English Artisans' Dwelling Act first real effort to meet housing problem among marginal groups	

Political	Social	Intellectual & Technological
	1875—Society for the Prevention of Cruelty to Children	
1876—Serbia declares war on Turkey Turks completely defeat Serbs	1876—Johns Hopkins University Insurrection in Bulgaria against Turkish rule	1876—Patents for manufacture of barbed wire Alexander G. Bell transmits first intelligible message by telephone Nikolaus Otto discovers principle of internal combustion engine Mark Twain, *The Adventures of Tom Sawyer*
1877—Russia declares war on Turkcy; Turks appeal to Europcan powers for mediation		1877—L. H. Morgan, *Ancient Society,* pioneer work in anthropology Henry James, *The American* Edison patents phonograph Development of hydroelectric power at Niagara Falls
1878—Turks request armistice from Russia Treaty of San Stefano between Russia and Turkey Congress of Berlin to settle issues of Russo-Turkish war German-Austrian alliance foundation of Bismarck's system	1878—William Booth establishes the Salvation Army Term "Solid South" enters American vocabulary	1878—C. F. Brush introduces arc light
1879—Agricultural depression and economic dislocation in England	1879—Formation of Standard Oil trust	1879—Henry George, *Progress and Poverty* Birth of Albert Einstein *Oct. 21* Edison perfects incandescent electric light Werner von Siemens introduces electric streetcar
	1880—English Employers' Liability Acts provide compensation to workers for injuries	1880—Charles Laveran discovers malaria parasite Henry Adams, *Democracy* Werner von Siemens constructs electric elevator in Germany

Political	Social	Intellectual & Technological
	1881—Alexander III, Czar of Russia, suppresses revolutionary movements	1881—Louis Pasteur discovers principle of immunization against disease through vaccination
	National Civil Service Reform League (U.S.) organized	
	American Red Cross Society organized; Clara Barton president	
	Tuskegee Institute for Negroes founded by Booker T. Washington	
1882 — Chinese Exclusion Act		1882—Robert Koch discovers tubercle bacillus
Triple Alliance: Germany, Austria, Italy		Igor Stravinsky born
1883—Beginning of German colonialism in Southwest Africa	1883—Germany establishes health insurance	1883—Brooklyn Bridge opened
1883–1945—Benito Mussolini	Fabian Society organizes in England	Lester F. Ward, *Dynamic Sociology*
	English Corrupt and Illegal Practices Act (control of election expenditures)	Northern Pacific, second American transcontinental railroad, completed
		Edwin Klebs identifies diphtheria bacillus
		José Clemente Orozco born
		Walter Gropius born
		1883–1924—Franz Kafka
1884 — Berlin Conference on African affairs	1884 — English Franchise Bill virtually establishes manhood suffrage	1884—Koch discovers cholera bacillus
	French Trade-Union Act legalizes unions	Charles Parsons perfects compound steam turbine
	German Accident Insurance Law passed	Dr. E. L. Trudeau introduces German sanatorium system for tuberculosis at Saranac Lake
	National Bureau of Labor (U.S.) created	W. D. Howells, *The Rise of Silas Lapham*
		Mark Twain, *The Adventures of Huckleberry Finn*
		1885—An electric street railway begins operation in Baltimore, Md.
		Pasteur develops inoculation against hydrophobia
		Ottmar Mergenthaler invents the linotype
		Woodrow Wilson, *Congressional Government*

Political	Social	Intellectual & Technological
	1886—Haymarket affair (Chicago)	1886—Gottlieb Daimler invents internal combustion engine using gasoline
	American Federation of Labor organized	Andrew Carnegie, *Triumphant Democracy*
		Diego Rivera born
	1887—Interstate Commerce Act	1887—Esperanto devised by Zamenhof
	Dawes Act designed to solve Indian problem	Michelson-Morley experiment, by two American scientists, later a basis for advance from Newtonian mechanics to twentieth-century physics and concept of relativity
		1887-1894 — European and American engineers develop early gasoline automobile
1888—William II becomes German Kaiser	1888 — Miners' Federation of Great Britain organized	1888—Edward Bellamy, *Looking Backward*
1889-1945—Adolf Hitler	1889—Hull-House founded in Chicago	1889—R. T. Ely, *Social Aspects of Christianity*
	General Federation of Women's Clubs (U.S.)	Thomas Hart Benton born
	German Old-Age and Invalidity Law passed	
	First Pan-American Congress meets	
	U.S. Department of Agriculture created	
1890—Dismissal of Bismarck by Kaiser William II	1890 — Ellis Island opens as immigration depot	
	Sherman Antitrust Act	
	1891—U.S. Forest Reserve Act initiates conservation policy	1891—William James, *Principles of Psychology*
	1891-1892—Denmark passes old-age and health insurance laws	
1892—Populist party formed	1892—Steel strike, Homestead, Penn.	1892—Rudolf Diesel patents engine
	1893 — English Independent Labour party, avowedly Socialist, founded	1893—First gasoline buggy tested by Charles F. Duryea in Springfield, Mass.
	Panic and depression in U.S.	

Political	Social	Intellectual & Technological
	1893—Woman suffrage is granted in New Zealand	1893—New York *World* uses color press
1894—Nicholas II, last of the czars, ascends Russian throne Sino-Japanese War over Korea begins	1894 — "General" Coxey leads his army of 20,000 unemployed into Washington, D. C.	1894—S. Kitasato discovers infectious agent of bubonic plague
1895—Venezuela boundary dispute between Great Britain and U.S.	1895—U.S. Supreme Court declares income tax law unconstitutional Anti-Saloon League of America formed	1895—Kiel Canal from North Sea to the Baltic Early work of Sigmund Freud on the subconscious Marconi invents wireless telegraphy Roentgen discovers X ray Gustav Le Bon, *Psychology of Crowds*
	1896 — Beginning of rural free delivery in U.S. First successful meeting of Olympic games, Athens	1896 — Antoine Henri Becquerel discovers the radioactivity of uranium Samuel P. Langley flies powered airplane model
1897 — Outbreak of war between Greece and Turkey		1897—Robert Koch demonstrates infectious agent of bubonic plague transmitted by fleas from rats
1898—*U.S.S. Maine* blows up in Havana Harbor; Spanish-American War Hawaii annexed to U.S. by joint resolution of Congress Peace treaty between Spain and U.S.	1898—Formation of Social Democratic party in Russia Universal manhood suffrage in Norway	1898—Ferdinand von Zeppelin describes principle of rigid airship Marie and Pierre Curie discover polonium and radium H. G. Wells, *The War of the Worlds* 1898–1937—George Gershwin
1899 — Outbreak of Boer War Open-door policy in Far East announced by John Hay 1900—Victor Emmanuel III becomes King of Italy Chinese Boxer nationalist movement U.S. forces join in suppression of Chinese Boxers	1899—First Hague Conference	1899—Mary Baker Eddy, *Science and Health* Thorstein Veblen, *Theory of the Leisure Class*

Political	Social	Intellectual & Technological
1901—Platt Amendment		1901—Andrew Carnegie, *The Gospel of Wealth* Planck advances hypothesis of quantum theory
1902—Boer War for independence suppressed British-Japanese alliance Filipino war for independence suppressed	1902—Theodore Roosevelt threatens seizure of mines to settle coal strike Woman suffrage is granted in Australia	1902—Jacob Riis, *The Battle with the Slum* William James, *Varieties of Religious Experience*
1903 — Panama revolution with U.S. intervention; canal treaty	1903 — Dreyfus case again focuses world attention on race prejudice Joint Department of Labor and Commerce established	1903—Pacific cable opened Wilbur and Orville Wright fly airplane at Kitty Hawk, N. C. John Dewey, *Studies in Logical Theory* Formation of Ford Motor Company
1904 — British-French entente		1904—Henry Adams, *Mont-Saint Michel and Chartres* Thorstein Veblen, *The Theory of Business Enterprise* First "sound moving picture"
1905 — U.S. protectorate over Santo Domingo Treaty of Portsmouth, influenced by U.S. President, concludes Russo-Japanese War	1905 — English Labour party emerging I.W.W. reflects tides of radical industrial unrest	1905—Alfred Binet develops intelligence tests Albert Einstein's theory of relativity Discovery of the syphilis spirochete
1906—Morocco crisis, Algeciras Conference Breach of U.S. isolation by participation at Algeciras	1906—English Trade Disputes Act equalizes collective bargaining U.S. Pure Food and Drugs Act Japanese immigration issue; U.S. exclusion policy Meat Inspection Act (U.S.) San Francisco earthquake and fire Rand School of Social Science	1906—Frederick A. Hopkins introduces new era of medicine by discovery of vitamins Upton Sinclair, *The Jungle* Henry Adams, *The Education of Henry Adams*

Political	Social	Intellectual & Technological
1907—Second Hague Conference First meeting of Philippine Assembly France occupies Morocco	1907—Russell Sage Foundation	1907—William G. Sumner, *Folkways* William James, *Pragmatism* Walter Rauschenbusch, *Christianity and the Social Crisis* Lee De Forest patents early vacuum tube
1908 — President Theodore Roosevelt displays U.S. strength by world naval cruise 1909—Payne-Aldrich tariff accentuates U.S. economic nationalism	1908—Conference of U.S. governors on natural resources	1908—Josiah Royce, *The Philosophy of Loyalty* 1909—Robert E. Peary reaches North Pole Freud's work appears in English Henry Ford inaugurates mass production methods with Model T Louis Blériot flies across English Channel T. H. Morgan formulates theory of the gene
1910 — Japan annexes Korea Portugal becomes a republic	1910 — French railroad strikes suppressed by Premier Briand Carnegie Endowment for International Peace Woman suffrage agitation in England	1910—William James, *Moral Equivalent of War* Norman Angell, *The Great Illusion* Paul Ehrlich introduces salvarsan as curative agent for syphilis
1911 — Parliament limits power of House of Lords Italo-Turkish War over Tripoli	1911 — Sun Yat-sen leads revolution in China	1911—First U.S. transcontinental air flight F. W. Taylor, *Principles of Scientific Management* Roald Amundsen reaches the South Pole Ernest Rutherford proposes nuclear theory of the structure of the atom
1912—Italy annexes Tripoli New Mexico and Arizona become states 1912–1913—Balkan Wars	1912 — English Minimum Wage Bill I.W.W. wins Lawrence strike	

Political	*Social*	*Intellectual &* *Technological*
1913 — U.S. Federal Reserve System created	1913—Rockefeller Foundation Parcel-post system begins in U.S. U.S. Income Tax Amendment goes into effect Labor acquires full departmental status in U.S. with a cabinet seat	1913—Charles Nicolle effects typhus control C. A. Beard, *Economic Interpretation of the Constitution* Woodrow Wilson, *The New Freedom* Wireless messages between Europe and the U.S.
1914—Wilson follows isolationist tradition; urges neutrality 1914–1918—World War I 1915—Sinking of *Lusitania*	1915—Seamen's Act (U.S.) 1915–1917 — U.S. shifts from debtor to creditor nation 1916-1917 — Woman suffrage is granted in Canada	1914—Panama Canal officially opens Louis Brandeis, *Other People's Money*
		1916—John Dewey, *Democracy and Education*
1917—Russian Revolution creates Soviet; Allies refuse to recognize U.S. enters World War I	1917—Literacy barrier to immigration voted by U.S. Congress over Wilson's veto	1917—Thorstein Veblen, *An Inquiry into the Nature of Peace*
1918—*Jan. 8* Wilson promulgates his Fourteen Points *Mar. 3* Treaty of Brest-Litovsk Kaiser abdicates Weimar Republic *Nov. 11* Armistice 1918–1920—Great Britain, U.S., and other allies embark upon armed intervention in Siberia	1918—Woman's suffrage in England achieved English Education Act passed	
1919—Paris Peace Conference; Versailles Treaty First attendance by an American President at an international peace conference; Wilson insists on a League of Nations program Ireland declares independence	1919—Prohibition Amendment becomes law in U.S. Committee for International Labor organization created (I.L.O.) American Legion organizes 1919–1924—Suppression of great strikes in U.S. revives injunctions	1919 — Ernest Rutherford performs the first successful experiment on the artificial disintegration of the nucleus J. W. Alcock and A. W. Brown make first transatlantic air crossing J. M. Keynes, *Economic Consequences of the Peace*

Political	Social	Intellectual & Technological
1920—First session of the Council of League of Nations	1920—Woman suffrage becomes effective in U.S.	1920—John Dewey, *Reconstruction in Philosophy*
Senate majority, but not two thirds, votes for Treaty and League		Early commercial radio broadcasting (Station KDKA)
First Reichstag election in Weimar Republic		
Nazis infiltrate German Workers' Party		
1921—Fascist party founded in Rome	1921 — Dutch neo-Malthusian League opens first mothers' clinic, London	1921—F. G. Banting, C. H. Best, J. W. MacLeod, and J. B. Collip devise method for extracting insulin from pancreas
Great Britain recognizes Irish Free State	American Birth Control League, Inc.	
1921–1922—Washington Armament Limitation Conference		
1922—World Court holds first session		1922—T. S. Eliot, *The Waste Land*
Fascist march on Rome makes Mussolini dictator		Sinclair Lewis, *Babbitt*
Fordney-McCumber tariff hits new peak of economic nationalism		John Dewey, *Human Nature and Conduct*
Fourteen Russian Republics form U.S.S.R.		James Joyce, *Ulysses*
1923—France occupies Ruhr	1923—U.S. Supreme Court holds a minimum wage law unconstitutional	1923—C. L. Morgan, *Emergent Evolution*
Primo de Rivera becomes dictator of Spain		
Turkish dictatorship established		
Beer hall *Putsch* in Munich		
1924—Dawes plan	1924—Ku Klux Klan claims 4 million members	1924—*American Mercury* founded
Teapot Dome oil scandal	U.S. Immigration Act adopts policy of nationalistic exclusion	*Saturday Review of Literature* commences publication
	English Labour party forms its first cabinet	First round-the-world air flight
		William Beveridge, *Insurance for All and Everything*
		N. Lenin, *Imperialism*
		A. Hitler, *Mein Kampf*
		H. J. Laski, *A Grammar of Politics*

Political	Social	Intellectual & Technological
1925—Locarno agreements strengthen European international cooperation		1925—J. T. Scopes is tried at Dayton, Tenn., for violation of antievolution law
		Theodore Dreiser, *An American Tragedy*
		1925–1928—"Talking" pictures introduced
1926—Weimar Germany admitted to League	1926—General strike in England	1926—*Mar.* 17 Wireless telephone between New York and London
Republic of Poland succumbs to Pilsudski dictatorship		*May 9* Richard E. Byrd circles North Pole in plane
		C. J. H. Hayes, *Essays on Nationalism*
1927—Kellogg-Briand Pact	1927—Great Britain's Trade Disputes Act regulates strikes and union finances	1927 — Charles A. Lindbergh's nonstop solo flight, New York to Paris
	Sacco and Vanzetti executed in Massachusetts	First television transmission, New York to Washington
		Transatlantic telephone service commences
		V. L. Parrington, *Main Currents in American Thought*
		H. L. Mencken, *Notes on Democracy*
		Stephen V. Benét, *John Brown's Body*
		Dictionary of American Biography begins to appear
		T. H. Morgan, *Theory of the Gene*
1928—Russia's first Five-Year Plan		
Salazar dictatorship overthrows Portugal's republic		
Chiang Kai-shek becomes President of China		
	1929—U.S. stock market crash; world depression begins	1929—Richard E. Byrd flies to South Pole
		Robert S. and Helen M. Lynd, *Middletown*
1930—London Naval Conference		1930—Sinclair Lewis receives Nobel Prize
Rhineland evacuated		
Briand urges federation of Europe		
Hawley-Smoot tariff		

Political	*Social*	*Intellectual & Technological*
1931—Spain establishes a republic Independence of British Commonwealths legally recognized Japan invades Manchuria Conservative party wins English election	1931–1932 — Hoover moratorium; war debts and reparations system collapse	1931—Lincoln Steffens, *Autobiography* Frank Lloyd Wright, *Modern Architecture* Empire State building opens M. R. Cohen, *Reason and Nature*
1932—League Commission reports on Manchuria; Japan's puppet government not "recognized"	1932—Bonus Army driven from Washington, D. C. Soviet turns on huge Dneprostroi plant U.S. Congress passes Norris-La Guardia Act 1932–1933—Huey Long's Share-Our-Wealth and Townsend Plan movements	1932—James Chadwick discovers the neutron Fritz Mietzsch and Josef Klarer issued patent for protonsil Harold C. Urey discovers heavy hydrogen isotope
1933—Hitler's cabinet dooms Weimar Republic Reichstag fire Japan secedes from League and invades north China Hitler's Reich sets up currency controls and trade restrictions . Germany secedes from League U.S. recognizes Soviet Russia	1933—Crash of U.S. banking system; "bank holiday" F.D.R. launches New Deal social program World Economic Conference fails Hull proposes multilateral trade reciprocity The TVA regional and social program begins Civilian Conservation Corps planned (U.S.) Formation of American Newspaper Guild	1933—A. A. Berle and Gardiner Means, *The Modern Corporation and Private Property*
1934—Russia admitted to League of Nations F.D.R. enunciates Good Neighbor policy; Platt Amendment abrogated Philippine Independence Act Japan denounces Washington Naval Treaty of 1922	1934—U.S. joins I.L.O. Reciprocity Act; Hull initiates bilateral trade agreements	

848

Political	Social	Intellectual & Technological
1935—Anglo-German Naval Agreement; early "appeasement" policy Saar Territory returned to Germany Mussolini invades Ethiopia 1935–1936—League fails to apply strong sanctions against Italian aggression	1935—Russia-U.S. reciprocal trade agreement signed *July 5* F.D.R. signs Wagner Labor Relations Act U.S. Social Security Act passed	1935—Pan-American Airways establishes transpacific commercial service Vilfredo Pareto, *The Mind and Society* Otto Klineberg, *Race Differences* James T. Farrell, *Studs Lonigan*
1936—King Leopold of Belgium adopts "neutrality" policy Léon Blum's Socialist government takes office in France Spanish Civil War starts	1936—American Labor Party organizes C.I.O. emerges from A.F. of L. Father Coughlin launches "Union for Social Justice" (U.S.)	1936—Eugene O'Neill receives Nobel Prize J. M. Keynes, *The General Theory of Employment, Interest and Money* Molecular theory of viruses announced
1937—Marco Polo Bridge "incident"; Japan begins undeclared war on China Italy secedes from League U.S. Neutrality Act passed		1937—John Dos Passos, *U.S.A.*
1938—*Sept. 29–30* Munich Conference; final appeasement *Oct. 1–3* Nazis occupy Czechoslovakia	1938—Fair Labor Standards Act enacted (U.S.) Mexico nationalizes petroleum industry "Ever-normal granary" program adopted in U.S.	1938—Church of England Commission reports Biblical "creation" symbolical
1939—Madrid surrenders to Franco and Axis forces *Feb. 27* France and England officially recognize Franco *May 22* Ten-year Axis pact between Germany and Italy *Aug. 24* Russo-German nonagression pact *Sept. 1* Nazis begin blitzkrieg in Poland *Sept. 3* Britain declares war on Germany; is followed by Australia, New Zealand, France, and Canada	1939—New York World's Fair	1939—O. Hahn and R. Strassman produce the fission of the uranium nucleus Scheduled transatlantic air service inaugurated John Steinbeck, *The Grapes of Wrath*

Political	Social	Intellectual & Technological
1939—*Sept. 27* Russia invades Poland		
Nov. 30 Russia invades Finland		
1940—*April 8–9* Germany invades Denmark and Norway	1940—The "America First" Committee organized	
May 10 Germany invades Holland, Belgium, and Luxemburg		
Churchill replaces Chamberlain as English prime minister		
May 29—June 4 Allied forces evacuated at Dunkirk		
June 10 Italy enters war and invades France		
June 22 Armistice between France and Germany signed		
Aug. 20 U.S. Administration gives England 50 destroyers for lease of Atlantic bases		
Sept. 16 U.S. Selective Service Act signed by President Roosevelt		
Sept. 27 Germany, Italy, and Japan sign ten-year pact		
Oct. 28 Fascist Italy launches air attack on Greece		
Nov. 5 F.D.R. elected President for third term		
1941—*Jan. 6* President Roosevelt defines the "Four Freedoms"	1941—*Aug. 12* House extends military service for year and a half by single vote	
March 10 Lend-Lease Bill becomes law	Office of Price Administration	
April 6 Germany invades Greece and Yugoslavia	FEPC established by President Roosevelt under wartime executive authority	
April 13 Japan signs five-year neutrality pact with Russia		
May 6 Stalin becomes Premier of Russia		
June 22 Germany and Rumania invade Russia		

Political	Social	Intellectual & Technological
1941—*Aug. 14* Atlantic Charter announced by Churchill and Roosevelt *Dec. 7* Japan declares war on U.S., Great Britain, and dominions. Sneak attacks on Pearl Harbor and the Philippines *Dec. 8* U.S. declares war on Japan *Dec. 11* U.S. declares war on Germany and Italy		
1942—*Jan. 1* Twenty-six countries issue Declaration of the United Nations *Feb. 15* Singapore surrenders to Japanese *June 4–6* Japanese invasion fleet defeated at Midway *Aug. 8* U.S. marines establish beachhead on Guadalcanal *Nov. 7–8* American-British invasion of North Africa	1942—Japanese removed from West Coast (U.S.) WPA liquidated by President Roosevelt	1942—Trans-Canada Highway opened Chicago's first subway U.S. "arsenal of democracy" begins unprecedented production
1943—*Jan. 14–24* Casablanca Conference *Feb. 2* Announcement of Stalingrad victory *May 12* German surrender in North Africa *July 25* Mussolini resigns *Sept. 3* Armistice signed between Allies and Italy *Oct. 30* Moscow Declaration pledges a permanent UN world organization *Nov. 9* United Nations create UNRRA	1943—Beveridge plan (England) "cradle-to-grave" social security House votes in U.S., 265–110, to abolish poll tax (defeated in Senate by filibuster) *May–June* UN Conference on Food and Agriculture at Hot Springs, Va.	

Political	Social	Intellectual & Technological
1943—*Nov. 21–26* Cairo Conference *Nov. 28–Dec. 2* Teheran Conference		
	1943—*Dec. 17* President Roosevelt signs bill repealing Chinese Exclusion Act	
1944—*June 6* Allies invade Normandy *Oct. 9* Conference of U.S., Great Britain, China, and Russia at Washington issues Dumbarton Oaks proposals for world organization *Oct. 20* Landing at Leyte *Oct. 22–27* Second Battle of the Philippines *Nov.* F.D.R. elected President for fourth term	1944—Right of Negroes to vote in primaries upheld by Supreme Court *July 1–22* UN Monetary and Financial Conference, Bretton Woods, N. H.	1944—William Beveridge, *Full Employment in a Free Society*
1945—*Feb. 3–11* Yalta Conference *Feb.–Mar.* Inter-American Conference (Chapultepuc) *April 1* U.S. invasion of Okinawa *April 12* Death of Franklin D. Roosevelt *April 21* Russians begin to storm Berlin *April 25–June 26* San Francisco Conference *May 8* Germany's unconditional surrender *June 26* San Francisco Conference issues Charter of United Nations *July 28* Senate ratifies Charter of United Nations *Aug. 8* Russia enters war against Japan *Aug. 14* Japan's unconditional surrender	1945—*Mar. 12* N. Y. State antidiscrimination bill *July 26* Labor victory in English elections; Churchill defeated *Aug. 6* Era of atomic warfare inaugurated by U.S. bombing of Hiroshima UN educational conference formally organizes UNESCO	1945—Gabriela Mistral (Chile) awarded Nobel prize in literature Vannevar Bush, *Science, the Endless Frontier* (the Bush Report)

Political	Social	Intellectual & Technological
1945—*Aug. 21* Russia ratifies Charter of United Nations *Aug. 21* Abrupt suspension of Lend-Lease by U.S. *Sept. 2* President Truman proclaims V-J day		
	1945—*Oct. 13* Japan extends suffrage to women *Oct. 16* UN conference at Quebec creates Food and Agricultural Organization *Oct. 18* Twenty-four Nazi leaders indicted as war criminals	
Nov. 29 Taft's UN amendments defeated in the Senate		
Dec. International Bank and Monetary Fund formally established	*Dec.* Shinto as national religion of Japan abolished; divinity of the Emperor disclaimed by Hirohito *Dec. 2* Bank of France nationalized	
1946—League of Nations expires *Jan.* First meeting of UN· Assembly, London, creates UN Atomic Energy Control Commission *March 25* First meeting of UN Security Council, N. Y.	1946—*Feb.* Senate filibuster kills permanent FEPC	1946—Synthetic penicillin achieved by Vincent du Vigneaud Biological warfare research equips U.S. with deadly botulinus toxin to decimate enemy peoples; accurate radar-guided missiles developed for all-weather bombing.
	June World Health Organization projected at UN health conference, N. Y. Negroes vote in Mississippi and Georgia primaries for first time U.S. Congress passes McMahon Act (Atomic Energy Commission)	
July 4 Philippine Republic achieves independence *Sept.* State Department issues proposed charter for International Trade Organization		

Political	Social	Intellectual & Technological
1946—*Nov.* Mid-term elections give control of Congress to Republican majorities *Dec.* Russia offers to accept atomic energy inspection if veto power retained 1947—*Mar. 31* U.S. Selective Service terminated	1946—*Nov.* First meeting of UNESCO, Paris, considers global cultural requirements	

INDEX

Man

Agriculture

Art